Funk & Wagnalls Hammond WORLD ATLAS

INCLUDING
UNITED STATES AND CANADA
RECREATION AND ROAD ATLAS

Funk & Wagnalls, Inc.
Publishers since 1876

CONTENTS

WORLD STATISTICS

WORLD MAP SECTION

CANADIAN MAP SECTION

MIDDLE AMERICA MAP SECTION

UNITED STATES MAP SECTION

THE FIFTY STATES

UNITED STATES AND CANADA RECREATION AND ROAD ATLAS

INDEX OF THE WORLD **193-208**

PRINTED IN THE UNITED STATES OF AMERICA

WORLD STATISTICAL TABLES

Elements of the Solar System

	Mean Distance from Sun: in Miles	in Kilometers	Period of Revolution around Sun	Period of Rotation on Axis	Equatorial Diameter: in Miles	in Kilometers	Surface Gravity (Earth = 1)	Mass (Earth = 1)	Mean Density (Water = 1)	Number of Satellites
MERCURY	35,990,000	57,900,000	87.97 days	59 days	3,032	4,880	0.38	0.055	5.5	0
VENUS	67,240,000	108,200,000	224.70 days	243 days†	7,523	12,106	0.90	0.815	5.25	0
EARTH	93,000,000	149,700,000	365.26 days	23h 56m	7,926	12,755	1.00	1.00	5.5	1
MARS	141,730,000	228,100,000	687.00 days	24h 37m	4,220	6,790	0.38	0.107	4.0	2
JUPITER	483,880,000	778,700,000	11.86 years	9h 50m	88,750	142,800	2.87	317.9	1.3	16
SATURN	887,130,000	1,427,700,000	29.46 years	10h 14m	74,580	120,020	1.32	95.2	0.7	17
URANUS	1,783,700,000	2,870,500,000	84.01 years	10h 49m†	31,600	50,900	0.93	14.6	1.3	5
NEPTUNE	2,795,500,000	4,498,800,000	164.79 years	15h 48m	30,200	48,600	1.23	17.2	1.8	3
PLUTO	3,667,900,000	5,902,800,000	247.70 years	6.39 days (?)	1,500	2,400	0.03 (?)	0.01 (?)	0.7(?)	1

†Retrograde motion

Facts About the Sun

Equatorial diameter	865,000 miles	1,392,000 kilometers
Period of rotation on axis	25-35 days*	
Orbit of galaxy	every 225 million years	
Surface gravity (Earth = 1)	27.8	
Mass (Earth = 1)	333,000	
Density (Water = 1)	1.4	
Mean distance from Earth	93,000,000 miles	149,700,000 kilometers

*Rotation of 25 days at Equator, decreasing to about 35 days at the poles.

Facts About the Moon

Equatorial diameter	2,160 miles	3,476 kilometers
Period of rotation on axis	27 days, 7 hours, 43 minutes	
Period of revolution around Earth (sidereal month)	27 days, 7 hours, 43 minutes	
Phase period between new moons (synodic month)	29 days, 12 hours, 44 minutes	
Surface gravity (Earth = 1)	0.16	
Mass (Earth = 1)	0.0123	
Density (Water = 1)	3.34	
Maximum distance from Earth	252,710 miles	406,690 kilometers
Minimum distance from Earth	221,460 miles	356,400 kilometers
Mean distance from Earth	238,860 miles	384,400 kilometers

Dimensions of the Earth

	Area in Sq. Miles	Sq. Kilometers
Superficial area	197,751,000	512,175,090
Land surface	57,970,000	150,142,300
Water surface	139,781,000	362,032,790

	Miles	Kilometers
Equatorial circumference	24,902	40,075
Polar circumference	24,860	40,007
Equatorial diameter	7,926.68	12,756.4
Polar diameter	7,899.99	12,713.4
Equatorial radius	3,963.34	6,378.2
Polar radius	3,949.99	6,356.7

Volume of the Earth	2.6×10^{11} cubic miles	10.84×10^{11} cubic kilometers
Mass or weight	6.6×10^{21} short tons	6.0×10^{21} metric tons
Maximum distance from Sun	94,600,000 miles	152,000,000 kilometers
Minimum distance from Sun	91,300,000 miles	147,000,000 kilometers

The Continents

	Area in: Sq. Miles	Sq. Km.	Percent of World's Land
Asia	17,128,500	44,362,815	29.5
Africa	11,707,000	30,321,130	20.2
North America	9,363,000	24,250,170	16.2
South America	6,875,000	17,806,250	11.8
Antarctica	5,500,000	14,245,000	9.5
Europe	4,057,000	10,507,630	7.0
Australia	2,966,136	7,682,300	5.1

Oceans and Major Seas

	Area in: Sq. Miles	Sq. Km.	Greatest Depth in: Feet	Meters
Pacific Ocean	64,186,000	166,241,700	36,198	11,033
Atlantic Ocean	31,862,000	82,522,600	28,374	8,648
Indian Ocean	28,350,000	73,426,500	25,344	7,725
Arctic Ocean	5,427,000	14,056,000	17,880	5,450
Caribbean Sea	970,000	2,512,300	24,720	7,535
Mediterranean Sea	969,000	2,509,700	16,896	5,150
Bering Sea	875,000	2,266,250	15,800	4,800
Gulf of Mexico	600,000	1,554,000	12,300	3,750
Sea of Okhotsk	590,000	1,528,100	11,070	3,370
East China Sea	482,000	1,248,400	9,500	2,900
Sea of Japan	389,000	1,007,500	12,280	3,740
Hudson Bay	317,500	822,300	846	258
North Sea	222,000	575,000	2,200	670
Black Sea	185,000	479,150	7,365	2,245
Red Sea	169,000	437,700	7,200	2,195
Baltic Sea	163,000	422,170	1,506	459

Major Ship Canals

	Length in: Miles	Kms.	Minimum Feet	Depth in: Meters
Volga-Baltic, U.S.S.R.	225	362	—	—
Baltic-White Sea, U.S.S.R.	140	225	16	5
Suez, Egypt	100.76	162	42	13
Albert, Belgium	80	129	16.5	5
Moscow-Volga, U.S.S.R.	80	129	18	6
Volga-Don, U.S.S.R.	62	100	—	—
Göta, Sweden	54	87	10	3
Kiel (Nord-Ostsee), W. Ger.	53.2	86	38	12
Panama Canal, Panama	50.72	82	41.6	13
Houston Ship, U.S.A.	50	81	36	11

Largest Islands

	Area in: Sq. Mi.	Sq. Km.
Greenland	840,000	2,175,600
New Guinea	305,000	789,950
Borneo	290,000	751,100
Madagascar	226,400	586,376
Baffin, Canada	195,928	507,454
Sumatra, Indonesia	164,000	424,760
Honshu, Japan	88,000	227,920
Great Britain	84,400	218,896
Victoria, Canada	83,896	217,290
Ellesmere, Canada	75,767	196,236
Celebes, Indonesia	72,986	189,034
South I., New Zealand	58,393	151,238
Java, Indonesia	48,842	126,501
North I., New Zealand	44,187	114,444
Newfoundland, Canada	42,031	108,860
Cuba	40,533	104,981
Luzon, Philippines	40,420	104,688
Iceland	39,768	103,000
Mindanao, Philippines	36,537	94,631
Ireland	31,743	82,214
Sakhalin, U.S.S.R.	29,500	76,405
Hispaniola, Haiti & Dom. Rep.	29,399	76,143
Hokkaido, Japan	28,983	75,066
Banks, Canada	27,038	70,028
Ceylon, Sri Lanka	25,332	65,610
Tasmania, Australia	24,600	63,710
Svalbard, Norway	23,957	62,049
Devon, Canada	21,331	55,247
Novaya Zemlya (north isl.), U.S.S.R.	18,600	48,200
Marajó, Brazil	17,991	46,597
Tierra del Fuego, Chile & Argentina	17,900	46,360
Alexander, Antarctica	16,700	43,250

World Statistics

Principal Mountains

	Feet	Meters
Everest, Nepal-China	29,028	8,848
Godwin Austen (K2), Pakistan-China	28,250	8,611
Kanchenjunga, Nepal-India	28,208	8,598
Lhotse, Nepal-China	27,923	8,511
Makalu, Nepal-China	27,824	8,481
Dhaulagiri, Nepal	26,810	8,172
Nanga Parbat, Pakistan	26,660	8,126
Annapurna, Nepal	26,504	8,078
Gasherbrum, Pakistan-China	26,740	8,068
Nanda Devi, India	25,645	7,817
Rakaposhi, Pakistan	25,550	7,788
Kamet, India	25,447	7,756
Gurla Mandhada, China	25,355	7,728
Kongur Shan, China	25,325	7,719
Tirich Mir, Pakistan	25,230	7,690
Gongga Shan, China	24,790	7,556
Muztagata, China	24,757	7,546
Communism Peak, U.S.S.R.	24,599	7,498
Pobeda Peak, U.S.S.R.	24,406	7,439
Chomo Lhari, Bhutan-China	23,997	7,314
Muztag, China	23,891	7,282
Cerro Aconcagua, Argentina	22,831	6,959
Ojos del Salado, Chile-Argentina	22,572	6,880
Bonete, Chile-Argentina	22,541	6,870
Tupungato, Chile-Argentina	22,310	6,800

	Feet	Meters
Pissis, Argentina	22,241	6,779
Mercedario, Argentina	22,211	6,770
Huascarán, Peru	22,205	6,768
Llullaillaco, Chile-Argentina	22,057	6,723
Nevada Ancohuma, Bolivia	21,489	6,550
Illampu, Bolivia	21,276	6,485
Chimborazo, Ecuador	20,561	6,267
McKinley, Alaska	20,320	6,194
Logan, Canada (Yukon)	19,524	5,951
Cotopaxi, Ecuador	19,347	5,897
Kilimanjaro, Tanzania	19,340	5,895
El Misti, Peru	19,101	5,822
Pico Cristóbal Colón, Colombia	19,029	5,800
Huila, Colombia	18,865	5,750
Citlaltépetl (Orizaba), Mexico	18,855	5,747
El'brus, U.S.S.R.	18,510	5,642
Damavand, Iran	18,376	5,601
St. Elias, Alaska-Canada (Yukon)	18,008	5,489
Vilcanota, Peru	17,999	5,486
Popocatépetl, Mexico	17,887	5,452
Dykhtau, U.S.S.R.	17,070	5,203
Kenya, Kenya	17,058	5,199
Ararat, Turkey	16,946	5,165
Vinson Massif, Antarctica	16,864	5,140
Margherita (Ruwenzori), Africa	16,795	5,119

	Feet	Meters
Kazbek, U.S.S.R.	16,512	5,033
Puncak Jaya, Indonesia	16,503	5,030
Tyree, Antarctica	16,289	4,965
Blanc, France	15,771	4,807
Klyuchevskaya Sopka, U.S.S.R.	15,584	4,750
Fairweather (Br. Col., Canada)	15,300	4,663
Dufourspitze (Mte. Rosa), Italy-Switzerland	15,203	4,634
Ras Dashan, Ethiopia	15,157	4,620
Matterhorn, Switzerland	14,691	4,478
Whitney, California, U.S.A.	14,494	4,418
Elbert, Colorado, U.S.A.	14,433	4,399
Rainier, Washington, U.S.A.	14,410	4,392
Shasta, California, U.S.A.	14,162	4,350
Pikes Peak, Colorado, U.S.A.	14,110	4,301
Finsteraarhorn, Switzerland	14,022	4,274
Mauna Kea, Hawaii, U.S.A.	13,796	4,205
Mauna Loa, Hawaii, U.S.A.	13,677	4,169
Jungfrau, Switzerland	13,642	4,158
Cameroon, Cameroon	13,350	4,069
Grossglockner, Austria	12,457	3,797
Fuji, Japan	12,389	3,776
Cook, New Zealand	12,349	3,764
Etna, Italy	11,053	3,369
Kosciusko, Australia	7,310	2,228
Mitchell, North Carolina, U.S.A.	6,684	2,037

Longest Rivers

	Length in: Miles	Kms.
Nile, Africa	4,145	6,671
Amazon, S. Amer.	3,915	6,300
Chang Jiang (Yangtze), China	3,900	6,276
Mississippi-Missouri-Red Rock, U.S.A.	3,741	6,019
Ob'Irtysh-Black Irtysh, U.S.S.R.	3,362	5,411
Yenisey-Angara, U.S.S.R.	3,100	4,989
Huang He (Yellow), China	2,877	4,630
Amur-Shilka-Onon, Asia	2,744	4,416
Lena, U.S.S.R.	2,734	4,400
Congo (Zaire), Africa	2,718	4,374
Mackenzie-Peace-Finlay, Canada	2,635	4,241
Mekong, Asia	2,610	4,200
Missouri-Red Rock, U.S.A.	2,564	4,125
Niger, Africa	2,548	4,101
Paraná-La Plata, S. Amer.	2,450	3,943
Mississippi, U.S.A.	2,348	3,778
Murray-Darling, Australia	2,310	3,718
Volga, U.S.S.R.	2,194	3,531
Madeira, S. Amer.	2,013	3,240
Purus, S. Amer.	1,995	3,211
Yukon, Alaska-Canada	1,979	3,185
St. Lawrence, Canada-U.S.A.	1,900	3,058
Rio Grande, Mexico-U.S.A.	1,885	3,034
Syrdar'ya-Naryn, U.S.S.R.	1,859	2,992

	Length in: Miles	Kms.
São Francisco, Brazil	1,811	2,914
Indus, Asia	1,800	2,897
Danube, Europe	1,775	2,857
Salween, Asia	1,770	2,849
Brahmaputra, Asia	1,700	2,736
Euphrates, Asia	1,700	2,736
Tocantins, Brazil	1,677	2,699
Xi (Si), China	1,650	2,655
Amudar'ya, Asia	1,616	2,601
Nelson-Saskatchewan, Canada	1,600	2,575
Orinoco, S. Amer.	1,600	2,575
Zambezi, Africa	1,600	2,575
Paraguay, S. Amer.	1,584	2,549
Kolyma, U.S.S.R.	1,562	2,514
Ganges, Asia	1,550	2,494
Ural, U.S.S.R.	1,509	2,428
Japurá, S. Amer.	1,500	2,414
Arkansas, U.S.A.	1,450	2,334
Colorado, U.S.A.-Mexico	1,450	2,334
Negro, S. Amer.	1,400	2,253
Dnieper, U.S.S.R.	1,368	2,202
Orange, Africa	1,350	2,173
Irrawaddy, Burma	1,325	2,132
Brazos, U.S.A.	1,309	2,107

	Length in: Miles	Kms.
Ohio-Allegheny, U.S.A.	1,306	2,102
Kama, U.S.S.R.	1,262	2,031
Red, U.S.A.	1,222	1,966
Don, U.S.S.R.	1,222	1,967
Columbia, U.S.A.-Canada	1,214	1,953
Saskatchewan, Canada	1,205	1,939
Peace-Finlay, Canada	1,195	1,923
Tigris, Asia	1,181	1,901
Darling, Australia	1,160	1,867
Angara, U.S.S.R.	1,135	1,827
Sungari, Asia	1,130	1,819
Pechora, U.S.S.R.	1,124	1,809
Snake, U.S.A.	1,000	1,609
Churchill, Canada	1,000	1,609
Pilcomayo, S. Amer.	1,000	1,609
Magdalena, Colombia	1,000	1,609
Uruguay, S. Amer.	994	1,600
Platte-N. Platte, U.S.A.	990	1,593
Ohio, U.S.A.	981	1,578
Pecos, U.S.A.	926	1,490
Oka, U.S.S.R.	918	1,477
Canadian, U.S.A.	906	1,458
Colorado, Texas, U.S.A.	894	1,439
Dniester, U.S.S.R.	876	1,410

Principal Natural Lakes

	Area in: Sq. Miles	Sq. Km.	Max. Depth in: Feet	Meters
Caspian Sea, U.S.S.R.-Iran	143,243	370,999	3,264	995
Lake Superior, U.S.A.-Canada	31,820	82,414	1,329	405
Lake Victoria, Africa	26,724	69,215	270	82
Aral Sea, U.S.S.R.	25,676	66,501	256	78
Lake Huron, U.S.A.-Canada	23,010	59,596	748	228
Lake Michigan, U.S.A.	22,400	58,016	923	281
Lake Tanganyika, Africa	12,650	32,764	4,700	1,433
Lake Baykal, U.S.S.R.	12,162	31,500	5,316	1,620
Great Bear Lake, Canada	12,096	31,328	1,356	413
Lake Nyasa (Malawi), Africa	11,555	29,928	2,320	707
Great Slave Lake, Canada	11,031	28,570	2,015	614
Lake Erie, U.S.A.-Canada	9,940	25,745	210	64
Lake Winnipeg, Canada	9,417	24,390	60	18
Lake Ontario, U.S.A.-Canada	7,540	19,529	775	244
Lake Ladoga, U.S.S.R.	7,104	18,399	738	225
Lake Balkhash, U.S.S.R.	7,027	18,200	87	27
Lake Maracaibo, Venezuela	5,120	13,261	100	31
Lake Chad, Africa	4,000-10,000	10,360-25,900	25	8
Lake Onega, U.S.S.R.	3,710	9,609	377	115

	Area in: Sq. Miles	Sq. Km.	Max. Depth in: Feet	Meters
Lake Eyre, Australia	3,500-0	9,000-0	—	—
Lake Titicaca, Peru-Bolivia	3,200	8,288	1,000	305
Lake Nicaragua, Nicaragua	3,100	8,029	230	70
Lake Athabasca, Canada	3,064	7,936	400	122
Reindeer Lake, Canada	2,568	6,651	—	—
Lake Turkana (Rudolf), Africa	2,463	6,379	240	73
Issyk-Kul', U.S.S.R.	2,425	6,281	2,303	702
Lake Torrens, Australia	2,230	5,776	—	—
Vänern, Sweden	2,156	5,584	328	100
Nettilling Lake, Canada	2,140	5,543	—	—
Lake Winnipegosis, Canada	2,075	5,374	38	12
Lake Mobutu Sese Seko (Albert), Africa	2,075	5,374	160	49
Kariba Lake, Zambia-Zimbabwe	2,050	5,310	295	90
Lake Nipigon, Canada	1,872	4,848	540	165
Lake Mweru, Zaire-Zambia	1,800	4,662	60	18
Lake Manitoba, Canada	1,799	4,659	12	4
Lake Taymyr, U.S.S.R.	1,737	4,499	85	26
Lake Khanka, China-U.S.S.R.	1,700	4,403	33	10
Lake Kioga, Uganda	1,700	4,403	25	8

This map has been prepared with the North Pole as the mathematical center. From it, distances to any part of the world may be measured. On Mercator's map of the world, the polar regions are so scattered that their relatively small area and availability for flight routes are disregarded. Today, with airplanes following great circle courses, often within the Arctic Circle, polar projection maps are indispensable to the people of this air-minded age.

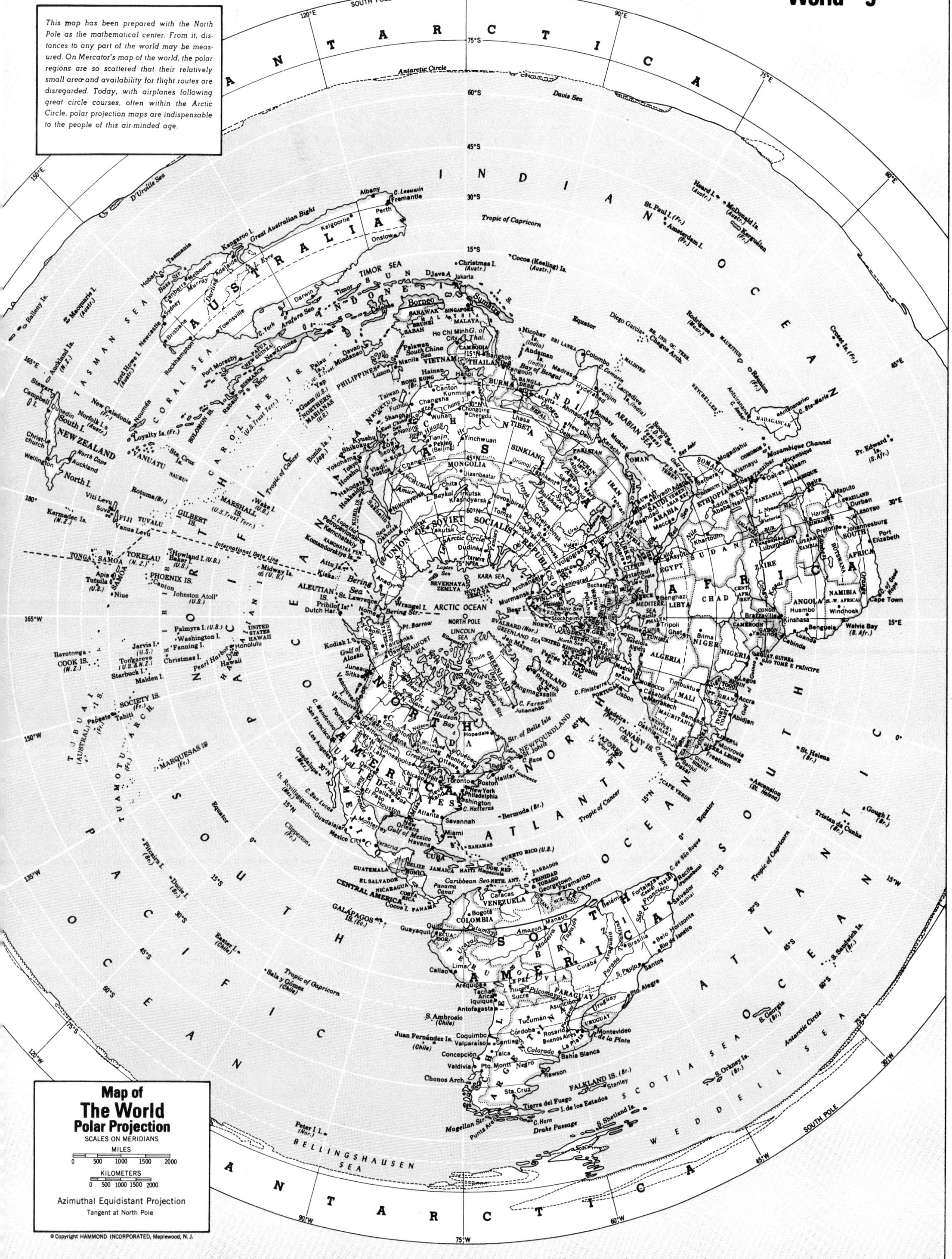
SOUTH POLE
ANTARCTICA
Antarctic Circle
Davis Sea
INDIAN OCEAN
Tropic of Capricorn
AUSTRALIA
Great Australian Bight
TASMAN SEA
CORAL SEA
TIMOR SEA
INDONESIA
NEW ZEALAND
PHILIPPINES
CHINA
MONGOLIA
UNION OF SOVIET SOCIALIST REPUBLICS
INDIA
ARABIAN SEA
Bay of Bengal
Equator
Tropic of Cancer
International Date Line
ARCTIC OCEAN
NORTH POLE
Arctic Circle
KARA SEA
Bering Sea
ALEUTIAN IS.
GREENLAND
ICELAND
EUROPE
AFRICA
SUDAN
EGYPT
LIBYA
ALGERIA
NIGER
CHAD
ZAIRE
ANGOLA
NAMIBIA
MADAGASCAR
NORTH AMERICA
CANADA
UNITED STATES
MEXICO
Gulf of Mexico
Caribbean Sea
CENTRAL AMERICA
SOUTH AMERICA
BRAZIL
ARGENTINA
CHILE
PERU
BOLIVIA
PARAGUAY
URUGUAY
VENEZUELA
COLOMBIA
NORTH PACIFIC OCEAN
SOUTH PACIFIC OCEAN
NORTH ATLANTIC OCEAN
SOUTH ATLANTIC OCEAN
SCOTIA SEA
WEDDELL SEA
BELLINGSHAUSEN SEA
Drake Passage
Cape Horn
FALKLAND IS.
HAWAII
FIJI
TONGA
SAMOA
TUBUAI (AUSTRAL)
TUAMOTU ARCH.
MARQUESAS IS.
105°E
90°E
75°E
60°E
45°E
30°E
15°E
0°
15°W
30°W
45°W
60°W
75°W
90°W
105°W
120°W
135°W
150°W
165°W
180°
165°E
150°E
120°E
75°S
60°S
45°S
30°S
15°S
15°N
30°N
45°N
60°N

Map of The World Polar Projection

SCALES ON MERIDIANS

MILES 0 500 1000 1500 2000

KILOMETERS 0 500 1000 1500 2000

Azimuthal Equidistant Projection

Tangent at North Pole

Europe
POLYCONIC PROJECTION
SCALE OF MILES
0 100 200 300 400
KILOMETERS
0 100 200 300 400
Capitals of Countries
Other Capitals
International Boundaries
Internal Boundaries
Canals
Denmark Strait
NORWEGIAN SEA
BARENTS SEA
WHITE SEA
NORTH SEA
ATLANTIC OCEAN
Bay of Biscay
English Channel
BALTIC SEA
BLACK SEA
ADRIATIC SEA
TYRRHENIAN SEA
IONIAN SEA
SEA OF AZOV
MEDITERRANEAN SEA
ICELAND
FINLAND
NORWAY
SWEDEN
UNITED KINGDOM
IRELAND
FRANCE
SPAIN
PORTUGAL
WEST GERMANY
EAST GERMANY
POLAND
CZECHOSLOVAKIA
AUSTRIA
SWITZERLAND
HUNGARY
ROMANIA
YUGOSLAVIA
BULGARIA
ITALY
GREECE
TURKEY
ALBANIA
UNION OF SOVIET SOCIALIST REPUBLICS
MOROCCO
ALGERIA
TUNISIA
AFRICA
CYPRUS
LEBANON
Longitude West of Greenwich 0° Longitude East of Greenwich

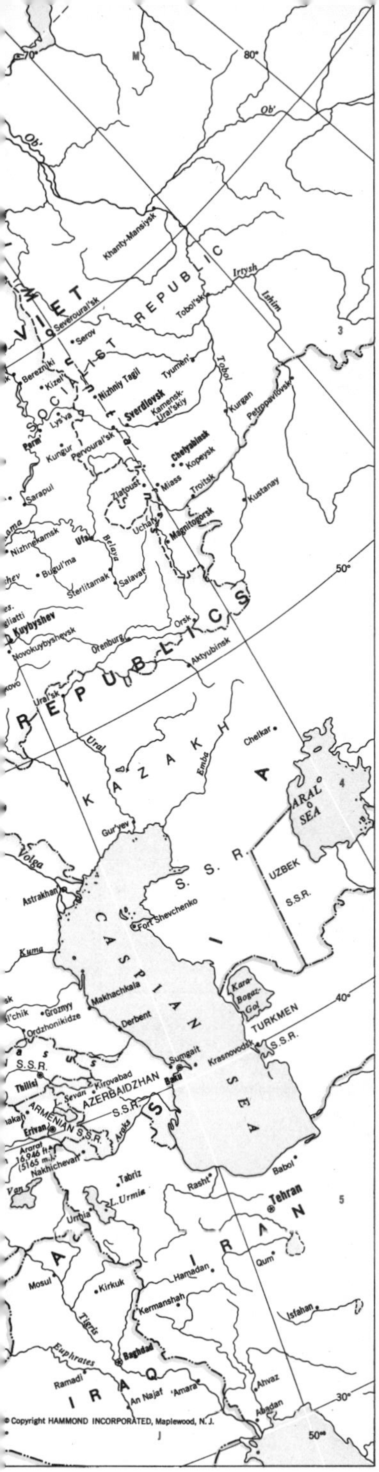

© Copyright HAMMOND INCORPORATED, Maplewood, N.J.

AREA 4,057,000 sq. mi. (10,507,630 sq. km.)
POPULATION 676,000,000
LARGEST CITY Paris
HIGHEST POINT El'brus 18,510 ft. (5,642 m.)
LOWEST POINT Caspian Sea -92 ft. (-28 m.)

Population Distribution

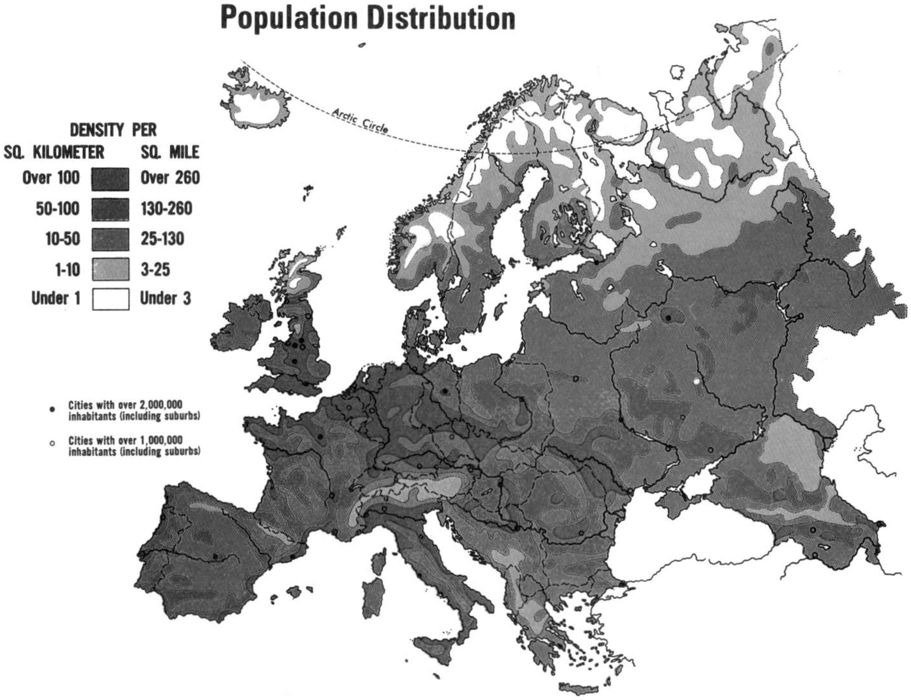

Vegetation

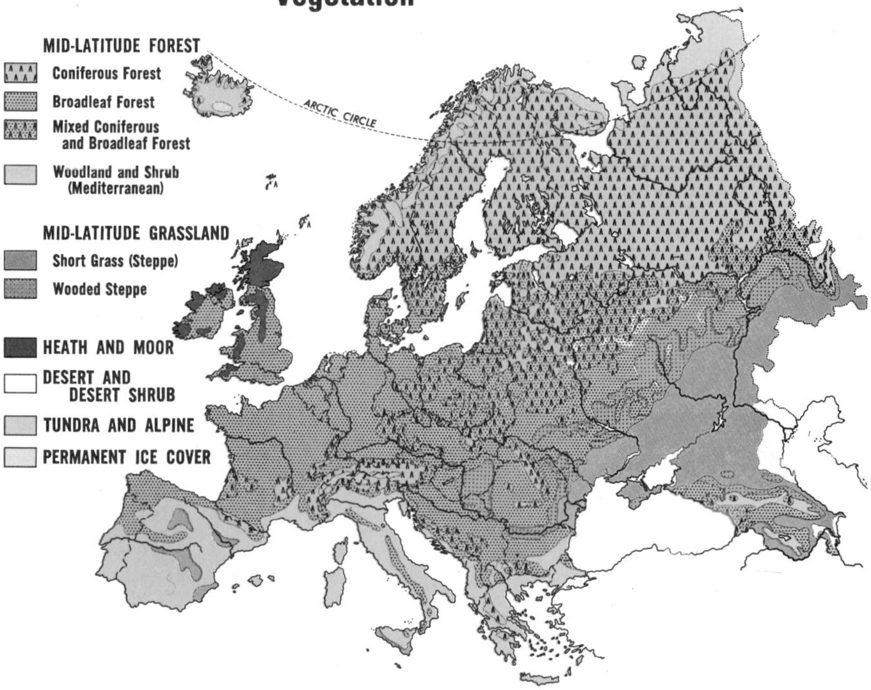

United Kingdom and Ireland
BONNE PROJECTION
SCALE OF MILES
SCALE OF KILOMETERS
Capitals of Countries
International Boundaries
Other Boundaries
Canals
Shetland Islands
Same scale as main map.
ATLANTIC OCEAN
NORTH SEA
IRISH SEA
ENGLISH CHANNEL
SCOTLAND
ENGLAND
WALES
NORTHERN IRELAND
IRELAND
FRANCE
OUTER HEBRIDES
INNER HEBRIDES
ORKNEY ISLANDS
SHETLAND ISLANDS
CHANNEL ISLANDS
GREATER LONDON
LONDON
Edinburgh
Glasgow
Dublin (Baile Átha Cliath)
Belfast
Cardiff
Aberdeen
Dundee
Inverness
Liverpool
Manchester
Birmingham
Leeds
Sheffield
Bristol
Newcastle upon Tyne
Cork
Limerick
Galway
Londonderry
Isle of Man
Isle of Wight
Bristol Channel
St. George's Channel
North Channel
Firth of Forth
Firth of Clyde
Solway Firth
The Wash
Strait of Dover
Bay of the Seine
Ben Nevis 4,406 ft. (1343 m.)
Snowdon 3,560 ft. (1085 m.)
Scafell Pike 3,210 ft. (978 m.)
Slieve Donard 2,796 ft. (852 m.)
Carrantuohill 3,415 ft. (1041 m.)
Longitude West of Greenwich

© Copyright HAMMOND INCORPORATED, Maplewood, N. J.

UNITED KINGDOM

AREA 94,399 sq. mi. (244,493 sq. km.)
POPULATION 55,672,000
CAPITAL London
LARGEST CITY London
HIGHEST POINT Ben Nevis 4,406 ft. (1,343 m.)
MONETARY UNIT pound sterling
MAJOR LANGUAGES English, Gaelic, Welsh
MAJOR RELIGIONS Protestantism, Roman Catholicism

IRELAND

AREA 27,136 sq. mi. (70,282 sq. km.)
POPULATION 3,440,427
CAPITAL Dublin
LARGEST CITY Dublin
HIGHEST POINT Carrantuohill 3,415 ft. (1,041 m.)
MONETARY UNIT Irish pound
MAJOR LANGUAGES English, Gaelic (Irish)
MAJOR RELIGION Roman Catholicism

UNITED KINGDOM

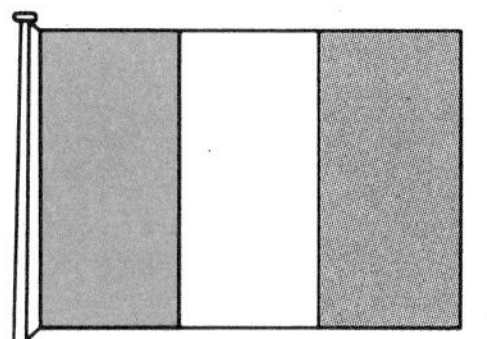

IRELAND

ENGLAND

COUNTIES

von, 920,200 . . . E 6
edfordshire, 491,700 . . . G 5
erkshire, 659,000 . . . F 6
uckinghamshire, 512,000 . . . G 6
ambridgeshire, 563,000 . . . G 5
heshire, 916,400 . . . E 4
leveland, 567,900 . . . F 3
ornwall, 405,200 . . . C 7
umbria, 473,600 . . . D 3
erbyshire, 887,600 . . . F 5
evon, 942,100 . . . D 7
orset, 575,800 . . . E 7
urham, 610,400 . . . F 3
ast Sussex, 655,600 . . . H 7
ssex, 1,426,200 . . . H 6
loucestershire, 491,500 . . . E 6
reater London, 7,028,200 . . . H 8
reater Manchester, 2,684,100 . . . H 2
ampshire, 1,456,100 . . . F 6
ereford and Worcester, 594,200 . . . E 5
ertfordshire, 937,300 . . . G 6
umberside, 848,600 . . . G 4
sle of Wight, 111,300 . . . F 7
sles of Scilly, 1,900 . . . A 7
ent, 1,448,100 . . . H 6
ancashire, 1,375,500 . . . E 4
eicestershire, 837,900 . . . F 5
ncolnshire, 524,500 . . . G 4
ondon, Greater, 7,028,200 . . . H 8
anchester, Greater, 2,684,100 . . . H 2
erseyside, 1,578,000 . . . G 2
orfolk, 662,500 . . . H 5
orthamptonshire, 505,900 . . . G 5
orthumberland, 287,300 . . . E 2
orth Yorkshire, 653,000 . . . F 3
ottinghamshire, 977,500 . . . F 4
Oxfordshire, 541,800 . . . F 6
Salop, 359,000 . . . E 5
Somerset, 404,400 . . . E 6
South Yorkshire, 1,318,300 . . . F 4
Staffordshire, 997,600 . . . E 5
Suffolk, 577,600 . . . H 5
Surrey, 1,002,900 . . . G 6
Sussex, East, 655,600 . . . H 7
Sussex, West, 623,400 . . . G 7
Tyne and Wear, 1,182,900 . . . H 3
Warwickshire, 471,000 . . . F 5
West Midlands, 2,743,300 . . . F 5
West Sussex, 623,400 . . . G 7
West Yorkshire, 2,072,500 . . . J 1
Wiltshire, 512,800 . . . E 6
Yorkshire, North, 653,000 . . . F 3
Yorkshire, South, 1,318,300 . . . F 4
Yorkshire, West, 2,072,500 . . . J 1

CITIES and TOWNS

Abingdon, 20,130 . . . F 6
Accrington, 36,470 . . . H 1
Adwick le Street, 17,650 . . . K 2
Aldeburgh, 2,750 . . . J 5
Aldershot, 33,750 . . . G 8
Aldridge Brownhills, 89,370 . . . E 5
Alfreton, 21,560 . . . F 4
Alnwick, 7,300 . . . F 2
Altrincham, 40,800 . . . H 2
Amersham, ⊙17,254 . . . G 7
Andover, 27,620 . . . F 6
Appleby, 2,240 . . . E 3
Arnold, 35,090 . . . F 4
Arundel, 2,390 . . . G 7
Ashford, 36,380 . . . H 6
Ashington, 24,720 . . . F 2
Ashton-under-Lyne, 48,500 . . . H 2
Axminster, ⊙4,515 . . . D 7
Aycliffe, ⊙20,203 . . . F 3
Aylesbury, 41,420 . . . G 7
Bacup, 14,990 . . . H 1
Bakewell, 4,100 . . . J 2
Banbury, 31,060 . . . F 5
Banstead, 44,100 . . . H 8
Barking, 153,800 . . . H 8
Barnet, 305,200 . . . H 7
Barnsley, 74,730 . . . J 2
Barnstaple, 17,820 . . . D 6
Barrow-in-Furness, 73,400 . . . D 3
Barton-upon-Humber, 7,750 . . . G 4
Basildon, 135,720 . . . J 8
Basingstoke, 60,910 . . . F 6
Bath, 83,100 . . . E 6
Batley, 41,630 . . . J 1
Battle, ⊙4,987 . . . H 7
Bebington, 62,500 . . . G 2
Bedford, 74,390 . . . G 5
Bedlington, 27,200 . . . F 2
Bedworth, 41,600 . . . F 5
Beeston and Stapleford, 65,360 . . . F 5
Benfleet, 49,180 . . . J 8
Bentley with Arksey, 22,320 . . . F 4
Berkhamsted, 15,920 . . . G 7
Beverley, 16,920 . . . G 4
Bexhill, 34,680 . . . H 7
Bexley, 213,500 . . . H 8
Biddulph, 18,720 . . . H 2
Birkenhead, 135,750 . . . G 2
Birmingham, 1,058,800 . . . F 5
Bishop Auckland, 32,940 . . . E 3
Bishop's Stortford, 21,720 . . . H 6
Blackburn, 101,670 . . . H 1
Blackpool, 149,000 . . . G 1
Blaydon, 31,940 . . . H 3
Blyth, 35,390 . . . F 2
Bodmin, 10,430 . . . C 7
Bognor Regis, 34,620 . . . G 7
Boldon, 24,430 . . . J 3
Bolton, 154,480 . . . H 2
Bootle, 71,160 . . . G 2
Boston, 26,700 . . . G 5
Bournemouth, 144,100 . . . F 7
Bracknell, ⊙34,067 . . . G 8
Bradford, 458,900 . . . J 1
Braintree and Bocking, 26,300 . . . H 6
Brent, 256,500 . . . H 8
Brentwood, 58,690 . . . J 8
Bridgwater, 26,700 . . . E 6
Bridlington, 26,920 . . . G 3
Bridport, 6,660 . . . E 7
Brigg, 4,870 . . . G 4
Brighowe, 35,320 . . . J 1
Brightlingsea, 7,170 . . . J 6
Brighton, 156,500 . . . G 7
Bristol, 416,300 . . . E 6
Broadstairs and Saint Peter's, 21,670 . . . J 6
Bromley, 299,100 . . . H 8
Bromsgrove, 41,430 . . . E 5
Buckfastleigh, 2,870 . . . C 7
Buckingham, 5,290 . . . G 6
Bude-Stratton, 5,750 . . . C 7
Bungay, 4,120 . . . J 5
Burgess Hill, 20,030 . . . G 7
Burnham-on-Crouch, 4,920 . . . H 6
Burnley, 74,300 . . . H 1
Burntwood, ⊙23,088 . . . F 5
Burton upon Trent, 49,480 . . . F 5
Bury, 69,550 . . . H 2
Bury Saint Edmunds, 26,800 . . . H 5
Bushey, 24,500 . . . H 7
Buxton, 20,050 . . . J 2
Caister-on-Sea, ⊙6,287 . . . J 5
Camborne-Redruth, 43,970 . . . B 7
Cambridge, 106,400 . . . G 5
Camden, 185,800 . . . H 8
Cannock, 56,440 . . . E 5
Canterbury, 115,600 . . . H 6
Canvey Island, 29,550 . . . J 8
Carlisle, 99,600 . . . D 3
Carlton, 46,690 . . . F 5
Caterham and Warlingham, 35,840 . H 8
Chatham, 59,550 . . . J 8
Cheadle and Gatley, 62,460 . . . H 2
Chelmsford, 58,320 . . . J 7
Cheltenham, 75,910 . . . E 6
Chertsey, 45,070 . . . G 8
Chesham, 20,830 . . . G 7
Cheshunt, 45,750 . . . H 7
Chester, 117,200 . . . G 2
Chesterfield, 69,480 . . . J 2
Chester-le-Street, 20,720 . . . J 3
Chichester, 20,940 . . . G 7
Chigwell, 54,220 . . . H 8
Chippenham, 18,550 . . . E 6
Chorley, 31,800 . . . G 2
Christchurch, 31,610 . . . F 7
Cirencester, 14,500 . . . E 6
Clacton, 39,380 . . . J 6
Clay Cross, 9,630 . . . J 2
Cleator Moor, ⊙7,686 . . . D 3
Cleethorpes, 37,200 . . . H 4
Clevedon, 15,140 . . . D 6
Clun, ⊙1,261 . . . D 6
Coalville, 28,740 . . . F 5
Cockermouth, 6,480 . . . D 3
Colchester, 79,600 . . . H 6
Colne, 19,030 . . . H 1
Colne Valley, 21,190 . . . J 2
Congleton, 21,500 . . . H 2
Consett, 35,080 . . . H 3
Corby, 48,850 . . . G 5
Coventry, 336,800 . . . F 5
Cowes, 19,190 . . . F 7
Crawley, 72,600 . . . G 6
Crewe and Nantwich, 98,100 . . . E 4
Cromer, 5,720 . . . J 5
Crook and Willington, 21,120 . . . E 3
Crosby, 56,750 . . . G 2
Croydon, 330,600 . . . H 8
Cuckfield, 26,500 . . . G 6
Darlington, 85,120 . . . F 3
Dartford, 44,130 . . . J 8
Darton, 15,710 . . . J 2
Darwen, 29,290 . . . H 1
Deal, 26,840 . . . J 6
Dearne, 24,780 . . . K 2
Denton, 38,110 . . . H 2
Derby, 213,700 . . . F 5
Dewsbury, 50,560 . . . J 1
Didcot, ⊙14,277 . . . F 6
Doncaster, 81,530 . . . F 4
Dorking, 22,410 . . . G 8
Dover, 34,160 . . . J 6
Downham Market, 4,120 . . . H 5
Droitwich, 13,950 . . . E 5
Dronfield, 20,000 . . . J 2
Dudley, 187,110 . . . E 5
Dunstable, 32,090 . . . G 6
Durham, 88,800 . . . J 3
Ealing, 293,800 . . . H 8
Eastbourne, 73,200 . . . H 7
East Grinstead, 19,420 . . . G 6
Eastleigh, 46,340 . . . F 7
East Retford, 18,260 . . . G 4
Egham, 30,320 . . . G 8
Egremont, ⊙7,253 . . . D 3
Eling, ⊙20,006 . . . F 7
Ellesmere, ⊙2,630 . . . E 5
Ellesmere Port, 63,870 . . . G 2
Enfield, 260,900 . . . H 7
Epsom and Ewell, 70,700 . . . G 8
Esher, 63,970 . . . H 8
Eston, ⊙46,219 . . . F 3
Eton, 4,950 . . . G 8
Evesham, 14,090 . . . F 5
Exeter, 93,300 . . . D 7
Exminster, ⊙3,181 . . . D 7
Exmouth, 26,840 . . . D 7
Falmouth, 17,530 . . . B 7
Fareham, 86,300 . . . F 7
Farnborough, 43,520 . . . G 8
Farnham, 33,140 . . . G 8
Farnworth, 26,110 . . . H 2
Faversham, 15,010 . . . H 6
Felixstowe, 19,460 . . . J 6
Felling, 38,990 . . . J 3
Filey, 5,660 . . . G 3
Fleet, 22,930 . . . G 8
Fleetwood, 30,070 . . . D 4
Folkestone, 45,610 . . . J 6
Formby, 24,850 . . . G 2
Framlingham, ⊙2,258 . . . J 5
Frimley and Camberley, 47,390 . . . G 8
Fulwood, 22,910 . . . G 1
Gainsborough, 17,440 . . . G 4
Gateshead, 91,230 . . . J 3
Gillingham, Dorset, ⊙4,050 . . . E 6
Gillingham, Kent, 93,900 . . . J 8
Glastonbury, 6,580 . . . E 6
Glossop, 24,820 . . . J 2
Gloucester, 91,600 . . . E 6
Godalming, 18,840 . . . G 8
Golborne, 28,720 . . . G 2
Goole, 17,920 . . . G 4
Gosport, 82,300 . . . F 7
Grange, 3,520 . . . E 3
Grantham, 27,830 . . . G 5
Gravesend, 53,500 . . . J 8
Great Baddow, ⊙18,755 . . . J 7
Great Torrington, 3,430 . . . C 7
Great Yarmouth, 49,410 . . . J 5
Greenwich, 207,200 . . . H 8
Grimsby, 93,800 . . . G 4
Guildford, 58,470 . . . G 8
Guisborough, 14,860 . . . F 3
Hackney, 192,500 . . . H 8
Hale, 17,080 . . . H 2
Halesowen, 54,120 . . . E 5
Halifax, 88,580 . . . J 1
Haltemprice, 54,850 . . . G 4
Haltwhistle, ⊙3,511 . . . E 2
Hammersmith, 170,000 . . . H 8
Haringey, 228,200 . . . H 8
Harlow, 79,160 . . . H 7
Harrogate, 64,620 . . . J 1
Harrow, 200,200 . . . G 8
Hartlepool, 97,100 . . . F 3
Harwich, 15,280 . . . J 6
Haslingden, 15,140 . . . H 1
Hastings, 74,600 . . . H 7
Hatfield, ⊙25,359 . . . H 7
Havant and Waterloo, 112,430 . . . G 7
Haverhill, 14,550 . . . H 5
Havering, 239,200 . . . J 8
Hayle, ⊙5,378 . . . B 7
Hazel Grove and Bramhall, 40,400 . . . H 2
Heanor, 24,590 . . . F 4
Hebburn, 23,150 . . . J 3
Hedon, 3,010 . . . G 4
Hemel Hempstead, 71,150 . . . G 7
Hereford, 47,800 . . . E 5
Hertford, 20,760 . . . H 7
Hetton, 16,810 . . . J 3
Hexham, 9,820 . . . E 3
Heywood, 31,720 . . . H 2
High Wycombe, 61,190 . . . G 8
Hillingdon, 230,800 . . . G 8
Hinckley, 49,310 . . . F 5
Hinderwell, ⊙2,551 . . . G 3
Hitchin, 29,190 . . . G 6
Hoddesdon, 27,510 . . . H 7
Holmfirth, 19,790 . . . J 2
Horley, ⊙18,593 . . . H 8
Hornsea, 7,280 . . . G 4
Horsham, 26,770 . . . G 6
Horwich, 16,670 . . . G 2
Houghton-le-Spring, 33,150 . . . J 3
Hounslow, 199,100 . . . G 8
Hove, 72,000 . . . G 7
Hoylake, 32,000 . . . G 2
Hoyland Nether, 15,500 . . . J 2
Hucknall, 27,110 . . . F 4
Huddersfield, 130,060 . . . J 2
Hugh Town, ⊙1,958 . . . A 8
Hull, 276,600 . . . G 4
Hunstanton, 4,140 . . . H 5
Huntingdon and Godmanchester, 17,200 . . . G 5
Huyton-with-Roby, 65,950 . . . G 2
Hyde, 37,040 . . . H 2
Ilfracombe, 9,350 . . . C 6
Ilkeston, 33,690 . . . F 5
Immingham, ⊙10,259 . . . G 4
Ipswich, 121,500 . . . J 5
Islington, 171,600 . . . H 8
Jarrow, 28,510 . . . J 3
Kendal, 22,440 . . . E 3
Kenilworth, 19,730 . . . F 5
Kensington and Chelsea, 161,400 . . G 8
Keswick, 4,790 . . . D 3
Kettering, 44,480 . . . G 5
Keynsham, 18,970 . . . E 6
Kidderminster, 49,960 . . . E 5
Kidsgrove, 22,690 . . . E 4
King's Lynn, 29,990 . . . H 5
Kingston upon Thames, 135,600 . . H 8
Kingswood, 30,450 . . . E 6
Kirkburton, 20,320 . . . J 2
Kirkby, 59,100 . . . G 2
Kirkby Lonsdale, ⊙1,506 . . . E 3
Kirkby Stephen, ⊙1,539 . . . E 3
Knutsford, 14,840 . . . H 2
Lambeth, 290,300 . . . H 8
Lancaster, 126,300 . . . E 3
Leatherhead, 40,830 . . . G 8
Leeds, 744,500 . . . J 1
Leek, 19,460 . . . H 2
Leicester, 289,400 . . . F 5
Leigh, 46,390 . . . H 2
Leighton-Linslade, 22,590 . . . F 7
Letchworth, 31,520 . . . G 6
Lewes, 14,170 . . . H 7
Lewisham, 237,300 . . . H 8
Leyland, 23,690 . . . G 1
Lichfield, 23,690 . . . F 5
Lincoln, 73,700 . . . G 4
Liskeard, 5,360 . . . C 7
Litherland, 23,530 . . . G 2
Littlehampton, 20,320 . . . G 7

(continued on following page)

ENGLAND

AREA 50,516 sq. mi. (130,836 sq. km.)
POPULATION 46,220,955
CAPITAL London
LARGEST CITY London
HIGHEST POINT Scafell Pike 3,210 ft. (978 m.)

WALES

AREA 8,017 sq. mi. (20,764 sq. km.)
POPULATION 2,790,462
LARGEST CITY Cardiff
HIGHEST POINT Snowdon 3,560 ft. (1,085 m.)

SCOTLAND

AREA 30,414 sq. mi. (78,772 sq. km.)
POPULATION 5,117,146
CAPITAL Edinburgh
LARGEST CITY Glasgow
HIGHEST POINT Ben Nevis 4,406 ft. (1,343 m.)

NORTHERN IRELAND

AREA 5,452 sq. mi. (14,121 sq. km.)
POPULATION 1,543,000
CAPITAL Belfast
LARGEST CITY Belfast
HIGHEST POINT Slieve Donard 2,796 ft. (852 m.)

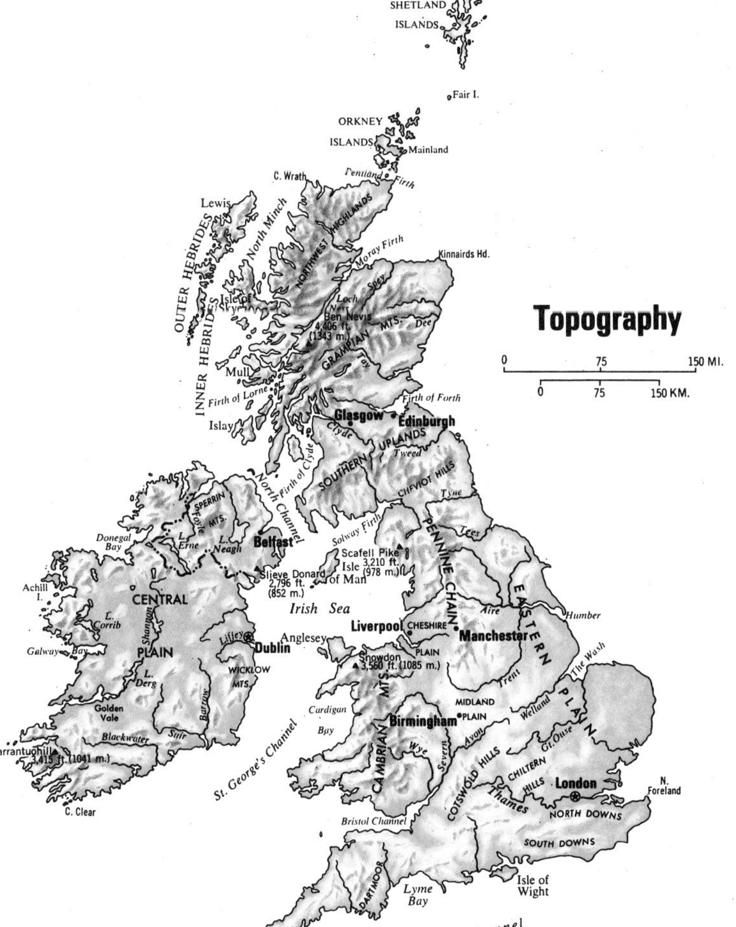

(continued)

Liverpool, 539,700 G 2
Loftus, 7,850 G 3
London (cap.), 7,028,200 H 8
London, ★12,332,900 H 8
Long Eaton, 33,560 F 5
Longbenton, 50,120 J 3
Looe, 4,060 C 7
Loughborough, 49,010 F 5
Lowestoft, 53,260 J 5
Ludlow, ⊙7,466 E 5
Luton, 164,500 G 6
Lydd, 4,670 H 7
Lyme Regis, 3,460 E 7
Lymington, 36,780 F 7
Lynton, 1,770 D 6
Lytham Saint Anne's, 42,120 G 1
Mablethorpe and Sutton, 6,750 H 4
Macclesfield, 45,420 H 2
Maidenhead, 48,210 G 8
Maidstone, 72,110 J 8
Maldon, 14,350 H 6
Malmesbury, 2,550 E 6
Malton, 4,010 G 3
Malvern, 30,420 E 5
Manchester, 490,000 H 2
Mangotsfield, 23,000 E 6
Mansfield, 58,450 K 2
Mansfield Woodhouse, 25,400 F 4
March, 14,560 H 5
Margate, 50,290 J 6
Market Harborough, 15,230 G 5
Marlborough, 6,370 F 6
Matlock, 20,300 J 2
Melton Mowbray, 20,680 G 5
Merton, 169,400 H 8
Middlesbrough, 153,900 F 3
Middleton, 53,340 H 2
Middlewich, 7,600 H 2
Mildenhall, ⊙9,269 H 5
Millom, ⊙7,101 D 3
Milton Keynes, 89,900 F 5
Minehead, 8,230 D 6
Moretonhampstead, ⊙1,440 C 7
Morpeth, 14,450 F 2
Mundesley, ⊙1,536 J 5
Nelson, 31,220 H 1
Neston, 18,210 G 2
Newark, 24,760 G 4
Newbury, 24,850 F 6
Newcastle upon Tyne, 295,800 H 3
Newcastle-under-Lyme, 75,940 E 4
Newham, 228,900 H 8
Newhaven, 9,970 H 7
Newport, 22,430 F 7
New Romney, 3,830 J 7
Newton Abbot, 19,940 D 7
Newton-le-Willows, 21,780 H 2
New Windsor, 29,660 G 8
Northallerton F 3
Northam, 8,310 C 6
Northampton, 128,290 F 5
Northfleet, 27,150 J 8
North Sunderland, ⊙1,725 F 2
Northwich, 17,710 H 2
Norton, 5,580 G 3
Norton-Radstock, 15,900 E 6
Norwich, 119,200 J 5
Nottingham, 280,300 F 5
Nuneaton, 69,210 F 5
Oadby, 20,700 F 5
Oakham, 7,280 G 5
Okehampton, 4,000 D 7
Oldham, 103,690 H 2
Ormskirk, 28,860 G 2
Oswaldtwistle, 14,270 H 1
Oxford, 117,400 F 6
Padstow, ⊙2,802 B 7
Penryn, 5,660 B 7
Penzance, 19,360 B 7
Peterborough, 118,900 G 5
Peterlee, ⊙21,846 J 3
Plymouth, 259,100 C 7
Polperro, ⊙1,491 C 7
Poole, 110,600 E 7
Porlock, ⊙1,290 D 6
Portishead, 9,680 E 6
Portland, 14,860 E 7
Portslade-by-Sea, 18,040 G 7
Portsmouth, 198,500 F 7
Potters Bar, 24,670 H 7
Poulton-le-Fylde, 16,340 G 1
Preston, 94,760 G 1
Prestwich, 32,850 H 2
Queenborough, 31,550 H 6
Radcliffe, 29,630 H 2
Ramsbottom, 16,710 H 2
Ramsgate, 40,090 J 6
Rawtenstall, 20,950 H 1
Rayleigh, 26,740 J 8
Reading, 131,200 G 8
Redbridge, 231,600 H 8
Redcar, ⊙46,325 F 3
Redditch, 44,750 E 5
Reigate, 55,600 H 8
Richmond upon Thames, 166,800 H 8
Rickmansworth, 29,030 G 8
Ripley, 18,060 F 4
Rochdale, 93,780 H 2
Rochester, 56,030 J 8
Rothbury, ⊙1,818 E 2
Rotherham, 84,770 K 2
Royal Leamington Spa, 44,950 F 5
Royal Tunbridge Wells, 44,800 H 6
Rugby, 60,380 F 5
Rugeley, 24,440 E 5
Runcorn, 42,730 G 2
Rushden, 21,840 G 5
Ryde, 23,170 F 7
Rye, 4,530 H 7
Ryton, 15,170 H 3
Saddleworth, 21,340 J 2
Saint Agnes, ⊙4,747 B 7
Saint Albans, 123,800 H 7
Saint Austell-with-Fowey, 32,710 C 7
Saint Columb Major, ⊙3,953 B 7
Saint Helens, 104,890 G 2
Saint Ives, Cornwall, 9,760 B 7
Saint Neots, 17,940 G 5
Salcombe, 2,370 D 7
Sale, 59,060 H 2
Salford, 261,100 H 2
Salisbury, 35,460 F 6
Saltburn and Marske-by-the-Sea, 21,170 G 3
Sandbach, 14,280 H 2
Sandown-Shanklin, 14,800 F 7
Sandwich, 4,420 J 6
Saxmundham, 1,820 J 5
Scarborough, 43,300 G 3
Scunthorpe, 68,100 G 4
Seaford, 18,020 H 7
Seaham, 22,470 J 3
Seascale, ⊙2,106 D 3
Seaton, 4,500 D 7
Seaton Valley, 35,880 J 3
Sedbergh, ⊙2,741 E 3
Selsey, ⊙6,491 G 7
Sevenoaks, 18,160 J 8
Shaftesbury, 4,180 E 7
Sheffield, 558,000 J 2
Sherborne, 9,230 E 7
Sheringham, 4,940 J 5
Shildon, 15,360 F 3
Shoreham-by-Sea, 19,620 G 7
Shrewsbury, 56,120 E 5
Silloth, ⊙2,662 D 3
Sittingbourne and Milton, 32,830 H 6
Skelmersdale, 35,850 G 2
Skelton and Brotton, 15,930 G 3
Sleaford, 8,050 G 5
Slough, 89,060 G 8
Solihull, 108,230 F 5
Southampton, 213,700 F 7
Southend-on-Sea, 159,300 H 6
Southport, 86,030 G 1
South Shields, 96,900 J 3
Southwark, 224,900 H 8
Southwold, 1,960 J 5
Sowerby Bridge, 15,700 H 1
Spalding, 17,040 G 5
Spenborough, 41,460 J 1
Spennymoor, 19,050 F 3
Stafford, 54,860 E 5
Staines, 56,380 G 8
Stamford, 14,980 G 5
Stanley, 42,280 H 3
Staveley, 17,620 K 2
Stevenage, 72,600 G 6
Stockport, 138,350 H 2
Stockton-on-Tees, 165,400 F 3
Stoke-on-Trent, 256,200 E 4
Stourbridge, 56,530 E 5
Stourport-on-Severn, 19,430 E 5
Stowmarket, 9,020 J 5
Stratford-upon-Avon, 20,080 F 5
Stretford, 52,450 H 2
Stroud, 19,600 E 6
Sudbury, 8,860 H 5
Sunbury-on-Thames, 40,070 G 8
Sunderland, 214,820 J 3
Sutton, 166,700 H 8
Sutton Bridge, ⊙3,113 H 5
Sutton in Ashfield, 40,330 K 2
Swadlincote, 21,060 F 5
Swanage, 8,000 E 7
Swindon, 90,680 F 6
Tamworth, 46,960 F 5
Taunton, 37,570 D 6
Tavistock, ⊙7,620 C 7
Telford, ⊙79,451 E 5
Tenbury, ⊙2,151 E 5
Tewkesbury, 9,210 E 6
Thetford, 15,690 H 5
Thirsk, ⊙2,884 F 3
Thornaby-on-Tees, ⊙42,385 F 3
Thorne, ⊙16,694 F 4
Thornton Cleveleys, 27,090 G 1
Thurrock, 127,700 J 8
Tiverton, 16,190 D 7
Todmorden, 14,540 H 1
Tonbridge, 31,410 H 8
Torbay, 109,900 D 7
Torpoint, 6,840 C 7
Tower Hamlets, 146,100 H 8
Tow Law, 2,460 H 4
Trowbridge, 20,120 E 6
Truro, 15,690 B 7
Turton, 22,800 H 2
Tynemouth, 67,090 J 3
Upton upon Severn, ⊙2,048 E 5
Urmston, 44,130 H 2
Uttoxeter, 9,100 E 5
Ventnor, 6,980 F 7
Wainfleet All Saints, ⊙1,116 H 4
Wakefield, 306,500 J 2
Wallasey, 94,520 G 2
Wallsend, 45,490 J 3
Walsall, 182,430 E 5
Waltham Forest, 223,700 H 8
Waltham Holy Cross, 14,810 H 7
Walton and Weybridge, 51,270 G 8
Walton-le-Dale, 27,660 G 1
Wandsworth, 284,600 H 8
Wantage, 8,490 F 6
Ware, 14,900 H 7
Wareham, 4,630 E 7
Warley, 161,260 E 5
Warminster, 14,440 E 6
Warrington, 65,320 G 2
Warwick, 17,870 F 5
Washington, 27,720 J 3
Watchet, 2,980 D 6
Watford, 77,000 H 7
Wellingborough, 39,570 G 5
Wells, 8,960 E 6
Wells-next-the-Sea, 2,450 H 5
Welwyn, 39,900 H 7
Wem, ⊙3,411 E 5
West Bridgford, 28,340 F 5
West Bromwich, 162,740 F 5
West Mersea, 4,730 H 6
Westminster, 216,100 H 8
Weston-super-Mare, 51,960 D 6
Weymouth and Melcombe Regis, 41,080 E 7
Whickham, 29,710 J 3
Whitchurch, ⊙7,142 E 5
Whitehaven, 26,260 D 3
Whitley Bay, 37,010 J 3
Widnes, 58,330 G 2
Wigan, 80,920 G 2
Wigston, 31,650 F 5
Wilmslow, 31,250 H 2
Wilton, 4,090 F 6
Winchester, 88,900 F 6
Windermere, 7,860 E 3
Winsford, 26,920 G 2
Wirral, 27,510 G 2
Wisbech, 16,990 H 5
Witham, 19,730 H 6
Withernsea, 6,300 H 4
Wivenhoe, 5,630 J 6
Woking, 79,300 G 8
Wokingham, 22,390 G 8
Wolverhampton, 266,400 E 5
Wombwell, 17,850 K 2
Woodhall Spa, 2,420 G 4
Woodley and Sandford, ⊙24,581 G 8
Woodstock, 2,070 F 6
Wooler, ⊙1,833 F 2
Worcester, 73,900 E 5
Workington, 28,260 D 3
Worksop, 36,590 F 4
Worsbrough, 15,180 J 2
Worsley, 49,530 H 2
Worthing, 89,100 G 7
Wymondham, 9,390 J 5
Yateley, ⊙16,505 G 8
Yeovil, 26,180 E 7
York, 101,900 F 4

OTHER FEATURES

Aire (riv.) F 4
Atlantic Ocean A 7
Avon (riv.) F 5
Avon (riv.) F 7
Axe Edge (mt.) H 2
Barnstaple (bay) C 6
Beachy (head) H 7
Bigbury (bay) C 7
Blackwater (riv.) H 6
Bristol (chan.) C 6
Brown Willy (mt.) C 7
Cheviot (hills) E 2
Cheviot, The (mt.) E 2
Chiltern (hills) G 6
Cleveland (hills) F 3
Colne (riv.) G 8
Cornwall (cape) B 7
Cotswold (hills) E 6
Cross Fell (mt.) E 3
Cumbrian (mts.) D 3
Dart (riv.) D 7
Dartmoor National Park C 7
Dee (riv.) D 4
Derwent (riv.) G 3
Derwent (riv.) H 3
Don (riv.) F 4
Dorset Heights (hills) E 7
Dove (riv.) J 2
Dover (str.) J 7
Dungeness (prom.) J 7
Dunkery (hill) D 6
Eddystone (rocks) C 7
Eden (riv.) E 3
English (chan.) D 8
Esk (riv.) D 2
Exe (riv.) D 7
Exmoor National Park D 6
Fens, The (reg.) G 5
Flamborough (head) G 3
Formby (head) G 2
Foulness Island (pen.) J 6
Gibraltar (pt.) H 4
Great Ouse (riv.) H 5
Hartland (pt.) C 6
High Willhays (mt.) C 7
Hodder (riv.) H 1
Holderness (pen.), 43,900 G 4
Holy (isl.), 189 F 2
Humber (riv.) G 4
Irish (sea) B 4
Kennet (riv.) F 6
Lake District National Park D 3
Land's End (prom.) B 7
Lea (riv.) G 6
Lincoln Wolds (hills) G 4
Lindisfarne (Holy) (isl.), 189 F 2
Liverpool (bay) D 4
Lizard, The (pen.), 7,371 B 8
Lundy (isl.), 49 C 6
Lune (riv.) E 3
Lyme (bay) D 7
Manacle (pt.) C 7
Medway (riv.) H 6
Mendip (hills) E 6
Mersea (isl.), 4,423 J 6
Mersey (riv.) G 2
Morecambe (bay) D 3
Mounts (bay) B 7
Naze, The (prom.) J 6
Nene (riv.) H 5
New (for.) F 6
North (sea) J 4
North Downs (hills) G 6
North Foreland (prom.) J 6
Northumberland National Park E 2
North York Moors National Park G 3
Orford Ness (prom.) J 5
Ouse (riv.) G 4
Ouse (riv.) G 6
Parrett (riv.) E 6
Peak District National Park F 4
Peak, The (mt.) J 2
Peel Fell (mt.) E 2
Pennine Chain (range) E 3
Plymouth (sound) C 7
Portland, Bill of (pt.) E 7
Prawle (pt.) D 7
Purbeck, Isle of (pen.), 39,500 F 7
Ribble (riv.) E 4
Saint Alban's (head) F 7
Saint Bees (head) D 3
Saint Martin's (isl.), 106 A 8
Saint Mary's (isl.), 1,958 A 8
Scafell Pike (mt.) D 3
Scilly (isls.), 1,900 A 7
Selsey Bill (prom.) G 7
Severn (riv.) E 6
Sheppey (isl.), 31,550 J 6
Sherwood (for.) F 4
Skiddaw (mt.) D 3
Solent (chan.) F 7
Solway (firth) D 3
South Downs (hills) G 7
Spithead (chan.) F 7
Spurn (head) H 4
Stonehenge (ruins) F 6
Stour (riv.) E 7
Stour (riv.) H 6
Stour (riv.) J 6
Swale (riv.) F 3
Tamar (riv.) C 7
Taw (riv.) D 7
Tees (riv.) F 3
Test (riv.) F 6
Thames (riv.) H 6
Tintagel (head) C 7
Torridge (riv.) C 7
Trent (riv.) G 4
Tresco (isl.), 246 A 8
Tweed (riv.) E 2
Tyne (riv.) F 3
Ure (riv.) F 3
Ver (riv.) H 7
Walney, Isle of (isl.), 11,241 D 3
Wash, The (bay) H 5
Weald, The (reg.) H 6
Wear (riv.) F 3
Weaver (riv.) G 2
Welland (riv.) G 5
Wey (riv.) G 6
Wharfe (riv.) E 3
Wirral (pen.), 432,900 G 2
Witham (riv.) G 4
Wolds, The (hills) G 4
Wye (riv.) D 5
Wyre (riv.) G 1
Yare (riv.) J 5
Yorkshire Dales National Park E 3

CHANNEL ISLANDS

CITIES and TOWNS

Saint Anne E 8
Saint Helier (cap.), Jersey, ⊙28,135 E 8
Saint Peter Port (cap.), Guernsey, ⊙16,303 E 8
Saint Sampson's, ⊙6,534 E 8

OTHER FEATURES

Alderney (isl.), 1,686 E 8
Guernsey (isl.), 51,351 E 8
Herm (isl.), 96 E 8
Jersey (isl.), 72,629 E 8
Sark (isl.), 590 E 8

ISLE of MAN

CITIES and TOWNS

Castletown, 2,820 C 3
Douglas (cap.), 20,389 C 3
Laxey, 1,170 C 3
Michael, 408 C 3
Onchan, 4,807 C 3
Peel, 3,081 C 3
Port Erin, 1,714 C 3
Port Saint Mary, 1,508 C 3
Ramsey, 5,048 C 3

OTHER FEATURES

Ayre (pt.) C 3
Calf of Man (isl.) C 3
Langness (prom.) C 3
Snaefell (mt.) C 3
Spanish (head) C 3

WALES

COUNTIES

Clwyd, 376,000 D 4
Dyfed, 323,100 C 6
Gwent, 439,600 D 6
Gwynedd, 225,100 C 4
Mid Glamorgan, 540,400 D 6
Powys, 101,500 D 5
South Glamorgan, 389,200 A 7
West Glamorgan, 371,900 D 6

CITIES and TOWNS

Aberaeron, 1,340 C 5
Abercarn, 18,370 B 6
Aberdare, 38,030 A 6
Abertillery, 20,550 B 6
Amlwch, 3,630 C 4
Bala, 1,650 D 5
Bangor, 16,030 C 4
Barmouth, 2,070 C 5
Barry, 42,780 B 7
Beaumaris, 2,090 C 4
Bedwellty, 25,460 B 6
Bethesda, 4,180 D 4
Betws-y-Coed, 720 D 4
Brecknock (Brecon), 6,460 D 6
Brecon, 6,460 D 6
Bridgend, 14,690 A 7
Brynmawr, 5,970 B 6
Builth Wells, 1,480 D 5
Burry Port, 5,990 C 6
Caernarfon, 8,840 C 4
Caerphilly, 42,190 B 6
Cardiff, 281,500 B 7
Cardigan, 3,830 C 5
Chepstow, 8,260 E 6
Chirk, ⊙3,564 D 5
Colwyn Bay, 25,370 D 4
Criccieth, 1,590 C 5
Cwmamman, 3,950 D 6
Cwmbran, 32,980 B 6
Denbigh, 8,420 D 4
Dolgellau, 2,430 D 5
Ebbw Vale, 25,670 B 6
Ffestiniog, 5,510 D 5
Fishguard and Goodwick, 5,020 B 5
Flint, 15,070 G 2
Gelligaer, 33,820 A 6
Harlech, ⊙332 C 5
Haverfordwest, 8,930 B 6
Hawarden, ⊙20,389 G 2
Hay, 1,200 D 5
Holywell, 8,570 G 2
Kidwelly, 3,090 C 6
Knighton, 2,190 D 5
Llandeilo, 1,780 C 6
Llandovery, 2,040 D 5
Llandrindod Wells, 3,460 D 5
Llandudno, 17,700 D 4
Llanelli, 25,870 C 6
Llanfairfechan, 3,800 D 4
Llangefni, 4,070 C 4
Llangollen, 3,050 D 5
Llanguicke, ⊙15,029 D 6
Llanidloes, 2,390 D 5
Llantrisant, ⊙27,490 A 7
Llanwrtyd Wells, 460 D 5
Llwchwr, 27,530 D 6
Machynlleth, 1,830 D 5
Maesteg, 21,100 D 6
Menai Bridge, 2,730 C 4
Merthyr Tydfil, 61,500 A 6
Milford Haven, 13,960 B 6
Mold, 8,700 G 2
Montgomery, 1,000 D 5
Mountain Ash, 27,710 A 6
Mynyddislwyn, 15,590 B 6
Narberth, 970 C 6
Neath, 27,280 D 6
Nefyn, ⊙2,086 C 5
Newcastle Emlyn, 690 C 5
Newport, Dyfed, ⊙1,062 C 5
Newport, Gwent, 110,090 B 6
New Quay, 760 C 5
Newtown, 6,400 D 5
Neyland, 2,690 B 6
Ogmore and Garw, 19,680 A 6
Pembroke, 14,570 C 6
Penarth, 24,180 B 7
Penmaenmawr, 4,050 C 4
Pontypool, 36,710 B 6
Pontypridd, 34,180 A 6
Porthcawl, 14,980 D 6
Porthmadog, 3,900 C 5
Port Talbot, 58,200 D 6
Prestatyn, 15,480 D 4
Presteigne, 1,330 D 5
Pwllheli, 4,020 C 5
Rhondda, 85,400 A 6
Rhyl, 22,150 D 4
Risca, 15,780 B 6
Ruthin, 4,780 D 4
Saint David's, ⊙1,638 B 6
Swansea, 190,800 C 6
Tenby, 4,930 C 6
Tredegar, 17,450 B 6
Tywyn, 3,850 C 5
Welshpool, 7,370 D 5
Wrexham, 39,530 E 4

OTHER FEATURES

Anglesey (isl.), 64,500 C 4
Aran Fawddwy (mt.) C 5
Bardsey (isl.), 9 C 5
Berwyn (mts.) D 5
Black (mts.) D 6
Braich-y-Pwll (prom.) C 5
Brecon Beacons (mt.) D 6
Brecon Beacons National Park D 6
Caldy (isl.), 70 C 6
Cambrian (mts.) D 5
Cardigan (bay) C 5
Carmarthen (bay) C 6
Cemmaes (head) C 5
Dee (riv.) D 4
Dovey (riv.) D 5
Ely (riv.) B 7
Gower (pen.), 17,220 C 6
Great Ormes (head) C 4
Holy (isl.), 13,715 C 4
Lleyn (pen.), 25,800 C 5
Menai (str.) C 4
Milford Haven (inlet) B 6
Pembrokeshire Coast National Park C 6
Plynlimon (mt.) D 5
Preseli (mts.) C 6
Radnor (for.) D 5
Rhymney (riv.) B 6
Saint Brides (bay) B 6
Saint David's (head) B 6
Saint George's (chan.) B 5
Saint Gowans (head) C 6
Severn (riv.) E 5
Snowdon (mt.) D 4
Snowdonia National Park D 4
Taff (riv.) B 7
Teifi (riv.) C 5
Towy (riv.) D 6
Tremadoc (bay) C 5
Usk (riv.) B 6
Wye (riv.) D 5
Ynys Môn (Anglesey) (isl.), 64,500 C 4

★Population of met. area.
⊙Population of parish.

SCOTLAND
(map on page 13)

REGIONS

Borders, 99,409 E 5
Central, 269,281 D 4
Dumfries and Galloway, 143,667 E 5
Fife, 336,339 E 4
Grampian, 448,772 F 3
Highland, 182,044 D 3
Lothian, 754,008 E 5
Orkney (islands area), 17,675 E 1
Shetland (islands area), 18,494 F 2
Strathclyde, 2,504,909 C 4
Tayside, 401,987 E 4
Western Isles (islands area) 29,615 A 3

CITIES and TOWNS

Aberchirder, 877 F 3
Aberdeen, 210,362 F 3
Aberdour, 1,576 D 1
Aberfeldy, 1,552 E 4
Aberfoyle, 793 D 4
Aberlady, 737 F 4
Aberlour, 842 E 3
Abernethy, 776 E 4
Aboyne, 1,040 F 3
Acharacle, ⊙764 C 4
Achiltibuie, ⊙1,564 C 3
Achnasheen, ⊙1,078 C 3
Ae, 239 E 5
Airdrie, 38,491 C 2
Alexandria, 9,758 A 1
Alford, 764 F 3
Alloa, 13,558 C 1
Alness, 2,560 D 3
Altnaharra, ⊙1,227 D 2
Alva, 4,593 C 1
Alyth, 1,738 E 4
Ancrum, 266 F 5
Annan, 6,250 E 6
Annat, ⊙550 C 3
Annbank Station, 2,530 D 5
Applecross, ⊙550 C 3
Arbroath, 22,706 F 4
Ardavasar, ⊙449 B 3
Ardersier, 942 E 3
Ardgay, 193 D 3
Ardrishaig, 946 C 4
Ardrossan, 11,072 D 5
Armadale, 7,200 C 2
Arrochar, 543 D 4
Ascog, 230 A 2
Auchenblae, 339 F 4
Auchencairn, 215 E 6
Auchinleck, 4,883 D 5
Auchterarder, 1,738 E 4
Auchtermuchty, 1,426 E 4
Auldearn, 405 E 3
Aviemore, 1,224 E 3
Avoch, 776 D 3
Ayr, 47,990 D 5
Ayton, 410 F 5
Bailivanish, 347 A 3
Baillieston, 7,671 B 2
Balallan, 283 B 2
Balerno, 3,576 D 2
Balfron, 1,149 B 1
Ballantrae, 262 C 5
Ballater, 981 F 3
Ballingry, 4,332 D 1
Ballinluig, 188 E 4
Balloch, Highland, 572 D 3
Balloch, Strathclyde, 1,484 B 1
Baltasound, 246 G 2
Banchory, 2,435 F 3
Banff, 3,832 F 3
Bankfoot, 868 E 4
Bankhead, 1,492 F 3
Bannockburn, 5,889 C 1
Barrhead, 18,736 B 2
Barrhill, 236 D 5
Barvas, 279 B 2
Bathgate, 14,038 C 2
Bayble, 543 B 2
Bearsden, 25,128 B 2
Beattock, 309 E 5
Beauly, 1,141 D 3
Beith, 5,859 D 5
Bellsbank, 3,066 D 5
Bellshill, 18,166 C 2
Berriedale, ⊙1,927 E 2
Bieldside, 1,137 F 3
Biggar, 1,718 E 5
Birnam, 659 E 4
Bishopbriggs, 21,570 B 2
Bishopton, 2,931 B 2
Blackburn, 7,636 C 2
Blackford, 529 E 4
Blair Atholl, 437 E 4
Blairgowrie and Rattray, 5,681 E 4
Blanefield, 835 B 1
Blantyre, 13,992 B 2
Blyth Bridge, ⊙441 E 5
Bo'ness, 12,959 C 1
Boat of Garten, 406 E 3
Boddam, 1,429 G 3
Bonar Bridge, 519 D 3
Bonhill, 4,385 B 1
Bonnybridge, 5,701 C 1
Bonnyrigg and Lasswade, 7,429 D 2
Bowmore, 947 B 5
Braemar, 394 E 3
Breasclete, 234 B 2
Brechin, 6,759 F 4
Bridge of Allan, 4,638 C 1
Bridge of Don, 4,086 F 3
Bridge of Weir, 4,724 A 2
Brightons, 3,106 C 1
Broadford, 310 B 3
Brodick, 630 C 5
Brora, 1,436 E 2
Broxburn, 7,776 D 1
Buchlyvie, 412 B 1
Buckhaven and Methil, 17,930 F 4
Buckie, 8,145 E 3
Bucksburn, 6,567 F 3
Bunessan, ⊙585 B 4
Burghead, 1,321 E 3
Burnmouth, 300 F 5
Burntisland, 5,626 D 1
Cairndow, ⊙874 D 4
Cairnryan, 199 D 6
Callander, 1,805 D 4
Cambuslang, 14,607 B 2
Campbeltown, 6,428 C 5
Cannich, 203 D 3
Canonbie, 234 F 5
Caol, 3,719 C 4
Carbost, ⊙772 B 3
Cardenden, 6,802 D 1
Carloway, 178 B 2
Carluke, 8,864 E 5
Carnoustie, 6,838 F 4
Carnwath, 1,246 E 5
Carradale, 262 C 5
Carrbridge, 416 E 3
Carron, 2,626 C 1
Carsphairn, 186 D 5
Castlebay, 284 A 4
Castle Douglas, 3,384 E 6
Castle Kennedy, 307 D 6
Castletown, 902 E 2
Catrine, 2,681 D 5
Cawdor, 111 E 3
Chirnside, 888 F 5
Chryston, 8,322 C 2
Clackmannan, 3,248 C 1
Clarkston, 8,404 B 2
Closeburn, 225 E 5
Clovulin, ⊙315 C 4
Clydebank, 47,538 B 2
Coalburn, 1,460 E 5
Coatbridge, 50,806 C 2
Cockburnspath, 233 F 5
Cockenzie and Port Seton, 3,539 D 1
Coldingham, 423 F 5
Coldstream, 1,393 F 5
Coll, 305 B 2
Colmonell, 218 D 5
Comrie, 1,119 E 4
Connel, 300 C 4
Cononbridge, 914 D 3
Corpach, 1,296 C 4
Coupar Angus, 2,010 E 4
Cove and Kilcreggan, 1,402 A 1
Cove Bay, 765 F 3
Cowdenbeath, 10,215 D 1
Cowie, 2,751 C 1
Craigellachie, 382 E 3
Craignure, ⊙544 C 4
Crail, 1,033 F 4
Crawford, 384 E 5
Creetown, 769 D 6
Crieff, 5,718 E 4
Crimond, 313 G 3
Crinan, ⊙462 C 4
Cromarty, 492 E 3
Crosshill, 535 D 5
Crossmichael, 317 D 6
Cruden Bay, 528 G 3
Cullen, 1,199 F 3
Culross, 504 C 1
Cults, 3,336 F 3
Cumbernauld, 41,200 C 1
Cumnock and Holmhead, 6,298 D 5
Cupar, 6,607 E 4
Currie, 6,764 D 2
Dailly, 1,258 D 5
Dalbeattie, 3,659 E 6
Daliburgh, 261 A 3
Dalkeith, 9,713 D 2
Dalmally, 283 D 4
Dalmellington, 1,949 D 5
Dalry, 5,833 D 5
Dalrymple, 1,336 D 5
Darvel, 3,177 D 5
Daviot, ⊙513 D 3
Denholm, 581 F 5
Denny and Dunipace, 10,424 C 1
Dervaig, ⊙1,081 B 4
Dingwall, 4,275 D 3
Dollar, 2,573 E 4
Dornoch, 880 D 3
Douglas, 1,843 E 5
Doune, 859 D 4
Drongan, 3,609 D 5
Drumbeg, ⊙833 C 2
Drummore, 336 D 6
Drumnadrochit, 359 D 3
Drymen, 659 B 1
Dufftown, 1,481 E 3
Dumbarton, 25,469 B 1
Dumfries, 29,259 E 5
Dunbar, 4,609 F 4
Dunbeath, 161 E 2
Dunbeg, 939 C 4
Dunblane, 5,222 E 4
Dundee, 194,732 F 4
Dundonald, 2,256 D 5
Dunfermline, 52,098 D 1
Dunkeld, 273 E 4
Dunning, 564 E 4
Dunoon, 8,759 A 2
Dunragit, 323 D 6
Duns, 1,812 F 5
Duntochter, 3,532 B 2
Dunure, 452 D 5
Dunvegan, 301 B 3
Dyce, 2,733 F 3
Eaglesfield, 581 E 5
Eaglesham, 2,788 D 5
Earlston, 1,415 F 5
East Calder, 2,690 D 2
East Kilbride, 71,200 B 2
East Linton, 882 F 5
Eastriggs, 1,455 E 5
Ecclefechan, 844 E 5
Edinburgh (cap.), 470,085 D 1
Edzell, 658 F 4
Elderslie, 5,204 B 2
Elgin, 17,042 E 3
Elie and Earlsferry, 807 F 4
Ellon, 2,855 F 3
Embo, 260 E 3
Errol, 762 E 4
Evanton, 562 D 3
Eyemouth, 2,704 F 5
Fairlie, 1,029 D 5
Falkirk, 36,901 C 1
Falkland, 998 E 4
Fallin, 3,159 C 1
Fauldhouse, 5,247 C 2
Ferness, ⊙287 E 3
Ferryden, 740 F 4
Findhorn, 664 E 3
Findochty, 1,229 E 3
Fintry, 296 B 1
Fochabers, 1,238 E 3
Forfar, 11,179 F 4
Forres, 5,317 E 3
Fort Augustus, 670 D 3
Forth, 2,929 C 2
Fortrose, 1,150 D 3
Fort William, 4,370 C 4
Foyers, 276 D 3
Fraserburgh, 10,930 G 3
Friockheim, 807 F 4
Furnace, 220 C 4
Fyvie, 405 F 3
Gairloch, 125 C 3
Galashiels, 12,808 F 5
Galston, 4,256 D 5
Gardenstown, 892 F 3
Garelochhead, 1,552 A 1
Gargunnock, 457 B 1
Garlieston, 385 D 6
Garmouth, 352 E 3
Garrabost, 307 B 2
Gartmore, 253 B 1
Gatehouse-of-Fleet, 835 D 6
Giffnock, 10,987 B 2
Gifford, 575 F 5
Girvan, 7,597 D 5
Glamis, 190 F 4
Glasgow, 880,617 B 2
Glasgow, ★1,674,789 B 2
Glenbarr, ⊙691 C 5
Glencaple, 275 E 5
Glencoe, 195 C 4
Glenelg, ⊙1,468 C 3
Glenluce, 725 D 6
Glenrothes, 31,400 E 4
Golspie, 1,374 E 3
Gordon, 320 F 5
Gorebridge, 3,426 D 2
Gourock, 11,192 A 1
Grangemouth, 24,430 C 1
Grantown-on-Spey, 1,578 E 3
Greenlaw, 574 F 5
Greenock, 67,275 A 2
Gretna, 1,907 E 5
Gullane, 1,701 F 4
Haddington, 6,767 F 5
Halkirk, 679 E 2
Hamilton, 45,495 C 2
Hamnavoe, 307 G 2
Harthill, 4,712 C 2
Hatton, 315 G 3
Hawick, 16,484 F 5
Heathhall, 1,365 E 5
Helensburgh, 13,327 A 1
Helmsdale, 727 E 2
Hill of Fearn, 233 D 3
Hillside, 692 F 4
Hillswick, ⊙696 G 2
Hopeman, 1,248 E 3
Huntly, 4,078 F 3
Hurlford, 4,294 D 5
Inchnadamph, ⊙833 D 2
Innellan, 922 A 2
Innerleithen, 2,293 E 5
Insch, 881 F 3
Inveraray, 473 C 4
Inverbervie, 853 F 4
Invercassley, ⊙1,067 D 3
Invergordon, 2,385 D 3
Invergowrie, 1,389 E 4
Inverie, ⊙1,468 C 3
Inverkeithing, 6,102 D 1
Inverness, 35,801 D 3
Inverurie, 5,534 F 3
Irvine, 48,500 D 5
Isle of Whithorn, 222 D 6
Jedburgh, 3,953 F 5
John O'Groats, 195 E 2
Johnshaven, 544 F 4
Johnstone, 23,251 B 2
Kames, 230 C 5
Keiss, 344 E 2
Keith, 4,192 F 3
Kelso, 4,934 F 5
Kelty, 6,573 D 1
Kemnay, 1,042 F 3
Kenmore, 211 E 4
Kilbarchan, 2,669 A 2
Kilbirnie, 8,259 A 2
Kilchoan, ⊙764 B 4
Kildonan, ⊙1,105 E 2
Killearn, 1,086 B 1
Killin, 600 D 4
Kilmacolm, 3,348 A 2
Kilmarnock, 50,175 D 5
Kilmaurs, 2,518 D 5
Kilninver, ⊙247 C 4
Kilrenny and Anstruther, 2,951 F 4
Kilsyth, 10,210 B 1
Kilwinning, 8,460 D 5
Kinbrace, ⊙1,105 E 2
Kincardine, 3,278 C 1
Kinghorn, 2,163 D 1
Kingussie, 1,036 D 3
Kinlochewe, ⊙1,794 C 3
Kinlochleven, 1,243 D 4
Kinloch Rannoch, 241 D 4
Kinloss, 2,378 E 3
Kinross, 2,829 E 4
Kintore, 970 F 3
Kippen, 529 B 1
Kirkcaldy, 50,207 D 1
Kirkcolm, 346 C 6
Kirkconnel, 3,318 E 5
Kirkcowan, 354 D 6
Kirkcudbright, 2,690 E 6
Kirkhill, 210 D 3
Kirkintilloch, 26,664 B 2
Kirkmuirhill, 2,575 E 5
Kirkton of Glenisla, ⊙331 E 4
Kirkwall, 4,777 E 2
Kirriemuir, 4,295 E 4
Kyleakin, 268 C 3
Kyle of Lochalsh, 687 C 3
Kylestrome, ⊙745 D 2
Ladybank, 1,216 E 4
Laggan, 393 D 3
Lairg, 572 D 2
Lamlash, 613 C 5
Lanark, 8,842 E 5
Langholm, 2,509 E 5
Larbert, 4,922 C 1
Largs, 9,461 A 2
Larkhall, 15,926 E 5
Lauder, 639 F 5
Laurencekirk, 1,416 F 4

(continued)

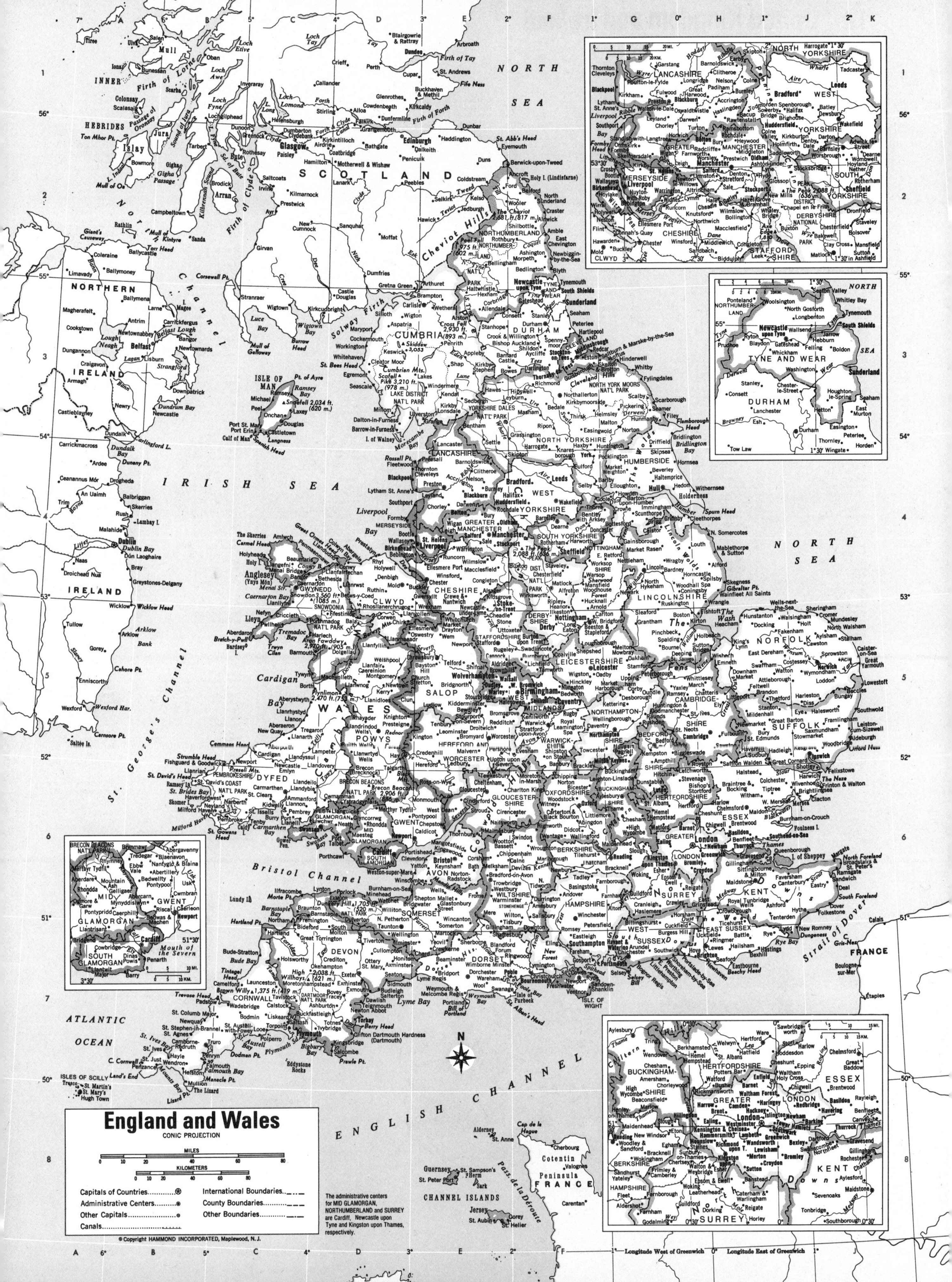
England and Wales
CONIC PROJECTION
MILES
KILOMETERS
Capitals of Countries
Administrative Centers
Other Capitals
Canals
International Boundaries
County Boundaries
Other Boundaries
The administrative centers for MID GLAMORGAN, NORTHUMBERLAND and SURREY are Cardiff, Newcastle upon Tyne and Kingston upon Thames, respectively.
© Copyright HAMMOND INCORPORATED, Maplewood, N. J.
NORTH SEA
IRISH SEA
ENGLISH CHANNEL
ATLANTIC OCEAN
SCOTLAND
WALES
FRANCE
Longitude West of Greenwich
Longitude East of Greenwich

12 United Kingdom and Ireland
(continued)

OTHER FEATURES

★Population of met. area
⊙Population of parish.

Agriculture, Industry and Resources

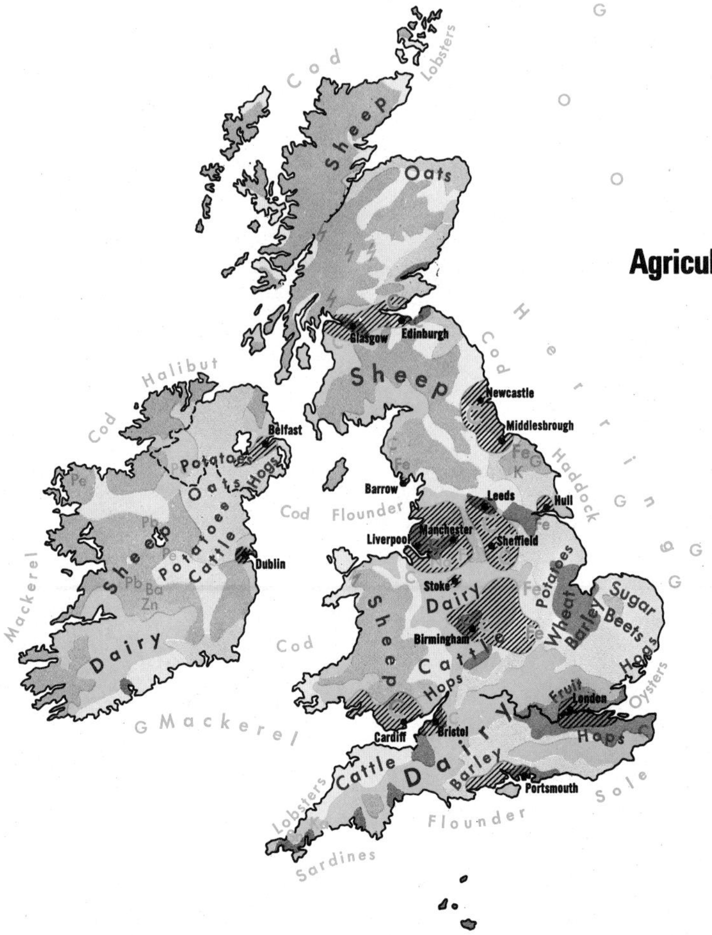

DOMINANT LAND USE

- Cereals (chiefly oats, barley)
- Truck Farming, Horticulture
- Dairy, Mixed Farming
- Livestock, Mixed Farming
- Pasture Livestock

MAJOR MINERAL OCCURRENCES

Ba	Barite	Na	Salt
C	Coal	O	Petroleum
F	Fluorspar	Pb	Lead
Fe	Iron Ore	Pe	Peat
G	Natural Gas	Sn	Tin
K	Potash	Zn	Zinc
Ka	Kaolin (china clay)		

ϟ Water Power

Major Industrial Areas

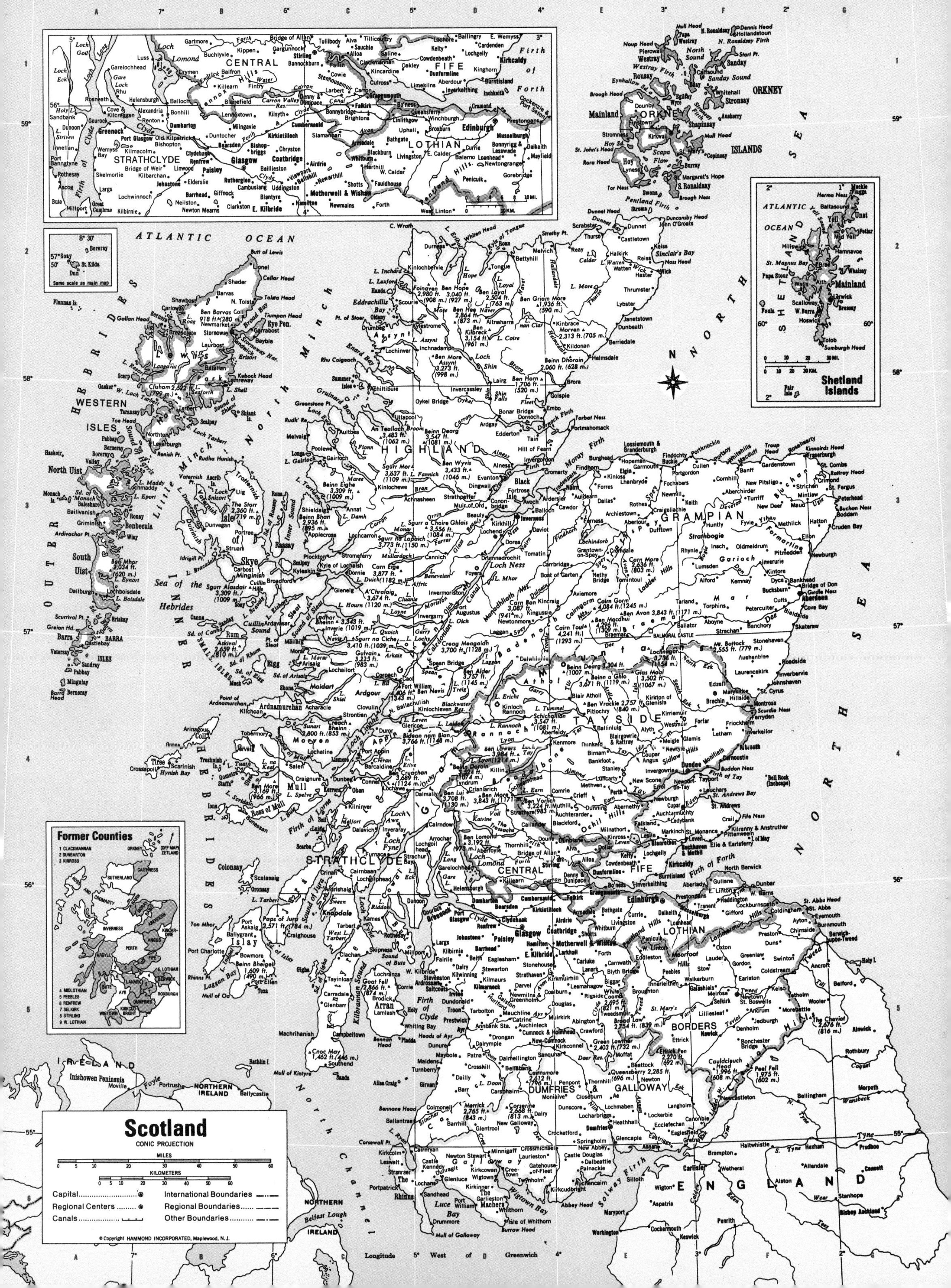
Scotland
CONIC PROJECTION
MILES
KILOMETERS
Capital
Regional Centers
Canals
International Boundaries
Regional Boundaries
Other Boundaries
© Copyright HAMMOND INCORPORATED, Maplewood, N. J.
Longitude 5° West of Greenwich
ATLANTIC OCEAN
NORTH SEA
HIGHLAND
GRAMPIAN
TAYSIDE
CENTRAL
FIFE
LOTHIAN
STRATHCLYDE
BORDERS
DUMFRIES & GALLOWAY
WESTERN ISLES
ORKNEY ISLANDS
Shetland Islands
ENGLAND
NORTHERN IRELAND
IRELAND
OUTER HEBRIDES
INNER HEBRIDES
North Minch
Little Minch
Sea of the Hebrides
North Channel
Firth of Clyde
Firth of Forth
Moray Firth
Solway Firth
Pentland Firth
Edinburgh
Glasgow
Aberdeen
Dundee
Inverness
Perth
Stirling
Former Counties
1 CLACKMANNAN
2 DUNBARTON
3 KINROSS
4 MIDLOTHIAN
5 PEEBLES
6 RENFREW
7 SELKIRK
8 STIRLING
9 W. LOTHIAN
Same scale as main map
St. Kilda

14 United Kingdom and Ireland
(continued)

IRELAND

COUNTIES

Carlow, 34,237 H 6
Cavan, 52,618 G 4
Clare, 75,008 D 6
Cork, 352,883 D 7
Donegal, 108,344 K 2
Dublin, 852,219 J 5
Galway, 149,223 D 5
Kerry, 112,772 B 7
Kildare, 71,977 H 5
Kilkenny, 61,473 G 6
Laoighis, 45,259 G 6
Leitrim, 28,360 E 3
Leix (Laoighis), 45,259 G 6
Limerick, 140,459 D 7
Longford, 28,250 F 4
Louth, 74,951 J 4
Mayo, 109,525 C 4
Meath, 71,729 H 4
Monaghan, 46,242 H 3
Offaly, 51,829 F 5
Roscommon, 53,519 E 4
Sligo, 50,275 D 3
Tipperary, 123,565 F 6
Waterford, 77,315 F 7
Westmeath, 53,570 G 5
Wexford, 86,351 H 7
Wicklow, 66,295 J 5

CITIES and TOWNS

Abbeydorney, 188 B 7
Abbeyfeale, 1,337 C 7
Abbeylara, ‡290 F 4
Abbeyleix, 1,033 G 6
Achill Sound, ‡1,163 B 4
Aclare, ‡336 D 3
Adare, 545 D 6
Aghada-Farsid-Rostellan, 461 E 8
Aghadoe, ‡497 B 7
Aghagower, ‡693 C 4
Ahascragh, 221 E 5
Annagry, 201 E 1
Annascaul, 236 B 7
An Uaimh, 4,605 H 4
An Uaimh, *6,665 H 4
Ardagh, Limerick, 213 C 7
Ardagh, Longford, ‡974 F 4
Ardara, 683 E 2
Ardee, *3,183 H 4
Ardee, 3,096 H 4
Ardfert, 286 B 7
Ardfinnan, 510 F 7
Ardmore, 233 F 8
Ardrahan, ‡239 D 5
Arklow, 6,948 J 6
Arthurstown, 1,188 H 7
Arva, 370 F 4
Ashford, 341 J 5
Askeaton, 844 D 6
Athboy, 705 H 4
Athea, 328 C 7
Athenry, 1,240 D 5
Athleague, ‡955 E 4
Athlone, 9,825 F 5
Athlone, *11,611 F 5
Athy, 4,270 H 6
Athy, *4,654 H 6
Aughrim, 451 J 6
Avoca, ‡620 J 6
Bagenalstown (Muinebeag), 2,321 H 6
Baile Átha Cliath (Dublin) (cap.), 567,866 K 5
Bailieborough, 1,293 G 4
Balbriggan, 3,741 J 4
Balla, 293 C 4
Ballaghaderreen, 1,121 E 4
Ballina, Mayo, 6,063 C 3
Ballina, *6,369 C 3
Ballina, Tipperary, 336 E 6
Ballinagh, 459 G 4
Ballinakill, 300 G 6
Ballineen D 8
Ballinamore, 808 F 3
Ballinasloe, 5,969 E 5
Ballincollig-Carrigrohane, 2,110 D 8
Ballindine, 232 C 4
Ballingarry, Limerick, 422 D 7
Ballingarry, Tipperary, ‡574 F 6
Ballinlough, 242 D 4
Ballinrobe, 1,272 C 4
Ballintober, ‡867 E 4
Ballintra, 197 E 2
Ballisodare, 486 E 3
Ballivor, 287 H 4
Ballybay, 754 G 3
Ballybay, *1,159 G 3
Ballybofey-Stranorlar, 2,214 F 2
Ballybunion, 1,287 B 7
Ballycanew, ‡460 J 6
Ballycarney, ‡294 J 6
Ballycastle, ‡724 C 3
Ballyconnell, 421 F 3
Ballycotton, 389 F 8
Ballydehob, 253 C 8
Ballyduff, 406 B 7
Ballygar, 359 E 4
Ballygeary, 725 J 7
Ballyhaise, 274 G 3
Ballyhaunis, 1,093 D 4
Ballyheigue, 450 B 7
Ballyjamesduff, 673 G 4
Ballylanders, 266 E 7
Ballylongford, 504 B 6
Ballymahon, 707 F 4
Ballymakeery, 272 C 8
Ballymore, ‡447 F 5
Ballymore Eustace, 433 J 5
Ballymote, 952 D 3
Ballyporeen, ‡810 E 7
Ballyragget, 519 G 6
Ballyroan, ‡478 G 6
Ballyshannon, 2,325 E 3
Ballytore, ‡580 H 5
Baltimore, 200 C 9
Baltinglass, 909 H 6
Baltray, 236 J 4
Banagher, 1,052 F 5
Bandon, 2,257 D 8
Bandon, *4,071 D 8
Bannow, ‡798 H 7
Bansha, 184 E 7
Bantry, 2,579 C 8
Barna, ‡1,734 C 5
Belmullet, 744 B 3
Belturbet, 1,092 G 3
Bennettsbridge, 367 G 6
Birr, 3,319 F 5
Birr, *3,881 F 5
Blanchardstown, 3,279 H 5
Blarney, 1,128 D 8
Blessington, 637 J 5
Boherbue, 372 C 7
Borris, 430 H 6
Borris-in-Ossory, 276 F 6
Borrisokane, 769 E 6
Borrisoleigh, 471 E 6
Boyle, 1,727 E 4
Boyle, *1,939 E 4
Bray, 14,467 K 5
Bray, *15,841 K 5
Brí Chualann (Bray), 14,467 K 5
Broadford, 226 C 7
Brosna, 250 C 7
Bruff, 547 D 7
Bruree, 243 D 7
Bunbeg-Derrybeg, 878 E 1
Bunclody-Carrickduff, 929 H 6
Buncrana, 2,955 G 1
Buncrana, *3,334 G 1
Bundoran, 1,337 E 3
Burtonport, ‡1,288 E 2
Buttevant, 1,045 D 7
Cahir, 1,747 F 7
Cahirciveen, 1,547 A 8
Callan, 1,283 G 7
Camolin, 306 J 6
Campile, 231 H 7
Cappamore, 567 E 6
Cappawhite, 305 E 6
Cappoquin, 872 F 7
Carbury, ‡894 H 5
Carlingford, 559 J 3
Carlow, 9,588 H 6
Carlow, *10,399 H 6
Carndonagh, 1,146 G 1
Carnew, 570 H 6
Carrickmacross, 2,100 H 4
Carrickmacross, *2,475 H 4
Carrick-on-Shannon, 1,854 F 4
Carrick-on-Suir, 5,006 F 7
Carrigaholt, ‡493 B 6
Carrigaline, 951 E 8
Carrigallen, 230 F 4
Carrigart, ‡753 F 1
Carrigtwohill, 622 E 8
Carrowkeel, ‡326 G 1
Cashel, 2,692 F 7
Castlebar, 5,979 C 4
Castlebar, *6,476 C 4
Castlebellingham, 407 J 4
Castleblayney, 2,118 H 3
Castleblayney, *2,395 H 3
Castlecomer-Donaguile, 1,244 G 6
Castledermot, 583 H 6
Castlefin, 610 F 2
Castlegregory, 216 A 7
Castleisland, 1,929 B 7
Castlemartyr, 491 E 8
Castlepollard, 693 G 4
Castlerea, 1,752 D 4
Castletown, ‡504 F 6
Castletownbere, 812 B 8
Castletownroche, 399 D 7
Castletownshend, 170 C 9
Causeway, 215 B 7
Cavan, 3,273 G 3
Cavan, *4,312 G 3
Ceanannus Mór, 2,391 G 4
Ceanannus Mór, *2,653 G 4
Celbridge, 1,568 H 5
Charlestown-Bellahy, 677 D 4
Charleville (Rathluirc), 2,232 D 7
Clara, 2,156 F 5
Claregalway, ‡594 D 5
Claremorris, 1,718 C 4
Clashmore, ‡379 F 8
Clifden, 790 B 5
Cloghan, 404 F 5
Clogh-Chatsworth, 324 G 6
Clogheen, 530 F 7
Clogherhead, 649 J 4
Clonakilty, 2,430 D 8
Clonaslee, 285 F 5
Clondalkin, 7,009 J 5
Clonegal, 202 H 6
Clones, 2,164 G 3
Clonfert, ‡430 E 5
Clonmany, ‡936 G 1
Clonmel, 11,622 F 7
Clonmel, *12,291 F 7
Clonmellon, 328 H 4
Clonroche, 222 H 7
Clontuskert, 351 E 4
Cloone, ‡460 F 4
Cloughjordan, 480 E 6
Cloyne, 654 E 8
Coachford, 290 D 8
Cóbh, 6,076 E 8
Cóbh, *7,141 E 8
Coill Dubh, 920 H 5
Collon, 262 J 4
Collooney, 546 E 3
Cong, 233 C 4
Convoy, 654 F 2
Coolaney, ‡352 D 3
Coolgreany, ‡603 J 6
Cootehill, 1,415 G 3
Cootehill, *1,542 G 3
Cork, 128,645 E 8
Cork, *134,430 E 8
Corofin, 342 C 6
Courtmacsherry, 210 D 8
Courtown Harbour, 291 J 6
Creeslough, 269 F 1
Crookhaven, ‡400 B 9
Croom, 756 D 6
Crosshaven, 1,222 E 8
Crossmolina, 1,077 C 3
Crusheen, ‡405 D 6
Culdaff, ‡621 G 1
Daingean, 492 G 5
Delvin, 223 G 4
Dingle, 1,401 A 7
Doaghbeg, ‡701 F 1
Donabate, 426 J 5
Donegal, 1,725 F 2
Doneraile, 799 D 7
Dooagh-Keel, 649 A 4
Doon, 387 E 6
Douglas, ‡4,448 D 8
Drimoleague, 415 C 8
Drishane, ‡1,548 C 7
Drogheda, 19,762 J 4
Drogheda, *20,095 J 4
Droichead Nua, 5,053 H 5
Droichead Nua, *6,444 H 5
Dromahair, 177 E 3
Drumcar, ‡1,215 J 4
Drumconrath, ‡1,044 H 4
Drumkeerin, ‡467 E 3
Drumlish, 205 F 4
Drumshanbo, 576 E 3
Dublin (cap.), 567,866 K 5
Dublin, *679,748 K 5
Duleek, 658 J 4
Duncannon, 228 H 7
Dundalk, 21,672 H 3
Dundalk, *23,816 H 3
Dunfanaghy, 303 F 1
Dungarvan, 5,583 F 7
Dungloe, 940 E 2
Dunkineely, 288 E 2
Dún Laoghaire, 53,171 K 5
Dún Laoghaire, *98,379 K 5
Dunlavin, 423 H 5
Dunleer, 855 J 4
Dunmanway, 1,392 C 8
Dunmore, 522 D 4
Dunmore East, 656 G 7
Dunshaughlin, ‡283 H 5
Durrow, Laoighis, 596 G 6
Durrow, Offaly, ‡441 F 5
Easky, 184 D 3
Edenderry, 2,953 G 5
Edenderry, *3,116 G 5
Elphin, 489 E 4
Emyvale, 281 G 3
Ennis, 5,972 D 6
Ennis, *10,840 D 6
Enniscorthy, 5,704 J 7
Enniscorthy, *6,642 J 7
Enniskerry, 772 J 5
Ennistymon, 1,013 C 6
Eyrecourt, 314 E 5
Fahan, ‡1,023 G 1
Falcarragh, 506 E 1
Feakle, ‡398 D 6
Fenit, 360 B 7
Ferbane, 1,064 F 5
Fermoy, 3,237 E 7
Fermoy, *4,033 E 7
Ferns, 712 J 6
Fethard, Tipperary, 1,064 F 7
Fethard, Wexford, ‡637 H 7
Foxford, 868 C 4
Foynes, 624 C 6
Frankford (Kilcormac), 1,089 F 5
Frenchpark, ‡693 E 4
Freshford, 585 G 6
Galbally, 258 E 7
Galway, 27,726 C 5
Galway, *29,375 C 5
Geashill, ‡751 G 5
Glandore, ‡695 C 8
Glanmire-Riverstown, 1,113 E 8
Glanworth, 335 E 7
Glenamaddy, 315 D 4
Glenbeigh, 266 B 7
Glencolumbkille, ‡787 D 2
Glengarriff, 244 C 8
Glenties, 734 E 2
Glenville, ‡264 D 7
Glin, 623 C 6
Golden, ‡640 F 7
Gorey, 2,946 J 6
Gorey, *3,024 J 6
Gormanston, ‡1,384 J 4
Gort, 975 D 5
Gowran, 402 G 6
Graiguenamanagh-Tinnahinch, 1,303 H 6
Granard, 1,054 F 4
Greencastle, 322 H 1
Greenore, 882 J 4
Greystones-Delgany, 4,517 K 5
Gurteen, 165 D 3
Hacketstown, 574 H 6
Headford, 673 C 5
Holycross, ‡902 F 6
Hospital, 525 E 7
Inchigeelagh, ‡516 C 8
Inishannon, 190 D 8
Inistioge, 179 G 7
Inniscrone, 582 C 3
Johnstown, 303 G 6
Kanturk, 2,063 D 7
Keel-Dooagh, 649 A 4
Kells, ‡423 G 6
Kells (Ceanannus Mór), 2,391 G 4
Kenmare, 903 B 8
Kilbaha, ‡471 B 6
Kilbeggan, 635 G 5
Kilcar, 273 D 2
Kilcock, 827 H 5
Kilconnell, ‡629 E 5
Kilcoole, 679 K 5
Kilcormac, 1,089 F 5
Kilcullen, 880 H 5
Kildare, 3,137 H 5
Kildysart, 239 C 6
Kilfenora, ‡441 C 6
Kilfinane, 561 D 7
Kilgarvan, 228 B 8
Kilkee, 1,287 B 6
Kilkelly, 225 D 4
Kilkenny, 9,838 G 6
Kilkenny, *13,306 G 6
Killala, 368 C 3
Killaloe, 871 D 6
Killarney, 7,184 C 7
Killarney, *7,541 C 7
Killavullen, 221 D 7
Killenaule, 592 F 6
Killeshandra, 432 F 3
Killimor, 221 E 5
Killinaboy, ‡297 C 6
Killorglin, 1,150 B 7
Killucan-Rathwire, 290 G 4
Killybegs, 1,094 E 2
Kilmacrennan, 274 F 1
Kilmacthomas, 396 G 7
Kilmallock, 1,170 D 7
Kilmeadan, ‡262 G 7
Kilmihill, 284 C 6
Kilmoganny, 181 G 7
Kilmore Quay, 273 H 7
Kilmurry, ‡387 C 6
Kilnaleck, 273 G 4
Kilronan, 243 B 5
Kilrush, 2,671 C 6
Kilsheelan, ‡665 F 7
Kiltimagh, 978 C 4
Kilworth, 360 E 7
Kingscourt, 1,016 H 4
Kingstown (Dún Laoghaire), 53,171 K 5
Kinlough, 160 E 3
Kinnegad, 362 G 5
Kinnitty, ‡420 F 5
Kinsale, 1,622 D 8
Kinsale, *1,989 D 8
Kinvara, 293 D 5
Knightstown, 236 A 8
Knock, ‡1,202 D 4
Knocklong, 248 D 7
Knocknagashel, 168 C 7
Labasheeda, ‡468 C 6
Laghey, ‡625 E 2
Lahinch, 455 C 6
Lanesborough-Ballyleague, 906 E 4
Laracor, ‡404 H 4
Laytown-Bettystown-Mornington, 1,882 J 4
Leenane, ‡271 B 4
Leighlindridge, 379 H 6
Leitrim, ‡544 F 3
Leixlip, 2,402 H 5
Letterkenny, 4,930 F 2
Letterkenny, *5,207 F 2
Lifford, 1,121 F 2
Limerick, 57,161 D 6
Limerick, *63,002 D 6
Liscarroll, 231 D 7
Lisdoonvarna, 459 C 5
Lismore, 884 F 7
Lismore, *1,041 F 7
Listowel, 3,021 C 7
Littleton, 322 F 6
Longford, 3,876 F 4
Longford, *4,791 F 4
Lorrha, ‡685 E 5
Loughrea, 3,075 E 5
Louisburgh, 310 B 4
Louth, 208 J 4
Lucan-Doddsborough, 4,245 J 5
Luimneach (Limerick), 57,161 D 6
Lusk, 553 J 4
Macroom, 2,256 C 8
Malahide, 3,834 J 5
Malin, ‡552 G 1
Mallow, 5,901 D 7
Mallow, *6,506 D 7
Manorhamilton, 858 E 3
Manulla, ‡660 C 4
Maryborough (Portlaoighise), 3,902 G 5
Maynooth, 1,296 H 5
Meathas Truim, 546 G 4
Midleton, 3,075 E 8
Midleton, *4,666 E 8
Milford, 763 F 1
Millstreet, 1,319 D 7
Milltown, 260 A 7
Miltown-Malbay, 677 C 6
Minard, ‡397 A 7
Mitchelstown, 2,783 E 7
Moate, 1,378 F 5
Mohill, 868 F 4
Monaghan, 5,256 G 3
Monasterevan, 1,619 H 5
Moneygall, 282 F 6
Monivea, ‡405 D 5
Mooncoin, 413 G 7
Mount Bellew, 275 D 5
Mountcharles, 445 E 2
Mountmellick, 2,595 G 5
Mountmellick, *2,864 G 5
Mountrath, 1,098 F 5
Moville, 1,089 G 1
Moycullen, ‡498 C 5
Moynalty, ‡583 H 4
Muff, 240 G 1
Muinebeag, 2,321 H 6
Mullagh, 293 H 4
Mullaghmore, ‡629 D 3
Mullinahone, 262 F 7
Mullinavat, 343 G 7
Mullingar, 6,790 G 4
Mullinger, *9,245 G 4
Naas, 5,078 H 5
Navan (An Uaimh), 4,605 H 4
Nenagh, 5,085 E 6
Nenagh, *5,174 E 6
Newbliss, ‡547 G 3
Newbridge (Droichead Nua), 5,053 H 5
Newcastle, 2,549 D 7
Newcastle, *2,680 D 7
Newmarket, 886 C 7
Newmarket-on-Fergus, 1,052 D 6
New Pallas, ‡1,271 E 6
Newport, Mayo, 420 C 4
Newport, Tipperary, 582 E 6
New Ross, 4,775 H 7
New Ross, *5,153 H 7
Newtownforbes, ‡495 F 4
Newtownmountkennedy, 882 J 5
Newtownsandes, 268 C 6
O'Briensbridge-Montpelier, 237 D 6
Oldcastle, 759 G 4
Old Leighlin, ‡309 G 6
Oola, 348 E 6
Oranmore, 440 D 5
Oughterard, 628 C 5
Passage East, 408 G 7
Passage West, 2,709 E 8
Patrickswell, 415 D 6
Pettigo, 332 F 2
Piltown, 456 G 7
Portarlington, 3,117 G 5
Portlaoighise, 3,902 G 5
Portlaoighise, *6,470 G 5
Portlaw, 1,166 G 7
Portmarnock, 1,726 J 5
Portumna, 913 E 5
Queenstown (Cóbh), 6,076 E 8
Rahan, ‡531 F 5
Ramelton, 807 F 1
Raphoe, 945 F 2
Rathangan, 868 G 5
Rathcoole, 1,740 J 5
Rathcormac, 191 E 7
Rathdowney, 892 F 6
Rathdrum, 1,141 J 6
Rathgormuck, ‡231 F 7
Rathkeale, 1,543 D 7
Rathluirc, 2,232 D 7
Rathmore, 437 J 5
Rathmullen, 486 F 1
Rathnew-Merrymeeting, 954 J 6
Rathowen, ‡294 F 4
Rathvilly, 230 H 6
Ratoath, 300 J 5
Riverstown, 236 E 3
Rockcorry, 233 H 3
Rosapenna, ‡822 F 1
Roscommon, 1,556 E 4
Roscommon, *2,821 E 4
Roscrea, 3,855 F 6
Rosscarbery, 309 C 8
Rosses Point, 464 D 3
Rosslare, 588 J 7
Rosslare Harbour (Ballygeary), 725 J 7
Roundstone, 204 A 5
Roundwood, 260 J 5
Rush, 2,633 J 4
Saint Johnston, 463 F 2
Scarriff, 619 E 6
Schull, 457 B 8
Scotstown, 264 H 3
Shanagolden, 231 C 6
Shannon Airport, 3,657 D 6
Shannon Bridge, 188 F 5
Shercock, 313 G 4
Shillelagh, 246 J 6
Shinrone, 365 F 5
Shrule, 288 C 4
Sixmilebridge, 567 D 6
Skerries, 3,044 J 4
Skibbereen, 2,104 C 8
Slane, 483 H 4
Sligo, 14,080 E 3
Sligo, *14,456 E 3
Sneem, 285 B 8
Spiddal, ‡819 C 5
Stepaside, 748 J 5
Stradbally, Laoighis, 891 G 5
Stradbally, Waterford, 158 F 7
Strokestown, 563 E 4
Swanlinbar, 257 F 3
Swinford, 1,105 C 4
Swords, 4,133 J 5
Taghmon, 369 H 7
Tallaght, 6,174 J 5
Tallow, 883 F 7
Tarbert, 485 C 6
Teltown, ‡739 H 4
Templemore, 2,174 F 6
Templetuohy, 197 F 6
Termonfeckin, 328 J 4
Thomastown, 1,270 G 7
Thurles, 6,840 F 6
Thurles, *7,087 F 6
Timoleague, 257 D 8
Tinahely, 450 H 6
Tipperary, 4,631 E 7
Tipperary, *4,717 E 7
Toomevara, 272 E 6
Tralee, 12,287 B 7
Tralee, *13,263 B 7
Tramore, 3,792 G 7
Trim, 1,700 H 4
Trim, *2,255 H 4
Tuam, 3,808 D 4
Tuam, *4,952 D 4
Tubbercurry, 959 D 3
Tulla, 415 D 6
Tullamore, 6,809 G 5
Tullamore, *7,474 G 5
Tullaroan, ‡301 G 6
Tullow, 1,838 H 6
Tullow, *1,945 H 6
Tynagh, ‡452 E 5
Tyrrellspass, 289 G 5
Urlingford, 652 F 6
Virginia, 583 G 4
Waterford, 31,968 G 7
Waterford, *33,676 G 7
Waterville, 547 A 8
Westport, 3,023 C 4
Wexford, 11,849 H 7
Wexford, *13,293 H 7
Whitegate, 370 E 8
Wicklow, 3,786 K 6
Wicklow, *3,915 K 6
Woodenbridge, ‡620 J 6
Woodford, 198 E 5
Youghal, 5,445 F 8
Youghal, *5,626 F 8

OTHER FEATURES

Achill (isl.), 3,129 A 4
Allen (lake) E 3
Allen, Bog of (marsh) H 5
Aran (isl.), 773 D 2
Aran (isls.), 1,499 B 5
Arklow (bank) K 6
Arrow (lake) E 3
Awbeg (riv.) D 7
Ballinskelligs (bay) A 8
Ballycotton (bay) F 8
Ballyheige (bay) B 7
Ballyhoura (hills) E 7
Ballyteige (bay) H 7
Bandon (riv.) D 8
Bann (riv.) J 6
Bantry (bay) B 8
Barrow (riv.) H 7
Baurtregaum (mt.) A 7
Bear (isl.), 288 B 8
Blacksod (bay) A 3
Blackstairs (mt.) H 6
Blackwater (riv.) D 7
Blackwater (riv.) H 4
Blasket (isls.) A 7
Bloody Foreland (prom.) E 1
Blue Stack (mts.) E 2
Boderg (lake) E 4
Boggeragh (mts.) D 7
Boyne (riv.) J 4
Brandon (head) A 7
Bride (riv.) E 7
Broad Haven (harb.) B 3
Brosna (riv.) F 5
Bull, The (isl.), 5 A 8
Caha (mts.) B 8
Carlingford (inlet) J 3
Carnsore (pt.) J 7
Carrantuohill (mt.) B 7
Clare (riv.) D 5
Clare (isls.), 168 A 4
Clear (cape) B 9
Clear (isl.), 192 C 9
Clew (bay) B 4
Comeragh (mts.) F 7
Conn (lake) C 3
Connacht (prov.), 390,902 C 4
Connemara (dist.), 7,599 B 5
Cork (harb.) E 8
Corrib (lake) C 5
Courtmacsherry (bay) D 8
Curragh, The H 5
Dee (riv.) H 4
Deel (riv.) D 7
Deele (riv.) F 2
Derg (lake) E 6
Derravaragh (lake) G 4
Derryveagh (mts.) E 2
Dingle (bay) A 7
Donegal (bay) D 3
Drum (hills) F 7
Dublin (bay) J 5
Dundalk (bay) J 4
Dunmanus (bay) B 8
Dursey (isl.), 38 A 8
Ennell (lake) G 5
Erne (riv.) E 3
Errigal (mt.) E 1
Erris (head) A 3
Fanad (head) F 1
Fastnet Rock (isl.), 3 B 9
Feale (riv.) C 7
Fergus (riv.) D 6
Finn (riv.) F 2
Finn (riv.) G 3
Flesk (riv.) C 7
Foyle (inlet) G 1
Foyle (riv.) G 2
Galley (head) D 9
Galtee (mts.) E 7
Galtymore (mt.) E 7
Galway (bay) C 5
Gara (lake) D 4
Garadice (lake) F 3
Gill (lake) E 3
Glyde (riv.) H 4
Golden Vale (plain) E 7
Gorumna (isl.), 1,108 B 5
Gowna (lake) G 4
Grand (canal) G 5
Greenore (pt.) J 7
Gweebarra (bay) D 2
Hags (head) B 6
Helvick (head) G 7
Hook (head) H 7
Horn (head) E 1
Iar Connacht (dist.), 10,774 C 5
Inishbofin (isl.), 236 A 4
Inishbofin (isl.), 103 E 1
Inisheer (isl.), 313 B 5
Inishmaan (isl.), 319 C 5
Inishmore (isl.), 864 B 5
Inishowen (head) H 1
Inishowen (pen.), 24,109 G 1
Inishtrahull (isl.), 3 G 1
Inishturk (isls.), 83 A 4
Inny (riv.) A 8
Inny (riv.) F 4
Inver (bay) E 2
Ireland's Eye (isl.) K 5
Irish (sea) K 4
Joyce's Country (dist.), 2,021 B 4
Kenmare (riv.) A 8
Kerry (head) A 7
Key (lake) E 3
Kilkieran (bay) B 5
Killala (bay) C 3
Killary (harb.) A 4
Kinsale (harb.) E 8
Kippure (mt.) J 5
Knockboy (mt.) B 8
Knockmealdown (mts.) F 7
Lady's Island Lake (inlet) J 7
Lambay (isl.), 24 K 4
Laune (riv.) B 7
Leane (lake) B 7
Leane (lake) G 4
Lee (riv.) D 8
Leinster (mt.) H 6
Leinster (prov.), 1,498,140 G 5
Lettermullan (isl.), 221 B 5
Liffey (riv.) H 5
Liscannor (bay) B 6
Long Island (bay) B 9
Loop (head) A 6
Lugnaquillia (mt.) J 5
Macgillicuddy's Reeks (mts.) B 7
Macnean (lake) F 3
Maigue (riv.) D 6
Maine (riv.) C 7
Malin (head) F 1
Mask (lake) C 4
Maumturk (mts.) B 5
Melvin (lake) E 3
Mizen (head) B 9
Moher (cliffs) B 6
Monavullagh (mts.) F 7
Moy (riv.) C 3
Mulkear (riv.) E 6
Mullaghareirk (mts.) C 7
Mulroy (bay) F 1
Munster (prov.), 882,002 D 7
Mweelrea (mt.) B 4
Mweenish (isl.), 198 B 5
Nagles (mts.) E 7
Nenagh (riv.) E 6
Nephin (mt.) C 3
Nore (riv.) G 7
North (sound) B 5
Omey (isl.), 34 A 5
Oughter (lake) G 3
Ovoca (riv.) J 6
Owenmore (riv.) D 3
Owey (isl.), 51 D 1
Paps, The (mt.) C 7
Partry (mts.) C 4
Pollaphuca (res.) J 5
Punchestown H 5
Rathlin O'Birne (isl.), 3 C 2
Ree (lake) F 5
Roaringwater (bay) B 9
Rosses (bay) D 1
Rosskeeragh (pt.) D 3
Royal (canal) G 4
Saint Finan's (bay) A 8
Saint George's (chan.) K 7
Saint John's (pt.) D 2
Saltee (isls.) H 7
Seven (heads) D 8
Seven Hogs, The (isls.) A 7
Shannon (riv.) E 6
Sheeffry (hills) B 4
Sheelin (lake) G 4
Sheep Haven (harb.) F 1
Sheeps (head) B 8
Sherkin (isl.), 82 C 9
Silvermine (mts.) E 6
Slaney (riv.) H 7
Slieve Aughty (mts.) D 5
Slieve Bloom (mts.) F 5
Slieve Gamph (mts.) D 3
Slievenaman (mt.) F 7
Sligo (bay) D 3
Slyne (head) A 5
South (sound) C 5
Stacks (mts.) B 7
Suck (riv.) E 5
Suir (riv.) G 7
Swilly (inlet) F 1
Tara (hill) H 4
Tory (isl.), 273 E 1
Tory (sound) E 1
Tralee (bay) B 7
Trawbreaga (bay) F 1
Ulster (part) (prov.), 207,204 G 2
Valencia (Valentia) (isl.), 770 A 8
Valentia (isl.), 770 A 8
Waterford (harb.) G 7
Wexford (bay) J 7
Wicklow (head) K 6
Wicklow (mts.) J 6
Youghal (bay) F 8

NORTHERN IRELAND

COUNTIES

Antrim, 37,600 J 2
Ards, 52,100 K 2
Armagh, 47,500 H 3
Ballymena, 52,200 J 2
Ballymoney, 22,700 J 1
Bainbridge, 28,800 J 3
Belfast, 368,200 J 2
Carrickfergus, 27,500 K 2
Castlereagh, 63,600 K 2
Coleraine, 44,900 H 1
Cookstown, 27,500 H 2
Craigavon, 71,200 J 3
Down, 48,800 K 3
Dungannon, 43,000 H 3
Fermanagh, 50,900 F 3
Larne, 29,000 K 2
Limavady, 25,000 H 1
Lisburn, 80,800 J 2
Londonderry, 86,600 G 2
Magherafelt, 32,200 H 2
Mourne (Newry and Mourne), 75,300 J 3
Moyle, 13,400 J 1
Newtownabbey, 71,500 J 2
North Down, 59,600 K 2
Omagh, 41,800 G 2
Strabane, 35,500 G 2

CITIES and TOWNS

Ahoghill, ‡1,929 J 2
Annalong, 1,001 K 3
Antrim, 8,351 J 2
Ardglass, 1,052 K 3
Armagh, 13,606 H 3
Armoy, ‡1,051 J 1
Augher, ‡1,986 G 3
Aughnacloy, ‡1,885 H 3
Ballycastle, 2,899 J 1
Ballyclare, 5,155 J 2
Ballygawley, ‡2,165 G 3
Ballykelly, 1,116 G 1
Ballymena, 23,386 J 2
Ballymoney, 5,697 J 1
Ballynahinch, 3,485 J 3
Banbridge, 7,968 J 3
Bangor, 35,260 K 2
Belfast (cap.), 353,700 J 2
Belfast, *551,940 J 2
Bellaghy, ‡2,265 H 2
Belleek, ‡2,487 E 3
Beragh, ‡2,137 G 2
Bessbrook, 2,619 J 3
Brookeborough, ‡2,534 G 3
Broughshane, 1,288 J 2
Bushmills, 1,288 J 1
Caledon, ‡1,828 H 3
Carnlough, 1,416 J 2
Carrickfergus, 16,603 K 2
Carrowdore, 2,548 K 2
Castledawson, 1,162 H 2
Castlederg, 1,766 F 2
Castlewellan, 1,488 K 3
Claudy, ‡2,507 G 2
Clogher, ‡1,888 G 3
Coalisland, 3,614 H 2
Coleraine, 16,354 H 1
Comber, 5,575 K 2
Cookstown, 6,965 H 2
Craigavon, 12,740 J 3
Crossgar, 1,098 K 3
Crossmaglen, 1,085 H 3
Crumlin, 1,450 J 2
Cullybackey, 1,649 J 2
Derrygonnelly, ‡2,539 F 3
Dervock, ‡1,191 J 1
Donaghadee, 4,008 K 2
Downpatrick, 7,918 K 3
Draperstown, ‡2,247 H 2
Dromore, Bainbridge, 2,848 J 3
Dromore, Omagh, ‡2,224 G 3
Drumquin, ‡1,982 F 2
Dundrum, ‡2,245 K 3
Dungannon, 8,190 H 3
Dungiven, 1,536 H 2
Dunnamanagh, ‡2,242 G 2
Ederny and Kesh, ‡2,497 F 2
Enniskillen, 9,679 F 3
Feeny, ‡1,459 H 2
Fintona, 1,190 G 3
Fivemiletown, ‡1,649 G 3
Garvagh, ‡2,363 H 2
Gilford, 1,592 J 3
Glenarm, ‡1,728 J 2
Glenavy, ‡2,360 J 2
Glynn, ‡1,872 K 2
Gortin, ‡2,033 G 2
Greyabbey, ‡2,646 K 2
Hillsborough, 1,021 J 3
Holywood, 9,892 K 2
Irvinestown, 1,457 F 3
Keady, 2,145 H 3
Kells, ‡2,560 J 2
Kesh, ‡2,497 F 3
Kilkeel, 4,090 K 3
Killough, ‡3,295 K 3
Killyleagh, 2,359 K 3
Kilrea, 1,196 H 2
Kircubbin, 1,075 K 3
Larne, 18,482 K 2
Limavady, 6,004 H 1
Lisburn, 31,836 J 2
Lisnaskea, 1,443 G 3
Londonderry, 51,200 G 2
Loughbrickland, ‡2,056 J 3
Maghera, 2,085 H 2
Magherafelt, 4,704 H 2
Markethill, ‡2,352 H 3
Millisle, 1,172 K 2
Moneymore, 1,178 H 2
Moy, ‡2,349 H 3
Moygashel, 1,086 H 3
Newcastle, 4,647 J 3
Newry, 20,279 J 3
Newtownabbey, 58,114 K 2
Newtownards, 15,484 K 2
Newtownbutler, ‡2,663 G 3
Newtownhamilton, ‡1,936 H 3
Newtownstewart, 1,433 G 2
Omagh, 14,594 G 2
Pomeroy, ‡1,786 H 2
Portaferry, 1,730 K 3
Portavogie, 1,310 K 3
Portglenone, ‡2,061 H 2
Portrush, 5,376 H 1
Portstewart, 5,085 H 1
Randalstown, 2,799 J 2
Rathfriland, 1,886 J 3
Rostrevor, 1,617 J 3
Saintfield, ‡2,198 K 3
Sion Mills, 1,588 G 2
Sixmilecross, ‡1,980 G 2
Stewartstown, ‡1,759 H 2
Strabane, 9,413 G 2
Strangford, ‡1,987 K 3
Tandragee, 1,725 J 3
Tempo, ‡2,282 G 3
Trillick, ‡2,167 G 3
Warrenpoint, 4,291 J 3
Whitehead, 2,642 K 2

OTHER FEATURES

Bann (riv.) H 2
Belfast (inlet) K 2
Blackwater (riv.) H 3
Bush (riv.) H 1
Derg (riv.) F 2
Divis (mt.) J 2
Dundrum (bay) K 3
Erne (lake) F 3
Foyle (inlet) G 1
Foyle (riv.) G 2
Giant's Causeway H 1
Lagan (riv.) K 2
Larne (inlet) K 2
Magee, Island (pen.), 1,581 K 2
Magilligan (pt.) H 1
Main (riv.) J 2
Mourne (mts.) J 3
Mourne (riv.) G 2
Neagh (lake) J 2
North (chan.) K 1
Rathlin (isl.), 109 J 1
Red (bay) K 1
Roe (riv.) H 1
Saint John's (pt.) K 3
Slieve Donard (mt.) K 3
Sperrin (mts.) G 2
Strangford (inlet) K 3
Torr (head) K 1
Ulster (part) (prov.), 1,537,200 G 2
Upper Lough Erne (lake) F 3

*City and suburbs.
‡Population of district.

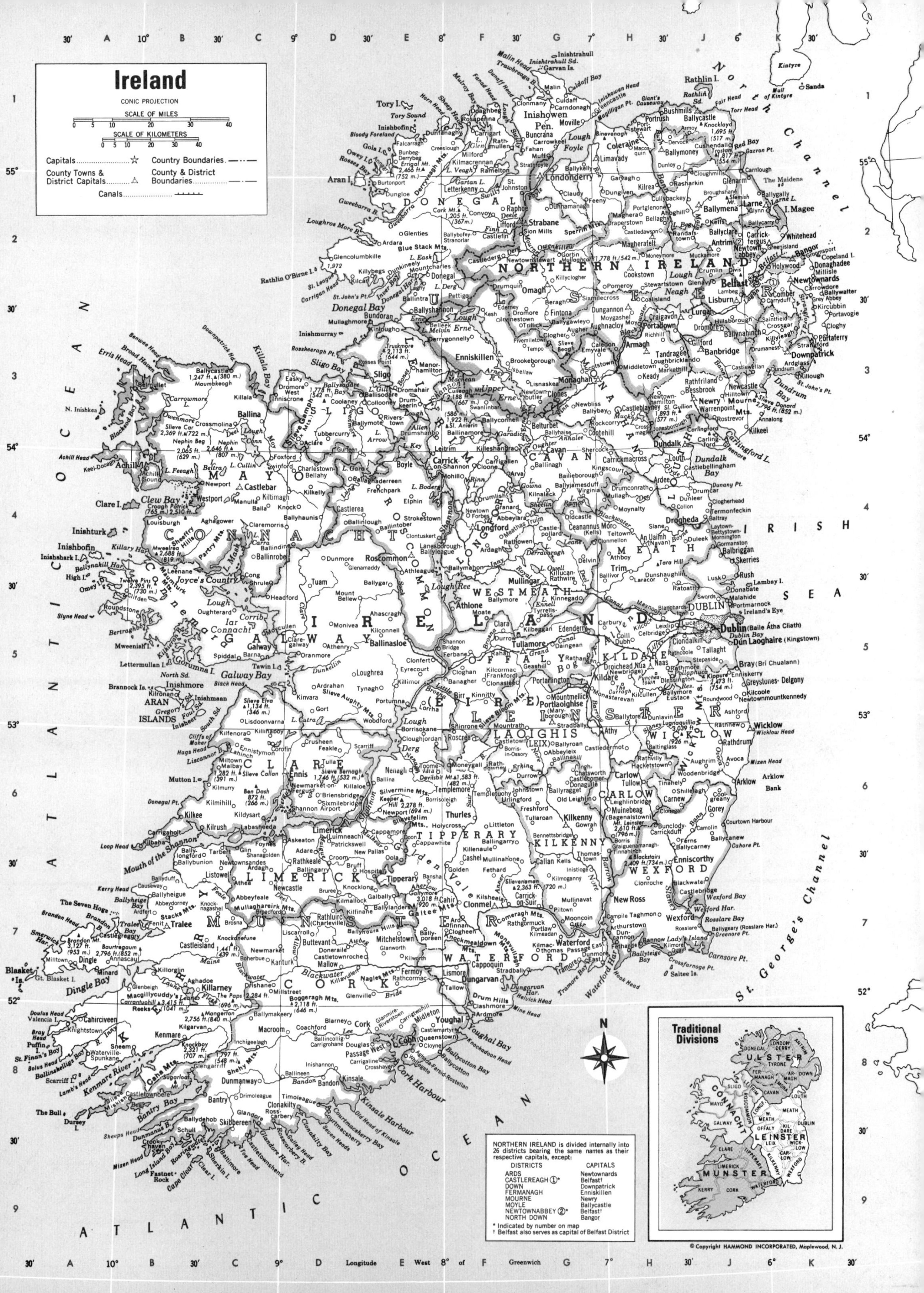
Ireland
CONIC PROJECTION
SCALE OF MILES
0 5 10 20 30 40
SCALE OF KILOMETERS
0 5 10 20 30 40
Capitals
Country Boundaries
County Towns & District Capitals
County & District Boundaries
Canals
NORTHERN IRELAND is divided internally into 26 districts bearing the same names as their respective capitals, except:
DISTRICTS / CAPITALS
ARDS / Newtownards
CASTLEREAGH ①* / Belfast†
DOWN / Downpatrick
FERMANAGH / Enniskillen
MOURNE / Newry
MOYLE / Ballycastle
NEWTOWNABBEY ②* / Belfast†
NORTH DOWN / Bangor
* Indicated by number on map
† Belfast also serves as capital of Belfast District
Traditional Divisions
ULSTER
CONNACHT
LEINSTER
MUNSTER
ATLANTIC OCEAN
IRISH SEA
North Channel
St. George's Channel
NORTHERN IRELAND
Longitude West 8° of Greenwich
© Copyright HAMMOND INCORPORATED, Maplewood, N. J.

Norway, Sweden, Finland and Denmark
CONIC PROJECTION
SCALE OF MILES
0 50 100 150
SCALE OF KILOMETERS
0 50 100 150 200
Capitals of Countries
Administrative Centers
International Boundaries
Internal Boundaries
Canals
SUBDIVISIONS Indicated by Numbers
Counties in NORWAY
1 Akershus G 6
2 Vestfold G 7
3 Østfold G 7
4 Oslo G 7
Oslo is the administrative center for Akershus and Oslo County.
Counties in SWEDEN
5 Göteborg och Bohus G 7
6 Västmanland K 7
7 Södermanland K 7
8 Östergötland J 7
9 Malmöhus H 9
10 Kristianstad J 8
Svalbard
NORWEGIAN SEA
STOCKHOLM
ARCTIC OCEAN
BARENTS SEA
NORWEGIAN SEA
ATLANTIC OCEAN
NORTH SEA
SKAGERRAK
KATTEGAT
BALTIC SEA
GULF OF BOTHNIA
Gulf of Finland
Gulf of Riga
DENMARK
WEST GERMANY
EAST GERMANY
POLAND
U. S. S. R.
OSLO
STOCKHOLM
COPENHAGEN
HELSINKI
LENINGRAD
BERLIN
WARSAW
© Copyright HAMMOND INCORPORATED, Maplewood, N. J.
Longitude East of Greenwich

AREA 125,053 sq. mi. (323,887 sq. km.)
POPULATION 4,092,000
CAPITAL Oslo
LARGEST CITY Oslo
HIGHEST POINT Glittertinden 8,110 ft. (2,472 m.)
MONETARY UNIT krone
MAJOR LANGUAGE Norwegian
MAJOR RELIGION Protestantism

AREA 173,665 sq. mi. (449,792 sq. km.)
POPULATION 8,320,000
CAPITAL Stockholm
LARGEST CITY Stockholm
HIGHEST POINT Kebnekaise 6,946 ft. (2,117 m.)
MONETARY UNIT krona
MAJOR LANGUAGE Swedish
MAJOR RELIGION Protestantism

AREA 130,128 sq. mi. (337,032 sq. km.)
POPULATION 4,788,000
CAPITAL Helsinki
LARGEST CITY Helsinki
HIGHEST POINT Haltiatunturi 4,343 ft. (1,324 m.)
MONETARY UNIT markka
MAJOR LANGUAGES Finnish, Swedish
MAJOR RELIGION Protestantism

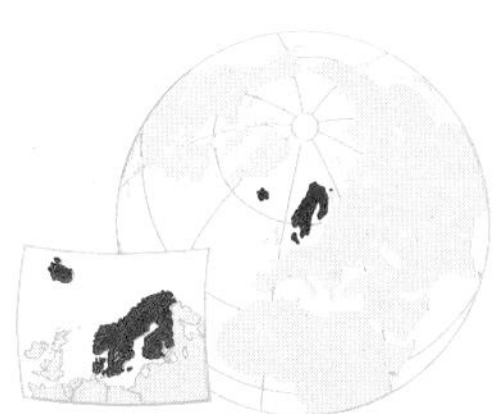

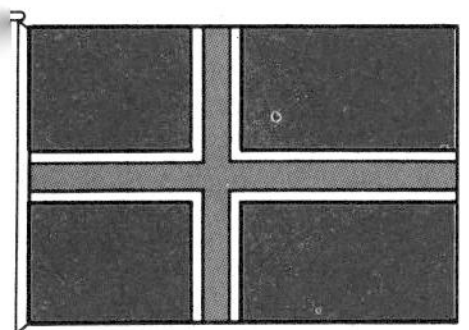

NORWAY

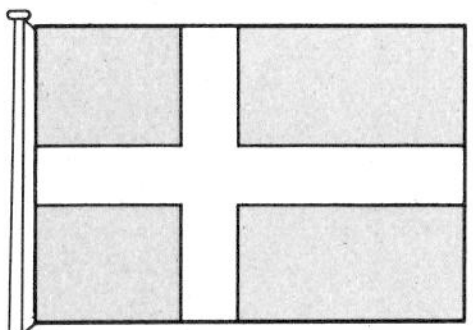

SWEDEN

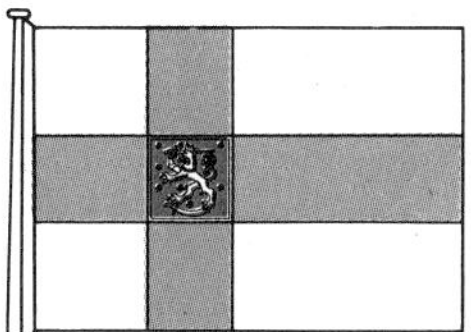

FINLAND

FINLAND

PROVINCES

venanmaa 22,380 ... L6
and (Ahvenanmaa) 22,380 ... L6
me 662,500 ... O6
ski-Suomi 241,770 ... O5
opio 252,023 ... P5
mi 346,478 ... Q6
ppi 196,792 ... P3
kkeli 211,453 ... P6
lu 406,309 ... P4
hjois-Karjala 179,065 ... Q5
rku ja Pori 697,988 ... N6
simaa 1,085,625 ... O6
asa 425,283 ... N5

CITIES and TOWNS

nekoski 10,725 ... O5
o (Turku) 164,857 ... N6
vus 10,285 ... N5
rgaå 18,740 ... O6
enäs 7,391 ... N6
Espoo 117,090 ... O6
Forssa 18,442 ... N6
Haapajärvi 7,791 ... O5
Hämeenlinna 40,761 ... O6
Hamina 11,055 ... P6
Hangö 10,374 ... N7
Hanko (Hangö) 10,374 ... N7
Harjavalta 8,445 ... M6
Heinola 15,350 ... P6
Helsinki (cap.) 502,961 ... O6
Helsinki* 794,746 ... O6
Huutokoski† 6,458 ... P5
Hyvinkää 35,865 ... O6
Iisalmi 21,159 ... P5
Ikaalinen 8,364 ... N6
Imatra 35,590 ... Q6
Ivalo 2,661 ... P2
Jakobstad 20,397 ... N5
Jämsä 12,526 ... O6
Järvenpää 16,259 ... O6
Joensuu 41,429 ... R5
Jyväskylä 61,209 ... O5
Jyväskylä* 84,185 ... O5
Kajaani 20,583 ... P4
Kalajoki 3,624 ... N4
Kankaanpää 12,564 ... M6
Karhula 21,834 ... P6
Karis 8,152 ... N6
Karjaa (Karis) 8,152 ... N6
Karkkila 8,678 ... N6
Kauniainien 6,219 ... O6
Kauttua 3,297 ... M6
Kelloselkä† 8,200 ... Q3
Kemi 27,893 ... O4
Kemijärvi 12,951 ... P3
Kerava 19,966 ... O6
Kokemäki 10,188 ... N6
Kokkola 22,096 ... N5
Kotka 34,026 ... P6
Kotka* 60,235 ... P6
Kouvola 29,383 ... P6
Kouvola* 59,507 ... P6
Kristiinankaupunki (Kristinestad) 9,331 ... N5
Kristinestad 9,331 ... N5
Kuhmo 4,150 ... Q4
Kuopio 71,684 ... Q5
Kurikka 11,177 ... M5
Kuusamo 4,449 ... Q4
Kuusankoski 22,342 ... P6
Lahti 94,864 ... O6
Lahti* 112,129 ... O6
Lappeenranta 52,682 ... P6
Lapua 15,189 ... N5
Lieksa 20,274 ... R5
Loimaa 6,575 ... N6
Lovisa 8,674 ... P6
Maarianhamina (Mariehamn) 9,574 ... M7
Mänttä 7,910 ... O6
Mariehamn 9,574 ... M7
Mikkeli 27,112 ... P6
Naantali 7,814 ... M6
Nokia 22,308 ... N6
Nurmes 11,721 ... Q5
Nykarleby 7,408 ... N5
Oulainen 7,322 ... O4
Oulu 93,707 ... O4
Oulu* 103,044 ... O4
Outokumpu 10,736 ... Q5
Parainen 10,170 ... M6
Parkano 8,518 ... N6
Pieksämäki 12,923 ... P5
Pietarsaari (Jakobstad) 20,397 ... N5
Pori 80,343 ... M6
Pori* 86,635 ... M6
Posio† 6,205 ... O3
Pudasjärvi† 12,594 ... P4
Raahe 15,379 ... O4
Raisio 14,271 ... M6
Rauma 29,081 ... M6
Riihimäki 24,106 ... O6
Rovaniemi 28,411 ... O3
Saarijärvi 2,714 ... O5
Salo 19,176 ... N6
Savonlinna 28,336 ... Q6
Seinäjoki 22,123 ... N5
Sodankylä 3,304 ... P3
Sotkamo 2,316 ... Q4
Suolahti 5,936 ... O5
Suonenjoki 9,286 ... P5
Tammisaari (Ekenäs) 7,391 ... N6
Tampere 168,118 ... N6
Tampere* 220,920 ... N6
Toijala 8,080 ... N6
Tornio 19,971 ... O4
Turku 164,857 ... N6
Turku* 217,423 ... N6
Turtola† 5,852 ... O3
Ulvila† 8,040 ... N6
Uusikaarlepyy (Nykarleby) 7,408 ... N5
Uusikaupunki 11,915 ... M6
Vaasa 54,402 ... M5
Vaasa* 58,224 ... M5
Valkeakoski 22,588 ... N6
Vammala 16,363 ... N6
Varkaus 24,450 ... Q5
Vasa (Vaasa) 54,402 ... M5
Vuotso† 10,186 ... P2
Ylivieska 10,827 ... O4

OTHER FEATURES

Åland (isls.) ... L6
Baltic (sea) ... K9
Bothnia (gulf) ... M5
Finland (gulf) ... P7
Hailuoto (isl.) ... O4
Haltiatunturi (mt.) ... M2
Hangöudd (prom.) ... N7
Haukivesi (lake) ... Q5
Iijoki (riv.) ... O4
Inari (lake) ... P2
Ivalojoki (riv.) ... P2
Juojärvi (lake) ... Q5
Kalajoki (riv.) ... O4
Kallavesi (lake) ... P5
Karlö (Hailuoto) (isl.) ... O4
Keitele (lake) ... O5
Kemijärvi (lake) ... Q3
Kemijoki (riv.) ... O3
Kiantajärvi (lake) ... Q4
Kilpisjärvi (lake) ... M2
Kitinen (riv.) ... P3
Kivijärvi (lake) ... O5
Koitere (lake) ... R5
Kuusamojärvi (lake) ... Q4
Längelmävesi (lake) ... O6
Lapland (reg.) ... O2
Lappajärvi (lake) ... O5
Lapuanjoki (riv.) ... N5
Lestijärvi (lake) ... O5
Lokka (res.) ... Q3
Muojärvi (lake) ... R4
Muonio (riv.) ... M2
Näsijärvi (lake) ... O6
Onkivesi (lake) ... P5
Orihvesi (lake) ... Q5
Oulujärvi (lake) ... P4
Oulujoki (riv.) ... O4
Ounasjoki (riv.) ... O3
Päijänne (lake) ... O6
Pielinen (lake) ... Q5
Puruvesi (lake) ... Q6
Puulavesi (lake) ... P5
Pyhäjärvi (lake) ... O5
Pyhäjärvi (lake) ... M6
Saimaa (lake) ... Q6
Siikajoki (riv.) ... O4
Simojärvi (lake) ... P3
Simojoki (riv.) ... O4
Tana (riv.) ... P2
Tornio (riv.) ... O3
Vallgrund (isl.) ... M5
Ylikitka (lake) ... Q3

NORWAY

COUNTIES

Akershus 355,196 ... G6
Aust-Agder 86,216 ... E7
Buskerud 209,684 ... F6
Finnmark 79,373 ... O2
Hedmark 183,465 ... G6
Hordaland 386,492 ... E6
Møre og Romsdal 231,944 ... E5
Nordland 243,233 ... J3
Nord-Trøndelag 122,886 ... H4
Oppland 178,259 ... F6
Oslo (city) 462,732 ... D3
Østfold 228,546 ... G7
Rogaland 287,653 ... E7
Sogn og Fjordane 103,135 ... E6
Sør-Trøndelag 241,361 ... G5
Telemark 158,853 ... F7
Troms 144,111 ... L2
Vest-Agder 131,659 ... E7
Vestfold 182,433 ... G7

CITIES and TOWNS

Ålesund 40,868 ... D5
Ålgård 2,322 ... D7
Alta 5,582 ... N2
Åndalsnes 2,574 ... F5
Årdalstangen 2,360 ... F6
Arendal 11,701 ... F7
Arendal* 21,228 ... F7
Årnes 2,267 ... G6
Askim 8,413 ... E4
Bamble† 7,031 ... F7
Barentsburg ... C2
Bergen 213,434 ... D6
Bodø 31,077 ... J3
Borge† 3,294 ... H2
Brønnøysund 3,130 ... G4
Dombås 1,114 ... F5
Drammen 50,777 ... C4
Drammen* 56,521 ... C4
Drøbak 4,538 ... D4
Eidsvoll 2,906 ... G6
Eigersund 11,379 ... D7
Elverum 7,391 ... G6
Farsund 8,908 ... E7
Flekkefjord 8,750 ... E7
Flora 8,822 ... D6
Fredrikstad 29,024 ... D4
Fredrikstad* 51,141 ... D4
Gjøvik 25,963 ... G6
Grimstad 13,091 ... F7
Halden 27,087 ... G7
Hamar 16,418 ... G6
Hamar* 25,138 ... G6
Hammerfest 7,610 ... N1
Hammerfest* 8,005 ... N1
Harstad 21,125 ... K2
Haugesund 27,386 ... D7
Haugesund* 29,277 ... D7
Hermansverk 706 ... E6
Holmestrand 8,246 ... C4
Hølmsbu 273 ... D4
Honningsvag 3,780 ... O1
Horten 13,746 ... D4
Horten* 17,246 ... D4
Kirkenes 4,466 ... Q2
Kongsberg 19,854 ... F7
Kongsvinger 16,146 ... H6
Kopervik 4,221 ... D7
Kornsjø† 6,079 ... G7
Kragerø 5,249 ... F7
Kristiansand 59,488 ... F8
Kristiansund 18,847 ... E5
Kvinnherad† 2,898 ... E6
Larvik 9,097 ... C4
Larvik* 19,202 ... C4
Lenvik† 11,098 ... L2
Levanger 5,068 ... G5
Lillehammer 21,248 ... F6
Lillesand 3,028 ... F7
Lillestrøm† 11,550 ... E3
Longyearbyen ... D2
Lysaker† 81,612 ... D3
Mandal 11,579 ... E7
Meråker† 2,907 ... G5
Mo 21,033 ... J3
Molde 20,334 ... E5
Mosjøen 9,341 ... H4
Moss 25,786 ... D4
Moss* 27,430 ... D4
Mysen 3,760 ... G7
Namsos 11,452 ... G4
Narvik 19,582 ... K2
Nesttun† 11,519 ... D6
Nittedal† 8,889 ... D3
Notodden 12,970 ... F7
Nøtterøy 11,944 ... D4
Ny-Ålesund ... C2
Odda 7,401 ... E6
Oppdal 2,173 ... F5
Orkanger 3,685 ... F5
Oslo (cap.) 462,732 ... D3
Oslo* 645,413 ... D3
Porsgrunn 31,709 ... G7
Rakkestad 2,392 ... G7
Ringerike 30,156 ... C3
Risør 6,560 ... F7
Rjukan 5,334 ... F7
Røros 3,041 ... G5
Sandefjord 33,350 ... C4
Sandnes 33,934 ... D7
Sandvika† 34,337 ... C3
Sarpsborg 12,889 ... D4
Sarpsborg* 36,449 ... D4
Selje† 3,386 ... D5
Ski 9,081 ... D4
Skien 47,105 ... F7
Stavanger 86,639 ... D7
Stavern 2,604 ... D4
Steinkjer 20,553 ... G4
Stor-Elvdal† 2,993 ... G6
Sunndalsøra 5,114 ... F5
Sveagruva ... D2
Svolvaer 3,942 ... J2
Tønsberg 9,964 ... D4
Tønsberg* 36,374 ... D4
Tromsø 43,830 ... L2
Trondheim 134,910 ... F5
Ullensvang† 2,326 ... E6
Vadsø 6,019 ... Q1
Vardø 3,875 ... R1
Vik 1,019 ... E6
Volda 3,511 ... E5
Voss 5,944 ... E6

OTHER FEATURES

Alsten (isl.) ... H4
Andøya (isl.) ... J2
Barduelv (riv.) ... L2
Bellsund ... C2
Bjørnafjorden (fjord) ... D6
Bjornøya (isl.) ... D3
Boknafjord (fjord) ... D7
Bremanger (isl.) ... D6
Dønna (isl.) ... H3
Dovrefjell (hills) ... F5
Edgeøya (isl.) ... E2
Femundsjø (lake) ... G5
Folda (fjord) ... G4
Folda (fjord) ... J3
Frohavet (bay) ... F5
Frøya (isl.) ... F5
Glittertinden (mt.) ... F6
Hardangervidda (plat.) ... E6
Hardangerfjord (fjord) ... D7
Hinlopenstreten (str.) ... C1
Hinnøya (isl.) ... K2
Hitra (isl.) ... F5
Hopen (isl.) ... E2
Isfjorden (fjord) ... C2
Jostedalsbreen (glac.) ... E6
Kjölen (mts.) ... K3
Kongsfjorden (fjord) ... B2
Kvaløya (isl.) ... O1
Lågen (riv.) ... G6
Laksefjorden (fjord) ... P1
Langøy (isl.) ... J2
Lapland (reg.) ... K2
Leka (isl.) ... G4
Lindesnes (cape) ... E8
Lista (pen.) ... E7
Lofoten (isls.) ... H2
Lopphavet (bay) ... M1
Magerøya (isl.) ... P1
Moskenesøya (isl.) ... H3
Namsen (riv.) ... H4
Nordaustlandet (isl.) ... D1
Nordfjord (fjord) ... E6
Nordkapp (pt.) ... C1
Nordkinn (headland) ... Q1
Nordkinn (pen.) ... P1
North Cape (Nordkapp) (pt.) ... P1
Norwegian (sea) ... F3
Ofotfjorden (fjord) ... K2
Oslofjord (fjord) ... D4
Otra (riv.) ... E7
Otterøya (isl.) ... E5
Pasvikelv (riv.) ... Q2
Platen, Kapp (pt.) ... D1
Porsangen (fjord) ... O1
Rana (fjord) ... H3
Rauma (riv.) ... F5
Ringvassøy (isl.) ... L2
Romsdalsfjorden (fjord) ... E5
Saltfjorden (fjord) ... J3
Seiland (isl.) ... N1
Senja (isl.) ... K2
Skagerrak (str.) ... F8
Smøla (isl.) ... E5
Sognafjorden (fjord) ... D6
Sørkapp (pt.) ... C2
Sorøya (isl.) ... N1
Spitsbergen (isl.) ... C2
Storfjorden (fjord) ... D2
Sulitjelma (mt.) ... J3
Svalbard (isls.) ... C3
Tana (riv.) ... P1
Tanafjord (fjord) ... Q1
Tokke (riv.) ... F7
Trondheimsfjorden (fjord) ... G5
Tyrifjord (lake) ... C3
Vaerøy (isl.) ... H3
Vagåvatn (lake) ... F6
Vannøy (isl.) ... L1
Varangerhalvøya (pen.) ... Q1
Varangerfjord (fjord) ... Q2
Vega (isl.) ... G4
Vesterålen (isls.) ... J2
Vestfjord (fjord) ... H3
Vestvågøya (isl.) ... H3
Vikna (isls.) ... G4

SWEDEN

COUNTIES

Älvsborg 418,150 ... H7
Blekinge 155,391 ... J8
Gävleborg 294,595 ... K6
Göteborg och Bohus 714,660 ... G7
Gotland 54,447 ... L8
Halland 219,767 ... H8
Jämtland 133,559 ... J5
Jönköping 301,905 ... H8
Kalmar 240,768 ... K8
Kopparberg 281,082 ... J6
Kristianstad 272,090 ... J8

(continued on following page)

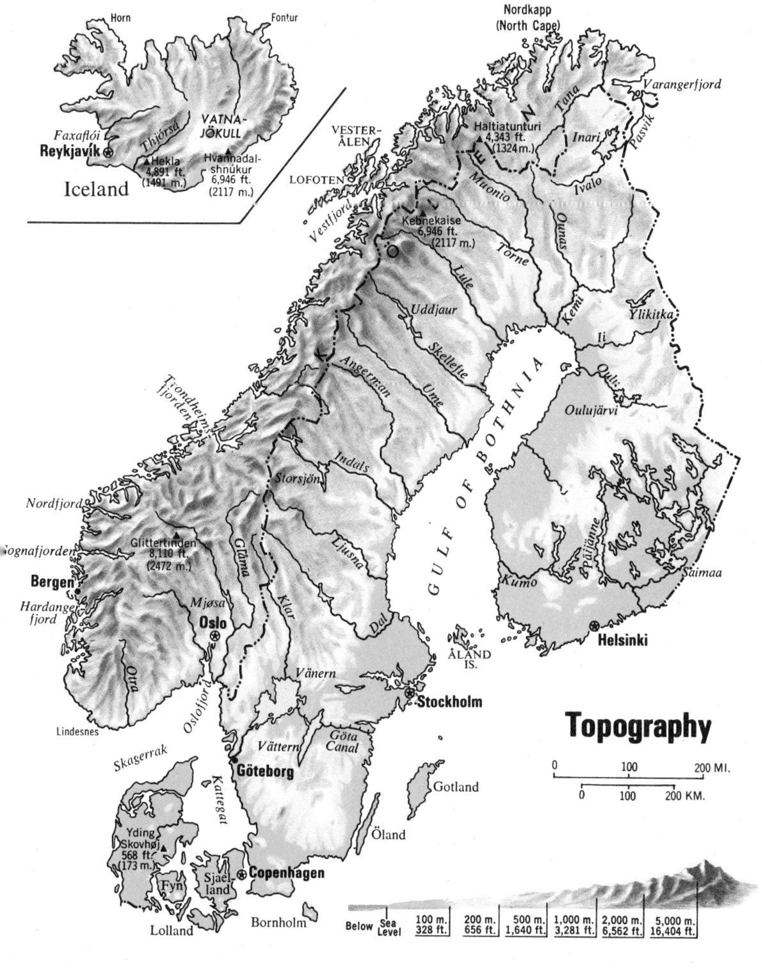

Norway, Sweden, Finland, Denmark and Iceland

(continued)

Kronoberg 169,454 J8
Malmöhus 740,137 H9
Norrbotten 264,215 L3
Örebro 273,994 J7
Östergötland 387,104 J7
Skaraborg 263,382 H7
Södermanland 252,030 K7
Stockholm 1,493,052 L7
Uppsala 229,879 K7
Värmland 284,442 H7
Västerbotten 236,367 K4
Västernorrland 268,202 K5
Västmanland 259,872 K7

CITIES and TOWNS

Åhus 6,125 J9
Alingsås 18,892 H7
Älmhult 7,390 H8
Alvesta 7,261 J8
Älvsbyn 4,707 M4
Åmål 9,556 H7
Ånge 3,760 J5
Ängelholm 16,016 H8
Arboga 11,819 J7
Arbrå 2,734 K6
Årjäng† 2,596 H7
Arvidsjaur 4,194 L4
Arvika 13,934 H7
Åseda 2,465 J8
Askim 17,609 G8
Åtvidaberg 8,436 K7
Avesta 19,095 J6
Bålsta 8,243 G1
Båstad 2,452 H8
Bengtsfors 3,535 H7
Boden 19,590 M4
Bollnäs 13,305 K6
Bollstabruk 3,548 L5
Borås 67,537 H8
Borås* 187,710 H8
Borgholm 2,789 K8
Borlänge 40,158 J6
Brunflo 3,460 J5
Dalby† 4,013 H6
Danderyd† 36,596 H1
Dannemora 291 K6
Edsbyn 4,388 J6
Eksjö 9,686 J8
Emmaboda 5,652 J8
Enköping 18,541 G1
Eskilstuna 66,409 K7
Eslöv 13,629 H9
Fagersta† 14,778 J6
Falkenberg 14,148 H8
Falköping 15,126 H7
Falun 30,073 J6
Färjestaden 2,995 K8
Filipstad 7,835 H7
Finspång 16,346 J7
Flen 6,770 K7
Forshaga 6,000 H7
Frösö 10,274 J5
Frövi 2,583 J7
Gällivare 8,669 M3
Gamleby 3,666 J8
Gävle 67,454 K6
Gimo 3,154 K6
Gislaved 8,564 H8
Gnesta 3,835 G2
Göteborg 444,540 G8
Göteborg* 690,767 G8
Hagfors 8,060 H6
Hällefors 7,862 J7
Hallsberg 6,799 J7
Hallstahammar 13,583 K7
Hallstavik 5,162 L6
Halmstad 49,558 H8
Haparanda 5,031 N4
Härnösand 18,971 L5
Hässleholm 16,813 H8
Hedemora 7,039 K6
Helsingborg 80,986 H8
Helsingborg* 215,894 H8
Hjo 4,615 J7
Hofors 11,459 K6
Höganäs 10,866 H8
Holmsund 5,467 M5
Hörnefors 2,441 L5
Huddinge 48,339 H1
Hudiksvall 15,004 K6
Hultsfred 5,763 K8
Husum 2,517 L5
Hyltebruk 3,469 H8
Iggesund 4,448 K6
Järna 6,237 G2
Jokkmokk 3,186 L3
Jönköping 78,650 H8
Jönköping* 131,499 H8
Kalix 7,668 N4
Kalmar 32,049 K8
Karlshamn 17,447 J8
Karlskoga† 35,425 J7
Karlskrona 33,414 J8
Karlstad 51,243 H7
Katrineholm 22,884 K7
Kinna 13,676 H8
Kiruna 25,410 L3
Kisa 4,323 J7
Köping 20,059 J7
Kopparberg 3,942 J7
Kramfors 7,719 L5
Kristianstad 30,780 J9
Kristinehamn 21,146 H7
Kumla 11,451 J7
Kungälv† 12,764 G8
Kungsbacka† 11,986 G8
Kvissleby 3,413 K5
Laholm 3,898 H8
Landskrona 29,486 H9
Långshyttan 2,744 K6
Laxå 5,166 J7
Leksand 4,410 J6
Lessebo 2,991 J8
Lidingö 30,098 H1
Lidköping 21,001 H7
Lindesberg 8,247 J7
Linköping 80,274 K7
Linköping* 132,839 K7
Ljungby 12,969 J8
Ljusdal 7,075 J6
Ljusne 3,578 K6
Ludvika 18,217 J6
Luleå 42,139 N4
Lund 55,047 H9
Lycksele 8,586 L4
Lysekil 7,815 G7
Malmberget 10,239 M3
Malmö 241,191 H9
Malmö* 453,339 H9
Malung 6,211 H6
Mariefred 2,553 F1
Mariestad 16,454 H7
Markaryd 4,266 H8
Märsta 17,066 K7
Marstrand 1,168 G8
Mellerud 3,579 H7
Mjölby 12,488 J7
Mölndal† 47,248 H8
Mönsterås 5,005 K8
Mora 8,772 J6
Motala 29,454 J7
Nacka 19,708 H1
Nässjö 18,634 J8
Nora 5,515 J7
Norberg 5,438 K6
Norrköping 85,244 K7
Norrköping* 163,206 K7
Norrtälje 12,784 L7
Nybro 13,010 J8
Nyköping 30,352 K7
Nynäshamn 11,070 L7
Ockelbo 2,810 K6
Olofström 10,096 J8
Örebro 117,877 J7
Örebro* 171,440 J7
Örnsköldsvik 29,514 L5
Orrefors 919 J8
Orsa 5,099 J6
Oskarshamn 19,021 K8
Östersund 40,056 J5
Östhammar 1,783 L6
Oxelösund 13,862 K7
Piteå 16,169 M4
Rättvik 4,087 J6
Rimbo 3,404 L7
Ronneby 12,086 J8
Säffle 11,428 H7
Sala 11,216 K7
Saltsjöbaden 8,113 J1
Sandviken 27,994 K6
Säter 4,297 J6
Sävsjö 4,913 J8
Sigtuna 4,780 H1
Simrishamn 5,834 J9
Skanör med Falsterbo 4,909 H9
Skara 10,138 H7
Skellefteå 29,353 M4
Skövde 29,945 H7
Skutskär 7,174 K6
Smedjebacken 8,418 J6
Söderhamn 14,673 K6
Söderköping 5,310 K7
Södertälje 58,408 G1
Sollefteå 8,923 K5
Sollentuna† 40,905 H1
Solna† 53,992 H1
Sölvesborg 7,292 J9
Stenungsund 8,361 G7
Stockholm (cap.) 665,550 G1
Stockholm* 1,357,183 G1
Storuman 2,587 K4
Storvik 2,748 K6
Strängnäs 10,255 F1
Strömstad 4,735 G7
Strömsund 4,119 K5
Sundbyberg† 27,058 G1
Sundsvall 52,268 K5
Sunne 4,273 H7
Surahammar 6,509 J7
Sveg 2,608 J5
Svenljunga 3,189 H8
Täby† 41,285 H1
Tibro 8,476 J7
Tidaholm 8,039 J7
Tierp 5,005 K6
Timrå 11,416 K5
Tomelilla 5,371 J9
Torsby 3,632 H6
Torshälla 8,231 K7
Tranås 14,854 J7
Trelleborg 22,559 H9
Trollhättan 42,499 H7
Trosa 3,128 K7
Uddevalla 32,700 G7
Ulricehamn 7,827 H8
Umeå 49,715 M5
Uppsala 101,850 K7
Uppsala* 157,202 L7
Vadstena 5,294 J7
Vaggeryd 3,974 J8
Valdemarsvik 3,558 K7
Vallentuna 10,477 H1
Vänersborg 20,510 G7
Vännäs 3,876 L5
Vansbro 2,708 H6
Vara 3,049 H7
Varberg 19,467 G8
Värnamo 15,726 J8
Västerås 98,858 K7
Västerås* 147,508 K7
Västerhaninge 14,125 H1
Västervik 21,239 K8
Vaxholm† 3,744 J1
Växjö 40,328 J8
Vetlanda 12,358 J8
Vilhelmina 4,060 K4
Vimmerby 7,405 J8
Virserum 2,495 J8
Visby 19,886 L8
Ystad 14,286 H9

OTHER FEATURES

Ångermanälven (riv.) K5
Åsnen (lake) J8
Baltic (sea) K9
Bolmen (lake) H8
Bothnia (gulf) N4
Dalälven (riv.) K6
Fårö (isl.) L8
Göta (canal) J7
Göta (riv.) H7
Gotland (isl.) L8
Gräsö (isl.) L6
Hanöbukten (bay) J9
Hjälmaren (lake) J7
Hoburgen (cliff) L8
Hornslandet (pen.) K6
Indalsälven (riv.) H5
Kalixälv (riv.) N3
Kalmarsund (sound) K8
Kattegat (str.) G8
Kebnekaise (mt.) L3
Kölen (mts.) K3
Klarälv (riv.) H6
Lapland (reg.) M2
Ljusnan (riv.) H5
Luleälv (riv.) M4
Mälaren (lake) G1
Muonioälv (riv.) M2
Öland (isl.) K8
Öresund (sound) H9
Ornö (isl.) J2
Österdalälven (riv.) H6
Piteälv (riv.) M4
Siljan (lake) J6
Skagerrak (str.) F8
Sommen (lake) J8
Stora Lulevatten (lake) L3
Storsjön (lake) J5
Sulitelma (mt.) K3
Torneälv (riv.) M3
Uddjaur (lake) L4
Umeälv (riv.) L4
Vänern (lake) H7
Västerdalälven (riv.) H6
Vättern (lake) J7

*City and suburbs.
†Population of commune.
†Population of parish.

DENMARK

COUNTIES

Århus 534,333 D5
Bornholm 47,241 F9
Copenhagen (commune) 622,612 F6
Faerøe Islands 41,969 B2
Frederiksberg (commune) 101,874 F6
Frederiksborg 260,825 E5
Fyn 433,765 D7
København (Copenhagen) (commune) 622,612 F6
Københaven 616,571 F6
Nordjylland 457,165 D4
Ribe 198,153 B7
Ringkøbing 242,006 B5
Roskilde 154,314 E6
Sønderjylland 238,502 C7
Storstrøm 252,780 E7
Vejle 306,809 C6
Vestsjaelland 259,484 E6
Viborg 221,002 C4

CITIES and TOWNS

Åbenrå 15,196 C7
Åbybro 2,897 C3
Åkirkeby 2,001 F9
Ålborg 154,582 D4
Ålestrup 1,926 C4
Århus 245,941 D5
Års 4,266 C4
Årup 1,675 D7
AErøskøbing 1,223 D8
Agerbaek 935 B6
Allingaåbro 1,385 D5
Allinge-Sandvig 1,991 F8
Ansager 1,157 B6
Arden 1,303 C4
Asaå 1,344 D3
Askov 904 C7
Asnaes 1,413 E6
Assens, Århus 1,341 D4
Assens, Fyn 5,139 D7
Augustenborg 2,628 D8
Auning 1,516 D5
Avlum 1,729 B5
Baelum 1,169 D4
Bagenkop 776 D8
Ballerup 50,673 F6
Bandholm 693 E8
Bedsted 965 B4
Birkerød 13,663 F6
Bjerringbro 4,761 C5
Bogense 2,861 D6
Bolderslev 774 C8
Børkop 1,410 C6
Borup 1,591 E7
Braedstrup 2,163 C6
Bramming 3,678 B7
Brande 4,784 B6
Bredebro 1,173 B7
Broager 2,143 C8
Brønderslev 10,247 C3
Brørup 2,584 C7
Brovst 4,200 C3
Bryrup 579 C5
Christiansfeld 1,994 C7
Copenhagen (cap.) 603,368 F6
Copenhagen* 1,327,940 F6
Dronninglund 4,661 D3
Dybvad 805 D3
Ebeltoft 3,017 D5
Egernsund 1,323 C8
Egtved 1,311 C6
Ejby 1,372 C7
Esbjerg 68,097 B7
Faåborg 6,495 D7
Fakse 2,720 F7
Fakse Ladeplads 1,799 F7
Farsø 2,821 C4
Farum 9,936 F6
Fjerritslev 2,134 C3
Fredensborg 4,709 F6
Fredericia 36,157 C6
Frederiksberg 101,874 F6
Frederikshavn 24,846 D3
Frederikssund 11,272 E6
Frederiksvaerk 8,903 E6
Fuglebjerg 1,094 E7
Gedser 1,200 F8
Gedsted 1,006 C4
Gelsted 1,307 C7
Gentofte 77,744 F6
Gilleleje 2,943 F5
Give 2,366 C6
Glamsbjerg 2,226 D7
Glostrup 28,326 F6
Glumsø 1,027 E7
Glyngøre 1,071 C4
Gørding 1,261 B7
Gørlev 1,542 E7
Graested 1,654 F5
Gram 2,061 C7
Graåsten 2,947 C8
Grenaå 12,569 D5
Grindsted 7,558 B6
Haårby 1,506 D7
Haderslev 20,042
Hadsten 3,914
Hadsund 3,652
Hals 1,654
Hammel 3,247
Hammerum 3,227
Hanstholm 1,716
Harboør 1,359
Haårlev 1,228
Hasle 18
Haslev 6,925
Havdrup 1,833
Hedensted 2,659
Hellebaek 2,911
Helsinge 3,613
Helsingør 42,425
Herning 32,973
Hillerød 23,963
Hinnerup 2,061
Hirtshals 6,861
Hjallerup 1,573
Hjerm 647
Hjørring 19,692
Hobro 8,737
Højer 1,416
Højslev 1,641
Holbaek 19,485
Holeby 1,434
Holstebro 25,006
Holsted 1,390
Høng 2,488
Hornslet 2,561
Horsens 44,120
Hørsholm 19,346
Hørve 1,139
Hov 635
Humlum 546
Hundested 5,443
Hurup 2,287
Hvidbjerg 994
Hvide Sande 2,129
Ikast 9,222
Jelling 1,540
Jerslev 798
Juelsminde 1,991
Jyderup 2,901
Kalundborg 12,248
Karise 1,184
Karup 1,694
Kastrup† 17,391
Kerteminde 5,007
Kibaek 1,279
Kjellerup 3,245
Klitmøller 542
København (Copenhagen) (cap.) 603,368
Køge 18,608
Kolding 41,602
Kolind 1,036
Korsør 15,502
Kvaerndrup 891
Langaå 2,320
Lem 1,026
Lemvig 6,448
Løgstør 3,633
Løgumkloster 2,091
Lohals 580
Løjt Kirkeby 1,203
Løkken 1,345
Løsning 1,967
Lundby 747
Lunderskov 1,494
Lyngby 61,516
Malling 1,584
Mariager 1,692
Maribo 5,287
Marstal 4,124
Middelfart 13,315

Agriculture, Industry and Resources

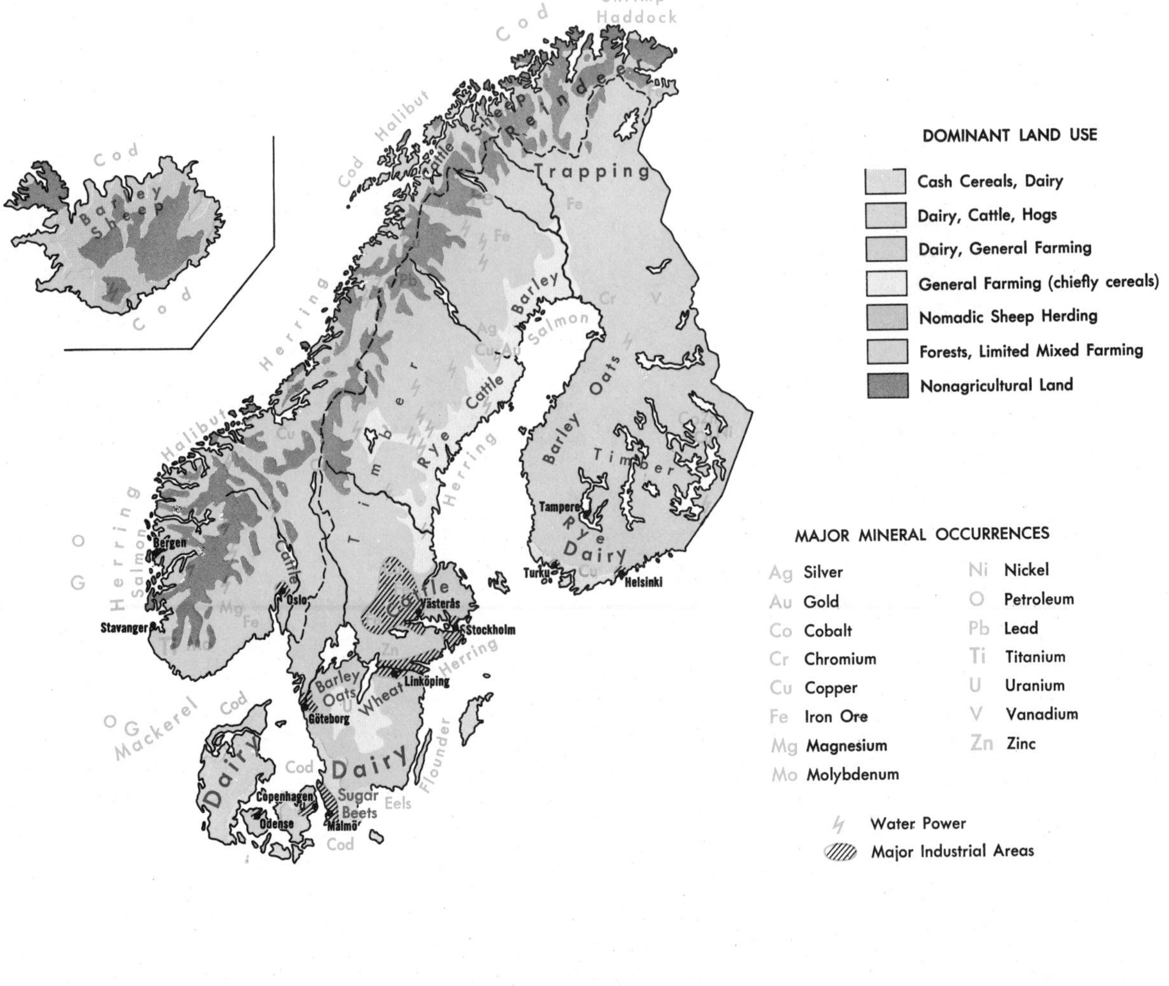

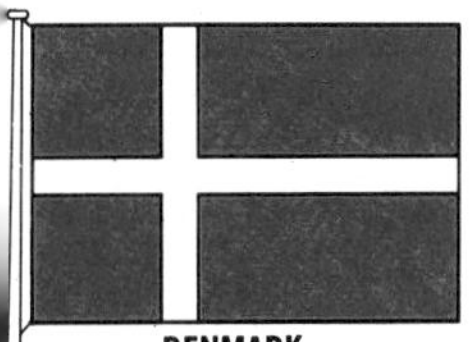

DENMARK

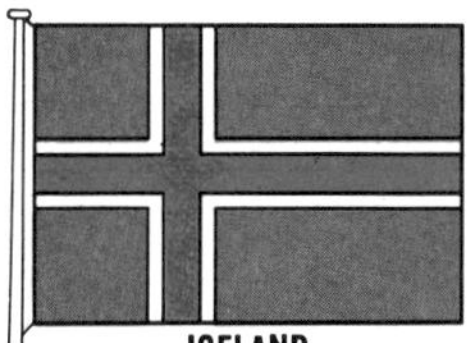

ICELAND

DENMARK

AREA 16,629 sq. mi. (43,069 sq. km.)
POPULATION 5,124,000
CAPITAL Copenhagen
LARGEST CITY Copenhagen
HIGHEST POINT Yding Skovhøj 568 ft. (173 m.)
MONETARY UNIT krone
MAJOR LANGUAGE Danish
MAJOR RELIGION Protestantism

ICELAND

AREA 39,768 sq. mi. (103,000 sq. km.)
POPULATION 228,785
CAPITAL Reykjavík
LARGEST CITY Reykjavík
HIGHEST POINT Hvannadalshnúkur 6,952 ft. (2,119 m.)
MONETARY UNIT króna
MAJOR LANGUAGE Icelandic
MAJOR RELIGION Protestantism

Møgeltønder 711 .... B8
Naestved 35,011 .... E7
Nakskov 16,393 .... E8
Neksø 3,527 .... F9
Nibe 2,796 .... C4
Nordborg 4,132 .... C7
Nordby, Ribe 2,084 .... B7
Nørre Åby 2,165 .... C7
Nørre Alslev 1,338 .... E8
Nørre Broby 904 .... D7
Nørre Nebel 901 .... B6
Nørre Snede 1,461 .... C6
Nørre Vorupør 644 .... B4
Nyborg 14,181 .... D7
Nykøbing, Storstrøm 20,059 .... F8
Nykøbing, Vestsjaelland 4,996 .... E6
Nykøbing, Viborg 9,066 .... B4
Nysted 1,229 .... E8
Odder 6,617 .... D6
Odense 168,178 .... D7
Ølgod 2,258 .... B6
Ørsted 1,093 .... D5
Øster Vrå 906 .... D3
Otterup 2,673 .... D7
Ovtrup 602 .... B6
Pandrup 1,525 .... C3
Praestø 2,789 .... F7
Ramme 506 .... B4
Randers 58,409 .... C5
Ranum 1,472 .... C4
Ribe 8,254 .... B7
Ringe 3,584 .... D7
Ringkøbing 6,298 .... A5
Ringsted 14,076 .... E7
Rødby 5,296 .... E8
Rødding 2,102 .... B7
Rødekro 2,246 .... C7
Rødkaersbro 1,098 .... C5
Rødvig 1,115 .... F7
Rømø 816 .... B7
Rønde 1,523 .... D5
Rønne 14,736 .... F9
Roskilde 44,248 .... E6
Roslev 1,058 .... B4
Rudkøbing 4,080 .... D8
Ruds Vedby 1,071 .... E7
Ry 2,699 .... C5
Ryomgård 1,000 .... D5
Saeby 5,430 .... D3
Sakskøbing 4,102 .... E8
Silkeborg 29,015 .... C5
Sindal 2,406 .... D3
Skaelskør 4,585 .... E7
Skaerbaek 2,483 .... B7
Skagen 11,620 .... D2
Skals 960 .... C4
Skanderborg 11,344 .... D5
Skårup 1,216 .... D7
Skibby 1,549 .... E6
Skive 17,015 .... B4
Skjern 6,056 .... B6
Skodborg 935 .... C7
Skørping 1,675 .... C4
Slagelse 26,851 .... E7
Slangerup 3,036 .... E6
Snedsted 1,105 .... B4
Søllested 960 .... F8
Sønderborg 24,526 .... C8
Sønder Omme 1,393 .... B6
Søndersø 885 .... D7
Sorø 8,683 .... E7
Stege 3,869 .... F8
Stenlille 1,014 .... E6
Stenstrup 1,245 .... D7
Stoholm 1,224 .... C5
Store Heddinge 2,630 .... F7
Støvring 2,366 .... C4
Strandby 1,017 .... D3
Struer 10,848 .... B5
Stubbekøbing 2,031 .... F8
Svaneke 1,193 .... F8
Svendborg 24,203 .... D7
Svinninge 1,797 .... E6
Tarm 3,150 .... B6
Tårnby 45,661 .... F6
Tåstrup 30,608 .... F6
Them 511 .... C5
Thisted 11,252 .... B4
Thyborøn 2,425 .... A4
Thyregod 1,001 .... C6
Tim 553 .... B5
Tinglev 1,531 .... C8
Tistrup 762 .... B6
Toftlund 2,147 .... B7
Tølløse 1,982 .... E6
Tommerup 1,439 .... D7
Tønder 7,469 .... B8
Tørring 1,537 .... C6
Tranebjerg 657 .... D6
Troense 771 .... D7
Trustrup 794 .... D5
Uldum 885 .... C6
Ulfborg 1,357 .... B5
Vamdrup 3,111 .... C7
Varde 11,615 .... B6
Vejen 6,213 .... C7
Vejle 43,976 .... C6
Vemb 989 .... B5
Vester Skerninge 603 .... D7
Vestervig 747 .... B4
Viborg 27,441 .... C5
Viby 1,549 .... F6
Videbaek 2,248 .... B5
Vig 1,037 .... E6
Vildbjerg 1,500 .... B5
Vinderup 2,284 .... B5
Vojens 5,595 .... C7
Vorbasse 791 .... B6
Vordingborg 11,639 .... E7
Vraå 2,652 .... C3

OTHER FEATURES

AErø (isl.) D8
Als (isl.) C8
Amager (isl.) F6
Anholt (isl.) E4
Årø (isl.) C7
Baågø (isl.) C7
Baltic (sea) E9
Bornholm (isl.) F9
Endelave (isl.) D6
Falster (isl.) F8
Fanø (isl.) B7
Fehmarn (str.) E8
Fejø (isl.) E8
Femø (isl.) E8
Frisian, North (isls.) B7
Fyn (isl.) D7
Gelsaå (riv.) C7
Gudenaå (riv.) C5
Isefjord (fjord) E6
Jutland (pen.) C5
Jylland (Jutland) (pen.) C5
Kattegat (str.) E4
Laesø (isl.) D3
Langeland (isl.) D8
Lille Baelt (chan.) C7
Limfjorden (fjord) A4
Løgstør Bredning (fjord) C4
Lolland (isl.) E8
Møn (isl.) F8
Mors (isl.) B4
North (sea) B9
North Frisian (isls.) B7
Omø (isl.) E7
Øresund (sound) F6
Rømø (isl.) B7
Samsø (isl.) D6
Sejerø (isl.) E6
Sjaelland (isl.) E6
Skagens Odde (cape) D2
Skagerrak (str.) C2
Skaw, The (Skagens Odde) (cape) D2
Storaå (riv.) B5
Store Baelt (chan.) D6
Susaå (riv.) E7
The Skaw (Skagens Odde) (cape) D2
Tranebjerg (mt.) C6
Yding Skovhøj (mt.) C6

FÆRØE ISLANDS

CITIES and TOWNS

Klaksvík 4,536 .... B2
Tórshavn (cap.), Faerøe Is. 11,618 .... A3

OTHER FEATURES

Faerøe (isls.) D2
Sandoy (isl.) B3
Streymoy (isl.) B3
Sudhuroy (isl.) B3

ICELAND

CITIES and TOWNS

Akranes 4,253 .... B1
Akureyri 10,755 .... C1
Hafnarfjördhur 9,696 .... B2
Húsavík 1,993 .... C1
Ísafjördhur 2,680 .... B1
Keflavík 5,663 .... B1
Kópavogur 11,105 .... D1
Nes (Neskaupstadhur) 1,552 .... D1
Neskaupstadhur 1,552 .... D1
Ólafsfjördhur 1,086 .... C1
Reykjavík (cap.) 81,693 .... B1
Reykjavík* 98,521 70
Saudhárkrókur 1,600 .... B1
Seydhisfjördhur 884 .... D1
Siglufjördhur 2,161 .... C1
Vestmannaeyjar 5,186 .... B2

OTHER FEATURES

Bjargtangar (pt.) A1
Breidhafjördhur (fjord) B1
Faxaflói (bay) B1
Fontur (pt.) D1
Gerpir (cape) D1
Grímsey (isl.) C1
Hekla (vol.) B1
Horn (cape) B1
Húnaflói (bay) B1
Hvannadalshnúkur (mt.) C1
North (Horn) (cape) B1
Reykjanestá (cape) A2
Surtsey (isl.) B2
Thjórsá (riv.) C1
Vatnajökull (glac.) C1

*City and suburbs

Germany
CONIC PROJECTION
SCALE OF MILES
SCALE OF KILOMETERS
Capitals of Countries
State and District Capitals
International Boundaries
State and District Boundaries
Canals
East Germany is divided into districts bearing the same name as their respective capitals.
DENMARK
BALTIC SEA
NORTH SEA
NORTH FRISIAN ISLANDS
EAST FRISIAN ISLANDS
WEST FRISIAN ISLANDS
SCHLESWIG-HOLSTEIN
MECKLENBURG
POMERANIA
BRANDENBURG
EAST GERMANY
LOWER SAXONY
NORTH RHINE-WESTPHALIA
HESSE
THURINGIA
SAXONY
RHINELAND-PALATINATE
SAARLAND
BADEN-WÜRTTEMBERG
BAVARIA
WEST GERMANY
NETHERLANDS
BELGIUM
LUXEMBOURG
FRANCE
SWITZERLAND
AUSTRIA
CZECHOSLOVAKIA
POLAND
BERLIN
HAMBURG
BREMEN
MUNICH
Berlin
WEST
EAST
Longitude East 10° of Greenwich
© Copyright HAMMOND INCORPORATED, Maplewood, N. J.

AREA 95,985 sq. mi. (248,601 sq. km.)
POPULATION 61,658,000
CAPITAL Bonn
LARGEST CITY Berlin (West)
HIGHEST POINT Zugspitze 9,718 ft. (2,962 m.)
MONETARY UNIT Deutsche mark
MAJOR LANGUAGE German
MAJOR RELIGIONS Protestantism, Roman Catholicism

AREA 41,768 sq. mi. (108,179 sq. km.)
POPULATION 16,737,000
CAPITAL Berlin (East)
LARGEST CITY Berlin (East)
HIGHEST POINT Fichtelberg 3,983 ft. (1,214 m.)
MONETARY UNIT East German mark
MAJOR LANGUAGE German
MAJOR RELIGIONS Protestantism, Roman Catholicism

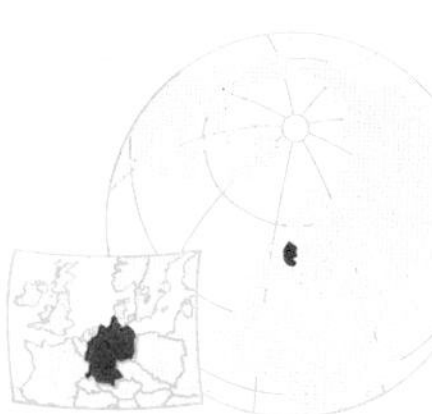

WEST GERMANY

EAST GERMANY

Topography

0 50 100 MI.
0 50 100 KM.

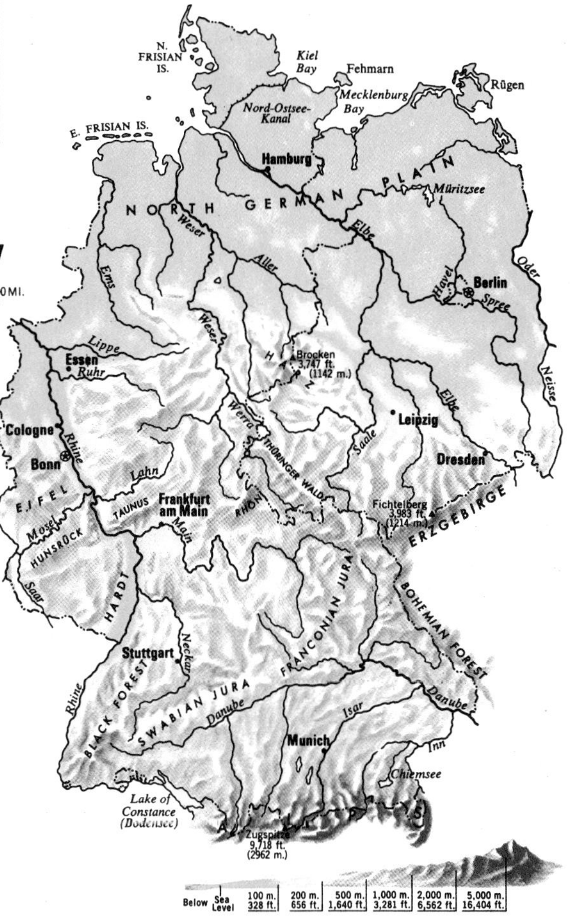

EAST GERMANY

DISTRICTS

in 1,094,147 ..... F4
bus 872,242 ..... F3
sden 1,845,459 ..... E3
rt 1,247,213 ..... D3
kfurt 688,637 ..... F2
a 738,847 ..... D3
e 1,890,187 ..... D3
-Marx-Stadt 1,994,115 ..... E3
zig 1,457,817 ..... E3
deburg 1,297,881 ..... D2
brandenburg 628,686 ..... E2
dam 1,124,892 ..... E2
ock 867,806 ..... E1
werin 592,334 ..... D2
l 550,497 ..... D3

CITIES and TOWNS

1 11,742 ..... D3
nburg 51,193 ..... E3
ermünde 11,786 ..... E2
lam 19,099 ..... E2
aberg-Buchholz 26,561 ..... E3
lda 28,649 ..... D3
stadt 29,462 ..... D3
hersleben 36,674 ..... D3
32,622 ..... E3
rbach 18,168 ..... E3
Doberan 12,541 ..... D1
Dürrenberg 15,192 ..... D3
Langensalza 166,282 ..... D3
Salzungen 17,277 ..... C3
h 12,069 ..... E1
tzen 45,851 ..... F3
gen 13,244 ..... E1
in, East (cap.) 1,094,147 ..... F4
nau bei Berlin 15,749 ..... E2
nburg 44,428 ..... D3
chofswerda 11,540 ..... F3
erfeld 27,062 ..... E3
kenburg am Harz 18,784 ..... D3
enburg an der Elbe 12,428 ..... D2
na 21,807 ..... E3
ndenburg 94,071 ..... E2
g bei Magdeburg 29,027 ..... D2
e 15,976 ..... D3
mnitz
Karl-Marx-Stadt) 303,811 ..... E3
wig, Dresden 22,149 ..... E3
wig, Halle 12,473 ..... E3
tbus 94,293 ..... F3
nmitschau 28,845 ..... E3
tzsch 24,076 ..... E3
nmin 17,270 ..... E2
sau 100,820 ..... E3
eln 27,624 ..... E3
sden 507,692 ..... E3
rsbach 12,694 ..... F3
rswalde-Finow 47,141 ..... E2
nburg 22,245 ..... E3
enach 49,954 ..... D3
enberg 13,450 ..... D3
enhüttenstadt 46,455 ..... F2
eben 29,297 ..... D3
urt 202,979 ..... D3
kensee 25,295 ..... E3
kenstein 14,367 ..... E3
sterwalde 22,466 ..... E3
st 28,084 ..... F3
nkfurt an der Oder 70,817 ..... F2
berg 50,815 ..... E3
tal 46,061 ..... E3
dland E2
stenwalde 31,065 ..... F2
delegen 12,987 ..... D2
nthin 15,916 ..... E2
a 113,108 ..... E3
uchau 30,927 ..... E3
litz 84,658 ..... F3
ha 59,243 ..... D3
ifswald 53,940 ..... E1
iz 37,612 ..... E3
vesmühlen 12,005 ..... D2
mma 17,100 ..... E3
mmen 14,571 ..... E1
ssenhain 18,712 ..... E3
ssräschen 12,889 ..... E3
oen
Wilhelm-Pieck-Stadt) 32,731 ..... F3
strow 36,824 ..... E2
berstadt 46,669 ..... D3
densleben 19,194 ..... D2
le 241,425 ..... D3
le-Neustadt 67,956 ..... D3
velberg D2
denau 21,315 ..... E3
ligenstadt 13,931 ..... D3
nnigsdorf bei Berlin 24,853 ..... E3
ttstedt 20,291 ..... D3
dburghausen 11,372 ..... D3
yerswerda 64,904 ..... F3
enau 22,021 ..... D3
na 99,431 ..... D3
hanngeorgenstadt 10,328 ..... E3
erbog 13,477 ..... E3
menz 18,221 ..... F3
l-Marx-Stadt 303,811 ..... E3
inmachnow 14,059 ..... E4
ngenthal 13,614 ..... E3
nigs Wusterhausen 11,825 ..... E2

Köpenick 130,987 ..... F4
Köthen 35,451 ..... E3
Kühlungsborn D1
Lauchhammer 26,939 ..... E3
Leipzig 570,972 ..... E3
Lichtenberg 192,063 ..... F4
Limbach-Oberfrohna 25,706 ..... E3
Löbau 18,077 ..... F3
Lübben 14,224 ..... E3
Lübbenau 22,350 ..... F3
Luckenwalde 28,544 ..... E2
Ludwigslust 13,280 ..... D2
Magdeburg 276,089 ..... D2
Markkleeberg 22,380 ..... E3
Meerane 25,037 ..... E3
Meiningen 26,134 ..... D3
Meissen 43,561 ..... E3
Merseburg 54,269 ..... D3
Meuselwitz 13,585 ..... E3
Mittweida 19,259 ..... E3
Mühlhausen (Thomas-Müntzer-Stadt) 44,106 ..... D3
Nauen 11,940 ..... E2
Naumburg 36,358 ..... D3
Neubrandenburg 59,971 ..... E2
Neuenhagen bei Berlin 12,603 ..... F4
Neuruppin 24,888 ..... E2
Neustrelitz 27,074 ..... E2
Nordhausen 44,442 ..... D3
Oelsnitz 15,084 ..... E3
Oelsnitz im Erzgebirge 16,063 ..... E3
Olbernhau 13,479 ..... E3
Oranienburg 24,452 ..... E2
Oschatz 18,974 ..... E3
Oschersleben 17,377 ..... D2
Pankow 136,527 ..... F3
Parchim 22,927 ..... D2
Pasewalk 15,099 ..... F2
Peenemünde E1
Perleberg 15,029 ..... D2
Pirna 49,771 ..... E3
Plauen 80,353 ..... E3
Pössneck 18,648 ..... D3
Potsdam 117,236 ..... E2
Prenzlau 22,738 ..... E2
Pritzwalk 11,887 ..... E2
Quedlinburg 29,796 ..... D3
Radeberg 18,528 ..... E3
Radebeul 38,383 ..... E3
Rathenow 32,011 ..... E2
Reichenbach 27,440 ..... E3
Ribnitz-Damgarten 17,254 ..... E1
Riesa 49,989 ..... E3
Rosslau 16,520 ..... E3
Rostock 210,167 ..... E1
Rudolstadt 31,698 ..... D3
Saalfeld 33,648 ..... D3
Salzwedel 21,741 ..... D2
Sangerhausen 32,721 ..... D3
Sassnitz 13,857 ..... E1
Schkeuditz 15,585 ..... E3
Schmalkalden 15,017 ..... D3
Schmölln 13,406 ..... E3
Schneeberg 20,376 ..... E3
Schönebeck 45,197 ..... D2
Schwedt 45,729 ..... F2
Schwerin 104,984 ..... D2
Sebnitz 13,470 ..... F3
Senftenberg 29,953 ..... F3
Sömmerda 20,712 ..... D3
Sondershausen 23,383 ..... D3
Sonneberg 29,193 ..... D3
Spremberg 22,862 ..... F3
Stassfurt 26,225 ..... D3
Stendal 39,647 ..... D2
Stralsund 72,167 ..... E1
Strausberg 21,334 ..... F2
Suhl 36,642 ..... D3
Tangermünde 12,898 ..... D2
Teltow 16,171 ..... E4
Templin 11,718 ..... E2
Thale 17,248 ..... D3
Thomas-Müntzer-Stadt 44,106 ..... D3
Torgau 21,613 ..... E3
Torgelow 14,320 ..... F2
Treptow 127,448 ..... F4
Ueckermünde 11,423 ..... F2
Waldheim 11,925 ..... E3
Waltershausen 13,893 ..... D3
Waren 22,921 ..... E2
Weida 11,816 ..... D3
Weimar 63,144 ..... D3
Weissenfels 43,191 ..... D3
Weissensee 78,451 ..... F3
Weisswasser 25,910 ..... F3
Werdau 22,249 ..... E3
Wernigerode 34,658 ..... D3
Wilhelm-Pieck-Stadt 32,731 ..... F3
Wismar 56,765 ..... D2
Wittenberg 51,364 ..... E3
Wittenberge 32,907 ..... D2
Wolfen 27,570 ..... E3
Wolgast 16,384 ..... E1
Wurzen 20,501 ..... E3
Zehdenick 12,651 ..... E2
Zeitz 44,582 ..... E3
Zella-Mehlis 16,301 ..... D3
Zerbst 19,356 ..... E3
Zeulenroda 13,452 ..... D3
Zittau 42,298 ..... F3
Zwickau 123,069 ..... E3

OTHER FEATURES

Altmark (reg.) D2
Arkona (cape) E1
Baltic (sea) E1
Black Elster (riv.) E3
Brandenburg (reg.) E2
Elbe (riv.) D2
Elde (riv.) D2
Elster, Black (riv.) E3
Elster, White (riv.) E3
Erzgebirge (mts.) E3
Fichtelberg (mt.) E3
Harz (mts.) D3
Havel (riv.) E2
Lusatia (reg.) F3
Mecklenburg (bay) D1
Mecklenburg (reg.) E2
Mulde (riv.) E3
Neisse (riv.) F3
Oder (riv.) F2
Peene (riv.) E2
Pomerania (reg.) E2
Pomeranian (bay) F1
Rhön (mts.) D3
Rügen (isl.) E1
Saale (riv.) D3
Saxony (reg.) E3
Spree (riv.) F3
Spreewald (for.) F3
Thüringer Wald (for.) D3
Thuringia (reg.) D3
Ücker (riv.) E2
Unstrut (riv.) D3
Usedom (isl.) F1
Warnow (riv.) D2
Werra (riv.) D3
White Elster (riv.) E3

WEST GERMANY

STATES

Baden-Württemberg 9,152,700 ..... C4
Bavaria 10,810,400 ..... D4
Berlin (West) (free city) 1,984,800 ..... E4
Bremen 716,800 ..... C2
Hamburg 1,717,400 ..... D2
Hesse 5,549,800 ..... C3
Lower Saxony 7,238,500 ..... C2
North Rhine-Westphalia 17,129,600 ..... B3
Rhineland-Palatinate 3,665,800 ..... B4
Saarland 1,096,300 ..... B4
Schleswig-Holstein 2,582,400 ..... C1

CITIES and TOWNS

Aachen 242,453 ..... B3
Aalen 64,735 ..... D4
Ahaus 27,126 ..... B2
Ahlen 54,214 ..... B3
Ahrensburg 24,964 ..... D2
Alfeld 24,273 ..... C2
Alsdorf 47,473 ..... B3
Alsfeld 18,091 ..... C3
Altena 26,753 ..... B3
Altona C2
Alzey 15,190 ..... C4
Amberg 46,934 ..... D4
Andernach 27,132 ..... B3
Ansbach 39,117 ..... D4
Arnsberg 80,287 ..... C3
Arolsen 15,619 ..... C3
Aschaffenburg 55,398 ..... C4
Augsburg 249,943 ..... D4
Aurich 34,194 ..... B2
Backnang 29,614 ..... C4
Bad Berleburg 20,415 ..... C3
Bad Driburg 17,478 ..... C3
Bad Dürkheim 16,133 ..... C4
Bad Ems 10,487 ..... B3
Baden-Baden 49,718 ..... C4
Bad Gandersheim 11,614 ..... D3
Bad Harzburg 25,786 ..... D3
Bad Hersfeld 29,248 ..... C3
Bad Homburg vor der Höhe 51,196 ..... C3
Bad Honnef 20,903 ..... B3
Bad Kissingen 22,279 ..... D3
Bad Kreuznach 42,588 ..... B4
Bad Lauterberg im Harz 14,715 ..... D3
Bad Mergentheim 19,895 ..... C4
Bad Münstereifel 14,340 ..... B3
Bad Nauheim 25,916 ..... C3
Bad Neuenahr-Ahrweiler 26,371 ..... B3
Bad Oldesloe 19,640 ..... D2
Bad Pyrmont 21,896 ..... C3
Bad Reichenhall 13,048 ..... E5
Bad Salzuflen 50,924 ..... C2
Bad Schwartau 18,696 ..... D2
Bad Segeberg 13,320 ..... D2
Bad Tölz 12,458 ..... D5
Bad Vilbel 25,012 ..... C3
Bad Waldsee 14,296 ..... C5
Bad Wildungen 15,418 ..... C3
Bad Wimpfen 5,536 ..... C4
Baiersbronn 14,845 ..... C4
Balingen 29,310 ..... C4
Bamberg 74,236 ..... D4
Barsinghausen 32,873 ..... C2
Bassum 14,113 ..... C2
Bayreuth 67,035 ..... D4
Bayrischzell 1,639 ..... E5
Bebra 15,740 ..... C3
Bendorf 15,943 ..... B3
Bensheim 32,653 ..... C4
Bentheim 13,681 ..... B2
Berchtesgaden 8,558 ..... E5
Bergisch Gladbach 99,517 ..... B3
Berleburg (Bad Berleburg) 20,415 ..... C3
Berlin (West) 1,984,837 ..... E4
Biberach an der Riss 28,891 ..... C4
Bielefeld 316,058 ..... C2
Bietigheim-Bissingen 34,042 ..... C4
Bingen 24,541 ..... B4
Birkenfeld 5,883 ..... B4
Blaubeuren 11,652 ..... C4
Böblingen 40,547 ..... C4
Bocholt 65,460 ..... B3
Bochum 414,842 ..... B3
Bonn (cap.) 283,711 ..... B3
Boppard 16,888 ..... B3
Borghorst 17,238 ..... B2
Borken 30,212 ..... B3
Bornheim 32,847 ..... B3
Bottrop 101,495 ..... B3
Brake 18,089 ..... C2
Bramsche 24,119 ..... B2
Braunschweig (Brunswick) 268,519 ..... D2
Breisach am Rhein 9,230 ..... B4
Bremen 572,969 ..... C2
Bremerhaven 143,836 ..... C2
Bremervörde 17,565 ..... C2
Bretten 22,140 ..... C4
Brilon 24,595 ..... C3
Bruchsal 38,929 ..... C4
Brühl 44,305 ..... B3
Brunsbüttel 11,451 ..... C2
Brunswick 268,519 ..... D2
Buchholz in der Nordheide 25,713 ..... C2
Bückeburg 21,393 ..... C2
Büdingen 16,846 ..... C3
Bühl 21,596 ..... C4
Bünde 40,021 ..... C2
Büren 17,352 ..... C3
Burg auf Fehmarn 5,874 ..... D1
Burghausen 16,892 ..... E4
Burgsteinfurt 31,367 ..... B2
Butzbach 20,592 ..... C3
Buxtehude 30,249 ..... C2
Castrop-Rauxel 82,373 ..... B3
Celle 74,347 ..... D2
Cham 12,423 ..... E4
Charlottenburg 201,732 ..... E4
Clausthal-Zellerfeld 16,690 ..... D3
Cloppenburg 19,757 ..... B2
Coburg 46,244 ..... D3
Coesfeld 30,617 ..... B3
Cologne 1,013,771 ..... B3
Crailsheim 24,506 ..... D4
Cuxhaven 60,353 ..... C2
Dachau 33,207 ..... D4
Dahlem E4
Darmstadt 137,018 ..... C4
Deggendorf 25,188 ..... E4
Delmenhorst 71,488 ..... C2
Detmold 65,629 ..... C3
Diepholz 14,201 ..... C2
Dillenburg 14,068 ..... C3
Dillingen 21,369 ..... B4
Dillingen an der Donau 11,601 ..... D4
Dingolfing 13,325 ..... E4
Dinkelsbühl 10,034 ..... D4
Donaueschingen 17,578 ..... C5
Donauwörth 17,077 ..... D4
Dorsten 65,718 ..... B3
Dortmund 630,609 ..... B3
Duderstadt 23,255 ..... D3
Dudweiler 27,877 ..... B4
Duisburg 591,635 ..... B3
Dülmen 37,013 ..... B3
Düren 87,774 ..... B3
Düsseldorf 664,336 ..... B3
Eberbach 15,834 ..... C4
Ebingen 22,594 ..... C4
Eckernförde 22,938 ..... D1
Ehingen 21,600 ..... C4
Eichstätt 13,080 ..... D4
Einbeck 29,821 ..... C3
Eiserfeld 22,346 ..... C3
Ellwangen 21,004 ..... D4
Elmshorn 41,355 ..... C2
Emden 53,509 ..... B2
Emmendingen 24,722 ..... B4
Emmerich 29,113 ..... B3
Emsdetten 30,195 ..... B2
Erlangen 100,671 ..... D4
Eschwege 24,882 ..... C3
Eschweiler 53,603 ..... B3
Espelkamp 22,670 ..... C2
Essen 677,568 ..... B3
Esslingen am Neckar 95,298 ..... C4
Ettlingen 35,159 ..... C4
Euskirchen 43,558 ..... B3
Eutin 17,701 ..... D1
Fellbach 42,501 ..... C4
Flensburg 93,213 ..... C1
Forchheim 23,430 ..... D4
Frankenberg-Eder 15,337 ..... C3
Frankenthal 43,684 ..... C4
Frankfurt am Main 636,157 ..... C3
Frechen 41,453 ..... B3
Freiburg im Breisgau 175,371 ..... B5
Freising 31,524 ..... D4
Freudenstadt 19,454 ..... C4
Friedberg 24,762 ..... C3
Friedrichshafen 51,544 ..... C5
Fritzlar 15,079 ..... C3
Fulda 58,976 ..... C3
Fürstenfeldbruck 27,194 ..... D4
Fürth 101,639 ..... D4
Füssen 10,506 ..... D5
Gaggenau 28,846 ..... C4
Garbsen 56,337 ..... C2
Garmisch-Partenkirchen 26,831 ..... D5
Gatow E4
Geesthacht 24,745 ..... D2
Geislingen an der Steige 28,693 ..... C4
Geldern 24,082 ..... B3
Gelnhausen 17,889 ..... C3
Gelsenkirchen 322,584 ..... B3
Georgsmarienhütte 30,259 ..... B2
Geretsried 17,330 ..... D5
Germersheim 12,041 ..... C4
Gerolstein 6,857 ..... B3
Gifhorn 31,635 ..... D2
Glückstadt 12,159 ..... C2
Goch 28,213 ..... B3
Göggingen 15,980 ..... D4
Göppingen 54,365 ..... C4
Goslar 53,957 ..... D3
Göttingen 123,797 ..... D3
Greven 27,479 ..... B2
Grevenbroich 56,392 ..... B3
Griesheim 18,548 ..... C4
Gronau 40,527 ..... B2
Gummersbach 49,316 ..... B3
Günzburg 13,528 ..... D4
Gunzenhausen 13,565 ..... D4
Gütersloh 77,128 ..... C3
Haar 18,824 ..... D4
Hagen 229,224 ..... B3
Haltern 29,750 ..... B3
Hamburg 1,717,383 ..... D2
Hameln 61,066 ..... C2
Hamm 172,210 ..... B3
Hammelburg 12,350 ..... C3
Hanau 86,676 ..... C3
Hannover 552,955 ..... C2
Harburg-Wilhelmsburg C2
Hassloch 17,752 ..... C4
Haunstetten 21,810 ..... D4
Hechingen 15,926 ..... C4
Heide 21,918 ..... C1
Heidelberg 129,368 ..... C4
Heidenheim an der Brenz 49,943 ..... D4
Heilbronn 113,177 ..... C4
Helmstedt 28,095 ..... D2
Hennef 27,815 ..... B3
Herford 64,385 ..... C2
Herne 190,561 ..... B3
Hildesheim 105,290 ..... D2
Hockenheim 16,890 ..... C4
Hof 54,357 ..... D3
Hofgeismar 13,380 ..... C3
Holzminden 23,650 ..... C3
Homburg 41,861 ..... B4
Horn-Bad Meinberg 16,927 ..... C3
Höxter 32,759 ..... C3
Hückelhoven 34,865 ..... B3
Hünfeld 13,873 ..... C3
Hürth 51,692 ..... B3
Husum 24,984 ..... C1
Hüttental 39,561 ..... C3
Ibbenbüren 42,202 ..... B2
Idar-Oberstein 37,179 ..... B4
Immenstadt im Allgäu 13,720 ..... C5
Ingolstadt 88,500 ..... D4
Iserlohn 96,174 ..... B3
Isny im Allgäu 12,367 ..... D5
Itzehoe 35,077 ..... C2
Jever 12,096 ..... B2
Jülich 31,564 ..... B3
Kaiserslautern 100,886 ..... B4
Karlsruhe 280,448 ..... C4
Kassel 205,534 ..... C3
Kaufbeuren 42,224 ..... D5
Kehl 29,861 ..... B4
Kelheim 11,996 ..... D4
Kempten 56,944 ..... D5
Kevelaer 20,971 ..... B3
Kiel 262,164 ..... D1
Kirchheim unter Teck 31,666 ..... C4
Kitzingen 19,116 ..... C4
Kleve 44,043 ..... B3
Koblenz 118,394 ..... B3
Köln (Cologne) 1,013,771 ..... B3
Königswinter 34,586 ..... B3
Konstanz 70,152 ..... C5
Korbach 22,998 ..... C3
Kornwestheim 27,771 ..... C4
Krefeld 228,463 ..... B3
Kreutztal 30,473 ..... C3
Kronach 11,538 ..... D3
Kulmbach 25,711 ..... D3
Lage 31,724 ..... C3
Lahnstein 19,725 ..... B3
Lahr 35,570 ..... B4
Lampertheim 31,993 ..... C4
Landau in der Pfalz 37,661 ..... C4
Landsberg am Lech 15,862 ..... D4
Landshut 55,858 ..... E4
Langen 30,227 ..... C4
Langenhagen 47,092 ..... C2
Lauenburg an der Elbe 11,077 ..... D2
Lauf an der Pegnitz 19,443 ..... D4
Lauingen 8,778 ..... D4
Lauterbach 15,007 ..... C3
Leer 32,785 ..... B2
Lehrte 38,272 ..... D2
Lemgo 39,664 ..... C2
Lengerich 20,836 ..... B2
Leverkusen 165,947 ..... B3
Lichtenfels 13,719 ..... D3
Limburg an der Lahn 28,606 ..... C3
Lindau 23,930 ..... C5

(continued on following page)

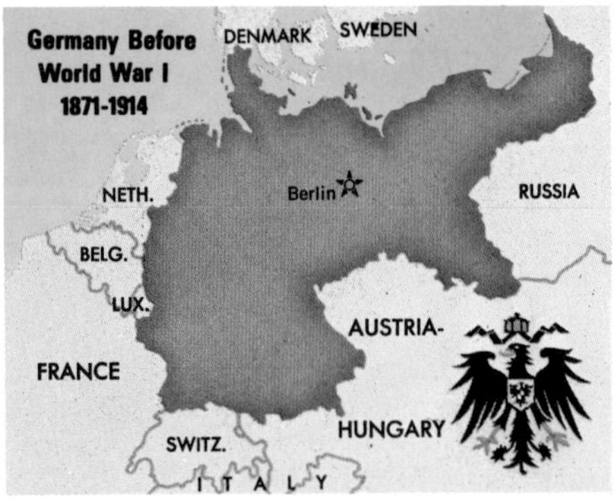

Lingen 43,785 .... B2
Lippstadt 63,040 .... C3
Löhne 17,859 .... C2
Lohr am Main 16,435 .... C4
Lörrach 44,179 .... B5
Lübeck 232,270 .... D2
Lüdenscheid 76,213 .... B3
Ludwigsburg 83,622 .... C4
Ludwigshafen am Rhein 170,374 .... C4
Lüneburg 64,586 .... D2
Lünen 85,685 .... B3
Mainz 183,880 .... C4
Mannheim 314,086 .... C4
Marbach am Neckar 12,131 .... C4
Marburg an der Lahn 72,458 .... C3
Marktredwitz 16,404 .... E4
Marl 91,930 .... B3
Mayen 21,018 .... B3
Mechernich 21,498 .... B3
Melle 41,339 .... C2
Melsungen 13,444 .... C3
Memmingen 34,612 .... D5
Meppen 27,308 .... B2
Merzig 30,197 .... B4
Meschede 32,472 .... C3
Metzingen 19,224 .... C4
Michelstadt 13,591 .... C4
Minden 78,887 .... C2
Mittenwald 8,831 .... D5
Mölln 15,780 .... D2
Mönchengladbach 261,367 .... B3
Moosburg an der Isar 12,196 .... D4
Mosbach 23,663 .... C4
Mühldorf am Inn 12,638 .... E4
Mülheim an der Ruhr 189,259 .... B3
Müllheim 12,183 .... B5
München (Munich) 1,314,865 .... D4
Münden 27,018 .... C3
Munich 1,314,865 .... D4
Münster 264,546 .... B3
Nagold 19,047 .... C4
Neckarsulm 20,112 .... C4
Neheim-Hüsten 36,373 .... C3
Neuburg an der Donau 19,400 .... D4
Neu-Isenburg 35,631 .... C3
Neumarkt in der
  Oberpfalz 29,713 .... D4
Neumünster 84,777 .... C1
Neunkirchen 54,992 .... B4
Neuss 148,198 .... B3
Neustadt an der
  Weinstrasse 51,011 .... B4
Neustadt bei Coburg 12,665 .... D3
Neustadt in Holstein 15,333 .... D1
Neu-Ulm 31,660 .... D4
Neuwied 62,029 .... B3
Nienburg 30,978 .... C2
Norden 24,207 .... B2
Nordenham 31,457 .... C2
Norderstedt 61,553 .... D2
Nordhorn 49,598 .... B2
Nördlingen 16,480 .... D4
Northeim 32,665 .... C3
Nuremberg 499,060 .... D4
Nürnberg (Nuremberg) 499,060 .... D4
Nürtingen 34,333 .... C4
Oberammergau 4,704 .... D5
Oberhausen 237,147 .... B3
Oberstdorf 11,687 .... D5
Oberursel 39,802 .... C3
Offenbach am Main 115,251 .... C3
Offenburg 51,553 .... B4
Oldenburg 134,706 .... C2
Oldenburg in Holstein 9,201 .... D1
Opladen 42,789 .... B3
Osnabrück 161,671 .... C2
Osterholz-Scharmbeck 22,734 .... C2
Osterode am Harz 29,668 .... D3
Paderborn 103,705 .... C3
Papenburg 27,039 .... B2
Passau 50,920 .... E4
Peine 49,450 .... D2
Pfaffenhofen an der Ilm 13,684 .... D4
Pforzheim 108,635 .... C4
Pfullingen 16,195 .... C4
Pinneberg 36,844 .... C2
Pirmasens 53,651 .... B4
Plettenberg 29,273 .... C3
Porz am Rhein 74,915 .... B3
Preetz 15,305 .... D1
Puttgarden D1
Radolfzell 23,274 .... C5
Rastatt 38,030 .... C4
Rastede 16,905 .... C2
Ratingen 86,028 .... B3
Ratzeburg 12,189 .... D2
Ravensburg 42,725 .... C5
Recklinghausen 122,437 .... B3
Regensburg 131,886 .... E4
Remagen 14,627 .... B3
Remscheid 133,145 .... B3
Rendsburg 34,407 .... C1
Reutlingen 95,289 .... C4
Rheda-Wiedenbrück 37,371 .... C3
Rheine 71,539 .... B2
Rheinfelden 27,500 .... B5
Rheydt 100,077 .... B3
Rietberg 22,421 .... C3
Rinteln 25,595 .... C2
Rosenheim 38,419 .... D5
Rotenburg 19,155 .... C2
Rotenburg an der Fulda 14,438 .... C3
Roth bei Nürnberg 17,782 .... D4
Rothenburg ob der
  Tauber 11,609 .... D4
Rottenburg am Neckar 30,583 .... C4
Rottweil 24,534 .... C4
Rüsselsheim 62,067 .... C4
Saarbrücken 205,336 .... B4
Saarlouis 39,974 .... B4
Säckingen 13,956 .... C5
Salzgitter 117,341 .... D2
Sankt Goar 3,511 .... B3
Sankt Ingbert 43,263 .... B4
Sankt Wendel 27,558 .... B4
Saulgau 15,403 .... C5
Schleswig 30,974 .... C1
Schlüchtern 13,801 .... C3
Schöneberg 169,835 .... E4
Schöningen 16,348 .... D2
Schramberg 19,677 .... C4
Schwabach 33,136 .... D4
Schwäbisch Gmünd 56,422 .... C4
Schwäbisch Hall 32,129 .... C4
Schwalmstadt 17,800 .... C3
Schwandorf im Bayern 22,547 .... E4
Schweinfurt 56,164 .... D3
Schwelm 31,850 .... B3
Schwetzingen 18,286 .... C4
Seesen 23,577 .... D3
Selb 16,723 .... E3
Sennestadt 20,187 .... C3
Siegburg 34,943 .... B3
Siegen 116,552 .... C3
Sigmaringen 15,437 .... C4
Sindelfingen 54,134 .... C4
Singen 45,566 .... C5
Soest 40,308 .... C3
Solingen 171,810 .... B3
Soltau 19,949 .... C2
Sonthofen 17,821 .... D5
Spandau 197,687 .... E3
Speyer 44,471 .... C4
Springe 30,968 .... C2
Stade 42,097 .... C2
Stadthagen 23,003 .... C2
Stolberg 57,379 .... B3
Straubing 43,774 .... E4
Stuttgart 600,421 .... C4
Sulzbach 22,133 .... B4
Sulzbach-Rosenberg 18,596 .... D4
Tailfingen 17,278 .... C4
Tegel E3
Telgte 15,165 .... B3
Tempelhof 159,730 .... F4
Timmendorfer Strand 10,690 .... D1
Traunstein 14,088 .... E5
Travemünde D2
Treuchtlingen 11,939 .... D4
Trier 100,338 .... B4
Troisdorf 56,402 .... B3
Tübingen 71,348 .... C4
Tuttlingen 32,342 .... C5
Übach-Palenberg 22,403 .... B3
Überlingen 17,735 .... C5
Uelzen 37,550 .... D2
Uetersen 16,330 .... C2
Ulm 98,237 .... C4
Uslar 17,251 .... C3
Varel 24,435 .... C2
Vechta 21,786 .... C2
Verden 24,247 .... C2
Viersen 84,220 .... B3
Villingen-Schwenningen 80,646 .... C4
Völklingen 47,271 .... B4
Waldkirch 19,009 .... B4
Waldkraiburg 20,140 .... E4
Waldshut-Tiengen 22,046 .... C5
Walsrode 23,423 .... C2
Wangen im Allgäu 23,127 .... C5
Wanne-Eickel 99,156 .... B3
Warburg 22,150 .... C3
Warendorf 32,273 .... B3
Wedel 30,045 .... C2
Weiden in der Oberpfalz 42,697 .... D4
Weilburg 12,652 .... C3
Weilheim im Oberbayern 15,347 .... D5
Weingarten 21,143 .... C5
Weinheim 41,005 .... C4
Weissenburg im Bayern 16,083 .... D4
Wertheim 20,942 .... C4
Wesel 56,584 .... B3
Westerland 9,652 .... C1
Westerstede 16,977 .... B2
Wiehl 19,004 .... B3
Wiesbaden 250,592 .... B3
Wildbad im Schwarzwald 11,611 .... C4
Wildeshausen 12,055 .... C2
Wilhelmshaven 103,417 .... B2
Witten 108,771 .... B3
Wittingen 12,189 .... D2
Wittlich 15,321 .... B3
Witzenhausen 16,877 .... C3
Wolfenbüttel 51,386 .... D2
Wolfsburg 126,298 .... D2
Worms 75,732 .... C4
Wunstorf 36,795 .... C2
Wuppertal 405,369 .... B3
Würzburg 112,584 .... C4
Xanten 15,688 .... B3
Zirndorf 13,661 .... D4
Zülpich 16,171 .... B3
Zweibrücken 35,978 .... B4
Zwischenahn 22,581 .... B2

OTHER FEATURES

Aller (riv.) C2
Allgäu (reg.) D5
Altmühl (riv.) D4
Ammersee (lake) D4
Amrum (isl.) C1
Baltrum (isl.) B2
Bavarian (for.) E4
Bavarian Alps (range) D5
Black (for.) C4
Bodensee (Constance) (lake) C5
Bohemian (for.) E4
Borkum (isl.) B2
Breisgau (reg.) B5
Chiemsee (lake) E5
Constance (lake) C5
Danube (riv.) C4
Donau (Danube) (riv.) C4
East Friesland (reg.) B2
East Frisian (isls.) B2
Eder (res.) C3
Elbe (riv.) C2
Ems (riv.) B2
Fehmarn (isl.) D1
Feldberg (mt.) C5
Fichtelgebirge (range) D3
Föhr (isl.) C1
Franconian Jura (range) D4
Frisian, East (isls.) B2
Frisian, North (isls.) B1
Grosser Arber (mt.) E4
Halligen (isls.) C1
Hardt (mts.) C4
Harz (mts.) D3
Hase (riv.) B2
Hegau (reg.) C5
Helgoland (bay) C1
Helgoland (isl.) B1
Hunsrück (mts.) B4
Hunte (riv.) C2
Iller (riv.) D4
Inn (riv.) E4
Isar (riv.) E4
Juist (isl.) B2
Kaiserstuhl (mt.) B4
Kiel (bay) D1
Kiel (Nord-Ostsee) (canal) C1
Königssee (lake) E5
Lahn (riv.) C3
Langeoog (isl.) B2
Lech (riv.) ....
Leine (riv.) ....
Lippe (riv.) ....
Lüneburger Heide (dist.) ....
Main (riv.) ....
Mecklenburg (bay) ....
Mosel (riv.) ....
Naab (riv.) ....
Neckar (riv.) ....
Norderney (isl.) ....
Nord-Ostsee (canal) ....
Nordstrand (isl.) ....
North (sea) ....
North Friesland (reg.) ....
North Frisian (isls.) ....
Odenwald (for.) ....
Oker (riv.) ....
Pellworm (isl.) ....
Regen (riv.) ....
Regnitz (riv.) ....
Rhine (riv.) ....
Rhön (mts.) ....
Ruhr (riv.) ....
Saar (riv.) ....
Sauer (riv.) ....
Sauerland (reg.) ....
Schneeberg (mt.) ....
Schwarzwald (Black) (for.) ....
Spessart (range) ....
Spiekeroog (isl.) ....
Starnbergersee (lake) ....
Swabian Jura (range) ....
Sylt (isl.) ....
Tauber (riv.) ....
Taunus (range) ....
Tegernsee (lake) ....
Teutoburger Wald (for.) ....
Vogelsberg (mts.) ....
Walchensee (lake) ....
Wangerooge (isl.) ....
Watzmann (mt.) ....
Weser (riv.) ....
Westerwald (for.) ....
Würmsee (Starnbergersee)
  (lake) ....
Zugspitze (mt.) ....

Agriculture, Industry and Resources

DOMINANT LAND USE

- Wheat, Sugar Beets
- Cereals (chiefly rye, oats, barley)
- Potatoes, Rye
- Dairy, Livestock
- Mixed Cereals, Dairy
- Truck Farming
- Grapes, Fruit
- Forests

MAJOR MINERAL OCCURRENCES

Ag	Silver	K	Potash
Ba	Barite	Lg	Lignite
C	Coal	Na	Salt
Cu	Copper	O	Petroleum
Fe	Iron Ore	Pb	Lead
G	Natural Gas	U	Uranium
Gr	Graphite	Zn	Zinc

Water Power
Major Industrial Areas

AREA 15,892 sq. mi. (41,160 sq. km.)
POPULATION 14,227,000
CAPITALS The Hague, Amsterdam
LARGEST CITY Amsterdam
HIGHEST POINT Vaalserberg 1,056 ft. (322 m.)
MONETARY UNIT guilder (florin)
MAJOR LANGUAGE Dutch
MAJOR RELIGIONS Protestantism, Roman Catholicism

AREA 11,781 sq. mi. (30,513 sq. km.)
POPULATION 9,855,110
CAPITAL Brussels
LARGEST CITY Brussels (greater)
HIGHEST POINT Botrange 2,277 ft. (694 m.)
MONETARY UNIT Belgian franc
MAJOR LANGUAGES French (Walloon), Flemish
MAJOR RELIGION Roman Catholicism

AREA 999 sq. mi. (2,587 sq. km.)
POPULATION 364,000
CAPITAL Luxembourg
LARGEST CITY Luxembourg
HIGHEST POINT Ardennes Plateau 1,825 ft. (556 m.)
MONETARY UNIT Luxembourg franc
MAJOR LANGUAGES Luxembourgeois (Letzeburgisch), French, German
MAJOR RELIGION Roman Catholicism

NETHERLANDS

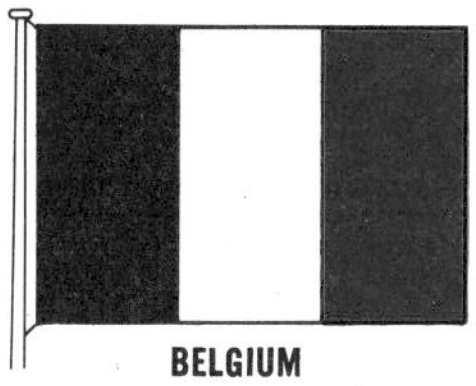

BELGIUM

LUXEMBOURG

BELGIUM

PROVINCES

…werp 1,533,249 .... F6
…ant 2,176,373 .... F7
… Flanders 1,310,117 .... D7
…aut 1,317,453 .... D7
…e 1,008,905 .... H7
…burg 652,547 .... G7
…embourg 217,310 .... G9
…ur 380,561 .... F8
…t Flanders 1,054,429 .... B7

CITIES and TOWNS†

…t 46,659 .... D7
…er 9,173 .... C6
…en (Arlon) 13,745 .... H9
…schot 12,474 .... F7
… (Ath) 11,842 .... D7
…n 8,677 .... G7
…t (Aalst) 46,659 .... D7
…y 7,617 .... G7
…enne 8,091 .... G8
…erlecht 103,796 .... B9
Anderlues 12,176 .... E8
Ans H7
Antoing 3,426 .... C7
Antwerp 224,543 .... E6
Antwerp* 928,000 .... E6
Antwerpen (Antwerp) 224,543 .... E6
Ardooie 7,081 .... C7
Arendonk 9,919 .... G6
Arlon 13,745 .... H9
As 5,496 .... H6
Asse 6,583 .... E7
Ath 11,842 .... D7
Attert H9
Aubange 3,761 .... H9
Audenarde (Oudenaarde) 26,615 .... D7
Auderghem 34,546 .... C9
Auvelais 8,287 .... F8
Aywaille 3,850 .... H8
Baerle-Hertog F6
Balen 15,110 .... G6
Basse-Sambre F8
Bastenaken (Bastogne) 6,816 .... H9
Bastogne 6,816 .... H9
Beernem C6
Beloeil D7
Berchem 50,241 .... F6
Berchem-Sainte-Agathe 19,087 .... B9
Bergen (Mons) 59,362 .... E8
Beringen G6
Bertogne H8
Bertrix 4,562 .... G9
Beveren 15,913 .... E6
Bilzen 7,178 .... G7
Binche 10,098 .... E8
Blankenberge 13,969 .... C6
Bocholt 6,497 .... H6
Boom 16,584 .... E6
Borgerhout 49,002 .... E6
Borgloon 3,412 .... G7
Borgworm (Waremme) 10,956 .... G7
Bourg-Léopold (Leopoldsburg) 9,593 .... G6
Boussu 11,474 .... D8
Braine-l'Alleud 18,531 .... E7
Braine-le-Comte 11,957 .... D7
Brecht F6
Bredene 9,244 .... B6
Bree 10,389 .... H6
Bruges 117,220 .... C6
Brugge (Bruges) 117,220 .... C6
Brussels (cap.)* 1,054,970 .... C9
Bruxelles (Brussels) (cap.)* 1,054,970 .... C9
Cerfontaine E8
Charleroi 23,689 .... E8
Charleroi* 458,000 .... E8
Chastre F7
Châtelet 14,752 .... F8
Chièvres 3,283 .... D7
Chimay 3,288 .... E8
Chiny G9
Ciney 7,536 .... G8
Comblain-au-Pont 3,582 .... G8
Comines 8,192 .... B7
Courcelles 17,015 .... E8
Courtrai (Kortrijk) 44,961 .... C7
Couvin 4,234 .... F8
Damme C6
De Haan C6
Deinze 16,711 .... C7
Denderleeuw 9,925 .... E7
Dendermonde 22,119 .... E6
De Panne 6,985 .... B6
Dessel 7,505 .... G6
Destelbergen D6
Deurne 80,766 .... F6
Diest 10,799 .... F7
Diksmuide 6,669 .... B6
Dilbeek 15,108 .... B9
Dilsen H6
Dinant 9,747 .... G8
Dison 8,466 .... H7
Dixmude (Diksmuide) 6,669 .... B6
Doische F8
Doornik (Tournai) 32,794 .... C7
Dour 10,059 .... D8
Drogenbos 4,840 .... B10
Duffel 13,802 .... F6
Durbuy H8
Ecaussinnes 6,630 .... E7
Edingen (Enghien) 4,115 .... D7
Eeklo 19,144 .... D6
Éghezée F7
Eigenbrakel (Braine-l'Alleud) 18,531 .... E7
Ekeren 27,648 .... E6
Ellezelles 3,556 .... D7
Enghien 4,115 .... D7
Érezée G8
Erquelinnes 4,471 .... E8
Esneux 6,183 .... H7
Essen 10,795 .... F6
Estampuis C7
Etterbeek 51,030 .... B9
Eupen 14,879 .... J7
Evere 26,957 .... C9
Evergem 12,886 .... D6
Farciennes E8
Fernelmont F7
Ferrières H8
Flémalle 8,135 .... G7
Fleurus 8,523 .... E8
Florennes 4,107 .... F8
Forest 55,135 .... B9
Fosses-La-Ville 3,972 .... F8
Frameries 11,224 .... D8
Froidchapelle E8
Furnes (Veurne) 9,496 .... B6
Ganshoren 21,147 .... B9
Geel 29,346 .... F6
Geldenaken (Jodoigne) 4,132 .... F7
Gembloux-sur-Orneau 11,249 .... F7
Genk 57,913 .... H7
Gent (Ghent) 148,860 .... D6
Geraardsbergen 17,533 .... D7
Gerpinnes F8
Ghent 148,860 .... D6
Ghent* 477,000 .... D6
Gistel B6
Gooik E7
Gouvy H8
Grammont (Geraardsbergen) 17,533 .... D7
Grez-Doiceau F7
Grimbergen E7
Haacht 4,436 .... F7
Habay H9
Hal (Halle) 20,017 .... E7
Halen 5,322 .... G7
Halle 20,017 .... E7
Hamme 17,559 .... E6
Hamois G8
Hamont-Achel 6,893 .... H6
Hannuit (Hannut) 7,232 .... G7
Hannut 7,232 .... G7
Harelbeke 18,498 .... C7
Hasselt 39,663 .... G7
Hastière F8
Heist-Knokke 27,582 .... C6
Heist-op-den-Berg 13,472 .... F6
Hensies D8
Herentals 18,639 .... F6
Herne E7
Herselt 7,412 .... F6
Herstal 29,600 .... H7
Herve 4,118 .... H7
Heuvelland B7
Hoboken 33,693 .... E6
Hoei (Huy) 12,736 .... G8
Hoeselt 6,884 .... G7
Honnelles D8
Hoogstraten 4,381 .... F6
Hotton G8
Huy 12,736 .... G8
Ichtegem B6
Ieper 20,825 .... B7
Ingelmunster 10,245 .... C7
Ittre E7
Ixelles 86,450 .... C9
Izegem 22,928 .... C7
Jabbeke C6
Jemappes 18,632 .... D8
Jette 40,013 .... B9
Jodoigne 4,132 .... F7
Kalmthout 12,724 .... F6
Kapellen 13,352 .... E6
Kasterlee F6
Kinrooi H6
Knokke-Heist 27,582 .... C6
Koekelare 7,807 .... B6
Koekelberg 17,570 .... B9
Koksijde B6
Kontich 14,432 .... E6
Kortemark 5,904 .... C6
Kortrijk 44,961 .... C7
Kraainem 11,390 .... C9
La Louvière 23,310 .... E8
La Louvière* 113,259 .... E8
Lanaken 8,659 .... H7
Landen 5,740 .... G7
Langemark-Poelkapelle 5,457 .... B7
Lasne F7
Lede 10,316 .... D7
Léglise H9
Leopoldsburg 9,593 .... G6
Le Roeulx E8
Lessen (Lessines) 8,906 .... D7
Lessines 8,906 .... D7
Leuven 30,623 .... F7
Leuze-en-Hainaut 7,185 .... D7
Libin G9
Libramont-Chevigny 2,975 .... G9
Lichtervelde 7,459 .... C6
Liedekerke 10,482 .... D7
Liège 145,573 .... H7
Liège* 622,000 .... H7
Lier 28,416 .... F6
Lierre (Lier) 28,416 .... F6
Limbourg 3,762 .... J7
Limburg (Limbourg) 3,762 .... J7
Linkebeek 4,265 .... C10
Linter G7
Lochristi D6
Lokeren 26,740 .... D6
Lommel 21,984 .... G6
Lontzen H9
Looz (Borgloon) 3,412 .... G7
Lo-Reninge B7
Louvain (Leuven) 30,623 .... F7
Luik (Liège) 145,573 .... H7
Lummen G7
Maaseik 8,622 .... H6
Maasmechelen H7
Machelen 7,057 .... C9
Maldegem 14,474 .... C6
Malines (Mechelen) 65,466 .... F6
Malmédy 6,464 .... J8
Manage E7
Manhay H8
Marche-en-Famenne 4,567 .... G8
Marchin 4,206 .... G8
Mechelen 65,466 .... F6
Meerhout 8,567 .... G6
Meise E7
Menen 22,037 .... C7
Menin (Menen) 22,037 .... C7
Merchtem 8,998 .... E7
Merelbeke 13,837 .... D7
Merksem 39,768 .... E6
Merksplas 5,065 .... F6
Messancy 3,150 .... H9
Mettet 3,372 .... F8
Meulebeke 10,458 .... C7
Middelkerke B6
Moeskroen (Mouscron) 37,311 .... C7
Mol 28,823 .... G6
Molenbeek-Saint-Jean 68,411 .... B9
Momignies E8
Mons 59,362 .... E8
Montigny-le-Tilleul E8
Moorslede B7
Mortsel 28,012 .... E6
Mouscron 37,311 .... C7
Namen (Namur) 32,269 .... F8
Namur 32,269 .... F8
Nassogne G8
Nazareth D7
Neerpelt 8,771 .... G6
Neufchâteau 2,670 .... G9
Nevele D6
Nieuport (Nieuwpoort) 8,273 .... B6
Nieuwpoort 8,273 .... B6
Nijvel (Nivelles) 16,126 .... E7
Ninove 12,428 .... D7
Nivelles 16,126 .... E7
Ohey G8
Onhaye F8
Oostende (Ostend) 71,227 .... B6
Oostkamp 8,999 .... C6
Opwijk 9,699 .... E7
Ostend 71,227 .... B6
Oudenaarde 26,615 .... D7
Oudenburg B6
Oud-Turnhout 9,245 .... F6
Oupeye H7
Overijse 16,181 .... F7
Overpelt 10,470 .... G6
Paliseul G9
Peer 7,201 .... G6
Péruwelz 7,878 .... D8
Philippeville 2,076 .... E8
Plombières F7
Pont-à-Celles E8
Poperinge 12,671 .... B7
Profondeville F8
Putte 6,953 .... F6
Quaregnon 17,688 .... D8
Quévy D8
Quiévrain 5,510 .... D8
Raeren 3,655 .... J7
Ravels G6
Rebecq 3,744 .... E7
Renaix (Ronse) 25,056 .... D7
Rendeux H8
Retie 6,619 .... G6
Rochefort 4,357 .... G8
Roeselare 40,428 .... C7
Ronse 25,056 .... D7
Roulers (Roeselare) 40,428 .... C7
Rouvroy G9
Ruislede C6
Sainte-Ode H8
Saint-Georges-sur-Meuse 6,003 .... G7
Saint-Gilles 55,055 .... B9
Saint-Hubert 3,091 .... G8
Saint-Josse-ten-Noode 23,633 .... C9
Saint-Nicolas G7
Saint-Trond (Sint-Truiden) 21,473 .... G7
Saint-Vith (Sankt Vith) 3,001 .... J8
Sankt Vith 3,001 .... J8
Schaerbeek 118,950 .... C9
Schoten 29,914 .... F6
Seraing 40,545 .... G7
's-Gravenbrakel (Braine-le-Comte) 11,957 .... D7
Sint-Laureins D6
Sint-Niklaas 49,214 .... E6

(continued on following page)

Agriculture, Industry and Resources

DOMINANT LAND USE

- Dairy, Truck Farming
- Cash Crops, Livestock
- Mixed Cereals, Dairy
- Specialized Horticulture
- Grapes, Wine
- Forests
- Sand Dunes

MAJOR MINERAL OCCURRENCES

C Coal
Fe Iron Ore
G Natural Gas
Na Salt
O Petroleum

Major Industrial Areas

24 Netherlands, Belgium and Luxembourg
(continued)

Sint-Pieters-Leeuw 16,856 B9
Sint-Truiden 21,473 G7
Soignies 12,006 D7
Somme-Leuze G8
Spa 9,504 H8
Sprimont H8
Staden 5,499 B7
Stavelot 4,723 H8
Steenokkerzeel 4,037 C9
Stekene E6
Stoumont H8
Tamise (Temse) 14,950 E6
Tellin G8
Temse 14,950 E6
Tenneville H8
Termonde (Dendermonde) 22,119 E6
Tessenderlo 11,778 G6
Theux 5,316 H8
Thuin 5,777 E8
Tielt 14,077 C7
Tielt-Winge 3,743 F7
Tienen 24,134 F7
Tintigny G9
Tirlemont (Tienen) 24,134 F7
Tongeren 20,136 G7
Tongres (Tongeren) 20,136 G7
Torhout 15,156 C6
Tournai 32,794 C7
Trois-Ponts H8
Tubeke (Tubize) 11,507 E7
Tubize 11,507 E7
Turnhout 38,007 F6
Uccle 78,909 B9
Ukkel (Uccle) 78,909 B9
Vaux-sur-Sûre H9
Verviers 33,587 H7
Veurne 9,496 B6
Vielsalm 3,587 H8
Vilvoorde 34,633 F7
Vilvorde (Vilvoorde) 34,633 F7
Viroinval F8
Virton 3,558 H9
Visé 6,880 H7
Vleteren B7
Vorst (Forest) 55,135 B9
Vresse-sur-Semois F9
Waarschoot 7,905 D6
Wachtebeke D6
Waregem 17,725 C7
Waremme 10,956 G7
Waterloo 17,764 E7
Watermaal-Bosvoorde
(Watermael-Boitsfort C9
Watermael-Boitsfort 25,123 C9
Waver (Wavre) 11,767 F7
Wavre 11,767 F7
Wellin G8
Wemmel 12,631 B9
Wervik 12,672 B7
Westerlo 14,173 F6
Westmalle F6
Wetteren 20,816 D7
Wezembeek-Oppem 10,899 D9
Wezet (Visé) 6,880 H7
Willebroek 15,726 E6
Wilrijk 43,485 E6
Wingene 7,140 C6
Woluwe-Saint-Lambert 47,360 C9
Woluwe-Saint-Pierre 40,884 C9
Ypres (Ieper) 20,825 B7
Zaventem 10,625 C9
Zedelgem C6
Zeebrugge C6
Zele 18,585 E6
Zelzate 12,785 D6
Zemst E7
Zinnik (Soignies) 12,006 D7
Zonhoven 13,484 G6
Zottegem 21,461 D7
Zuienkerke C6

OTHER FEATURES

Albert, (canal) F6
Ardennes, (for.) F9
Botrange, (mt.) J8
Dender, (riv.) D7
Deûle, (riv.) B7
Dyle, (riv.) F7
Hohe Venn, (plat.) H8
Lesse, (riv.) F8
Lys, (riv.) B7
Mark, (riv.) F6
Meuse, (riv.) F8
Nethe, (riv.) F6
North, (sea) D4
Ourthe, (riv.) G8
Rupel, (riv.) F7
Sambre, (riv.) D8
Schelde (Scheldt), (riv.) C7
Scheldt, (riv.) C7
Schnee Eifel, (plat.) J8
Semois, (riv.) G9
Senne, (riv.) E7
Vaalserberg, (mt.) J7
Vesdre, (riv.) H7
Weisserstein, (mt.) J8
Yser, (riv.) B7
Zitterwald, (plat.) J8

LUXEMBOURG

CITIES and TOWNS

Clervaux 916 J8
Diekirch† 5,059 J9
Differdange 9,287 H9
Dudelange† 14,615 J10
Echternach† 3,792 J9
Esch-sur-Alzette† 27,574 J9
Ettelbruck† 5,990 J9
Grevenmacher† 2,918 J9
Luxembourg (cap.) 78,272 J9
Mamer 3,123 H9
Mersch 1,869 J9
Pétange 6,234 H9
Remich† 12,138 J9
Viandent† 1,520 J9
Wiltz 1,601 H9

OTHER FEATURES

Alzette, (riv.) J9
Clerf, (riv.) J8
Eisling, (mts.) H9
Mosel, (riv.) J9
Our, (riv.) J9
Sauer, (riv.) J9

NETHERLANDS

PROVINCES

Drenthe 405,924 K3
Dronten 15,343 H4
Friesland 560,614 H2
Gelderland 1,639,997 H4
Groningen 540,062 K2
Limburg 1,051,620 H6
North Brabant 1,967,261 F5
North Holland 2,295,875 F3
Overijssel 985,569 J4
South Holland 3,048,648 E5
Utrecht 867,909 G4
Zeeland 332,286 D6
Zuidelijke
IJsselmeerpolders 14,231 H4

CITIES and TOWNS†

Aalsmeer 20,779 F4
Aalten 17,486 K5
Aardenburg 3,869 C6
Akkrum 5,044 H2
Alkmaar 65,199 F3
Almelo 62,634 K4
Alphen aan de Rijn 46,065 F4
Amersfoort 87,784 G4
Amstelveen 71,803 B5
Amsterdam (cap.) 751,156 B4
Amsterdam* 987,205 B4
Andijk 5,301 G3
Apeldoorn 134,055 H4
Apeldoorn* 237,231 H4
Appingedam 13,295 K2
Arnhem 126,051 H4
Arnhem* 281,126 H4
Assen 43,783 K3
Asten 12,295 H6
Axel 12,072 D6
Baarle-Nassau 5,583 F6
Baarn 25,045 G4
Barneveld 34,189 H4
Bath E6
Beilen 12,948 K3
Bemmel 14,218 H5
Bergeijk 9,009 G6
Bergen 14,306 F3
Bergen op Zoom 40,770 E5
Bergum 28,047 H2
Berkel 9,367 F5
Berkhout 5,167 F3
Beverwijk 37,551 F4
Blerick J6
Bloemendaal 17,940 E4
Blokzijl H3
Bodegraven 15,848 F4
Bolsward 9,934 H2
Borculo 9,859 J4
Borger 12,017 K3
Borne 18,216 K4
Boskoop 12,985 F4
Boxmeer 12,662 H5
Boxtel 22,465 G5
Breda 118,086 F5
Breda* 151,182 F5
Breezand F3
Breskens C6
Brielle 10,620 E5
Brouwershaven 3,263 D5
Brummen 20,460 J4
Brunssum 26,116 J7
Buiksloot C4
Bussum 37,848 G4
Capelle 36,696 F5
Coevorden 13,089 K3
Colijnsplaat D5
Culemborg 17,682 G5
Cuyk 15,366 H5
Dalen 5,084 K3
De Bilt 32,588 G4
Dedemsvaart 12,975 J3
De Koog F2
Delft 86,103 E4
Delfzijl 23,316 K2
Den Burg 12,132 F2
Denekamp 11,533 L4
Den Helder 60,421 F3
Deurne 26,539 H6
Deventer 65,557 J4
Didam 14,263 J5
De Wijk 4,631 J3
Diemen 13,704 C5
Dieren J4
Diever 3,162 J3
Dinxperlo 7,296 K5
Dirksland 6,495 E5
Doesburg 9,759 J4
Doetinchem 34,915 J5
Dokkum 11,203 H2
Domburg 3,874 C5
Dongen 19,219 F5
Doorn 11,966 G4
Dordrecht 101,840 F5
Dordrecht* 186,793 F5
Drachten 45,390 J2
Driebergen 17,022 G4
Dronten 16,544 H3
Druten 11,113 H5
Echt 17,035 H6
Edam-Volendam 21,507 G4
Ede 79,897 H4
Egmond aan Zee 5,734 E3
Eindhoven 192,562 G6
Eindhoven* 358,234 G6
Elburg 18,082 H4
Elst 16,686 H5
Emmeloord 34,467 H3
Emmen 86,700 K3
Enkhuizen 13,430 G3
Enschede 141,597 K4
Enschede* 239,015 K4
Epe 32,267 H4
Erica K3
Ermelo 23,835 H4
Etten-Leur 26,167 F5
Europoort E5
Flushing 43,806 C6
Franeker 11,415 H2
Geertruidenberg 6,185 F5
Geldermalsen 8,952 G5
Geldrop 25,879 H6
Geleen 35,910 H7
Gemert 15,267 H5
Gendringen 19,086 J5
Genemuiden 6,058 H3
Gennep 14,773 H5
Giessendam-Hardinxveld 15,523 F5
Giethoorn J3
Gilze 19,603 F5
Goes 28,505 D6
Goirle 13,447 G5
Goor 11,435 K4
Gorinchem 28,337 G5
Gorredijk J2
Gouda 56,403 F4
Graauw E6
Gramsbergen 5,866 K3
Grave 9,492 H5
Groenlo 8,693 K4
Groesbeek 18,094 H5
Groningen 163,357 K2
Groningen* 201,662 K2
Grouw 8,567 H2
Haamstede 4,575 D5
Haarlem 164,672 F4
Haarlem* 232,048 F4
Haarlemmermeer
(Hoofddorp) 72,046 F4
Hague, The (cap.) 479,369 E4
Hague, The* 682,452 E4
Halfweg 4,456 B4
Hallum H2
Hardenberg 28,489 J3
Harderwijk 28,508 H4
Hardinxveld-Giessendam 15,523 G5
Harlingen 14,533 G2
Hasselt 5,817 J3
Hattem 11,074 H4
Heemskert 31,728 F3
Heemstede 27,376 F4
Heer H7
Heerde 16,833 H4
Heerenveen 34,948 H3
Heerhugowaard 26,019 F3
Heerlen 71,500 J7
Heesch 8,659 G5
Heiloo 20,524 F3
Hellendoorn 32,068 J4
Hellevoetsluis 14,186 E5
Helmond 59,249 H6
Hengelo, Gelderland 8,015 J4
Hengelo, Overijssel 72,281 K4
Heusden 5,542 G5
Hillegom 17,489 E4
Hilvarenbeek 8,408 G6
Hilversum 94,041 G4
Hilversum* 110,498 G4
Hippolytushoef 7,847 G3
Hoek D6
Hoek van Holland (Hook of
Holland) D4
Hoensbroek 22,441 H7
Holijsloot C4
Hollum H2
Holwerd H2
Hoofddorp
(Haarlemmermeer) 72,046 F4
Hoogeveen 42,673 J3
Hoogezand-Sappemeer 33,860 K2
Hoogkarspel 5,112 G3
Hook of Holland D4
Hoorn 24,609 G3
Horst 16,242 H6
Huissen 11,049 H5
Huizen 25,603 G4
Hulst 17,283 E6
IJmuiden 6,633 E4
IJsselstein 15,450 F4
Ilpendam 3,310 C4
Joure 14,329 H3
Kampen 29,488 H3
Katwijk aan Zee 37,437 E4
Kerkdriel 7,584 G5
Kerkrade 46,609 J7
Kesteren 8,257 G5
Klazienaveen 9,520 L3
Kollum 11,887 J2
Krimpen aan den IJssel 26,396 F5
Landsmeer 8,082 C4
Laren 13,615 G4
Leek 15,713 J2
Leerdam 15,030 F5
Leeuwarden 85,074 H2
Leiden 99,891 E4
Leiden* 167,554 E4
Lelystad H3
Lemmer 10,013 H3
Lisse 19,182 F4
Lith 5,088 G5
Lochem 17,274 J4
Lonneker K4
Loon op Zand 18,000 G5
Losser 20,688 L4
Maarssen 18,346 F4
Maasbree 9,462 H6
Maassluis 28,170 E5
Maastricht 111,044 H7
Maastricht* 145,862 H7
Margraten 3,318 H7
Medemblik 6,432 G3
Meerssen 8,414 H7
Meppel 21,057 J3
Middelburg 36,372 C6
Middelharnis 14,245 E5
Middenmeer F3
Millingen aan den Rijn 5,035 J5
Moerdijk F5
Monnickendam 8,127 C4
Montfoort 3,442 G4
Muiden 6,567 G4
Muntendam 4,147 K2
Naaldwijk 24,117 E4
Naarden 17,319 G4
Nagele H3
Neede 10,842 K4
Nes 3,012 H2
Nieuwegein 22,648 G4
Nieuwe-Pekela 5,086 L2
Nieuwkoop 8,923 F4
Nieuw-Schoonebeek 7,556 L3
Nijkerk 21,615 H4
Nijmegen 148,493 H5
Nijmegen* 213,981 H5
Noordwijk 22,386 E4
Norg 6,041 J2
Numansdorp 7,072 E5
Nunspeet 21,340 H4
Odoorn 11,973 K3
Oisterwijk 16,263 G5
Oldenzaal 26,624 K4
Olst 8,480 J4
Ommen 16,136 J3
Onstwedde K2
Oostburg 18,461 C6
Oosterhout 40,077 F5
Ooosterwolde 5,845 J2
Oostmahorn J2
Oostzaan 6,336 C4
Ootmarsum 3,901 K4
Oss 45,643 H5
Otterlo H4
Oud-Beijerland 14,251 E5
Ouddorp 9,091 D5
Oudenbosch 11,061 E5
Oude-Pekela 8,067 K2
Oudewater 6,870 F4
Purmerend 32,614 F4
Putten 18,243 H4
Raalte 23,598 J4
Renkum 34,547 H5
Reusel 6,901 G6
Rheden 49,755 J4
Rhenen 16,893 H5
Ridderkerk 45,069 F5
Rijnsburg 10,698 F4
Rijssen 20,008 J4
Rijswijk 54,123 E4
Roden 16,437 J2
Roermond 36,695 J6
Roosendaal 51,685 F5
Rotterdam 614,767 E5
Rotterdam* 1,016,505 E5
Rutten H3
Ruurlo 7,557 J4
Sappemeer-Hoogezand 33,860 K2
Schagen 13,929 F3
Scheveningen E4
Schiedam 78,068 E5
Schijndel 18,658 G5
Schiphol B5
Schoonhoven 10,753 F5
's Gravendeel 7,242 E5
's Gravenhage (The Hague)
(cap.) 479,369 E4
's Gravenhage* 682,452 E4
's Gravenzande 15,833 E4
's Heerenberg 18,326 J5
's Hertogenbosch 86,184 G5
Simpelveld 6,783 H7
Sint Annaland E5
Sint Jacobiparochie H2
Sittard 34,278 H6
Sliedrecht 21,839 F5
Slochteren 13,447 K2
Sloten, North Holland B5
Sloterdijk B4
Sluis 3,140 C6
Smilde 8,247 K3
Sneek 28,123 H2
Soest 40,165 G4
Soesterberg G4
Stadskanaal 13,946 L3
Staphorst 11,608 J3
Steenbergen 12,930 E5
Steenwijk 20,721 J3
Stiens 7,711 H2
Swifterbant H3
Tegelen 18,386 J6
Ter Apel L3
Termunten 4,803 K2
Terneuzen 33,731 D6
Tholen 17,213 E5
Tiel 24,974 G5
Tilburg 151,513 G5
Tilburg* 212,510 G5
Twello 22,542 J4
Uden 28,946 H5
Uithoorn 22,812 F4
Uithuizen 5,194 K2
Ulrum 3,665 J2
Urk 9,397 H3
Utrecht 250,887 G4
Utrecht* 464,357 G4
Vaals 11,057 H7
Vaassen 7,225 H4
Valkenswaard 27,121 H6
Veendam 26,168 K2
Veenendaal 35,845 G4
Veenhuizen J2
Veere 4,252 D5
Veghel 22,308 H5
Veldhoven 30,030 G6
Velp J5
Velsen 64,035 F4
Venlo 61,659 J6
Venraij 31,526 H6
Vianen 12,821 G5
Vlaardingen 78,311 E5
Vlagtwedde 16,719 L3
Vlijmen 13,515 G5
Vlissingen (Flushing) 43,806 C6
Volendam-Edam 21,507 G4
Voorburg 45,209 E4
Voorst 22,542 J4
Vorden 7,276 J4
Vriezenveen 16,025 K4
Vught 23,261 G5
Waalre 13,219 G6
Waalwijk 25,977 F5
Wageningen 28,659 H5
Wamel 8,979 H5
Warmenhuizen 3,818 F3
Weert 36,850 H6
Weesp 17,037 C5
West-Terschelling 4,542 G2
Wierden 20,618 K4
Wijhe 6,888 J4
Wijk bij Duurstede 7,927 G5
Wijk en Aalburg 9,266 F5
Winschoten 19,760 L2
Winsum 5,007 K2
Winterswijk 27,413 K5
Woensdrecht 9,101 E6
Woerden 22,064 F4
Wolvega 22,812 J3
Workum 4,135 G3
Zaandam (Zaanstad) 124,795 B4
Zaandam (Zaanstad)* 137,371 B4
Zaltbommel 8,010 G5
Zandvoort 16,289 E4
Zeist 58,630 G4
Zevenaar 26,560 J5
Zevenbergen 13,307 E5
Zierikzee 8,816 D5
Zundert 12,444 F6
Zutphen 29,188 J4
Zwartsluis 4,391 H3
Zwijndrecht 38,271 E5
Zwolle 77,826 J3

OTHER FEATURES

Alkmaardermeer (lake) F3
Ameland (isl.) H2
Bergumermeer (lake) J2
Beulaker Wijde (lake) H3
Borndiep (chan.)
De Fluessen (lake)
De Honte (bay)
De Peel (reg.)
De Twente (reg.)
De Zaan (riv.)
Dollard (bay)
Dommel (riv.)
Duiveland (isl.)
Eastern Scheldt (est.)
Eems (riv.)
Eijerlandsche Gat (str.)
Flevoland Polders 35,618
Friesche Gat (chan.)
Frisian, West (isls.)
Galgenberg (hill)
Goeree (isl.)
Grevelingen (str.)
Griend (isl.)
Groninger Wad (sound)
Groote IJ Polder
Haarlemmermeer Polder 72,046
Haringvliet (str.)
Het IJ (est.)
Hoek van Holland (cape)
Hondsrug (hills)
Houtrak Polder
Hunse (riv.)
IJmeer (bay)
IJssel (riv.)
IJsselmeer (lake)
Lauwers (chan.)
Lauwers Zee (bay)
Lek (riv.)
Lemelerberg (hill)
Lower Rhine (riv.)
Maas (riv.)
Mark (riv.)
Marken (isl.)
Markerwaard Polder
Marsdiep (chan.)
North (sea)
North Beveland (isl.)
North East Polder 34,467
North Holland (canal)
North Sea (canal)
Old Rhine (riv.)
Oostzaan Polder 6,336
Orange (canal)
Overflakkee (isl.)
Pinke Gat (chan.)
Regge (riv.)
Rhine (riv.)
Roer (riv.)
Rottumeplaat (isl.)
Rottumeroog (isl.)
Schiermonnikoog (isl.)
Schouwen (isl.)
Slotermeer (lake)
Sneekermeer (lake)
South Beveland (isl.)
Terschelling (isl.)
Texel (isl.)
Tjeukemeer (lake)
Tjonger (riv.)
Vaalserberg (mt.)
Vecht (riv.)
Vechte (riv.)
Veersche Meer (lake)
Veluwe (reg.)
Vlieland (isl.)
Vliestroom (str.)
Voorne (isl.)
Waal (riv.)
Waddenzee (sound)
Walcheren (isl.)
Wester Eems (chan.)
Western Scheldt (De Honte)
(bay)
West Frisian (isls.)
Westgat (chan.)
Wieringermeer Polder 11,870
Wilhelmina (canal)
Willems (canal)

*City and suburbs.
†Population of cities in Belgium & Netherlands are communes

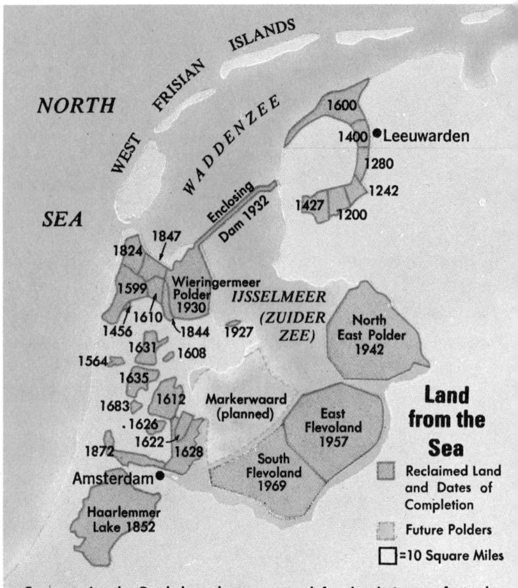

For centuries the Dutch have been renowned for the drainage of marshes and the construction of polders, i.e., arable land reclaimed from the sea. Future projects will convert much of the present IJsselmeer to agricultural land.

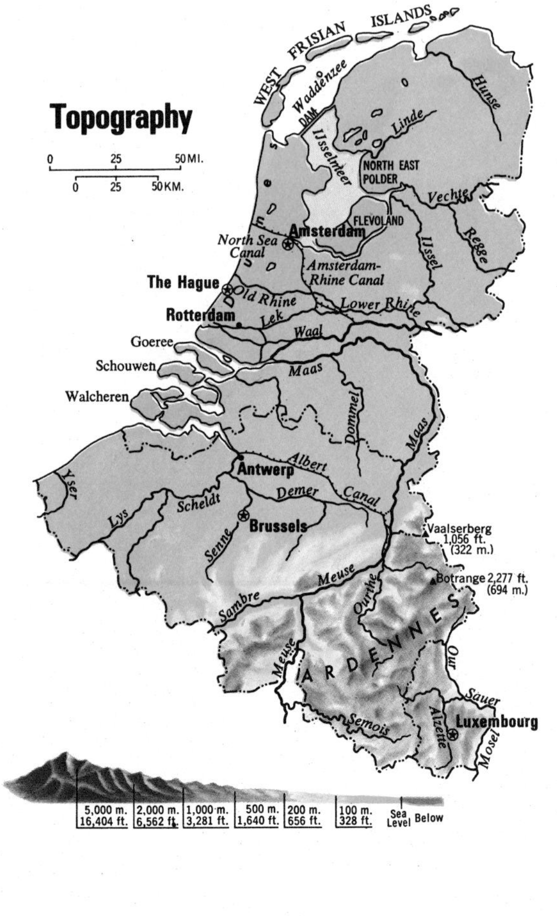

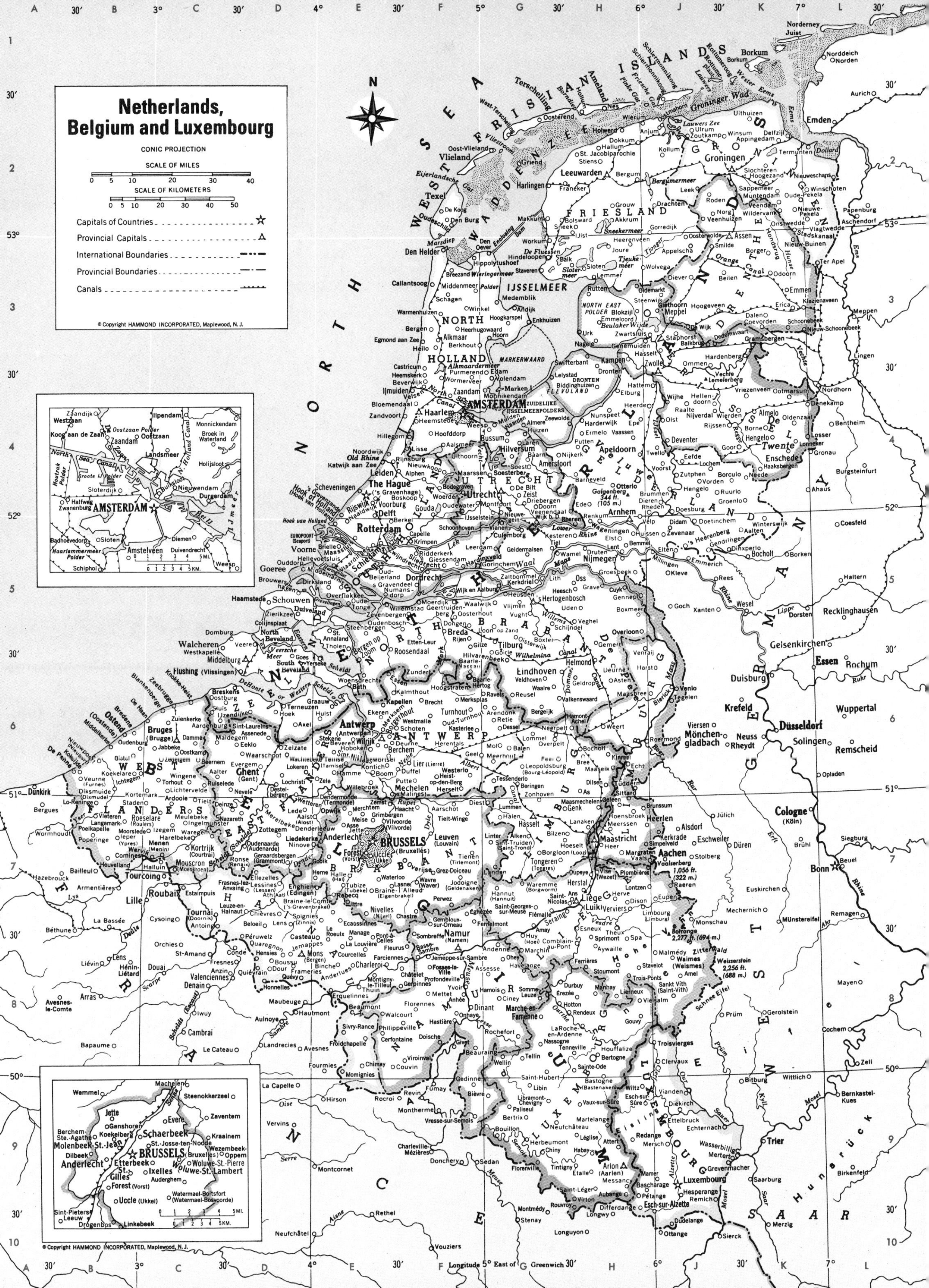
Netherlands, Belgium and Luxembourg
CONIC PROJECTION
SCALE OF MILES
0 5 10 20 30 40
SCALE OF KILOMETERS
0 5 10 20 30 40 50
Capitals of Countries
Provincial Capitals
International Boundaries
Provincial Boundaries
Canals
© Copyright HAMMOND INCORPORATED, Maplewood, N. J.
NORTH SEA
WEST FRISIAN ISLANDS
WADDEN ZEE
IJSSELMEER
GRONINGEN
FRIESLAND
DRENTHE
OVERIJSSEL
GELDERLAND
NORTH HOLLAND
SOUTH HOLLAND
UTRECHT
FLEVOLAND
ZEELAND
NORTH BRABANT
LIMBURG
WEST FLANDERS
EAST FLANDERS
ANTWERP
BRABANT
HAINAUT
NAMUR
LIÈGE
LUXEMBOURG
GERMANY
FRANCE
AMSTERDAM
The Hague ('s Gravenhage)
Rotterdam
Utrecht
Groningen
Leeuwarden
Arnhem
Nijmegen
Eindhoven
Maastricht
Antwerp (Antwerpen)
Ghent (Gent)
Bruges (Brugge)
BRUSSELS (Bruxelles)
Liège (Luik)
Namur (Namen)
Mons (Bergen)
Charleroi
Luxembourg
Arlon (Aarlen)
Lille
Aachen
Cologne (Köln)
Düsseldorf
Trier
Emden
Longitude 5° East of Greenwich
Zaandijk
Westzaan
Koog aan de Zaan
Zaandam
Oostzaan
Ilpendam
Monnickendam
Broek in Waterland
Landsmeer
Holijsloot
Sloterdijk
Halfweg
Zwanenburg
AMSTERDAM
Nieuwendam
Durgerdam
Badhoevedorp
Sloten
Diemen
Haarlemmermeer Polder
Amstelveen
Duivendrecht
Schiphol
Weesp
0 1 2 3 4 5 MI.
0 1 2 3 4 5 KM.
Wemmel
Machelen
Steenokkerzeel
Jette
Ganshoren
Evere
Zaventem
Berchem-Ste.-Agathe
Koekelberg
Schaerbeek
Kraainem
Molenbeek-St.-Jean
St.-Josse-ten-Noode
Wezembeek-Oppem
Dilbeek
BRUSSELS (Bruxelles)
Woluwe-St.-Pierre
Anderlecht
Etterbeek
Ixelles
Woluwe-St.-Lambert
St.-Gilles
Auderghem
Forest (Vorst)
Watermael-Boitsfort (Watermaal-Bosvoorde)
Uccle (Ukkel)
Sint-Pieters-Leeuw
Drogenbos
Linkebeek
© Copyright HAMMOND INCORPORATED, Maplewood, N. J.

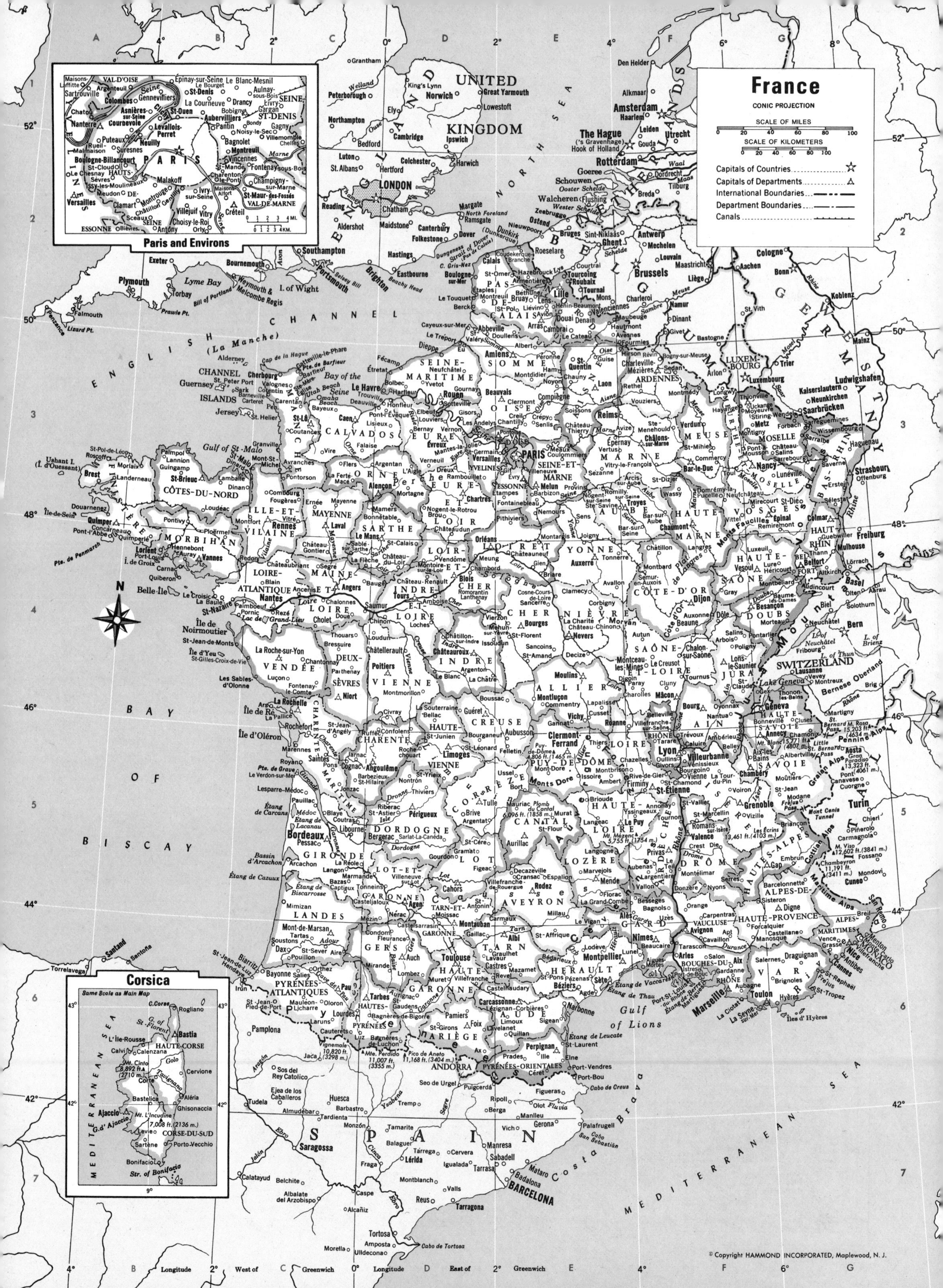
France
CONIC PROJECTION
SCALE OF MILES
0 20 40 60 80 100
SCALE OF KILOMETERS
0 20 40 60 80 100
Capitals of Countries
Capitals of Departments
International Boundaries
Department Boundaries
Canals
Paris and Environs
VAL-D'OISE
SEINE-ST-DENIS
PARIS
HAUTS-DE-SEINE
VAL-DE-MARNE
ESSONNE
Versailles
Nanterre
St-Denis
Créteil
Corsica
Same Scale as Main Map
HAUTE-CORSE
CORSE-DU-SUD
Bastia
Ajaccio
Corte
Calvi
Bonifacio
Porto-Vecchio
Str. of Bonifacio
MEDITERRANEAN SEA
UNITED KINGDOM
LONDON
NORTH SEA
NETHERLANDS
Amsterdam
The Hague
Rotterdam
BELGIUM
Brussels
Antwerp
LUXEMBOURG
Luxembourg
GERMANY
SWITZERLAND
Geneva
Basel
Bern
ITALY
Turin
SPAIN
BARCELONA
Saragossa
ANDORRA
MONACO
ENGLISH CHANNEL
(La Manche)
CHANNEL ISLANDS
BAY OF BISCAY
Gulf of Lions
MEDITERRANEAN SEA
Costa Brava
PARIS
Lille
Amiens
Rouen
Le Havre
Caen
Cherbourg
Brest
Rennes
Nantes
Angers
Le Mans
Orléans
Tours
Bordeaux
Toulouse
Montpellier
Marseille
Nice
Toulon
Lyon
Grenoble
St-Étienne
Dijon
Besançon
Strasbourg
Metz
Nancy
Reims
Clermont-Ferrand
Limoges
Poitiers
La Rochelle
Perpignan
Avignon
Nîmes
Bay of the Seine
Gulf of St-Malo
Longitude West of Greenwich
Longitude East of Greenwich

DEPARTMENTS

n 376,477 F4
sne 533,862 E3
lier 378,406 E4
pes-de-Haute-Provence 112,178 G5
pes-Maritimes 816,681 G6
rdèche 257,065 F5
rdennes 309,306 F3
riège 137,857 D6
ube 284,823 E3
ude 272,366 E6
veyron 278,306 E5
as-Rhin 882,121 G3
elfort (terr.) 128,125 G4
ouches-du-Rhône 1,632,974 F6
alvados 560,967 C3
antal 166,549 E5
harente 337,064 D5
harente-Maritime 497,859 C5
her 316,350 E4
orrèze 240,363 D5
orse du Sud 128,634 B6
ôte-d'Or 456,070 F4
ôtes-du-Nord 525,556 B3
reuse 146,214 D4
eux-Sèvres 335,829 C4
ordogne 373,179 D5
oubs 471,082 G4
rôme 361,847 F5
ssonne 923,063 E3
ure 422,952 D3
ure-et-Loir 335,151 D3
nistère 804,088 A3
ard 494,575 F6
ers 175,366 D6
ironde 1,061,480 C5
aute-Corse 161,208 B6
aute-Garonne 777,431 D6
aute-Loire 205,491 E5
aute-Marne 212,304 F3
autes-Alpes 97,358 G5
aute-Saône 222,254 G4
aute-Savoie 447,795 G5
autes-Pyrénées 227,222 D6
aute-Vienne 352,149 D5
aut-Rhin 635,209 G4
auts-de-Seine 1,438,930 A2
érault 648,202 E6
le-et-Vilaine 702,199 C3
ndre 248,523 D4
ndre-et-Loire 478,601 D4
sère 860,339 F5
ura 238,856 F4
andes 288,323 C5
oire 742,396 F5
oire-Atlantique 934,499 C4
oiret 490,189 E4
oir-et-Cher 283,686 D4
ot 150,778 D5
ot-et-Garonne 292,616 D5
ozère 74,825 E5
aine-et-Loire 629,849 C4
anche 451,662 C3
arne 530,399 F3
ayenne 261,789 C3
eurthe-et-Moselle 722,588 G3
euse 203,904 F3
orbihan 563,588 B4
oselle 1,006,373 G3
ièvre 245,212 E4
ord 2,510,738 E2
ise 606,320 E3
rne 293,523 C3
aris (city) 2,299,830 B2
as-de-Calais 1,403,035 E2
uy-de-Dôme 580,033 E5
yrénées-Atlantiques 534,748 C6
yrénées-Orientales 299,506 E6
hône 1,429,647 F5
aône-et-Loire 569,810 F4
arthe 490,385 D3
avoie 305,118 G5
eine et Marne 755,762 E3
eine-Saint-Denis 1,322,127 C1
omme 538,462 E3
arn 338,024 E6
arn-et-Garonne 183,314 D5
al-de-Marne 1,215,713 C1
al-d'Oise 840,885 E3
ar 626,093 G6
aucluse 390,446 F6
Vendée 450,641 C4
Vienne 357,366 D4
Vosges 397,957 G3
Yonne 299,851 E4
Yvelines 1,082,255 D3

CITIES and TOWNS

Abbeville 25,252 D2
Agde 9,856 E6
Agen 33,763 D5
Aix-en-Provence 91,665 F6
Aix-les-Bains 21,884 G5
Ajaccio 47,065 B7
Albert 11,746 E2
Albertville 16,630 G5
Albi 43,942 E6
Alençon 32,917 D3
Alès 33,315 E5
Ambérieu-en-Bugey 9,294 F5
Amboise 10,498 D4
Amiens 129,453 D3
Ancenis 6,689 C4
Angers 136,603 C4
Angoulême 46,293 D5
Annecy 53,058 G5
Annonay 19,234 F5
Antibes 44,226 G6
Antony 57,450 B2
Apt 9,735 F6
Arcachon 13,856 C5
Argentan 16,063 D3
Argenteuil 101,542 A1
Arles 37,337 F6
Armentières 23,850 E2
Arras 45,804 E2
Asnières-sur-Seine 75,328 A1
Aubagne 26,145 F6
Aubenas 11,967 F5
Aubervilliers 72,859 B1
Auch 18,767 D6
Audincourt 18,570 G4
Aulnay-sous-Bois 77,982 B1
Auray 10,006 B4
Aurignac 744 D6
Aurillac 29,458 E5
Autun 19,441 F4
Auxerre 36,039 E4
Auxonne 6,414 F4
Avallon 8,518 E4
Avignon 73,482 F6
Avion 22,860 E2
Avranches 10,128 C3
Ax-les-Thermes 1,456 D6
Bagnères-de-Bigorre 9,080 D6
Bagnolet 35,858 B2
Bagnols-sur-Cèze 13,111 F5
Barbizon 1,189 E3
Barcelonnette 2,523 G5
Barfleur 701 C3
Bar-le-Duc 19,188 F3
Bar-sur-Aube 7,227 F3
Bastia 45,387 B6
Bayeux 13,381 C3
Bayonne 41,281 C6
Beaucaire 10,189 F6
Beaune 16,386 F4
Beauvais 53,493 E3
Belfort 54,469 G4
Belley 6,612 F5
Berck 14,104 D2
Bergerac 25,488 D5
Bernay 9,928 D3
Besançon 119,803 G4
Béthune 26,208 E2
Béziers 79,213 E6
Biarritz 27,453 C6
Blois 49,134 D4
Bobigny 43,041 B1
Bogny-sur-Meuse 6,845 F3
Bolbec 12,347 D3
Bondy 48,285 B1
Bonneville 6,717 G4
Bordeaux 220,830 C5
Boulogne-Billancourt 103,527 A2
Boulogne-sur-Mer 48,309 D2
Bourg-en-Bresse 40,052 F4
Bourges 75,200 E4
Bourgoin-Jallieu 18,504 F5
Bressuire 9,778 C4
Brest 163,940 A3
Briançon 8,523 G5
Brignoles 8,784 G6
Brioude 7,756 E5
Brive-la-Gaillarde 49,276 D5
Bruay-en-Artois 25,544 E2
Caen 116,987 C3
Cahors 19,288 D5
Calais 73,009 D2
Caluire-et-Cuire 43,024 F5
Cambrai 38,706 E2
Cannes 70,226 G6
Carcassonne 38,887 D6
Carmaux 11,970 E5
Carpentras 20,169 F5
Castelnaudary 8,947 E6
Castelsarrasin 6,562 D6
Castres 41,037 E6
Cavaillon 17,383 F6
Châlons-sur-Marne 50,870 F3
Chalon-sur-Saône 55,495 F4
Chambéry 52,286 F5
Chambord 166 D4
Chamonix-Mont-Blanc 6,246 G5
Champigny-sur-Marne 80,189 C2
Chantilly 10,517 E3
Charenton-le-Pont 20,383 B2
Charleville-Mézières 59,513 F3
Chartres 38,574 D3
Châteaubriant 12,417 C4
Château-du-Loir 5,598 D4
Châteaudun 14,634 D3
Château-Gontier 8,301 C4
Châteauroux 53,166 D4
Château-Thierry 13,379 E3
Châtellerault 33,811 D4
Châtillon 26,562 B2
Châtillon-sur-Seine 7,367 F4
Chatou 26,415 A1
Chaumont 26,568 F3
Chauny 14,324 E3
Chelles 24,192 C1
Cherbourg 31,333 C3
Chinon 5,378 D4
Choisy-le-Roi 38,629 B2
Cholet 49,887 C4
Clamart 52,881 A2
Clermont 7,834 E3
Clermont-Ferrand 153,379 E5
Clichy 47,731 B1
Cluny 4,335 F4
Cluses 12,713 G4
Cognac 21,567 C5
Colmar 58,585 G3
Colombes 83,241 A1
Commentry 8,074 E4
Commercy 6,918 F3
Compiègne 37,009 E3
Concarneau 15,096 A4
Cosne-Cours-sur-Loire 9,768 E4
Coudekerque-Branche 24,702 E2
Coulommiers 11,363 E3
Courbevoie 54,391 A1
Coutances 8,286 C3
Creil 31,893 E3
Crépy-en-Valois 10,001 E3
Créteil 58,665 B2
Cusset 13,672 E4
Dax 18,019 C6
Deauville 5,655 C3
Decazeville 9,318 E5
Decize 6,853 E4
Denain 26,096 E2
Dieppe 25,607 D3

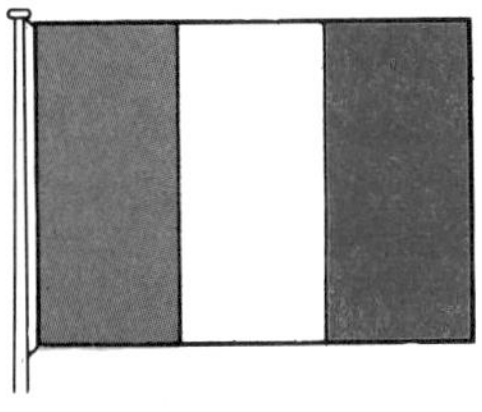

AREA 210,038 sq. mi. (543,998 sq. km.)
POPULATION 53,788,000
CAPITAL Paris
LARGEST CITY Paris
HIGHEST POINT Mont Blanc 15,771 ft. (4,807 m.)
MONETARY UNIT franc
MAJOR LANGUAGE French
MAJOR RELIGION Roman Catholicism

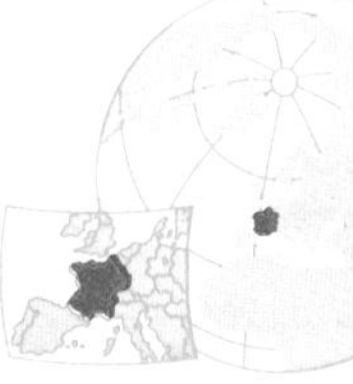

Topography

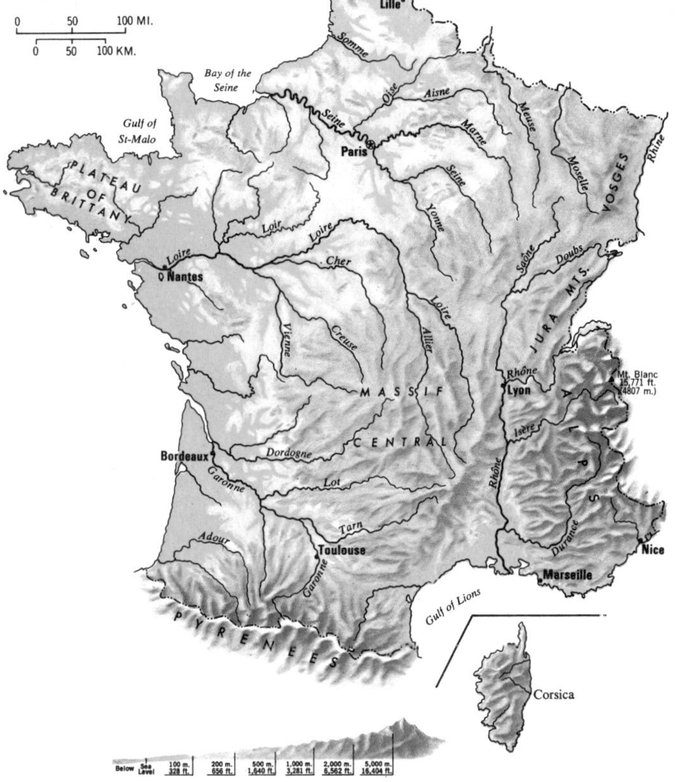

Historic Provinces

A resident of the city of Caen thinks of himself as a Norman rather than as a citizen of the modern department of Calvados. In spite of the passing of nearly two centuries, the historic provinces which existed before 1790 command the local patriotism of most Frenchmen.

Digne 13,140 G5
Digoin 10,449 F4
Dijon 149,899 F4
Dinan 13,303 B3
Dinard 9,211 B3
Dôle 28,109 F4
Domrémy-la-Pucelle 190 F3
Douai 43,954 E2
Douarnenez 17,851 A3
Doullens 6,806 E2
Draguignan 19,653 G6
Drancy 64,258 B1
Dreux 31,503 D3
Dunkirk (Dunkerque) 78,171 E2
Elbeuf 18,642 D3
Épernay 29,286 E3
Épinal 39,000 G3
Épinay-sur-Seine 46,458 B1
Erstein 6,494 G3
Étampes 18,810 E3
Étaples 10,423 D2
Eu 8,349 D3
Évreux 46,181 D3
Évry 15,300 E3
Falaise 8,133 C3
Fécamp 20,835 D3
Figeac 8,675 D5
Firminy 23,776 F5
Flers 18,590 C3
Foix 9,569 D6
Fontainebleau 16,436 E3
Fontenay-le-Comte 12,301 C4
Fontenay-sous-Bois 46,200 C2
Forbach 24,812 G3
Fougères 26,260 C3
Fourmies 15,318 F2
Fréjus 27,805 G6
Gagny 36,714 C1
Gaillac 7,653 D6
Gap 24,962 G5
Gardanne 8,175 F6
Gennevillers 50,154 B1
Gentilly 16,843 B2
Gex 3,959 G4
Gien 13,817 E4
Gif 10,866 E3
Gisors 7,591 D3
Givet 7,787 F2
Givors 19,356 F5
Granville 12,869 C3
Grasse 24,260 G6
Graulhet 11,099 E6
Gray 8,718 F4
Grenoble 165,431 F5
Guebwiller 10,477 G4
Guéret 14,418 D4
Guingamp 9,269 B3
Guise 6,642 E3
Haguenau 23,023 G3
Harfleur 9,857 D3
Hautmont 19,130 F2
Hayange 8,479 F3
Hazebrouck 18,867 E2
Hendaye 9,404 C6
Hénin-Beaumont 26,296 E2
Hennebont 8,978 B4
Héricourt 8,481 G4
Hirson 11,909 F3
Honfleur 8,995 D3
Hyères 29,366 G6
Issoire 13,560 E5
Issoudun 15,065 D4
Issy-les-Moulineaux 47,355 A2
Istres 10,127 F6
Ivry-sur-Seine 62,804 B2
Joigny 10,825 E3
La Baule-Escoublac 13,854 B4
La Ciotat 29,290 F6
La Courneuve 37,917 B1
La Flèche 12,743 C4
La Grand-Combe 9,406 E5
L'Aigle 9,198 D3
Landerneau 13,983 B3
Langres 10,745 F4
Lannion 13,692 B3
Laon 27,420 E3
La Pallice C4
La Rochelle 72,936 C4
La Roche-sur-Yon 40,789 C4
La Seyne-sur-Mer 50,059 F6
Laval 50,734 C3
Lavelanet 9,278 E6
Le Blanc 7,431 D4
Le Blanc-Mesnil 49,062 B1
Le-Bourget 10,520 B1
Le Cateau 8,680 E2
Le Chesnay 24,590 A2
Le Creusot 31,643 F4
Le Havre 216,917 C3
Le Mans 150,289 C3
Lens 39,973 E2
Le Puy 24,793 F5
Les Andelys 7,524 D3
Les Sables-d'Olonne 17,157 B4
Le Teil 7,993 F5
Le Tréport 6,463 D2
Levallois-Perret 52,460 A1
Lézignan-Corbières 6,929 E6
Libourne 21,265 C5
Liévin 33,040 E2
Lille 171,010 E2
Limoges 136,059 D5
Limoux 9,595 E6
Lisieux 24,972 D3
Livry-Gargan 32,879 C1
Lodève 7,131 E6
Longwy 20,107 F3
Lons-le-Saunier 20,897 F4
Lorient 68,655 B4
Loudéac 7,173 B3
Loudun 7,060 D4
Lourdes 17,685 C6
Louviers 17,919 D3
Luçon 8,834 C4
Lunel 12,392 E6
Lunéville 22,438 G3
Lure 8,538 G4
Luxeuil-les-Bains 10,061 G4
Lyon 454,265 F5
Mâcon 39,130 F4
Maisons-Alfort 53,963 B2
Maisons-Laffitte 23,465 A1
Malakoff 34,100 A2
Manosque 17,256 G6
Mantes-la-Jolie 42,403 D3
Marmande 13,223 C5
Marseille 901,421 F6
Martigues 26,850 F6
Maubeuge 34,152 F2
Mayenne 11,278 C3
Mazamet 13,148 E6
Meaux 41,831 E3
Mehun-sur-Yèvre 6,533 E4
Melun 36,913 E3
Mende 10,040 E5
Menton 24,736 G6
Metz 110,939 G3
Meudon 31,294 A2
Millau 20,401 E5
Mimizan 6,826 C5
Mirecourt 7,160 G3
Moissac 7,403 D5
Montargis 18,021 E3
Montauban 35,344 D5
Montbard 7,477 F4
Montbéliard 29,968 G4
Montbrison 9,945 E5
Montceau-les-Mines 28,093 F4
Mont-de-Marsan 24,812 C6
Mont-Dore 2,074 E5
Montélimar 25,422 F5
Montfort 2,701 C3
Montigny-les-Metz 24,208 G3
Montluçon 56,337 E4
Montmédy 1,859 F3
Montpellier 178,136 E6
Montreuil,
Seine-Saint-Denis 96,441 B2
Montrouge 40,189 B2
Mont-Saint-Michel 88 C3
Morlaix 15,919 B3
Morteau 6,515 G4
Moulins 25,856 E4
Moyeuvre-Grande 12,448 G3
Mulhouse 116,494 G4
Muret 13,041 D6
Nancy 106,906 G3
Nanterre 94,441 A1
Nantes 252,537 C4
Narbonne 36,525 F6
Nemours 11,159 E3
Neufchâteau 8,582 F3
Neuilly-sur-Seine 65,941 A1
Nevers 45,122 E4
Nice 331,002 G6
Nîmes 123,914 F6
Niort 59,297 C4
Nogent-le-Rotrou 12,284 D3
Noisy-le-Sec 37,674 B1
Noyon 13,784 E3
Oloron-Sainte-Marie 11,616 C6
Orange 19,847 F5
Orléans 88,503 D3
Orly 26,090 B2
Orthez 9,639 C6
Oullins 27,731 F5
Oyonnax 22,548 F4
Pamiers 12,906 D6
Pantin 42,651 B1
Paray-le-Monial 11,523 F4
Paris (cap.) 2,291,554 B2
Parthenay 12,549 C4
Pau 81,560 C6
Périgueux 34,779 D5
Péronne 8,358 E3
Perpignan 101,198 E6
Pessac 50,333 C5
Pézenas 6,768 E6
Pithiviers 9,976 E3
Poitiers 78,739 D4
Pont-à-Mousson 14,461 G3
Pontarlier 17,778 G4
Pontivy 9,478 B3
Pont-l'Abbe 6,618 A4
Pontoise 26,702 E3
Port-de-Bouc 20,448 F6
Port-Saint-Louis-du-Rhône 9,649 F6
Port-Vendres 5,448 E6
Privas 9,385 F5
Provins 12,281 E3
Puteau 35,366 A2
Quimper 50,856 A4
Quimperlé 9,783 B4
Rambouillet 18,446 D3
Redon 9,528 C4
Reims 177,320 E3
Remiremont 10,250 G3
Rennes 194,094 C3

(continued on following page)

(continued)

Rethel 8,189 .... F3
Révin 11,459 .... F3
Rezé 35,512 .... C4
Rive-de-Gier 17,369 .... F5
Roanne 54,999 .... E4
Rochechouart 2,953 .... D5
Rochefort 27,264 .... C4
Rodez 24,898 .... E5
Romans-sur-Isère 30,974 .... F5
Romilly-sur-Seine 17,276 .... F3
Romorantin-Lanthenay 15,727 .... D4
Roubaix 109,473 .... E2
Rouen 113,536 .... D3
Royan 17,978 .... C5
Rueil-Malmaison 62,504 .... A2
Sablé-sur-Sarthe 9,913 .... C4
Saint-Affrique 6,842 .... E6
Saint-Amand-Mont-Rond 11,896 .... E4
Saint-Brieuc 51,838 .... B3
Saint-Chamond 39,236 .... F5
Saint-Claude 12,651 .... F4
Saint-Cloud 28,052 .... A2
Saint-Denis 95,808 .... B1
Saint-Dié 22,834 .... G3
Saint-Dizier 36,377 .... F3
Sainte-Mère-Église 1,041 .... C3
Saintes 24,946 .... C5
Sainte-Savine 10,526 .... E3
Saint-Étienne 218,289 .... F5
Saint-Florent-sur-Cher 6,385 .... E4
Saint-Flour 6,900 .... E5
Saint-Gaudens 12,103 .... D6
Saint-Germain-en-Laye 35,351 .... D3
Saint-Gilles-Croix-de-Vie 6,569 .... B4
Saint-Girons 7,259 .... D6
Saint-Jean-d'Angély 8,801 .... C4
Saint-Jean-de-Luz 10,921 .... C6
Saint-Jean-de-Maurienne 9,525 .... G5
Saint-Jean-Pied-de-Port 1,725 .... C6
Saint-Junien 9,281 .... D5
Saint-Lô 21,670 .... C3
Saint-Malo 43,277 .... B3
Saint-Mandé 20,714 .... B2
Saint-Marcellin 6,768 .... F5
Saint-Maur-des-Fossés 80,797 .... B2
Saint-Mihiel 5,544 .... F3
Saint-Nazaire 65,228 .... B4
Saint-Omer 16,419 .... E2
Saint-Ouen 43,569 .... B1
Saint-Pol-de-Léon 6,571 .... A3
Saint-Quentin 69,956 .... E3
Saint-Raphaël 19,499 .... G6
Saint-Tropez 4,484 .... G6
Saint-Vallier 10,000 .... F5
Salon-de-Provence 31,783 .... F6
Sancerre 2,029 .... E4
Sarlat-La-Canéda 8,191 .... D5
Sarrebourg 12,442 .... G3
Sarreguemines 24,570 .... G3
Sartrouville 42,092 .... A1
Saumur 30,984 .... D4
Saverne 10,015 .... G3
Sceaux 19,651 .... A2
Sedan 23,867 .... F3
Sélestat 15,209 .... G3
Senlis 13,481 .... E3
Sens 25,621 .... E3
Sète 39,075 .... E6
Sèvres 21,100 .... A2
Sisteron 6,434 .... G5
Soissons 29,694 .... E3
Sotteville-les-Rouen 30,393 .... D3
Stiring-Wendel 12,665 .... G3
Strasbourg 251,520 .... H3
Suresnes 37,456 .... A2
Tarare 11,931 .... F5
Tarascon 8,522 .... F6
Tarbes 54,286 .... D6
Thann 8,508 .... G4
Thiers 14,534 .... E5
Thionville 37,943 .... G3
Thonon-les-Bains 24,673 .... G4
Thouars 11,835 .... C4
Tonneins 7,256 .... D5
Toul 16,141 .... F3
Toulon 180,508 .... F6
Toulouse 371,143 .... D6
Tourcoing 102,092 .... E2
Tournon 8,568 .... F5
Tournus 7,284 .... F4
Tours 139,560 .... D4
Troyes 71,600 .... F3
Tulle 18,375 .... D5
Uckange 11,552 .... G3
Ussel 9,816 .... E5
Uzès 6,470 .... F5
Valence 67,101 .... F5
Valenciennes 41,976 .... E2
Vannes 36,722 .... B4
Vence 7,332 .... G6
Vendôme 17,828 .... D4
Vénissieux 74,264 .... F5
Verdun-sur-Meuse 22,889 .... F3
Vernon 21,184 .... D3
Versailles 93,359 .... A2
Vesoul 17,883 .... F4
Vichy 32,107 .... E4
Vienne 25,981 .... F5
Vierzon 33,057 .... D4
Villefranche 6,600 .... G6
Villefranche-de-Rouergue 10,848 .... E5
Villefranche-sur-Saône 29,996 .... F4
Villejuif 53,884 .... B2
Villemomble 28,684 .... C1
Villeneuve-Saint-Georges 31,378 .... E3
Villeneuve-sur-Lot 17,818 .... D5
Villeurbanne 115,913 .... F5
Vincennes 44,256 .... B2
Vire 12,832 .... C3
Vitré 10,989 .... C3
Vitry-le-François 19,075 .... F3
Vitry-sur-Seine 87,119 .... B2
Vittel 6,791 .... F3
Vizille 6,810 .... F5
Voiron 17,879 .... F5
Wissembourg 6,679 .... G3
Yvetot 10,088 .... D3

OTHER FEATURES

Adour (riv.) C6
Ain (riv.) F4
Aisne (riv.) E3
Ajaccio (gulf) B7
Allier (riv.) E5
Aube (riv.) F3
Auvergne (mts.) E5
Belle-Île (isl.) B4
Biscay (bay) B5
Blanc (mt.) G5
Bonifacio (str.) B7
Calais (Dover) (str.) D2
Causses (reg.) D5
Cévennes (mts.) E5
Charente (riv.) C5
Cher (riv.) D4
Corse (cape) B6
Corsica (isl.) B6
Côte-d'Or (mts.) F4
Cotentin (pen.) C3
Cottian Alps (range) G5
Creuse (riv.) D4
Dordogne (riv.) D5
Dore Alps (mts.) E5
Doubs (riv.) G4
Drôme (riv.) F5
Dronne (riv.) D5
Durance (riv.) F6
English (chan.) B3
Eure (riv.) D3
Faucilles (mts.) G3
Forez (mts.) E5
Fréjus (pass) G5
Gard (riv.) F5
Garonne (riv.) C5
Gave de Pau (riv.) C6
Geneva (lake) G4
Gers (riv.) D6
Gironde (riv.) C5
Graian Alps (range) G5
Groix (isl.) B4
Hague (cape) C3
Hérault (riv.) E6
Hyères (isls.) G6
Indre (riv.) D4
Isère (riv.) F5
Isle (riv.) D5
Langres (plat.) F4
Limousin (reg.) D5
Lions (gulf) F6
Little Saint Bernard (pass) G5
Loir (riv.) D4
Loire (riv.) C4
Lot (riv.) D5
Manche, La (English) (chan.) B3
Maritime Alps (range) G5
Marne (riv.) C2
Mayenne (riv.) C4
Mediterranean (sea) E7
Médoc (reg.) C5
Meuse (riv.) F3
Mont Cenis (tunnel) G5
Morvan (plat.) F4
Moselle (riv.) G3
Noirmoutier (isl.) B4
North (sea) E1
Oise (riv.) E3
Oléron (isl.) C5
Omaha (beach) C3
Orb (riv.) E6
Orne (riv.) C3
Ouessant (isl.) A3
Penmarch (pt.) A4
Perche (reg.) D3
Puy-de-Dôme (mt.) E5
Pyrenees (range) C6
Ré (isl.) C4
Rhine (riv.) G3
Rhône (riv.) F5
Risle (riv.) D3
Riviera (reg.) G6
Saint-Florent (gulf) B6
Saint-Malo (gulf) B3
Saône (riv.) F4
Sarthe (riv.) D4
Sein (isl.) A3
Seine (bay) C3
Seine (riv.) D3
Sologne (reg.) E4
Somme (riv.) D2
Tarn (riv.) E6
Ushant (Ouessant) (isl.) A3
Utah (beach) C3
Vaccarès (lag.) F6
Vienne (riv.) D4
Vilaine (riv.) C4
Vosges (mts.) G3
Yonne (riv.) E3

MONACO

CITIES and TOWNS

Monte Carlo 11,599 .... G6

* City and suburbs

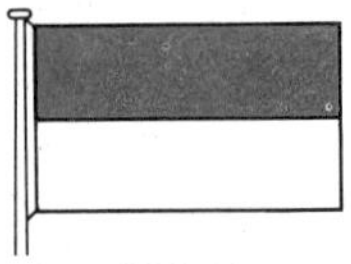

MONACO

AREA 368 acres (149 hectares)
POPULATION 25,029

Wine Regions

Climate, soil and variety of grape planted determine the quality of wine. Long, hot and fairly dry summers with cool, humid nights constitute an ideal climate. The nature of the soil is such a determining influence that identical grapes planted in Bordeaux, Burgundy and Champagne, will yield wines of widely different types.

Agriculture, Industry and Resources

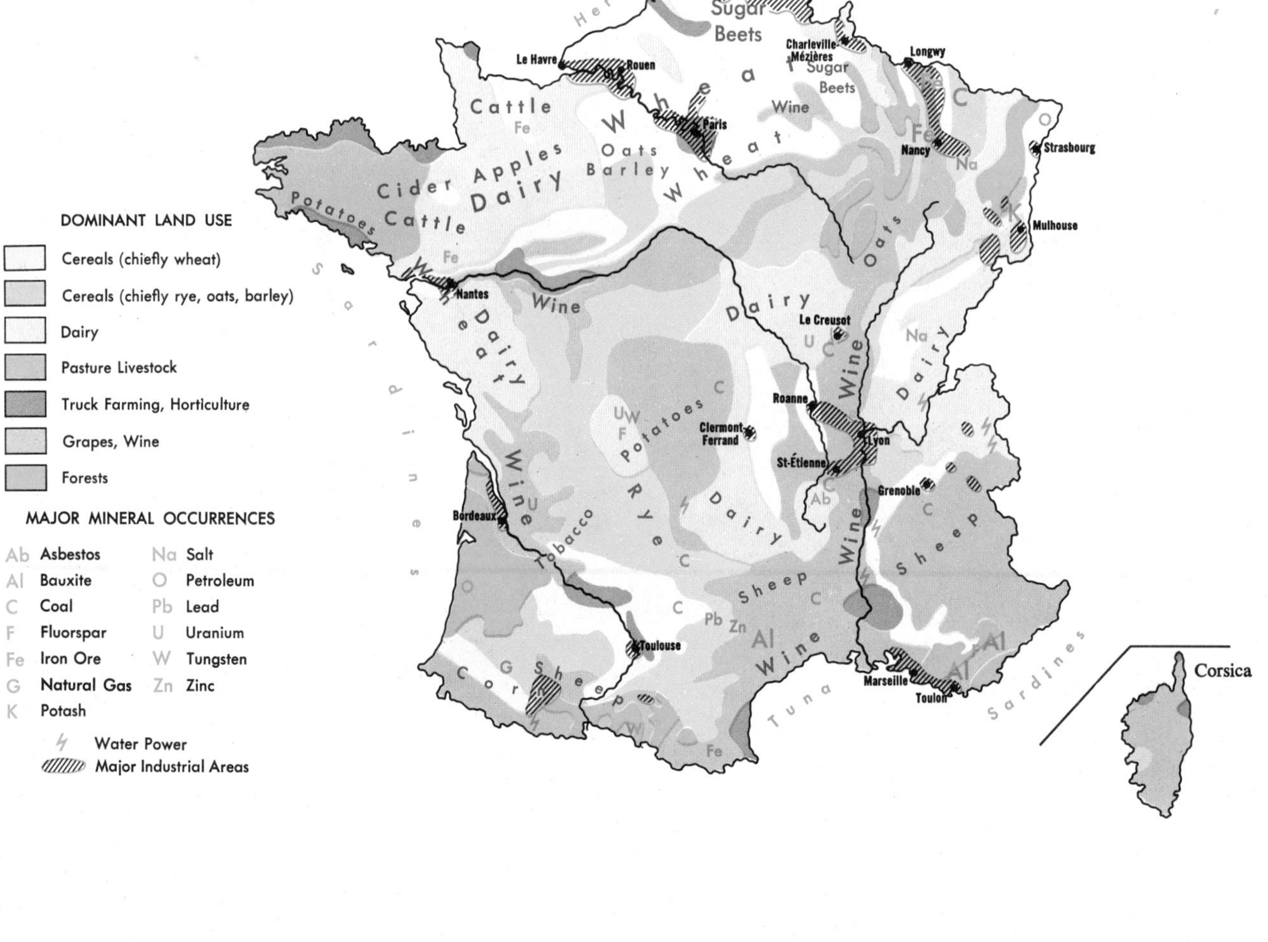

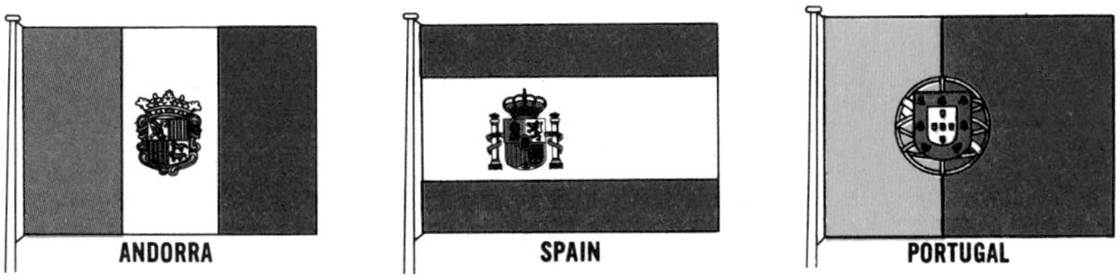

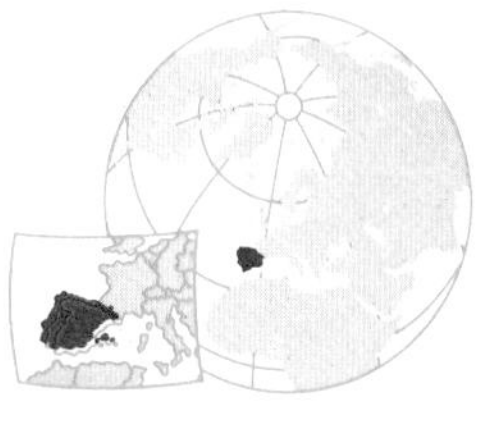

SPAIN

AREA 194,881 sq. mi. (504,742 sq. km.)
POPULATION 37,430,000
CAPITAL Madrid
LARGEST CITY Madrid
HIGHEST POINT Pico de Teide 12,172 ft. (3,710 m.) (Canary Is.); Mulhacén 11,411 ft. (3,478 m.) (mainland)
MONETARY UNIT peseta
MAJOR LANGUAGES Spanish, Catalan, Basque, Galician, Valencian
MAJOR RELIGION Roman Catholicism

PORTUGAL

AREA 35,549 sq. mi. (92,072 sq. km.)
POPULATION 9,933,000
CAPITAL Lisbon
LARGEST CITY Lisbon
HIGHEST POINT Malhão da Estrela 6,532 ft. (1,991 m.)
MONETARY UNIT escudo
MAJOR LANGUAGE Portuguese
MAJOR RELIGION Roman Catholicism

ANDORRA

AREA 188 sq. mi. (487 sq. km.)
POPULATION 31,000
CAPITAL Andorra la Vella
MONETARY UNITS French franc, Spanish peseta
MAJOR LANGUAGE Catalan
MAJOR RELIGION Roman Catholicism

GIBRALTAR

AREA 2.28 sq. mi. (5.91 sq. km.)
POPULATION 29,760
CAPITAL Gibraltar
MONETARY UNIT pound sterling
MAJOR LANGUAGES English, Spanish
MAJOR RELIGION Roman Catholicism

SPAIN

PROVINCES

ava 204,323 E1
bacete 335,026 E3
icante 920,105 F3
imería 375,004 E4
vila 203,798 D2
adajoz 687,599 C3
aleares 558,287 H3
arcelona 3,929,194 G2
urgos 358,075 E1
áceres 457,777 C3
ádiz 885,433 D4
astellón 385,823 G2
iudad Real 507,650 D3
órdoba 724,116* D3
uenca 247,158 E2
erona 414,397 H1
ranada 733,375 E4
uadalajara 147,732 E2
uipúzcoa 631,003 E1
uelva 397,683 C4
uesca 222,238 F1
aén 661,146 E4
a Coruña 1,004,188 B1
as Palmas 579,710 C4
eón 548,721 C1
érida 347,015 G2
ogroño 235,713 E1
ugo 415,052 C1
ladrid 3,792,561 E2
lálaga 867,330 D4
lurcia 832,313 F4
avarra 464,867 F1
rense 413,733 C1
viedo 1,045,635 C1
alencia 198,763 D1
ontevedra 750,701 B1
alamanca 371,607 C2
anta Cruz de Tenerife 590,514 B5
antander 467,138 D1
egovia 162,770 D2
evilla 1,327,190 D4
oria 114,956 E2
arragona 431,961 G2
eruel 170,284 F2
oledo 468,925 D3
alencia 1,767,327 F3
alladolid 412,572 D2
izcaya 1,043,310 E1
amora 251,934 D2
aragoza 760,186 F2

CITIES and TOWNS

dra 10,851 E4
guilar 12,893 D4
guilas 15,525 F4
lagón 5,114 F2
layor 5,124 J3
lbacete 82,607 F3
lbox 5,072 E4
lburquerque 7,530 C3
lcalá de Guadaira 28,781 D4
lcalá de Henares 59,783 G4
lcalá de los Gazules 5,262 D4
lcalá la Real 9,849 E4
lcanar 5,961 G2
lcañiz 10,229 F2
lcantarilla 19,895 F4
lcaudete 8,557 E4
lcázar de San Juan 24,620 E3
lcira 30,493 F3
lcora 6,711 F2
lcoy 61,371 F3
lfaro 8,766 F1
lgeciras 74,754 D4
lgemesí 21,158 F3
lhama de Granada 6,148 E4
lhama de Murcia 9,274 F4
licante 177,918 F3
lmadén 10,713 D3
lmagro 9,066 E3
lmansa 16,965 F3
lmendralejo 21,929 C3
lmería 104,008 E4
lmodóvar del Campo 7,310 D3
lmonte 9,960 C4
lmuñécar 7,812 E4
lora 8,209 D4
ltea 7,262 G3
mposta 11,767 G2
ndorra 6,485 F2
ndújar 25,962 D3
ntequera 28,039 D4
racena 5,390 C4
randa de Duero 18,183 E2
ranjuez 28,559 E2
rchena 7,118 F3
rchidona 6,084 D4
rcos de la Frontera 16,217 D4
renas de San Pedro 5,225 D2
renys de Mar 8,325 H2
révalo 5,807 D2
rgamasilla de Alba 6,192 E3
rganda 11,876 G4
rnedo 9,809 E1
rrecife 21,310 C4
rroyo de la Luz 8,130 C3
rtá 5,284 H3
rucas 9,095 B5
spe 13,229 F3
storga 11,791 C1
vila de los Caballeros 30,958 D2
vilés 67,186 C1
yamonte 9,897 C4
yora 5,249 F3
zpeitia 7,835 E1
zuaga 10,719 D3
Badajoz 80,793 C3
Badalona 162,888 H2
Baena 16,496 D4
Baeza 12,607 E4
Bailén 13,207 E3
Balaguer 11,676 G2
Bañolas 9,807 H1
Baracaldo 108,757 E1
Barbastro 13,243 F1
Barcarrota 5,012 C3
Barcelona 1,741,144 H2
Barcelona‡ 2,000,000 H2
Baza 14,290 E4
Beas de Segura 6,592 E3
Béjar 16,804 D2
Bélmez 5,161 D3
Benavente 11,779 D1
Benicarló 12,831 G2
Berga 11,163 G1
Berja 7,081 E4
Bermeo 16,714 E1
Betanzos 7,283 B1
Bilbao 393,179 E1
Bilbao‡ 450,000 E1
Binéfar 6,821 G2
Blanes 15,810 H2
Borjas Blancas 4,991 G2
Bujalance 8,236 D4
Bullas 8,131 F4
Burgos 118,366 E1
Burriana 21,298 G3
Cabeza del Buey 8,704 D3
Cabra 16,177 D4
Cáceres 53,108 C3
Cádiz 135,743 C4
Calahorra 16,315 E1
Calasparra 7,238 F3
Calatayud 16,524 F2
Calella 9,696 H2
Callosa de Ensarriá 5,701 G3
Calzada de Calatrava 5,751 E3
Campanario 7,722 D3
Campillos 7,014 D4
Campo de Criptana 12,604 E3
Candás 5,517 D1
Candeleda 5,153 D2
Cangas de Narcea 4,826 C1
Caniles 5,099 E4
Caravaca de le Cruz 10,411 E3
Carballo 5,542 B1
Carcagente 18,223 F3
Carmona 22,832 D4
Cartagena 52,312 F4
Caspe 8,766 G2
Cassá de la Selva 5,248 H2
Castellón de la Plana 79,773 G2
Castro del Río 10,087 D4
Castro-Urdiales 8,369 E1
Castuera 8,060 D3
Caudete 7,332 F3
Cazalla de la Sierra 5,382 D4
Cazorla 6,938 E4
Cehegín 9,661 F3
Cervera 5,693 G2
Ceuta 60,639 D5
Chiclana de la Frontera 22,986 C4
Chiva 5,394 F3
Ciempozuelos 9,185 F5
Cieza 22,929 F3
Ciudadela 13,701 H2
Ciudad Real 39,931 D3
Ciudad-Rodrigo 11,694 C2
Cocentaina 8,375 F3
Coín 14,190 D4
Colmenar de Oreja 4,930 G5
Colmenar Viejo 12,886 F4
Constantina 10,227 D4
Consuegra 10,026 E3
Córdoba 216,049 D4
Corella 5,850 F1
Coria 8,083 C3
Coria del Río 18,085 C4
Corral de Almaguer 8,006 E3
Crevillente 15,749 F3
Cuéllar 6,118 D2
Cuenca 33,980 E2
Cullera 15,128 F3
Daimiel 17,710 E3
Denia 14,514 G3
Dolores 5,420 F3
Don Benito 21,351 C3
Dos Hermanas 36,921 D4
Durango 20,403 E1
Écija 27,295 D4
Eibar 36,729 E1
Ejea de los Caballeros 9,766 F1
El Arahal 14,703 D4
Elche 101,271 F3
Elda 41,404 F3
Elizondo 2,516 F1
El Puerto de Santa María 36,451 C4
Espejo 5,925 D4
Estella 10,371 E1
Estepa 9,376 D4
Estepona 18,560 D4
Felanitx 9,100 H3
Ferrol del Caudillo 75,464 B1
Figueras 22,087 H1
Fraga 9,665 G2
Fregenal de la Sierra 6,826 C3
Fuengirola 20,597 D4
Fuente de Cantos 5,967 C3
Fuenterrabiá 2,350 E1
Fuentes de Andalucía 8,257 D4
Gandía 30,702 F3
Gerona 37,095 H2
Getafe 68,680 F4
Gijón 159,806 D1
Granada 185,799 E4
Granollers 30,066 H2
Guadalajara 30,924 E2
Guadix 15,311 E4
Guareña 7,706 C3
Guernica y Luno 12,046 E1
Haro 8,393 E1
Hellín 15,934 F3
Herencia 8,212 E3
Hinojosa del Duque 9,873 D3
Hortaleza G4
Hospitalet 241,978 H2
Huelma 5,260 E4
Huelva 96,689 C4
Huercal-Overa 5,158 F4
Huesca 33,076 F1
Huéscar 6,384 E4
Ibiza 16,943 G3
Igualada 27,941 G2
Inca 16,930 H3
Irún 38,014 F1
Iscar 5,192 D2
Isla Cristina 11,402 C4
Iznalloz 4,814 E4
Jaca 9,936 F1
Jaén 71,145 E4
Jaraíz de la Vera 6,379 D2
Játiva 20,934 F3
Jávea 6,228 G3
Jerez de la Frontera 112,411 C4
Jerez de los Caballeros 8,607 C3
Jijona 8,117 F3
Jódar 11,973 E4
Jumilla 16,407 F3
La Almunia de Doña Godina 4,835 F2
La Bañeza 8,480 C1
La Bisbal 6,374 H1
La Carolina 13,138 E3
La Coruña 184,372 B1
La Granja (San Ildefonso) 3,198 E2
La Guardia 4,967 B2
La Línea de la Concepción 51,021 D4
La Orotava 8,246 B4
La Palma del Condado 9,256 C4
La Puebla 9,923 H3
La Puebla de Montalbán 6,629 D3
La Rambla 6,525 D4
Laredo 9,114 E1
La Roda 11,460 E3
La Solana 13,894 E3
Las Palmas de Gran Canaria 260,368 B4
Las Pedroñeras 5,846 E3
La Unión 9,998 F4
Lebrija 15,081 D4
Leganés 57,537 F4
León 99,702 D1
Lérida 73,148 G2
Linares 45,330 E3
Liria 11,323 F3
Llerena 5,728 C3
Llivia 801 G1
Llodio 15,587 E1
Lluctmayor 9,630 H3
Logroño 83,117 E1
Loja 11,549 D4
Lora del Río 15,741 D4
Lorca 25,208 F4
Los Santos de Maimona 7,899 C3
Los Yébenes 5,477 E3
Lucena 21,527 D4
Lugo 53,504 C1
Madrid (cap.) 3,146,071 F4
Madrid‡ 3,500,000 F4
Madridejos 9,948 E3
Madroñera 5,397 D3
Mahón 17,802 J3
Málaga 334,988 D4
Málaga‡ 400,000 D4
Malagón 7,732 E3
Malpartida de Cáceres 5,054 C3
Manacor 20,266 H3
Mancha Real 7,547 E4
Manlleu 13,169 H1
Manresa 52,526 G2
Manzanares 15,024 E3
Marbella 19,648 D4
Marchena 16,227 D4
Marín 10,948 B1
Martos 16,395 E4
Mataró 73,129 H2
Medina del Campo 16,345 D2
Medina de Rioseco 4,874 D2
Medina-Sidonia 7,523 D4
Mérida 36,916 C3
Miajadas 8,042 D3
Mieres 22,790 D1
Minas de Ríotinto 3,939 C4
Miranda de Ebro 29,355 E1
Moguer 7,629 C4
Mollerusa 6,685 G2
Monesterio 5,923 C3
Monforte 14,002 C1
Monóvar 9,071 F3
Montehermoso 5,952 C2
Montellano 6,658 D4
Montijo 11,931 C3
Montilla 18,670 D4
Montoro 9,295 D3
Monzón 14,089 G2
Mora 10,523 E3
Moratalla 5,101 E3
Morón de la Frontera 25,662 D4
Mota del Cuervo 5,130 E3
Motril 26,121 E4
Mula 9,168 F3
Munera 5,003 E3
Murcia 102,242 F4
Navalcarnero 6,212 F4
Navalmoral de la Mata 9,650 D3
Nerja 7,413 E4
Nerva 10,830 C4
Novelda 16,867 F3
Nules 9,027 F3
Ocaña 5,603 E3
Oliva 16,717 F3
Oliva de la Frontera 8,560 C3
Olivenza 7,616 C3
Olot 18,062 H1
Olvera 9,825 D4
Onda 13,012 F3
Onteniente 23,685 F3
Orense 63,542 C1
Orihuela 17,610 F3
Osuna 17,384 D4
Oviedo 130,021 C1
Padul 6,377 E4
Palafrugell 10,421 H2
Palamós 7,679 H2
Palencia 58,327 D2
Palma 191,416 H3
Palma del Río 15,075 D4
Pamplona 142,686 F1
Pego 8,861 F3
Peñafiel 4,794 E2
Peñaranda de Bracamonte 6,094 D2
Peñarroya-Pueblonuevo 15,649 D3
Pinos-Puente 7,634 E4
Plasencia 26,897 C2
Pola de Lena 5,760 D1
Pollensa 7,625 H3
Ponferrada 22,838 C1
Pontevedra 27,118 B1
Porcuna 8,169 D4
Port-Bou 2,230 H1
Portugalete 45,589 E1
Posadas 7,245 D4
Pozoblanco 13,280 D3
Pozuelo de Alarcón 14,041 D2
Priego de Córdoba 12,676 D4
Puente-Genil 22,888 D4
Puertollano 50,609 D3
Puerto Real 13,993 D4
Puigcerdá 4,418 G1
Quesada 6,965 E4
Quintana de la Serena 5,171 D3
Quintanar de la Orden 7,764 E3
Reinosa 10,863 D1
Requena 9,836 F3
Reus 47,240 G2
Ripoll 9,283 H1
Ronda 22,094 D4
Roquetas 5,617 G2
Rosas 5,448 H1
Rota 20,021 C4
Rute 8,294 D4
Sabadell 148,223 H2
Sagunto 17,052 F3
Salamanca 125,132 D2
Sallent 7,118 H2
Salobreña 5,961 E4
Salt 5,572 H1
Sama 9,863 D1
San Carlos de la Rápita 8,946 G2
San Clemente 6,016 E3
San Feliu de Guíxols 12,006 H2
San Fernando 59,309 C4
San Ildefonso 3,198 E2

Agriculture, Industry and Resources

DOMINANT LAND USE

- Cereals (chiefly wheat)
- Livestock (chiefly sheep, goats)
- Mixed Cereals, Livestock
- Olives, Fruit
- Grapes, Fruit, Nuts, Mixed Cereals
- Forests
- Nonagricultural Land

MAJOR MINERAL OCCURRENCES

Ag	Silver	Na	Salt
C	Coal	O	Petroleum
Cu	Copper	Pb	Lead
Fe	Iron Ore	Py	Pyrites
G	Natural Gas	Sb	Antimony
Hg	Mercury	Sn	Tin
K	Potash	U	Uranium
Lg	Lignite	W	Tungsten
Mg	Magnesium	Zn	Zinc

Water Power
Major Industrial Areas

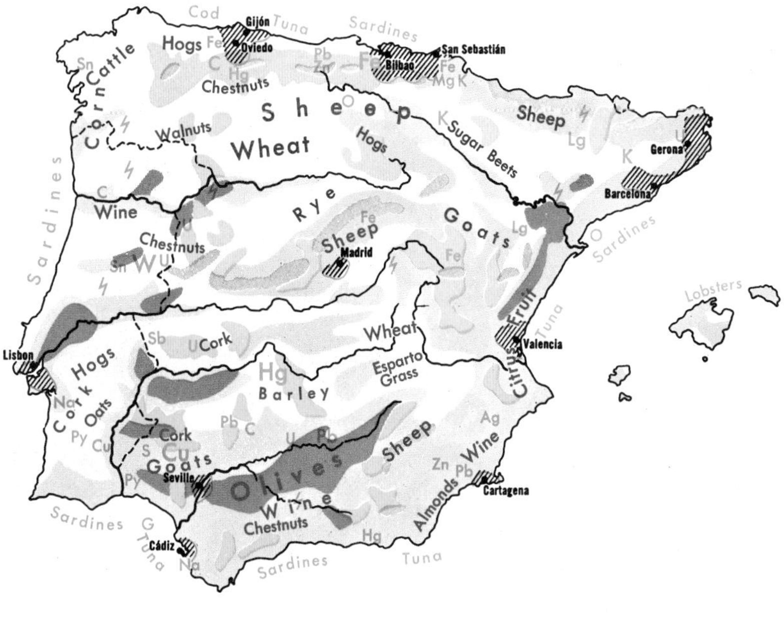

(continued on following page)

(continued)

San Lorenzo de El Escorial 8,098 .... E2
Sanlúcar de Barrameda 29,483 .... C4
Sanlúcar la Mayor 6,121 .... C4
San Roque 8,224 .... D4
San Sebastián 159,557 .... E1
Santa Cruz de la Palma 10,393 .... B4
Santa Cruz de Mudela 6,354 .... E3
Santa Cruz de Tenerife 74,910 .... B4
Santa Eugenia 5,946 .... B1
Santa Fé 8,990 .... E4
Santander 130,019 .... D1
Santiago 51,620 .... B1
Santo Domingo de la Calzada 5,638 .... E1
Santoña 9,546 .... E1
San Vicente de Alcántara 7,006 .... C3
Saragossa 449,319 .... F2
Saragossa‡ 500,000 .... F2
Segorbe 6,962 .... F3
Segovia 41,880 .... D2
Seo de Urgel 6,604 .... G1
Seville 511,447 .... D4
Seville‡ 560,000 .... D4
Sitges 8,906 .... G2
Socuéllamos 12,610 .... E3
Sóller 6,470 .... H3
Solsona 5,346 .... G2
Sonseca 6,594 .... D3
Soria 24,744 .... E2
Sotrondio 5,914 .... D1
Sueca 20,019 .... F3
Tabernes de Valldigna 13,962 .... G3
Tafalla 8,858 .... F1
Talavera de la Reina 39,889 .... D2
Tarancón 8,238 .... E3
Tarazona 11,067 .... E2
Tarazona de la Mancha 5,952 .... F3
Tarifa 9,201 .... D4
Tarragona 53,548 .... G2
Tarrasa 134,481 .... G2
Tárrega 9,036 .... G2
Tauste 6,832 .... F2
Telde 13,257 .... B5
Teruel 20,614 .... F2
Tobarra 5,887 .... F3
Toledo 43,905 .... D3
Tolosa 15,164 .... F1
Tomelloso 26,041 .... E3
Tordesillas 5,815 .... D2
Toro 8,455 .... D2
Torredonjimeno 12,507 .... D4
Torrejón de Ardoz 21,081 .... G4
Torrelavega 19,933 .... D1
Torremolinos 20,484 .... D4
Torrente 38,397 .... F3
Torrevieja 9,431 .... F4
Torrijos 6,362 .... D2
Torrox 5,583 .... E4
Tortosa 20,030 .... G2
Totana 12,714 .... F4
Trigueros 6,280 .... C4
Trujillo 9,024 .... D3
Tudela 20,942 .... F1
Úbeda 28,306 .... E3
Ubrique 13,166 .... D4
Utiel 9,168 .... F3
Utrera 28,287 .... D4
Valdemoro 6,263 .... F4
Valdepeñas 24,018 .... E3
Valencia 626,675 .... F3
Valencia‡ 700,000 .... F3
Valencia de Alcántara 5,963 .... C3
Valladolid 227,511 .... D2
Vall de Uxó 23,976 .... F3
Vallecas G4
Valls 14,189 .... G2
Valverde del Camino 10,566 .... C4
Vejer de la Frontera 6,184 .... C4
Vélez-Málaga 20,794 .... E4
Vendrell 7,951 .... G2
Vera 4,903 .... F4
Vergara 11,541 .... E1
Vicálvaro G4
Vich 23,449 .... H2
Vigo 114,526 .... B1
Vilafranca del Penedés 16,875 .... G2
Villacañas 9,883 .... E3
Villacarrillo 9,452 .... E3
Villafranca de los Barros 12,610 .... C3
Villagarcía 6,601 .... B1
Villajoyosa 12,573 .... F3
Villanueva de Córdoba 11,270 .... D3
Villanueva del Arzobispo 8,076 .... E3
Villanueva de la Serena 16,687 .... D3
Villanueva de los Infantes 8,154 .... E3
Villanueva y Geltrú 35,714 .... G2
Villarreal de los Infantes 29,482 .... G3
Villarrobledo 19,698 .... E3
Villarrubia de los Ojos 9,144 .... E3
Villaverde F4
Villena 23,483 .... F3
Vinaroz 13,727 .... G2
Vitoria 124,791 .... E1
Yecla 19,352 .... F3
Zafra 11,583 .... C3
Zalamea de la Serena 6,017 .... D3
Zamora 48,791 .... D2
Zaragoza (Saragossa) 449,319 .... F2

OTHER FEATURES

Alborán (isl.) E5
Alcaraz, Sierra de (range) E3
Alcudia (bay) H3
Almanzor (mt.) D2
Almanzora (riv.) F4
Andalusia (reg.) C4
Aneto (peak) G1
Aragón (reg.) F2
Arosa, Ria de (est.) B1
Asturias (reg.) C1
Balaitous (mt.) F1
Balearic (Baleares) (isls.) H3
Barbate (riv.) D4
Biscay (bay) E1
Cabrera (isl.) H3
Cádiz (gulf) C4
Cala Burras (pt.) D4
Canary (isls.) B4
Cantabrian (range) C1
Catalonia (reg.) G2
Cinca (riv.) G2
Columbretes (isls.) G3
Costa Brava (reg.) H2
Costa de Sola (Costa del Sol) (reg.) D4
Creus (cape) H1
Cuenca, Sierra de (range) F3
Demanda, Sierra de la (range) E1
Douro (riv.) C2
Duero (Douro) (riv.) C2
Ebro (riv.) G2
Eresma (riv.) D2
Esla (riv.) D2
Estats (peak) G1
Estremadura (reg.) C3
Finisterre (cape) B1
Formentera (isl.) G3
Formentor (cape) H2
Fuerteventura (isl.) C4
Galicia (reg.) B1
Gata (cape) F4
Gata (mts.) C2
Genil (riv.) D4
Gibraltar (str.) D5
Gomera (isl.) B5
Gran Canaria (isl.) B5
Gredos, Sierra de (range) D2
Guadalimar (riv.) E3
Guadalquivir (riv.) C4
Guadarrama, Sierra de (range) E2
Guadarrama (riv.) F4
Guadiana (riv.) D3
Gúdar, Sierra de (range) F2
Henares (riv.) G4
Hierro (isl.) A5
Ibiza (isl.) G3
Jalón (riv.) E2
Jarama (riv.) E2
Júcar (riv.) F3
Lanzarote (isl.) C4
La Palma (isl.) A4
León (reg.) C1
Llobregat (riv.) H2
Majorca (isl.) H3
Mallorca (Majorca) (isl.) H3
Mancha, La (reg.) E3
Manzanares (riv.) F4
Marismas, Las (marsh) C4
Mar Menor (lag.) F4
Mayor (cape) E1
Menorca (Minorca) (isl.) J2
Miño (riv.) B1
Minorca (isl.) J2
Moncayo, Sierra de (range) F2
Montserrat (mt.) G2
Morena, Sierra (range) E3
Mulhacén (mt.) E4
Murcia (reg.) F3
Nao (cape) G3
Navia (riv.) C1
Nevada, Sierra (mts.) E4
New Castile (reg.) E3
Odiel (riv.) C4
Old Castile (reg.) D2
Órbigo (riv.) D1
Palos (cape) F4
Peñalara (mt.) E2
Peñas (cape) D1
Peña Vieja (mt.) D1
Penibética, Sistema (range) E4
Perdido (mt.) G1
Pyrenees (range) F1
Rosas (gulf) H1
San Jorge (gulf) G2
Segre (riv.) G2
Segura (riv.) F3
Sil (riv.) C1
Tagus (riv.) D3
Tajo (Tagus) (riv.) D3
Teide, Pico de (peak) B5
Tenerife (isl.) B5
Ter (riv.) H1
Tinto (riv.) C4
Toledo (mts.) E3
Tortosa (cape) G2
Trafalgar (cape) C4
Turia (riv.) F3
Ulla (riv.) B1
Urgel, Llanos de (plain) G2
Valencia (gulf) G3
Valencia (reg.) F3
Valencia, Albufera de (lag.) G3
Vascongadas (reg.) E1

PORTUGAL

DISTRICTS

Aveiro 545,230 .... B2
Beja 204,440 .... C3
Braga 609,415 .... B2
Bragança 180,395 .... C2
Castelo Branco 254,355 .... C3
Coimbra 399,380 .... B2
Évora 178,475 .... C3
Faro 268,040 .... B4
Funchal 251,135 .... A2
Guarda 210,720 .... C2
Leiria 376,940 .... B3
Lisbon 1,568,020 .... A1
Oporto (Porto) 1,309,560 .... B2
Portalegre 145,545 .... C3
Porto 1,309,560 .... B2
Santarém 427,995 .... B3
Sétubal 469,555 .... B3
Viano do Castelo 250,510 .... B2
Vila Real 265,605 .... C2
Viseu 410,795 .... C2

CITIES and TOWNS

Abrantes 11,775 .... B3
Águeda 9,343 .... B2
Albufeira 7,479 .... B4
Alcácer do Sal 13,187 .... B3
Alcântara 23,699 .... A1

Topography

0 50 100 MI.
0 50 100 KM.
Cape Finisterre
CANTABRIAN MTS.
Bilbao
PYRENEES
Pico de Aneto 11,168 ft. (3404 m.)
Porto
Douro
Saragossa
Barcelona
Madrid
SA. DE GUADARRAMA
SA. DA ESTRELA
SA. DE GATA
Malhão de Estrela 6,532 ft. (1991 m.)
Lisbon
Tagus
Valencia
Júcar
Gulf of Valencia
Majorca
Minorca
Ibiza
BALEARIC ISLANDS
C. de la Nao
SIERRA MORENA
Córdoba
Seville
Guadalquivir
Genil
Cape St. Vincent
Gulf of Cadiz
Mulhacén 11,411 ft. (3478 m.)
SA. NEVADA
Málaga
Europa Pt.
Below Sea Level
100 m. 328 ft.
200 m. 656 ft.
500 m. 1,640 ft.
1,000 m. 3,281 ft.
2,000 m. 6,562 ft.
5,000 m. 16,404 ft.

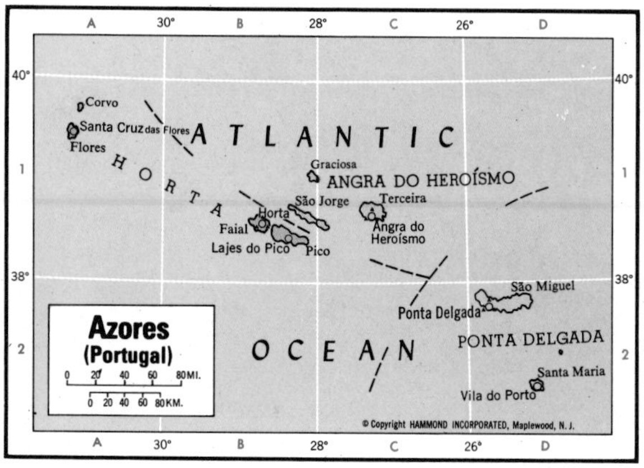

Azores (Portugal)
ATLANTIC
OCEAN
Corvo
Santa Cruz das Flores
Flores
HORTA
ANGRA DO HEROÍSMO
Graciosa
São Jorge
Terceira
Horta
Faial
Pico
Lajes do Pico
Angra do Heroísmo
São Miguel
Ponta Delgada
PONTA DELGADA
Santa Maria
Vila do Porto
0 20 40 60 80 MI.
0 20 40 60 80 KM.
© Copyright HAMMOND INCORPORATED, Maplewood, N. J.

AZORES

INTERNAL DIVISIONS

Angra do Heroísmo (dist.) 83,500 .... C1
Horta (dist.) 38,700 .... A1
Ponta Delgada (dist.) 153,700 .... D2

CITIES and TOWNS

Angra do Heroísmo 13,795 .... C1
Horta 6,145 .... B1
Lajes do Pico 2,147 .... B1
Ponta Delgada 20,195 .... C2
Santa Cruz das Flores 1,880 .... A1
Vila do Porto 4,149 .... D2

OTHER FEATURES

Azores (isls.) A2
Corvo (isl.) A1
Faial (isl.) B1
Flores (isl.) A1
Graciosa (isl.) C1
Pico (isl.) C1
Santa Maria (isl.) D2
São Jorge (isl.) B1
São Miguel (isl.) D2
Terceira (isl.) C1

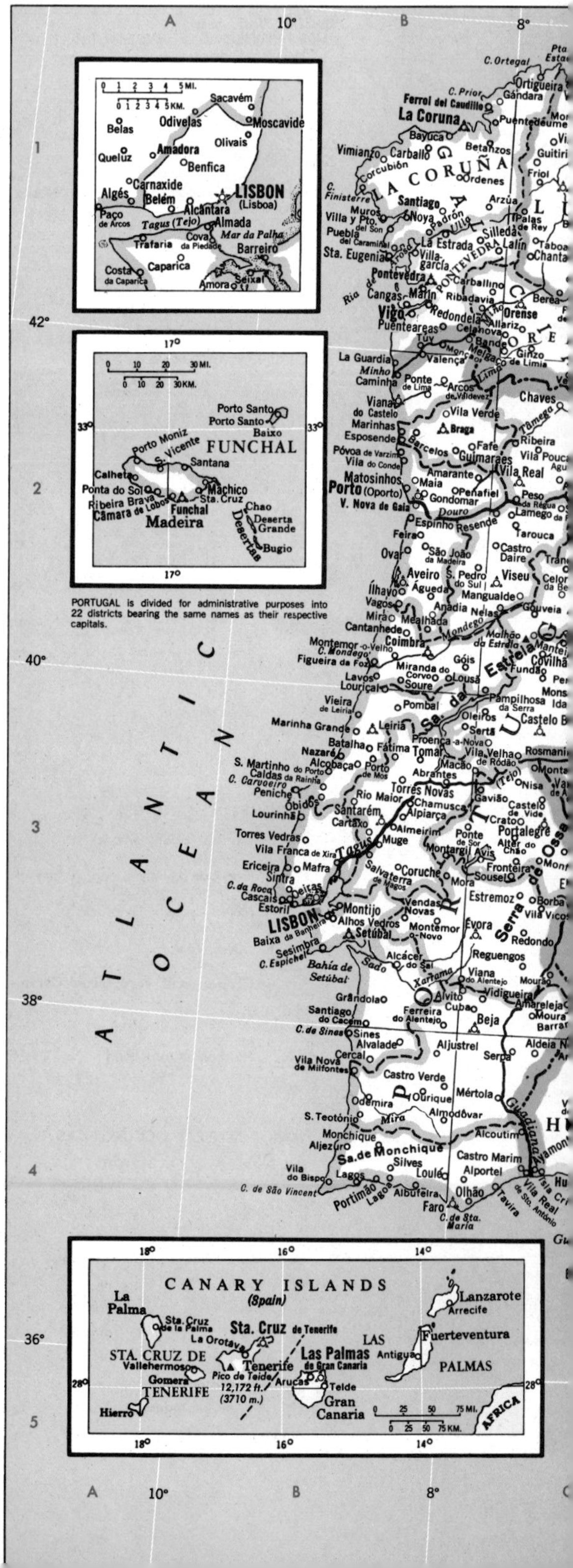

ATLANTIC OCEAN
LISBON (Lisboa)
FUNCHAL
Madeira
PORTUGAL is divided for administrative purposes into 22 districts bearing the same names as their respective capitals.
CANARY ISLANDS (Spain)
La Palma
Santa Cruz de la Palma
Lanzarote
Fuerteventura
STA. CRUZ DE TENERIFE
Las Palmas de Gran Canaria
LAS PALMAS
Gran Canaria
Gomera
Hierro
Pico de Teide 12,172 ft. (3710 m.)
AFRICA
La Coruña
Vigo
Porto (Oporto)
Coimbra
Lisbon
Setúbal
Faro

Alcobaça 4,799 .... B3
Aldeia Nova de São Bento 5,228 .... C4
Algés 18,010 .... A1
Alhos Vedros 7,915 .... B3
Aljustrel 7,473 .... B4
Almada 38,990 .... A1
Almeirim 8,780 .... B3
Alpiarça 7,623 .... B3
Alportel 7,632 .... C4
Amadora 65,870 .... A1
Amarante 6,067 .... B2
Amora 10,330 .... A1
Aveiro 19,905 .... B2
Avis 1,686 .... C3
Baixa da Banheira 18,550 .... B3
Barreiro 53,690 .... B1
Batalha 6,673 .... B3
Beja 14,760 .... C3
Belas 12,001 .... A1
Belém 19,043 .... A1
Benfica 39,459 .... A1
Borba 4,879 .... C3
Braga 48,735 .... B2
Bragança 9,310 .... C2
Caldas da Rainha 13,070 .... B3
Câmara de Lobos 14,068 .... A2
Campo Maior 7,405 .... C3
Cantanhede 6,734 .... B2
Caparica 13,315 .... A1
Carnaxide 38,309 .... A1
Cartaxo 6,628 .... B3
Cascais 14,925 .... B3
Castelo Branco 18,740 .... C3
Cercal 5,021 .... B4
Chaves 11,465 .... C2
Coimbra 55,985 .... B2
Coruche 17,461 .... B3
Cova da Piedade 21,000 .... A1
Covilhã 26,530 .... C2
Elvas 10,305 .... C3
Espinho 11,745 .... B2
Estoril 15,740 .... B3
Estremoz 9,565 .... C3
Évora 23,665 .... C3
Fafe 8,142 .... B2
Faro 20,470 .... B4
Fátima 6,433 .... B3
Feira 5,222 .... B2
Ferreira do Alentejo 6;153 .... B3
Figueira da Foz 10,485 .... B2
Funchal 38,340 .... A2
Fundão 5,081 .... C2
Gondomar 14,105 .... B2
Grândola 9,698 .... B3
Guarda 9,735 .... C2
Guimarães 24,280 .... B2
Ílhavo 11,083 .... B2
Lagoa 5,694 .... B4
Lagos 10,359 .... B4
Lamego 10,350 .... C2
Lavos 5,051 .... B2
Leiria 7,540 .... B3
Lisbon (Lisboa) (cap.) 769,410 .... A1
Lisbon‡ 1,100,000 .... A1
Loulé 12,777 .... B4
Louriçal 6,087 .... B3
Lourinhã 7,340 .... B3
Lousã 7,341 .... B2
Machico 10,905 .... A2
Mafra 7,149 .... B3
Mangualde 4,839 .... C2
Marinha Grande 18,548 .... B3
Matosinhos 22,505 .... B2
Mira 12,740 .... B2
Mirandela 5,203 .... C2
Monchique 8,155 .... B4
Montargil 5,070 .... B3
Montemor-o-Novo 9,284 .... B3
Montijo 26,730 .... B3
Moscavide 21,765 .... A1
Moura 9,351 .... C3
Nazaré 8,553 .... B3
Odemira 6,793 .... B4
Odivelas 26,020 .... A1
Oeiras 14,880 .... B3
Olhão 11,155 .... C4
Olivais 55,138 .... A1
Oporto (Porto) 300,925 .... B2
Ovar 16,004 .... B2
Paço de Arcos 11,791 .... A1
Penafiel 6,463 .... B2
Peniche 12,555 .... B3
Peso da Régua 5,376 .... C2
Pombal 12,508 .... B3
Ponta do Sol 5,599 .... A2
Ponte de Sor 9,951 .... C3
Portalegre 10,970 .... C3
Portimão 10,300 .... B4
Porto 300,925. .... B2
Póvoa de Varzim 17,415 .... B2
Proença-a-Nova 4,792 .... B3
Queluz 25,845 .... A1
Redondo 6,858 .... C3
Reguengos de Monsaraz 5,806 .... C3
Ribeira Brava 7,416 .... A2
Rio Maior 10,206 .... B3
Sacavém 12,625 .... A1
Salvaterra de Magos 6,265 .... B3
Santa Cruz 6,348 .... A2
Santarém 16,850 .... B3
Santiago do Cacem 5,887 .... B3
São Brás de Alportel (Alportel) 7,632 .... C4
São João da Madeira 14,225 .... B2
São Teotónio 6,146 .... B4
São Vicente 5,147 .... A2
Serpa 7,991 .... C4
Sertã 6,043 .... B3
Sesimbra 16,614 .... B3
Setúbal 49,670 .... B3
Silves 9,493 .... B4
Sines 6,996 .... B4
Sintra 15,994 .... B3
Soure 7,620 .... B2
Tavira 10,263 .... C4
Tomar 10,905 .... B3
Torres Novas 13,806 .... B3
Torres Vedras 14,833 .... B3
Trafaria 6,145 .... A1
Vagos 5,088 .... B2
Vendas Novas 8,979 .... B3
Viana do Castelo 12,510 .... B2
Vila do Conde 16,485 .... B2
Vila Franca de Xira 13,070 .... B3
Vila Nova de Gaia Gaia 50,805 .... B2
Vila Real Real 10,050 .... C2
Vila Real de Santo Antonio 10,320 .... C4
Viseu 16,140 .... C2

OTHER FEATURES

Atlantic Ocean A3
Carvoeiroeiro (cape) B3
Desertasrtas (isls.) A2
Douro (riv.) B2
Espichel (cape) B3
Estrela, Serra da (mts.) C2
Guadiana (riv.) C4
Lima (riv.) B2
Madeira (isl.) ....
Madeira (isls.) A2
Minho (riv.) B2
Mira (riv.) B4
Monchique, Serra de (mts.) B4
Mondego (riv.) B2
Monsanto (mt.) A1
Ossa, Serra da (mts.) C3
Palha, Mar da (bay) A1
Porto Santo (isl.) B2
Roca (cape) B3
Sadu (riv.) B3
São Vincent (cape) B4
Santa Marla (cape) C4
Setúbal (bay) B3
Tagus (riv.) B3
Tâmega (riv.) C2
Tejo (Tagus) (riv.) B3
Xarrama (riv.) B3

ANDORRA

CITIES and TOWNS

Andorra la Vella (cap.) 12,000 .... G1

GIBRALTAR

Gibraltar 29,760 .... D4

PHYSICAL FEATURES

Europa (pt.) D4

‡Population of metropolitan area.

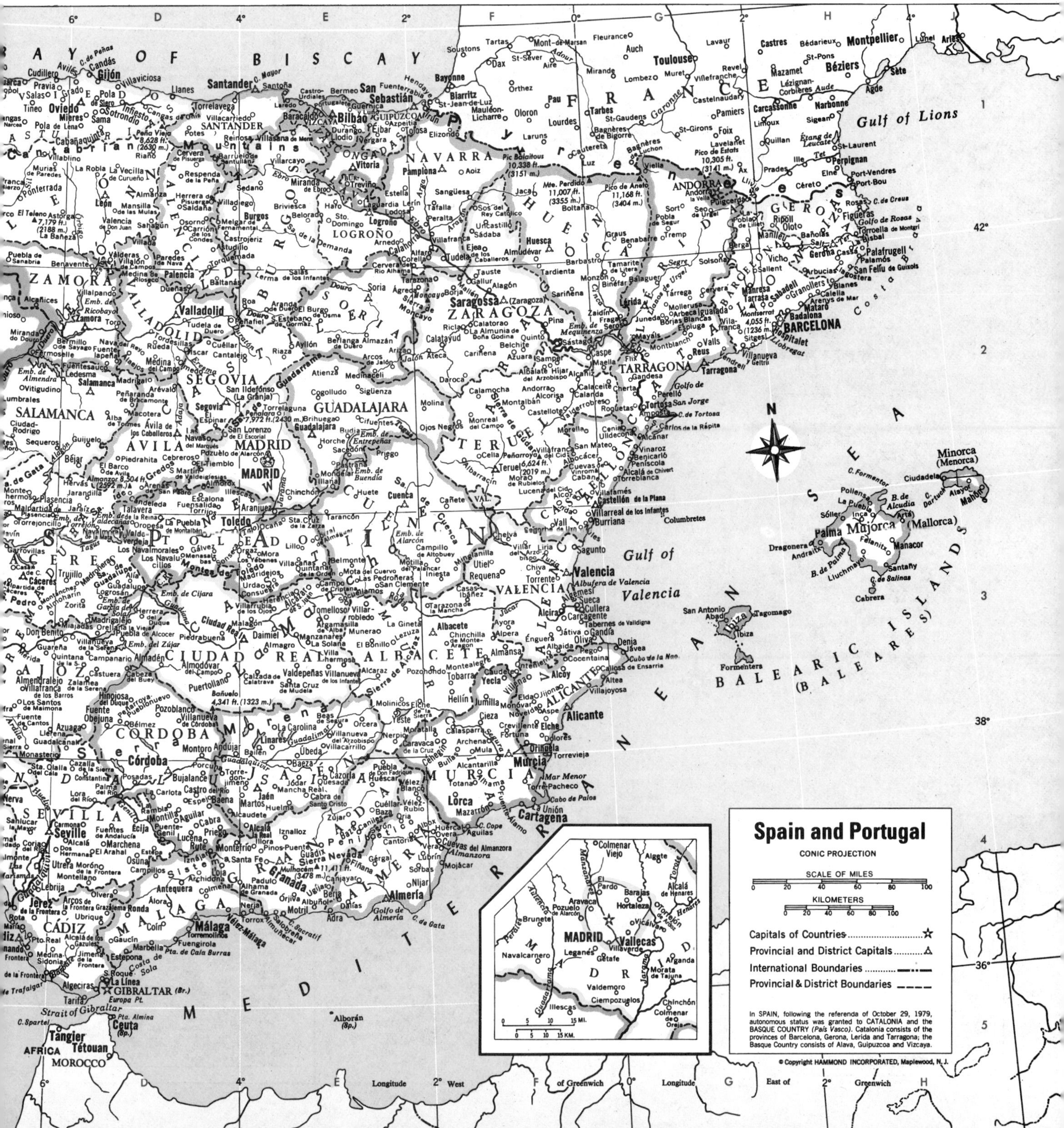

Spain and Portugal
CONIC PROJECTION
SCALE OF MILES
0 20 40 60 80 100
KILOMETERS
0 20 40 60 80 100
Capitals of Countries
Provincial and District Capitals
International Boundaries
Provincial & District Boundaries
In SPAIN, following the referenda of October 29, 1979, autonomous status was granted to CATALONIA and the BASQUE COUNTRY (País Vasco). Catalonia consists of the provinces of Barcelona, Gerona, Lerida and Tarragona; the Basque Country consists of Alava, Guipuzcoa and Vizcaya.
© Copyright HAMMOND INCORPORATED, Maplewood, N. J.
BAY OF BISCAY
FRANCE
Gulf of Lions
MADRID
BARCELONA
ANDORRA
Gulf of Valencia
BALEARIC ISLANDS (BALEARES)
MEDITERRANEAN SEA
Strait of Gibraltar
AFRICA
MOROCCO
Tangier
Tétouan
Ceuta (Sp.)
Minorca (Menorca)
Majorca (Mallorca)
Ibiza
Formentera
Longitude West of Greenwich
Longitude East of Greenwich

Italy
CONIC PROJECTION
SCALE OF MILES
0 20 40 60 80 100
SCALE OF KILOMETERS
0 20 40 60 80 100
Capitals of Countries
Regional Capitals
Provincial Capitals
International Boundaries
Regional Boundaries
The regions are subdivided into provinces bearing the same names as their respective capitals, except:
PROVINCE
CAPITAL
MASSA-CARRARA
Massa
PESARO-URBINO
Pesaro
Vatican City
Rome and Environs
WEST GERMANY
AUSTRIA
SWITZERLAND
YUGOSLAVIA
FRANCE
TUNISIA
CORSICA
SARDINIA
SICILIA
MALTA
ADRIATIC SEA
LIGURIAN SEA
TYRRHENIAN SEA
IONIAN SEA
MEDITERRANEAN SEA
ROME
MILAN
NAPLES
Gulf of Taranto
Strait of Sicily
Malta Channel
Longitude 12° East of Greenwich
© Copyright HAMMOND INCORPORATED, Maplewood, N. J.

VATICAN CITY

AREA 108.7 acres (44 hectares)
POPULATION 728

SAN MARINO

AREA 23.4 sq. mi. (60.6 sq. km.)
POPULATION 19,149

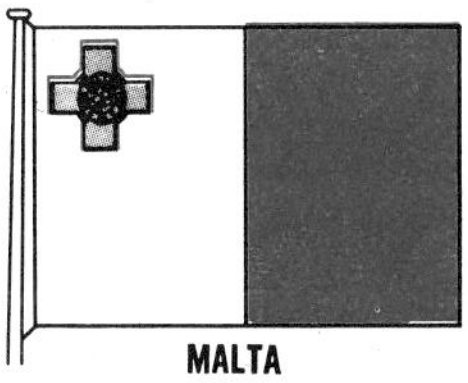

MALTA

AREA 122 sq. mi. (316 sq. km.)
POPULATION 343,970
CAPITAL Valletta
LARGEST CITY Sliema
HIGHEST POINT 787 ft. (240 m.)
MONETARY UNIT Maltese pound
MAJOR LANGUAGES Maltese, English
MAJOR RELIGION Roman Catholicism

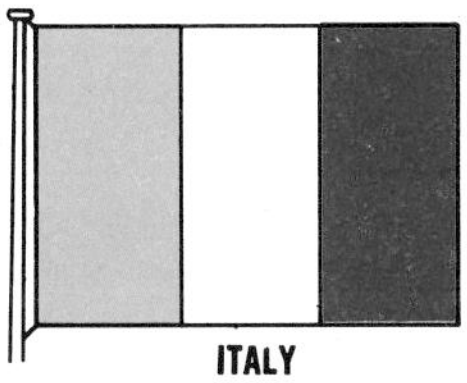

ITALY

AREA 116,303 sq. mi. (301,225 sq. km.)
POPULATION 57,140,000
CAPITAL Rome
LARGEST CITY Rome
HIGHEST POINT Dufourspitze (Mte. Rosa) 15,203 ft. (4,634 m.)
MONETARY UNIT lira
MAJOR LANGUAGE Italian
MAJOR RELIGION Roman Catholicism

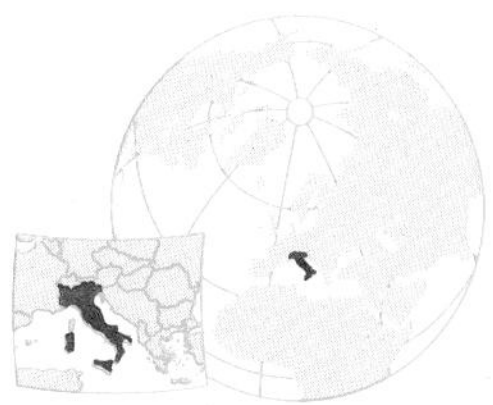

ITALY

REGIONS

Abruzzi 1,166,664 .... D3
Aosta 109,150 .... A2
Apulia (Puglia) 3,582,787 .... F4
Basilicata 603,064 .... F4
Calabria 1,988,051 .... F5
Campania 5,059,348 .... E4
Emilia-Romagna 3,846,755 .... C2
Friuli-Venezia Giulia 1,213,532 .... D1
Latium (Lazio) 4,689,482 .... D3
Liguria 1,853,578 .... B2
Lombardy 8,543,657 .... B2
Marche 1,359,907 .... D3
Molise 319,807 .... E4
Piedmont 4,432,313 .... A2
Sardinia 1,473,800 .... B4
Sicily 4,680,715 .... D6
Trentino-Alto Adige 841,886 .... C1
Tuscany 3,473,097 .... C3
Umbria 775,783 .... D3
Veneto 2,109,502 .... D3

PROVINCES

Agrigento 454,045 .... D6
Alessandria 483,183 .... B2
Ancona 416,611 .... D3
Aosta 109,150 .... A2
Arezzo 306,340 .... C3
Ascoli Piceno 340,758 .... D3
Asti 218,547 .... B2
Avellino 427,509 .... E4
Bari 1,351,288 .... F4
Belluno 221,155 .... D1
Benevento 286,499 .... E4
Bergamo 829,019 .... B2
Bologna 918,844 .... C2
Bolzano-Bozen 414,041 .... C1
Brescia 957,686 .... C2
Brindisi 366,027 .... G4
Cagliari 802,888 .... B5
Caltanissetta 282,069 .... D6
Campobasso 227,641 .... E4
Caserta 677,959 .... E4
Catania 938,273 .... E6
Catanzaro 718,069 .... F5
Chieti 351,567 .... E3
Como 720,463 .... B2
Cosenza 691,659 .... F5
Cremona 334,281 .... B2
Cuneo 540,504 .... A2
Enna 202,131 .... E6
Ferrara 383,639 .... C2
Florence 1,146,367 .... C3
Foggia 657,292 .... E4
Forlì 565,470 .... D2
Frosinone 422,630 .... D4
Genoa 1,087,973 .... B2
Gorizia 142,412 .... D2
Grosseto 216,315 .... C3
Imperia 225,127 .... B3
Isernia 92,166 .... E4
L'Aquila 293,066 .... D3
La Spezia 244,435 .... B2
Latina 376,238 .... D4
Lecce 696,503 .... G4
Leghorn 335,265 .... C3
Lucca 380,356 .... C3
Macerata 286,155 .... D3
Mantua 376,892 .... C2
Massa-Carrara 200,955 .... C2
Matera 194,629 .... F4
Messina 654,703 .... E5
Milan 3,903,685 .... B2
Modena 553,852 .... C2
Naples 2,709,929 .... E4
Novara 496,811 .... B2
Nuoro 273,021 .... B4
Padua 762,998 .... C2
Palermo 1,124,015 .... D5
Parma 395,497 .... C2
Pavia 526,389 .... B2
Perugia 552,936 .... D3
Pesaro e Urbino 316,383 .... D3
Pescara 264,981 .... E3
Piacenza 284,881 .... B2
Pisa 375,933 .... C3
Pistoia 254,335 .... C2
Pordenone 253,906 .... D2
Potenza 408,435 .... E4
Ragusa 255,047 .... E6
Ravenna 351,876 .... D2
Reggio di Calabria 578,323 .... E5
Reggio nell'Emilia 392,696 .... C2
Rieti 143,162 .... D3
Rome 3,490,377 .... F6
Rovigo 251,908 .... C2
Salerno 957,452 .... E4
Sassari 397,891 .... B4
Savona 296,043 .... B2
Siena 257,221 .... C3
Sondrio 169,149 .... B1
Syracuse 365,039 .... E6
Taranto 511,677 .... F4
Teramo 257,080 .... D3
Terni 222,847 .... D3
Trapani 405,393 .... D5
Trento 427,845 .... C1
Treviso 668,620 .... D2
Trieste 300,304 .... E2
Turin 2,287,016 .... A2
Udine 516,910 .... D1
Varese 725,823 .... B2
Venice 807,251 .... D2
Vercelli 406,252 .... B2
Verona 733,595 .... C2
Vicenza 677,884 .... C2
Viterbo 257,075 .... C3

CITIES and TOWNS

Acireale 34,081 .... E6
Acqui Terme 20,099 .... B2
Acri 8,150 .... F5
Adrano 31,988 .... E6
Adria 11,951 .... D2
Agira 11,262 .... E6
Agnone 3,965 .... E4
Agrigento 40,513 .... D6
Agropoli 9,413 .... E4
Alassio 13,512 .... A2
Alatri 5,710 .... D4
Alba 23,522 .... B2
Albano Laziale 15,561 .... F7
Albenga 13,397 .... B3
Albino 8,837 .... B2
Alcamo 41,448 .... D6
Alessandria 78,644 .... B2
Alghero 28,454 .... B4
Altamura 44,879 .... F4
Amalfi 4,205 .... E4
Amantea 6,132 .... E5
Amelia 4,331 .... D3
Ancona 88,427 .... D3
Andria 76,405 .... F4
Anguillara Sabazia 3,241 .... F6
Anzio 14,966 .... D4
Aosta 35,053 .... A2
Aprilia 18,412 .... D4
Aragona 11,213 .... D6
Arezzo 56,693 .... C3
Argenta 6,682 .... D2
Ariano Irpino 9,796 .... E4
Ariccia 7,287 .... F7
Artena 5,034 .... F7
Ascoli Piceno 43,041 .... D3
Assisi 4,630 .... D3
Asti 62,277 .... B2
Atessa 3,079 .... E3
Atri 4,686 .... D3
Augusta 32,501 .... E6
Avellino 44,750 .... E4
Aversa 46,536 .... E4
Avezzano 26,456 .... D3
Avigliano 5,400 .... E4
Avola 29,089 .... E6
Bagheria 32,465 .... D5
Barcellona Pozzo di Gotto 25,280 .... E5
Bari 339,110 .... F4
Barletta 75,116 .... F4
Bassano del Grappa 33,002 .... C2
Bellagio 3,258 .... B2
Belluno 22,180 .... D1
Benevento 48,523 .... E4
Bergamo 127,553 .... B2
Biancavilla 18,743 .... E6
Biella 46,453 .... B2
Bisceglie 45,014 .... F4
Bitonto 39,714 .... F4
Bitti 4,606 .... B4
Bologna 493,282 .... C2
Bolzano (Bolzen) 102,806 .... C1
Bondeno 7,451 .... C2
Bonorva 5,232 .... B4
Bordighera 8,994 .... A3
Borgo 4,013 .... C1
Borgomanero 16,655 .... B2
Bôrgo San Lorenzo 7,699 .... C2
Bosa 8,045 .... B4
Boves 3,896 .... A2
Bra 18,399 .... A2
Bracciano 7,681 .... C3
Brescia 189,092 .... C2
Bressanone 12,261 .... C1
Brindisi 76,612 .... G4
Bronte 17,823 .... E6
Brunico 5,175 .... D1
Budrio 5,635 .... C2
Busto Arsizio 72,400 .... B2
Cagli 4,356 .... D3
Cagliari 211,015 .... B5
Caltagirone 34,444 .... E6
Caltanissetta 52,838 .... D6
Camaiore 8,578 .... C3
Camerino 4,644 .... D3
Campobasso 35,551 .... E4
Campo Tures 1,325 .... C1
Canicatti 28,761 .... E6
Canosa di Puglia 30,263 .... E4
Cantù 28,617 .... B2
Capua 13,938 .... E4
Caravaggio 11,298 .... B2
Carbonia 23,031 .... B5
Carini 14,255 .... D5
Carloforte 6,671 .... B5
Carmagnola 16,469 .... A2
Carpi 41,789 .... C2
Carrara 56,236 .... C2
Casale Monferrato 35,156 .... B2
Casalmaggiore 6,374 .... C2
Cascina-Navacchio 28,263 .... C3
Caserta 51,621 .... E4
Cassano allo Ionio 9,661 .... F5
Cassino 14,747 .... D4
Castelfranco Veneto 16,042 .... D2
Castel Gandolfo 2,965 .... F7
Castellammare del Golfo 13,144 .... D5
Castellammare di Stabia 64,341 .... E4
Castel San Pietro Terme 6,985 .... C2
Castelvetrano 29,167 .... D6
Castiglion Fiorentino 3,797 .... C3
Castrovillari 15,207 .... F5
Catania 403,390 .... E6
Catanzaro 52,054 .... F5
Caulonia 3,402 .... F5
Cava de'Tirreni 33,868 .... E4
Cavarzere 7,917 .... D2
Cecina 19,415 .... C3
Cefalù 11,043 .... E5
Ceglie Messapico 17,512 .... F4
Celano 9,531 .... D3
Cerignola 44,648 .... E4
Cernobbio 8,026 .... B2
Cerveteri 5,239 .... E6
Cesano 2,883 .... F6
Cesena 49,915 .... D2
Cesenatico 12,805 .... D2
Chiari 12,017 .... C2
Chiavari 29,950 .... B2
Chieri 27,548 .... A2
Chieti 31,895 .... E3
Chioggia 24,044 .... D2
Chivasso 21,369 .... A2
Ciampino 36,728 .... F7
Cittadella 9,321 .... C2
Città di Castello 18,880 .... C3
Cittanova 11,045 .... F5
Cividale del Friuli 8,345 .... D1
Civitavecchia 41,305 .... C3
Clusone-Fiorine 6,428 .... C2
Codroipo 6,117 .... D2
Colle di Val d'Elsa 8,657 .... C3
Comacchio 10,437 .... D2
Comiso 24,508 .... E6
Como 73,257 .... B2
Conegliano 28,635 .... D2
Conversano 16,805 .... F4
Corato 38,163 .... F4
Cori 6,829 .... F7
Corigliano Calabro 14,518 .... F5
Corleone 11,057 .... D6
Correggio 11,415 .... C2
Cortina d'Ampezzo 7,285 .... D1
Cortona 3,482 .... C3
Cosenza 94,565 .... F5
Courmayeur 1,401 .... A2
Crema 26,061 .... B2
Cremona 75,988 .... B2
Crotone 44,081 .... F5
Cuneo 41,633 .... A2
Cuorgnè 6,752 .... A2
Desenzano del Garda 14,624 .... C2
Diano Marina 6,001 .... B3
Domodossola 18,562 .... A1
Dorgali 6,714 .... B4
Eboli 19,787 .... E4
Edolo 3,707 .... C1
Empoli 30,526 .... C3
Enna 27,351 .... E6
Este 12,992 .... C2
Fabriano 18,355 .... D3
Faenza 36,241 .... D2
Fano 31,238 .... D3
Fasano 21,247 .... F4
Favara 27,940 .... D6
Feltre 11,806 .... C1
Fermo 17,521 .... D3
Ferrandina 8,372 .... F4
Ferrara 97,507 .... C2
Fidenza 18,064 .... B2
Fiesole 3,772 .... C3
Finale Emilia 7,474 .... C2
Finale Ligure 11,461 .... B2
Firenze (Florence) 441,654 .... C3
Fiumicino 13,180 .... F7
Florence 441,654 .... C3
Floridia 16,562 .... E6
Foggia 136,436 .... E4
Foligno 26,887 .... D3
Fondi 16,472 .... D4
Forlì 83,303 .... D2
Formia 18,978 .... D4
Fossano 15,857 .... A2
Fossombrone 5,882 .... D3
Francavilla Fontana 30,347 .... F4
Frascati 14,217 .... F7
Frosinone 34,066 .... D4
Gaeta 21,973 .... D4
Galatina 22,137 .... G4
Galatone 13,880 .... F4
Gallarate 43,773 .... B2
Gallipoli 16,878 .... F4
Garessio 3,359 .... A2
Gela 66,845 .... E6
Gemona 6,863 .... D1
Genoa 787,011 .... B2
Genova (Genoa) 787,011 .... B2
Genzano di Roma 14,147 .... F7
Giarre 18,233 .... E6
Gioia del Colle 23,299 .... F4
Gioiosa Ionica 3,811 .... F5
Giovinazzo 17,768 .... F4
Giulianova 17,926 .... E3
Gorizia 35,912 .... D2
Gravina in Puglia 32,006 .... F4
Grosseto 48,309 .... C3
Grottaferrata 10,639 .... F7
Grottaglie 23,556 .... F4
Guardiagrele 4,122 .... E3
Guastalla 7,639 .... C2
Gubbio 12,371 .... D3
Guidonia 8,413 .... F6
Iglesias 24,472 .... B6
Imola 42,111 .... C2
Imperia 37,585 .... B3
Isernia 12,290 .... E4
Ivrea 26,530 .... B2
Jesi 33,011 .... D3
Ladispoli 6,625 .... E6
Lagonegro 5,613 .... E4
La Maddalena 10,405 .... B4
Lanciano 19,652 .... E3
Lanusei 5,508 .... B5
Lanuvio 2,970 .... F7
L'Aquila 36,233 .... D3
Larino 5,166 .... E4
La Spezia 121,254 .... B2
Latina 53,003 .... D4
Lauria 4,927 .... F4
Lavello 11,486 .... E4
Lecce 80,114 .... G4
Lecco 53,165 .... B2
Leghorn 170,369 .... C3
Legnago 15,534 .... C2
Lendinara 7,079 .... C2
Lentini 31,429 .... E6
Leonforte 16,317 .... E6
Lerici 5,407 .... B2
Licata 40,997 .... D6
Lido di Ostia 61,492 .... F7
Lido di Venezia 18,794 .... D2
Lipari 3,886 .... E5
Livigno 2,135 .... C1
Livorno (Leghorn) 170,369 .... C3
Lodi 42,489 .... B2
Lonigo 6,368 .... C2
Lucca 54,280 .... C3
Lucera 29,355 .... E4
Lugo 19,497 .... D2
Macerata 33,470 .... D3
Macomer 9,433 .... B4
Maglie 13,326 .... G4
Manduria 25,194 .... F4
Manfredonia 44,463 .... F4
Mantua 59,529 .... C2
Marino 12,135 .... F7
Marsala 34,150 .... D6
Marsciano 5,372 .... D3
Martina Franca 31,811 .... F4
Massa 56,591 .... C2
Massafra 22,610 .... F4
Massa Marittima 6,438 .... C3
Matera 43,026 .... F4
Mazara del Vallo 37,441 .... D6
Mazzarino 14,981 .... E6
Melfi 13,355 .... E4
Menfi 12,386 .... D6
Merano 30,951 .... C1
Mesagne 26,955 .... G4
Messina 203,937 .... E5
Mestre 184,818 .... D2
Milan 1,724,557 .... B2
Milazzo 18,576 .... E5
Minturno 2,428 .... D4
Mirandola 11,551 .... C2
Mira Taglio 10,194 .... D2
Mistretta 6,631 .... E6
Modena 149,029 .... C2
Modica 31,074 .... E6
Mola di Bari 23,778 .... F4
Molfetta 63,250 .... F4
Moncalieri 49,953 .... A2
Mondovì Breo 12,524 .... A2
Monfalcone 29,589 .... D2
Monopoli 29,776 .... F4
Monreale 19,348 .... D5
Monselice 9,047 .... C2
Montalto Uffugo 3,173 .... E5
Montebelluna 9,573 .... D2
Montefiascone 6,885 .... D3
Montepulciano 4,069 .... C3
Monterotondo 15,869 .... F6
Monte Sant'Angelo 17,756 .... F4
Montevarchi 16,849 .... C3
Monza 110,735 .... B2
Mortara 13,929 .... B2
Naples 1,214,775 .... E4
Nardò 24,142 .... F4
Narni 6,213 .... D3
Naro 13,171 .... D6
Nettuno 20,927 .... D4
Nicastro 27,206 .... F5
Nicosia 13,982 .... E6
Niscemi 23,925 .... E6
Nizza Monferrato 7,532 .... B2
Nocera Inferiore 44,415 .... E4
Noto 21,606 .... E6
Novara 92,634 .... B2
Novi Ligure 29,944 .... B2
Nuoro 30,551 .... B4
Olbia 20,998 .... B4
Oliena 7,030 .... B4
Orbetello 6,884 .... C3
Oristano 20,966 .... B5
Ortona 11,966 .... E3
Orvieto 8,813 .... D3
Osimo 12,034 .... D3
Ostia Antica 2,583 .... F7
Ostuni 27,241 .... F4
Otranto 3,707 .... G4
Ozieri 9,149 .... B4
Pachino 20,427 .... E6
Padua 210,950 .... C2
Palazzolo Acreide 8,981 .... E6
Palermo 556,374 .... D5
Palestrina 9,239 .... F7
Palma di Montechiaro 22,381 .... D6
Palmi 14,405 .... E5
Palombara Sabina 5,292 .... F6
Pantelleria 3,116 .... C6
Paola 11,330 .... E5
Parma 151,967 .... C2
Partanna 10,303 .... D6
Partinico 25,447 .... D6
Paterno 41,504 .... F6
Patti 7,500 .... E5
Pavia 80,639 .... B2
Pavullo nel Frignano 5,026 .... C2
Penne 5,889 .... D3
Pergine Valsugana 6,248 .... C1
Pergola 3,866 .... D3
Perugia 65,975 .... D3
Pesaro 72,104 .... D3
Pescara 125,391 .... E3
Pescia 9,918 .... C3
Piacenza 100,001 .... B2
Piazza Armerina 21,754 .... E6
Pietrasanta 6,620 .... B3
Pinerolo 33,935 .... A2
Piombino 35,641 .... C3
Piove di Sacco 7,035 .... C2
Pisa 91,156 .... C3
Pisticci 11,239 .... F4
Pistoia 55,403 .... C2
Poggibonsi 21,271 .... C3
Pomezia 11,915 .... F7
Pont Canavese 4,075 .... A2
Pontecorvo 5,986 .... D4
Pontinia 3,166 .... D4
Pontremoli 5,222 .... B2
Popoli 5,372 .... E3
Pordenone 43,230 .... D2
Portocivitanova 25,773 .... D3
Porto Empedocle 15,986 .... D6
Portoferraio 7,579 .... C3
Portofino 720 .... B2
Portogruaro 12,258 .... D2
Portomaggiore 6,343 .... C2
Porto Recanati 5,389 .... D3
Porto Torres 15,422 .... B4
Potenza 46,869 .... E4
Pozzallo 12,199 .... E6
Pozzuoli 53,546 .... D4
Prato 108,385 .... C3
Prima Porta 11,393 .... F6
Priverno 9,950 .... D4
Putignano 19,290 .... F4
Quartu Sant'Elena 29,715 .... B5
Ragusa 55,751 .... E6
Rapallo 22,272 .... B2
Ravenna 75,153 .... D2
Recanati 10,176 .... D3
Reggio di Calabria 110,291 .... E5
Reggio nell'Emilia 102,337 .... C2
Rho 39,206 .... B2
Riesi 15,855 .... E6
Rieti 26,775 .... D3
Rimini 101,579 .... D2
Rionero in Vulture 11,230 .... E4
Riva del Garda 8,513 .... C2
Roccastrada 2,629 .... C3
Rome (cap.) 2,535,018 .... F6
Ronciglione 5,900 .... C3
Rossano 12,119 .... F5
Rovereto 26,827 .... C2
Rovigo 31,124 .... C2
Ruvo di Puglia 23,133 .... F4

(continued on following page)

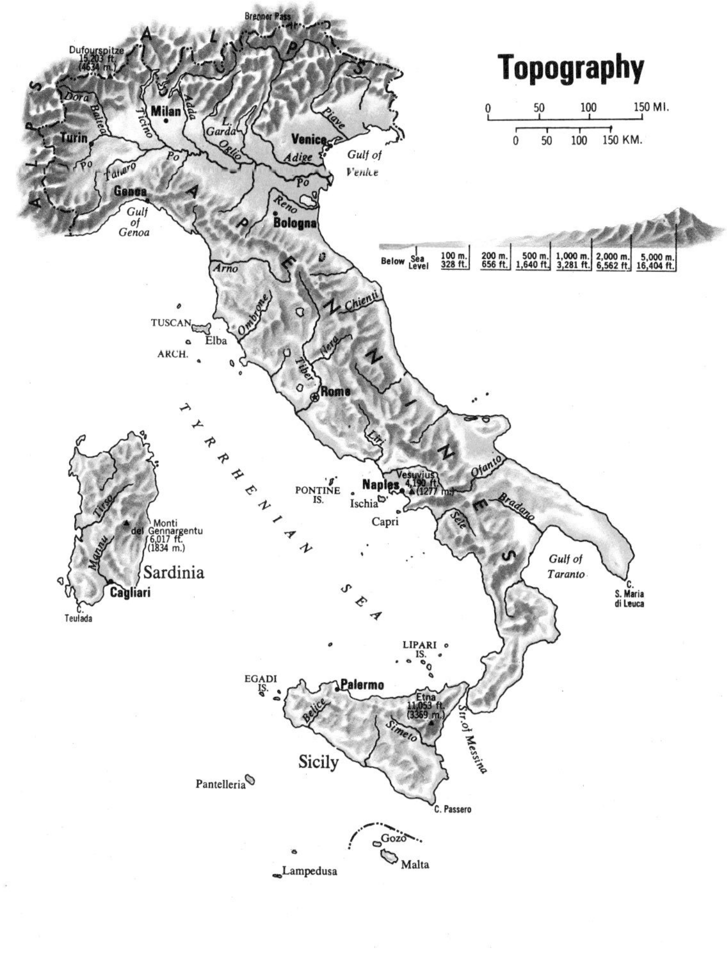

(continued)

Sabaudia 4,501 D4
Saint Vincent 3,737 A2
Sala Consilina 8,177 E4
Salemi 10,180 D6
Salerno 146,534 E4
Salsomaggiore Terme 13,677 B2
Saluzzo 13,929 A2
Sambiase 10,567 F5
San Bartolomeo in Galdo 6,943 E4
San Benedetto del Tronto 40,108 E3
San Cataldo 19,609 D6
San Giovanni in Fiore 16,116 F5
San Giovanni in Persiceto 12,151 C2
San Marco in Lamis 15,817 E4
San Miniato 3,245 C3
Sannicandro Garganico 17,939 E4
San Remo 47,684 A3
Sansepolcro 11,443 C3
San Severino Marche 6,447 D3
San Severo 49,622 E4
Santa Maria Capua Vetere 31,077 E4
Sant'Elpidio a Mare 4,446 E3
Santeramo in Colle 19,758 F4
San Vito 3,901 B5
San Vito al Tagliamento 6,328 D2
San Vito dei Normanni 18,447 F4
San Vito Romano 3,256 F6
Saronno 32,477 B2
Sarroch 3,560 B5
Sassari 94,312 B4
Sassuolo 33,451 C2
Savigliano 14,036 A2
Savona 76,274 B2
Schio 27,890 C2
Sciacca 29,803 D6
Scicli 18,405 E6
Segni 7,193 F7
Senigallia 25,413 D3
Sesto Fiorentino 41,636 C3
Sestri Levante 18,331 B2
Settebagni 5,022 F6
Sezze 7,043 D4
Siderno 8,023 F5
Siena 56,539 C3
Siniscola 6,149 B4
Sinnai 8,499 B5
Siracusa (Syracuse) 93,006 E6
Sondrio 19,724 B1
Sora 14,031 D4
Soresina 9,300 C2
Sorrento 13,078 E4
Sorso 10,741 B4
Spoleto 18,013 D3
Squinzano 14,053 G4
Stresa 3,758 B2
Sulmona 18,221 D3
Susa 5,773 A2
Suzzara 12,013 C2
Syracuse 93,006 E6
Taormina 6,696 E6
Taranto 205,158 F4
Tarquinia 10,300 C3
Taurianova 12,198 E5
Tempio Pausania 10,382 B4
Teramo 31,163 D3
Termini Imerese 24,085 D6
Termoli 13,986 E3
Terni 75,873 D3
Terracina 24,092 D4
Terralba 8,551 B5
Tirano 7,413 C1
Tivoli 28,393 F6
Todi 5,705 D3
Tolentino 11,642 D3
Torino (Turin) 1,181,698 A2
Torre Annunziata 71,068 E4
Torre del Greco 74,752 E4
Torremaggiore 16,171 E4
Tortona 24,165 B2
Trani 40,508 F4
Trapani 90,305 D5
Trento 64,272 C1
Treviglio 21,920 B2
Treviso 87,447 D2
Tricase 10,481 G5
Trieste 257,259 E2
Trino 8,722 B2
Turin 1,181,698 A2
Udine 97,544 D2
Umbertide 6,640 D3
Urbino 7,735 D3
Valdagno 20,342 C2
Valenza 20,533 B2
Valmontone 6,543 F7
Varallo Pombia 3,118 B2
Varazze 11,676 B2
Varese 65,978 B2
Vasto 17,295 E3
Velletri 22,020 F7
Venafro 5,156 E4
Venezia (Venice) 108,082 D2
Venice 108,082 D2
Venosa 10,993 E4
Ventimiglia 20,343 A3
Verbania 29,894 B2
Vercelli 54,934 B2
Veroli 2,793 D4
Verona 227,032 C2
Viadana 6,667 C2
Viareggio 49,965 C3
Vibo Valentia 18,005 F5
Vicenza 99,451 C2
Vicovaro 3,005 F6
Vigevano 62,855 B2
Villacidro 12,651 B5
Villafranca di Verona 11,762 C2
Viterbo 39,291 C3
Vittoria 43,673 E6
Vittorio Veneto 25,476 D1
Vizzini 8,583 E6
Voghera 37,316 B2
Volterra 10,732 C3
Zagarolo 4,232 F7

OTHER FEATURES

Adda (riv.) B2
Adige (riv.) C2
Adriatic (sea) E3
Alicudi (isl.) E5
Apennines, Central (range) D3
Apennines, Northern (range) B2
Apennines, Southern (range) E4
Arno (riv.) C3
Asinara (isl.) B4
Bernina, Piz (peak) B1
Blanc (mt.) A2
Bolsena (lake) C3
Bonifacio (str.) B4
Bracciano (lake) D3
Brenner (pass) C1
Capraia (isl.) B3
Capri (isl.) E4
Carbonara (cape) B5
Carnic Alps (range) D1
Castellammare (gulf) D5
Circeo (cape) D4
Como (lake) B1
Cottian Alps (range) A2
Dolomite Alps (range) C1
Dora Baltea (riv.) A2
Dora Riparia (riv.) A2
Egadi (isls.) C6
Elba (isl.) C3
Etna (vol.) E6
Favignana (isl.) D6
Filicudi (isl.) E5
Gaeta (gulf) D4
Garda (lake) C2
Gennargentu, Monti del (mt.) B5
Genoa (gulf) B2
Giannutri (isl.) C3
Giglio (isl.) C3
Gorgona (isl.) B3
Graian Alps (range) A2
Gran Paradiso (mt.) A2
Great Saint Bernard (pass) A2
Ionian (sea) F6
Ischia (isl.) D4
Julian Alps (range) D1
Lampedusa (isl.) D7
Lepontine Alps (range) B1
Levanzo (isl.) D5
Ligurian (sea) B3
Linosa (isl.) D7
Lipari (isl.) E5
Lipari (isls.) E5
Maggiore (lake) B1
Manfredonia (gulf) F4
Marettimo (isl.) C6
Maritime Alps (range) A2
Marmolada (mt.) C1
Mediterranean (sea) B6
Messina (str.) E6
Metauro (riv.) D3
Mincio (riv.) C2
Montecristo (isl.) C3
Nera (riv.) D3
Oglio (riv.) C2
Ombrone (riv.) C3
Oristano (gulf) B5
Orosei (gulf) B4
Ortles (range) C1
Otranto (str.) G5
Ötztal Alps (range) C1
Panarea (isl.) E5
Panaro (riv.) C2
Pantelleria (isl.) D6
Pelagie (isls.) D7
Pennine Alps (range) A2
Pianosa (isl.) C3
Piave (riv.) D2
Po (riv.) C2
Pompeii (ruins) E4
Pontine (isls.) D4
Ponza (isl.) D4
Rosa (mt.) A1
Salina (isl.) E5
Salso (riv.) D6
San Pietro (isl.) B5
Santa Maria di Leuca (cape) G5
Sant'Antioco (pen.) B5
Sant'Eufemia (gulf) F5
Sardinia (isl.) B4
Sicily (isl.) E6
Sicily (str.) D6
Simplon (tunnel) A1
Spartivento (cape) B5
Spartivento (cape) F6
Squillace (gulf) F5
Stromboli (isl.) E5
Tagliamento (riv.) D1
Tanaro (riv.) B2
Taranto (gulf) F5
Testa del Gargano (cape) F4
Tiber (riv.) D3
Trasimeno (lake) D3
Tremiti (isls.) E3
Trieste (gulf) D2
Tuscan (arch.) B3
Tyrrhenian (sea) C4
Ustica (isl.) D5
Vaticano (cape) E5
Venice (gulf) D2
Ventotene (isl.) D4
Vesuvius (vol.) E4
Viso (mt.) A2
Volturno (riv.) E4
Vulcano (isl.) E5

MALTA

CITIES and TOWNS

Sliema 20,095 E7
Valletta (cap.) 14,042 E7
Victoria 5,249 E6

SAN MARINO

CITIES and TOWNS

San Marino (cap.) 4,628 D3
San Marino* 5,410 D3

VATICAN CITY

Vatican City 728 B6

*City and suburbs.

Agriculture, Industry and Resources

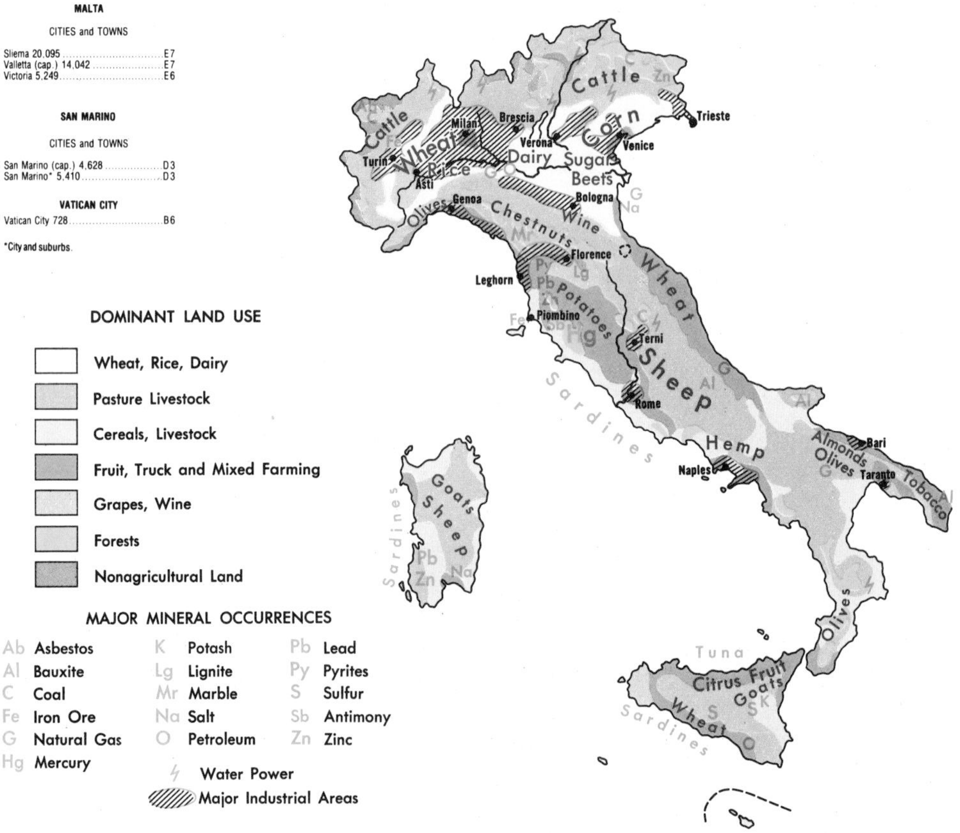

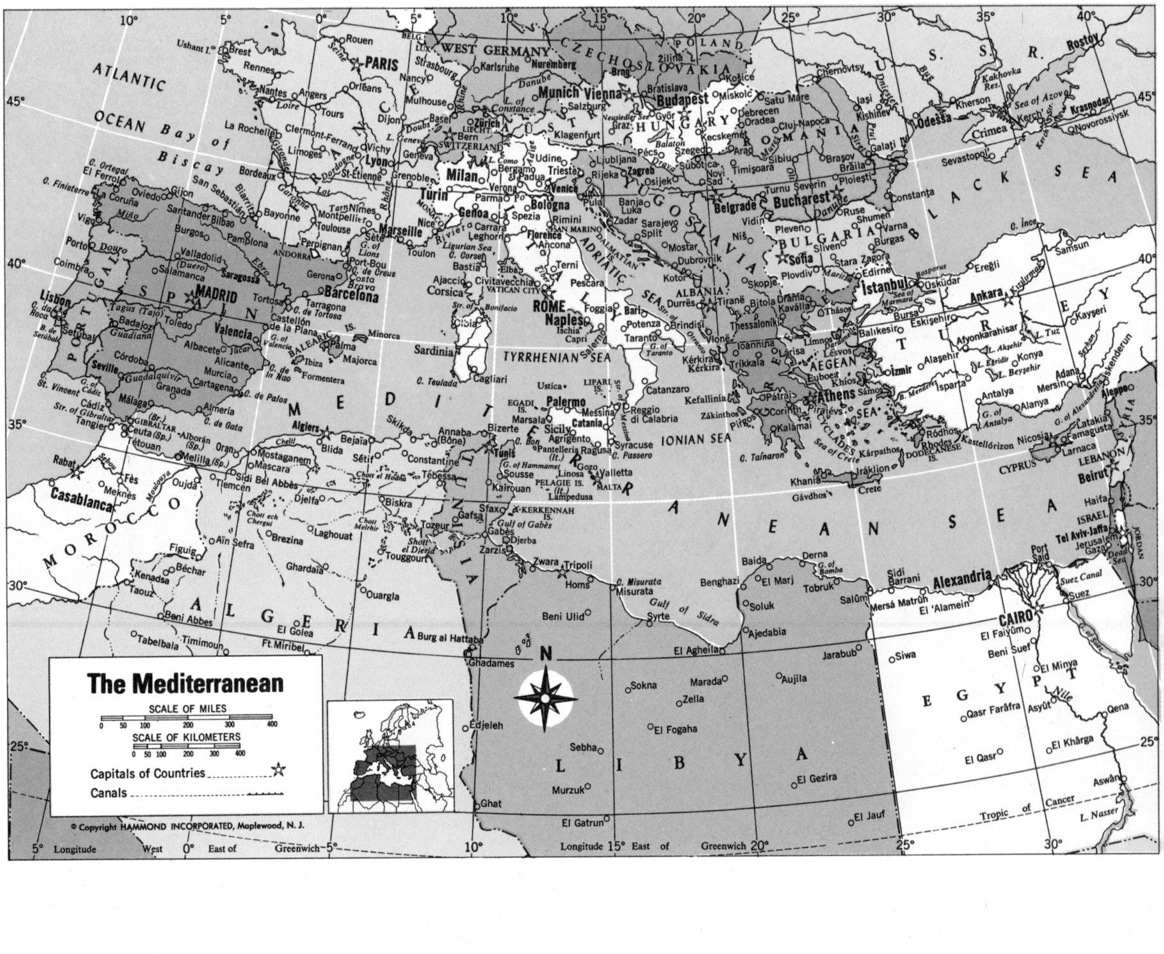

SWITZERLAND
AREA 15,943 sq. mi. (41,292 sq. km.)
POPULATION 6,365,960
CAPITAL Bern
LARGEST CITY Zürich
HIGHEST POINT Dufourspitze (Mte. Rosa) 15,203 ft. (4,634 m.)
MONETARY UNIT Swiss franc
MAJOR LANGUAGES German, French, Italian, Romansch
MAJOR RELIGIONS Protestantism, Roman Catholicism

LIECHTENSTEIN
AREA 61 sq. mi. (158 sq. km.)
POPULATION 25,220
CAPITAL Vaduz
LARGEST CITY Vaduz
HIGHEST POINT Grauspitze 8,527 ft. (2,599 m.)
MONETARY UNIT Swiss franc
MAJOR LANGUAGE German
MAJOR RELIGION Roman Catholicism

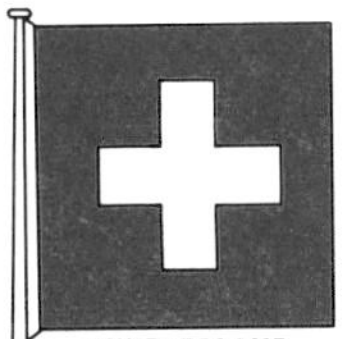
SWITZERLAND

LIECHTENSTEIN

Languages

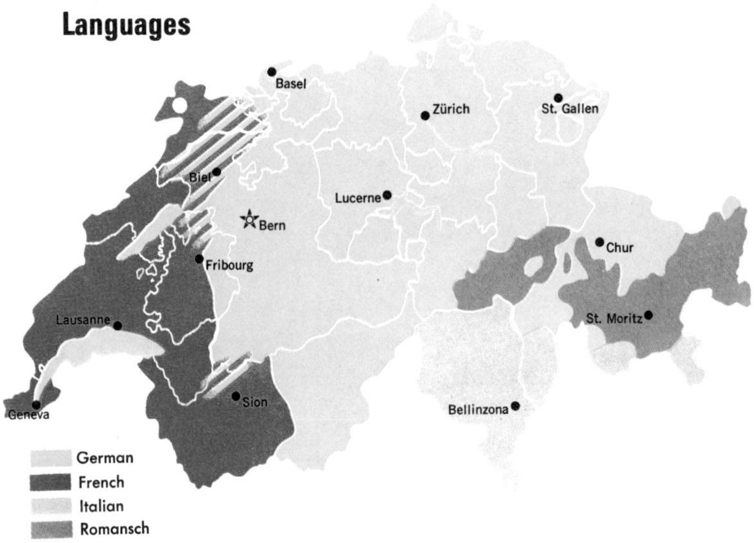
Basel
Zürich
St. Gallen
Biel
Lucerne
Bern
Chur
Fribourg
Lausanne
St. Moritz
Sion
Geneva
Bellinzona
German
French
Italian
Romansch

Switzerland is a multilingual nation with four official languages. 70% of the people speak German, 19% French, 10% Italian and 1% Romansch.

SWITZERLAND

CANTONS

Aargau 442,400 ..... F2
Appenzell, Ausser Rhoden 46,700 ..... H2
Appenzell, Inner Rhoden 13,500 ..... H2
Baselland 219,500 ..... E2
Baselstadt 209,700 ..... E1
Bern 920,900 ..... D2
Fribourg 181,600 ..... D3
Geneva (Genève) 338,600 ..... B4
Glarus 35,700 ..... H3
Graubünden (Grisons) 164,300 ..... H3
Grisons (Graubünden) 164,300 ..... H3
Jura 67,200 ..... D2
Lucerne (Luzern) 292,900 ..... F2
Luzern 292,900 ..... F2
Neuchâtel 162,200 ..... C3
Nidwalden 26,900 ..... F3
Obwalden 25,400 ..... F3
Sankt Gallen 385,000 ..... H2
Schaffhausen 69,300 ..... G1
Schwyz 93,100 ..... G2
Soleure (Solothurn) 221,800 ..... E2
Solothurn 221,800 ..... E2
Thurgau 183,500 ..... H1
Ticino 264,400 ..... G4
Uri 34,000 ..... G3
Valais 214,000 ..... D4
Vaud 523,500 ..... B3
Zug 73,600 ..... C2
Zürich 1,117,300 ..... G2

CITIES and TOWNS

Aadorf 3,022 ..... G2
Aarau 16,881 ..... F2
Aarau* 51,800 ..... F2
Aarberg 3,122 ..... D2
Aarburg 5,943 ..... E2
Adelboden 3,326 ..... E3
Adliswil 15,920 ..... F2
Aeschi bei Spiez 1,402 ..... E3
Affoltern am Albis 7,363 ..... F2
Affoltern im Emmental 1,223 ..... E2
Aigle 6,532 ..... C4
Airolo 2,140 ..... G3
Alle 1,615 ..... D2
Allschwil 17,638 ..... D1
Alpnach 3,277 ..... F3
Altdorf 8,647 ..... G3
Altstätten 9,084 ..... J2
Amriswil 7,601 ..... H1
Andelfingen 1,453 ..... G1
Andermatt 1,589 ..... G3
Appenzell 5,217 ..... H2
Arbedo-Castione 2,456 ..... G4
Arbon 12,227 ..... H1
Arbon* 15,400 ..... H1
Ardon 1,498 ..... D4
Arosa 2,717 ..... J3
Arth 7,580 ..... F2
Ascona 4,086 ..... G4
Attalens 1,116 ..... C3
Au 4,944 ..... J2
Aubonne 1,983 ..... B4
Avenches 2,235 ..... D3
Baar 14,074 ..... F2
Baden 14,115 ..... F2
Baden* 66,800 ..... F2
Dad Ragaz 3,713 ..... H2
Balerna 3,885 ..... G5
Balsthal 5,607 ..... E2
Bäretswil 2,733 ..... G2
Basel 199,600 ..... E1
Basel* 379,700 ..... E1
Bassecourt 2,985 ..... D2
Bätterkinden 1,757 ..... E2
Bauma 3,159 ..... G2
Beatenberg 1,263 ..... E3
Beinwil am See 2,520 ..... F2
Belfaux 1,075 ..... D3
Bellinzona 16,979 ..... H4
Bellinzona* 31,000 ..... H4
Belp 6,981 ..... D3
Berg 1,039 ..... H1
Bern (cap.) 154,700 ..... D3
Bern* 285,300 ..... D3
Beromünster 1,552 ..... F2
Bettlach 4,046 ..... D2
Béx 5,069 ..... D4
Biasca 4,696 ..... H4
Biberist 7,769 ..... D2
Biel 63,400 ..... D2
Biel**89,900 ..... D2
Bière 1,252 ..... B3
Binningen 15,344 ..... D1
Bischofszell 4,233 ..... H1
Blumenstein 1,049 ..... E3
Bodio 1,425 ..... G4
Bolligen 26,121 ..... E3
Boltigen 1,519 ..... D3
Bonaduz 1,289 ..... H3
Boncourt 1,528 ..... C2
Bönigen 1,738 ..... E3
Boswil 1,904 ..... F2
Boudry 4,372 ..... C3
Bourg Saint-Pierre 236 ..... D5
Breil-Brigels 1,215 ..... H3
Breitenbach 2,455 ..... E2
Bremgarten 4,873 ..... F2
Brienz 2,796 ..... F3
Brig 5,191 ..... F4
Brissago 2,120 ..... G4
Brittnau 2,888 ..... E2
Broc 1,842 ..... D3
Brugg 8,635 ..... F2
Brusio 1,344 ..... K4
Bubendorf 2,070 ..... E2
Bubikon 3,244 ..... G2
Buchs 8,454 ..... H2
Bülach 11,043 ..... G1
Bulle 7,556 ..... D3
Buochs 3,232 ..... F3
Büren an der Aare 3,085 ..... D2
Burgdorf 15,888 ..... E2
Burgdorf* 18,400 ..... E2
Bürglen, Thurgau 1,920 ..... H1
Bürglen, Uri 3,401 ..... G3
Bussigny-près-Lausanne 4,509 ..... B3
Bütschwil 3,270 ..... H2
Carouge 14,055 ..... B4
Castagnola 4,430 ..... G4
Cazis 1,687 ..... H3
Cernier 1,717 ..... C2
Chalais 1,651 ..... E4
Cham 8,209 ..... F2
Chamoson 2,049 ..... D4
Charmey 1,155 ..... D3
Château-d'Oex 3,203 ..... D4
Châtel-Saint-Denis 2,842 ..... C3
Chêne-Bougeries 8,670 ..... B4
Chavornay 1,521 ..... C3
Chexbres 1,607 ..... C3
Chiasso 8,868 ..... G5
Chippis 1,561 ..... E4
Chur 32,400 ..... J3
Churwalden 1,052 ..... J3
Claro 1,143 ..... G4
Collombey-Muraz 2,279 ..... C4
Collonge-Bellerive 3,541 ..... B4
Conthey 4,259 ..... D4
Coppet 1,097 ..... B4
Corcelles-près-Payerne 1,256 ..... C3
Corgémont 1,645 ..... D2
Cossonay 1,529 ..... B3
Courgenay 1,954 ..... D2
Courrendlin 2,656 ..... D2
Courroux 1,788 ..... D2
Courtelary 1,462 ..... C2
Courtételle 1,864 ..... D2
Couvet 3,481 ..... C3
Cully 1,535 ..... C4
Davos 10,238 ..... J3
Degersheim 3,400 ..... H2
Delémont 11,797 ..... D2
Derendingen 4,917 ..... E2
Dielsdorf 2,691 ..... F1
Diemtigen 1,913 ..... D3
Diepoldsau 3,311 ..... J2
Diessenhofen 2,532 ..... G1
Dietikon 22,705 ..... F2
Disentis-Mustér 2,319 ..... G3
Domat-Ems 5,701 ..... H3
Dombresson 1,109 ..... C2
Dornach 5,258 ..... E2
Döttingen 3,380 ..... F1
Dübendorf 19,639 ..... G2
Düdingen 4,932 ..... D3
Dürnten 4,820 ..... G2
Dürrenroth 1,084 ..... E2
Ebnat-Kappel 5,131 ..... H2
Echallens 1,643 ..... C3
Ecublens 6,379 ..... B3
Egg 5,250 ..... G2
Eggiwil 2,391 ..... E3
Eglisau 2,160 ..... G1
Egnach 3,466 ..... H1

(continued on following page)

Agriculture, Industry and Resources

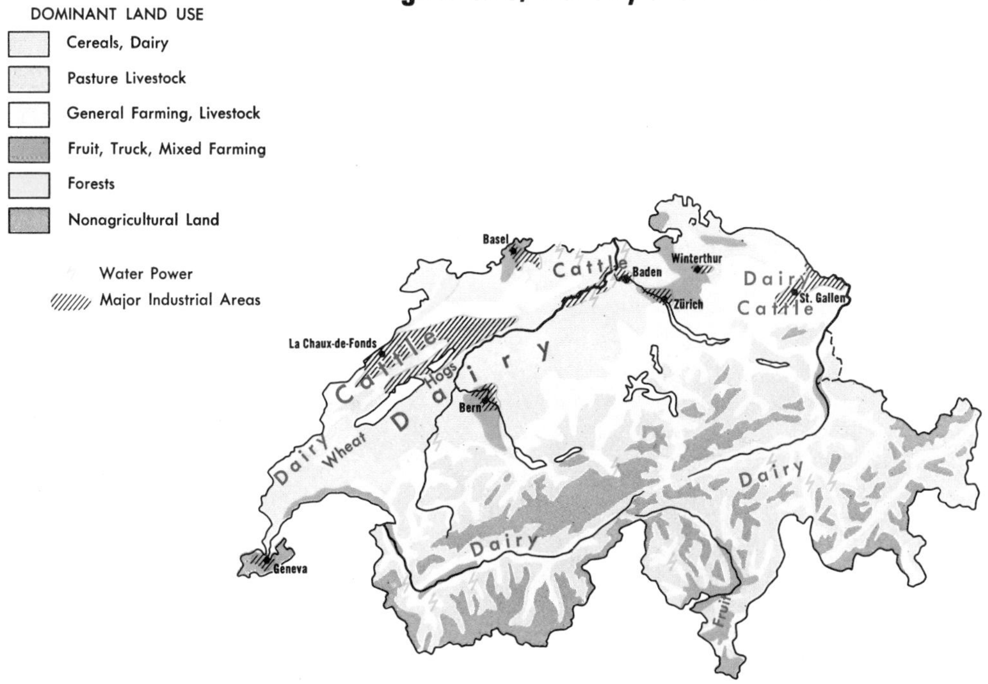
DOMINANT LAND USE
Cereals, Dairy
Pasture Livestock
General Farming, Livestock
Fruit, Truck, Mixed Farming
Forests
Nonagricultural Land
Water Power
Major Industrial Areas
Basel
Winterthur
Baden
Zürich
St. Gallen
La Chaux-de-Fonds
Bern
Geneva
Cattle
Dairy
Wheat
Hogs
Fruit

Switzerland and Liechtenstein

(continued)

Topography

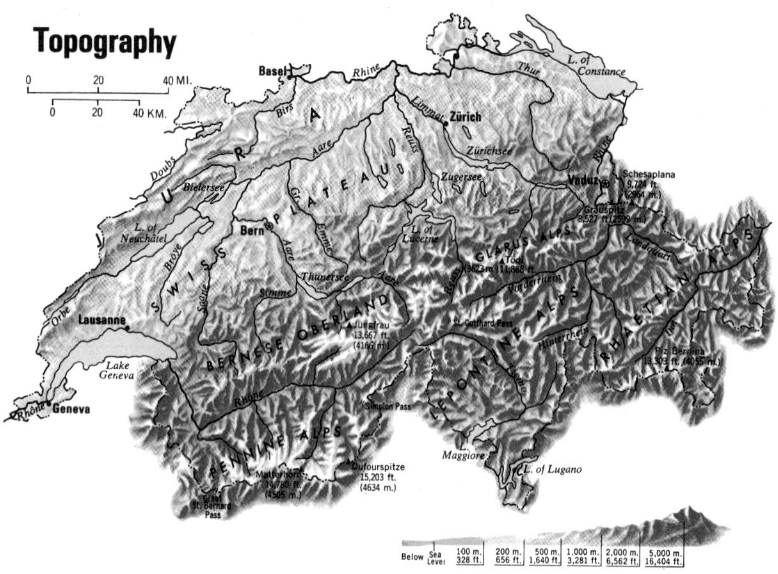

Einsiedeln 10,020 G2
Elgg 2,970 G2
Emmen 22,040 F2
Engelberg 2,841 F3
Ennenda 2,762 H2
Entlebuch 3,310 F3
Erlach 1,052 D2
Erlenbach im Simmental 1,436 E3
Ermatingen 1,787 H1
Erstfeld 4,516 G3
Eschenbach 3,387 G2
Escholzmatt 3,161 E3
Estavayer-le-Lac 3,439 C3
Evolène 1,403 D4
Faido 1,866 G4
Felsberg 1,321 H3
Feuerthalen 3,118 G1
Flawil 8,474 H2
Fleurier 4,124 C3
Flims 1,936 H3
Flüelen 1,731 G3
Flums 4,474 H2
Frauenfeld 17,576 G1
Freienbach 8,429 G2
Fribourg 41,600 D3
Fribourg* 53,500 D3
Frick 3,112 E1
Frutigen 5,796 E3
Fully 3,643 D4
Gais 2,344 H2
Gelterkinden 5,157 E2
Geneva (Genève) 163,100 B4
Geneva (Genève)* 320,200 B4
Gersau 1,753 G2
Gimel 1,205 B3
Giornico 1,389 G4
Giswil 2,760 F3
Giubiasco 5,796 H4
Gland 2,404 B4
Glarus 6,189 H2
Glattfelden 2,857 F1
Glis 3,389 E4
Gordola 2,586 G4
Gossau 12,793 H2
Grabs 4,245 H2
Grächen 1,063 E4
Grandson 2,135 C3
Grenchen 20,051 D2
Grenchen* 28,300 D2
Grindelwald 3,511 E3
Grosswangen 2,213 F2
Gruyères 1,234 D3
Gstaad D4
Gsteig 865 D4
Guggisberg 1,739 D3
Gurtnellen 1,048 G3
Guttingen 1,060 H1
Hallau 1,836 F1
Heiden 3,716 H2
Heimberg 3,046 E3
Hérémence 1,484 D4
Hergiswil 4,364 F3
Herisau 14,597 H2
Herzogenbuchsee 5,140 E2
Hilterfingen 3,647 E3
Hinwil 6,547 G2
Hitzkirch 1,468 F2
Hochdorf 5,222 F2
Horgen 15,691 G2
Huttwil 4,800 E2
Igis 5,283 J3
Ilanz 1,783 H3
Illnau 13,693 G2
Ingenbohl 5,111 G2
Innertkirchen 1,064 F3
Ins 2,435 D2
Interlaken 4,735 E3
Jegenstorf 2,858 D2
Jenaz 1,124 J3
Jona 9,286 G2
Jungfraujoch E3
Kaltbrunn 2,751 H2
Kandersteg 957 E4
Kerns 3,807 F3
Kerzers 2,688 D3
Kirchberg, Bern 3,595 E2
Kirchberg, St. Gallen 6,309 G2
Kleinlützel 1,271 D2
Klingnau 2,545 F1
Klosters Dorf 3,534 J3
Kloten 16,388 G2
Koblenz 1,439 F1
Kölliken 3,219 F2
Köniz 33,800 D3
Konolfingen 4,137 E3
Kreuzlingen 15,760 H1
Kriens 20,409 F2
Krummenau 1,904 H2
Küsnacht 12,193 G2
Küssnacht am Rigi 7,956 F2
Küttigen 4,181 F2
L'Abbaye 1,319 B3
La Chaux-de-Fonds 42,500 C2
Lachen 4,914 G2
Lancy 20,523 B4
La Neuveville 3,917 D2
Langenthal 13,077 E2
Langenthal* 22,100 E2
Langnau am Albis 4,879 G2
Langnau in Emmental 8,950 E3
La Roche 1,069 D3
La Sarraz 1,190 C3
La Tour-de-Peilz 8,864 C4
Läufelfingen 1,243 E2
Laufen 4,723 D2
Laufenburg 2,128 F1
Laupen 2,139 D3
Lauperswil 2,542 E3
Lausanne 136,100 C3
Lausanne* 228,700 C3
Lauterbrunnen 3,431 E3
Le Brassus 5,465 B3
Le Châble 4,541 D4
Le Chenit (Le Brassus) 5,465 B3
Le Landeron 2,768 C2
Le Locle 14,452 C2
Le Mont-sur-Lausanne 2,692 C3
Lengau 4,736 D2
Lenk 1,876 D4
Le Noirmont 1,516 C2
Lens 2,052 D4
Lenzburg 7,594 F2
Les Bois 1,110 C2
Les Ponts-de-Martel 1,327 C2
Leuk 2,796 E4
Leukerbad 1,056 E4
Leysin 2,752 C4
Liechtensteig 2,131 H2
Liestal 12,500 E2
Liestal-Sissach* 40,800 E2
Linthal 1,458 H3
Littau 13,495 F2
Locarno 14,143 G4
Locarno* 39,200 G4
Lodrino 1,075 G4
Lotzwil 2,323 E2
Lucens 2,144 C3
Lucerne 70,200 F2
Lucerne* 158,600 F2
Lugano 22,280 G4
Lugano* 64,200 G4
Lungern 1,813 F3
Luthern 1,706 E2
Lutry 4,994 C3
Lützelflüh 3,842 E3
Luzern (Lucerne) 70,200 F2
Lyss 8,131 D2
Maienfeld 1,542 J2
Malans 1,294 J3
Malleray 1,969 D2
Malters 5,100 F2
Malvaglia 1,099 H4
Männedorf 7,419 G2
Marbach 1,265 E3
Martigny 10,478 C4
Meilen 9,881 G2
Meiringen 3,759 F3
Melide 1,315 G5
Mellingen 3,211 F2
Mels 5,969 H2
Mendrisio 6,223 G5
Menzingen 3,483 G2
Menznau 2,185 E2
Mesocco 1,376 H4
Meyrin 14,255 B4
Minusio 5,027 G4
Möhlin 6,003 E1
Mollis 2,628 H2
Montana 1,725 D4
Monthey 10,114 C4
Montreux 20,421 C4
Morges 11,931 B3
Morges* 17,200 B3
Moudon 3,773 C3
Moutier 8,794 D2
Müllheim 1,620 G1
Mümliswil-Ramiswil 2,702 E2
Münchenbuchsee 6,459 E2
Münsingen 8,350 E3
Muotathal 2,763 G3
Muri 4,853 F2
Muri bei Bern 3,057 E3
Mürren E3
Murten 4,256 D3
Muttenz 15,518 E1
Näfels 3,739 H2
Naters 5,517 E4
Nebikon 1,378 F2
Nendaz 4,051 D4
Nesslau 1,934 H2
Netstal 2,771 H2
Neuchâtel 38,400 C3
Neuchâtel* 61,700 C3
Neuenegg 3,452 D3
Neuhausen am Rheinfall 12,103 G1
Neunkirch 1,239 F1
Nidau 7,962 D2
Niederbipp 3,293 E2
Niederurnen 3,354 G2
Nunningen 1,450 E2
Nyon 11,424 B4
Oberägeri 2,992 G2
Oberburg 3,015 E2
Oberdiessbach 2,145 E3
Oberdorf 1,953 E2
Oberriet 6,123 J2
Obersiggenthal 6,623 F1
Oberzwil 4,659 H2
Oensingen 3,387 E2
Oftringen 9,189 E2
Ollon 4,470 D4
Olten 21,209 E2
Olten* 49,000 E2
Opfikon 11,115 G2
Orbe 4,522 C3
Orsières 2,470 D4
Ouchy C4
Paradiso 3,101 G5
Payerne 6,899 C3
Penthalaz 1,701 C3
Péry 1,486 D2
Peseux 5,578 C3
Pfaffnau 2,584 E2
Pieterlen 3,485 D2
Plaffeien 1,448 D3
Pontresina 1,646 J3
Porrentruy 7,827 C2
Port-Valais 1,363 C4
Poschiavo 3,563 J4
Prangins 1,466 B4
Pratteln 15,127 E1
Pully 15,917 C4
Quinto 1,490 G3
Rafz 2,215 G1
Ramsen 1,217 G1
Rapperswil 8,713 G2
Raron 1,257 E4
Regensdorf 8,566 F2
Reichenbach im Kandertal 2,900 E3
Reiden 3,275 F2
Reinach in Aargau 5,862 F2
Reinach in Baselland 13,419 E2
Renan 1,094 C2
Renens 17,391 C3
Rheinau 2,075 G1
Rheineck 3,275 J2
Rheinfelden 6,866 E1
Richterswil 7,380 G2
Riehen 21,026 E1
Riggisberg 2,193 E3
Riva San Vitale 1,607 G5
Rivera 1,146 G4
Roggwil 3,403 E2
Rolle 3,658 B4
Romanshorn 8,329 H1
Romont 3,276 C3
Rorschach 11,963 H2
Rorschach* 24,200 H2
Rosenlaui F3
Rothrist 5,883 E2
Roveredo 2,037 H4
Rüeggisberg 1,857 E3
Rumlang 5,677 G2
Rüschegg 1,346 D3
Ruswil 4,756 F2
Rüthi 1,493 J2
Rüti, Zürich 9,546 G2
Saanen 5,840 D4
Sachseln 3,059 F3
Saignelégier 1,745 D2
Saint-Aubin-Sauges 2,058 C3
Saint-Blaise 2,586 D2
Sainte-Croix 6,240 B3
Saint-Imier 6,740 D2
Saint-Légier-La Chiésaz 2,230 C4
Saint-Martin 1,120 E4
Saint-Maurice 3,808 C4
Saint Moritz 5,699 J3
Saint Niklaus 2,043 E4
Saint-Prex 2,306 B4
Saint Stephan 1,213 D3
Saint-Ursanne 1,073 D2
Samedan 2,574 J3
Sankt Gallen 81,900 H2
Sankt Gallen* 90,400 H2
Sankt Margrethen 5,101 J2
Sargans 4,058 H2
Sarnen 6,952 F3
Satigny 1,877 A4
Savièse 3,585 D4
Saxon 2,409 D4
Schaffhausen 36,800 G1
Schaffhausen* 55,800 G1
Schänis 2,355 H2
Schattdorf 3,292 G3
Scherzingen 1,420 H1
Schiers 2,342 J3
Schinznach-Dorf 1,154 F2
Schleitheim 1,544 G1
Schlieren 11,869 F2
Schönenwerd 4,793 E2
Schübelbach 4,395 G2
Schüpfheim 3,773 F3
Schwanden 2,823 H2
Schwyz 12,194 G2
Scuol 1,686 K3
Sempach 1,619 F2
Seon 3,628 F2
Seuzach 3,258 G1
Sevelen 2,742 H2
Sierre 11,017 D4
Signau 2,642 E3
Sigriswil 3,540 E3
Silenen 2,338 G3
Sils im Domleschg 762 H3
Silvaplana 714 J4
Sins 2,435 F2
Sion 21,925 D4
Sirnach 3,706 G2
Sissach 4,938 E2
Solothurn (Soleure) 17,708 E2
Solothurn* 35,600 E2
Somvix 1,555 G3
Sonvico 1,129 G4
Spiez 9,911 E3
Stäfa 9,937 G2
Stalden 1,121 E4
Stans 5,180 F3
Steckborn 3,752 G1
Steffisburg 12,621 E3
Stein 1,763 E1
Stein am Rhein 2,751 G1
Suhr 7,223 F2
Sulgen 1,834 H1
Sumiswald 5,334 E2
Sursee 7,052 F2
Tafers 2,021 D3
Täuffelen 1,761 D2
Tavannes 3,869 D2
Tavetsch 1,273 G3
Teufen 5,300 H2
Thal 4,919 J2
Thalwil 13,591 G2
Thayngen 3,640 G1
Therwil 5,412 E1
Thun 37,000 E3
Thun* 63,600 E3
Thunstetten 2,483 E2
Thusis 2,381 H3
Trachselwald 1,199 E2
Tramelan 5,549 D2
Trimmis 1,109 J3
Troistorrents 2,208 C4
Trub 1,833 E3
Trun 1,607 G3
Turbenthal 2,939 G2
Uetendorf 3,132 E3
Unterägeri 4,671 G2
Unteriberg 1,344 G2
Unterkulm 2,596 F2
Unterseen 4,192 E3
Untervaz 1,230 H3
Urnäsch 2,313 H2
Uster 21,819 G2
Utzenstorf 3,193 E2
Uznach 3,984 H2
Uzwil 9,133 H2
Vallorbe 4,028 B3
Vaz-Obervaz 2,003 J3
Vechigen 3,595 E3
Vernayaz 1,356 D4
Versoix 5,627 B4
Vevey 17,957 C4
Vevey-Montreux* 62,300 C4
Villeneuve 3,705 C4
Visp 5,252 E4
Vouvry 1,851 C4
Vuadens 1,278 C3
Wädenswil 15,695 G2
Wahlern 4,832 D3
Wald 8,185 G2
Waldenburg 1,449 E2
Waldkirch 2,669 H2
Walenstadt 3,446 H2
Wallisellen 10,415 G2
Walzenhausen 2,082 J2
Wangen an der Aare 2,013 E2
Wängi 2,730 H1
Wartau 3,604 H2
Wattwil 8,566 H2
Weesen 1,308 H2
Weggis 2,517 F2
Weinfelden 8,621 H1
Wettingen 19,900 F2
Wetzikon 13,469 G2
Wil 14,646 H2
Wil* 20,500 H2
Wilchingen 1,066 F1
Wilderswil 1,666 E3
Wildhaus 1,104 H2
Willisau 2,728 F2
Wimmis 1,833 E3
Windisch 7,444 F1
Winterthur 93,500 G1
Winterthur* 110,100 G1
Wohlen 12,024 F2
Wohlen* 16,000 F2
Wohlen bei Bern 4,190 D3
Wolfenschiessen 1,470 F3
Wolhusen 3,556 F2
Worb 9,526 E3
Wünnewil 3,652 D3
Wynigen 1,986 E2
Yverdon 20,538 C3
Yvonand 1,321 C3
Zell, Luzern 1,590 E2
Zell, Zürich 4,008 G2
Zermatt 3,101 E4
Zizers 1,913 J3
Zofingen 9,292 F2
Zollikofen 9,069 E3
Zollikon 12,117 G2
Zug 22,972 G2
Zug* 51,300 G2
Zuoz 1,165 J3
Zürich 401,600 F2
Zürich* 718,100 F2
Zurzach 3,098 F1
Zweisimmen 2,738 D3

OTHER FEATURES

Aa (riv.) F3
Aare (riv.) E3
Ägerisee (lake) G2
Aiguille d'Argentière (mt.) C5
Aletschhorn (mt.) F4
Aroser Rothorn (mt.) J3
Ault (peak) H3
Balmhorn (mt.) E4
Bernese Oberland (reg.) E3
Bernina (peak) J4
Bernina (pass) K4
Bielersee (lake) D2
Bietschhorn (mt.) E4
Birs (riv.) D2
Blinnenhorn (mt.) F4
Blümlisalp (mt.) E3
Bodensee (Constance) (lake) H1
Borgne (riv.) D4
Breithorn (mt.) E5
Breithorn (mt.) E4
Brienzer Rothorn (mt.) F3
Brienzersee (lake) F3
Broye (riv.) C3
Buchegg (mts.) D2
Buin (peak) K3
Campo Tencia (peak) G4
Chasseron (mt.) C3
Churfirsten (mt.) H2
Clariden (mt.) G3
Constance (lake) H1
Cornettes de Bise (mts.) C4
Dammastock (mt.) F3
Davos (valley) J3
Dent Blanche (mt.) E4
Dent de Lys (mt.) D4

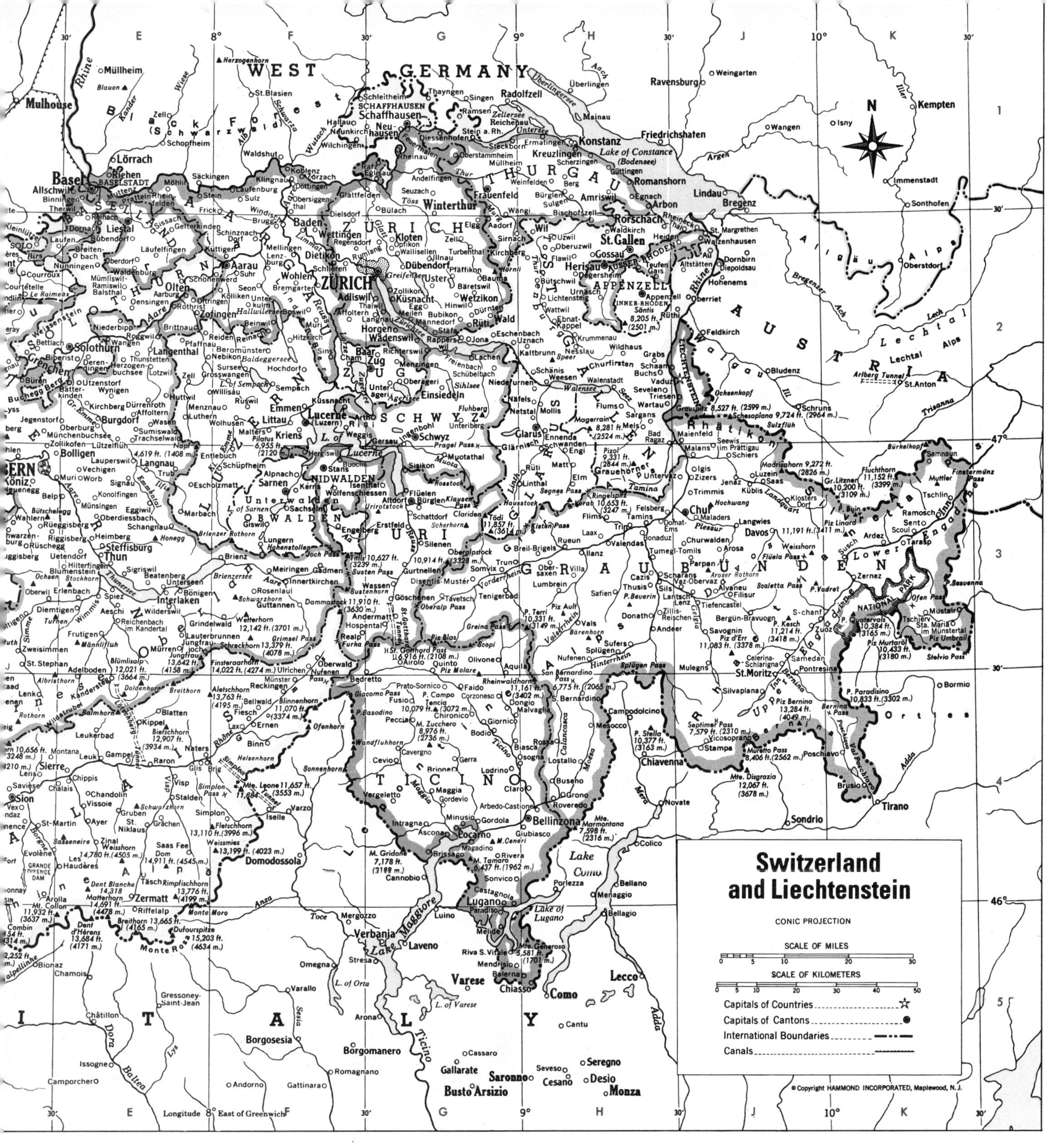

LIECHTENSTEIN

CITIES and TOWNS

OTHER FEATURES

*City and suburbs.

AUSTRIA

PROVINCES

Burgenland 272,119 D3
Carinthia 525,728 B3
Lower Austria 1,414,161 C2
Salzburg 401,766 B3
Styria 1,192,442 C3
Tirol 540,771 A3
Upper Austria 1,223,444 B2
Vienna (city) 1,614,841 D2
Vorarlberg 271,473 A3

CITIES and TOWNS†

Admont 3,126 C3
Allentsteig 2,783 C2
Altheim 4,766 B2
Althofen 3,886 C3
Amstetten 13,330 C2
Andau 3,058 D3
Arnoldstein 6,740 B3
Aspang Markt 2,316 D3
Attnang-Puchheim 7,837 B2
Bad Aussee 5,039 B3
Baden 22,631 D2
Badgastein 5,228 B3
Bad Goisern 6,360 B3
Bad Hofgastein 5,525 B3
Bad Ischl 12,740 B3
Bad Leonfelden 2,712 C2
Bad Sankt-Leonhard im Lavanttal 4,882 C3
Berndorf 8,371 C3
Bischofshofen 9,417 B3
Bludenz 12,050 A3
Bramberg am Wildkogel 3,129 B3
Braunau am Inn 16,432 B2
Bregenz 22,839 A3
Bruck an der Leitha 7,506 D2
Bruck an der Mur 16,359 C3
Deutsch Feistritz 3,820 C3
Deutschkreutz 3,673 D3
Deutsch Landsberg 6,614 C3
Deutsch Wagram 4,481 D2
Dornbirn 33,810 A3
Ebenfurth 2,272 D3
Ebensee 9,413 B3
Eferding 3,014 B2
Eggenburg 3,730 C2
Ehrwald 2,198 A3
Horn 6,264 C2
Hüttenberg 3,251 C3
Imst 5,855 A3
Innsbruck 115,800 A3
Innsbruck* 167,200 A3
Jenbach 5,868 A3
Jennersdorf 4,210 C3
Judenburg 11,346 C3
Kapfenberg 26,001 C3
Kappl 2,156 A3
Kaprun 2,604 B3
Kindberg 6,128 C3
Kirchdorf an der Krems 3,471 C3
Kitzbühel 7,995 B3
Klagenfurt 74,326 C3
Klagenfurt* 112,600 C3
Klosterneuburg 21,912 D2
Knittelfeld 14,517 C3
Köflach 12,612 C3
Königswiesen 2,921 C2
Korneuburg 8,892 D2
Kössen 2,764 B3
Kötschach-Mauthen 3,740 B3
Krems an der Donau 21,733 C2
Kufstein 12,766 A3
Kundl 3,020 A3
Laa an der Thaya 5,455 D2
Laakirchen 7,664 B3
Lambach 3,301 C2
Landeck 7,388 A3
Längenfeld 2,838 A3
Langenlois 4,957 C2
Langenwang 4,071 C3
Lavamünd 4,120 C3
Leibnitz 6,646 C3
Lenzing 5,385 B3
Leoben 35,153 C3
Lienz 11,696 B3
Liezen 6,244 C3
Lilienfeld 3,126 C3
Linz 205,700 C2
Linz* 356,500 C2
Lustenau 15,239 A3
Mannersdorf am Leithagebirge 4,012 D3
Marchegg 2,678 D2
Mariazell 2,298 C3
Matrei in Osttirol 4,003 B3
Mattersburg 5,417 D3
Mattighofen 4,344 B2
Mauerkirchen 2,237 B2
Mautern in Steiermark 2,536 C3
Sankt Valentin 8,715 C2
Sankt Veit an der Glan 11,047 C3
Sankt Wolfgang im Salzkammergut 2,746 B3
Schärding 5,874 B2
Scheibbs 4,419 C2
Schladming 3,460 B3
Schrems 3,393 C2
Schruns 3,607 A3
Schwarzach im Pongau 3,616 B3
Schwaz 10,253 A3
Schwechat 14,997 D2
Schwertberg 3,881 C2
Sierning 8,162 C2
Sillian 1,988 B3
Solbad Hall in Tirol 12,335 A3
Spital am Pyhrn 2,315 C3
Spittal an der Drau 13,690 B3
Steinach 2,698 A3
Steyr 40,578 C2
Stockerau 12,634 D2
Strassburg 2,850 C3
Tamsweg 5,060 B3
Telfs 6,589 A3
Ternitz 10,287 D3
Traiskirchen 8,878 D2
Traun 20,843 C2
Trieben 4,639 C3
Trofaiach 8,731 C3
Tulln 7,705 D2
Velden am Wörthersee 7,306 C3
Vienna (cap.) 1,700,000 D2
Vienna* 1,858,700 D2
Villach 50,979 B3
Vöcklabruck 10,627 B2
Voitsberg 11,094 C3
Völkermarkt 10,772 C3
Vordernberg 2,508 C3
Waidhofen an der Thaya 4,200 C2
Waidhofen an der Ybbs 5,218 C3
Weitensfeld-Flattnitz 5,206 B3
Weitra 3,250 C2
Weiz 8,241 C3
Wels 47,279 C2
Weyer Markt 2,518 C3
Wien (Vienna) (cap.) 1,700,000 D2
Wiener Neustadt 34,774 D3
Wildon 2,002 C3
Wilhelmsburg 6,307 C2
Wolfsberg 31,176 C3
Wörgl 7,811 A3
Ybbs an der Donau 6,422 C2
Zams 3,120 A3
Zell am See 7,456 B3
Zell am Ziller 1,882 A3
Zeltweg 8,431 C3
Zirl 4,157 A3
Zistersdorf 3,412 D2
Zwettl-Niederösterreich 11,624 C2

OTHER FEATURES

AllgÄu Alps (mts.) A3
Bavarian Alps (mts.) A3
Bodensee (Constance) (lake) A3
Brenner (pass) A3
Carnic Alps (mts.) B3
Constance (lake) A3
Danube (riv.) C2
Donau (Danube) (riv.) D2
Drau (riv.) C3
Enns (riv.) C3
Grossglockner (mt.) B3
Hohe Tauern (range) B3
Inn (riv.) B2
Karawanken (range) C3
March (riv.) D2
Mühlviertel (reg.) C2
Mur (riv.) C3
Neusiedler See (lake) D3
Niedere Tauern (range) B3
Ötztal Alps (mts.) A3
Raab (riv.) C3
Rhine (riv.) A3
Salzach (riv.) B2
Salzkammergut (reg.) B3
Semmering (pass) C3
Thaya (riv.) C2
Traun (riv.) C2
Wildspitze (mt.) A3
Zugspitze (mt.) A3

CZECHOSLOVAKIA

REPUBLICS

Czech Socialist Rep. 9,964,338 B1
Slovak Socialist Rep. 4,670,409 E2

REGIONS

Bratislava (city) 333,000 D2
Jihočeský 662,002 C2
Jihomoravský 1,966,850 D2
Praha (city) 1,161,200 C1
Severočeský 1,122,035 C1
Severomoravský 1,849,286 D2
Středočeský 1,193,041 C2
Středoslovenský 1,436,351 E2
Východočeský 1,214,581 C1
Východoslovenský 1,298,481 F2
Západočeský 865,094 B2
Západoslovenský 1,610,542 D2

CITIES and TOWNS

Aš 120,000 B1
Austerlitz (Slavkov) D2
Bánovce nad Bebravou 11,400 E2
Banská Bystrica 53,000 E2
Banská štiavnica 7,486 E2
Bardejov 17,400 F2
Benešov 11,100 C2
Beroun 17,600 B2
Bílina 17,800 B1
Blansko 13,800 D2
Boskovice 8,531 D2
Brandýs nad Labem-Stará Boleslavv 333,000 C1
Bratislava 333,000 D2
Břeclav 21,100 D2
Brezno 14,800 E2
Brno 335,700 D2
Broumov 7,782 D1
Bruntál 12,300 D2
Bystřice nad Pernštejnem 6,471 D2
Bystřice pod Hostýnem 6,681 D2
Bytča 6,922 E2
Čadca 16,800 E2
Čalovo 6,591 D3
Čáslav 10,200 C2
Česká Lípa 18,600 C1
Česká Třebová 14,700 D2
České Budějovice 80,800 C2
Český Brod 6,640 C1
Český Krumlov 12,000 C2
Český Těšín 17,200 E2
Cheb 27,000 B1
Choceň 8,198 D1
Chodov 14,400 B1
Chomutov 44,200 B1
Chotěboř 6,692 C2
Chrudim 18,800 C2
Čierny Balog 6,435 E2
Děčín 46,500 C1
Detva 13,100 E2
Dobříš 6,378 C2
Dobruška 5,779 D1
Dolný Kubín 9,900 E2
Domažlice 9,100 B2
Dubnica nad Váhom 11,300 E2
Duchcov 9,712 B1
Dunajská Streda 13,000 D3
Dvory nad Žitavou 5,847 E3
Dvů Králové nad Labem 16,800 C1
Falknov (Sokolov) 23,900 B1
Fil'akovo 7,822 E2
Frenštát pod Radhoštěm 8,516 E2
Frýdek-Místek 43,800 E2
Frýdlant v. Čechách 5,948 C1
Frýdlant nad Ostravicí 6,250
Galanta 12,300
Gottwaldov 84,300
Handlová 16,200
Havířov 85,000
Havlíčkův Brod 19,200
Hlinsko 8,890
Hlohovec 15,200
Hlučín 15,300
Hnúšt'a-Likier
Hodonín 22,600
Holešov 9,091
Holíč 7,602
Holice 6,151
Horažd'ovice
Hořice v Podkrkonoší 7,715
Horná Štubňa
Horní Benešov
Horní Libina
Hořovice 5,665
Horšovský Týn
Hostinné
Hradec Králové 85,600
Hranice 13,300
Hrinova 7,800
Hronov 9,767
Hrušovany
Humenné 22,200
Humpolec 7,810
Hurbanovo
Hustopeče
Ilava
Ivančice 7,314

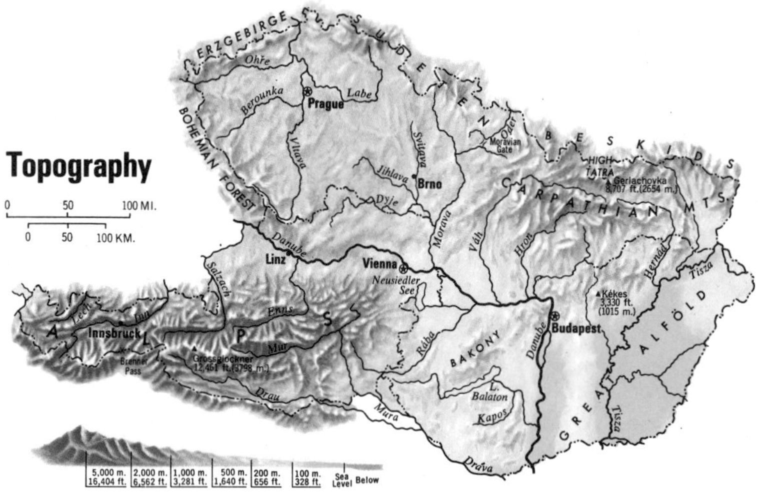

Topography

0 50 100 MI.
0 50 100 KM.

AREA 32,375 sq. mi. (83,851 sq. km.)
POPULATION 7,507,000
CAPITAL Vienna
LARGEST CITY Vienna
HIGHEST POINT Grossglockner 12,457 ft. (3,797 m.)
MONETARY UNIT schilling
MAJOR LANGUAGE German
MAJOR RELIGION Roman Catholicism

AREA 49,373 sq. mi. (127,876 sq. km.)
POPULATION 15,276,799
CAPITAL Prague
LARGEST CITY Prague
HIGHEST POINT Gerlachovka 8,707 ft. (2,654 m.)
MONETARY UNIT koruna
MAJOR LANGUAGES Czech, Slovak
MAJOR RELIGIONS Roman Catholicism, Protestantism

AREA 35,919 sq. mi. (93,030 sq. km.)
POPULATION 10,709,536
CAPITAL Budapest
LARGEST CITY Budapest
HIGHEST POINT Kékes 3,330 ft. (1,015 m.)
MONETARY UNIT forint
MAJOR LANGUAGE Hungarian
MAJOR RELIGIONS Roman Catholicism, Protestantism

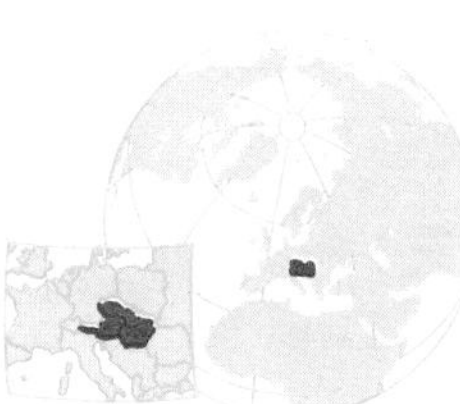

AUSTRIA

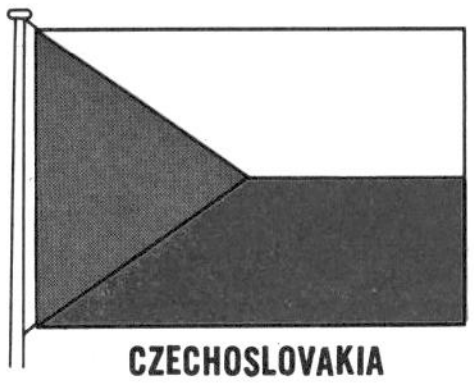
CZECHOSLOVAKIA

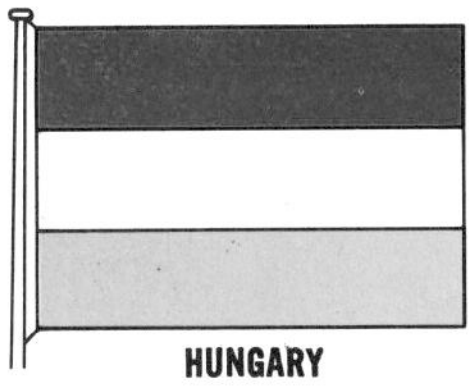
HUNGARY

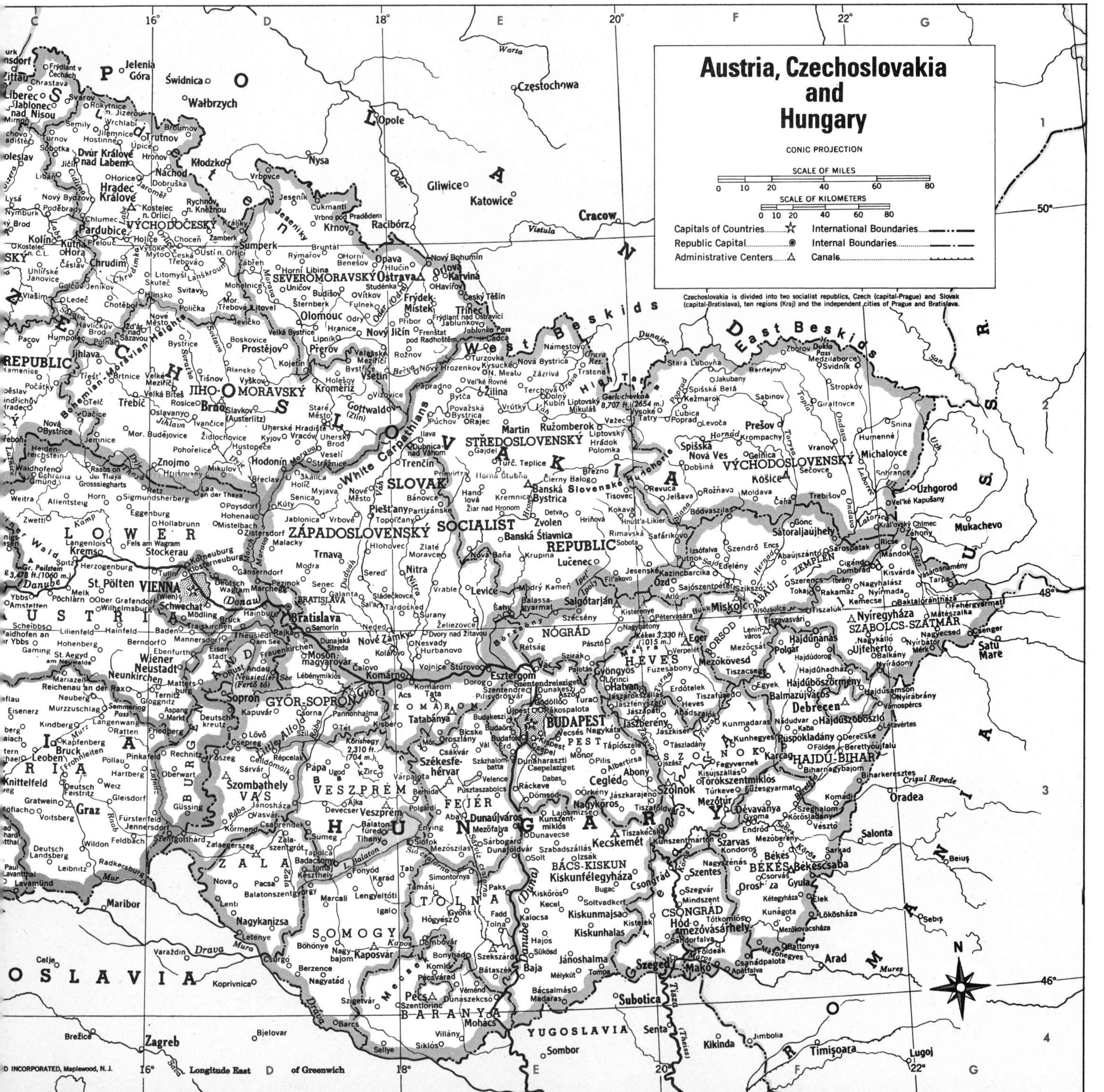

40 Austria, Czechoslovakia and Hungary
(continued)

Jablonec nad Nisou 36,300 C1
Jablonica D2
Jablunkov 9,405 E2
Jáchymov B1
Jakubany F2
Jaroměř 11,600 C1
Jelšava F2
Jemnice C2
Jeseník 10,900 D1
Jesenské F2
Jevíčko D2
Jičín 13,200 C1
Jihlava 44,500 C2
Jilemnice C1
Jindřichův Hradec 15,700 C2
Jiřkov 11,400 B1
Kadaň 18,100 B1
Kamenice C2
Kaplice C2
Karlovy Vary 43,300 B1
Karviná 79,100 E2
Kdyně B2
Kežmarok 11,000 F2
Kladno 61,200 B1
Klatovy 18,500 B2
Kojetín 5,852 D2
Kokava nad Rimavicou 5,391 E2
Kolárovo 10,500 D3
Kolín 29,100 C1
Komárno 28,200 D3
Košice 169,100 F2
Kostelec nad Orlicí 5,575 D1
Král'ovský Chlmec 5,329 G2
Kralupy nad Vltavou 16,900 C1
Kraslice 6,733 B1
Kremnica 5,941 E2
Krnov 25,000 D1
Kroměříž 23,200 D2
Krompachy 6,332 F2
Krupina 6,627 E2
Krupka 8,301 B1
Kutná Hora 19,200 C2
Kyjov 10,700 D2
Kynšperk 5,524 B1
Kysucké Nové Mesto 11,700 E2
Lanškroun 8,683 D2
Levice 19,000 E2
Levoča 10,100 F2
Libáň C1
Liberec 75,600 C1

Moravě 6,581 D2
Nové Město nad
Váhom 15,900 D2
Nové Strašecí B1
Nové Zámky 27,300 D3
Nový Bohumín 16,700 E2
Nový Bor 7,621 C1
Nový Bydžov 6,824 C1
Nový Hrozenkov E2
Nový Jičín 21,400 E2
Nymburk 13,600 C1
Nýřany 6,204 B2
Nýrsko B2
Odry D2
Olomouc 82,800 D2
Opava 53,800 E2
Orlová 25,500 E2
Ostrava 293,500 E2
Ostrov 18,200 B1
Pardubice 78,500 C1
Partizánske 15,100 E2
Pelhřimov 11,900 C2
Pezinok 13,100 D2
Piešt'any 25,400 D2
Písek 25,100 C2
Plzeň 155,000 B2
Počátky C2
Podbořany B1
Poděbrady 13,400 C1
Pohořelice D2
Polička 6,529 D2
Polná C2
Polomka E2
Poprad 25,800 F2
Považská Bystrica 19,300 E2
Prachatice 7,900 B2
Prague (Praha) (cap.) 1,161,200 C1
Přelouč 6,251 C1
Přerov 43,500 D2
Prešov 61,000 F2
Přeštice B2
Příbor 7,726 E2
Příbram 31,300 B2
Prievidza 30,900 E2
Prostějov 44,200 D2
Protivín C2
Púchov 9,306 E2
Radnice B2
Rajec E2
Rakovník 14,200 B1

Štúrovo 8,287 E3
Šumperk 25,900 D1
Šurany 6,693 E2
Sušice 10,300 B2
Svárov C1
Svidník 4,600 F2
Svitavy 15,000 D2
Tábor 28,100 C2
Tachov 11,400 B2
Telč 5,285 C2
Teplice 52,300 B1
Tišnov 8,263 D2
Topol'čany 17,500 D2
Třebíč 23,900 C2
Trebišov 13,700 F2
Třeboň 6,068 C2
Trenčín 38,800 E2
Třešt' 5,053 C2
Třinec 32,000 E2
Trnava 48,600 D2
Trutnov 24,500 D1
Turnov 13,600 C1
Turzovka 6,107 E2
Uherské Hradiště 32,100 D2
Uherský Brod 12,800 D2
Uničov 10,800 D2
Úpice 6,323 C1
Ústí nad Labem 74,900 C1
Ústí nad Orlicí 13,700 D2
Valašské
Meziříčí 19,400 D2
Varnsdorf 14,700 C1
Važec E2
Vejprty B1
Velká Bíteš D2
Velká Bystřice D2
Vel'ké Kapušany G2
Velké Meziříčí 7,590 D2
Vel'ké Rovné E2
Veselí nad Lužnicí C2
Veselí nad Moravou 11,500 D2
Vimperk 5,749 B2
Vítkov 5,138 D2
Vizovice D2
Vlašim 8,873 C2
Vodňany 5,620 C2
Vojnice E3
Volary B2
Volyně B2
Votice C2

Jablunka (pass) E2
Jeseníky (mts.) D1
Jihlava (riv.) D2
Krušné Hory (Erzgebirge)
(mts.) B1
Labe (riv.) C1
Lipno (res.) C2
Lužnice (riv.) C2
Moldau (Vltava) (riv.) C2
Morava (riv.) D2
Nitra (riv.) E2
Oder (Odra) (riv.) D2
Ohře (riv.) B1
Ondava (riv.) F2
Orava (riv.) E2
Orlická (res.) C2
Sázava (riv.) C2
Slovenské Rudohorie (mts.) E2
Sudeten (mts.) C1
Svitava (riv.) D2
Svratka (riv.) D2
Tatra, High (mts.) E2
Torysa (riv.) F2
Úhlava (riv.) B2
Váh (riv.) D2
Vltava (riv.) C2
White Carpathians (mts.) E2

HUNGARY

COUNTIES

Bács-Kiskun 568,532 E3
Baranya 434,030 E4
Békés 436,987 F3
Borsod-Abaúj-Zemplén 808,924 F2
Budapest (city) 2,060,170 E3
Csongrád 456,862 F3
Fejér 421,568 E3
Győr-Sopron 428,476 D3
Hajdú-Bihar 552,417 F3
Heves 350,874 F3
Komárom 321,579 E3
Nógrád 239,907 E3
Pest 973,486 E3
Somogy 360,308 D3
Szabolcs-Szatmár 593,746 G3
Szolnok 446,379 F3
Tolna 266,414 E3
Vas 285,527 D3

Csenger 4,792 G3
Csepel 71,693 E3
Csepreg 4,079 D3
Csongrád 22,202 E3
Csorna 12,131 D3
Csorvás 6,826 F3
Csurgó 5,463 D3
Dabas 13,075 E3
Debrecen 192,484 F3
Derecske 9,579 F3
Dévaványa 11,208 F3
Devecser 5,482 D3
Dombóvár 19,917 E3
Dombrád 6,328 F2
Dömsöd 6,545 E3
Dorog 10,754 E3
Dunaföldvár 10,318 E3
Dunaharaszti 15,788 E3
Dunakeszi 25,187 E3
Dunaszekcső 2,999 E3
Dunaújváros 60,694 E3
Dunavecse 4,521 E3
Edelény 9,559 F2
Eger 61,283 F3
Egyek 7,956 F3
Elek 6,032 F3
Enes 2,565 F2
Endrőd 8,136 F3
Enying 7,518 E3
Érd 41,210 E3
Erdőtelek 4,250 F3
Esztergom 30,476 E3
Fadd 4,805 E3
Fegyvernek 8,421 F3
Fehérgyarmat 6,729 G3
Földeák 3,855 F3
Földes 5,293 F2
Fonyód 3,957 D3
Füzesabony 6,965 F3
Füzesgyarmat 7,097 F3
Gödöllő 28,057 E3
Gönc 2,875 F2
Gyoma 10,392 F3
Gyöngyös 36,927 E3
Gyönk 2,507 E3
Győr 123,618 D3
Gyula 34,514 F3
Hajdúböszörmény 32,145 F3
Hajdúdorog 10,118 F3
Hajdúhadház 13,626 F3

Körmend 11,787 D3
Körösladány 6,565 F3
Kőszeg 12,705 D3
Kunágota 4,622 F3
Kunhegyes 10,116 F3
Kunmadaras 7,343 F3
Kunszentmárton 11,103 F3
Kunszentmiklós 7,952 E3
Lajosmizse 12,872 E3
Lébénymiklós 6,190 D3
Lengyeltóti 3,389 D3
Leninváros 18,667 F3
Lenti 8,106 D3
Létavértes 9,106 G3
Letenye 4,395 D3
Lőkösháza 2,514 F3
Lőrinci 10,679 E3
Madaras 4,519 E3
Makó 29,943 F3
Mándok 5,093 G2
Marcali 12,485 D3
Mátészalka 17,709 G3
Mélykút 7,640 E3
Mérk 3,211 G3
Mezőberény 12,702 F3
Mezőcsát 6,729 F3
Mezőfalva 5,008 E3
Mezőhegyes 8,631 F3
Mezőkovácsháza 7,473 F3
Mezőkövesd 18,435 F3
Mezőszilas 2,792 E3
Mezőtúr 22,018 F3
Mindszent 8,730 F3
Miskolc 206,727 F2
Mohács 21,385 E4
Monor 16,838 E3
Mór 12,066 E3
Mosonmagyaróvár 29,732 D3
Nádudvar 9,447 F3
Nagyatád 12,946 D3
Nagybajom 4,402 D3
Nagyecsed 8,225 G3
Nagyhalász 6,437 F2
Nagykálló 11,282 F3
Nagykanizsa 48,494 D3
Nagykáta 11,922 E3
Nagykőrös 27,900 E3
Nagyszénás 7,124 F3
Nyírábrány 4,509 G3
Nyíradony 7,146 G3

Szarvas 20,598
Szécsény 5,690
Százhalombatta 13,963
Szeged 171,342
Szeghalom 9,736
Szegvár 6,395
Székesfehérvár 103,197
Szekszárd 34,592
Szendrő 4,098
Szentendre 16,844
Szentes 35,326
Szentgotthárd 5,837
Szentlőrinc 3,926
Szerencs 8,612
Szigetvár 12,114
Szikszó 6,419
Szil 2,073
Szolnok 75,203
Szombathely 82,830
Tab 3,922
Tamási 7,602
Tápiószele 5,575
Tapolca 17,161
Tarpa 3,436
Tata 24,114
Tatabánya 75,942
Tét 4,441
Tiszacsege 6,263
Tiszaföldvár 12,560
Tiszafüred 12,259
Tiszakécske 12,378
Tiszalök 6,230
Tiszavasvári 13,292
Tokaj 4,845
Tolna 8,997
Tompa 5,365
Törökszentmiklós 25,551
Tótkomlós 8,803
Tura 8,235
Túrkeve 11,393
Újfehértó 14,412
Újpest 80,384
Újszász 7,098
Vác 34,837
Vál 2,488
Vámospércs 5,213
Várpalota 28,293
Vásárosnamény 8,637
Vasvár 4,275
Vecsés 19,193

Agriculture, Industry and Resources

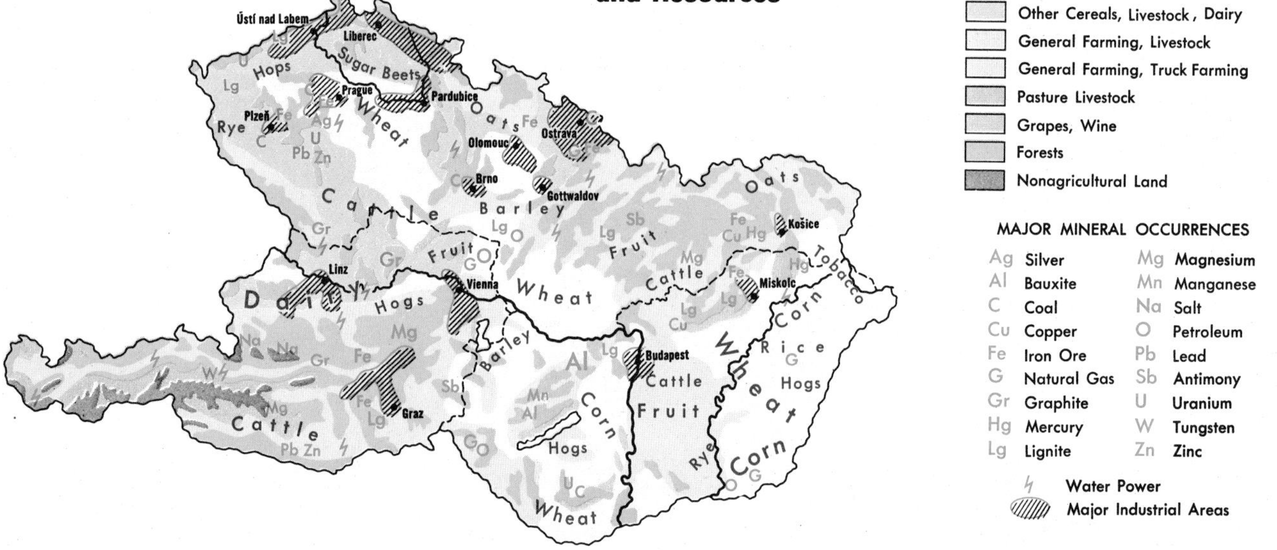

Ústí nad Labem
Liberec
Hops
Sugar Beets
Prague
Pardubice
Plzeň
Rye
Wheat
Oats
Ostrava
Olomouc
Brno
Gottwaldov
Cattle
Barley
Oats
Košice
Fruit
Linz
Vienna
Dairy
Hogs
Wheat
Cattle
Miskolc
Tobacco
Corn
Rice
Barley
Budapest
Cattle
Fruit
Hogs
Graz
Cattle
Corn
Hogs
Wheat
Rye
Corn
Wheat
DOMINANT LAND USE
Cereals (chiefly wheat, corn)
Other Cereals, Livestock, Dairy
General Farming, Livestock
General Farming, Truck Farming
Pasture Livestock
Grapes, Wine
Forests
Nonagricultural Land
MAJOR MINERAL OCCURRENCES
Ag Silver
Al Bauxite
C Coal
Cu Copper
Fe Iron Ore
G Natural Gas
Gr Graphite
Hg Mercury
Lg Lignite
Mg Magnesium
Mn Manganese
Na Salt
O Petroleum
Pb Lead
Sb Antimony
U Uranium
W Tungsten
Zn Zinc
Water Power
Major Industrial Areas

Lidice C1
Lipník nad Bečvou 7,358 D2
Liptovský Mikuláš 19,400 E2
Litoměřice 19,700 C1
Litomyšl 8,112 D2
Litovel 5,805 D2
Litvínov 23,300 B1
Lomnice C2
Louny 15,200 B1
Lovosice 9,323 C1
L'ubica F2
Lučenec 23,300 E2
Lysá nad Labem 9,920 C1
Malacky 13,200 D2
Mariánské Lázně 14,600 B2
Martin 47,800 E2
Medzilaborce F2
Mělník 17,800 C1
Michalovce 23,600 G2
Mikulov 6,267 D2
Milevsko 7,091 C2
Mimoň 6,773 C1
Mladá Boleslav 36,900 C1
Mladá Vožice C2
Mnichovo Hradiště 5,239 C1
Modra 7,219 D2
Modrý Kameň 6,200 E2
Mohelnice 6,050 D2
Moldava nad Bodvou 5,397 F2
Moravská Třebová 9,052 D2
Moravské Budějovice 5,576 D2
Most 59,400 B1
Myjava 6,657 D2
Náchod 19,300 D1
Námestovo E2
Neded D2
Nejdek 8,187 B1
Nepomuk B2
Nesvady 5,453 E3
Netolice C2
Nitra 50,000 E2
Nová Baňa 6,218 E2
Nová Bystrica E2
Nová Bystřice C2
Nové Hrady C2
Nové Město na Moravě 6,581 D2

Revúca 5,901 F2
Říčany u Prahy 8,407 C2
Rimavská Sobota 5,800 E2
Rokycany 12,800 B2
Rokytnice nad Jizerou C1
Rosice D2
Roudnice nad Labem 11,800 C1
Rožňava 12,400 F2
Rožnov pod
Radhoštěm 11,600 E2
Rumburk C1
Ružomberok 22,600 E2
Rychnov nad Kněžnou 7,500 D1
Rýmařov 7,522 D2
Sabinov 5,473 F2
Šafárikovo F2
Šahy 5,049 E2
Šal'a 15,200 D2
Samorín 8,287 D2
Sečovce 5,744 F2
Sedlčany C2
Semily 8,200 C1
Senec 8,544 D2
Senica 12,300 D2
Sered' 12,500 D2
Skalica 11,100 D2
Skuteč D2
Sládečkovce 5,598 D2
Slaný 13,200 C1
Slavkov D2
Snina 10,900 G2
Soběslav 6,140 C2
Sobotka C1
Sobrance G2
Sokolov 23,900 B1
Spišská Belá F2
Spišská Nová Ves 26,100 F2
Stará L'ubovňa 5,800 F2
Staré Město 6,293 D2
Šternberk 13,700 D2
Stod B2
Strakonice 19,000 B2
Strážnice 5,482 D2
Stříbro B2
Stropkov 5,645 F2
Studénka 9,744 D2

Vráble E2
Vracov D2
Vranov nad Teplou 14,700 F2
Vrbno pod Pradědem 5,594 D1
Vrbovce D1
Vrbové D2
Vrchlabí 11,700 C1
Vrútky 5,756 E2
Vsetín 24,100 D2
Vyškov 15,100 D2
Vysoké Mýto 8,830 D2
Vysoké Tatry F2
Vyšší Brod C2
Zábřeh 11,300 D2
Žamberk 5,040 D1
Žatec 17,400 B1
Zázrivá E2
Zbiroh B2
Zborov F2
Žd'ár nad Sázavou 17,800 C2
Želiezovce 5,478 E2
Žiar nad Hronom 14,800 E2
Židlochovice D2
Žilina 56,000 E2
Zlaté Moravce 10,300 E2
Zlín (Gottwaldov) 84,300 D2
Žlutice B1
Znojmo 28,500 D2
Zvolen 29,000 E2

OTHER FEATURES

Berounka (riv.) C2
Beskids, East (mts.) F1
Beskids, West (mts.) E2
Bohemian (for.) B2
Bohemian-Moravian Heights
(hills) C2
Danube (riv.) C2
Dunajec (riv.) F2
Dyje (riv.) D2
Erzgebirge (mts.) B1
Gerlachovka (mt.) E2
Hornád (riv.) F2
Hron (riv.) E2
Ipel' (riv.) E2

Veszprém 386,740 D3
Zala 316,610 D3

CITIES and TOWNS

Aba 4,271 E3
Abádszalók 6,386 F3
Abaújszántó 4,209 F2
Abony 15,624 E3
Ács 8,423 E3
Ajka 29,601 D3
Albertirsa 11,252 E3
Alsózsolca 5,045 F2
Arló 4,203 F2
Aszód 6,218 E3
Bácsalmás 9,025 E3
Badacsonytomaj 2,933 D3
Baja 38,456 E3
Baktalórántháza 3,736 G2
Balassagyarmat 18,534 E2
Balatonfüred 12,599 D3
Balkány 7,667 G3
Balmazújváros 17,371 F3
Barcs 11,448 D4
Bátaszék 7,274 E3
Battonya 9,324 F3
Békés 22,287 F3
Békéscsaba 67,266 F3
Berettyóújfalu 16,406 F3
Berzence 3,406 D3
Bicske 10,720 E3
Biharkeresztes 4,788 F3
Biharnagybajom 4,093 F3
Böhönye 3,215 D3
Bonyhád 14,841 E3
Budafok 40,623 E3
Budaörs 13,958 E3
Budakeszi 10,429 E3
Budapest (cap.) 2,060,170 E3
Bugak 4,989 E3
Cegléd 40,567 E3
Celldömölk 12,533 D3
Cigánd 4,767 F2
Csabrendek 3,045 D3
Csákvár 5,238 E3
Csanádpalota 4,642 F3

Hajdúnánás 18,146 F3
Hajdúsámson 7,492 F3
Hajdúszoboszló 23,374 F3
Hajós 5,113 E3
Hatvan 24,790 E3
Heves 10,943 F3
Hódmezővásárhely 54,481 F3
Hőgyész 3,534 E3
Ibrány 7,037 F2
Izsák 7,686 E3
Izsófalva 6,816 F2
Jánoshalma 12,534 E3
Jánosháza 3,274 D3
Jászapáti 10,424 E3
Jászárokszállás 10,139 E3
Jászberény 31,347 E3
Jászfényszaru 6,869 E3
Jászkarajenő 4,101 E3
Jászkisér 6,816 F3
Jászladány 7,823 F3
Kaba 6,654 F2
Kalocsa 18,613 E3
Kaposvár 72,330 D3
Kapuvár 11,243 D3
Karád 2,754 D3
Karcag 25,264 F3
Kazincbarcika 37,481 F2
Kecel 10,493 E3
Kecskemét 91,929 E3
Kemecse 4,583 F2
Keszthely 21,671 D3
Kétegyháza 4,728 F3
Kisbér 4,562 D3
Kiskőrös 15,499 E3
Kiskunfélegyháza 35,339 E3
Kiskunhalas 30,552 E3
Kiskunmajsa 14,439 E3
Kispest 65,106 E3
Kistelek 8,544 E3
Kisterenye 6,844 E2
Kisújszállás 13,699 F3
Kisvárda 17,828 G2
Komádi 8,765 F3
Komárom 19,955 E3
Komló 30,301 E3
Kondoros 7,319 F3

Nyírbátor 13,388 G3
Nyíregyháza 108,156 F3
Nyírmada 4,744 F2
Örkény 5,013 E3
Orosháza 36,243 F3
Oroszlány 20,604 E3
Ózd 48,521 F2
Pacsa 1,984 D3
Paks 19,514 E3
Pannonhalma 3,731 D3
Pápa 32,202 D3
Pásztó 7,962 E3
Pécs 168,788 E3
Pécsvárad 3,672 E3
Pétervására 2,753 F3
Pilis 9,055 E3
Pilisvörösvár 10,217 E3
Polgár 9,429 F3
Polgárdi 5,767 E3
Püspökladány 15,730 F3
Pusztaszabolcs 5,794 E3
Putnok 7,103 F2
Ráckeve 7,534 E3
Rajka 2,448 D3
Rakamaz 5,407 F2
Rákospalota 60,983 E3
Répcelak 1,997 D3
Ricse 2,992 G2
Sajószentpéter 13,992 F2
Salgótarján 49,320 E2
Sándorfalva 5,949 F3
Sárbogárd 11,178 E3
Sarkad 11,937 F3
Sárospatak 15,316 F2
Sárvár 15,126 D3
Sátoraljaújhely 19,252 F2
Sellye 2,804 D4
Siklós 10,567 E4
Simontornya 4,892 E3
Siófok 20,084 E3
Solt 6,911 E3
Soltvadkert 7,934 E3
Sopron 53,930 D3
Sükösd 4,430 E3
Sümeg 6,229 D3
Szabadszállás 8,223 E3

Velence 3,463
Vémend 2,293
Verpelét 4,622
Veszprém 54,898
Vésztő 9,815
Villány 2,764
Záhony 3,049
Zalaegerszeg 39,671
Zalaszentgrót 5,346
Zirc 5,980

OTHER FEATURES

Bakony (mts.)
Balaton (lake)
Berettyó (riv.)
Bükk (mts.)
Csepelsziget (isl.)
Danube (riv.)
Dráva (riv.)
Duna (Danube) (riv.)
Fertő tó (Neusiedler See)
(lake)
Great Alföld (plain)
Hernád (riv.)
Kapos (riv.)
Kékes (mt.)
Körös (riv.)
Maros (riv.)
Mátra (mts.)
Mecsek (mts.)
Mura (riv.)
Rába (riv.)
Sajó (riv.)
Sárviz csatorna (canal)
Sió csatorna (canal)
Szentendreisziget (isl.)
Tisza (riv.)
Zala (riv.)

*City and suburbs.
†Population of Austrian cities are communes.

YUGOSLAVIA

AREA 98,766 sq. mi. (255,804 sq. km.)
POPULATION 22,471,000
CAPITAL Belgrade
LARGEST CITY Belgrade
HIGHEST POINT Triglav 9,393 ft. (2,863 m.)
MONETARY UNIT Yugoslav dinar
MAJOR LANGUAGES Serbo-Croatian, Slovenian, Macedonian, Montenegrin, Albanian
MAJOR RELIGIONS Eastern Orthodoxy, Roman Catholicism, Islam

ALBANIA

AREA 11,100 sq. mi. (28,749 sq. km.)
POPULATION 2,590,600
CAPITAL Tiranë
LARGEST CITY Tiranë
HIGHEST POINT Korab 9,026 ft. (2,751 m.)
MONETARY UNIT lek
MAJOR LANGUAGE Albanian
MAJOR RELIGIONS Islam, Eastern Orthodoxy, Roman Catholicism

ROMANIA

AREA 91,699 sq. mi. (237,500 sq. km.)
POPULATION 22,048,305
CAPITAL Bucharest
LARGEST CITY Bucharest
HIGHEST POINT Moldoveanul 8,343 ft. (2,543 m.)
MONETARY UNIT leu
MAJOR LANGUAGES Romanian, Hungarian
MAJOR RELIGION Eastern Orthodoxy

BULGARIA

AREA 42,823 sq. mi. (110,912 sq. km.)
POPULATION 8,862,000
CAPITAL Sofia
LARGEST CITY Sofia
HIGHEST POINT Musala 9,597 ft. (2,925 m.)
MONETARY UNIT lev
MAJOR LANGUAGE Bulgarian
MAJOR RELIGION Eastern Orthodoxy

GREECE

AREA 50,944 sq. mi. (131,945 sq. km.)
POPULATION 9,599,000
CAPITAL Athens
LARGEST CITY Athens
HIGHEST POINT Olympus 9,570 ft. (2,917 m.)
MONETARY UNIT drachma
MAJOR LANGUAGE Greek
MAJOR RELIGION Eastern (Greek) Orthodoxy

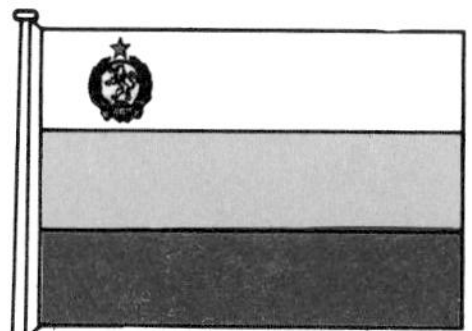

BULGARIA

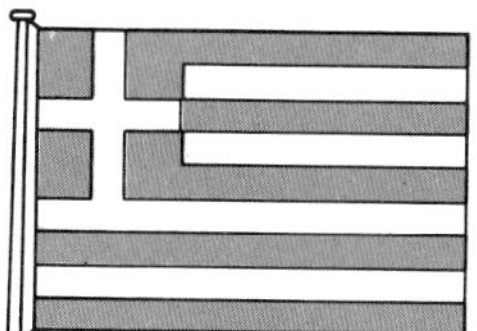

GREECE

YUGOSLAVIA

ALBANIA

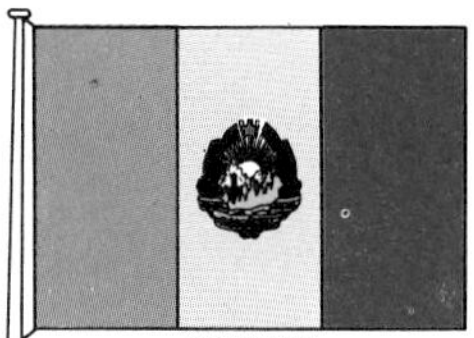

ROMANIA

Agriculture, Industry and Resources

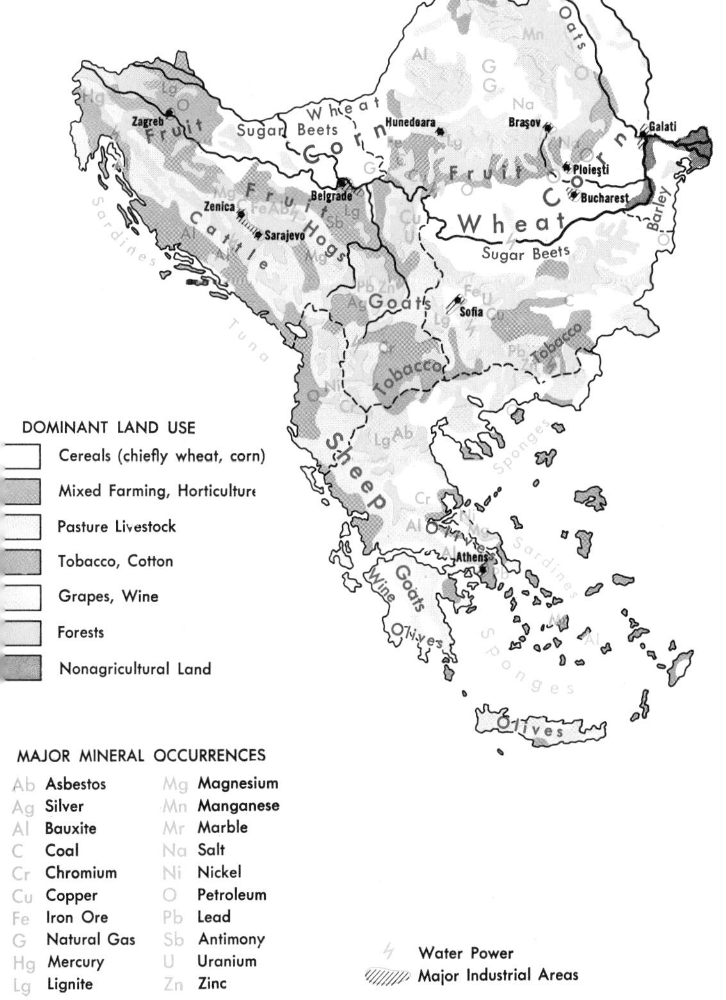
Zagreb
Belgrade
Hunedoara
Braşov
Galati
Ploieşti
Bucharest
Zenica
Sarajevo
Sofia
Athens
Wheat
Corn
Fruit
Sugar Beets
Oats
Barley
Cattle
Hogs
Goats
Sheep
Tobacco
Wine
Olives
Sardines
Tuna
Sponges
DOMINANT LAND USE
Cereals (chiefly wheat, corn)
Mixed Farming, Horticulture
Pasture Livestock
Tobacco, Cotton
Grapes, Wine
Forests
Nonagricultural Land
MAJOR MINERAL OCCURRENCES
Ab Asbestos
Ag Silver
Al Bauxite
C Coal
Cr Chromium
Cu Copper
Fe Iron Ore
G Natural Gas
Hg Mercury
Lg Lignite
Mg Magnesium
Mn Manganese
Mr Marble
Na Salt
Ni Nickel
O Petroleum
Pb Lead
Sb Antimony
U Uranium
Zn Zinc
Water Power
Major Industrial Areas

ALBANIA

CITIES and TOWNS

Berat 25,700 D5
Çorovodë E5
Burrel D5
Delvinë 6,000 D6
Durrës (Durazzo) 53,800 D5
Elbasan 41,700 E5
Ersekë E5
Fier 23,000 D5
Gjirokastër 17,100 D5
Kavajë 18,700 D5
Korçë 47,300 E5
Krujë 7,900 D5
Kuçovë (Stalin) 14,000 D5
Kukës 6,100 E4
Leskovik E5
Lezhë D5
Lushnje 18,900 D5
Memaliaj D5
Peqin D5
Përmet E5
Peshkopi 6,600 F5
Pogradec 10,100 E5
Pukë E4
Sarandë 8,700 E6
Shëngjin D5
Shijak 6,200 D5
Shkodër 55,300 D5
Stalin 14,000 D5
Tepelenë D5
Tiranë (Tirana) (cap.) 171,300 E5
Vlorë 50,000 D5

OTHER FEATURES

Adriatic (sea) B4
Drin (riv.) E4
Korab (mt.) E5
Ohrid (lake) E5
Otranto (str.) D5
Prespa (lake) E5
Sazan (isl.) D5
Scutari (lake) D4
Vijosë (riv.) D5

BULGARIA

CITIES and TOWNS

Akhtopol 938 H4
Alfatar 3,249 H4
Ardino 5,080 G5
Asenovgrad 43,049 G5
Aytos 20,967 H4
Balchik 11,070 H4
Bansko 10,011 F5
Belogradchik 6,892 F4
Berkovitsa 16,253 F4
Blagoevgrad 50,043 F5
Botevgrad 17,789 F4
Bregovo 5,567 F3
Breznik 4,699 F4
Burgas 144,449 H4
Byala 10,564 G4
Byala Slatina 15,788 F4
Chirpan 20,595 G4
Devin 7,120 G5
Dimitrovgrad 45,596 G4
Dobrich (Tolbukhin) 86,184 H4
Dryanovo 9,804 G4
Elena 7,008 G4
Elin Pelin 5,499 F4
Elkhovo 12,397 H4
Gabrovo 75,034 G4
General-Toshevo 8,928 H4
Godech 5,225 F4
Gorna Oryakhovitsa 34,157 G4
Gotse Delchev 17,015 F5
Grudovo 9,871 H4
Ikhtiman 11,482 F4
Isperikh 10,500 H4
Ivaylovgrad 3,900 H5
Karapelit H4
Karlovo 25,472 G4
Karnobat 21,480 H4
Kavarna 10,872 J4
Kazanlŭk 53,607 G4
Kharmanli 19,240 H5
Khaskovo 75,031 G5
Kotel 8,229 H4
Krumovgrad 5,211 G5
Kubrat 9,826 H4
Kula 5,667 F4
Kŭrdzhali 47,757 G5
Kyustendil 48,239 F4
Lom 30,538 F4
Lovech 43,858 G4
Lukovit 10,400 G4
Malko Tŭrnovo 4,233 H4
Maritsa 8,664 H4
Michurin 4,434 H4
Mikhaylovgrad 40,064 F4
Momchilgrad 8,185 G5
Nesebŭr 6,768 H4
Nikopol 5,563 G4
Nova Zagora 21,872 H4
Novi Pazar 15,751 H4
Omurtag 9,067 H4
Oryakhovo 14,012 F4
Panagyurishte 20,649 F4
Pazardzhik 65,577 G4
Pernik 87,432 F4
Peshtera 16,882 G4
Petrich 24,381 F5
Pirdop 8,248 G4
Pleven 107,567 G4
Plovdiv 300,242 G4
Pomorie 11,960 H4
Popina H3
Popovo 19,428 H4
Provadiya 15,143 H4
Radomir 10,436 F4
Razgrad 42,486 H4
Răzlog 13,690 F5
Rositsa H4
Ruse 160,351 H4
Samokov 25,763 F4
Sandanski 19,003 F5
Sevlievo 24,421 G4
Shabla 4,471 J4
Shumen 83,525 H4
Silistra 58,270 H3
Simeonovgrad (Maritsa) 8,664 H4
Sliven 90,137 H4
Smolyan 29,032 G5
Smyadovo 3,020 H4
Sofia (cap.) 965,728 F4
Sozopol 3,877 H4
Stanke Dimitrov 42,034 F4
Stara Zagora 122,200 G4
Svilengrad 15,150 G5
Svishtov 29,412 G4
Teteven 12,555 G4
Tolbukhin 86,184 H4
Topolovgrad 7,230 H4
Troyan 23,692 G4
Trŭn 3,435 F4
Tŭrgovishte 38,796 H4
Tutrakan 11,447 H4
Varna 251,654 J4
Veliko Tŭrnovo 56,497 G4
Vidin 63,030 F4
Vratsa 61,265 F4
Yambol 75,861 H4
Zimnitsa H4
Zlatograd 7,732 G5

OTHER FEATURES

Balkan (mts.) G4
Black (sea) J4
Danube (riv.) H4
Dunav (Danube) (riv.) H4
Emine (cape) J4
Iskŭr (riv.) G4
Kaliakra (cape) J4
Maritsa (riv.) G4
Mesta (riv.) F5
Midzhur (mt.) F4
Musala (mt.) F4
Osŭm (riv.) G4
Rhodope (mts.) G5
Rujen (mt.) F4
Struma (riv.) F5
Timok (riv.) F3
Tundzha (riv.) G4
Vit (riv.) G4

GREECE

REGIONS

Aegean Islands 417,813 G6
Athens, Greater 2,566,775 F7
Áyion Óros (aut. dist.) 1,732 G5
Central Greece and Euboea 966,543 F6
Crete 456,642 G8
Epirus 310,334 E6
Ionian Islands 184,443 D6
Macedonia 1,888,952 E5
Pelopónnisos 986,912 F7
Thessaly 659,913 F6
Thrace 329,582 G5

CITIES and TOWNS

Agrínion 30,973 E6
Alyina 5,704 F7
Alyion 18,829 F6
Alexandroúpolis 22,995 H5
Alivérion 4,414 G6
Almirós 5,680 F6
Amaliás 14,177 E7
Amfilokhía 4,668 E6
Ámfissa 6,605 F6
Ándissa 1,762 H6
Andravídha 3,046 E6
Ándros 1,827 G7
Áno Viánnos 1,431 G8
Anóyia 2,750 G8
Ardhéa 3,555 F5
Areópolis 674 F7
Argalastí 1,621 F6
Árgos 18,890 F7
Argostólion 7,060 E6
Arkhángelos 3,016 J7
Arnaia 2,424 F5
Árta 19,498 E6
Astipálaia 787 H7
Atalándi 4,581 F6
Athens (cap.) 867,023 F7
Athens* 2,566,775 F7
Ayiá 3,241 F6
Áyios Kírikos 1,083 H7
Áyios Matthaíos 1,596 D6
Áyios Nikólaos 5,002 G8
Candia (Iráklion) 77,506 G8
Canea (Khaniá) 40,564 G8
Corinth 20,773 F7
Delfí 1,185 F6
Delvinákion 1,067 E6
Dhidhimótikhon 8,388 H5
Dhíkaia 1,222 H5
Dhimitsána 996 F7
Dhomokós 1,991 F6
Dráma 29,692 F5
Édhessa 13,967 F5
Elassón 7,200 F6
Elevtheroúpolis 4,888 G5
Ermoúpolis 13,502 G7
Fársala 6,967 F6
Filiátes 2,579 E6
Filiatrá 5,919 E7
Filippiás 3,248 E6
Flórina 11,164 E5
Gargaliánoi 5,888 E7
Grevená 8,106 E5
Ídhra 2,381 F7
Ierápetra 7,055 G8
Igoumenítsa 4,109 E6
Ioánnina 40,130 E6
Íos 1,270 G7
Iráklion 77,506 G8
Istiaía 4,059 F6
Itháki 2,293 E6
Kalámai 39,133 F7
Kalampáka 5,453 E6
Kalávrita 1,948 F6
Kálimnos 6,492 H7
Kándanos 403 F8
Kardhítsa 25,685 E6
Kariá 1,350 E6
Kariaí 301 G5
Káristos 3,550 G6
Kárpathos 1,363 H8
Karpenísion 4,414 E6
Kastéllion (Kíssamos) 2,996 F8
Kastéllion 1,152 G8
Kastoría 15,407 E5
Katákolon 690 E7
Kateríni 28,808 F5
Kaválla 46,234 G5
Kéa 693 G7
Kérkira 28,630 D6
Khalkís 36,300 F6
Khaniá 40,564 G8
Khíos 24,084 G6
Khóra Sfakíon 246 G8
Kiáton 7,392 F6
Kilkís 10,538 F5
Kími 2,772 F6
Kiparissía 3,882 E7
Kíssamos 2,996 G8
Kíthira 349 F7
Komotiní 28,896 G5
Kónitsa 3,150 E5
Koropí 9,367 G7
Kos 7,828 H7
Kozáni 23,240 F5
Kranídhion 3,657 F7
Lagkadia 1,350 E7
Lamía 37,872 F6
Langadhás 6,707 F5
Langádhia F7
Lárisa 72,336 F6
Lávrion 8,283 G7
Leonídhion 3,181 F7
Levádhia 15,445 F6
Levkás 6,818 E6
Limenária 1,507 G5

(continued on following page)

(continued)

Topography

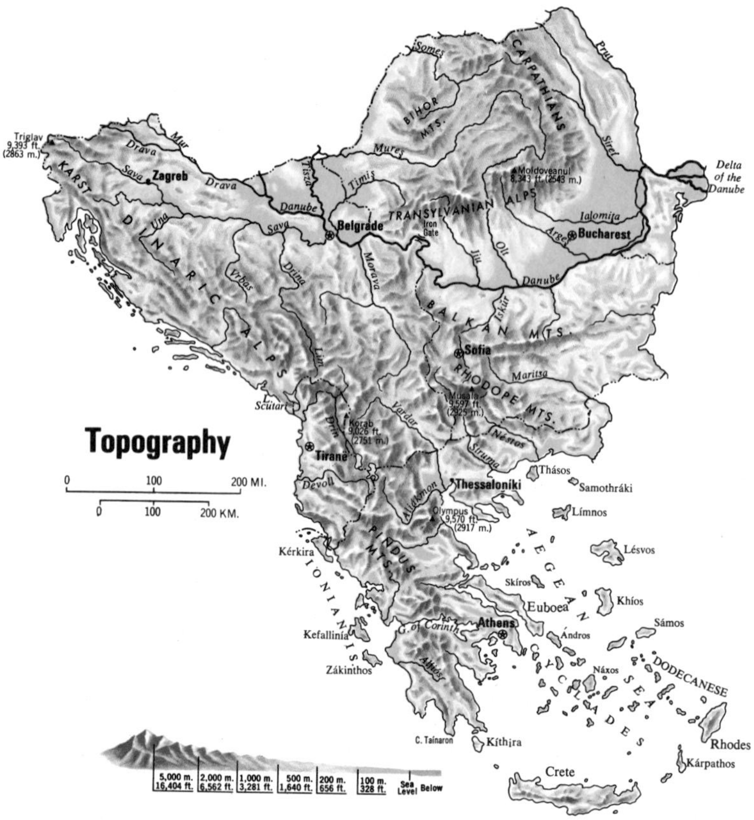

Límni 2,394 F6
Líndos 700 J7
Litókhoron 5,561 F5
Lixoúrion 3,364 E6
Loutrá Aidhipsoú 2,195 F6
Marathón 1,976 G6
Megalópolis 3,357 E7
Mégara 17,294 F6
Meligalá 1,724 F7
Mesolóngion 11,614 E6
Messíni 6,625 E7
Métsovon 2,823 E6
Mikínai 390 F7
Mílos 850 G7
Mírina 3,982 G6
Míthimna 1,414 G6
Mitilíni 23,426 H6
Moírai 2,948 G8
Moláoi 2,484 F7
Monólithos 247 H7
Moúdhros 1,024 G6
Náousa 17,375 F5
Návpaktos 8,170 F6
Návplion 9,281 F7
Náxos 2,892 G7
Neápolis 3,070 F7
Neméa 4,356 F7
Néon Karlóvasi 4,401 H7
Nestórion 1,143 E5
Nigríta 7,301 F5
Oinóï 188 F6
Orestías 10,727 H5
Paramithía 2,747 E6
Pátrai 111,607 E6
Pérdika 1,198 E6
Péta 2,116 E6
Pílos 2,258 E7
Piraiévs (Piraeus) 187,362 F7
Pírgos 20,599 E7
Piryí 1,455 G6
Píthion 1,047 H5
Plomárion 4,353 H6
Políkastron 5,279 F5
Políkhnitos 4,152 G6
Políyiros 3,707 F5
Póros 4,051 F7
Préveza 11,439 E6
Psakhná 4,650 F6
Psári 622 E7
Ptolemaís 16,588 E5
Réthimnon 14,969 G8
Rhodes (Ródhos) 32,092 J7
Salamís 18,256 F6
Salonika
(Thessaloníki) 345,799 F5
Sámi 957 E6
Sámos 5,146 H7
Samothráki 508 G5
Sápai 2,456 G5
Sérrai 39,897 F5
Sérvia 3,834 F5
Siátista 4,852 E5
Sidhirókastron 6,363 F5
Sími 2,344 H7
Sitía 6,167 H8
Skíathos 3,707 F6
Skíros 1,925 G6
Skópelos 2,545 F6
Souflíon 5,637 H5
Sparta 10,549 F7
Spétsai 3,427 F7
Spíli 789 G8
Stavrós 1,700 F5
Stílis 4,427 F6
Thásos 2,052 G5
Thessaloníki 345,799 F5
Thessaloníki* 482,361 F5
Thíra 1,322 G7
Thívai 15,971 F6
Timbákion 3,229 G8
Tínos 3,423 G7
Tírnavos 10,451 F6
Tríkkala 34,794 E6
Trípolis 20,209 F7
Vámos 652 F8
Vartholomión 3,015 E7
Vathí 2,491 H7
Velvendós 4,063 F5
Vérroia 29,528 F5
Vólos 51,290 F6
Vónitsa 3,324 E6
Vrondádhes 4,253 G6
Xánthi 24,867 G5
Yerolimín 73 F7
Yiannitsá 18,151 F5
Yíthion 4,915 F7
Zákinthos 9,339 E7
Zante (Zákinthos) 9,339 E7

OTHER FEATURES

Aegean (sea) G6
Akrítas (cape) E7
Aktí (pen.) G5
Amorgós (isl.) G7
Anáfi (isl.) G7
Andikíthira (isl.) F8
Ándros (isl.) G7
Árda (riv.) G5
Argolís (gulf) F7
Astipálaia (isl.) H7
Áthos (mt.) G5
Áyios Evstrátios
(isl.) G6
Áyios Yeóryios (cape) G5
Cephalonia (Kefallinía)
(isl.) E6
Corfu (Kérkira) (isl.) D6
Corinth (gulf) F6
Crete (isl.) G8
Crete (sea) G7
Cyclades (isls.) G7
Día (isl.) G8
Dodecanese (isls.) H8
Euboea (Évvoia)
(isl.) G6
Évros (riv.) H5
Évvoia (isl.) G6
Gávdhos (isl.) F8
Ídhi (mt.) G8
Ikaría (isl.) G7
Ionian (sea) D7
Íos (isl.) G7
Itháki (Ithaca) (isl.) E6
Kafirévs (cape) G6
Kálimnos (isl.) H7
Kárpathos (isl.) H8
Kásos (isl.) H8
Kassándra (pen.) F6
Kéa (isl.) G7
Kefallinía (isl.) E6
Kérkira (isl.) D6
Khálki (isl.) H7
Khaniá (gulf) G8
Khíos (isl.) G6
Kímolos (isl.) G7
Kiparissía (gulf) E7
Kíthira (isl.) F7
Kíthnos (isl.) G7
Kos (isl.) H7
Kriós (cape) F8
Kríti (Crete) (isl.) G8
Lakonía (gulf) F7
Léros (isl.) H7
Lésvos (isl.) G6
Levítha (isl.) H7
Levkás (isl.) E6
Límnos (isl.) G6
Maléa (cape) F7
Matapan (Taínaron) (cape) F7
Merabéllou (gulf) H8
Mesará (gulf) G8
Messíni (gulf) E7
Míkonos (isl.) G7
Mílos (isl.) G7
Mirtóön (sea) F7
Náxos (isl.) G7
Néstos (riv.) G5
Nísiros (isl.) H7
Northern Sporades (isls.) F6
Olympia (isls.) E7
Olympus (mt.) F5
Parnassus (mt.) F6
Páros (isl.) G7
Pátmos (isl.) H7
Paxoí (isl.) D6
Pindus (mts.) E6
Piniós (riv.) E6
Prespa (lake) E5
Psará (isl.) G6
Psevdhókavos (cape) G6
Rhodes (isl.) H7
Rhodope (mts.) G5
Salonika (Thermaic) (gulf) F6
Sámos (isl.) H7
Samothráki (isl.) G5
Saría (isl.) H8
Saronic (gulf) F7
Sérifos (isl.) G7
Sídheros (cape) H8
Sífnos (isl.) G7
Sími (isl.) H7
Síros (isl.) G7
Sithoniá (pen.) F5
Skíros (isl.) G6
Spátha (cape) F8
Strimón (gulf) G5
Strofádhes (isls.) E7
Taínaron (cape) F7
Thásos (isl.) G5
Thermaic (gulf) F6
Thíra (isl.) G7
Tílos (isl.) H7
Tínos (isl.) G7
Toronaic (gulf) F5
Vardar (riv.) E5
Voïvís (lake) F6
Vólvi (lake) F5
Voúxa (cape) F8
Zákinthos (Zante)
(isl.) E7

ROMANIA

CITIES and TOWNS

Aiud 25,173 F2
Alba Iulia 44,552 F2
Alexandria 38,296 G3
Anina 11,594 E3
Arad 161,568 E2
Babadag 8,423 J3
Bacău 131,413 H2
Baia de Aramă 5,065 F3
Baia Mare 112,893 F2
Băile Herculane 4,606 F3
Băilești 21,246 F3
Balș 16,091 G3
Beiuș 9,992 F2
Berești Tîrg H2
Bicaz 9,490 G2
Bîrlad 59,059 H2
Bistrița 47,562 G2
Bivolari H2
Blaj 21,678 F2
Borșa 25,287 G2
Botoșani 69,881 H2
Brad 18,391 F2
Brăila 203,983 H3
Brașov 259,108 G3
Bucharest (București)
(cap.) 1,832,015 G3
Bucharest* 1,960,097 G3
Buhuși 20,204 H2
Buzău 106,738 H3
Buziaș 8,310 E3
Calafat 16,421 F3
Călărași 58,960 H3
Caracal 31,159 G3
Caransebeș 27,429 F3
Carei 24,496 F2
Cernavodă 14,686 J3
Chișineu Criș 9,344 E2
Cîmpeni 7,722 F2
Cîmpia Turzii 23,745 F2
Cîmpina 33,259 H3
Cîmpulung 33,448 G3
Cîmpulung Moldovenesc 19,270 G2
Cisnădie 21,114 G3
Cluj-Napoca 274,095 F2
Cogealac J3
Comanești 18,177 H2
Constanța 279,308 J3
Corabia 20,454 G4
Costești 10,446 G3
Craiova 220,893 F3
Cujmir F3
Curtea de Argeș 23,555 G3
Dăbuleni F4
Dăeni J3
Darabani 12,207 H1
Dej 35,396 F2
Deta 6,956 E3
Deva 68,290 F3
Dorohoi 23,121 H2
Drăgănești Olt 11,606 G3
Drăgășani 16,290 F3
Drobeta-Turnu Severin 80,114 F3
Făgăraș 34,762 G3
Fălciu J2
Fălticeni 22,463 H2
Făurei 3,620 H3
Fetești 28,730 H3
Focșani 62,275 H3
Foltești H3
Găești 13,384 G3
Galați 252,884 H3
Gheorghe Gheorghiu-Dej 41,297 H2
Gheorghieni 20,592 G2
Gherla 19,303 G2
Giurgiu 53,241 G3
Hațeg 9,706 F3
Hîrlău 8,135 H2
Hîrșova 8,434 J3
Huedin 8,557 F2
Hunedoara 83,159 F3
Huși 24,329 J2
Iași 262,493 H2
Ineu 10,414 E2
Isaccea 5,283 J3
Jibou F2
Jimbolia 15,325 E3
Lipova 12,427 E2
Luduș 15,771 G2
Lugoj 48,558 F3
Lupeni 28,251 F3
Mangalia 27,263 J4
Medgidia 43,691 J3
Mediaș 68,442 G2
Miercurea Ciuc 38,097 G2
Mizil 14,294 H3
Mociu G2
Moinești 21,015 H2
Moldova Nouă 18,498 E3
Moreni 17,743 G3
Nădlac 8,407 E2
Năsăud 8,646 G2
Negrești 7,435 H2
Ocna Mureș 16,381 G2
Odobești 8,440 H3
Odorheiu Secuiesc 33,392 G2
Oltenița 25,536 H3
Oradea 175,400 E2
Orăștie 18,769 F3
Oravița 13,628 E3
Orșova 14,873 F3
Panciu 7,772 H3
Pașcani 26,937 H2
Pătulele F3
Pechea H3
Pecica E2
Periam E2
Petrila 25,087 F3
Petroșeni 42,316 F3
Piatra Neamț 84,192 G2
Pincota 7,494 E2
Pitești 125,029 G3
Plenița F3
Ploiești 207,009 H3
Poenari Burchi G3
Poiana Mare F4
Pucioasa 14,056 G3
Rădăuți 24,222 G2
Reghin 31,948 G2
Reșița 90,698 E3
Rîmnicu Sărat 29,815 H3
Rîmnicu Vîlcea 75,070 G3
Roman 56,466 H2
Roșiori de Vede 28,832 G3
Săcele 29,391 G3
Salonta 19,698 E2
Satu Mare 108,152 F2
Săveni 7,913 H1
Sebeș 27,448 F3
Sebiș 6,401 F2
Segarcea 8,783 F3
Sfîntu Gheorghe 51,210 G3
Sfîntu Gheorghe J3
Sibiu 156,854 G3
Sighetu Marmației 38,879 F2
Sighișoara 32,296 G2
Șimleul Silvaniei 14,780 F2
Sinaia 14,215 G3
Sînnicolaul Mare 13,565 E2
Siret 6,677 G1
Slănic 8,017 G3
Slatina 54,954 G3
Slobozia 35,207 H3
Solca 4,835 G2
Sovata 10,745 G2
Ștefănești H2
Strehaia 11,431 F3
Suceava 66,857 G2
Sulina 5,240 J3
Tășnad 10,441 F2
Techirghiol 11,228 J3
Tecuci 37,928 H3
Timișoara 281,320 E3
Tinca F2
Tîrgoviște 71,533 G3
Tîrgu Cărbunești 7,536 F3
Tîrgu Frumos 6,428 H2
Tîrgu Jiu 70,629 F3
Tîrgu Mureș 129,284 G2
Tîrgu Neamț 15,756 G2
Tîrgu Ocna 12,960 H2
Tîrgu Secuiesc 18,265 H2
Tîrnăveni 27,799 F2
Toplița 14,347 G2
Tulcea 67,091 J3
Turda 57,972 F2
Turnu Măgurele 30,003 G4
Urlața 10,900 H3
Urziceni 13,500 H3
Vasile Roaită J3
Vaslui 44,134 H2
Vatra Dornei 16,748 G2
Videle 11,323 G3
Vișeul de Sus 20,697 F2
Viziru H3
Zalău 36,158 F2
Zărnești 23,378 G3
Zimnicea 15,111 G4

OTHER FEATURES

Argeș (riv.) G3
Bîrlad (riv.) H2
Black (sea) J4
Brăila (marshes) H3
Buzău (riv.) H3
Carpathian (mts.) G2
Crișul Alb (riv.) F2
Crișul Repede (riv.) F2
Danube (delta) J3
Danube (riv.) H4
Ialomița (marshes) J3
Ialomița (riv.) H3
Jijia (riv.) H2
Jiu (riv.) F3
Moldoveanul (mt.) G3
Mureș (riv.) E2
Olt (riv.) G3
Peleaga (mt.) F3
Pietrosul (mt.) G2
Prut (riv.) J2
Siret (riv.) H2
Someș (riv.) F2
Timiș (riv.) E3
Tîrnava Mare (riv.) G2
Transylvanian Alps (mts.) G3

YUGOSLAVIA

INTERNAL DIVISIONS

Bosnia and Hercegovina
(rep.) 3,710,965 C3
Croatia (rep.) 4,396,397 C3
Kosovo (aut. reg.) 1,240,919 E4
Macedonia (rep.) 1,623,598 E5
Montenegro (rep.) 527,207 D4
Serbia (rep.) 8,401,673 E3
Slovenia (rep.) 1,697,068 B2
Vojvodina (aut.
prov.) 1,953,980 D3

CITIES and TOWNS

Aleksinac 11,943 E4
Apatin 17,501 D3
Arendjelovac 15,659 E3
Bačka Topola 16,028 D3
Bakar B3
Banja Luka 85,786 C3
Bar 3,594 D4
Bečej 26,616 E3
Bela Crkva 11,137 E3
Belgrade (cap.) 727,945 E3
Beli Manastir 7,325 D3
Beograd (Belgrade)
(cap.) 727,945 E3
Berovo 5,053 F5
Bihać 24,155 B3
Bijeljina 24,888 D3
Bijelo Polje 9,298 D4
Bileća 4,083 D4
Biograd 3,595 B4
Bitola 64,467 E5
Bjelovar 21,019 C3
Blato 5,591 C4
Bled 4,710 A2
Bor 27,520 E3
Bosanska Dubica 9,191 C3
Bosanska Gradiška 9,742 C3
Bosanska Kostajnica 2,535 B3
Bosanska Krupa 8,947 C3
Bosanski Brod 10,113 D3
Bosanski Novi 9,861 C3
Bosanski Petrovac 4,113 C3
Bosanski Šamac 4,949 D3
Brčko 25,575 D3
Brežice 3,271 B3
Budva 2,483 D4
Bugojno 9,079 C3
Čačak 38,890 E4
Čakovec 11,766 C2
Čapljina 4,677 C4
Caribrod (Dimitrovgrad) 5,449 F4
Cazin 1,213 B3
Celje 30,827 B2
Cetinje 12,089 D4
Ćuprija 17,691 E4
Daruvar 8,478 C3
Debar 8,597 E5
Derventa 11,887 C3
Dimitrovgrad 5,449 F4
Djakovica 29,499 E4
Djakovo 15,833 D3
Doboj 18,073 C3
Donji Vakuf 4,928 C3
Drvar 6,237 C3
Dubrovnik 31,213 C4
Fiume (Rijeka) 128,883 B3
Foča 9,370 D4
Gacko 1,641 D4
Gevgelija 9,319 F5
Glamoč 2,627 C3
Gnjilane 21,359 E4
Gornji Milanovac 11,114 D3
Gornji Vakuf 2,429 C4
Gospić 8,238 B3
Gostivar 18,805 E5
Gračac 3,228 B3
Gračanica 9,302 D3
Gradačac 7,571 D3
Grubišno Polje 2,771 C3
Gusinje 2,616 D4
Herceg Novi 6,645 D4
Ivangrad 11,373 E4
Ivanjica 5,719 E4
Jajce 9,221 C3
Jesenice 16,163 A2
Kanjiža 11,348 D2
Karlovac 47,046 B3
Kavadarci 17,974 E5
Kičevo 14,189 E5
Kikinda 37,392 E3
Kladanj 3,255 D3
Ključ 3,466 C3
Knin 7,279 C3
Knjaževac 11,734 F4
Kočani 16,611 F5
Kočevje 7,277 B3
Kolašin 2,111 D4
Konjic 9,161 D4
Koper 16,683 A3
Koprivnica 16,398 C2
Kosovska Mitrovica 42,526 E4
Kostajnica 9,161 C3
Kotor 5,728 D4
Kragujevac 72,080 E3
Kraljevo 28,065 E4
Kranj 26,341 B2
Križevci 8,501 C2
Krk 1,500 B3
Krško 4,451 B3
Kruševac 29,902 E4
Kulen Vakuf 1,078 B3
Kumanovo 44,791 E4
Kutina 10,892 C3
Leskovac 46,050 E4
Livno 7,223 C4
Ljubinje 785 D4
Ljubljana 169,064 B3
Ljubuški 2,891 C4
Loznica 13,513 D3
Maglaj 5,869 D3
Makarska 6,589 C4
Maribor 94,976 B2
Modriča 7,406 D3
Mostar 47,821 D4
Murska Sobota 9,665 C2
Našice 5,836 C3
Negotin 11,325 F3
Nevesinje 3,077 D4
Nikšić 28,940 D4
Nin 1,782 B3
Niš 128,231 F4
Nova Gorizia A2
Nova Gradiška 11,765 C3
Novi 2,682 B3
Novi Pazar 28,696 E4
Novi Sad 143,591 D3
Novo Mesto 9,553 B3
Novska 5,168 C3
Ogulin 9,975 B3
Ohrid 26,352 E5
Omiš 3,515 C4
Opatija 9,238 A3
Osijek 94,989 D3
Pag 2,318 B3
Pančevo 53,979 E3
Paraćin 21,555 E4
Peć 41,783 E4
Petrinja 12,296 B3
Piran 5,485 A3
Pirot 29,658 F4
Plav 3,072 D4
Pljevlja 14,459 D4
Ploče 4,257 C4
Pola (Pula) 47,117 A3
Poreč 4,512 A3
Postojna 6,085 B3
Požarevac 33,336 E3
Preševo 7,634 E4
Priboj 12,556 D4
Prijedor 22,379 C3
Prijepolje 7,960 D4
Prilep 48,045 E5
Priština 71,264 E4
Prizren 41,875 E4
Prokuplje 20,617 E4
Prozor 1,420 C4
Ptuj 9,245 C2
Pula 47,117 A3
Rab 1,675 B3
Radoviš 9,373 F5
Ragusa (Dubrovnik) 31,213 C4
Raška 3,935 E4
Ravne na Koroškem 6,529 B2
Rijeka 128,883 B3
Rogatica 4,801 D4
Rovinj 8,998 A3
Rožaj E4
Ruma 24,180 D3
Šabac 43,539 D3
Samobor 7,821 B3
Sanski Most 8,718 C3
Sarajevo 245,058 D4
Senj 4,927 B3
Senta 24,694 D3
Šibenik 29,619 C4
Šid 11,867 D3
Sinj 4,705 C4
Sisak 37,215 C3
Sjenica 9,118 E4
Škofja Loka 4,971 A2
Skopje 308,117 E5
Skradin 893 B4
Slavonska Požega 18,160 C3
Slavonski Brod 38,829 D3
Smederevo 39,200 E3
Smederevska Palanka 18,837 E3
Sombor 44,210 D3
Split 150,739 C4
Srebrenica 3,101 D3
Sremska Mitrovica 32,569 D3
Štip 27,218 F5
Stolac 3,862 D4
Ston 407 C4
Struga 11,369 E5
Strumica 22,770 F5
Subotica 89,476 D2
Surdulica 7,048 F4
Svetozarevo 27,812 E4
Svilajnac 7,848 E3
Teslić 4,940 C3
Tetovo 35,293 E5
Titograd 54,639 D4
Titovo Užice 35,465 D4
Titov Veles 35,583 E5
Travnik 12,745 C3
Trbovlje 16,393 B2
Trebinje 3,553 D4
Trogir 6,162 C4
Trstenik 7,167 E4
Tržič 4,435 B2
Tuzla 53,836 D3
Ub 3,785 E3
Ulcinj 7,472 D5
Umag 3,228 A3
Uroševac E4
Valjevo 26,655 D3
Varaždin 34,662 B2
Vareš 7,632 D3
Velenje 11,225 B2
Velika Plana E3
Veliki Bečkerek
(Zrenjanin) 60,201 E3
Vinkovci 29,257 D3
Virovitica 16,389 C3
Višegrad 4,753 D4
Visoko 9,365 D4
Vlasenica 4,033 D3
Vranje 25,909 F4
Vrbas 22,502 D3
Vršac 33,573 E3
Vučitrn 11,701 E4
Vukovar 29,500 D3
Žabljak 1,023 D4
Zadar 43,588 B3
Zagreb 561,773 C3
Zaječar 27,724 E4
Zara (Zadar) 43,588 B3
Zenica 49,522 C3
Žepče 3,177 D3
Zrenjanin 60,201 E3
Zvornik 8,498 D3

OTHER FEATURES

Adriatic (sea) B4
Bobotov Kuk (mt.) D4
Bosna (riv.) D3
Brač (isl.) C4
Cazma (riv.) C3
Cres (isl.) B3
Čvrsnica (mt.) C4
Dalmatia (reg.) C4
Danube (riv.) E3
Dinaric Alps (mts.) B3
Drava (riv.) C3
Drina (riv.) D3
Dugi Otok (isl.) B3
Hvar (isl.) C4
Ibar (riv.) E4
Istria (pen.) A3
Kamenjak (cape) A3
Kladovo F3
Korab (mt.) E5
Korčula (isl.) C4
Kornat (isl.) B4
Krk (isl.) B3
Kupa (riv.) B3
Kvarner (gulf) B3
Lastovo (Lagosta) (isl.) C4
Lim (riv.) D4
Lošinj (isl.) B3
Midzhur (mt.) F4
Mljet (isl.) C4
Morava (riv.) E3
Mur (riv.) B2
Neretva (riv.) D4
Ohrid (lake) E5
Pag (isl.) B3
Palagruža (Pelagosa) (isl.) C4
Prespa (lake) E5
Rab (isl.) B3
Rujen (mt.) F4
Sava (riv.) D3
Scutari (lake) D4
Slavonia (reg.) C3
Šolta (isl.) C4
Tara (riv.) D4
Timok (riv.) F3
Tisa (riv.) E3
Triglav (mt.) A2
Una (riv.) C3
Vardar (riv.) E5
Vis (isl.) C4
Vrbas (riv.) C3
Žirje (isl.) B4

*City and suburbs.

The Balkan States
CONIC PROJECTION
SCALE OF MILES
0 25 50 75 100 125 150 175
SCALE OF KILOMETERS
0 25 50 75 100 125 150 175
Capitals of Countries
Administrative Centers
International Boundaries
Major Internal Boundaries
Minor Internal Boundaries
Canals
BULGARIA and GREECE are divided into counties and departments, respectively. Because of the scale no attempt has been made to delimit and name these subdivisions; their administrative centers have, however, been designated.
The larger divisions named in Greece are well-known geographical regions, without administrative function.
ROMANIA consists of thirty-nine counties and three cities of regional status, Bucharest, Constanța and Petroșeni. Scale does not permit delimiting these counties.
ALBANIA is divided into twenty-seven districts. Scale does not permit the delimitation of these divisions.
YUGOSLAVIA is a federation of six republics. The Serbian republic includes an autonomous province (Vojvodina), and an autonomous region (Kosovo).
POLAND
CZECHOSLOVAKIA
WEST GERMANY
AUSTRIA
HUNGARY
U.S.S.R.
ROMANIA
YUGOSLAVIA
BULGARIA
ALBANIA
GREECE
TURKEY
ITALY
ADRIATIC SEA
IONIAN SEA
AEGEAN SEA
BLACK SEA
SEA OF MARMARA
TYRRHENIAN SEA
MEDITERRANEAN SEA
SEA OF CRETE
Longitude East of Greenwich
© Copyright HAMMOND INCORPORATED, Maplewood, N. J.

Topography

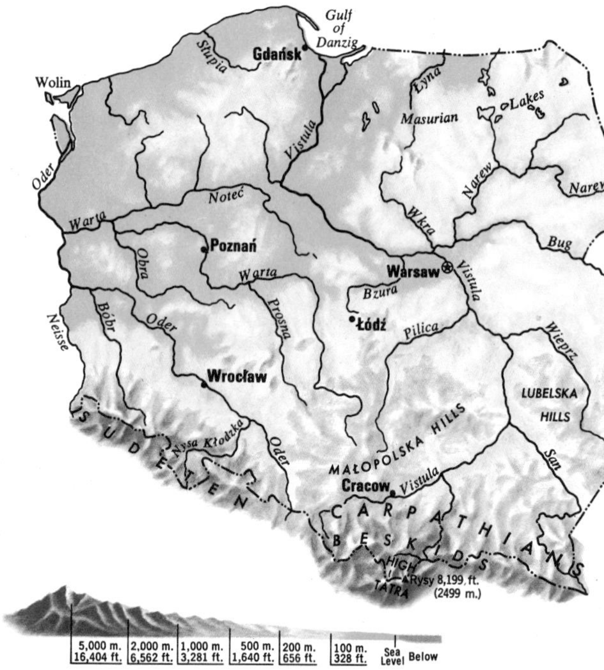

PROVINCES

Biata Podlaska 283,200	F3
Białystok 613,800	F2
Bielsko 765,500	D4
Bydgoszcz 982,100	C2
Chełm 221,000	F3
Ciechanów 398,500	E2
Cracow (Kraków) 1,097,600	E4
Cracow (city) 651,300	E4
Częstochowa 723,200	D3
Elbląg 419,800	D1
Gdańsk 1,312,300	D1
Gorzów 428,700	B2
Jelenia Góra 483,400	B3
Kalisz 640,300	D3
Katowice 3,439,700	D3
Kielce 1,030,400	E3
Konin 423,700	D2
Koszalin 428,500	C1
Krosno 418,000	E4
Legnica 405,600	C4
Leszno 340,600	C3
Łódź 1,063,700	D3
Łódź (city) 777,800	D3
Łomza 320,600	F2
Lublin 875,300	F3
Nowy Sącz 600,300	E4
Olsztyn 654,400	E2
Opole 961,600	C3
Ostrołęka 360,700	E2
Piła 414,000	C2
Piotrków 581,900	D3
Płock 479,700	D2
Poznań 1,156,500	C2
Przemyśl 373,100	F4
Radom 674,400	E3
Rzeszów 602,200	F4
Siędlce 602,100	F2
Sieradz 388,000	D3
Skierniewice 388,300	E3
Słupsk 352,900	C1
Suwałki 412,700	F1
Szczecin 841,400	B2
Tarnobrzeg 532,200	E3
Tarnów 573,900	E4
Toruń 580,500	D2
Wałbrzych 709,600	C3
Warsaw 2,117,700	E2
Warsaw (city) 1,377,100	E2
Włocławek 402,000	D2
Wrocław 1,014,600	C3
Zamość 472,300	F3
Zielona Góra 575,000	B3

CITIES and TOWNS

Aleksandrów Kujawski 9,600	
Aleksandrów Łódzki 14,400	
Allenstein (Olsztyn) 94,119	
Andrespol 12,400	
Andrychów 14,300	
Augustów 19,784	
Auschwitz (Oświęcim) 39,600	
Bartoszyce 15,500	
Będzin 42,787	
Beuthen (Bytom) 186,993	
Biała Podlaska 26,100	
Białogard 20,500	
Białystok 166,619	
Bielawa 30,900	
Bielsk Podlaski 14,000	
Bielsko-Biała 105,601	
Biłgoraj 12,888	
Błonie 12,500	
Bochnia 14,500	
Bogatynia 11,800	
Boguszów-Gorce 11,900	
Bolesławiec 30,500	

Poland 1938

0 50 100 MILES

Agriculture, Industry and Resources

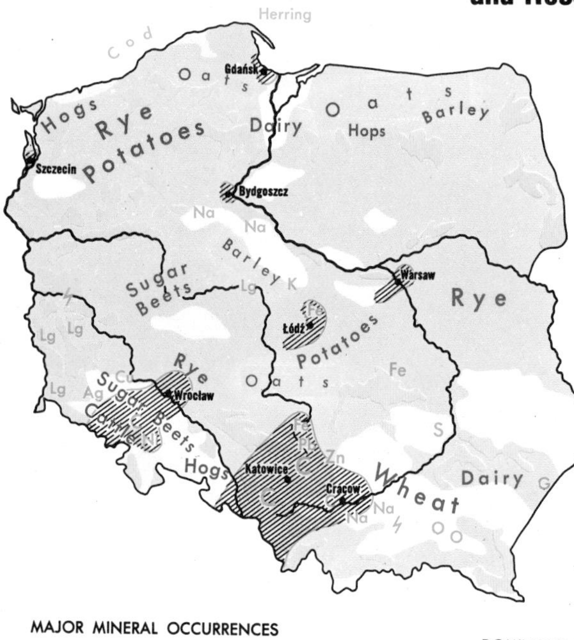

MAJOR MINERAL OCCURRENCES

Ag	Silver	Na	Salt
C	Coal	Ni	Nickel
Cu	Copper	O	Petroleum
Fe	Iron Ore	Pb	Lead
G	Natural Gas	S	Sulfur
K	Potash	Zn	Zinc
Lg	Lignite		

Water Power

Major Industrial Areas

DOMINANT LAND USE

- Cereals (chiefly wheat)
- Rye, Oats, Barley, Potatoes
- General Farming, Livestock
- Forests

Poland 1945

0 50 100 MILES

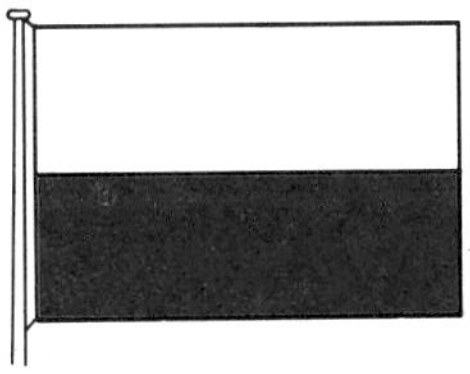

AREA 120,725 sq. mi. (312,678 sq. km.)
POPULATION 35,815,000
CAPITAL Warsaw
LARGEST CITY Warsaw
HIGHEST POINT Rysy 8,199 ft. (2,499 m.)
MONETARY UNIT zloty
MAJOR LANGUAGE Polish
MAJOR RELIGION Roman Catholicism

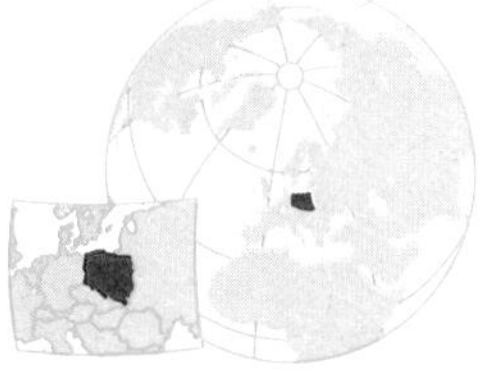

Braniewo 12,100 D1
Breslau (Wrocław) 461,900 C3
Brieg (Brzeg) 30,780 C3
Brodnica 17,300 D2
Brzeg 30,780 C3
Brzeg Dolny 10,800 C3
Brzesko 9,701 E3
Busko Zdrój 11,100 E3
Bydgoszcz 280,460 C2
Bytom 186,993 A3
Bytów 10,642 C1
Chełm 38,789 F3
Chełmno 17,906 D2
Chełmza 14,200 D2
Chodziez 14,100 C2
Chojnice 23,500 C2
Chojnów 11,000 B3
Chorzów 151,338 B4
Choszczno 9,800 B2
Chrzanów 29,300 B4
Ciechanów 28,500 E2
Cieplice Śląskie-Zdrój 15,400 B3
Cieszyn 25,234 D4
Cracow 651,300 E4
Czechowice-Dziedzice 25,400 D4
Czeladź 31,843 B4
Częstochowa 187,613 D3
Dąbrowa Górnicza 61,660 B3
Danzig (Gdańsk) 364,285 D1
Darłowo 11,200 C1
Dębica 22,900 E3
Dęblin 14,600 E3
Dębno 10,700 B2
Działdowo 10,100 E2
Dzierzoniów 32,800 C3
Elbing (Elblag) 89,835 D1
Ełk 27,188 F2
Gdańsk 364,285 D1
Gdynia 190,125 D1
Gizycko 18,200 E1
Gleiwitz (Gliwice) 170,912 A4
Głogów (Glogau) 20,226 C3
Głowno 12,800 D2
Głubczyce 11,300 C3
Głuchołazy 13,200 C3
Gniezno 50,643 C2
Goleniów 14,600 B2
Gorlice 15,200 E4
Gorzów Wielkopolski 74,267 B2
Gostyń 13,000 C3
Gostynin 12,000 D2
Grajewo 11,200 F2
Grodzisk Mazowiecki 20,400 E2
Grójec 10,300 E3
Grudziądz 75,511 D2
Grünberg (Zielona Góra) 59,700 B3
Gryfice 13,200 B2
Guben (Gubin) 14,600 B3
Hajnowka m4,345 F2
Hindenburg (Zabrze) 199,400 A4
Hirschberg (Jelenia Góra) 55,720 B3
Hrubieszów 14,999 F3
Iława 16,400 D2
Inowrocław 54,817 D2
Jarocin 18,100 C3
Jarosław 29,000 F4
Jasło 17,025 E4
Jastrzębie Zdroj 34,400 D3
Jaworzno 63,271 B4
Jędrzejów 13,264 E3
Jelenia Góra 55,720 B3
Kalisz 81,227 D3
Kamienna Góra 21,000 B3
Kartuzy 10,558 C1
Katowice 303,264 B4
Kedzierzyn-Koźle 45,600 C3
Kępno 10,151 C3
Kętrzyn 19,300 E1
Kielce 125,952 E3
Kłobuck 12,600 D3
Kłodzko 26,000 C3
Kluczbork 18,000 D3
Knurów 28,400 A4
Kolberg (Kołobrzeg) 25,419 B1
Koło 13,100 D2
Kołobrzeg 25,419 B1
Konin 40,600 D2
Końskie 13,100 E3
Konstantynów Łódzki 12,800 D3
Kościan 18,700 C2
Kościerzyna 18,914 C1
Köslin (Koszalin) 64,414 C1
Kostrzyń 11,200 B2
Koszalin 64,414 C1
Kraków (Cracow) 651,300 E4
Krapkowice 13,800 D3
Kraśnik Fabryczny 14,600 F3
Krasnystaw 12,495 F3
Krosno 26,500 E4
Krotoszyn 21,900 C3
Krynica 10,200 E4
Küstrin 11,200 B2
Kutno 30,000 D2
Kwidzin 23,104 D2
Łancut 12,049 F3
Landsberg (Gorzów Wielkepolski) 74,267 B2
Łaziska Górne 10,800 A4
Lębork 25,000 C1
Łęczyca 13,900 D2
Legionowo 20,800 E2
Legnica 75,843 C3
Leszcyny 12,200 A4
Leszno 33,890 C3
Libiaz 10,600 D3
Lidzbark Warmiński 12,900 E1
Liegnitz (Legnica) 75,843 C3
Lipno 10,900 D2
Łódź 777,800 D3
Łomza 25,500 F2
Łowicz 20,400 D2
Lubań 17,200 B3
Lubartów 10,000 F3
Lubin 28,400 C3
Lublin 235,937 F3
Lubliniec 19,800 D3
Luboń 16,400 C2
Lubsko 12,600 B3
Łuków 15,500 F3
Malbork (Marienburg) 30,900 D1
Międzyrzec Podlaski 13,500 F3
Międzyrzecz 14,900 B2
Mielec 26,800 E3
Mikłów 21,300 B4
Mińsk Mazowiecki 24,200 E2
Mława 20,007 E2
Mońki 9,560 F2
Morąg 9,681 E2
Mrągowo 13,400 E2
Myślenice 12,100 E4
Mysłowice 44,737 C4
Myszków 18,000 D3
Nakło nad Notecia 16,800 C2
Namysłów 11,076 C3
Neisse (Nysa) 31,837 C3
Nidzica 9,642 E2
Nisko 10,000 E3
Nowa Ruda 18,100 C3
Nowa Sól 33,300 B3
Nowy Dwór Mazowiecki 16,900 E2
Nowy Sącz 41,103 E4
Nowy Targ 21,900 E4
Nysa 31,837 C3
Oborniki 10,200 C2
Oława 17,746 C3
Oleśnica 27,500 C3
Olkusz 15,800 D3
Olsztyn 94,119 E2
Opoczno 12,168 E3
Opole 86,510 C3
Oppeln 86,510 C3
Orzesze 9,600 A4
Ostróda 21,300 D2
Ostrołęka 21,981 E2
Ostrów Mazowiecka 15,000 E2
Ostrów Wielkopolski 49,530 C3
Ostrowiec Świętokrzyski 49,958 E3
Oświęcim 39,600 D3
Otwock 39,863 E2
Ozorków 18,200 D3
Pabianice 62,275 D3
Piekary Śląskie 36,300 B4
Piła 43,778 C2
Pionki 13,600 E3
Piotrków Trybunalski 59,683 D3
Pisz 11,100 E2
Pleszew 13,348 C3
Płock 71,727 D2
Płońsk 11,619 E2
Police 12,700 B2
Poznań 469,085 C2
Prudnik 20,300 C3
Pruszcz Gdanski 13,000 D1
Pruszków 42,961 E2
Przasnysz 11,100 E2
Przemyśl 53,228 F4
Puck 9,500 D1
Puławy 34,800 F3
Pułtusk 12,600 E2
Rabka 10,700 D4
Racibórz 40,418 C3
Radom 158,640 E3
Radomsko 31,179 D3
Ratibor (Racibórz) 40,418 C3
Rawa Mazowiecka 9,800 E3
Rawicz 14,100 C3
Ruda Śląska 142,407 B4
Rumia 23,300 D1
Rybnik 43,415 D3
Rypin 10,029 D2
Rzeszów 82,192 F4
Sandomierz 16,800 E3
Sanok 21,600 F4
Schneidemühl (Piła) 36,600 C2
Schweidnitz (Świdnica) 47,542 C3
Siedlce 38,983 F2
Siemianowice Śląskie 67,278 B4
Sieradz 18,500 D3
Sierpc 12,700 D2
Skarzysko-Kamienna 39,194 E3
Skawina 15,900 D4
Skierniewice 25,590 E2
Sławno 10,700 C1
Słubice 12,000 B2
Słupsk 68,311 C1
Sochaczew 20,500 E2
Sokółka 10,023 F2
Sokołów Podlaski 9,569 F2
Sopot 47,573 D1
Sosnowiec 144,652 B4
Śrem 15,600 C2
Środa Śląska 10,259 C3
Środa Wielkopolska 14,800 C2
Stalowa Wola 29,768 F3
Starachowice 42,807 E3
Stargard Szeciński 44,400 B2
Starogard Gdański 33,400 D2
Stary Sacz 57,400 E4
Stettin (Szćzecin) 337,294 B2
Stolp (Słupsk) 68,311 C1
Strzegom 14,000 C3
Strzelce Opolskie 14,700 D3
Strzelin 9,800 C3
Sulechów 10,200 B2
Suwałki 25,360 F1
Swarzędz 12,100 C2
Świdnica 47,542 C3
Świdnik 21,900 F3
Świdwin 12,500 B2
Świebodzice 18,500 C3
Świebodzin 14,900 B2
Świecie 17,900 D2
Świętochłowice 57,633 A4
Świnoujście (Swinemünde) 27,900 B1
Szamotuły 14,600 G2
Szczecin 337,204 B2
Szczecinek 28,600 C2
Szczytno 17,371 E2
Szprotawa 11,200 B3
Tarnobrzeg 18,800 E3
Tarnów 85,514 E4
Tarnowskie Góry 34,200 A3
Tczew 40,794 D1
Tomaszów Lubelski 12,329 F3
Tomaszów Mazowiecki 54,911 E3
Toruń 129,152 D2
Trzcianka 10,900 C2
Trzebinia-Siersza C4
Turek 18,500 D2
Tychy 71,384 B4
Ustka 9,900 C1
Wąbrzeźno 11,800 D2
Wadowice 11,700 D4
Wągrowiec 15,600 C2
Wałbrzych 125,048 C3
Wałcz 18,900 C2
Waldenburg (Wałbrzych) 125,048 C3
Warsaw (Warszawa) (cap.) 1,377,100 E2
Wejherowo 33,600 D1
Wieliczka 13,600 E3
Wieluń 14,300 D3
Wisła 9,800 D4
Włocławek 77,169 D2
Wodzisław Śląski 25,600 D4
Wolin 35,458 B2
Wołomin 24,000 E2
Wołów 10,500 C3
Wrocław 523,318 C3
Września 17,800 C2
Wschowa 10,000 C3
Wyszków E2
Ząbki 16,000 E2
Ząbkowice Śląskie 13,800 C3
Zabrze 197,214 A4
Zagań 21,400 B3
Zakopane 27,039 D4
Zambrów 14,082 E2
Zamość 34,734 F3
Zary 28,300 B3
Zawiercie 39,410 D3
Zduńska Wola 29,066 D3
Zgierz 42,838 D3
Zgorzelec 28,400 B3
Ziębice 9,700 C3
Zielona Góra 73,156 B3
Złocieniec 10,100 C2
Złotoryja 12,200 C3
Złotów 11,600 C2
Znin 9,600 C2
Zyrardów 33,196 E2
Zywiec 22,400 D4

OTHER FEATURES

Baltic (sea) B1
Beskids (range) D4
Brda (riv.) C2
Brynica (riv.) B4
Bug (riv.) F2
Danzig (Gdańsk) (gulf) D1
Dukla (pass) E4
Dunajec (riv.) E4
Gwda (riv.) C2
Hel (pen.) D1
High Tatra (range) D4
Kłodnica (riv.) A4
Łyna (riv.) E1
Mamry, Jezioro (lake) E1
Masurian (lkes) E2
Narew (riv.) E2
Neisse (riv.) B3
Noteć (riv.) B2
Nysa Kłodzka (riv.) C3
Nysa Łuzycka (Neisse) (riv.) B3
Oder (riv.) B2
Orava (res.) D4
Pilica (riv.) D3
Pomeranian (bay) B1
Prosna (riv.) C3
Przemsza (riv.) B4
Rysy (mt.) D4
San (riv.) F3
Słupia (riv.) C1
Śniardwy, Jezioro (lake) E2
Sudeten (range) B3
Uznam (Usedom) (isl.) B1
Vistula (riv.) D2
Warmia (reg.) D1
Warta (riv.) B2
Wieprz (riv.) F3
Wisła (Vistula) (riv.) D2
Wkra (riv.) E2
Wolin (Wollin) (isl.) B2

Poland
CONIC PROJECTION
SCALE OF MILES
SCALE OF KILOMETERS
Capitals of Countries
Other Capitals
International Boundaries
Internal Boundaries
Canals
Poland is divided into 49 provinces (bearing the same name as their capitals) and the autonomous cities of Warsaw, Łódź and Cracow.
BALTIC SEA
Gulf of Danzig
Pomeranian Bay
DENMARK
EAST GERMANY
U. S. S. R.
CZECHOSLOVAKIA
Warsaw
Gdańsk
Kraków
Łódź
Wrocław
Poznań
Szczecin
Berlin
Kaliningrad
L'vov
Dnieper
Gerlachovka 8,707 ft. (2654 m.)
Rysy 8,199 ft. (2499 m.)
Longitude East of Greenwich
© Copyright HAMMOND INCORPORATED, Maplewood, N. J.

Union of Soviet Socialist Republics

UNION REPUBLICS

- Armenian S.S.R. 3,031,000 .... E6
- Azerbaidzhan S.S.R. 6,028,000 .... E5
- Estonian S.S.R. 1,466,000 .... C4
- Georgian S.S.R. 5,015,000 .... D5
- Kazakh S.S.R. 14,684,000 .... G5
- Kirgiz S.S.R. 3,529,000 .... H5
- Latvian S.S.R. 2,521,000 .... C4
- Lithuanian S.S.R. 3,398,000 .... C4
- Moldavian S.S.R. 3,947,000 .... C5
- Russian S.F.S.R. 137,551,000 .... D4
- Tadzhik S.S.R. 3,801,000 .... H6
- Turkmen S.S.R. 2,759,000 .... F6
- Ukrainian S.S.R. 49,755,000 .... C5
- Uzbek S.S.R. 15,391,000 .... G5
- White Russian S.S.R. 9,560,000 .... C4

INTERNAL DIVISIONS

- Abkhaz A.S.S.R. 505,000 .... E5
- Adygey Aut. Obl. 405,000 .... D5
- Adzhar A.S.S.R. 354,000 .... E5
- Aginsk Buryat Aut. Okr. 69,000 .... M4
- Bashkir A.S.S.R. 3,849,000 .... F4
- Buryat A.S.S.R. 900,000 .... M4
- Chechen-Ingush A.S.S.R. 1,154,000 .... E5
- Chukchi Aut. Okr. 133,000 .... R3
- Chuvash A.S.S.R. 1,292,000 .... E4
- Dagestan A.S.S.R. 1,628,000 .... E5
- Evenki Aut. Okr. 16,000 .... K3
- Gorno-Altay Aut. Obl. 172,000 .... J4
- Gorno-Badakhshan Aut. Obl. 127,000 .... H6
- Jewish Aut. Obl. 190,000 .... O5
- Kabardin-Balkar A.S.S.R. 674,000 .... E5
- Kalmuck A.S.S.R. 294,000 .... E5
- Karachay-Cherkess Aut. Obl. 368,000 .... E5
- Karakalpak A.S.S.R. 904,000 .... G5
- Karelian A.S.S.R. 736,000 .... D3
- Khakass Aut. Obl. 500,000 .... J4
- Khanty-Mansi Aut. Okr. 569,000 .... H3
- Komi A.S.S.R. 1,119,000 .... F3
- Komi-Permyak Aut. Okr. 173,000 .... F4
- Koryak Aut. Okr. 34,000 .... R3
- Mari A.S.S.R. 703,000 .... E4
- Mordvinian A.S.S.R. 991,000 .... E4
- Nagorno-Karabakh Aut. Obl. 161,000 .... E5
- Nakhichevan' A.S.S.R. 239,000 .... E6
- Nenets Aut. Okr. 47,000 .... F3
- North Ossetian A.S.S.R. 597,000 .... E5
- South Ossetian Aut. Obl. 98,000 .... E5
- Tatar A.S.S.R. 3,436,000 .... F4
- Taymyr Aut. Okr. 44,000 .... K2
- Tuvinian A.S.S.R. 267,000 .... K4
- Udmurt A.S.S.R. 1,494,000 .... F4
- Ust'-Ordynskiy Buryat Aut. Okr. 133,000 .... L4
- Yakut A.S.S.R. 839,000 .... N3
- Yamal-Nenets Aut. Okr. 158,000 .... H3

CITIES and TOWNS

- Abakan 128,000 .... K4
- Abay 34,245 .... H5
- Abaza 15,202 .... J4
- Achinsk 117,000 .... K4
- Agata K3
- Aginskoye 7,922 .... M4
- Akmolinsk (Tselinograd) 234,000 .... H4
- Aksay 10,010 .... F4
- Aktas G5
- Aktash J4
- Aktyubinsk 191,000 .... F4
- Aldan 17,689 .... N4
- Aleksandrovsk-Sakhalinskiy 20,342 .... P5
- Alekseyevka 18,041 .... H4
- Aleysk 32,487 .... J4
- Alga 12,000 .... F5
- Aliskerovo R3
- Allakh-Yun' O3
- Alma-Ata 910,000 .... H5
- Almaznyy M3
- Ambarchik R3
- Amderma F3
- Amursk 24,010 .... O4
- Anadyr' 7,703 .... S3
- Andizhan 230,000 .... H5
- Angarsk 239,000 .... L4
- Angren H5
- Anzhero-Sudzhensk 105,000 .... J4
- Aral'sk 37,722 .... G5
- Archangel (Arkhangel'sk) 385,000 .... E3
- Arkalyk 15,108 .... G4
- Armavir 162,000 .... E5
- Arsen'yev 60,000 .... O5
- Artem 69,000 .... O5
- Artemovskiy M4
- Arys' 26,414 .... G5
- Arzamas 93,000 .... E4
- Asbest 79,000 .... G4
- Ashkhabad 312,000 .... F6
- Asino 29,395 .... J4
- Astrakhan' 461,000 .... E5
- Atbasar 37,228 .... G4
- Atka Q3
- Ayaguz 35,827 .... J5
- Ayan O4
- Aykhal M3
- Bagdarin M4
- Baku 1,022,000 .... F5
- Baku* 1,550,000 .... F5
- Balakovo 152,000 .... E4
- Balashov 93,000 .... E4
- Baley 27,215 .... M4
- Balkhash 78,000 .... H5
- Balykshi 22,397 .... F5
- Bam N4
- Barabinsk 37,274 .... H4
- Baranovichi 131,000 .... C4
- Barnaul 533,000 .... J4
- Batagay 10,000 .... O3
- Batumi 123,000 .... E5
- Baykit K3
- Baykonyr G5
- Bayram-Ali 31,987 .... G6
- Belgorod 240,000 .... D4
- Belogorsk 63,000 .... N4
- Belomorsk 16,595 .... D3
- Beloretsk 71,000 .... F4
- Belovo 112,000 .... J4
- Berdichev 80,000 .... C5
- Berdsk 67,000 .... J4
- Berezniki 185,000 .... F4
- Berezovo 6,000 .... G3
- Beringovskiy T3
- Bikin 17,473 .... O5
- Bira O5
- Birobidzhan 69,000 .... O5
- Biruni G5
- Biysk 212,000 .... J4
- Blagoveshchensk 172,000 .... N4
- Bobruysk 192,000 .... C4
- Bodaybo 19,000 .... M4
- Borisoglebsk 68,000 .... E4
- Borzya 27,815 .... M4
- Bratsk 214,000 .... L4
- Brest 177,000 .... C4
- Brindakit O4
- Bryansk 394,000 .... D4
- Bugul'ma 80,000 .... F4
- Bukachacha 10,000 .... M4
- Bukhara 185,000 .... G5
- Bulun N2
- Buzuluk 76,000 .... F4
- Chadan K4
- Chapayevsk 85,000 .... F4
- Chara M4
- Chardzhou 140,000 .... G6
- Charsk 10,100 .... J5
- Cheboksary 308,000 .... E4
- Chegdomyn 16,499 .... O4
- Chelkar 19,377 .... F5
- Chelyabinsk 1,030,000 .... G4
- Cheremkhovo 77,000 .... L4
- Cherepovets 266,000 .... D4
- Cherkessk 91,000 .... E5
- Chernigov 238,000 .... D4
- Chernogorsk 71,000 .... K4
- Chernovtsy 219,000 .... C5
- Chernyshevsk 10,000 .... M4
- Cherskiy Q3
- Chimbay 18,899 .... F5
- Chimkent 322,000 .... H5
- Chirchik 132,000 .... H5
- Chita 303,000 .... M4
- Chokurdakh P2
- Chumikan O4
- Dal'negorsk 33,506 .... O5
- Dal'nerechensk 28,224 .... O5
- Daugavpils 116,000 .... C4
- Denau G6
- Dikson J2
- Dimitrovgrad 106,000 .... F4
- Dnepropetrovsk 1,066,000 .... D5
- Donetsk 1,021,000 .... D5
- Drogobych 66,000 .... C5
- Druzhba J5
- Druzhina P3
- Dudinka 19,701 .... J3
- Dushanbe 494,000 .... G6
- Dzerzhinsk 257,000 .... E4
- Dzhalal-Abad 55,000 .... H5
- Dzhalinda N4
- Dzhambul 264,000 .... H5
- Dzhelinda M2
- Dzhetygara 32,169 .... G4
- Dzhezkazgan 89,000 .... G5
- Dzhusaly 20,658 .... G5
- Egvekinot S3
- Ekibastuz 66,000 .... H4
- Ekimchan O4
- El'dikan O3
- Elista 70,000 .... E5
- Emba 17,820 .... F5
- Engel's 161,000 .... E4
- Erivan 1,019,000 .... E6
- Evensk Q3
- Fergana 176,000 .... H5
- Fort-Shevchenko 12,000 .... F5
- Frolovo 33,398 .... E5
- Frunze 533,000 .... H5
- Gasan-Kuli F6
- Gol'chikha J2
- Gomel' 383,000 .... D4
- Gor'kiy 1,344,000 .... E4
- Gorno-Altaysk 34,413 .... J4
- Gornyak 16,643 .... J4
- Grodno 195,000 .... C4
- Groznyy 375,000 .... E5
- Gubakha 33,243 .... F4
- Gulistan 30,879 .... G5
- Gur'yev 131,000 .... F5
- Gusinoozersk 10,000 .... L4
- Gyda H2
- Igarka 15,624 .... J3
- Igrim G3
- Ilanskiy 22,852 .... K4
- Indiga E3
- Inta 51,000 .... G3
- Iolotan' 10,000 .... G6
- Irkutsk 550,000 .... L4
- Ishim 63,000 .... H4
- Isil'kul' 25,958 .... H4
- Iul'tin T3
- Ivano-Frankovsk 150,000 .... C5
- Ivanovo 465,000 .... E4
- Ivdel 15,308 .... G3
- Izhevsk 549,000 .... F4
- Izmail 83,000 .... C5
- Kachug L4
- Kagan 34,117 .... G6
- Kalachinsk 20,809 .... H4
- Kalakan M4
- Kalinin 412,000 .... D4
- Kaliningrad 355,000 .... B4
- Kalmykovo F5
- Kaluga 265,000 .... D4
- Kamen'-na-Obi 35,604 .... H4

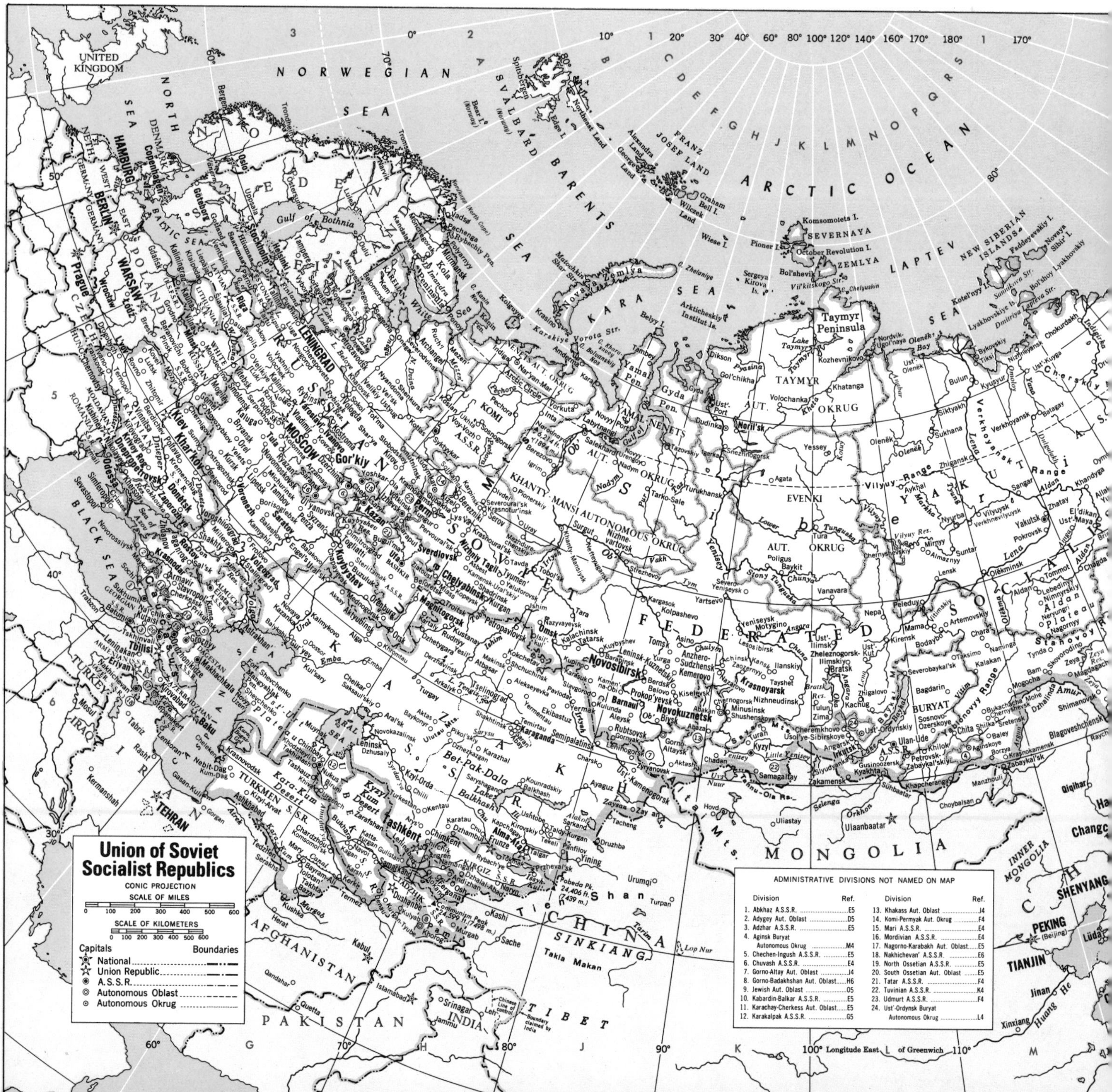

AREA 8,649,490 sq. mi. (22,402,179 sq. km.)
POPULATION 262,436,227
CAPITAL Moscow
LARGEST CITY Moscow
HIGHEST POINT Communism Peak 24,599 ft. (7,498 m.)
MONETARY UNIT ruble
MAJOR LANGUAGES Russian, Ukrainian, White Russian, Uzbek, Azerbaidzhani, Tatar, Georgian, Lithuanian, Armenian, Yiddish, Latvian, Mordvinian, Kirgiz, Tadzhik, Estonian, Kazakh, Moldavian (Romanian), German, Chuvash, Turkmenian, Bashkir
MAJOR RELIGIONS Eastern (Russian) Orthodoxy, Islam, Judaism, Protestantism (Baltic States)

menskoye	R3
mensk-Ural'skiy 187,000	G4
myshin 112,000	E4
ndalaksha 42,656	C3
nsk 101,000	K4
pchagay	H5
ra	G3
raganda 572,000	H5
rasuk 22,637	H4
ratau 26,962	H5
razhal 17,702	H5
rgasok	J4
rpinsk	F4
rshi 108,000	G6
rtaly 42,801	G4
tangli	P4
ttakurgan 53,000	G5
unas 370,000	C4
Kavalerovo 16,415	O5
Kazan' 993,000	F4
Kem' 21,025	D3
Kemerovo 471,000	J4
Kentau 52,000	G5
Kerki 10,000	G6
Khabarovsk 528,000	O5
Khandyga	O3
Khanty-Mansiysk 24,754	H3
Khar'kov 1,444,000	D4
Khatanga	L2
Kherson 319,000	D5
Khilok 17,000	M4
Khiva 24,139	F5
Khodzheyli 36,435	F5
Kholmsk 37,412	P5
Khorog 12,295	H6
Kiev 2,144,000	D4

UNION REPUBLICS

	AREA (sq. mi.)	AREA (sq. km.)	POPULATION	CAPITAL and LARGEST CITY
RUSSIAN S.F.S.R.	6,592,812	17,075,400	137,551,000	Moscow 7,831,000
KAZAKH S.S.R.	1,048,300	2,715,100	14,684,000	Alma-Ata 910,000
UKRAINIAN S.S.R.	233,089	603,700	49,755,000	Kiev 2,144,000
TURKMEN S.S.R.	188,455	488,100	2,759,000	Ashkhabad 312,000
UZBEK S.S.R.	173,591	449,600	15,391,000	Tashkent 1,780,000
WHITE RUSSIAN S.S.R.	80,154	207,600	9,560,000	Minsk 1,262,000
KIRGIZ S.S.R.	76,641	198,500	3,529,000	Frunze 533,000
TADZHIK S.S.R.	55,251	143,100	3,801,000	Dushanbe 494,000
AZERBAIDZHAN S.S.R.	33,436	86,600	6,028,000	Baku 1,022,000
GEORGIAN S.S.R.	26,911	69,700	5,015,000	Tbilisi 1,066,000
LITHUANIAN S.S.R.	25,174	65,200	3,398,000	Vilna 481,000
LATVIAN S.S.R.	24,595	63,700	2,521,000	Riga 835,000
ESTONIAN S.S.R.	17,413	45,100	1,466,000	Tallinn 430,000
MOLDAVIAN S.S.R.	13,012	33,700	3,947,000	Kishinev 503,000
ARMENIAN S.S.R.	11,506	29,800	3,031,000	Erivan 1,019,000

Kirensk 10,000	L4
Kirov 390,000	E4
Kirovabad 232,000	E5
Kirovograd 237,000	D5
Kirovskiy	H5
Kiselevsk 122,000	J4
Kishinev 503,000	C5
Kizel 46,264	F4
Kizyl-Arvat 21,671	F6
Klaipeda 176,000	B4
Kokand 153,000	H5
Kokchetav 103,000	H4
Kolomna 147,000	D4
Kolpashevo 24,911	J4
Komsomol'sk 15,385	G4
Komsomol'sk-na-Amure 264,000	O4
Kondopoga 27,908	D3
Kopeysk 146,000	G4
Korf	R3
Korsakov 38,210	P5
Koslan	E3
Kostroma 255,000	E4
Kotlas 61,000	E3
Kovel' 33,351	C4
Kovrov 143,000	E4
Kozhevnikovo	L2
Krasino	F2
Krasnodar 560,000	E5
Krasnokamensk 51,000	M4
Krasnokamsk 56,000	F4
Krasnotur'insk 61,000	G3
Krasnoural'sk 39,743	G4
Krasnovodsk 53,000	F5
Krasnoyarsk 796,000	K4
Kremenchug 210,000	D5
Krivoy Rog 650,000	D5
Kudymkar 26,350	F4
Kul'sary 16,427	F5
Kulunda 15,264	H4
Kulyab 55,000	H6
Kum-Dag 10,000	F6
Kungur 80,000	F4
Kupino 20,799	H4
Kurgan 310,000	G4
Kurgan-Tyube 34,620	G6
Kursk 375,000	D4
Kushka	G6
Kustanay 165,000	G4
Kutaisi 194,000	E5
Kuybyshev 1,216,000	F4
Kuybyshev 40,166	H4
Kyakhta 15,316	L4
Kyusyur	N2
Kyzyl 66,000	K4
Kzyl-Orda 156,000	G5
Labytnangi	G3
Lebedinyy	N4
Leninabad 130,000	G5
Leninakan 207,000	E5
Leningrad 4,073,000	D4
Leningrad* 4,588,000	D4
Leninogorsk 54,000	J5
Leninsk	G5
Leninsk-Kuznetskiy 132,000	J4
Leninskoye	O5
Lenkoran' 35,505	E6
Lensk 16,758	M3
Lesosibirsk	K4
Lesozavodsk 34,957	O5
Liepāja 108,000	B4
Lipetsk 396,000	E4
Luga 31,905	D4
Lutsk 137,000	C4
L'vov 667,000	C4
Lys'va 75,000	F4
Magadan 121,000	P4
Magdagachi 15,059	N4
Magnitogorsk 406,000	G4
Makhachkala 251,000	E5
Makinsk 22,850	H4
Mama	M4
Markovo	S3
Mary (Merv) 74,000	G6
Maykop 128,000	D5
Mednogorsk 38,024	F4
Medvezh'yegorsk 17,465	D3
Mezen'	E3
Miass 150,000	G4
Michurinsk 101,000	E4
Millerovo 34,627	E5
Minsk 1,262,000	C4
Minsk* 1,276,000	C4
Minusinsk 56,000	K4
Mirnyy 23,826	M3
Mogilev 290,000	D4
Mogocha 17,884	N4
Molodechno 73,000	C4
Monchegorsk 51,000	C3
Moscow (cap.) 7,831,000	D4
Moscow* 8,011,000	D4
Motygino 10,000	K4
Mozyr' 73,000	C4
Murgab	H6
Murmansk 381,000	D3
Muynak 12,000	F5
Mys Shmidta	T3
Nadym	H3
Nagornyy	N4
Nakhichevan' 33,279	E6
Nakhodka 133,000	O5
Nal'chik 207,000	F5
Namangan 227,000	H5
Naminga	M4
Nar'yan-Mar 16,864	F3
Naryn 21,098	H5
Navoi 84,000	G6
Nazarovo 54,000	K4
Nazyvayevsk 15,792	H4
Nebit-Dag 71,000	F6
Nefteyugansk 52,000	H3
Nel'kan	O4
Nepa	L4
Neryungri	N4
Nevel'sk 20,726	P5
Nikolayev 440,000	D5
Nikolayevsk-na-Amure 30,082	P4
Nikol'skoye	R4
Nizhneudinsk 39,743	K4
Nizhnevartovsk 109,000	H3
Nizhneyansk	O3
Nizhniy Tagil 398,000	G4
Nordvik-Ugol'naya	M2
Noril'sk 180,000	J3
Novaya Kazanka	F5
Novgorod 186,000	D4
Novokazalinsk 34,815	G5
Novokuznetsk 541,000	J4
Novomoskovsk 147,000	E4
Novorossiysk 159,000	D5
Novosibirsk 1,312,000	J4
Novozybkov 34,433	D4
Novyy Port	G3
Novyy Uzen' 18,073	F5
Novyy Urengoy	H3
Nukus 109,000	G5

Topography

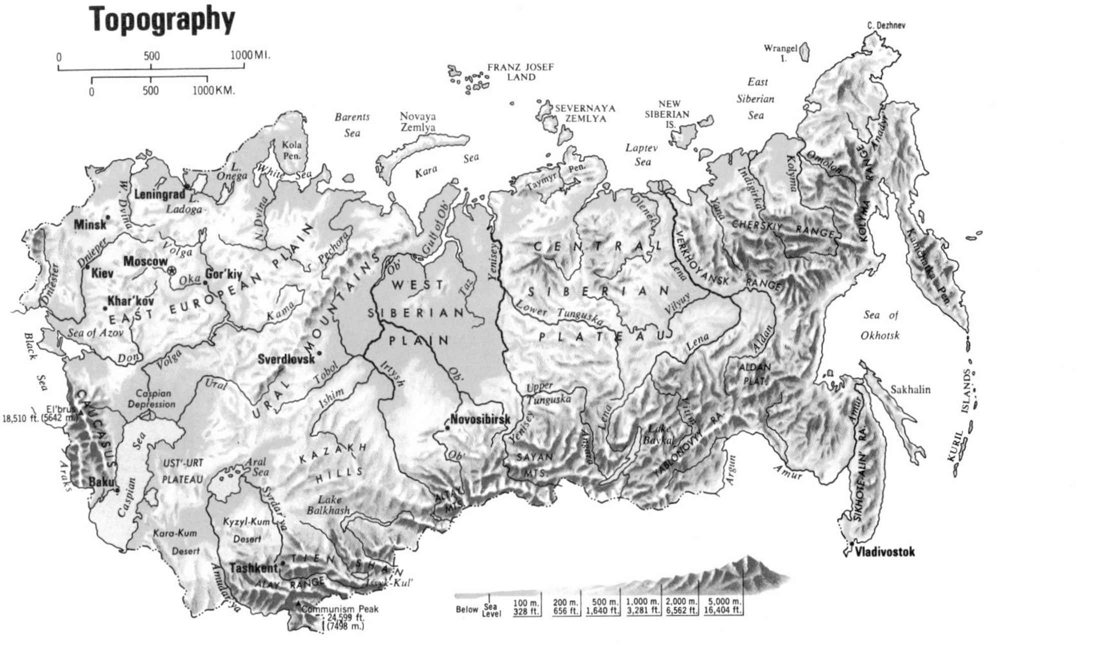

(continued)

OTHER FEATURES

*City and suburbs.

Agriculture, Industry and Resources

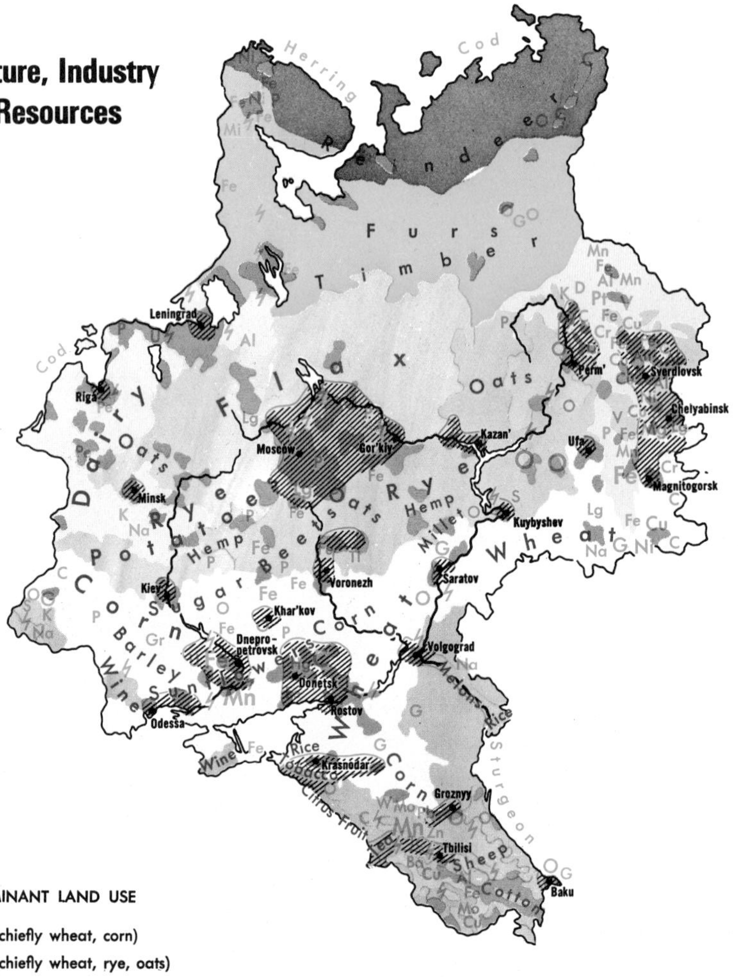

DOMINANT LAND USE

- Cereals (chiefly wheat, corn)
- Cereals (chiefly wheat, rye, oats)
- Dairy, Hogs, Livestock
- Livestock, Dairy
- Pasture Livestock
- Truck Farming, Potatoes, Vegetables, Dairy
- Flax, Dairy, Potatoes
- Cotton
- Vineyards, Orchards, Horticulture
- Sheep Herding, Limited Agriculture
- Forests
- Nonagricultural Land

MAJOR MINERAL OCCURRENCES

Ab	Asbestos	Hg	Mercury	Pb	Lead
Al	Bauxite	K	Potash	Pe	Peat
Au	Gold	Lg	Lignite	Pt	Platinum
Ba	Barite	Mg	Magnesium	S	Sulfur, Pyrite
C	Coal	Mi	Mica	Tc	Talc
Cr	Chromium	Mn	Manganese	Ti	Titanium
Cu	Copper	Mo	Molybdenum	U	Uranium
D	Diamonds	Na	Salt	V	Vanadium
Fe	Iron Ore	Ni	Nickel	W	Tungsten
G	Natural Gas	O	Petroleum	Zn	Zinc
Gr	Graphite	P	Phosphates		

Water Power

Major Industrial Areas

Agriculture, Industry and Resources

DOMINANT LAND USE

- Cereals (chiefly wheat, corn)
- Livestock, Dairy
- Truck Farming, Potatoes, Vegetables, Dairy
- Cotton
- Sheep Herding, Limited Agriculture
- Forests
- Nonagricultural Land

MAJOR MINERAL OCCURRENCES

Ab	Asbestos	Cu	Copper	Mi	Mica	Pt	Platinum
Au	Silver	D	Diamonds	Mn	Manganese	S	Sulfur, Pyrites
Al	Bauxite	F	Fluorspar	Mo	Molybdenum	Sb	Antimony
Au	Gold	Fe	Iron Ore	Na	Salt	Sn	Tin
Be	Beryl	G	Natural Gas	Ni	Nickel	U	Uranium
C	Coal	Hg	Mercury	O	Petroleum	W	Tungsten
Co	Cobalt	Ka	Kaolin	P	Phosphates	Zn	Zinc
Cr	Chromium	Lg	Lignite	Pb	Lead		

Water Power   Major Industrial Areas

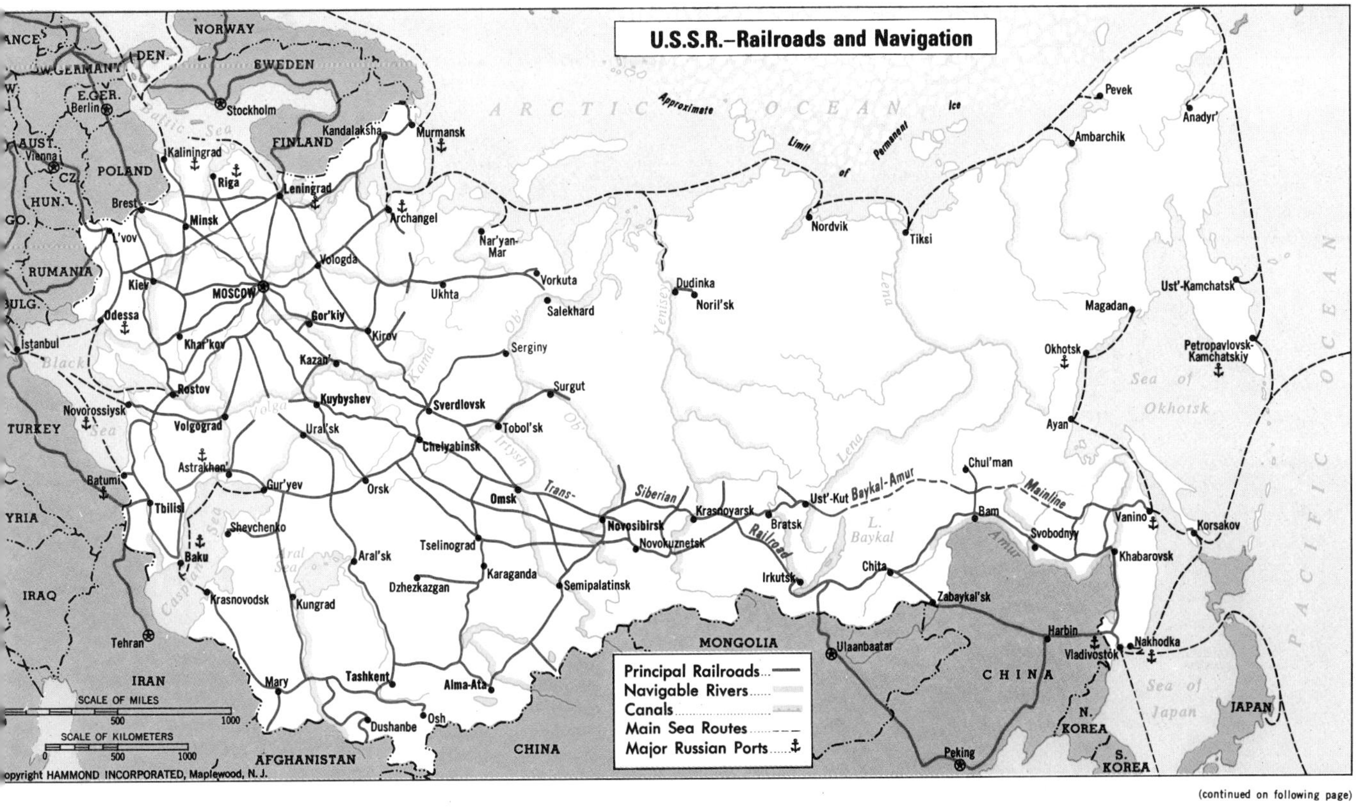

(continued on following page)

Union of Soviet Socialist Republics
European Part
CONIC PROJECTION
SCALE OF MILES
0 50 100 200 300
SCALE OF KILOMETERS
0 50 100 200 300
National Capitals
Capitals of Union Republics
Administrative Centers
International boundaries
Union Republic boundaries
A.S.S.R., Oblast, Kray boundaries
Autonomous Oblast boundaries
Autonomous Okrug boundaries
The government of the United States has not recognized the incorporation of Estonia, Latvia and Lithuania into the Soviet Union.
ARCTIC OCEAN
BARENTS SEA
KARA SEA
PECHORA SEA
WHITE SEA
BALTIC SEA
BLACK SEA
CASPIAN SEA
Sea of Azov
Administrative Divisions bear same names as their respective Capitals or Centers, except:
Abkhaz A.S.S.R. Sukhumi F6
Adygey Aut. Oblast Maykop F6
Adzhar A.S.S.R. Batumi F6
Bashkir A.S.S.R. Ufa J4
Chechen-Ingush A.S.S.R. Groznyy G6
Chuvash A.S.S.R. Cheboksary G3
Crimean Oblast Simferopol' D6
Dagestan A.S.S.R. Makhachkala G6
Kabardin-Balkar A.S.S.R. Nal'chik F6
Kalmuck A.S.S.R. Elista F5
Karachay-Cherkess Aut. Obl. Cherkessk F6
Karelian A.S.S.R. Petrozavodsk D2
Komi A.S.S.R. Syktyvkar H2
Komi-Permyak Aut. Okrug Kudymkar H3
Mari A.S.S.R. Yoshkar-Ola G3
Mordvinian A.S.S.R. Saransk G4
Nagorno-Karabakh Aut. Obl. Stepanakert G7
Nenets Aut. Okrug Nar'yan-Mar H1
North Ossetian A.S.S.R. Ordzhonikidze F6
South Ossetian Aut. Obl. Tskhinvali F6
Tatar A.S.S.R. Kazan' G3
Trans-Carpathian Oblast Uzhgorod B5
Udmurt A.S.S.R. Izhevsk H3
Volyn Oblast Lutsk C4
© Copyright HAMMOND INCORPORATED, Maplewood, N. J.
Longitude East of Greenwich

U.S.S.R. — EUROPEAN

UNION REPUBLICS

enian S.S.R. 3,031,000 F6
rbaidzhan S.S.R. 6,028,000 G6
onian S.S.R 1,466,000 C3
rgian S.S.R. 5,015,000 F6
vian S.S.R 2,521,000 B3
uanian S.S.R. 3,398,000 B3
ldavian S.S.R. 3,947,000 C5
ssian S.F.S.R. 137,551,000 F3
ainian S.S.R. 49,755,000 D5
ite Russian S.S.R. 9,560,000 C4

INTERNAL DIVISIONS

khaz A.S.S.R. 505,000 F6
ygey Aut. Obl. 405,000 F6
har A.S.S.R. 354,000 F6
shkir A.S.S.R. 3,849,000 J4
echen-Ingush
A.S.S.R. 1,154,000 G6
uvash A.S.S.R. 1,292,000 G3
mean Oblast 2,183,000 D6
gestan A.S.S.R. 1,628,000 G6
bardin-Balkar
A.S.S.R. 674,000 F6
muck A.S.S.R. 294,000 F5
achav-Cherkess Aut. Obl. 368,000 F6
elian A.S.S.R. 736,000 D2
mi A.S.S.R. 1,119,000 H2
mi-Permyak Aut. Okr. 173,000 H3
ri A.S.S.R. 703,000 G3
rdvinian A.S.S.R. 991,000 G4
gorno-Karabakh Aut.
Obl. 161,000 G7
khichevan' A.S.S.R. 239,000 F7
nets Aut. Okr. 47,000 H1
rth Ossetian
A.S.S.R. 597,000 F6
uth Ossetian Aut.
Obl. 98,000 F6
ar A.S.S.R. 3,436,000 G3
ns-Carpathian
Oblast 1,155,000 B5
murt A.S.S.R. 1,494,000 H3
yn Oblast 1,015,000 C4

CITIES and TOWNS

dulino 26,010 H4
dam 21,277 G6
ryz 19,267 H3
haltsikhe 18,972 F6
htubinsk 43,466 G5
hty G6
htyrka 41,354 E4
kerman
(Belgorod-Dnestrovskiy) 32,928 D5
gir 18,161 F6
tyr' 43,499 G4
verdi 21,311 F6
eksandriya 82,000 D5
eksandrovsk 18,286 J3
ekseyevka 25,562 E4
eksin 67,000 E4
-Bayramly 33,828 G7
met'yevsk 110,000 H3
ushta 22,016 D6
nderma K1
apa 29,900 E6
atity 62,000 D1
sheronsk 32,867 F6
changel
(Arkhangel'sk) 385,000 F2
mavir 162,000 F5
zamas 93,000 F3
tara G7
trakhan' 461,000 G5
karsk 28,881 G4
ov 75,000 E5
khchisaray 15,912 D6
ku 1,022,000 H6
ku* 1,550,000 H6
lakhna 36,542 F3
laklava D6
lakovo 152,000 G4
lashov 93,000 F4
ltiysk 20,300 A4
ranovichi 131,000 C4
rysh 20,792 G4
taysk 90,000 E5
tumi 123,000 F6
laya Tserkov' 151,000 C5
lebey 32,460 H4
lev 17,733 E4
lgorod 240,000 F4
lgorod-Dnestrovskiy 32,928 D5
lomorsk 16,595 D2
lorechensk 35,970 E6
loretsk 71,000 J4
lozersk E3
l'tsy 125,000 C5
lush'ya Guba H1
ndery 101,000 C5
rdichev 80,000 C5
rdyansk 122,000 E5
regovo 27,308 B5
rezniki 185,000 J3
slan 26,893 F6
zhetsk 30,030 E3
rsk 29,607 J3
brov 17,977 F4
bruysk 192,000 C4
logoye 33,949 D3
r 63,000 F3
rislav 33,800 B5
risoglebsk 68,000 F4
risov 112,000 C4
rovichi 60,000 D3
est 177,000 B4
yansk 394,000 D4
gul'ma 80,000 H4
guruslan 54,000 H4
turlinovka 21,643 F4
y 29,946 F3
ynaksk 37,946 G6
zuluk 76,000 H4
khov 17,371 C4
sis 17,696 C3
hadyr-Lunga 20,474 C5
hapayevsk 85,000 G4
haykovskiy 48,034 H3
heboksary 308,000 G3
herdyn' J2
herepovets 266,000 E3
herkassy 228,000 D5
herkessk 91,000 F6
hernigov 238,000 D4
hernovtsy 219,000 C5
hernushka 21,106 J3
hervonograd 55,000 B4
hiatura 25,474 F6
histopol' 64,000 H3
hortkov 19,183 B5
hudovo D3
husovoy 56,000 J3
anilov 17,500 E3
ankov 20,030 E4
augavpils 116,000 C3
avlekanovo 20,123 H4
erbent 70,000 G6
imitrovgrad 106,000 G4
neprodzerzhinsk 250,000 D5
nepropetrovsk 1,066,000 D5
obrush 16,809 D4
obryanka 18,349 J3
onetsk 1,021,000 E5
rogobych 66,000 B5
ubna 55,000 E3
ubna E4

Dubno 25,442 C4
Dvinsk (Daugavpils) 116,000 C3
Dyat'kovo 26,825 D4
Dzerzhinsk 257,000 F3
Dzhankoy 43,459 D5
Dzhul'fa G7
Echmiadzin 31,819 F6
Elektrostal' 139,000 E3
Elista 70,000 F5
El'ton G5
Engel's 161,000 G4
Erivan 1,019,000 F6
Fastov 51,000 C4
Feodosiya 76,000 D5
Frolovo 33,398 F5
Furmanov 40,155 F3
Gagra 23,025 E6
Galich 19,374 F3
Gandzha (Kirovabad) 232,000 G6
Gatchina 75,000 C3
Gay 28,250 J4
Gaysin 23,741 C5
Gdov C3
Gelendzhik 29,086 E6
Genichesk 20,031 E5
Georgiu-Dezh 52,000 E4
Glazov 81,000 H3
Glubokoye C3
Glukhov 27,096 D4
Gomel' 383,000 D4
Gori 56,000 F6
Gorki 22,117 D4
Gor'kiy 1,344,000 F3
Gorlovka 336,000 E5
Gorodets 34,229 F3
Gremikha E1
Gremyachinsk 29,975 J3
Grodno 195,000 B4
Groznyy 375,000 G6
Gryazi 41,292 F4
Gubakha 33,243 J3
Gubkin 65,000 E4
Gudauta F6
Gudermes 32,445 G6
Gukovo 68,000 F5
Gus'-Khrustal'nyy 72,000 F3
Imishli 17,839 G7
Inta 51,000 K1
Inza 19,060 G4
Ishimbay 57,000 J4
Ivano-Frankovsk 150,000 B5
Ivanovo 465,000 E3
Izberbash 17,299 G6
Izhevsk 549,000 H3
Izmail 83,000 C5
Izyum 61,000 E5
Jēkabpils 22,440 C3
Jelgava 68,000 B3
Jurmala 61,000 B3
Kadiyevka (Stakhanov) 108,000 E5
Kafan 29,916 G7
Kagul 26,249 C5
Kakhovka 28,472 D5
Kalach 18,475 F4
Kalach-na-Donu 20,795 F5
Kalinin 412,000 E3
Kaliningrad,
Kaliningrad 355,000 B4
Kaliningrad, Moscow
Oblast 133,000 E3
Kalinkovichi 23,918 C4
Kaluga 265,000 E4
Kalush 60,000 B5
Kamenets-Podol'skiy 81,000 C5
Kamenka, Penza 30,067 F4
Kamensk-Shakhtinskiy 72,000 F5
Kamyshin 112,000 F4
Kanash 40,682 G3
Kandalaksha 42,656 D1
Kapsukas 28,763 B4
Karachayevsk F6
Karachev 15,972 E4
Kashin 17,678 E3
Kasimov 33,066 F4
Kaspiysk 38,990 G6
Kaunas 370,000 B4
Kazan' 993,000 G3
Kazatin 26,649 C5
Kem' 21,025 D2
Kerch' 157,000 E5
Keret' D1
Khachmas 22,313 G6
Khadyzhensk 17,856 E6
Khar'kov 1,444,000 E5
Khasavyurt 65,000 G6
Khashuri 24,469 F6
Kherson 319,000 D5
Khmel'nitskiy 172,000 C5
Khotin C5
Khust 23,810 B5
Khvalynsk 16,249 G4
Kiev 2,144,000 D4
Kiliya 24,276 C5
Kimovsk 44,490 E4
Kimry 58,000 E3
Kinel' 39,373 H4
Kineshma 101,000 F3
Kirishi 27,252 D3
Kirov, Kaluga 29,355 D4
Kirov, Kirov 390,000 G3
Kirovabad 232,000 G6
Kirovakan 146,000 G6
Kirovo-Chepetsk 71,000 H3
Kirovograd 237,000 D5
Kirovsk 38,484 D1
Kirsanov 21,795 F4
Kishinev 503,000 C5
Kislovodsk 101,000 F6
Kizel 46,264 J3
Kizlyar 29,745 G6
Klaipeda 176,000 B3
Klintsy 67,000 D4
Kobrin 24,935 B4
Kobuleti 18,051 F6
Kohtla-Järve 73,000 C3
Kolomiya 52,000 B5
Kolomna 147,000 E4
Kolpino 114,000 D3
Kommunarsk 120,000 E5
Komrat 21,369 C5
Komsomol'skiy 17,078 K1
Kondopoga 27,908 D2
Königsberg
(Kaliningrad) 355,000 B4
Konotop 82,000 D4
Konstantinovka 112,000 E5
Korenovsk 26,323 E5
Korosten' 65,000 C4
Korostyshev 21,153 C4
Koryazhma 33,230 G2
Kostopol' 17,548 C4
Kostroma 255,000 F3
Kotel'nich 29,196 G3
Kotel'nikovo 19,063 F5
Kotlas 61,000 G2
Kotovo 20,553 G4
Kotovsk, Odessa 36,463 C5
Kotovsk, Tambov 33,347 F4
Kovel' 33,351 C4
Kovrov 143,000 F3
Kovylkino 17,300 F4
Kramatorsk 178,000 E5
Krasnoarmeysk 60,000 G4
Krasnodar 560,000 E6
Krasnograd 18,386 E5
Krasnokamsk 56,000 H3
Krasnoslobodsk 17,749 G5
Krasnovishersk J2
Krasnyy Kut 17,087 G4
Krasnyy Luch 106,000 E5

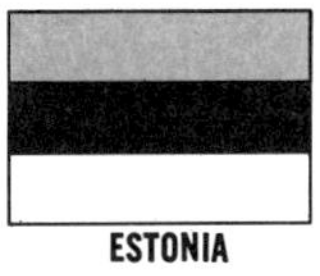

ESTONIA

LATVIA

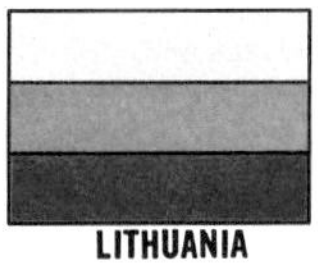

LITHUANIA

The government of the United States has not recognized the incorporation of Estonia, Latvia and Lithuania into the Soviet Union, nor does it recognize other post-war territorial changes shown on this map. The flags shown here were the official flags of the independent Baltic States prior to 1939.

The Baltic States

SCALE OF MILES 0 25 50 75 100
SCALE OF KILOMETERS 0 30 60 90 120 150 180

Capitals ☆
International Boundaries —·—
Union Republic Boundaries —·—
Prewar boundaries of the Baltic States where divergent from present boundaries ....

BALTIC STATES

Alytus 55,000 C3
Biržai 11,400 C2
Cēsis 17,696 C2
Daugava (Western Dvina)
(riv.) D2
Daugavpils 116,000 D3
Dobele 10,100 B2
Druskininkai 11,200 C3
Dvina, Western (riv.) C2
Finland (gulf) D1
Gauja (riv.) C2
Haapsalu 11,483 B1
Hiiumaa (isl.) B1
Jēkabpils 22,400 C2
Jelgava 68,000 B2
Jonava 14,400 C3
Jurmala 61,000 B2
Kapsukas 28,763 B3
Kaunas 370,000 C3
Kedainiai 19,677 C3
Kihnu (isl.) B1
Kingisepp (Kuressaare) 12,140 B1
Kiviõli 11,153 D1
Klaipeda 176,000 A3
Kohtla-Järve 73,000 D1
Kretinga 13,000 A3
Kuldīga 12,300 A2
Kuressaare 12,140 B1
Kuršenai 11,500 B2
Liepāja 108,000 A2
Lubāna (lake) D2
Mažeikiai 13,400 A2
Memel (Klaipeda) 176,000 A3
Muhu (isl.) B1
Narva 73,000 E1
Naujoji-Akmene 10,200 B2
Niemen (riv.) A3
Ogre 15,708 C2
Panevežys 102,000 C3
Pärnu 51,000 C1
Peipus (lake) D1
Plunge 13,600 B3
Radviliškis 16,841 B3
Rakvere 17,891 D1
Rēzekne 30,803 D2
Riga (cap.), Latvia 835,000 C2
Riga (gulf) B2
Saaremaa (isl.) B1
Saldus 10,000 B2
Šiauliai 118,000 B3
Sillamäe 13,505 D1
Šilute 12,400 A3
Tallinn (cap.),
Estonia 430,000 C1
Tapa 10,037 C1
Tartu 105,000 D1
Taurage 19,461 B3
Telšiai 20,220 B2
Tukums 14,800 B2
Ukmerge 21,663 C3
Utena 13,300 C3
Valga 16,795 D2
Valmiera 20,331 C2
Venta (riv.) B2
Ventspils 40,467 A2
Viliya (riv.) C3
Viljandi 20,814 C1
Vilna (Vilnius) (cap.)
Lithuania 481,000 C3
Vormosi (isl.) B1
Võrtsjärv (lake) D1
Võru 15,398 D2
Western Dvina (riv.) C2

Krasnyy Sulin 41,684 F5
Kremenchug 210,000 D5
Krichev 25,682 D4
Krivoy Rog 650,000 D5
Krolevets 18,307 D4
Kronshtadt 39,477 C3
Kropotkin 70,000 F5
Krymsk 41,430 E5
Kuba 18,871 G6
Kudymkar 26,350 H3
Kulebaki 46,252 F3
Kumertau 52,000 J4
Kunda C3
Kungur 80,000 J3
Kupyansk 30,055 E5
Kuressaare 12,140 B3
Kursk 375,000 E4
Kutaisi 194,000 F6
Kuvandyk 22,914 J4
Kuybyshev 1,216,000 H4
Kuznetsk 94,000 G4
Kuzomen' E1
Labinsk 54,000 F6
Lakhdenpokh'ya C2
Lebedin 29,240 D4
Leninakan 207,000 F6
Leningrad 4,073,000 C3
Leningrad* 4,588,000 C3
Leninogorsk 54,000 H4
Lenkoran' 35,505 G7
L'gov 25,110 E4
Lida 66,000 C4
Liepāja 108,000 B3
Likhoslavl' E3
Lipetsk 396,000 E4
Lisichansk 110,000 E5
Livny 37,290 E4
Lodeynoye Pole 19,632 D2
Lozovaya 53,000 E5
Lubny 54,000 D4
Luga 31,905 C3
Lutsk 137,000 B4
L'vov (Lwów) 667,000 B5
Lys'va 75,000 J3
Lyubertsy 160,000 E3
Lyubotin 33,324 E4
Lyudinovo 33,871 D4
Makeyevka 436,000 E5
Makhachkala 251,000 G6
Makharadze 21,679 F6
Malaya Vishera 15,381 D3
Malgobek 20,548 F6
Manturovo 21,510 F3
Marganets 50,000 E5
Mariupol' (Zhdanov) 503,000 E5
Marks 17,132 G4
Maykop 128,000 F6
Mednogorsk 38,024 J4
Medvezh'yegorsk 17,465 D2
Melenki 18,545 F3
Meleuz 24,851 J4
Melitopol' 161,000 D5
Memel (Klaipeda) 176,000 B3
Merefa 29,985 E5
Mezen' F1
Michurinsk 101,000 F4
Mikhaylovka 58,000 F4
Millerovo 34,627 F5
Mineral'nye Vody 67,000 F6
Mingechaur 60,000 G6
Minsk 1,262,000 C4
Minsk* 1,276,000 C4
Mirgorod 28,407 D5
Mogilev 290,000 C4
Mogilev-Podol'skiy 26,051 C5
Molodechno 73,000 C4
Molotov (Perm') 999,000 J3
Monchegorsk 51,000 D1
Morshansk 44,245 F4
Moscow (Moskva)
(cap.) 7,831,000 E3
Moscow* 8,011,000 E3
Mozhaysk 20,321 E3
Mozhga 38,930 H3
Mozyr' 73,000 C4
Mtsensk 27,833 E4
Mukachevo 72,000 B5
Murmansk 381,000 D1
Murom 114,000 F3
Mytishchi 141,000 E3
Naberezhnye Chelny 301,000 H3
Nakhichevan' 33,279 F7
Nal'chik 207,000 F6
Narva 73,000 C3
Nar'yan-Mar 16,864 H1
Neftekamsk 70,000 J3
Nelidovo 29,813 D3
Nerekhta 25,722 F3
Nevel' 17,804 D3
Nevinnomyssk 104,000 F6

Nezhin 70,000 D4
Nikel' 21,299 C1
Nikolayev 440,000 D5
Nikol'sk 20,740 G4
Nikopol' 146,000 D5
Nizhnekamsk 134,000 H3
Nizhniy Lomov 17,460 F4
Nizhniy Novgorod
(Gor'kiy) 1,344,000 F3
Nosovka 19,430 D4
Novaya Kakhovka 52,000 D5
Novgorod 186,000 D3
Novgorod-Severskiy D4
Novoanninskiy 20,461 F4
Novocherkassk 183,000 F5
Novograd-Volynskiy 41,194 C4
Novogrudok 19,374 C4
Novokuybyshevsk 109,000 G4
Novomoskovsk 147,000 E4
Novopolotsk 67,000 C3
Novorossiysk 159,000 E6
Novoshakhtinsk 104,000 E5
Novotroitsk 95,000 J4
Novoukrainka 19,554 D5
Novouzensk G4
Novovolynsk 41,187 B4
Novovyatsk 26,408 G3
Novozybkov 34,433 D4
Nurlat 17,533 H4
Nyandoma 23,366 F2
Nytva 17,491 H3
Nyuvchim H2
Obninsk 73,000 E3
Ochamchira 18,718 F6
Odessa 1,046,000 D5
Oktyabr'sk 33,081 G4
Oktyabr'skiy 88,000 H4
Okulovka 19,194 D3
Olenegorsk 21,485 D1
Olonets D2
Omutninsk 28,777 H3
Onega 25,047 E2
Ordzhonikidze 279,000 F6
Orel 305,000 E4
Orenburg 459,000 J4
Orgeyev 25,798 C5
Orsha 112,000 C4
Orsk 247,000 J4
Osa 15,038 J3
Osipenko (Berdyansk) 122,000 E5
Osipovichi 19,705 C4
Ostashkov 23,419 D3
Ostrogozhsk 29,921 E4
Ostrov 22,369 C3
Otradnyy 44,426 H4
Panevežys 102,000 B3
Pärnu 51,000 C3
Pavlograd 107,000 E5
Pavlovo 68,000 F3
Pechenga D1
Pechora 56,000 J1
Penza 483,000 G4
Perm' 999,000 J3
Pervomaysk 72,000 D5
Petrokrepost' D3
Petrovsk 30,953 G4
Petrozavodsk 234,000 D2
Petsamo (Pechenga) D1
Pinsk 90,000 C4
Podol'sk 202,000 E3
Podporozh'ye 21,545 D2
Pokhvistnevo 26,125 H4
Polonnoye 22,484 C4
Polotsk 71,000 C3
Poltava 279,000 D5
Polyarnyy 15,321 D1
Ponoy F1
Poti 45,979 F6
Povenets E2
Povorino 20,591 F4
Prikumsk 35,768 F6
Priluki 65,000 D4
Primorsk C2
Primorsko-Akhtarsk 25,981 E5
Priozersk 16,652 D2
Privolzhskiy 23,041 G4
Priyutovo 21,051 H4
Prokhladnyy 40,074 F6
Pskov 176,000 C3
Pugachev 33,963 G4
Pushkin 90,000 C3
Pyatigorsk 110,000 F6
Rabocheostrovsk D1
Rakhov B5
Rakvere 17,891 C3
Rasskazovo 40,038 F4
Razdan 26,833 G6
Rechitsa 60,000 C4
Reni 19,625 C5
Revel (Tallinn) 430,000 B3

Rēzekne 30,803 C3
Riga 835,000 B3
Romny 53,000 D4
Roslavl' 56,000 D4
Rossosh' 36,438 E4
Rostov 30,815 E3
Rostov-na-Donu 934,000 F5
Rovno 179,000 C4
Rtishchevo 37,146 F4
Rubezhnoye 66,000 E5
Rustavi 129,000 G6
Ruzayevka 41,084 F4
Ryazan' 453,000 E4
Ryazhsk 25,425 F4
Rybinsk 239,000 E3
Rybnitsa 32,266 C5
Rzhev 69,000 D3
Safonovo 53,000 D3
Saki 24,208 D5
Salavat 137,000 H4
Sal'sk 57,000 F5
Sal'yany 24,228 G7
Samara (Kuybyshev) 1,216,000 H4
Sambor 29,253 B5
Saransk 263,000 G4
Sarapul 107,000 H3
Saratov 856,000 G4
Sasovo 27,228 F4
Segezha 28,810 D2
Semenov 23,633 F3
Semiluki 18,221 E4
Sengiley G4
Serdobol (Sortavala) 22,188 D2
Serdobsk 33,783 F4
Sergach 22,509 F3
Serpukhov 140,000 E4
Sevastopol' 301,000 D6
Severodonetsk 113,000 E5
Severodvinsk 197,000 E2
Severomorsk 50,000 D1
Shakhty 209,000 F5
Shakhun'ya 20,009 G3
Shar'ya 25,788 G3
Shchekino 70,000 E4
Shchigry 17,133 E4
Sheki 43,158 G6
Shemakha 17,986 G6
Shepetovka 38,707 C4
Shostka 82,000 D4
Shpola 19,806 D5
Shumerlya 33,816 G3
Shuya 72,000 F3
Šiauliai 118,000 B3
Sibay 37,656 J4
Simferopol' 302,000 D6
Skadovsk D5
Skopin 24,429 F4
Slantsy 41,146 C3
Slavuta 25,573 C4
Slavyansk 140,000 E5
Slavyansk-na-Kubani 54,000 E5
Slobodskoy 34,374 H3
Slonim 30,279 B4
Slutsk 35,609 C4
Smela 62,000 D5
Smolensk 276,000 D4
Sochi 287,000 E6
Sokol 48,243 F3
Soligorsk 65,000 C4
Solikamsk 101,000 J3
Sol'-Iletsk 22,227 J4
Sorochinsk 23,235 H4
Soroki 21,924 C5
Sortavala 22,188 D2
Sosnogorsk 24,688 H2
Sovetsk (Tilsit) 38,456 B4
Sovetsk 17,027 G3
Stakhanov 108,000 E5
Stalingrad (Volgograd) 929,000 F5
Staraya Russa 34,577 D3
Staryy Oskol 115,000 E4
Stavropol' 258,000 F5
Stepanakert 30,293 G7
Sterlitamak 220,000 J4
Stupino 70,000 E4
Sudak E6
Sukhumi 114,000 F6
Sumgait 190,000 G6
Sumy 228,000 E4
Svetlogorsk 55,000 C4
Svetlograd 40,265 F5
Syktyvkar 171,000 H2
Syzran' 178,000 G4
Taganrog 276,000 E5
Tallinn 430,000 B3
Tambov 270,000 F4
Tartu 105,000 C3
Taurage 19,461 B3
Tbilisi 1,066,000 F6
Telavi 21,179 G6

Telšiai 20,220 B3
Temryuk 23,172 E5
Ternopol' 144,000 C5
Teykovo 41,607 E3
Tiflis (Tbilisi) 1,066,000 F6
Tighina (Bendery) 101,000 C5
Tikhoretsk 64,000 F5
Tikhvin 59,000 D3
Tilsit (Sovetsk) 38,456 B4
Timashevsk 29,055 E5
Tiraspol' 139,000 D5
Togliatti (Tol'yatti) 502,000 G4
Tokmak 59,000 E5
Toropets 16,863 D3
Torzhok 45,443 D3
Troitsko-Pechorsk J2
Tskhinvali 30,311 F6
Tuapse 60,000 E6
Tukums 14,800 B3
Tula 514,000 E4
Tutayev 16,839 E3
Tuymazy 37,021 H4
Tver (Kalinin) 412,000 E3
Tyrnyauz 18,253 F6
Uchaly 21,808 J4
Ufa 969,000 J4
Uglich 35,463 E3
Ukmerge 21,663 C3
Ul'yanovsk 464,000 G4
Uman' 79,000 D5
Unecha 21,749 D4
Ungeny 17,228 C5
Uryupinsk 38,192 F4
Usinsk J1
Usman' 20,150 E4
Uvarovo 31,046 F4
Uzhgorod 91,000 B5
Uzlovaya 65,000 E4
Valga 16,795 C3
Valmiera 20,331 C3
Valuyki 29,093 E4
Vasil'kov 26,741 D4
Velikiye Luki 102,000 D3
Velikiy Ustyug 36,737 F2
Vel'sk 21,899 F2
Ventspils 40,467 B3
Vereshchagino 23,585 H3
Vichuga 52,000 F3
Viipuri (Vyborg) 76,000 C2
Vileyka C4
Vilna (Vilnius) 481,000 C4
Vinnitsa 314,000 C5
Vinogradov 20,580 B5
Vitebsk 297,000 C3
Vladimir 296,000 F3
Vladimir-Volynskiy 28,412 B4
Volgodonsk 91,000 F5
Volgograd 929,000 F5
Volkhov 47,025 D3
Volkovysk 28,266 B4
Vologda 237,000 F3
Vol'sk 66,000 G4
Volzhsk 52,000 G3
Volzhskiy 209,000 G5
Vorkuta 100,000 K1
Voronezh 783,000 E4
Voroshilovgrad 463,000 E5
Voskresensk 76,000 E3
Votkinsk 90,000 H3
Voznesensk 36,457 D5
Vyatskiye Polyany 32,729 H3
Vyaz'ma 52,000 D3
Vyborg 76,000 C2
Vyksa 54,000 F3
Vyshniy Volochek 72,000 D3
Yalta 80,000 D6
Yanaul 20,115 J3
Yaroslavl' 597,000 E3
Yartsevo 36,662 D3
Yefremov 53,000 E4
Yelabuga 31,728 H3
Yelets 112,000 E4
Yenakiyevo 114,000 E5
Yershov 21,731 G4
Yessentuki 78,000 F6
Yevlakh 29,462 G6
Yevpatoria 93,000 D5
Yeysk 71,000 E5
Yoshkar-Ola 201,000 G3
Yur'yevets 20,144 F3
Zagorsk 107,000 E3
Zapolyarnyy 22,084 D1
Zaporozh'ye 781,000 E5
Zelenodol'sk 85,000 G3
Zelenokumsk 29,691 F6
Zernograd 20,324 F5
Zhdanov 503,000 E5
Zheleznodorozhnyy 76,000 H2
Zheleznogorsk 65,000 E4
Zhigulevsk 52,130 G4

Zhitomir 244,000 C4
Zhlobin 25,359 D4
Zhmerinka 36,195 C5
Zhodino 22,083 C4
Zhovtnevoye 31,102 D5
Znamenka 27,393 D5
Zolotonosha 27,639 D5
Zugdidi 39,896 F6
Zuyevka 17,001 H3

OTHER FEATURES

Apsheron (pen.) H6
Araks (riv.) G7
Azov (sea) E5
Baltic (sea) B3
Barents (sea) E1
Belaya (riv.) H3
Beloye (lake) E2
Black (sea) D6
Bug (riv.) B4
Bug (riv.) D5
Caspian (sea) G6
Caucasus (mts.) F6
Crimea (pen.) D5
Desna (riv.) D4
Dnieper (riv.) D5
Dniester (riv.) C5
Don (riv.) F5
Donets (riv.) E5
Dvina (bay) E2
Dvina, Northern (riv.) F2
Dvina, Western (riv.) C3
Dykh-Tau (mt.) F6
El'brus (mt.) F6
Finland (gulf) C3
Hiiumaa (isl.) B3
Il'men' (lake) D3
Imandra (lake) D1
Kakhovka (res.) D5
Kama (riv.) H2
Kandalaksha (gulf) D1
Kanin (pen.) G1
Kara (sea) K1
Karskiye Vorota (str.) J1
Kazbek (mt.) F6
Khoper (riv.) F4
Kola (pen.) E1
Kolguyev (isl.) G1
Kuban' (riv.) E5
Kura (riv.) G6
Kuybyshev (res.) G4
Ladoga (lake) D2
Lapland (reg.) D1
Mezen' (riv.) G1
Moksha (riv.) F4
Narodnaya (mt.) J1
Niemen (riv.) B4
Novaya Zemlya (isls.) H1
Oka (riv.) F4
Onega (bay) E2
Onega (lake) E2
Onega (riv.) E2
Pechora (riv.) H1
Peipus (lake) C3
Pripet (marshes) C4
Pripyat' (riv.) C4
Prut (riv.) C5
Riga (gulf) B3
Rybachiy (pen.) D1
Rybinsk (res.) E3
Saaremaa (isl.) B3
Samara (riv.) H4
Sevan (lake) G6
Seym (riv.) D4
Sura (riv.) G4
Svir' (riv.) D2
Timan (ridge) G1
Tsil'ma (riv.) H1
Tsimlyansk (res.) F5
Tuloma (riv.) D1
Ural (mts.) J2
Ural (riv.) J4
Usa (riv.) K1
Valday (hills) D3
Vaygach (isl.) K1
Velikaya (riv.) C3
Volga (riv.) G5
Volga-Don (canal) F5
Volgograd (res.) G5
Volkhov (riv.) D3
Vorskla (riv.) E4
Vyatka (riv.) H3
Vychegda (riv.) G2
Vyg (lake) E2
White (sea) E1
Yamantau (mt.) J4
Yugorskiy (pen.) K1

*City and suburbs.

ALGERIA

AREA 919,591 sq. mi. (2,381,740 sq. km.)
POPULATION 17,422,000
CAPITAL Algiers
LARGEST CITY Algiers
HIGHEST POINT Tahat 9,852 ft. (3,003 m.)
MONETARY UNIT Algerian dinar
MAJOR LANGUAGES Arabic, Berber, French
MAJOR RELIGION Islam

ANGOLA

AREA 481,351 sq. mi. (1,246,700 sq. km.)
POPULATION 7,078,000
CAPITAL Luanda
LARGEST CITY Luanda
HIGHEST POINT Mt. Moco 8,593 ft. (2,620 m.)
MONETARY UNIT kwanza
MAJOR LANGUAGES Mbundu, Kongo, Lunda, Portuguese
MAJOR RELIGIONS Tribal religions, Roman Catholicism

BENIN

AREA 43,483 sq. mi. (112,620 sq. km.)
POPULATION 3,338,240
CAPITAL Porto-Novo
LARGEST CITY Cotonou
HIGHEST POINT Atakora Mts. 2,083 ft. (635 m.)
MONETARY UNIT CFA franc
MAJOR LANGUAGES Fon, Somba, Yoruba, Bariba, French, Mina, Dendi
MAJOR RELIGIONS Tribal religions, Islam, Roman Catholicism

BOTSWANA

AREA 224,764 sq. mi. (582,139 sq. km.)
POPULATION 819,000
CAPITAL Gaborone
LARGEST CITY Francistown
HIGHEST POINT Tsodilo Hill 5,922 ft. (1,805 m.)
MONETARY UNIT pula
MAJOR LANGUAGES Setswana, Shona, Bushman, English, Afrikaans
MAJOR RELIGIONS Tribal religions, Protestantism

BURUNDI

AREA 10,747 sq. mi. (27,835 sq. km.)
POPULATION 4,021,910
CAPITAL Bujumbura
LARGEST CITY Bujumbura
HIGHEST POINT 8,858 ft. (2,700 m.)
MONETARY UNIT Burundi franc
MAJOR LANGUAGES Kirundi, French, Swahili
MAJOR RELIGIONS Tribal religions, Roman Catholicism, Islam

CAMEROON

AREA 183,568 sq. mi. (475,441 sq. km.)
POPULATION 8,503,000
CAPITAL Yaoundé
LARGEST CITY Douala
HIGHEST POINT Cameroon 13,350 ft. (4,069 m.)
MONETARY UNIT CFA franc
MAJOR LANGUAGES Fang, Bamileke, Fulani, Duala, French, English
MAJOR RELIGIONS Tribal religions, Christianity, Islam

CAPE VERDE

AREA 1,557 sq. mi. (4,033 sq. km.)
POPULATION 324,000
CAPITAL Praia
LARGEST CITY Praia
HIGHEST POINT 9,281 ft. (2,829 m.)
MONETARY UNIT Cape Verde escudo
MAJOR LANGUAGE Portuguese
MAJOR RELIGION Roman Catholicism

CENTRAL AFRICAN REPUBLIC

AREA 242,000 sq. mi. (626,780 sq. km.)
POPULATION 2,284,000
CAPITAL Bangui
LARGEST CITY Bangui
HIGHEST POINT Gao 4,659 ft. (1,420 m.)
MONETARY UNIT CFA franc
MAJOR LANGUAGES Banda, Gbaya, Sangho, French
MAJOR RELIGIONS Tribal religions, Christianity, Islam

CHAD

AREA 495,752 sq. mi. (1,283,998 sq. km.)
POPULATION 4,309,000
CAPITAL N'Djamena
LARGEST CITY N'Djamena
HIGHEST POINT Emi Koussi 11,204 ft. (3,415 m.)
MONETARY UNIT CFA franc
MAJOR LANGUAGES Arabic, Bagirmi, French, Sara, Massa, Moudang
MAJOR RELIGIONS Islam, tribal religions

COMOROS

AREA 719 sq. mi. (1,862 sq. km.)
POPULATION 290,000
CAPITAL Moroni
LARGEST CITY Moroni
HIGHEST POINT Karthala 7,746 ft. (2,361 m.)
MONETARY UNIT CFA franc
MAJOR LANGUAGES Arabic, French, Swahili
MAJOR RELIGION Islam

CONGO

AREA 132,046 sq. mi. (342,000 sq. km.)
POPULATION 1,537,000
CAPITAL Brazzaville
LARGEST CITY Brazzaville
HIGHEST POINT Leketi Mts. 3,412 ft. (1,040 m.)
MONETARY UNIT CFA franc
MAJOR LANGUAGES Kikongo, Bateke, Lingala, French
MAJOR RELIGIONS Christianity, tribal religions, Islam

DJIBOUTI

AREA 8,880 sq. mi. (23,000 sq. km.)
POPULATION 386,000
CAPITAL Djibouti
LARGEST CITY Djibouti
HIGHEST POINT Moussa Ali 6,768 ft. (2,063 m.)
MONETARY UNIT Djibouti franc
MAJOR LANGUAGES Arabic, Somali, Afar, French
MAJOR RELIGIONS Islam, Roman Catholicism

EGYPT

AREA 386,659 sq. mi. (1,001,447 sq. km.)
POPULATION 41,572,000
CAPITAL Cairo
LARGEST CITY Cairo
HIGHEST POINT Jeb. Katherina 8,651 ft. (2,637 m.)
MONETARY UNIT Egyptian pound
MAJOR LANGUAGE Arabic
MAJOR RELIGIONS Islam, Coptic Christianity

EQUATORIAL GUINEA

AREA 10,831 sq. mi. (28,052 sq. km.)
POPULATION 244,000
CAPITAL Malabo
LARGEST CITY Malabo
HIGHEST POINT 9,868 ft. (3,008 m.)
MONETARY UNIT ekuele
MAJOR LANGUAGES Fang, Bubi, Spanish
MAJOR RELIGIONS Tribal religions, Christianity

ETHIOPIA

AREA 471,776 sq. mi. (1,221,900 sq. km.)
POPULATION 31,065,000
CAPITAL Addis Ababa
LARGEST CITY Addis Ababa
HIGHEST POINT Ras Dashan 15,157 ft. (4,620 m.)
MONETARY UNIT birr
MAJOR LANGUAGES Amharic, Gallinya, Tigrinya, Somali, Sidamo, Arabic, Ge'ez
MAJOR RELIGIONS Coptic Christianity, Islam

GABON

AREA 103,346 sq. mi. (267,666 sq. km.)
POPULATION 551,000
CAPITAL Libreville
LARGEST CITY Libreville
HIGHEST POINT Ibounzi 5,165 ft. (1,574 m.)
MONETARY UNIT CFA franc
MAJOR LANGUAGES Fang and other Bantu languages, French
MAJOR RELIGIONS Tribal religions, Christianity, Islam

GAMBIA

AREA 4,127 sq. mi. (10,689 sq. km.)
POPULATION 601,000
CAPITAL Banjul
LARGEST CITY Banjul
HIGHEST POINT 100 ft. (30 m.)
MONETARY UNIT dalasi
MAJOR LANGUAGES Mandingo, Fulani, Wolof, English, Malinke
MAJOR RELIGIONS Islam, tribal religions, Christianity

GHANA

AREA 92,099 sq. mi. (238,536 sq. km.)
POPULATION 11,450,000
CAPITAL Accra
LARGEST CITY Accra
HIGHEST POINT Togo Hills 2,900 ft. (884 m.)
MONETARY UNIT cedi
MAJOR LANGUAGES Twi, Fante, Dagbani, Ewe, Ga, English, Hausa, Akan
MAJOR RELIGIONS Tribal religions, Christianity, Islam

GUINEA

AREA 94,925 sq. mi. (245,856 sq. km.)
POPULATION 5,143,284
CAPITAL Conakry
LARGEST CITY Conakry
HIGHEST POINT Nimba Mts. 6,070 ft. (1,850 m.)
MONETARY UNIT syli
MAJOR LANGUAGES Fulani, Mandingo, Susu, French
MAJOR RELIGIONS Islam, tribal religions

GUINEA-BISSAU

AREA 13,948 sq. mi. (36,125 sq. km.)
POPULATION 777,214
CAPITAL Bissau
LARGEST CITY Bissau
HIGHEST POINT 689 ft. (210 m.)
MONETARY UNIT Guinea-Bissau escudo
MAJOR LANGUAGES Balante, Fulani, Crioulo, Mandingo, Portuguese
MAJOR RELIGIONS Islam, tribal religions, Roman Catholicism

IVORY COAST

AREA 124,504 sq. mi. (322,465 sq. km.)
POPULATION 7,920,000
CAPITAL Abidjan
LARGEST CITY Abidjan
HIGHEST POINT 5,745 ft. (1,751 m.)
MONETARY UNIT CFA franc
MAJOR LANGUAGES Bale, Bete, Senufu, French, Dioula
MAJOR RELIGIONS Tribal religions, Islam

KENYA

AREA 224,960 sq. mi. (582,646 sq. km.)
POPULATION 15,327,061
CAPITAL Nairobi
LARGEST CITY Nairobi
HIGHEST POINT Kenya 17,058 ft. (5,199 m.)
MONETARY UNIT Kenya shilling
MAJOR LANGUAGES Kikuyu, Luo, Kavirondo, Kamba, Swahili, English
MAJOR RELIGIONS Tribal religions, Christianity, Hinduism, Islam

LESOTHO

AREA 11,720 sq. mi. (30,355 sq. km.)
POPULATION 1,339,000
CAPITAL Maseru
LARGEST CITY Maseru
HIGHEST POINT 11,425 ft. (3,482 m.)
MONETARY UNIT loti
MAJOR LANGUAGES Sesotho, English
MAJOR RELIGIONS Tribal religions, Christianity

LIBERIA

AREA 43,000 sq. mi. (111,370 sq. km.)
POPULATION 1,873,000
CAPITAL Monrovia
LARGEST CITY Monrovia
HIGHEST POINT Wutivi 5,584 ft. (1,702 m.)
MONETARY UNIT Liberian dollar
MAJOR LANGUAGES Kru, Kpelle, Bassa, Vai, English
MAJOR RELIGIONS Christianity, tribal religions, Islam

LIBYA

AREA 679,358 sq. mi. (1,759,537 sq. km.)
POPULATION 2,856,000
CAPITAL Tripoli
LARGEST CITY Tripoli
HIGHEST POINT Bette Pk. 7,500 ft. (2,286 m.)
MONETARY UNIT Libyan dinar
MAJOR LANGUAGES Arabic, Berber
MAJOR RELIGION Islam

MADAGASCAR

AREA 226,657 sq. mi. (587,041 sq. km.)
POPULATION 8,742,000
CAPITAL Antananarivo
LARGEST CITY Antananarivo
HIGHEST POINT Maromokotro 9,436 ft. (2,876 m.)
MONETARY UNIT Madagascar franc
MAJOR LANGUAGES Malagasy, French
MAJOR RELIGIONS Tribal religions, Roman Catholicism, Protestantism

MALAWI

AREA 45,747 sq. mi. (118,485 sq. km.)
POPULATION 5,968,000
CAPITAL Lilongwe
LARGEST CITY Blantyre
HIGHEST POINT Mulanje 9,843 ft. (3,000 m.)
MONETARY UNIT Malawi kwacha
MAJOR LANGUAGES Chichewa, Yao, English, Nyanja, Tumbuka, Tonga, Ngoni
MAJOR RELIGIONS Tribal religions, Islam, Christianity

MALI

AREA 464,873 sq. mi. (1,204,021 sq. km.)
POPULATION 6,906,000
CAPITAL Bamako
LARGEST CITY Bamako
HIGHEST POINT Hombori Mts. 3,789 ft. (1,155 m.)
MONETARY UNIT Mali franc
MAJOR LANGUAGES Bambara, Senufu, Fulani, Soninke, French
MAJOR RELIGIONS Islam, tribal religions

MAURITANIA

AREA 419,229 sq. mi. (1,085,803 sq. km.)
POPULATION 1,634,000
CAPITAL Nouakchott
LARGEST CITY Nouakchott
HIGHEST POINT 2,972 ft. (906 m.)
MONETARY UNIT ouguiya
MAJOR LANGUAGES Arabic, Wolof, Tukolor, French
MAJOR RELIGION Islam

MAURITIUS

AREA 790 sq. mi. (2,046 sq. km.)
POPULATION 959,000
CAPITAL Port Louis
LARGEST CITY Port Louis
HIGHEST POINT 2,711 ft. (826 m.)
MONETARY UNIT Mauritian rupee
MAJOR LANGUAGES English, French, French Creole, Hindi, Urdu
MAJOR RELIGIONS Hinduism, Christianity, Islam

AFRICA

AREA 11,707,000 sq. mi. (30,321,130 sq. km.)
POPULATION 469,000,000
LARGEST CITY Cairo
HIGHEST POINT Kilimanjaro 19,340 ft. (5,895 m.)
LOWEST POINT Lake Assal, Djibouti -512 ft. (-156 m.)

MAYOTTE

AREA 144 sq. mi. (373 sq. km.)
POPULATION 47,300
CAPITAL Dzaoudzi

REUNION

AREA 969 sq. mi. (2,510 sq. km.)
POPULATION 491,000
CAPITAL St-Denis

MOROCCO

AREA 172,414 sq. mi. (446,550 sq. km.)
POPULATION 20,242,000
CAPITAL Rabat
LARGEST CITY Casablanca
HIGHEST POINT Jeb. Toubkal 13,665 ft. (4,165 m.)
MONETARY UNIT dirham
MAJOR LANGUAGES Arabic, Berber, French
MAJOR RELIGIONS Islam, Judaism, Christianity

MOZAMBIQUE

AREA 303,769 sq. mi. (786,762 sq. km.)
POPULATION 12,130,000
CAPITAL Maputo
LARGEST CITY Maputo
HIGHEST POINT Mt. Binga 7,992 ft. (2,436 m.)
MONETARY UNIT metical
MAJOR LANGUAGES Makua, Thonga, Shona, Portuguese
MAJOR RELIGIONS Tribal religions, Roman Catholicism, Islam

NAMIBIA (SOUTH-WEST AFRICA)

AREA 317,827 sq. mi. (823,172 sq. km.)
POPULATION 1,200,000
CAPITAL Windhoek
LARGEST CITY Windhoek
HIGHEST POINT Brandberg 8,550 ft. (2,606 m.)
MONETARY UNIT rand
MAJOR LANGUAGES Ovambo, Hottentot, Herero, Afrikaans, English
MAJOR RELIGIONS Tribal religions, Protestantism

NIGER

AREA 489,189 sq. mi. (1,267,000 sq. km.)
POPULATION 5,098,427
CAPITAL Niamey
LARGEST CITY Niamey
HIGHEST POINT Banguezane 6,234 ft. (1,900 m.)
MONETARY UNIT CFA franc
MAJOR LANGUAGES Hausa, Songhai, Fulani, French, Tamashek, Djerma
MAJOR RELIGIONS Islam, tribal religions

NIGERIA

AREA 357,000 sq. mi. (924,630 sq. km.)
POPULATION 82,643,000
CAPITAL Lagos
LARGEST CITY Lagos
HIGHEST POINT Dimlang 6,700 ft. (2,042 m.)
MONETARY UNIT naira
MAJOR LANGUAGES Hausa, Yoruba, Ibo, Ijaw, Fulani, Tiv, Kanuri, Ibibio, English, Edo
MAJOR RELIGIONS Islam, Christianity, tribal religions

RWANDA

AREA 10,169 sq. mi. (26,337 sq. km.)
POPULATION 4,819,317
CAPITAL Kigali
LARGEST CITY Kigali
HIGHEST POINT Karisimbi 14,780 ft. (4,505 m.)
MONETARY UNIT Rwanda franc
MAJOR LANGUAGES Kinyarwanda, French, Swahili
MAJOR RELIGIONS Tribal religions, Roman Catholicism, Islam

SÃO TOMÉ E PRÍNCIPE

AREA 372 sq. mi. (963 sq. km.)
POPULATION 85,000
CAPITAL São Tomé
LARGEST CITY São Tomé
HIGHEST POINT Pico 6,640 ft. (2,024 m.)
MONETARY UNIT dobra
MAJOR LANGUAGES Bantu languages, Portuguese
MAJOR RELIGIONS Tribal religions, Roman Catholicism

SENEGAL

AREA 75,954 sq. mi. (196,720 sq. km.)
POPULATION 5,508,000
CAPITAL Dakar
LARGEST CITY Dakar
HIGHEST POINT Futa Jallon 1,640 ft. (500 m.)
MONETARY UNIT CFA franc
MAJOR LANGUAGES Wolof, Peul (Fulani), French, Mende, Mandingo, Dida
MAJOR RELIGIONS Islam, tribal religions, Roman Catholicism

SEYCHELLES

AREA 145 sq. mi. (375 sq. km.)
POPULATION 63,000
CAPITAL Victoria
LARGEST CITY Victoria
HIGHEST POINT Morne Seychellois 2,993 ft. (912 m.)
MONETARY UNIT Seychellois rupee
MAJOR LANGUAGES English, French, Creole
MAJOR RELIGION Roman Catholicism

SIERRA LEONE

AREA 27,925 sq. mi. (72,325 sq. km.)
POPULATION 3,470,000
CAPITAL Freetown
LARGEST CITY Freetown
HIGHEST POINT Loma Mts. 6,390 ft. (1,947 m.)
MONETARY UNIT leone
MAJOR LANGUAGES Mende, Temne, Vai, English, Krio (pidgin)
MAJOR RELIGIONS Tribal religions, Islam, Christianity

SOMALIA

AREA 246,200 sq. mi. (637,658 sq. km.)
POPULATION 3,645,000
CAPITAL Mogadishu
LARGEST CITY Mogadishu
HIGHEST POINT Surud Ad 7,900 ft. (2,408 m.)
MONETARY UNIT Somali shilling
MAJOR LANGUAGES Somali, Arabic, Italian, English
MAJOR RELIGION Islam

SOUTH AFRICA

AREA 455,318 sq. mi. (1,179,274 sq. km.)
POPULATION 23,771,970
CAPITALS Cape Town, Pretoria
LARGEST CITY Johannesburg
HIGHEST POINT Injasuti 11,182 ft. (3,408 m.)
MONETARY UNIT rand
MAJOR LANGUAGES Afrikaans, English, Xhosa, Zulu, Sesotho
MAJOR RELIGIONS Protestantism, Roman Catholicism, Islam, Hinduism, tribal religions

SUDAN

AREA 967,494 sq. mi. (2,505,809 sq. km.)
POPULATION 18,691,000
CAPITAL Khartoum
LARGEST CITY Khartoum
HIGHEST POINT Jeb. Marra 10,073 ft. (3,070 m.)
MONETARY UNIT Sudanese pound
MAJOR LANGUAGES Arabic, Dinka, Nubian, Beja, Nuer
MAJOR RELIGIONS Islam, tribal religions

SWAZILAND

AREA 6,705 sq. mi. (17,366 sq. km.)
POPULATION 547,000
CAPITAL Mbabane
LARGEST CITY Manzini
HIGHEST POINT Emlembe 6,109 ft. (1,862 m.)
MONETARY UNIT lilangeni
MAJOR LANGUAGES siSwati, English
MAJOR RELIGIONS Tribal religions, Christianity

TANZANIA

AREA 363,708 sq. mi. (942,003 sq. km.)
POPULATION 17,527,560
CAPITAL Dar es Salaam
LARGEST CITY Dar es Salaam
HIGHEST POINT Kilimanjaro 19,340 ft. (5,895 m.)
MONETARY UNIT Tanzanian shilling
MAJOR LANGUAGES Nyamwezi-Sukuma, Swahili, English
MAJOR RELIGIONS Tribal religions, Christianity, Islam

TOGO

AREA 21,622 sq. mi. (56,000 sq. km.)
POPULATION 2,472,000
CAPITAL Lomé
LARGEST CITY Lomé
HIGHEST POINT Agou 3,445 ft. (1,050 m.)
MONETARY UNIT CFA franc
MAJOR LANGUAGES Ewe, French, Twi, Hausa
MAJOR RELIGIONS Tribal religions, Roman Catholicism, Islam

TUNISIA

AREA 63,378 sq. mi. (164,149 sq. km.)
POPULATION 6,367,000
CAPITAL Tunis
LARGEST CITY Tunis
HIGHEST POINT Jeb. Chambi 5,065 ft. (1,544 m.)
MONETARY UNIT Tunisian dinar
MAJOR LANGUAGES Arabic, French
MAJOR RELIGION Islam

UGANDA

AREA 91,076 sq. mi. (235,887 sq. km.)
POPULATION 12,630,076
CAPITAL Kampala
LARGEST CITY Kampala
HIGHEST POINT Margherita 16,795 ft. (5,119 m.)
MONETARY UNIT Ugandan shilling
MAJOR LANGUAGES Luganda, Acholi, Teso, Nyoro, Soga, Nkole, English, Swahili
MAJOR RELIGIONS Tribal religions, Christianity, Islam

UPPER VOLTA

AREA 105,869 sq. mi. (274,200 sq. km.)
POPULATION 6,908,000
CAPITAL Ouagadougou
LARGEST CITY Ouagadougou
HIGHEST POINT 2,352 ft. (717 m.)
MONETARY UNIT CFA franc
MAJOR LANGUAGES Mossi, Lobi, French, Samo, Gourounsi
MAJOR RELIGIONS Islam, tribal religions, Roman Catholicism

WESTERN SAHARA

AREA 102,703 sq. mi. (266,000 sq. km.)
POPULATION 76,425
HIGHEST POINT 2,700 ft. (823 m.)
MAJOR LANGUAGE Arabic
MAJOR RELIGION Islam

ZAIRE

AREA 905,063 sq. mi. (2,344,113 sq. km.)
POPULATION 28,291,000
CAPITAL Kinshasa
LARGEST CITY Kinshasa
HIGHEST POINT Margherita 16,795 ft. (5,119 m.)
MONETARY UNIT zaire
MAJOR LANGUAGES Tshiluba, Mongo, Kikongo, Kingwana, Zande, Lingala, Swahili, French
MAJOR RELIGIONS Tribal religions, Christianity

ZAMBIA

AREA 290,586 sq. mi. (752,618 sq. km.)
POPULATION 5,679,808
CAPITAL Lusaka
LARGEST CITY Lusaka
HIGHEST POINT Sunzu 6,782 ft. (2,067 m.)
MONETARY UNIT Zambian kwacha
MAJOR LANGUAGES Bemba, Tonga, Lozi, Luvale, Nyanja, English
MAJOR RELIGIONS Tribal religions

ZIMBABWE

AREA 150,803 sq. mi. (390,580 sq. km.)
POPULATION 7,360,000
CAPITAL Harare
LARGEST CITY Harare
HIGHEST POINT Mt. Inyangani 8,517 ft. (2,596 m.)
MONETARY UNIT Zimbabwe dollar
MAJOR LANGUAGES English, Shona, Ndebele
MAJOR RELIGIONS Tribal religions, Protestantism

Topography

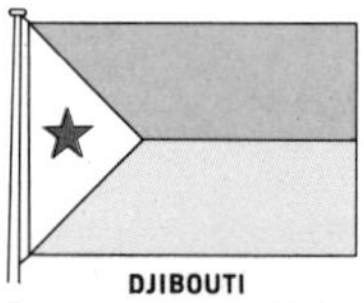

DJIBOUTI

ZIMBABWE

ALGERIA

CITIES and TOWNS

Ain Sefra 22,400	G5
Algiers (cap.) 1,365,400	G4
Annaba 255,900	H4
Béchar 72,800	F5
Bejaïa 89,500	G4
Biskra 90,500	H5
Blida 160,900	G4
Bou Saâda 50,000	G5
Constantine 335,100	H4
Djelfa 51,000	G5
El Asnam 106,100	G4
El Bayadh 38,500	G5
El Oued 72,100	H5
Ghardaïa 70,500	G5
Jijel 49,800	H4
Laghouat 59,200	G5
Mascara 62,300	G4
Mostaganem 101,600	F4
Oran 491,900	F4
Ouargla 77,400	G5
Saïda 62,100	G4
Sétif 144,200	H4
Sidi Bel Abbès 116,000	F4
Skikda 107,700	H4
Tamanrasset 23,200	H7
Tébessa 67,200	H4
Tiaret 62,900	G4
Tizi Ouzou 73,100	G4
Tlemcen 109,400	F5
Touggourt 75,600	G5

OTHER FEATURES

Ahaggar (range)	H7
Grand Erg Occidental (des.)	G5
Grand Erg Oriental (des.)	H5
Sahara (des.)	EM7
Tanezrouft (des.)	G7

ANGOLA

CITIES and TOWNS

Benguela 40,996	J14
Bié 18,941	K14
Cabinda 21,124	J13
Lobito 59,528	J14
Luanda (cap.) 475,328	J13
Lubango 31,674	J14
Malange 31,599	K13
Moçâmedes 12,076	J15
Saurimo 12,901	L13

OTHER FEATURES

Cubango (riv.)	K14
Cunene (riv.)	J15

BENIN

CITIES and TOWNS

Abomey 38,000	G10
Cotonou 178,000	G10
Parakou 21,000	G10
Porto-Novo (cap.) 104,000	G10

BOTSWANA

CITIES and TOWNS

Francistown 22,000	M16
Gaborone (cap.) 21,000	M16
Kayne 10,664	L6
Mahalapye 12,056	M16
Serowe 15,723	M16

OTHER FEATURES

Kalahari (des.)	L16
Makgadikgadi (salt pan)	L16
Ngami (lake)	L16
Okovanggo (swamps)	L14

BURUNDI

CITIES and TOWNS

Bujumbura (cap.) 141,040	N12
Gitega 19,500	N12

CAMEROON

CITIES and TOWNS

Buea 24,584	H11
Douala 458,426	J11
Ebolowa 24,000	J11
Foumban 33,944	J10
Garoua 63,900	J10
Maroua 67,187	J9
Ngaoundéré 38,992	J10
N'Kongsamba 71,298	J11
Yaoundé (cap.) 313,706	J11

OTHER FEATURES

Biafra (bight)	H11
Cameroon (mt.)	H11
Sanaga (riv.)	J11

CENTRAL AFRICAN REPUBLIC

CITIES and TOWNS

Bambari 31,285	L
Bangassou 21,773	L
Bangui (cap.) 279,792	K
Berberati 27,285	K
Bossangoa 25,150	K
Bouar 29,528	K

OTHER FEATURES

Lobaye (riv.)	K
Shinko (riv.)	L

CHAD

CITIES and TOWNS

Abéché 28,100	
Bongor 14,300	
Faya-Largeau 6,800	
Moundou 39,600	K
N'Djamena (cap.) 179,000	

OTHER FEATURES

Baguirmi (reg.)	
Chad (lake)	
Emi Koussi (mt.)	
Ennedi (plat.)	
Sahara (des.)	E
Shari (riv.)	
Sudan (reg.)	E
Tibesti (mts.)	
Wadai (reg.)	

COMOROS

CITIES and TOWNS

Moroni (cap.) 12,000	P

OTHER FEATURES

Anjouan (isl.)	P
Grand Comoro (isl.)	P
Mohéli (isl.)	P

CONGO

CITIES and TOWNS

Brazzaville (cap.) 298,967	J
Impfondo	K
Ouesso	K

FLAGS OF AFRICA

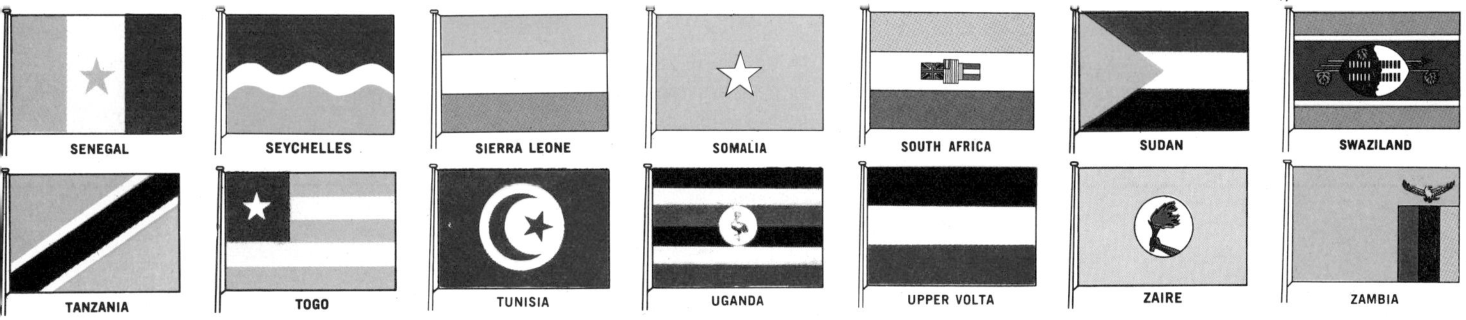

nte-Noire 141,700 .... J12

OTHER FEATURES

go (riv.) K12
ngi (riv.) K11

DJIBOUTI

CITIES and TOWNS

bouti (cap.) 96,000 .... P9
ock P9

EGYPT

CITIES and TOWNS

xandria 2,318,655 .... M5
wân 144,377 .... N7
/ût 213,983 .... N6
i Suef 118,148 .... N6
ro (cap.) 5,084,463 .... N5
mietta (Dumyat) 93,546 .... N5
'lamein M5
aiyûm 167,081 .... M6
Khârga 26,375 .... N6
Minya 146,423 .... M6
nailia 145,978 .... N5
or 92,748 .... N6
rsá Matrûh 27,857 .... M5
rt Said 262,620 .... N5
na 94,013 .... N6
i Barrani 1,574 .... M5
Suez 194,001 .... N6
Tanta 284,636 .... N5

OTHER FEATURES

Aqaba (gulf) O6
Arabian (des.) N6
Aswân (dam) N7
Banas (cape) O7
Farâfra (oasis) M6
Khârga (oasis) N6
Libyan (des.) M6
Nasser (lake) N7
Nile (riv.) N7
Qattara (depr.) M5
Sahara (des.) EM7
Sinai (pen.) N6
Siwa (oasis) M6
Suez (canal) N5
Suez (gulf) N6

EQUATORIAL GUINEA

CITIES and TOWNS

Bata 270,241 .... H11
Malabo (cap.) 37,237 .... A3

OTHER FEATURES

Annobón (isl.) G12
Bioko (Fernando Po)
(isl.) H11
Elobey (isl.) H11
Río Muni (terr.) 203,000 .... J11

ETHIOPIA

CITIES and TOWNS

Addis Ababa (cap.)
1,196,300 .... O10
Adwa 16,400 .... O9
Aksum 12,800 .... O9
Asmara 393,800 .... O9
Assab 16,000 .... P9
Debra Markos 30,260 .... O9
Dessye 49,750 .... O9
Dire Dawa 63,700 .... P10
Gondar 38,600 .... O9
Harar 48,440 .... P10
Jimma 47,360 .... O10
Makale 30,780 .... P9
Massawa 19,800 .... O8
Soddu 11,900 .... O10
Yirga-Alam 14,500 .... O10

OTHER FEATURES

Abay (Blue Nile) (riv.) O9
Dahlak (arch.) P8
Danakil (reg.) P9
Dashan, Ras (mt.) O9
Eritrea (reg.) O8
Mandeb, Bab el (str.) R9
Ogaden (reg.) P10
Tana (lake) O9

GABON

CITIES and TOWNS

Franceville 9,345 .... J12
Lambaréné 17,770 .... H12
Libreville (cap.) 105,080 ..... H11
Mouila 15,016 .... J12
Oyem 12,455 .... J11
Port-Gentil 48,190 .... H12
Tchibanga 14,001 .... J12

OTHER FEATURES

Lopez (cape) H12
Ogooué (riv.) J12

GAMBIA

CITIES and TOWNS

Banjul (Bathurst)
(cap.) 39,476 .... C9
Georgetown 2,510 .... C9

GHANA

CITIES and TOWNS

Accra (cap.) 564,194 .... G11
Axim 8,107 .... F11
Cape Coast 51,653 .... F11
Ho 24,199 .... G10
Keta 14,446 .... G10
Koforidua 46,235 .... F10
Kumasi 260,286 .... F10
Obuasi 31,005 .... F10
Oda 20,957 .... F10
Sekondi 33,713 .... F11
Sekondi-Takoradi*
160,868 .... F11
Takoradi 58,161 .... F11
Tamale 83,653 .... F10
Tarkwa 14,702 .... F10
Tema 60,767 .... G10
Wa 21,374 .... F9
Winneba 30,778 .... F11
Yendi 22,072 .... F10

OTHER FEATURES

Ashanti (reg.) F10
Volta (riv.) F10

GUINEA

CITIES and TOWNS

Beyla E10
Conakry (cap.)* 525,671 .... D10
Dabola D9
Kankan 85,310 .... E9
Kindia 79,861 .... D9
Labé 79,670 .... D9
N'Zérékoré 23,000 .... E10
Siguiri E9

GUINEA-BISSAU

CITIES and TOWNS

Bissau (cap.) 109,486 .... D9
Bolama○ 9,133 .... D9
Cacheu○ 15,194 .... C9

IVORY COAST

CITIES and TOWNS

Abidjan (cap.) 685,828 .... E10
Agboville 27,192 .... F10
Bingerville 18,218 .... F10
Bondoukou 19,111 .... F10
Bouaké 173,248 .... F10
Dabou 23,870 .... F11
Daloa 60,958 .... E10
Dimbokro 30,986 .... F10
Ferkessédougou 25,307 .... E10
Gagnoa 42,362 .... E10
Grand-Bassam 25,808 .... F11
Katiola 21,559 .... E10
Korhogo 47,657 .... E10
Man 50,315 .... E10
Port-Bouet 72,616 .... F11
Sassandra 9,404 .... E11
Seguéla 12,587 .... E10

OTHER FEATURES

Cavally (riv.) E10
Sassandra (riv.) E10

KENYA

CITIES and TOWNS

Eldoret 18,196 .... O11
Kisumu 32,431 .... N12
Lamu 7,403 .... P12
Malindi 10,757 .... P12
Mombasa 247,073 .... P12
Nairobi (cap.) 509,286 .... O12
Nakuru 47,151 .... O11
Nanyuki 11,624 .... O11

OTHER FEATURES

Elgon (mt.) N11
Kenya (mt.) O12
Turkana (Rudolf) (lake) O11

LESOTHO

CITIES and TOWNS

Maseru (cap.) 71,500 .... M17

LIBERIA

CITIES and TOWNS

Buchanan 23,999 .... D10
Greenville 8,462 .... E11
Harper 10,627 .... E11
Marshall D10

(continued on following page)

Agriculture, Industry and Resources

DOMINANT LAND USE

- Cereals, Horticulture, Livestock
- Cash Crops, Mixed Cereals
- Cotton, Cereals
- Diversified Tropical Crops
- Plantation Agriculture
- Oases
- Pasture Livestock
- Nomadic Livestock Herding
- Forests
- Nonagricultural Land

MAJOR MINERAL OCCURRENCES

Ab	Asbestos	Mi	Mica
Ag	Silver	Mn	Manganese
Al	Bauxite	Na	Salt
Au	Gold	O	Petroleum
Be	Beryl	P	Phosphates
C	Coal	Pb	Lead
Co	Cobalt	Pt	Platinum
Cr	Chromium	Sb	Antimony
Cu	Copper	Sn	Tin
D	Diamonds	So	Soda Ash
Fe	Iron Ore	Ti	Titanium
G	Natural Gas	U	Uranium
Gp	Gypsum	V	Vanadium
Gr	Graphite	W	Tungsten
K	Potash	Zn	Zinc

Water Power

Major Industrial Areas

Monrovia (cap.) 166,507 ...... D10

OTHER FEATURES

Palmas (cape) E11

LIBYA

CITIES and TOWNS

Ajedabia○ 53,170 .... L5
Baida○ 59,765 .... L5
Benghazi○ 286,943 .... K5
Brak○ 12,507 .... J6
Derna○ 44,145 .... L5
El Azizia○ 34,077 .... J5
El Jauf○ 6,481 .... L7
El Marj (Barce)○ 55,444 .... L5
Ghadames○ 6,172 .... J6
Gharian○ 65,224 .... J5
Ghat○ 6,924 .... J6
Homs○ 66,890 .... J5
Misurata○ 102,439 .... K5
Murzuk○ 22,185 .... J6
Nalut○ 23,535 .... J5
Sebha○ 35,879 .... K6
Shahat○ 17,157 .... L5
Syrte○ 22,797 .... K5
Tobruk○ 58,384 .... L5
Tripoli (cap.)○ 550,438 .... J5
Ubari○ 19,132 .... J6
Waddan○ 5,347 .... K6
Zella○ 72,092 .... K6
Zliten○ 58,981 .... K5
Zwara○ 15,078 .... J5

OTHER FEATURES

Cyrenaica (reg.) L6
Fezzan (reg.) J6
Idehan (des.) J6
Kufra (oasis) L7
Sahara (des.) EM7
Sidra (gulf) L5
Tripolitania (reg.) J5

MADAGASCAR

CITIES and TOWNS

Ambanja 12,258 .... R14
Ambatondrazaka 18,044 ...... R15
Ambilobe 9,415 .... R14
Ambositra 16,780 .... R16
Antalaha 17,541 .... S14
Antananarivo 451,808 .... R15
Antsirabe 32,979 .... R16
Antsiranana
(Diego-Suarez) 40,443 ..... R14
Arivonimamo 8,497 .... R15
Faradofay
(Fort-Dauphin) 13,805 ..... R17
Farafangana 10,817 .... R16
Fenoarivo 7,696 .... R16
Fianarantsoa 68,054 .... R16
Maevatanana 7,197 .... R15
Maintirano 6,375 .... P15
Majunga 65,864 .... R15
Manakara 19,768 .... R16
Mananjary 14,638 .... R16
Marovoay 20,253 .... R15
Moramanga 10,806 .... R15
Morondava 19,061 .... P16
Sambava 6,215 .... S14
Tamatave 77,395 .... S15
Toliary 45,676 .... P16

OTHER FEATURES

Bobaomby (Amber) (cape) S15
Mozambique (chan.) O16
Nossi-Bé (isl.) R14
Tsiafajavona (mt.) R15
Vohimena (Ste Marie)
(cape) P17

MALAWI

CITIES and TOWNS

Blantyre 222,153 .... N15
Karonga 11,873 .... N13
Lilongwe (cap.) 102,924 ...... N14
Nkhotakota 10,312 .... N14
Zomba 21,000 .... N15

OTHER FEATURES

Nyasa (lake) N14
Shire (riv.) N15

MALI

CITIES and TOWNS

Bamako (cap.) 404,022 .... E9
Bougouni 17,246 .... E9
Djenné 10,251 .... F9
Gao 30,714 .... G8
Goundam 10,262 .... F8
Kati 24,991 .... E9
Kayes 44,736 .... D9
Kita 17,538 .... E9
Koulikoro 16,376 .... E9
Koutiala 27,497 .... F9
Mopti 53,885 .... F9
Nioro 11,617 .... E8
San 22,962 .... F9
Ségou 64,890 .... E9
Sikasso 47,030 .... E9
Timbuktu 20,483 .... F8

OTHER FEATURES

Adrar des Iforas (plat.) G7
Niger (riv.) G9
Sahara (des.) EM7

MAURITANIA

CITIES and TOWNS

Atar 16,326 .... D7
Bir Mogreïn D6
Bogué 8,056 .... D8
Boutilimit 7,261 .... D8
Fdérik 2,160 .... D7
Kaédi 20,248 .... D8
Kiffa 10,629 .... D8
Néma 8,232 .... E8
Nouadhibou 21,961 .... C7
Nouakchott (cap.) 134,986 ..... C8
Rosso 16,466 .... C8
Tidjikja 7,870 .... D8

OTHER FEATURES

Adrar (reg.) D7
Blanc (cape) C7
Hodh (reg.) E8
Sahara (des.) EM7
Senegal (riv.) D8
Tagant (reg.) D8

MAURITIUS

CITIES and TOWNS

Curepipe 52,709 .... S19
Mahébourg 15,463 .... T19
Port Louis (cap.) 141,022 ..... S19

MAYOTTE

CITIES AND TOWNS

Mamoutzou (cap.) 196 .... R14

MOROCCO

CITIES and TOWNS

Agadir 61,192 .... D5
Al Hoceima 18,686 .... F4
Casablanca 1,506,373 .... E5
El Jadida 55,501 .... E5
Essaouira 30,061 .... D5
Fès 325,327 .... F5
Kenitra 139,206 .... E5
Khenifra 25,526 .... F5
Larache 45,710 .... E4
Marrakech 332,741 .... E5
Meknès 248,369 .... E5
Ouezzane 33,267 .... E5
Oujda 175,532 .... F5
Rabat (cap.) 367,620 .... E5
Safi 129,113 .... E5
Salé 155,557 .... E5
Settat 42,325 .... E5
Tangier (Tanger) 187,894 .... E4
Taroudant 22,272 .... E5
Taza 55,157 .... F5
Tétouan 139,105 .... F4

OTHER FEATURES

Atlas (mts.) E5
Beddouza, Ras el (cape) E5
Draa, Wadi (dry riv.) E6
Juby (cape) D5

MOZAMBIQUE

CITIES and TOWNS

Bartolomeu Dias○ 6,102 ...... O16
Beira 46,293 .... O15
Chibuto 23,763 .... N16
Chimoio 4,507 .... N15
Homoíne 1,122 .... O16
Ibo 1,015 .... P14
Inhambane 4,975 .... O16
Magude 1,502 .... N16
Maniamba 7,634 .... O14
Maputo (cap.) 755,300 .... N17
Marromeu 1,330 .... O15
Massangena○ 3,301 .... N16
Meconta 1,051 .... O14
Moçambique 1,730 .... P15
Mocímboa da Praia 935 .... P14
Mocuba 2,293 .... O15
Nacala 4,601 .... P14
Nampula 23,072 .... P15
Pemba 3,629 .... P14
Quelimane 10,522 .... O15
Songo 1,350 .... N15
Tete 4,549 .... N15
Vila de Sena○ 21,074 .... N15
Vila Fontes 1,363 .... N15
Xai-Xai 5,234 .... N16

OTHER FEATURES

Angoche (isl.) O16
Delagoa (bay) N17
Delgado (cape) P14
Mozambique (chan.) O16
Nyasa (chan.) N14
Rovuma (riv.) O14
Save (riv.) N16

NAMIBIA

CITIES and TOWNS

Bethanie 1,207 .... K17
Gobabis 4,428 .... K16
Grootfontein 4,627 .... K15
Karasburg 2,693 .... K17
Karibib 1,653 .... K16
Keetmanshoop 10,297 .... K17
Lüderitz 6,642 .... J17
Mariental 4,629 .... K16
Omaruru 2,783 .... K16
Oranjemund 2,594 .... K17
Otjiwarongo 8,018 .... K16
Outjo 2,545 .... K15
Rehoboth 5,363 .... K16
Swakopmund 5,681 .... J16
Tsumeb 12,338 .... K15
Usakos 2,334 .... K16
Windhoek (cap.) 61,369 .... K16

OTHER FEATURES

Caprivi Strip (reg.) L15
Cubango (riv.) K15
Cunene (riv.) J15
Damaraland (reg.) K16
Etosha Pan (salt pan) J15
Fish (riv.) K17
Fria (cape) J15
Great Namaland (reg.) K17
Kalahari (des.) L16
Namib (des.) J15
Okovanggo (riv.) K15
Orange (riv.) K17
Ovamboland (reg.) K15

NIGER

CITIES and TOWNS

Agadès 11,000 .... H8
Bilma J8
Birni-N'Konni 10,000 .... H9
Gaya 5,000 .... G9
Iférouane J9
Maradi 45,852 .... H9
N'Guigmi J9
Niamey (cap.) 225,314 .... G9
Tahoua 31,265 .... H9
Zinder 58,436 .... H9

OTHER FEATURES

Air (mts.) H8
Djado (plat.) J7
Niger (riv.) G9
Sahara (des.) EM7
Ténéré (des.) J8

NIGERIA

CITIES and TOWNS

Aba 177,000 .... H10
Abeokuta 253,000 .... G10
Benin City 136,000 .... H10
Bonny H11
Calabar 103,000 .... H10
Enugu 187,000 .... H10
Ibadan 847,000 .... G10
Ife 176,000 .... G10
Ilorin 282,000 .... G10
Kaduna 202,000 .... H9
Kano 399,000 .... H9
Katsina 109,424 .... H9
Lagos (cap.) 1,060,848 .... G10
Maiduguri 189,000 .... J9
Ogbomosho 432,000 .... H10
Onitsha 220,000 .... H10
Oshogbo 282,000 .... H10
Oyo 152,000 .... G10
Port Harcourt 242,000 .... H11
Sokoto H9
Yola J10
Zaria 224,000 .... H9

OTHER FEATURES

Adamawa (reg.) J10
Benin (bight) G11
Benue (riv.) H10
Chad (lake) K9
Gongola (riv.) J9
Kaduna (riv.) H9
Niger (riv.) G9

RÉUNION

CITIES and TOWNS

Le Port 21,564 .... P20
Le Tampon 17,089 .... P20
Saint-Denis (cap.) 80,075 .... P19
Saint-Louis 10,252 .... P20
Saint-Pierre 21,817 .... P20

OTHER FEATURES

Bassas da India (isl.) O16
Europa (isl.) P16
Glorioso (isls.) R14
Juan de Nova (isl.) P15
Piton des Neiges (mt.) P20

RWANDA

CITIES and TOWNS

Kigali (cap.) 117,749 .... N12

SÃO TOMÉ E PRÍNCIPE

CITIES and TOWNS

São Tomé (cap.) 7,681 .... H11

OTHER FEATURES

Príncipe (isl.) H11
São Tomé (isl.) H11

SENEGAL

CITIES and TOWNS

Dagana 10,506 .... D8
Dakar (cap.) 798,792 .... C9
Diourbel 50,618 .... C9
Kaolack 106,899 .... C9
Louga 35,063 .... C8
Matam 10,002 .... D8
M'Bour 37,663 .... C9
Saint-Louis 88,404 .... C8
Tambacounda 25,147 .... D9
Thiès 117,333 .... C9
Ziguinchor 72,726 .... C9

OTHER FEATURES

Senegal (riv.) D8
Verde (cape) C9

SEYCHELLES

OTHER FEATURES

Aldabra (isls.) P13
Assumption (isl.) R14
Cerf (isl.) S13
Cosmoledo (isls.) R13
Farquhar (isl.) S14
Providence (isl.) S13
Saint Pierre 47 ....

SIERRA LEONE

CITIES and TOWNS

Bo 42,216 .... D10
Bonthe 6,230 .... D10
Freetown (cap.) 274,000 .... D10
Makeni 28,684 .... D10

OTHER FEATURES

Sherbro (isl.) D10

SOMALIA

CITIES and TOWNS

Afmadu 2,580 .... P11
Barawa (Brava) 6,167 .... P11
Baydhabo 14,962 .... P
Belet Weyne 11,426 .... P
Berbera 12,219 ....
Borama 3,244 ....
Bosaso ....
Brava 6,167 .... P
Bulo Burti 5,247 .... P
Burao 12,617 .... R
Chisimayu 17,872 .... P
Eil .... S
Erigabo 4,279 ....
Galcaio .... R
Giohar 13,156 .... R
Hargeysa 40,254 .... P
Jilib 3,232 .... P
Las Anod 2,441 .... R
Marka 17,708 .... R
Mogadishu (cap.) 371,000 .... R
Oddur .... P
Zeila 1,226 ....

OTHER FEATURES

Asèr, Ras (cape) ....
Chiambone, Ras (cape) .... P
Giuba (Juba) (riv.) P1
Mijirtein (reg.) R1
Mudugh (reg.) R1
Wabi Shebelle (riv.) R1

SOUTH AFRICA

INTERNAL DIVISIONS

Bophuthatswana (aut.
rep.) 1,200,000 .... L1
Cape of Good Hope
(prov.) 5,543,506 .... L1
Ciskei (aut. rep.) M1
Natal (prov.) 5,722,215 .... N1
Orange Free State
(prov.) 1,833,216 .... M1
Transkei (aut.
rep.) 2,000,000 .... M1
Transvaal (prov.) 10,673,033 M1
Venda (aut. rep.) 450,000 ...... N1

CITIES and TOWNS

Aliwal North 12,311 .... M1
Beaufort West 17,862 .... L1
Bellville 49,026 .... G1
Benoni□ 164,543 .... M1
Bethlehem 29,918 .... M1
Bisho M1
Bloemfontein□ 182,329 .... L1
Calvinia 6,386 .... K1
Cape Town (cap.)□ 833,731 .. F1
Ceres 9,230 .... H1
Cradock 20,822 .... M1
De Aar 18,057 .... L1
Durban□ 975,494 .... N1
East London□ 126,671 .... M1
George 24,625 .... L1
Germiston□ 293,257 .... M1
Goodwood 31,592 .... G1
Graaff-Reinet 22,392 .... L1
Grahamstown 41,302 .... M1
Johannesburg□ 1,417,818 .. M1
Kimberley 105,258 .... L1
King William's Town 15,798 .. M18
Knysna 13,479 .... L18
Kraaifontein 10,286 .... G19
Kroonstad 51,988 .... M17
Ladysmith 28,920 .... N17
Louis Trichardt 8,906 .... M16
Malmesbury 9,314 .... G18
Messina 21,121 .... M16
Middelburg, C. of
G.H. 11,121 .... M18
Middelburg, Transv. 26,942 .. N17
Mmabatho L17
Moorreesburg 4,945 .... K18
Mossel Bay 17,574 .... L18
Newcastle 14,407 .... N17
Oudtshoorn 26,907 .... L18
Paarl 49,244 .... H19
Parow 60,768 .... G19
Pietermaritzburg□ 174,179 .. N17
Pietersburg 27,174 .... N16
Pinelands 11,769 .... G19
Port Elizabeth□ 413,961 .... M18
Port Nolloth 2,893 .... K17
Port Shepstone 5,581 .... N18
Potchefstroom 57,443 .... M17
Pretoria (cap.)□ 573,283 ...... M17
Prieska 8,521 .... L17
Queenstown 39,304 .... M18
Richards Bay 598 .... N17
Saldanha 4,994 .... K18
Simonstown 12,137 .... F19
Somerset West 11,828 .... G19
Stellenbosch 29,955 .... G19
Strand 24,503 .... G19
Thohoyandou N16
Uitenhage 70,517 .... M18
Umtata 25,216 .... M18
Upington 28,632 .... L17
Vryburg 16,916 .... L17
Walvis Bay 21,725 .... J16
Wellington 17,092 .... H18
Worcester 41,198 .... H18

OTHER FEATURES

Agulhas (cape) K19
Algoa (bay) M18
Cape (pt.) F20
False (bay) G20
Good Hope (cape) F20
Hangklip (cape) G20
Kalahari (des.) L16
Limpopo (riv.) N16
Maclear (cape) F20
Molopo (riv.) L17
Nossob (riv.) L17
Orange (riv.) K17

ıben (isl.) F19
ıt Helena (bay) K18
down (bay)....................G20
le (bay) F19
ıe (mt.) F19
l (riv.)...........................M17
ıland□ 756,707 ....N17

SUDAN

CITIES and TOWNS

ara 66,000......................N8
ıgola 6,000 ....M8
Damazin 12,000 ....N9
Dueim 27,000 ....N9
asher 52,000..................M9
ieneina 33,000 ....L9
beid 90,000......................N9
Nahud 23,000 ....M9
daref 92,000 ....O9
a 57,000.........................N10
dugli 18,000 ....M9
ssala 99,000 ....O8
artoum (cap.) 334,000 ....N8
artoum North 151,000........N8
sti 57,000 ....N9
lakal 35,000 ....N10
ala 60,000..........................L9
durman 299,000 ....N8
t Sudan 133,000...............O8
di Halfa N7
d Medani 107,000 ....N9
u 53,000.......................N10

OTHER FEATURES

ab, Bahr el (riv.)...............M10
ara (riv.) O8
e Nile (riv.)........................N9
zira, El (reg.) N9
roe (ruin).........................N8
sser (lake) N7
e (riv.)...............................N7
bian (des.) N7
hara (des.) EM7
bat (riv.) N10
dan (reg.) FM9
ite Nile (riv.) N10

SWAZILAND

CITIES and TOWNS

babane (cap.) 23,109 .... N17

TANZANIA

CITIES and TOWNS

usha 55,281 .... O12
gamoyo 5,112 .... O13
koba 20,430 .... N12
ake Chake 4,862 .... P13
r es Salaam
(cap.) 757,346 ....P1
doma 45,703 .... N13
ita 3,066 .... N12
ıga 57,182 .... O13
goma-Ujiji 50,044 .... N12
osa 4,458......................... O13
wa Kivinje 2,790 .... P13
ndoa 4,514........................ O12
di 27,308 .... O14
shoto 1,803 .... O12
beya 76,606 .... N13
orogoro 61,890 .... O13
oshi 52,223 .... O12
twara-Mikindani 48,510..... P14
usoma 32,658.................. N12
wadui 7,383 .... N12
wanza 110,611 .... N12
chingwea 3,751 .... O14
ngani 2,955 .... O13
inyanga 21,703 .... N12
ngida 29,252 .... N12
ngea 17,954 .... O14
bora 67,392 .... N12
nga 103,409 .... O12
nzibar 110,669.............. P13

OTHER FEATURES

eat Ruaha (riv.) O13
limanjaro (mt.) O12
afia (isl.)........................ P13
atron (lake) O12
yasa (lake) N14
angani (riv.) O12
emba (isl.) P13
ufiji (riv.) O13
ukwa (lake) N13

Tanganyika (lake)............... N13
Victoria (lake) N12
Zanzibar (isl.) P13

TOGO

CITIES and TOWNS

Anécho 10,889 .... G10
Kpalimé 19,801 .... G10
Lomé (cap.) 148,443 .... G10
Sokodé 29,623 .... G10

TUNISIA

CITIES and TOWNS

Bizerte 62,856 .... J4
Gabès 40,585 ....H5
Gafsa 42,225.......................H5
Kairouan 54,546..................H4
Mahdia 25,711...................... J4
Menzel Bourguiba 42,111 ....H4
Moknine 26,035 .... J4
Sfax 171,297....................... J5
Sousse 69,530..................... J4
Tunis (cap.) 550,404 .... J4

OTHER FEATURES

Bon (cape)......................... J4
Djerba (isl.)........................ J5
Djerid, Shott el (salt lake) H5
Gabès (gulf) J5

UGANDA

CITIES and TOWNS

Arua 10,837 .... N11
Entebbe 21,096................. N12
Jinja 52,509 .... N11
Kabale 8,234 .... N12
Kampala (cap.) 478,895....... N11
Mbarara 16,078 .... N12
Soroti 8,130...................... N11

OTHER FEATURES

Albert (lake) M11
Edward (lake) M12
Kioga (lake)...................... N11
Ruwenzori (range).............. N11
Victoria (lake) N12

UPPER VOLTA

CITIES and TOWNS

Bobo Dioulasso 115,063 .... F9
Koudougou 36,838 .... F9
Ouagadougou (cap.) 172,661 .. F9
Ouahigouya 25,690 .... F9

OTHER FEATURES

Black Volta (riv.) F9
Red Volta (riv.).................... F9

Sudan (reg.) FM9
White Volta (riv.)................. F9

WESTERN SAHARA

CITIES and TOWNS

Dakhla C7
Laayoune 24,519.................D6

OTHER FEATURES

Blanc (cape) C7
Bojador (cape) C6

ZAIRE

CITIES and TOWNS

Aketi 17,200 ....L11
Bandundu□...................... K12
Beni 22,800 ....M11
Boma 61,100 ....J13
Bukavu 134,861 ....M12
Bumba 34,700....................L11
Bunia 28,800..................... N11
Butembo 27,800 ....M11
Demba 22,000...................L13
Dilolo 14,000 ....L13
Gemena 37,300 ....L11
Goma 48,600 ....M12
Ilebo 32,200 ....L12
Isiro 49,300 ....M11
Kalemie 62,300 ....M13
Kamina 56,300 ....L13
Kananga 428,960 ....L13
Kasongo 37,800................M12
Kikwit 111,960.................. K13
Kinshasa (cap.) 1,323,039.... K12
Kisangani 229,596 ....M11
Kolwezi 81,600 ....L14
Lubumbashi 318,000..........M14
Luebo 21,800.....................L13
Manono 44,500 ....M13
Matadi 110,436...................J13
Mbandaka 107,910 .... K11
Mbanza-Ngungu 55,800 ...... K11
Mbuji-Mayi 256,154 ....L13
Mwene Ditu 71,200 ....L13
Panda-Likasi 146,394 ....M14
Port Kindu 42,800...............L12
Tshikapa 38,900..................L13
Virunga 21,900 ....M13
Watsa 21,300....................M11
Yangambi 22,600 ....L11

OTHER FEATURES

Albert (lake) M11
Aruwimi (riv.) M11
Bomu (riv.).........................L11
Boyama (Stanley) (falls) M11
Congo (riv.) K12
Edward (lake) M12
Kasai (riv.)........................ K12
Kivu (reg.) M12
Lualaba (riv.).....................M13
Luapula (riv.).....................M14
Lulua (riv.) L13
Mweru (lake) M13
Ruwenzori (range)............. N11
Stanley (falls) M11
Stanley Pool (lake)............. K12
Tanganyika (lake).............. N13
Ubangi (riv.)..................... K11
Uele (riv.) L11
Zaire (Congo) (riv.) K12

ZAMBIA

CITIES and TOWNS

Broken Hill (Kabwe) 143,635 .M14
Choma 17,943...................M15
Kabwe 143,635..................M14
Kasama 38,093.................. N13
Livingstone 71,987.............M15
Lusaka (cap.) 538,469.........M15
Mazabuka 29,602 ....M15
Mongu 24,919....................L15
Mpika 25,880 .... N14
Ndola 282,439...................M14
Senanga 7,204...................L15
Solwezi 15,032 ....M14

OTHER FEATURES

Bangweulu (lake) N14
Kafue (riv.) M15
Kariba (lake).....................M15
Mweru (lake) M13
Victoria (falls) M15
Zambezi (riv.) M15

ZIMBABWE

CITIES and TOWNS

Bulawayo 359,000 ....M16
Fort Victoria 22,000 .... N15
Gatooma 32,000 ....M15
Gwaai○ 2,710...................M15
Gwelo 68,000 ....M15
Harare (Salisbury)
(cap.) 601,000 .... N15
Hartley 12,000 ....M15
Kariba 3,943 ....M15
Matopos○ 11,330 ....M16
Salisbury (Harare)
(cap.) 601,000 .... N15
Selukwe 8,387 ....M15
Sinoia 25,000 ....M15
Umtali 61,000.................... N15
Wankie 33,000...................M15

OTHER FEATURES

Kariba (lake).....................M15
Limpopo (riv.) N16
Victoria (falls) M15
Zambezi (riv.) M15

*City and suburbs.
○Population of sub-district or division.
□Population of urban area.

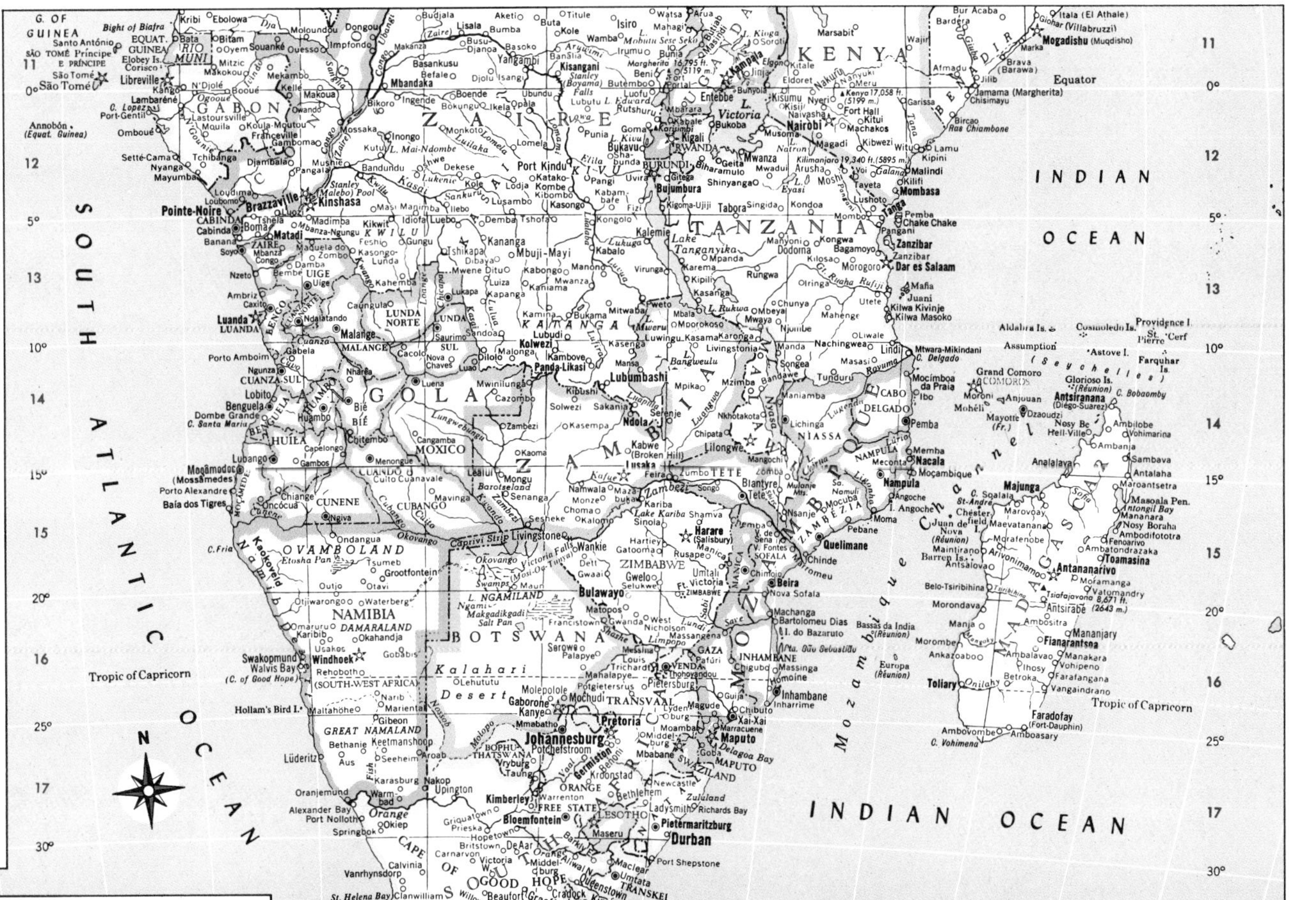

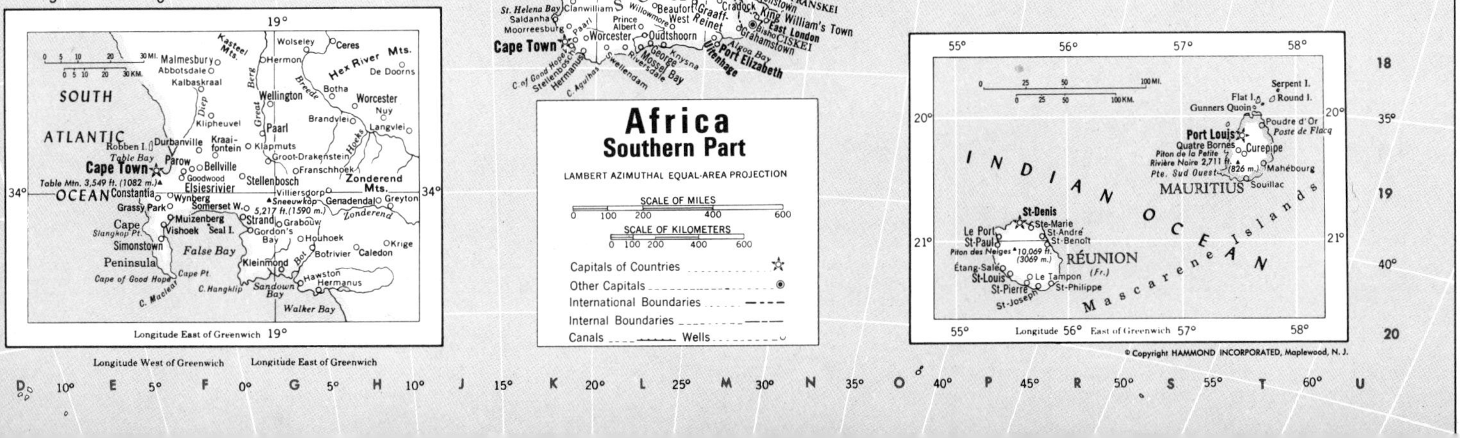

Asia
LAMBERT AZIMUTHAL EQUAL-AREA PROJECTION
SCALE OF MILES
0 100 200 400 600 800 1000 1200
SCALE OF KILOMETERS
0 200 400 600 800 1000 1200
Capitals of Countries
Other Capitals
International Boundaries
Other Boundaries
Canals
© Copyright HAMMOND INCORPORATED, Maplewood, N. J.
ATLANTIC OCEAN
ARCTIC OCEAN
North Pole
Longitude East of Greenwich
NORWEGIAN SEA
BARENTS SEA
KARA SEA
LAPTEV SEA
EAST SIBERIAN SEA
CHUKCHI SEA
BERING SEA
NORTH AMERICA
UNITED STATES
ALASKA
SEA OF OKHOTSK
PACIFIC OCEAN
SEA OF JAPAN
EAST CHINA SEA
SOUTH CHINA SEA
PHILIPPINE SEA
PHILIPPINES
SULU SEA
CELEBES SEA
MOLUCCA SEA
BANDA SEA
FLORES SEA
JAVA SEA
TIMOR SEA
AUSTRALIA
Great Sandy Desert
Great Victoria Desert
Tropic of Capricorn
Tropic of Cancer
Equator
INDIAN OCEAN
ARABIAN SEA
BAY OF BENGAL
ANDAMAN SEA
MEDITERRANEAN SEA
BLACK SEA
CASPIAN SEA
RED SEA
Arctic Circle
UNION OF SOVIET SOCIALIST REPUBLICS
RUSSIAN SOVIET FEDERATED SOCIALIST REPUBLIC
Siberia
KAZAKH S.S.R.
UZBEK S.S.R.
TURKMEN S.S.R.
KIRGIZ S.S.R.
MONGOLIA
Gobi
Inner Mongolia
CHINA
Sinkiang
Tibet
Takla Makan
Tien Shan
Kunlun
Altun Shan
Qilian Shan
INDIA
PAKISTAN
AFGHANISTAN
IRAN
IRAQ
SAUDI ARABIA
Rub' al Khali
OMAN
TURKEY
SYRIA
JORDAN
ISRAEL
LEBANON
CYPRUS
EGYPT
SUDAN
ETHIOPIA
SOMALIA
DJIBOUTI
YEMEN ARAB REP.
PEOPLE'S DEM. REP. OF YEMEN
KUWAIT
BAHRAIN
QATAR
UNITED ARAB EMIRATES
NEPAL
BHUTAN
BANGLADESH
BURMA
THAILAND
LAOS
VIETNAM
CAMBODIA
MALAYSIA
SINGAPORE
BRUNEI
INDONESIA
Borneo
Sumatra
Celebes
Java
SRI LANKA (CEYLON)
MALDIVES
N. KOREA
S. KOREA
JAPAN
TAIWAN
HONG KONG
MADAGASCAR
SEYCHELLES
MAURITIUS
BRITISH INDIAN OCEAN TERRITORY
SUNDA ISLANDS
Moscow
Leningrad
Peking (Beijing)
Shanghai
Tokyo
Seoul
Manila
Bangkok
Rangoon
Calcutta
Bombay
Madras
New Delhi
Karachi
Tehran
Baghdad
Kabul
Ulaanbaatar
Hanoi
Ho Chi Minh City (Saigon)
Jakarta
Kuala Lumpur
Canton (Guangzhou)
Lhasa
Kathmandu
Dhaka
Colombo
Novosibirsk
Vladivostok
Mt. Everest 29,028 ft. (8848 m.)
Hindu Kush
Pamirs
Great Khingan Range
Stanovoy Range
Verkhoyansk Range
Cherskiy Range
Kolyma Range
Yablonovyy Range
Lake Baykal
Lop Nur
Aral Sea
Lake Balkhash

Population Distribution

DENSITY PER

SQ. KILOMETER	SQ. MILE
Over 100	Over 260
50-100	130-260
10-50	25-130
1-10	3-25
Under 1	Under 3

• Cities with over 2,000,000 inhabitants (including suburbs)

∘ Cities with over 1,000,000 inhabitants (including suburbs)

AREA 17,128,500 sq. mi. (44,362,815 sq. km.)
POPULATION 2,633,000,000
LARGEST CITY Tokyo
HIGHEST POINT Mt. Everest 29,028 ft. (8,848 m.)
LOWEST POINT Dead Sea -1,296 ft. (-395 m.)

Vegetation

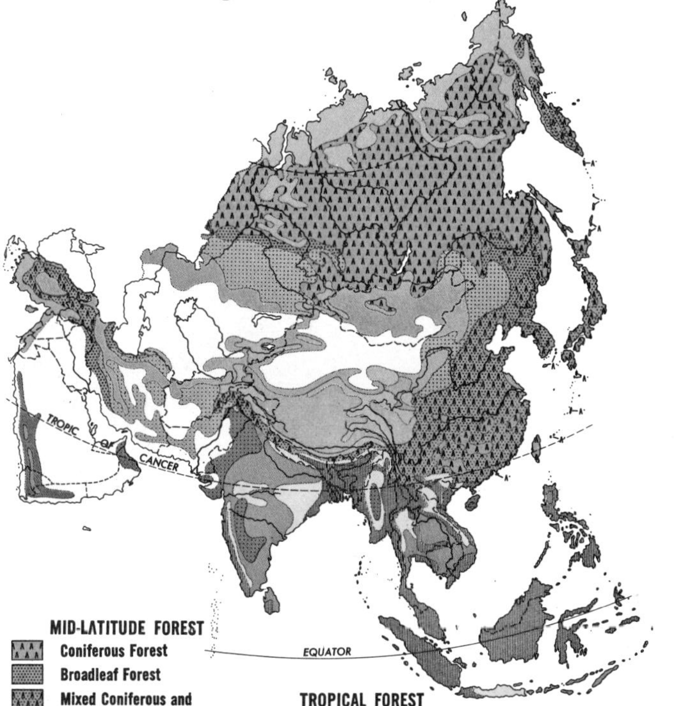

MID-LATITUDE FOREST
- Coniferous Forest
- Broadleaf Forest
- Mixed Coniferous and Broadleaf Forest
- Woodland and Shrub (Mediterranean)

MID-LATITUDE GRASSLAND
- Short Grass (Steppe)
- Wooded Steppe

DESERT AND DESERT SHRUB

TROPICAL FOREST
- Tropical Rainforest
- Light Tropical Forest
- Woodland and Shrub

TROPICAL GRASSLAND
- Grass and Shrub (Savanna)
- Wooded Savanna

TUNDRA AND ALPINE

UNCLASSIFIED HIGHLANDS

SAUDI ARABIA

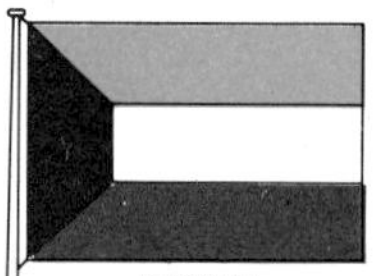

KUWAIT

YEMEN ARAB REPUBLIC

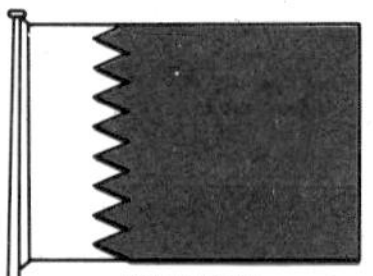

BAHRAIN

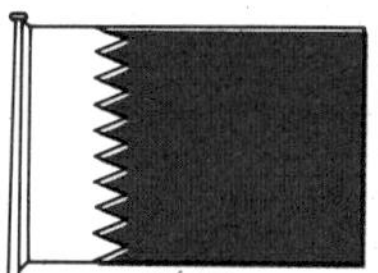

QATAR

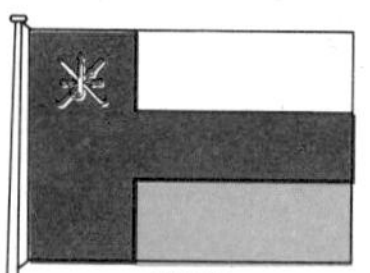

OMAN

PEOPLE'S DEM. REP. OF YEMEN

AFGHANISTAN

CITIES and TOWNS

Anar Darreh	H3
Andkhvoy	H2
Aqcheh	J2
Aybak 33,016	J2
Baghlan 75,130	J2
Balkh	J2
Bamian 7,355	J3
Baraki Barak	J3
Belcheragh	J2
Chahar Borjak	H3
Charikar 25,093	J2
Dowlat Yar	J3
Dowlatabad	H3
Dowshi	J2
Farah 18,797	H3
Farsi	H3
Feyzabad 10,142	K2
Gardez 11,415	J3
Gereshk	H3
Ghazni 30,425	J3
Ghurian	H3
Gizab	J3
Hazar Qadam	J3
Herat 163,960	H3
Jalalabad 56,384	K3
Jorm	K2
Kabul (cap.) 905,108	J3
Kalat (Qalat) 5,946	J3
Kandahar (Qandahar) 178,409	J3
Khanabad	J2
Khugiani	J3
Kowst	J3
Kuhestan	H3
Landay	H3
Lash-e Joveyn	H3
Lashkar Gah 26,646	H3
Mar'uf	J3
Mazar-e Sharif 122,567	J2
Meymaneh 54,954	H2
Mirabad	H3
Moqor	J3
Now Zad	H3
Owbeh	H3
Panjab	J3
Pol-e Khomri	J2
Qalat 5,946	J3
Qale'h-ye Now 5,340	H3
Qale'h-ye Panjeh	K2
Qandahar 178,409	J3
Qonduz 107,191	J2
Rostaq	J2
Rudbar	H3
Sakhar	J3
Sar-e Pol	J2
Shah Juy	J3
Sheberghan 54,870	H
Shindand	H
Spin Buldak	J
Tagab	J
Taloqan 46,202	J2
Teyvareh	H
Tulak	H
Zaranj 6,477	H
Zibak	K2

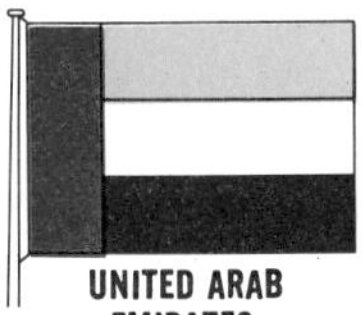

UNITED ARAB EMIRATES

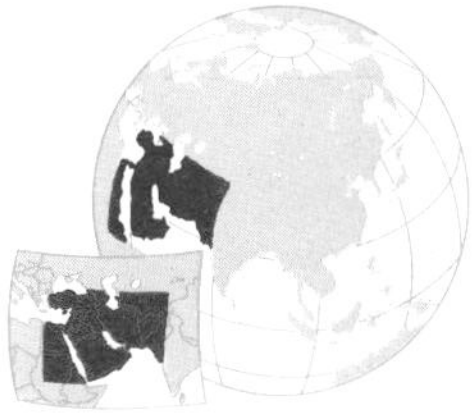

OTHER FEATURES

'ah Rud (riv.) H3
wd-e Zerreh (depr.) H4
rirud (riv.) H3
lmand (riv.) J3
ndu Kush (mts.) J2
bul (riv.) K3
nar (riv.) K2
rah (riv.) J3
Margow, Dasht-e (des.) H3
Murghab (riv.) H2
Namaksar (salt lake) H3
Paropamisus (mts.) H3
Rigestan (reg.) H3

BAHRAIN

CITIES and TOWNS

Manama (cap.) 88,785 ..... F4
Muharraq 37,732 ..... F4

GAZA STRIP

CITIES and TOWNS

Gaza* 118,272 ..... B3

IRAN

CITIES and TOWNS

Abadan 296,081 ..... E3
Abadeh 16,000 ..... F3
Abarqu 8,000 ..... F3
Ahvaz 329,006 ..... E3
Amol 68,782 ..... F2
Anar 463 ..... G3
Anarak 2,038 ..... F3
Arak 114,507 ..... E3
Ardabil 147,404 ..... E2
Ardestan 5,868 ..... F3
Asterabad (Gorgan) 88,348 ..... F2
Babol 67,790 ..... F2
Bafq 5,000 ..... G3
Baft 6,000 ..... G4

(continued on following page)

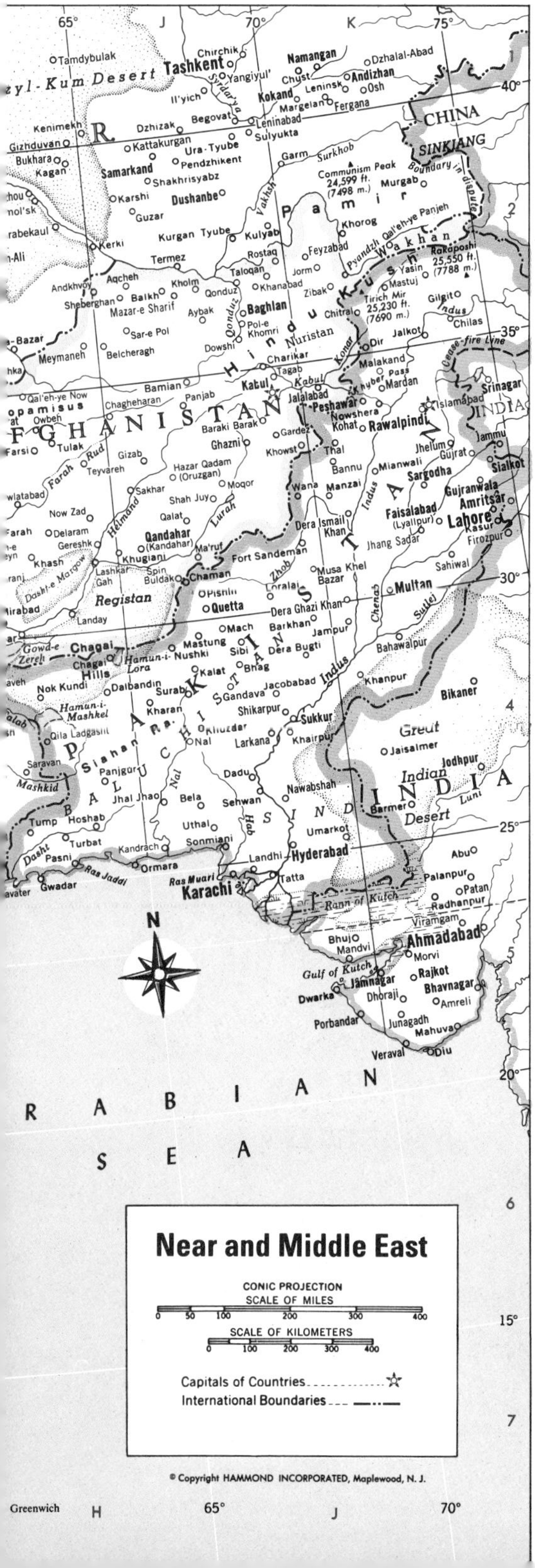

SAUDI ARABIA

AREA 829,995 sq. mi. (2,149,687 sq. km.)
POPULATION 8,367,000
CAPITAL Riyadh
MONETARY UNIT Saudi riyal
MAJOR LANGUAGE Arabic
MAJOR RELIGION Islam

YEMEN ARAB REPUBLIC

AREA 77,220 sq. mi. (200,000 sq. km.)
POPULATION 6,456,189
CAPITAL San'a
MONETARY UNIT Yemeni rial
MAJOR LANGUAGE Arabic
MAJOR RELIGION Islam

QATAR

AREA 4,247 sq. mi. (11,000 sq. km.)
POPULATION 220,000
CAPITAL Doha
MONETARY UNIT Qatari riyal
MAJOR LANGUAGE Arabic
MAJOR RELIGION Islam

PEOPLE'S DEM. REP. OF YEMEN

AREA 111,101 sq. mi. (287,752 sq. km.)
POPULATION 1,969,000
CAPITAL Aden
MONETARY UNIT Yemeni dinar
MAJOR LANGUAGE Arabic
MAJOR RELIGION Islam

KUWAIT

AREA 6,532 sq. mi. (16,918 sq. km.)
POPULATION 1,355,827
CAPITAL Al Kuwait
MONETARY UNIT Kuwaiti dinar
MAJOR LANGUAGE Arabic
MAJOR RELIGION Islam

BAHRAIN

AREA 240 sq. mi. (622 sq. km.)
POPULATION 358,857
CAPITAL Manama
MONETARY UNIT Bahraini dinar
MAJOR LANGUAGE Arabic
MAJOR RELIGION Islam

OMAN

AREA 120,000 sq. mi. (310,800 sq. km.)
POPULATION 891,000
CAPITAL Muscat
MONETARY UNIT Omani rial
MAJOR LANGUAGE Arabic
MAJOR RELIGION Islam

UNITED ARAB EMIRATES

AREA 32,278 sq. mi. (83,600 sq. km.)
POPULATION 1,040,275
CAPITAL Abu Dhabi
MONETARY UNIT dirham
MAJOR LANGUAGE Arabic
MAJOR RELIGION Islam

Topography

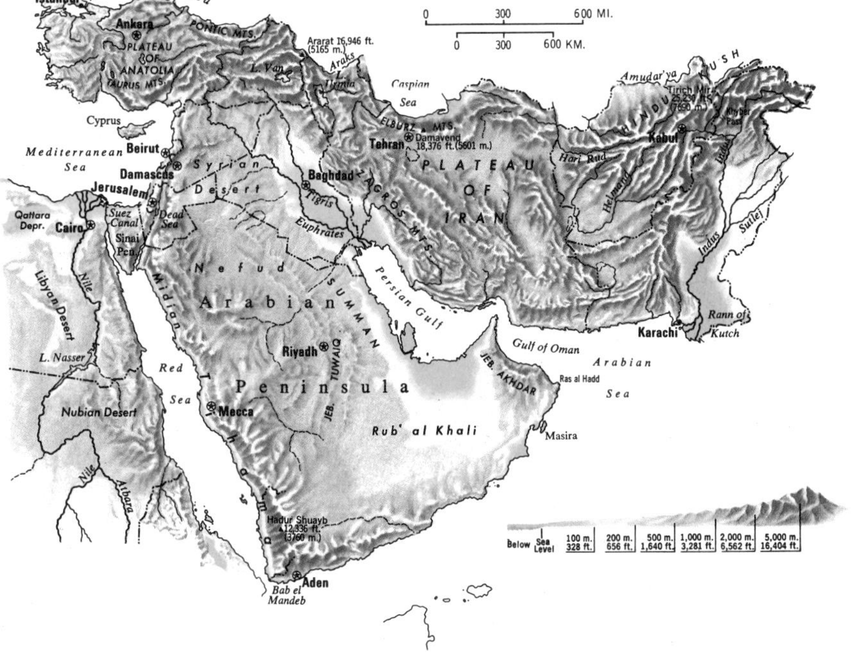

(continued)

Bam 22,000 ... G4
Bampur 1,585 ... H4
Bandar 'Abbas 89,103 ... G4
Bandar-e Lengeh 4,920 ... F4
Bandar-e Pahlavi
(Enzeli) 55,978 ... E2
Bandar-e Rig 1,889 ... F4
Bandar-e Torkaman 13,000 ... F2
Bandar Khomeini 6,000 ... E3
Bejestan 3,823 ... G3
Bir Bala 103 ... G4
Birjand 25,854 ... G3
Bojnurd 31,248 ... G2
Borazjan 20,000 ... F4
Borujerd 100,103 ... E3
Bushehr 57,681 ... F4
Chah Bahar 1,800 ... H4
Chalus 15,000 ... F2
Damghan 13,000 ... F2
Darab 13,000 ... G4
Dashtiari ... H4
Dezful 110,287 ... E3
Dezh Shahpur 1,384 ... E2
Enzeli 55,978 ... E2
Estahbanat 18,187 ... F4
Fahrej (Iranshahr) 5,000 ... H4
Fasa 19,000 ... F4
Ferdows 11,000 ... G3
Gach Saran ... F3
Garmsar 4,723 ... F2
Golpayegan 20,515 ... F3
Gonabad 8,000 ... gg3
Gorgan 88,348 ... F2
Hamadan 155,846 ... E3
Iranshahr 5,000 ... H4
Isfahan 617,825 ... F3
Jahrom 38,236 ... F4
Jask 1,078 ... G4
Kangan 2,682 ... F4
Kangavar 9,414 ... E3
Kashan 84,545 ... F3
Kashmar 17,000 ... G2
Kazerun 51,309 ... F4
Kerman 140,309 ... G3
Kermanshah 290,861 ... E3
Khash 7,439 ... H4
Khorramabad 104,928 ... E3
Khorramshahr 146,709 ... E3
Khvor 2,912 ... G3
Khvoy 70,040 ... E2
Lar 22,000 ... F4
Mahabad 28,610 ... E2
Maragheh 60,820 ... E2
Marand 24,000 ... E2
Meshed 670,180 ... H2
Mianeh 28,447 ... E2
Minab 4,228 ... G2
Mirjaveh 11,000 ... H4
Nahavand 24,000 ... E3
Na'in 5,925 ... F3
Najafabad 76,236 ... F3
Nasratabad (Zabol) 20,000 ... H3
Natanz 4,370 ... F3
Nehbandan 2,130 ... G3
Neyshabur 59,101 ... G2
Nikshahr ... H4
Pahlevi (Enzeli) 55,978 ... E2
Qasr-e Qand 1,879 ... H4
Qayen 6,000 ... G3
Qazvin 138,527 ... E2
Qom 246,831 ... F3
Quchan 29,133 ... G2
Qum (Qom) 246,831 ... F3
Rafsanjan 21,000 ... G3
Rasht 187,203 ... E2
Ravar 5,074 ... G3
Rey 102,825 ... F2
Reza'iyeh (Urmia) 163,991 ... D2
Sabzevar 69,174 ... G2
Sabzvaran 7,000 ... G4
Sai'dabad 20,000 ... G4
Sanandaj 95,834 ... E2
Saqqez 17,000 ... E2
Saravan ... H4
Sari 70,936 ... F2
Saveh 17,565 ... F2
Semnan 31,058 ... F2
Shahdad 2,777 ... G3
Shahreza 34,220 ... F3
Shahrud 30,767 ... G2
Shahsavar 12,000 ... F2
Shiraz 416,408 ... F4
Shirvan 11,000 ... G2
Shustar 24,000 ... E3
Sirjan (Sai'dabad) 20,000 ... G4
Susangerd 21,000 ... E3
Tabas 10,000 ... G3
Tabas-Masina (Tabas) 466 ... H3
Tabriz 598,576 ... E2
Tarom 394 ... G4
Tehran (cap.) 4,496,159 ... F2
Torbat-e Heydariyeh 30,106 ... G2
Torbat-e Jam 13,000 ... H2
Torud 721 ... F2
Turan ... G2
Turbat-i-Shaikh Jam 13,000 ... H2
Urmia 163,991 ... D2
Yazd 135,978 ... F3
Yazdan ... H3
Zabol 20,000 ... H3
Zahedan 92,628 ... H4
Zanjan 99,967 ... E2
Zarand 5,000 ... G3

OTHER FEATURES

Araks (riv.) ... E2
Atrek (riv.) ... G2
Bazman, Kuh-e (mt.) ... H4
Damavand (mt.) ... F2
Dez (riv.) ... E3
Elburz (mts.) ... F2
Gavkhuni (lake) ... F3
Gorgan (riv.) ... F2
Halil (riv.) ... G4
Jaz Murian, Hamun-e (marsh) ... G4
Karun (riv.) ... E3
Kavir, Dasht-e (salt des.) ... G3
Kavir-e Namak (salt des.) ... G3
Lut, Dasht-e (des.) ... G3
Maidani, Ras (cape) ... G4
Mand Rud (riv.) ... F4
Mashkid (riv.) ... H4
Mehran (riv.) ... F4
Namak, Daryacheh-ye
(salt lake) ... F3
Namaksar (salt lake) ... H3
Namakzar-e Shahdad
(salt lake) ... G3
Oman (gulf) ... G5
Persian (gulf) ... F4
Qeys (isl.) ... F4
Qezel Owzan (riv.) ... E2
Qeshm (isl.) ... G4
Safidar, Kuh-e (mt.) ... F4
Shaikh Shua'ib (isl.) ... F4
Shir Kuh (mt.) ... F3
Taftan, Kuh-e (mt.) ... H4
Talab (riv.) ... H4
Tashk (lake) ... F4
Urmia (lake) ... E2
Zagros (mts.) ... E3

IRAQ

CITIES and TOWNS

Al'Aziziya 7,450 ... E3
Al Falluja 38,072 ... D3
Al Fatha† 15,329 ... D2
Al Musaiyib 15,955 ... D3
Al Qurna 5,638 ... E3
'Amadiya 2,578 ... D2
'Amara 64,847 ... E3
'Ana 15,729 ... D3
An Najaf 128,096 ... D3
An Nasiriya 60,405 ... E3
Arbela (Erbil) 90,320 ... D2
Ar Rahhaliya 1,579 ... D3
As Salman 3,584 ... E3
Baghdad (cap.) 502,503 ... E3
Baghdad* 1,745,328 ... E3
Baq'uba 34,575 ... D3
Basra 313,327 ... E3
Erbil 90,320 ... D2
Habbaniya 14,405 ... D3
Haditha 6,870 ... D3
Hai 16,988 ... E3
Hilla 84,717 ... D3
Hit 9,131 ... D3
Karbal'a 83,301 ... D3
Khanaqin 23,522 ... D3
Kirkuk 167,413 ... D2
Kirkuk* 176,794 ... D2
Kut 42,116 ... E3
Maidan 354 ... E3
Mosul 315,157 ... D2
Qala' Sharqat 2,434 ... D2
Ramadi 28,723 ... D3
Rutba 5,091 ... D3
Samarra 24,746 ... D3
Samawa 33,473 ... D3
Shithatha 2,326 ... D3
Sulaimaniya 86,822 ... E2
Tikrit 9,921 ... D3

OTHER FEATURES

'Aneiza, Jebel (mt.) ... C3
'Ara'r, Wadi (dry riv.) ... D3
Batin, Wadi al (dry riv.) ... E4
Euphrates (riv.) ... E3
Hauran, Wadi (dry riv.) ... D3
Mesopotamia (reg.) ... D3
Syrian (El Hamad) (des.) ... D3
Tigris (riv.) ... E3

KUWAIT

CITIES and TOWNS

Al Kuwait (cap.) 181,774 ... E4
Mina al Ahmadi ... E4
Mina Saud ... E4

OTHER FEATURES

Bubiyan (isl.) ... E4
Persian (gulf) ... F4

OMAN

CITIES and TOWNS

Adam ... G5
Buraimi ... G5
Dhank ... G5
Ibra ... G5
I'bri ... G5
Juwara ... G6
Kamil ... G5
Khaluf ... G5
Khasab ... G4
Manah ... G5
Masqat (Muscat) (cap.) 7,500 ... G5
Matrah 15,000 ... G5
Mina al Fahal ... G5
Murbat ... G6
Muscat (cap.) 7,500 ... G5
Nizwa ... G5
Quryat ... G5
Raysut (Risut) ... F6
Salala 4,000 ... F6
Sarur ... G5
Shinas ... G5
Sohar ... G5
Sur ... G5
Suwaiq ... G5

OTHER FEATURES

Akhdar, Jebel (range) ... G5
Batina (reg.) ... G5
Dhofar (reg.) ... F6
Hadd, Ras al (cape) ... G5
Jibsh, Ras (cape) ... G5
Kuria Muria (isls.) ... G6
Madraka, Ras (cape) ... G6
Masira (gulf) ... G6
Masira (isl.) ... G5
Musandam, Ras (cape) ... G4
Nus, Ras (cape) ... G6
Oman (gulf) ... G5
Oman (reg.) ... G5
Ruus al Jibal (dist.) ... G4
Sauqira (bay) ... G6
Sauqira, Ras (cape) ... G6
Sham, Jebel (mt.) ... G5
Sharbatat, Ras (cape) ... G6

QATAR

CITIES and TOWNS

Doha (cap.) 150,000 ... F4
Dukhan ... F4
Umm Sai'd ... F5

OTHER FEATURES

Persian (gulf) ... F4
Rakan, Ras (cape) ... F4

SAUDI ARABIA

CITIES and TOWNS

Aba as Sau'd 47,501 ... D6
'Abaila ... F5
Abha 30,150 ... D6
Abqaiq ... E4
Abu 'Arish ... D6
Abu Hadriya ... E4
'Ain al Mubarrak ... C5
Al 'Ain ... C4
Al 'Ala ... C4
Al 'Auda ... E4
Al Birk ... D6
Al Hilla ... E5
Al Lidam ... D5
Al Lith ... C5
Al Muadhdam ... C4
'Anaiza ... D4
Artawiya ... E4
'Ashaira ... D5
Ayun ... D4
Badr ... C5
Buraida 69,940 ... D4
Dam ... D5
Dammam 127,844 ... F4
Dar al Hamra ... C4
Dhaba ... C4
Dhahran ... E4
Dharma ... E5
Dilam ... E5
Doqa ... D6
Duwadami ... D5
Er Ras ... D4
Faid ... D4
Gail ... E5
Haddar ... E5
Hadiya ... C4
Hafar al Batin ... E4
Hail 40,502 ... D4
Hamar ... E5
Hamda ... D6
Hanakiya ... D5
Haql ... C4
Harad ... E5
Haraja ... D6
Hariq ... E5
Hofuf 101,271 ... E4
Jabrin ... E5
Jauf ... C4
Jidda 561,104 ... C5
Jizan (Qizan) 32,812 ... D6
Jubail ... F4
Jubba ... D4
Junaina ... D5
Kaf ... C3
Khaibar, 'Asir ... D5
Khaibar, Hejaz ... C4
Khamis Mushait 49,581 ... D6
Khay ... D6
Khurma ... D5
Laila ... E5
Majmaa' ... D4
Maqna ... C4
Marib ... E6
Mastaba ... C5
Mastura ... C5
Mecca 366,801 ... C5
Medain Salih ... C4
Medina 198,186 ... D5
Mendak ... D5
Mina Sau'd ... E4
Mubarraz 54,325 ... E4
Mudhnib ... D4
Muwailih ... C4
Najran (Aba as Sau'd) 47,501 ... D6
Nisab ... D4
O'qair ... E4
Qadhima ... C5
Qafar ... D4
Qasr al Haiyanya ... D4
Qatif ... E4
Qizan 32,812 ... D6
Qunfidha ... D6
Qusaiba ... D4
Rabigh ... C5
Ra's al Khafji ... E4
Ras Tanura ... F4
Riyadh (cap.) 666,840 ... E5
Rumah ... E4
Sabya ... D6
Sakaka ... D4
Salwa ... F5
Shaqra ... D4
Shuqaiq ... D6
Sufeina ... D5
Sulaiyil ... E5
Taif 204,857 ... D5
Taima ... C4
Tamra ... E5
Tathlith ... D6
Tebuk (Tabuk) 74,825 ... C4
Truba ... D4
Turaba ... D5
Umm Lajj ... C4
Wejh ... C4
Yamama ... E5
Yenbo ... C5
Zahran ... D6
Zalim ... D5
Zilfi ... E4

OTHER FEATURES

Abu-Mad, Ras (cape) ... C5
'Aneiza, Jebel (mt.) ... C3
'Aqaba (gulf) ... C4
Arafat, Jebel (mt.) ... D5
'Ara'r, Wadi (dry riv.) ... D3
Arma (plat.) ... E4
Aswad, Ras al (cape) ... C5
Bahr es Safi (des.) ... E6
Barida, Ras (cape) ... C5
Bisha, Wadi (dry riv.) ... D5
Dahana (des.) ... E4
Dawasir, Wadi (dry riv.) ... E5
Dawasir, Hadhb (range) ... D5
Farasan (isls.) ... D6
Hatiba, Ras (cape) ... C5
Jafura (des.) ... F5
Mashabi (isl.) ... C4
Midian (dist.) ... C4
Mishaa'b, Ras (cape) ... E4
Nefud (des.) ... D4
Nefud Dahi (des.) ... D5
Persian (gulf) ... F4
Ranya, Wadi (dry riv.) ... D5
Red (sea) ... C5
Rima, Wadi (dry riv.) ... D4
Rimal, Ar (des.) ... F5
Rub al Khali (des.) ... F5
Safaniya, Ras (cape) ... E4
Salma, Jebel (mts.) ... D4
Shaibara (isl.) ... C4
Shammar, Jebel (plat.) ... D4
Sirhan, Wadi (dry riv.) ... C3
Subh, Jebel (mt.) ... C5
Summan (plat.) ... E4
Tihama (reg.) ... C5
Tiran (isl.) ... C4
Tiran (str.) ... C4
Tuwaiq, Jebel (range) ... E5

UNITED ARAB EMIRATES

CITIES and TOWNS

Abu Dhabi (cap.) 347,000 ... F5
'AJman ... G4
'Aradah ... F5
Buraimi ... G5
Dubai ... F4
Fujairah ... G4
Jebel Dhanna ... F5
Ras al Khaimah ... G4
Ruwais ... F5
Sharjah ... F4
Umm al Qaiwain ... G4

OTHER FEATURES

Das (isl.) ... F4
Oman (gulf) ... G5
Yas (isl.) ... F5
Zirko (isl.) ... F5

WEST BANK

CITIES and TOWNS

Hebron 38,309 ... C3

OTHER FEATURES

Dead (sea) ... C3

YEMEN ARAB REP.

CITIES and TOWNS

'Amran
Bait al Faqih
Dhamar 19,467
El Beida 5,975
Hajja 5,814
Harib
Hodeida 80,314
Huth
Ibb 19,066
Luhaiya
Marib 292
Mocha
Saa'da 4,252
Sana' (cap.) 134,588
Sheikh Sai'd
Tai'zz 78,642
Yarim
Zabid

OTHER FEATURES

Hanish (isls.)
Manar, Jebel (mt.)
Mandeb, Bab el (str.)
Red (sea)
Sabir, Jebel (mt.)
Tihama (reg.)
Zuqar (isl.)

YEMEN, PEOPLE'S DEM. REPUBLIC O

CITIES and TOWNS

Aden (cap.) 240,370
Ahwar
Balhaf
Bir 'Ali
Damqut
Ghaida
Habban
Hadibu
Hajarain
Haura
Hureidha
I'rqa
Lahej
Leijun
Lodar
Madinat ash Shab'
Meifa
Mukalla 45,000
Nisab
Nuqub
Qishn
Riyan
Saihut
Seiyun 20,000
Shabwa
Shibam
Shihr
Shuqra
Tarim
Yeshbum
Zinjibar

OTHER FEATURES

Fartak, Ras (cape)
Hadhramaut (dist.)
Hadhramaut, Wadi (dry riv.)
Kamaran (isl.)
Perim (isl.)
Socotra (isl.)

*City and suburbs.

Agriculture, Industry and Resources

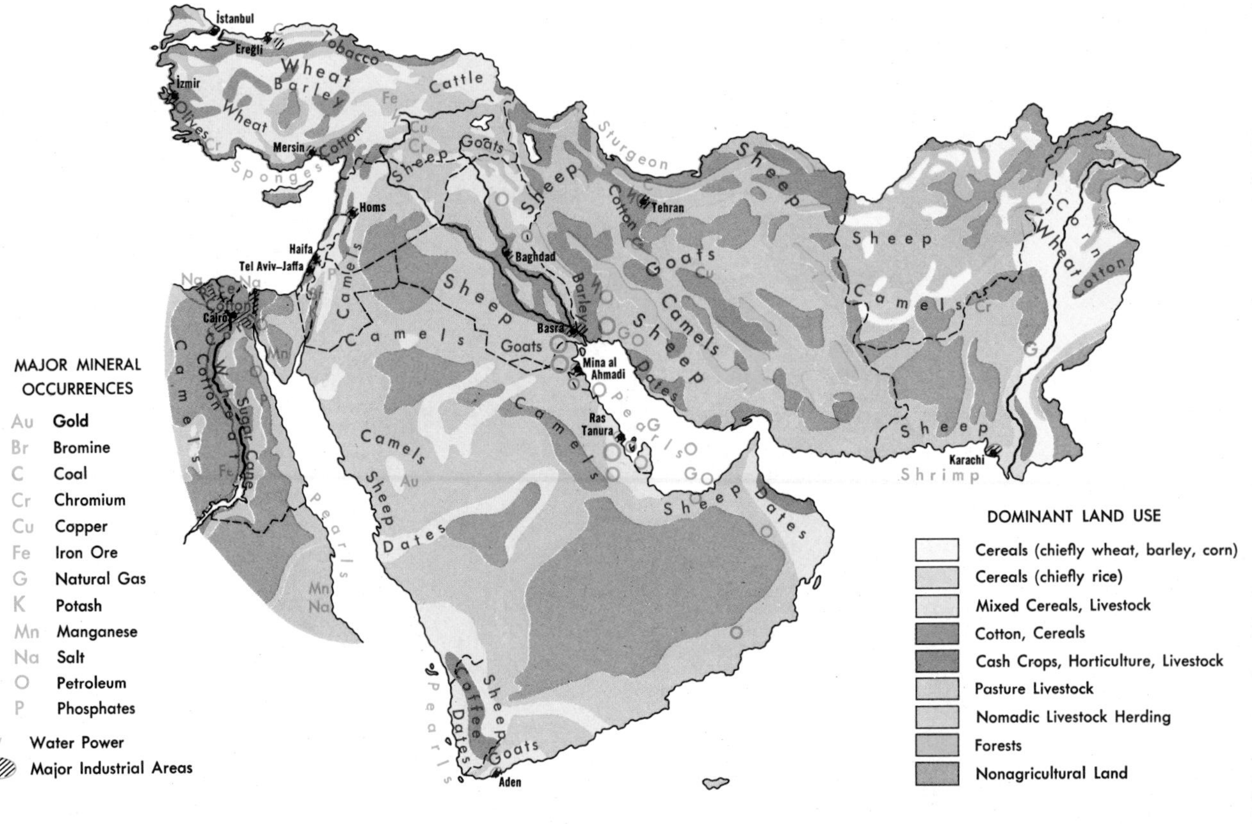

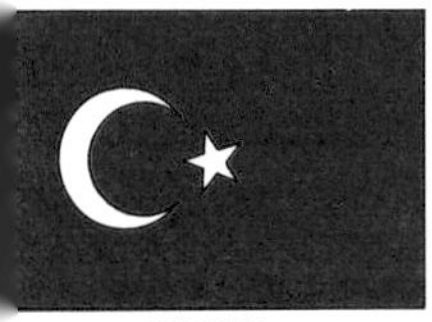

TURKEY

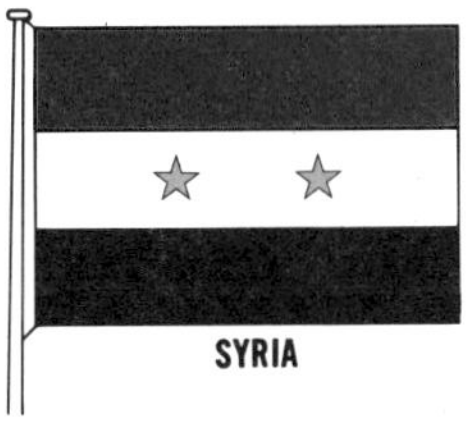

SYRIA

LEBANON

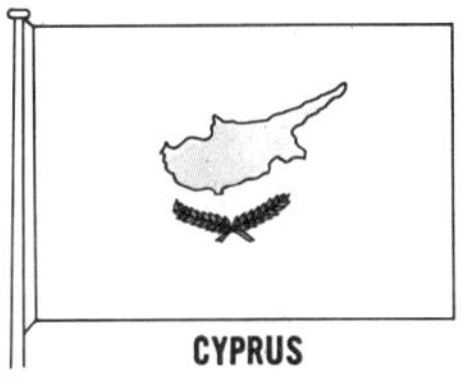

CYPRUS

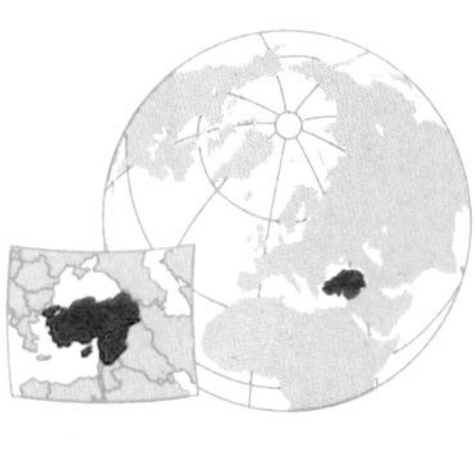

AREA 300,946 sq. mi. (779,450 sq. km.)
POPULATION 45,217,556
CAPITAL Ankara
LARGEST CITY Istanbul
HIGHEST POINT Ararat 16,946 ft. (5,165 m.)
MONETARY UNIT Turkish lira
MAJOR LANGUAGE Turkish
MAJOR RELIGION Islam

AREA 71,498 sq. mi. (185,180 sq. km.)
POPULATION 8,979,000
CAPITAL Damascus
LARGEST CITY Damascus
HIGHEST POINT Hermon 9,232 ft. (2,814 m.)
MONETARY UNIT Syrian pound
MAJOR LANGUAGES Arabic, French, Kurdish, Armenian
MAJOR RELIGIONS Islam, Christianity

AREA 4,015 sq. mi. (10,399 sq. km.)
POPULATION 3,161,000
CAPITAL Beirut
LARGEST CITY Beirut
HIGHEST POINT Qurnet es Sauda 10,131 ft. (3,088 m.)
MONETARY UNIT Lebanese pound
MAJOR LANGUAGES Arabic, French
MAJOR RELIGIONS Christianity, Islam

AREA 3,473 sq. mi. (8,995 sq. km.)
POPULATION 629,000
CAPITAL Nicosia
LARGEST CITY Nicosia
HIGHEST POINT Troödos 6,406 ft. (1,953 m.)
MONETARY UNIT Cypriot pound
MAJOR LANGUAGES Greek, Turkish, English
MAJOR RELIGIONS Eastern (Greek) Orthodoxy, Islam

CYPRUS

CITIES and TOWNS

hali 2,970 ... E5
iskopi 2,150 ... E5
magusta 38,960 ... F5
ima ... E5
yrenia 3,892 ... E5
ythrea 3,400 ... E5
apithos 3,600 ... E5
arnaca 19,608 ... E5
efka 3,650 ... E5
imassol 79,641 ... E5
orphou 9,040 ... E5
icosia (cap.) 115,718 ... E5
aphos 8,984 ... E5
olis 2,200 ... E5
izokarpasso 3,600 ... F5
ialousa 2,750 ... E5

OTHER FEATURES

ndreas (cape) ... F5
rnauti (cape) ... E5
ata (cape) ... E5
reco (cape) ... F5
ormakiti (cape) ... E5
roodos (mt.) ... E5

LEBANON

CITIES and TOWNS

A'leih 18,630 ... F6
Amyun 7,926 ... F5
Baa'lbek 15,560 ... G5
Batrun 5,976 ... F5
Beirut (cap.) 474,870 ... F6
Beirut* 938,940 ... F6
Hermil 2,652 ... G5
Merj U'yun 9,318 ... F6
Rasheiya 6,731 ... F6
Rayak 1,480 ... G6
Saida 32,200 ... F6
Sidon (Saida) 32,200 ... F6
Sur 16,483 ... F6
Tripoli (Tarabulus) 127,611 ... F5
Tyre (Sur) 16,483 ... F6
Zahle 53,121 ... F6
Zegharta 18,210 ... G5

OTHER FEATURES

Lebanon (mts.) ... F6
Leontes (Litani) (riv.) ... F6
Litani (riv.) ... F6
Sauda, Qurnet es (mt.) ... G5

SYRIA

PROVINCES

Aleppo 1,316,872 ... G4
Damascus 1,457,934 ... G6
Deir ez Zor 292,780 ... H5
Dera' 230,481 ... G6
El Quneitra 16,490 ... F6
Es Suweida 139,650 ... G6
Hama 514,748 ... G5
Haseke 468,506 ... J4
Homs 546,176 ... G5
Idlib 383,695 ... G5
Latakia 389,552 ... G5
Rashid 243,736 ... H5
Tartus 302,065 ... G5

CITIES and TOWNS

Abu Kemal 6,907 ... J5
A'in el A'rab 4,529 ... H4
Aleppo 639,428 ... G4
Azaz 13,923 ... G4
Baniyas 8,537 ... F5
Busra ... G6
Damascus (cap.) 836,668 ... G6
Damascus* 923,253 ... G6
Deir ez Zor 66,164 ... H5
Dera' 27,651 ... G6
Dimashq (Damascus) (cap.) 836,668 ... G6
Duma 30,050 ... G6
El Bab 27,366 ... G4
El Haseke 32,746 ... J4
El Ladhiqiya (Latakia) 125,716 ... F5
El Quryatein ... G5
El Quneitra 17,752 ... F6
El Rashid 37,151 ... H5
En Nebk 16,334 ... G5
Es Suweide 29,524 ... G6
Et Tell el Abyad ... H4
Haffe 4,656 ... G5
Haleb (Aleppo) 639,428 ... G4
Hama 137,421 ... G5
Harim 6,837 ... G4
Homs 215,423 ... G5
Idlib 34,515 ... G5
Izra 3,226 ... G6
Jeble 15,715 ... F5
Jerablus 8,610 ... G4
Jisr esh Shughur 13,131 ... G5
Khan Sheikhun ... G5
Latakia 125,716 ... F5
Masyaf 7,058 ... G5
Membij 13,796 ... G4
Meskene ... H5
Meyadin 12,515 ... J5
Qala't es Salihiye ... J5
Qamishliye 31,448 ... J4
Quteife 4,993 ... G6
Raqqa (El Rashid) 37,151 ... H5
Sabkha 3,375 ... H5
Safita 9,650 ... G5
Selemiya 21,677 ... G5
Tadmur 10,670 ... H5
Tartus 29,842 ... F5
Telkalakh 6,242 ... F5
Zebdani 10,010 ... G6

OTHER FEATURES

A'mrit (ruins) ... F5
Arwad (Ruad) (isl.) ... F5
A'si (Orontes) (riv.) ... G5
Druz, Jebel ed (mts.) ... G6
El Furat (riv.) ... H4
Euphrates (El Furat) (riv.) ... H4
Hermon (mt.) ... F6
Khabur (riv.) ... J5
Orontes (riv.) ... G5
Palmyra (Tadmor) (ruins) ... H5
Ruwaq, Jebel er (mts.) ... G5

TURKEY

PROVINCES

Adana 1,240,475 ... F4
Adiyaman 346,892 ... H4
Afyonkarahisar 579,171 ... D3
Ağri 330,201 ... K3
Amasya 322,806 ... F2
Ankara 2,585,293 ... E3
Antalya 669,357 ... D4
Artvin 228,026 ... J2
Aydin 609,869 ... B4
Balikesir 789,255 ... B3
Bilecik 137,120 ... D2
Bingöl 210,804 ... J3
Bitlis 218,305 ... J3
Bolu 428,704 ... D2
Burdur 222,896 ... D4
Bursa 961,639 ... C2
Çanakkale 369,385 ... B2
Çankiri 265,468 ... E2
Çorum 547,580 ... F2
Denizli 560,916 ... C4
Diyarbakir 651,233 ... H4
Edirne 340,732 ... B2
Elâziğ 417,924 ... H3
Erzincan 283,683 ... H3
Erzurum 746,666 ... J3
Eskişehir 495,097 ... D3
Gaziantep 715,939 ... G4
Giresun 463,587 ... H2
Gümüşhane 293,673 ... H2
Hakkâri 126,036 ... K4
Hatay 744,113 ... G4
Içel 714,817 ... F4
Isparta 322,685 ... D4
Istanbul 3,904,588 ... C2
Izmir 1,673,966 ... B3
Kahramanmaraş 641,480 ... G4
Kars 707,398 ... K2
Kastamonu 438,243 ... E2
Kayseri 676,809 ... F3
Kirklareli 268,399 ... B2
Kirşehir 232,853 ... F3
Kocaeli 477,736 ... C2
Konya 1,422,461 ... E4
Kütahya 470,423 ... C3
Malatya 574,558 ... H3
Manisa 872,375 ... B3
Mardin 519,687 ... J4
Muğla 400,796 ... C4
Muş 267,203 ... J3
Nevşehir 249,308 ... F3
Niğde 463,121 ... F4
Ordu 664,290 ... G2
Rize 336,278 ... J2
Sakarya 495,649 ... D2
Samsun 906,381 ... F2
Siirt 381,503 ... J4
Sinop 267,605 ... F2
Sivas 741,713 ... G3
Tekirdağ 319,987 ... B2
Tokat 599,166 ... G2
Trabzon 719,008 ... H2
Tunceli 164,591 ... H3
Urfa 597,277 ... H4
Uşak 229,679 ... C3
Van 386,314 ... K3
Yozgat 500,371 ... F3
Zonguldak 836,156 ... D2

CITIES and TOWNS

Acigöl 3,934 ... F3
Acipayam 5,046 ... C4
Adalia (Antalya) 130,774 ... D4
Adana 475,384 ... F4
Adapazari 114,130 ... D2
Adilcevaz 9,022 ... K3
Adiyaman 43,782 ... H4
Afşin 18,231 ... G3
Afyonkarahisar 60,150 ... D3
Ağlasun 4,288 ... D4
Ağli 3,399 ... E2
Ağri (Karaköse) 35,284 ... K3
Ahlat 7,995 ... K3
Akçaabat 10,756 ... H2
Akçadağ 7,366 ... G3
Akçakoca 9,066 ... D2
Akdağmadeni 7,909 ... F3
Akhisar 53,357 ... B3
Aksaray 45,564 ... F3
Akşehir 35,544 ... D3
Akseki 5,141 ... D4
Akviran 3,799 ... E4
Akyazi 12,438 ... D2
Alaca 12,552 ... F2
Alacahan 2,321 ... G3
Alaçam 10,013 ... F2
Alanya 18,520 ... D4
Alaşehir 23,243 ... C3
Alexandretta (Iskenderun) 107,437 ... G4
Aliağa 5,727 ... B3
Alibeyköyü 33,387 ... D6
Almus 4,225 ... G2
Alpu 3,718 ... D3
Altindağ 512,392 ... E2
Altinova 6,980 ... B3
Altintaş 3,386 ... C3
Altinözü 5,158 ... G4
Alucra 7,070 ... H2
Amasra 4,369 ... E2
Amasya 41,496 ... G2
Anamur 21,475 ... E4
Andirin 5,018 ... G4
Ankara (cap.) 1,701,004 ... E3
Antakya 77,518 ... G4
Antalya 130,774 ... D4
Antioch (Antakya) 77,518 ... G4
Araç 3,594 ... E2
Aralik 4,155 ... L3
Arapkir 8,436 ... H3
Ardahan 16,285 ... K2
Ardeşen 7,980 ... J2
Ardanuç 2,942 ... K2
Arguvan 2,461 ... H3
Arhavi 6,311 ... J2
Arpaçay 2,651 ... K2
Arsin 6,557 ... H2
Artova 2,813 ... G2
Artvin 13,390 ... J2
Aşkale 10,817 ... J3
Avanos 8,635 ... F3
Ayancik 7,202 ... F1
Ayaş 4,575 ... E2
Aybasti 13,180 ... G2
Aydin 59,579 ... B4
Aydincik 6,739 ... E4
Ayranci 2,664 ... E4
Ayvacik 3,120 ... B3
Ayvalik 18,041 ... B3
Babadağ 5,890 ... C4
Babaeski 17,090 ... B2
Bafra 34,288 ... F2
Bahçe 10,212 ... G4
Bakirköy 200,942 ... D6
Baklan 3,327 ... C4
Balâ 4,107 ... E3
Balikesir 99,443 ... B3
Balya 2,362 ... B3
Banaz 6,264 ... C3
Bandirma 45,752 ... B2
Bartin 18,409 ... E2
Başkale 8,558 ... K3
Başmakçi 5,925 ... C4
Batman 64,384 ... J4
Bayat 4,671 ... F2
Bayburt 20,156 ... J2
Bayindir 14,078 ... B3
Baykan 2,690 ... J3
Bayramiç 6,385 ... B3
Bergama 29,749 ... B3
Beşiktaş 174,931 ... D6
Beşiri 4,165 ... J4
Besni 16,313 ... G4
Beykoz 76,804 ... D5
Beyoğlu 230,532 ... D6
Beypazari 14,963 ... D2
Beyşehir 15,060 ... D4
Beytüşşebap 2,766 ... K4
Biga 15,188 ... B2
Bigadiç 7,535 ... C3
Bilecik 11,269 ... D2
Bingöl (Çapakçur) 22,047 ... J3
Birecik 20,104 ... H4
Bismil 12,775 ... J4
Bitlis 25,054 ... J3
Bodrum 7,858 ... B4
Boğazliyan 10,329 ... F3
Bolu 32,812 ... D2
Bolvadin 29,218 ... D3
Bor 16,560 ... F4
Borçka 4,636 ... J2
Bornova 45,096 ... B3
Boyabat 13,139 ... F2
Bozdoğan 7,218 ... C4
Bozkir 5,294 ... E4
Bozkurt 2,948 ... F2
Bozova 5,462 ... H4
Bozüyük 15,197 ... C3
Bucak 15,090 ... D4
Bulancak 14,153 ... H2
Bulanik 8,296 ... K3
Buldan 11,115 ... C3
Bünyan 12,277 ... G3
Burdur 36,633 ... D4
Burhaniye 12,800 ... B3
Bursa 346,103 ... C2
Büyükada ... D6
Büyükdere ... D5
Çal 3,274 ... C3
Çala 2,450 ... K2
Çaldiran 3,366 ... K3

(continued on following page)

Agriculture, Industry and Resources

DOMINANT LAND USE

- Cereals (chiefly wheat, barley), Livestock
- Cash Crops, Horticulture, Livestock
- Pasture Livestock
- Nomadic Livestock Herding
- Forests
- Nonagricultural Land

MAJOR MINERAL OCCURRENCES

Ab	Asbestos	Na	Salt
Al	Bauxite	O	Petroleum
C	Coal	P	Phosphates
Cr	Chromium	Pb	Lead
Cu	Copper	Py	Pyrites
Fe	Iron Ore	Sb	Antimony
Hg	Mercury	Zn	Zinc
Mg	Magnesium		

Water Power
Major Industrial Areas

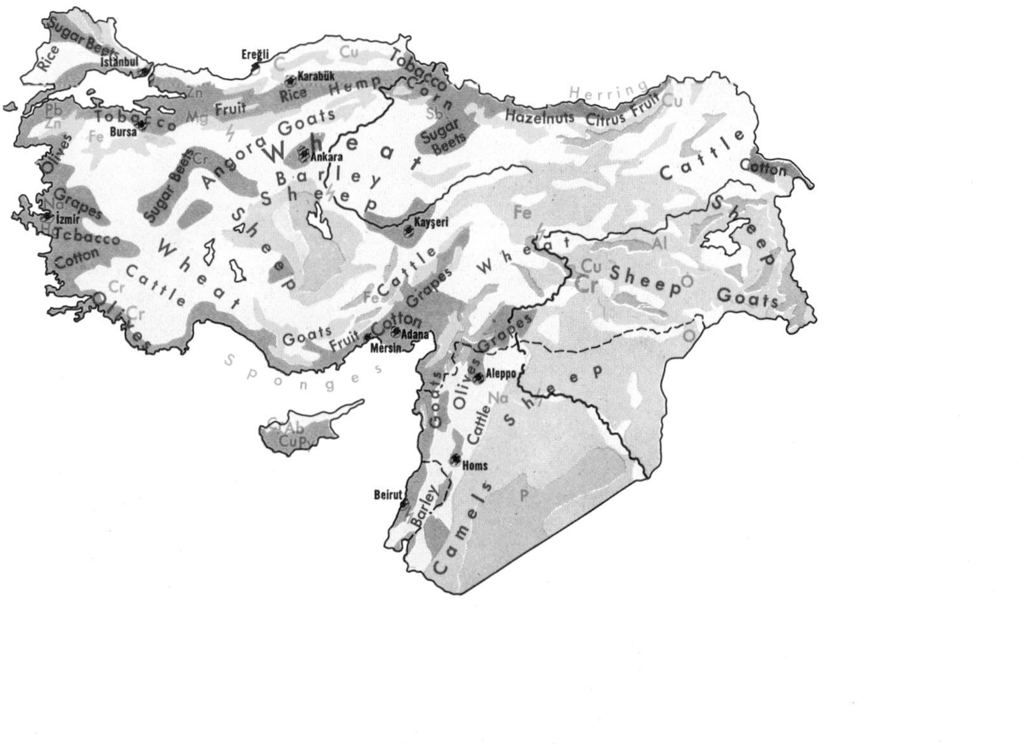

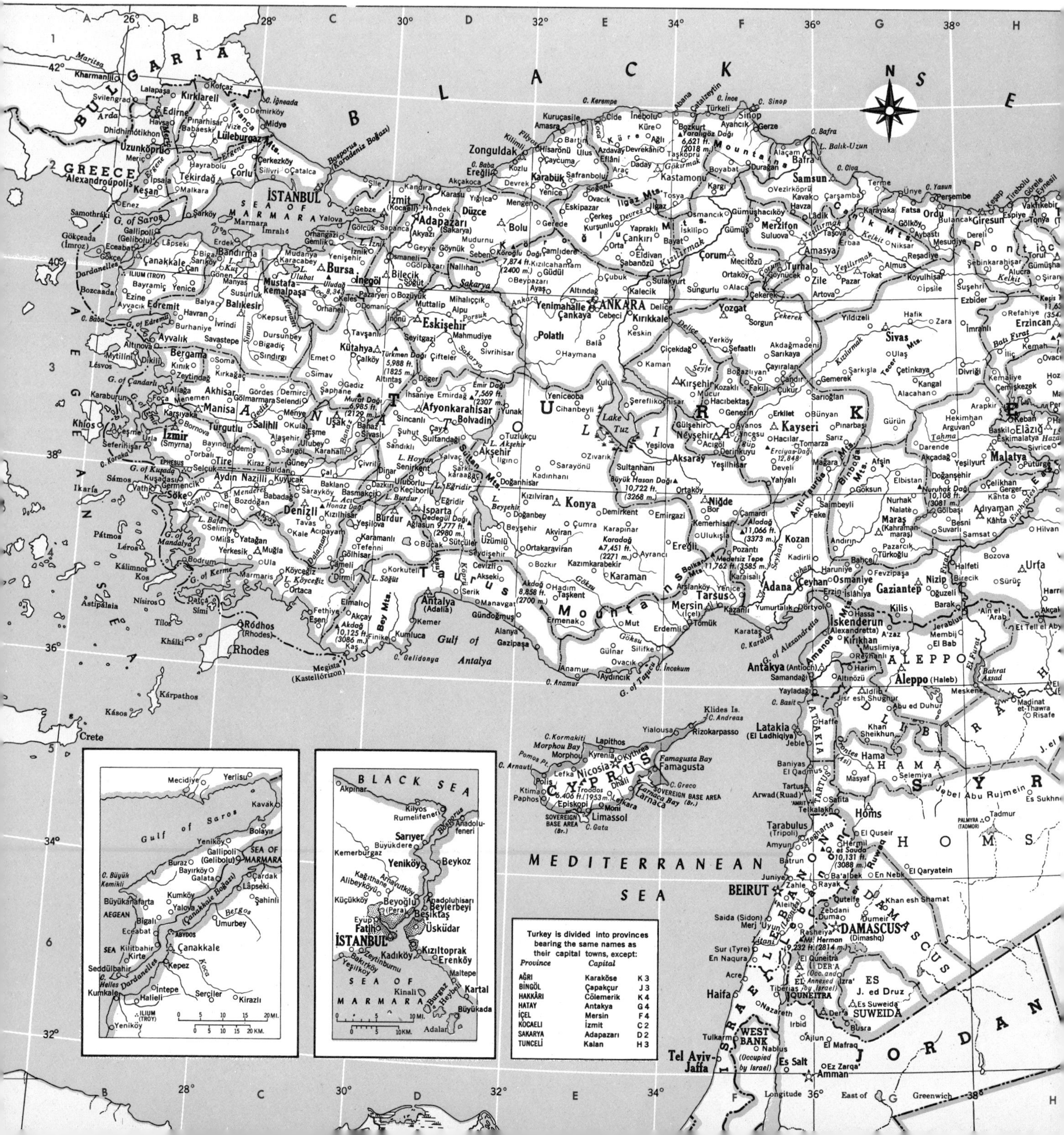

Turkey is divided into provinces bearing the same names as their capital towns, except:

Province	Capital	
AĞRI	Karaköse	K 3
BİNGÖL	Çapakçur	J 3
HAKKÂRI	Cölemerik	K 4
HATAY	Antakya	G 4
İÇEL	Mersin	F 4
KOCAELİ	İzmit	C 2
SAKARYA	Adapazarı	D 2
TUNCELİ	Kalan	H 3

'abolu 12,331 ..... B2
o 4,896 ..... J3
mhan 11,818 ..... G3
dek 15,291 ..... D2
an 6,473 ..... H4
s 10,226 ..... J3
rönü 4,485 ..... E2
n 2,545 ..... K3
a 9,089 ..... J2
asan 7,724 ..... K2
at 5,796 ..... H3
(Mersin) 152,236 ..... F4
4,862 ..... J4
r 29,542 ..... K3
z 6,624 ..... E2
11,830 ..... D3
8,947 ..... J3
anli 5,667 ..... H2
su 7,089 ..... F3
olu 6,824 ..... E2
öl 37,805 ..... C2
ü 4,152 ..... D3
la 6,829 ..... B2
e 2,328 ..... G2
nderun 107,437 ..... G4
ip 16,588 ..... F2
Islâhiye 20,683 ..... G4
Isparta 62,870 ..... D4
Ispir 3,929 ..... J2
Istanbul 2,547,364 ..... D6
Ivrindi 3,730 ..... B3
Izmir 636,834 ..... B3
Izmit 165,483 ..... D2
Iznik 11,614 ..... C2
Kadiköy 354,957 ..... D6
Kadinhani 11,802 ..... E3
Kadirli 34,779 ..... F4
Kağithane 164,448 ..... D6
Kağizman 11,517 ..... K2
Kâhta 15,602 ..... H4
Kalan 11,637 ..... H3
Kale 3,399 ..... C4
Kalecik 4,707 ..... E2
Kaman 16,516 ..... E3
Kandira 10,187 ..... D2
Kangal 5,937 ..... G3
Karabük 69,182 ..... E2
Karacabey 21,648 ..... C2
Karahalli 5,539 ..... C3
Karaisali 2,316 ..... F4
Karakoçan 5,604 ..... H3
Karaköse (Ağri) 35,284 ..... K3

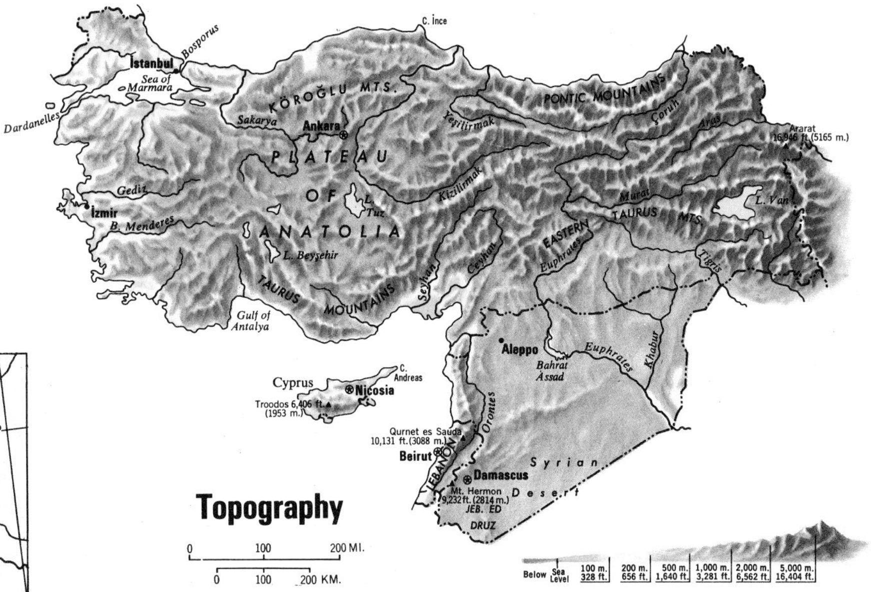

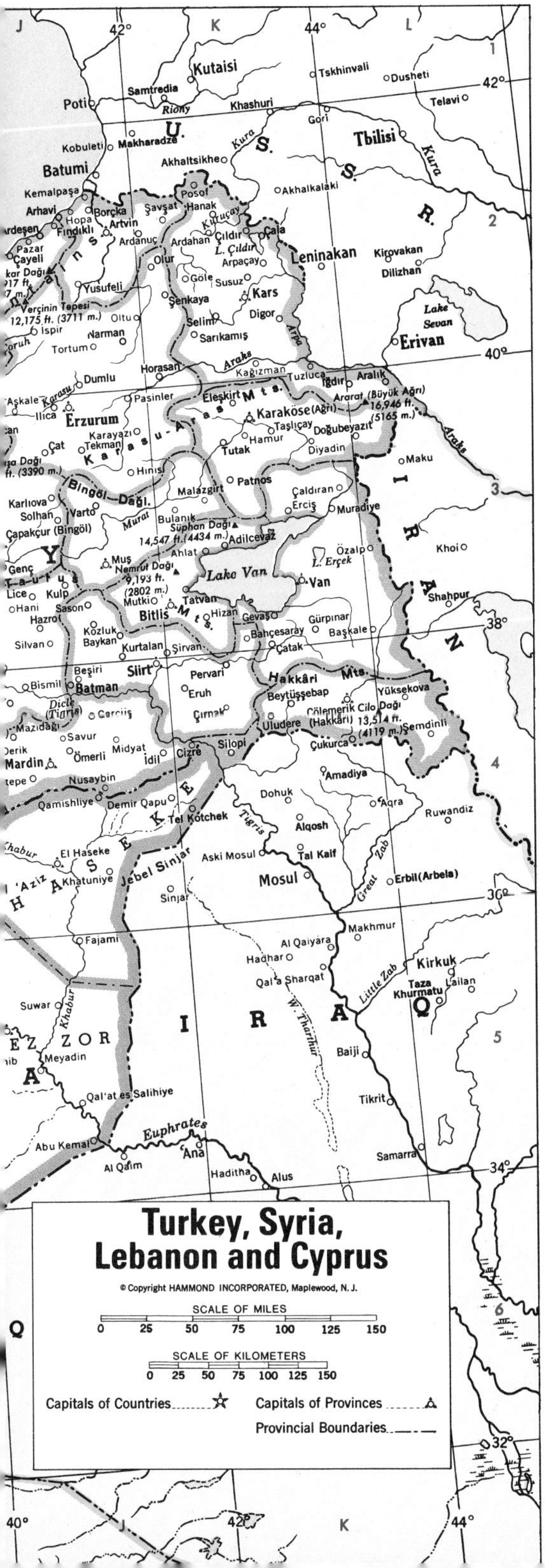

Karaman 43,759 ..... E4
Karamanli 5,904 ..... C4
Karapinar 19,589 ..... E4
Karasu 11,600 ..... D2
Karataş 5,598 ..... F4
Karayaka 4,242 ..... G2
Karayazi 3,595 ..... J3
Kargi 5,021 ..... F2
Karliova 3,631 ..... J3
Kars 54,892 ..... K2
Karşiyaka 171,600 ..... B3
Kartal 53,073 ..... D6
Kaş 2,493 ..... C4
Kastamonu 29,993 ..... F2
Kavak, Çanakkale 3,932 ..... C5
Kavak, Samsun 3,964 ..... F2
Kayseri 207,037 ..... F3
Kazanli 4,461 ..... F4
Kazimkarabekir 4,086 ..... E4
Keban 5,800 ..... H3
Keçiborlu 7,096 ..... D4
Keles 2,423 ..... C3
Kelkit 6,928 ..... H2
Kemah 3,038 ..... H3
Kemaliye 3,014 ..... H3
Kemalpaşa 7,572 ..... J2
Kemerburgaz 7,234 ..... D5
Kemirhisar 6,205 ..... F4
Kepsut 4,704 ..... C3
Keşan 27,088 ..... B2
Keşap 5,264 ..... H2
Keskin 10,540 ..... E3
Kiği 5,598 ..... J3
Kilimli 26,649 ..... D2
Kilis 54,055 ..... G4
Kinik 11,785 ..... B3
Kiraz 5,204 ..... C0
Kirikhan 38,118 ..... G4
Kirikkale 137,874 ..... E3
Kirkağaç 15,078 ..... B3
Kirklareli 33,265 ..... B2
Kirşehir 41,415 ..... F3
Kizilcahamam 7,050 ..... E2
Kizilhisar 11,119 ..... C4
Kiziltepe 21,531 ..... J4
Kizilviran 3,260 ..... E4
Kocaeli (Izmit) 165,483 ..... D2
Koçarli 5,182 ..... B4
Konya 246,727 ..... E4
Korkuteli 10,334 ..... D4
Köyceğiz 4,612 ..... C4
Koyulhisar 3,861 ..... G2
Kozakli 6,200 ..... F3
Kozan 32,045 ..... F4
Kozlu 27,322 ..... D2
Kozluk 6,197 ..... J3
Küçükköy 56,411 ..... C6
Kula 10,807 ..... C3
Kulp 4,474 ..... J3
Kulu 11,707 ..... E3
Kumkale 1,752 ..... B6
Kumluca 7,704 ..... D4
Küre 2,378 ..... E2
Kurşunlu 6,562 ..... E2
Kurtalan 7,001 ..... J3
Kuşadasi 10,269 ..... B4
Kütahya 82,442 ..... C3
Kuyucak 6,039 ..... C4
Lâdik 6,785 ..... G2
Lâpseki 3,727 ..... C6
Lice 8,625 ..... J3
Lüleburgaz 32,401 ..... B2
Maden 15,151 ..... H3
Mağara 4,314 ..... G3
Mahmudiye 5,240 ..... D3
Malatya 154,505 ..... H3
Malazgirt 13,094 ..... K3
Malkara 14,399 ..... B2
Maltepe 66,343 ..... D6
Manavgat 10,804 ..... D4
Manisa 78,114 ..... B3
Manyas 4,410 ..... B3
Maraş
(Kahramanmaraş) 135,782 ..... G4
Mardin 36,629 ..... J4
Marmaris 5,596 ..... C4
Mazgirt 3,141 ..... H3
Mazidaği 4,842 ..... J4
Mecitözü 6,066 ..... F2
Menemen 18,464 ..... B3
Mengen 2,459 ..... D2
Meriç 3,922 ..... B2
Mersin 152,236 ..... F4
Merzifon 30,801 ..... F2
Mesudiye 4,294 ..... F4
Midyat 16,905 ..... J4
Midye 2,003 ..... C2
Mihaliççik 4,004 ..... D3
Milâs 17,929 ..... B4
Mucur 9,398 ..... F3
Mudanya 8,399 ..... C2
Mudurnu 3,905 ..... D2
Muğla 24,178 ..... C4
Muradiye 6,334 ..... K3
Muş 27,761 ..... J3
Mustafakemalpaşa 27,706 ..... C3
Mut 11,466 ..... E4
Mutki 2,815 ..... J3
Muttalip 3,917 ..... D3
Nallihan 7,883 ..... D2
Narman 4,607 ..... J2
Nazilli 52,176 ..... C4
Nevşehir 30,203 ..... F3
Niğde 31,844 ..... F4
Niksar 19,156 ..... G2
Nizip 36,190 ..... G4
Nurhak 5,330 ..... G4
Nusaybin 23,684 ..... J4
Ödemiş 37,364 ..... C3
Of 10,376 ..... J2
Oğuzeli 7,194 ..... G4
Oltu 10,093 ..... J2
Ömerli 4,738 ..... J4
Ordu 47,481 ..... G2
Orhaneli 3,335 ..... C3
Orhangazi 12,181 ..... C2
Orta 3,596 ..... E2
Ortaca 8,604 ..... C4
Ortakaraviran 3,856 ..... E4
Ortaköy, Çorum 2,657 ..... F2
Ortaköy, Niğde 6,371 ..... F3
Osmancik 11,921 ..... F2
Osmaneli 4,789 ..... D2
Osmaniye 61,581 ..... G4
Ovacik, Tunceli 2,248 ..... H3
Özalp 4,188 ..... K3
Palu 5,489 ..... H3
Pasinler 14,267 ..... J3
Patnos 16,010 ..... K3
Pazar, Rize 8,856 ..... J2
Pazar, Tokat 4,337 ..... G2
Pazarcik 15,943 ..... G4
Pazaryeri 5,633 ..... C3
Pera (Beyoğlu) 230,532 ..... D6
Perşembe 6,701 ..... G2
Pertek 4,176 ..... H3
Pervari 4,126 ..... K4
Pinarbaşi 9,503 ..... G3
Pinarhisar 10,523 ..... B2
Polatli 35,267 ..... E3
Posof 2,209 ..... K2
Pozanti 5,408 ..... F4
Pülümür 3,442 ..... H3
Pütürge 4,878 ..... H3
Refahiye 6,570 ..... H3
Reşadiye 9,022 ..... G2
Reyhanli 25,749 ..... G4
Rize 36,044 ..... J2
Şabanözü 3,442 ..... E2
Safranbolu 14,793 ..... E2
Saimbeyli 3,622 ..... G4
Sakarya (Adapazari) 114,130 ..... D2
Salihli 45,514 ..... C3
Samandaği 22,540 ..... F4
Samsat 2,083 ..... H4
Samsun 168,478 ..... F2
Sandikli 13,181 ..... D3
Sapanca 9,040 ..... D2
Şaphane 3,919 ..... C3
Sarayköy 10,513 ..... C4
Sarayönü 8,946 ..... E3
Sarigöl 6,979 ..... C3
Sarikamiş 21,262 ..... K2
Sarikaya 5,160 ..... F3
Sariköy 4,695 ..... B2
Sarioğlan 3,245 ..... G3
Sariyer 79,329 ..... D5
Sariz 3,591 ..... G3
Şarkikaraağaç 4,772 ..... D3
Şarkişla 12,763 ..... G3
Şarköy 5,396 ..... B2
Sason 3,211 ..... J3
Savaştepe 7,179 ..... B3
Şavşat 3,078 ..... K2
Savur 4,983 ..... J4
Seben 2,471 ..... D2
Şebinkarahisar 10,214 ..... H2
Şefaatli 6,769 ..... F3
Seferihisar 6,484 ..... B3
Selçuk 12,251 ..... B3
Selendi 4,457 ..... C3
Selim 3,569 ..... K2
Selimiye 2,989 ..... B4
Senirkent 8,247 ..... D3
Şenkaya 3,190 ..... K2
Şereflikoçhisar 20,523 ..... E3
Serik 14,161 ..... D4
Seydişehir 25,651 ..... D4
Seyitgazi 2,819 ..... D3
Siirt 35,654 ..... J4
Şile 4,062 ..... C2
Silifke 19,257 ..... E4
Silivri 8,525 ..... C2
Silopi 4,460 ..... K4
Silvan 29,599 ..... J3
Simav 11,601 ..... C3
Sincanli 3,847 ..... D3
Sindirgi 7,818 ..... C3
Sinop 16,098 ..... F2
Şiran 5,048 ..... H2
Şirnak 10,587 ..... K4
Şirvan 5,166 ..... K3
Sivas 149,201 ..... G3
Sivasli 4,394 ..... C3
Siverek 40,990 ..... H4
Sivrihisar 8,713 ..... D3
Smyrna (Izmir) 636,834 ..... B3
Söğüt 5,329 ..... D3
Söke 35,407 ..... B4
Solhan 7,014 ..... J3
Soma 23,713 ..... B3
Sorgun 14,081 ..... F3
Şuhut 8,154 ..... D3
Sulakyurt 4,311 ..... E2
Sultandaği 4,017 ..... D3
Sultanhani 5,112 ..... E3
Suluova 21,278 ..... F2
Sungurlu 21,641 ..... F2
Sürmene 8,096 ..... J2
Sürüç 20,395 ..... H4
Suşehri 10,863 ..... H2
Susurluk 14,000 ..... C3
Susuz 5,006 ..... K2
Sütçüler 2,721 ..... D4
Tarsus 102,186 ..... F4
Taşkent 7,098 ..... E4
Taşköprü 8,146 ..... F2
Taşliçay 3,684 ..... K3
Taşova 6,516 ..... F4
Tatvan 29,271 ..... K3
Tavas 9,729 ..... C4
Tavşanli 19,575 ..... C3
Tefenni 4,280 ..... C4
Tekirdağ 41,257 ..... B2
Tercan 6,068 ..... J3
Terme 15,660 ..... G2
Tire 30,694 ..... B3
Tirebolu 7,385 ..... H2
Tokat 48,588 ..... G2
Tomarza 6,548 ..... F3
Tömük 7,660 ..... F4
Tonya 10,544 ..... H2
Torbali 17,237 ..... B3
Tortum 4,110 ..... J2
Torul 3,221 ..... H2
Tosya 17,515 ..... F2
Trabzon 97,210 ..... H2
Trebizond (Trabzon) 97,210 ..... H2
Tunceli (Kalan) 11,637 ..... H3
Turgutlu 47,009 ..... B3
Turhal 39,170 ..... F2
Türkeli 2,194 ..... F2
Türkoğlu 9,207 ..... G4
Tutak 4,325 ..... K3
Tuzluca 5,209 ..... K3
Tuzlukçu 4,613 ..... D3
Ula 5,117 ..... C4
Ulaş 2,469 ..... G3
Ulubey 4,214 ..... C3
Uluborlu 10,016 ..... D3
Uludere 4,050 ..... K4
Ulukişla 6,336 ..... F4
Umurbey 2,754 ..... C6
Ünye 23,366 ..... G2
Urfa 132,934 ..... H4
Ürgüp 6,758 ..... F3
Urla 13,903 ..... B3
Uşak 58,578 ..... C3
Üsküdar 202,957 ..... D6
Üzümlü 4,365 ..... D4
Uzunköprü 27,005 ..... B2
Vakfikebir 12,556 ..... H2
Van 63,663 ..... K3
Varto 5,572 ..... J3
Vezirköprü 11,705 ..... F2
Viranşehir 26,244 ..... H4
Vize 8,203 ..... B2
Yahyali 13,738 ..... F3
Yalova, Istanbul 27,289 ..... C2
Yalvaç 18,305 ..... D3
Yaprakli 3,020 ..... E2
Yatağan 4,903 ..... C4
Yayladaği 4,471 ..... F5
Yenice, Çanakkale 4,004 ..... B3
Yenice, Içel 4,106 ..... F4
Yenice, Zonguldak 5,791 ..... E2
Yeniceoba 5,740 ..... E3
Yeniköy, Istanbul D6
Yenimahalle 198,643 ..... E3
Yenişehir 15,188 ..... C2
Yerkesik 2,381 ..... C4
Yerköy 19,927 ..... F3
Yeşilhisar 10,409 ..... F3
Yeşilköy D6
Yeşilova, Burdur 3,685 ..... C4
Yeşilova, Niğde 5,237 ..... E3
Yeşilyurt 7,451 ..... H3
Yildizeli 7,043 ..... G3
Yozgat 32,501 ..... F3
Yüksekova 7,329 ..... L4
Yumurtalik 2,442 ..... F4
Yunak 6,187 ..... D3
Yusufeli 3,050 ..... J2
Zara 10,376 ..... G3
Zeytinburnu 123,548 ..... D6
Zeytindağ 3,517 ..... B3
Zile 32,157 ..... G2
Zivarik 2,703 ..... E3
Zonguldak 90,221 ..... D2

OTHER FEATURES

Abydos (ruins) B6
Aci (lake) C4
Adalar (isl.) D6
Aegean (sea) A3
Ağri, Büyuk (Ararat)
(mt.) L3
Akdağ (mt.) C4
Aladağ (mt.) F4
Alexandretta (gulf) F4
Amanos (mts.) G4
Anamur (cape) E5
Anatolia (reg.) D3
Ankara (riv.) D3
Antalya (gulf) D4
Anti-Taurus (mts.) G3
Araks (riv.) K2
Ararat (mt.) L3
Arpa (riv.) K2
Baba (cape) A3
Bati Firat (riv.) H3
Beyşehir (lake) D4
Black (sea) E1
Bosporus (str.) C2
Bozcaada (isl.) A3
Burgaz (isl.) D6
Büyük Ağri (Ararat)
(mt.) L3
Çanakkale Boğazi (Dardanelles) (str.) B6
Çandarli (gulf) B3
Canik (mts.) G2
Ceyhan (riv.) F4
Cilo Daği (mt.) K4
Çoruh (riv.) J2
Dardanelles (str.) B6
Dicle (riv.) J4
Eastern Taurus (mts.) J3
Ephesus (ruins) B3
Erciyas Daği (mt.) F3
Ergene (riv.) B2
Euphrates (Firat) (riv.) G4
Firat (riv.) G4
Gediz (riv.) C3
Gelidonya (cape) D4
Gökçeada (isl.) A2
Göksu (riv.) E4
Helles (cape) B6
Heybeli (isl.) D6
Ilium (ruins) B6
Imroz (Gökçeada)
(isl.) A2
Ince (cape) F1
Istranca (mts.) B2
Kaçkar Daği (mt.) J2
Karadeniz Boğazi (Bosporus)
(str.) C2
Karasu-Aras (mts.) J3
Kelkit (riv.) G2
Kerme (gulf) B4
Keşiş Tepesi (mt.) H3
Kizilirmak (riv.) F2
Koca (riv.) C3
Köroğlu (mts.) E2
Küre (mts.) E2
Mandalya (gulf) B4
Marmara (isl.) B2
Marmara (sea) C2
Menderes, Büyük (riv.) C4
Meriç (riv.) B2
Murat (riv.) H3
Pontic (mts.) H2
Porsuk (riv.) D3
Prinkipo (Adalar) (isl.) D6
Sakarya (riv.) D2
Saros (gulf) B2
Seyhan (riv.) F4
Simav (riv.) C3
Sinop (cape) F1
Sultan (mts.) D3
Süphan Daği (mt.) K3
Taurus (mts.) D4
Tigris (Dicle) J4
Troy (Ilium) (ruins) B6
Tuz (lake) E3
Van (lake) K3
Yeşilirmak (riv.) G2

* City and suburbs

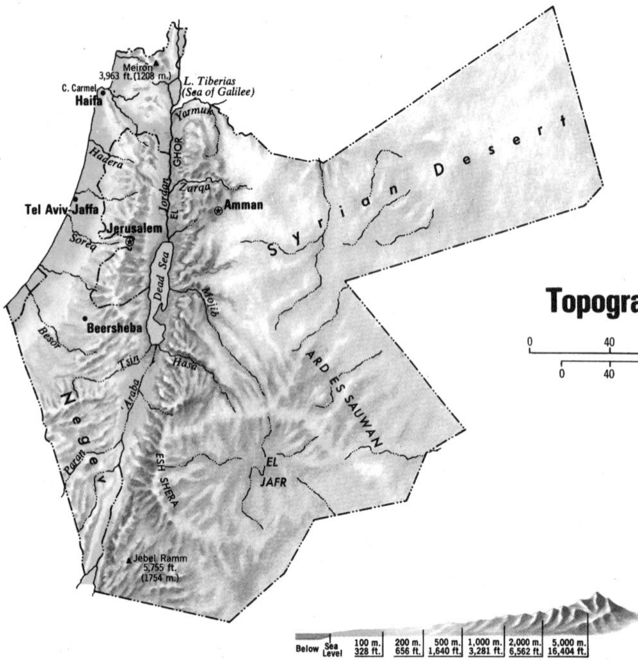
Meiron
3,963 ft. (1208 m.)
C. Carmel
Haifa
L. Tiberias
(Sea of Galilee)
Yarmuk
Hadera
GHOR
Jordan
Zarqa
Tel Aviv-Jaffa
Jerusalem
Amman
Soreq
EL
Dead Sea
Syrian Desert
Mojib
Beersheba
Besor
Tsin
Hasa
Negev
Araba
ARD ES SAUWAN
Paran
ESH SHERA
EL
JAFR
Jebel Ramm
5,755 ft.
(1754 m.)
Below Sea Level
100 m. 328 ft.
200 m. 656 ft.
500 m. 1,640 ft.
1,000 m. 3,281 ft.
2,000 m. 6,562 ft.
5,000 m. 16,404 ft.

Topography

0 40 80 MI.
0 40 80 KM.

ISRAEL

DISTRICTS

- Central 572,300 .... B3
- Haifa 480,800 .... C2
- Jerusalem 338,600 .... B4
- Northern 473,700 .... C2
- Southern 351,300 .... B5
- Tel Aviv 905,100 .... B3

CITIES and TOWNS

- Acre 34,400 .... C2
- Afiqim 1,243 .... D2
- 'Afula 17,400 .... C2
- Ahuzzam 407 .... B4
- Akko (Acre) 34,400 .... C2
- Arad 5,400 .... C5
- 'Arrabe 6,000 .... C2
- Ashdod 40,500 .... B4
- Ashdot Yaa'qov 1,197 .... D2
- Ashqelon 43,100 .... A4
- Atlit 1,516 .... B2
- Avihayil 579 .... B3
- Bat Shelomo 218 .... B2
- Bat Yam 124,100 .... B3
- Be'eri 390 .... A5
- Be'er Menuha D5
- Beersheba (Be'er Sheva) 101,000 .... B5
- Be'er Tuveya 602 .... B4
- Beit Guvrin B4
- Bene Beraq 74,100 .... B3
- Bet Qama 228 .... B5
- Bet She'an 11,300 .... D3
- Bet Shemesh 10,100 .... B4
- Binyamina 2,701 .... B2
- Carmiel C2
- Dafna 577 .... D1
- Dalyat al-Karmel 6,200 .... B2
- Dan 498 .... D1
- Dimona 23,700 .... D4
- Dor 195 .... B2
- E'in Gedi C5
- E'in Harod 1,372 .... C2
- Elat D6
- Elath (Elat) 12,800 .... D6
- El 'Auja D5
- Elyakim 568 .... C2
- Elyashiv 435 .... B3
- Even Yehuda 3,464 .... B3
- Gal'on 356 .... B4
- Gat 430 .... B4
- Gedera 5,400 .... B4
- Gerofit D5
- Gesher 360 .... C2
- Gesher Haziv 238 .... C1
- Gevara'm 283 .... B4
- Gilat 561 .... B5
- Ginnosar 473 .... D2
- Giv'atayim 48,500 .... B3
- Giva't Brenner 1,505 .... B4
- Giv'at Hayyim 1,360 .... B3
- Habonim 189 .... B2
- Hadera 31,900 .... B3
- Haifa 227,800 .... B2
- Haifa* 367,400 .... B2
- Hatseva D5
- Hazerim 127 .... B5
- Hazor Hagelilit D2
- Helez 466 .... B4
- Herzeliyya 41,200 .... B3
- Hod Hasharon 13,500 .... B3
- Hodiyya 400 .... B4
- Holon 121,200 .... B3
- Iksal 2,156 .... C2
- Jerusalem (cap.) 376,000 .... C4
- Jish 1,498 .... C1
- Kafar Kanna 5,200 .... C2
- Kafr Yasif 2,975 .... C2
- Karkur-Pardes Hanna 13,600 .... C3
- Kefar Blum 565 .... D1
- Kefar Gila'di 701 .... C1
- Kefar Ruppin 306 .... D3
- Kefar Sava 26,500 .... B3
- Kefar Vitkin 808 .... B3
- Kefar Zekhariya 420 .... B4
- Kinneret 909 .... D2
- Lod (Lydda) 30,500 .... B4
- Lydda 30,500 .... B4
- Magen 149 .... A5
- Maa'lot-Tarshiha C1
- Malkiya D1
- Mash 'Abbe Sade 238 .... B6
- Mavqii'm 177 .... B4
- Megiddo C2
- Metula 261 .... D1
- Migdal 688 .... C2
- Migdal Ha E'meq C2
- Mikhmoret 608 .... B3
- Mishmar Hanegev 336 .... B5
- Mishmar Hayarden D1
- Mivtahim 398 .... A5
- Mizpe Ramon 331 .... D5
- Moza Illit 219 .... C4
- Mughar 4,010 .... C2
- Muqeible 459 .... C2
- Nahariyya 24,000 .... C1
- Nazareth 33,300 .... C2
- Nazerat I'llit C2
- Negba 453 .... B4
- Nes Ziyyona 11,700 .... B4
- Netanya 70,700 .... B3
- Netivot B5
- Nevatim 436 .... B5
- Newe Yam 211 .... B2
- Newe Zohar C5
- Nir Yitzhaq 209 .... A5
- Nizzanim 479 .... B4
- Ofaqim B5
- O'mer B5
- Oron C6
- Or Yehuda B4
- Pardes Hanna-Karkur 13,600 .... B2
- Peduyim 361 .... B5
- Petah Tiqwa 112,000 .... B3
- Qadima 2,937 .... B3
- Qalansuwa B3
- Qedma 157 .... B4
- Qiryat Atta C2
- Qiryat Bialik 18,000 .... C2
- Qiryat Gat 19,200 .... B4
- Qiryat Mal'akhi B4
- Qiryat Motzkin 17,600 .... C2
- Qiryat Shemona 15,200 .... C1
- Qiryat Tivo'n 9,800 .... C2
- Qiryat Yam 19,800 .... C2
- Raa'nana 14,900 .... B3
- Ramat Gan 120,900 .... B3
- Ramat Hasharon 20,100 ....
- Rame 2,986 ....
- Ramla 34,100 ....
- Rehovot 39,200 ....
- Rei'm 155 ....
- Revadim 175 ....
- Revivim 258 ....
- Rishon Le Ziyyon 51,900 ....
- Rosh Ha 'Ayin ....
- Rosh Pinna 700 ....
- Ruhama 497 ....
- Saa'd 418 ....
- Safad (Zefat) 13,600 ....
- Sakhnin 8,400 ....
- Sede Boqer ....
- Sederot ....
- Sedom ....
- Sedot Yam 511 ....
- Shave Ziyyon 269 ....
- Shefara'm 11,800 ....
- Shefayim 614 ....
- Shoval 393 ....
- Tayibe 11,700 ....
- Tel Aviv-Jaffa 343,300 ....
- Tel Aviv-Jaffa* 1,219,900 ....
- Tiberias 23,800 ....
- Tirat Hakarmel 14,400 ....
- Tirat Zevi 353 ....
- Tur'an 2,304 ....
- Umm el Fahm 13,300 ....
- Urim 203 ....
- Uzza 487 ....
- Yad Mordekhai 416 ....
- Yagur 1,266 ....
- Yahav ....
- Yavne 10,100 ....
- Yavne'el 1,580 ....
- Yehud 8,900 ....
- Yeroham 5,800 ....
- Yesodot 293 ....
- Yesud Hamaa'la 428 ....
- Yiftah ....
- Yirka 2,715 ....
- Yotvata ....
- Zavdi'el 396 ....
- Ze'elim 148 ....
- Zefat 13,600 ....
- Zikhron Yaa'qov 6,500 ....
- Zippori 241 ....

OTHER FEATURES

- Aqaba (gulf) ....
- 'Araba, Wadi (valley) ....
- Beer Sheva' (dry riv.) ....
- Besor (riv.) ....
- Carmel (cape) ....
- Carmel (mt.) ....
- Dead (sea) ....
- Galilee, Sea of (Tiberias) (lake) ....
- Galilee (reg.) ....
- Gerar (dry riv.) ....
- Hadera (dry riv.) ....
- Haniqra, Rosh (cape) ....
- Jordan (riv.) ....
- Judaea (reg.) ....
- Lakhish (dry riv.) ....
- Meiron (mt.) ....
- Negev (reg.) ....

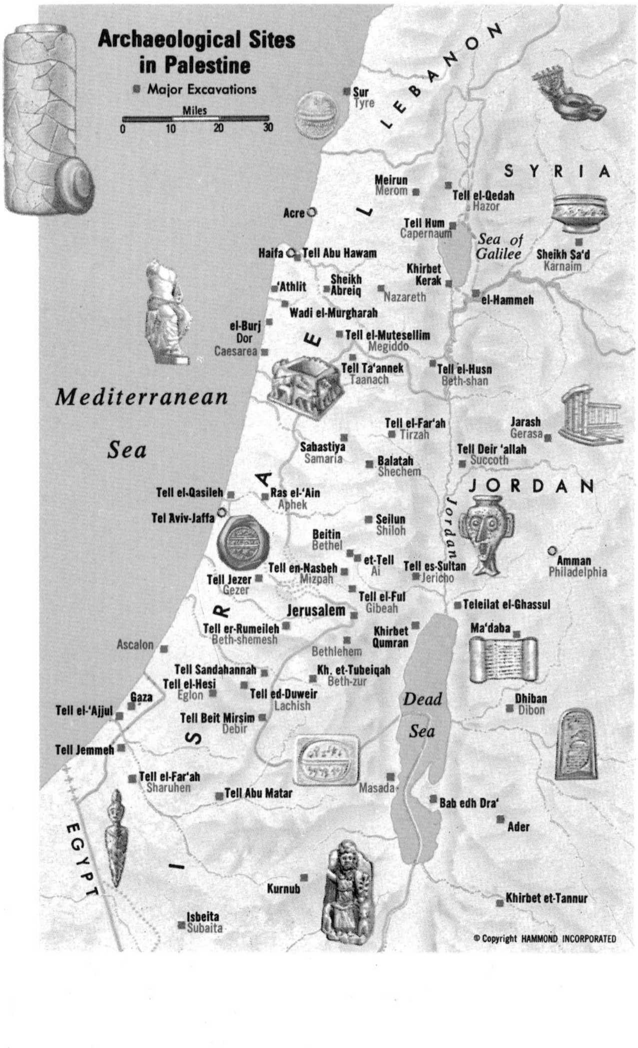
Archaeological Sites in Palestine
Major Excavations
Miles
0 10 20 30
Sur
Tyre
LEBANON
SYRIA
Meirun
Merom
Tell el-Qedah
Hazor
Acre
Tell Hum
Capernaum
Sea of Galilee
Sheikh Sa'd
Karnaim
Haifa
Tell Abu Hawam
'Athlit
Sheikh Abreiq
Khirbet Kerak
Nazareth
el-Hammeh
Wadi el-Murgharah
el-Burj
Dor
Caesarea
Tell el-Mutesellim
Megiddo
Tell Ta'annek
Taanach
Tell el-Husn
Beth-shan
Mediterranean
Sea
Tell el-Far'ah
Tirzah
Jarash
Gerasa
Sabastiya
Samaria
Balatah
Shechem
Tell Deir 'allah
Succoth
Tell el-Qasileh
Ras el-'Ain
Aphek
JORDAN
Tel Aviv-Jaffa
Seilun
Shiloh
Beitin
Bethel
Jordan
et-Tell
Ai
Tell es-Sultan
Jericho
Amman
Philadelphia
Tell Jezer
Gezer
Tell en-Nasbeh
Mizpah
Tell el-Ful
Gibeah
Jerusalem
Teleilat el-Ghassul
Tell er-Rumeileh
Beth-shemesh
Ascalon
Khirbet Qumran
Ma'daba
Bethlehem
Tell Sandahannah
Kh. et-Tubeiqah
Beth-zur
Tell el-Hesi
Eglon
Gaza
Tell ed-Duweir
Lachish
Dead Sea
Dhiban
Dibon
Tell el-'Ajjul
Tell Beit Mirsim
Debir
Tell Jemmeh
Tell el-Far'ah
Sharuhen
Tell Abu Matar
Masada
Bab edh Dra'
Ader
EGYPT
ISRAEL
Kurnub
Khirbet et-Tannur
Isbeita
Subaita

Agriculture, Industry and Resources

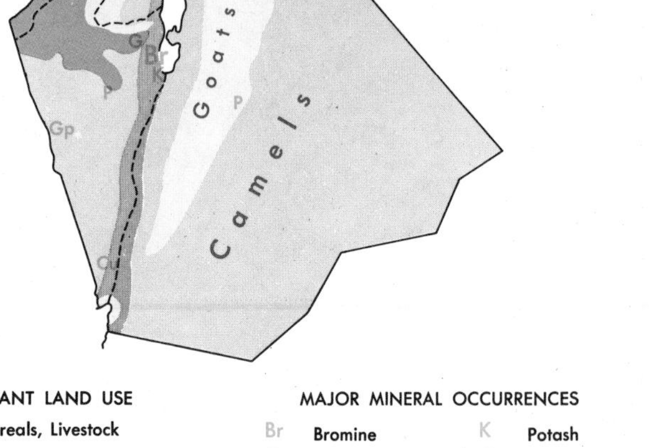
Acre
Haifa
Netanya
Tel Aviv-Jaffa
Jerusalem
Citrus Fruit
Olives
Wheat
Wine
Sheep
Goats
Camels
Br
K
P
Gp

DOMINANT LAND USE

- Cereals, Livestock
- Cash Crops, Horticulture
- Nomadic Livestock Herding
- Nonagricultural Land

MAJOR MINERAL OCCURRENCES

- Br Bromine
- Cu Copper
- G Natural Gas
- Gp Gypsum
- K Potash
- O Petroleum
- P Phosphates
- Major Industrial Areas

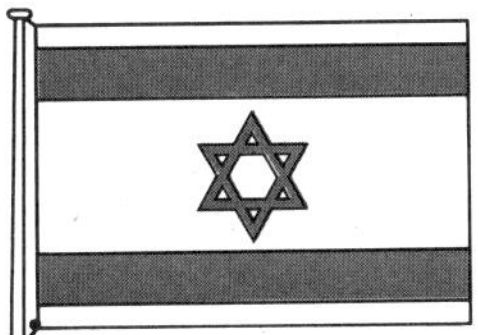

ISRAEL

JORDAN

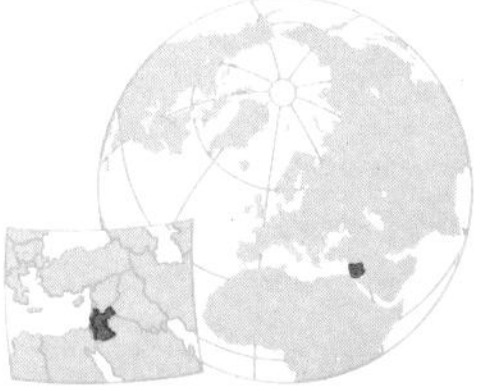

ISRAEL

AREA 7,847 sq. mi. (20,324 sq. km.)
POPULATION 3,878,000
CAPITAL Jerusalem
LARGEST CITY Tel Aviv-Jaffa
HIGHEST POINT Meiran 3,963 ft. (1,208 m.)
MONETARY UNIT shekel
MAJOR LANGUAGES Hebrew, Arabic
MAJOR RELIGIONS Judaism, Islam, Christianity

JORDAN

AREA (East Bank) 35,000 sq. mi. (90,650 sq. km.)
POPULATION 2,152,273
CAPITAL Amman
LARGEST CITY Amman
HIGHEST POINT Jeb. Ramm 5,755 ft. (1,754 m.)
MONETARY UNIT Jordanian dinar
MAJOR LANGUAGE Arabic
MAJOR RELIGION Islam

GAZA STRIP

CITIES and TOWNS

WEST BANK

CITIES AND TOWNS

OTHER FEATURES

JORDAN

GOVERNORATES

CITIES and TOWNS

OTHER FEATURES

*City and suburbs.
⊙Population of subdivision.

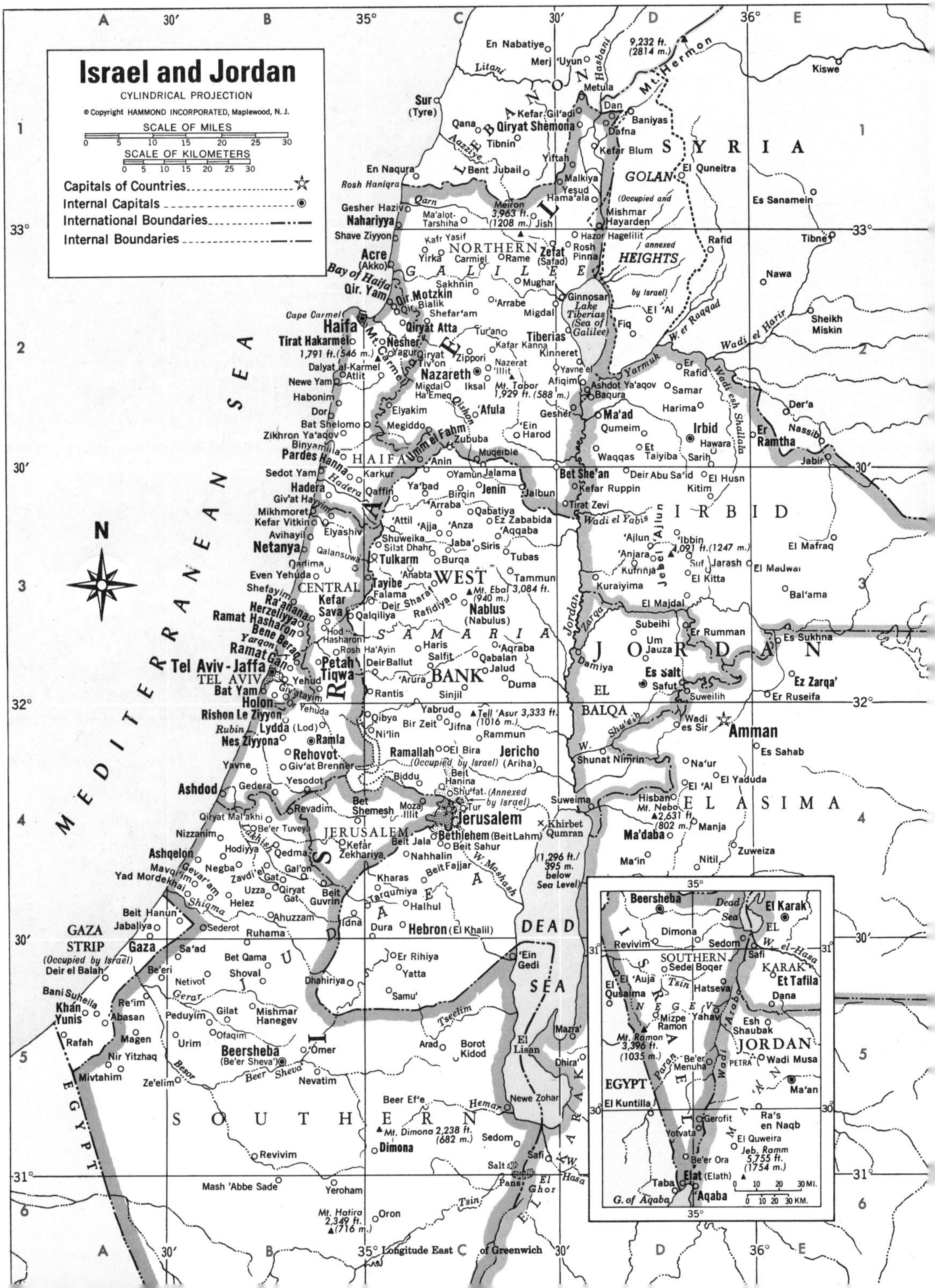

Iran and Iraq

IRAN

INTERNAL DIVISIONS

Azerbaijan, East (prov.) 3,194,543 .... E1
Azerbaijan, West (prov.) 1,404,875 .... D1
Bakhtiari (governorate) 394,300 .... F4
Boyer Ahmediyeh and Kohkiluyeh (governor 244,750 .... G5
Bushehr (prov.) 345,427 .... G6
Central (Markazi) (prov.) 6,921,283 .... G3
Esfahan (Isfahan) (prov.) 1,974,938 .... H4
Fárs (prov.) 2,020,947 .... H6
Gilan (prov.) 1,577,800 .... F2
Hamadan (governorate) 1,086,512 .... F3
Hormozgan (prov.) 463,419 .... J7
Ilam (governorate) 244,222 .... E4
Isfahan (prov.) 1,974,938 .... H4
Kerman (prov.) 1,088,045 .... K6
Kermanshahan (prov.) 1,016,199 .... E3
Khorasan (prov.) 3,266,650 .... K3
Khuzestan (prov.) 2,176,612 .... F5
Kordestan (Kurdistan) (prov.) 781,889 .... E3
Lorestan (Luristan) (governorate) 924,848 .... F4
Mazandaran (prov.) 2,384,226 .... H2
Semnan (governorate) 485,875 .... J3
Sistan and Baluchestan (prov.) 659,297 .... M6
Yazd (governorate) 356,218 .... J5
Zanjan (governorate) 579,000 .... F2

CITIES and TOWNS

Abadan 296,081 .... F5
Abadeh 16,000 .... H5
Abarqu 8,000 .... H5
Abhar 24,000 .... F2
Agha Jari 24,195 .... F5
Ahar 24,000 .... E1
Ahvaz (Ahwaz) 329,006 .... F5
Amol 68,782 .... H2
Anarak 2,038 .... H4
Andimeshk 16,000 .... F4
Aradan 8,978 .... H3
Arak 114,507 .... F3
Ardabil 147,404 .... F1
Ardestan 5,868 .... H4
Asadabad 7,000 .... F3
Asterabad (Gorgan) 88,348 .... J2
Babol 67,790 .... H2
Babol Sar 7,237 .... H2
Bafq 5,000 .... J5
Baft 6,000 .... K6
Bahramabad (Rafsanjan) 21,000 .... K5
Bajgiran 1,151 .... L2
Bam 22,000 .... L6
Bampur 1,585 .... M7
Bandar A'bbas 89,103 .... J7
Bandar-e Deylam 3,691 .... G5
Bandar-e Lengeh 4,920 .... J7
Bandar-e Mas'hur 17,000 .... F5
Bandar-e Pahlavi (Enzeli) 55,978 .... F2
Bandar-e Rig 1,889 .... G6
Bandar-e Torkaman 13,000 .... H2
Bandar Khomeini 6,000 .... F5
Bandar Shahpur 6,000 .... F5
Bastak 2,473 .... J7
Bastam 3,296 .... J2
Behbehan 39,874 .... G5
Behshahr 26,032 .... H2
Bejestan 3,823 .... K3
Bijar 12,000 .... E3
Birjand 25,854 .... L4
Bojnurd 31,248 .... K2
Borazjan 20,000 .... G6
Borujerd 100,103 .... F4
Bostan 4,619 .... F5
Bowkan 9,000 .... E2
Bushehr (Bushire) 57,681 .... G6
Chah Bahar 1,800 .... M8
Chalus 15,000 .... G2
Damavand 5,319 .... H3
Damghan 13,000 .... J2
Darab 13,000 .... J6
Daran 4,609 .... G4
Darreh Gaz 11,000 .... L2
Deheq 4,115 .... G4
Dehkhvareqan 6,000 .... D2
Delijan 6,000 .... G4
Dezful 110,287 .... F4
Dizful (Dezful) 110,287 .... F4
Duzdab (Zahedan) 92,628 .... M6
Enzeli 55,978 .... F2
Esfahan (Isfahan) 671,820 .... G4
Estahbanat 18,187 .... J6
Evaz 6,064 .... J7
Ezna 5,000 .... F4
Fahrej (Iranshahr) 5,000 .... M7
Fariman 8,000 .... L3
Farrashband 3,532 .... G6
Fasa 19,000 .... H6
Ferdows 11,000 .... K3
Firuzabad 8,718 .... H6
Firuzkuh 4,684 .... H3
Fowman 9,000 .... F2
Gach Saran G5
Ganaveh 9,000 .... G6
Garmsar 4,723 .... H3
Gavater M8
Golpayegan 20,515 .... G4
Golshan (Tabas) 10,000 .... K4
Gomishan 6,000 .... J2
Gonabad 8,000 .... L3
Gonbad-e Kavus 59,868 .... J2
Gorgan (Gurgan) 88,348 .... J2
Haft Gel 10,000 .... F5
Hamadan 155,846 .... F3
Hashtpar 5,000 .... F2
Herowabad 5,422 .... F2
Homayunshahr 46,836 .... G4
Hormoz 2,569 .... J7
Hoveyzeh 4,722 .... F5
Ilam 15,000 .... E4
Iranshahr 5,000 .... M7
Isfahan 671,825 .... G4
Izeh 1,983 .... F5
Jahrom 38,236 .... H6
Jajarm 3,641 .... K2
Jask 1,078 .... K8
Kakhk 4,043 .... L3
Kangan 2,682 .... G7
Kangavar 9,414 .... F3
Karaj 138,774 .... G3
Kashan 84,545 .... G3
Kashmar 17,000 .... L3
Kazerun 51,309 .... G6
Kazvin (Qazvin) 138,527 .... F2
Kerman 140,309 .... K5
Kermanshah 290,861 .... E3
Khaf 5,000 .... L3
Khash 7,439 .... M6
Khiyav 9,000 .... E1
Khoman 3,054 .... F2
Khorramabad 104,928 .... F4
Khorramshahr 146,709 .... F5
Khvaf 5,000 .... L3
Khvonsar 10,947 .... F4
Khvor 2,912 .... J4
Khvoy (Khoi) 70,040 .... D1
Kord Kuy 9,855 .... J2
Lahijan 25,725 .... G2
Lar 22,000 .... J7
Mahabad 28,610 .... D2
Mahallat 12,000 .... G4
Mahan 8,000 .... K5
Maku 7,000 .... D1
Malamir (Izeh) 1,983 .... F5
Malayer 28,434 .... F3
Maragheh 60,820 .... E2
Marand 24,000 .... D1
Marv Dasht 25,498 .... H6
Mashhad (Meshed) 670,180 .... L2
Masjed Soleyman 77,161 .... F5
Mehran 664 .... E4
Meshed 670,180 .... L2
Meybod 15,000 .... J4
Meshed-i-Sar (Babol Sar) 12,000 .... H2
Miandowab 19,000 .... E2
Mianeh 28,447 .... E2
Minab 4,228 .... K7
Mirjaveh 11,000 .... M6
Naft-e Shah 3,043 .... D4
Nahavand 24,000 .... F3
Nain 5,925 .... H4
Najafabad 76,236 .... G4
Naraq 2,725 .... G3
Nasratabad (Zabol) 20,000 .... M5
Natanz 4,370 .... H4
Neyriz 16,114 .... J6
Neyshabur 59,101 .... L2
Nishapur (Neyshabur) 59,101 .... L2
Nosratabad 20,000 .... L6
Now Shahr 8,000 .... G2
Oshnoviyeh 5,000 .... D2
Pahlevi (Enzeli) 55,978 .... F2
Pazanan 81 .... F5
Qasr-e-Shirin 15,094 .... E3
Qayen 6,000 .... L4
Qazvin 138,527 .... F2
Qom 246,831 .... G3
Qorveh 2,929 .... E3
Quchan 29,133 .... L2
Qum (Qom) 246,831 .... G3
Rafsanjan 21,000 .... K5
Ramhormoz 9,000 .... F5
Ramsar 12,000 .... G2
Rasht 187,203 .... F2
Ravar 5,074 .... K5
Resht (Rasht) 187,203 .... F2
Rey 102,825 .... G3
Rezaiyeh (Urmia) 163,991 .... D2
Rigan 8,255 .... L6
Rud Sar 7,460 .... G2
Sabzevar 69,174 .... K2
Sabzvaran 7,000 .... K6
Sai'dabad 20,000 .... J6
Sanandaj 95,834 .... E3
Sang-e Sar 9,000 .... H3
Saqqez 17,000 .... E2
Sarab 16,000 .... E2
Sarakhs 3,461 .... M2
Saravan 4,012 .... N7
Sar Dasht 6,000 .... D2
Sar Eskand Khan 3,153 .... E2
Sari 70,936 .... H2
Savanat (Estahbanat) 18,187 .... J6
Saveh 17,565 .... G3
Semnan 31,058 .... H3
Shadegan 6,000 .... F5
Shahabad 12,000 .... E3
Shahdad 2,777 .... K5
Shahi 63,289 .... H2
Shahin Dezh 4,195 .... E2
Shahistan (Saravan) 4,012 .... M
Shahpur 13,161 .... D
Shahreza 34,220 .... H
Shahr Kord 24,000 .... G
Shahrud 30,767 .... J
Shahsavar 12,000 .... G
Sharafkhaneh 1,260 .... D
Shiraz 416,408 .... H
Shirvan 11,000 .... K
Shush 1,433 .... F
Shushtar 24,000 .... F
Sinneh (Sanandaj) 95,834 .... E
Sirjan (Sai'dabad) 20,000 .... J
Sivand 1,811 .... H
Songor 10,433 .... E
Sufian 2,914 .... E
Sultanabad (Kashmar) 17,000 L
Susangerd 21,000 .... F
Tabas 10,000 .... K
Tabriz 598,576 .... D
Taft 7,000 .... J
Tajrish 157,486 .... G
Takestan 13,485 .... F
Tehran (cap.) 4,496,159 .... G
Torbat-e-Heydariyeh 30,106 L
Torbat-e Jam 13,000 .... M
Tun (Ferdows) 11,000 .... K
Turbat-i-Shaikh Jam 13,000 .... M
Tuysarkan 12,000 .... F
Urmia 163,991 .... D
Varamin 11,183 .... G
Yazd (Yezd) 135,978 .... J
Yazd-e Khvasat 3,544 .... H
Zabol 20,000 .... M
Zahedan 92,628 .... M
Zanjan 99,967 .... K
Zarand 5,000 .... H
Zarqam 7,000 .... H
Zenjan (Zanjan) 99,967 .... F

OTHER FEATURES

Chai (riv.) ... E1
rabi (isl.) ... G7
aks (Aras) (riv.) ... E1
rak (Atrek) (riv.) ... J2
khtegan (lake) ... J6
luchistan (reg.) ... M7
mpur (riv.) ... M7
histun (ruins) ... E3
spian (sea) ... G1
mavend (Demavend) (mt.) ... G3
z (riv.) ... F4
burz (mts.) ... G2
rsi (isl.) ... G7
organ (riv.) ... J2
ari Rud (riv.) ... M3
arkheh (riv.) ... E4
arun (riv.) ... F5
ashaf Rud (riv.) ... M2
ark (Kharg) (isl.) ... G6
h (cape) ... K8
rang (riv.) ... G4
ristan (reg.) ... J7
akran (reg.) ... M8
and Rud (riv.) ... G6
ehran (riv.) ... J7
maksar (lake) ... M4
zwar (mt.) ... H3
man (gulf) ... M8
sargadae (ruins) ... H5
rsepolis (ruins) ... H6
rsian (gulf) ... F6
areh Su (riv.) ... E1
areh Su (riv.) ... G3
eshm (isl.) ... J7
ezel Owzam (riv.) ... F2
fid Rud (riv.) ... F2
Shaikh Shua'ib (isl.) ... H7
Shelagh (riv.) ... M5
Shirvan (riv.) ... E3
Shur (riv.) ... J7
Siah Kuh (mt.) ... L3
Silup (riv.) ... M8
Susa (ruins) ... F4
Talab (riv.) ... N6
Tashk (lake) ... J6
Urmia (lake) ... D2
Zagros (mts.) ... E4
Zarineh (riv.) ... E2
Zilbir (riv.) ... D1
Zohreh (riv.) ... F5

IRAQ

GOVERNORATES

Anbar ... B4
An Najaf ... C5
Babil ... D4
Baghdad ... D4
Basra ... E5
Dhi Qar ... E5
Diyala ... D4
Dohuk ... C2
Erbil ... C3
Karbala ... B4
Maysan ... E5
Muthanna ... D5
Ninawa ... B3
Qadisiya ... D4
Salahuddin ... C3
Sulaimaniya ... D3
Tamin ... D3
Wasit ... D4

CITIES and TOWNS

Ad Diwaniya 60,553 ... D5
A'faq 5,390 ... D4
Al A'ziziya 7,450 ... D4
Al Falluja 38,072 ... C4
Al Fatha† 15,329 ... C3
A'li Gharbi 15,456 ... E4
A'li Sharqi 8,398 ... E4
Al Kufa 30,862 ... D4
Al Musaiyib 15,955 ... D4
Al Q'aim 3,372 ... B3
Al Qaiyara 3,060 ... C3
Al Qosh 3,863 ... C2
Al Qurna 5,638 ... E5
A'madiya 2,578 ... C2
A'mara 64,847 ... E5
A'na 15,729 ... B3
An Najaf 128,096 ... D5
An Nasiriya 60,405 ... D5
A'qra 8,659 ... D2
Arbela (Erbil) 90,320 ... D2
Aski Mosul 643 ... C2
As Salman 1,789 ... D5
Az Zubair 41,408 ... E5
Badra 3,564 ... D4
Baghdad (cap.) 502,503 ... D4
Baghdad* 1,745,328 ... D4
Baiji 6,785 ... C3
Baq'uba 34,575 ... D4
Basra 313,327 ... E5
Dohuk 16,998 ... C2
Erbil 90,320 ... D2
Fao 15,399 ... F6
Habbaniya 14,405 ... C4
Haditha 6,870 ... C3
Hai 16,988 ... E4
Halabja 11,206 ... D3
Hilla 84,717 ... D4
Hindiya 16,436 ... C4
Hit 9,131 ... C4
Karbal'a 83,301 ... C4
Khanaqin 23,522 ... D3
Kifri 8,500 ... D3
Kirkuk 167,413 ... D3
Kirkuk* 176,794 ... D3
Kubaisa 4,023 ... C4
Kut 42,116 ... D4
Makhmur 2,556 ... C3
Mandali 11,262 ... D4
Mosul 315,157 ... C2
Muqdadiyah 12,181 ... D4
Naft Kaneh ... D3
Na'maniya 11,943 ... D4
Qal'at Diza 6,250 ... D2
Ramadi 28,723 ... C4
Rania 4,090 ... D2
Refai' 7,681 ... E5
Rumaitha 10,222 ... D5
Rutba 5,091 ... B4
Ruwandiz 5,801 ... D2
Sad'iya 5,285 ... D3
Samarra 24,746 ... C3
Samawa 33,473 ... D5
Shaikh Saa'd 2,958 ... E4
Shaqlawa 6,814 ... D2
Shatra 18,822 ... E5
Sinjar 7,942 ... B2
Sulaimaniya 86,822 ... D3
Tal Kaif 7,482 ... C2
Taza Khurmatu 2,681 ... D3
Tikrit 9,921 ... C3
Tuz Khurmatu 13,860 ... D3
Zakho 14,790 ... C2

OTHER FEATURES

Adhaim (riv.) ... D3
Aneiza, Jebel (mt.) ... A4
A'rab, Shatt-al- (riv.) ... F5
A'ra'r, Wadi (dry riv.) ... B5
Babylon (ruins) ... D4
Batin, Wadi al (dry riv.) ... E6
Ctesiphon (ruins) ... D4
Darbandikhan (dam) ... D3
Euphrates (riv.) ... D4
Great Zab (riv.) ... C2
Hauran, Wadi (dry riv.) ... B4
Little Zab (riv.) ... C3
Mesopotamia (reg.) ... B3
Nineveh (ruins) ... C2
Sad'iya, Hor (lake) ... E4
Saniya, Hor (lake) ... E5
Shai'b Hisb, Wadi (dry riv.) ... C5
Sinjar, Jebel (mts.) ... B2
Siyah Kuh (mt.) ... D2
Syrian (des.) ... B4
Tigris (riv.) ... E4
Ubaiyidh, Wadi (dry riv.) ... B5
Ur (ruins) ... E5

*City and suburbs.
†Population of commune.

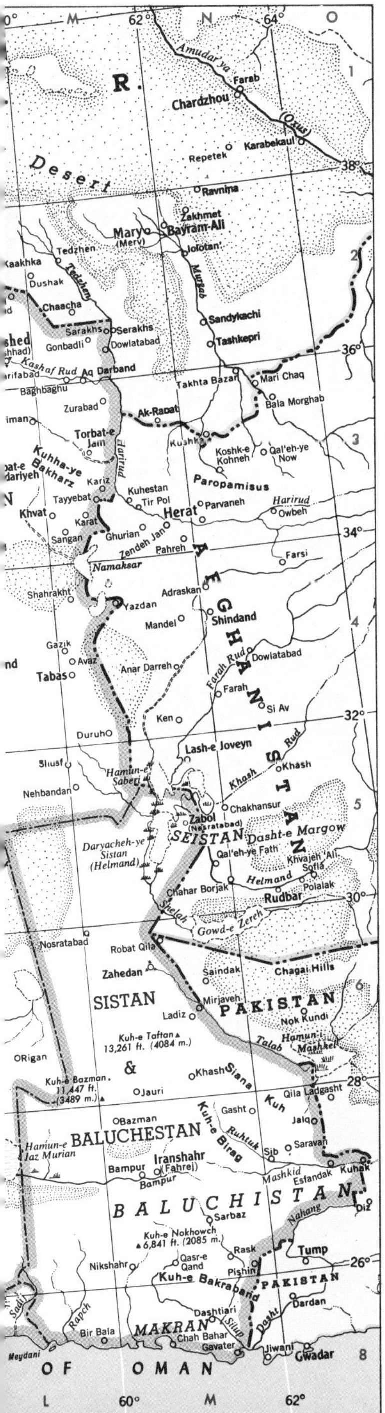

IRAN

IRAQ

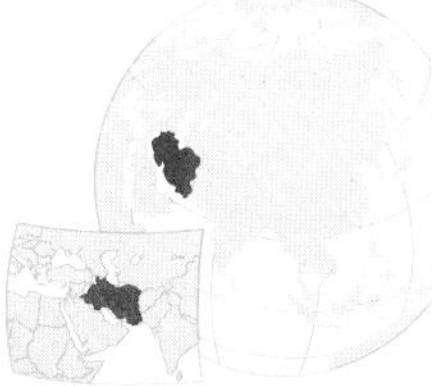

AREA 636,293 sq. mi. (1,648,000 sq. km.)
POPULATION 37,447,000
CAPITAL Tehran
LARGEST CITY Tehran
HIGHEST POINT Damavand 18,376 ft. (5,601 m.)
MONETARY UNIT Iranian rial
MAJOR LANGUAGES Persian, Azerbaijani, Kurdish
MAJOR RELIGION Islam

AREA 172,476 sq. mi. (446,713 sq. km.)
POPULATION 12,767,000
CAPITAL Baghdad
LARGEST CITY Baghdad
HIGHEST POINT Haji Ibrahim 11,811 ft. (3,600 m.)
MONETARY UNIT Iraqi dinar
MAJOR LANGUAGES Arabic, Kurdish
MAJOR RELIGION Islam

Topography

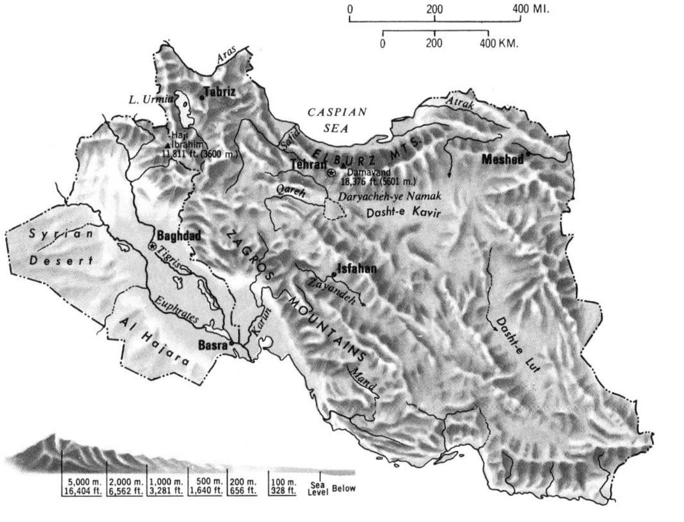

Agriculture, Industry and Resources

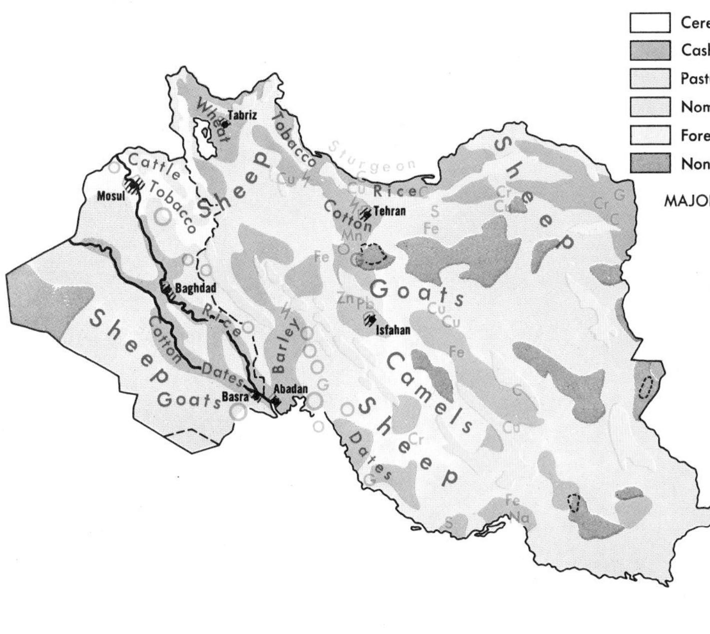

DOMINANT LAND USE

- Cereals, Livestock
- Cash Crops, Horticulture, Livestock
- Pasture Livestock
- Nomadic Livestock Herding
- Forests
- Nonagricultural Land

MAJOR MINERAL OCCURRENCES

- C Coal
- Cr Chromium
- Cu Copper
- Fe Iron Ore
- G Natural Gas
- Mn Manganese
- Na Salt
- O Petroleum
- Pb Lead
- S Sulfur, Pyrites
- Zn Zinc

- Water Power
- Major Industrial Areas

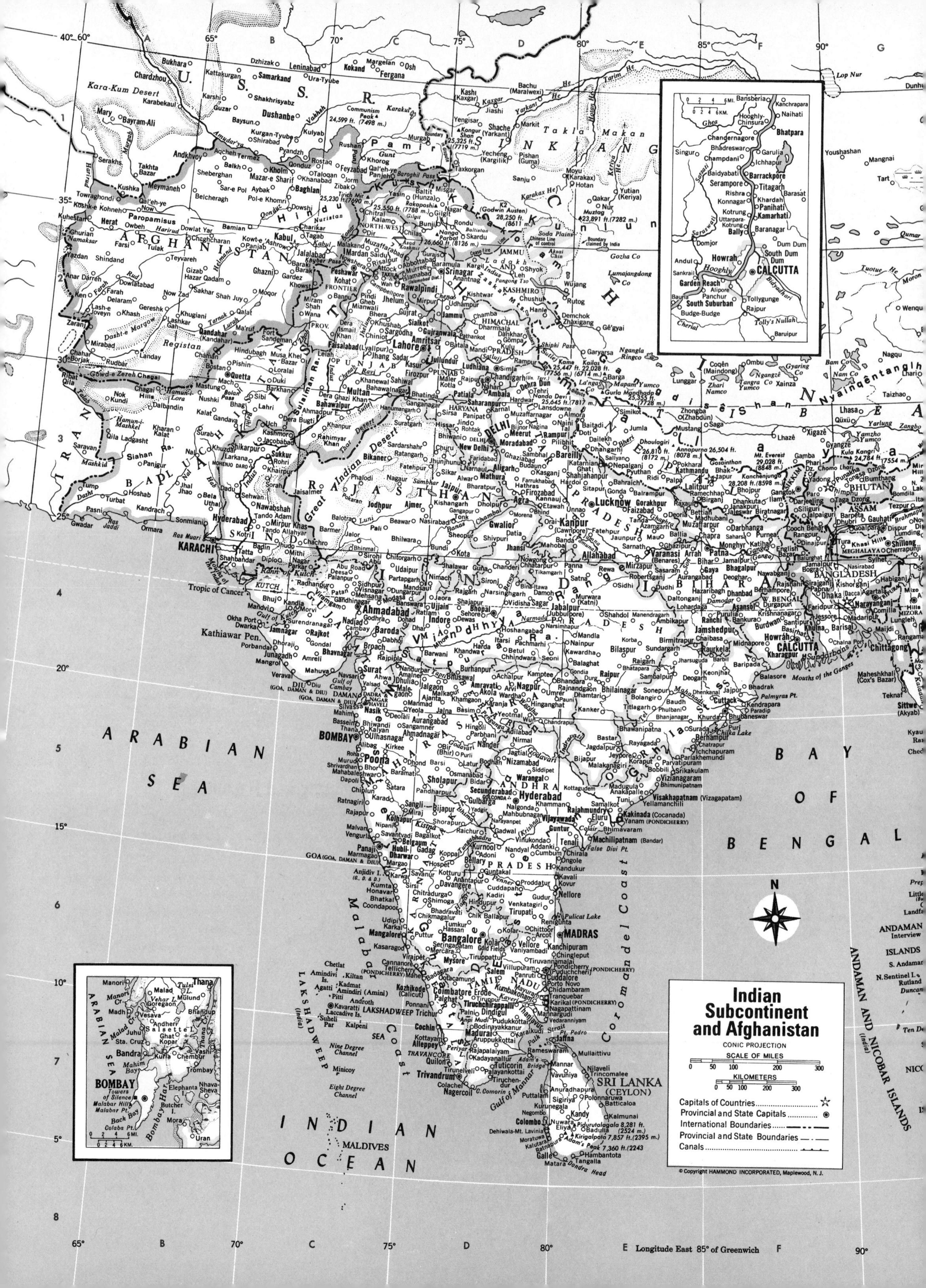

Indian Subcontinent and Afghanistan
CONIC PROJECTION
SCALE OF MILES
0 50 100 200 300
KILOMETERS
0 50 100 200 300
Capitals of Countries
Provincial and State Capitals
International Boundaries
Provincial and State Boundaries
Canals
© Copyright HAMMOND INCORPORATED, Maplewood, N. J.
U. S. S. R.
AFGHANISTAN
IRAN
BALUCHISTAN
SIND
PUNJAB
KASHMIR
SINKIANG
TIBET
NEPAL
BHUTAN
BANGLADESH
SRI LANKA (CEYLON)
ARABIAN SEA
BAY OF BENGAL
INDIAN OCEAN
MALDIVES
ANDAMAN AND NICOBAR ISLANDS (India)
LAKSHADWEEP (India)
Tropic of Cancer
Longitude East 85° of Greenwich
Kara-Kum Desert
Pamir
Hindu Kush
Karakoram
Takla Makan
Great Indian Desert
Thar Desert
Kathiawar Pen.
Malabar Coast
Coromandel Coast
Mouths of the Ganges
Gulf of Mannar
Palk Strait
Kabul
Herat
Kandahar (Qandahar)
Quetta
Karachi
Hyderabad
Multan
Lahore
Peshawar
Rawalpindi
Srinagar
Amritsar
Delhi
New Delhi
Jaipur
Agra
Lucknow
Kanpur
Allahabad
Varanasi (Benares)
Patna
Kathmandu
Calcutta
Dhaka (Dacca)
Chittagong
Ahmadabad
Bhopal
Nagpur
Bombay
Poona
Hyderabad
Madras
Bangalore
Mysore
Cochin
Trivandrum
Colombo
Jaffna
Mt. Everest 29,028 ft. (8848 m.)
K2 (Godwin Austen) 28,250 ft. (8611 m.)
Bombay
Calcutta
Howrah
Thana
Salsette I.
Elephanta

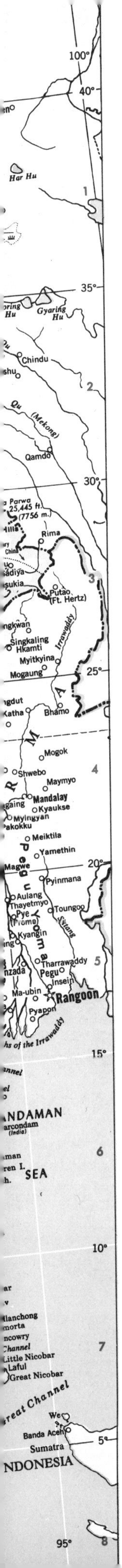

INDIA

AREA 1,269,339 sq. mi. (3,287,588 sq. km.)
POPULATION 683,810,051
CAPITAL New Delhi
LARGEST CITY Calcutta (greater)
HIGHEST POINT Nanda Devi 25,645 ft. (7,817 m.)
MONETARY UNIT Indian rupee
MAJOR LANGUAGES Hindi, English, Bihari, Telugu, Marathi, Bengali, Tamil, Gujarati, Rajasthani, Kanarese, Malayalam, Oriya, Punjabi, Assamese, Kashmiri, Urdu
MAJOR RELIGIONS Hinduism, Islam, Christianity, Sikhism, Buddhism, Jainism, Zoroastrianism, Animism

PAKISTAN

AREA 310,403 sq. mi. (803,944 sq. km.)
POPULATION 83,782,000
CAPITAL Islamabad
LARGEST CITY Karachi
HIGHEST POINT K2 (Godwin Austen) 28,250 ft. (8,611 m.)
MONETARY UNIT Pakistani rupee
MAJOR LANGUAGES Urdu, English, Punjabi, Pushtu, Sindhi, Baluchi, Brahui
MAJOR RELIGIONS Islam, Hinduism, Sikhism, Christianity, Buddhism

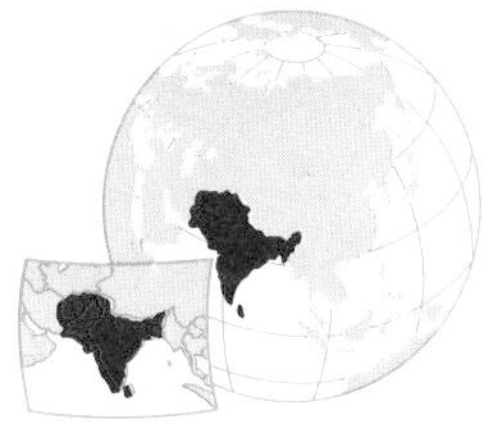

SRI LANKA (CEYLON)

AREA 25,332 sq. mi. (65,610 sq. km.)
POPULATION 14,850,001
CAPITAL Colombo
LARGEST CITY Colombo
HIGHEST POINT Pidurutalagala 8,281 ft. (2,524 m.)
MONETARY UNIT Sri Lanka rupee
MAJOR LANGUAGES Sinhala, Tamil, English
MAJOR RELIGIONS Buddhism, Hinduism, Christianity, Islam

AFGHANISTAN

AREA 250,775 sq. mi. (649,507 sq. km.)
POPULATION 15,540,000
CAPITAL Kabul
LARGEST CITY Kabul
HIGHEST POINT Nowshak 24,557 ft. (7,485 m.)
MONETARY UNIT afghani
MAJOR LANGUAGES Pushtu, Dari, Uzbek
MAJOR RELIGION Islam

NEPAL

AREA 54,663 sq. mi. (141,577 sq. km.)
POPULATION 14,179,301
CAPITAL Kathmandu
LARGEST CITY Kathmandu
HIGHEST POINT Mt. Everest 29,028 ft. (8,848 m.)
MONETARY UNIT Nepalese rupee
MAJOR LANGUAGES Nepali, Maithili, Tamang, Newari, Tharu
MAJOR RELIGIONS Hinduism, Buddhism

MALDIVES

AREA 115 sq. mi. (298 sq. km.)
POPULATION 143,046
CAPITAL Male
LARGEST CITY Male
HIGHEST POINT 20 ft. (6 m.)
MONETARY UNIT Maldivian rupee
MAJOR LANGUAGE Divehi
MAJOR RELIGION Islam

BHUTAN

AREA 18,147 sq. mi. (47,000 sq. km.)
POPULATION 1,298,000
CAPITAL Thimphu
LARGEST CITY Thimphu
HIGHEST POINT Kula Kangri 24,784 ft. (7,554 m.)
MONETARY UNIT ngultrum
MAJOR LANGUAGES Dzongka, Nepali
MAJOR RELIGIONS Buddhism, Hinduism

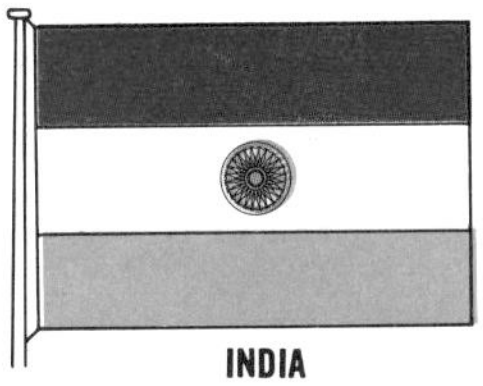
INDIA

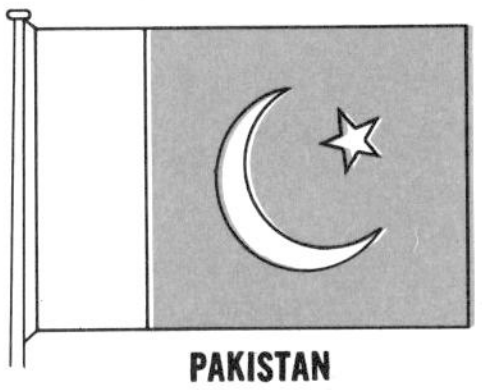
PAKISTAN

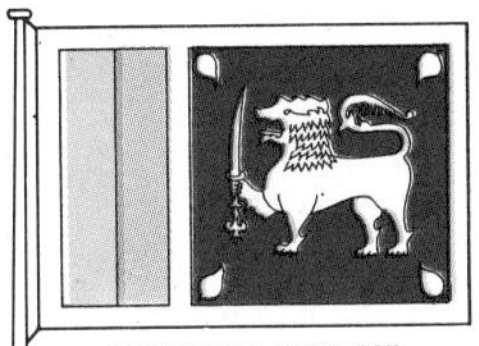
SRI LANKA (CEYLON)

BHUTAN

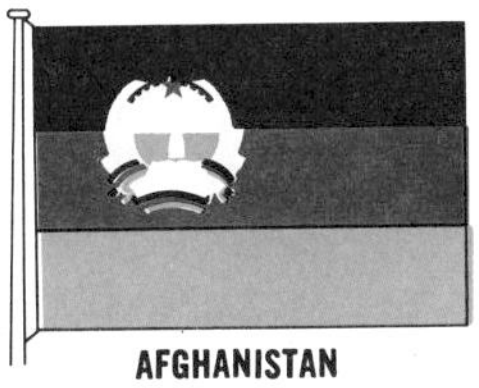
AFGHANISTAN

MALDIVES

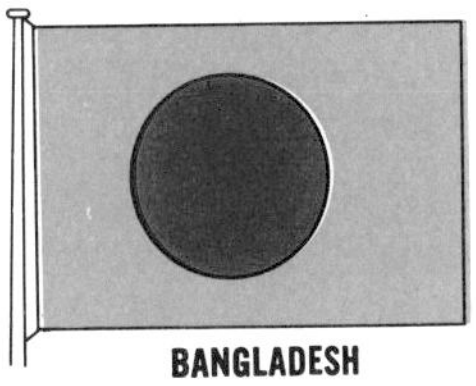
BANGLADESH

NEPAL

BANGLADESH

AREA 55,126 sq. mi. (142,776 sq. km.)
POPULATION 87,052,024
CAPITAL Dhaka
LARGEST CITY Dhaka
HIGHEST POINT Keokradong 4,034 ft. (1,230 m.)
MONETARY UNIT taka
MAJOR LANGUAGES Bengali, English
MAJOR RELIGIONS Islam, Hinduism, Christianity

AFGHANISTAN

CITIES and TOWNS

Bala Murghab 10,000 .... A1
Balkh 15,000 .... B1
Chahardeh B2
Girishk 10,000 .... A2
Kabul (cap.) 318,094 .... B2
Kabul* 534,350 .... B2
Kuhsan A2
Kushk 10,000 .... A1
Landi Muhammad Amin Khan 1,000 .... A2
Panjao 3,000 .... B2
Qaleh-i-Kang 17,400 .... A2
Sabzawar 5,000 .... A2
Shindand (Sabzawar) 5,000 .... A2
Taiwara 5,000 .... A2

OTHER FEATURES

Farah Rud (riv.) A2
Hari Rud (riv.) A1
Helmand (riv.) B2
Hindu Kush (mts.) B1
Jam (mt.) A2
Kabul (riv.) C2
Kunar (riv.) C1
Kunduz (riv.) B1
Lora (riv.) B2
Margo, Dasht-i- (des.) A2
Namaksar (salt lake) A2
Paropamisus (range) A2
Registan (reg.) B2

BANGLADESH

CITIES and TOWNS

Chittagong 416,733 .... G4
Cox's Bazar (Maheshkhali) ... G4
Dhaka (Dacca) (cap.) 1,310,976 .... G4
Dhaka (Dacca)□ 2,539,991 . G4
Habiganj G4
Jamalpur F4
Khulna 436,000 .... F4
Kishorganj G4
Madaripur G4
Maheshkhali G4
Narayanganj 176,879 .... G4
Nawabganj F4
Noakhali 19,874 .... G4
Rangamati 6,416 .... G4

OTHER FEATURES

Bengal, Bay of (sea) F5
Brahmaputra (riv.) G3
Ganges (riv.) F3
Sundarbans (reg.) F4

BHUTAN

CITIES and TOWNS

Bumthang 10,000 .... G3
Punakha 12,000 .... G3
Taga Dzong 18,000 .... G3
Tongsa Dzong 2,500 .... G3

OTHER FEATURES

Chomo Lhari (mt.) F3
Himalaya (mts.) E2
Kula Kangri (mt.) G3

INDIA

INTERNAL DIVISIONS

Andaman and Nicobar Isls. (terr.) 115,133 .... G6
Andhra Pradesh (state) 43,502,708 .... D5
Arunachal Pradesh (terr.) 467,511 .... G3
Assam (state) 14,625,152 .. G3
Bihar (state) 56,353,369 .... F4
Chandigarh (terr.) 257,251 .... D2
Dadra and Nagar Haveli (terr.) 74,170 .... C4
Delhi (terr.) 4,065,698 ...... D3
Goa, Daman and Diu (terr.) 857,771 .... C4
Gujarat (state) 26,697,475 .. C4
Haryana (state) 10,036,808 . D3
Himachal Pradesh (state) 3,460,434 .... D2
Jammu and Kashmir (state) 4,616,632 .... D2
Karnataka (state) 29,299,014 .... D6
Kerala (state) 21,347,375 ... D6
Lakshadweep (terr.) 31,810 .... C6
Madhya Pradesh (state) 41,654,119 .... D4
Maharashtra (state) 50,412,235 .... C5
Manipur (state) 1,072,753 .. G4
Meghalaya (state) 1,011,699 .... G3
Mizoram (terr.) 332,390 .... G4
Nagaland (state) 516,449 .... G3

(continued on following page)

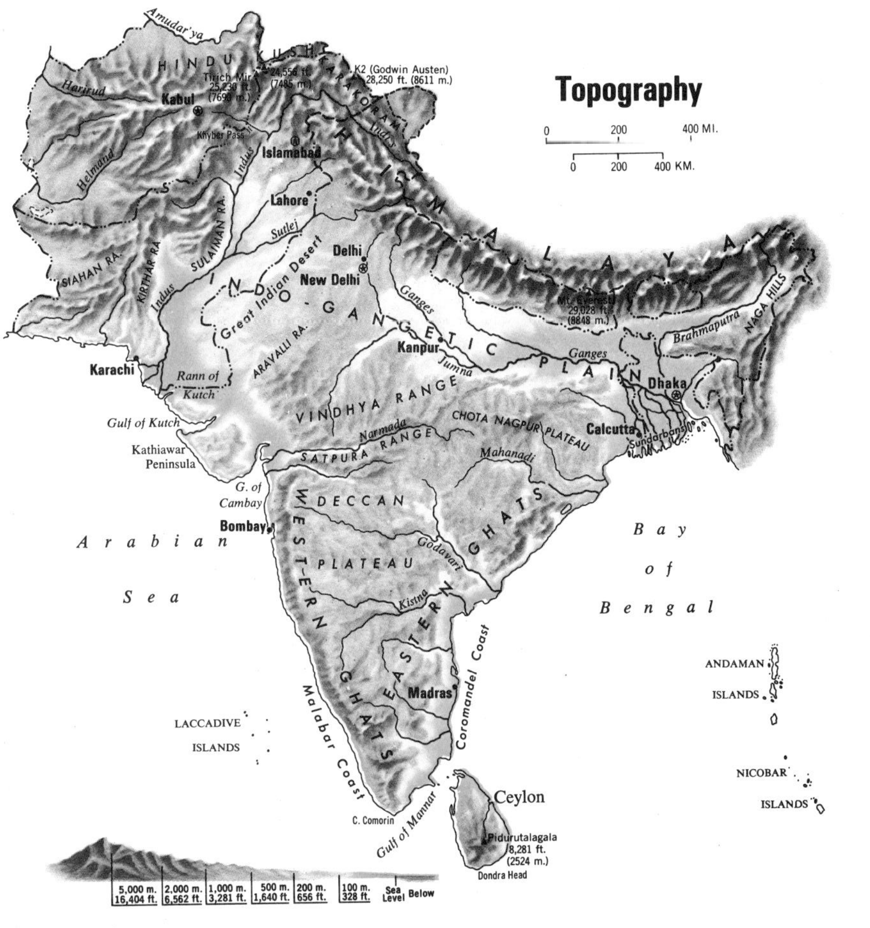

- Orissa (state) 21,944,615 ... E5
- Pondicherry (terr.) 471,707 ... E6
- Punjab (state) 13,551,060 ... D2
- Rajasthan (state) 25,765,806 ... C3
- Sikkim (state) 209,843 ... F3
- Tamil Nadu (state) 41,199,168 ... D6
- Tripura (state) 1,556,342 ... G4
- Uttar Pradesh (state) 88,341,144 ... D3
- West Bengal (state) 44,312,011 ... F4

CITIES and TOWNS

- Abu 9,840 ... C4
- Agra 591,917 ... D3
- Agra☐ 634,622 ... D3
- Ahmadabad 1,591,832 ... C4
- Ahmadabad☐ 1,741,522 ... C4
- Ajanta ... D4
- Ajmer 262,851 ... C3
- Akola 168,438 ... D4
- Alibag 11,913 ... C5
- Aligarh 252,314 ... D3
- Allahabad 490,622 ... E3
- Allahabad☐ 513,036 ... E3
- Alleppey 160,166 ... D7
- Almora 19,671 ... D3
- Ambikapur 23,087 ... E4
- Amravati 193,800 ... D4
- Amritsar 407,628 ... C2
- Amritsar☐ 458,029 ... C2
- Asansol 155,968 ... F4
- Aurangabad, Maharashtra 150,483 ... D5
- Baltit ... C1
- Bandra ... B7
- Bangalore 1,540,741 ... D6
- Bangalore☐ 1,653,779 ... D6
- Bareilly 296,248 ... D3
- Baroda 466,696 ... C4
- Baroda☐ 467,487 ... C4
- Barwani 22,099 ... D4
- Belgaum 192,427 ... C5
- Benares (Varanasi) 583,856 ... E3
- Bhagalpur 172,202 ... F4
- Bhatpara 204,750 ... F1
- Bhavnagar 225,358 ... C4
- Bhawanipatna 22,808 ... E5
- Bhilai 157,173 ... E4
- Bhopal 298,022 ... D4
- Bikaner 188,518 ... C3
- Bombay (Greater)* 5,970,575 ... B7
- Bunji ... C1
- Calcutta 3,148,746 ... F2
- Calcutta☐ 7,031,382 ... F2
- Calicut (Kozhikode) 333,979 ... D6
- Cawnpore (Kanpur) 1,154,388 ... E3
- Chamba 11,814 ... D2
- Chanderi 10,294 ... D4
- Chandigarh 218,743 ... D2
- Chembur ... B7
- Chilas ... C1
- Chushul ... D2
- Cocanada (Kakinada) 164,200 ... E5
- Cochin 439,066 ... D6
- Coimbatore 356,368 ... D6
- Coimbatore☐ 736,203 ... D6
- Colachel 18,819 ... D7
- Cuttack 194,068 ... F4
- Dehra Dun 166,073 ... D2
- Delhi 3,287,883 ... D3
- Delhi☐ 3,647,023 ... D3
- Dhanbad☐ 434,031 ... F4
- Dharmsala 10,939 ... D2
- Dharwar-Hubli 379,166 ... C5
- Diphu 10,200 ... G3
- Dispur 1,725 ... G3
- Dungarpur 19,773 ... C4
- Durgapur 206,638 ... F4
- Dwarka 17,801 ... B4
- Gangtok 12,000 ... F3
- Garden Reach 154,913 ... F2
- Gaya 179,884 ... F4
- Gilgit ... C1
- Gorakhpur 230,911 ... E3
- Goregaon ... B7
- Guntur 269,991 ... D5
- Gwalior 384,772 ... D3
- Gwalior☐ 406,140 ... D3
- Haflong 5,197 ... G3
- Honavar 12,444 ... C6
- Howrah 737,877 ... F2
- Hubli-Dharwar 379,166 ... C5
- Hunza (Baltit) ... C1
- Hyderabad 1,607,396 ... D5
- Hyderabad☐ 1,796,339 ... D5
- Ichchapuram 15,850 ... F5
- Indore 543,381 ... D4
- Indore☐ 560,936 ... D4
- Itanagar⊙ 18,787 ... G3
- Jabalpur 426,224 ... D4
- Jabalpur☐ 534,845 ... D4
- Jaipur 615,258 ... D3
- Jaipur☐ 636,768 ... D3
- Jaisalmer 16,578 ... C3
- Jajpur 16,707 ... F4
- Jalor 15,478 ... C3
- Jammu 155,338 ... D2
- Jamnagar 214,816 ... B4
- Jamnagar☐ 227,640 ... B4
- Jamshedpur 341,576 ... F4
- Jamshedpur☐ 456,146 ... F4
- Jhansi 173,292 ... D3
- Jodhpur 317,612 ... C3
- Jubbulpore (Jabalpur) 426,224 ... D4
- Juhu ... B7
- Jullundur 296,106 ... D2
- Kakinada 164,200 ... E5
- Kamarhati 169,404 ... F1
- Kandla 17,995 ... C4
- Kanpur 1,154,388 ... E3
- Kanpur☐ 1,275,242 ... E3
- Kargil 2,390 ... D2
- Katarnian Ghat ... E3
- Kavaratti 4,420 ... C6
- Kendrapara 20,079 ... F4
- Kohima 21,545 ... G3
- Kolhapur 259,050 ... C5
- Koraput 21,505 ... E5
- Kota 212,991 ... D3
- Kozhikode 333,979 ... D6
- Kumta 19,112 ... C6
- Kurla ... B7
- Leh 5,519 ... D2
- Lucknow 749,239 ... E3
- Lucknow☐ 813,982 ... E3
- Ludhiana 397,850 ... D2
- Ludhiana☐ 401,176 ... D2
- Madras 2,469,449 ... E6
- Madras☐ 3,169,930 ... E6
- Madurai 549,114 ... D7
- Madurai☐ 711,501 ... D7
- Mahabaleshwar 7,318 ... C5
- Mahe 8,972 ... D6
- Malad ... B6
- Malegaon 191,847 ... C4
- Malvan 17,579 ... C5
- Mandi 16,849 ... D2
- Mandla 24,406 ... E4
- Mangalore 165,174 ... C6
- Meerut 270,993 ... D3
- Mercara 19,357 ... D6
- Mirpur ... C2
- Moradabad 258,590 ... D3
- Mulund ... B6
- Muzaffarabad ... C2
- Mysore 355,685 ... D6
- Nagar ... D1
- Nagpur 866,076 ... D4
- Nagpur☐ 930,459 ... D4
- Nahan 16,017 ... D2
- Naini Tal 23,986 ... D3
- Nasik 176,091 ... C5
- New Delhi (cap.) 301,801 ... D3
- Okha Port 10,687 ... B4
- Pachmarhi 1,212 ... D4
- Panna 22,316 ... E4
- Pasighat 5,116 ... G3
- Patna 473,001 ... F3
- Patna☐ 491,217 ... F3
- Poona 856,105 ... C5
- Poona☐ 1,135,034 ... C5
- Porto Novo 17,412 ... E6
- Raipur 174,518 ... E4
- Rajahmundry 165,912 ... E5
- Rajapur 9,017 ... C5
- Rajkot 300,612 ... C4
- Rameswaram 16,755 ... D7
- Rampur, Uttar Pradesh 161,417 ... D3
- Ranchi 175,934 ... F4
- Raxaul 12,064 ... E3
- Sadiya⊙ 64,252 ... H3
- Saharanpur 225,396 ... D3
- Salem 308,716 ... D6
- Salem☐ 416,440 ... D6
- Santa Cruz ... B7
- Sarnath ... E3
- Secunderabad 250,636 ... D5
- Seringapatam 14,100 ... D6
- Sholapur 398,361 ... D5
- Sidhi 8,341 ... E4
- Silvassa ... C4
- Sirohi 18,774 ... C4
- Skardu ... D1
- South Suburban 272,600 ... F2
- Srinagar 403,413 ... D2
- Srinagar☐ 423,253 ... D2
- Sundargarh 17,244 ... E4
- Surat 471,656 ... C4
- Surat☐ 493,001 ... C4
- Tehri 5,480 ... D2
- Thana 170,675 ... B6
- Tiruchchirappalli 307,400 ... D6
- Tiruchchirappalli☐ 464,624 ... D6
- Tiruchendur 18,126 ... D7
- Tollygunge ... F2
- Tranquebar 17,318 ... E6
- Trivandrum 409,627 ... D7
- Trombay ... B7
- Tura 15,489 ... G3
- Tuticorin 155,310 ... D7
- Udaypur 161,278 ... C4
- Udhampur 16,392 ... D2
- Ujjain 203,278 ... D4
- Ulhasnagar 168,462 ... C5
- Varanasi 583,856 ... E3
- Varanasi☐ 606,721 ... E3
- Vellore☐ 178,554 ... D6
- Vengurla 11,805 ... C5
- Vijayawada 317,258 ... D5
- Visakhapatnam 352,504 ... E5
- Vizagapatam (Visakhapatnam) 352,504 ... E5
- Warangal 207,520 ... D5
- Yanam 8,291 ... E5
- Yasin ... C1

OTHER FEATURES

- Abor (hills) ... G3
- Adam's Bridge (sound) ... D7
- Agatti (isl.) ... C6
- Amindiri (isl.) ... C6
- Amindivi (isls.) ... C6
- Amini (Amindiri) (isl.) ... C6
- Andaman (isls.) ... G6
- Andaman (sea) ... G6
- Androth (isl.) ... C6
- Angedeva (isl.) ... C6
- Anjidiv (Angedeva) (isl.) ... C6
- Arabian (sea) ... B5
- Back (bay) ... B7
- Baltistan (reg.) ... D1
- Bengal, Bay of (sea) ... F5
- Berar (reg.) ... D4
- Brahmaputra (riv.) ... G3
- Butcher (isl.) ... B7
- Cambay (gulf) ... C4
- Car Nicobar (isl.) ... G7
- Chambal (riv.) ... D3
- Chenab (riv.) ... C2
- Chetlat (isl.) ... C6
- Chilka (lake) ... F5
- Coco (chan.) ... G6
- Colaba (pt.) ... B7
- Colair (lake) ... E5
- Comorin (cape) ... D7
- Coromandel Coast (reg.) ... E6
- Daman (dist.) ... C4
- Damodar (riv.) ... F4
- Deccan (plat.) ... D6
- Diu (dist.) ... C4
- Eastern Ghats (mts.) ... D6
- Elephanta (isl.) ... B7
- Ganga (Ganges) (riv.) ... F3
- Ganges, Mouths of the (delta) ... F4
- Ganges (riv.) ... F3
- Ghaghara (riv.) ... E3
- Goa (dist.) ... C5
- Godavari (riv.) ... D5
- Godwin Austen (K2) (mt.) ... D1
- Golconda (ruins) ... D5
- Great (chan.) ... G7
- Great Indian (des.) ... C3
- Great Nicobar (isl.) ... G7
- Himalaya (mts.) ... D2
- Hindu Kush (mts.) ... C1
- Hooghly (riv.) ... F2
- Indus (riv.) ... B3
- Jhelum (riv.) ... C2
- Jumna (riv.) ... E3
- K2 (mt.) ... D1
- Kadmat (isl.) ... C6
- Kalpeni (isl.) ... C7
- Kamet (mt.) ... D2
- Kanchenjunga (mt.) ... F3
- Karakoram (mts.) ... D1
- Kaveri (riv.) ... D6
- Khasi (hills) ... G3
- Kiltan (isl.) ... C6
- Kistna (riv.) ... D5
- Krishna (Kistna) (riv.) ... D5
- Kunlun (range) ... D1
- Kutch (gulf) ... B4
- Kutch, Rann of (salt marsh) ... B4
- Laccadive (isls.) ... C6
- Ladakh (reg.) ... D2
- Little Andaman (isl.) ... G6
- Little Nicobar (isl.) ... G7
- Mahanadi (riv.) ... E4
- Malabar (hill) ... B7
- Malabar Coast (reg.) ... C6
- Mannar (gulf) ... D7
- Middle Andaman (isl.) ... G6
- Minicoy (isl.) ... C7
- Miri (hills) ... G3
- Mishmi (hills) ... H3
- Nancowry (isl.) ... G7
- Nanda Devi (mt.) ... D2
- Nanga Parbat (mt.) ... D1
- Narmada (riv.) ... D4
- Nicobar (isls.) ... G7
- North Andaman (isl.) ... G6
- Palk (str.) ... D7
- Penganga (riv.) ... D5
- Periyar (lake) ... D7
- Pitti (isl.) ... C6
- Pulicat (lake) ... E6
- Rakaposhi (mt.) ... C1
- Salsette (isl.) ... B7
- Sambhar (lake) ... C3
- Satpura (range) ... D4
- Shipki (pass) ... D2
- South Andaman (isl.) ... G6
- Sundarbans (reg.) ... F4
- Sutlej (riv.) ... C3
- Ten Degree (chan.) ... G7
- Towers of Silence ... B7
- Travancore (reg.) ... D7
- Tungabhadra (riv.) ... D5
- Vindhya (range) ... D4
- Western Ghats (mts.) ... C5
- Zaskar (mts.) ... D2

MALDIVES

- Maldives 136,000 ... C7

NEPAL

CITIES and TOWNS

- Dhangarhi ... E3
- Jumla⊙ 122,753 ... E3
- Kathmandu⊙ 353,752 ... E3
- Lalitpur⊙ 154,998 ... E3
- Mukhtinath ... E3
- Mustang⊙ 26,944 ... E3
- Nepalganj 23,523 ... E3
- Pokhara 20,611 ... E3
- Pyuthan⊙ 137,338 ... E3
- Ridi ... E3
- Sallyana⊙ 141,457 ... E3

OTHER FEATURES

- Annapurna (mt.) ... E3
- Bheri (riv.) ... E3
- Dhaulagiri (mt.) ... E3
- Everest (mt.) ... F3
- Himalaya (mts.) ... D2
- Kanchenjunga (mt.) ... F3

PAKISTAN

PROVINCES

- Baluchistan 2,409,000 ... B3
- Federal Capital Territory 235,000 ... C2
- North-West Frontier 10,909,000 ... C2
- Punjab 37,374,000 ... C2
- Sind 13,965,000 ... B3

CITIES and TOWNS

- Attock ... C2
- Bela 3,139 ... B3
- Campbellpore 19,041 ... C2
- Chaman 12,208 ... B2
- Chitral ... C1
- Dadu 19,142 ... B3
- Diplo ... B4
- Dir ... C1
- Fort Sandeman 8,058 ... B2
- Gujranwala 360,419 ... C2
- Gwadar 8,146 ... A4
- Hyderabad 628,310 ... B3
- Hyderabad* 834,000 ... B3
- Kalat 5,321 ... B3
- Karachi 3,498,634 ... B4
- Karachi* 3,650,000 ... B4
- Kharan Kalat 2,692 ... A3
- Lahore 2,165,372 ... C2
- Loralai 5,519 ... B2
- Lyallpur 822,263 ... C2
- Lyallpur* 1,104,000 ... C2
- Mach 4,921 ... B3
- Malakand ... C2
- Mastung 5,962 ... B3
- Miram Shah ... C2
- Multan 542,195 ... C2
- Multan* 723,000 ... C2
- Nal ... B3
- Nok Kundi 861 ... A3
- Nushki 3,153 ... B3
- Ormara ... A3
- Pasni 7,483 ... A3
- Peshawar 268,366 ... C2
- Quetta 156,000 ... B2
- Rawalpindi 615,392 ... C2
- Risalpur 11,291 ... C2
- Rohri 19,072 ... B3
- Saidu 15,920 ... C2
- Sargodha 201,407 ... C2
- Sialkot 203,779 ... C2
- Sibi 13,327 ... B3
- Sonmiani ... B3
- Sukkur 158,876 ... B3
- Tatta 12,786 ... B4
- Turbat 4,578 ... A3
- Uch 5,483 ... B3
- Umarkot 5,878 ... B3
- Wana ... C2

OTHER FEATURES

- Arabian (sea) ... B5
- Bolan (pass) ... B3
- Chagai (hills) ... A3
- Chenab (riv.) ... C2
- Hindu Kush (mts.) ... B1
- Indus (riv.) ... B3
- Jhelum (riv.) ... C2
- Khyber (pass) ... C2
- Kunar (riv.) ... C1
- Kutch, Rann of (salt marsh) ... B4
- Mashkel (riv.) ... A3
- Mohenjo Daro (ruins) ... B3
- Muari, Ras (cape) ... B4
- Ravi (riv.) ... C2
- Siahan (range) ... A3
- Sulaiman (range) ... C3
- Sutlej (riv.) ... C3
- Talab (riv.) ... A3
- Taxila (ruins) ... C2
- Tirich Mir (mt.) ... C1
- Zhob (riv.) ... B2

SRI LANKA (CEYLON)

CITIES and TOWNS

- Colombo (cap.) 618,000 ... D7
- Colombo* 852,098 ... D7
- Hambantota 6,908 ... E7
- Kalmunai 19,176 ... E7
- Mannar 11,157 ... E7
- Mullaittivu 4,930 ... E7
- Nuwara Eliya 16,347 ... E7
- Polonnaruwa 9,551 ... E7
- Puttalam 17,982 ... D7
- Sigiriya 1,446 ... E7
- Vavuniya 15,639 ... E7

OTHER FEATURES

- Adam's (peak) ... E7
- Adam's Bridge (shoals) ... D7
- Dondra (head) ... E7
- Kirigalpota (mt.) ... E7
- Mannar (gulf) ... D7
- Palk (str.) ... D7
- Pedro (pt.) ... E6
- Pidurutalagala (mt.) ... E7

*City and suburbs.
⊙Population of district.
☐Population of urban areas.

Agriculture, Industry and Resources

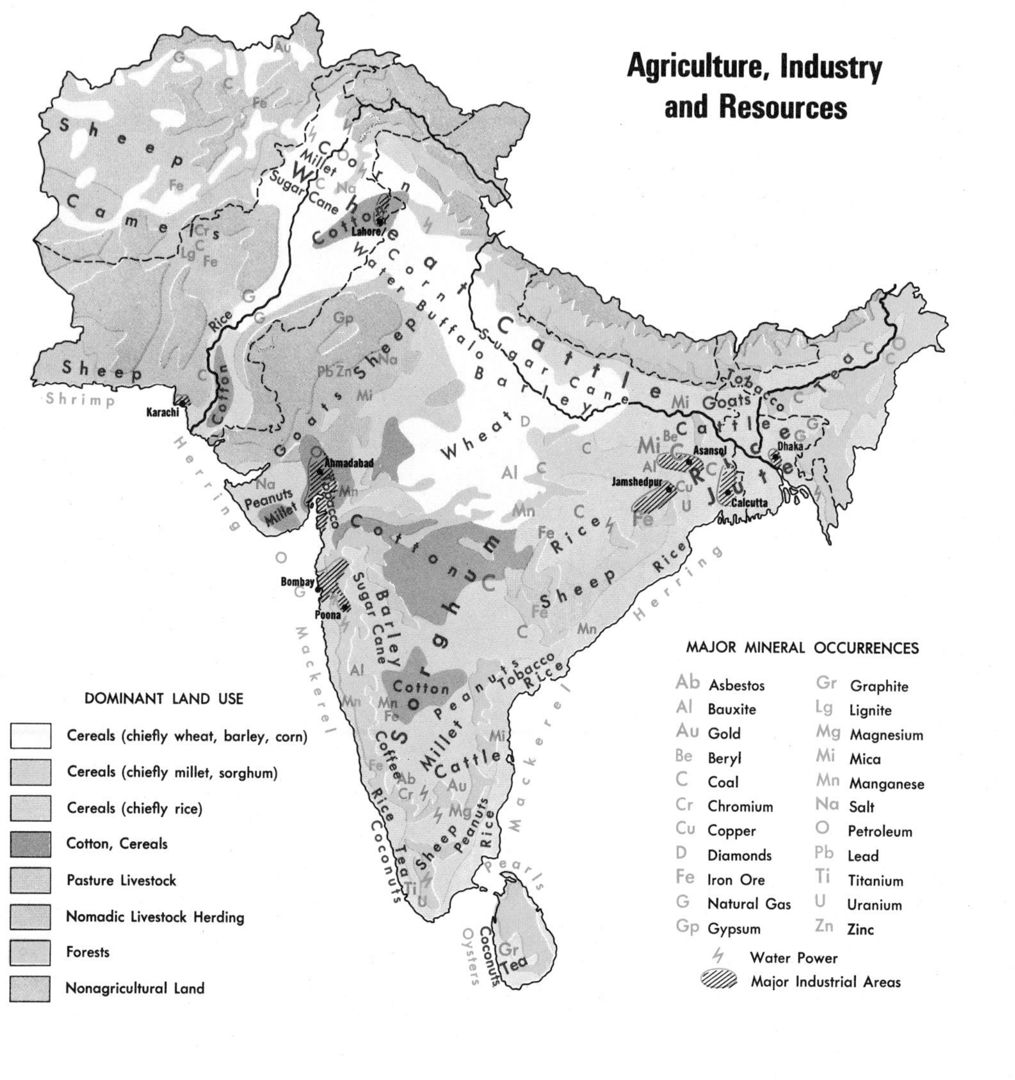

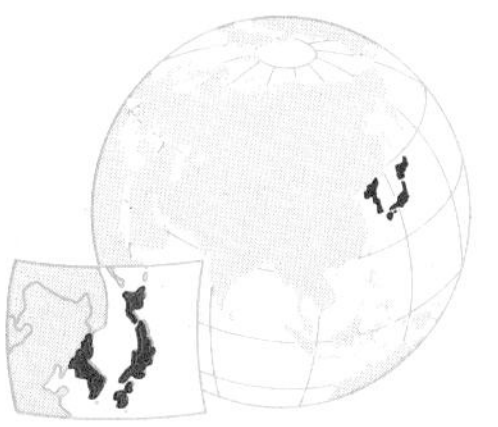

AREA 145,730 sq. mi. (377,441 sq. km.)
POPULATION 117,057,485
CAPITAL Tokyo
LARGEST CITY Tokyo
HIGHEST POINT Fuji 12,389 ft. (3,776 m.)
MONETARY UNIT yen
MAJOR LANGUAGE Japanese
MAJOR RELIGIONS Buddhism, Shintoism

AREA 46,540 sq. mi. (120,539 sq. km.)
POPULATION 17,914,000
CAPITAL P'yŏngyang
LARGEST CITY P'yŏngyang
HIGHEST POINT Paektu 9,003 ft. (2,744 m.)
MONETARY UNIT won
MAJOR LANGUAGE Korean
MAJOR RELIGIONS Confucianism, Buddhism, Ch'ondogyo

AREA 38,175 sq. mi. (98,873 sq. km.)
POPULATION 37,448,836
CAPITAL Seoul
LARGEST CITY Seoul
HIGHEST POINT Halla 6,398 ft. (1,950 m.)
MONETARY UNIT won
MAJOR LANGUAGE Korean
MAJOR RELIGIONS Confucianism, Buddhism, Ch'ondogyo, Christianity

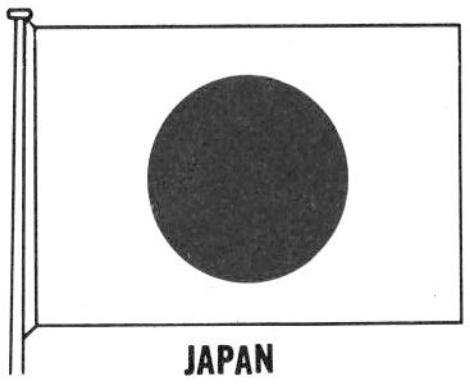

JAPAN

NORTH KOREA

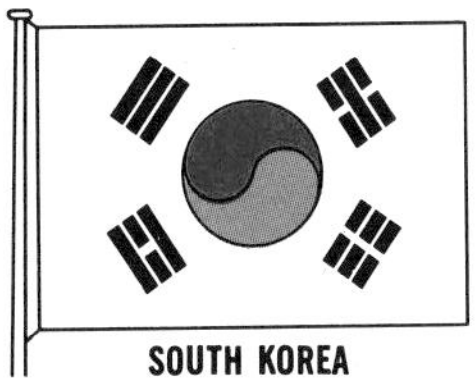

SOUTH KOREA

JAPAN

PREFECTURES

5,923,569 ..... H6
1,232,481 ..... J4
ri 1,468,646 ..... K3
4,149,147 ..... P2
e 1,465,215 ..... F7
773,599 ..... G5
oka 4,292,963 ..... D7
shima 1,970,616 ..... K5
1,867,978 ..... H6
na 1,756,480 ..... J5
hima 2,646,324 ..... E6
aido 5,338,206 ..... K2
o 4,992,140 ..... H7
ki 2,342,198 ..... K5
awa 1,069,872 ..... H5
1,385,563 ..... K4
wa 961,292 ..... G6
shima 1,723,902 ..... E8
gawa 6,397,748 ..... O2
i 808,397 ..... F7
amoto 1,715,273 ..... E7
o 2,424,856 ..... J7
1,626,002 ..... H6
gi 1,955,267 ..... K4
zaki 1,085,055 ..... E8
no 2,017,564 ..... J5
saki 1,571,912 ..... D7
1,077,491 ..... J8
ta 2,391,938 ..... J5
1,190,314 ..... E7
ama 1,814,305 ..... F6
awa 1,042,572 ..... N6
a 8,278,925 ..... J8
837,674 ..... E7
Saitama 4,821,340 ..... O2
Shiga 985,621 ..... J7
Shimane 768,886 ..... F6
Shizuoka 3,308,799 ..... H6
Tochigi 1,698,003 ..... K5
Tokushima 805,166 ..... G7
Tokyo 11,673,554 ..... O2
Tottori 581,311 ..... G6
Toyama 1,070,791 ..... H5
Wakayama 1,072,118 ..... G6
Yamagata 1,220,302 ..... K4
Yamaguchi 1,555,218 ..... E6
Yamanashi 783,050 ..... J6

CITIES and TOWNS

Abashiri 43,825 ..... M1
Ageo 146,358 ..... O2
Aikawa 13,546 ..... H4
Aizuwakamatsu 108,650 ..... J5
Ajigasawa 18,086 ..... J3
Akashi 234,905 ..... H8
Aki 24,480 ..... F7
Akita 261,246 ..... J4
Akkeshi 16,778 ..... M2
Akune 30,295 ..... E7
Amagasaki 545,783 ..... H8
Amagi 42,725 ..... E7
Anan 60,439 ..... G7
Aomori 264,222 ..... K3
Asahi 34,028 ..... K6
Asahikawa 320,526 ..... L2
Ashibetsu 36,520 ..... L2
Ashikaga 162,359 ..... J5
Ashiya 76,211 ..... H8
Atami 51,437 ..... J6
Atsugi 108,955 ..... O2
Awaji 9,623 ..... H8
Ayabe 43,490 ..... G6
Beppu 133,894 ..... E7
Bibai 38,416 ..... L2
Biratori 9,331 ..... L2
Chiba 659,356 ..... P2
Chichibu 61,798 ..... J5
Chigasaki 152,023 ..... O3
Chitose 61,031 ..... K2
Chofu 175,924 ..... O2
Choshi 90,374 ..... K6
Daito 110,829 ..... J8
Ebetsu 77,624 ..... K2
Eniwa 39,884 ..... K2
Esashi, Hokkaido 10,172 ..... L1
Esashi, Hokkaido 14,409 ..... J3
Esashi, Iwate 36,336 ..... K4
Fuchu, Hiroshima 50,217 ..... F6
Fuchu, Tokyo 182,474 ..... O2
Fuji 199,195 ..... J6
Fujieda 90,358 ..... J6
Fujisawa 265,975 ..... O3
Fukagawa 36,000 ..... L2
Fukuchiyama 60,003 ..... G6
Fukue 32,018 ..... D7
Fukui 231,364 ..... G5
Fukuoka 1,002,201 ..... D7
Fukushima 246,531 ..... K5
Fukuyama 329,714 ..... F6
Funabashi 423,101 ..... P2
Furukawa 54,356 ..... K4
Gifu 408,707 ..... H6
Gobo 30,272 ..... G7
Gose 37,554 ..... J8
Gosen 39,376 ..... J5
Goshogawara 49,040 ..... K3
Gotsu 27,992 ..... F6
Habikino 94,160 ..... J8
Haboro 13,624 ..... K1
Hachinohe 224,366 ..... K3
Hachioji 322,580 ..... O2
Hadano 103,663 ..... O3
Hagi 52,724 ..... E6
Hakodate 307,453 ..... K3
Hakui 28,726 ..... H5
Hamada 50,316 ..... E6
Hamamatsu 468,884 ..... H6
Hanamaki 65,826 ..... K4
Hanno 55,926 ..... O2
Haramachi 43,483 ..... K5
Hayama 24,026 ..... O3
Higashiosaka 524,750 ..... J8
Hikone 85,066 ..... H6
Himeji 436,086 ..... G6
Himi 61,789 ..... H5
Hino 126,847 ..... O2
Hirakata 297,618 ..... J7
Hirara 29,301 ..... L7
Hirata 30,942 ..... F6
Hiratsuka 195,635 ..... O3
Hiroo 11,399 ..... L2
Hirosaki 164,911 ..... K3
Hiroshima 852,611 ..... E6
Hitachi 202,383 ..... K5
Hitachiota 35,322 ..... K5
Hitoyoshi 41,118 ..... E7
Hofu 105,540 ..... E6
Hondo 40,432 ..... E7
Honjo 40,488 ..... J4
Hyuga 53,448 ..... E7
Ibaraki 210,286 ..... J7
Ibusuki 32,339 ..... E8
Ichihara 194,068 ..... P3
Ichikawa 319,291 ..... P2
Ichinohe 21,433 ..... K3
Ichinomiya 238,463 ..... H6
Ichinoseki 59,122 ..... K4
Ide 9,112 ..... J7
Iida 77,112 ..... H6
Iizuka 75,417 ..... E7
Ikeda, Hokkaido 12,306 ..... L2
Ikeda, Osaka 100,268 ..... H7
Ikoma 48,848 ..... J8
Ikuno 6,658 ..... G6
Imabari 119,726 ..... F6
Imari 60,913 ..... D7
Imazu 11,519 ..... G6
Ina 54,468 ..... H6
Isahaya 73,341 ..... D7
Ise 104,957 ..... H6
Ishigaki 34,657 ..... L7
Ishige 19,220 ..... P2
Ishinomaki 115,085 ..... K4
Ishioka 43,679 ..... K5
Itami 171,978 ..... H7
Ito 68,072 ..... J6
Itoigawa 36,646 ..... H5
Itoman 39,363 ..... N6
Iwaizumi 20,219 ..... K4
Iwaki 330,213 ..... K5
Iwakuni 111,069 ..... E6
Iwami 16,063 ..... G6
Iwamizawa 72,305 ..... L2
Iwanai 25,823 ..... K2
Iwasaki 4,437 ..... J3
Iwata 67,665 ..... H6
Iwatsuki 83,825 ..... O2
Iyo 27,805 ..... F7
Izuhara 18,460 ..... D6
Izumi 118,237 ..... J8
Izumiotsu 66,250 ..... J8
Izumisano 86,139 ..... G6
Izumo 71,568 ..... F6
Joetsu 123,418 ..... H5
Joyo 58,923 ..... J7
Kadoma 143,238 ..... J7
Kaga 61,599 ..... H5
Kagoshima 456,827 ..... E8
Kaizuka 79,506 ..... H8
Kakogawa 169,293 ..... G6
Kamaishi 68,981 ..... L4
Kamakura 165,552 ..... O3
Kameoka 58,184 ..... J7
Kamiisco 27,229 ..... K3
Kaminoyama 37,858 ..... J4
Kamiyaku 8,668 ..... E8
Kamo 8,953 ..... J7
Kanazawa 395,263 ..... H5
Kanonji 44,131 ..... F6
Kanoya 67,951 ..... E8
Kanuma 81,799 ..... J5
Karatsu 75,224 ..... D7
Kaseda 24,969 ..... D8
Kashihara 95,701 ..... J8
Kashiwa 203,065 ..... P2
Kashiwara 63,586 ..... J8
Kashiwazaki 80,351 ..... J5
Kasugai 213,857 ..... H6
Kasukabe 121,639 ..... O2
Katsuta 79,996 ..... K5
Katsuura 26,755 ..... K6
Kawachinagano 66,936 ..... J8
Kawagoe 225,465 ..... O2
Kawaguchi 345,538 ..... J6
Kawanishi 115,773 ..... H7
Kawasaki 1,014,951 ..... O2
Kesennuma 66,616 ..... K4
Kikonai 10,034 ..... K3
Kimitsu 76,016 ..... O3
Kiryu 134,239 ..... J5
Kisarazu 96,840 ..... P3
Kishiwada 174,952 ..... J8
Kitaibaraki 44,332 ..... K5
Kitakami 48,759 ..... K4
Kitakata 37,471 ..... J5
Kitakyushu 1,058,058 ..... E6
Kitami 91,519 ..... L2
Kizu 11,890 ..... J7
Kobayashi 38,325 ..... E8
Kobe 1,360,605 ..... H7
Kochi 280,962 ..... F7
Kodaira 156,181 ..... O2
Kofu 193,879 ..... J6
Koga 55,973 ..... J5
Koganei 102,714 ..... O2
Kokubu 31,660 ..... E8
Komagane 30,318 ..... H6
Komatsu 100,273 ..... H5
Koriyama 264,628 ..... K5
Koshigaya 195,917 ..... P2
Koyama 16,394 ..... E8
Kubohama 17,817 ..... F7
Kuji 38,122 ..... K3
Kuki 45,797 ..... O2
Kumagaya 131,485 ..... J5
Kumamoto 488,166 ..... E7
Kumano 27,026 ..... G7
Kumiyama 11,540 ..... J7
Kurashiki 392,755 ..... F6
Kurayoshi 50,785 ..... F6
Kure 242,655 ..... F6
Kuroiso 42,349 ..... K5
Kurume 204,474 ..... E7
Kushikino 30,456 ..... E8
Kushima 30,038 ..... E8
Kushimoto 18,997 ..... G7
Kushiro 206,840 ..... M2
Kyonan 13,067 ..... O3
Kyoto 1,461,059 ..... J7
Machida 255,305 ..... O2
Maebashi 250,241 ..... J5
Maihara 12,845 ..... G6
Maizuru 97,780 ..... G6
Makubetsu 18,444 ..... L2
Makurazaki 29,685 ..... O3
Mashike 9,312 ..... K2
Masuda 50,734 ..... E6
Matsubara 132,662 ..... H8
Matsue 127,440 ..... F6
Matsumae 18,307 ..... J3
Matsumoto 185,595 ..... H5
Matsusaka 108,893 ..... H6
Matsuto 36,170 ..... H5
Matsuyama 367,323 ..... F7
Mihara 83,679 ..... F6
Miki 53,731 ..... H7
Mikuni 21,602 ..... G5
Minamata 36,782 ..... E7
Minobu 10,345 ..... J6
Minoo 79,621 ..... J7
Misawa 37,437 ..... K3
Mitaka 164,950 ..... O2
Mito 197,953 ..... K5
Mitsukaido 38,820 ..... P2
Miura 47,888 ..... O3
Miyako 61,912 ..... L4
Miyakonojo 118,289 ..... E8
Miyazaki 234,347 ..... E8
Miyazu 30,194 ..... G6
Miyoshi 37,193 ..... F6
Mizusawa 52,266 ..... K4
Mobara 64,942 ..... K6
Mombetsu 32,825 ..... L1
Monbetsu 15,029 ..... L2
Mooka 47,345 ..... K5
Mori 17,030 ..... K2
Moriguchi 178,383 ..... J7
Morioka 216,223 ..... K4
Motobu 17,823 ..... N6
Muko 45,886 ..... J7
Murakami 32,939 ..... J4
Muroran 158,715 ..... K2
Muroto 26,660 ..... G7
Musashino 139,508 ..... O2
Mutsu 44,646 ..... K3
Nachikatsuura 23,596 ..... H7
Nagahama, Ehime 13,144 ..... F7
Nagahama, Shiga 54,064 ..... H6
Nagano 306,637 ..... J5
Nagaoka, Kyoto 65,557 ..... J7
Nagaoka, Niigata 171,742 ..... J5
Nagaokakyo 65,557 ..... J7
Nagasaki 450,194 ..... D7
Nagato 27,327 ..... E6
Nago 45,210 ..... N6
Nagoya 2,079,740 ..... H6
Naha 295,006 ..... N6
Nakaminato 33,147 ..... K5
Nakamura 34,437 ..... F7
Nakasato 14,248 ..... K3
Nakatsu 59,111 ..... E7
Nanao 49,493 ..... H5
Nankoku 42,832 ..... F7
Nara 257,538 ..... J8
Narashino 117,852 ..... P2
Nayoro 35,145 ..... L1
Naze 46,359 ..... O5
Nemuro 45,817 ..... M2
Neyagawa 254,311 ..... J7
Nichinan 52,171 ..... E8
Niigata 423,188 ..... J5
Niihama 131,712 ..... F6
Niimi 30,014 ..... F6
Niitsu 58,970 ..... J5
Nishinomiya 400,622 ..... H8

(continued on following page)

Agriculture, Industry and Resources

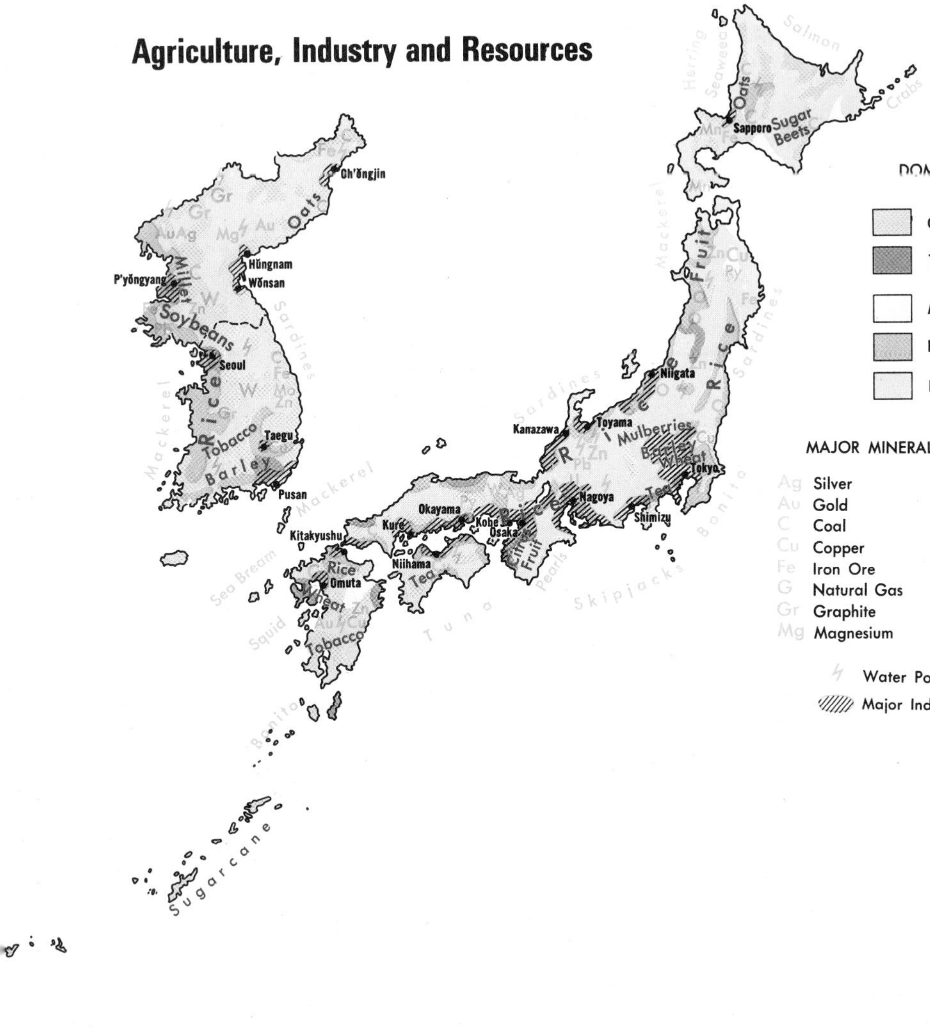

DOMINANT LAND USE

Cereals, Cash Crops
Truck Farming, Horticulture
Mixed Farming, Dairy
Rice
Forests, Scrub

MAJOR MINERAL OCCURRENCES

Ag Silver
Au Gold
C Coal
Cu Copper
Fe Iron Ore
G Natural Gas
Gr Graphite
Mg Magnesium
Mn Manganese
Mo Molybdenum
O Petroleum
Pb Lead
Py Pyrites
U Uranium
W Tungsten
Zn Zinc

Water Power
Major Industrial Areas

(continued)

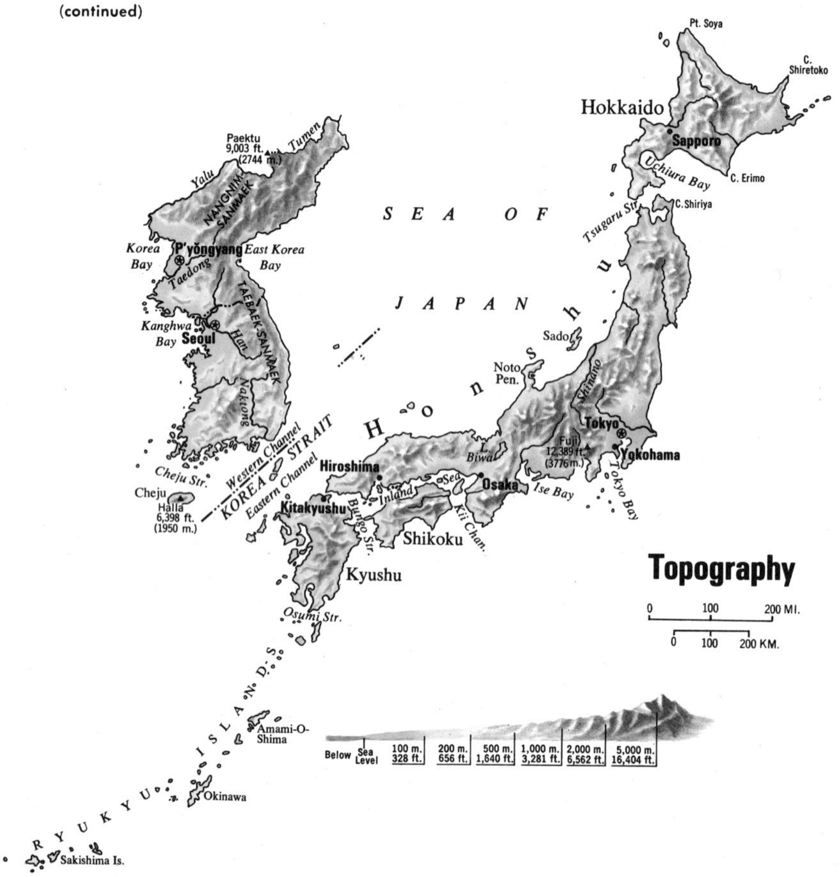

Okhotsk (sea) M1
Oki (isls.) F5
Okinawa (isl.) N6
Okinawa (isls.) N6
Okinoerabu (isl.) N5
Okushiri (isl.) J2
Oma (cape) K3
Omono (riv.) J4
Ono (riv.) E7
Ontake (mt.) H6
Osaka (bay) H8
O-Shima (isl.) J6
Osumi (isls.) E8
Osumi (pen.) E8
Osumi (str.) E8
Otakine (mt.) K5
Rikuchu-Kaigan National Park L4
Rishiri (isl.) K1
Ryukyu (isls.) L7
Sado (isl.) J4
Sagami (bay) O3
Sagami (riv.) O2
Sagami (sea) J6
Saikai National Park D7
Sakishima (isls.) K7
San'in Kaigan National Park ....
Sata (cape) ....
Setonaikai National Park ....
Shikoku (isl.) ....
Shikotan (isl.) ....
Shikotsu (lake) ....
Shikotsu-Toya National Park ....
Shimane (pen.) ....
Shimokita (pen.) ....
Shinano (riv.) ....
Shiono (cape) ....
Shiragami (cape) ....
Shirane (mt.) ....
Shirane (mt.) ....
Shiretoko (cape) ....
Shiriya (cape) ....
Soya (pt.) ....
Suo (sea) ....
Suruga (bay) ....
Suwanose (isl.) ....
Suzu (pt.) ....
Takeshima (isls.) ....
Tama (riv.) ....
Tanega (isl.) ....
Tappi (cape) ....

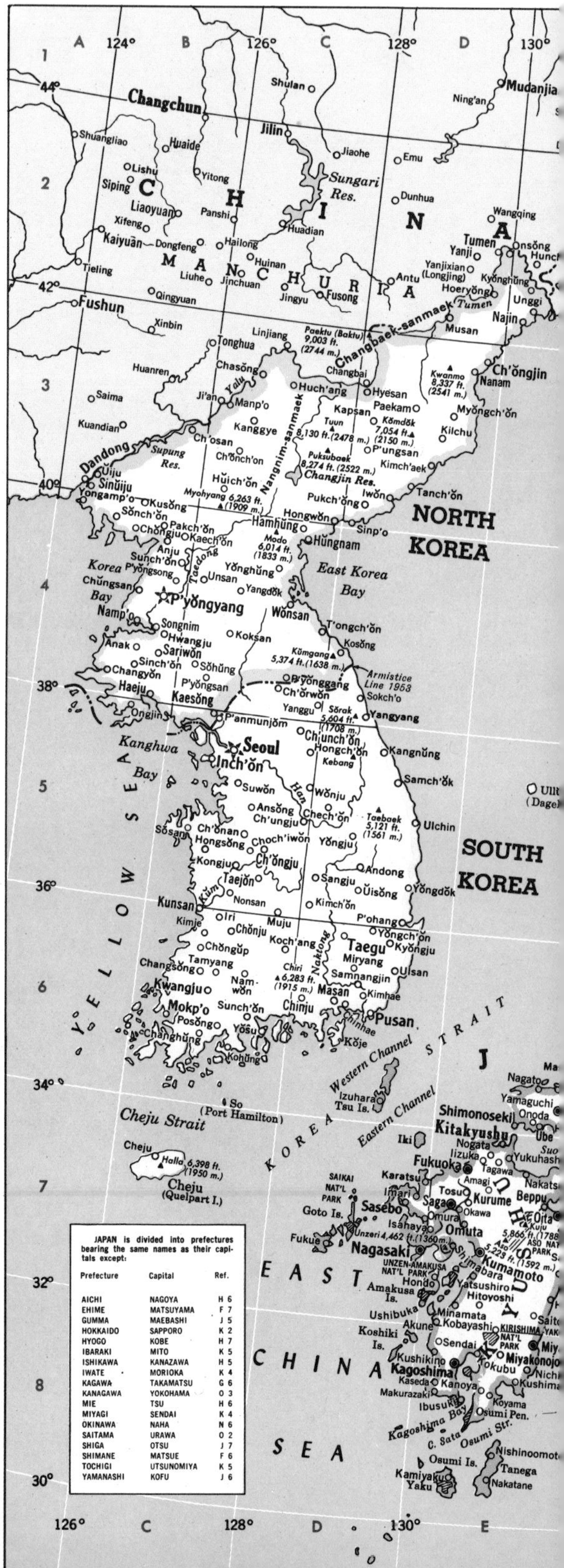

Nishinoomote 24,266 .... E8
Nobeoka 134,521 .... E7
Noboribetsu 50,885 .... K2
Noda 78,193 .... P2
Nogata 58,551 .... E7
Nose 9,749 .... J7
Noshiro 59,215 .... J3
Noto 15,815 .... H5
Numata 45,255 .... J5
Numazu 199,325 .... J6
Obama 33,890 .... G6
Obihiro 141,774 .... L2
Oda 37,449 .... F6
Odate 71,828 .... K3
Odawara 173,519 .... J6
Ofunato 39,632 .... K4
Oga 39,619 .... J4
Ogaki 140,424 .... H6
Ogi 4,717 .... J5
Ohata 12,632 .... K3
Oita 320,237 .... E7
Ojiya 44,375 .... J5
Okawa 50,395 .... E7
Okaya 61,776 .... H5
Okayama 513,471 .... F6
Okazaki 234,510 .... H6
Omagari 40,581 .... K4
Omiya 327,698 .... O2
Omu 7,407 .... L1
Omura, Bonin Is. 1,5C7 .... M3
Omura, Nagasaki 60,919 .... E7
Omuta 165,969 .... E7
Onagawa 16,945 .... K4
Ono 41,918 .... H6
Onoda 43,804 .... E6
Onomichi 102,951 .... F6
Osaka 2,778,987 .... J8
Ota 110,723 .... J5
Otaru 184,406 .... K2
Otawara 42,332 .... K5
Otofuke 26,933 .... L2
Otsu 191,481 .... J7
Owase 31,797 .... H6
Oyabe 35,791 .... H5
Oyama 120,264 .... J5
Ozu 37,294 .... F7
Rausu 8,249 .... M1
Rikuzentakata 29,439 .... K4
Rumoi 36,882 .... K2
Ryotsu 22,110 .... J4
Ryugasaki 40,565 .... P2
Sabae 57,252 .... H5
Saga 152,258 .... E7
Sagamihara 377,398 .... O2
Saigo 14,409 .... F5
Saiki 52,863 .... E7
Saito 37,054 .... E7
Sakado 51,232 .... O2
Sakai, Ibaraki 24,347 .... P1
Sakai, Osaka 750,688 .... J8
Sakaide 67,624 .... G6
Sakaiminato 35,821 .... F6
Sakata 97,723 .... J4
Saku 56,143 .... J5
Sakurai 54,314 .... J8
Sanda 35,261 .... H7
Sanjo 81,806 .... J5
Sapporo 1,240,613 .... K2
Sarufutsu 3,552 .... L1
Sasebo 250,729 .... D7
Satte 43,083 .... O1
Sawara 48,670 .... K6
Sayama 98,548 .... O2
Sendai, Kagoshima 61,788 .... E8
Sendai, Miyagi 615,473 .... K4
Setouchi 15,290 .... O5
Settsu 76,704 .... J8
Shari 15,996 .... M2
Shibata 74,025 .... J5
Shibetsu 30,028 .... M2
Shimabara 45,179 .... E7
Shimamoto 22,404 .... J7
Shimizu 243,049 .... J6
Shimoda 31,700 .... J6
Shimonoseki 266,593 .... E6
Shingu 39,023 .... H7
Shinjo 42,227 .... K4
Shiogama 59,235 .... K4
Shirakawa 42,685 .... K5
Shiranuka 14,897 .... M2
Shiroishi 40,862 .... K4
Shizunai 24,833 .... L2
Shizuoka 446,952 .... H6
Shobara 23,867 .... F6
Soka 167,177 .... O2
Soma 37,551 .... K5
Sonobe 14,827 .... J7
Suita 300,956 .... J7
Sukagawa 54,922 .... K5
Sukumo 25,340 .... F7
Sumoto 44,137 .... G6
Sunagawa 26,023 .... K2
Susaki 31,019 .... F7
Suttsu 6,511 .... J2
Suwa 49,594 .... H6
Suzu 28,238 .... H5
Suzuka 141,829 .... H6
Tachikawa 138,129 .... O2
Tagawa 61,464 .... E7
Tajimi 68,901 .... H6
Takaishi 66,824 .... H8
Takamatsu 298,999 .... F6
Takaoka 169,621 .... H5
Takarazuka 162,624 .... H7
Takasaki 211,348 .... J5
Takatsuki 330,570 .... J7
Takayama 60,504 .... H5
Takefu 65,012 .... G6
Takikawa 50,090 .... K2
Tanabe, Kyoto 30,022 .... J7
Tanabe, Wakayama 66,999 .... G7
Tateyama 56,139 .... K6
Tendo 48,082 .... K4
Tenri 62,909 .... J8
Teshio 6,509 .... K1
Toba 29,346 .... H6
Tobetsu 17,351 .... K2
Togane 33,406 .... K6
Toi 6,983 .... J6
Tojo 13,796 .... F6
Tokamachi 50,211 .... J5
Tokorozawa 196,870 .... O2
Tokunoshima 35,391 .... O5
Tokushima 239,281 .... G7
Tokuyama 106,967 .... F6
Tokyo (cap.) 8,646,520 .... O2
Tokyo* 11,673,554 .... O2
Tomakomai 132,477 .... K2
Tomiyama 7,389 .... O3
Tondabayashi 91,393 .... J8
Tosa 30,679 .... F7
Tosashimizu 24,856 .... F7
Tosu 50,733 .... E7
Tottori 122,312 .... G6
Towada 54,365 .... K3
Toyama 290,143 .... H5
Toyohashi 284,585 .... H6
Toyonaka 398,384 .... J7
Toyooka 46,210 .... G6
Toyota 248,774 .... H6
Tsu 139,538 .... H6
Tsubame 43,265 .... J5
Tsuchiura 104,028 .... J5
Tsuruga 60,205 .... G6
Tsuruoka 95,932 .... J4
Tsuyama 79,907 .... F6
Ube 161,969 .... E6
Ueda 105,151 .... J5
Ugo 21,956 .... K4
Uji 133,405 .... J7
Uozu 48,419 .... H5
Urakawa 20,213 .... L2
Urawa 331,145 .... O2
Ushibuka 24,250 .... D7
Usuki 39,163 .... F7
Utsunomiya 344,420 .... K5
Uwajima 70,428 .... F7
Wajima 33,234 .... H5
Wakasa 6,989 .... G6
Wakayama 389,717 .... G6
Wakkanai 55,464 .... K1
Warabi 76,311 .... O2
Yaizu 94,102 .... J6
Yakumo 19,260 .... J2
Yamagata 219,773 .... K4
Yamaguchi 106,099 .... E6
Yamato 145,881 .... O2
Yamatokoriyama 71,001 .... J8
Yamatotakada 58,637 .... J8
Yao 261,639 .... J8
Yatabe 22,225 .... P2
Yatsushiro 103,691 .... E7
Yawata 50,132 .... J7
Yawatahama 45,259 .... F7
Yoichi 25,816 .... K2
Yokawa 8,015 .... H7
Yokkaichi 247,001 .... H6
Yokohama 2,621,771 .... O3
Yokosuka 389,557 .... O3
Yokote 43,030 .... K4
Yonago 118,332 .... F6
Yonezawa 91,974 .... K5
Yono 71,044 .... O2
Yubari 50,131 .... L2
Yubetsu 6,693 .... L1
Yukuhashi 53,750 .... E7
Yuzawa 38,005 .... K4
Zushi 56,298 .... O3

OTHER FEATURES

Abashiri (riv.) M1
Abukuma (riv.) K4
Agano (riv.) J4
Akan National Park M2
Amakusa (isls.) D7
Amami (isls.) N5
Amami-O-Shima (isl.) N5
Ara (riv.) O2
Asahi (mt.) J4
Asama (mt.) J5
Ashizuri (cape) F7
Aso (mt.) E7
Aso National Park E7
Atsumi (bay) H6
Awa (isl.) J4
Awaji (isl.) H8
Bandai (mt.) K5
Bandai-Asahi National Park J4
Biwa (lake) H6
Bonin (isls.) M3
Boso (pen.) K6
Bungo (str.) F7
Chichi (isl.) M3
Chichibu-Tama National Park J6
Chokai (mt.) J4
Chubu-Sangaku National Park H5
Dai (mt.) F6
Daimanji (mt.) F5
Daio (cape) H6
Daisen-Oki National Park F6
Daisetsu (mt.) L2
Daisetsu-Zan National Park L2
Dogo (isl.) F5
Dozen (isls.) F5
East China (sea) C8
Edo (riv.) P2
Erimo (cape) L3
Esan (pt.) K3
Fuji (mt.) J6
Fuji (riv.) J6
Fuji-Hakone-Izu National Park H6
Gassan (mt.) J4
Goto (isls.) D7
Habomai (isls.) N2
Hachiro (lag.) J3
Haha (isl.) M3
Hakken (mt.) H6
Haku (mt.) H5
Hakusan National Park H5
Harima (sea) G6
Hida (riv.) H6
Hodaka (mt.) H5
Hokkaido (isl.) L2
Honshu (isl.) J5
Ie (isl.) N6
Iheya (isl.) N6
Iki (isl.) D7
Ina (riv.) H7
Inawashiro (lake) K5
Inubo (cape) K6
Iriomote (isl.) K7
Iro (cape) J6
Ise (bay) H6
Ise-Shima National Park H6
Ishigaki (isl.) L7
Ishikari (bay) K2
Ishikari (riv.) L2
Ishizuchi (mt.) F7
Iwaki (mt.) K3
Iwate (mt.) K4
Iwo (isl.) M4
Iyo (sea) E7
Izu (isls.) J6
Izu (pen.) J6
Japan (sea) G4
Joshinetsu-Kogen National Park J5
Kagoshima (bay) E8
Kamui (cape) K2
Kariba (mt.) K2
Kasumiga (lag.) K5
Kazan-retto (Volcano) (isls.) M4
Kerama (isls.) M6
Kii (chan.) G7
Kikai (isl.) O5
Kino (riv.) G6
Kirishima-Yaku National Park E7
Kita Iwo (isl.) M4
Kitakami (riv.) K4
Komaga (mt.) K2
Koshiki (isls.) D8
Kuchino (isl.) O4
Kuju (mt.) E7
Kume (isl.) M6
Kutcharo (lake) M2
Kyushu (isl.) E7
Meakan (mt.) L2
Minami Iwo (isl.) M5
Miura (pen.) O3
Miyako (isl.) L7
Miyako (isls.) L7
Mogami (riv.) K4
Motsuta (cape) J2
Muko (isl.) M3
Muko (riv.) H7
Muroto (pt.) G7
Mutsu (bay) K3
Naka (riv.) K5
Nampo-Shoto (isls.) M3
Nansei Shoto (Ryukyu) (isls.) M6
Nantai (mt.) J5
Nasu (mt.) J5
Nemuro (str.) M1
Nii (isl.) J6
Nikko National Park J5
Nishino (isl.) M3
Nojima (cape) K6
Nosappu (pt.) N2
Noto (pen.) H5
Nyudo (cape) J4
Oani (riv.) K3
Obitsu (riv.) P3
Oga (pen.) J4
Ogasawara-gunto (Bonin) (isls.) M3

ma (isl.) L7
wa (lake) K4
io (mt.) L1
io (riv.) L1
(isl.) J4
achi (mt.) L2
achi (riv.) L2
ara (isls.) O5
uno (isl.) O5
yo (bay) O2
e (riv.) K6
(bay) F7
ada (lake) K3
ada-Hachimantai National ark K3
(lake) K2
ama (bay) H5
(isls.) D6
garu (str.) K3
rugi (mt.) G7
iura (bay) K2
en (mt.) D7
en-Amakusa National Park D7
cano (isls.) M4
kasa (bay) G6
Yaeyama (isls.) K7
Yaku (isl.) E8
Yodo (riv.) J7
Yonaguni (isl.) K7
Yoron (isl.) N6
Yoshino (riv.) G6
Yoshino-Kumano National Park H7
Zao (mt.) K5

KOREA (NORTH)

CITIES and TOWNS

Ch'ŏngjin 306,000 ..... E3
Chŏngju B4
Haeju 140,000 ..... B4
Hamhŭng 484,000 ..... C4
Heijo (P'yŏngyang) (cap.) 1,250,000 ..... C4
Hongwŏn C3
Huch'ang C3
Hŭich'ŏn C3
Hyesan D3
Iwŏn D3
Kaech'ŏn B4
Kaesŏng 175,000 ..... C4
Kanggye C3
Kapsan C3
Kilchu D3
Kimch'aek 100,000 ..... D3
Najin E2
Namp'o 140,000 ..... B4
Onsŏng E2
P'anmunjŏm C5
P'yŏngyang (cap.) 1,250,000 ..... C4
Sariwŏn B4
Sinŭiju 300,000 ..... B3
Songnim B4
Wŏnsan 275,000 ..... C4

OTHER FEATURES

Baktu (Paektu) (mt.) C3
Changjin (res.) C3
East Korea (bay) D4
Japan (sea) G4
Kanghwa (bay) B5
Kŏmdŏk (mt.) D3
Kŭmgang (mt.) D4
Kwanmo (mt.) D3
Myohyang (mt.) C3
Nangnim-sanmaek (range) C3
Paektu (mt.) C3
Puksubaek (mt.) C3
Sasu (mt.) C4
Supung (res.) B3
Taedong (riv.) C4
Tumen (riv.) D2
Tuun (mt.) C3
Yalu (riv.) C3
Yellow (sea) B6

KOREA (SOUTH)

CITIES and TOWNS

Andong 95,364 ..... D5
Ansŏng 27,723 ..... C5
Changhŭng 22,227 ..... C6
Changsŏng 26,266 ..... C6
Chech'ŏn 74,239 ..... D5
Cheju 135,081 ..... C7
Chinhae 103,640 ..... D6
Chinju 154,646 ..... D6
Choch'iwŏn 29,198 ..... C5
Ch'ŏnan 96,766 ..... C5
Ch'ŏngju 192,707 ..... C5
Chŏngŭp 54,864 ..... C6
Chŏnju 311,393 ..... C6
Ch'ŏrwŏn 8,180 ..... C4
Ch'unch'ŏn 140,530 ..... D5
Ch'ungju 105,274 ..... C5
Hongch'ŏn 29,499 ..... D5
Hongsŏng 26,995 ..... C5
Inch'ŏn 800,007 ..... C5
Iri 117,155 ..... C6
Kangnŭng 84,981 ..... D5
Kimch'ŏn 67,078 ..... D5
Kimje 221,414 ..... C6
Kimhae 203,428 ..... D6
Koch'ang 23,721 ..... C6
Kohŭng 217,446 ..... C6
Kongju 39,756 ..... C5
Kunsan 154,780 ..... C6
Kwangju 607,011 ..... C6
Kyŏngju 108,431 ..... D6
Masan 371,917 ..... D6
Miryang 42,951 ..... D6
Mokp'o 192,958 ..... C6
Muju 18,130 ..... C6
Namwŏn 50,857 ..... C6
Nonsan 226,429 ..... C5
P'anmunjŏm C5
P'ohang 134,418 ..... D5
Posŏng 20,256 ..... C6
Pusan 2,453,173 ..... D6
Samch'ŏk 42,526 ..... D5
Samnangjin 19,374 ..... D6
Sangju 52,839 ..... D5
Seoul (cap.) 6,889,502 ..... C5
Sokch'o 71,387 ..... D4
Sŏsan 38,081 ..... C5
Sunch'ŏn 108,063 ..... C6
Suwŏn 224,145 ..... C5
Taegu 1,310,768 ..... D6
Taejŏn 506,708 ..... C5
Tamyang 15,494 ..... C6
Ŭisŏng 26,480 ..... D5
Ulchin 27,607 ..... D5
Ulsan 252,570 ..... D6
Wŏnju 120,276 ..... D5
Yanggu 277,986 ..... C4
Yangyang 10,819 ..... D4
Yŏngch'on 50,765 ..... D6
Yŏngdŏk 18,671 ..... D5
Yŏngju 70,793 ..... D5
Yŏsu 130,623 ..... C6

OTHER FEATURES

Cheju (isl.) C7
Cheju (str.) C7
Chiri (mt.) C6
Dagelet (Ullŭng) (isl.) E5
East China (sea) C8
Halla (mt.) C7
Han (riv.) C5
Japan (sea) G4
Kanghwa (bay) B5
Kebang (mt.) D5
Kŏje (isl.) D6
Korea (str.) D6
Kŭm (riv.) C5
Naktong (riv.) D6
Port Hamilton (So) (isl.) C6
Quelpart (Cheju) (isl.) C7
So (isl.) C6

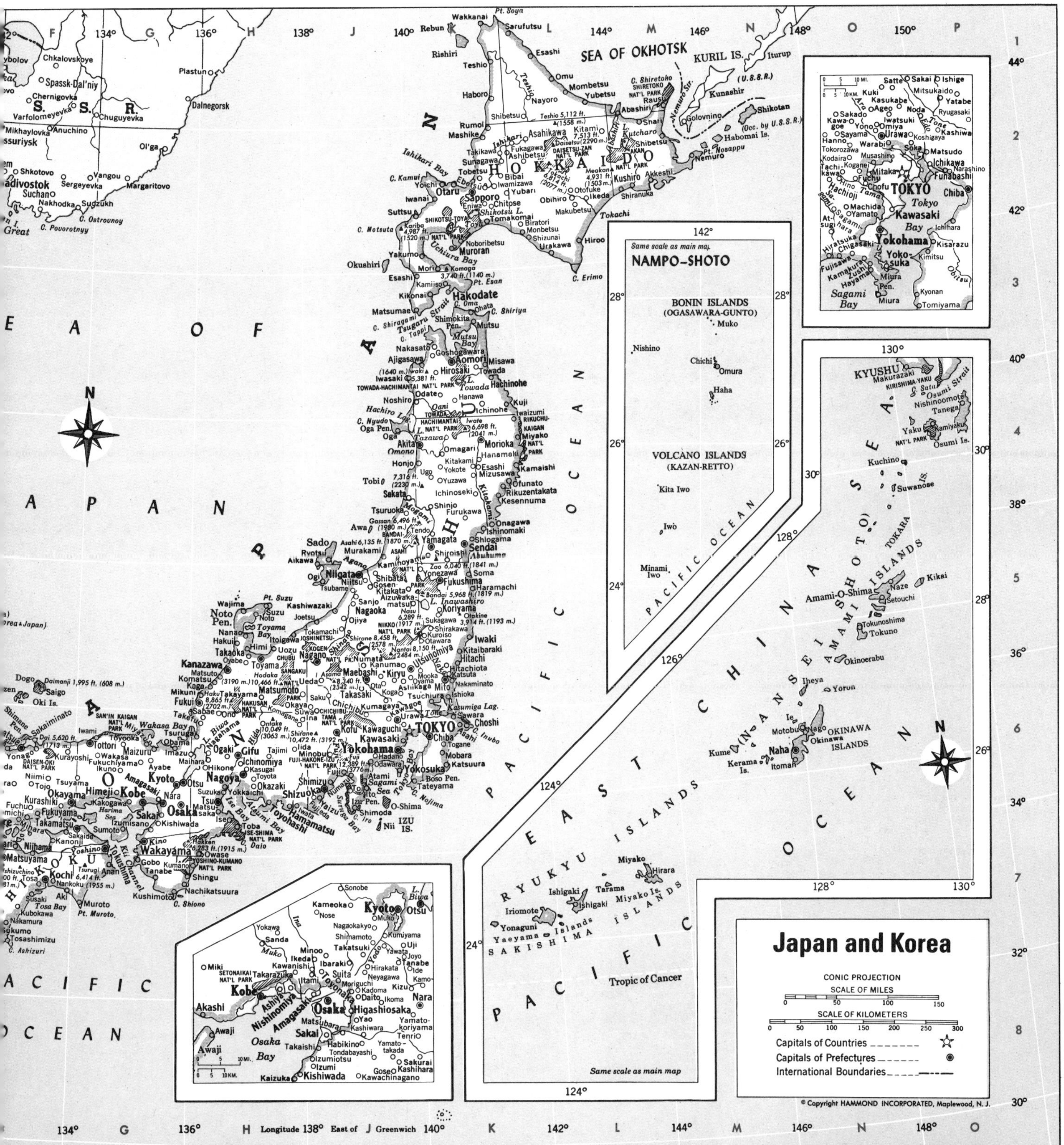
Japan and Korea
CONIC PROJECTION
SCALE OF MILES
SCALE OF KILOMETERS
Capitals of Countries
Capitals of Prefectures
International Boundaries
SEA OF OKHOTSK
SEA OF JAPAN
PACIFIC OCEAN
EAST CHINA SEA
HOKKAIDO
HONSHU
SHIKOKU
KYUSHU
NAMPO-SHOTO
BONIN ISLANDS (OGASAWARA-GUNTO)
VOLCANO ISLANDS (KAZAN-RETTO)
RYUKYU ISLANDS
SAKISHIMA ISLANDS
OKINAWA ISLANDS
AMAMI ISLANDS
TOKYO
Tropic of Cancer
Same scale as main map
Longitude 138° East of Greenwich
© Copyright HAMMOND INCORPORATED, Maplewood, N. J.

China and Mongolia

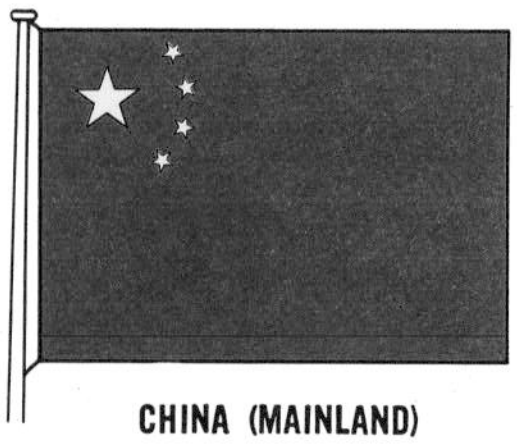

CHINA (MAINLAND)

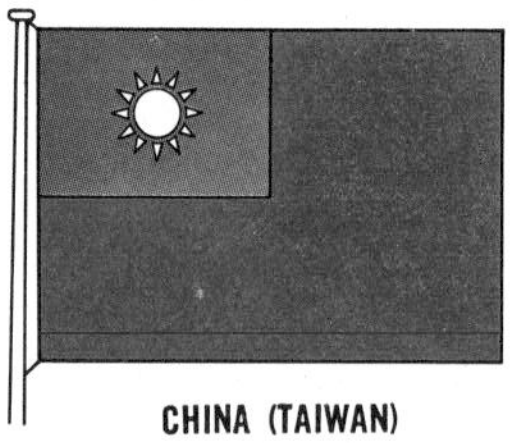

CHINA (TAIWAN)

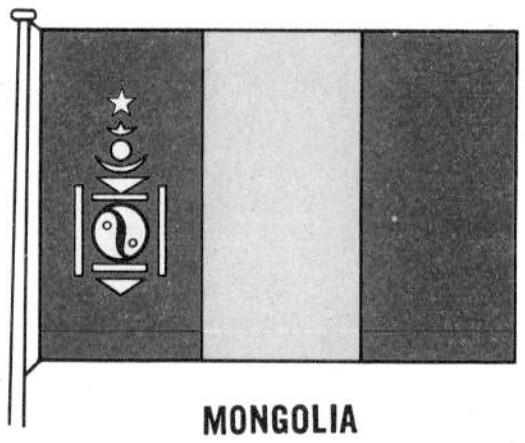

MONGOLIA

CHINA (MAINLAND)

AREA 3,691,000 sq. mi. (9,559,690 sq. km.)
POPULATION 958,090,000
CAPITAL Peking (Beijing)
LARGEST CITY Shanghai
HIGHEST POINT Mt. Everest 29,028 ft. (8,848 m.)
MONETARY UNIT yuan
MAJOR LANGUAGES Chinese, Chuang, Uigur, Yi, Tibetan, Miao, Mongol, Kazakh
MAJOR RELIGIONS Confucianism, Buddhism, Taoism, Islam

Topography

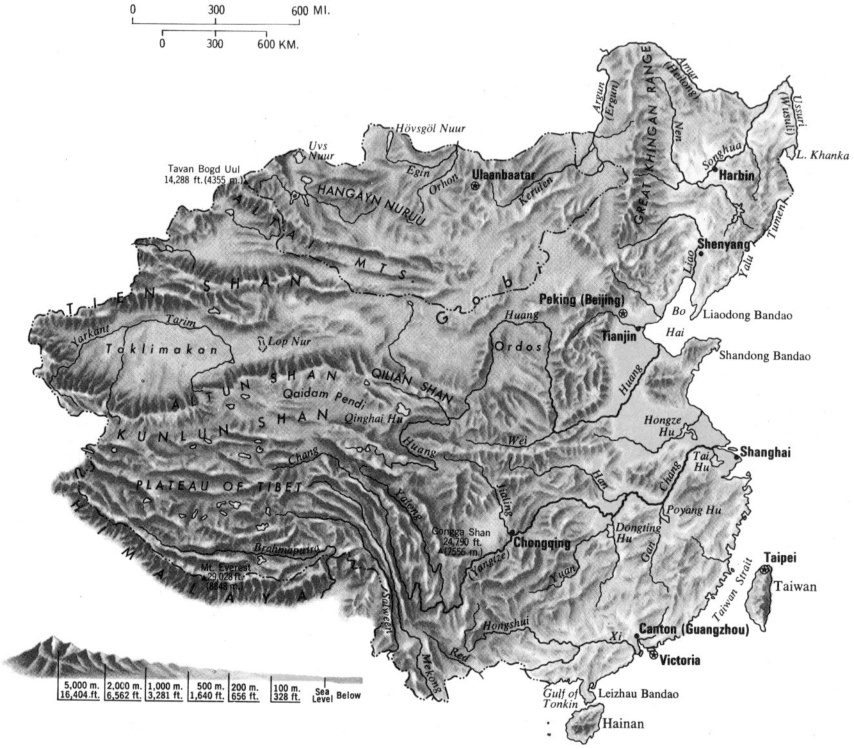

CHINA†

PROVINCES

Anhui (Anhwei) 47,130,000 .... J5
Fujian (Fukien) 24,500,000 ..... J6
Gansu (Kansu) 18,730,000 ..... E3
Guangdong (Kwangtung) 55,930,000 .... H7
Guangxi Zhuangzu (Kwangsi Chuang Autonomous Reg. 34,020,000 .... G7
Guizhou (Kweichow) 26,860,000 .... G6
Heilongjiang (Heilungkiang) 33,760,000 .. K2
Hebei (Hopei) 50,570,000 ...... J4
Henan (Honan) 70,660,000 ..... H5
Hubei (Hupei) 45,750,000 ...... H5
Hunan 51,660,000 .... H6
Jiangsu (Kiangsu) 58,340,000 . K5
Jiangxi (Kiangsi) 31,830,000 ... J6
Jilin (Kirin) 24,740,000 .... L3
Liaoning 37,430,000 .... K3
Nei Monggol (Inner Mongolian Aut. Reg.) 8,900,000 .... H3
Ningxia Huizu (Ningsia Hui Aut. Reg.) 3,660,000 .... F3
Qinghai (Tsinghai) 3,650,000 .. E4
Shaanxi (Shensi) 27,790,000 ... G5
Shanxi (Shansi) 24,340,000 .... H4
Shandong (Shantung) 71,600,000 ...... J4
Sichuan (Szechwan) 97,070,000 ..... F5
Taiwan 16,609,961 .... K7
Xinjiang Uygur (Sinkiang-Uigur Aut. Reg.) 12,330,000 .... B3
Xizang (Tibet Aut. Reg.) 1,790,000 .... B5
Yunnan 30,920,000 .... F7
Zhejiang (Chekiang) 37,510,000 ...... K6

CITIES AND TOWNS

Aihui (Aigun) (Heihe) L1
Amoy (Xiamen) 400,000 .... J7
Anqing (Anking) 160,000 .... J5
Anshan 1,500,000 .... K3
Anyang 225,000 .... H4
Aqsu (Aksu) B3
Baicheng K2
Baoding (Paoting) 350,000 ..... J4
Baoji (Paoki) 275,000 .... G5
Baoshan E7
Baotou (Paotow) 800,000 .... G3
Bei'an (Pehan) 130,000 .... L2
Beihai (Pakhoi) 175,000 .... G7
Beijing (Peking) (cap.)○ 8,500,000 .... J3
Bengbu (Pengpu) 400,000 ...... J5
Benxi (Penki) 750,000 .... K3
Canton (Guangzhou) 2,300,000 .... H7
Chamdo (Qamdo) E5
Changchun 1,500,000 .... K3
Changde (Changteh) 225,000 .. H6
Changhua 137,236 .... K7
Changsha 850,000 .... H6
Changzhi (Changchih) H4
Changzhou (Changchow) 400,000 .... K5
Chankiang (Zhanjiang) 220,000 .... H7
Chao'an (Chaochow) J7
Charkhlīa (Ruoqiang) C4
Chefoo (Yantai) 180,000 .... K4
Chengchow (Zhengzhou) 1,500,000 ...... H5
Chengde (Chengteh) 200,000 .. J3
Chengdu (Chengtu) 2,000,000 . F5
Cherchen (Qiemo) C4
Chiai 238,713 .... K7
Chinchow (Jinzhou) 750,000 ... K3
Chinkiang (Zhenjiang) 250,000 .... J5
Chinwangtao (Qinhuangdao) 400,000 ...... K4
Chongqing (Chungking) 3,500,000 ...... G6
Chüanchow (Quanzhou) 130,000 .... J7
Chuchow (Zhuzhou) 350,000 ... H6
Chuguchak (Tacheng) B2
Chungshan (Zhongshan) 135,000 .... H7
Dandong (Tantung) 450,000 ... K3
Dali E6
Datong (Tatung), Shanxi 300,000 .... H3
Erenhot H3
Foshan (Fatshan) H7
Fushun 1,700,000 .... K3
Fuxin (Fusin) 350,000 .... K3
Fuzhou (Foochow) 900,000 ..... J6
Ganzhou (Kanchow) 135,000 ... H6
Garyarsa (Gartok) B5
Gejiu (Kokiu) 250,000 .... F7
Golmud (Golmo) D4
Guangzhou (Canton) 2,300,000 H7
Guilin (Kweilin) 225,000 .... G6
Guiyang (Kweiyang) 1,500,000 G6
Gulja (Yining) 160,000 .... B3
Gyangzê C6
Haikou (Hoihow) 500,000 .... H7
Hailar J2
Hami (Kumul) D3
Handan (Hantan) 500,000 .... H4
Hangzhou (Hangchow) 1,100,000 ...... J5
Hanzhong (Hanchung) 120,000 G5
Harbin 2,750,000 .... L2
Hefei (Hofei) 400,000 .... J5
Hegang (Hokang) 350,000 ...... L2
Heihe (Aihui) (Aigun) L1
Hengyang 310,000 .... H6
Hohhot (Huhehot) 700,000 ..... H3
Horqin Youyi Qianqi (Ulanhot) 100,000 .... K2
Hotan B4
Huainan 350,000 .... J5
Huangshi 200,000 .... J5
Ichang (Yichang) 150,000 ...... H5
Ichun (Yichun) 200,000 .... L2
Ipin (Yibin) 275,000 .... F6
Jiamusi (Kiamusze) 275,000 .. M2
Ji'an (Kian) 100,000 .... J6
Jiangmen (Kongmoon) 150,000 H7
Jiaozuo (Tsiaotso) 300,000 ..... H4
Jilin (Kirin) 1,200,000 .... L3
Jinan (Tsinan) 1,500,000 .... J4
Jingdezhen (Kingtehchen) 300,000 .... J6
Jining (Tsining) 160,000 .... H3
Jinshi (Tsingshih) 100,000 ...... H6
Jinzhou (Chinchow) 750,000 ... K3
Jiujiang (Kiukiang) 120,000 ..... J6
Jixi (Kisi) 350,000 .... M2
Juichin (Ruijin) J6
Kaifeng 330,000 .... H5
Kalgan (Zhangjiakou) 1,000,000 .... J3
Kanchow (Ganzhou) 135,000 ... H6
Kaohsiung 1,028,334 .... J7
Karakax (Kara Kash) (Moyu) A4
Karamay B2
Karghalik (Yecheng) A4
Kashi (Kashgar) 175,000 .... A4
Kaxgar (Kashi) 175,000 .... A4
Keelung 342,604 .... K6
Keriya (Yutian) B4
Khotan (Hotan) B4
Kiamusze (Jiamusi) 275,000 .. M2
Kian (Ji'an) 100,000 .... J6
Kingtehchen (Jingdezhen) 300,000 .... J6
Kirin (Jilin) 1,200,000 .... L3
Kisi (Jixi) 350,000 .... M2
Kiukiang (Jiujiang) 120,000 ..... J6
Kokiu (Gejiu) 250,000 .... F7
Kongmoon (Jiangmen) 150,000H7
Kuldja (Yining) 160,000 .... B3
Kunming 1,700,000 .... F6
Kwangchow (Canton) 2,300,000H7
Kweilin (Guilin) 225,000 .... G6
Kweisui (Hohhot) 700,000 ...... H3
Kweiyang (Guiyang) 1,500,000 G6
Lanzhou (Lanchow) 1,500,000. F4
Leshan (Loshan) 250,000 .... F6
Lhasa 175,000 .... D6
Lhazê (Lhatse) C6
Lianyungang (Lienyünkang) 300,000 ...... J5
Liaoyang 250,000 .... K3
Liaoyuan 300,000 .... K3
Linqing (Lintsing) J4
Linxia (Linsia) F4
Liuzhou (Liuchow) 250,000 .... G7
Lopnur (Yuli) C3
Lüda (Lüta) 4,000,000 .... K4

On this map Chinese place-names have been rendered according to the Pinyin spelling system within the area controlled by the People's Republic of China. Alphabetically listed below are selected Chinese place-names spelled in the traditional manner, followed by the equivalent Pinyin form.

Amoy (Hsiamen)	Xiamen	Kirin	Jilin	Sian	Xi'an
Anhwei	Anhui	Kiukiang	Jiujiang	Siangtan	Xiangtan
Canton (Kwangchow)	Guangzhou	Kwangsi Chuang	Guangxi Zhuangzu	Sining	Xining
Chefoo (Yentai)	Yantai	Kwangtung	Guangdong	Sinkiang-Uighur	Xinjiang Uygur
Chekiang	Zhejiang	Kweichow	Guizhou	Soochow	Suzhou
Chengchow	Zhengzhou	Kweilin	Guilin	Süchow	Xuzhou
Chengtu	Chengdu	Kweiyang	Guiyang	Swatow	Shantou
Chinchow	Jinzhou	Lanchow	Lanzhou	Szechuan	Sichuan
Chungking	Chongqing	Liuchow	Liuzhou	Tachai	Dazhai
Foochow	Fuzhou	Loyang	Luoyang	Tatung	Datong
Fukien	Fujian	Lüta	Lüda	Tibet	Xizang
Hangchow	Hangzhou	Mutankiang	Mudanjiang	Tientsin	Tianjin
Heilungkiang	Heilongjiang	Nanking	Nanjing	Tsinan	Jinan
Hofei	Hefei	Ningpo	Ningbo	Tsinghai	Qinghai
Honan	Henan	Ningsia Hui	Ningxia Huizu	Tsingtao	Qingdao
Hopei	Hebei	Paoting	Baoding	Tsining	Jining
Huhehot	Hohhot	Paotow	Baotou	Tsitsihar	Qiqihar
Hupeh	Hubei	Penki	Benxi	Tsunyi	Zunyi
Hwainan	Huainan	Peking	Beijing	Tungchwan	Tongchuan
Inner Mongolia	Nei Monggol	Pengpu	Bengbu	Tzepo	Zibo
Kansu	Gansu	Shansi	Shanxi	Urumchi	Ürümqi
Kiangsi	Jiangxi	Shantung	Shandong	Wusih	Wuxi
Kiangsu	Jiangsu	Shensi	Shaanxi	Yenan	Yan'an
Kingtehchen	Jingdezhen	Shihkiachwang	Shijiazhuang	Yinchwan	Yinchuan

CHINA (TAIWAN)

A 13,971 sq. mi. (36,185 sq. km.)
ULATION 16,609,961
ITAL Taipei
GEST CITY Taipei
HEST POINT Yü Shan 13,113 ft. (3,997 m.)
IETARY UNIT new Taiwan yüan (dollar)
OR LANGUAGES Chinese, Formosan
OR RELIGIONS Confucianism, Buddhism, Taoism, Christianity, tribal religions

MONGOLIA

AREA 606,163 sq. mi. (1,569,962 sq. km.)
POPULATION 1,594,800
CAPITAL Ulaanbaatar
LARGEST CITY Ulaanbaatar
HIGHEST POINT Tabun Bogdo 14,288 ft. (4,355 m.)
MONETARY UNIT tughrik
MAJOR LANGUAGES Khalkha Mongolian, Kazakh (Turkic)
MAJOR RELIGION Buddhism

HONG KONG

AREA 403 sq. mi. (1,044 sq. km.)
POPULATION 5,022,000
CAPITAL Victoria
MONETARY UNIT Hong Kong dollar
MAJOR LANGUAGES Chinese, English
MAJOR RELIGIONS Confucianism, Buddhism, Christianity

MACAU

AREA 6 sq. mi. (16 sq. km.)
POPULATION 271,000
CAPITAL Macau
MONETARY UNIT pataca
MAJOR LANGUAGES Chinese, Portuguese
MAJOR RELIGIONS Confucianism, Buddhism, Taoism, Christianity

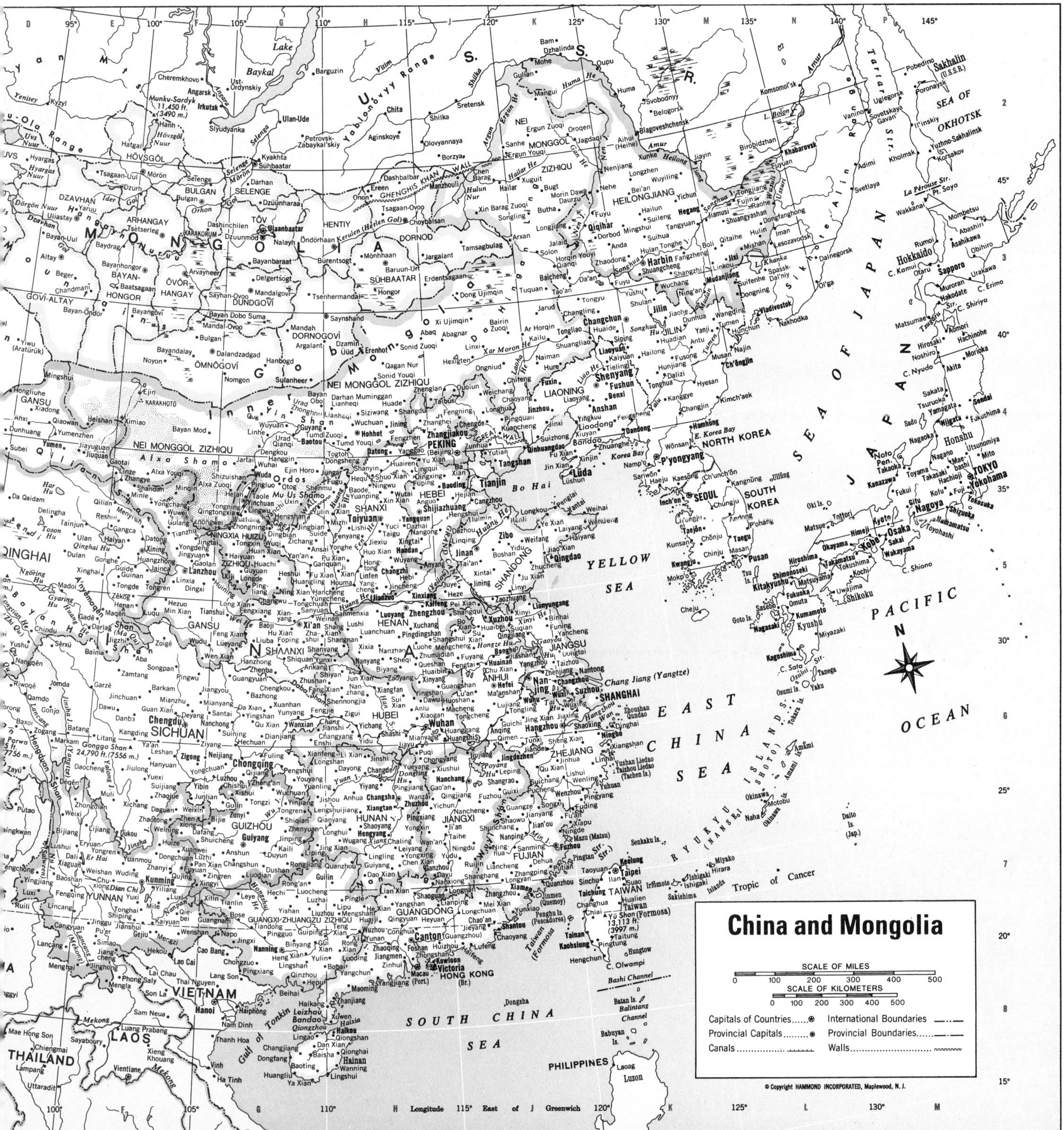

(continued)

Luoyang (Loyang) 750,000 ..... H5
Lüshun K4
Luzhou (Luchol) 225,000 ..... G6
Ma'anshan J5
Manzhouli (Manchouli) J2
Maoming (Mowming) H7
Mengzi F7
Mianyang G5
Minfeng (Niya) B4
Moyu (Karakax) A4
Mudanjiang
(Mutankiang) 400,000 ..... M3
Mukden (Shenyang) 3,750,000 K3
Nanchang 900,000 ..... J6
Nanchong (Nanchung) 275,000 G5
Nanjing (Nanking) 2,000,000 ... J5
Nanning 375,000 ..... G7
Nanping J6
Nantong 300,000 ..... K5
Nanyang H5
Neijiang (Neikiang) 240,000 ..... G6
Nenjiang L2
Ningbo (Ningpo) 350,000 ..... K6
Ningsia (Yinchuan,
Yinchwan) 175,000 ..... G4
Paicheng (Baicheng) K2
Pakhoi (Beihai) 175,000 ..... G7
Paoki (Baoji) 275,000 ..... G5
Paoting (Baoding) 350,000 ..... J4
Paotow (Baotou) 800,000 ..... G3
Pehan (Bei'an) 130,000 ..... L2
Peking (Beijing)
(cap.)○ 8,500,000 ..... J3
Pengpu (Bengbu) 400,000 ..... J5
Penki (Benxi) 750,000 ..... K3
Pingdingshan H5
Pingliang G4
Pingtung 165,360 ..... K7
Pingxiang, Guangxi
Zhuangzu G7
Pingxiang, Jiangxi H6
Piqan (Shanshan) D3
Qamdo E5
Qarkilik (Ruoqiang) C4
Qiemo (Qarqan) C4
Qingdao (Tsingtao) 1,900,000 . K4
Qingjiang 110,000 ..... J5
Qinhuangdao
(Chinwangtao) 400,000 ..... K4
Qiqihar
(Tsitsihar) 1,500,000 ..... K2
Qitai C3
Qoqek (Tacheng) B2
Quanzhou
(Chüanchow) 130,000 ..... J7
Ruijin (Juichin) J6
Ruoqiang (Qarkilik) C4
Shache (Yarkand) A4
Shanghai○ 10,980,000 ..... K5
Shangqui (Shangkiu) 250,000 .. J5
Shangrao (Shangjao) 100,000 . J6
Shangshui 100,000 ..... J5
Shanshan (Piqan) D3
Shantou (Swatow) 400,000 ..... J7
Shaoguan (Shiukwan) 125,000 H7
Shaoxing (Shaohing) 225,000 .. K5
Shaoyang 275,000 ..... H6
Shashi 125,000 ..... H5
Shenyang (Mukden) 3,750,000 K3
Shigatse (Xigazê) C6
Shihezi (Shihhotzu) C3
Shijiazhuang
(Shihkiachwang) 1,500,000 . J4
Shiyan H5
Shizuishan (Shihsuishan) G4
Shuangcheng L2
Shuangyashan 150,000 ..... M2
Siakwan (Xiaguan) E6
Sian (Xi'an) 1,900,000 ..... G5
Siangfan (Xiangfan) 150,000 ... H5
Siangtan (Xiangtan) 300,000 ... H6
Sienyang (Xianyang) 125,000 .. G5
Simao (Fusingchen) F7
Sinchu 208,038 ..... K7
Singtai (Xingtai) H4
Sining (Xining) 250,000 ..... F4
Sinsiang (Xinxiang) 300,000 ..... H4
Sinyang (Xinyang) 125,000 ..... H5
Siping (Szeping) 180,000 ..... K3
Soche (Shache) A4
Suao K7
Süchow (Xuzhou) 1,500,000 ... J5
Suifenhe M3
Suihua L2
Suining G5
Suzhou (Soochow) 1,300,000 . K5
Swatow (Shantou) 400,000 ..... J7
Tacheng (Qoqek) B2
Tai'an J4
Taichung 565,255 ..... K7
Tainan 541,390 ..... J7
Taipei 2,108,193 ..... K7
Taitung K7
Taiyuan 2,725,000 ..... H4
Taizhou (Taichow) 275,000 ..... K5
Tali (Dali) E6
Tangshan 1,200,000 ..... J4
Tantung (Dandong) 450,000 ... K3
Tao'an K2
Taoyuan 105,841 ..... K6
Tatung (Datong) 300,000 ..... H3
Tehchow (Dezhou) J4
Tianjin (Tientsin)○ 7,210,000 ... J4
Tianshui 100,000 ..... F5
Tieling K3
Tientsin (Tianjin)○ 7,210,000 ... J4
Tongchuan (Tungchwan) G5
Tonghua (Tunghwa) 275,000 ... L3
Tongjiang (Tungkiang) M2
Tongliao K3
Tongling J5
Tsiaotso (Jiaozuo) 300,000 ..... H4
Tsinan (Jinan) 1,500,000 ..... J4
Tsingkiang
(Qingjiang) 110,000 ..... J5
Tsingshih (Jinshi) 100,000 ..... H6
Tsingtao (Qingdao) 1,900,000 . K4
Tsining (Jining) 160,000 ..... H3
Tsitsihar
(Qiqihar) 1,500,000 ..... K2
Tsunyi (Zunyi) 275,000 ..... G6
Tumen M3
Tunxi (Tunki) J6
Turpan (Turfan) C3
Tzekung (Zigong) 350,000 ..... F6
Tzepo (Zibo) 1,750,000 ..... J4
Uch Turfan (Wushi) A3
Ulanhot (Horquin Youyi
Qianqi) 100,000 ..... K2
Ulughchat (Wuqia) A4
Ürümqi
(Urumchi) 500,000 ..... C3
Usu B3
Wanxian (Wanhsien) 175,000 .. G5
Weifang 260,000 ..... J4
Weihai (Weihaiwei) K4
Wenzhou 250,000 ..... J6
Wuda G4
Wuhan 4,250,000 ..... H5
Wuhu 300,000 ..... J5
Wuqi G4
Wuqia A4
Wushi A3
Wuxi (Wusih) 900,000 ..... K5
Wuxing (Wuhing) 160,000 ..... K5
Wuzhong (Wuchung) G4
Wuzhou (Wuchow) 150,000 ..... H7
Xiaguan (Siakwan) E6
Xiamen (Amoy) 400,000 ..... J7
Xi'an (Sian) 1,900,000 ..... G5
Xiangfan (Siangfan) 150,000 ... H5
Xiangtan (Siangtan) 300,000 ... H6
Xianyang (Sienyang) 125,000 .. G5
Xiapu (Siapu) K6
Xichang (Sichang) F6
Xigazê (Shigatse) C6
Xingtai (Singtai) H4
Xining (Sining) 250,000 ..... F4
Xinxiang (Sinsiang) 300,000 ..... H4
Xinyang (Sinyang) 125,000 ..... H5
Xuzhou (Süchow) 1,500,000 ... J5
Ya'an 100,000 ..... F6
Yadong C6
Yan'an (Yenan) G4
Yanji (Yenki) 130,000 ..... L3
Yangquan
(Yangchüan) 350,000 ..... H4
Yangzhou (Yangchow)
210,000 ..... J5
Yantai (Chefoo) 180,000 ..... K4
Yarkand (Shache) A4
Ya Xian G8
Yecheng A4
Yenan (Yan'an) G4
Yibin (Ipin) 275,000 ..... F6
Yichang (Ichang) 150,000 ..... H5
Yichun 200,000 ..... L2
Yinchuan (Ningsia) 175,000 ..... G4
Yingkou 215,000 ..... K3
Yining 160,000 ..... B3
Yiyang H6
Yuci (Yütze) H4
Yuli (Lopnur) C3
Yumen 325,000 ..... E4
Yungkia (Wenzhou) 250,000 ... J6
Yutian B4
Zhangjiakou
(Kalgan) 1,000,000 ..... J3
Zhangzhou (Changchow) J7
Zhanjiang
(Chankiang) 220,000 ..... H7
Zhaoqing H7
Zhengzhou
(Chengchow) 1,500,000 ..... H5
Zhenjiang
(Chinkiang) 250,000 ..... J5
Zhongshan
(Chungshan) 135,000 ..... H7
Zhuzhou (Chuchow) 350,000 ... H6
Zibo (Tzepo) 1,750,000 ..... J4
Zigong (Tzekung) 350,000 ..... F6
Zunyi (Tsunyi) 275,000 ..... G6

OTHER FEATURES

Altun Shan (range) C4
Alxa Shamo (des.) F4
Amur (Heilong Jiang) (riv.) L2
A'nyêmaqên Shan (mts.) E5
Argun' (Ergun He) (riv.) K1
Bashi (chan.) K7
Bayan Har Shan (range) E5
Bo Hai (gulf) J4
Bosten (Bagrax) Hu (lake) C3
Chang Jiang (Yangtze) (riv.) K5
Da Hingan Ling (range) J3
Dian Chi (lake) F7
Dongsha (isl.) J7
Dongting Hu (riv.) H6
East China (sea) L6
Ergun He (Argun') (riv.) K1
Er Hai (lake) F6
Everest (mt.) C6
Formosa (Taiwan) (str.) J7
Gangdisê Shan (range) B5
Ghenghis Khan Wall (ruin) H2
Gobi (des.) G3
Grand (canal) J4
Great Wall (ruins) G4,J
Gurla Mandhada (mt.) B5
Hainan (isl.) H8
Hangzhou Wan (bay) K5
Heilong Jiang (Amur) (riv.) L2
Himalaya (mts.) C6
Hotan He (riv.) B4
Huang He (Yellow) (riv.) J4
Hulun Nur (lake) J2
Inner Mongolia (reg.) H3
Jinmen (Quemoy) (isl.) J7
Jinsha Jiang (Yangtze) (riv.) E5
Junggar Pendi (desert
basin) C2
Karakhoto (ruins) F3
Karamiran Shankou (pass) C4
Keriya Shankou (pass) B4
Khanka (lake) M3
Kongur Shan (mt.) A4
Künes He (riv.) B3
Kunlun Shan (range) B4
Kuruktag Shan (range) C3
Lancang Jiang (riv.) F7
Leizhau Bandao (pen.) G7
Liaodong Bandao (pen.) K3
Liao He (riv.) K3
Lop Nor (Lop Nur) (lake) D3
Manas He (riv.) C3
Mazu (Matsu) (isl.) K6
Mekong (Lancang Jiang)
(riv.) F7
Muztag (mt.) B4
Muztagata (mt.) A4
Nam Co (lake) D5
Namzha Parwa (mt.) E6
Nan Ling (mts.) H6
Nu Jiang (riv.) E6
Nyainqêntanglha Shan
(range) D5
Olwampi (cape) K7
Ordos (reg.) G4
Penghu (Pescadores) (isls.) J7
Pobeda (peak) A3
Poyang Hu (lake) J6
Pratas (Dongsha) (isl.) J7
Qaidam Pendi (basin)
(swamp) D4
Qarqan He (riv.) C4
Qilian Shan (range) E4
Qinghai Hu (lake) E4
Qiongzhou Haixia (str.) G7
Quemoy (Jinmen) (isl.) J7
Salween (Nu Jiang) (riv.) E6
Siling Co (lake) C5
Songhua Jiang (Sungari)
(riv.) M2
South China (sea) J7
Tai Hu (lake) J5
Taiwan (Formosa) (str.) J7
Taizhou (Tachen) (isls.) K6
Takla Makan (Taklimakan Shamo)
(des.) B4
Tanggula Shan (range) D5
Tangra Yumco (lake) C5
Tarim Pendi (basin) B4
Tian Shan (range) C3
Tibet (reg.) B5
Tongtian He (Zhi Qu) (riv.) E5
Tonkin (gulf) G7
Tumen (riv.) L3
Ulu Muztag (mt.) C4
Ussuri (Wusuli Jiang) (riv.) M2
Wei He (riv.) G5
Wusuli Jiang (Ussuri) (riv.) M2
Xiang Jiang (riv.) .....
Xi Jiang (riv.) .....
Yalong Jiang (riv.) .....
Yalu (riv.) .....
Yangtze (Chang Jiang) (riv.) ...
Yarkant He (riv.) .....
Yellow (Huang He) (riv.) .....
Yellow (sea) .....
Yü Shan (mt.) .....

HONG KONG

CITIES and TOWNS

Kowloon* 2,378,480 .....
Victoria (cap.)* 1,026,870 .....

MACAU (MACAO)

CITIES and TOWNS

Macau (Macao (cap.) 226,880

MONGOLIA

CITIES and TOWNS

Tamsagbulag .....
Ulaanbaatar (Ulan Bator)
(cap.) 345,000 .....

OTHER FEATURES

Altai (mts.) .....
Dzavhan Gol (riv.) .....
Hangayn Nuruu (mts.) .....
Har Us Nuur (lake) .....
Herlen Gol (Kerulen)
(riv.) .....
Hovd Gol (riv.) .....
Hövsgöl Nuur (lake) .....
Hyargas Nuur (lake) .....
Karakorum (ruins) .....
Kerulen (riv.) .....
Munku-Sardyk (mt.) .....
Orhon Gol (riv.) .....
Selenge Mörön (riv.) .....
Tannu-Ola (range) .....
Tavan Bogd Uul (mt.) .....
Uvs Nuur (lake) .....

○Population of municipality. *City and suburbs †Populations of mainland cities excluding Peking (Beijing), Shanghai and Tianjin (Tientsin), courtesy of Kingsley Davis, Office of Int'l Population and Urban Research, Institute of Int'l Studies, Univ. of California.

Agriculture, Industry and Resources

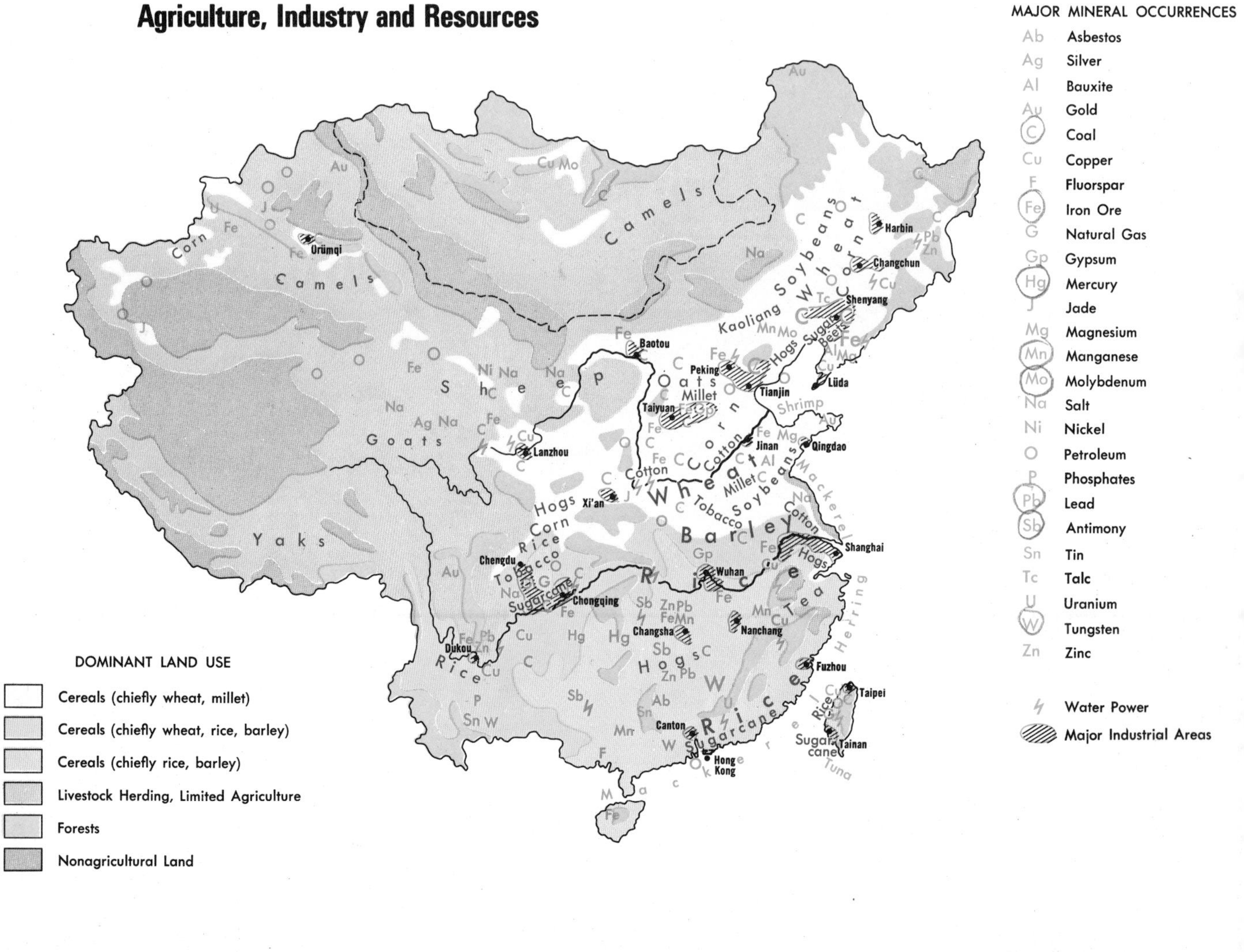

BURMA

THAILAND

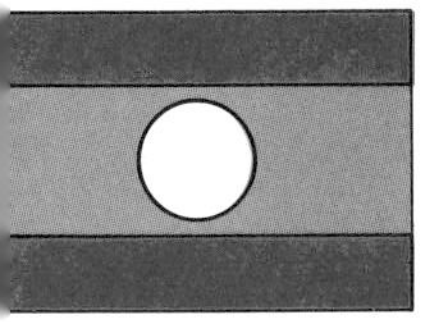

LAOS

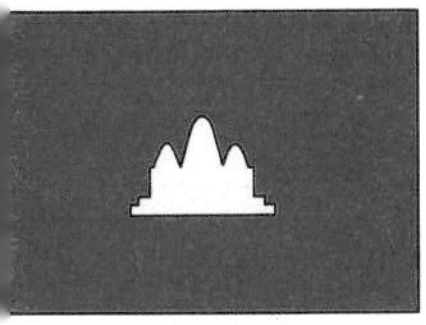

CAMBODIA

VIETNAM

MALAYSIA

SINGAPORE

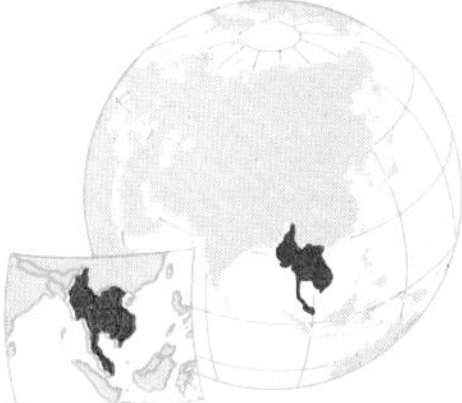

BURMA

AREA 261,789 sq. mi. (678,034 sq. km.)
POPULATION 32,913,000
CAPITAL Rangoon
LARGEST CITY Rangoon
HIGHEST POINT Hkakabo Razi 19,296 ft. (5,881 m.)
MONETARY UNIT kyat
MAJOR LANGUAGES Burmese, Karen, Shan, Kachin, Chin, Kayah, English
MAJOR RELIGIONS Buddhism, tribal religions

THAILAND

AREA 198,455 sq. mi. (513,998 sq. km.)
POPULATION 46,455,000
CAPITAL Bangkok
LARGEST CITY Bangkok
HIGHEST POINT Doi Inthanon 8,452 ft. (2,576 m.)
MONETARY UNIT baht
MAJOR LANGUAGES Thai, Lao, Chinese, Khmer, Malay
MAJOR RELIGIONS Buddhism, tribal religions

LAOS

AREA 91,428 sq. mi. (236,800 sq. km.)
POPULATION 3,721,000
CAPITAL Vientiane
LARGEST CITY Vientiane
HIGHEST POINT Phou Bia 9,252 ft. (2,820 m.)
MONETARY UNIT kip
MAJOR LANGUAGE Lao
MAJOR RELIGIONS Buddhism, tribal religions

CAMBODIA

AREA 69,898 sq. mi. (181,036 sq. km.)
POPULATION 5,200,000
CAPITAL Phnom Penh
LARGEST CITY Phnom Penh
HIGHEST POINT 5,948 ft. (1,813 m.)
MONETARY UNIT riel
MAJOR LANGUAGE Khmer (Cambodian)
MAJOR RELIGION Buddhism

VIETNAM

AREA 128,405 sq. mi. (332,569 sq. km.)
POPULATION 52,741,766
CAPITAL Hanoi
LARGEST CITY Ho Chi Minh City (Saigon)
HIGHEST POINT Fan Si Pan 10,308 ft. (3,142 m.)
MONETARY UNIT dong
MAJOR LANGUAGES Vietnamese, Thai, Muong, Meo, Yao, Khmer, French, Chinese, Cham
MAJOR RELIGIONS Buddhism, Taoism, Confucianism, Roman Catholicism, Cao-Dai

MALAYSIA

AREA 128,308 sq. mi. (332,318 sq. km.)
POPULATION 13,435,588
CAPITAL Kuala Lumpur
LARGEST CITY Kuala Lumpur
HIGHEST POINT Mt. Kinabalu 13,455 ft. (4,101 m.)
MONETARY UNIT ringgit
MAJOR LANGUAGES Malay, Chinese, English, Tamil, Dayak, Kadazan
MAJOR RELIGIONS Islam, Confucianism, Buddhism, tribal religions, Hinduism, Taoism, Christianity, Sikhism

SINGAPORE

AREA 226 sq. mi. (585 sq. km.)
POPULATION 2,413,945
CAPITAL Singapore
LARGEST CITY Singapore
HIGHEST POINT Bukit Timah 581 ft. (177 m.)
MONETARY UNIT Singapore dollar
MAJOR LANGUAGES Chine·e, Malay, Tamil, English, Hindi
MAJOR RELIGIONS Confucianism, Buddhism, Taoism, Hinduism, Islam, Christianity

Topography

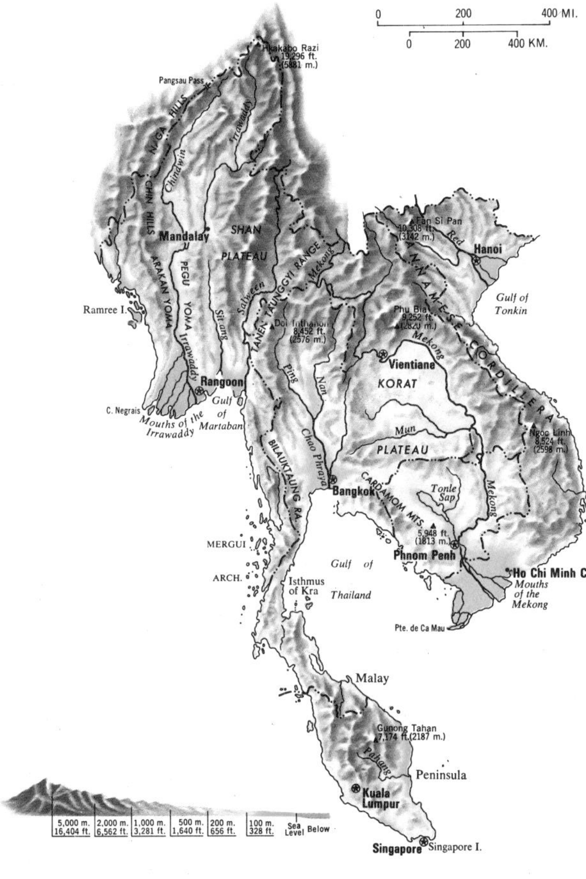

BURMA

INTERNAL DIVISIONS

Arakan (state) 1,710,913 ..... B3
Chin (state) 323,094 ..... B2
Irrawaddy (div.) 4,152,521 ..... B3
Kachin (state) 735,144 ..... C1
Karen (state) 065,210 ..... C3
Kayah (state) 126,492 ..... C3
Magwe (div.) 2,632,144 ..... B2
Mandalay (div.) 3,662,312 ..... B2
Mon (state) 1,313,111 ..... C3
Pegu (div.) 3,174,109 ..... C3
Rangoon (div.) 3,186,886 ..... C3
Sagaing (div.) 3,115,502 ..... B1
Shan (state) 3,178,214 ..... C2
Tenasserim (div.) 717,607 ..... C4

CITIES and TOWNS

Akyab (Sittwe) 42,329 ..... B2
Allanmyo 15,580 ..... B3
Amarapura 11,268 ..... B2
Amherst 6,000 ..... C3
An B3
Anin C4
Bassein 126,045 ..... B3
Bhamo 9,821 ..... C1
Chauk 24,466 ..... B2
Danubyu B3
Falam B2
Fort Hertz (Putao) C1
Gawai C1
Gokteik C2
Gwa B3
Gyobingauk 9,922 ..... C3
Haka B2
Henzada 61,972 ..... B3
Hmawbi 23,032 ..... C3
Homalin B1
Hsenwi C2
Hsipaw C2
Htawgaw C1
Insein 143,625 ..... C3
Kamaing C1
Karathuri C5
Katha 7,648 ..... C1
Kawludo C3
Kawthaung 1,520 ..... C5
Keng Hkam C2
Keng Tung C2
Koma C4
Kunlong C2
Kyaikto 13,154 ..... C3
Kya-in Seikkyi C3
Kyangin 6,073 ..... B3
Kyaukme C2
Kyaukpadaung 5,480 ..... B2
Kyaukpyu 7,335 ..... B3
Kyaukse 8,659 ..... C2
Labutta 12,982 ..... B3
Lai-hka C2
Lamu B3
Lashio C2
Lenya C5
Letpadan 15,896 ..... C3
Lewe B3
Loi-kaw C3
Lonton B1
Magwe 13,270 ..... B2
Maingkwan C1
Maliwun C5
Mandalay 418,008 ..... C2
Man Hpang C2
Martaban 5,661 ..... C3
Ma-ubin 23,362 ..... B3
Maungdaw 3,772 ..... B2
Mawkmai C2
Mawlaik 2,993 ..... B2
Mawlu C1
Maymyo 22,287 ..... C2
Meiktila 19,474 ..... B2
Mergui 33,697 ..... C4
Minbu 9,096 ..... B2
Minhla 6,470 ..... B3
Mogaung 2,920 ..... C1
Mogok 8,334 ..... C2
Mohnyin C1
Möng Hsat C2
Möng Maü C3
Möng Mit C2
Möng Pan C2
Möng Ꮛi C2
Möng Tön C2
Möng Tung C2
Monywa 26,279 ..... B2
Moulmein 171,977 ..... C3
Mudon 20,136 ..... C3
Myanaung 11,155 ..... B3
Myaungmya 24,532 ..... B3
Myingyan 36,439 ..... B2
Myitkyina 12,382 ..... C1
Myohaung 6,534 ..... B2
Naba B1
Namhkam C2
Namlan C2
Namtu C2
Natmauk B2
Okkan 14,443 ..... B3
Okpo 12,155 ..... C3
Pakokku 30,943 ..... B2
Palaw 5,596 ..... C4
Paletwa B2
Pantha B2
Papun C3
Pasawng C3
Paungde 17,286 ..... B3
Pegu 47,378 ..... C3
Prome (Pye) 36,997 ..... B3
Putao C1
Pyapon 19,174 ..... B3
Pye 36,997 ..... B3
Pyinmana 22,025 ..... C3
Pyu 10,443 ..... C3
Rangoon (cap.) 1,586,422 ..... C3
Rangoon* 2,055,365 ..... C3
Rathedaung 2,969 ..... B2
Sadon C1
Sagaing 15,382 ..... B2
Samka C2
Sandoway 5,172 ..... B3
Shingbwiyang B1
Shwebo 17,827 ..... B2
Shwenyaung C2
Singkaling Hkamti B1
Singu 4,027 ..... C2
Sinlumkaba C1
Sittwe 42,329 ..... B2
Sumprabum C1
Syriam 15,296 ..... C3
Taungdwingyi 16,233 ..... C2
Taunggyi C2
Tavoy 40,312 ..... C4
Tharrawaddy 8,977 ..... C3
Thaton 38,047 ..... C3
Thaungdut B1
Thayetmyo 11,649 ..... B3
Thazi 7,531 ..... C2
Thongwa 10,829 ..... C3
Toungoo 31,589 ..... C3
Wakema 20,716 ..... B3
Yamethin 11,167 ..... C2
Yandoon 15,245 ..... B3
Ye 12,852 ..... C4
Yenangyaung 24,416 ..... B2
Yesagyo 7,880 ..... B2
Ye-u 5,307 ..... B2
Ywathit C3
Zadi C4
Zalun 899 ..... B3

OTHER FEATURES

Amya (pass) C4
Andaman (sea) B4
Arakan Yoma (mts.) B3
Ataran (riv.) C4
Bengal, Bay of (sea) B3
Bentinck (isl.) C5

(continued on following page)

(continued)

Agriculture, Industry and Resources

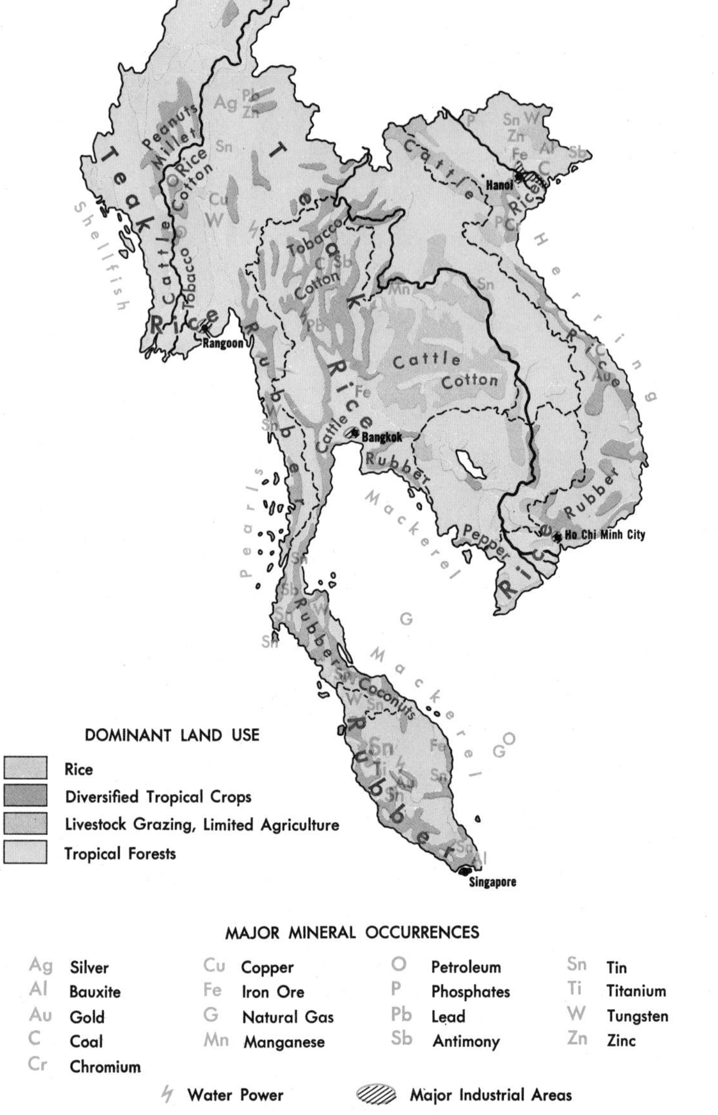

Bilauktaung (range) C4
Chaukan (pass) C1
Cheduba (isl.) B3
Chin (hills) B2
Chindwin (riv.) B2
Coco (chan.) B4
Combermere (bay) B3
Daung Kyun (isl.) C4
Dawna (range) C3
Great Coco (isl.) B4
Great Tenasserim (riv.) C4
Heinze Chaung (bay) C4
Heywood (chan.) B3
Hka, Nam (riv.) C2
Hkakabo Razi (mt.) C1
Indawgyi (lake) C1
Inle (lake) C2
Irrawaddy (riv.) B3
Irrawaddy, Mouths of the (delta) B4
Kadan Kyun (isl.) C4
Kaladan (riv.) B2
Kalegauk (isl.) C4
Khao Luang (mt.) C5
Lanbi Kyun (isl.) C5
Launglon Bok (isls.) C4
Loi Leng (mt.) C2
Manipur (riv.) B2
Martaban (gulf) C4
Mekong (riv.) D2
Mergui (arch.) C5
Mon (riv.) B2
Mu (riv.) B2
Negrais (cape) B3
Pakchan (riv.) C5
Pangsau (pass) C1
Pawn, Nam (riv.) C2
Pegu Yoma (mts.) B3
Preparis (isl.) B4
Ramree (isl.) B3
Salween (riv.) C3
Shan (plat.) C2
Sittang (riv.) C3
Taungthonton (mt.) B1
Tavoy (pt.) C4
Tenasserim (isl.) C4
Teng, Nam (riv.) C2
Three Pagodas (pass) C4
Victoria (mt.) B2

CAMBODIA (KAMPUCHEA)

CITIES and TOWNS

Batdambang (Battambang) D4
Choam Khsant E4
Kampong Cham E4
Kampong Chhnang D4
Kampong Khleang E4
Kampong Saom D5
Kampong Spoe E5
Kampong Thum E4
Kampong Trabek E5
Kampot E5
Kaoh Nhek E4
Kracheh E4
Krong Kaoh Kong D4
Krong Keb E5
Kulen E4
Lumphat E4
Moung Roessei D4
Pailin D4
Paoy Pet D4
Phnom Penh (cap.) c. 300,000 E5
Phnum Tbeng Meanchey E4
Phsar Ream D5
Phumi Banam E5
Phumi Phsar E4
Phumi Prek Kak E4
Phumi Samraong D4
Pouthisat D4
Prek Pouthi E5
Prey Veng E5
Pursat (Pouthisat) D4
Rovieng Tbong E4
Sambor E4
Senmonoron E4
Siempang E4
Siemreab D4
Sisophon D4
Sre Ambel D5
Sre Khtum E4
Stoeng Treng E4
Suong E5
Svay Rieng E5
Takev E5
Virochey E4

OTHER FEATURES

Angkor Wat (ruins) E4
Dangrek (mts.) D4
Drang, Ia (riv.) E4
Joncs (plain) E5
Khong, Se (riv.) E4
Kong, Kaoh (isl.) D5
Mekong (riv.) E4
Rung, Kaoh (isl.) D5
San, Se (riv.) E4
Sen, Stoeng (riv.) E4
Srepok (riv.) E4
Tang, Kaoh (isl.) D5
Thailand (gulf) D5
Tonle Sap (lake) D4
Wai, Poulo (isls.) D5

LAOS

CITIES and TOWNS

Attapu 2,750 E4
Ban Khon E4
Ban Lahanam E3
Borikan D3
Champasak 3,500 E4
Dônghén E3
Khamkeut⊙ 31,206 E3
Louang Namtha 1,459 D2
Louangphrabang 7,596 D3
Muang Hinboun 1,750 E3
Muang Kènthao D3
Muang Khammoun 5,500 E3
Muang Không 1,750 E4
Muang Khôngxédôn 2,000 E4
Muang Khoua D2
Muang May E4
Muang Ou Tai D2
Muang Paktha D2
Muang Phin E3
Muang Tahoi E3
Muang Vapi E4
Muang Xaignabouri (Sayaboury) 2,500 D3
Mounlapamôk E4
Napè E3
Nong Het E3
Pakxé 8,000 E4
Phiafai⊙ 17,216 E4
Phôngsali 2,500 D2
San Nua (Sam Neua) 3,000 E2
Saravan 2,350 E4
Savannakhét 8,500 E3
Sayaboury (Muang Xaignabouri) 2,500 D3
Thakhek (Muang Khammouan) 5,500 E3
Tourakom D3
Viangchan (Vientiane) 132,253 D3
Vientiane (cap.) 132,253 D3
Xiangkhoang 3,500 D3

OTHER FEATURES

Bolovens (plat.) E4
Hou, Nam (riv.) D2
Jars (plain) D3
Mekong (riv.) D3
Ou, Nam (riv.) D2
Phou Bia (mt.) D3
Phou Cô Pi (mt.) E3
Phou Loi (mt.) D2
Rao Co (mt.) E3
Se Khong (riv.) E4
Tha, Nam (riv.) D2
Xianghoang (plat.) D3

MALAYA, MALAYSIA*

STATES

Federal Territory 937,875 D7
Johor (Johore) 1,601,504 D7
Kedah 1,102,200 D6
Kelantan 877,575 D6
Melaka 453,153 D7
Negeri Sembilan 563,955 D7
Pahang 770,644 D7
Perak 1,762,288 D6
Perlis 147,726 D6
Pinang (Penang) 911,586 D6
Selangor 1,467,441 D7
Terengganu 542,280 D6

CITIES and TOWNS

Alor Gajah 2,222 D7
Alor Setar 66,260 D6
Bandar Maharani (Muar) 61,218 D7
Bandar Penggaram (Batu Pahat) 53,291 D7
Batu Gajah 10,692 D6
Batu Pahat 53,291 D7
Bentong 22,683 D7
Butterworth 61,187 D6
Chukai 12,514 D6
Gemas 5,214 D7
George Town (Pinang) 269,603 C6
Ipoh 247,953 D6
Johor Baharu (Johore Bharu) 136,234 F5
Kampar 26,591 D6
Kangar 8,758 D6
Kelang 113,611 D7
Keluang 43,272 D7
Kota Baharu 55,124 D6
Kota Tinggi 8,725 F5
Kuala Dungun 17,560 D6
Kuala Lipis 9,270 D6
Kuala Lumpur (cap.) 451,977 D7
Kuala Lumpur* 937,875 D7
Kuala Pilah 12,508 D7
Kuala Rompin 1,384 D7
Kuala Selangor 3,132 D7
Kuala Terengganu 53,320 D6
Kuantan 43,358 D7
Kulai 11,841 F5
Lumut 3,255 D6
Malacca (Melaka) 87,160 D7
Mawai F5
Melaka 87,160 D7
Mersing 18,246 E7
Muar 61,218 D7
Pekan 4,682 D7
Pekan Nanas 9,003 E5
Pinang (George Town) 269,603 C6
Pontian Kechil 8,349 E5
Port Dickson 10,300 D7
Port Kelang D7
Port Weld 3,233 D6
Raub 18,433 D7
Segamat 17,796 D7
Seremban 80,921 D7
Sungai Petani 35,959 C6
Taiping 54,645 D6
Tanah Merah 7,012 D6
Telok Anson 44,524 D6
Tumpat 10,673 D6

OTHER FEATURES

Aur, Pulau (isl.) E7
Belumut, Gunong (mt.) D7
Gelang, Tanjong (pt.) D6
Johor, Sungai (riv.) F5
Johore (str.) E6
Kelantan, Sungai (riv.) D6
Langkawi, Pulau (isl.) C6
Ledang, Gunong (mt.) D7
Lima, Pulau (isl.) F6
Malacca (str.) D7
Malay (pen.) D6
Pahang, Sungai (riv.) D7
Pangkor, Pulau (isl.) D6
Perak, Gunong (mt.) D6
Perhentian, Kepulauan (isls.) D6
Pulai, Sungai (riv.) E5
Ramunia, Tanjong (pt.) F6
Redang, Pulau (isl.) D6
Sedili Kechil, Tanjong (pt.) F5
Tahan, Gunong (mt.) D6
Temiang, Bukit (mt.) D6
Tenggol, Pulau (isl.) D6
Tinggi, Pulau (isl.) E7

SINGAPORE

CITIES and TOWNS

Jurong 50,974 E6
Nee Soon 37,641 F6
Serangoon 89,558 F6
Singapore (cap.) 2,413,945 F6

OTHER FEATURES

Keppel (harb.) F6
Main (str.) F6
Singapore (str.) F6
Tekong Besar, Pulau (isl.) F6

THAILAND (SIAM)

CITIES and TOWNS

Ang Thong 7,267 C4
Ayutthaya (Phra Nakhon Si Ayutthaya) 37,213 D4
Ban Aranyaprathet 12,276 D4
Bangkok (cap.) 1,867,297 D4
Bangkok* 2,495,312 D4
Bang Lamung D4
Bang Saphan C5
Ban Kantang 9,247 C6
Ban Kapong C5
Ban Khlong Yai D5
Ban Kui Nua D4
Ban Ngon D3
Ban Pak Phanang 13,590 D5
Banphot Phisai C3
Ban Pua D3
Ban Sattahip D4
Ban Tha Uthen D3
Bua Chum D4
Buriram 16,431 D4
Chachoengsao 22,106 D4
Chai Badan D4
Chai Buri D3
Chainat 9,944 D4
Chaiya C5
Chaiyaphum 12,540 D4
Chang Khoeng C3
Chanthaburi 15,479 D4
Chiang Dao C3
Chiang Khan D3
Chiang Mai 83,729 C3
Chiang Rai 13,927 C3
Chiang Saen C2
Chon Buri 39,367 D4
Chumphon 11,643 C5
Den Chai C3
Hat Yai 47,953 C6
Hot C3
Hua Hin 21,426 D4
Kalasin 14,960 D3
Kamphaeng Phet 12,378 C3
Kanchanaburi 16,397 C4
Khanu C3
Khemmarat E4
Khon Kaen 29,431 D3
Khorat (Nakhon Ratchasima) 66,071 D4
Krabi 8,764 C5
Krung Thep (Bangkok) (cap.) 1,867,297 D4
Kumphawapi D3
Lae D3
Lampang 40,100 C3
Lamphun 11,309 C3
Lang Suan 4,020 C5
Loei 10,137 D3
Lom Sak 10,597 D3
Lop Buri 23,112 D4
Mae Hong Son 3,981 C3
Maha Sarakham 19,707 D3
Mukdahan E3
Nakhon Nayok 8,185 D4
Nakhon Pathom 34,300 C4
Nakhon Phanom 20,385 D3
Nakhon Ratchasima 66,071 D4
Nakhon Sawan 46,853 D4
Nakhon Si Thammarat 40,671 D5
Nan 17,738 D3
Nang Rong D4
Narathiwat 21,256 D6
Ngao D3
Nong Khai 21,150 D3
Pattani 21,938 D6
Phanat Nikhom 10,514 D4
Phangnga 5,738 C5
Phatthalung 13,336 D6
Phayao 20,346 C3
Phet Buri 27,755 C4
Phetchabun 6,240 D3
Phichai D3
Phichit 10,814 D3
Phitsanulok 33,883 D3
Phon Phisai D3
Phrae 17,555 D3
Phra Nakhon Si Ayutthaya 37,213 D4
Phuket 34,362 C6
Phutthaisong D4
Prachin Buri 14,167 D4
Prachuap Khiri Khan 9,075 D5
Pran Buri D4
Rahaeng (Tak) 16,317 C3
Ranong 10,301 C5
Rat Buri 32,271 C4
Rayong 14,846 D4
Roi Et 20,242 D4
Rong Kwang D3
Sakon Nakhon 18,943 E3
Samut Prakan 46,632 D4
Samut Sakhon 33,619 D4
Samut Songkhram 23,574 C4
Sara Buri 25,025 D4
Satun 7,315 C6
Sawankhalok 8,387 C3
Selaphum E3
Sing Buri 9,050 D4
Singora (Songkhla) 41,193 D6
Sisaket 13,662 E4
Songkhla 41,193 D6
Sukhothai 15,488 D3
Suphan Buri 18,768 C4
Surat Thani 24,923 C5
Surin 16,342 D4
Suwannaphum D4
Tak 16,317 C3
Takua Pa 7,825 C5
Thoen C3
Thon Buri 628,015 D4
To Mo D6
Trang 32,985 C6
Trat 7,917 D4
Ubon 40,650 E4
Udon Thani 56,218 D3
Uthai Thani 10,525 C4
Uttaradit 12,022 D3
Warin Chamrap 21,520 E4
Yala 30,051 D6
Yasothon 12,079 D4

OTHER FEATURES

Amya (pass) C4
Bilauktaung (range) C4
Chang, Ko (isl.) D4
Chao Phraya, Mae Nam (riv.) D4
Chi, Mae Nam (riv.) D3
Dangrek (Dong Rak) (mts.) D4
Doi Inthanon (mt.) C3
Doi Pha Hom Pok (mt.) C2
Doi Pia Fai (mt.) D4
Kao Prawa (mt.) C3
Khao Luang (mt.) C5
Khwae Noi, Mae Nam (riv.) C4
Kra (isth.) C5
Kut, Ko (isl.) D5
Laem Pho (cape) D6
Laem Talumphuk (cape) D5
Lanta, Ko (isl.) C6
Luang (mt.) C5
Mae Klong, Mae Nam (riv.) C4
Mekong (riv.) E3
Mun, Mae Nam (riv.) D4
Nan, Mae Nam (riv.) D3
Nong Lahan (lake) D3
Pakchan (riv.) C5
Pa Sak, Mae Nam (riv.) D4
Phangan, Ko (isl.) D5
Phuket, Ko (isl.) C5
Ping, Mae Nam (riv.) C3
Samui (str.) D5
Samui, Ko (isl.) D5
Siam (Thailand) (gulf) D5
Tao, Ko (isl.) C5
Tapi, Mae Nam (riv.) C5
Terutao, Ko (isl.) C6
Tha Chin, Mae Nam (riv.) C4
Thale Luang (lag.) D6
Thalu, Ko (isls.) C5
Three Pagodas (pass) C4
Wang, Mae Nam (riv.) C3

VIETNAM

CITIES and TOWNS

An Loc (Binh Long) 15,276 E5
An Nhon F4
An Tuc (An Khe) F4
Ap Long Ha F5
Ap Vinh Hao F5
Bac Can E2
Bac Giang E2
Bac Lieu 53,841 E5
Bac Ninh 22,560 E2
Ba Don E3
Bai Thuong E3
Ban Me Thuot 68,771 F4
Bao Ha D2
Bao Lac E2
Bien Hoa 87,135 E5
Binh Long (An Loc) 15,276 E5
Binh Son F4
Bo Duc E4
Bong Son (Hoai Nhon) F4
Cam Ranh 118,111 F5
Can Tho 182,424 E5
Cao Bang E2
Cao Lanh 16,482 E5
Chau Phu 37,175 E5
Chu Lai F4
Con Cuong E3
Cua Rao E3
Da Lat 105,072 F5
Dam Doi E5
Da Nang 492,194 E3
Dien Bien Phu D2
Dong Hoi E3
Duong Dong D5
Gia Dinh E5
Go Cong 33,191 E5
Ha Giang E2
Haiphong* 1,279,067 E2
Hanoi (cap.)* 2,570,905 E2
Ha Tien E5
Ha Tinh E3
Hau Bon E4
Hoa Binh E2
Hoa Da F5
Hoai Nhon F4
Ho Chi Minh City (Saigon)* 3,419,678 E5
Hoi An 45,059 F4
Hoi Xuan E2
Hon Chong E5
Hon Gai 100,000 E2
Hue 209,043 E3
Huong Khe E3
Ke Bao E2
Khanh Hoa F4
Khanh Hung 59,015 E5
Khe Sanh E3
Kien Hung E5
Kontum 33,554 E4
Lac Giao (Ban Me Thuot) 68,771 E4
Lai Chau D2
Lang Son 15,071 E2
Lao Cai E2
Loc Ninh E5
Long Xuyen 72,658 E5
Mo Duc F4
Mong Cai E2
Muong Khuong E2
My Tho 119,892 E5
Nam Dinh E2
Nghia Lo D2
Nha Trang 216,227 F4
Ninh Binh E3
Phan Rang 33,377 F5
Phan Thiet 80,122 F5
Phu Cuong 28,267 E5
Phu Lang Thuong (Bac Giang) E2
Phuc Loi E3
Phu Dien E3
Phu Ly E2
Phu My F4
Phu Qui E3
Phu Rieng E5
Phu Tho 10,888 E2
Phu Vinh 48,485 E5
Pleiku 23,720 E4
Quang Nam E4
Quang Ngai 14,119 F4
Quang Tri 15,874 E3
Quang Yen E2
Quan Long 59,331 E5
Qui Nhon 213,757 F4
Rach Gia 104,161 E5
Ron E3
Sa Dec 51,867 E5
Saigon (Ho Chi Minh City)* 3,419,678 E5
Song Cau F4
Son Ha F4
Son La D2
Son Tay 19,213 E2
Tam Ky 38,532 F4
Tam Quan F4
Tan An 38,082 E5
Tay Ninh 22,957 E5
Thai Binh 14,739 E2
Thai Nguyen E2
Thanh Hoa 31,211 E3
Thanh Tri E5
That Khe E2
Tien Yen E2
Tra Vinh (Phu Vinh) 48,485 E5
Truc Giang 68,629 E5
Trung Khanh Phu E2
Tuyen Quang E2
Tuy Hoa 63,552 F4
Van Hoa E2
Van Ninh F4
Van Yen E2
Vinh 43,954 E3
Vinh Long 30,667 E5
Vinh Yen E2
Vu Liet E3
Vung Tau 108,436 E5
Xuan Loc
Yen Bai

OTHER FEATURES

Bach Long Vi, Dao (isl.)
Ba Den, Nui (mt.)
Bai Bung, Mui (Ca Mau) (pt.)
Black (riv.)
Ca Mau (Mui Bai Bung) (pt.)
Cam Ranh, Vinh (bay)
Cat Ba, Dao (isl.)
Chon May, Vung (bay)
Cu Lao, Hon (isls.)
Deux Frères, Les (isls.)
Dinh, Mui (cape)
Fan Si Pan (mt.)
Ia Drang (riv.)
Joncs (plain)
Kontum (plat.)
Khoai, Hon (isl.)
Lang Bian, Nui (mts.)
Lay, Mui (cape)
Mekong, Mouths of the (delta)
Nam Tram, Mui (cape)
Nightingale (Bach Long Vi) (isl.)
Panjang, Hon (Hon Tho Chau) (isl.)
Phu Quoc, Dao (isl.)
Rao Co (mt.)
Red (riv.)
Se San (riv.)
Sip Song Chau Thai (mts.)
Song Ba (riv.)
Song Ca (riv.)
Song Cai (riv.)
South China (sea)
Tonkin (gulf)
Varella, Mui (cape)
Wai, Poulo (isls.)
Yang Sin, Chu (mt.)

*See Southeast Asia, p. 84 for other part of Malaysia.

*City and suburbs.
⊙Population of district.

Burma, Thailand, Indochina and Malaya
CONIC PROJECTION
SCALE OF MILES
0 50 100 150 200
SCALE OF KILOMETERS
0 50 100 200 300
International Boundaries
Division and State Boundaries
Capitals of Countries
Division and State Capitals
Longitude East 96° of Greenwich
© Copyright HAMMOND INCORPORATED, Maplewood, N. J.
BHUTAN
INDIA
BANGLADESH
CHINA
BURMA
THAILAND
LAOS
VIETNAM
CAMBODIA
MALAYA
MALAYSIA
SUMATRA
INDONESIA
SINGAPORE
BAY OF BENGAL
ANDAMAN SEA
GULF OF THAILAND
GULF OF TONKIN
SOUTH CHINA SEA
Strait of Malacca
Tropic of Cancer
KACHIN STATE
SHAN STATE
SAGAING
MANDALAY
CHIN STATE
KAYAH STATE
KAREN STATE
IRRAWADDY
RANGOON
Mandalay
Rangoon
Moulmein
Bangkok (Krung Thep)
Vientiane (Viangchan)
Louangphrabang
Hanoi
Haiphong
Hue
Da Nang
Ho Chi Minh City (Saigon)
Phnom Penh
Kuala Lumpur
George Town
Kunming
Nanning
Hainan
Paracel Is.
North Andaman
Middle Andaman
South Andaman
Port Blair
ANDAMAN IS. (India)
NICOBAR IS. (India)
Car Nicobar
Great Nicobar
Isthmus of Kra
Mergui Arch.
Tenasserim
Plateau des Bolovens
Mouths of the Mekong
Mouths of the Irrawaddy
Anambas Is.
JOHOR
Johor Baharu
Singapore Str.
N

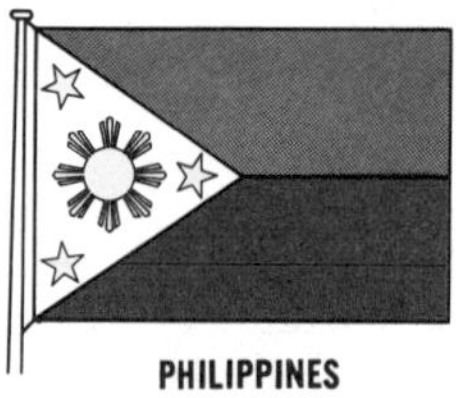

PHILIPPINES

AREA 115,707 sq. mi. (299,681 sq. km.)
POPULATION 47,914,017
CAPITAL Manila
LARGEST CITY Manila
HIGHEST POINT Apo 9,692 ft. (2,954 m.)
MONETARY UNIT piso
MAJOR LANGUAGES Pilipino (Tagalog), English, Spanish, Bisayan, Ilocano, Bikol
MAJOR RELIGIONS Roman Catholicism, Islam, Protestantism, tribal religions

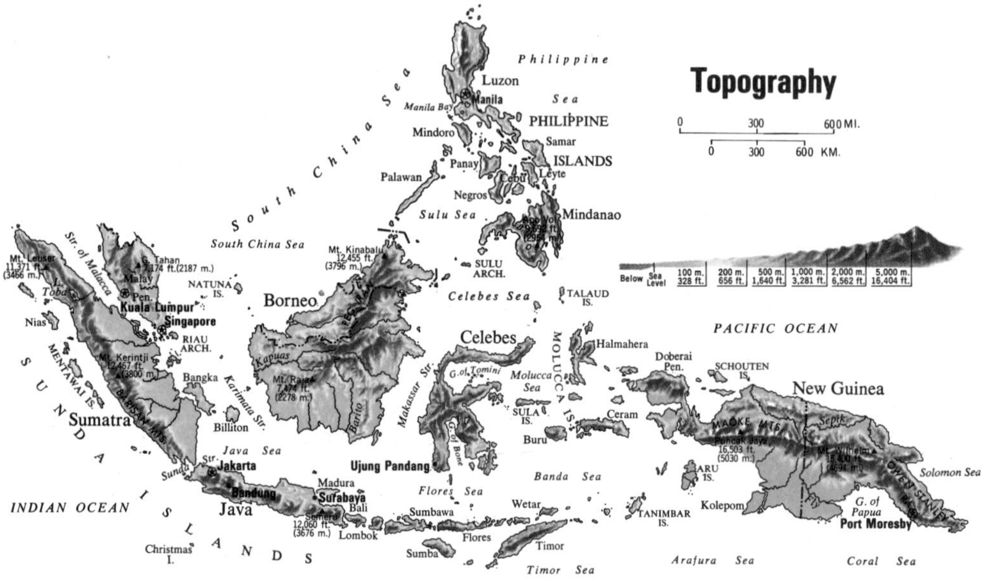

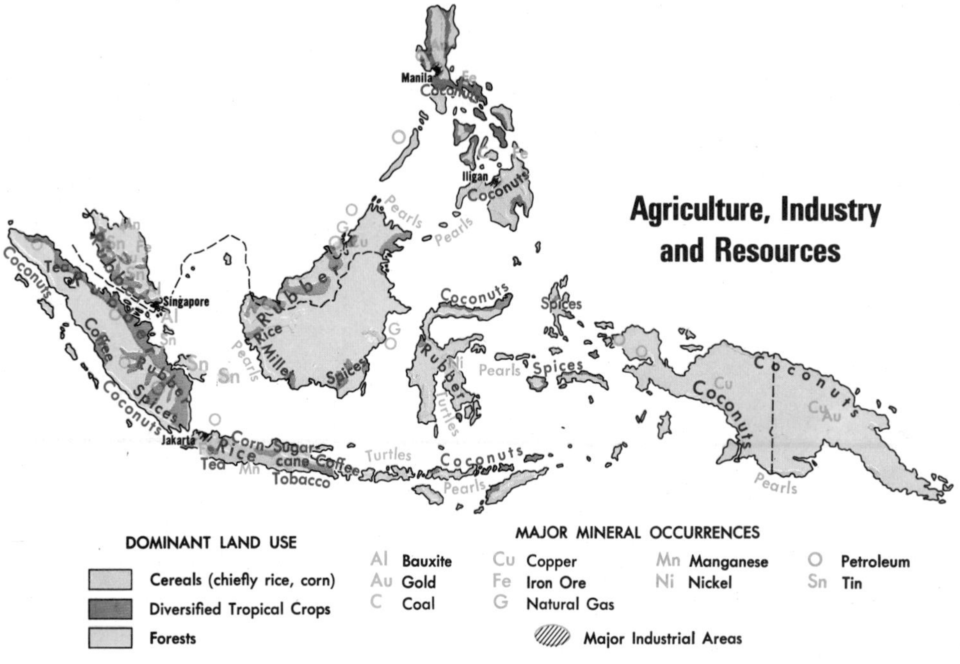

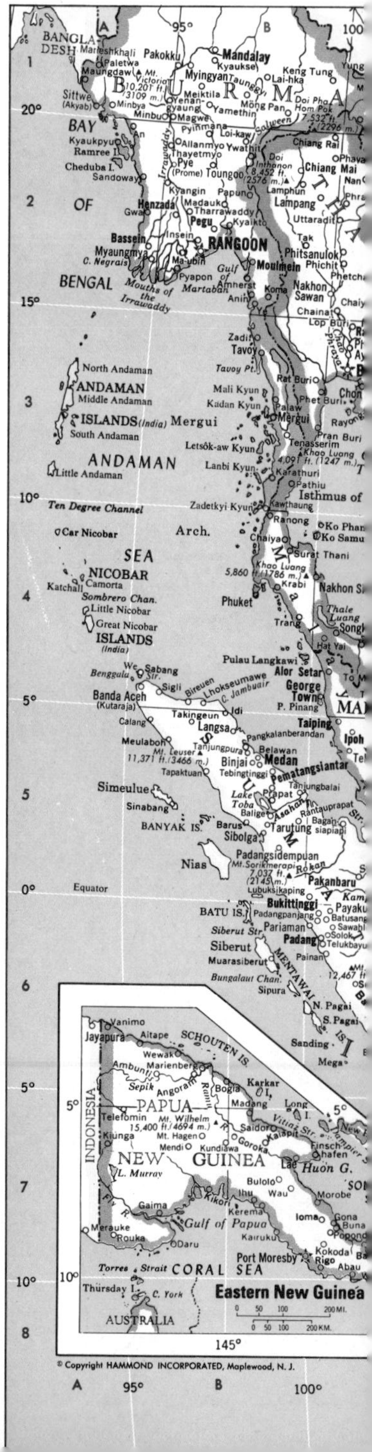

INDONESIA

AREA 788,430 sq. mi. (2,042,034 sq. km.)
POPULATION 147,383,075
CAPITAL Jakarta
LARGEST CITY Jakarta
HIGHEST POINT Puncak Jaya 16,503 ft. (5,030 m.)
MONETARY UNIT rupiah
MAJOR LANGUAGES Bahasa Indonesia, Indonesian and Papuan languages, English
MAJOR RELIGIONS Islam, tribal religions, Christianity, Hinduism

PAPUA NEW GUINEA

AREA 183,540 sq. mi. (475,369 sq. km.)
POPULATION 3,006,799
CAPITAL Port Moresby
LARGEST CITY Port Moresby
HIGHEST POINT Mt. Wilhelm 15,400 ft. (4,694 m.)
MONETARY UNIT kina
MAJOR LANGUAGES pidgin English, Hiri Motu, English
MAJOR RELIGIONS Tribal religions, Christianity

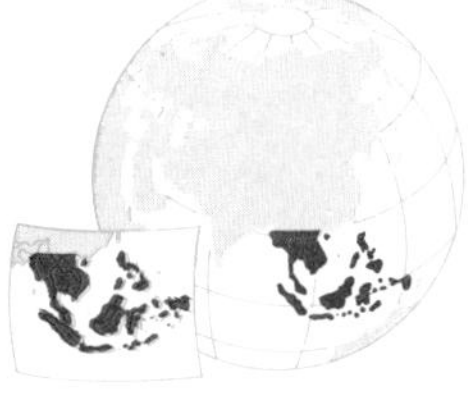

BRUNEI

AREA 2,226 sq. mi. (5,765 sq. km.)
POPULATION 212,840
CAPITAL Bandar Seri Begawan

84 Southeast Asia
(continued)

BRUNEI

CITIES and TOWNS

Bandar Seri Begawan 36,987 E4
Seria E5

CHINA

OTHER FEATURES

Amphitrite (isls.) E2
Crescent (isls.) E2
Duncan (isls.) E2
Lincoln (isl.) E2
Money (isl.) E2
Paracel (isls.) E2
Robert (isl.) E2
Triton (isl.) E2
Xisha (isls.) E2
Woody (isl.) E2

INDONESIA

CITIES and TOWNS

Agats K7
Ambon (Amboina) 79,636 H6
Amurang G5
Baa G8
Bagansiapiapi C5
Balikpapan 137,340 F6
Banda Aceh 53,668 A4
Bandanaira H6
Bandung 1,201,730 H2
Banggai G6
Bangil⊙ 49,438 K2
Bangkalan⊙ 41,639 K2
Banjarmasin 281,673 E6
Bantul⊙ 40,585 J2
Banyumas J2
Banyuwangi⊙ 76,596 L2
Barabai⊙ 33,688 F6
Barus⊙ 46,120 B5
Batang⊙ 69,577 J2
Batavia (Jakarta)
(cap.) 4,576,009 H1
Baturaja⊙ 48,350 C6
Bekasi⊙ 123,264 H2
Belawan B5
Bengkalis⊙ 14,072 C5
Bengkayang⊙ 15,404 E5
Bengkulu 31,866 C6
Beo H5
Biak K6
Binjai 59,882 B5
Bintuhan C6
Bitung⊙ 59,507 H5
Blitar 67,856 K2
Blora⊙ 67,853 K2
Bogor 195,882 H2
Bojonegoro⊙ 74,241 J2
Bondowoso⊙ 50,317 L2
Bonthain⊙ 30,377 F7
Brebes⊙ 87,918 H2
Bukittinggi 63,132 B6
Bula J6
Bulukumba⊙ 63,932 G7
Bumiayu⊙ 65,403 H2
Buntok F6
Ciamis⊙ 105,434 H2
Cianjur⊙ 132,058 H2
Cijulang⊙ 44,487 H2
Cilacap⊙ 118,815 H2
Cimahi⊙ 157,222 H2
Cirebon 178,529 H2
Curup⊙ 71,965 C6
Demak⊙ 57,676 J2
Demta L6
Denpasar⊙ 98,005 E7
Dili H7
Djakarta (Jakarta)
(cap.) 4,576,009 H1
Djambi (Jambi) 158,559 C6
Djokjakarta
(Yogyakarta) 342,267 J2
Dobo J7
Dompu⊙ 14,103 F7
Donggala F6
Fakfak J6
Galela⊙ 11,554 H5
Garut⊙ 93,340 H2
Gorontalo 82,320 G5
Gresik⊙ 48,561 K2
Hollandia (Jayapura)⊙
45,786 K6
Indramayu⊙ 69,441 H2
Jailolo⊙ 17,243 H5
Jakarta (cap.) 4,576,009 H1
Jambi 158,559 C6
Jayapura⊙ 45,786 L6
Jember⊙ 115,201 K2
Jeneponto⊙ 6,883 F7
Jepara⊙ 75,124 J2
Jogjakarta
(Yogyakarta) 342,267 J2
Jombang⊙ 80,643 K2
Kaimana J6
Kayuagung⊙
37,319 D6
Kalianda⊙ 42,609 D7
Kampung Baru
(Tolitoli)⊙ 10,071 G5
Karangasem⊙ 15,177 F7
Kebumen⊙ 81,571 J2
Kediri 178,865 K2
Kendal⊙ 32,544 J2
Kendari⊙ 28,628 G6
Kepi K7
Ketapang E6
Klaten⊙ 58,870 J2
Kokonau K6
Kolaka⊙ 10,384 G6
Kolonodale G6
Kotaagung⊙ 20,154 C7
Kotabaharu E6
Kotabaru⊙ 23,443 F6
Kotawaringin E6
Kragan⊙ 33,389 K2
Krawang⊙ 99,552 H2
Kudus⊙ 79,186 J2
Kumai⊙ 13,564 E6
Kuningan⊙ 105,255 H2
Kupang⊙ 49,354 G8
Kutaraja (Banda
Aceh) 53,668 A4
Kutoarjo⊙ 52,989 J2
Labuha H6
Labuhan⊙ 34,274 G2
Lahat⊙ 48,136 C6
Laiwui H6
Lamongan⊙ 38,897 K2
Langsa⊙ 58,060 B5
Larantuka G7
Lawang⊙ 59,071 K2
Lekitobi G6
Longiram F5
Lubuklinggau⊙ 43,011 C6
Lubuksikaping⊙ 24,244 B5
Lumajang⊙ 79,641 K2
Madiun 136,147 K2
Majalengka⊙ 80,999 H2
Magelang 110,308 J2
Magetan⊙ 59,507 K2
Makassar (Ujung
Pandang) 434,766 F7
Malang 422,428 K2
Malili G6
Malinau⊙ 14,130 F5
Mamuju⊙ 17,345 F6
Manado 169,684 G5
Manokwari J6
Martapura⊙ 55,011 F6
Masamba⊙ 16,571 G6
Mataram⊙ 46,846 F7
Maumere G7
Medan 635,562 B5
Menggala⊙ 20,878 D6
Merauke⊙ 21,366 K7
Mindiptana L7
Mojokerto 60,013 K2
Muarabungo⊙ 26,304 C6
Muarasiberut B6
Muntok⊙ 31,719 D6
Nangapinoh⊙ 19,983 E6
Negara⊙ 65,762 E7
Ngabang⊙ 33,190 D5
Pacitan⊙ 51,993 J2
Padang 196,339 B6
Padangpanjang 30,711 B6
Padangsidempuan⊙ 134,611 B5
Pakanbaru 145,030 C5
Palangkaraya 27,132 E6
Palaumerak⊙ 58,655 G1
Paleleh⊙ 7,603 G5
Palembang 582,961 D6
Pamangkat⊙ 62,402 D5
Pamekasan⊙ 55,409 L2
Pameungpeuk⊙ 41,449 H2
Panarukan⊙ 37,482 K2
Pandeglang⊙ 35,550 G1
Pangkalanberandan⊙ 60,299 B5
Pangkalanbuun E6
Pangkalpinang 74,733 D6
Pare⊙ 107,806 K2
Parepare 72,538 F6
Pariaman⊙ 44,428 B6
Pasangkayu F6
Pasuruan 75,266 K2
Pati⊙ 75,397 J2
Payakumbuh 63,388 C6
Pekalongan 111,537 J2
Pemalang⊙ 110,206 J2
Pematangsiantar 129,232 B5
Perabumulih⊙ 88,031 C6
Pinrang F6
Plaju D6
Ponorogo⊙ 58,321 J2
Pontianak 217,555 D6
Prapat⊙ 7,723 B5
Praya⊙ 89,266 F7
Probolinggo 82,008 K2
Purbolinggo⊙ 41,031 J2
Purwakarta⊙ 93,016 H2
Purwodadi⊙ 75,713 J2
Purwokerto⊙ 125,464 H2
Purworejo⊙ 28,663 J2
Putussibau⊙ 12,408 E5
Raha G6
Rangkasbitung⊙ 78,685 G2
Rantauprapat C5
Rembang⊙ 33,610 K2
Rengat⊙ 33,559 C6
Ruteng⊙ 12,294 G7
Sabang, Weh 17,625 B4
Salatiga 69,831 J2
Samarinda 137,521 F6
Sambas⊙ 48,253 D5
Sampang⊙ 60,136 K2
Sampit E6
Sanggau⊙ 7,040 E5
Sangkulirang⊙ 8,769 F5
Sarmi K6
Sawahlunto 12,427 C6
Seba G8
Semarang 646,590 J2
Semitau⊙ 7,165 E5
Serang⊙ 79,675 G1
Serui K6
Sibolga 42,223 B5
Sidoharjo⊙ 59,942 K2
Sigli⊙ 10,623 B4
Sinabang B5
Sindangbarang⊙ 70,603 D7
Singaraja F7
Singkawang⊙ 93,650 D5
Sintang⊙ 24,842 E5
Situbondo⊙ 36,094 L2
Solo (Surakarta) 414,285 J2
Solok 24,771 C6
Sorong⊙ 23,763 J6
Sragen⊙ 50,515 J2
Subang⊙ 35,077 H2
Sukabumi 96,242 H2
Sukadana⊙ 9,741 E6
Sumedang H2
Sumenep⊙ 46,659 L2
Surabaya 1,556,255 K2
Surakarta 414,285 J2
Tanahmerah K7
Tanjungbalai 33,604 C5
Tanjungkarang 198,986 C7
Tanjungpandan⊙ 61,225 D6
Tanjungpinang C5
Tanjungpriok⊙ 147,824 H1
Tanjungpura⊙ 30,992 B5
Tanjungselor F5
Tarakan⊙ 31,118 F5
Tasikmalaya⊙ 135,919 H2
Tebingtinggi 30,314 B5
Tegal 105,752 J2
Telukbayur C6
Temanggung⊙ 85,492 J2
Tenggarong⊙ 15,081 F6
Tepa H7
Terempa D5
Ternate⊙ 34,539 H5
Tjilatjap (Cilacap)⊙ 118,815 H2
Tjirebon (Cirebon) 178,529 H2
Tolitoli⊙ 10,071 G5
Tondano⊙ 35,978 H5
Trenggalek⊙ 49,065 K2
Tuban⊙ 54,212 K2
Tulungagung⊙ 53,880 K2
Turen⊙ 76,018 K2
Ujung Pandang 434,766 F7
Vila Arminda Monteiro H7
Vila Salazar H7
Viquique H7
Wahai H6
Wajabula H5
Weda H5
Wonogiri⊙ 56,435 J2
Wonosobo⊙ 47,650 J2
Wonreli H7
Yogyakarta 342,267 J2

OTHER FEATURES

Adi (isl.) J6
Adonara (isl.) G7
Alas (str.) F7
Alor (isl.) G7
Ambelau (isl.) H6
Anambas (isls.) D5
Arafura (sea) J8
Aru (isls.) K7
Asahan (riv.) B5
Asia (isls.) J5
Ayu (isls.) J5
Babar (isl.) H7
Babar (isls.) H7
Bacan (isls.) H6
Balabalagan (isls.) F6
Bali (isl.) F7
Bali (sea) F7
Bali (str.) E7
Banda (isls.) H6
Banda (sea) H7
Banggai (arch.) G6
Bangka (isl.) D6
Bangka (str.) C6
Banyak (isls.) B5
Barbar (isls.) J7
Barisan (mts.) C6
Barito (riv.) E6
Batu (isls.) B6
Bawean (isl.) K1
Belitung (Billiton) (isl.) D6
Benggala (str.) A4
Berau (bay) J6
Berhala (str.) C6
Biak (isl.) K6
Billiton (isl.) D6
Binongko (isl.) G7
Bintan (isl.) C5
Blackwood (Ngundju) (cape) F8
Boano (isl.) H6
Bone (gulf) G7
Borneo (isl.) E5
Bosch, van den (cape) J6
Bungalaut (chan.) B6
Bunguran (Great Natuna)
(isl.) D5
Bunguran (Natuna) (isls.) D5
Bunyu (isl.) F5
Buru (isl.) H6
Buru (sea) H6
Butung (isl.) G6
Celebes (Sulawesi) (isl.) G5
Celebes (sea) G5
Cenderawasih (bay) K6
Ceram (isl.) H6
Ciremay (mt.) H2
Damar (isl.) H7
Damar (isls.) H7
Dampier (str.) J6
Dempo (mt.) C6
Digul (riv.) K7
Doberai (pen.) J6
Enggano (isl.) C7
Ewab (Kai) (isls.) J7
Fatagar Tuting (cape) J6
Flores (isl.) G7
Flores (sea) F7
Frederik Hendrik (Kolepom)
(isl.) K7
Gebe (isl.) H6
Gede (mt.) H2
Geelvink (Cenderawasih)
(bay) K6
Gorong (isl.) J6
Gorong (isls.) J6
Great Kai (isl.) J7
Great Natuna (isl.) D5
Gunungapi (isl.) H7
Halmahera (isl.) H5
Halmahera (sea) H5
Hari (riv.) C6
Indian Ocean E8
Indramayu (pt.) H1
Irian Jaya (reg.) J6
Jambuair (cape) B4
Jamursba (cape) J5
Java (head) C7
Java (isl.) J2
Java (sea) D6
Jaya, Puncak (mt.) K6
Jayawijaya (range) K6
Jemaja (isl.) D5
Kabaena (isl.) G7
Kahayan (riv.) E6
Kai (isls.) J7
Kalao (isl.) G7
Kalaotoa (isl.) G5
Kalimantan (reg.) E5
Kampar (riv.) C5
Kangean (isl.) F7
Kangean (isls.) F7
Kapuas (riv.) D6
Karakelong (isl.) H5
Karimata (arch.) D6
Karimata (isl.) D6
Karimata (str.) D6
Karimunjawa (isls.) J1
Kawi (mt.) K2
Kawio (isls.) G5
Kayan (riv.) F5
Kelasa (str.) D6
Kengah (isls.) F7
Kerinci (mt.) C6
Kisar (isl.) H7
Kobroor (isl.) K7
Kolepom (isl.) K7
Komodo (isl.) F7
Komoran (isl.) K7
Krakatau (Rakata) (isl.) C7
Kur (isl.) J7
Lakor (isl.) H7
Larat (isl.) J7
Laurot (Laut Kecil)
(isls.) E7
Laut (isl.) F6
Laut (North Natuna) (isl.) D5
Laut Kecil (isls.) E7
Lawu (mt.) J2
Leti (isls.) H7
Leuser (mt.) B5
Lima (isls.) F7
Lingga (arch.) D5
Lingga (isl.) D6
Little Kai (isl.) J7
Liukang Tenggaja (isls.) F7
Lomblen (isl.) G7
Lombok (isl.) F7
Lombok (str.) E7
Macan (isls.) G7
Madura (isl.) K2
Madura (str.) K2
Maffin (bay) K6
Mahakam (riv.) F6
Makassar (str.) F6
Malacca (str.) C5
Malangka (cape) G5
Mamberamo (riv.) K6
Mandar (cape) F6
Mangkalihat (cape) F5
Mangole (il.) H6
Manipa (str.) H6
Manui (isl.) G6
Maoke (mts.) K6
Mapia (isls.) J5
Maras (mt.) D6
Maratua (isl.) F5
Masela (isl.) H7
Mega (isl.) C6
Mentawai (isls.) B6
Misool (isl.) J6
Moa (isl.) H7
Molucca (sea) H6
Moluccas (isls.) H6
Morotai (isl.) H5
Muli (str.) K7
Müller (mts.) E5
Muna (isl.) G7
Muryo (mt.) J2
Musi (riv.) C6
Natuna (isls.) D5
Ngunju (cape) F8
Nias (isl.) B5
Nila (isl.) H7
North Natuna (isl.) D4
North Pagai (isl.) C6
Numfoor (isl.) J6
Nusa Barung (isl.) K3
Obi (isl.) H6
Obi (isls.) H6
Ombai (str.) H7
Panaitan (isl.) C7
Pantar (isl.) G7
Patuha (mt.) H2
Pegun (isl.) J5
Pelabuhan Ratu (bay) G2
Peleng (isl.) G6
Pembuang (riv.) E6
Penyu (isls.) H7
Perkam (cape) K6
Pujut (pt.) G1
Puting, Borneo (cape) E6
Puting, Sumatra (cape) C7
Raja Ampat Group (isls.) H6
Rakata (isl.) C7
Rangasa (cape) F6
Rantekombola (mt.) F6
Raung (mt.) L2
Raya (mt.) E6
Rewataya (reef) F7
Riau (arch.) C5
Rokan (riv.) C5
Romang (isl.) H7
Roti (isl.) G8
Rupat (isl.) C5
Sabra (cape) J6
Salabangka (isls.) G6
Salawati (isl.) J6
Sandalwood (Sumba) (isl.) F7
Sanding (isl.) C6
Sangeang (isl.) F7
Sanggabuwana (mt.) G2
Sangihe (isl.) H5
Sangihe (isls.) G5
Saweba (cape) J6
Sawu (isl.) G8
Sawu (isls.) G8
Sawu (sea) G7
Schouten (isls.) K6
Schwaner (mts.) E6
Sebatik (isl.) F5
Sebuku (bay) F5
Selaru (isl.) J7
Selatan (cape) E6
Selayar (isl.) G7
Semeru (mt.) K2
Sera (isl.) J7
Serasan (isl.) D5
Sermata (isl.) H7
Serua (isl.) H7
Siak (riv.) C5
Siau (isl.) H5
Siberut (isl.) B6
Siberut (str.) B6
Simeulue (isl.) A5
Singkep (isl.) D6
Sipura (isl.) B6
Sisi (cape) F6
Slamet (mt.) J2
Solor (isl.) G7
Sopi (cape) H5
Sorikmerapi (mt.) B5
South China (sea) D4
South Natuna (isls.) D5
South Pagai (isl.) C6
Subi Besar (isl.) D5
Sudirman (range) K6
Sula (isls.) H6
Sulawesi (isl.) G6
Sumatra (isl.) B5
Sumba (isl.) F7
Sumba (str.) F7
Sumbawa (isl.) F7
Sumbing (mt.) J2
Sunda (str.) C7
Supiori (isl.) K6
Tahulandang (isl.) H5
Talaud (isls.) H5
Taliabu (isl.) G6
Tambelan (isls.) D5
Tanimbar (isls.) J7
Tariku (riv.) K6
Taritatu (riv.) K6
Tidore (isl.) H5
Tiger (Macan) (isls.) G7
Timor (reg.) H7
Timor (sea) H7
Toba (lake) B5
Togian (isls.) G6
Tolo (gulf) G6
Tomini (gulf) G6
Torawitan (cape) G5
Towuti (lake) G6
Trangan (isl.) J7
Tukangbesi (isls.) G7
Turtle (Penju) (isls.) H7
Vals (cape) K7
Vogelkop (Doberai) (pen.) J6
Waigeo (isl.) J5
Wakde (isl.) K6
Wangiwangi (isl.) G7
Watubela (isls.) J6
We (isl.) B4
Wetar (isl.) H7
Wokam (isl.) K7
Workai (isl.) K7
Wowoni (isl.) G6
Yamdena (isl.) J7
Yapen (isl.) K6
Yapen (str.) K6

MALAYSIA

STATES

North Borneo
(Sabah) 1,002,608 F3
Sabah 1,002,608 F4
Sarawak 1,294,753 E5

CITIES and TOWNS

Beaufort 2,709 F4
Bintulu 4,424 E5
Kabone E5
Kampong Sibuti E5
Keningau 2,037 F4
Kota Kinabalu 40,939 F4
Kuching 63,535 E5
Kudat 5,089 F4
Kupir 1,929 E5
Labuan 7,216 E4
Lahad Datu 5,169 F5
Lamag F4
Marudi 4,700 E5
Miri 35,702 E5
Mukah 1,717 E5
Papar 1,855 F4
Ranau 2,024 F4
Sandakan 42,413 F4
Semporna 3,371 F5
Serian 2,209 E5
Sibu 50,635 E5
Suai F5
Simanggang 8,445 E5
Tawau 24,247 F5
Weston F4

OTHER FEATURES

Balambangan (isl.) F4
Banggi (isl.) F4
Barut, Tanjong (cape) E5
Borneo (isl.) E5
Iran (mts.) E5
Kinabalu (mt.) F4
Labuan (isl.) E4
Labuk (bay) F4
Malay (pen.) B4
Rajang (riv.) E5
Sebatik (isl.) F5
Sirik (cape) E5
South China (sea) D4

PAPUA NEW GUINEA

CITIES and TOWNS

Abau C7
Aitape 3,366 B6
Ambunti○ 989 B6
Angoram 1,830 B6
Baniara C7
Bogia○ 678 B6
Bulolo 6,801 B7
Buna C7
Daru 7,149 B7
Finschhafen C7
Gaima B7
Gehua C8
Gona C7
Goroka 18,797 B7
Ioma C7
Kairuku B7
Kerema 3,354 B7
Kikori 670 B7
Kiunga○ 1,113 B7
Kokoda C7
Kundiawa 4,298 B7
Lae 61,682 B7
Madang 21,332 B7
Mendi 4,131 B7
Morobe C7
Mount Hagen 13,642 B7
Popondetta 6,343 C7
Port Moresby (cap.)
122,761 B7
Rigo C7
Saidor B7
Samarai○ 1,948 C8
Tufi C7
Vanimo 3,051 B6
Wau 2,374 B7
Wewak 19,554 B6

OTHER FEATURES

Coral (sea) B7
Dampier (str.) C7
D'Entrecasteaux (isls.) C7
Fly (riv.) A7
Huon (gulf) C7
Karkar (isl.) B6
Kiriwina (isl.) C7
Long (isl.) B7
Louisiade (arch.) D8
Milne (bay) C8
Misima (isl.) C8
Murray (lake) B7
New Britain (isl.) C7
Ramu (riv.) B7
Rossel (isl.) D8
Schouten (isls.) B6
Sepik (riv.) B6
Solomon (sea) C7
Tagula (isl.) C8
Torres (str.) A7
Trobriand (isls.) C7
Vitiaz (str.) B7
Wilhelm (mt.) B7
Woodlark (isl.) C7

PHILIPPINES

CITIES and TOWNS

Aparri 14,597 G
Bacolod 266,604 G
Baguio 118,611 G
Bangued 10,482 G
Bangui 2,085 G
Batangas 143,554 G
Baybay 11,989 H
Bayombong 11,697 G
Bislig 26,625 H
Bontoc 3,336 G
Butuan 172,404 H
Cabanatuan 138,297 G
Cagayan de Oro 228,409 G
Calapan 11,376 G
Catbalogan 18,413 H
Cateel 2,736 H
Cavite 87,813 G
Cebu 489,208 G
Cotabato 88,486 G
Daet 23,739 G
Davao 611,311 H
Dumaguete 63,411 G
Glan 5,837 G
Iba 4,486 F
Iloilo 244,211 G
Laoag 69,648 F
Legazpi 100,488 G
Lingayen 15,333 F
Lucena 107,872 G
Manila (cap.) 1,626,249 G
Marawi 53,198 G
Mati 16,186 H
Mondragon⊙ 4,941 H
Naga 90,712 G
Oroquieta 47,176 G
Palanan⊙ 7,518 G
Puerto Princesa 59,347 F
Roxas 81,183 G
San Jose 10,388 G
Siocon (Siokun) 3,023 G
Sorsogon 19,008 G
Surigao 78,235 H
Tacloban 102,609 H
Tarlac 23,547 G
Tay Tay 1,241 G
Tuguegarao 14,116 G
Vigan 30,252 F
Zamboanga 344,275 G

OTHER FEATURES

Babuyan (isls.) G
Balabac (isl.) F
Balabac (str.) F
Basilan (isl.) G
Batan (isls.) G
Bohol (isl.) G
Bugsuk (isl.) F
Buliluyan (cape) F
Busuanga (isl.) F
Cagayan (isls.) F
Cagayan Sulu (isl.) F
Calamian Group
(isls.) F
Catanduanes (isl.) H
Cebu (isl.) G
Cuyo (isls.) G
Davao (gulf) H
Dinagat (isl.) H
Dumaran (isl.) G
Espiritu Santo (cape) H
Jolo (isl.) G
Leyte (isl.) H
Lubang (isls.) F
Luzon (isl.) G
Masbate (isl.) G
Matutum (mt.) [illegible]
Mindanao (isl.) H
Mindanao (sea) G
Mindoro (isl.) G
Mindoro (str.) F
Moro (gulf) G
Negros (isl.) G
Olutanga (isl.) G
Palawan (isl.) F
Palawan (passage) F
Panay (isl.) G
Pangutaran Group
(isls.) G
Philippine (sea) G
Polillo (isl.) G
Samar (isl.) H
San Agustin (cape) H
San Miguel (isls.) F
Sarangani (isls.) G
Siargao (isl.) H
Sibutu (passage) F
Sibuyan (isl.) G
Sibuyan (sea) G
South China (sea) D
Sulu (arch.) G
Sulu (sea) G
Tagolo (pt.) G
Tapul Group (isls.) G
Tawitawi Group
(isls.) G
Tinaca (pt.) H
Tubbataha (reefs) G
Visayan (sea) G

*City and suburbs.
⊙Population of district.
○Population of sub-district or divisi

AUSTRALIA

REA 2,966,136 sq. mi. (7,682,300 sq. km.)
OPULATION 13,548,448
APITAL Canberra
ARGEST CITY Sydney
IGHEST POINT Mt. Kosciusko 7,310 ft. (2,228 m.)
OWEST POINT Lake Eyre -39 ft. (-12 m.)
ONETARY UNIT Australian dollar
AJOR LANGUAGE English
AJOR RELIGIONS Protestantism, Roman Catholicism

NEW ZEALAND

AREA 103,736 sq. mi. (268,676 sq. km.)
POPULATION 3,167,357
CAPITAL Wellington
LARGEST CITY Auckland
HIGHEST POINT Mt. Cook 12,349 ft. (3,764 m.)
MONETARY UNIT New Zealand dollar
MAJOR LANGUAGES English, Maori
MAJOR RELIGIONS Protestantism, Roman Catholicism

AUSTRALIA   NEW ZEALAND

AUSTRALIA

STATES and TERRITORIES

more and Cartier Is., Terr. ..C2
tralian Capital Territory 203,300 ....H7
al Sea Islands Territory H2
v South Wales 4,914,300 ...H6
folk Island 2,180 ....L5
thern Territory 97,090 ....E3
eensland 2,111,700 ....G4
ith Australia 1,261,600 ....F6
mania 402,866 ....H8
toria 3,746,000 ....G7
stern Australia 1,169,800 ...B5

CITIES and TOWNS

elaide (cap.), S. Aust. 857,196 ....D8
any, W. Aust. 12,616 ....B6
ury, N.S.W. 31,954 ....H7
e Springs, N. Terr. 14,149 ....E4
na, Vic. 30,272 ....J3
rat, Vic. 8,288 ....G7
nidale, N.S.W. 19,711 ....J6
nfield, N.S.W. 42,322 ....K4
urn, N.S.W. 47,556 ....K4
, Queens. 8,606 ....H3
nsdale, Vic. 9,130 ....H7
larat, Vic. 37,863 ....G7
nkstown, N.S.W. 155,843 ...K4
hurst, N.S.W. 18,589 ....H6
ja, N.S.W. 4,253 ....J7
ndigo, Vic. 32,573 ....G7
ckall, Queens. 1,618 ....H4
Blacktown, N.S.W. 159,734 ....K4
Blue Mountains, N.S.W. 45,798 ....J6
Bordertown, S. Aust. 1,983 ....F7
Botany, N.S.W. 35,739 ....L4
Boulder, W. Aust. 19,041 ....C6
Bourke, N.S.W. 3,534 ....H6
Bowen, Queens. 6,707 ....H3
Box Hill, Vic. 50,280 ....K2
Brighton, S. Aust. 21,407 ....D8
Brighton, Vic. 35,783 ....K3
Brisbane (cap.), Queens. 696,740 ....K3
Brisbane Water, N.S.W. 54,819 ....J6
Broadmeadows, Vic. 108,744 ..J2
Broken Hill, N.S.W. 27,647 ....G6
Broome, W. Aust. 2,920 ....C3
Brunswick, Vic. 46,192 ....K2
Bunbury, W. Aust. 19,513 ....B6
Bundaberg, Queens. 31,189 ....J4
Burnie-Somerset, Tas. 19,465 ....H8
Burnside, S. Aust. 38,461 ....E8
Burwood, N.S.W. 29,045 ....K4
Busselton, W. Aust. 5,550 ....A6
Cairns, Queens. 39,305 ....H3
Camberwell, Vic. 89,865 ....K2
Campbelltown, S. Aust. 41,252 ....E8
Canberra (cap.), A.C.T.‡ 197,622 ....H7
Canterbury, N.S.W. 128,710 ...K4
Carnarvon, W. Aust. 5,341 ....A4
Casino, N.S.W. 9,456 ....J5
Caulfield, Vic. 73,630 ....K2
Ceduna, S. Aust. 2,327 ....E6
Cessnock-Bellbird, N.S.W. 16,256 ....J6
Charleville, Queens. 3,802 ....H5
Charters Towers, Queens. 7,914 ....H4
Chelsea, Vic. 26,357 ....K3
Clermont, Queens. 1,644 ....H4
Cloncurry, Queens. 2,079 ....G4
Cobar, N.S.W. 3,339 ....H6
Coburg, Vic. 58,379 ....K2
Coffs Harbour, N.S.W. 12,197 ....J6
Collie, W. Aust. 7,540 ....B6
Collinsville, Queens. 2,403 ....H4
Concord, N.S.W. 24,598 ....K4
Condobolin, N.S.W. 3,273 ....H6
Coober Pedy, S. Aust. 1,903 ...E5
Cooma, N.S.W. 7,353 ....H7
Coonamble, N.S.W. 3,054 ....H6
Cootamundra, N.S.W. 6,384 ...H6
Cowra, N.S.W. 7,734 ....H6
Croydon, Vic. 5,162 ....L2
Cunnamulla, Queens. 1,897 ....H5
Dalby, Queens. 8,997 ....J5
Dandenong, Vic. 48,444 ....L3
Darwin (cap.), N. Terr. 39,193 ....E2
Deniliquin, N.S.W. 6,865 ....G7
Derby, W. Aust. 2,411 ....C3
Devonport, Tas. 19,399 ....H8
Doncaster and templestowe, Vic. 82,090 ....K2
Drummoyne, N.S.W. 31,516 ...K4
Dubbo, N.S.W. 20,149 ....H6
Echuca, Vic. 7,873 ....G7
Elizabeth, S. Aust. 33,721 ....E7
Eltham, Vic. 28,631 ....K2
Enfield, S. Aust. 73,505 ....D7
Esperance, W. Aust. 5,262 ....C6
Essendon, Vic. 51,133 ....J2
Fairfield, N.S.W. 114,603 ....K4
Footscray, Vic. 51,774 ....J2
Forbes, N.S.W. 7,754 ....H6
Fremantle, W. Aust. 23,497 ....B6
Gawler, S. Aust. 8,596 ....F6
Geelong, Vic. 15,727 ....G7
Geraldton, W. Aust. 18,773 ....A5
Gladstone, Queens. 18,591 ....J4
Glen Innes, N.S.W. 5,953 ....J5
Glenorchy, Tas. 42,437 ....H8
Gold Coast, Queens. 87,510 ....J5
Goondiwindi, Queens. 3,741 ...H5
Goulburn, N.S.W. 21,735 ....J6
Grafton, N.S.W. 16,516 ....J5
Griffith, N. S. 11,930 ....H6
Gunnedah, N.S.W. 8,689 ....H6
Gympie, Queens. 11,205 ....J5
Hamilton, Vic. 9,504 ....G7
Hawthorne, Vic. 32,505 ....K2
Hay, N.S.W. 2,872 ....H6
Heidelberg, Vic. 66,108 ....K2
Hindmarsh, S. Aust. 8,691 ....D8
Hobart (cap.), Tas. 50,384 ....H8
Holyroyd, N.S.W. 79,867 ....K4
Home Hill, Queens. 3,330 ....H3
Hornsby, N.S.W. 104,110 ....K3
Horsham, Vic. 11,647 ....G7
Hughenden, Queens. 1,811 ....G4
Hurstville, N.S.W. 66,450 ....K4
Ingham, Queens. 5,868 ....H3
Innisfail, Queens. 7,933 ....H3
Inverell, N.S.W. 9,432 ....J5
Kadina, S. Aust. 2,849 ....F6
Kalgoorlie, W. Aust. 9,067 ....C6
Katanning, W. Aust. 4,162 ....B6
Katherine, N. Terr. 3,127 ....E2
Keilor, Vic. 20,597 ....J2
Kempsey, N.S.W. 8,881 ....J6
Kensington and Norwood, S. Aust. 13,476 ....E8
Kew, Vic. 29,683 ....K2
Kingaroy, Queens. 5,088 ....J5
Knox, Vic. 74,456 ....L2
Kogarah, N.S.W. 46,721 ....K4
Kwinana-Newtown, W. Aust. 10,981 ....B2
Lane Cove, N.S.W. 29,341 ....L4
Launceston, Tas. 32,953 ....H8
Leichhardt, N.S.W. 62,520 ....L4
Lismore, N.S.W. 22,082 ....J5
Lithgow, N.S.W. 12,703 ....J6
Liverpool, N.S.W. 89,682 ....K4
Longreach, Queens. 3,354 ....G4
Mackay, Queens. 31,522 ....H4
Maitland, N.S.W. 36,030 ....J6
Malvern, Vic. 45,566 ....K2
Mandurah, W. Aust. 7,050 ....B3
Mareeba, Queens. 5,776 ....G3
Marion, S. Aust. 67,283 ....D8
Maroochydore-Mooloolaba, Queens. 10,283 ....J5
Marrickville, N.S.W. 87,821 ....L4
Maryborough, Queens. 21,521 J5
Maryborough, Vic. 7,569 ....G7
Melbourne (cap.), Vic. 64,970 ....K2
Merredin, W. Aust. 3,661 ....B6
Mildura, Vic. 14,417 ....G6
Mitcham, S. Aust. 59,887 ....D8
Moorabbin, Vic. 103,059 ....K3
Mordialloc, Vic. 28,615 ....K3
Moree, N.S.W. 9,359 ....H5
Mossman, Queens. 1,598 ....G3
Mount Gambier, S. Aust. 17,858 ....G7
Mount Isa, Queens. 25,377 ....F4
Mount Morgan, Queens. 3,246 J4
Mudgee, N.S.W. 5,724 ....J6
Murray Bridge, S. Aust. 7,476 ....F7
Murwillumbah, N.S.W. 7,294 ..J5
Muswellbrook, N.S.W. 7,805 ..J6
Naracoorte, S. Aust. 4,571 ....F7
Narrabri, N.S.W. 6,951 ....J6
Narrandera, N.S.W. 4,984 ....H6
Narrogin, W. Aust. 4,812 ....B6
Narromine, N.S.W. 2,802 ....H6
Nedlands, W. Aust. 20,974 ....B2
Newcastle, N.S.W. 138,718 ....J6
New Norfolk, Tas. 6,679 ....H8
Northam, W. Aust. 6,866 ....B6
Northcote, Vic. 54,881 ....K2
North Sydney, N.S.W. 48,536 .L4
Nowra-Bomaderry, N.S.W. 15,496 ....J6
Nunawading, Vic. 94,325 ....K2
Nyngan, N.S.W. 2,359 ....H6
Oakleigh, Vic. 54,532 ....K2
Orange, N.S.W. 26,254 ....H6
Orbost, Vic. 2,789 ....H7
Parkes, N.S.W. 8,905 ....H6
Parramatta, N.S.W. 131,659 ...K4
Penrith, N.S.W. 79,043 ....J6
Perth (cap.), W. Aust. 87,598 ....B2
Peterborough, S. Aust. 2,760 ....F6
Port Adelaide, S. Aust. 36,024 ....D7
Port Augusta, S. Aust. 13,092 ....F6
Port Hedland, W. Aust. 11,144 ....B3
Portland, Vic. 6,368 ....G7
Port Lincoln, S. Aust. 9,809 ....E6
Port Melbourne, Vic. 9,356 ....K2
Port Macquarie, N.S.W. 13,362 ....J6
Port Pirie, S. Aust. 15,005 ....F6
Prahan, Vic. 48,462 ....K2
Preston, Vic. 88,384 ....K2
Proserpine, Queens. 3,012 ....H4
Queenstown, Tas. 4,520 ....H8
Randwick, N.S.W. 119,500 ....L4
Red Cliffe, Queens. 39,073 ....J5
Renmark, S. Aust. 6,247 ....G6
Richmond, Vic. 26,179 ....K2
Ringwood, Vic. 37,085 ....K2
Rockdale, N.S.W. 83,797 ....K4
Rockhampton, Queens. 50,132 H4
Rockingham, W. Aust. 17,693 .B2
Roma, Queens. 5,898 ....H5
Ryde, N.S.W. 89,137 ....K4
Saint George, Queens. 2,095 ...H5
Saint Kilda, Vic. 52,154 ....K2
Sale, Vic. 12,111 ....H7
Salisbury, S. Aust. 77,477 ....E7
Sandringham, Vic. 32,698 ....K3
Sarina, Queens. 2,832 ....H4
Seymour, Vic. 6,240 ....H7
Shepparton, Vic. 25,848 ....G7
South Sydney, N.S.W. 33,145 .L4
Springvale, Vic. 72,474 ....K3
Stanthorpe, Queens. 3,927 ....J5
Stirling, W. Aust. 162,313 ....B2
Strathfield, N.S.W. 26,301 ....K4
Sunshine, Vic. 88,167 ....J2
Sutherland, N.S.W. 156,754 ...K5
Swan Hill, Vic. 7,857 ....G7
Sydney (cap.), N.S.W. 2,765,040 ....L4
Tamworth, N.S.W. 27,231 ....J6
Taree, N.S.W. 13,440 ....J6
Tea Tree Gully, S. Aust. 56,050 ....E7
Temora, N.S.W. 4,324 ....H6
Tennant Creek, N. Terr. 2,236 ....E3
Tenterfield, N.S.W. 3,563 ....J5
Thursday Island, Queens. 2,336 ....G2
Toowoomba, Queens. 63,956 ..J5
Townsville, Queens. 78,653 ....H3
Tully, Queens. 2,793 ....H3
Tumut, N.S.W. 5,569 ....H7
Unley, S. Aust. 37,016 ....D8
Victor Harbor, S. Aust. 4,279 ....F7
Wagga Wagga, N.S.W. 32,984 H7
Wagin, W. Aust. 1,658 ....B6
Walgett, N.S.W. 2,253 ....H6
Wangaratta, Vic. 16,157 ....H7
Warren, N.S.W. 2,077 ....H6
Warrnambool, Vic. 20,195 ....G7
Warwick, Queens. 9,169 ....J5
Waverley, N.S.W. 61,693 ....L4
Waverley, Vic. 117,144 ....K2
Werribee, Vic. 31,790 ....G7
West Torrens, S. Aust. 47,992 ....D8
Williamstown, Vic. 26,348 ....J2
Willoughby, N.S.W. 51,541 ....K3
Wollongong, N.S.W. 197,127 .J6
Wonthaggi, Vic. 4,021 ....G7
Woodville, S. Aust. 75,276 ....D7
Woollahra, N.S.W. 53,259 ....L4
Woomera, S. Aust. 2,958 ....F6
Wynyard, Tas. 4,348 ....H8
Young, N.S.W. 6,459 ....H6

OTHER FEATURES

Adele (isl.), W. Aust. C3
Admiralty (gulf), W. Aust. D2
Albatross (bay), Queens. G2
Alberga, The (riv.), S. Aust. E5
Altona (bay), Vic. J3
Amadeus (lake), N. Terr. E4
Anson (bay), N. Terr. D2
Arafura (sea) E2

(continued on following page)

DOMINANT LAND USE

- Cereals (chiefly wheat), Livestock
- Dairy, Truck Farming
- Cash Crops, Horticulture, Fruit
- Pasture Livestock
- Range Livestock
- Forests
- Nonagricultural Land

Agriculture, Industry and Resources

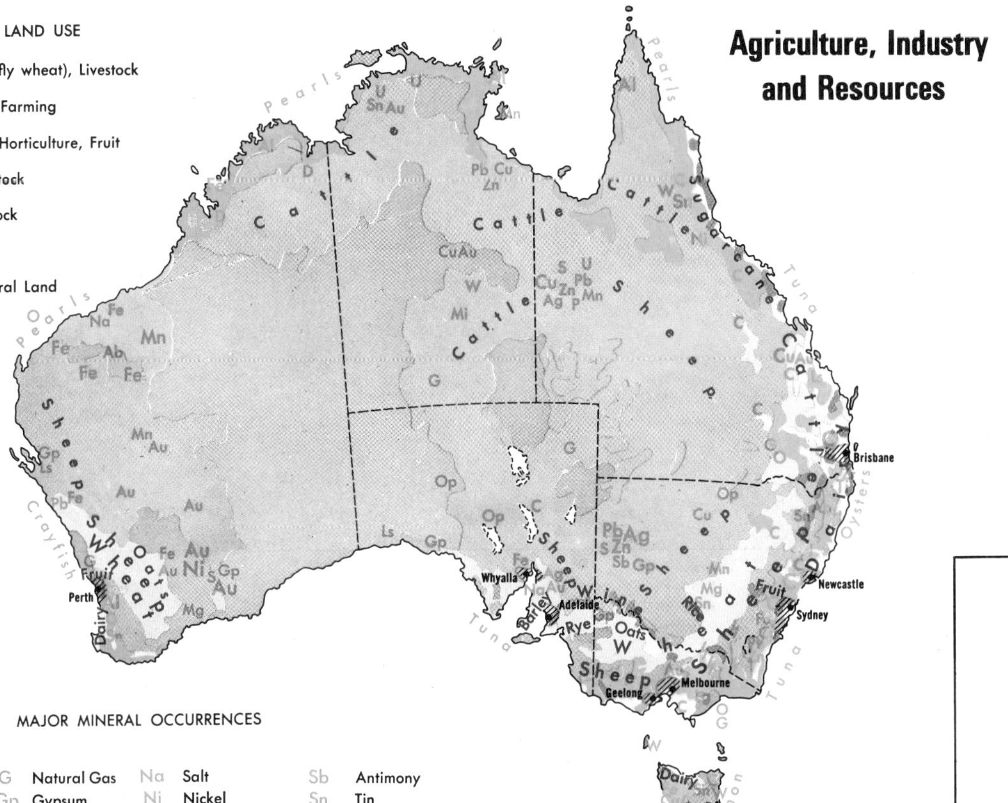

MAJOR MINERAL OCCURRENCES

	Asbestos	G	Natural Gas	Na	Salt	Sb	Antimony
	Silver	Gp	Gypsum	Ni	Nickel	Sn	Tin
	Bauxite	Lg	Lignite	O	Petroleum	Ti	Titanium
	Gold	Ls	Limestone	Op	Opals	U	Uranium
	Coal	Mg	Magnesium	P	Phosphates	W	Tungsten
	Copper	Mi	Mica	Pb	Lead	Zn	Zinc
	Diamonds	Mn	Manganese	S	Sulfur, Pyrites	Zr	Zirconium
	Iron Ore						

Water Power
Major Industrial Areas

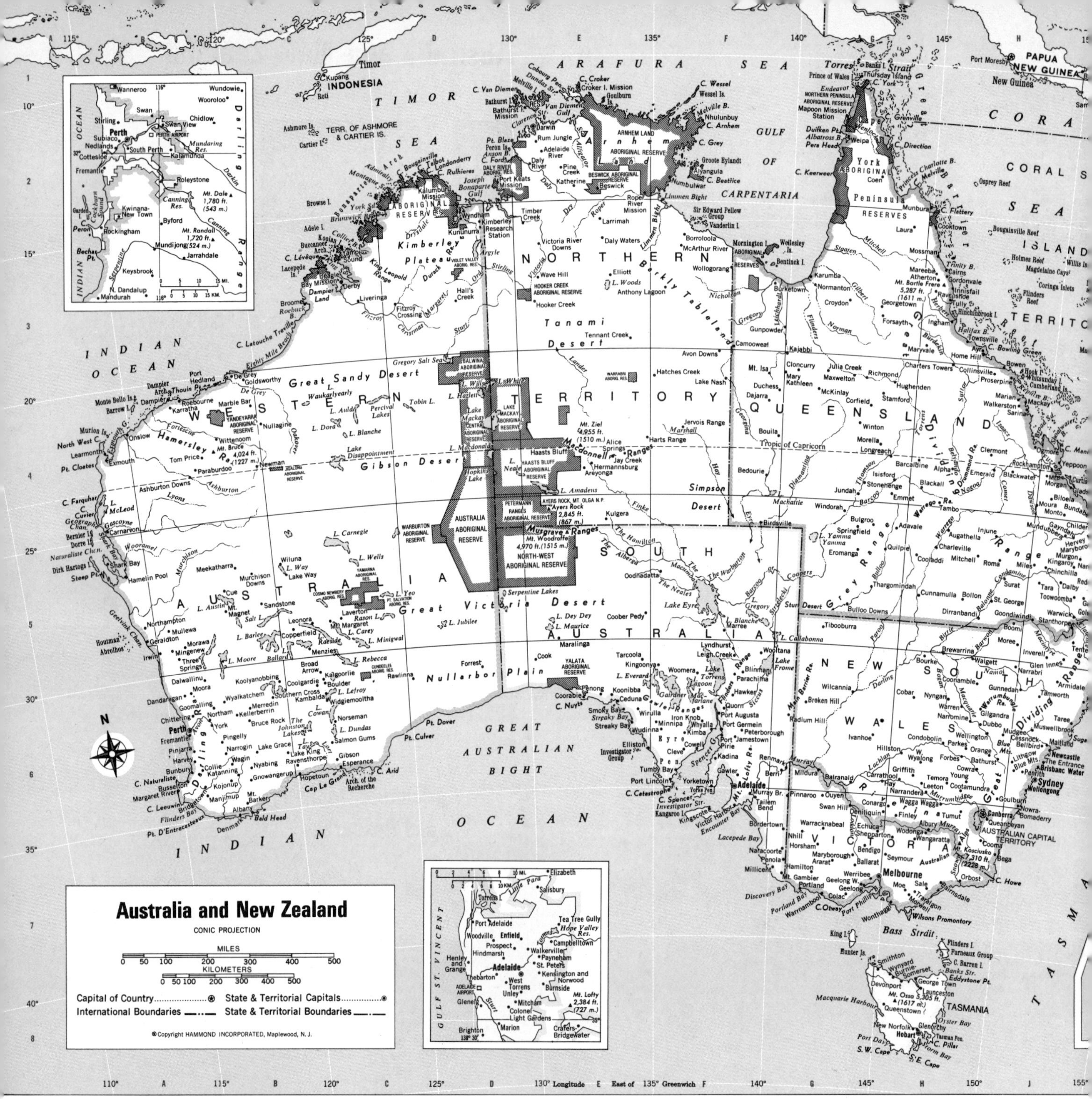
Australia and New Zealand
CONIC PROJECTION
MILES
0 50 100 200 300 400 500
KILOMETERS
0 50 100 200 300 400 500
Capital of Country
State & Territorial Capitals
International Boundaries
State & Territorial Boundaries
©Copyright HAMMOND INCORPORATED, Maplewood, N. J.
110° A 115° B 120° C 125° D 130° Longitude E East of 135° Greenwich F 140° G 145° H 150° J 155°

Arid (cape), W. Aust. C6
Arnhem (cape), N. Terr. F2
Arnhem Land (reg.), N. Terr. 4,563 E2
Ashburton (riv.), W. Aust. B4
Australian Alps (mts.), Vic. H7
Avon (riv.), W. Aust. B6
Ayers Rock (mt.), N. Terr. E5
Bald (head), W. Aust. B7
Balonne (riv.), Queens. H5
Banks (str.), Tas. H8
Barcoo (creek), S. Aust. F5
Barkly Tableland, N. Terr. F3
Barlee (lake), W. Aust. B5
Barrow (isl.), W. Aust. A4
Barwon (riv.) H5
Bass (str.) H7
Bathurst (isl.), N. Terr. D2
Beatrice (cape), N. Terr. F2
Bentinck (isl.), Queens. F3
Blanche (lake), S. Aust. F5
Blue (mts.), N.S.W. H6
Botany (bay), N.S.W. L4
Bougainville (cape), W. Aust. D2
Bougainville (reef), Coral Sea Is. Terr. H3
Bowling Green (cape), Queens. H3
Broad (sound), Queens. H4
Bruce (mt.), W. Aust. B4
Brunswick (bay), W. Aust. C3
Buccaneer (arch.), W. Aust. C3
Bulloo (riv.), Queens. G5
Burdekin (riv.), Queens. H3
Cape Barren (isl.), Tas. H8
Capricorn Group (isls.), Queens. J4
Carey (lake), W. Aust. C5
Carnegie (lake), W. Aust. C5
Carpentaria (gulf) F2
Cartier (isl.) C2
Clarence (str.), N. Terr. E2
Cobourg (pen.), N. Terr. E2
Collier (bay), W. Aust. C3
Comet (riv.), Queens. H4
Coopers (Barcoo) (creek), S. Aust. G5
Coral (sea) H2
Coringa (isls.), Coral Sea Is. Terr. H3
Cowan (lake), W. Aust. C6
Croker (cape), N. Terr. E2
Dale (mt.), W. Aust. B2
Daly (riv.), N. Terr. E2
Dampier (arch.), W. Aust. B4
Dampier Land (reg.), W. Aust. C3
Darkin (riv.), W. Aust. B2
Darling (range), W. Aust. B6
Darling (riv.), N.S.W. G6
Dawson (riv.), Queens. H4
De Grey (riv.), W. Aust. C4
D'Entrecasteaux (pt.), W. Aust. B7
Diamantina (riv.), Queens. G4
Direction (cape), Queens. G2
Dirk Hartogs (isl.), W. Aust. A5
Disappointment (lake), W. Aust. C4
Discovery (bay) E7
Dorre (isl.), W. Aust. A5
Dover (pt.), W. Aust. D6
Drysdale (riv.), W. Aust. D3
Duifken (pt.), Queens. G2
Dundas (str.), N. Terr. E2
Durack (range), W. Aust. D3
Eddystone (pt.), Tas. H8
Encounter (bay), S. Aust. F7
Endeavor (str.), Queens. G2
Everard (lake), S. Aust. E6
Exmouth (gulf), W. Aust. A4
Eyre (lake), S. Aust. F5
Eyre (pen.), S. Aust. F6
Fitzroy (riv.), Queens. J4
Fitzroy (riv.), W. Aust. C3
Flattery (cape), Queens. H2
Flinders (bay), W. Aust. oa6
Flinders (isl.), Tas. H7
Flinders (range), S. Aust. F6
Flinders (riv.), Queens. G3
Ford (cape), N. Terr. D2
Fortescue (riv.), W. Aust. B4
Fraser (isl.), Queens. J4
Frome (lake), S. Aust. G6
Furneaux Group (isls.), Tas. H8
Gairdner (lake), S. Aust. F6
Garden (isl.), W. Aust. A2
Gascoyne (riv.), W. Aust. A4
Gawler (ranges), S. Aust. F6
Geelvink (chan.), W. Aust. A5
Geographe (chan.), W. Aust. A4
Georges (riv.), N.S.W. K4
Georgina (riv.), Queens. F4
Gibson (des.), W. Aust. C4
Gilbert (riv.), Queens. G3
Goulburn (isls.), N. Terr. E2
Great Australian (bight) D6
Great Barrier (reef) H2
Great Dividing (range), N.S.W. J6
Great Sandy (des.), W. Aust. C4
Great Sandy (Fraser) (isl.), Queens. J5
Great Victoria (des.) D5
Gregory (lake), S. Aust. F5
Gregory (riv.), Queens. F3
Grenville (cape), Queens. G2
Groote (isl.), N. Terr. F2
Hamersley (range), W. Aust. B4
Hay (dry riv.), N. Terr. F4
Hervey (bay), Queens. J4
Hinchinbrook (isl.), Queens. H3
Holmes (reef), Coral Sea Is. Terr. H3
Hook (isl.), Queens. H4
Hope Valley (res.), S. Aust. E7
Houtman Abrolhos (isls.), W. Aust. A5
Howe (cape) J7
Investigator (str.), S. Aust. F7
Isaacs (riv.), Queens. H4
Joseph Bonaparte (gulf) D2
Kangaroo (isl.), S. Aust. 3,156 F7
Kimberley (plat.), W. Aust. D3
King (isl.), Tas. G7
King (sound), W. Aust. C3
King Leopold (range), W. Aust. D3
Kosciusko (mt.), N.S.W. H7
Lacepede (range), W. Aust. D3
Lachlan (riv.), N.S.W. G6
Latouche Treville (cape), W. Aust. C3
Leeuwin (cape), W. Aust. A6
Lefroy (lake), W. Aust.
Leichhardt (riv.), Queens.
Lévêque (cape), W. Aust.
Lihou (cays), Coral Sea Is. Terr.
Limmen Bight (riv.), N. Terr.
Little Para (riv.), S. Aust.
Lofty (mt.), S. Aust.
Londonderry (cape), W. Aust.
Macdonald (lake), W. Aust.
Macdonnell (ranges), N. Terr.
Mackay (lake), N. Terr.
Macquarie (harb.), Tas.
Macumba (riv.), S. Aust.
Magdelaine (cays), Coral Sea Is. Terr.
Main Barrier (range), N.S.W.
Manifold (cape), Queens.
Margaret (riv.), W. Aust.

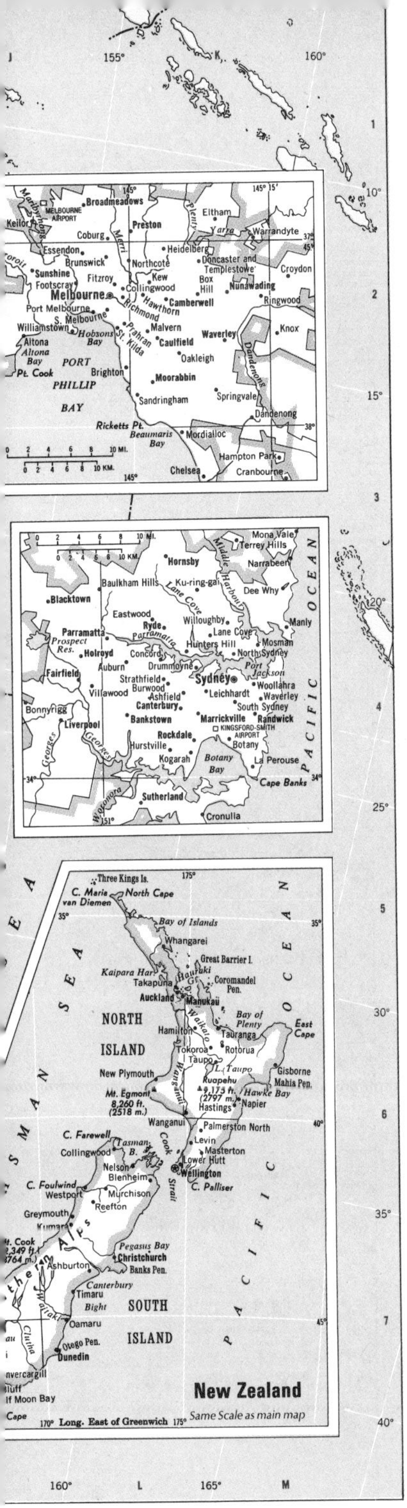

Population Distribution

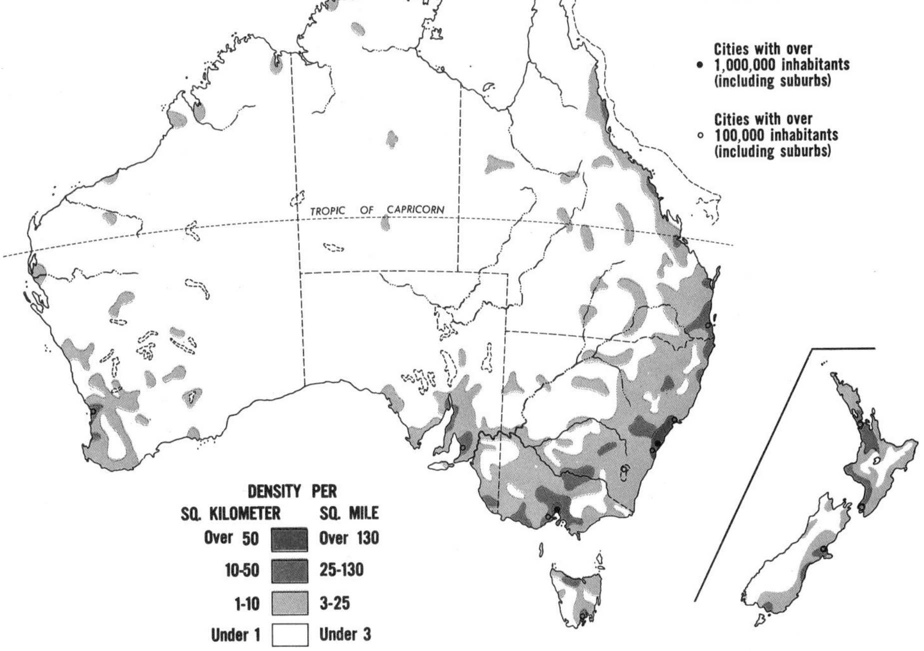

Topography

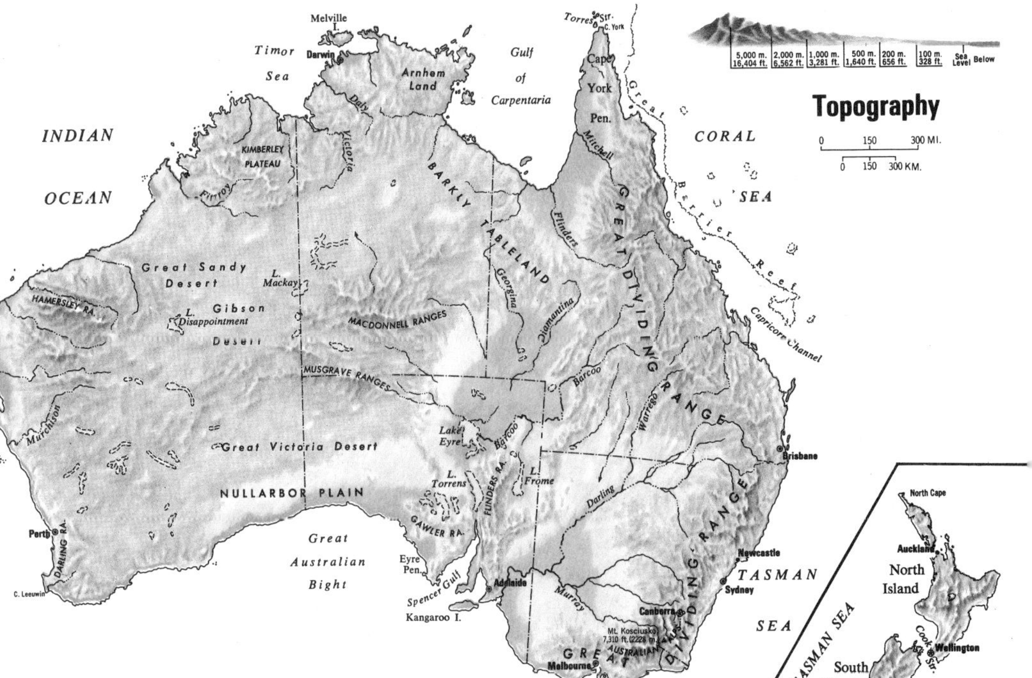

NEW ZEALAND

CITIES and TOWNS

OTHER FEATURES

‡Population of metropolitan area.

FIJI

AREA 7,055 sq. mi. (18,272 sq. km.)
POPULATION 588,068
CAPITAL Suva
LARGEST CITY Suva
HIGHEST POINT Tomaniivi 4,341 ft. (1,323 m.)
MONETARY UNIT Fijian dollar
MAJOR LANGUAGES Fijian, Hindi, English
MAJOR RELIGIONS Protestantism, Hinduism

KIRIBATI

AREA 291 sq. mi. (754 sq. km.)
POPULATION 56,213
CAPITAL Bairiki (Tarawa)
HIGHEST POINT (on Banaba I.) 285 ft. (87 m.)
MONETARY UNIT Australian dollar
MAJOR LANGUAGES I-Kiribati, English
MAJOR RELIGIONS Protestantism, Roman Catholicism

NAURU

AREA 7.7 sq. mi. (20 sq. km.)
POPULATION 7,254
CAPITAL Yaren (district)
MONETARY UNIT Australian dollar
MAJOR LANGUAGES Nauruan, English
MAJOR RELIGION Protestantism

SOLOMON ISLANDS

AREA 11,500 sq. mi. (29,785 sq. km.)
POPULATION 221,000
CAPITAL Honiara
HIGHEST POINT Mount Popomanatseu 7,647 ft. (2,331 m.)
MONETARY UNIT Solomon Islands dollar
MAJOR LANGUAGES English, pidgin English, Melanesian dialects
MAJOR RELIGIONS Tribal religions, Protestantism, Roman Catholicism

TONGA

AREA 270 sq. mi. (699 sq. km.)
POPULATION 90,128
CAPITAL Nuku'alofa
LARGEST CITY Nuku'alofa
HIGHEST POINT 3,389 ft. (1,033 m.)
MONETARY UNIT pa'anga
MAJOR LANGUAGES Tongan, English
MAJOR RELIGION Protestantism

TUVALU

AREA 9.78 sq. mi. (25.33 sq. km.)
POPULATION 7,349
CAPITAL Fongafale (Funafuti)
HIGHEST POINT 15 ft. (4.6 m.)
MONETARY UNIT Australian dollar
MAJOR LANGUAGES English, Tuvaluan
MAJOR RELIGION Protestantism

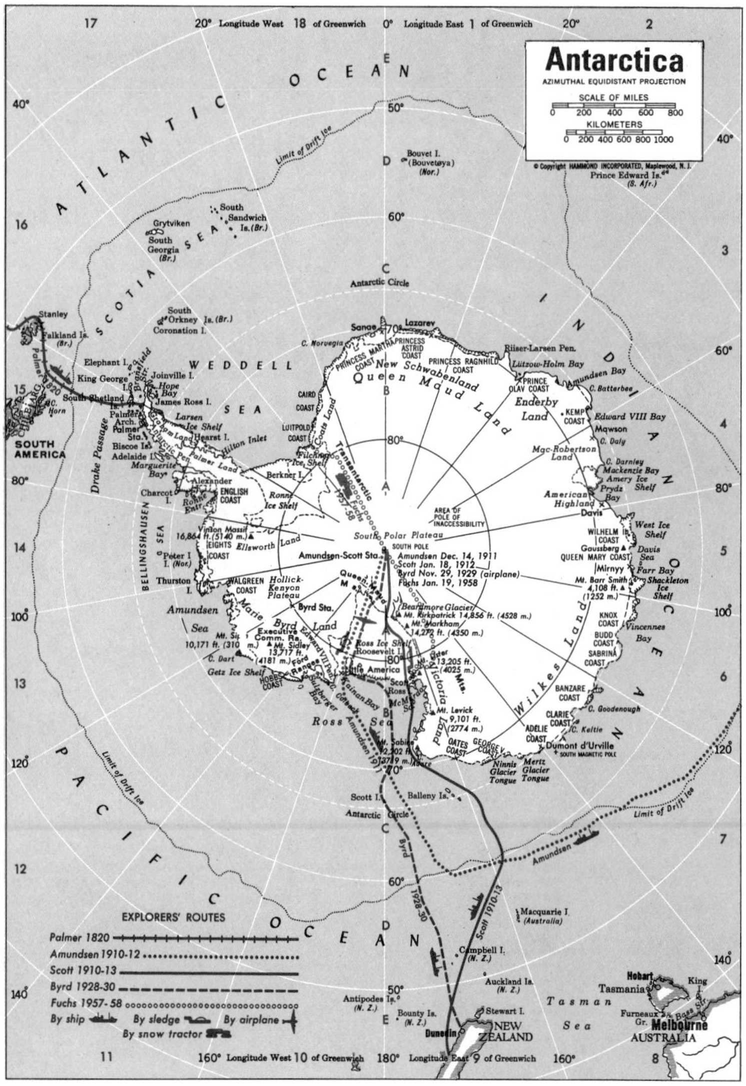

Hawaiian (isls.) 769,913 .... J3
Henderson (isl.) O8
Hikueru (atoll) M7
Hivaoa (isl.) 1,159 .... N6
Honiara (cap.), Solomon Is. 14,942 .... F6
Hoorn (isls.) 3,173 .... J7
Howland (isl.) J5
Huahine (isl.) 3,140 .... L7
Hull (isl.) J6
Huon (gulf) E6
Huon (isls.) G7
Ifalik (atoll) E5
Iwo (isl.) E3
Jaluit (atoll) G5
Jarvis (isl.) K6
Johnston (atoll) 339 .... K4
Kadavu (Kandavu) (isl.) 8,699 .... H7
Kanton (Canton) (isl.) J6
Kapingamarangi (atoll) F5
Kavieng 4,566 .... E6
Kermadec (isls.) 11 .... J9
Kieta 3,445 .... F6
Kili (isl.) G5
Kimbe 4,680 .... F6
Kingman (reef) K5
Kiribati 57,500 .... J6
Kita Iwo (isl.) D3

VANUATU

AREA 5,700 sq. mi. (14,763 sq. km.)
POPULATION 112,596
CAPITAL Vila
HIGHEST POINT Mt. Tabwemasana 6,165 ft. (1,879 m.)
MONETARY UNIT vatu
MAJOR LANGUAGES Bislama, English, French
MAJOR RELIGIONS Christian, animist

WESTERN SAMOA

AREA 1,133 sq. mi. (2,934 sq. km.)
POPULATION 151,983
CAPITAL Apia
LARGEST CITY Apia
HIGHEST POINT Mt. Silisili 6,094 ft. (1,857 m.)
MONETARY UNIT tala
MAJOR LANGUAGES Samoan, English
MAJOR RELIGIONS Protestantism, Roman Catholicism

*City and suburbs.
○Population of sub-district or division.
□Population of urban area.

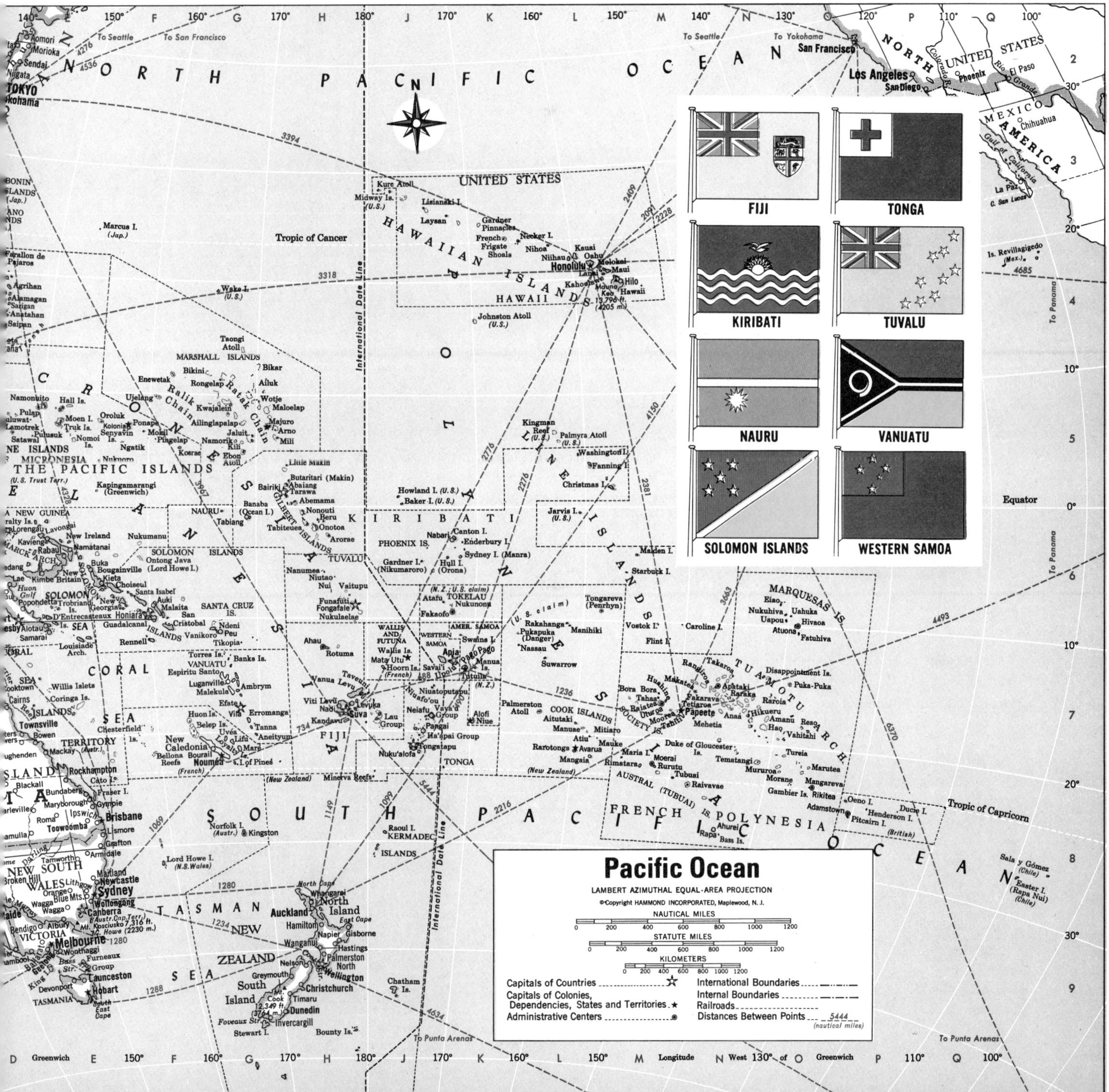

NORTH PACIFIC OCEAN
SOUTH PACIFIC OCEAN
FIJI
TONGA
KIRIBATI
TUVALU
NAURU
VANUATU
SOLOMON ISLANDS
WESTERN SAMOA
Tropic of Cancer
Tropic of Capricorn
Equator
International Date Line
Pacific Ocean
LAMBERT AZIMUTHAL EQUAL-AREA PROJECTION
©Copyright HAMMOND INCORPORATED, Maplewood, N. J.
NAUTICAL MILES
STATUTE MILES
KILOMETERS
Capitals of Countries
Capitals of Colonies, Dependencies, States and Territories
Administrative Centers
International Boundaries
Internal Boundaries
Railroads
Distances Between Points 5444 (nautical miles)
Longitude West 130° of Greenwich

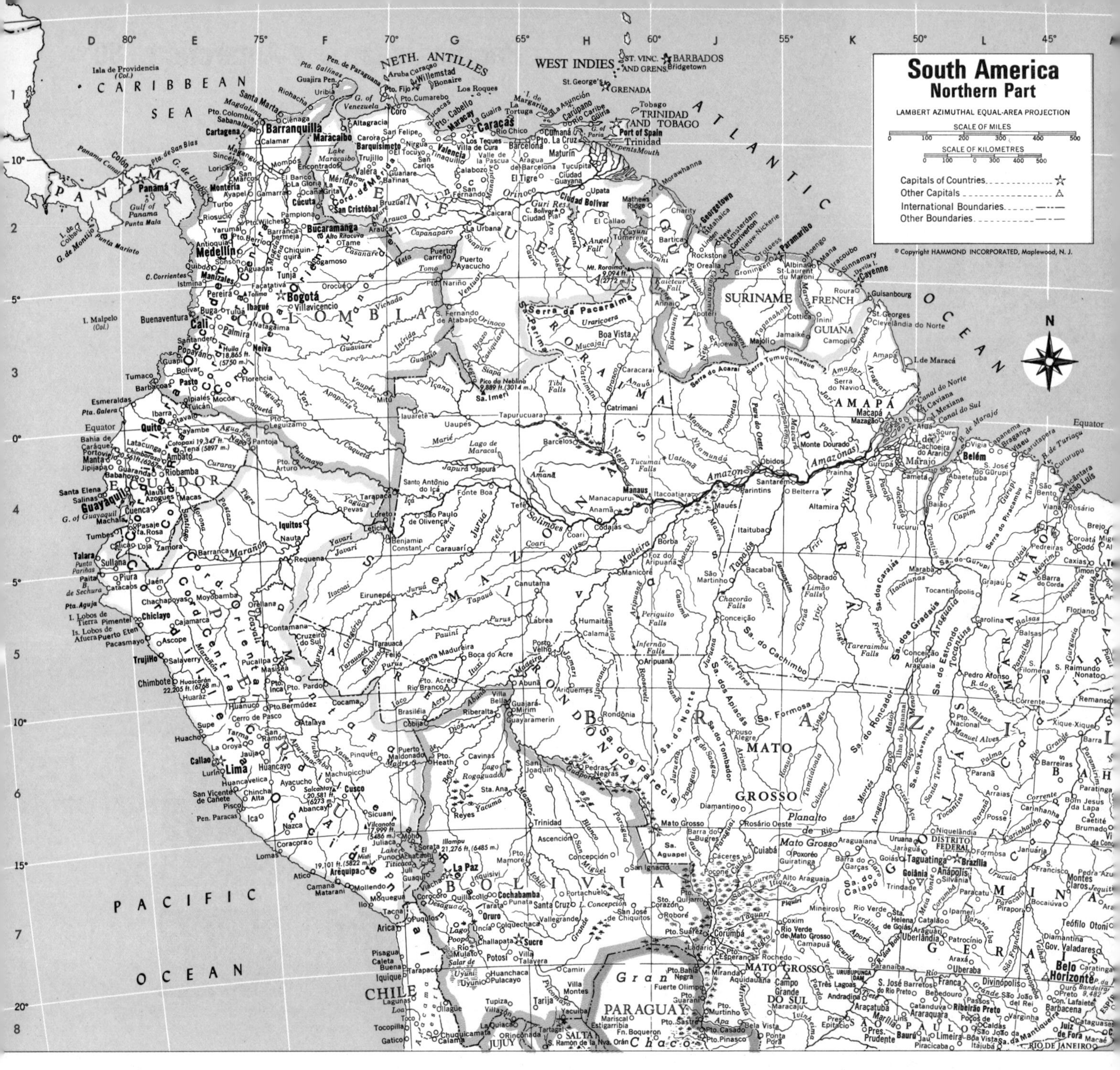
South America
Northern Part
LAMBERT AZIMUTHAL EQUAL-AREA PROJECTION
SCALE OF MILES
SCALE OF KILOMETRES
Capitals of Countries
Other Capitals
International Boundaries
Other Boundaries
© Copyright HAMMOND INCORPORATED, Maplewood, N. J.
CARIBBEAN SEA
ATLANTIC OCEAN
PACIFIC OCEAN

ARGENTINA

PROVINCES

Buenos Aires 10,796,036 ..... H11
Catamarca 206,204 .... G9
Chaco 692,410 .... H9
Chubut 262,196 .... G12
Córdoba 2,407,135 .... H10
Corrientes 657,716 .... J9
Distrito Federal 2,908,001 .... O12
Entre Ríos 902,241 .... J10
Formosa 292,479 .... H8
Jujuy 408,514 .... G8
La Pampa 207,132 .... G11
La Rioja 163,342 .... G9
Mendoza 1,187,305 .... G10
Misiones 579,579 .... K9
Neuquén 241,904 .... G11
Río Negro 383,896 .... G12
Salta 662,369 .... G8
San Juan 469,973 .... G10
San Luis 212,837 .... G10
Santa Cruz 114,479 .... G13
Santa Fe 2,457,188 .... H9
Santiago del Estero 652,318 .... H9
Tierra del Fuego, Antártida, e Islas del Atlántico Sur (terr.) 29,451 .... G14
Tucumán 968,066 .... G9

CITIES and TOWNS

Azul 36,023 .... J11
Bahía Blanca 182,158 .... H11
Balcarce 26,461 .... J11
Bell Ville 22,528 .... H10
Bolívar 18,643 .... H11
Buenos Aires (cap.) 2,908,001 .... H10
Campana 33,919 .... H10
Catamarca 64,410 .... H9
Chivilcoy 37,190 .... H11
Comodoro Rivadavia 72,906 . G13
Concepción del Uruguay 38,967 .... J10
Concordia 72,136 .... J10
Córdoba 790,508 .... G10
Corrientes 136,924 .... J9
Cruz del Eje 23,401 .... H10
Curuzú Cuatiá 20,636 .... J9
El Turbio F14
Embarcación 7,207 .... G8
Esperanza 17,636 .... H10
Formosa 61,071 .... J9
Gaimán 1,702 .... G12
Gastre G12
General Alvear 17,277 .... G11
General Pico 21,897 .... H11
General Roca 29,320 .... G11
Godoy Cruz 112,481 .... G10
Goya 39,367 .... J9
Jachal 6,815 .... G10
Jujuy 82,637 .... G8
La Plata 478,666 .... J11
La Rioja 46,090 .... G9
Lincoln 17,391 .... H10
Maquinchao 1,495 .... G12
Mar del Plata 302,282 .... J11
Mendoza 470,896 .... G10
Mercedes 40,052 .... G10
Miramar 10,512 .... J11
Necochea 39,868 .... J11
Neuquén 43,070 .... G11
Olavarría 52,453 .... H11
Paraná 127,635 .... J10
Pehuajó 21,078 .... H11
Pergamino 56,078 .... H10
Plaza Huincul 4,714 .... G11
Posadas 97,514 .... J9
Presidencia Roque Sáenz Peña 38,620 .... J9
Puerto Madryn 6,115 .... G12
Punta Alta 36,805 .... H11
Rafaela 43,695 .... H10
Rawson 7,229 .... H12
Reconquista 25,333 .... H9
Resistencia 142,848 .... J9
Rinconada G8
Río Cuarto 88,852 .... H10
Río Gallegos 27,833 .... G14
Río Grande G14
Rosario 806,942 .... H10
Rosario de la Frontera 9,075 .... H9
Salta 176,216 .... G8
San Antonio de los Cobres 1,947 .... G8
San Carlos de Bariloche 26,799 .... F12
San Francisco 48,896 .... H10
San Juan 217,514 .... G10
San Julián 3,589 .... G13
San Luis 50,771 .... G10
San Miguel de Tucumán 366,392 .... H9
San Nicolás 64,730 .... J10
San Rafael 58,237 .... G10
Santa Cruz 1,448 .... G14
Santa Fe 244,655 .... H10
Santa Rosa 33,649 .... H11
Santiago del Estero 105,127 .... H9
Tandil 65,876 .... J9
Tartagal 23,696 .... H8
Trelew 24,214 .... G12
Trenque Lauquen 18,169 ...... H11
Tres Arroyos 37,991 .... J11
Ushuaia 5,373 .... G14
Valcheta 1,776 .... G12
Venado Tuerto 35,677 .... H10
Viedma 12,888 .... H12
Villa Dolores 19,010 .... G10
Villa María 56,087 .... H10

OTHER FEATURES

Aconcagua (mt.) G10
Andes de Patagonia (mts.) F14
Argentino (lake) G14
Bermejo (riv.) H9
Colorado (riv.) H11
Estados, Los (isl.) H14
Gran Chaco (reg.) H8
Iguassú (falls) K9
Magellan (str.) G14
Maipo (mt.) G10
Nàhuel Huapi (lake) F12
Negro (riv.) H11
Ojos del Salado (mt.) G9
Pampas (plain) H11
Patagonia (reg.) F12
Plata, Río de la (est.) J11
Salado (riv.) G11
Salado (riv.) H9
San Antonio (cape) J11
San Martín (lake) F13
San Matías (gulf) H12
Staten (Los Estados) (isl.) H14
Tierra del Fuego (isl.) G14
Tres Puntas (cape) H13
Uruguay (riv.) J9
Valdés (pen.) H12

BOLIVIA

CITIES and TOWNS

Cochabamba 204,684 .... G7
Guaqui 2,266 .... G7
Guayamerin 1,470 .... G6
Huanchaca G8
La Paz (cap.) 635,283 .... G7
Oruro 124,213 .... G7
Potosí 77,397 .... G7
Puerto Suárez 1,159 .... J7
Santa Cruz 254,682 .... H7
Sucre (cap.) 63,625 .... H7
Tarija 38,916 .... H8

OTHER FEATURES

Abuná (riv.) G6
Beni (riv.) G6
Desaguadero (riv.) G7
Grande (riv.) H7
Guaporé (riv.) H6
Illampu (mt.) G7
Mamoré (riv.) H6
Poopó (lake) G7
Real, Cordillera (mts.) G7
Titicaca (lake) F7

BRAZIL

STATES

Acre 216,200 .... F5
Alagoas 1,579,605 .... N5
Amapá (terr.) 114,687 .... K3
Amazonas 955,394 .... G5
Bahia 7,508,779 .... M6
Ceará 4,366,970 .... N5
Distrito Federal 538,351 .... L7
Espírito Santo 1,600,305 ...... M8
Goiás 2,941,107 .... L6
Guanabara 4,252,009 .... N15
Maranhão 2,997,576 .... L5
Mato Grosso 1,600,494 .... J6
Mato Grosso do Sul 1,300,000 .... J8
Minas Gerais 11,497,574 ...... M7
Pará 2,161,316 .... K4
Paraíba 2,384,615 .... N5
Paraná 6,936,743 ....
Pernambuco 5,166,554 ....
Piauí 1,680,954 ....
Rio de Janeiro 4,746,848 ....
Rio Grande do Norte 1,552,158 ....
Rio Grande do Sul 6,670,382 ....
Rondônia (terr.) 113,659 ....
Roraima (terr.) 40,915 ....
Santa Catarina 2,903,360 ....
São Paulo 17,775,889 ....
Sergipe 901,618 ....

CITIES and TOWNS

Alagoinhas 53,891 ....
Alcobaça 2,257 ....
Alegrete 45,522 ....
Amapá 1,923 ....
Amarante 4,410 ....
Anápolis 89,405 ....
Andradina 43,465 ....
Aracaju 179,512 ....
Araçatuba 85,660 ....
Araguari 48,702 ....
Arapiraca 43,875 ....
Araraquara 82,607 ....
Araxá 31,498 ....
Bacabal 29,251 ....
Bagé 57,036 .... K
Bahia (Salvador) 998,258 ....
Barbacena 57,766 ....
Barcelos 821 ....

AREA 6,875,000 sq. mi. (17,806,250 sq. km.)
POPULATION 245,000,000
LARGEST CITY São Paulo
HIGHEST POINT Cerro Aconcagua 22,831 ft. (6,959 m.)
LOWEST POINT Salina Grande -131 ft. (-40 m.)

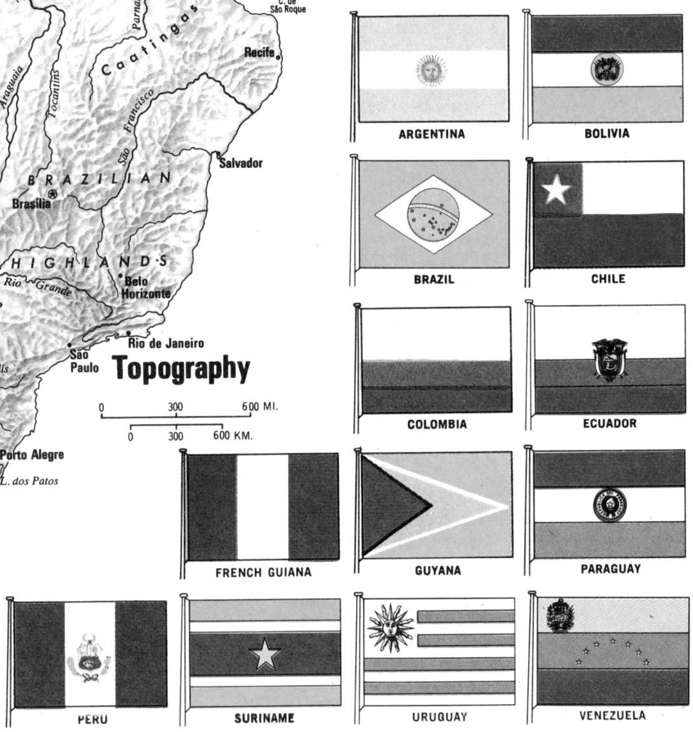

ARGENTINA
AREA 1,072,070 sq. mi. (2,776,661 sq. km.)
POPULATION 27,862,771
CAPITAL Buenos Aires
LARGEST CITY Buenos Aires
HIGHEST POINT Cerro Aconcagua 22,831 ft. (6,959 m.)
MONETARY UNIT Argentine peso
MAJOR LANGUAGE Spanish
MAJOR RELIGION Roman Catholicism

BOLIVIA
AREA 424,163 sq. mi. (1,098,582 sq. km.)
POPULATION 5,600,000
CAPITALS La Paz, Sucre
LARGEST CITY La Paz
HIGHEST POINT Nevada Ancohuma 21,489 ft. (6,550 m.)
MONETARY UNIT Bolivian peso
MAJOR LANGUAGES Spanish, Quechua, Aymara
MAJOR RELIGION Roman Catholicism

BRAZIL
AREA 3,284,426 sq. mi. (8,506,663 sq. km.)
POPULATION 119,024,600
CAPITAL Brasília
LARGEST CITY São Paulo (greater)
HIGHEST POINT Pico da Neblina 9,889 ft. (3,014 m.)
MONETARY UNIT cruzeiro
MAJOR LANGUAGE Portuguese
MAJOR RELIGION Roman Catholicism

CHILE
AREA 292,257 sq. mi. (756,946 sq. km.)
POPULATION 11,198,789
CAPITAL Santiago
LARGEST CITY Santiago
HIGHEST POINT Ojos del Salado 22,572 ft. (6,880 m.)
MONETARY UNIT Chilean escudo
MAJOR LANGUAGE Spanish
MAJOR RELIGION Roman Catholicism

COLOMBIA
AREA 439,513 sq. mi. (1,138,339 sq. km.)
POPULATION 27,520,000
CAPITAL Bogotá
LARGEST CITY Bogotá
HIGHEST POINT Pico Cristóbal Colón 19,029 ft. (5,800 m.)
MONETARY UNIT Colombian peso
MAJOR LANGUAGE Spanish
MAJOR RELIGION Roman Catholicism

ECUADOR
REA 109,483 sq. mi. (283,561 sq. km.)
OPULATION 8,354,000
APITAL Quito
RGEST CITY Guayaquil
GHEST POINT Chimborazo 20,561 ft. (6,267 m.)
ONETARY UNIT sucre
AJOR LANGUAGES Spanish, Quechua
AJOR RELIGION Roman Catholicism

FRENCH GUIANA
AREA 35,135 sq. mi. (91,000 sq. km.)
POPULATION 64,000
CAPITAL Cayenne
LARGEST CITY Cayenne
HIGHEST POINT 2,723 ft. (830 m.)
MONETARY UNIT French franc
MAJOR LANGUAGE French
MAJOR RELIGIONS Roman Catholicism, Protestantism

GUYANA
AREA 83,000 sq. mi. (214,970 sq. km.)
POPULATION 820,000
CAPITAL Georgetown
LARGEST CITY Georgetown
HIGHEST POINT Mt. Roraima 9,094 ft. (2,772 m.)
MONETARY UNIT Guyana dollar
MAJOR LANGUAGES English, Hindi
MAJOR RELIGIONS Christianity, Hinduism, Islam

PARAGUAY
AREA 157,047 sq. mi. (406,752 sq. km.)
POPULATION 2,973,000
CAPITAL Asunción
LARGEST CITY Asunción
HIGHEST POINT Amambay Range 2,264 ft. (690 m.)
MONETARY UNIT guaraní
MAJOR LANGUAGES Spanish, Guaraní
MAJOR RELIGION Roman Catholicism

PERU
REA 496,222 sq. mi. (1,285,215 sq. km.)
OPULATION 17,031,221
APITAL Lima
RGEST CITY Lima
GHEST POINT Huascarán 22,205 ft. (6,768 m.)
ONETARY UNIT sol
AJOR LANGUAGES Spanish, Quechua, Aymara
AJOR RELIGION Roman Catholicism

SURINAME
AREA 55,144 sq. mi. (142,823 sq. km.)
POPULATION 352,041
CAPITAL Paramaribo
LARGEST CITY Paramaribo
HIGHEST POINT Julianatop 4,200 ft. (1,280 m.)
MONETARY UNIT Suriname guilder
MAJOR LANGUAGES Dutch, Hindi, Indonesian
MAJOR RELIGIONS Christianity, Islam, Hinduism

URUGUAY
AREA 72,172 sq. mi. (186,925 sq. km.)
POPULATION 2,899,000
CAPITAL Montevideo
LARGEST CITY Montevideo
HIGHEST POINT Mirador Nacional 1,644 ft. (501 m.)
MONETARY UNIT Uruguayan peso
MAJOR LANGUAGE Spanish
MAJOR RELIGION Roman Catholicism

VENEZUELA
AREA 352,143 sq. mi. (912,050 sq. km.)
POPULATION 13,913,000
CAPITAL Caracas
LARGEST CITY Caracas
HIGHEST POINT Pico Bolívar 16,427 ft. (5,007 m.)
MONETARY UNIT Bolívar
MAJOR LANGUAGE Spanish
MAJOR RELIGION Roman Catholicism

OTHER FEATURES

CHILE

CITIES and TOWNS

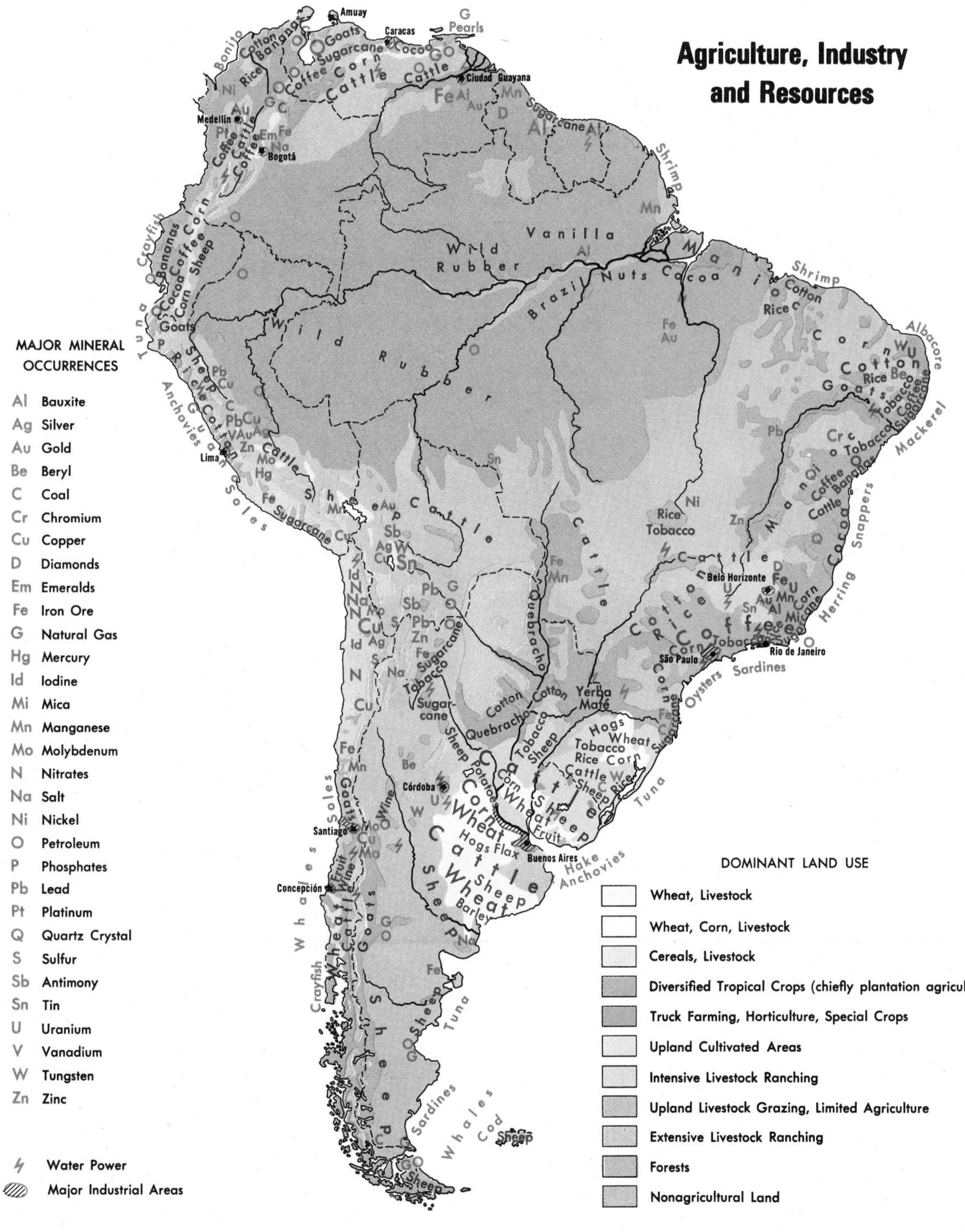
Agriculture, Industry and Resources
MAJOR MINERAL OCCURRENCES
Al Bauxite
Ag Silver
Au Gold
Be Beryl
C Coal
Cr Chromium
Cu Copper
D Diamonds
Em Emeralds
Fe Iron Ore
G Natural Gas
Hg Mercury
Id Iodine
Mi Mica
Mn Manganese
Mo Molybdenum
N Nitrates
Na Salt
Ni Nickel
O Petroleum
P Phosphates
Pb Lead
Pt Platinum
Q Quartz Crystal
S Sulfur
Sb Antimony
Sn Tin
U Uranium
V Vanadium
W Tungsten
Zn Zinc
Water Power
Major Industrial Areas
DOMINANT LAND USE
Wheat, Livestock
Wheat, Corn, Livestock
Cereals, Livestock
Diversified Tropical Crops (chiefly plantation agriculture)
Truck Farming, Horticulture, Special Crops
Upland Cultivated Areas
Intensive Livestock Ranching
Upland Livestock Grazing, Limited Agriculture
Extensive Livestock Ranching
Forests
Nonagricultural Land
Amuay
Caracas
Pearls
Ciudad Guayana
Medellín
Bogotá
Lima
Córdoba
Santiago
Buenos Aires
Concepción
Belo Horizonte
São Paulo
Rio de Janeiro
Vanilla
Wild Rubber
Brazil Nuts
Shrimp
Sardines
Anchovies
Whales
Tuna
Yerba Maté
Quebracho
Cattle
Sheep
Wheat
Cotton
Coffee
Cocoa

via 82,300 ... F11
nar 26,800 ... F9
raíso 250,400 ... F10
del Mar 182,000 ... F10

OTHER FEATURES

es (mts.) ... F10
ama (des.) ... G8
é (isl.) ... E12
ovado (gulf) ... F12
nados (gulf) ... F12
(cape) ... G15
illaco (vol.) ... G8
riv.) ... F8
ellan (str.) ... E14
o (mt.) ... O10
rino (isl.) ... G14
ggins (lake) ... F13
del Salado (mt.) ... G9
s (gulf) ... E13
o (pen.) ... E13
a del Fuego (isl.) ... G14

COLOMBIA

CITIES and TOWNS

ca 7,613 ... F2
ancabermeja 87,191 ... F2
anquilla 661,009 ... F1
otá (cap.) 2,696,270 ... F3
aramanga 291,661 ... F2
naventura 115,770 ... E3
a 71,016 ... E3
898,253 ... E3
agena 292,512 ... E1
uinquirá 21,727 ... F2
aga 42,546 ... F1
uta 219,772 ... F2
anco 20,756 ... F2
ativá 27,892 ... F3
encia 31,817 ... E3
ué 176,223 ... F3
es 30,871 ... E3
cia 6,285 ... F4
angué 34,396 ... E2
izales 199,904 ... E2
ellín 1,070,924 ... E2
1,637 ... F3
oa 6,221 ... E3
nterla 89,583 ... E2
a 105,476 ... F3
a 38,352 ... F2
nira 140,481 ... E3
nplona 31,817 ... F2
to 119,339 ... E3
eira 174,128 ... E3
ayán 77,669 ... E3
rto Carreño 2,172 ... G2
rto Wilches 5,282 ... F2
dó 28,040 ... E2
ta Marta 102,484 ... F1
celejo 68,797 ... E2
amoso 48,891 ... F2
á 86,736 ... E3
aco 38,742 ... E3
já 51,620 ... F2
avicencio 82,869 ... F3
umal 21,333 ... E2

OTHER FEATURES

Ritacuva (mt.) ... F2
uporis (riv.) ... F3
uca (riv.) ... G2
uetá (riv.) ... F4
anare (riv.) ... F2
ca (riv.) ... E2
ntral, Cordillera (mts.) ... E2
inía (riv.) ... G3
jira (pen.) ... F1
aviare (riv.) ... F3
a (mt.) ... E3
ida (riv.) ... G3
gdalena (riv.) ... F2
ta (riv.) ... G2
cidental, Cordillera (mts.) ... E3
ental, Cordillera (mts.) ... F2
noco (riv.) ... G2
umayo (riv.) ... F3
ima (mt.) ... E3
upés (riv.) ... F3
hada (riv.) ... F3

ECUADOR

CITIES and TOWNS

bato 77,955 ... E4
bahoyo 28,914 ... D4
querizo Moreno 1,311 ... D7
enca 104,470 ... E4
meraldas 60,364 ... D3
ayaquil 823,219 ... D4
rra 41,335 ... E3
ijapa 19,996 ... D4
acunga 21,921 ... E4
a 47,697 ... E4
cas 1,934 ... E4
chala 69,170 ... D4
nta 64,519 ... D4
saje 20,790 ... E4
rtoviejo 59,550 ... D4
erto Villamil ... D7
ito (cap.) 599,828 ... E4
obamba 58,087 ... E4
nta Elena 7,687 ... D4
nta Rosa 19,696 ... E4
na ... E4
lcán 24,398 ... E3

OTHER FEATURES

imborazo (mt.) ... E4
topaxi (mt.) ... E4

Guayaquil (gulf) ... D4
Morona (riv.) ... E4
Napo (riv.) ... F4
Occidental, Cordillera (mts.) ... E4
Pastaza (riv.) ... E4
Real, Cordillera (mts.) ... E4
Santiago (riv.) ... E4

FALKLAND ISLANDS

CITIES and TOWNS

Stanley (cap.) ... J14

OTHER FEATURES

East Falkland (isl.) ... J14
Falkland (sound) ... H14
West Falkland (isl.) ... H14

FRENCH GUIANA

CITIES and TOWNS

Cayenne (cap.) 28,888 ... K2
Guisanbourg ... K3
Iracoubo 715 ... K2
Mana 659 ... K2
Saint-Georges 668 ... K3

OTHER FEATURES

Devils (isl.) ... K2
Maroni (riv.) ... K3
Oyapock (riv.) ... K3

GUYANA

CITIES and TOWNS

Georgetown (cap.) 63,184 ... J2
Morawhanna○ 292 ... J2

New Amsterdam 17,782 ... J2

OTHER FEATURES

Courantyne (riv.) ... J3
Cuyuni (riv.) ... H2
Essequibo (riv.) ... J2
Kaieteur (falls) ... J3
Mazaruni (riv.) ... H2
Roraima (mt.) ... H2
Rupununi (riv.) ... J3

PARAGUAY

CITIES and TOWNS

Asunción (cap.) 387,676 ... J9
Concepción 19,392 ... J8
Encarnación 23,343 ... J9
Fuerte Olimpo 3,063 ... J8
Mariscal Estigarribia 3,150 ... H8
Puerto Casado 4,078 ... J8
Puerto Guaraní 302 ... J8
Puerto Sastre 160 ... J8
Villarrica 17,687 ... J9

OTHER FEATURES

Gran Chaco (reg.) ... H8
Paraguay (riv.) ... J8
Paraná (riv.) ... K9
Pilcomayo (riv.) ... H8

PERU

CITIES and TOWNS

Arequipa 304,653 ... F7
Ayacucho 43,304 ... F6
Cajamarca 37,608 ... E5
Callao 296,220 ... E6
Catacaos 19,155 ... D5
Cerro de Pasco 47,178 ... E6
Chiclayo 189,685 ... E5
Chimbote 159,045 ... E5
Chincha Alta 28,785 ... E6
Coracora 4,508 ... F7
Cusco 120,881 ... F6
Huacho 36,697 ... E6
Huancavelica 15,916 ... E6
Huancayo 115,693 ... F6
Huánuco 41,123 ... E6
Ica 73,883 ... E6
Ilo 21,551 ... F7
Iquitos 111,327 ... F4
Jauja 13,936 ... E6
Juliaca 38,475 ... F7
La Oroya 25,908 ... E6
Lima (cap.) 354,292 ... E6
Machupicchu 235 ... F6
Matarani ... F7
Mollendo 15,573 ... F7
Moquegua 16,959 ... F7
Nazca 21,025 ... F6
Pacasmayo 15,381 ... D5
Paita 14,875 ... D5
Pisco 41,429 ... E6
Piura 126,702 ... D5
Pucallpa 57,525 ... E5
Puno 41,166 ... F7
Sullana 60,112 ... D4
Supe 15,623 ... E6
Tacna 55,752 ... F7
Talara 29,884 ... D4
Tarma 28,100 ... E6
Trujillo 241,882 ... E5
Tumbes 32,972 ... D4

OTHER FEATURES

Aguja (pt.) ... D5
Altiplano (plat.) ... F7
Apurímac (riv.) ... F6
Central, Cordillera (mts.) ... E5
Huascarán (mt.) ... E5
Madre de Dios (riv.) ... G6
Marañón (riv.) ... E4
Misti, El (mt.) ... F7
Montaña, La (reg.) ... F5
Napo (riv.) ... F4
Occidental, Cordillera (mts.) ... F6
Oriental, Cordillera (mts.) ... E5
Paracas (pen.) ... E6
Putumayo (riv.) ... F4
Real, Cordillera (mts.) ... F6
Sechura (bay) ... D5
Titicaca (lake) ... F7
Ucayali (riv.) ... E5
Urubamba (riv.) ... F6
Vilcanota (mt.) ... F6

SURINAME

CITIES and TOWNS

Albina 1,000 ... K3
Groningen 600 ... J2
Moengo 2,100 ... K3
Paramaribo (cap.) 102,297 ... K2
Totness 1,300 ... J2

OTHER FEATURES

Coeroeni (riv.) ... J3
Tapanahoni (riv.) ... J3

URUGUAY

CITIES and TOWNS

Artigas 29,256 ... J10
Canelones 15,938 ... J10
Colonia 16,895 ... J10
Durazno 25,811 ... J10
Florida 25,030 ... J10
Fray Bentos 19,569 ... J10
Maldonado 22,159 ... K11
Melo 38,260 ... K10
Mercedes 34,667 ... J10
Minas 35,433 ... K10
Montevideo (cap.) 1,173,254 ... J11
Paysandú 62,412 ... J10
Rivera 49,013 ... J10
Rocha 21,612 ... K10
Salto 72,948 ... J10
San José 28,427 ... J10
Tacuarembó 34,152 ... J10
Treinta y Tres 25,757 ... K10
Trinidad 17,598 ... J10

OTHER FEATURES

Mirim (lag.) ... K10
Negro (riv.) ... J10
Plata, Río de la (est.) ... J11
Uruguay (riv.) ... J9

VENEZUELA

CITIES and TOWNS

Barcelona 78,201 ... H2
Barinas 56,329 ... G2
Barquisimeto 330,815 ... F2
Bruzual 941 ... G2
Calabozo 37,282 ... G2
Caracas (cap.) 1,035,499 ... G1
Carora 36,115 ... F1
Carúpano 50,935 ... H1
Ciudad Bolívar 103,728 ... H2
Ciudad Piar 3,965 ... H2
Coro 68,701 ... G1
Cumaná 119,751 ... H1
El Tigre 49,801 ... H2
El Tocuyo 19,351 ... G2
Guanare 34,148 ... G2
La Guaira 20,344 ... G1
Los Teques 63,106 ... G1
Maracaibo 651,574 ... F1
Maracay 255,134 ... G1
Maturín 98,188 ... H2
Mérida 74,214 ... F2
Puerto Cabello 72,103 ... G1
Puerto La Cruz 63,276 ... H1
San Carlos 21,029 ... G2
San Cristóbal 151,717 ... F2
San Felipe 43,801 ... G1
San Fernando 38,960 ... G2
Trujillo 25,921 ... F2
Tucacas 4,780 ... G1
Tucupita 21,417 ... H2
Valencia 367,171 ... G2
Valera 76,740 ... F2
Valle de la Pascua 36,809 ... G2
Villa de Cura 27,832 ... G2

OTHER FEATURES

Angel (fall) ... H2
Arauca (riv.) ... G2
Apure (riv.) ... F2
Bolívar (mt.) ... F2
Caroní (riv.) ... H3
Casiquiare, Brazo (riv.) ... G3
Maracaibo (lake) ... F2
Margarita (isl.) ... H1
Mérida (mts.) ... F2
Orinoco (riv.) ... G2
Paraguana (pen.) ... F1
Paria (gulf) ... H1
Serpents Mouth (str.) ... H2
Tortuga, La (isl.) ... G1
Venezuela (gulf) ... F1

†Population of commune.
○Population of sub-district or division.

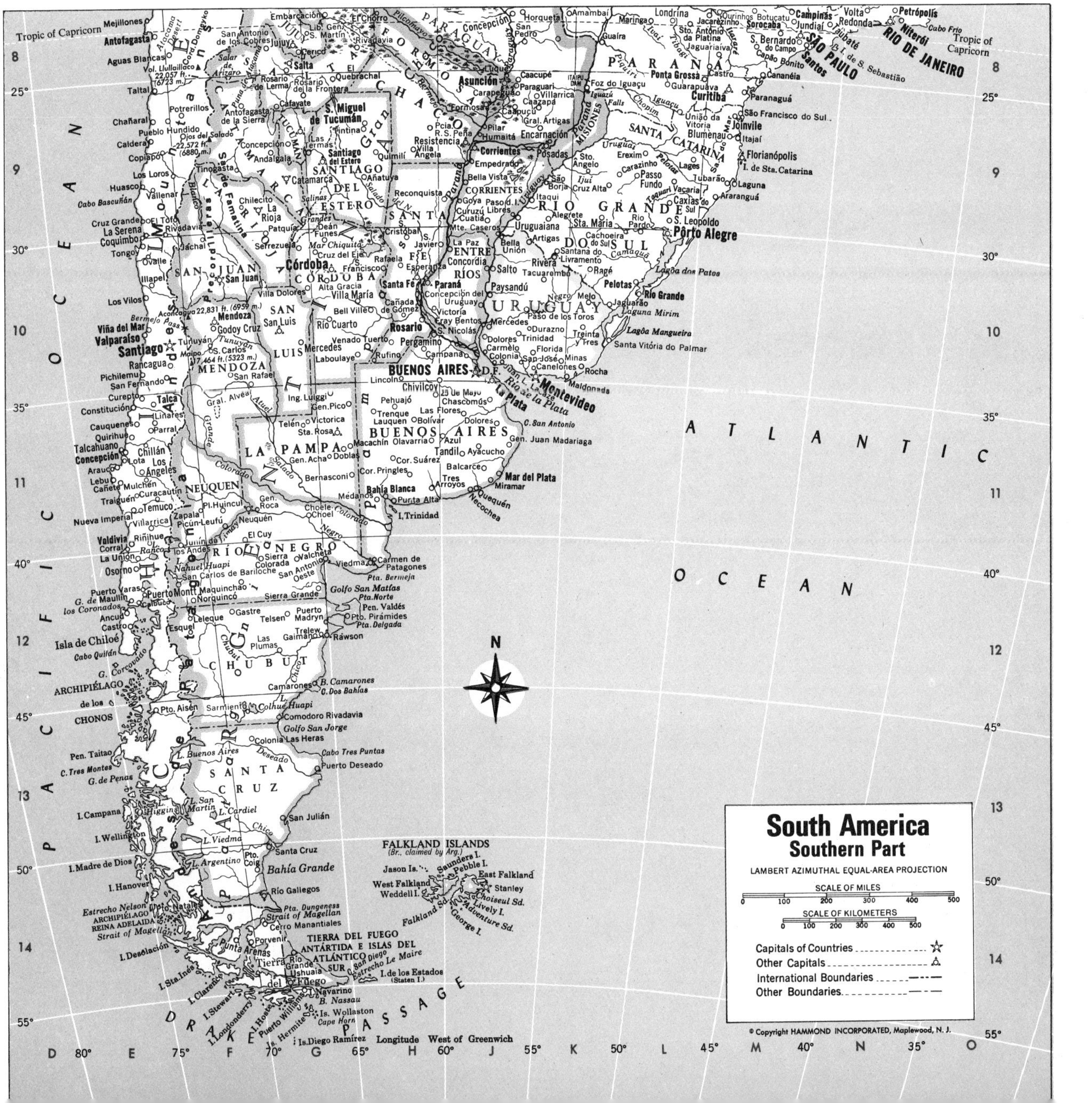

North America
LAMBERT AZIMUTHAL EQUAL-AREA PROJECTION
MILES
0 100 200 400 600 800
KILOMETERS
0 100 200 400 600 800
Capitals of Countries
Other Capitals
International Boundaries
Other Boundaries
© Copyright HAMMOND INCORPORATED, Maplewood, N. J.
Longitude West 90° of Greenwich
ARCTIC OCEAN
PACIFIC OCEAN
ATLANTIC OCEAN
GREENLAND
ICELAND
ASIA
U.S.S.R.
EUROPE
UNITED STATES
ALASKA
CANADA
MEXICO
SOUTH AMERICA
Gulf of Mexico
CARIBBEAN SEA
Hudson Bay
Baffin Bay
BERING SEA
BEAUFORT SEA
LABRADOR SEA
GREENLAND SEA
NORWEGIAN SEA
Gulf of Alaska
WEST INDIES
BAHAMAS
CUBA
VENEZUELA
COLOMBIA
ECUADOR
PERU
BRAZIL
BOLIVIA
Tropic of Cancer
Equator
NORTH POLE

Population Distribution

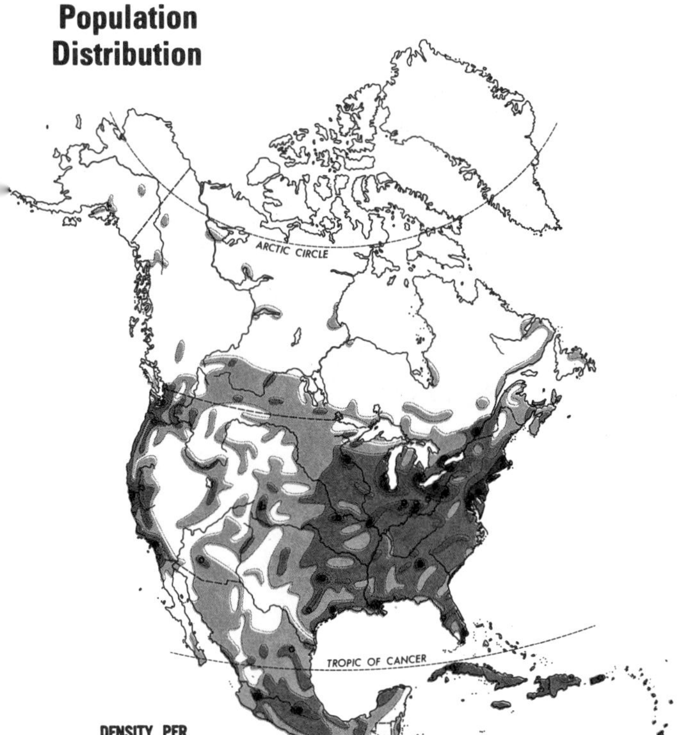

DENSITY PER

SQ. KILOMETER	SQ. MILE
Over 100	Over 260
50-100	130-260
10-50	25-130
1-10	3-25
Under 3	Under 1

• Cities with over 2,000,000 inhabitants (including suburbs)

○ Cities with over 1,000,000 inhabitants (including suburbs)

AREA 9,363,000 sq. mi. (24,250,170 sq. km.)
POPULATION 370,000,000
LARGEST CITY New York
HIGHEST POINT Mt. McKinley 20,320 ft. (6,194 m.)
LOWEST POINT Death Valley -282 ft. (-86 m.)

Vegetation

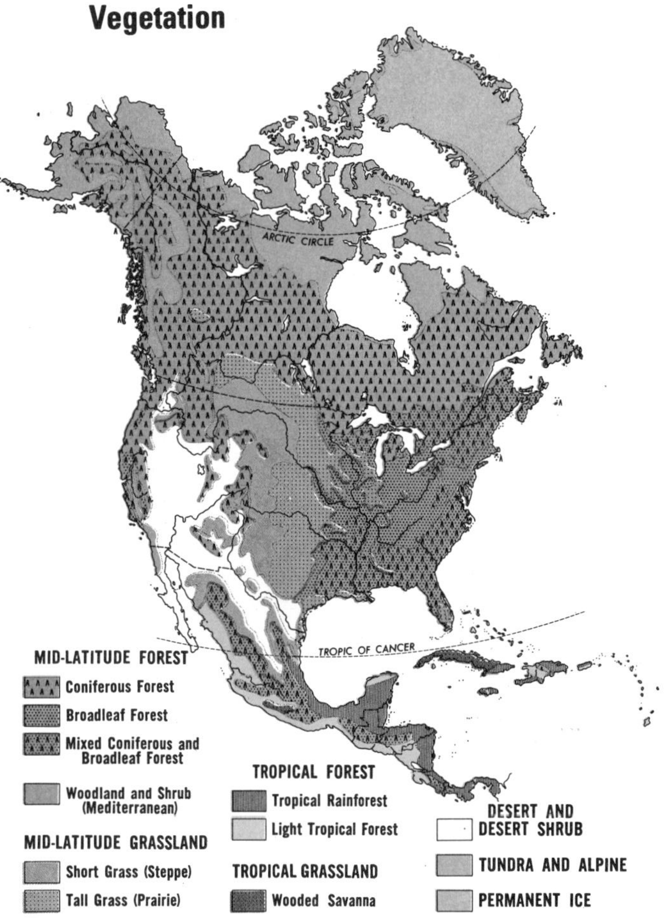

ulco de Juárez, Mexico ... H8
n, Ohio ... K5
ma (state), U.S. ... K6
a (gulf) ... D4
a (pen.), Alaska ... C4
a (state), U.S. ... C3
y (cap.), N.Y. ... L5
ta (prov.) Canada ... G4
querque, N. Mex. ... H6
illo, Texas ... H6
orage, Alaska ... D3
nagssalik, Greenland ... Q3
illa (isl.) ... M8
ua (isl.) ... M8
c (ocean) ... B2
na (state), U.S. ... G6
nsas (riv.), U.S. ... J6
nsas (state), U.S. ... J6
basca (lake), Canada ... H4
ta (cap.), Ga. ... K6
sta, Ga. ... K6
sta (cap.), Maine ... M5
n (cap.), Texas ... J6
n (bay) ... M2
n (isl.), N.W.T. ... L2
mas ... L7
rsfield, Calif. ... G6
more, Md. ... L6
ados ... N8
ow (pt.), Alaska ... C2
n Rouge (cap.), La. ... J6
fort (sea) ... D2
e ... K8
e Isle (str.), Canada ... N5
nopan (cap.), Belize ... K8
ng (sea) ... A3
ng (str.) ... B3
muda (isls.) ... M6
ingham, Ala. ... K6
narck (cap.), N. Dak. ... H5
e (cap.), Idaho ... G5
ton (cap.), Mass. ... L5
sh Columbia (prov.), anada ... F4
alo, N.Y. ... L5
e, Mont. ... G5
ary (cap.), Alta. ... G4
fornia (gulf), Mexico ... G7
fornia (state), U.S. ... G6
ada ... G4
adian (riv.), U.S. ... H6
averal (cape), Fla. ... L7
bbean (sea) ... K8
son City (cap.), Nev. ... G6
cade (range), U.S. ... F5
rleston, S.C. ... L6
rleston (cap.), W. Va. ... K6
rlotte, N.C. ... K6
rlottetown (cap.), P.E.I. ... M5
ttanooga, Tenn. ... K6
sapeake (bay), U.S. ... L6
yenne (cap.), Wyo. ... H5
ago, Ill. ... K5
uahua, Mexico ... H7
cinnati, Ohio ... K6
dad Juárez, Mexico ... H6
veland, Ohio ... K5
perton (isl.) ... H8
st (mts.), Br. Col. ... E4
st (ranges), U.S. ... F5

Cocos (isl.), C. Rica ... K9
Cod (cape), Mass. ... M5
Colón, Pan. ... K9
Colorado (riv.), Texas ... H6
Colorado (riv.), U.S. ... G6
Colorado (state), U.S. ... H6
Colorado Springs, Colo. ... H6
Columbia (cap.), S.C. ... K6
Columbia (riv.), U.S. ... F5
Columbus, Ga. ... K6
Columbus (cap.), Ohio ... K6
Concord (cap.), N.H. ... L5
Connecticut (state), U.S. ... L5
Costa Rica ... K8
Cuba ... L7
Dallas, Texas ... J6
Dayton, Ohio ... K6
Delaware (state), U.S. ... L6
Denmark (str.) ... S3
Denver (cap.), Colo. ... H6
Des Moines (cap.), Iowa ... J5
Detroit, Mich. ... K5
District of Columbia ... L6
Dominica ... M8
Dominican Republic ... L8
Dover (cap.), Del. ... L6
Duluth, Minn. ... J5
Edmonton, Alta. ... G4
Ellesmere (isl.), N.W.T. ... K1
El Paso, Texas ... H6
El Salvador ... J8
Erie (lake) ... K5
Fairbanks, Alaska ... D3
Farewell (cape), Greenland ... P4
Flin Flon, Man. ... H4
Florida (state), U.S. ... K7
Florida (strs.) ... K7
Fort McPherson, N.W.T. ... E3
Fort Smith, Ark. ... J6
Fort Worth, Texas ... J6
Foxe (basin), N.W.T. ... L3
Frankfort (cap.), Ky. ... K6
Fraser (riv.), Br. Col. ... F4
Fredericton, N. Br. ... M5
Fresno, Calif. ... G6
Georgia (state), U.S. ... K6
Godhavn, Greenland ... N3
Godthåb (Nûk) (cap.), Greenland ... N3
Goose Bay, Newf. ... M4
Gracias a Dios (cape), Nic. ... K8
Grand Bahama (isl.), Bahamas ... L7
Grand Rapids, Mich. ... K5
Great Bear (lake), N.W.T. ... F3
Greater Antilles (isls.) ... K7
Great Falls, Mont. ... G5
Great Salt (lake), Utah ... G6
Great Slave (lake), N.W.T. ... H3
Green Bay, Wis. ... J5
Greenland ... P2
Greenland (sea) ... T2
Grenada ... M8
Guadalajara, Mexico ... H7
Guadeloupe (isl.) ... M8
Guantánamo, Cuba ... L7
Guatemala ... J8
Guatemala (cap.), Guat. ... J8
Haiti ... L8
Halifax (cap.), N.S. ... M5
Hamilton, Ont. ... K5

Harrisburg (cap.), Pa. ... L5
Hartford (cap.), Conn. ... L5
Hatteras (cape), N.C. ... L6
Havana (cap.), Cuba ... K7
Helena (cap.), Mont. ... G5
Hispaniola (isl.) ... L7
Honduras ... K8
Honduras (gulf) ... K8
Houston, Texas ... J7
Hudson (bay), Canada ... K3
Hudson (str.), Canada ... L3
Huron (lake) ... K5
Idaho (state), U.S. ... G5
Illinois (state), U.S. ... K6
Indiana (state), U.S. ... K6
Indianapolis (cap.), Ind. ... K5
Inuvik, N.W.T. ... E3
Iowa (state), U.S. ... J5
Jackson (cap.), Miss. ... K6
Jacksonville, Fla. ... K6
Jamaica ... L8
James (bay), Canada ... K4
Jefferson City (cap.), Mo. ... J6
Juan de Fuca (str.) ... F5
Juneau, Alaska ... E4
Kansas (state), U.S. ... J6
Kansas City, Mo. ... J6
Kentucky (state), U.S. ... K6
Ketchikan, Alaska ... E4
Key West, Fla. ... K7
Kingston (cap.), Jamaica ... L8
Kingston, Ont. ... L5
Knoxville, Tenn. ... K6
Kodiak (isl.), Alaska ... C4
Labrador (reg.), Newf. ... M4
Lansing (cap.), Mich. ... K5
Lesser Antilles (isls.) ... M8
Lexington, Ky. ... K6
Liard (riv.), Canada ... F3
Limón, C. Rica ... K8
Linçoln (cap.), Nebr. ... J5
Lincoln (sea) ... M1
Little Rock (cap.), Ark. ... J6
London, Ont. ... K5
Los Angeles, Calif. ... G6
Louisiana (state), U.S. ... J6
Louisville, Ky. ... K6
Lower California (pen.), Mexico ... G7
Mackenzie (riv.), N.W.T. ... F3
Macon, Ga. ... K6
Madison (cap.), Wis. ... K5
Maine (state), U.S. ... M5
Managua (cap.), Nic. ... K8
Manitoba (prov.), Canada ... J4
Manitoba (lake), Man. ... H4
Marquette, Mich. ... K5
Martinique (isl.) ... M8
Maryland (state), U.S. ... L6
Massachusetts (state), U.S. ... L5
Matanzas, Cuba ... K7
Mazatlán, Mexico ... H7
McKinley (mt.), Alaska ... C3
Mead (lake), U.S. ... G6
Medicine Hat, Alta. ... H4
Memphis, Tenn. ... K6
Mendocino (cape), Calif. ... F5
Mérida, Mexico ... J7
Mexico ... H7
Mexico (gulf) ... K7

Mexico City (cap.), Mexico ... J7
Miami, Fla. ... K7
Michigan (lake), U.S. ... K5
Michigan (state), U.S. ... K5
Milwaukee, Wis. ... K5
Minneapolis, Minn. ... J5
Minnesota (state), U.S. ... J5
Mississippi (riv.), U.S. ... J6
Mississippi (state), U.S. ... K6
Missouri (riv.), U.S. ... J5
Missouri (state), U.S. ... J6
Mobile, Ala. ... K6
Montana (state), U.S. ... H5
Monterrey, Mexico ... J7
Montgomery (cap.), Ala. ... K6
Montpelier (cap.), Vt. ... L5
Montréal, Que. ... L5
Moose Jaw, Sask. ... H4
Nares (str.) ... L2
Nashville (cap.), Tenn. ... K6
Nassau (cap.), Bahamas ... L7
Nebraska (state), U.S. ... J5
Nelson (riv.), Man. ... J4
Netherlands Antilles ... M8
Nevada (state), U.S. ... G6
New Brunswick (prov.), Canada ... M5
Newfoundland (prov.), Canada ... M4
New Hampshire (state), U.S. ... L5
New Jersey (state), U.S. ... L5
New Mexico (state), U.S. ... H6
New Orleans, La. ... K7
New York, N.Y. ... L5
New York (state), U.S. ... L5
Nicaragua ... K8
Nicaragua (lake), Nic. ... K8
Nome, Alaska ... B3
Norfolk, Va. ... L6
North Bay, Ont. ... L5
North Carolina (state), U.S. ... K6
North Dakota (state), U.S. ... H5
North Saskatchewan (riv.), Canada ... G4
Northwest Territories (prov.), Canada ... G3
Nova Scotia (prov.), Canada ... M5
Nûk (cap.), Greenland ... N3
Oakland, Calif. ... F6
Oaxaca, Mexico ... J8

Ohio (riv.), U.S. ... K6
Ohio (state), U.S. ... K5
Oklahoma (state), U.S. ... J6
Oklahoma City (cap.), Okla. ... J6
Olympia (cap.), Wash. ... F5
Omaha, Nebr. ... J5
Ontario (lake) ... L5
Ontario (prov.), Canada ... K4
Oregon (state), U.S. ... F5
Ottawa (cap.), Canada ... L5
Ottawa (riv.), Canada ... L5
Panama ... K9
Panama (canal), Pan. ... L8
Panamá (cap.), Pan. ... L9
Panamá (gulf), Pan. ... L9
Parry (chan.), N.W.T. ... G2
Peace (riv.), Canada ... G4
Pennsylvania (state), U.S. ... L5
Pensacola, Fla. ... K6
Philadelphia, Pa. ... L6
Phoenix (cap.), Ariz. ... G6
Pierre (cap.), S. Dak. ... J5
Pittsburgh, Pa. ... K5
Port-au-Prince (cap.), Haiti ... L8
Portland, Maine ... M5
Portland, Oreg. ... F5
Prince Edward Island (prov.), Canada ... M5
Providence (cap.), R.I. ... L5
Prudhoe (bay), Alaska ... D2
Puebla, Mexico ... J8
Puerto Rico ... M8
Québec (cap.), Que. ... L5
Québec (prov.), Que. ... L4
Queen Charlotte (isls.), Br. Col. ... E4
Queen Elizabeth (isls.), N.W.T. ... G2
Raleigh (cap.), N.C. ... L6
Red (riv.) ... J5
Red (riv.), U.S. ... J6
Regina (cap.), Sask. ... H4
Reno, Nev. ... G6
Rhode Island (state), U.S. ... M5
Richmond (cap.), Va. ... L6
Rio Grande (riv.) ... H7
Rochester, N.Y. ... L5
Rocky (mts.) ... F4
Sable (cape), N.S. ... M5

Sacramento (cap.), Calif. ... F6
Saint Augustine, Fla. ... K7
Saint John (cap.), N. Br. ... M5
Saint John's (cap.), Newf. ... N5
Saint Lawrence (gulf) ... M5
Saint Lawrence (riv.) ... L5
Saint Louis, Mo. ... K6
Saint Lucia ... M8
Saint Paul (cap.), Minn. ... J5
Saint Pierre and Miquelon (isls.) ... N5
Saint Vincent and the Grenadines ... M8
Salem (cap.), Oreg. ... F5
Salt Lake City (cap.), Utah ... G6
Saltillo, Mexico ... H7
San Antonio, Texas ... J7
San Diego, Calif. ... G6
San Francisco, Calif. ... F6
San José (cap.), C. Rica ... K9
San Juan (cap.), P. Rico ... M8
San Salvador (cap.), El Salvador ... J8
Santa Fe (cap.), N. Mex. ... H6
Santiago de Cuba, Cuba ... L8
Santo Domingo (cap.), Dom. Rep. ... L8
Saskatchewan (prov.), Canada ... H4
Saskatoon, Sask. ... H4
Sault Ste. Marie, Ont. ... K5
Savannah, Ga. ... K6
Seattle, Wash. ... F5
Shreveport, La. ... J6
Sierra Madre Occidental (mts.), Mexico ... H7
Sierra Nevada (range), Calif. ... F6
Sioux City, Iowa ... J5
Sioux Falls, S. Dak. ... J5
Sitka, Alaska ... E4
Slave (riv.), Canada ... G3
Snake (riv.), U.S. ... G5
South Carolina (state), U.S. ... K6
South Dakota (state), U.S. ... H5
South Platte (riv.), U.S. ... H6
South Saskatchewan (riv.), Canada ... G4
Springfield (cap.), Ill. ... J6
Sudbury, Ont. ... K5

Superior (lake) ... K5
Sverdrup (isls.), N.W.T. ... J2
Tacoma, Wash. ... F5
Tallahassee (cap.), Fla. ... K6
Tampa, Fla. ... K7
Tampico, Mexico ... J7
Tegucigalpa (cap.), Hond. ... K8
Tennessee (state), U.S. ... K6
Texas (state), U.S. ... J6
Thule, Greenland ... M2
Thunder Bay, Ont. ... K5
Toledo, Ohio ... K5
Topeka (cap.), Kansas ... J6
Toronto (cap.), Ont. ... K5
Trenton (cap.), N.J. ... L5
Trinidad and Tobago ... N8
Tucson, Ariz. ... G6
Tulsa, Okla. ... J6
Ungava (bay), Canada ... M4
United States ... H5
Utah (state), U.S. ... G6
Vancouver, Br. Col. ... F4
Vancouver (isl.), Br. Col. ... F5
Veracruz, Mexico ... J8
Vermont (state), U.S. ... L5
Victoria (cap.), Br. Col. ... F5
Victoria (isl.), N.W.T. ... G2
Virgin Islands (isls.) ... M8
Virginia (state), U.S. ... L6
Washington (state), U.S. ... F5
Washington, D.C. (cap.), U.S. ... L6
West Indies (isls.) ... M7
West Virginia (state), U.S. ... K6
Whitehorse (cap.), Yukon ... E3
Wichita, Kansas ... J6
Windward (passg.) ... L8
Winnipeg (cap.), Man. ... J5
Winnipegosis (lake), Man. ... H4
Wisconsin (state), U.S. ... K5
Woods (lake) ... J5
Wyoming (state), U.S. ... H5
Yellowknife, N.W.T. ... G3
Yucatán (pen.), Mexico ... K7
Yukon (riv.) ... C3
Yukon Territory (terr.), Canada ... E3

Canada
CONIC PROJECTION
SCALE OF MILES
0 50 100 200 300
SCALE OF KILOMETERS
0 50 100 200 300 400 500
Capitals of Countries
Provincial & Territorial Capitals
International Boundaries
Provincial Boundaries
© Copyright HAMMOND INCORPORATED, Maplewood, N. J.

Abitibi (lake), Ont. H6
Aklavik, N.W.T. 781 .... C2
Albany (riv.), Ont. H5
Alberta (prov.) 1,838,037 .... E5
Amherst, N.S. 10,263 .... K6
Amos, Que. 9,213 .... J6
Anticosti (isl.), Que. K6
Arctic Bay, N.W.T. 388 .... H1
Arctic Red River, N.W.T. 120 .... C2
Athabasca, Alta. 1,759 .... E5
Athabasca (lake) F4
Athabasca (riv.), Alta. E4
Atikokan, Ont. 5,668 .... G6
Axel Heiburg (isl.), N.W.T. N3
Baffin (bay), N.W.T. J1
Baffin (isl.), N.W.T. J1
Baie-Saint-Paul, Que. 4,062 .... J6
Baker Lake, N.W.T. 856 .... G3
Banff, Alta. 3,410 .... E5
Banff Nat'l Park, Alta. 3,849 .... E5
Banks (isl.), N.W.T. D1
Baskatong (res.), Que. J6
Bathurst, N. Br. 16,301 .... K6
Battleford, Sask. 2,569 .... E5
Belle Isle (str.), Newf. L5
Biggar, Sask. 2,491 .... F5
Big River, Sask. 827 .... F5
Blind River, Ont. 3,142 .... H6
Boissevain, Man. 1,584 .... G6
Bonavista, Newf. 4,299 .... L6
Boothia (pen.), N.W.T. G1
Bow (riv.), Alta. E5
Brandon, Man. 34,901 .... F6
Bridgewater, N.S. 6,010 .... K7
British Columbia
(prov.) 2,466,608 .... D4
Burns Lake, Br. Col. 1,433 .... D5
Cabot (str.) K6
Calgary, Alta. 469,917 .... E5
Callander, Ont. 1,058 .... H6
Cambridge Bay, N.W.T. 612 .... F2
Campbellton, N. Br. 9,282 .... K6
Camrose, Alta. 10,104 .... E5
Cap-Chat, Que. 3,617 .... K6
Cape Breton (isl.), N.S. K6
Cardston, Alta. 3,043 .... E6
Carman, Man. 2,272 .... G6
Cartwright, Newf. 675 .... L5
Chandler, Que. 4,011 .... K6
Channel-Port aux Basques,
Newf. 6,187 .... L6
Chapleau, Ont. 3,253 .... H6
Charlottetown (cap.),
P.E.I. 17,063 .... K6
Chatham, N. Br. 7,601 .... K6
Chesterfield Inlet,
N.W.T. 241 .... G3
Chibougamu, Que. 10,536 .... J6
Chicoutimi, Que. 57,737 .... J6
Chidley (cape), Newf. K3
Chilliwack, Br. Col. 8,634 .... D6
Churchill, Man. 1,699 .... G4
Clyde, N.W.T. 348 .... J1
Coast (mts.) C4
Cobalt, Ont. 2,056 .... H6
Cochrane, Ont. 4,974 .... H6
Coleman, Alta. 1,543 .... E6
Coppermine, N.W.T. 755 .... E2
Corner Brook, Newf. 25,198 .... K6
Cornwall, Ont. 46,121 .... J7
Courtenay, Br. Col. 7,733 .... D6
Cranbrook, Br. Col. 13,510 .... E6
Cree (lake), Sask. F4
Dartmouth, N.S. 65,341 .... K7
Dauphin, Man. 9,109 .... F5
Davis (str.), N.W.T. K1
Dawson, Yukon 838 .... C3
Devon (isl.), N.W.T. M3
Didsbury, Alta. 2,153 .... E5
Drumheller, Alta. 6,154 .... E5
Edmogton (cap.), Alta. 461,361 .... E5
Edmundston, N. Br. 12,710 .... K6
Edson, Alta. 4,038 .... E5
Ellesmere (isl.), N.W.T. N3
Emerson, Man. 756 .... G6
Englehart, Ont. 1,767 .... H6
Eskimo Point, N.W.T. 835 .... G3
Estevan, Sak. 8,847 .... F6
Eston, Sask. 1,354 .... F5
Fernie, Br. Col. 4,608 .... E6
Finlay (riv.), Br. Col. D4
Flin Flon, Man.-Sask. 9,560 .... F4
Fogo (isl.), Newf. 1,103 .... L6
Fort-Chimo, Que. 867 .... K4
Fort Frances, Ont. 9,325 .... G6
Fort Franklin, N.W.T. 422 .... D3
Fort-George, Que. 1,074 .... J5
Fort Good Hope, N.W.T. 440 .... D2
Fort Liard, N.W.T. 296 .... D3
Fort Macleod, Alta. 3,067 .... E6
Fort McMurray, Alta. 15,424 .... E4
Fort McPherson, N.W.T. 704 .... C2
Fort Nelson, Br. Col. 2,916 .... D4
Fort Norman, N.W.T. 230 .... D3
Fort Providence, N.W.T. 598 .... E3
Fort Resolution, N.W.T. 497 .... E3
Fort Saskatchewan, Alta. 8,304 .... E5
Fort Simpson, N.W.T. 1,136 .... D3
Fort Smith, N.W.T. 2,288 .... E3
Foxe (basin), N.W.T. J2
Franklin (dist.), N.W.T. H1
Fraser (riv.), Br. Col. D5
Fredericton, N. Br. 45,248 .... K6
Frobisher Bay, N.W.T. 2,320 .... K3
Fundy (bay) K7
Gagnon, Que. 3,423 .... K5
Gander, Newf. 9,301 .... L6
Gaspé, Que. 16,842 .... K6
Georgian (bay), Ont. H6
Geraldton, Ont. 3,127 .... H6
Gjoa Haven, N.W.T. 416 .... G2
Glace Bay, N.S. 21,836 .... L6
Goose Bay, Newf. 8,075 .... K5
Gouin (res.), Que. J6
Grand Falls, Newf. 8,729 .... L6
Grande Prairie, Alta. 17,626 .... E4
Great Bear (lake), N.W.T. D2
Great Slave (lake), N.W.T. E3
Guelph, Ont. 67,538 .... H7
Halifax (cap.), N.S. 117,882 .... K7
Hamilton, Ont. 312,003 .... H7
Hanna, Alta. 2,627 .... E5
Harbour Grace, Newf. 2,937 .... L6
Havre-St-Pierre, Que. 3,208 .... K5
Hay River, N.W.T. 3,268 .... E3
Hearst, Ont. 5,195 .... H6
Hecate (str.), Br. Col. C5
High River, Alta. 3,598 .... E5
Hope, Br. Col. 2,963 .... D6
Hopedale, Newf. 447 .... L4
Hull, Que. 61,039 .... J6
Humboldt, Sask. 4,265 .... F5
Indian Head, Sask. 1,720 .... F5
Inuvik, N.W.T. 3,116 .... C2
Inverness, N.S. 1,980 .... K6
Iroquois Falls, Ont. 6,887 .... H6
Jasper, Alta. 3,404 .... E5
Jasper Nat'l Park, Alta. E5
Jonquière, Que. J6
Juan de Fuca (str.), Br.
Col. D6
Kamloops, Br. Col. 58,311 .... D5
Kamsack, Sask. 2,726 .... F5
Kane (basin), N.W.T. N3
Kapuskasing, Ont. 12,676 .... H6
Keewatin (dist.), N.W.T. 3,978 .... G3
Kelowna, Br. Col. 51,955 .... E6
Kenora, Ont. 10,565 .... G5
Killarney, Man. 2,348 .... G6
Kindersley, Sask. 3,523 .... F5
Kingston, Ont. 56,032 .... J7
Kirkland Lake, Ont. 13,567 .... H6
Kitimat, Br. Col. 11,791 .... D5
Kluane (lake), Yukon C3
Kootenay (lake), Br. Col. E5
Labrador (reg.), Newf. K4
Labrador (sea) L4
Lac La Biche, Alta. 1,954 .... E5
Lacombe, Alta. 3,888 .... E5
Lake Harbour, N.W.T. 233 .... J3
Lake Louise, Alta. 140 .... E5
Lancaster (sound), N.W.T. H1
La Sarre, Que. 4,978 .... J6
La Tuque, Que. 12,067 .... J6
Leduc, Alta. 8,576 .... E5
Lesser Slave (lake), Alta. E4
Lethbridge, Alta. 46,752 .... E6
Liard (riv.) D3
Lillooet, Br. Col. 2,218 .... D5
Lloydminster,
Alta.-Sask. 10,311 .... E5
Logan (mt.), Yukon B3
London, Ont. 240,392 .... H7
Lunenburg, N.S. 3,024 .... K7
Lynn Lake, Man. 2,568 .... G4
Mackenzie (dist.), N.W.T. E3
Mackenzie (riv.), N.W.T. C2
Magdalen (isls.), Que. K6
Manicouagan (riv.), Que. K5
Manitoba (lake), Man. G5
Manitoba (prov.) G5
Manitoulin (isl.), Ont. H6
Maple Creek, Sask. 2,330 .... F6
Marathon, Ont. 2,250 .... H6
Mattawa, Ont. 2,849 .... J6
Mayo, Yukon 448 .... C3
M'Clintock (chan.), N.W.T. F1
Medicine Hat, Alta. 32,811 .... E5
Melfort, Sask. 5,141 .... F5
Melville, Sask. 5,149 .... F5
Melville (isl.), N.W.T. E1
Merritt, Br. Col. 5,680 .... D5
Minto (lake), Que. J4
Mistassibi (riv.), Que. J5
Mistassini (lake), Que. J5
Moncton, N. Br. 55,934 .... K6
Mont-Joli, Que. 6,508 .... K6
Mont-Laurier, Que. 8,565 .... J6
Montréal, Que. 1,080,546 .... J7
Moose Jaw, Sask. 32,581 .... F6
Moosomin, Sask. 2,449 .... F5
Moosonee, Ont. 1,349 .... H5
Morden, Man. 3,886 .... G6
Nain, Newf. 812 .... K4
Nanaimo, Br. Col. 40,336 .... D6
Nares (str.), N.W.T. N3
Nelson, Br. Col. 9,235 .... E6
Nelson (riv.), Man. G4
New Brunswick (prov.) 677,250 .... K6
Newcastle, N. Br. 6,423 .... K6
Newfoundland (isl.) L6
Newfoundland (prov.) 557,725 .... L5
New Liskeard, Ont. 5,601 .... H6
New Westminster, Br. Col. D6
Noranda, Que. 9,809 .... J6
Norman Wells, N.W.T. 364 .... D2
North Battleford, Sask. 13,158 .... F5
North Bay, Ont. 51,639 .... J6
North Vancouver, Br.
Col. 63,471 .... D6
Northwest Territories 21,836 .... E2
Nottaway (riv.), Que. J5
Nova Scotia (prov.) 828,571 .... K7
Okanagan (lake), Br. Col. D6
Ontario (prov.) 8,264,465 .... H5
Ottawa (cap.), Canada 304,462 .... J6
Ottawa (riv.) J6
Owen Sound, Ont. 19,525 .... H7
Pangnirtung, N.W.T. 807 .... K2
Parry (chan.), N.W.T. E-H1
Parry Sound, Ont. 5,501 .... J6
Peace (riv.), Alta. E4
Peace River, Alta. 4,840 .... E4
Peel (riv.) C2
Pelly (riv.), Yukon C3
Pembroke, Ont. 14,927 .... J6
Péribonca (riv.),
Que. 59,683 .... J5
Peterborough, Ont. 59,683 .... J7
Pincher Creek, Br. Col. 3,448 .... E6
Pond Inlet, N.W.T. 500 .... J1
Portage la Prairie,
Man. 12,555 .... G5
Port-Cartier, Que. 8,139 .... K5
Port Radium, N.W.T. 51 .... E2
Poste-de-la-Baleine, Que. 718 .... J4
Povungnituk, Que. J3
Prince Albert, Sask. 28,631 .... F5
Prince Albert Nat'l Park,
Sask. F5
Prince Edward Island
(prov.) 118,229 .... K6
Prince George, Br. Col. 59,929 .... D5
Prince Patrick (isl.),
N.W.T. M3
Prince Rupert, Br. Col. 14,754 .... C5
Québec (cap.), Que. 177,082 .... J6
Québec (prov.) 6,234,445 .... J5
Queen Charlotte (isls.), Br.
Col. C5
Queen Elizabeth (isls.),
N.W.T. M3
Quesnel, Br. Col. 7,637 .... D5
Race (cape), Newf. L6
Radville, Sask. 1,008 .... F6
Rae-Edzo, N.W.T. 1,158 .... E3
Rainy (lake), Ont. G6
Rainy River, Ont. 1,092 .... G6
Ray (cape), Newf. K6
Raymond, Alta. 2,290 .... E6
Red Deer, Alta. 32,184 .... E5
Regina (cap.), Sask. 149,593 .... F5
Reindeer (lake) F4
Renfrew, Ont. 8,617 .... J6
Revelstoke, Br. Col. 4,615 .... E5
Riding Mountain Nat'l Park,
Man. F5
Rigolet, Newf. 238 .... L5
Rimouski, Que. 27,897 .... K6
Rivière-du-Loup, Que. 13,103 .... K6
Roberval, Que. 8,543 .... J6
Robson (mt.), Br. Col. D5
Rocky (mts.) D4
Rocky Mountain House,

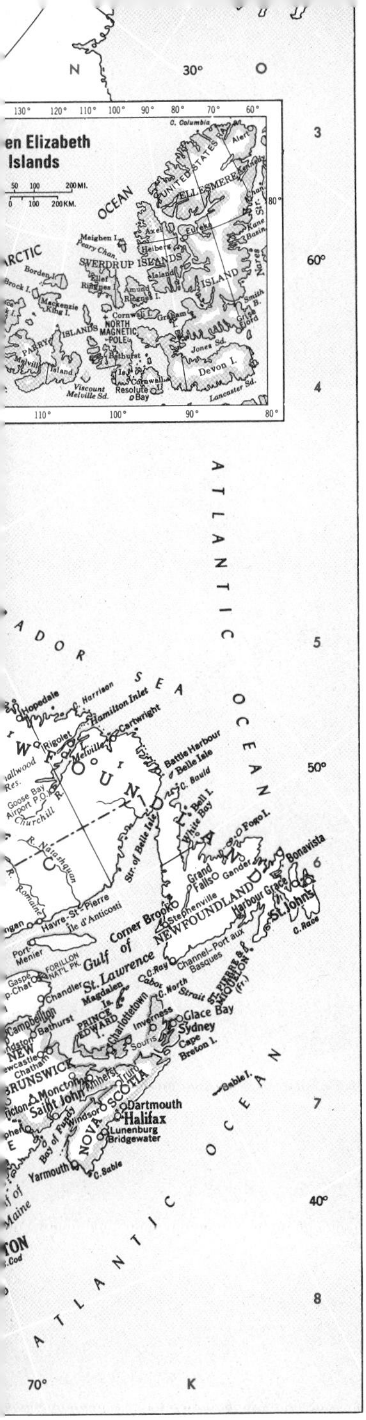
en Elizabeth
Islands
ATLANTIC OCEAN
ATLANTIC OCEAN
Gulf of St. Lawrence
NEWFOUNDLAND
NOVA SCOTIA
PRINCE EDWARD IS.
NEW BRUNSWICK
Halifax
Dartmouth
Sydney
Glace Bay
Charlottetown
Saint John
Moncton
St. John's
Corner Brook
Grand Falls
Gander
Yarmouth
Lunenburg
Bridgewater
Cape Breton I.
Sable I.
C. Sable
Bay of Fundy
Churchill
Goose Bay
Hamilton Inlet
Cartwright
Battle Harbour
Belle Isle
Str. of Belle Isle
White Bay
Fogo I.
Bonavista
C. Race
Stephenville
Channel-Port aux Basques
Cabot Strait
Magdalen Is.
Gaspé
Bathurst
Campbellton
Chatham
Newcastle
Truro
Windsor
Amherst
Inverness
Souris
North
C. Ray
C. North
Havre-St.-Pierre
Île d'Anticosti
Hopedale
Rigolet
Melville
Harrison
30°
60°
50°
40°
70°
N
O
K
3
4
5
6
7
8

AREA 3,851,787 sq. mi. (9,976,139 sq. km.)
POPULATION 24,105,163
CAPITAL Ottawa
LARGEST CITY Montréal
HIGHEST POINT Mt. Logan 19,524 ft. (5,951 m.)
MONETARY UNIT Canadian dollar
MAJOR LANGUAGES English, French
MAJOR RELIGIONS Protestantism, Roman Catholicism

Population Distribution

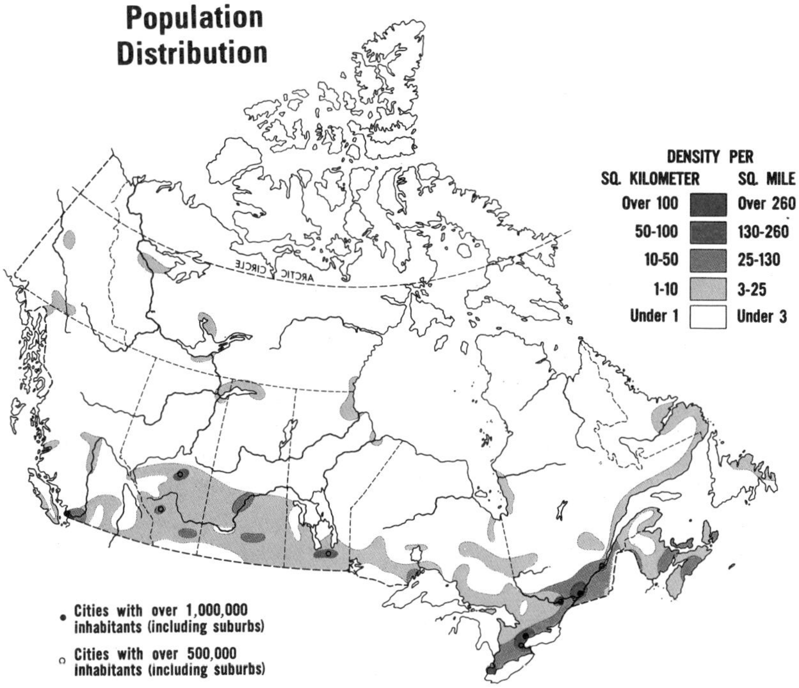
ARCTIC CIRCLE
DENSITY PER
SQ. KILOMETER
SQ. MILE
Over 100
Over 260
50-100
130-260
10-50
25-130
1-10
3-25
Under 1
Under 3
Cities with over 1,000,000 inhabitants (including suburbs)
Cities with over 500,000 inhabitants (including suburbs)

Vegetation

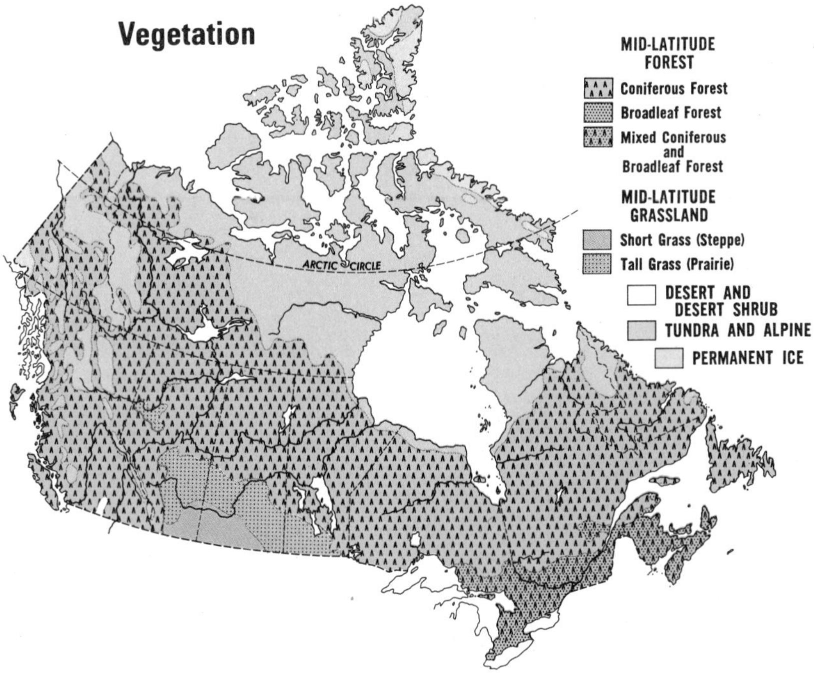
ARCTIC CIRCLE
MID-LATITUDE FOREST
Coniferous Forest
Broadleaf Forest
Mixed Coniferous and Broadleaf Forest
MID-LATITUDE GRASSLAND
Short Grass (Steppe)
Tall Grass (Prairie)
DESERT AND DESERT SHRUB
TUNDRA AND ALPINE
PERMANENT ICE

Alta. 3,432 ..... E5
osetown, Sask. 2,551 ..... F5
ossland, Br. Col. 3,716 ..... E6
osthern, Sask. 1,604 ..... F5
ouyn, Que. 17,678 ..... J6
able (cape), N.S. K7
able (isl.), N.S. L7
aint Elias (mt.), Yukon B3
aint John, N. Br. 85,956 ..... K6
aint John's (cap.),
Newf. 86,576 ..... L6
aint Lawrence (riv.) K6
aint Paul, Alta. 4,337 ..... E5
aint Pierre & Miquelon
(isls.) 5,840 ..... L6
aint Stephen, N. Br. 5,264 ..... K6
aint Walburg, Sask. 718 ..... F5
arnia, Ont. 55,576 ..... H7
askatchewan (prov.) 921,323 ..... F5
askatchewan (riv.) F5
askatoon, Sask. 133,750 ..... F5
ault Sainte Marie,
Ont. 81,048 ..... H6
chefferville, Que. 3,429 ..... K5
elkirk, Man. 9,862 ..... G5
ept-Îles (Seven Is.),
Que. 30,617 ..... K5
haunavon, Sask. 2,183 ..... F6
hawinigan, Que. 24,921 ..... J6
herbrooke, Que. 76,804 ..... J7
herridon, Man. 187 ..... G4
ioux Lookout, Ont. 3,108 ..... G5
keena (riv.), Br. Col. D5
lave (riv.) E3
mallwood (res.), Newf. K5
mithers, Br. Col. 3,783 ..... D5
now Lake, Man. 1,585 ..... G5
ouris, Man. 1,712 ..... F6
ouris, P.E.I. 1,447 ..... K6
outhampton (isl.), N.W.T. H2
tettler, Alta. 4,182 ..... E5
tewart (riv.), Yukon C3
Stikine (riv.), Br. Col. C4
Sturgeon Falls, Ont. 6,400 ..... H6
Sudbury, Ont. 97,604 ..... H6
Swan River, Man. 3,443 ..... F5
Swift Current, Sask. 14,262 ..... F5
Sydney, N.S. 30,645 ..... K6
Tadoussac, Que. 998 ..... J6
Terrace, Br. Col. 7,576 ..... D5
The Pas, Man. 6,602 ..... F5
Thessalon, Ont. 1,824 ..... H6
Thompson, Man. 17,291 ..... G4
Thunder Bay, Ont. 111,476 ..... H6
Timmins, Ont. 44,747 ..... H6
Tisdale, Sask. 3,026 ..... F5
Toronto (cap.), Ont. 633,318 ..... H7
Trail, Br. Col. 9,976 ..... E6
Trois-Rivières, Que. 52,518 ..... J6
Truro, N.S. 12,840 ..... K6
Tuktoyaktuk, N.W.T. 590 ..... C2
Uranium City, Sask. 1,765 ..... F4
Val-d'Or, Que. 19,915 ..... J6
Vancouver, Br. Col. 410,188 ..... D6
Vancouver (isl.), Br. Col. D6
Vanderhoof, Br. Col. 1,990 ..... D5
Vègreville, Alta. 4,158 ..... E5
Vernon, Br. Col. 17,546 ..... E5
Victoria (cap.), Br.
Col. 62,551 ..... D6
Victoria (isl.), N.W.T. E1
Wabush, Newf. 3,769 ..... K5
Waterton-Glacier International Peace
Par 194 ..... E6
Wetaskiwin, Alta. 6,754 ..... E5
Weyburn, Sask. 8,892 ..... F6
Whitehorse (cap.),
Yukon 13,311 ..... C3
Williams Lake, Br. Col. 6,199 ..... D5
Williston (lake), Br. Col. D4
Windsor, N.S. 3,702 ..... K7
Windsor, Ont. 196,526 ..... H7
Winnipeg (cap.), Man. 560,874 ..... G6
Winnipeg (lake), Man. G5

Topography

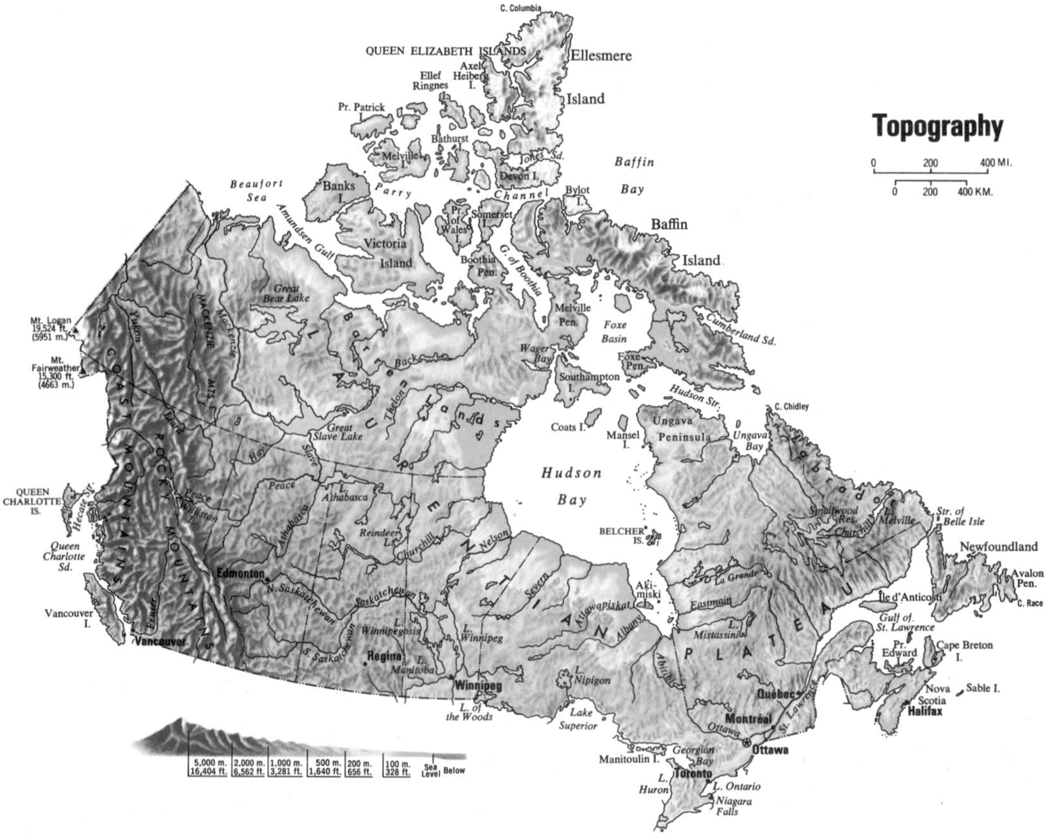

Agriculture, Industry and Resources

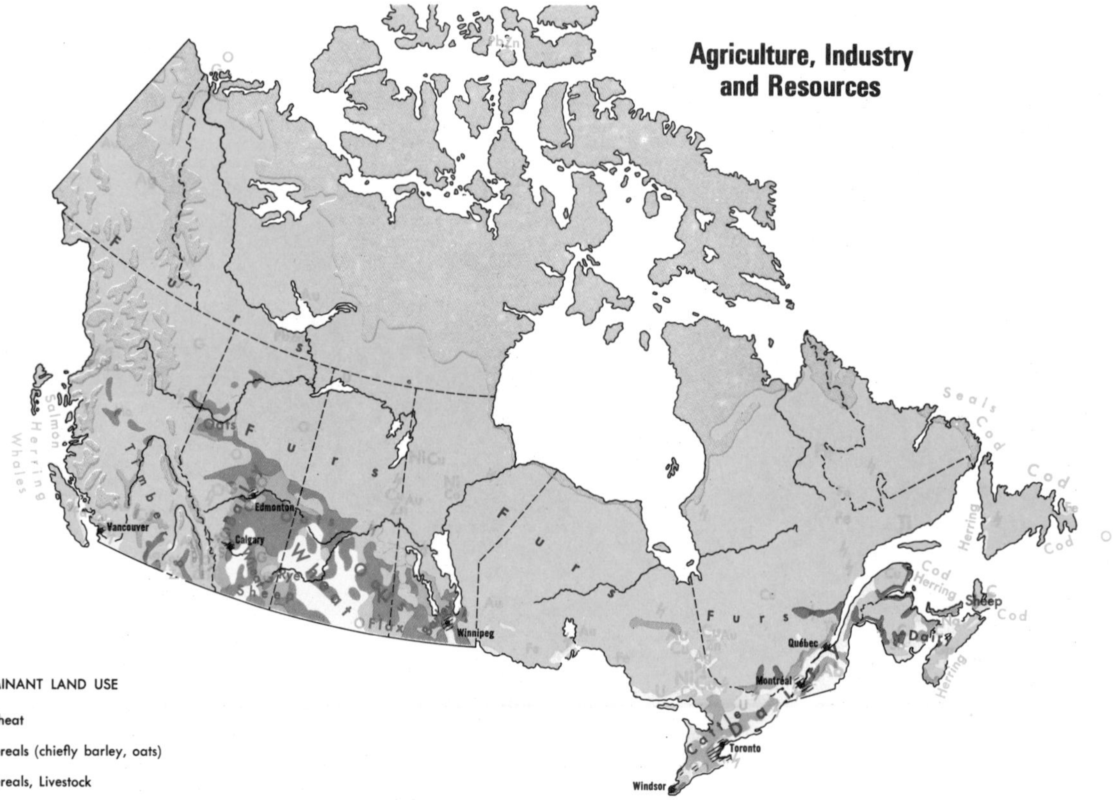

DOMINANT LAND USE

- Wheat
- Cereals (chiefly barley, oats)
- Cereals, Livestock
- General Farming, Livestock
- Dairy
- Fruit, Vegetables
- Pasture Livestock
- Range Livestock
- Forests
- Nonagricultural Land

MAJOR MINERAL OCCURRENCES

Ab	Asbestos	Fe	Iron Ore	Ni	Nickel	Sb	Antimony
Ag	Silver	G	Natural Gas	O	Petroleum	Ti	Titanium
Au	Gold	Gp	Gypsum	Pb	Lead	U	Uranium
C	Coal	K	Potash	Pt	Platinum	W	Tungsten
Co	Cobalt	Mo	Molybdenum	S	Sulfur	Zn	Zinc
Cu	Copper	Na	Salt				

Water Power
Major Industrial Areas

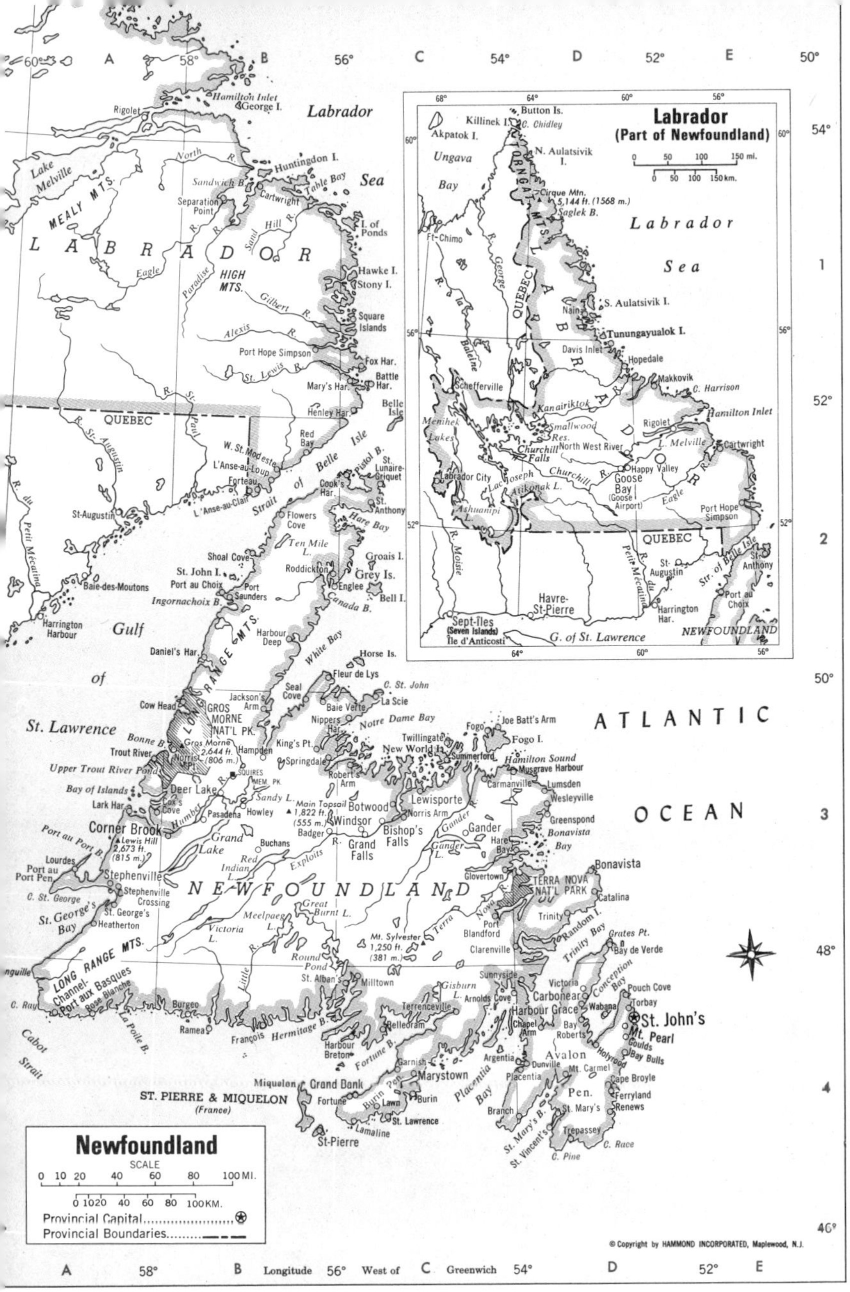

Newfoundland 99

AREA 156,184 sq. mi. (404,517 sq. km.)
POPULATION 561,996
CAPITAL St. John's
LARGEST CITY St. John's
HIGHEST POINT in Torngat Mountains 5,420 ft. (1,652 m.)
SETTLED IN 1610
ADMITTED TO CONFEDERATION 1949
PROVINCIAL FLOWER Pitcher Plant

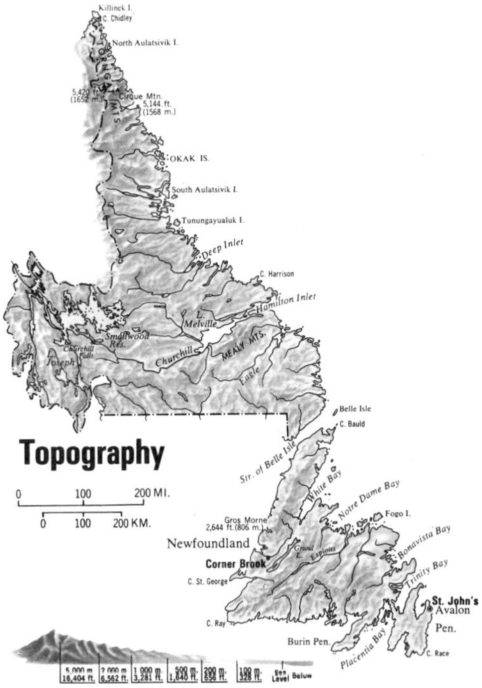

Topography

Agriculture, Industry and Resources

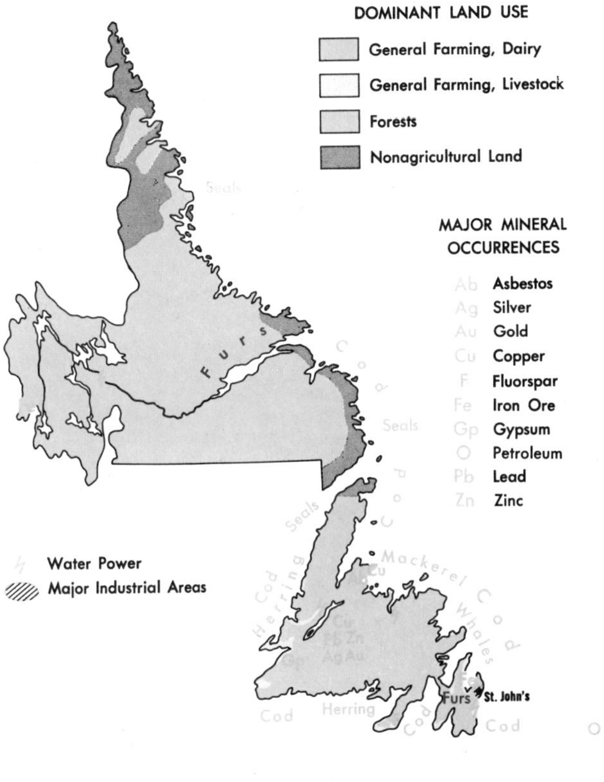

NOVA SCOTIA

COUNTIES

Annapolis 23,208 ....C4
Antigonish 17,573 ....F3
Cape Breton 128,229 ....H3
Colchester 41,771 ....E3
Cumberland 35,914 ....D3
Digby 20,932 ....C4
Guysborough 12,825 ....F3
Halifax 278,531 ....E4
Hants 32,383 ....D4
Inverness 21,773 ....G2
Kings 47,977 ....D4
Lunenburg 42,388 ....D4
Pictou 49,076 ....F3
Queens 12,947 ....C4
Richmond 12,447 ....H3
Shelburne 16,970 ....C5
Victoria 8,417 ....H2
Yarmouth 25,210 ....C5

CITIES and TOWNS

Alder Point........................H2
Aldershot..........................D3
Amherst⊙ 10,263 ....D3
Annapolis Royal⊙ 738 ....C4
Antigonish⊙ 5,442 ....F3
Arichat⊙ 893 ....H3
Baddeck⊙ 943 ....H2
Bear River 716 ....C4
Beaverbank 1,294..............E4
Berwick 1,701 ....D4
Bible Hill 4,266..................E3
Bridgetown 1,037...............C4
Bridgewater 6,010..............D4
Brookfield 892....................E3
Brooklyn 1,179 ....D4
Cambridge Station 922 ....D3
Canso 1,173.......................H3
Cape North 136 ....H2
Centreville, Kings 736 ....D3
Chester 1,121 ....D4
Chéticamp 1,027 ....G2
Church Point 377 ....B4
Clark's Harbour 1,077 ....C5
Dartmouth 65,341 ....E4
Digby⊙ 2,542 ....C4
Dominion 2,938 ....J2
Donkin 1,087 ....J2
Echo Lake 1,048 ....E4
Elmsdale 944 ....E4
Elmsvale 132 ....E3
Enfield 1,234 ....E4
Fall River 1,060 ....E4
Falmouth 1,017 ....D3
Florence 2,111 ....H2
Glace Bay 21,836 ....J2
Guysborough⊙ 514............G3
Halifax (cap.)⊙ 117,882 .....E4
Hantsport 1,423 ....D3
Harrietsfield 949 ....E4
Herring Cove 1,363............E4
Hilden 1,076......................E3
Ingonish 407 ....H2
Inverness 1,980 ....G2
Judique 770 ....G3
Kentville⊙ 5,056 ....D3
Kingston 1,562 ....D4
Lakeside 1,831 ....E4
Lantz 769 ....E4
Liverpool⊙ 3,336 ....D4
Lockeport 1,030 ....C5
Louisbourg 1,519 ....J3
Louisdale 1,026..................G3
Lower West Pubnico 778.....C5
Lunenburg⊙ 3,024 ....D4
Mahone Bay 1,236 ....D4
Meteghan 761 ....B4
Middleton 1,823 ....C4
Milton 1,918 ....D4
Mira Road 1,496 ....H2
Mulgrave 1,206 ....G3
New Germany 910..............D4
New Glasgow 10,672..........F3
New Minas 2,873...............D3
New Road 1,151 ....E4
New Victoria 1,345............H2
New Waterford 9,223 ....J2
North Sydney 8,319...........H2
Oxford 1,498 ....E3
Parrsboro 1,857 ....D3
Petit-de-Grat 762 ....H3
Pictou⊙ 4,588 ....F3
Porters Lake 991................E4
Port Hastings 719 ....G3
Port Hawkesbury 4,008 ......G3
Port Hood⊙ 769 ....G2
Port Morien 763.................J2
Port Williams 993 ....D3
Pugwash 746 ....E3
Reserve Mines 2,394 ....H2
River Hébert 861 ....D3
Sackville 14,590 ....E4
Saint Peters 705 ....H3
Salmon River, Colchester 1,889 ....E3
Scotchtown 2,086 ....H2
Sheet Harbour 762.............F4
Shelburne⊙ 2,511 ....C5
Springhill 5,220 ....E3
Stellarton 5,366 ....F3
Stewiacke 1,174 ....E3
Sydney⊙ 30 645 ....H2
Sydney Mines 8,965 ....H2
Sydney River 2,468 ....H2
Terence Bay 1,087.............E4
Thorburn 965 ....F3
Three Mile Plains 950.........D4
Timberlea 1,657.................E4
Trenton 3,224 ....F3
Truro⊙ 12,840 ....E3
Waterville 1,215 ....D3
Waverley 1,142 ....E4
Wedgeport 797 ....C5
Western Shore 1,242 ....D4
Westmount 2,080 ....H2
Westville 4,251 ....F3
Wileville 890......................D4
Windsor⊙ 3,702 ....D3
Wolfville 3,073...................D3
Yarmouth⊙ 7,801 ....B5

OTHER FEATURES

Advocate, (bay) D3
Ainslie, (lake) ....G
Amet, (sound)...................E
Andrew, (isl.) ....H
Annapolis, (basin) C
Annapolis, (riv.) C
Antigonish, (harb.) ....G
Argos, (cape) ....G
Aspy, (bay) ....H
Avon, (riv.) ....D
Baccaro, (pt.) C
Baddeck, (riv.) ....H
Barachois, (pt.) ....G
Barren, (isl.) ....G
Barrington, (bay) C
Bedford, (basin).................E
Berry, (head).....................G
Boularderie, (isl.)...............H
Bras d'Or, (lake).................H
Breton, (cape) ....J
Brier, (isl.).........................B
Canso, (cape) ....H
Canso, (str.) ....G
Cap d'Or, (cape).................D

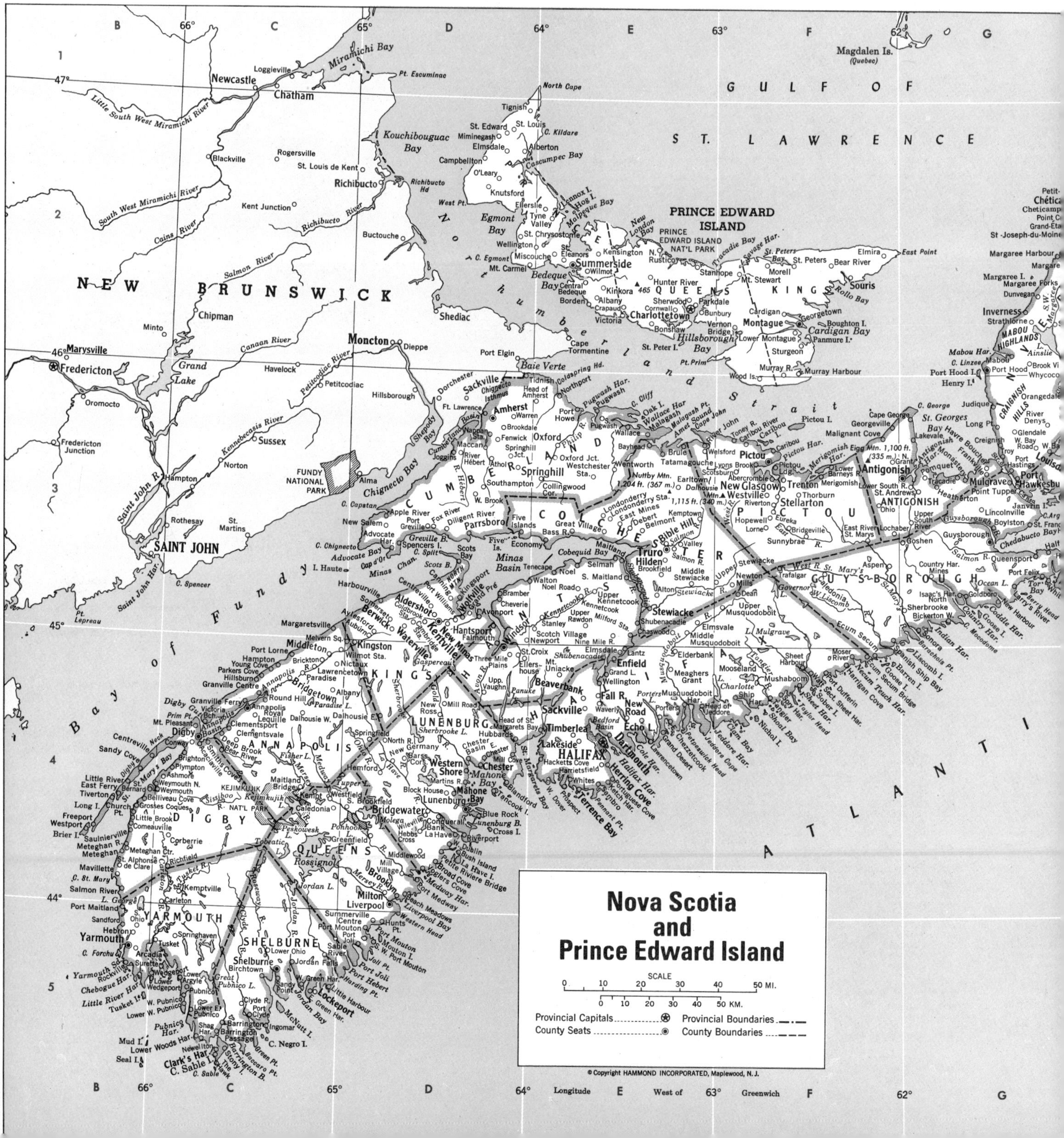
Nova Scotia and Prince Edward Island
SCALE
0 10 20 30 40 50 MI.
0 10 20 30 40 50 KM.
Provincial Capitals
County Seats
Provincial Boundaries
County Boundaries
© Copyright HAMMOND INCORPORATED, Maplewood, N.J.
Longitude West of Greenwich
GULF OF ST. LAWRENCE
PRINCE EDWARD ISLAND
NEW BRUNSWICK
Northumberland Strait
Bay of Fundy
ATLANTIC
Magdalen Is. (Quebec)
Charlottetown
Summerside
Fredericton
SAINT JOHN
Moncton
HALIFAX
Dartmouth
Truro
Yarmouth
Amherst
New Glasgow
Antigonish
Minas Basin
Chignecto Bay
FUNDY NATIONAL PARK
KEJIMKUJIK NAT'L PARK

ˑ Breton (isl.) J2
ˑ Breton Highlands Nat'l
ark........................H2
ˑ Negro (isl.) C5
ˑ Sable (isl.) C5
stan (cape)...............D3
oou (isl.)................F3
eton (riv.)...............C4
lotte (lake)..............F4
oogue (harb.).............B5
dabucto (bay).............G3
icamp (isl.)..............G2
necto (bay)...............D3
necto (cape)..............C3
necto (isth.).............D3
ı (bay)...................F4
(cape)....................E3
e (riv.)..................C5
equid (bay)...............E3
dle (harb.)...............G3
spring (head).............E3
(harb.)...................E4
ntry (harb.)..............G3
Craignish (hills) G3
Cross (isl.) D4
Cumberland (basin) D3
Dalhousie (mt.) E3
Dauphin (cape)................H2
Digby Gut (chan.) C4
Digby Neck (pen.) B4
East (bay).....................H3
East (riv.) F3
East Bay (hills)................H3
Egmont (cape) H2
Eigg (mt.) F3
Fisher (lake) C4
Five (isls.) D3
Forchu (bay)...................H3
Forchu (cape) B5
Framboise Cove (bay)........H3
Fundy (bay).....................C3
Gabarus (bay) H3
Gabarus (cape) J3
Gaspereau (lake)..............D4
George (cape)..................G3
George (lake) B5

PRINCE EDWARD ISLAND

AREA 2,184 sq. mi. (5,657 sq. km.)
POPULATION 121,328
CAPITAL Charlottetown
LARGEST CITY Charlottetown
HIGHEST POINT 465 ft. (142 m.)
SETTLED IN 1720
ADMITTED TO CONFEDERATION 1873
PROVINCIAL FLOWER Lady's Slipper

NOVA SCOTIA

AREA 21,425 sq. mi. (55,491 sq. km.)
POPULATION 837,789
CAPITAL Halifax
LARGEST CITY Halifax
HIGHEST POINT Cape Breton Highlands 1,747 ft. (532 m.)
SETTLED IN 1605
ADMITTED TO CONFEDERATION 1867
PROVINCIAL FLOWER Trailing Arbutus or Mayflower

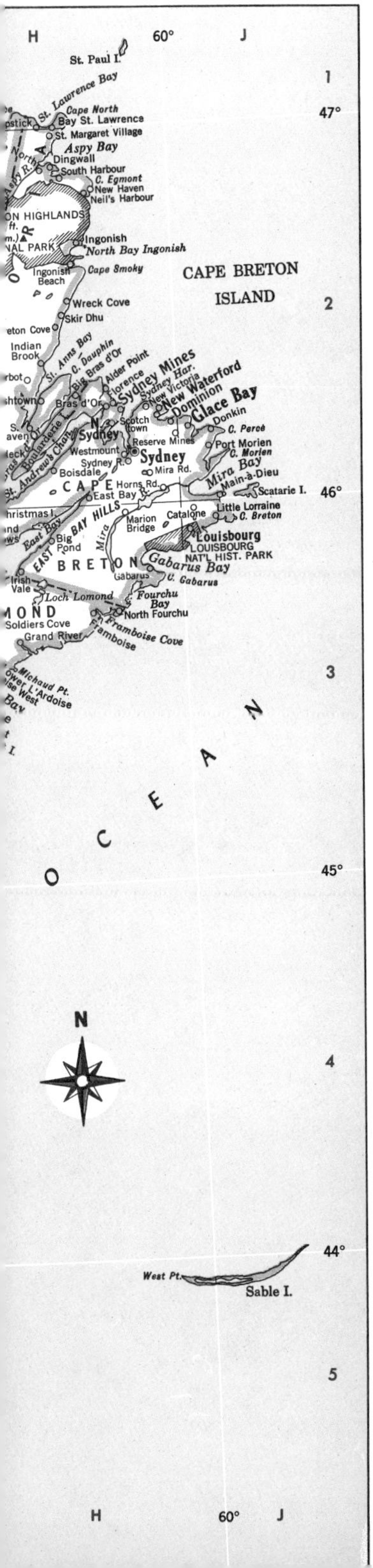

Gold (riv.) D4
Goose (isl.) F4
Goose (isl.).....................G3
Governor (lake)................F3
Great Bras d'Or (chan.) H2
Great Pubnico (lake) C5
Green (pt.).......................C5
Greville (bay)...................D3
Guysborough (riv.)............G3
Halifax (harb.).................E4
Harding (pt.) D5
Haute (isl.)......................C3
Hébert (riv.) D3
Henry (isl.) G3
Indian (harb.) G3
Ingonish North (bay).........H2
Janvrin (isl.)....................G3
Jeddore (cape) E4
Jeddore (harb.).................F4
John (cape).....................E3
Joli (pt.) D5
Jordan (bay)....................C5
Jordan (lake) C4
Jordan (riv.) C5
Kejimkujik (lake) C4
Kejimkujik Nat'l Park C4
Kennetcook (riv.) E3
La Have (isl.)...................D4
La Have (riv.) D4
Linzee (cape)...................G2
Liscomb (isl.) G4
Little River (harb.)............B5
Liverpool (bay).................D5
Lomond Loch, (lake).........H3
Long (isl.) B4
Louisbourg Nat'l Hist. Park J3
Lunenburg (bay)...............D4
Mabou (harb.) G2
Mabou Highlands, (hills) G2
Madame (isl.) H3
Mahone (bay) D4
Malagash (pt.)..................E3
Margaree (isl.)..................F4
McNutt (isl.)....................C5
Medway (harb.)................D4
Medway (riv.) C4
Merigomish (harb.) F3
Mersey (riv.) C4
Michaud (pt.) H3
Minas (basin) D3
Minas (chan.) D3
Mira (bay)........................J2
Mira (riv.)........................H3
Mocodome (cape) G3
Molega (lake)...................D4
Morien (cape)...................J2
Mouton (isl.) D5
Mud (isl.) B5
Mulgrave (lake).................F3
Musquodoboit (riv.) E4
Necum Teuch (harb.).........F4
Nichol (isl.) F4
North (cape).....................H1
North (mt.) D3
North Aspy (riv.) H2
North Bay Ingonish (bay) ...H2
North East Margaree (riv.) H2
Northumberland (str.)........E2
Nuttby (mt.) E3
Oak (isl.)........................E3
Ocean (lake) G3
Ohio (riv.) D4
Panuke (lake)...................D4
Paradise (lake) C4
Pennant (pt.) E4
Percé (cape) J2
Peskowesk (lake) C4
Petit-de-Grat (isl.) H3
Petpeswick (head) E4
Philip (riv.).....................E3
Pictou (harb.)...................F3
Pictou (isl.) F3
Pleasant (bay)..................H2
Ponhook (lake).................D4
Porters (lake)...................E4
Port Hebert (harb.)...........D5
Port Hood (isl.)................G2
Port Joli (harb.) D5
Port Mouton (harb.) D5
Poulet Cove (bay) H2
Prim (pt.)........................C4
Pubnico (harb.)................C5
Pugwash (harb.) E3
Roseway (riv.) C4
Rossignol (lake)...............C4
Sable (cape) C5
Sable (isl.) J5
Saint Andrews (chan.).......H2
Saint Anns (bay)...............H2
Saint Georges (bay)..........G3
Saint Lawrence (bay) H1
Saint Lawrence (cape) H1
Saint Margarets (bay)........E4
Saint Mary (cape).............B4
Saint Marys (bay).............B4
Saint Mary's (riv.) F3
Saint Patrick (chan.) G3
Saint Paul (isl.) H1
Saint Peters (bay) H3

Topography

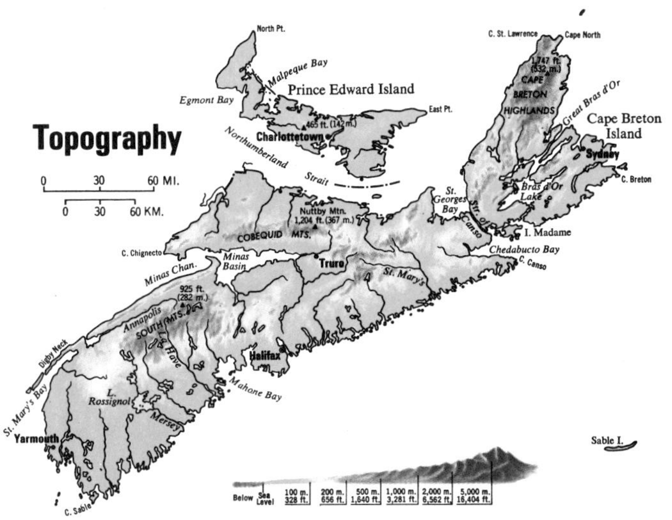

Salmon (riv.) E3
Salmon (riv.)...................G3
Scatarie (isl.) J2
Scots (bay) D3
Seal (isl.) B5
Sheet (harb.) F4
Sherbrooke (lake).............D4
Sherbrooke (riv.) D4
Shoal (bay)......................F4
Shubenacadie (lake) E4
Shubenacadie (riv.)...........E3
Sissiboo (riv.) C4
Smoky (cape) H2
Sober (isl.).....................F4
South West Margaree (riv.) G2
Split (cape) D3
Spry (harb.).....................F4
Stewiacke (riv.) E3
Sydney (harb.).................H2
Tangier (riv.)....................F4
Taylor (head) F4
Tobeatic (lake) C4
Tor (bay).........................G3
Tupper (lake) D4
Tusket (isl.).....................B5
Tusket (riv.) C4
Verte (bay)......................D2
Wallace (harb.)................E3
West (bay).......................G3
West (pt.)........................H5
West (riv.) F3
Western (head) D5
West Liscomb (riv.) F3
West Saint Mary's (riv.) F3
Whitehaven (harb.)...........G3
Yarmouth (sound) B5

PRINCE EDWARD ISLAND

COUNTIES

Kings 18,578 ....F2
Prince 43,237 ....D2
Queens 56,414 ....E2

CITIES and TOWNS

Alberton 1,062 ....E2
Borden 589 ....E2
Bunbury 759 ....F2
Charlottetown (cap.)⊙ 17,063 ....E2
Cornwall 1,256 ....E2
Georgetown⊙ 732 ....F2
Kensington 1,150 ....E2
Miscouche 748..................D2
Montague 1,827.................F2
North Rustico 727 ....E2
O'Leary 805 ....D2
Parkdale 2,172 ....E2
Saint Eleanors 2,495 ....E2
Sherwood 5,602 ....E2
Souris 1,447.....................F2
Stanhope 200....................E2
Summerside⊙ 8,592 ....E2
Tignish 1,077 ....D2
Victoria 164......................E2
Wilmot 1,183.....................E2

OTHER FEATURES

Bedeque (bay)...................E2
Boughton (isl.) F2
Cardigan (bay)...................F2
Cascumpeque (bay) E2
East (pt.)........................G2
Egmont (bay)....................D2
Egmont (cape) D2
Hillsborough (bay) E2
Hog (isl.)........................E2
Kildare (cape)...................E2
Lennox (isl.) E2
Malpeque (bay)..................E2
New London (bay) E2
North (pt.) E1
Northumberland (str.) D2
Panmure (isl.) F2
Prim (pt.) E2
Prince Edward Island Nat'l Park E2
Rollo (bay) F2
Saint Lawrence (gulf).........F2
Saint Peters (bay).............F2
Saint Peters (isl.) E2
Savage (harb.)..................F2
Tracadie (bay) F2
West (pt.)........................D2
Wood (isls.) F3

⊙County seat.

Agriculture, Industry and Resources

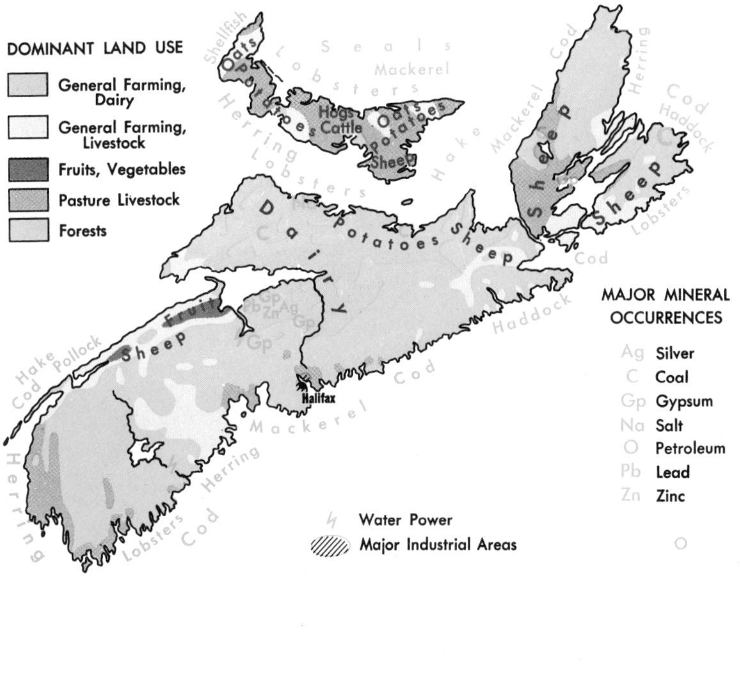

COUNTIES

Albert 22,159 .... F3
Carleton 24,561 .... C2
Charlotte 25,423 .... C3
Gloucester 81,025 .... E1
Kent 28,987 .... E2
King's 43,588 .... E3
Madawaska 34,892 .... B1
Northumberland 53,894 .... D2
Queen's 12,720 .... D3
Restigouche 40,620 .... C1
Saint John 90,103 .... E3
Sunbury 21,190 .... D3
Victoria 20,932 .... C1
Westmorland 105,725 .... F2
York 71,431 .... C3

CITIES and TOWNS

Acadie Siding 88 .... E2
Acadieville 179 .... E2
Adamsville 119 .... E2
Albert Mines 102 .... F3
Alcida 148 .... E1
Aldouane E2
Allardville 529 .... E1
Alma 334 .... F3
Anagance 100 .... E3
Anse-Bleue 490 .... E1
Apohaqui 354 .... E3
Argyle 46 .... C2
Armstrong Brook 231 .... E1
Aroostook 464 .... C2
Arthurette 199 .... C2
Astle 180 .... D2
Atholville 1,862 .... D1
Aulac 109 .... F3
Back Bay 393 .... D3
Baie-Sainte-Anne 701 .... F1
Baie-Verte 168 .... F2
Bairdsville 70 .... C2
Baker Brook 499 .... B1
Balmoral 1,722 .... D1
Barachois 588 .... F2
Barnaby River E2
Barnettville 123 .... E2
Bartibog Bridge 129 .... E1
Bas-Caraquet 1,728 .... F1
Bass River 99 .... E2
Bath 882 .... C2
Bathurst⊙ 16,301 .... E1
Bathurst Mines 34 .... E1
Bayfield 105 .... G2
Bayside 180 .... C3
Beaubois 68 .... E1
Beaver Brook Station 132 .... E1
Beaver Harbour 302 .... D3
Beechwood 123 .... C2
Beersville 41 .... E2
Belledune 747 .... E1
Bellefleur 95 .... C1
Bellefond 205 .... E1
Belleisle Creek 168 .... E3
Benjamin 77 .... D1
Ben Lomond 418 .... E3
Benton 101 .... C3
Beresford 3,199 .... E1
Berry Mills 148 .... E2
Bertrand 1,203 .... E1
Berwick 138 .... E3
Black Point 124 .... D1
Black River 96 .... E3
Black River Bridge E2
Blacks Harbour 1,619 .... D3
Blackville 924 .... E2
Blissfield 127 .... D2
Bloomfield Ridge 184 .... D2
Bloomfield Station 94 .... E3
Bocabec 29 .... C3
Boiestown 326 .... D2
Bonny River D3
Bossé 178 .... B1
Bourgeois 214 .... F2
Brantville 984 .... E1
Breau-Village 277 .... F2
Brest 116 .... E2
Brewers Mills 373 .... C2
Bridgedale F3
Briggs Corner 74 .... E2
Bristol 860 .... C2
Brockway 70 .... C3
Browns Flat 263 .... D3
Buctouche 2,556 .... F2
Burnsville 157 .... E1
Burton⊙ 294 .... D3
Burtts Corner 429 .... D2
Cambridge-Narrows 406 .... E3
Campbellton 9,282 .... D1
Canaan 84 .... E2
Canaan Forks 67 .... E2
Canaan Road 80 .... E2
Canterbury 501 .... C3
Cap-Bateau 433 .... F1
Cape Tormentine 239 .... G2
Cap Lumière 255 .... F2
Cap-Pelé 2,287 .... F2
Caraquet 3,950 .... E1
Carlingford 203 .... C2
Carlisle 40 .... C2
Caron Brook 178 .... B1
Carrolls Crossing 109 .... D2
Castalia 126 .... D4
Central Blissville 100 .... D3
Centre-Saint-Simon 365 .... E1
Centreville 606 .... C2
Chance Harbour 203 .... D3
Charlo 1,302 .... D1
Chatham 7,601 .... E1
Chatham Head 1,196 .... E2
Chipman 1,999 .... E2
Clair 792 .... B1
Clarendon 63 .... D3
Cliffordvale 85 .... C2
Clifton 140 .... E1
Coal Branch 93 .... E2
Coal Creek 40 .... E2
Cocagne 325 .... F2
Cocagne Cape 245 .... F2
Codys 124 .... E3
Coldstream 182 .... C2
Coles Island 150 .... E3
College Bridge 590 .... F3
Collette 212 .... E2
Connell 70 .... C2
Connors 82 .... B1
Cork 70 .... D3
Cornhill 167 .... E3
Coughlan 183 .... E2
Cross Creek 216 .... D2
Cumberland Bay 217 .... E2
Dalhousie⊙ 5,640 .... D1
Dalhousie Junction 123 .... D1
Darlington 624 .... D1
Daulnay 533 .... E1
Dawsonville 234 .... C1
Debec 226 .... C2
Dieppe 7,460 .... F2
Dipper Harbour 162 .... D3
Doaktown 1,022 .... D2
Dorchester⊙ 1,125 .... F3
Dorchester Crossing 568 .... F2
Douglas Harbour 55 .... D3
Douglastown 1,032 .... E1
Drummond 675 .... C1
Duguayville 358 .... E1
Dumbarton 40 .... C3
Dumfries 98 .... C3
Dupuis Corner 269 .... F2
Durham Bridge 255 .... D2
Edmundston⊙ 12,710 .... B1
Eel River Bridge 348 .... F1
Eel River Crossing 811 .... D1
Elgin 275 .... E3
Enniskillen 66 .... D3
Escuminac 210 .... F1
Evandale 58 .... D3
Evangeline 373 .... F1
Everett 56 .... C1
Fairfield 198 .... E3
Fairhaven 137 .... C4
Fairisle 569 .... E1
Fairvale 3,258 .... E3
Ferry Road 291 .... E1
Fielding 173 .... C2
Five Fingers 157 .... C1
Flatlands 250 .... D1
Florenceville 768 .... C2
Fontaine 13 .... F
Forest City 40 C
Fosterville 84 C
Four Falls 79 C
Fredericton (cap.)⊙ 45,248 D
Fredericton Junction 630 .... D
Gagetown⊙ 655 .... D
Gardner Creek 40 .... E
Geary 892 .... D
Germantown 27 .... F
Gillespie 63 C
Glassville 114 C
Glencoe 142 .... D
Glenlivet 273 .... D
Gloucester Junction 33 .... E
Gondola Point 1,846 .... D
Grafton 409 C
Grand Bay 2,947 .... D
Grande-Anse 765 .... E
Grand Falls 6,223 C
Grand Falls Hill 93 C
Grand Harbour 527 .... D
Gray Rapids 273 .... E
Hammondvale 77 .... E
Hampstead 100 .... D
Hampton⊙ 2,641 .... E
Harcourt 119 .... E
Hardwicke 96 .... E
Hardwood Ridge 173 .... D
Hartland 974 C

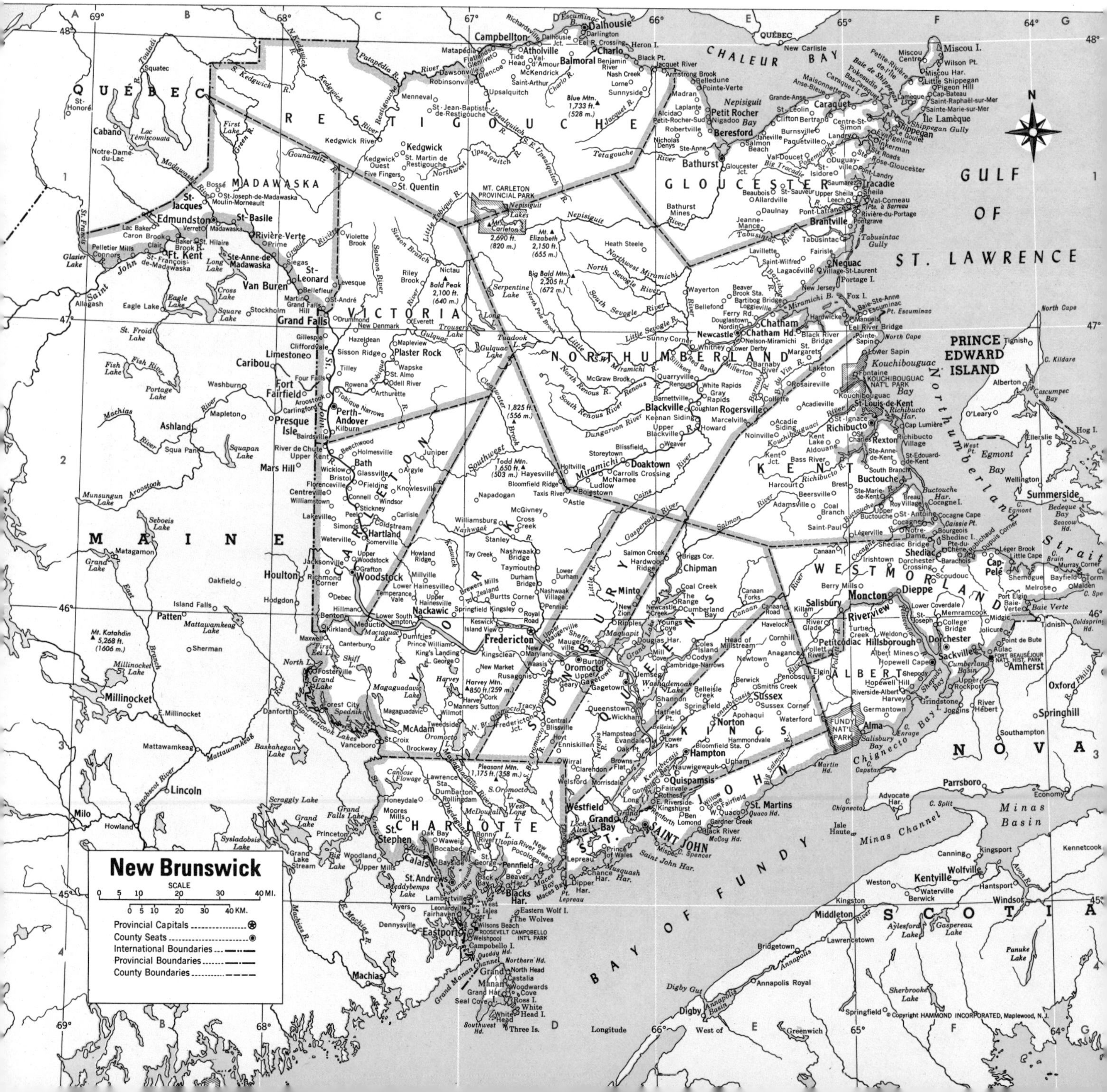
New Brunswick
SCALE
0 5 10 20 30 40 MI.
0 5 10 20 30 40 KM.
Provincial Capitals
County Seats
International Boundaries
Provincial Boundaries
County Boundaries
RESTIGOUCHE
MADAWASKA
GLOUCESTER
VICTORIA
NORTHUMBERLAND
CARLETON
YORK
SUNBURY
QUEENS
KENT
WESTMORLAND
ALBERT
KINGS
CHARLOTTE
SAINT JOHN
QUÉBEC
MAINE
NOVA SCOTIA
PRINCE EDWARD ISLAND
GULF OF ST. LAWRENCE
CHALEUR BAY
BAY OF FUNDY
Northumberland Strait
Fredericton
Saint John
Moncton
Longitude West of Greenwich
© Copyright HAMMOND INCORPORATED, Maplewood, N.J.

vey, Albert 75 ....F3
vey, York 376.............D3
field Point 179............E3
elock 351 ....E3
esville 130.................D2
eldean 130.................C2
d of Millstream 79 ....E3
th Steele D1
man 80 ....C2
sborough 1,153 ....F3
mesville 136 ....C2
tville 229 ....D2
eydale 72 ....C3
ewell Cape⊙ 129 ....F3
ewell Hill 178 ....F3
ward 152.....................E2
wland Ridge 67 ....C2
t D3
erman 324 ....F1
town 232 ....F2
nd View 260.................D3
ksonville 328 ....C2
quet River 735 ....E1
eville 192.....................E1
nne Mance 97 ....E1
seg 188 ....D3
cure 87 ....F3
iper 572.......................C2
gwick 1,271 ....C1
gwick Ouest 21 ....C1
gwick River 15...............C1
nan Siding 91 ....E2
t Junction 104 ....E2
t Lake E2
wick 288.......................D3
urn 111 ....C2
am 65 ....E2
gsclear 178 ....D3
gsley 129 ....D2
g's Landing C3
dland 63 ....C3
wlesville 64 ....C2
chibouguac 97 ....F2
Baker 325......................B1
acéville 220...................E1
e George 172..................C3
eton 109 ....E2
eville 530 ....C2
bertville 153 ....C3
nèque 973 ....F1
dry 94 ....E1
lante 222.......................E1
illette 580 ....E1
vrence Station 187 ....C3
ch 574...........................E1
er Brook 423 ....F2
erville 183......................F2
Goulet 1,059 ....F1

Leonardville 138 ....C4
Lepreau 183 ....D3
Levesque 76 ....C1
Little Cape 550 ....F2
Little Shippegan 111...........F1
Loggieville 784 ....E1
Lorne 987.........................D1
Lower Cloverdale 576 ....F2
Lower Derby 209 ....E2
Lower Durham 55 ....D2
Lower Hainesville 99 ....C2
Lower Kars 32...................E3
Lower Millstream 176 ....E3
Lower Sapin 201 ....F2
Lower Southampton 88 ....C2
Ludlow 97 ....D2
Maces Bay 117 ....D3
Madran 255.......................E1
Magaguadavic 98 ....C3
Maisonnette 714 ....E1
Malden 80 ....G2
Manners Sutton 187 ....D3
Manuels 330......................F1
Mapleview 110 ....C2
Marcelville 51....................E2
Martin 105 ....C1
Maugerville 266.................D3
Mэxwell 47 ....C3
McAdam 1,985...................C3
McGivney 175....................D2
McGraw Brook D2
McKendrick 547 ....D1
McNamee 154....................D2
Meductic 170.....................C3
Melrose 97 ....F2
Memramcook 262...............F2
Menneval 111 ....C1
Midgic Station 170.............F3
Mill Cove 50......................D3
Millerton 144 ....E2
Millville 308.......................C2
Minto 3,714 ....D2
Miscou Centre 519.............F1
Miscou Harbour 97 ....F1
Mispec 152 ....E3
Moncton 55,934 ....F2
Moores Mills 106 ....C3
Morrisdale 188...................D3
Moulin-Morneault 433 ....B1
Murray Corner 162.............G2
Nackawic 1,341 ....C2
Napadogan 103 ....D2
Nash Creek 183.................D1
Nashwaak Bridge 161.........D2
Nashwaak Village 275.........D2
Nauwigewauk 201 ....E3
Neguac 1,733 ....E1
Nelson-Miramichi 1,543 ......E2

Newcastle⊙ 6,423 ....E2
Newcastle Creek 235..........D2
New Denmark 100.............C1
New Jersey 176 ....E1
New Market 110 ....D3
New Maryland 481 ....D3
New River Beach 43 ....D3
Newtown 108....................E3
New Zion 152 ....D2
Nicholas Denys 174 ....D1
Nictau 29.........................C1
Nigadoo 799 ....E1
Noinville E2
Nordin 350.......................E1
North Head 647 ....D4
Norton 1,285 ....E3
Notre-Dame 282................F2
Oak Bay 254.....................C3
Oak Point 106...................D3
Odell River 28 ....C2
Oromocto 10,276...............D3
Paquetville 601 ....E1
Peel 98 ....C2
Pelletier Mills 85 ....B1
Pennfield 305 ....D3
Penniac 176 ....D2
Penobsquis 275 ....E3
Perth-Andover⊙ 1,973 ....C2
Petitcodiac 1,472 ....E3
Petite-Rivière-de-l'Île 539 .....F1
Petit Rocher 1,790 ....E1
Petit Rocher Sud 310 ....E1
Pigeon Hill 527 ....F1
Plaster Rock 1,368 ....C2
Pocologan 65 ....D3
Point de Bute 147..............F3
Pointe-du-Chêne 468 ....F2
Pointe-Verte 617 ....E1
Pointe-Sapin 326 ....F2
Pollett River 57..................E3
Pontgrave 215 ....F1
Pont-Lafrance 806 ....E1
Pont-Landry 322 ....F1
Port Elgin 492 ....F2
Prime 87 ....B1
Prince of Wales D3
Prince William 242 ....C3
Quarryville 213 ....E2
Queenstown 98 ....D3
Quispamsis 4,968 ....E3
Red Bank 161 ....E2
Renforth 1,572..................E3
Renous 161.......................E2
Rexton 872.......................F2
Richardsville 819 ....D1
Richibucto⊙ 1,909.............E2
Richibucto Village 432 ....F2
Richmond Corner 79...........C2

Riley Brook 111 ....C1
Ripples 192.......................D3
River de Chute 42 ....C2
River Glade 264 ....E3
Rivière-du-Portage 672........F1
Riverside-Albert 467 ....F3
Riverview 14,177 ....F2
Rivière Verte 1,009............B1
Robertville 628 ....E1
Robichaud 392 ....F2
Robinsonville 211..............C1
Rogersville 1,138 ....E2
Rollingdam 81...................C3
Rosaireville 73...................E2
Rothesay 1,283 ....E3
Rowena 78........................C2
Roy 147 ....F2
Royal Road 65 ....D2
Rusagonis 195 ....D3
Sackville 5,755 ....F3
Saint Almo 26 ....C2
Saint-André 310.................C1
Saint Andrews⊙ 1,711 ....C3
Saint-Antoine 1,062 ....F2
Saint Arthur 391 ....D1
Saint Basile 3,072 ....B1
Saint-Charles 310 ....F2
Saint Croix C3
Sainte-Anne 321 ....E1
Sainte-Anne-de-Kent 142 .....F2
Sainte-Anne-de-Madawaska
1,341 ....B1
Saint-Édouard-de-Kent 163 ...F2
Sainte-Marie-de-Kent 250.....F2
Sainte-Marie-sur-Mer 563 ....F1
Sainte-Rose-Gloucester 412 F1
Saint François de
Madawaska 650 ....B1
Saint George 1,148 ....D3
Saint Hilaire 168 ....B1
Saint-Ignace.....................F2
Saint-Isidore 286...............E1
Saint-Jacques 1,374 ....B1
Saint-Jean-Baptiste-de-
Restigouche 227 ....C1
Saint John⊙ 85,956 ....E3
Saint-Joseph 741 ....F3
Saint-Joseph-de-Madawaska
188.................................B1
Saint-Léolin 770................E1
Saint Leonard 1,593 ....C1
Saint-Louis-de-Kent 1,278....F2
Saint Margarets 77 ....E2
Saint Martin de
Restigouche 158 ...,..........C1
Saint Martins 544..............E3
Saint-Paul 341..................E2
Saint Quentin 2,246 ....C1
Saint-Raphaël-sur-Mer 373 ...F1
Saint Sauveur 299 ....E1
Saint Stephen 5,264 ....C3
Saint Wilfred 360 ....E1
Salisbury 1,410 ....E2
Salmon Beach 275..............E1
Salmon Creek 39................E2
Saumarez 238 ....E1
Scoudouc 171 ....F2
Seal Cove 526...................D4
Shannon 30.......................E3
Shediac 4,216 ....F2
Shediac Bridge 424 ....F2
Sheffield 109 ....D3
Sheila 753.........................F1
Shemogue 197 ....F2
Shepody 72 ....F3
Shippegan 2,344 ....F1
Siegas 227.........................C1
Sillikers 313 ....E2
Simonds 201 ....C2
Sisson Ridge 134................C2
Six Roads 118....................F1
Smiths Creek 141...............E3
Somerville 326 ....C2
South Branch 111...............F2
Springfield, King's 138 ....E3
Springfield, York 138 ....C2
Stanley 435.......................D2
Stickney 223......................C2
Storeytown 144..................D2
Sunny Corner 369 ....E2
Sunnyside 98.....................D1
Sussex 3,938......................E3
Sussex Corner 864 ....E3
Tabusintac 304...................E1
Taxis River 103 ....D2

Tay Creek 161...................D2
Taymouth 287...................D2
Temperance Vale 331 ....C2
The Range 53 ....E2
Thibault 280 ....C1
Tide Head 897 ....D1
Tilley 177 ....C2
Tobique Narrows 129 ....C2
Tracadie 2,591 ....F1
Tracy 662.........................D3
Turtle Creek 127 ....F3
Tweedside 75....................C3
Upham 94.........................E3
Upper Blackville 93 ....E2
Upper Buctouche 138 ....F2
Upper Gagetown 200 ....D3
Upper Hainesville 185.........C2
Upper Kent 190 ....C2
Upper Maugerville 554........D3
Upper Mills 138.................C3
Upper Rockport 18 ....F3
Upper Sheila 764 ....E1
Upper Woodstock 291 ....C2
Upsalquitch 173 ....D1
Val-Comeau 489.................F1
Val d'Amour 489 ....D1
Val Doucet 521 ....E1
Verret 244 ....B1
Village-Saint-Laurent 210.....E1
Violette Brook C1
Waasis 273 ....D3
Wapske 206 ....C2
Waterford 95 ....E3
Waterville 155...................C2
Waweig 113 ....C3
Wayerton 153 ....E1
Weaver E2
Weldon 215.......................F3
Welsford 231 ....D3
Welshpool 200 ....D4
Westfield 1;048 ....D3
West Quaco 29 ....E3
White Head 183.................D4
White Rapids 212...............E2
Whitney 234 ....E2
Wickham 65......................D3
Wicklow 104......................C2
Williamsburg 261 ....D2
Williamstown 160...............C2
Willow Grove 402...............E3
Wilmot 66.........................C3
Wilson Point 49 ....F1
Wilsons Beach 915.............D4
Windsor 59 ....C2
Wirral 95..........................D3

Woodstock⊙ 4,869 ....C2
Woodwards Cove 120 ....D4
Youngs Cove 76 ....E3
Zealand 466 ....D2

OTHER FEATURES

Bald (mt.).........................C1
Baritbog (riv.) E1
Bay du Vin (riv.) E2
Big Tracadie (riv.) E1
Buctouche (harb.)..............F2
Buctouche (riv.) F2
Campobello (isl.) D4
Canaan (riv.)....................E2
Carleton (mt.)...................D1
Chaleur (bay) E1
Chignecto (bay) F3
Chiputneticook (lkes)..........C3
Cocagne (isl.)...................F2
Cumberland (basin)............F3
Deer (isl.).........................D4
Digdeguash (riv.) C3
Escuminac (bay)................D1
Escuminac (pt.) F1
Fundy (bay)......................E3
Fundy Nat'l Park E3
Gaspereau (riv.) D2
Grand (bay)......................D3
Grand (lake) C3
Grand (lake) D3
Grande (riv.)....................C1
Grand Manan (chan.) C4
Grand Manan (isl.) D4
Green (riv.) B1
Hammond (riv.).................E3
Harvey (lake) C3
Heron (isl.) D1
Kedgwick (riv.)..................C1
Kennebecasis (riv.) E3
Keswick (riv.) C2
Kouchibouguac (bay) F2
Kouchibouguacis (riv.) E2
Kouchobouguac Nat'l Park F2
Lamèque (isl.) F1
Lepreau (riv.) D3
Little (riv.) D2
Long (isl.) D3
Long Reach (inlet).............D3
Maces (bay) D3
Mactaquac (lake)...............C3
Madawaska (riv.) B1
Magaguadavic (lake) C3
Magaguadavic (riv.) C3
Miramichi (bay) E1

Miscou (isl.) F1
Miscou (pt.) F1
Mount Carleton Prov. Park D1
Musquash (harb.) D3
Nashwaak (riv.) D2
Nepisiguit (bay) E1
Nepisiguit (riv.) D1
Nerepis (riv.) D3
Northern (head) D4
North Sevogle (riv.) D1
Northumberland (str.) F2
Northwest Miramichi (riv.) ...D1
Oromocto (lake)................C3
Oromocto (riv.) D3
Passamaquoddy (bay) C3
Patapédia (riv.).................C1
Petitcodiac (riv.) F3
Pokemouche (riv.) E1
Pokesudie (isl.).................F1
Pollett (riv.).....................E3
Quaco (head) E3
Renous (riv.) D2
Restigouche (riv.) C1
Richibucto (harb.) F2
Richibucto (riv.)................E2
Roosevelt Campobello Int'l
Park D4
Saint Croix (riv.) C3
Saint Francis (riv.).............A1
Saint John (harb.) E3
Saint John (riv.) C2
Saint Lawrence (gulf)..........F1
Salisbury (bay) F3
Salmon (riv.) C1
Salmon (riv.) E2
Shediac (isl.) F2
Shepody (bay) F3
Shippegan (bay)................E1
Shippegan (gully) F1
South Sevogle (riv.)...........D1
Southwest (head)...............D4
Southwest Miramichi (riv.)...D2
Spear (cape).....................G2
Spednik (lake)...................C3
Spencer (cape) E3
Tabusintac (gully) F1
Tabusintac (riv.) E1
Tetagouche (riv.) D1
Tobique (riv.)....................C2
Upsalquitch (riv.) D1
Utopia (lake).....................D3
Verte (bay).......................G2
Washademoak (lake) E3
West (isls.) D4
White Head (isl.) D4

⊙ County seat.

AREA 28,354 sq. mi. (73,437 sq. km.)
POPULATION 688,926
CAPITAL Fredericton
LARGEST CITY Saint John
HIGHEST POINT Mt. Carleton 2,690 ft. (820 m.)
SETTLED IN 1611
ADMITTED TO CONFEDERATION 1867
PROVINCIAL FLOWER Purple Violet

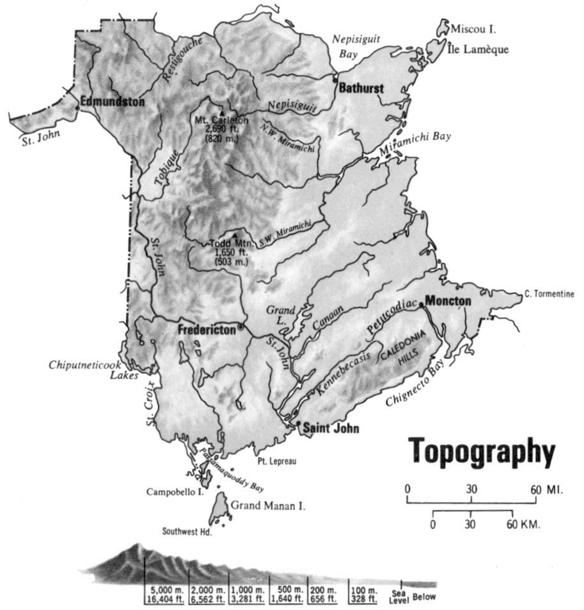

Topography

Agriculture, Industry and Resources

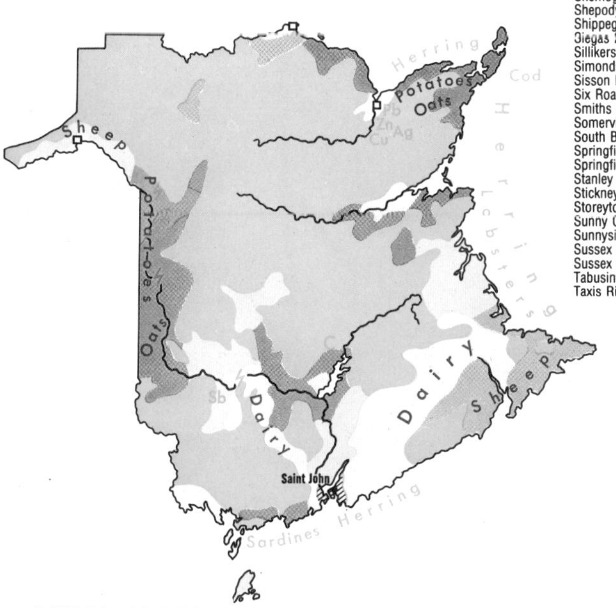

DOMINANT LAND USE

- Cereals, Livestock
- Dairy
- Potatoes
- General Farming, Livestock
- Pasture Livestock
- Forests

MAJOR MINERAL OCCURRENCES

- Ag Silver
- C Coal
- Cu Copper
- Pb Lead
- Sb Antimony
- Zn Zinc
- Water Power
- Major Industrial Areas

Topography

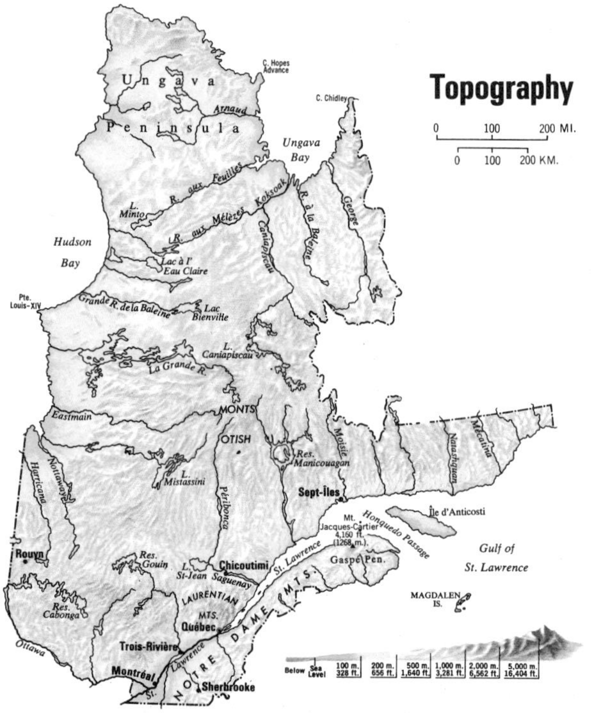

COUNTIES

Argenteuil 31,654 ... C4
Arthabaska 54,176 ... E4
Bagot 24,791 ... E4
Beauce 67,083 ... G3
Beauharnois 53,026 ... C4
Bellechasse 22,908 ... G3
Berthier 28,465 ... C3
Bonaventure 40,724 ... C2
Brome 16,410 ... E4
Chambly 286,130 ... J4
Champlain 114,078 ... E2
Charlevoix-Est 17,085 ... G2
Charlevoix-Ouest 13,601 ... G2
Châteauguay 57,252 ... D4
Chicoutimi 165,859 ... G1
Compton 20,512 ... F4
Deux-Montagnes 58,568 ... C4
Dorchester 32,396 ... C3
Drummond 66,122 ... E4
Frontenac 26,203 ... G4
Gaspé-Est 40,720 ... D1
Gaspé-Ouest 19,238 ... C1
Gatineau 52,193 ... B3
Hull 134,518 ... B4
Huntingdon 16,653 ... C4
Iberville 21,296 ... D4
Île-de-Montréal 1,869,641 ... H4
Île-Jésus 246,243 ... H4
Joliette 55,524 ... C3
Kamouraska 27,740 ... H2
Labelle 31,065 ... B3
Lac-Saint-Jean-Est 45,558 ... F1
Lac-Saint-Jean-Ouest 57,556 E1
Laprairie 84,217 ... H4
L'Assomption 84,967 ... D4
Lévis 75,916 ... J3
L'Islet 22,223 ... G2
Lotbinière 27,780 ... F3
Maskinongé 20,879 ... D3
Matane 28,954 ... B1
Matapédia 24,063 ... B2
Mégantic 56,566 ... F3
Missisquoi 34,853 ... D4
Montcalm 23,534 ... C3
Montmagny 26,622 ... G3
Montmorency No. 1 20,712 ... F2
Montmorency No. 2 5,869 ... G3
Napierville 12,595 ... D4
Nicolet 31,102 ... E3
Papineau 36,275 ... B4
Pontiac 20,559 ... A3
Portneuf 51,643 ... E3
Québec 449,633 ... F3
Richelieu 49,944 ... D4
Richmond 39,895 ... E4
Rimouski 64,768 ... J1
Rivière-du-Loup 39,339 ... H2
Rouville 36,672 ... D4
Saguenay 115,736 ... H1
Saint-Hyacinthe 52,417 ... D4
Saint-Jean 50,587 ... D4
Saint-Maurice 106,023 ... D3
Shefford 65,528 ... E4
Sherbrooke 109,589 ... E4
Soulanges 13,254 ... C4
Stanstead 36,737 ... F4
Témiscouata 52,871 ... J2
Terrebonne 164,502 ... H4
Vaudreuil 44,257 ... C4
Verchères 49,298 ... J4
Wolfe 15,254 ... F4
Yamaska 14,490 ... E3

CITIES and TOWNS

Acton Vale 4,326 ... E4
Albanel 889 ... E1
Alma⊙ 25,638 ... F1
Amqui⊙ 3,949 ... B2
Ancienne-Lorette 11,694 ... H3
Angers ... B4
Anjou 36,596 ... H4
Annaville 586 ... E3
Armagh 966 ... G3
Arthabaska⊙ 5,907 ... F3
Arvida ... F1
Asbestos 9,075 ... F4
Ascot Corner 895 ... F4
Audet 674 ... G4
Ayer's Cliff⊙ 873 ... E4
Aylmer 25,714 ... B4
Baie-Comeau 11,911 ... A1
Baie-des-Sables 588 ... A1
Baie-d'Urfé 3,955 ... G4
Baie-Saint-Paul⊙ 4,062 ... G2
Baie-Trinité 802 ... B1
Beaconsfield 20,417 ... H4
Beauceville 4,276 ... G3
Beauharnois⊙ 7,665 ... D4
Beaumont 635 ... F3
Beauport 55,539 ... J3
Beaupré 2,821 ... G2
Bécancour⊙ 9,043 ... E3
Bedford⊙ 3,010 ... E4
Beebe Plain 1,155 ... E4
Bélair 10,716 ... H3
Beloeil 15,913 ... D4
Bernierville 2,182 ... F3
Berthier-en-Bas 576 ... G3
Berthierville⊙ 4,249 ... D3
Bic 2,670 ... J1
Biencourt 818 ... J2
Black Lake 4,051 ... F3
Blainville 12,517 ... H4
Boischatel 2,279 ... J3
Bois-des-Filion 4,346 ... H4
Bolduc 1,593 ... G4
Bonaventure 1,195 ... C2
Boucherville 25,530 ... J4
Boulanger 953 ... E1
Bromont 2,505 ... E4
Bromptonville 2,992 ... F4
Brossard 37,641 ... H4
Brownsburg 3,114 ... C4
Buckingham 14,328 ... B4
Cabano 3,193 ... J2
Cacouna 1,083 ... H2
Calumet 708 ... C4
Candiac 7,166 ... J4
Cap-à-l'Aigle 712 ... G2
Cap-Chat 3,617 ... B1
Cap-de-la-Madeleine 32,126 ... E3
Cap-des-Rosiers 691 ... D1
Cap-Saint-Ignace 1,312 ... G2
Cap-Santé⊙ 1,312 ... F3
Carignan 3,585 ... J4
Carleton 2,538 ... C2
Caughnawaga 3,708 ... H4
Causapscal 2,743 ... B2
Chambly 11,815 ... J4
Chambord 1,058 ... E1
Champlain 548 ... E3
Chandler 4,011 ... D2
Charette 538 ... D3
Charlemagne 4,025 ... H4
Charlesbourg 63,147 ... J3
Charny 6,416 ... J3
Châteauguay 36,329 ... H4
Châteauguay-Centre ... H4
Château-Richer⊙ 3,075 ... F3
Chénéville 699 ... B4
Chicoutimi⊙ 57,737 ... G1
Chicoutimi-Nord ... F1
Chute-aux-Outardes 2,103 ... A1
Clermont 3,518 ... G2
Cloridorme 553 ... D1
Coaticook 6,392 ... F4
Coleraine 1,485 ... F4
Compton 584 ... F4
Contrecoeur ... D4
Cookshire⊙ 1,453 ... F4
Coteau-du-Lac 1,248 ... C4
Coteau-Landing⊙ 1,106 ... C4
Côte-Saint-Luc 25,721 ... H4
Courcelles 677 ... G4
Courville ... J3
Cowansville 11,902 ... E4
Crabtree 1,942 ... D4
Danville 2,367 ... E4
Daveluyville 1,321 ... E3
Deauville 804 ... E4
Dégelis 3,304 ... J2
Delisle 1,249 ... F1
Delson 4,241 ... H4
Desbiens 1,673 ... E1
Deschambault 1,018 ... E3
Deschênes ... B4
Deux-Montagnes 8,957 ... H4
Didyme 759 ... E1
Disraëli 3,306 ... F4
Dixville 534 ... F4
Dolbeau 8,451 ... E1
Dollard-des-Ormeaux 36,837 H4
Donnacona 5,800 ... F3
Dorion 5,843 ... C4
Dorval 19,131 ... H4
Douville ... D4
Drummondville⊙ 29,286 ... E4
Drummondville-Nord 2,298 ... E4
Drummondville-Sud 9,420 ... E4
Dunham 2,505 ... E4
Durham-Sud 1,040 ... E4
East Angus 4,417 ... F4
East Broughton 1,371 ... F3
East Broughton Station 1,191 F3
Eastman 557 ... E4
Escoumins 2,324 ... H1
Farnham 6,476 ... E4
Ferme-Neuve 2,113 ... B3
Forestville 1,819 ... H1
Frampton 759 ... G3
Francoeur 1,389 ... F3
Gaspé 16,842 ... D1
Gatineau 73,479 ... B4
Giffard ... J3
Girardville 1,035 ... E1
Godbout 593 ... B1
Gracefield 927 ... A3
Granby 37,132 ... E4
Grande-Rivière 4,390 ... D2
Grandes-Bergeronnes 779 ... H1
Grande-Vallée 632 ... D1
Grand'Mère 15,999 ... E3
Greenfield Park 18,430 ... J4
Grenville 1,517 ... C4
Gros-Morne 584 ... C1
Hampstead 7,562 ... H4
Ham-Sud⊙ 67 ... F4
Hauterive 14,724 ... A1
Hébertville 1,520 ... F1
Hébertville-Station 1,362 ... F1
Hemmingford 763 ... D4
Henryville 590 ... D4
Howick 660 ... D4
Huberdeau 679 ... C4
Hudson 4,480 ... C4
Hull⊙ 61,039 ... B4
Huntingdon⊙ 3,098 ... C4
Iberville⊙ 8,897 ... D4
Île-Bizard 2,985 ... H4
Île-Perrot 5,272 ... G4
Inverness⊙ 365 ... F3
Joliette⊙ 18,118 ... D3
Jonquière 60,691 ... F1
Kingsey Falls 601 ... E4
Kirkland 7,476 ... H4
La Baie 20,116 ... G1
La Baie-de-Shawinigan 632 ... E3
Labelle 2,007 ... C3
Lac-Alouette 738 ... D4
Lac-au-Saumon 1,309 ... B2
Lac-aux-Sables 818 ... E3
Lac-Beauport ... F3
Lac-Bouchette 1,685 ... E1
Lac-Carré 687 ... C3
Lac-des-Aigles 787 ... J2
Lac-des-Écorces 638 ... B3
Lac-Drolet 1,015 ... G4
Lac-Etchemin 2,746 ... G3
Lachenaie 7,118 ... D4
Lachine 41,503 ... H4
Lachute⊙ 11,928 ... C4
Lac-Mégantic⊙ 6,457 ... G4
Lacolle 1,193 ... D4
Lac-Saint-Charles 3,285 ... H3
La Durantaye 763 ... G3
Lafontaine 4,442 ... C4
La Guadeloupe 1,804 ... F4
La Malbaie⊙ 4,069 ... G2
Lambton 777 ... F4
Lamartine 675 ... G2
L'Ange-Gardien 1,838 ... F3
Langlais 1,197 ... F1
L'Annonciation 2,186 ... C3
Lanoraie 1,362 ... D4
La Pérade 1,032 ... E3
La Pêche 4,662 ... B4
La Pocatière 4,319 ... H2
La Prairie⊙ 9,173 ... J4
La Providence ... E4
La Rédemption 808 ... B2
Larouche 549 ... F1
La Salle 76,713 ... H4
L'Ascension, Lac-St-Jean E. 1,090 ... F1
L'Assomption⊙ 4,832 ... D4
La Station-du-Coteau 869 ... C4
Laterrière 693 ... F1
La Trinité-des-Monts 592 ... J1
La Tuque 12,067 ... E2
Laurentides 1,804 ... D4
Laurier-Station 1,260 ... F3
Laurierville 867 ... F3
Lauzon 12,663 ... J3
Laval 246,243 ... H4
Lavaltrie 1,473 ... D4
Lawrenceville 528 ... E4
Le Moyne 7,202 ... J4
Lennoxville 3,682 ... F4
L'Épiphanie 2,912 ... D4
Léry 2,201 ... H4
Les Becquets 577 ... E3
Les Éboulements 1,190 ... G2
Les Méchins 1,049 ... B1
Lévis 17,819 ... J3
Linière 1,176 ... G3
L'Islet 1,113 ... G2
L'Islet-sur-Mer 817 ... G2
L'Isle-Verte 1,201 ...
Longueuil⊙ 122,429 ...
Loretteville⊙ 14,767 ...
Lorraine 5,388 ...
Louiseville⊙ 3,993 ...
Lucerne 8,000 ...
Luceville 1,513 ...
Lyster 811 ...
Magog 13,290 ...
Maniwaki⊙ 5,969 ...
Manseau 656 ...
Mansonville 590 ...
Maple Grove 1,857 ...
bmarbleton 551 ...
Maria 1,016 ...
Marieville⊙ 4,853 ...
Marsoui 541 ...
Mascouche 14,266 ...
Maskinongé 1,001 ...
Masson ...
Massueville ...
Matane⊙ 12,726 ...
Matapédia 581 ...
Melocheville 1,660 ...
Mercier 4,957 ...
Metabetchouan 3,016 ...
Mirabel⊙ 13,486 ...
Mistassini 5,473 ...
Montauban 903 ...
Mont-Carmel 852 ...
Montcerf 587 ...
Montebello 1,276 ...
Mont-Joli 6,508 ...
Mont-Laurier⊙ 8,565 ...

Agriculture, Industry and Resources

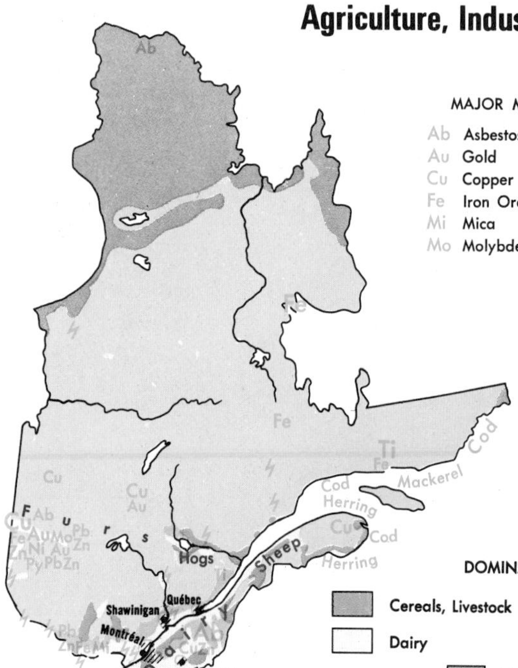

MAJOR MINERAL OCCURRENCES

- Ab Asbestos
- Au Gold
- Cu Copper
- Fe Iron Ore
- Mi Mica
- Mo Molybdenum
- Ni Nickel
- Pb Lead
- Py Pyrites
- Ti Titanium
- Zn Zinc

Water Power
Major Industrial Areas

DOMINANT LAND USE

- Cereals, Livestock
- Dairy
- Pasture Livestock, Dairy
- Forests
- Nonagricultural Land

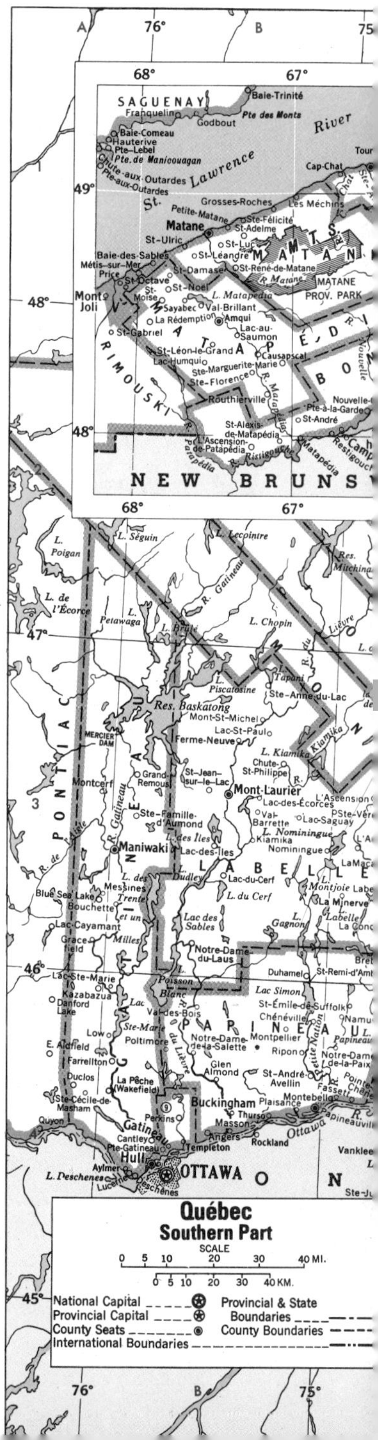

ıtmagny⊙ 12,326 .... G3
ıtréal⊙ 1,080,546 .... H4
ıtréal-Est 4,372 .... J4
ıtréal-Nord 97,250 .... H4
ıt-Rolland 1,591 .... C4
ıt-Royal 20,514 .... H4
ıt-Saint-Hilaire 7,688 .... D4
ʳdochville 3,704 .... C1
ierville⊙ 2,166 .... D4
ville 918 .... F3
v Carlisle⊙ 1,403 .... D2
vport 558 .... D2
v Richmond 4,295 .... C2
ɔlet 4,818 .... E3
nininque 757 .... B3
mandin 1,874 .... E1
th Hatley 788 .... F4
re-Dame-de-la-Doré
19 .... E1
re-Dame-des-Anges 903 . E3
re-Dame-des-Laurentides H3
re-Dame-des-Prairies
714 .... D3
re-Dame-du-Bon-Conseil
1,023 .... E4
re-Dame-du-Lac⊙ 2,153 . J2
ıvelle 682 .... C2
1,483 .... C4
erville 1,308 .... E4
ıstown 1,503 .... D4
ainville H3
ɜrburn Park 4,159 .... D4
remont 27,089 .... H4
ɔs 1,018 .... D2
Pabos-Mills 1,512 .... D2
Packington 700 .... J2
Papineauville⊙ 1,509 .... C4
Paspébiac 1,807 .... D2
Percé⊙ 5,198 .... D1
Perkins 3,551 .... B4
Petit Cap 1,028 .... D1
Petite-Matane 920 .... B1
Petit-Saguenay (Saint-François
-d'Assis 680 .... G1
Pierrefonds 35,402 .... H4
Pierreville 1,311 .... E3
Pincourt 7,892 .... D4
Plaisance 634 .... B4
Plessisville 7,238 .... F3
Pohénégamooke 3,627 .... H2
Pointe-à-la-Croix 1,515 .... C2
Pointe-au-Pic 1,066 .... G2
Pointe-aux-Outardes 968 .... A1
Pointe-aux-Trembles 35,618 . J4
Pointe-Claire 25,917 .... H4
Pointe-du-Lac 2,737 .... E3
Pointe-Gatineau B4
Pointe-Lebel 1,302 .... A1
Pont-Rouge 3,342 .... F3
Port-Alfred G1
Portneuf 1,320 .... F3
Price 2,461 .... A1
Princeville 3,852 .... F3
Proulxville 608 .... E3
Québec (cap.) 177,082 .... H3
Quyon A4
Rawdon 2,808 .... D3
Repentigny 26,698 .... J4
Richelieu 1,755 .... D4
Richmond⊙ 4,021 .... E4
Rigaud 2,203 .... C4
Rimouski⊙ 27,897 .... J1
Rimouski-Est 2,328 .... J1
Rivière-à-Pierre 604 .... E3
Rivière-au-Renard 1,772 .... D1
Rivière-du-Loup⊙ 13,103 ... H2
Rivière-du-Moulin G1
Rivière-Éternité 709 .... G1
Rivière-Portneuf 959 .... H1
Robertsonville 1,666 .... F3
Roberval⊙ 8,543 .... E1
Rock Forest 652 .... F4
Rock Island 1,230 .... E4
Rosemère 7,112 .... H4
Rougemont 933 .... D4
Roxboro 7,106 .... H4
Roxton Falls 1,215 .... E4
Saint-Adelme 738 .... B1
Saint-Adelphe 1,220 .... E3
Saint-Adolphe-d'Howard
1,315 .... C4
Saint-Agapitville 1,672 .... F3
Saint-Aimé-des-Lacs 805 .... G2
Saint-Alban 726 .... E3
Saint-Alexandre-de-Kamouraska
966 .... H2
Saint-Alexis-des-Monts
1,815 .... D3
Saint-Amable 1,557 .... J4
Saint-Ambroise 3,169 .... F1
Saint-Anaclet 1,009 .... J1
Saint-André-Avellin 1,088 .... B4
Saint-André-Est 1,206 .... C4
Saint-Anselme 1,735 .... F3
Saint-Antoine 6,872 .... H4
Saint-Aubert 881 .... G2
Saint-Augustin-de-Québec
3,904 .... E3
Saint-Basile-le-Grand 5,843 . J4
Saint-Basile-Sud 1,649 .... F3
Saint-Benjamin 1,072 .... G3
Saint-Bernard 562 .... F3
Saint-Boniface-de-Shawinigan
2,680 .... D3
Saint-Bruno 2,259 .... F1
Saint-Bruno-de-Montarville
21,272 .... J4
Saint-Camille-de-Bellechasse
1,235 .... G3
Saint-Casimir 1,184 .... E3
Saint-Césaire 2,701 .... D4
Saint-Charles,
Bellechasse 1,027 .... G3
Saint-Charles-de-Mandeville
847 .... D3
Saint-Charles-Garnier 558 .... J1
Saint-Chrysostome 1,065 .... D4
Saint-Côme 839 .... D3
Saint-Constant 7,659 .... H4
Saint-Cyprien 791 .... J2
Saint-Cyrille 1,059 .... E4
Saint-Damien-de-Buckland
1,676 .... G3
Saint-David 4,386 .... J3
Saint-David-de-Falardeau
1,692 .... F1

AREA 594,857 sq. mi. (1,540,680 sq. km.)
POPULATION 6,377,518
CAPITAL Québec
LARGEST CITY Montréal
HIGHEST POINT Mont D'Iberville 5,420 ft. (1,652 m.)
SETTLED IN 1608
ADMITTED TO CONFEDERATION 1867
PROVINCIAL FLOWER White Garden Lily

Saint-Denis 888 .... D4
Saint-Dominique 1,772 .... E4
Saint-Donat-de-Montcal
1,460 .... C3
Sainte-Adèle 4,186 .... C4
Sainte-Agathe 727 .... F3
Sainte-Agathe-des-Monts
5,435 .... C3
Sainte-Agnes-de-Charlevoix
551 .... G2
Sainte-Anne-de-Beaupré
3,284 .... F2
Sainte-Anne-de-Bellevue
3,738 .... H4
Sainte-Anne-des-Monts⊙
5,945 .... C1
Sainte-Anne-des-Plaines
2,329 .... H4
Sainte-Aurélie 1,103 .... G3
Sainte-Blandine 1,008 .... J1
Sainte-Catherine 901 .... F3
Sainte-Claire 1,528 .... G3
Sainte-Croix⊙ 1,719 .... F3
Sainte-Émélie-de-l'Énergie
558 .... D3
Sainte-Félicité 762 .... B1
Sainte-Foy 71,237 .... H3
Sainte-Françoise 647 .... H1
Sainte-Geneviève 2,869 .... H4
Sainte-Geneviève-de-Batiscan⊙
412 .... E3
Sainte-Hedwidge-de-Roberval
966 .... E1
Sainte-Hélène-de-Kamouraska
658 .... H2
Sainte-Hénédine⊙ 561 .... F3
Sainte-Julie-de-Verchères
8,666 .... J4
Sainte-Julienne⊙ 809 .... D4
Sainte-Justine 1,116 .... G3
Saint-Éleuthère 1,033 .... H2
Saint-Élie 601 .... E3
Sainte-Louise 851 .... G2
Saint-Elzéar 643 .... F3
Saint-Elzéar-de-Bonaventure
617 .... C2
Sainte-Marie, Beauce 4,462 . G3
Sainte-Martine⊙ 1,957 .... D4
Saint-Émile 4,205 .... H3
Sainte-Monique,
Lac-St-Jean-E. 596 .... F1
Sainte-Perpétue-de-L'Islet
1,269 .... H2
Saint-Éphrem-de-Tring 880 .. G3

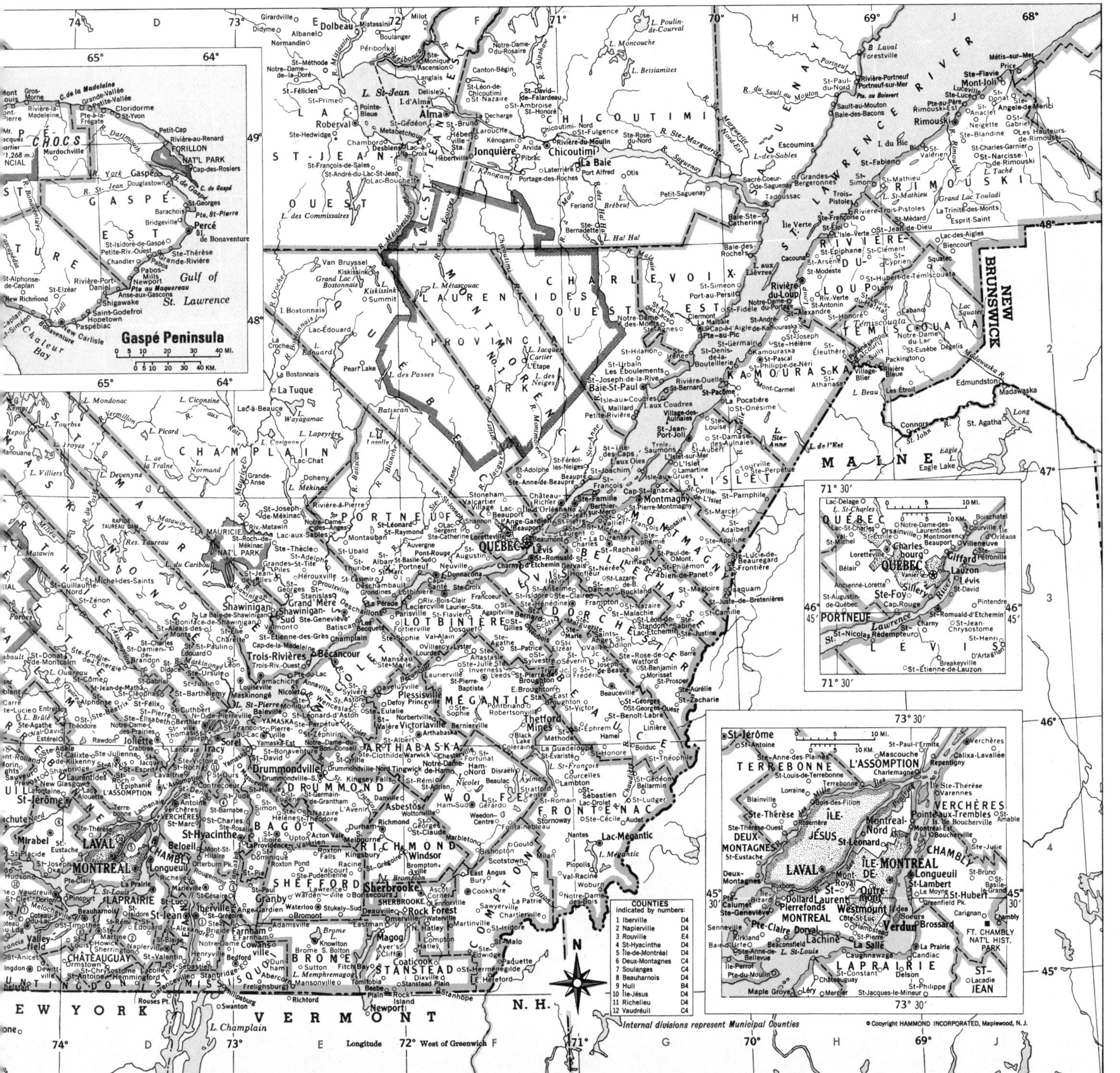

Gaspé Peninsula
Gulf of St. Lawrence
Chaleur Bay
NEW BRUNSWICK
MAINE
NEW YORK
VERMONT
N. H.
LAURENTIDES PROVINCIAL PARK
MONTMORENCY PROVINCIAL No. 1 PARK
ST. LAWRENCE RIVER
QUÉBEC
MONTREAL
LAVAL
COUNTIES
indicated by numbers:
1 Iberville D4
2 Napierville D4
3 Rouville E4
4 St-Hyacinthe D4
5 Île-de-Montréal D4
6 Deux-Montagnes C4
7 Soulanges C4
8 Beauharnois D4
9 Hull B4
10 Île-Jésus D4
11 Richelieu D4
12 Vaudréuil C4
Internal divisions represent Municipal Counties
Longitude 72° West of Greenwich
© Copyright HAMMOND INCORPORATED, Maplewood, N. J.

(continued)

Sainte-Pudentienne 802 ...... E4
Saint-Esprit 948 .... D4
Sainte-Thècle 1,761 .... E3
Sainte-Thérèse 17,479 .... H4
Saint-Étienne-de-Grès 728 ... E3
Saint-Eustache 21,248 .... H4
Saint-Évariste-de-Forsyth
787 .... F4
Saint-Fabien 1,458 .... J1
Saint-Félicien 4,985 .... E1
Saint-Félix-de-Valois 1,495 .. D3
Saint-Flavien 693 .... F3
Saint-François-d'Assise 680 . G1
Saint-François-de-Sales 803 . E1
Saint-François-du-Lac⊙ 971 .E3
Saint-Fulgence 966 .... G1
Saint-Gabriel 3,271 .... D3
Saint-Gédéon,
Frontenac 1,292 .... G4
Saint-Gédéon,
Lac-St-Jean-E. 697 .... F1
Saint-Georges, Beauce 8,605G3
Saint-Georges, Champlain
2,707 .... E3
Saint-Georges-Ouest 6,478 .. G3
Saint-Germain-de-Grantham
1,289 .... E4
Saint-Gervais 780 .... G3
Saint-Gilles 905 .... F3
Saint-Grégoire-de-Greenlay
622 .... E4
Saint-Henri J3
Saint-Honoré, Beauce 1,115 G4
Saint-Honoré,
Chicoutimi 1,546 .... F1
Saint-Honoré-de-Témiscouata
539 .... H2
Saint-Hubert 49,706 .... J4
Saint-Hubert-de-Témiscouata
539 .... J2
Saint-Hyacinthe⊙ 37,500 .... D4
Saint-Isidore 768 .... F3
Saint-Isidore-de-Laprairie
846 .... D4
Saint-Jacques 2,095 .... D4
Saint-Jacques-le-Mineur
1,086 .... H4
Saint-Jean⊙ 34,363 .... D4
Saint-Jean-Chrysostome
3,606 .... J3
Saint-Jean-de-Dieu 1,261 .... J1
Saint-Jean-de-Matha 947 .... D3
Saint-Jean-Port-Joli⊙ 1,844 G2
Saint-Jérôme,
Terrebonne⊙ 25,175 ...... H4
Saint-Joachim 943 .... G2
Saint-Joseph-de-Beauce
3,213 .... G3
Saint-Joseph-de-Sorel 2,811 D3
Saint-Jovite 3,595 .... C3
Saint-Lambert 20,318 .... J4
Saint-Laurent 64,404 .... H4
Saint-Lazare 558 .... G3
Saint-Léonard 78,452 .... H4
Saint-Léonard-d'Aston 1,049 E3
Saint-Léonard-de-Portneuf
555 .... E3
Saint-Léon-de-Standon 855 .. G3
Saint-Léon-le-Grand 1,325 ... B2
Saint-Liboire⊙ 648 .... E4
Saint-Louis-de-Terrebonne
8,479 .... H4
Saint-Louis-du-Ha Ha 672 ... H2
Saint-Luc 7,103 .... D4
Saint-Luc-de-Matane 609 .... B1
Saint-Marc-des-Carrières
2,625 .... E3
Saint-Méthode-de-Frontenac
898 .... F3
Saint-Michel-de-Bellechasse
960 .... G3
Saint-Michel-des-Saints
1,966 .... D3
Saint-Nazaire-de-Chicoutimi
938 .... F1
Saint-Nérée 907 .... G3
Saint-Noël 777 .... B1
Saint-Odilon 697 .... G3
Saint-Omer 569 .... C2
Saint-Ours 742 .... D4
Saint-Pacôme 1,167 .... G2
Saint-Pamphile 3,450 .... H3
Saint-Pascal⊙ 2,552 .... H2
Saint-Paul 544 .... E4
Saint-Paul-de-Montminy 691 G3
Saint-Paulin 734 .... D3
Saint-Paul-l'Ermite 6,107 .... J4
Saint-Petronille 801 .... J3
Saint-Philippe-de-Néri 732 .. H2
Saint-Pie 1,720 .... E4
Saint-Pierre,
Île-de-Mont. 6,039 .... H4
Saint-Pierre, Joliette 679 ..... D3
Saint-Pierre-d'Orléans 619 ... G3
Saint-Polycarpe 540 .... C4
Saint-Prime 2,266 .... E1
Saint-Prosper-de-Dorchester
1,878 .... G3
Saint-Raphaël⊙ 1,328 .... G3
Saint-Raymond 3,742 .... F3
Saint-Rédempteur 3,031 ..... J3
Saint-Régis C4
Saint-Rémi 4,866 .... D4
Saint-Roch-de-l'Achigan
1,052 .... D4
Saint-Roch-de-Richelieu 614 D4
Saint-Romuald-d'Etchemin⊙
9,160 .... J3
Saint-Sauveur-des-Monts
1,999 .... C4
Saint-Siméon 1,163 .... G2
Saint-Siméon-de-Bonaventure
650 .... C2
Saint-Simon 675 .... H1
Saint-Thomas-de-Joliette 577D3
Saint-Timothée 1,927 .... D4
Saint-Tite 3,128 .... E3
Saint-Tite-des-Caps 609 ...... G2
Saint-Ubald E3
Saint-Ulric 804 .... B1
Saint-Urbain-de-Charlevoix
1,076 .... G2
Saint-Victor 1,044 .... G3
Saint-Zacharie 1,300 .... G3
Saint-Zotique 1,519 .... C4
Sault-au-Mouton 914 .... H1
Sawyerville 878 .... F4
Sayabec 1,818 .... B2
Scotstown 827 .... F4
Scott-Jonction 571 .... F3
Senneville 1,333 .... G4
Shawbridge 831 .... C4
Shawinigan 24,921 .... E3
Shawinigan-Sud 11,155 ...... E3
Shawville 1,724 .... A4
Sherbrooke⊙ 76,804 .... E4
Sillery 13,580 .... J3
Sorel⊙ 19,666 .... D4
Squatec 920 .... J2
Stanstead Plain 1,163 .... F4
Sully 833 .... H2
Sutton 1,655 .... E4
Tadoussac⊙ 998 .... H1
Terrebonne 11,204 .... H4
Thetford Mines 20,874 .... F3
Thurso 3,066 .... B4
Tourville 669 .... H2
Tracy 12,284 .... D3
Tring-Jonction 1,248 .... F3
Trois-Pistoles 4,554 .... H1
Trois-Rivières 52,518 .... E3
Trois-Rivières-Ouest 10,564 . E3
Upton 822 .... E4
Val-Brillant 677 .... B1
Valcourt 2,566 .... E4
Val-David 2,073 .... C3
Vallée-Jonction 1,288 .... G3
Valleyfield 29,716 .... C4
Vanier 10,683 .... J3
Varennes 6,469 .... J4
Vaudreuil⊙ 5,630 .... C4
Verchères⊙ 3,586 .... J4
Verdun 68,013 .... H4
Victoriaville 21,825 .... F3
Villeneuve J3
Warwick 2,865 .... F4
Waterloo⊙ 4,746 .... E4
Waterville 1,458 .... F4
Weedon-Centre 1,264 .... F4
Westmount 22,153 .... H4
Windsor 5,637 .... F4
Woburn 542 .... G4
Wottonville 700 .... F4
Yamachiche⊙ 1,202 .... E3

OTHER FEATURES

Alma (isl.) F1
Aylmer (lake) F4
Baskatong (res.) B3
Batiscan (riv.) E2
Bécancour (riv.) F3
Bonaventure (isl.) D1
Bonaventure (riv.) C1
Brome (lake) E4
Brompton (lake) E4
Cascapédia (riv.) C1
Chaleur (bay) C2
Champlain (lake) D4
Chaudière (riv.) G4
Chic-Chocs (mts.) C1
Chicoutimi (riv.) F2
Coudres (isl.) G2
Deschênes (lake) A4
Deux Montagnes (lake) C4
Ditton (riv.) F4
Forillon Nat'l Park D1
Fort Chambly Nat'l Hist.
Park J4
Gaspé (bay) D1
Gaspé (cape) D1
Gaspé (pen.) D2
Gaspésie Prov. Park C1
Gatineau (riv.) B3
Îles (lake) B3
Jacques-Cartier (mt.) C1
Jacques-Cartier (riv.) F2
Kénogami (lake) F1
Kiamika (lake) B3
La Maurice Nat'l Park D3
Laurentides Prov. Park F2
Lièvre (riv.) B4
Lièvres (isl.) H2
Maskinongé (riv.) D3
Matane (riv.) B1
Matane Prov. Park B1
Matapédia (riv.) B2
Mégantic (lake) G4
Memphremagog (lake) E4
Mercier (dam) A3
Métabetchouane (riv.) F1
Mille Îles (riv.) H4
Montmorency (riv.) F2
Mont-Tremblant Prov. Park . C3
Nicolet (riv.) E3
Nominingue (lake) B3
Nord (riv.) C4
Orléans (isl.) F3
Ottawa (riv.) B4
Ouareau (riv.) D3
Patapédia (riv.) B2
Péribonca (riv.) F1
Petite Nation (riv.) B4
Prairies (riv.) H4
Rimouski (riv.) J1
Ristigouche (riv.) B2
Saguenay (riv.) G1
Sainte-Anne (riv.) F3
Sainte-Anne (riv.) G2
Saint-François (lake) F4
Saint-François (riv.) E4
Saint-Jean (lake) E1
Saint Lawrence (gulf) D2
Saint Lawrence (riv.) H1
Saint-Louis (lake) H4
Saint-Maurice (riv.) E2
Saint-Pierre (lake) E3
Shawinigan (riv.) E3
Shipshaw (riv.) F1
Soeurs (isl.) H4
Témiscouata (lake) H2
Tremblant (lake) C3
Trente et un Milles (lake) B3
Verte (isl.) H1
Yamaska (riv.) E4
York (riv.) D1

QUÉBEC, NORTHERN

INTERNAL DIVISIONS

Abitibi (county) 88,229 .... B2
Abitibi (terr.) B3
Berthier (county) 28,465 ..... B3
Bonaventure (county) 40,724D3
Champlain (county) 114,078 C3
Charlevoix-Est (county)
17,065 .... C3
Charlevoix-Ouest
(county) 13,601 .... C3
Chicoutimi (county) 165,859 C2
Gaspé-Est (county) 40,720 ... E3
Gaspé-Ouest (county) 19,238D3
Gatineau (county) 52,193 .... B3
Joliette (county) 55,524 ...... B3
Lac-Saint-Jean-Est
(county) 45,558 .... C3
Lac-Saint-Jean-Ouest
(county) 57,556 .... C2
Maskinongé (county) 20,879 C3
Matane (county) 28,954 ...... D3
Matapédia (county) 24,063 D3
Mistassini (terr.) B2
Montcalm (county) 23,534 ... B3
Montmorency No. I
(county) 20,712 .... C3
Nouveau-Québec
(terr.) 38,982 .... E1
Pontiac (county) 20,559 ...... B3
Portneuf (county) 51,643 .... C3
Québec (county) 449,633 .... C3
Rimouski (county) 64,768 ... D3
Saguenay (county) 115,736 D2
Saint-Maurice (county)
106,023 .... C3
Témiscamingue
(county) 52,871 .... B3

CITIES and TOWNS

Alma⊙ 25,638 .... C3
Amos⊙ 9,213 .... B3
Baie-Comeau 11,911 .... D3
Baie-du-Poste C2
Chibougamau 10,536 .... C3
Chicoutimi⊙ 57,737 .... C3
Gaspé 16,842 .... E3
Hauterive 14,724 .... D3
Jonquière 60,691 .... C3
La Tuque 12,067 .... C3
Lévis 17,819 .... C3
Manicouagan D2
Matane⊙ 12,726 .... D3
Mistassini (Baie-du-Poste) ... C2
Montmagny⊙ 12,326 .... C3
New Carlisle⊙ 1,403 .... E3
Noranda 9,809 .... B3
Nouveau-Comptoir B2
Percé⊙ 5,198 .... E3
Port-Cartier-Ouest 1,171 ..... D3
Port-Menier⊙ 438 .... E3
Povungnituk E1
Québec (cap.)⊙ 177,082 .... C3
Rimouski⊙ 27,897 .... D3
Rivière-au-Tonnerre ....
Rivière-du-Loup⊙ 13,103 ...
Rouyn 17,678 ....
Sept-Îles 30,617 ....
Seven Islands
(Sept-Îles) 30,617 ....
Shawinigan 24,921 ....
Tadoussac⊙ 998 ....
Val d'Or 19,915 ....
Ville-Marie⊙ 2,274 ....

OTHER FEATURES

Allard (lake) ....
Anticosti (isl.) ....
Baleine, Grand Rivière de la
(riv.) ....
Bell (riv.) ....
Betsiamites (riv.) ....
Bienville (lake) ....
Broadback (riv.) ....
Cabonga (res.) ....
Caniapiscau (riv.) ....
Eastmain (riv.) ....
Eau Claire (lake) ....
Feuilles (riv.) ....
Gaspésie Prov. Park ....
George (riv.) ....
Gouin (res.) ....
Grande Rivière, La (riv.) .....
Honguedo (passage) ....
Hudson (bay) ....
Hudson (str.) ....
Jacques-Cartier (passage) ....
James (bay) ....
Koksoak (riv.) ....
Laurentides Prov. Park ....
Louis-XIV (pt.) ....
Manicouagan (res.) ....
Minto (lake) ....
Mistassibi (riv.) ....
Mistassini (lake) ....
Moisie (riv.) ....
Mont-Tremblant Prov. Park ..
Natashquan (riv.) ....
Nottaway (riv.) ....
Nouveau-Québec (crater) .....
Otish (mts.) ....
Ottawa (riv.) ....
Péribonca (riv.) ....
Plétipi (lake) ....
Saguenay (riv.) ....
Saint-Jean (lake) ....
Saint Lawrence (gulf) ....
Saint Lawrence (riv.) ....
Ungava (pen.) ....

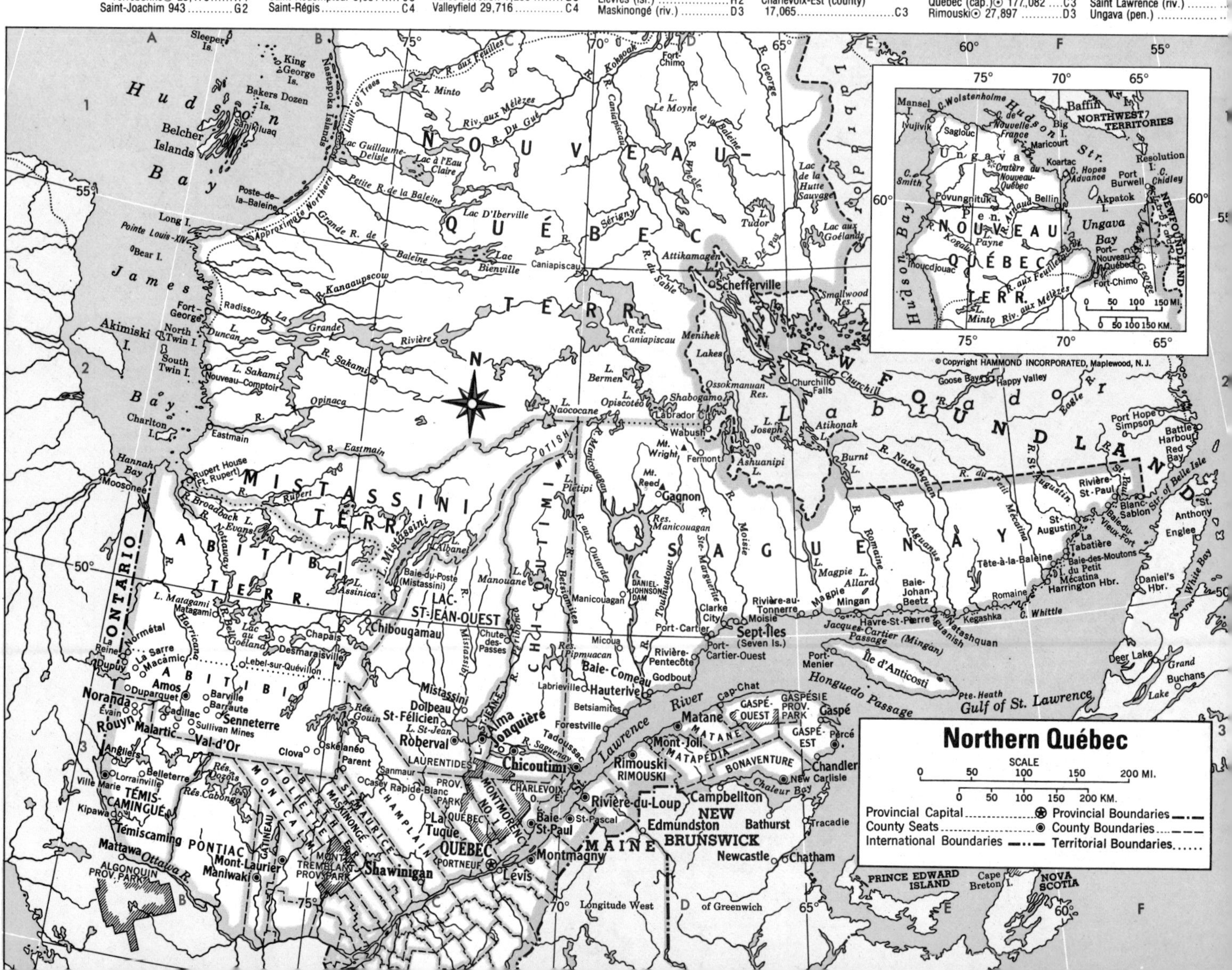

AREA 412,580 sq. mi. (1,068,582 sq. km.)
POPULATION 8,551,733
CAPITAL Toronto
LARGEST CITY Toronto
HIGHEST POINT in Timiskaming Dist. 2,275 ft. (693 m.)
SETTLED IN 1749
ADMITTED TO CONFEDERATION 1867
PROVINCIAL FLOWER White Trillium

ONTARIO, NORTHERN

INTERNAL DIVISIONS

Algoma (terr. dist.) 122,883 D3
Cochrane (terr. dist.) 96,825 D2
Kenora (terr. dist.) 57,980 .. C2
Manitoulin (terr. dist.) 10,893 .... D3
Nipissing (terr. dist.) 81,739 E3
Parry Sound (terr. dist.) 32,654 .... E3
Rainy River (terr. dist.) 24,768 .... B3
Renfrew (county) 89,099 .... E3
Sudbury (reg. munic.) 167,705 .... D3
Sudbury (terr. dist.) 27,287. D3
Thunder Bay (terr. dist.) 150,647 .... C3
Timiskaming (terr. dist.) 43,760 .... D3

CITIES and TOWNS

Chalk River 1,095 .... E3
Fort Albany D2
Huntsville 11,123 .... E3
Kapuskasing 12,676 .... D3
Kenora⊙ 10,565 .... B3
Kirkland Lake 13,567 .... D3
Moose Factory 554 .... D2
Moosonee 1,349 .... D2
Nickel Centre 13,157 .... D3
North Bay⊙ 51,639 .... E3
Pembroke⊙ 14,927 .... E3
Sault Sainte Marie⊙ 81,048 D3
Sudbury 97,604 .... D3
Thunder Bay⊙ 111,476 .... C3
Timmins 44,747 .... D3
Valley East 19,591 .... D3
Walden 10,453 .... D3

OTHER FEATURES

Abitibi (lake) E3
Abitibi (riv.) D2
Albany (riv.) C2
Algonquin Prov. Park E3
Asheweig (riv.) C2
Attawapiskat (lake) C2
Attawapiskat (riv.) C2
Basswood (lake) B3
Berens (riv.) A2
Big Trout (lake) B2
Black Duck (riv.) C1
Bloodvein (riv.) A2
Caribou (isl.) C3
Cobham (riv.) A2
Eabamet (lake) C2
Ekwan (riv.) C2
English (riv.) B2
Fawn (riv.) C2
Finger (lake) B2
Georgian (bay) D3
Hannah (bay) D2
Henrietta Maria (cape) D1
Hudson (bay) D1
Huron (lake) D3
James (bay) D2
Kapiskau (riv.) D2
Kapuskasing (riv.) D3
Kenogami (riv.) C2
Kesagami (lake) E2
Lake of the Woods (lake) B3
Lake Superior Prov. Park ... D3
Little Current (riv.) C2
Long (lake) C3
Manitoulin (isl.) D3
Mattagami (riv.) D3
Michipicoten (isl.) C3
Mille Lacs (lake) B3
Missinaibi (lake) D3
Missinaibi (riv.) D2
Missisa (lake) D2
Nipigon (lake) C3
Nipissing (lake) E3
North (chan.) D3
North Caribou (lake) B2
Nungesser (lake) B2
Ogidaki (mt.) D3
Ogoki (riv.) C2
Opazatika (riv.) D3
Opinnagau (riv.) D2
Otoskwin (riv.) B2
Ottawa (riv.) E3
Pipestone (riv.) B2
Polar Bear Prov. Park D2
Pukaskwa Prov. Park C3
Quetico Prov. Park B3
Rainy (lake) B3
Red (lake) B2
Sachigo (riv.) B2
Saganaga (lake) B3
Saint Ignace (isl.) C3
Saint Joseph (lake) B2
Sandy (lake) B2
Savant (lake) B2
Seine (riv.) B3
Seul (lake) B2
Severn (lake) B2
Severn (riv.) B2
Shamattawa (riv.) C2
Shibogama (lake) C2
Sibley Prov. Park C3
Slate (isls.) C3
Stout (lake) B2
Superior (lake) C3
Sutton (lake) D2
Sutton (riv.) D2
Timagami (lake) D3
Timiskaming (lake) E3
Trout (lake) B2
Wabuk (pt.) D1
Winisk (lake) C2
Winisk (riv.) C2
Winnipeg (riv.) A2
Woods (lake) B3

ONTARIO

INTERNAL DIVISIONS

Algoma (terr. dist.) 122,883 J5
Brant (county) 99,950 .... D4
Bruce (county) 57,472 .... C3
Cochrane (terr. dist.) 96,825 J4
Dufferin (county) 28,528 ..... D3
Dundas (county) 18,507 ...... J2
Durham (reg. munic.) 247,473 .... F3
Elgin (county) 69,092 .... C5
Essex (county) 310,362 ...... B5
Frontenac (county) 108,052 H3
Glengarry (county) 19,270 ... K2
Grenville (county) 26,025 ..... J3
Grey (county) 72,176 .... D3
Haldimand-Norfolk (reg. munic.) 89,252 .... E5
Haliburton (county) 10,795 ... F2
Halton (reg. munic.) 128,497 E4
Hamilton-Wentworth (reg. munic.) 409,490 .... D4
Hastings (county) 105,837 ... G3
Huron (county) 56,007 .... C4
Kenora (terr. dist.) 57,980 ... G5
Kent (county) 106,130 .... B5
Lambton (county) 120,576 ... B5
Lanark (county) 44,197 ...... H3
Leeds (county) 52,579 .... H3
Lennox and Addington (county) 32,633 .... G3
Manitoulin (terr. dist.) 10,893 .... B2
Middlesex (county) 303,745 C4
Muskoka (dist. munic.) 36,691 .... E3
Niagara (reg. munic.) 365,438 E4
Nipissing (terr. dist.) 81,739 F2
Northumberland (county) 64,441 .... G3
Ottawa-Carleton (reg. munic.) 520,533 .... J2
Oxford (county) 85,337 ...... D4
Parry Sound (terr. dist.) 32,654 .... D2
Peel (reg. munic.) 375,910 . E4
Perth (county) 66,279 .... C4
Peterborough (county) 99,930 .... F3
Prescott (county) 29,100 .... K2
Prince Edward (county) 22,559 .... G3
Rainy River (terr. dist.) 24,768 .... G5
Renfrew (county) 89,099 .... G2
Russell (county) 19,735 ..... J2
Simcoe (county) 210,691 .... E3
Stormont (county) 61,173 ... K2
Sudbury (reg. munic.) 167,705 .... K6
Sudbury (terr. dist.) 27,287. J5
Thunder Bay (terr. dist.) 150,647 .... H5
Timiskaming (terr. dist.) 43,760 .... K5
Toronto (metro. munic.) 2,124,291 .... K4
Victoria (county) 43,543 ..... F3
Waterloo (reg. munic.) 289,129 .... D4
Wellington (county) 123,736 D4
York (reg. munic.) 203,915 . E4

CITIES and TOWNS

Ailsa Craig 701 .... C4
Ajax 20,774 .... E4
Alban 351 .... D1
Alcona Beach 861 .... E3
Alexandria 3,498 .... K2
Alfred 1,105 .... K2
Alliston 4,155 .... E3
Alma 271 .... D4
Almonte 3,693 .... H2
Alvinston 672 .... B5
Amherstburg 5,566 .... A5
Amherst View 5,295 .... H3
Ancaster 14,255 .... D4
Angus 3,494 .... E3
Apple Hill 271 .... K2
Apsley 281 .... F3
Arkona 458 .... C4
Armstrong 323 .... H4
Arnprior 6,111 .... H2
Arthur 1,660 .... D4
Astorville 373 .... E1
Athens 1,054 .... J3
Atherley 367 .... E3
Atikokan 5,668 .... G5
Atwood 720 .... D4
Aurora 14,249 .... J3
Avonmore 300 .... K2
Aylmer 5,125 .... C5
Ayr 1,331 .... D4
Ayton 450 .... D3
Baden 824 .... D4
Bala 536 .... E2
Bancroft 2,332 .... G2
Barrie⊙ 34,389 .... E3
Barry's Bay 1,256 .... G2
Batawa 484 .... G3
Bath 762 .... H3
Bayfield 549 .... C4
Bayside 3,356 .... G3
Beachburg 649 .... H2
Beachville 988 .... D4
Beardmore 656 .... H5
Beaverton 1,737 .... E3
Beeton 1,604 .... E3
Belle River 3,254 .... B5
Belleville⊙ 35,311 .... G3
Belmont 739 .... C5
Bethany 314 .... F3
Bewdley 475 .... F3
Binbrook 465 .... E4
Blackstock 767 .... F3
Blenheim 3,804 .... C5
Blind River 3,142 .... J5
Bloomfield 756 .... G4
Blyth 866 .... C4
Bobcaygeon 1,562 .... F3
Bonfield 722 .... E1
Bothwell 899 .... C5
Bourget 949 .... J2
Bracebridge⊙ 8,428 .... E2
Bradford 5,080 .... E3
Braeside 538 .... H2
Brampton⊙ 103,459 .... J4
Brantford⊙ 66,950 .... D4
Bridgenorth 1,368 .... F3
Brigden 548 .... B5
Brighton 3,199 .... G3
Brights Grove 1,113 .... B4
Britt 468 .... D2
Brockville⊙ 19,903 .... J3
Bruce Mines 517 .... J5
Brussels 1,043 .... C4
Burford 1,051 .... D4
Burgessville 289 .... D4
Burk's Falls 871 .... E2
Burlington 104,314 .... E4
Cache Bay 691 .... D1
Caesarea 547 .... F3
Calabogie 289 .... H2
Caledon 22,434 .... E4
Callander 1,058 .... E1
Cambridge 72,383 .... D4
Campbellford 3,487 .... G3
Cannington 1,419 .... E3
Capreol 4,089 .... K5
Caramat 382 .... H5
Cardinal 1,867 .... J3
Carleton Place 5,256 .... H2
Carlisle 565 .... D4
Carlsbad Springs 478 .... J2
Carp 681 .... H2
Cartier 673 .... J5
Casselman 1,422 .... J2
Castleton 326 .... F3
Cedar Springs 281 .... B5
Chalk River 1,095 .... G1
Chapleau 3,253 .... J5
Charing Cross 441 .... B5
Chatham⊙ 38,685 .... B5
Chatsworth 394 .... D3
Cherry Valley 273 .... G4
Chesley 1,839 .... C3
Chesterville 1,324 .... J2
Chute-à-Blondeau 350 .... K2
City View J2
Clarence Creek 395 .... J2
Clarksburg 481 .... D3
Clifford 641 .... D4
Clinton 3,151 .... C4
Cobalt 2,056 .... K5
Cobden 1,025 .... H2
Coboconk 377 .... F3
Cobourg⊙ 11,421 .... F4
Cochrane⊙ 4,974 .... K5
Codes Corner 407 .... H3
Colborne 1,724 .... G4
Colchester 990 .... B6
Coldwater 803 .... E3
Collingwood 11,114 .... D3
Collins Bay 6,897 .... H3
Comber 649 .... B5
Consecon 363 .... G3
Cookstown 874 .... E3
Cornwall⊙ 46,121 .... K2
Corunna 3,723 .... B5
Cottam 514 .... B5
Courtland 602 .... D5
Coverdale 1,573 .... F4
Crediton 439 .... C4
Creemore 1,089 .... D3
Crysler 490 .... J2
Cumberland 550 .... J2
Cumberland Beach 686 .... E3
Dashwood 434 .... C4
Deep River 5,565 .... G1
Delaware 346 .... C5
Delhi 3,929 .... D5
Delta 310 .... H3
Denbigh 294 .... G2
Deseronto 1,893 .... G3
Dorchester 2,756 .... C5
Douglas 291 .... H2
Drayton 801 .... D4
Dresden 2,484 .... B5
Drumbo 397 .... D4
Dryden 6,799 .... G4
Dublin 282 .... C4
Dubreuilville 818 .... J5
Dundalk 1,165 .... D3
Dundas 19,179 .... D4
Dunnville 11,642 .... E5
Durham 2,501 .... D3
Dutton 1,036 .... C5
Earlton 1,008 .... K5
East York 106,950 .... J4
Echo Bay 745 .... J5
Eden Mills 332 .... D4
Eganville 1,328 .... G2
Egmondville 120 .... C4
Elgin 292 .... H3
Elk Lake 564 .... K5
Elliot Lake 8,849 .... B1
Elmira 7,034 .... D4
Elmvale 1,176 .... E3
Elmwood 423 .... C3
Elora 2,589 .... D4
Embro 800 .... C4
Embrun 1,763 .... J2
Emeryville B5
Emo 792 .... F5
Englehart 1,767 .... K5
Enterprise 295 .... H3
Erieau 453 .... C5
Erin 2,007 .... D4
Espanola 5,926 .... J5
Essex 5,577 .... B5
Etobicoke 297,109 .... J4
Everett 438 .... E3
Exeter 3,494 .... C4
Fauquier 620 .... J5
Fenelon Falls 1,637 .... F3
Fergus 6,001 .... D4
Field 568 .... E1
Finch 407 .... J2
Fingal 345 .... C5
Fitzroy Harbour 431 .... H2
Flesherton 568 .... D3
Foleyet 538 .... J5
Fordwich 412 .... C4
Forest 2,557 .... C4
Formosa 395 .... C3
Fort Erie 24,031 .... E5
Fort Frances⊙ 9,325 .... F5
Foxboro 560 .... G3
Frankford 1,851 .... G3
Fraserdale 385 .... J5
Freelton 310 .... D4
Gananoque 5,103 .... H3
Garden Village 265 .... E1
Geraldton 3,127 .... H5
Glencoe 1,818 .... C5
Glen Miller 605 .... G3
Glen Robertson 312 .... K2
Glen Walter 662 .... K2
Goderich⊙ 7,385 .... C4
Gogama 702 .... J5

(continued on following page)

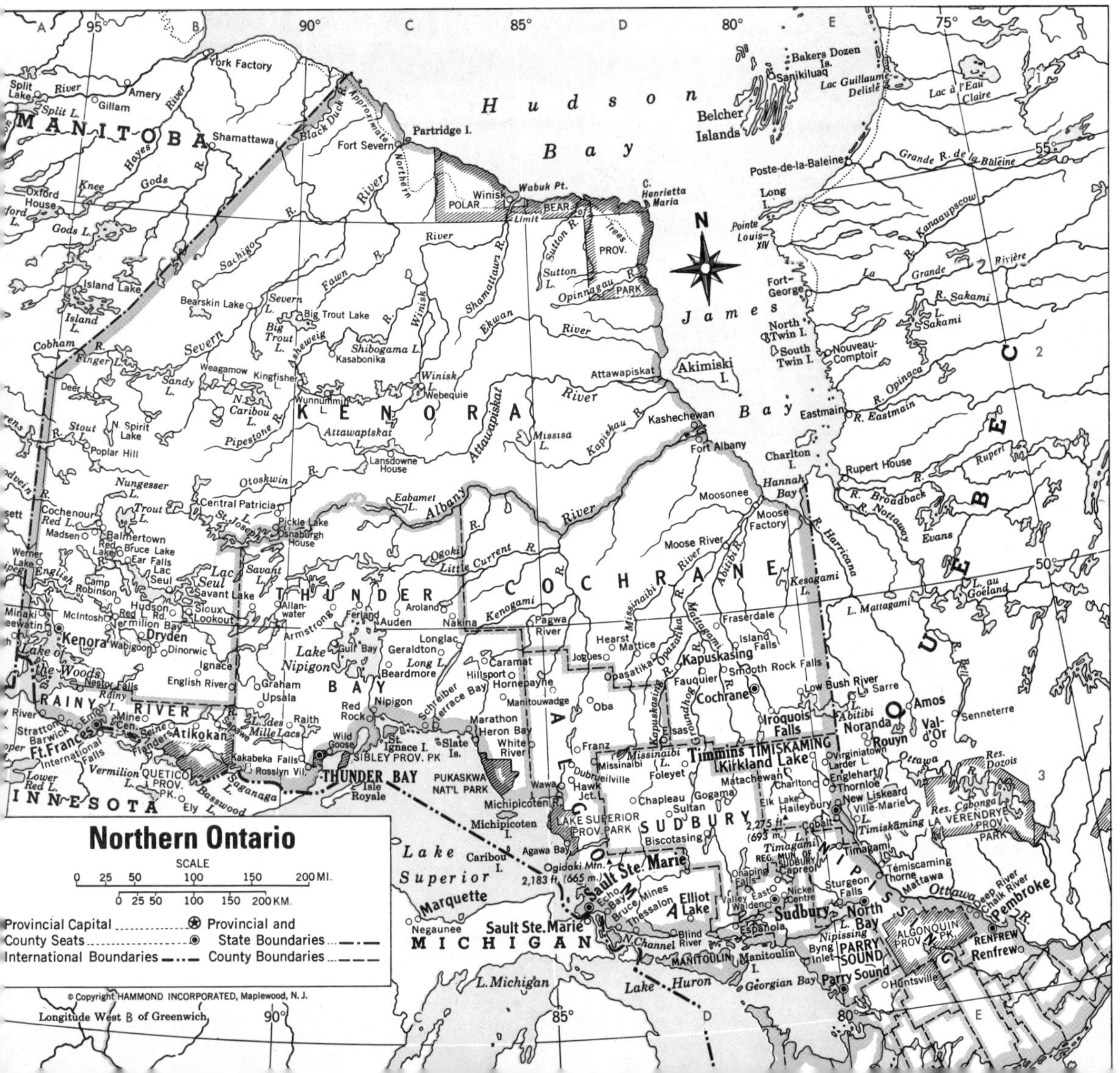

Northern Ontario
SCALE
0 25 50 100 150 200 MI.
0 25 50 100 150 200 KM.
Provincial Capital ⊛ Provincial and
County Seats ⊙ State Boundaries
International Boundaries County Boundaries
© Copyright HAMMOND INCORPORATED, Maplewood, N.J.
Longitude West of Greenwich
Hudson Bay
James Bay
MANITOBA
KENORA
COCHRANE
THUNDER BAY
SUDBURY
TIMISKAMING
NIPISSING
PARRY SOUND
RENFREW
ALGONQUIN PROV. PK.
QUÉBEC
MICHIGAN
MINNESOTA
Lake Superior
Lake Huron
L. Michigan
Georgian Bay
Belcher Islands
Akimiski I.
York Factory
Fort Severn
Moosonee
Moose Factory
Kapuskasing
Cochrane
Timmins
Kirkland Lake
Sudbury
North Bay
Pembroke
Sault Ste. Marie
Elliot Lake
Thunder Bay
Kenora
Dryden
Atikokan
Ft. Frances
Nipigon
Geraldton
Hearst
Chapleau
Wawa
Michipicoten
Marquette

(continued)

Gore Bay⊙ 767 .... B2
Gorrie 424 .... C4
Grafton 402 .... G4
Grand Bend 750 .... C4
Grand Valley 1,096 .... D4
Granton 313 .... C4
Gravenhurst 7,986 .... E3
Greely 509 .... J2
Green Valley 478 .... K2
Grimsby 15,567 .... E4
Guelph⊙ 67,538 .... D4
Haileybury⊙ 4,939 .... K5
Haldimand 16,375 .... E5
Haliburton 1,124 .... F2
Halton Hills 34,477 .... E4
Hamilton⊙ 312,003 .... E4
Hanover 5,691 .... C3
Harriston 1,872 .... D4
Harrow 1,936 .... B5
Harrowsmith 533 .... H3
Harwood 262 .... F3
Hastings 990 .... G3
Havelock 1,280 .... G3
Hawkesbury 9,789 .... K2
Hawkestone 309 .... E3
Hawk Junction 363 .... J5
Hearst 5,195 .... J5
Hensall 993 .... C4
Hepworth 377 .... C3
Heyden 316 .... J5
Highgate 418 .... C5
Hillsburgh 819 .... D4
Hillsdale 274 .... E3
Holland Landing 1,782 .... E3
Honey Harbour 289 .... E3
Hornepayne 1,694 .... J5
Hudson 565 .... G4
Huntsville 11,123 .... E2
Huron Park 1,341 .... C4
Ignace 515 .... G5
Ilderton 330 .... C4
Ingersoll 8,198 .... C4
Ingleside 1,106 .... J2
Innerkip 655 .... D4
Inverhuron 275 .... C3
Iron Bridge 790 .... A1
Iroquois 1,278 .... J3
Iroquois Falls 6,887 .... J5
Jasper 374 .... H3
Johnstown 560 .... J3
Kakabeka Falls 367 .... G5
Kaladar 262 .... H3
Kanata 6,304 .... J2
Kapuskasing 12,676 .... J5
Kars 409 .... J2
Kearney 285 .... E2
Keene 275 .... F3
Keewatin 1,954 .... F5
Kemptville 2,544 .... J2
Kenora⊙ 10,565 .... F4
Keswick 1,217 .... E3
Killaloe Station 699 .... G2
Killarney 445 .... C2
Kincardine 4,182 .... C3
King City 2,182 .... J3
Kingston⊙ 56,032 .... H3
Kingsville 4,692 .... B6
Kinmount 270 .... F3
Kirkland Lake 13,567 .... K5
Kitchener⊙ 131,870 .... D4
Komoka 812 .... C5
Lakefield 2,240 .... F3
Lambeth 2,876 .... C5
Lanark 803 .... H2
Lancaster 540 .... K2
Langton 421 .... D5
Lansdowne 542 .... H3
Larder Lake 1,238 .... K5
Latchford 457 .... K5
Leamington 11,169 .... B5
Lefroy 534 .... E3
Limoges 616 .... J2
Lincoln 14,460 .... E4
Linden Beach 484 .... B6
Lindsay⊙ 13,062 .... F3
Linwood 455 .... D4
Lion's Head 500 .... C2
Listowel 5,126 .... D4
Little Britain 359 .... F3
Little Current 1,476 .... B2
London⊙ 240,392 .... C5
Longlac 1,923 .... H5
Long Sault 1,096 .... K2
L'Orignal⊙ 1,380 .... K2
Lucan 1,377 .... C4
Lucknow 1,127 .... C4
Lyn 562 .... J3
Lynden 457 .... D4
Lynhurst 429 .... C5
Macdiarmid 444 .... H5
MacGregor's Bay 885 .... G2
MacTier 690 .... E2
Madawaska 288 .... F2
Madoc 1,363 .... G3
Maitland 584 .... J3
Mallorytown 290 .... J3
Manitouwadge 3,551 .... H5
Manitowaning 373 .... C2
Manotick 1,410 .... J2
Marathon 2,250 .... H5
Markdale 1,361 .... D3
Markham 56,206 .... K4
Markstay 521 .... D1
Marmora 1,326 .... G3
Martintown 366 .... K2
Massey 1,345 .... C1
Matachewan 619 .... J5
Matheson 703 .... K5
Mattawa 2,849 .... F1
Mattice 816 .... J5
Maxville 852 .... K2
Maynooth 281 .... G2
McGregor 810 .... B5
McKerrow 323 .... C1
Meaford 4,319 .... D3
Melbourne 339 .... C5
Merlin 722 .... B5
Merrickville 932 .... J3
Metcalfe 681 .... J2
Midhurst 626 .... E3
Midland 11,568 .... D3
Mildmay 990 .... C3
Milford Bay 320 .... E2
Millbank 383 .... D4
Millbrook 898 .... F3
Milton⊙ 20,756 .... E4
Milverton 1,393 .... D4
Mindemoya 407 .... B2
Minden⊙ 590 .... F3
Mississauga 250,017 .... J4
Mitchell 2,742 .... C4
Monkton 550 .... C4
Moonbeam 925 .... J5
Moorefield 304 .... D4
Moose Creek 382 .... K2
Morpeth 305 .... C5
Morrisburg 2,188 .... J3
Mount Albert 909 .... E3
Mount Brydges 1,573 .... C5
Mount Elgin 289 .... D5
Mount Forest 3,376 .... D4
Mount Hope 687 .... E4
Mount Pleasant 545 .... D4
Munster 1,119 .... J2
Nairn 457 .... C1
Nakina 602 .... H4
Nanticoke 19,489 .... E5
Napanee⊙ 4,844 .... G3
Neustadt 543 .... D3
Newburgh 628 .... H3
Newbury 388 .... C5
Newcastle 31,928 .... F4
New Hamburg 3,628 .... D4
Newington 278 .... K2
New Liskeard 5,601 .... K5
Newmarket⊙ 24,795 .... E3
Niagara Falls 69,423 .... E4
Niagara-on-the-Lake 12,485 .... E4
Nickel Centre 13,157 .... D1
Nipigon 2,724 .... H5
Nobel 291 .... D2
Nobleton 1,537 .... J3
Noelville 665 .... D1
North Bay⊙ 51,639 .... E1
North Brook 409 .... G3
North Gower 625 .... J2
North York 558,398 .... J4
Norwich 1,891 .... D5
Norwood 1,243 .... F3
Nottawa 326 .... D3
Oakville 68,950 .... E4
Oakwood 382 .... F3
Odessa 877 .... H3
Oil Springs 618 .... B5
Omemee 790 .... F3
Onaping Falls 6,776 .... J5
Opasatika 798 .... J5
Orangeville⊙ 12,021 .... D4
Orillia 24,412 .... E3
Orleans 4,316 .... J2
Osgoode 984 .... J2
Oshawa 107,023 .... F4
Ottawa (cap.), Canada⊙ 304,462 .... J2
Otterville 785 .... D5
Owen Sound⊙ 19,525 .... D3
Paincourt 403 .... B5
Painswick 785 .... E3
Paisley 1,033 .... C3
Pakenham 1,322 .... H2
Palmerston 1,961 .... D4
Paris 6,173 .... D4
Parkhill 1,300 .... C4
Parry Sound⊙ 5,501 .... E2
Pefferlaw 750 .... E3
Pelham 10,071 .... E4
Pembroke⊙ 14,927 .... G2
Penetanguishene 6,221 .... D3
Perkinsfield 342 .... E3
Perth⊙ 5,675 .... H3
Petawawa 5,815 .... G2
Peterborough⊙ 59,683 .... F3
Petrolia 4,393 .... B5
Pickering 27,879 .... K4
Picton⊙ 4,649 .... G3
Plantagenet 919 .... K2
Plattsville 498 .... D
Point Edward 2,524 .... B
Pontypool 497 .... F
Port Burwell 726 .... D
Port Carling 628 .... E
Port Colborne 20,536 .... E
Port Elgin 5,069 C
Port Hope 9,788 .... F
Port Lambton 716 .... B
Portland 282 .... H
Port McNicoll 1,522 .... E
Port Perry 3,917 .... E
Port Rowan 806 .... D
Port Stanley 1,707 C
Pottageville 298 .... J
Powassan 1,238 .... E
Prescott⊙ 4,975 .... J
Princeton 480 .... D
Rainy River 1,092 .... F
Ramore 335 .... K
Rayside-Balfour 16,035 .... K
Red Rock 1,244 .... H
Renfrew 8,617 .... H
Richards Landing 313 .... J
Richmond 2,667 .... J
Richmond Hill 34,716 .... J
Ridgetown 3,100 C
Ripley 577 C
Rockcliffe Park 2,117 .... J
Rockland 3,930 .... J
Rockwood 959 .... D
Rodney 983 C
Rolphton 290 .... G
Rosseau 260 .... E
Rosslyn Village 320 .... G
Russell 857 .... J

LAKE HURON
GEORGIAN BAY
LAKE ERIE
LAKE ONTARIO
North Channel
ALGOMA
MANITOULIN
PARRY SOUND
MUSKOKA
HALIBURTON
ALGONQUIN PROVINCIAL PARK
RENFREW
PETERBOROUGH
VICTORIA
SIMCOE
GREY
BRUCE
DUFFERIN
YORK
DURHAM
PEEL
HALTON
WELLINGTON
HURON
PERTH
WATERLOO
OXFORD
BRANT
MIDDLESEX
LAMBTON
ELGIN
KENT
ESSEX
HALDIMAND-NORFOLK
NIAGARA
NORTHUMBERLAND
HASTINGS
FRONTENAC
LENNOX AND ADDINGTON
PRINCE EDWARD
QUÉBEC
MICHIGAN
NEW YORK
PA.
Sudbury
North Bay
Parry Sound
Owen Sound
Orillia
Barrie
Peterborough
Kingston
Belleville
Oshawa
TORONTO
MISSISSAUGA
Brampton
Hamilton
Kitchener
Guelph
Cambridge
Brantford
Stratford
LONDON
St. Thomas
Sarnia
Port Huron
Chatham
WINDSOR
DETROIT
St. Catharines
Niagara Falls
BUFFALO
Pembroke
Alpena
Oswego
Ontario
Central Part
Kenora
Dryden
Fort Frances
Thunder Bay
KENORA
RAINY RIVER
THUNDER BAY
MINN.
WIS.
LAKE SUPERIOR
© Copyright HAMMOND INCORPORATED, Maplewood, N.J.
Longitude
West of
Greenwich

ıthven 384 .... B6
ıint Catharines⊙ 123,351 E4
ıint Charles 347 .... D1
ıint Clair Beach 1,953 .... B5
ıint Clements 954 .... D4
ıint-Eugène 493 .... K2
ıint George 930 .... D4
ıint Isidore de Prescott 689 K2
ıint Jacobs 852 .... D4
ıint Mary's 4,843 .... C4
ıint Thomas⊙ 27,206 .... C5
ıint Williams 458 .... D5
ılem 743 .... D4
ırnia⊙ 55,576 .... B5
ıuble Beach 769 .... C3
ıult Sainte Marie⊙ 81,048 J5
ıarborough 387,149 .... K4
ıhomberg 782 .... J3
ıhreiber 1,982 .... H5
ıotland 687 .... D4
ıaforth 2,084 .... C4
ıarchmont 390 .... J5
ıbringville 534 .... C4
ıeleys Bay 452 .... H3
ıakespeare 606 .... D4
ıallow Lake 411 .... C3
ıannonville 299 .... G3
ıanty Bay 333 .... E3
ıarbot Lake 296 .... H3
ıedden 346 .... C5
ıelburne 2,928 .... D3
ımcoe⊙ 14,189 .... D5
ıoux Lookout 3,108 .... G4
ımithfield 357 .... G3
ımiths Falls 9,279 .... H3
ımithville 1,737 .... E4
Smooth Rock Falls 2,446 .... J5
Sombra 439 .... B5
Southampton 2,734 .... C3
South River 1,094 .... E2
Spanish 1,082 .... J5
Spencerville 434 .... J3
Springfield 558 .... C5
Springford 279 .... D5
Stayner 2,454 .... E3
Stirling 1,571 .... G3
Stittsville 2,703 .... J2
Stoney Creek 30,294 .... E4
Stoney Point 1,041 .... B5
Straffordville 759 .... D5
Stratford⊙ 25,657 .... C4
Strathroy 7,769 .... C5
Stroud 892 .... E3
Sturgeon Falls 6,400 .... E1
Sudbury⊙ 97,604 .... K5
Sultan 274 .... J5
Sunderland 769 .... E3
Sundridge 692 .... E2
Sutton 3,655 .... E3
Sydenham 528 .... H3
Tamworth 350 .... H3
Tara 717 .... C3
Tavistock 1,783 .... D4
Tecumseh 5,326 .... B5
Teeswater 988 .... C3
Terrace Bay 2,088 .... H5
Thamesford 1,872 .... C4
Thamesville 1,003 .... C5
Thedford 715 .... C4
Thessalon 1,824 .... J5
Thornbury 1,326 .... D3
Thorndale 476 .... C4
Thornton 421 .... E3
Thorold 14,944 .... E4
Thunder Bay⊙ 111,476 .... H5
Tilbury 4,248 .... B5
Tillsonburg 9,404 .... D5
Timagami 518 .... K5
Timmins 44,747 .... J5
Tiverton 825 .... C3
Tobermory 317 .... C2
Toronto (cap.)⊙ 633,318 .... K4
Tottenham 2,747 .... E3
Trenton 15,465 .... G3
Trout Creek 623 .... E2
Turkey Point 369 .... D5
Tweed 1,654 .... G3
Udora 310 .... E3
Union 462 .... C5
Uxbridge 4,354 .... E3
Valley East 19,591 .... J5
Vanier 19,812 .... J2
Vankleek Hill 1,568 .... K2
Vars 564 .... J2
Vaughan 17,782 .... J4
Vermilion Bay 570 .... G4
Verner 1,055 .... D1
Vernon 305 .... J2
Verona 991 .... H3
Victoria Harbour 1,310 .... E3
Vienna 398 .... D5
Virginiatown 1,189 .... K5
Vittoria 425 .... D5
Wabigoon 362 .... G5
Walden 10,453 .... J5
Walkerton⊙ 4,626 .... C3
Wallaceburg 11,132 .... B5
Wallacetown 266 .... C5
Wardsville 448 .... C5
Warkworth 552 .... G3
Warren 612 .... D1
Wasaga Beach 4,985 .... D3
Washago 442 .... E3
Waterdown 2,737 .... D4
Waterloo 46,623 .... D4
Watford 1,365 .... C5
Waubaushene 820 .... E3
Wawa 4,272 .... J5
Webbwood 464 .... C1
Welland 45,047 .... E5
Wellesley 842 .... D4
Wellington 1,057 .... G4
Wendover 362 .... J2
West Lorne 1,171 .... C5
Westmeath 275 .... H2
Westport 644 .... H3
Wheatley 1,637 .... B5
Whitby⊙ 28,173 .... F4
Whitchurch-Stouffville 12,884 J3
White River 754 .... J5
Whitney 767 .... F2
Wiarton 2,144 .... C3
Wikwemikong 941 .... C2
Wilberforce 266 .... F3
Williamsburg 407 .... J3
Williamsford 264 .... D3
Williamstown 336 .... K2
Winchester 1,745 .... J2
Windsor⊙ 196,526 .... B5
Wingham 2,871 .... C4
Wolfe Island 331 .... H3
Woodstock⊙ 26,779 .... D4
Woodville 573 .... F3
Wroxeter 287 .... C4
Wyoming 1,646 .... B5
Yarker 365 .... H3
York 141,367 .... J4
Zurich 753 .... C4

OTHER FEATURES

Abitibi (riv.) J5
Algonquin Prov. Park F2
Amherst (isl.) H3
Balsam (lake) F3
Barrie (isl.) B1
Bays (lake) F2
Big Rideau (lake) H3
Black (riv.) E3
Bruce (pen.) C2
Buckhorn (lake) F3
Cabot (head) C2
Charleston (lake) J3
Christian (isl.) D3
Clear (lake) F3
Cockburn (isl.) A2
Couchiching (lake) E3
Croker (cape) D3
Don (riv.) J4
Doré (lake) G2
Douglas (pt.) C3
Erie (lake) E5
Flowerpot (isl.) C2
French (riv.) D1
Georgian (bay) D2
Georgina (isl.) E3
Grand (riv.) D4
Humber (riv.) J3
Hurd (cape) C2
Huron (lake) B3
Ipperwash Prov. Park C4
Joseph (lake) E2
Killarney Prov. Park C1
Killbear Point Prov. Park D2
Lake of the Woods (lake) F5
Lake Superior Prov. Park J5
Lonely (isl.) C2
Long (pt.) D5
Long Point (bay) D5
Madawaska (riv.) G2
Magnetawan (riv.) D2
Main (chan.) C2
Manitou (lake) C2
Manitoulin (isl.) B2
Mattagami (riv.) J5
Michipicoten (isl.) H5
Missinaibi (riv.) J5
Mississagi (riv.) A1
Mississippi (lake) H2
Muskoka (lake) E2
Niagara (riv.) E4
Nipigon (lake) H5
Nipissing (lake) E1
North (chan.) A1
Nottawasaga (bay) D3
Ogidaki (mt.) J5
Ontario (lake) G4
Opeongo (lake) F2
Ottawa (riv.) H2
Owen (sound) D3
Panache (lake) C1
Parry (isl.) D2
Parry (sound) D2
Pelee (pt.) B6
Petre (pt.) G4
Point Pelee Nat'l Park B5
Presqu'Ile Prov. Park G4
Pukaskwa Prov. Park H5
Quetico Prov. Park G5
Rainy (lake) G5
Rice (lake) F3
Rideau (lake) H3
Rondeau Prov. Park C5
Rosseau (lake) E2
Saint Clair (lake) B5
Saint Clair (riv.) B5
Saint Lawrence (lake) K3
Saint Lawrence (riv.) J3
Saint Lawrence Is. Nat'l Park J3
Saugeen (riv.) C3
Scugog (lake) F3
Seul (lake) G4
Severn (riv.) E3
Sibley Prov. Park H5
Simcoe (lake) E3
South (bay) C2
Spanish (riv.) C1
Stony (lake) G3
Superior (lake) H5
Sydenham (riv.) B5
Thames (riv.) B5
Theano (pt.) J5
Thousand (isls.) H3
Timagami (lake) K5
Trout (lake) E1
Vernon (lake) E2
Walpole (isl.) B5
Welland (canal) E5
Woods (lake) F5

⊙County seat.

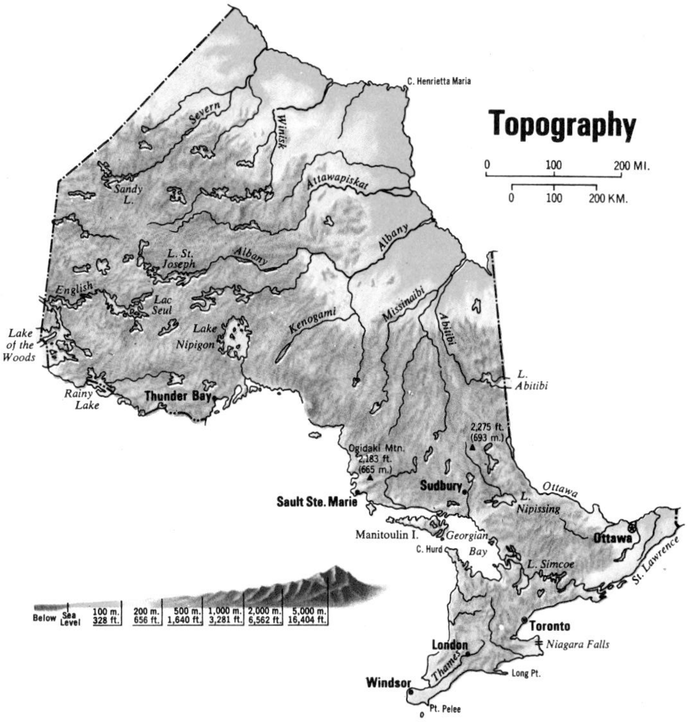

Agriculture, Industry and Resources

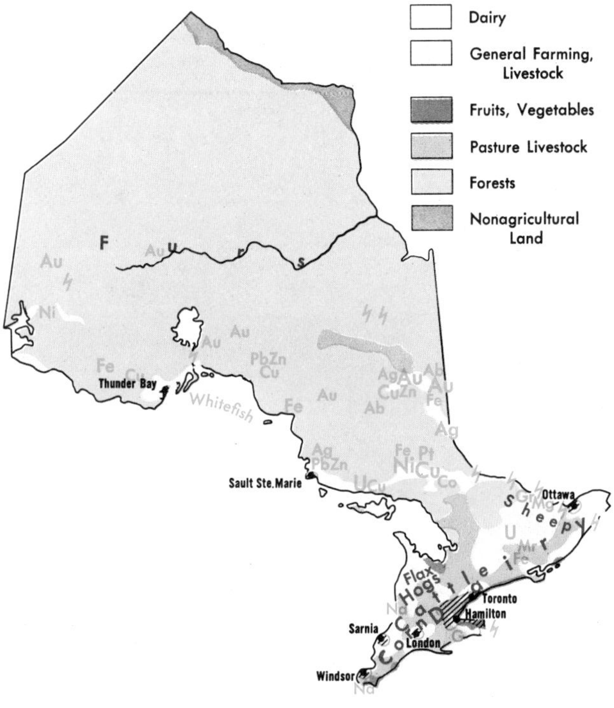

DOMINANT LAND USE

- Cereals, Cash Crops, Livestock
- Dairy
- General Farming, Livestock
- Fruits, Vegetables
- Pasture Livestock
- Forests
- Nonagricultural Land

MAJOR MINERAL OCCURRENCES

Ab	Asbestos	Mg	Magnesium
Ag	Silver	Mr	Marble
Au	Gold	Na	Salt
Co	Cobalt	Ni	Nickel
Cu	Copper	Pb	Lead
Fe	Iron Ore	Pt	Platinum
G	Natural Gas	U	Uranium
Gr	Graphite	Zn	Zinc

- Water Power
- Major Industrial Areas

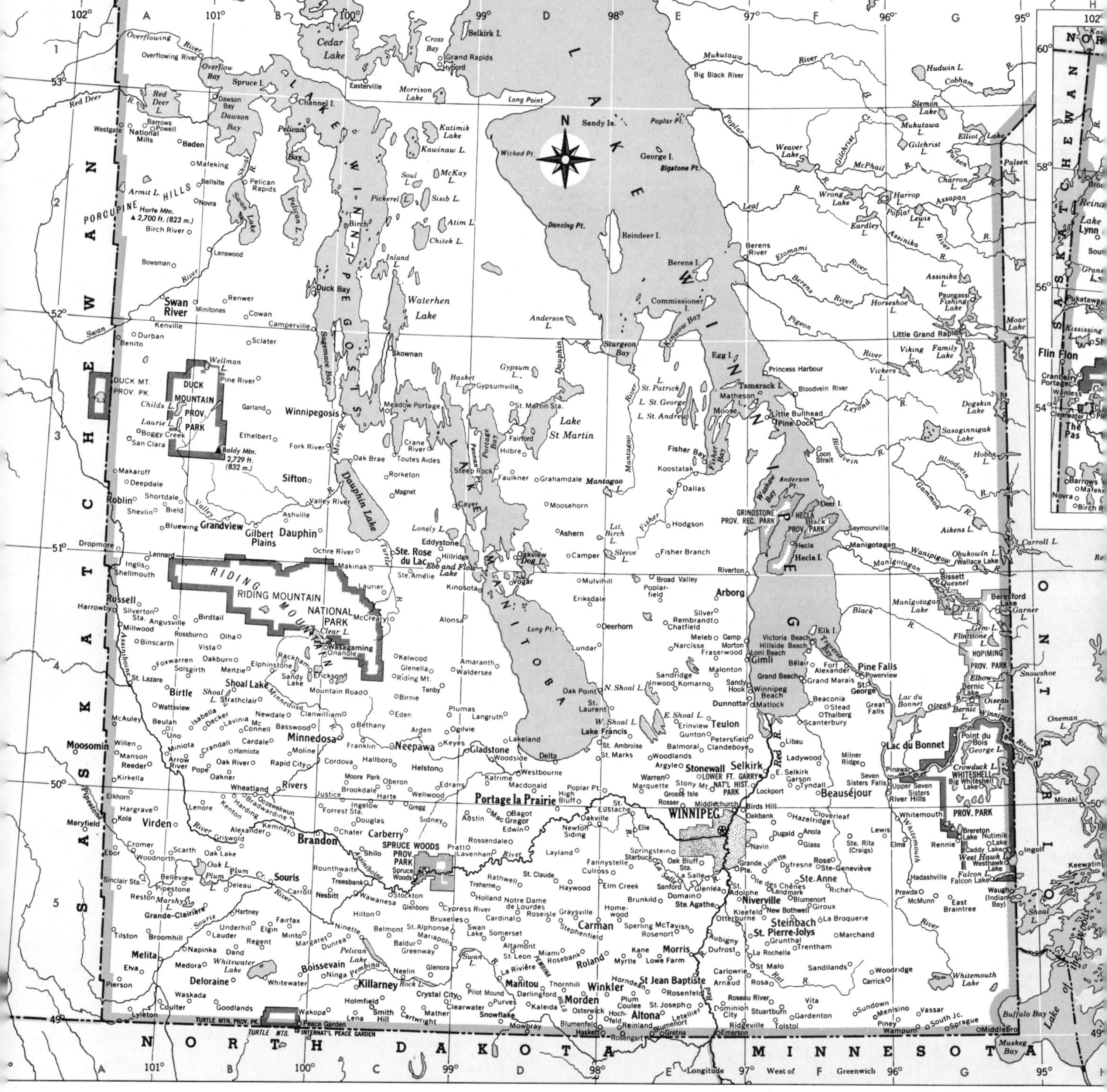

LAKE WINNIPEG
LAKE WINNIPEGOSIS
LAKE MANITOBA
Cedar Lake
Lake St. Martin
Dauphin Lake
Waterhen Lake
WINNIPEG
Brandon
Portage la Prairie
Selkirk
RIDING MOUNTAIN NATIONAL PARK
DUCK MOUNTAIN PROV. PARK
SPRUCE WOODS PROV. PARK
PORCUPINE HILLS
SASKATCHEWAN
NORTH DAKOTA
MINNESOTA
ONTARIO
Longitude West of Greenwich

CITIES and TOWNS

Alexander 280 .... B5
Altona 2,480 .... E5
Amaranth 248 .... D4
Arborg 861 .... E4
Arden 160 .... C4
Ashern 642 .... D3
Austin 421 .... D5
Baldur 378 .... C5
Barrows 219 .... A2
Beauséjour 2,422 .... F4
Belmont 317 .... C5
Benito 507 .... A3
Berens River 899 .... F2
Binscarth 430 .... A4
Birch River 617 .... A2
Birds Hill 631 .... F4
Birtle 821 .... B4
Bloodvein River 416 .... F3
Blumenort 379 .... F5
Boissevain 1,584 .... C5
Bowsman 483 .... A2
Brandon 34,901 .... C5
Camperville 530 .... B2
Carberry 1,423 .... C5
Carman 2,272 .... D5
Cartwright 361 .... C5
Churchill 1,699 .... K2
Cormorant 378 .... H3
Cranberry Portage 861 .... H3
Crane River 252 .... C3
Crystal City 513 .... C5
Cypress River 255 .... D5
Darlingford 158 .... D5
Dauphin 9,109 .... B3
Deloraine 1,019 .... B5
Dominion City 385 .... E5
Douglas 164 .... C5
Duck Bay 535 .... B2
Dugald 328 .... F5
Dunnottar 219 .... E4
Easterville 565 .... C1
East Selkirk 901 .... F4
Elgin 163 .... B5
Elie 372 .... E5
Elkhorn 527 .... A5
Elm Creek 296 .... E5
Elphinstone 237 .... B4
Emerson 756 .... E5
Erickson 558 .... C4
Eriksdale 303 .... D4
Ethelbert 493 .... B3
Fairford 616 .... D3
Fisher Branch 529 .... E3
Flin Flon 8,152 .... H3
Fort Alexander 1,492 .... F4
Fort Churchill 201 .... K2
Foxwarren 178 .... A4
Garson 290 .... F4
Gilbert Plains 847 .... B3
Gillam 2,365 .... K2
Gimli 1,659 .... F4
Gladstone 976 .... D4
Glenboro 720 .... C5
Glenella 164 .... C4
Gods River 198 .... K3
Grand Marais 220 .... F4
Grand Rapids 503 .... C1
Grandview 1,013 .... B3
Great Falls 267 .... F4
Gretna 510 .... E5
Grunthal 537 .... F5
Hamiota 765 .... B4
Hartney 484 .... B5
Hillridge 251 .... C3
Hochfeld 197 .... E5
Holland 405 .... D5
Île des Chênes 689 .... F5
Ilford 199 .... J2
Inglis 255 .... A4
Inwood 171 .... E4
Island Lake 2,929 .... J3
Jenpeg 336 .... J2
Kelwood 249 .... C4
Kenton 176 .... B5
Killarney 2,348 .... C5
Kleefeld 173 .... F5
La Broquerie 565 .... F5
Lac du Bonnet 971 .... G4
Landmark 465 .... F5
La Rivière 218 .... D5
La Salle 190 .... E5
Laurier 229 .... C4
Letellier 181 .... E5
Little Grand Rapids 510 .... G2
Lockport 275 .... F4
Long Spruce 376 .... K2
Lorette 755 .... F5
Lowe Farm 286 .... E5
Lundar 688 .... D4
Lynn Lake 2,568 .... H2
MacGregor 789 .... D5
Mafeking 276 .... B2
Manibridge 232 .... J2
Manigotagan 172 .... F3
Manitou 883 .... D5
Mariapolis 177 .... C5
McCreary 614 .... C4
Melita 1,169 .... A5
Miami 375 .... D5
Middlechurch 348 .... E4
Miniota 206 .... B4
Minitonas 605 .... B2
Minnedosa 2,718 .... B4
Moosehorn 183 .... D3
Moose Lake 514 .... H3
Morden 3,886 .... D5
Morris 1,572 .... E5
Neepawa 3,508 .... C4
New Bothwell 207 .... F5
Newdale 217 .... B4
Ninette 307 .... C5
Niverville 1,251 .... F5
Norway House 676 .... J3
Notre Dame de Lourdes 651 D5
Oakbank 221 .... F5
Oakburn 290 .... B4
Oak Lake 367 .... B5
Oak Point 201 .... B5
Oak River 221 .... D4
Oakville 398 .... D5
Ochre River 298 .... C3
Onanole 334 .... C4
Oozewekwun 887 .... B5
Otterburne 161 .... E5
Oxford House J3
Paungassi 222 .... G2
Pelican Rapids 226 .... B2
Petersfield 181 .... E4
Pierson 221 .... A5
Pikwitonei 202 .... J3
Pilot Mound 730 .... D5
Pinawa 2,080 .... G4
Pine Falls 945 .... F4
Pine River 398 .... B3
Plumas 289 .... D4
Plum Coulee 477 .... E5
Point du Bois 164 .... G4
Poplar Point 250 .... D4
Portage la Prairie 12,555 .... D4
Powerview 668 .... F4
Rapid City 412 .... B4
Red Sucker Lake 345 .... K3
Reston 539 .... A5
Richer 307 .... F5
Riding Mountain 193 .... C4
Rivers 1,185 .... B4
Riverton 685 .... E3
Roblin 1,971 .... A3
Roland 302 .... D5
Rorketon 248 .... C3
Rosenfeld 270 .... E5
Rossburn 652 .... B4
Russell 1,524 .... A4
Saint Adolphe 617 .... E5
Saint Ambroise 314 .... E4
Saint Claude 612 .... D5
Sainte Agathe 317 .... E5
Sainte Anne 1,174 .... F5
Sainte Rose du Lac 1,038 .... C3
Saint Eustache 344 .... E5
Saint George 540 .... F4
Saint Jean Baptiste 562 .... E5
Saint Lazare 476 .... A4
Saint Malo 731 .... F5
Saint Pierre-Jolys 906 .... F5
Sandy Lake 351 .... B4
Sanford 347 .... E5
Selkirk 9,862 .... F4
Sherridon 187 .... H3
Shoal Lake 865 .... B4
Sifton 207 .... B3
Snow Lake 1,585 .... H3
Somerset 625 .... D5
Souris 1,712 .... B5
South Indian Lake 668 .... H2
Split Lake 869 .... J2
Starbuck 235 .... E5
Steinbach 5,979 .... F5
Stonewall 1,826 .... E4
Stony Mountain 1,334 .... E4
Strathclair 396 .... B4

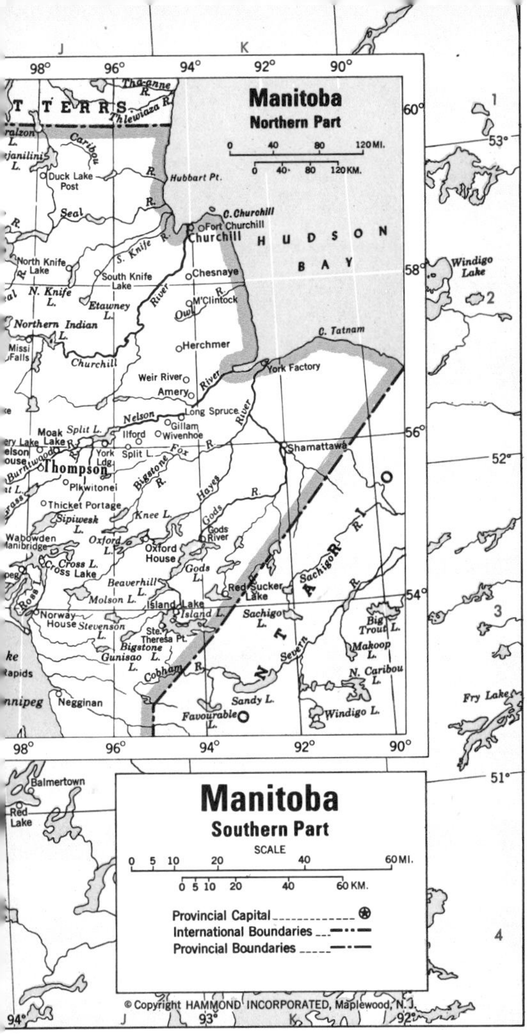
Manitoba
Northern Part
HUDSON BAY
Churchill
York Factory
Thompson
C. Churchill
C. Tatnam
Manitoba
Southern Part
SCALE
0 5 10 20 40 60 MI.
0 5 10 20 40 60 KM.
Provincial Capital
International Boundaries
Provincial Boundaries
© Copyright HAMMOND INCORPORATED, Maplewood, N.J.

AREA 250,999 sq. mi. (650,087 sq. km.)
POPULATION 1,017,323
CAPITAL Winnipeg
LARGEST CITY Winnipeg
HIGHEST POINT Baldy Mtn. 2,729 ft. (832 m.)
SETTLED IN 1812
ADMITTED TO CONFEDERATION 1870
PROVINCIAL FLOWER Prairie Crocus

Swan Lake 338 ....D5
Swan River 3,443 ....A2
Teulon 873......................E4
The Pas 6,602 ....H3
Thicket Portage 255 ....J3
Thompson 17,291 ....J2
Treherne 706 ....D5
Tyndall 411 ....F4
Virden 2,936 ....A5
Vita 213 ....F5
Wabowden 847.................J3
Wanless 252 ....H3
Warren 302 ....E4
Waskada 257....................B5
Wawanesa 487 ....C5
Whitemouth 314 ....G5
Whitewater 885 ....B5
Winkler 3,749 ....E5
Winnipeg (cap.) 560,874 .....E5
Winnipeg Beach 582...........F4
Winnipegosis 893..............B3
Woodridge 175 ....G5
York Landing 198..............J2

OTHER FEATURES

Aikens (lake) G3
Anderson (lake)...............D2
Anderson, (pt.)..................F3
Armit (lake)......................A2
Assapan (riv.)...................G2
Assiniboine (riv.) C5
Assinika (lake) G2
Assinika (riv.) G2
Atim (lake).......................C2
Baldy (mt.) B3
Baralzon (lake)..................J1
Basket (lake)....................C3
Beaverhill (lake) J3
Berens (isl.) E2
Berens (riv.) F2
Bernic (lake).....................G4
Big Sand (lake) H2
Bigstone (lake) J3
Bigstone (pt.)....................E2
Bigstone (riv.) J3
Birch (isl.) C2
Black (isl.) F3
Black (riv.) F4
Bloodvein (riv.)..................F3
Bonnet (lake)....................G4
Buffalo (bay) G5
Burntwood (riv.) J2
Caribou (riv.) J1
Carroll (lake) G3
Cedar (lake)......................B1
Channel (isl.)....................B2
Charron (lake)...................G2
Childs (lake) A3
Chitek (lake) C2
Churchill (cape) K2
Churchill (riv.)...................J2
Clear (lake) C4
Clearwater Lake Prov. Park H3
Cobham (riv.)....................G1
Cochrane (riv.)..................H2
Commissioner (isl.) E2
Cormorant (lake)...............H3
Cross (bay) C1
Cross (lake)......................J3
Crowduck (lake) G4
Dancing (pt.)....................D2
Dauphin (lake)..................C3
Dauphin (riv.) D3
Dawson (bay) B2
Dog (lake) D3
Dogskin (lake)..................G3
Duck Mountain Prov. Park ...B3
Eardley (lake) F2
East Shoal (lake) E4
Ebb and Flow (lake) C3
Egg (isl.) E3
Elbow (lake) G4
Elk (isl.) F4
Elliot (lake) G2
Etawney (lake) J2
Etomami (riv.) F2
Falcon (lake).....................G5
Family (lake).....................G3
Fisher (bay) E3
Fisher (riv.) E3
Fishing (lake)....................G2
Flintstone (lake)................G4
Fox (riv.)..........................K2
Gammon (riv.) G3
Garner (lake) G4
Gem (lake).......................G4
George (isl.) E2
George (lake)....................G4
Gilchrist (creek) F2
Gilchrist (lake) G2
Gods (lake) K3
Gods (riv.)........................K3
Granville (lake).................H2
Grass (riv.).......................J3
Grass River Prov. Park H3
Grindstone Prov. Rec. Park F3
Gunisao (lake) J3
Gypsum (lake) D3
Harrop (lake) G2
Harte (mt.).......................A2
Hayes (riv.) K3
Hecla (isl.) F3
Hecla Prov. Park F3
Hobbs (lake).....................G3
Horseshoe (lake)...............G2
Hubbart (pt.) K2
Hudson (bay)....................K2
Hudwin (lake) G1
Inland (lake) C2
International Peace Garden...B5
Island (lake) K3
Katimik (lake)...................C2
Kawinaw (lake) C2
Kinwow (bay)...................E2
Kississing (lake) H2
Knee, (lake) J3
Lake of the Woods (lake) ...H5
La Salle (riv.)....................E5
Laurie (lake) A3
Leaf (riv.) F2
Lewis (lake) G2
Leyond (riv.).....................F3
Little Birch (lake)...............E3
Lonely (lake).....................C3
Long (lake) G4
Long (pt.) D1
Long (pt.).........................D4
Manigotagan (lake) G4
Manigotagan (riv.).............G3
Manitoba (lake) D4
Mantagao (lake) E3
Mantagao (riv.).................E3
Marshy (lake)....................B5
McKay (lake) C2
McPhail (riv.) F2
Minnedosa (riv.) B4
Moar (lake) G2
Molson (lake)....................J3
Moose (isl.) B3
Morrison (lake)..................C1
Mossy (riv.) C3
Mukutawa (riv.) E1
Muskeg (bay) G6
Nejanilini (lake).................J1
Nelson (riv.) J2
Nopiming Prov. Park..........G4
Northern Indian (lake) J2
North Knife (lake) J2
North Seal (riv.) H2
North Shoal (lake) E4
Nueltin (lake)....................H1
Oak (lake).........................B5
Obukowin (lake) G3
Oiseau (lake) G4
Oiseau (riv.).....................G4
Overflow (bay) A1
Overflowing (riv.) A1
Owl (riv.).........................K2
Oxford (lake).....................J3
Paint (lake).......................J2
Palsen (riv.) G2
Pelican (bay) B2
Pelican (lake) B2
Pelican (lake) C5
Pembina (hills)..................D5
Pembina (riv.)...................C5
Peonan (pt.).....................D3
Pickerel (lake) C2
Pigeon (riv.) F2
Pipestone (creek) A5
Plum (creek).....................B5
Plum (lake) B5
Poplar (pt.) E2
Poplar (riv.).....................E2
Porcupine (hills) A2
Portage (bay)...................D3
Punk (isl.)........................F3
Quesnel (lake)..................G4
Rat (riv.) F5
Red (riv.).........................F4
Red Deer (lake) A2
Red Deer (riv.).................A2
Reindeer (isl.) E2
Reindeer (lake).................H2
Riding (mt.) B4
Riding Mountain Nat'l Park B4
Rock (lake) C5
Ross (isl.).........................J3
Sagemace (bay)................B3
Saint Andrew (lake)...........E3
Saint George (lake) E3
Saint Martin (lake)............D3
Saint Patrick (lake) E3
Sale (riv.) E5
Sandy (isls.).....................D2
Sasaginnigak (lake)...........G3
Seal (riv.) J2
Selkirk (isl.) C1
Setting (lake)....................H3
Shoal (lake)......................B4
Shoal (lake)......................G5
Shoal (riv.) B2
Sipiwesk (lake) J3
Sisib (lake).......................C2
Sleeve (lake)....................E3
Slemon (lake) G1
Snowshoe (lake)...............G4
Soul (lake) C2
Souris (riv.) B5
Southern Indian (lake) H2
South Knife (riv.) J2
South Seal (riv.) J2
Split (lake) J2
Spruce (isl.) B1
Spruce Woods Prov. Park....C5
Stevenson (lake) J3
Sturgeon (bay) E3
Swan (lake)......................B2
Swan (lake)......................D5
Swan (riv.).......................A3
Tadoule (lake) J2
Tamarack (isl.) F3
Tatnam (cape)..................K2
Traverse (bay) F4
Turtle (mts.).....................B5
Turtle (riv.) C3
Turtle Mountain Prov. Park B5
Valley (riv.) B3
Vickers (lake) F3
Viking (lake).....................G3
Wanipigow (riv.)...............G3
Washow (bay) F3
Waterhen (lake) C2
Weaver (lake)...................F2
Wellman (lake) B3
West Hawk (lake)..............G5
West Shoal (lake).............E4
Whitemouth (lake).............G5
Whitemouth (riv.) G5
Whiteshell Prov. Park.........G4
Whitewater (lake) B5
Wicked (pt.).....................D2
Winnipeg (lake) E2
Winnipeg (riv.).................G4
Winnipegosis (lake) C2
Woods (lake)....................H5
Wrong (lake).....................F2

Topography

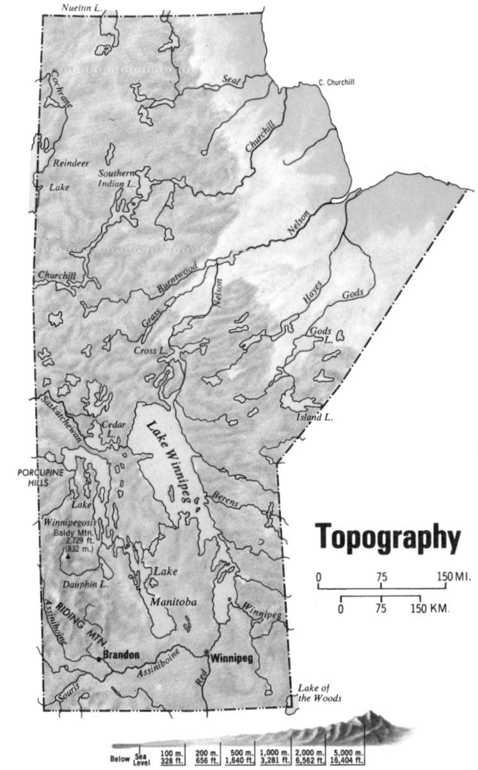
Lake Winnipeg
Lake Manitoba
Winnipeg
Brandon
RIDING MTN.
PORCUPINE HILLS
Baldy Mtn. 2,729 ft. (832 m.)
0 75 150 MI.
0 75 150 KM.
Below Sea Level
100 m. 328 ft.
200 m. 656 ft.
500 m. 1,640 ft.
1,000 m. 3,281 ft.
2,000 m. 6,562 ft.
5,000 m. 16,404 ft.

Agriculture, Industry and Resources

DOMINANT LAND USE

- Cereals (chiefly barley, oats)
- Cereals, Livestock
- Dairy
- Livestock
- Forests
- Nonagricultural Land

MAJOR MINERAL OCCURRENCES

Au	Gold	Ni	Nickel
Co	Cobalt	O	Petroleum
Cu	Copper	Pb	Lead
Na	Salt	Pt	Platinum
		Zn	Zinc

Water Power
Major Industrial Areas

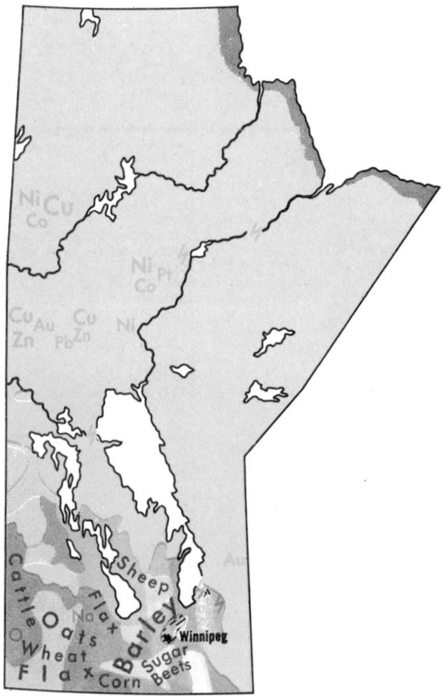
Winnipeg
Sheep
Flax
Barley
Cattle
Oats
Wheat
Flax
Corn
Sugar Beets

Topography

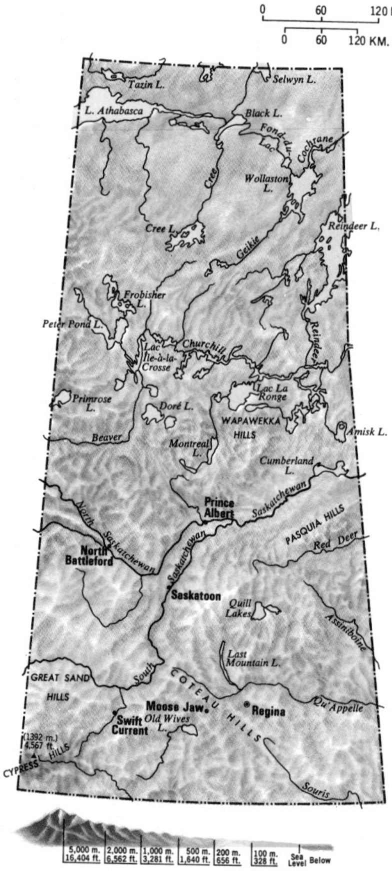
0 60 120 MI.
0 60 120 KM.
Tazin L.
Selwyn L.
L. Athabasca
Black L.
Fond du Lac
Cochrane
Wollaston L.
Cree
Cree L.
Reindeer L.
Geikie
Frobisher L.
Peter Pond L.
Churchill
Lac Île-à-la-Crosse
Reindeer
Primrose L.
Doré L.
Lac La Ronge
WAPAWEKKA HILLS
Beaver
Montreal L.
Amisk L.
Cumberland L.
Prince Albert
Saskatchewan
North Saskatchewan
PASQUIA HILLS
Red Deer
North Battleford
Saskatoon
Quill Lakes
Assiniboine
South Saskatchewan
Last Mountain L.
GREAT SAND HILLS
COTEAU HILLS
Moose Jaw
Regina
Qu'Appelle
Swift Current
Old Wives L.
(1392 m.) 4,567 ft.
CYPRESS HILLS
Souris
5,000 m. 16,404 ft.
2,000 m. 6,562 ft.
1,000 m. 3,281 ft.
500 m. 1,640 ft.
200 m. 656 ft.
100 m. 328 ft.
Sea Level
Below

CITIES and TOWNS

Abbey 259 ... C5
Aberdeen 373 ... E3
Abernethy 299 ... H5
Air Ronge 348 ... M3
Alameda 319 ... J6
Alida 163 ... K6
Allan 720 ... E4
Alsask 734 ... B4
Aneroid 153 ... D6
Annaheim 187 ... G3
Antelope 150 ... C5
Arborfield 400 ... H2
Archerwill 272 ... H3
Arcola 547 ... J6
Asquith 416 ... D3
Assiniboia 2,738 ... E6
Avonlea 415 ... G5
Aylsham 153 ... H2
Balcarres 729 ... H5
Balgonie 715 ... G5
Batoche ... E3
Battleford 2,569 ... C3
Beauval 518 ... L3
Beechy 344 ... D5
Bellevue 145 ... F3
Bengough 603 ... F6
Bethune 317 ... F5
Bienfait 807 ... J6
Biggar 2,491 ... C3
Big River 827 ... D2
Birch Hills 752 ... F3
Bjorkdale 248 ... H3
Blaine Lake 631 ... D3
Borden 195 ... D3
Bredenbury 441 ... K5
Broadview 861 ... J5
Brock 183 ... C4
Broderick 135 ... E4
Bruno 762 ... F3
Buchanan 434 ... J4
Buffalo Narrows 837 ... L3
Burstall 548 ... B5
Cabri 631 ... C5
Cadillac 203 ... D6
Calder 158 ... K4
Cando 144 ... C3
Canoe Lake 155 ... L3
Canora 2,689 ... J4
Carievale 245 ... K6
Carlyle 1,057 ... J6
Carnduff 1,071 ... K6
Carrot River 1,020 ... H2
Central Butte 518 ... E5
Ceylon 259 ... G6
Chaplin 382 ... E5
Chitek Lake 172 ... D2
Choiceland 535 ... G2
Christopher Lake 193 ... F2
Churchbridge 928 ... J5
Climax 277 ... C6
Cochin 221 ... C2
Codette 214 ... H2
Coleville 398 ... B4
Colonsay 542 ... F4
Connaught Heights 162 ... G3
Conquest 265 ... D4
Consul 160 ... B6
Coronach 386 ... F6
Craik 543 ... F4
Craven 185 ... G5
Creelman 178 ... H6
Creighton 1,746 ... N4
Crooked River 155 ... H3
Cudworth 907 ... F3
Cumberland House 796 ... J2
Cupar 611 ... G5
Cut Knife 530 ... B3
Dalmeny 602 ... E3
Davidson 1,092 ... E4
Debden 381 ... E2
Delisle 783 ... D4
Delmas 153 ... C3
Denare Beach 308 ... M4
Denzil 230 ... B3
Deschambault Lake 372 ... M3
Dinsmore 398 ... D4
Dodsland 312 ... C4
Domremy 188 ... F3
Dorintosh 159 ... L4
Drake 251 ... G4
Dubuc 142 ... J5
Duck Lake 683 ... E3
Dundurn 409 ... E4
Dysart 236 ... H5
Earl Grey 242 ... G5
Eastend 771 ... C6
Eatonia 553 ... B4
Ebenezer 155 ... J4
Edam 348 ... C2
Edenwold 134 ... G5
Elbow 286 ... E4
Elfros 213 ... H4
Elrose 614 ... D4
Elstow 146 ... E4
Endeavour 220 ... J3
Englefeld 258 ... G3
Esterhazy 2,894 ... K5
Estevan 8,847 ... J6
Eston 1,354 ... C4
Eyebrow 198 ... E5
Fillmore 350 ... H6
Fleming 164 ... K5
Flin Flon 408 ... N4
Foam Lake 1,387 ... H4
Fond du Lac 449 ... L2
Fort Qu'Appelle 1,764 ... H5
Fox Valley 429 ... B5
Francis 150 ... H5
Frobisher 187 ... J6
Frontier 385 ... C6
Gainsborough 311 ... K6
Gerald 139 ... K5
Glaslyn 383 ... C2
Glenavon 295 ... J5
Glen Ewen 143 ... K6
Goodeve 134 ... H4
Goodsoil 217 ... L4
Govan 323 ... G4
Gravelbourg 1,326 ... E6
Grayson 260 ... J5
Green Acres 165 ... F2
Green Lake 616 ... L4
Grenfell 1,363 ... J5
Guernsey 222 ... F4
Gull Lake 1,053 ... C5
Hafford 515 ... D3
Hague 530 ... E3
Hanley 446 ... E4
Harris 233 ... D4
Hawarden 133 ... E4
Hepburn 352 ... E3
Herbert 986 ... D5
Hodgeville 332 ... E5
Holdfast 312 ... F5
Hudson Bay 2,280 ... J3
Humboldt 4,265 ... F3
Hyas 190 ... J4
Île-à-la-Crosse 821 ... L3
Imperial 456 ... F4
Indian Head 1,720 ... H5
Invermay 397 ... J4
Ituna 910 ... H4
Jansen 209 ... G4
Kamsack 2,726 ... K4
Kelliher 411 ... H4
Kelvington 1,053 ... H3
Kenaston 352 ... E4
Kennedy 241 ... J5
Kenosee Park 135 ... J6
Kerrobert 1,100 ... C4
Killaly 137 ... J5
Kincaid 245 ... D6
Kindersley 3,523 ... B4
Kinistino 763 ... F3
Kipling 949 ... J5
Kisbey 252 ... J6
Kuroki 145 ... H4
Kyle 499 ... C5
Lafleche 639 ... E6
Laird 201 ... E3
Lake Lenore 385 ... G3
La Loche 1,651 ... L3
Lampman 720 ... J6
Lancer 171 ... C5
Landis 285 ... C3
Lang 189 ... G6
Langenburg 1,197 ... K5
Langham 729 ... E3
Lanigan 1,646 ... F4
La Ronge 1,714 ... L3
Lashburn 517 ... B2
Leader 1,160 ... B5
Leask 446 ... E2
Lebret 268 ... H5
Lemberg 417 ... H5
Leoville 404 ... D2
Leroy 436 ... G4
Lestock 414 ... G4
Limerick 166 ... E6
Lintlaw 225 ... H3
Lipton 353 ... H5
Lloydminster 4,493 ... A2
Loon Lake 365 ... B1
Loreburn 224 ... E4
Lucky Lake 340 ... D5
Lumsden 1,116 ... G5
Luseland 682 ... B3
Macdowall 146 ... E2
Macklin 873 ... A3
MacNutt 141 ... K4
Macoun 163 ... H6
Maidstone 747 ... B2
Major 150 ... B4
Manitou Beach 136 ... F4
Mankota 406 ... D6
Manor 348 ... K6
Maple Creek 2,330 ... B6
Marcelin 273 ... E3
Margo 178 ... H4
Marsden 211 ... B3
Marshall 326 ... B2
Martensville 960 ... E3
Maryfield 408 ... K6
Maymont 172 ... D3
McLean 184 ... G5
Meacham 184 ... F3
Meadow Lake 3,662 ... C1
Meath Park 298 ... F2
Medstead 197 ... C2
Melfort 5,141 ... G3
Melville 5,149 ... J5
Meota 248 ... C2
Mervin 174 ... C2
Midale 572 ... H6
Middle Lake 270 ... F3
Milden 234 ... D4
Milestone 511 ... G5
Minton 159 ... G6
Mistatim 139 ... H3
Molanosa 248 ... M4
Montmartre 534 ... H5
Montreal Lake 306 ... F1
Moose Jaw 32,581 ... F5
Moosomin 2,449 ... K5
Morse 435 ... D5
Mortlach 278 ... E5
Mossbank 444 ... E6
Muenster 333 ... F3
Naicam 739 ... G3
Neilburg 369 ... B3
Neudorf 394 ... J5
Neuhorst 146 ... E3
Nipawin 4,317 ... H2
Nokomis 535 ... F4
Norquay 520 ... J4
North Battleford 13,158 ... C3
North Portal 157 ... J6
Odessa 203 ... H5
Ogema 432 ... G6
Ormiston 144 ... F6
Osler 225 ... E3
Outlook 1,687 ... E4
Oxbow 1,221 ... J6
Paddockwood 179 ... F2
Pangman 208 ... G6
Paradise Hill 395 ... B2
Patuanak 136 ... L3
Paynton 186 ... B2
Pelican Narrows 212 ... N3
Pelly 354 ... K4
Pennant 216 ... C5
Pense 356 ... G5
Perdue 393 ... D3
Pierceland 358 ... K4
Pilot Butte 585 ... G5
Pine House 528 ... M3
Plenty 193 ... C4
Plunkett 139 ... F4
Ponteix 760 ... D6
Porcupine Plain 935 ... H3
Preeceville 1,170 ... J4
Prelate 337 ... B5
Prince Albert 28,631 ... F2
Prud'homme 239 ... F3
Punnichy 400 ... G4
Qu'Appelle 551 ... H5
Quill Lake 534 ... G3
Quinton 189 ... G4
Rabbit Lake 166 ... D2
Radisson 432 ... D3
Radville 1,008 ... G6
Rama 163 ... H4
Raymore 562 ... G4
Redvers 843 ... K6
Regina (cap.) 149,593 ... G5
Regina Beach 488 ... F5
Reserve 187 ... J3
Rhein 284 ... J4
Richmound 174 ... B5
Ridgedale 147 ... H2
Riverhurst 182 ... E5
Rocanville 872 ... K5
Rockglen 508 ... F6
Rosetown 2,551 ... D4
Rose Valley 534 ... H3
Rosthern 1,604 ... E3
Rouleau 380 ... G5
Saint Benedict 164 ... F3
Saint Brieux 362 ... G3
Saint Gregor 144 ... G3
Saint Louis 394 ... F3
Saint Philips 636 ... K4
Saint Walburg 718 ... B2
Saltcoats 488 ... J4
Sandy Bay 555 ... N3
Saskatoon 133,750 ... E3
Sceptre 204 ... B5
Scott 209 ... C3
Sedley 289 ... H5
Semans 343 ... G4
Shaunavon 2,183 ... C6
Sheho 311 ... H4
Shellbrook 1,098 ... E2
Shell Lake 217 ... D2
Simmie 174 ... C6
Simpson 223 ... F4
Sintaluta 213 ... H5
Smeaton 275 ... G2
Southey 604 ... G5
Spalding 375 ... G3
Speers 135 ... D3
Spiritwood 841 ... D2
Springside 474 ... J4
Spy Hill 351 ... K5
Squaw Rapids 1,024 ... H2
Star City 539 ... G3
Stenen 182 ... J4
Stockholm 329 ... J5
Stony Rapids 526 ... M2
Storthoaks 152 ... K6
Stoughton 705 ... J6
Strasbourg 812 ... G4
Sturgis 705 ... J4
Swift Current 14,264 ... D5
Tantallon 186 ... K5
Theodore 463 ... J4
Tisdale 3,026 ... H3
Togo 197 ... K4
Tompkins 274 ... C5
Torquay 344 ... H6
Tramping Lake 200 ... B3
Tugaske 179 ... E5
Turnor Lake 190 ... L3
Turtleford 442 ... B2
Unity 2,244 ... B3
Uranium City 1,765 ... L2
Val Marie 253 ... D6
Vanguard 286 ... D6
Vanscoy 276 ... D4
Veregin 140 ... K4
Vibank 305 ... H5
Viscount 424 ... F4
Vonda 311 ... F3
Wadena 1,377 ... H4
Wakaw 1,031 ... F3
Waldeck 196 ... D5
Waldheim 647 ... E3
Wapella 453 ... K5
Warman 1,117 ... E3
Waskesiu Lake 176 ... E2
Watrous 1,520 ... F4
Watson 940 ... G3
Wawota 619 ... J6
Weekes 166 ... J3
Weirdale 160 ... F2
Weldon 272 ... F2
Welwyn 180 ... K5
Weyburn 8,892 ... H6
White City 340 ... G5
White Fox 380 ... H2
Whitewood 1,072 ... J5
Wilcox 175 ... G5
Wilkie 1,604 ... C3
Willow Bunch 417 ... F6
Windthorst 215 ... J5
Wiseton 201 ... D4
Wishart 238 ... H4
Wollaston Lake 263 ... N2
Wolseley 883 ... H5
Wymark 148 ... D5
Wynyard 2,045 ... G4
Yarbo 139 ...
Yellow Creek 166 ...
Yellow Grass 461 ...
Yorkton 14,119 ...
Young 495 ...
Zealandia 150 ...
Zenon Park 313 ...

OTHER FEATURES

Allan (hills) ...
Amisk (lake) ...
Antelope (lake) ...
Antler (riv.) ...
Arm (riv.) ...
Assiniboine (riv.) ...
Athabasca (lake) ...
Bad (lake) ...
Bad (hills) ...
Basin (lake) ...
Batoche Nat'l Hist. Site ...
Battle (creek) ...
Battle (riv.) ...
Bear (hills) ...
Beaver (hills) ...
Beaver (riv.) ...
Beaverlodge (lake) ...
Big Muddy (lake) ...
Bigstick (lake) ...
Birch (lake) ...
Bitter (lake) ...
Black (lake) ...

Lloydminster
Kindersley
Maple Creek
Leader
Kerrobert
Wilkie
Meadow Lake
Ministikwan L.
Frog L.
Manito L.
Bigstick L.
Cypress L.
Crane L.
GREAT SAND HILLS
CYPRESS HILLS PROV. PARK
FT. WALSH NATIONAL HIST. PARK
STELLE NARROWS HIST. PARK
BOUNDARY PLATEAU
4,567 ft. (1392 m.)

Agriculture, Industry and Resources

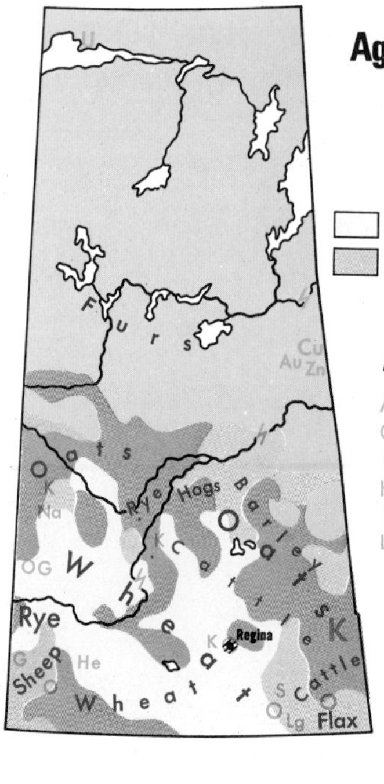
Furs
Wheat
Oats
Barley
Rye
Hogs
Cattle
Sheep
Flax
Regina

DOMINANT LAND USE

- Wheat
- Cereals (chiefly barley, oats)
- Cereals, Livestock
- Livestock
- Forests

MAJOR MINERAL OCCURRENCES

- Au Gold
- Cu Copper
- G Natural Gas
- He Helium
- K Potash
- Lg Lignite
- Na Salt
- O Petroleum
- S Sulfur
- U Uranium
- Zn Zinc
- Water Power
- Major Industrial Areas

undary (plat.) B6
ghtsand (lake) B2
onson (lake) B2
ffalo Pound Prov. Park F5
ori (lake) B4
ctus (hills) F5
ndle (lake) F2
nnington Manon Hist. Park J6
noe (lake) L3
rrot (riv.) J2
aplin (lake) E5
ipman (riv.) M2
itek (lake) D2
urchill (riv.) M3
earwater (riv.) L3
chrane (riv.) N2
teau (hills) D4
wan (lake) D2
ane (lake) B5
ean (lake) E1
ee (lake) L3
ee (riv.) M2
imberland (lake) J1
press (hills) B6
press (lake) B6
press Hills Prov. Park B6
nielson Prov. Park E4
elaronde (lake) E1
efenbaker (lake) E4
ré (lake) L3
uglas Prov. Park E4
ick Lake Hist. Park E3
Duck Mountain Prov. Park K4
Eagle (hills) C3
Eaglehill (creek) D4
Ear (lake) B3
Echo Valley Prov. Park G5
Etomami (riv.) J3
Eyebrow (lake) E5
Eyehill (creek) B3
Fife (lake) E6
File (hills) H5
Fir (riv.) J2
Fond du Lac (riv.) M2
Forrest (lake) L3
Fort Battleford Nat'l Hist. Park C3
Fort Carlton Hist. Park E3
Fort Pitt Hist. Park B2
Fort Walsh Nat'l Hist. Park A6
Foster (riv.) M3
Frenchman (riv.) C6
Frobisher (lake) L3
Gap (creek) B6
Gardiner (dam) D4
Geikie (riv.) M3
Good Spirit (lake) J4
Goodspirit Lake Prov. Park J4
Great Sand (hills) B5
Green (lake) D1
Greenwater Lake Prov. Park H3
Haultain (riv.) L3
Île-à-la-Crosse (lake) L3
Ironspring (creek) G3
Jackfish (lake) C2
Katepwa Prov. Park H5
Kingsmere (lake) E1
Kiyiu (lake) C4
Lac La Ronge Prov. Park M3
Lanigan (creek) F4
Last Mountain (lake) F4
Leaf (lake) J2
Leech (lake) J4
Lenore (lake) G3
Little Manitou (lake) F4
Lodge (creek) B6
Long (creek) H6
Loon (creek) G4
Makwa (lake) B1
Makwa (riv.) B1
Manito (lake) B3
Maple (creek) B5
McFarlane (riv.) L2
Meadow (lake) C1
Meadow Lake Prov. Park K4
Meeting (lake) D2
Midnight (lake) C2
Ministikwan (lake) B1
Missouri Coteau (hills) F5
Montreal (lake) F1
Moose (mt.) J6
Moose Jaw (riv.) G5
Moose Mountain (creek) J6
Moose Mountain Prov. Park J6
Mossy (riv.) H1
Muddy (lake) B3
Mudjatik (riv.) L3
Nipawin Prov. Park G1
North Saskatchewan (riv.) D3
Notukeu (creek) D6
Oldman (riv.) L2
Old Wives (lake) E5
Opuntia (lake) C4
Overflowing (riv.) K2
Pasquia (hills) J2
Pasquia (riv.) K2
Pelican (lake) E5
Peter Pond (lake) L3
Pheasant (hills) J5
Pine Lake Prov. Park E4
Pinto (creek) D6
Pipestone (creek) K6
Pipestone (riv.) L2
Ponass (lkes) H3
Poplar (riv.) E6
Porcupine (hills) K3
Primrose (lake) L3
Primrose Lake Air Weapons Range L3
Prince Albert Nat'l Park E1
Qu'Appelle (riv.) J5
Quill (lkes) G4
Red Deer (riv.) A5
Red Deer (riv.) K3
Reindeer (lake) N3
Reindeer (riv.) M3
Riou (lake) M2
Rivers (lake) F6

AREA 251,699 sq. mi. (651,900 sq. km.)
POPULATION 957,025
CAPITAL Regina
LARGEST CITY Regina
HIGHEST POINT Cypress Hills 4,567 ft. (1,392 m.)
SETTLED IN 1774
ADMITTED TO CONFEDERATION 1905
PROVINCIAL FLOWER Prairie Lily

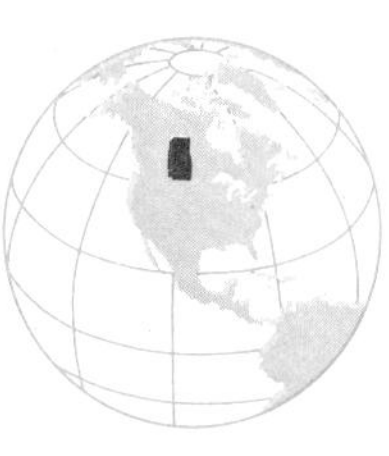

Ronge, La (lake) M3
Rowans Ravine Prov. Park F4
St. Victor Petroglyths Hist. Park E6
Saskatchewan (riv.) H2
Saskatchewan Landing Prov. Park C5
Saskeram (riv.) K2
Scott (lake) M2
Selwyn (lake) M2
Souris (riv.) H6
South Saskatchewan (riv.) C5
Steele Narrows Hist. Park B2
Stripe (lake) C4
Sturgeon (riv.) E2
Swan (riv.) J3
Swift Current (creek) D5
Tazin (lake) L2
The Battlefords Prov. Park C2
Thickwood (hills) D2
Thunder (hills) L4
Tobin (lake) H2
Torch (riv.) H2
Touchwood (hills) G4
Tramping (lake) C3
Trout (riv.) L2
Turtle (lake) C2
Twelvemile (lake) E6
Vermilion (hills) E5
Wapawekka (hills) M4
Waskana (creek) G5
Waskesiu (lake) E2
Wathaman (riv.) M3
Weed (hills) J5
White Fox (riv.) G2
White Gull (creek) G2
Whiteshore (lake) C3
Whiteswan (lkes) F1
William (riv.) L2
Willow Bunch (lake) F6
Witchekan (lake) D2
Wollaston (lake) N2
Wood (mt.) E6
Wood (riv.) E6
Wood Mountain Hist. Park E6

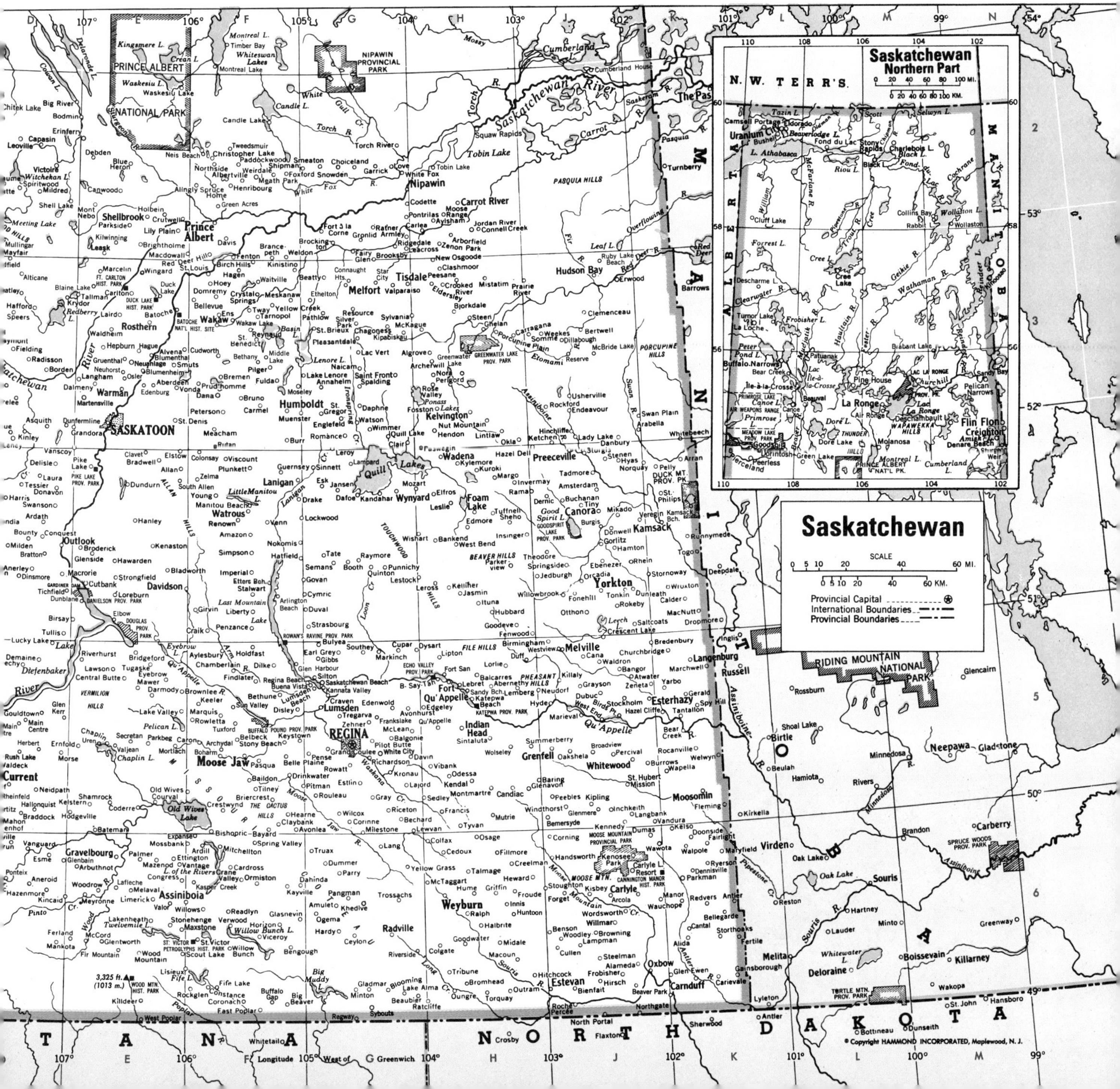

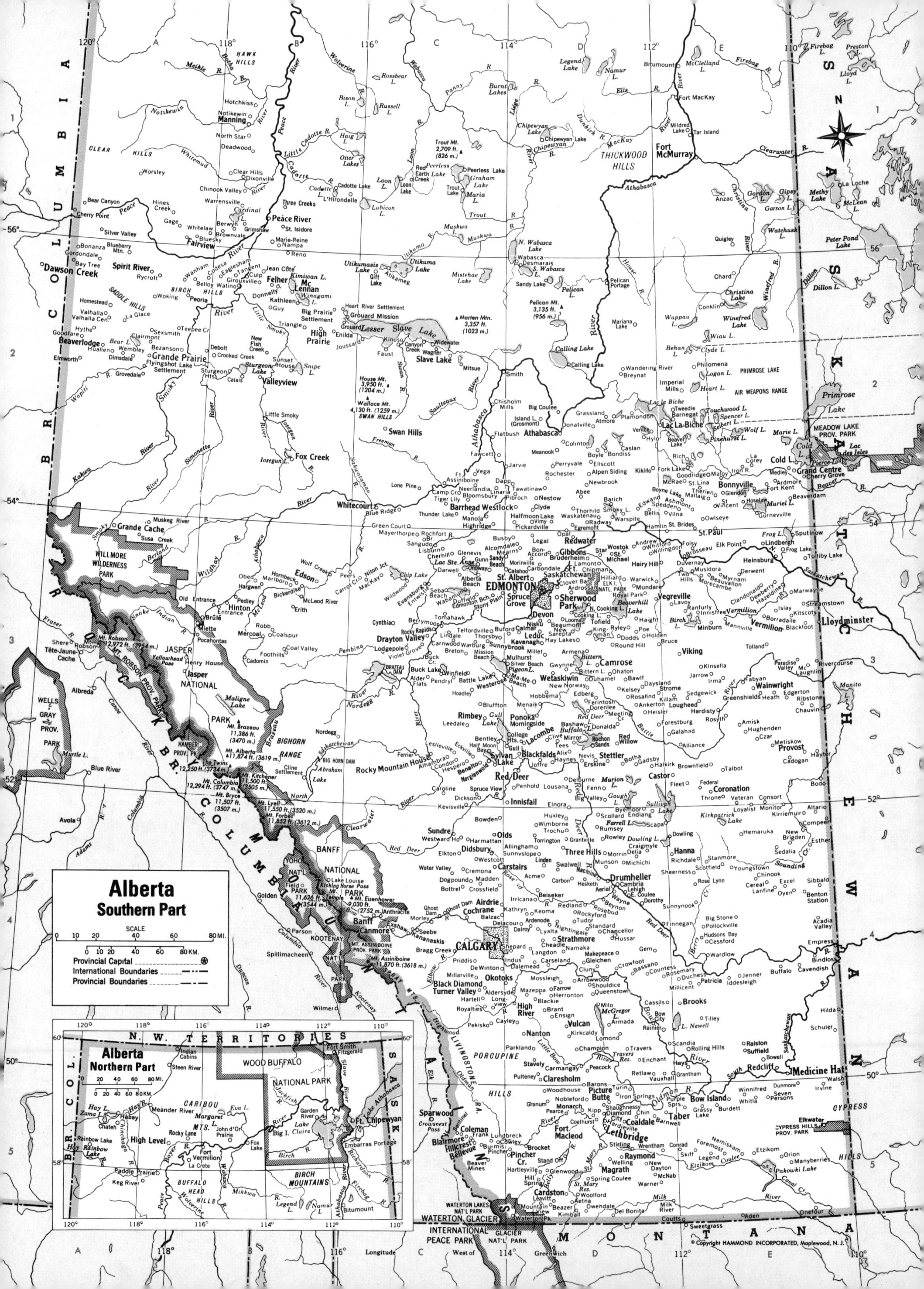

Alberta
Southern Part
SCALE
0 10 20 40 60 80 MI.
0 10 20 40 60 80 KM.
Provincial Capital
International Boundaries
Provincial Boundaries
Alberta
Northern Part
N. W. TERRITORIES
WOOD BUFFALO
NATIONAL PARK
CARIBOU MTS.
BIRCH MOUNTAINS
BUFFALO HEAD HILLS
High Level
Fort Vermilion
Fort Smith
Ft. Chipewyan
Lake Athabasca
BRITISH COLUMBIA
SASKATCHEWAN
MONTANA
EDMONTON
CALGARY
Red Deer
Lethbridge
Medicine Hat
Fort McMurray
Grande Prairie
Peace River
Lesser Slave Lake
Lac La Biche
Lloydminster
Camrose
Wetaskiwin
Drumheller
Banff
Jasper
JASPER NATIONAL PARK
BANFF NATIONAL PARK
WILLMORE WILDERNESS PARK
WATERTON LAKES NAT'L PARK
WATERTON GLACIER INTERNATIONAL PEACE PARK
GLACIER NAT'L PARK
CYPRESS HILLS PROV. PARK
MEADOW LAKE PROV. PARK
PRIMROSE LAKE AIR WEAPONS RANGE
THICKWOOD HILLS
SWAN HILLS
PORCUPINE HILLS
LIVINGSTONE RA.
Mt. Robson 12,972 ft. (3954 m.)
Mt. Columbia 12,294 ft. (3747 m.)
Mt. Alberta 11,874 ft. (3619 m.)
Mt. Assiniboine 11,870 ft. (3618 m.)
Longitude West of Greenwich
© Copyright HAMMOND INCORPORATED, Maplewood, N.J.

Topography

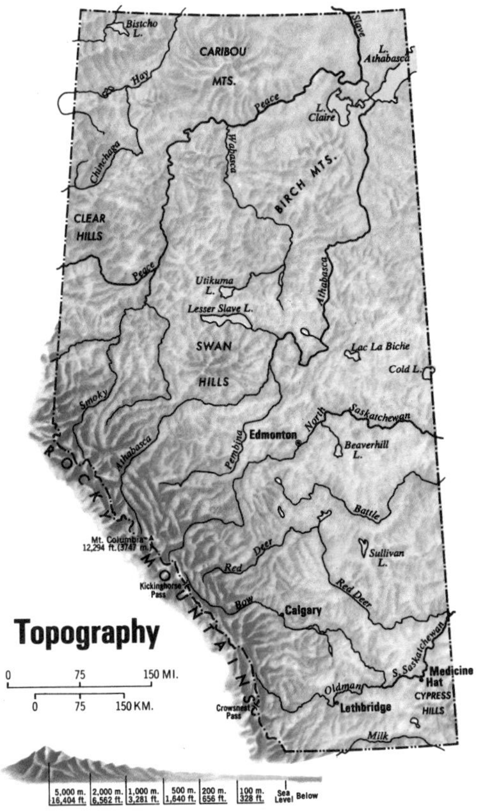

AREA 255,285 sq. mi. (661,185 sq. km.)
POPULATION 2,207,856
CAPITAL Edmonton
LARGEST CITY Edmonton
HIGHEST POINT Mt. Columbia 12,294 ft. (3,747 m.)
SETTLED IN 1861
ADMITTED TO CONFEDERATION 1905
PROVINCIAL FLOWER Wild Rose

CITIES and TOWNS

me 351 .... D4
drie 1,408 .... C4
erta Beach 432 .... C3
x 669 .... D3
iance 228 .... E3
drew 486 .... D3
dmore 238 .... E2
habasca 1,759 .... D2
nff 3,410 .... C4
rons 283 .... D4
rrhead 2,944 .... C2
shaw 773 .... D3
ssano 999 .... D4
aumont 851 .... D3
averlodge 1,332 .... A2
iseker 486 .... D4
llevue 1,186 .... C5
ntley 730 .... C3
rwyn 433 .... B1
g Valley 344 .... D3
ack Diamond 1,242 .... C4
ackfalds 1,024 .... D3
ackie 223 .... D4
airmore 2,321 .... C5
n Accord 882 .... D3
nnyville 2,885 .... E2
wden 661 .... C4
w Island 1,296 .... E5
yle 576 .... D2
agg Creek 384 .... C4
eton 424 .... C3
ocket 405 .... D5
ooks 6,339 .... E4
uce 93 .... E3
uderheim 484 .... D3
rdett 214 .... E5
lgary 469,917 .... C4
lmar 872 .... D3
mrose 10,104 .... D3
nmore 1,927 .... C4
rbon 435 .... D4
rdston 3,043 .... D5
rmangay 263 .... D4
roline 385 .... C3
rstairs 1,059 .... D4
stor 1,207 .... D3
real 231 .... E4
ampion 300 .... D4
ateh 400 .... A5
auvin 296 .... E3
ipman 296 .... D3
airmont 599 .... A2
aresholm 3,276 .... D4
ive 254 .... D3
yde 312 .... D2
aldale 3,654 .... D5
alhurst 473 .... D5
chrane 1,450 .... C4
old Lake 1,317 .... E2
leman 1,543 .... C5
ollege Heights 332 .... D3
nsort 609 .... E3
Cooking Lake 237 .... D3
Coronation 1,198 .... E3
Coutts 387 .... D5
Cowley 284 .... D5
Cremona 227 .... C4
Crossfield 777 .... C4
Daysland 615 .... D3
Delburne 417 .... D3
Delia 232 .... D4
Devon 2,786 .... D3
Didsbury 2,153 .... C4
Donnelly 278 .... B2
Drayton Valley 4,303 .... C3
Drumheller 6,154 .... D4
Duchess 343 .... E4
Eaglesham 229 .... B2
East Coulée 261 .... D4
Eckville 774 .... C3
Edgerton 324 .... E3
Edmonton (cap.) 461,361 .... D3
Edmonton Beach 243 .... C3
Edson 4,038 .... B3
Elk Point 807 .... E3
Elkton 226 .... C4
Elnora 211 .... D3
Empress 238 .... E4
Entwistle 380 .... C3
Erskine 234 .... D3
Evansburg 671 .... C3
Exshaw 389 .... C4
Fairview 2,248 .... A1
Falher 1,120 .... B2
Faust 298 .... C2
Foremost 534 .... E5
Forestburg 808 .... E3
Fort Assiniboine 185 .... C2
Fort Chipewyan 1,179 .... C5
Fort Macleod 3,067 .... D5
Fort McMurray 15,424 .... E1
Fort Saskatchewan 8,304 .... D3
Fort Vermilion 729 .... B5
Fox Creek 1,625 .... B2
Fox Lake 482 .... B5
Gibbons 1,093 .... D3
Gift Lake 432 .... C2
Girouxville 303 .... B2
Gleichen 339 .... D4
Glendon 370 .... E2
Grand Centre 2,780 .... E2
Grande Cache 4,116 .... A3
Grande Prairie 17,626 .... A2
Granum 413 .... D5
Grimshaw 1,665 .... B1
Grouard Mission 213 .... C2
Gunn 223 .... C3
Hanna 2,627 .... E4
Hardieville 546 .... D5
Hardisty 534 .... E3
Hay Lakes 236 .... D3
High Level 1,562 .... A5
High Prairie 2,281 .... B2
High River 3,598 .... D4
Hillcrest 653 .... C5
Hines Creek 503 .... A1
Hinton 6,731 .... B3
Holden 393 .... D3
Hughenden 236 .... E3
Hythe 460 .... A2
Innisfail 2,897 .... D3
Innisfree 265 .... E3
Irma 428 .... E3
Irricana 264 .... D4
Irvine 221 .... E5
Jasper 3,404 .... B3
John d'Or Prairie 326 .... B5
Joussard 270 .... B2
Killam 887 .... E3
Kinuso 305 .... C2
Kitscoty 391 .... E3
Lac La Biche 1,954 .... E2
Lacombe 3,888 .... D3
La Crete 349 .... B5
Lake Louise 140 .... B4
Lamont 997 .... D3
Leduc 8,576 .... D3
Legal 874 .... D3
Lethbridge 46,752 .... D5
Linden 296 .... D4
Lloydminster 5,818 .... E3
Lougheed 213 .... E3
Magrath 1,315 .... D5
Mallaig 339 .... E2
Manning 1,050 .... B1
Mannville 681 .... E3
Marwayne 376 .... E3
Mayerthorpe 1,018 .... C3
McLennan 1,133 .... B2
Medicine Hat 32,811 .... E4
Midlandvale 449 .... D4
Milk River 814 .... D5
Millet 762 .... D3
Mirror 335 .... D3
Morinville 2,097 .... D3
Morrin 230 .... D4
Mundare 555 .... D3
Myrnam 396 .... E3
Nacmine 330 .... D4
Nampa 286 .... B1
Nanton 1,152 .... D4
New Norway 276 .... D3
New Sarepta 237 .... D3
Nobleford 417 .... D5
Okotoks 1,795 .... C4
Olds 3,658 .... D4
Onoway 444 .... C3
Oyen 962 .... E4
Peace River 4,840 .... B1
Penhold 773 .... D3
Picture Butte 1,164 .... D5
Pincher Creek 3,448 .... D5
Plamondon 228 .... D2
Pollockville 29 .... E4
Ponoka 4,636 .... D3
Provost 1,532 .... E3
Rainbow Lake 434 .... A5
Ralston 465 .... E4
Raymond 2,290 .... D5
Redcliff 3,006 .... E4
Red Deer 32,184 .... D3
Redwater 1,493 .... D3
Rimbey 1,452 .... C3
Rockyford 276 .... D4
Rocky Mountain House 3,432 .... C3
Rosemary 273 .... E4
Rycroft 533 .... A2
Ryley 432 .... D3
Saint Albert 24,129 .... D3
Saint Paul 4,337 .... E3
Sangudo 409 .... C3
Sedgewick 825 .... E3
Sexsmith 770 .... A2
Shaughnessy 299 .... D5
Sherwood Park 26,534 .... D3
Slave Lake 3,561 .... C2
Smith 353 .... D2
Smoky Lake 925 .... D2
Spirit River 1,020 .... A2
Spruce Grove 6,907 .... D3
Standard 305 .... D4
Stavely 432 .... D4
Stettler 4,182 .... D3
Stirling 543 .... D5
Stony Plain 2,717 .... C3
Strathmore 1,561 .... D4
Strome 227 .... E3
Sundre 1,099 .... C4
Swan Hills 2,012 .... C2
Sylvan Lake 1,837 .... C3
Taber 5,296 .... E5
Thorhild 533 .... D2
Thorsby 657 .... C3
Three Hills 1,564 .... D4
Tilley 329 .... E4
Tofield 1,120 .... D3
Trochu 752 .... D4
Turner Valley 1,132 .... C4
Two Hills 943 .... E3
Valleyview 1,716 .... B2
Vauxhall 954 .... D4
Vegreville 4,158 .... E3
Vermilion 3,182 .... E3
Veteran 279 .... E3
Viking 1,217 .... E3
Vilna 348 .... E2
Vulcan 1,442 .... D4
Wabamun 581 .... C3
Wabasca 528 .... D2
Wainwright 3,890 .... E3
Wanham 225 .... A2
Warburg 408 .... C3
Warner 434 .... D5
Waskatenau 271 .... D2
Wayne 255 .... D4
Wembley 507 .... A2
Westlock 3,721 .... C2
Wetaskiwin 6,754 .... D3
Whitecourt 3,878 .... C2
Wildwood 360 .... C3
Willingdon 308 .... E3
Youngstown 272 .... E4

OTHER FEATURES

Abranam (lake) B3
Alberta (mt.) B3
Assiniboine (mt.) C4
Athabasca (lake) C5
Athabasca (riv.) D1
Banff Nat'l Park 3,849 .... B4
Battle (riv.) D3
Bear (lake) A2
Beaver (riv.) E2
Beaverhill (lake) D3
Behan (lake) E2
Belly (riv.) D5
Berland (riv.) A3
Berry (creek) E4
Biche (lake) E2
Big (isl.) B5
Big Horn (dam) B3
Bighorn (range) B3
Birch (hills) A2
Birch (lake) E3
Birch (mts.) B5
Birch (riv.) B5
Bison (lake) B1
Bittern (lake) D3
Botha (riv.) B1
Bow (riv.) D4
Boyer (riv.) A5
Brazeau (dam) C3
Brazeau (mt.) B3
Brazeau (riv.) B3
Buffalo (lake) D3
Buffalo Head (hills) B5
Burnt (lkes) C1
Cadotte (lake) B1
Cadotte (riv.) B1
Calling (lake) D2
Canal (creek) E5
Cardinal (lake) B1
Caribou (mts.) B5
Chinchaga (riv.) A5
Chip (lake) C3
Chipewyan (lake) D1
Chipewyan (riv.) D1
Christina (lake) E2
Christina (riv.) E1
Claire (lake) B5
Clear (hills) A1
Clearwater (riv.) C4
Clearwater (riv.) E1
Clyde (lake) E2
Cold (lake) E2
Columbia (mt.) B3
Crowsnest (pass) C5
Cypress (hills) E5
Cypress Hills Prov. Park E5
Dillon (riv.) E2
Dowling (lake) D4
Dunkirk (riv.) D1
Eisenhower (mt.) C4
Elbow (riv.) C4
Elk Island Nat'l Park 33 .... D3
Ells (riv.) D1
Etzikom Coulee (riv.) E5
Eva (lake) B5
Farrell (lake) D4
Firebag (riv.) E1
Forbes (mt.) B4
Freeman (riv.) C2
Frog (lake) E3
Garson (lake) E1
Gipsy (lake) E1
Gordon (lake) E1
Gough (lake) D3
Graham (lake) C1
Gull (lake) C3
Haig (lake) B1
Hawk (hills) B1
Hay (lake) A5
Hay (riv.) A5
Heart (lake) E2
Highwood (riv.) C4
House (mt.) C2
House (riv.) D2
Iosegun (lake) B2
Iosegun (riv.) B2
Jackfish (riv.) B5
Jasper Nat'l Park 3,602 .... A3
Kakwa (riv.) A2
Kickinghorse (pass) B4
Kimiwan (lake) B2
Kirkpatrick (lake) E4
Kitchener (mt.) B3
Legend (lake) D1
Lesser Slave (lake) C2
Liége (riv.) D1
Little Bow (riv.) D4
Little Cadotte (riv.) B1
Little Smoky (riv.) B2
Livingstone (range) C4
Logan (lake) E2
Loon (lake) C1
Loon (riv.) C1
Lubicon (lake) C1
Lyell (mt.) B4
MacKay (riv.) D1
Maligne (lake) B3
Margaret (lake) B5
Marie (lake) E2
Marion (lake) D3
Marten (mt.) C2
McClelland (lake) E1
McGregor (lake) D4
McLeod (riv.) B3
Meikle (riv.) A1
Mikkwa (riv.) B5
Milk (riv.) D5
Mistehae (lake) C2
Muriel (lake) E2
Muskwa (lake) C1
Muskwa (riv.) C1
Namur (lake) D1
Newell (lake) E4
Nordegg (riv.) C3
North Saskatchewan (riv.) E3
North Wabasca (lake) D1
Notikewin (riv.) A1
Oldman (riv.) D5
Otter (lkes) B1
Pakowki (lake) E5
Panny (riv.) C1
Peace (riv.) B1
Peerless (lake) C1
Pelican (lake) D2
Pelican (mt.) D2
Pelican (mts.) D2
Pembina (riv.) C3
Pigeon (lake) D3
Pinehurst (lake) E2
Porcupine (hills) C4
Primrose (lake) E2
Rainbow (lake) A5
Red Deer (lake) D3
Red Deer (riv.) D4
Richardson (riv.) C5
Rocky (mts.) C4
Rosebud (riv.) D4
Rossbear (lake) C1
Russell (lake) C1
Saddle (hills) A2
Sainte Anne (lake) C3
Saint Mary (res.) D5
Saint Mary (riv.) D5
Sakwatamau (riv.) C2
Saulteaux (riv.) C2
Seibert (lake) E2
Simonette (riv.) A2
Slave (riv.) C5
Smoky (riv.) A2
Snake Indian (riv.) A3
Snipe (lake) B2
Sounding (creek) E4
South Saskatchewan (riv.) E4
South Wabasca (lake) D2
Spencer (lake) E2
Spray (mts.) C4
Sturgeon (lake) B2
Sullivan (lake) D3
Swan (hills) C2
Swan (riv.) C2
Temple (mt.) B4
The Twins (mt.) B3
Thickwood (hills) D1
Touchwood (lake) E2
Travers (res.) D4
Trout (mt.) C1
Trout (riv.) C1
Utikuma (lake) C2
Utikuma (riv.) C1
Utikumasis (lake) C2
Vermilion (riv.) E3
Wabasca (riv.) C1
Wallace (mt.) C2
Wapiti (riv.) A2
Wappau (lake) E2
Watchusk (lake) E1
Waterton-Glacier Int'l Peace Park 194 .... C5
Waterton Lakes Nat'l Park 194 .... C5
Whitemud (riv.) A1
Wiau (lake) E2
Wildhay (riv.) B3
Willmore Wilderness Prov. Park A3
Winagami (lake) B2
Winefred (lake) E2
Winefred (riv.) E2
Wolf (lake) E2
Wolverine (riv.) B1
Wood Buffalo Nat'l Park 199 .... B5
Yellowhead (pass) A3
Zama (lake) A5

Agriculture, Industry and Resources

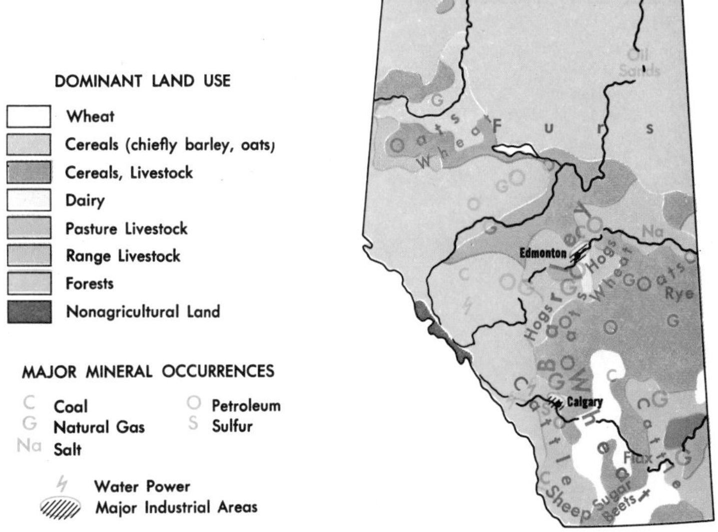

Topography

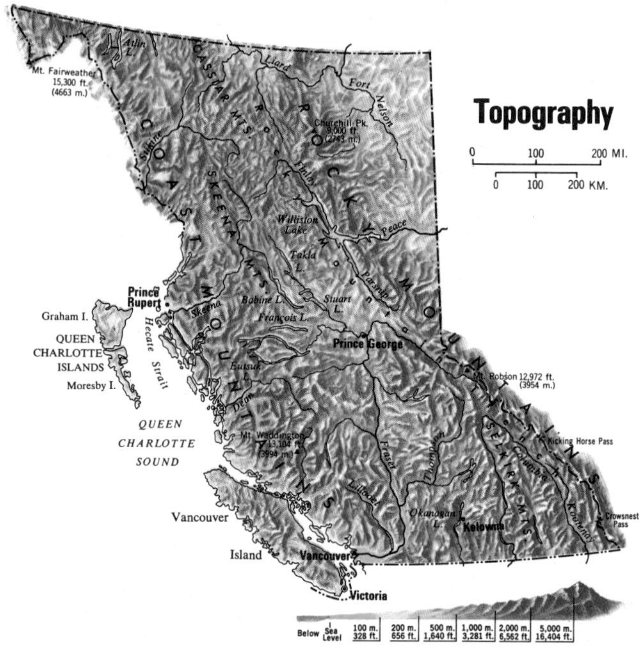

CITIES and TOWNS

Abbotsford 9,507 .... L3
Alert Bay 605 .... D5
Armstrong 2,260 .... H5
Ashcroft 2,032 .... G5
Barrière 835 .... H4
Bear Lake 431 .... F3
Big Eddy 833 .... H4
Blueberry Creek 660 .... J5
Blue River 425 .... H4
Boston Bar 602 .... G5
Brackendale 1,410 .... F5
Britannia Beach 431 .... K2
Burnaby• 131,599 .... K3
Burns Lake 1,433 .... D3
Cache Creek 1,050 .... G5
Campbell River 11,781 .... E5
Canal Flats 832 .... K5
Cassiar 801 .... K2
Castlegar 6,255 .... J5
Central Saanich• 7,413 .... K3
Chase 1,425 .... H5
Chemainus 2,129 .... J3
Cherry Creek 496 .... G5
Chetwynd 1,487 .... G2
Chilliwack 8,634 .... M3
Clearbrook 4,849 .... L3
Clearwater 766 .... G4
Clinton 808 .... G4
Coldstream• 4,995 .... H5
Comox 5,359 .... H2
Coquitlam• 55,464 .... K3
Courtenay 7,733 .... E5
Cranbrook 13,510 .... K5
Creston 3,552 .... J5
Crofton 1,143 .... J3
Cultus Lake 470 .... M3
Cumberland 1,697 .... E5
Dawson Creek 10,528 .... G2
Delta• 64,492 .... K3
Duncan 4,106 .... J3
East Kelowna 607 .... H5
Edgewater 424 .... J5
Elkford 1,873 .... K5
Enderby 1,482 .... H5
Erickson 1,008 .... J5
Errington 466 .... J3
Esquimalt• 15,053 .... K4
Falkland 456 .... H5
Fernie 4,608 .... K5
Fort Fraser 443 .... E3
Fort Langley 2,072 .... L3
Fort Nelson 2,916 .... M2
Fort Saint James 2,110 .... E3
Fort Saint John 8,947 .... G2
Fraser Lake 1,430 .... E3
Fraser Mills• 663 .... K3
Fruitvale 1,481 .... J5
Gabriola 1,169 .... J3
Galiano 480 .... K3
Ganges 444 .... K3
Gibsons 2,074 .... K3
Gillies Bay 560 .... H2
Golden 3,282 .... J4
Gold River 1,942 .... D5
Grand Forks 3,096 .... H6
Granisle 1,210 .... D3
Greenwood 931 .... H5
Haney 2,441 .... L3
Harrison Hot Springs 572 .... M3
Hatzic 1,140 .... L3
Hedley 480 .... G5
Holberg 421 .... C5
Honeymoon Bay 501 .... J3
Hope 2,963 .... M3
Hornby Island 411 .... H2
Houston 1,266 .... D3
Hudson Hope 981 .... F2
Invermere 1,194 .... J5
Kaleden 789 .... H5
Kamloops 58,311 .... G5
Kaslo 756 .... J5
Kelowna 51,955 .... H5
Kent• 2,924 .... M3
Keremeos 702 .... G5
Kimberley 7,111 .... K5
Kitimat 11,791 .... C3
Ladysmith 4,004 .... J3
Lake Cowichan 2,369 .... J3
Langley 10,123 .... L3
Lantzville 813 .... J3
Lillooet 2,218 .... G5
Lion's Bay 785 .... K3
Logan Lake 1,388 .... G5
Lumby 1,081 .... H5
Lytton 468 .... G5
Mackenzie• 5,338 .... F2
Mackenzie 5,266 .... F2
Maple Bay 578 .... K3
Maple Ridge• 29,462 .... L3
Masset 1,563 .... B3
Matsqui• 31,178 .... L3
Mayne 480 .... K3
McBride 619 .... G3
Merritt 5,680 .... G5
Metchosin 517 .... K4
Mica Creek 738 .... H4
Midway 589 .... H6
Mill Bay 566 .... K3
Mission• 14,997 .... L3
Mission City 8,278 .... L3
Montrose 1,197 .... J5
Nakusp 1,416 .... J5
Nanaimo 40,336 .... J3
Naramata 741 .... H5
Nelson 9,235 .... J5
New Denver 668 .... J5
New Hazelton 462 .... D2
New Westminster 33,393 .... K3
Nootka D5
North Cowichan• 15,956 .... J3
North Pender Island 709 .... K3
North Saanich• 4,697 .... K3
North Vancouver• 63,471 .... K3
North Vancouver 31,934 .... K3
Oak Bay• 17,658 .... K4
Ocean Falls 985 .... D4
Okanagan Falls 874 .... H5
Okanagan Landing 825 .... H5
Old Barkerville 9 .... G3
Oliver 1,641 .... H5
One Hundred Mile House 1,584 .... G4
Osoyoos 2,100 .... H5
Oyama 460 .... H5
Parksville 3,187 .... J3
Peachland• 2,286 .... G5
Penticton 21,344 .... H5
Pitt Meadows• 4,689 .... L3
Port Alberni 19,585 .... H3
Port Alice 1,497 .... D5
Port Clements 409 .... B3
Port Coquitlam 23,926 .... L3
Port Edward 1,189 .... B3
Port Hammond 1,353 .... L3
Port Hardy• 3,653 .... D5
Port McNeill 1,480 .... D5
Port Moody 11,649 .... L3
Pouce-Coupé 776 .... G2
Powell River• 13,694 .... E5
Prince George 59,929 .... F3
Prince Rupert 14,754 .... B3
Princeton 3,132 .... G5
Qualicum Beach 1,724 .... J3
Queen Charlotte 727 .... A3
Quesnel 7,637 .... F4
Revelstoke 4,615 .... J5
Richmond• 80,034 .... K3
Roberts Creek 711 .... J3
Robson 1,044 .... J5
Rossland 3,716 .... H6
Royston 635 .... H2
Rutland 1,283 .... H5
Saanich• 73,383 .... K3
Salmo 1,089 .... J5
Salmon Arm• 9,391 .... H5
Salmon Arm 1,876 .... H5
Saltair 1,339 .... J3
Sandspit 598 .... B3
Sardis 1,430 .... M3
Saseenos 772 .... J3
Savona 609 .... G5
Sechelt 822 .... J2
Shoreacres 426 .... J5
Sicamous 809 .... H5
Sidney 6,732 .... K3
Slocan Park 446 .... J5
Smithers 3,783 .... D3
Sointula 546 .... D5
Sooke 650 .... J4
South Hazelton 578 .... D2
South Wellington 606 .... J3
Spallumcheen 3,378 .... H5
Sparwood 3,081 .... K5
Sproat Lake 408 .... H3
Squamish 1,611 .... F5
Stewart• 1,382 .... C2
Summerland• 6,724 .... G5
Surrey• 116,497 .... K3
Tahsis 1,663 .... D5
Taylor 649 .... G2
Telkwa 691 .... D3
Terrace• 10,251 .... C3
Terrace 7,576 .... C3
Thornhill 3,938 .... C3
Tofino 612 .... E5
Trail 9,976 .... J6
Ucluelet 1,180 .... E6
Union Bay 513 .... H2
Valemount 878 .... H4
Vananda 407 .... E5
Vancouver 410,188 .... K3
Vancouver (Greater)• 1,085,242 .... K3
Vanderhoof 1,990 .... E3
Vavenby 845 .... H4
Vernon 17,546 .... H5
Victoria (cap.) 62,551 .... K4
Victoria‡ 230,592 .... K4
Warfield 1,957 .... J5
Wasa 403 .... K5
Westbank 1,067 .... H5
West Vancouver• 37,144 .... K3
Westwold 451 .... G5
Whistler 531 .... F5
White Rock 12,497 .... K3
Williams Lake 6,199 .... F4
Wilson Creek 417 .... J2
Windermere 635 .... K5
Winfield 1,033 .... H5
Winlaw 444 .... J5
Woss Lake 408 .... D5
Wynndel 528 .... J5
Yarrow 1,070 .... M3
Youbou 1,064 .... J3

OTHER FEATURES

Adams (lake) H4
Adams (riv.) H4
Alberni (inlet) H3
Alsek (riv.) H1
Aristazabal (isl.) C4
Assiniboine (mt.) K5
Atlin (lake) J1
Azure (lake) G4
Babine (lake) E3
Babine (riv.) D2
Banks (isl.) B3
Barkley (sound) E6
Beale (cape) E6
Bear (lake) D2
Beatton (riv.) G1
Bella Coola (riv.) D4
Bell-Irving (riv.) C2
Bennett, W.A.C. (dam) F2
Birkenhead Lake Prov. Park F5
Bowron Lake Prov. Park G3
Bowser (lake) C2
Brooks (pen.) D5
Browning Entrance (str.) B3
Bryce (mt.) J4
Bugaboo Glacier Prov. Park J5
Bulkley (riv.) D2
Burke (chan.) D4
Burnaby (isl.) B4
Bute (inlet) E5
Caamaño (sound) C4
Calvert (isl.) C4
Canim (lake) G4
Canoe (riv.) H4
Cariboo (mts.) G3
Carpenter (lake) F5
Carp Lake Prov. Park F3
Cassiar (mts.) K2
Castle (mt.) A2
Cathedral Prov. Park H5
Charlotte (lake) E4
Chatham (sound) B3
Chehalis (lake) L3
Chilcotin (riv.) E4
Chilko (lake) F4
Chilko (riv.) E4
Chilkoot (pass) J1
Chuchi (lake) E2
Churchill (peak) L2
Clayoquot (sound) D5
Clearwater (lake) G4
Clearwater (riv.) G4
Coast (mts.) D3
Columbia (lake) K5
Columbia (mt.) J4
Columbia (riv.) H4
Cook (cape) C5
Cowichan (lake) J3
Crowsnest (pass) K5
Cypress Prov. Park K3
Dean (chan.) D4
Dean (riv.) D4
Dease (lake) K2
Dease (riv.) K2
Devils Thumb (mt.) A1
Dixon Entrance (chan.) A3
Douglas (chan.) C3
Duncan (riv.) J5
Dundas (isl.) B3
Elk (riv.) K5
Elk Lakes Prov. Park K5
Eutsuk (lake) D3
Fairweather (mt.) H1
Finlay (riv.) E1
Fitzhugh (sound) D4
Flathead (riv.) K6
Flores (isl.) D5
Fontas (riv.) M2
Forbes (mt.) J4
Fort Nelson (riv.) M2
François (lake) D3
Fraser (lake) E3
Fraser (riv.) F4
Fraser Reach (chan.) C3
Galiano (isl.) K3
Gardner (canal) C3
Garibaldi Prov. Park F5
Georgia (str.) J3
Germansen (lake) E2
Gil (isl.) C3
Glacier Nat'l Park J4
Golden Ears Prov. Park L2
Gordon (riv.) H3
Graham (isl.) A3
Graham Reach (chan.) C3
Grenville (chan.) C3
Halfway (riv.) F2
Hamber Prov. Park H4
Harrison (lake) M2
Hawkesbury (isl.) C3
Hazelton (mts.) C2
Hecate (str.) B3
Hobson (lake) H4
Homathko (riv.) E4
Horsefly (lake) G4
Howe (sound) K2

Agriculture, Industry and Resources

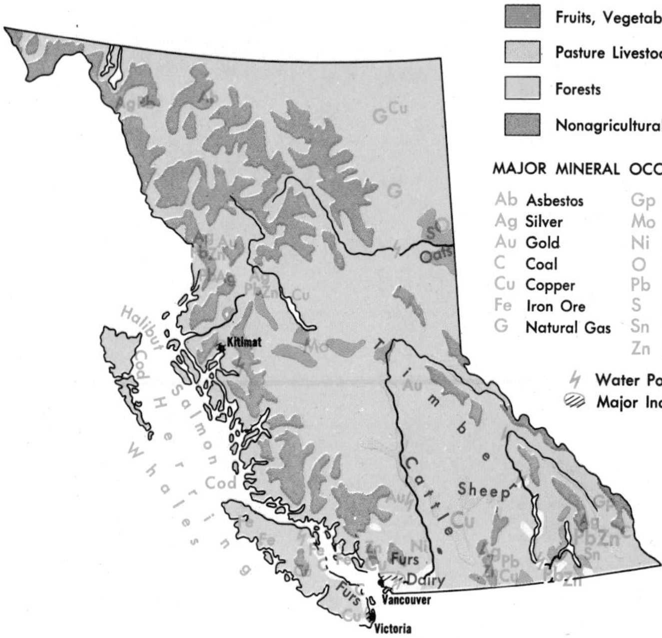

DOMINANT LAND USE

- Cereals, Livestock
- Dairy
- Fruits, Vegetables
- Pasture Livestock
- Forests
- Nonagricultural Land

MAJOR MINERAL OCCURRENCES

Ab	Asbestos	Gp	Gypsum
Ag	Silver	Mo	Molybdenum
Au	Gold	Ni	Nickel
C	Coal	O	Petroleum
Cu	Copper	Pb	Lead
Fe	Iron Ore	S	Sulfur
G	Natural Gas	Sn	Tin
		Zn	Zinc

Water Power
Major Industrial Areas

ter (isl.) C4
n (riv.) J2
na (lake) E3
c (lake) G3
t (riv.) B2
is (inlet) E5
n Jay (mt.) B2
nstone (str.) D5
n de Fuca (str.) J4
s Needle (mt.) A1
nika (riv.) L2
ney (dam) E3
le (riv.) H5
ing Horse (pass) J4
(isl.) D4
atinaw (riv.) G2
aklini (riv.) E4
ch (lake) E2
ght (inlet) E5
x (cape) A3
anee Glacier Prov. Park J5
canusa (lake) K6
tenay (lake) J5
tenay (riv.) K5
tenay Nat'l Park J4
cho (lake) M2
cho (riv.) M2
ghit (isl.) B4
quot (sound) D5
gara (isl.) A3
edo (sound) C4
d (riv.) L2
poet (riv.) F5

Louise (isl.) B4
Lower Arrow (lake) H5
Lyell (isl.) B4
Lyell (mt.) J4
Mabel (lake) H5
Mahood (lake) G4
Malaspina (str.) J2
Manning Prov. Park G5
Masset (inlet) A3
McCauley (isl.) B3
McGregor (riv.) G3
Meziadin (lake) C2
Milbanke (sound) C4
Moberly (lake) F2
Monashee (mts.) H4
Moresby (isl.) B4
Morice (lake) D3
Morice (riv.) D3
Mount Assiniboine Prov. Park K5
Mount Edziza Prov. Park and Rec. Area B1
Mount Revelstoke Nat'l Park H4
Mount Robson Prov. Park H3
Muncho Lake Prov. Park L2
Murray (riv.) G3
Murtle (lake) H4
Muskwa (riv.) M2
Nanika (dam) D3
Nanika (lake) D3
Nass (riv.) C2
Nation (riv.) F2
Nechako (riv.) E3
Nitinat (lake) H3

Nootka (isl.) D5
Nootka (sound) D5
North Thompson (riv.) G4
Observatory (inlet) C2
Okanagan (lake) H5
Okanagan Mtn. Prov. Park G5
Okanogan (riv.) H6
Omineca (mts.) E2
Omineca (riv.) E2
Ootsa (lake) D3
Owikeno (lake) D4
Pacific Rim Nat'l Park E6
Parsnip (riv.) F3
Peace (riv.) G2
Pend Oreille (riv.) J6
Petitot (riv.) M2
Pinchi (lake) E3
Pine (riv.) G2
Pitt (isl.) C3
Pitt (lake) L2
Porcher (isl.) B3
Portland (canal) B2
Portland (inlet) C3
Price (isl.) C4
Princess Royal (isl.) C3
Principe (chan.) C3
Prophet (riv.) M2
Purcell (mts.) J5
Quatsino (sound) C5
Queen Charlotte (isls.) B3
Queen Charlotte (sound) C4
Queen Charlotte (str.) D5
Queens (sound) C4

Quesnel (lake) G4
Quesnel (riv.) F4
Rivers (inlet) D4
Robson (mt.) H3
Rocky (mts.) F2
Roderick (isl.) C4
Rose (pt.) B3
Saint James (cape) B4
Salmon (riv.) F3
Salmon Arm (inlet) J2
San Juan (riv.) J3
Schoen Lake Prov. Park E5
Scott (cape) C5
Scott (isls.) C5
Seechelt (inlet) J2
Seechelt (pen.) J2
Selkirk (mts.) J4
Seymour (inlet) D4
Sheslay (riv.) J2
Shuswap (lake) H4
Sikanni Chief (riv.) F1
Silver Star Prov. Park H5
Sir Sandford (mt.) H4
Skagit (riv.) G6
Skeena (mts.) C2
Skeena (riv.) C3
Skidegate (inlet) B3
Slocan (lake) J5
Smith (sound) C4
South Bentinck Arm (inlet) D4
Stave (lake) L3
Stephens (isl.) B3
Stikine (riv.) B1

AREA 366,253 sq. mi. (948,596 sq. km.)
POPULATION 2,716,301
CAPITAL Victoria
LARGEST CITY Vancouver
HIGHEST POINT Mt. Fairweather 15,300 ft. (4,663 m.)
SETTLED IN 1806
ADMITTED TO CONFEDERATION 1871
PROVINCIAL FLOWER Dogwood

Stone Mountain Prov. Park L2
Strathcona Prov. Park E5
Stuart (lake) E3
Sustut (riv.) D2
Tagish (lake) J1
Tahtsa (lake) D3
Takla (lake) D2
Taku (riv.) J2
Tatlatui (lake) D2
Tatlayoko (lake) E4
Tchentlo (lake) E2
Teslin (lake) K1
Tetachuck (lake) E3
Texada (isl.) J2
Tezzeron (lake) E3

Thompson (riv.) G5
Three Guardsmen (mt.) H1
Thutade (lake) D2
Tiedemann (mt.) E4
Toad (riv.) L2
Toba (inlet) E5
Tochcha (lake) E3
Top Of The World Prov. Park K5
Trembleur (lake) E3
Troitsa (lake) D3
Tumeka (lake) C1
Turnagain (riv.) K2
Tuya (riv.) K2
Tweedsmuir Prov. Park D3
Unuk (riv.) B2

Upper Arrow (lake) H5
Valdes (isl.) K3
Vancouver (isl.) D5
Virago (sound) A3
Waddington (mt.) E4
Wapiti (riv.) H3
Wells Gray Prov. Park H4
West Road (riv.) E3
Whitesail (lake) D3
Williston (lake) F2
Work (chan.) C3
Yellowhead (pass) H4
Yoho Nat'l Park J4

•Population of municipality.

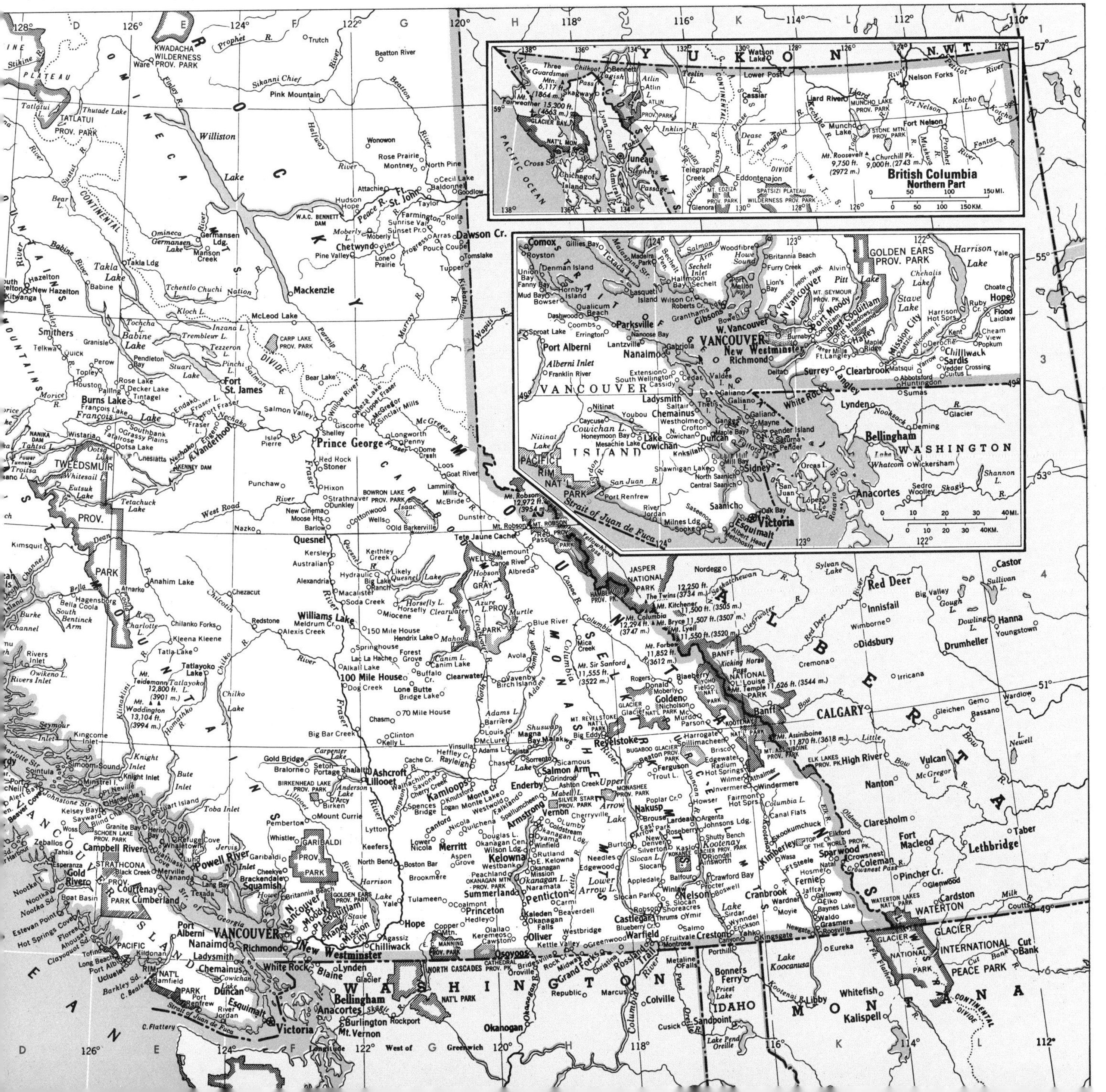

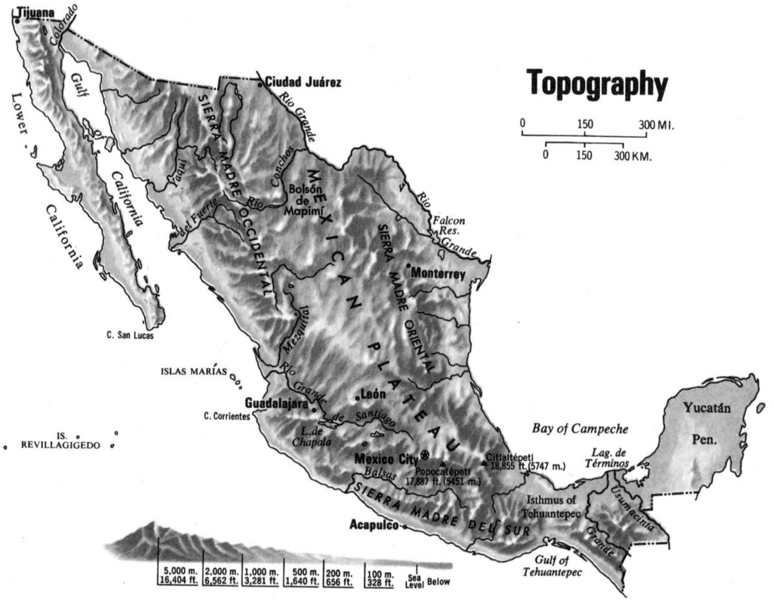

STATES

Aguascalientes 504,300 .... H6
Baja California 1,227,400 .... B1
Baja California Sur 221,000 .... C3
Campeche 371,800 .... O7
Chiapas 2,097,500 .... N8
Chihuahua 1,935,100 .... F2
Coahuila 1,561,000 .... H3
Colima 339,400 .... G7
Distrito Federal 9,377,300 .... L1
Durango 1,160,300 .... G4
Guanajuato 3,045,600 .... J6
Guerrero 2,174,200 .... J8
Hidalgo 1,518,200 .... K6
Jalisco 4,296,500 .... H6
México 7,542,300 .... K7
Michoacán 3,049,400 .... H7
Morelos 931,400 .... K7
Nayarit 729,500 .... G6
Nuevo León 2,463,500 .... K4
Oaxaca 2,517,500 .... L8
Puebla 3,285,300 .... L7
Querétaro 730,900 .... J6
Quintana Roo 209,900 .... P7
San Luis Potosí 1,669,900 .... J5
Sinaloa 1,882,200 .... F4
Sonora 1,498,100 .... D2
Tabasco 1,150,000 .... N7
Tamaulipas 1,924,900 .... K4
Tlaxcala 548,500 .... N1
Veracruz 5,263,800 .... L7
Yucatán 1,034,300 .... P6
Zacatecas 1,144,700 .... H5

CITIES and TOWNS

Acala 11,483 .... N8
Acámbaro 32,257 .... J7
Acaponeta 11,844 .... G5
Acapulco de Juárez 309,254 .... K8
Acatlán de Osorio 7,624 .... K7
Acatzingo de Hidalgo 6,905 .... N2
Acayucan 21,173 .... M8
Aconchi 1,596 .... D2
Actopan, Hidalgo 11,037 .... K6
Actopan, Veracruz 2,265 .... Q1
Agua Dulce 21,060 .... M7
Agualeguas 2,502 .... J3
Agua Prieta 20,754 .... E1
Aguascalientes 181,277 .... H6
Aguililla 5,715 .... H7
Ahome 4,182 .... E4
Ahuacatitlán 6,436 .... L1
Ahuacatlán 5,350 .... G6
Ahumada 6,466 .... F1
Ajalpan 8,238 .... L7
Alamo 9,954 .... L6
Álamos 4,269 .... E3
Aldama, Chihuahua 6,047 .... G2
Aldama, Tamaulipas 3,033 .... L5
Aljojuca 3,204 .... O1
Allende, Coahuila 11,076 .... J2
Allende, Nuevo León 9,914 .... J4
Almoloya del Río 3,714 .... K1
Altamira 6,053 .... L5
Altar 2,519 .... D1
Altepexi 6,661 .... L7
Alto Lucero 3,698 .... P1
Altotonga 6,754 .... P1
Alvarado 15,592 .... M7
Amatlán de los Reyes 3,664 .... P2
Amealco 2,960 .... K6
Ameca 21,018 .... H6
Amecameca de Juárez 16,276 .... L1
Amozoc de Mota 9,203 .... N2
Anáhuac, Chihuahua 10,886 .... F2
Anáhuac, Nuevo León 8,168 .... J3
Angostura 2,663 .... E4
Antiguo Morelos 1,569 .... K5
Apan 13,705 .... M1
Apatzingán de la Constitución 44,849 .... H7
Apizaco 21,189 .... N1
Aquiles Serdán 2,565 .... G2
Aramberri 1,786 .... J5
Arandas 18,934 .... H6
Arcelia 10,024 .... J7
Ario de Rosales 8,774 .... J7
Arizpe 1,736 .... D1
Armería 10,616 .... G7
Arriaga 13,193 .... N8
Arteaga 5,324 .... H7
Ascensión 4,104 .... E1
Asunción Nochixtlán 3,235 .... L8
Atlixco 41,967 .... M2
Atotonilco el Alto 16,271 .... H6
Atoyac de Álvarez 8,874 .... J8
Autlán de Navarro 20,398 .... G7
Axochiapan 8,283 .... M2
Ayutla de los Libres 3,618 .... K8
Azcapotzalco 534,554 .... L1
Azoyú 3,446 .... K8
Bacadéhuachi 1,514 .... E2
Bacalar 2,121 .... P7
Bachíniva 1,809 .... F2
Bácum 2,668 .... D3
Bahía Tortugas 1,457 .... B3
Balancán de Domínguez 3,669 .... O8
Bamoa 5,866 .... E4
Banderilla 3,488 .... P1
Baviácora 2,049 .... E2
Benjamín Hill 5,366 .... D1
Bernardino de Sahagún 12,327 .... M1
Boca del Río 2,354 .... Q2
Bolonchén de Rejón 2,342 .... O7
Buenaventura 3,924 .... F2
Burgos 673 .... K4
Cabo San Lucas 1,534 .... E5
Cacahoatán 5,079 .... N9
Cadereyta Jiménez 13,586 .... K4
Calkiní 6,870 .... O6
Calnali 3,318 .... K6
Calpulálpan 8,659 .... M1
Calvillo 6,453 .... H6
Campeche 69,506 .... O7
Cananea 17,518 .... D1
Canatlán 5,983 .... G4
Cancún 326 .... Q6
Candela 1,689 .... J3
Candelaria 1,982 .... O7
Cañitas de Felipe Pescador 4,885 .... H5
Capulhuac de Mirafuentes 8,289 .... K1
Carbo 2,804 .... D2
Cárdenas, San Luis Potosí 12,020 .... K6
Cárdenas, Tabasco 15,643 .... N8
Carichic 1,520 .... F2
Castaños 8,996 .... J3
Catemaco 11,786 .... M7
Ceballos 2,937 .... H3
Cedral 4,057 .... J5
Celaya 79,977 .... J6
Celestún 1,490 .... O6
Cerritos 10,421 .... J5
Cerro Azul 20,259 .... L6
Chahuites 5,218 .... M8
Chalchihuites 1,894 .... G5
Chalco de Díaz Covarrubias 12,172 .... M1
Champotón 6,606 .... O7
Charcas 10,491 .... J5
Chetumal 23,685 .... Q7
Chiapa de Corzo 8,571 .... N8
Chiautempan 12,327 .... N1
Chietla 4,602 .... M2
Chignahuapan 3,805 .... N1
Chihuahua 327,313 .... F2
Chilapa de Álvarez 9,204 .... K8
Chilpancingo de los Bravos 36,193 .... K8
China, Nuevo León 4,958 .... K4
Chocomán 5,114 .... P2
Choix 2,503 .... E3
Cholula de Rivadavia 15,399 .... M1
Cihuatlán 9,451 .... G7
Cintalapa de Figueroa 12,036 .... N8
Ciudad Acuña (Villa Acuña) 30,276 .... J2
Ciudad Altamirano 8,694 .... J7
Ciudad Camargo, Chihuahua 24,030 .... G3
Ciudad Camargo, Tamaulipas 5,953 .... K3
Ciudad del Carmen 34,656 .... N7
Ciudad Delicias 52,446 .... G2
Ciudad del Maíz 5,241 .... K5
Ciudad de Río Grande 11,651 .... H5
Ciudad Guerrero 3,110 .... F2
Ciudad Guzmán 48,166 .... H7
Ciudad Hidalgo, Chiapas 4,105 .... N9
Ciudad Hidalgo, Michoacán 24,692 .... J7
Ciudad Juárez 424,135 .... F1
Ciudad Lerdo 19,803 .... H4
Ciudad Madero 115,302 .... L5
Ciudad Mante 51,247 .... K5
Ciudad Mendoza 18,696 .... O2
Ciudad Miguel Alemán 11,259 .... K3
Ciudad Obregón 144,795 .... E3
Ciudad Río Bravo 39,018 .... K4
Ciudad Satélite 35,083 .... L1
Ciudad Serdán 9,581 .... O2
Ciudad Valles 47,587 .... K5
Ciudad Victoria 83,897 .... K5
Coalcomán de Matamoros 4,875 .... H7
Coatepec 21,542 .... P1
Coatetelco 5,268 .... L2
Coatzacoalcos 69,753 .... M7
Coatzingo 3,038 .... N2
Cocorit 4,478 .... E3
Colima 58,450 .... H7
Colón 3,346 .... K6
Colotlán 6,135 .... H5
Comala 5,592 .... H7
Comalcalco 14,963 .... N7
Comitán de Domínguez 21,249 .... O8
Compostela 9,801 .... G6
Concepción del Oro 8,144 .... J4
Concordia 3,947 .... G5
Contla 7,517 .... N1
Copala 3,783 .... K8
Coquimatlán 6,212 .... G7
Córdoba 78,495 .... P2
Cosalá 2,279 .... F4
Cosamaloapan de Carpio 19,766 .... M7
Cosautlán de Carvajal 2,039 .... P1
Coscomatepec de Bravo 6,023 .... P2
Coslo 2,680 .... H5
Costa Rica 11,795 .... F4
Cotija de la Paz 9,178 .... H7
Coyoacán 339,446 .... L1
Coyotepec 8,888 .... L1
Coyuca de Benítez 6,328 .... J8
Coyuca de Catalán 2,926 .... J7
Coyutla 3,726 .... L6
Cozumel 5,858 .... Q6
Creel 2,449 .... E3
Cuatrociénagas de Carranza 5,523 .... H3
Cuauhtémoc 26,598 .... F2
Cuautepec de Hinojosa 5,501 .... K6
Cuautitlán de Romero Rubio 11,439 .... L1
Cuautla Morelos 13,946 .... L2
Cuencamé de Ceniceros 3,774 .... H4
Cuernavaca 239,813 .... L2
Cuicatlán 2,733 .... L8
Cuitlahuac 4,813 .... P2
Culiacán 228,001 .... F4
Cumpas 2,395 .... E1
Cunduacán 4,397 .... N7
Dimas 2,194 .... F5
Doctor Arroyo 4,290 .... K5
Dolores Hidalgo de la Independencia Naci 16,849 .... J6
Durango 182,633 .... G1
Dzibalchén 1,917 .... P7
Dzidzantún 7,064 .... P6
Dzitbalché 4,393 .... P6
Ebano 17,489 .... K5
Ecatepec de Morelos 11,899 .... L1
Ejutla de Crespo 5,263 .... L8
Eldorado 8,115 .... E4
El Fuerte 7,179 .... E3
El Porvenir 3,030 .... G1
El Potosí 2,032 .... J4
El Salto 7,818 .... G5
El Zacatón 2,686 .... J5
Empalme 24,927 .... D2
Encarnación de Díaz 10,474 .... H6
Ensenada 77,687 .... A1
Escalón 2,998 .... G3
Escarcega 7,248 .... O7
Escuinapa de Hidalgo 16,442 .... G5
Escuintla 4,111 .... N9
Esperanza, Puebla 4,258 .... O2
Esperanza, Sonora 11,762 .... E3
Espita 5,394 .... Q6
Esqueda 1,458 .... E1
Etchojoa 4,398 .... E3
Ezequiel Montes 3,139 .... K6
Fortín de las Flores 9,358 .... P2
Francisco I. Madero 12,613 .... H4
Fresnillo de González Echererría 44,475 .... H5
Frontera 10,066 .... N7
Galeana, Nuevo León 3,429 .... J4
General Bravo 2,894 .... K4
General Cepeda 3,486 .... J4
General Terán 5,354 .... K4
Gómez Farías 3,030 .... F2
Gómez Palacio 79,650 .... G4
González 6,440 .... K5
Guadalajara 1,478,383 .... H6
Guadalajara* 2,343,034 .... H6
Guadalupe, Nuevo León 51,899 .... K4
Guadalupe, Zacatecas 13,246 .... H5
Guadalupe Bravo 3,333 .... F1
Guadalupe Victoria, Durango 7,931 .... H4
Guadalupe Victoria, Puebla 3,946 .... O1
Guamúchil 17,151 .... E4
Guanajuato 36,809 .... J6
Guasave 26,080 .... E4
Guaymas 57,492 .... D3
Gustavo Díaz Ordaz 10,154 .... K3
Gutiérrez Zamora 9,099 .... L6
Halachó 4,804 .... O6
Hecelchakán 4,279 .... O6
Hermosillo 232,691 .... D2
Heroica Caborca 20,771 .... C1
Heroica Nogales 52,108 .... D1
Hidalgo, Tamaulipas 2,450 .... K4
Hidalgo del Parral (Parral) 57,619 .... G3
Hopelchén 3,699 .... P7
Huajuapan de León 13,822 .... L8
Huamantla 15,565 .... N1
Huaquechula 2,294 .... M2
Huatabampo 18,506 .... D3
Huatusco de Chicuellar 9,501 .... P2
Huauchinango 16,826 .... L6
Huautla de Jiménez 6,132 .... L7
Huehuetlán el Chico 2,667 .... M2
Huejotzingo 8,552 .... M1
Huejutla 6,854 .... K6
Huetamo 9,333 .... J7
Hueyotlipan de Hidalgo 2,353 .... M1
Huimanguillo 7,075 .... N8
Huitzilán 3,573 .... O1
Huitzuco de los Figueroa 9,406 .... K7
Huixcolotla 4,039 .... N2
Huixtepec 5,927 .... L8
Huixtla 15,737 .... N9
Hunucmá 8,020 .... O6
Ignacio de la Llave 3,962 .... Q2
Iguala de la Independencia 45,355 .... K7
Imuris 1,958 .... D1
Irapuato 135,596 .... J6
Isla Mujeres 2,663 .... Q6
Isla, Veracruz 8,075 .... M7
Ixmiquilpan 6,048 .... K6
Ixtapa J8
Ixtapalapa 522,095 .... L1
Ixtenco 5,035 .... N1
Ixtepec 14,025 .... M8
Ixtlán del Río 10,986 .... G6
Izamal 9,749 .... P6
Izúcar de Matamoros 21,164 .... M2
Jala 4,535 .... G6
Jalacingo 3,427 .... P1
Jalapa Enríquez 161,352 .... P1
Jalpa 9,904 .... H6
Jalpa de Méndez 4,785 .... N7
Jalpan 1,878 .... K6
Jáltipan de Morelos 15,170 .... M8
Jantetelco 2,015 .... L2
Jaumave 3,072 .... K5
Jerez de García Salinas 20,325 .... H5
Jico 7,269 .... P1
Jilotepec de Abasolo 4,252 .... K7
Jiménez, Chihuahua 18,095 .... G3
Joachín 3,918 .... Q2
Jojutla de Juárez 14,438 .... L2
Jonacatepec 3,868 .... M2
Jonuta 2,746 .... N7
José Cardel 5,396 .... Q1
Juan Aldama 9,667 .... H4
Juchipila 6,328 .... H6
Juchitán de Zaragoza 30,218 .... M8
Kantunilkin 1,970 .... Q6
La Barca 18,055 .... H6
La Barra de Navidad 1,829 .... G7
La Concordia 3,559 .... N9
La Cruz, Sinaloa 4,218 .... F5
Lagos de Moreno 33,782 .... J6
La Huerta 4,328 .... G7
La Paz, Baja California Sur 46,011 .... D5
La Paz, San Luis Potosí 3,735 .... J5
La Piedad Cavadas 34,963 .... H6
Las Choapas 20,166 .... M7
Las Hadas G7
Las Nieves 2,262 .... G3
Las Rosas 7,658 .... N8
León 468,887 .... J6
Lerdo de Tejada 11,628 .... M8
Lerma 4,158 .... O7
Libres 4,830 .... O1
Linares 24,456 .... K4
Llera de Canales 3,564 .... K5
Loma Bonita 15,804 .... M7
Loreto, Baja California 2,570 .... D4
Loreto, Zacatecas 7,132 .... J5
Los Mochis 67,953 .... E4
Los Reyes de Salgado 19,452 .... H7
Macuspana 12,293 .... N8
Madera 9,759 .... F2
Magdalena de Kino 10,281 .... D1
Maltrata 5,457 .... O2
Manzanillo 20,777 .... G7
Mapastepec 5,907 .... N9
Mapimí 2,737 .... G4
Martínez de la Torre 17,203 .... L6
Mascota 5,674 .... G6
Matamoros, Coahuila 15,125 .... H4
Matamoros, Tamaulipas 165,124 .... L4
Matehuala 28,799 .... J5
Matías Romero 13,200 .... M8
Maxcanú 6,505 .... O6
Mazatlán 147,010 .... F5
Melchor Múzquiz 18,868 .... H3
Melchor Ocampo del Balsas 4,766 .... H8
Meoquí 12,308 .... G2
Mérida 233,912 .... P6
Metepec 4,625 .... M2
Metlatonoc 1,870 .... K8
Mexicali 317,228 .... B1
Mexico City (cap.) 9,377,300 .... L1
Mexico City* 13,993,866 .... L1
Miacatlán 3,980 .... K2
Mier 5,636 .... K3
Miguel Auza 9,303 .... H4
Minatitlán 68,397 .... M8
Mineral del Monte 8,887 .... K6
Miquihuana 1,971 .... J5
Misantla 8,799 .... P1
Miahuatlán de Porfirio Díaz 5,714 .... L8
Mocorito 3,993 .... F4
Moctezuma, San Luis Potosí 1,734 .... J5
Moctezuma, Sonora 2,700 .... E2
Monclova 78,134 .... J3
Montemorelos 18,642 .... K4
Monterrey 1,006,221 .... J4
Monterrey* 1,923,402 .... J4
Morelia 199,099 .... J7
Morelos 4,241 .... J2
Morelos Cañada 2,288 .... O2
Moroleón 25,620 .... J6
Motozintla de Mendoza 4,682 .... N9
Motul de Felipe Carillo Puerto 12,949 .... P6
Muna 5,491 .... P6
Naco 3,580 .... D1
Nacozari 2,976 .... E1
Nadadores 2,461 .... H3
Naica 7,190 .... G2
Namiquipa 4,875 .... F2
Nanaçamilpa 6,356 .... M1
Naolinco de Victoria 4,365 .... P1
Naranjos 14,732 .... L6
Naucalpan de Juárez 9,425 .... L1
Nautla 1,935 .... L6
Nava 4,097 .... J2
Navojoa 43,817 .... E3
Navolato 12,799 .... E4
Nazas 2,881 .... G4
Netzahualcóyotl 580,436 .... L1
Nieves 3,966 .... H5
Nochistlán 8,780 .... H6
Nogales 14,254 .... P2
Nombre de Dios 3,188 .... G5
Nopalucan de la Granja 3,002 .... O1
Nueva Casas Grandes 20,023 .... F1
Nueva Ciudad Guerrero 3,300 .... K3
Nueva Italia de Ruiz 14,718 ....
Nueva Rosita 34,706 ....
Nuevo Ideal 5,252 ....
Nuevo Laredo 184,622 ....
Oaxaca de Juárez 114,948 ....
Ocampo, Coahuila 1,613 ....
Ocampo, Tamaulipas 4,801 ....
Ocosingo 2,946 ....
Ocotlán 35,361 ....
Ocotlán de Morelos 5,882 ....
Ojinaga 12,757 ....
Ojocaliente 7,582 ....
Ometepec 7,342 ....
Oriental 6,009 ....
Orizaba 105,150 ....
Otumba de Gómez Farías 3,198 ....
Oxkutzcab 8,182 ....
Ozuluama 2,851 ....
Ozumba de Alzate 6,876 ....
Pachuca de Soto 83,892 ....
Padilla 4,581 ....
Palenque 2,595 ....
Palizada 2,332 ....
Palomas 2,129 ....

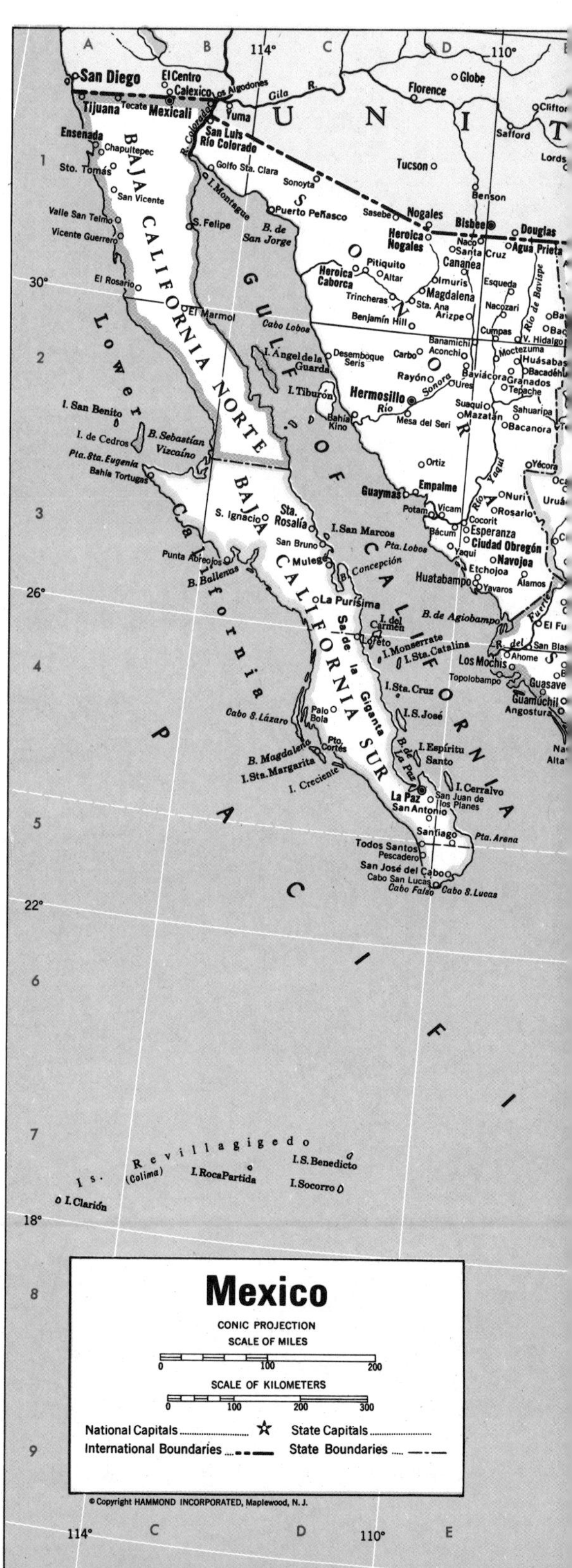

(continued on following page)

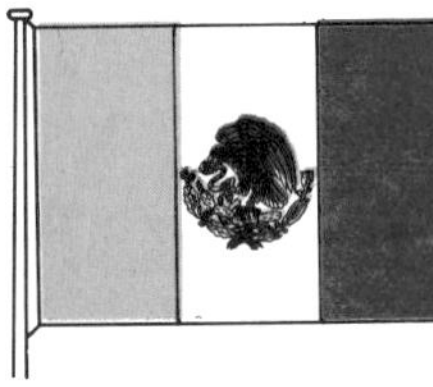

AREA 761,601 sq. mi. (1,972,546 sq. km.)
POPULATION 67,395,826
CAPITAL Mexico City
LARGEST CITY Mexico City
HIGHEST POINT Citlaltépetl 18,855 ft. (5,747 m.)
MONETARY UNIT Mexican peso
MAJOR LANGUAGE Spanish
MAJOR RELIGION Roman Catholicism

(continued)

Rosario, Sinaloa 10,276 ....G5
Rosario, Sonora 1,887 ....E3
Ruiz 8,954 ....G6
Sabancuy 1,819 ....O7
Sabinas 20,538 ....J3
Sabinas Hidalgo 17,439 ....J3
Sahuaripa 4,710 ....E2
Sahuayo de Díaz 28,727 ....H7
Sain Alto 3,628 ....H5
Salamanca 61,039 ....J6
Salina Cruz 22,004 ....M9
Salinas 7,471 ....J5
Saltillo 200,712 ....J4
Salvatierra 18,975 ....J6
San Andrés Tuxtla 24,267 ....M7
San Blas, Nayarit 3,443 ....G6
San Blas, Sinaloa 6,222 ....E3
San Buenaventura 9,188 ....J3
San Carlos, Coahuila 1,960 ....J2
San Cristóbal de las Casas 25,700 ....N8
San Felipe, Baja California 160 ....B1
San Felipe, Guanajuato 10,129 ....J6
San Fernando, Tamaulipas 27,656 ....L4
San Francisco del Oro 12,116 ....F3
San Francisco del Rincón 27,079 ....H6
San Gabriel Chilac 6,707 ....K7
San Ignacio, Sinaloa 1,804 ....F5
San Jerónimo de Juárez 5,204 ....J8
San José del Cabo 2,571 ....D5
San Juan 15,422 ....K6
San Juan de los Lagos 19,570 ....H6
San Juan Xiutetelco 3,306 ....O1
San Luis de la Paz 12,654 ....J6
San Luis del Cordero 2,203 ....H4
San Luis Potosí 271,123 ....J5
San Luis Río Colorado 49,990 ....B1
San Marcos 5,861 ....K8
San Martín de las Pirámides 4,575 ....M1
San Martín Texmelucan 23,355 ....M1
San Miguel de Allende 24,286 ....J6
San Nicolás de los Garza 28,803 ....J3
San Pedro de las Colonias 26,882 ....H4
San Pedro Pochutla 4,395 ....L9
San Rafael 8,974 ....M1
San Salvador el Seco 7,729 ....O1
Santa Ana 7,020 ....D1
Santa Ana Chiautempan (Chiautempan) 12,327 ....N1
Santa Bárbara 16,978 ....F3
Santa Clara 3,449 ....H4
Santa María del Oro 4,231 ....G3
Santa María del Río 4,972 ....J6
Santa María del Tule 1,674 ....L8
Santander Jiménez 3,586 ....K4
Santa Rosalía 7,356 ....C3
Santiago Ixcuintla 17,321 ....G6
Santiago Jamiltepec 5,280 ....K8
Santiago Juxtlahuaca 2,923 ....K8
Santiago Miahuatlán 4,917 ....O2
Santiago Papasquiaro 6,636 ....F4
Santiago Pinotepa Nacional 9,382 ....K8
Santiago Tuxtla 9,426 ....M7
Saucillo 8,467 ....G2
Sayula 14,339 ....H7
Sayula de Alemán 4,896 ....M8
Seybaplaya 4,439 ....O7
Silao 31,825 ....J6
Simojovel de Allende 3,779 ....N8
Sinaloa de Leyva 1,998 ....E4
Soledad de Doblado 6,612 ....Q2
Soledad Díez Gutiérrez 9,622 ....J5
Sombrerete 11,077 ....H5
Sonoyta 2,463 ....C1
Sotuta 3,772 ....P6
Tabasco 3,197 ....H6
Tacámbaro de Codallos 9,695 ....J7
Tacotalpa 2,019 ....N8
Tala 15,744 ....H6
Talpa de Allende 4,264 ....G6
Tamazulapan del Progreso 2,870 ....L8
Tamazunchale 12,302 ....K6
Tamiahua 6,264 ....L6
Tampico 212,188 ....L5
Tamuín 7,251 ....K6
Tantoyuca 11,902 ....L6
Tapachula 60,620 ....N9
Taxco de Alarcón 27,089 ....K7
Tayoltita 2,697 ....G4
Teapa 6,534 ....N8
Tecamachalco 3,319 ....O2
Tecate 14,738 ....A1
Tecomán 31,625 ....H7
Tecpan de Galeana 8,095 ....J8
Tecuala 12,461 ....G5
Tehuacán 47,497 ....L7
Tehuantepec 16,179 ....M8
Tekax de Álaro Obregón 10,326 ....P6
Teloloapan 10,335 ....J7
Temax 4,915 ....P6
Temósachic 1,738 ....E2
Tenabo 3,278 ....P6
Tenancingo de Degollado 12,807 ....K7
Tenango de Río Blanco 12,302 ....O2
Tenosique de Pino Suárez 11,393 ....O8
Teocaltiche 13,745 ....H6
Teocelo 4,572 ....P1
Teotihuacán de Arista 2,238 ....L1
Teotitlán del Camino 3,106 ....L8
Tepache 1,591 ....E2
Tepalcingo 5,968 ....M2
Tepatitlán de Morelos 29,292 ....H6
Tepeaca 7,466 ....N2
Tepeapulco 7,027 ....M1
Tepehuanes 2,531 ....G4
Tepeji del Río 10,365 ....L1
Tepexi de Rodríguez 2,618 ....N2
Tepic 108,924 ....G6
Tepoztlán 6,851 ....L1
Tequixquitla 4,825 ....O1
Terán 5,215 ....N8
Terrenate 1,515 ....N1
Texcoco de Mora 18,044 ....M1
Teziutlán 23,948 ....O1
Tezonapa 3,506 ....P2
Tezontepec 2,762 ....M1
Ticul 14,341 ....P6
Tierra Blanca 22,727 ....L7
Tila 2,633 ....N8
Tijuana 363,154 ....A1
Tixtla de Guerrero 10,334 ....K8
Tizayuca 6,262 ....L1
Tizimín 18,343 ....Q6
Tlachichuca 3,721 ....O1
Tlacolula de Matamoros 8,300 ....L8
Tlacotepec de Mejiá 1,595 ....P1
Tlahualilo de Zaragoza 8,951 ....H3
Tlalancaneca 5,090 ....M1
Tlalixcoyan 3,211 ....Q2
Tlalmanalco de Velásquez 5,744 ....L1
Tlalnepantla de Comonfort 45,575 ....L1
Tlalpan 130,719 ....L1
Tlaltenango de Sánchez Román 7,698 ....H6
Tlaltizapan 6,384 ....L2
Tlapacoyan 13,172 ....P1
Tlapa de Comonfort 6,676 ....K8

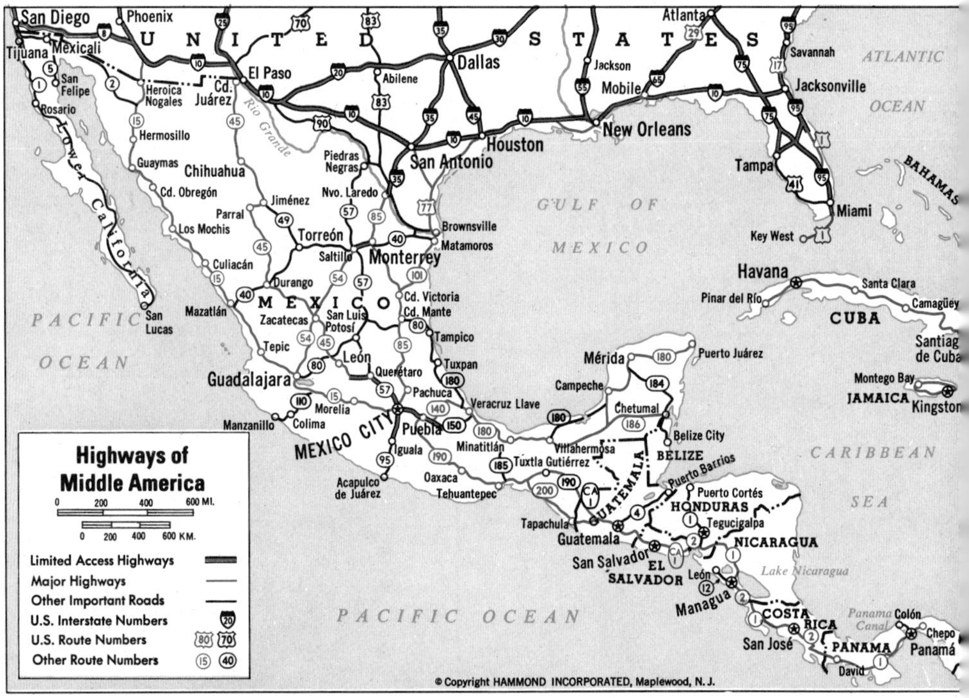

Tlaquepaque 59,760 ....G6
Tlatlauquitepec 4,272 ....O1
Tlaquiltenango 8,625 ....L2
Tlaxcala de Xicotencatl 9,972 ....M1
Tlaxco 4,969 ....N1
Tlaxiaco 4,477 ....L8
Tlayacapan 3,538 ....L1
Tochimilco 3,190 ....M2
Todos Santos 2,400 ....D5
Toluca de Lerdo 136,092 ....K7
Tomatlán 2,695 ....G6
Tonalá 15,611 ....N8
Topolobampo 4,685 ....E4
Torreón 244,309 ....H4
Tula, Tamaulipas 5,407 ....K5
Tula de Allende 10,720 ....K6
Tulancingo 35,799 ....K7
Tulcingo del Valle 2,983 ....M2
Tultepec 8,321 ....L1
Tuxpan, Jalisco 14,693 ....H7
Tuxpan, Nayarit 20,322 ....G6
Tuxpan de Rodríguez Cano 33,901 ....L6
Tuxtepec 17,701 ....L7
Tuxtla Gutiérrez 66,851 ....N8
Tzucabab 4,876 ....P7
Umán 8,371 ....P6
Unión de Tula 6,399 ....G7
Unión Hidalgo 8,658 ....M8
Ures 3,681 ....D2
Ursulo Galván 2,637 ....Q1
Uruapan del Progreso 108,124 ....H7
Valladolid 14,663 ....P6
Valle de Allende 4,973 ....G3
Valle de Bravo 7,628 ....J7
Valle Hermoso 19,278 ....L4
Vanegas 2,042 ....J5
Venado 2,790 ....J5
Venustiano Carranza 23,624 ....N8
Veracruz 255,646 ....Q1
Vicam 4,104 ....D3
Vicente Guerrero, Durango 8,451 ....G5
Victor Rosales 7,629 ....H5
Viesca 2,923 ....H4
Villa Acuña 30,276 ....J2
Villa Cuauhtémoc 6,611 ....L5
Villa de Cos 1,850 ....H5
Villa de Guadelupe Hidalgo 88,537 ....L1
Villa Frontera 25,761 ....J3
Villa García 2,765 ....J5
Villahermosa 133,181 ....N8
Villa Hidalgo, Sonora 2,126 ....E1
Villaldama 2,350 ....J3
Villa Matamoros 1,998 ....G3
Villanueva 5,895 ....H5
Villa Unión, Coahuila 4,058 ....J2
Villa Unión, Durango 4,042 ....H5
Villa Unión, Sinaloa 6,789 ....F5
Villa Vicente Guerrero 18,280 ....N1
Xaltocan 2,524 ....N1
Xicoténcatl 6,374 ....K5
Xicotepec de Juárez 12,656 ....L6
Xochihuehuetlán 3,268 ....K8
Xochimilco 116,493 ....L1
Xochitlán 3,312 ....N2
Yajalón 4,506 ....N8
Yaqui 8,061 ....D3
Yanga 3,843 ....P2
Yautepec 13,952 ....L2
Yavaros 1,959 ....E3
Yécora E2
Yecuatla 2,816 ....P1
Yehualtepec 2,558 ....O2
Zaachila 7,270 ....L8
Zacapoaxtla 4,527 ....O1
Zacapu 31,989 ....J7
Zacatepec 16,839 ....L2
Zacatecas 50,251 ....H5
Zacatelco 14,117 ....N1
Zacatlán 7,909 ....N1
Zacoalco de Torres 11,343 ....H6
Zamora de Hidalgo 5,775 ....H7
Zaragoza, Coahuila 6,797 ....J2
Zaragoza, Chihuahua 3,984 ....F1
Zaragoza, Puebla 4,754 ....O1
Zempoala 5,064 ....Q1
Zihuantanejo 4,879 ....J8
Zimatlán de Álvarez 5,746 ....L8
Zitácuaro 36,911 ....J7
Zongolica 2,378 ....P2
Zumpango de Ocampo 12,923 ....L1
Zumpango del Río 8,162 ....J8

OTHER FEATURES

Agiobampo (bay) E3
Aguanaval (riv.) H4
Amistad (res.) J2
Ángel de la Guarda (isl.) C2
Antigua (riv.) Q1
Arena (pt.) E5
Arenas (cay) O5
Atoyac (riv.) N2
Atoyac (riv.) Q2
Babia (riv.) J2
Bacalar (lake) P7
Ballenas (bay) C3
Balsas (riv.) J7
Banderas (bay) G6
Bavispe, Río de (riv.) E1
Blanco (riv.) Q2
Bravo (Grande) (riv.) G2
Burro (mts.) J2
California (gulf) D3
Campeche (bank) O6
Campeche (bay) N7
Candelaria (riv.) O8
Carmen (isl.) D3
Casas Grandes (riv.) F1
Catoche (cape) Q6
Cedros (isl.) B2
Cerralvo (isl.) E4
Chamela (bay) G7
Chapala (lake) H6
Chetumal (bay) P8
Chichén-Itzá (ruin) P6
Citlaltépetl (mt.) O2
Clarión (isl.) B7
Colorado (riv.) B1
Conchos (riv.) G2
Corrientes (cape) F6
Coyuca (riv.) O1
Creciente (isl.) D5
Cuitzeo (lake) J7
Delgada (pt.) L7
Dzibichaltún (ruin) P6
El Azúcar (res.) K3
Espíritu Santo (isl.) D4
Falcón (res.)
Falso (cape)
Fuerte (riv.)
Giganta, Sierra de la (mts.)
Grande (riv.)
Grande (riv.)
Grande de Santiago (riv.)
Grijalva (riv.)
Guzmán (lake)
Herrero (pt.)
Hondo (riv.)
Jesús María (reef)
La Boquilla (res.)
La Paz (bay)
Lobos (cape)
Lobos (pt.)
Lower California (pen.)
Madre (lag.)
Madre del Sur, Sierra (mts.)
Madre Occidental, Sierra (mts.)
Madre Oriental, Sierra (mts.)
Magdalena (bay)
Maldonado (pt.)
Mapimí (depr.)
María Cleófas (isl.)
María Madre (isl.)
María Magdalena (isl.)
Mexico (gulf)
Mezquital (riv.)
Mita (pt.)
Mitla (ruin)
Moctezuma (riv.)
Monserrate (isl.)
Montague (isl.)
Muerto, Mar (lag.)
Nauhcampatépetl (mt.)
Nayarit, Sierra (mts.)
Nazas (riv.)
Nuevo, Bajo (reef)
Orizaba (Citlaltépetl) (mt.)
Palenque (ruin)
Palmito de la Virgen (isl.)
Palmito del Verde (isl.)
Pánuco (riv.)
Paricutín (vol.)
Pátzcuaro (lake)
Pérez (isl.)
Petacalco (bay)
Popocatépetl (mt.)
Ramos (riv.)
Revillagigedo (isls.)
Roca Partida (isl.)
Sabinas (riv.)
San Antonio (reef)
San Benedicto (isl.)
San Benito (isl.)
San Jorge (bay)
San José (isl.)
San Lázaro (cape)
San Lucas (cape)
San Marcos (isl.)
San Rafael (reef)
Santa Ana (reef)
Santa Catalina (isl.)
Santa Cruz (isl.)
Santa Eugenia (pt.)
Santa Margarita (isl.)
Santa María (lake)
Santa María (riv.)
Santiaguillo (lake)
Sebastián Vizcaíno (bay)
Socorro (isl.)
Sonora (riv.)
Superior (lag.)
Teacapán (inlet)
Tehuantepec (gulf)
Tehuantepec (isth.)
Teotihuacán (ruin)
Términos (lag.)
Tiburón (isl.)
Triángulo Este (isl.)
Triángulo Oeste (isl.)
Tula (riv.)
Urique (riv.)
Usumacinta (riv.)
Uxmal (ruins)
Valsequillo (res.)
Verde (riv.)
Verde (riv.)
Yaqui (riv.)

*City and suburbs.

Agriculture, Industry and Resources

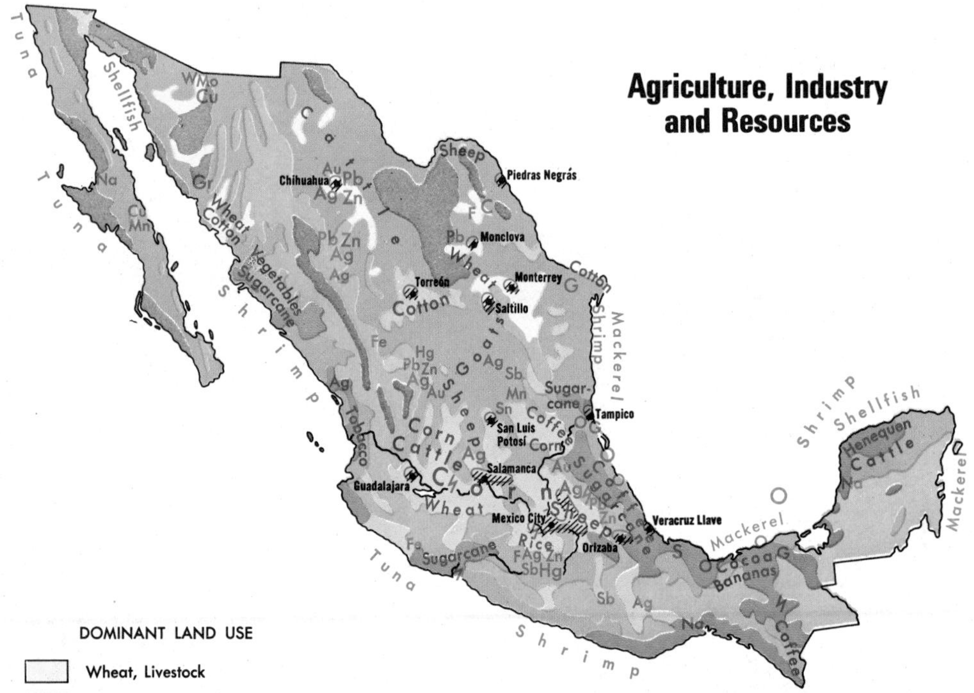

DOMINANT LAND USE

- Wheat, Livestock
- Cereals (chiefly corn), Livestock
- Diversified Tropical Cash Crops
- Cotton, Mixed Cereals
- Livestock, Limited Agriculture
- Range Livestock
- Forests
- Nonagricultural Land

Water Power

Major Industrial Areas

MAJOR MINERAL OCCURRENCES

Ag	Silver	G	Natural Gas	O	Petroleum
Au	Gold	Gr	Graphite	Pb	Lead
C	Coal	Hg	Mercury	S	Sulfur
Cu	Copper	Mn	Manganese	Sb	Antimony
F	Fluorspar	Mo	Molybdenum	Sn	Tin
Fe	Iron Ore	Na	Salt	W	Tungsten
				Zn	Zinc

GUATEMALA

REA 42,042 sq. mi. (108,889 sq. km.)
OPULATION 7,262,419
APITAL Guatemala
ARGEST CITY Guatemala
HIGHEST POINT Tajumulco 13,845 ft. (4,220 m.)
MONETARY UNIT quetzal
MAJOR LANGUAGES Spanish, Quiché
MAJOR RELIGION Roman Catholicism

BELIZE

AREA 8,867 sq. mi. (22,966 sq. km.)
POPULATION 144,857
CAPITAL Belmopan
LARGEST CITY Belize City
HIGHEST POINT Victoria Peak 3,681 ft. (1,122 m.)
MONETARY UNIT Belize dollar
MAJOR LANGUAGES English, Spanish, Mayan
MAJOR RELIGIONS Roman Catholicism, Protestantism

EL SALVADOR

AREA 8,260 sq. mi. (21,393 sq. km.)
POPULATION 4,813,000
CAPITAL San Salvador
LARGEST CITY San Salvador
HIGHEST POINT Santa Ana 7,825 ft. (2,385 m.)
MONETARY UNIT colón
MAJOR LANGUAGE Spanish
MAJOR RELIGION Roman Catholicism

HONDURAS

AREA 43,277 sq. mi. (112,087 sq. km.)
POPULATION 3,691,000
CAPITAL Tegucigalpa
LARGEST CITY Tegucigalpa
HIGHEST POINT Las Minas 9,347 ft. (2,849 m.)
MONETARY UNIT lempira
MAJOR LANGUAGE Spanish
MAJOR RELIGION Roman Catholicism

NICARAGUA

AREA 45,698 sq. mi. (118,358 sq. km.)
POPULATION 2,703,000
CAPITAL Managua
LARGEST CITY Managua
HIGHEST POINT Cerro Mocotón 6,913 ft. (2,107 m.)
MONETARY UNIT córdoba
MAJOR LANGUAGE Spanish
MAJOR RELIGION Roman Catholicism

COSTA RICA

AREA 19,575 sq. mi. (50,700 sq. km.)
POPULATION 2,245,000
CAPITAL San José
LARGEST CITY San José
HIGHEST POINT Chirripó Grande 12,530 ft. (3,819 m.)
MONETARY UNIT colón
MAJOR LANGUAGE Spanish
MAJOR RELIGION Roman Catholicism

PANAMA

AREA 29,761 sq. mi. (77,082 sq. km.)
POPULATION 1,830,175
CAPITAL Panamá
LARGEST CITY Panamá
HIGHEST POINT Vol. Baru 11,401 ft. (3,475 m.)
MONETARY UNIT balboa
MAJOR LANGUAGE Spanish
MAJOR RELIGION Roman Catholicism

Agriculture, Industry and Resources

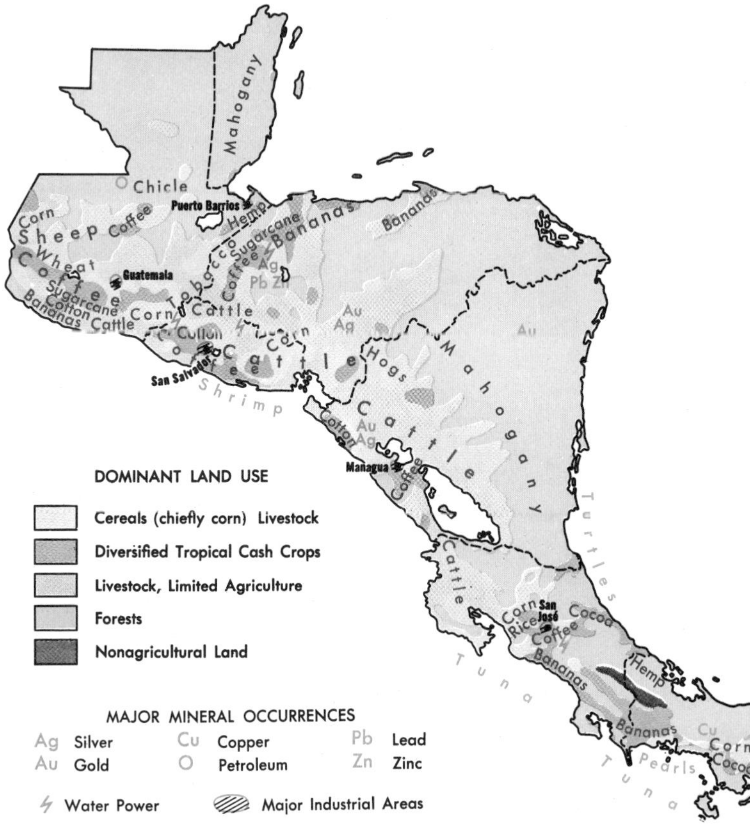

GUATEMALA

HONDURAS

BELIZE

NICARAGUA

EL SALVADOR

COSTA RICA

PANAMA

BELIZE

CITIES and TOWNS

elize City 39,887 .... C2
elize City* 50,925 .... C2
elmopan (cap.) 2,932 .... C2
orozal Town 6,862 .... C1
attieville 904 .... C2
Libertad 856 .... C1
Orange Walk Town 8,441 .... C1
Punta Gorda 2,219 .... C2
San Ignacio 5,606 .... C2
Stann Creek Town 6,627 .... C2

OTHER FEATURES

Ambergris (cay) D1
Belize (riv.) C2
Bokel (cay) D2
Glover (reef) D2
Half Moon (cay) D2
Hondo (riv.) C1
Honduras (gulf) D2
Mauger (cay) D2
New (riv.) C2
Saint Georges (cay) D2
Sarstún (riv.) C3
Turneffe (isls.) D2

COSTA RICA

CITIES and TOWNS

Alajuela 33,122 .... E6
Atenas 1,728 .... E6
Bagaces 2,129 .... E5
Boruca⊙ 1,892 .... F6
Buenos Aires⊙ 302 .... F6
Cañas 6,053 .... E5
Cartago 21,753 .... F6
Ciudad Quesada 9,754 .... E5
Esparta 4,699 .... E5
Filadelfia 2,958 .... E5
Golfito 6,962 .... F6
Grecia 8,355 .... E5
Guácimo 1,168 .... F5
Guápiles 3,524 .... F5
Heredia 22,700 .... E5
Las Juntas 1,129 .... E5
Liberia 10,802 .... E5
Limón 29,621 .... F6
Miramar 1,673 .... E5
Nicoya 7,474 .... E5
Orotina 3,170 .... E6
Palmares 3,083 .... F6
Paralso 8,446 .... F6
Puerto Cortés 2,070 .... F6
Puntarenas 26,331 .... E6
Quepos 2,155 .... E6
San José (cap.) 215,441 .... F5
San José* 391,107 .... F5
San Marcos 917 .... E6
San Ramón 9,245 .... E5
Santa Cruz 5,777 .... E5
Santo Domingo 5,148 .... F6
Siquirres 4,361 .... F5
Turrialba 12,151 .... F6

(continued on following page)

OTHER FEATURES

Blanca (pt.) F5
Blanco (cape) E6
Blanco (peak) F6
Burica (pt.) F6
Cahuita (pt.) F6
Caño (isl.) F6
Carreta (pt.) F6
Chirripó Grande (mt.) F6
Coronada (bay) F6
Cuilapa Miravalles (vol.) E5
Dulce (gulf) F6
Góngora (mt.) E5
Guionos (pt.) E6
Irazú (mt.) F6
Judas (pt.) E6
Llerena (pt.) F6
Matapalo (cape) F6
Nicoya (gulf) E6
Nicoya (pen.) E6
Papagayo (gulf) E5
Salinas (bay) D5
San Juan (riv.) E5
Santa Elena (cape) D5
Talamanca (range) F6
Velas (cape) D5

EL SALVADOR

CITIES and TOWNS

Acajutla 8,598 .... B4
Ahuachapán 17,242 .... B4
Atiquizaya 7,035 .... C3
Chalatenango 7,633 .... C3
Chinameca 6,303 .... C4
Cojutepeque 20,615 .... C4
Estanzuelas 2,548 .... C4
Ilobasco 6,572 .... C4
Intipucá 3,469 .... D4
Jucuarán 1,443 .... C4
La Libertad C4
La Palma 1,998 .... C3
La Unión 17,207 .... D4
Metapán 7,704 .... C3
Nueva San Salvador 35,106 .... C4
Puerto de la Concordia C4
San Francisco Gotera 4,725 .... C4
San Miguel 59,304 .... D4
San Salvador (cap.) 337,171 .... C4
Santa Ana 96,306 .... C4
Santa Rosa de Lima 5,707 .... D4
San Vicente 18,872 .... C4
Sensuntepeque 7,226 .... C4
Sonsonate 33,562 .... C4
Suchitoto 5,540 .... C4
Texistepeque 1,722 .... C3
Usulután 19,616 .... C4
Zacatecoluca 15,718 .... C4

OTHER FEATURES

Fonseca (gulf) D4
Güija (lake) C3
Lempa (riv.) C4
Remedios (pt.) B4
Santa Ana (mt.) C4

GUATEMALA

CITIES and TOWNS

Amatitlán 15,251 .... B3
Antigua 17,994 .... B3
Asunción Mita 7,477 .... C3
Cahabón 1,344 .... C3
Chajul 4,329 .... B3
Champerico 5,722 .... A3
Chichicastenango 2,635 .... B3
Chimaltenango 12,860 .... B3
Chiquimula 16,126 .... C3
Coatepeque 15,979 .... A3
Cobán 11,418 .... B3
Comalapa 10,980 .... B3
Cubulco 2,021 .... B3
Cuilapa 4,287 .... B3
Cuilco 862 .... B3
Dolores 973 .... C2
El Estor 2,324 .... C3
El Progreso 4,009 .... B3
Escuintla 33,205 .... B3
Flores 1,477 .... C2
Gualán 5,169 .... C3
Guatemala (cap.) 700,538 .... B3
Huehuetenango 12,570 .... B3
Ipala 3,386 .... C3
Iztapa 1,237 .... B4
Jacaltenango 4,517 .... B3
Jalapa 13,788 .... B3
Jutiapa 8,210 .... B3
La Gomera 2,394 .... B3
La Libertad 908 .... B2
Livingston 2,898 .... C3
Los Amates 1,383 .... C3
Masagua 1,178 .... B3
Mazatenango 23,285 .... B3
Momostenango 5,210 .... B3
Morales 2,113 .... C3
Ocós 741 .... A3
Panzós 1,643 .... C3
Puerto Barrios 22,598 .... C3
Quezaltenango 53,021 .... B3
Quezaltepeque 2,222 .... C3
Rabinal 4,625 .... B3
Retalhuleu 19,060 .... B3
Río Hondo 1,416 .... C3
Sacapulas 1,439 .... B3
Salamá 5,529 .... B3
San Andrés 1,066 .... B2
San Felipe 3,210 .... B3
San José 9,402 .... B4
San Luis 1,136 .... C2
San Luis Jilotepeque 6,055 .... C3
San Marcos 5,700 .... B3
San Martín Jilotepeque 3,770 .... B3
San Mateo Ixtatán 1,834 .... B3
San Pedro Carchá 4,465 .... B3
Santa Cruz del Quiché 7,651 .... B3
Santa Rosa de Lima 1,161 .... B3
Sololá 3,960 .... B3
Tacaná 1,280 .... A3
Tejutla 1,205 .... B3
Tikal C2
Totonicapán 8,568 .... B3
Zacapa 12,688 .... C3

OTHER FEATURES

Atitlán (lake) B3
Atitlán (vol.) B3
Azul (riv.) C2
Chixoy (riv.) B2
Güija (lake) C3
Honduras (gulf) D2
Izabal (lake) C3
Minas (mts.) C3
Motagua (riv.) C3
Pasión (riv.) ....
Petén-Itzá (lake) ....
San Pedro (riv.) ....
Sarstún (riv.) ....
Tacaná (vol.) ....
Tajumulco (vol.) ....
Tres Puntas (cape) ....
Usumacinta (riv.) ....

HONDURAS

CITIES and TOWNS

Amapala 2,274 ....
Brus Laguna 933 ....
Catacamas 9,134 ....
Cedros 917 ....
Choloma 961 ....
Choluteca 26,152 ....
Comayagua 15,941 ....
Corquín 2,629 ....
Danlí 10,825 ....
El Dulce Nombre 1,297 ....

Paraíso, Copán 2,164 C3
Paraíso, El
Paraíso 6,709 D4
Porvenir 1,076 D3
Progreso 28,105 D3
Triunfo 2,925 D4
oascorán 996 D4
racias 2,299 C3
uaimaca 3,953 D3
uanaja 1,947 E2
uayape 804 D3
iona 26 E2
acaleapa 1,609 D3
esús de Otoro 2,976 C3
utiapa 1,126 D3
uticalpa 10,075 D3
a Ceiba 38,788 D3
a Esperanza 2,146 C3
a Paz 6,811 D3
imón 1,704 E3
Aanto 689 D3
Aarcala 3,183 C3
Aorazán 4,367 D3
Aorocelí 1,442 D3
Aacaome 6,159 D4
Namasigüe 816 D4
Naranjito 2,770 C3
Nueva Armenia 670 D4
Nueva Ocotepeque 4,724 C3
Olanchito 7,411 D3
Omoa 9,161 C3
Pespire 1,895○ D4
Puerto Castilla D3
Puerto Cortés 25,817 D2
Puerto Lempira 727 F3
Roatán 1,943 D2
Sabanagrande 1,446 D4
Salado D3
San Francisco 1,557 D3
San Francisco de la Paz 2,291 D3
San Juan de Flores 1,184 D3
San Luis 2,237 C3
San Marcos 2,499 C3
San Pedro Sula 150,991 C3
Santa Bárbara 5,883 C3
Santa Cruz de Yojoa 1,848 D3
Santa Rita 5,298 D3
Santa Rosa de Aguán 1,622 E2
Santa Rosa de Copán 12,413 C3
Siguatepeque 12,456 D3

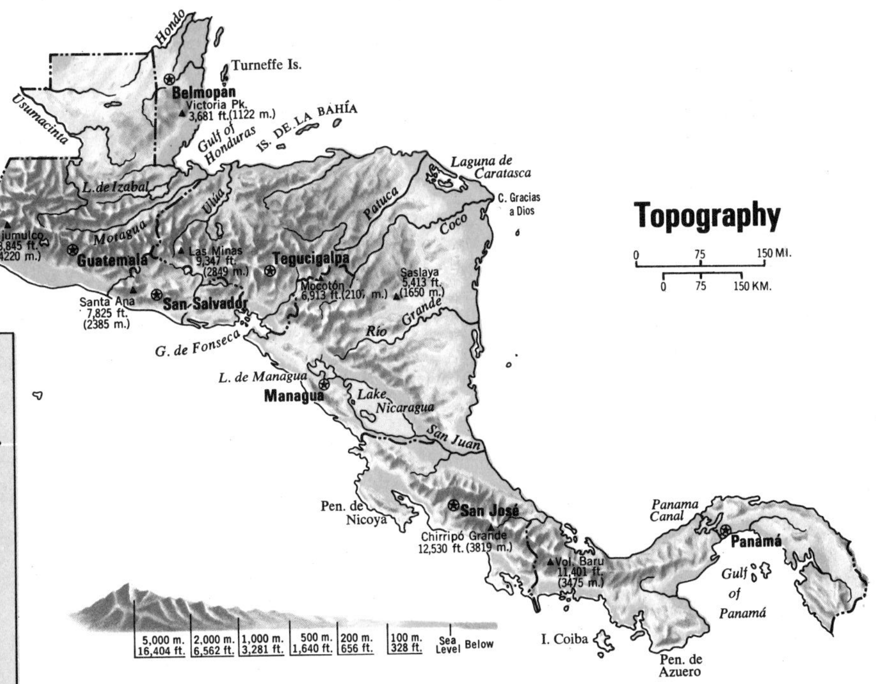

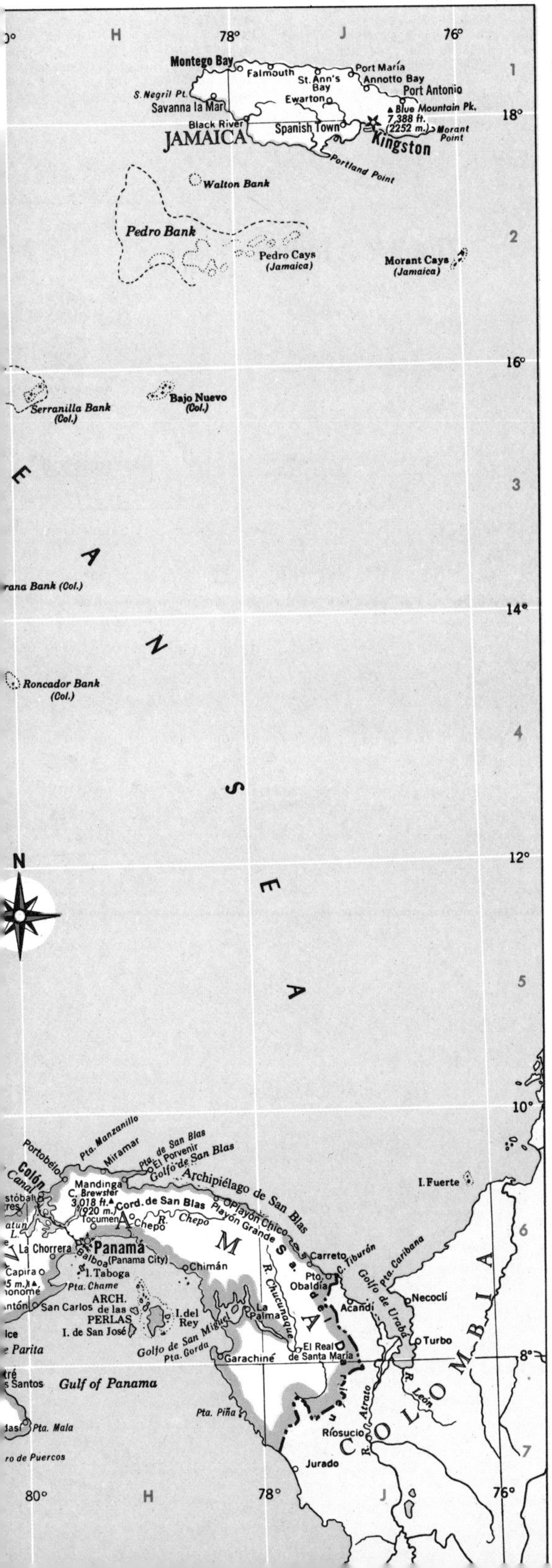

Sinuapa 831 C3
Sonaguera 2,264 D3
Sulaco 1,121 D3
Tegucigalpa (cap.) 273,894 D3
Tegucigalpa* 305,387 D3
Tela 19,055 D3
Teupasenti 2,003 D3
Tocoa 2,803 E3
Trinidad 1,598 C3
Trujillo 3,961 E3
Utila 1,177 D2
Villa de San Antonio 2,359 D3
Yorito 770 D3
Yoro 4,449 D3
Yuscarán 1,835 D4

OTHER FEATURES

Aguán (riv.) D3
Bahía (isls.) D2
Bonacca (Guanaja) (isl.) E2
Brus (lag.) E2
Camarón (cape) E2
Caratasca (cays) F2
Caratasca (lag.) F3
Choluteca (riv.) D4
Cisne (isls.) F2
Coco (riv.) E3
Colón (mts.) E3
Esperanza (mts.) E3
Falso (cape) F3
Fonseca (gulf) D4
Gorda (bank) F3
Guanaja (isl.) E2
Honduras (cape) E2
Honduras (gulf) D2
Patuca (pt.) E3
Patuca (riv.) E3
Paulaya (riv.) E3
Pija, Sierra de (mts.) D3
Roatán (isl.) D2
San Pablo, Sierra (mts.) E3
Segovia (Coco) (riv.) E3
Sico (riv.) E3
Sulaco (riv.) D3
Swan (Cisne) (isls.) F2
Ulúa (riv.) D3
Utila (isl.) D2
Wanks (Coco) (riv.) E3
Yojoa (lake) D3

NICARAGUA

CITIES and TOWNS

Acoyapa 2,588 E5
Barra de Río Grande F4
Bluefields 14,252 F4
Boaco 6,372 E4
Bonanza E4
Bragman's Bluff (Puerto Cabezas) 5,457 F3
Cabo Gracias a Dios○ 3,846 F3
Camoapa 4,385 E4
Chichigalpa 14,498 D4
Chinandega 30,441 D4
Ciudad Darío 5,304 D4
Condega 3,414 D4
Corinto 13,404 D4
Diriamba 10,085 D5
El Jícaro 1,669 E4
El Limón E4
El Realejo 2,229 D4
El Sauce 3,202 D4
El Viejo 8,507 D4
Esquipulas 2,232 E4
Estelí 20,222 D4
Granada 34,976 E5
Greytown (San Juan del Norte) 294 F5
Jalapa 3,633 E4
Jinotega 9,506 E4
Jinotepe 12,473 D5
Juigalpa 8,497 E4
La Cruz 150 E4
La Libertad 1,286 E4
La Paz Central 6,175 D4
La Paz de Oriente 957 E5
La Trinidad 3,548 D4
León 55,625 D4
Managua (cap.) 398,514 D4
Managua* 404,634 D4
Masatepe 6,307 D5
Masaya 30,753 D5
Matagalpa 21,385 E4
Mateare 1,405 D4
Morrito 368 E5
Moyogalpa 1,551 E5
Muy Muy 1,373 E4
Nagarote 7,185 D4
Nandaime 5,631 E5
Ocotal, Segovia 8,215 D4
Poneloya D4
Prinzapolka 8,979 F4
Puerto Cabezas 5,457 F3
Quilalí 1,245 E4
Rama 1,341 E4
Rivas 10,125 E5
San Carlos 2,022 E5
San Jorge 2,874 E5
San Juan del Norte 294 F5
San Juan del Sur 2,393 D5
San Miguelito 1,312 E5
San Rafael del Norte 1,938 E4
San Rafael del Sur 2,914 D5
San Ramón 477 E4
Santo Domingo 1,949 E4
Santo Tomás 2,309 E5
Siuna E4
Somotillo 1,864 D4
Somoto 5,847 D4
Telpaneca 991 D4
Terrabona 904 E4
Teustepe 1,060 E4
Tipitapa 5,758 E4
Waspán 1,246 E3

OTHER FEATURES

Coco (riv.) E3
Cosegüina (pt.) D4
Dariense, Cordillera (range) E4
Dipilto, Cordillera (range) D4
Escondido (riv.) F4
Fonseca (gulf) D4
Gorda (pt.) F5
Gracias a Dios (cape) F3
Grande (riv.) E4
Great Corn (isl.) F4
Huapí (mts.) E4
Isabelia, Cordillera (range) E4
King (cays) F4
Kukalaya (riv.) F4
Little Corn (isl.) F4
Maíz Grande (Great Corn) (isl.) F4
Maíz Pequeña (Little Corn) (isl.) F4
Managua (lake) E4
Miskitos (cays) F3
Monkey (pt.) F5
Mosquitos, Costa de (reg.) E4
Nicaragua (lake) E5
Ometepe (isl.) E5
Pearl (cays) F4
Perlas (pt.) F4
Prinzapolca (riv.) F4
Salinas (bay) D5
San Juan (riv.) E5
San Juan del Norte (bay) F5
Solentiname (isls.) E5
Tuma (riv.) E4
Tyra (cays) F4
Waspuk (riv.) E3
Wawa (riv.) E3
Zapatera (isl.) E5

PANAMA

CITIES and TOWNS

Aguadulce 10,659 G6
Alanje 866 F6
Almirante 4,664 F6
Antón 4,259 G6
Bajo Boquete 2,831 F6
Balboa 1,952 H6
Bocas del Toro 2,515 F6
Cañazas 1,526 G6
Capira 1,749 G6
Changuinola 9,528 F6
Chepo 4,529 H6
Chiriquí Grande F6
Chitré 17,156 G7
Coclé del Norte G6
Colón 59,832 H6
Cristóbal⊙ 7,959 G6
David 50,621 F6
Dolega 1,019 F6
El Real de Santa María 912 J6
Garachiné 1,116 H6
Gualaca 1,510 F6
Horconcitos 1,090 F6
La Chorrera 36,971 H6
La Concepción 10,460 F6
La Palma 1,634 H6
La Pintada 1,100 G6
Las Palmas 738 G6
Las Tablas 5,230 G7
Los Santos 4,644 G7
Mandinga 81 H6
Montijo 1,152 G6
Natá 5,603 G6
Nuevo Chagres 306 G6
Ocú 2,353 G7
Panamá (cap.) 388,638 H6
Panamá* 498,624 H6
Parita 1,010 00
Pedasí 934 G7
Penonomé 7,389 G6
Playón Chico 1,395 H6
Portobelo 551 H6
Puerto Armuelles 12,488 F6
Puerto Obaldía 491 J6
San Francisco 990 G6
Santa Fe 490 G6
Santiago 21,809 G6
Soná 4,471 G6
Tocumen⊙ 21,745 H6
Tolé 1,052 G6
Tonosí 891 G7

OTHER FEATURES

Azuero (pen.) G7
Bastimentos (isl.) G6
Brewster, Cerro (mt.) H6
Burica, Punta (cape) F6
Cébaco (isl.) G7
Chepo (riv.) H6
Chiriquí (gulf) F7
Chiriquí (lag.) G6
Chucunaque (riv.) J6
Coiba, Isla de (isl.) F7
Colón, Isla de (isl.) G6
Contreras (isls.) F7
Darién (mts.) J6
Escudo de Veraguas (isl.) G6
Gatun (lake) G6
Gorda (pt.) H6
Jicarón (isl.) F7
Ladrones (isls.) F7
Manzanillo (pt.) H6
Montijo (gulf) G7
Mosquitos, Golfo de los (gulf) G6
Panama (gulf) H7
Pando, Cerro (mt.) F6
Parida (isl.) F6
Parita (bay) G6
Perlas (arch.) H6
Puercos, Morro de (head) H7
Rey (isl.) H6
Rincón (pt.) G6
San Blas, Golfo de (bay) H6
San Blas, Pta. de (pt.) H6
San Blas, Cordillera de (mts.) H6
San José (isl.) H6
San Miguel, Golfo de (bay) H6
Santiago, Cerro (mt.) G6
Secas (isls.) G7
Tabasará (mts.) G6
Taboga (isl.) H6
Tiburón (pt.) J6
Valiente (pen.) G6

*City and suburbs.
○Population of sub-district or division.
⊙Population of district.

BAHAMAS

AREA 5,382 sq. mi. (13,939 sq. km.)
POPULATION 223,455
CAPITAL Nassau
LARGEST CITY Nassau
HIGHEST POINT Mt. Alvernia 206 ft. (63 m.)
MONETARY UNIT Bahamian dollar
MAJOR LANGUAGE English
MAJOR RELIGIONS Roman Catholicism, Protestantism

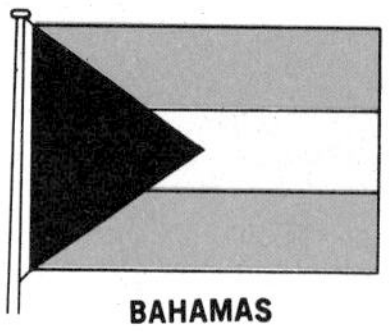
BAHAMAS

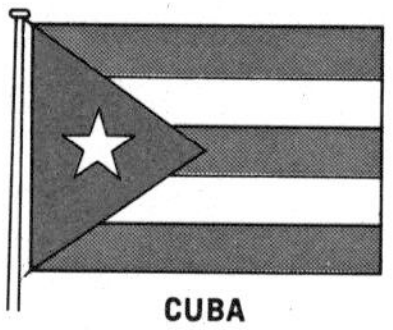
CUBA

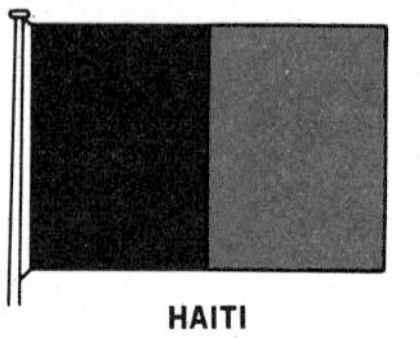
HAITI

DOMINICAN REPUBLIC

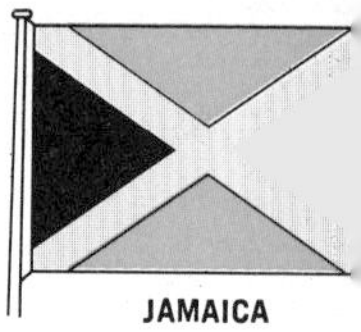
JAMAICA

CUBA

AREA 44,206 sq. mi. (114,494 sq. km.)
POPULATION 9,706,369
CAPITAL Havana
LARGEST CITY Havana
HIGHEST POINT Pico Turquino 6,561 ft. (2,000 m.)
MONETARY UNIT Cuban peso
MAJOR LANGUAGE Spanish
MAJOR RELIGION Roman Catholicism

JAMAICA

AREA 4,411 sq. mi. (11,424 sq. km.)
POPULATION 2,161,000
CAPITAL Kingston
LARGEST CITY Kingston
HIGHEST POINT Blue Mountain Peak 7,402 ft. (2,256 m.)
MONETARY UNIT Jamaican dollar
MAJOR LANGUAGE English
MAJOR RELIGIONS Protestantism, Roman Catholicism

GRENADA

AREA 133 sq. mi. (344 sq. km.)
POPULATION 110,000
CAPITAL St. George's
LARGEST CITY St. George's
HIGHEST POINT Mt. St. Catherine 2,757 ft. (840 m.)
MONETARY UNIT East Caribbean dollar
MAJOR LANGUAGES English, French patois
MAJOR RELIGIONS Roman Catholicism, Protestantism

DOMINICA

AREA 290 sq. mi. (751 sq. km.)
POPULATION 74,089
CAPITAL Roseau
HIGHEST POINT Morne Diablotin 4,747 ft. (1,447 m.)
MONETARY UNIT Dominican dollar
MAJOR LANGUAGES English, French patois
MAJOR RELIGIONS Roman Catholicism, Protestantism

SAINT VINCENT AND THE GRENADINES

AREA 150 sq. mi. (388 sq. km.)
POPULATION 124,000
CAPITAL Kingstown
HIGHEST POINT Soufrière 4,000 ft. (1,219
MONETARY UNIT East Caribbean dollar
MAJOR LANGUAGE English
MAJOR RELIGIONS Protestantism, Roman Catholicism

HAITI

AREA 10,694 sq. mi. (27,697 sq. km.)
POPULATION 5,009,000
CAPITAL Port-au-Prince
LARGEST CITY Port-au-Prince
HIGHEST POINT Pic La Selle 8,793 ft. (2,680 m.)
MONETARY UNIT gourde
MAJOR LANGUAGES Creole French, French
MAJOR RELIGION Roman Catholicism

TRINIDAD AND TOBAGO

AREA 1,980 sq. mi. (5,128 sq. km.)
POPULATION 1,067,108
CAPITAL Port of Spain
LARGEST CITY Port of Spain
HIGHEST POINT Mt. Aripo 3,084 ft. (940 m.)
MONETARY UNIT Trinidad and Tobago dollar
MAJOR LANGUAGES English, Hindi
MAJOR RELIGIONS Roman Catholicism, Protestantism, Hinduism, Islam

DOMINICAN REPUBLIC

AREA 18,704 sq. mi. (48,443 sq. km.)
POPULATION 5,431,000
CAPITAL Santo Domingo
LARGEST CITY Santo Domingo
HIGHEST POINT Pico Duarte 10,417 ft. (3,175 m.)
MONETARY UNIT Dominican peso
MAJOR LANGUAGE Spanish
MAJOR RELIGION Roman Catholicism

BARBADOS

AREA 166 sq. mi. (430 sq. km.)
POPULATION 249,000
CAPITAL Bridgetown
LARGEST CITY Bridgetown
HIGHEST POINT Mt. Hillaby 1,104 ft. (336 m.)
MONETARY UNIT Barbadian dollar
MAJOR LANGUAGE English
MAJOR RELIGION Protestantism

SAINT LUCIA

AREA 238 sq. mi. (616 sq. km.)
POPULATION 115,783
CAPITAL Castries
HIGHEST POINT Mt. Gimie 3,117 ft. (950
MONETARY UNIT East Caribbean dollar
MAJOR LANGUAGES English, French patoi
MAJOR RELIGIONS Roman Catholicism, Protestantism

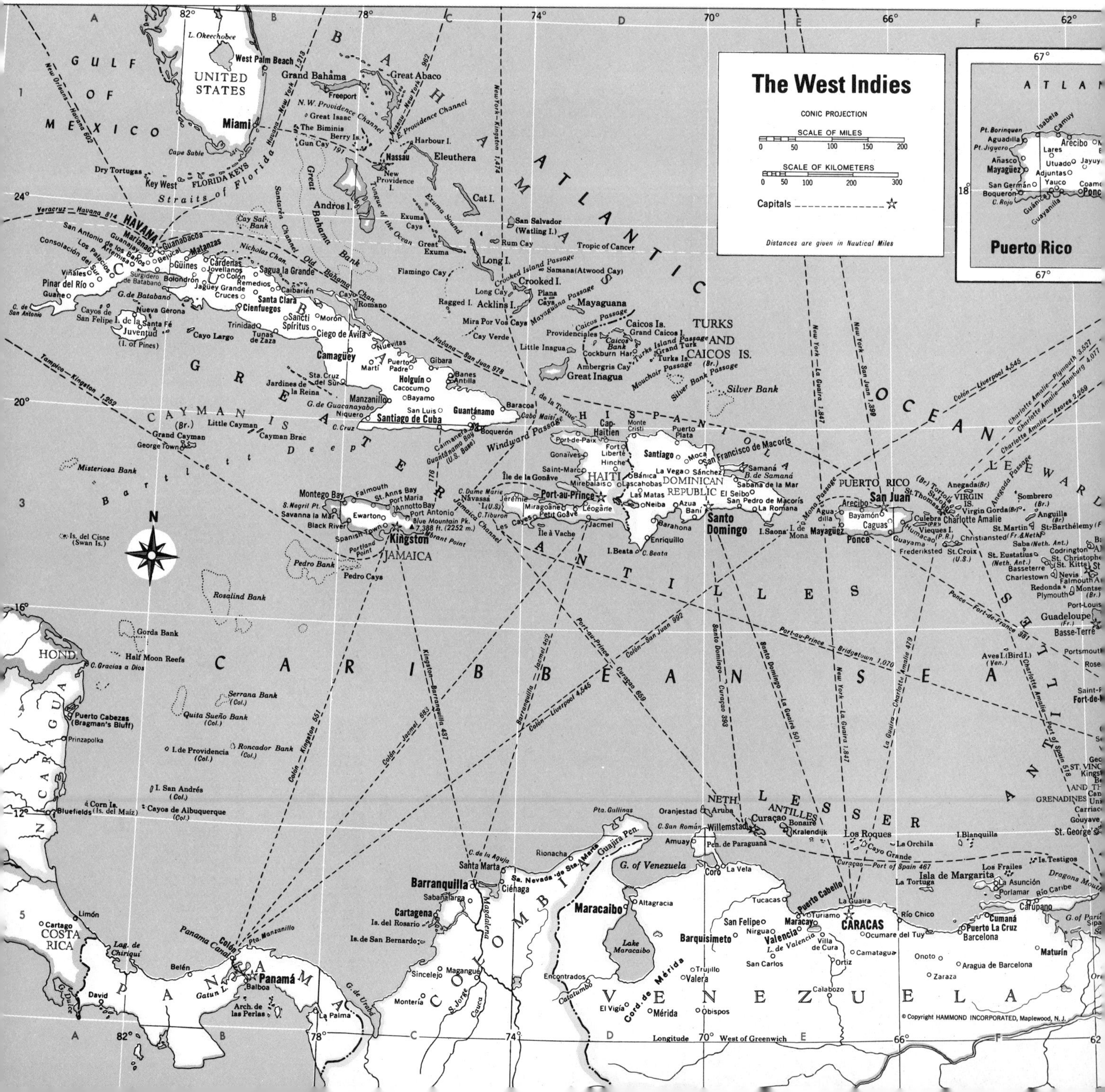

BARBADOS

TRINIDAD & TOBAGO

DOMINICA

ANTIGUA AND BARBUDA

·171 sq. mi. (443 sq. km.)
ULATION 72,000
ITAL St. John's
EST POINT Boggy Peak 1,319 ft. (402 m.)
ETARY UNIT East Caribbean dollar
OR LANGUAGE English
OR RELIGION Protestantism

Agriculture, Industry and Resources

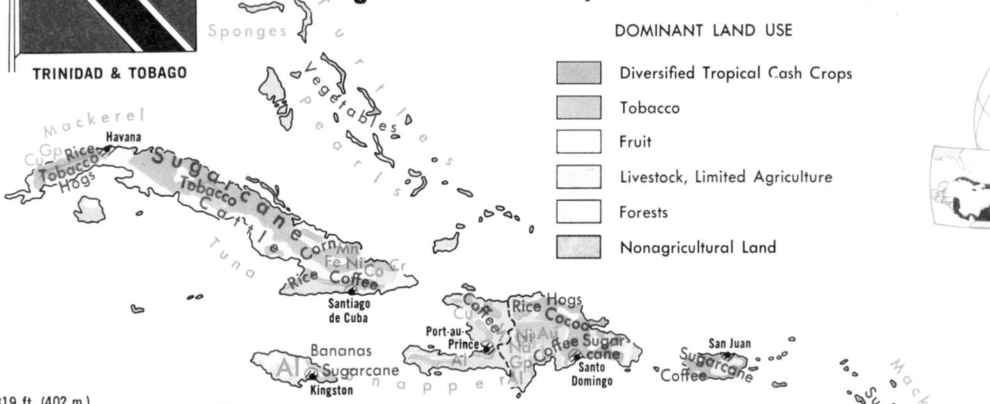

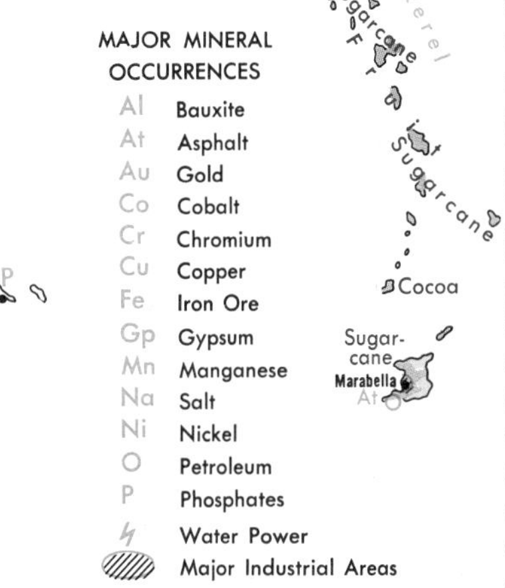

SAINT LUCIA

SAINT VINCENT & THE GRENADINES

GRENADA

ANTIGUA AND BARBUDA

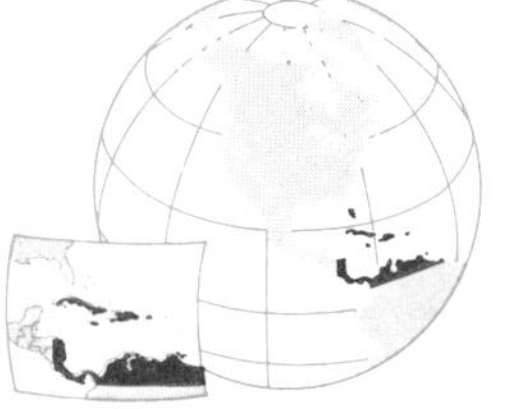

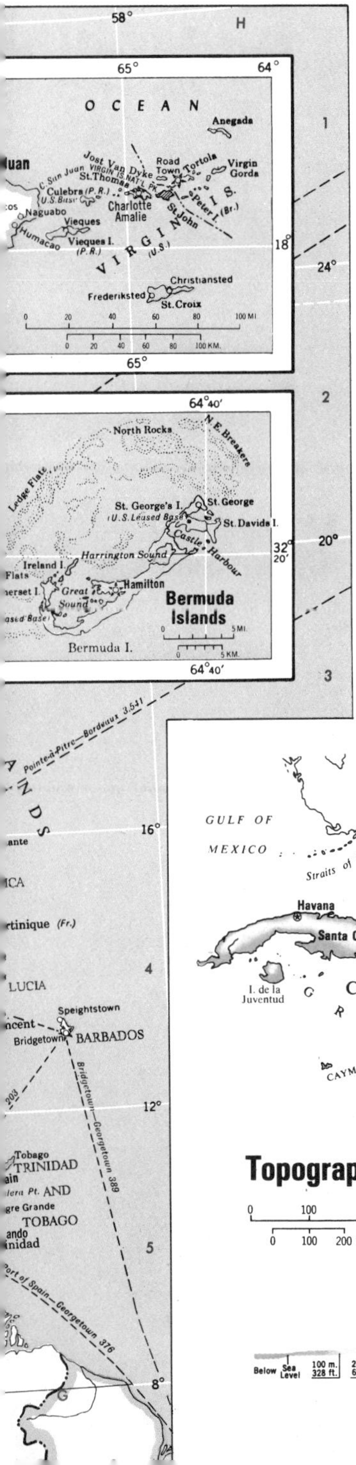

⊙Population of district.
●Population of municipality.

Topography

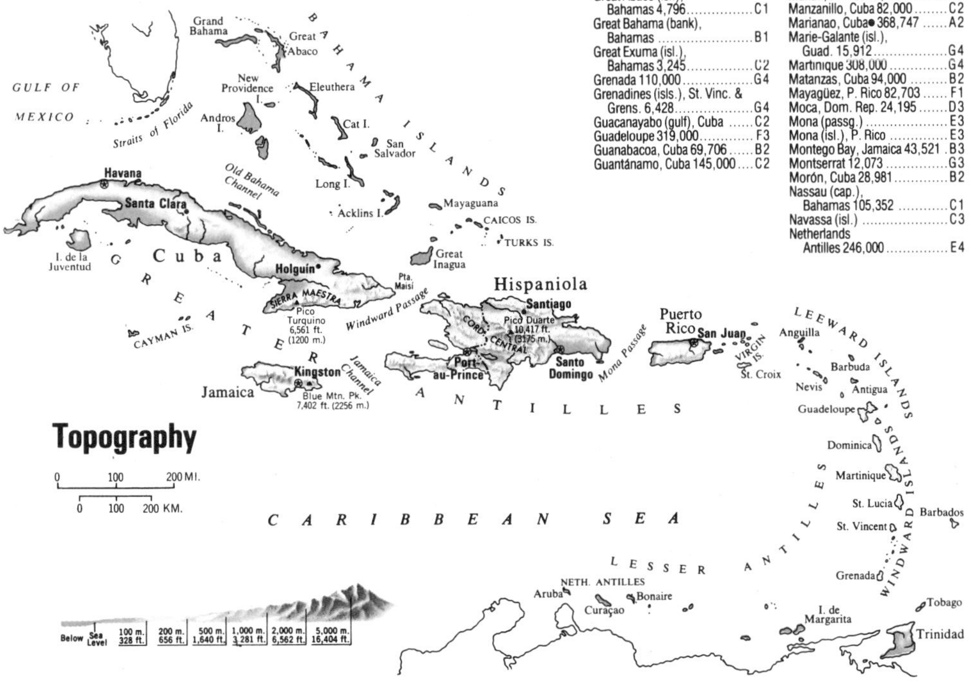

United States
POLYCONIC PROJECTION
SCALE OF MILES
SCALE OF KILOMETERS
Capitals of Countries
State Capitals
International Boundaries
© Copyright HAMMOND INCORPORATED, Maplewood, N. J.
Longitude 95° West of Greenwich 90°
PACIFIC OCEAN
GULF OF MEXICO
CANADA
MEXICO
Gulf of California
ARCTIC OCEAN
PACIFIC OCEAN
Same scale as Alaska map
Tropic of Cancer

Akron, Ohio‡ 660,328 .... K2
Alabama (state) 3,890,061 .... J4
Alaska (state) 400,481 .... C5
Alaska (gulf), Alaska D6
Alaska (range), Alaska C6
Albany (cap.), N.Y.‡ 795,019 .... M2
Albuquerque, N. Mex.‡ 454,499 .... E3
Aleutian (isls.), Alaska D6
Allentown, Pa.‡ 636,714 .... L2
Anchorage, Alaska‡ 173,017 .... D6
Annapolis (cap.), Md. 31,740 .... L3
Ann Arbor, Mich.‡ 264,748 .... K2
Appalachian (mts.) K3
Appleton, Wis.‡ 291,325 .... J2
Arizona (state) 2,717,866 .... D4
Arkansas (state) 2,285,513 .... H3
Arkansas (riv.) H3
Atlanta (cap.), Ga.‡ 2,029,618 .... K4
Atlantic City, N.J.‡ 194,119 .... M3
Attu (isl.), Alaska D6
Augusta, Ga.‡ 327,372 .... K4
Augusta (cap.), Maine 21,819 .... N2
Austin (cap.), Texas‡ 536,450 .... G4
Bakersfield, Calif.‡ 403,089 .... C3
Baltimore, Md.‡ 2,174,023 .... L3
Baton Rouge (cap.), La.‡ 493,973 .... H4
Beaumont, Texas‡ 375,497 .... H4
Bering (sea), Alaska C6
Bering (str.), Alaska C5
Bighorn (riv.) E2
Binghamton, N.Y.‡ 301,336 .... L2
Birmingham, Ala.‡ 847,360 .... J4
Bismarck (cap.), N. Dak.‡ 79,988 .... G1
Bitterroot (range) D1
Black Hills (mts.) F2
Boise (cap.), Idaho‡ 173,076 .... C2
Borah (peak), Idaho D2
Boston (cap.), Mass.‡ 2,763,357 .... M2
Bridgeport, Conn.‡ 395,455 .... M2
Brazos (riv.), Texas G4
Brooks (range), Alaska C5
Buffalo, N.Y.‡ 1,242,573 .... L2
California (state) 23,668,562 .... B3
Canadian (riv.) F3
Canaveral (Kennedy) (cape), Fla. L5
Canton, Ohio‡ 404,421 .... K2
Cape Fear (riv.), N.C. L4
Carson City (cap.), Nev. 32,022 .... C3
Cascade (range) B1
Cedar Rapids, Iowa‡ 169,775 .... H2
Champlain (lake) M2
Charleston, S.C.‡ 430,301 .... L4
Charleston (cap.), W. Va.‡ 269,595 .... K3
Charlotte, N.C.‡ 637,218 .... L3
Chattahoochee (riv.) K4
Chattanooga, Tenn.‡ 426,540 .... J3
Chesapeake (bay) L3
Cheyenne (cap.), Wyo. 47,283 .... E2
Cheyenne (riv.) F2
Chicago, Ill.‡ 7,102,328 .... J2
Cimarron (riv.) G3
Cincinnati, Ohio‡ 1,401,403 .... K3
Cleveland, Ohio‡ 1,898,720 .... K2
Coast (ranges) B2
Cod (cape), Mass. N2
Colorado (state) 2,888,834 .... E3
Colorado (riv.) D4
Colorado (riv.), Texas G4
Colorado Springs, Colo.‡ 317,458 .... F3
Columbia (cap.), S.C.‡ 408,176 .... K4
Columbia (riv.) B1
Columbus, Ga.‡ 239,196 .... K4
Columbus (cap.), Ohio‡ 1,093,293 .... K3
Concord (cap.), N.H. 30,400 .... M2
Connecticut (state) 3,107,576 .... M2
Connecticut (riv.) M2
Corpus Christi, Texas‡ 326,228 .... G5
Cumberland (riv.) J3
Dallas, Texas‡ 2,974,878 .... G4
Davenport, Iowa‡ 383,958 .... H2
Dayton, Ohio‡ 830,070 .... K3
Death Valley (depr.), Calif. C3
Delaware (state) 595,225 .... L3
Delaware (bay) M3
Denver (cap.), Colo.‡ 1,619,921 .... F3
Des Moines (cap.), Iowa‡ 338,048 .... H2
Detroit, Mich.‡ 4,352,762 .... K2
District of Columbia 637,651 .... L3
Dover (cap.), Del. 23,512 .... L3
Duluth, Minn.‡ 266,650 .... H1
Durham, N.C.‡ 530,673 .... L3
Elbert (mt.), Colo. E3
El Paso, Texas‡ 479,899 .... E4
Erie, Pa.‡ 279,780 .... K2
Erie (lake) K2
Eugene, Oreg.‡ 275,226 .... B2
Evansville, Ind.‡ 309,408 .... J3
Everglades, The (swamp), Fla. K5
Fayetteville, N.C.‡ 247,160 .... L3
Flint, Mich.‡ 521,589 .... K2
Florida (state) 9,739,992 .... K5
Florida (keys), Fla. K6
Fort Smith, Ark.‡ 203,269 .... H3
Fort Wayne, Ind.‡ 382,961 .... J2
Fort Worth, Texas 385,141 .... G4
Frankfort (cap.), Ky. 25,973 .... K3
Fresno, Calif.‡ 515,013 .... C3
Galveston, Texas‡ 195,940 .... H5
Gary, Ind.‡ 642,781 .... J2
Georgia (state) 5,464,265 .... K4
Gila (riv.) D4
Glacier Nat'l Park, Mont. D1
Golden Gate (chan.), Calif. B3
Grand Canyon Nat'l Park, Ariz. D3
Grand Rapids, Mich.‡ 601,680 .... K2
Great Salt (lake), Utah D2
Greensboro, N.C.‡ 827,385 .... K3
Greenville, S.C.‡ 568,758 .... K4
Hamilton, Ohio‡ 258,787 .... K3
Harrisburg (cap.), Pa.‡ 446,072 .... L2
Hartford (cap.), Conn.‡ 726,114 .... M2
Hatteras (cape), N.C. M3
Havasu (lake) D4
Hawaii (state) 965,000 .... F5
Hawaii (isl.), Hawaii F6
Helena (cap.), Mont. 23,938 .... D1
Honolulu (cap.), Hawaii‡ 762,874 .... F5
Houston, Texas‡ 2,905,350 .... G5
Huntington, W. Va.‡ 311,350 .... K3
Huntsville, Ala.‡ 308,593 .... J4
Huron (lake), Mich. K2
Idaho (state) 943,935 .... D2
Illinois (state) 11,418,461 .... J3
Indiana (state) 5,490,179 .... J3
Aleutian (isls.), Alaska D6
Iowa (state) 2,913,387 .... H2
Jackson (cap.), Miss.‡ 320,425 .... J4
Jacksonville, Fla.‡ 737,519 .... K4
Jefferson City (cap.), Mo. 33,619 .... H3
Jersey City, N.J.‡ 556,972 .... M2
Johnstown, Pa.‡ 664,506 .... L2
Juneau (cap.), Alaska 19,528 .... E6
Kalamazoo, Mich.‡ 279,192 .... J2
Kansas (state) 2,363,208 .... G3
Kansas City, Kans.-Mo.‡ 1,327,020 .... G3
Kauai (isl.), Hawaii E5
Kentucky (state) 3,661,433 .... J3
Kentucky (lake) J3
Knoxville, Tenn.‡ 476,517 .... K3
Lancaster, Pa.‡ 362,346 .... L2
Lansing (cap.), Mich.‡ 476,517 .... K2
Las Vegas, Nev.‡ 461,816 .... C3
Lawrence, Mass.‡ 281,981 .... M2
Lexington, Ky.‡ 318,136 .... K3
Lima, Ohio‡ 218,244 .... K2
Lincoln (cap.), Nebr.‡ 192,884 .... G2
Little Rock (cap.), Ark.‡ 393,494 .... H4
Long (isl.), N.Y. M2
Long Beach, Calif. 361,334 .... C4
Los Angeles, Calif.‡ 7,477,657 .... C4
Louisiana (state) 4,203,972 .... H4
Louisvillle, Ky.‡ 906,240 .... J3
Lowell, Mass.‡ 233,410 .... M2
Lubbock, Texas‡ 211,651 .... F4
Macon, Ga.‡ 254,623 .... K4
Madison (cap.), Wis.‡ 323,545 .... H2
Maine (state) 1,124,660 .... N1
Maryland (state) 4,216,446 .... L3
Massachusetts (state) 5,737,037 .... M2
Maui (isl.), Hawaii F5
Mauna Kea (mt.), Hawaii G6
Mauna Loa (mt.), Hawaii G6
May (cape), N.J. M3
McKinley (mt.), Alaska D5
Memphis, Tenn.‡ 912,887 .... J3
Mendocino (cape), Calif. A2
Mexico (gulf) J5
Miami, Fla.‡ 1,625,979 .... K5
Michigan (state) 9,258,344 .... J1
Michigan (lake) J2
Milwaukee, Wis.‡ 1,397,143 .... J2
Minneapolis, Minn.‡ 2,114,256 .... H1
Minnesota (state) 4,077,148 .... H1
Mississippi (state) 2,520,638 .... J4
Mississippi (riv.) H4
Missouri (state) 4,917,444 .... H3
Missouri (riv.) H3
Mitchell (mt.), N.C. K3
Mobile, Ala.‡ 442,819 .... J4
Montana (state) 786,690 .... E1
Montgomery (cap.), Ala.‡ 272,687 .... J4
Nantucket (isl.), Mass. N2
Nashville (cap.), Tenn.‡ 850,505 .... J3
Nebraska (state) 1,570,006 .... F2
Nevada (state) 799,184 .... C3
Newark, N.J.‡ 1,965,304 .... L2
New Hampshire (state) 920,610 .... M2
New Haven, Conn.‡ 417,592 .... M2
New Jersey (state) 7,364,158 .... M3
New Mexico (state) 1,299,968 .... E4
New Orleans, La.‡ 1,186,725 .... H5
Newport News, Va.‡ 364,449 .... L3
New York (state) 17,557,288 .... L2
New York, N.Y.‡ 9,119,737 .... M2
Norfolk, Va.‡ 806,691 .... L3
North Carolina (state) 5,874,429 .... L3
North Dakota (state) 652,695 .... F1
Oahu (isl.), Hawaii F5
Oakland, Calif.‡ 3,252,721 .... B3
Ohio (state) 10,797,419 .... K2
Ohio (riv.) J3
Oklahoma (state) 3,025,266 .... G3
Oklahoma City (cap.), Okla.‡ 834,088 .... G3
Olympia (cap.), Wash.‡ 124,264 .... B1
Olympic Nat'l Park, Wash. A1
Omaha, Nebr.‡ 570,399 .... G2
Ontario (lake), N.Y. L2
Oregon (state) 2,632,663 .... B2
Orlando, Fla.‡ 700,699 .... K5
Ozark (mts.) H3
Paterson, N.J.‡ 447,585 .... M2
Pennsylvania (state) L2
Pensacola, Fla.‡ 289,782 .... J4
Peoria, Ill.‡ 365,864 .... J2
Philadelphia, Pa.‡ 4,716,818 .... M2
Phoenix (cap.), Ariz.‡ 1,508,030 .... D4
Pierre (cap.), S. Dak. 11,793 .... F2
Pikes (peak), Colo. E3
Pittsburgh, Pa.‡ 2,263,894 .... L2
Platte (riv.), Nebr. G2
Pontchartrain (lake), La. J5
Portland, Maine‡ 183,625 .... N2
Portland, Oreg.‡ 1,242,187 .... B1
Potomac (riv.) L3
Providence (cap.), R.I.‡ 919,216 .... M2
Racine, Wis.‡ 173,132 .... J2
Raleigh (cap.), N.C.‡ 530,673 .... L3
Rainier (mt.), Wash. B1
Reading, Pa.‡ 312,509 .... L2
Red (riv.) H4
Red River of the North (riv.) G1
Rhode Island (state) 947,154 .... M2
Richmond (cap.), Va.‡ 632,015 .... L3
Rio Grande (riv.) F5
Roanoke, Va.‡ 218,244 .... K3
Rochester, N.Y.‡ 971,079 .... L2
Rockford, Ill.‡ 279,514 .... J2
Rocky (mts.) E3
Sacramento (cap.), Calif.‡ 1,014,002 .... B3
Saginaw, Mich.‡ 224,548 .... K2
Saint Clair (lake), Mich. K2
Saint Lawrence (riv.), N.Y. N1
Saint Louis, Mo.‡ 2,355,276 .... H3

AREA 3,623,420 sq. mi. (9,384,658 sq. km.)
POPULATION 226,504,825
CAPITAL Washington
LARGEST CITY New York
HIGHEST POINT Mt. McKinley 20,320 ft. (6,194 m.)
MONETARY UNIT U.S. dollar
MAJOR LANGUAGE English
MAJOR RELIGIONS Protestantism, Roman Catholicism, Judaism

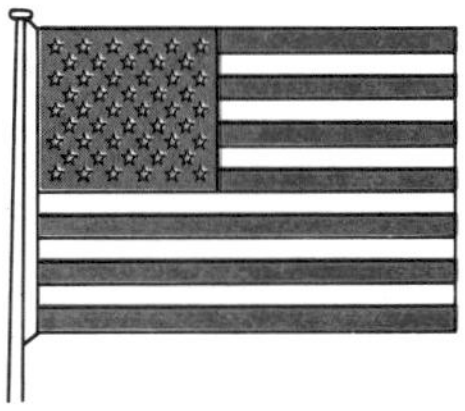

Population Distribution

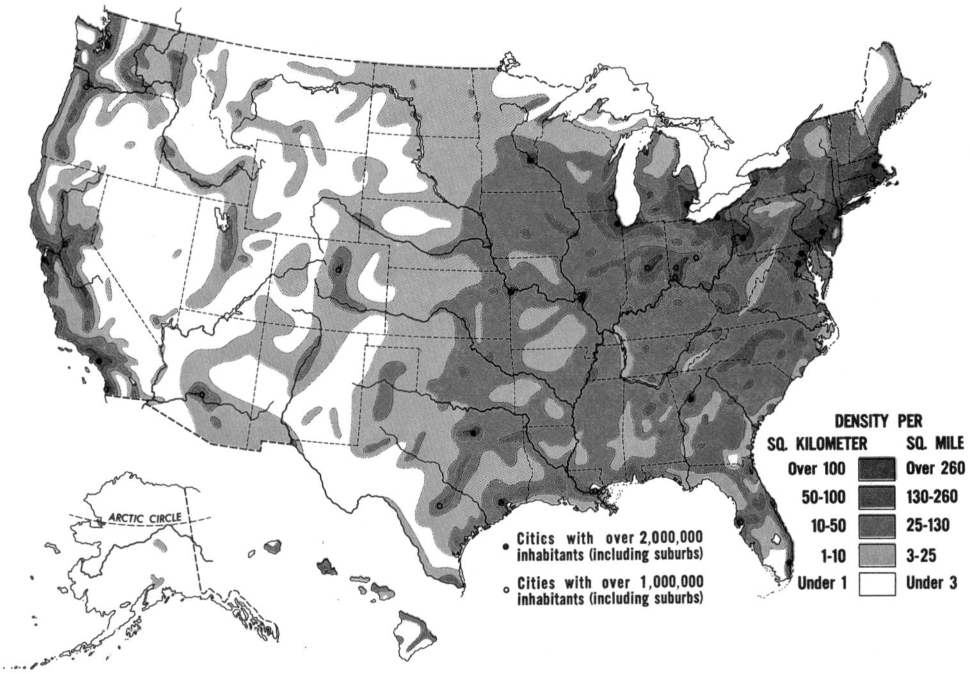

Vegetation

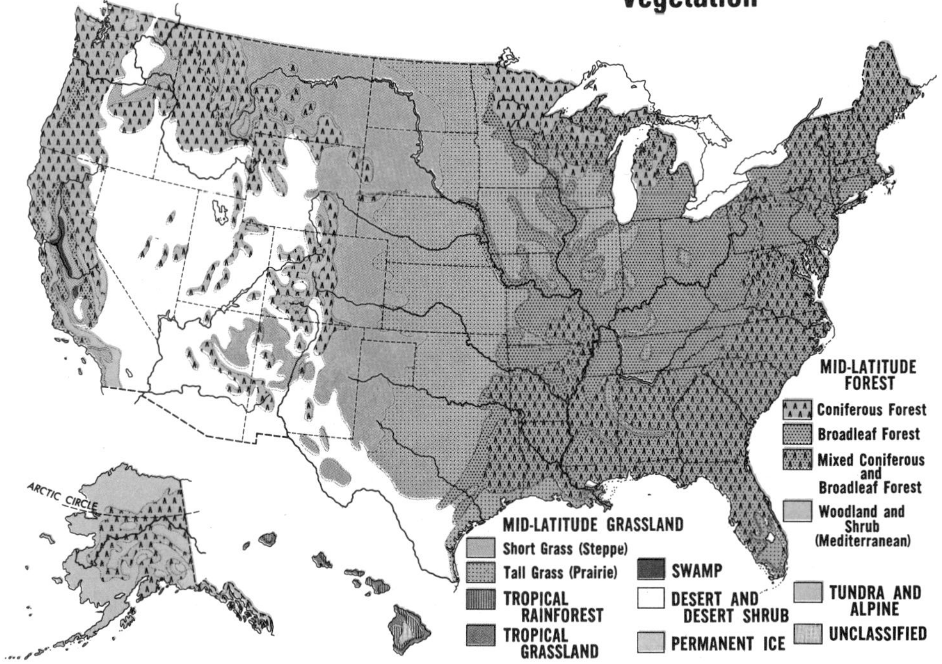

Saint Paul (cap.), Minn. 270,230 .... H1
Sakakawea (lake), N. Dak. F1
Salem (cap.), Oreg.‡ 249,895 .... B1
Salinas, Calif.‡ 290,444 .... B3
Salt Lake City (cap.), Utah‡ 936,255 .... D2
Salton Sea (lake), Calif. C4
San Antonio, Texas‡ 1,071,954 .... G5
San Bernardino, Calif.‡ 1,557,080 .... C4
San Diego, Calif.‡ 1,861,846 .... C4
San Francisco, Calif.‡ 325,721 .... B3
San Joaquin (riv.), Calif. C3
San Jose, Calif.‡ 1,295,071 .... B3
Santa Ana, Calif.‡ 1,931,570 .... C4
Santa Barbara, Calif.‡ 298,660 .... C4
Santa Fe (cap.), N. Mex. 48,899 .... E3
Savannah, Ga.‡ 228,178 .... K4
Scranton, Pa. 88,117 .... L2
Seattle, Wash.‡ 1,606,765 .... B1
Shasta (mt.), Calif. B2
Shreveport, La.‡ 376,646 .... H4
Sierra Nevada (mts.) B3
Snake (riv.) C1
South Bend, Ind.‡ 280,772 .... J2
Spokane, Wash.‡ 341,835 .... C1
South Carolina (state) 3,119,208 .... K4
South Dakota (state) 690,178 .... F2
Springfield (cap.), Ill.‡ 187,338 .... H3
Springfield, Mass.‡ 530,668 .... M2
Springfield, Mo.‡ 207,704 .... H3
Springfield, Ohio‡ 183,885 .... K2
Stockton, Calif.‡ 347,342 .... B3
Superior (lake) J1
Syracuse, N.Y.‡ 642,375 .... L2
Tacoma, Wash.‡ 485,643 .... B1
Tahoe (lake) C3
Tallahassee (cap.), Fla.‡ 159,542 .... K4
Tampa, Fla.‡ 1,569,492 .... K5
Tennessee (state) 4,590,750 .... J3
Terre Haute, Ind.‡ 176,583 .... J3
Texas (state) 14,228,383 .... G4
Toledo, Ohio‡ 791,599 .... K2
Topeka (cap.), Kans.‡ 185,442 .... G3
Trenton (cap.), N.J.‡ 307,863 .... M2
Tucson, Ariz.‡ 531,263 .... D4
Tulsa, Okla.‡ 689,628 .... G3
Utah (state) 1,461,037 .... D3
Utica, N.Y.‡ 320,180 .... M2
Vermont (state) 511,456 .... M2
Virginia (state) 5,346,279 .... L3
Wabash (riv.) J3
Washington (state) 4,130,163 .... B1
Washington, D.C. (cap.), U.S.‡ 3,060,240 .... L3
Waterbury, Conn.‡ 228,059 .... M2
Waterloo, Iowa 75,985 .... H2
West Palm Beach, Fla.‡ 573,125 .... K5
West Virginia (state) 1,949,644 .... K3
Wheeling, W. Va.‡ 185,566 .... K2
Whitney (mt.), Calif. C3
Wichita, Kans.‡ 411,313 .... G3
Wilkes-Barre, Pa. 51,551 .... L2
Wilmington, Del.‡ 524,108 .... M3
Wisconsin (state) 4,705,335 .... J2
Woods (lake), Minn. G1
Worcester, Mass.‡ 372,940 .... M2
Wyoming (state) 470,816 .... E2
Yellowstone Nat'l Park, Wyo. E2
York, Pa.‡ 381,255 .... L3
Yosemite Nat'l Park, Calif. C3
Youngstown, Ohio‡ 531,350 .... K2
Yukon (riv.), Alaska C5

‡ Population of metropolitan area.

Topography

Agriculture, Industry and Resources

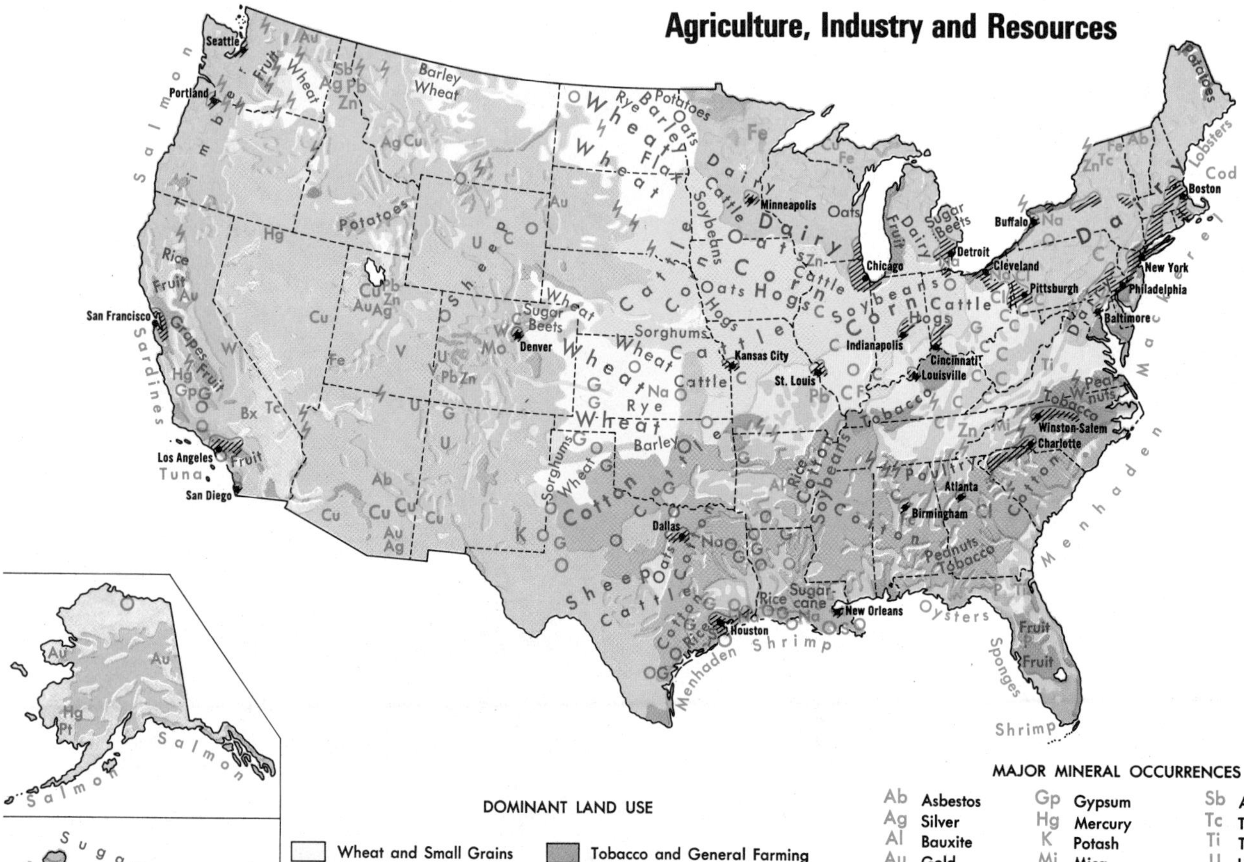

DOMINANT LAND USE

- Wheat and Small Grains
- Feed Grains and Livestock
- Dairy
- General Farming
- Cotton
- Fruit, Truck and Mixed Farming
- Tobacco and General Farming
- Special Crops and General Farming
- Range Livestock
- Forests
- Swampland
- Nonagricultural Land

MAJOR MINERAL OCCURRENCES

Ab	Asbestos	Gp	Gypsum	Sb	Antimony
Ag	Silver	Hg	Mercury	Tc	Talc
Al	Bauxite	K	Potash	Ti	Titanium
Au	Gold	Mi	Mica	U	Uranium
Bx	Borax	Mo	Molybdenum	V	Vanadium
C	Coal	Na	Salt	W	Tungsten
Cl	Clay	O	Petroleum	Zn	Zinc
Cu	Copper	P	Phosphates		
F	Fluorspar	Pb	Lead	ϟ	Water Power
Fe	Iron Ore	Pt	Platinum		Major Industrial Areas
G	Natural Gas	S	Sulfur		

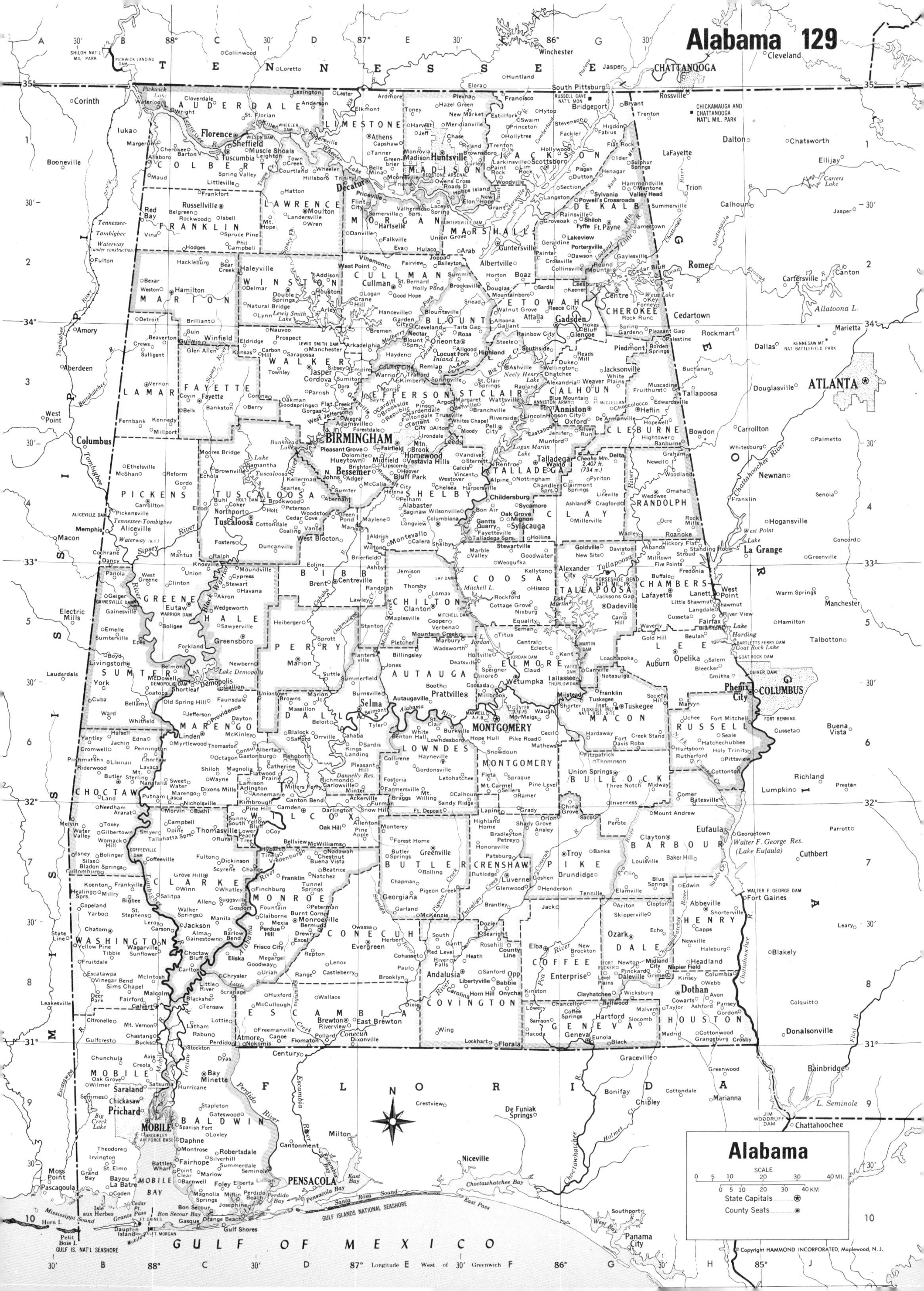
TENNESSEE
MISSISSIPPI
GEORGIA
FLORIDA
GULF OF MEXICO
LAUDERDALE
LIMESTONE
MADISON
JACKSON
COLBERT
LAWRENCE
MORGAN
MARSHALL
DE KALB
FRANKLIN
MARION
WINSTON
CULLMAN
BLOUNT
ETOWAH
CHEROKEE
LAMAR
FAYETTE
WALKER
JEFFERSON
ST. CLAIR
CALHOUN
CLEBURNE
PICKENS
TUSCALOOSA
SHELBY
TALLADEGA
CLAY
RANDOLPH
GREENE
HALE
BIBB
CHILTON
COOSA
TALLAPOOSA
CHAMBERS
SUMTER
PERRY
AUTAUGA
ELMORE
LEE
MARENGO
DALLAS
LOWNDES
MONTGOMERY
MACON
RUSSELL
CHOCTAW
WILCOX
BUTLER
CRENSHAW
PIKE
BULLOCK
BARBOUR
CLARKE
MONROE
CONECUH
COFFEE
DALE
HENRY
WASHINGTON
ESCAMBIA
COVINGTON
GENEVA
HOUSTON
MOBILE
BALDWIN
BIRMINGHAM
MONTGOMERY
Huntsville
Mobile
Tuscaloosa
Gadsden
Anniston
Dothan
CHATTANOOGA
ATLANTA
COLUMBUS
PENSACOLA
Alabama
SCALE
0 5 10 20 30 40 MI.
0 5 10 20 30 40 KM.
State Capitals
County Seats
Longitude West of Greenwich
© Copyright HAMMOND INCORPORATED, Maplewood, N. J.

Alaska and Hawaii

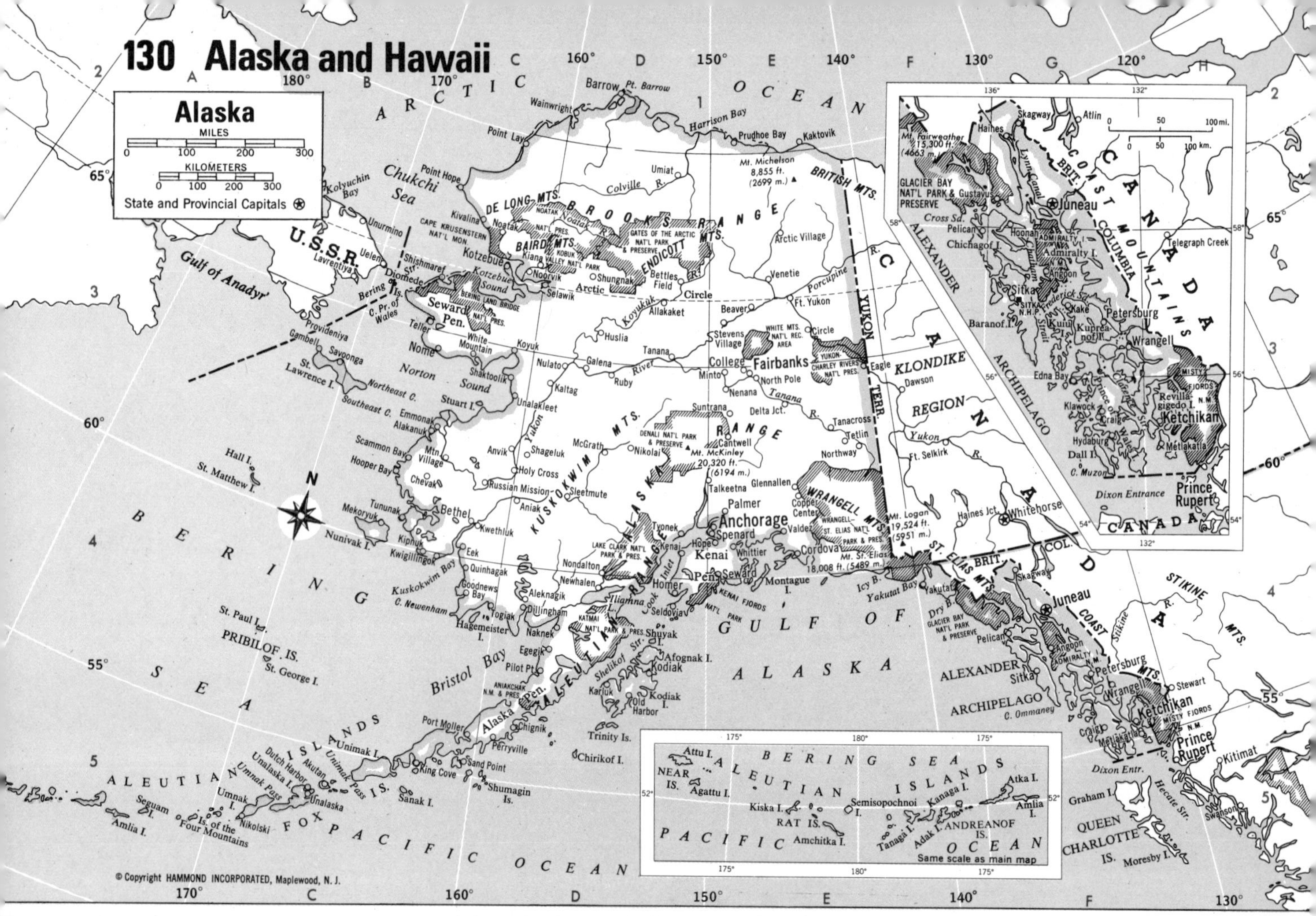
Alaska
MILES
0 100 200 300
KILOMETERS
0 100 200 300
State and Provincial Capitals
ARCTIC OCEAN
Barrow
Pt. Barrow
Wainwright
Point Lay
Harrison Bay
Prudhoe Bay
Kaktovik
Point Hope
Chukchi Sea
Kotzebue
Kivalina
Noatak
DE LONG MTS.
BROOKS RANGE
BAIRD MTS.
ENDICOTT MTS.
CAPE KRUSENSTERN NAT'L MON.
GATES OF THE ARCTIC NAT'L PARK & PRESERVE
KOBUK VALLEY NAT'L PARK
Kiana
Noorvik
Shungnak
Selawik
Kotzebue Sound
Umiat
Colville R.
Mt. Michelson 8,855 ft. (2699 m.)
BRITISH MTS.
Arctic Village
Venetie
Bettles Field
Allakaket
Circle
Ft. Yukon
Porcupine R.
Beaver
Stevens Village
WHITE MTS. NAT'L REC. AREA
YUKON-CHARLEY RIVERS NAT'L PRES.
Eagle
College
Fairbanks
North Pole
Nenana
Tanana R.
Delta Jct.
Tanacross
Tetlin
Northway
Minto
Tanana
Galena
Ruby
Koyukuk
Nulato
Huslia
Kaltag
Unalakleet
Shaktoolik
Norton Sound
Nome
Teller
White Mountain
Seward Pen.
BERING LAND BRIDGE NAT'L PRES.
Shishmaref
Bering Str.
Diomede Is.
C. Pr. of Wales
U.S.S.R.
Uelen
Lavrentiya
Unurmino
Kolyuchin Bay
Gulf of Anadyr'
Provideniya
Gambell
Savoonga
St. Lawrence I.
Northeast C.
Southeast C.
Stuart I.
Emmonak
Alakanuk
Scammon Bay
Hooper Bay
Mtn. Village
Chevak
Hall I.
St. Matthew I.
Anvik
Shageluk
Holy Cross
McGrath
Nikolai
Russian Mission
Sleetmute
Aniak
Bethel
Tununak
Mekoryuk
Nunivak I.
Kipnuk
Kwigillingok
Kwethluk
Eek
Quinhagak
Goodnews Bay
C. Newenham
Kuskokwim Bay
KUSKOKWIM MTS.
ALASKA RANGE
DENALI NAT'L PARK & PRESERVE
Mt. McKinley 20,320 ft. (6194 m.)
Suntrana
Cantwell
Talkeetna
Glennallen
Palmer
Anchorage
Spenard
Tyonek
Kenai
Hope
Whittier
Valdez
Cordova
Copper Center
WRANGELL MTS.
WRANGELL-ST. ELIAS NAT'L PARK & PRES.
Mt. Sanford
Mt. St. Elias 18,008 ft. (5489 m.)
Mt. Logan 19,524 ft. (5951 m.)
Seward
Homer
Seldovia
KENAI FJORDS NAT'L PARK
Montague I.
Icy B.
Yakutat Bay
LAKE CLARK NAT'L PARK & PRES.
Nondalton
Newhalen
Iliamna L.
Cook Inlet
Aleknagik
Dillingham
Togiak
Naknek
Hagemeister I.
Egegik
Pilot Pt.
KATMAI NAT'L PARK & PRES.
ANIAKCHAK N.M. & PRES.
Shuyak I.
Afognak I.
Kodiak
Kodiak I.
Old Harbor
Karluk
Shelikof Str.
Bristol Bay
BERING SEA
St. Paul I.
PRIBILOF IS.
St. George I.
ALEUTIAN RANGE
Alaska Pen.
Port Moller
Chignik
Perryville
Trinity Is.
Chirikof I.
Sand Point
King Cove
Shumagin Is.
Sanak I.
Unimak I.
Unimak Pass
Akutan
Dutch Harbor
Unalaska
Unalaska I.
Umnak I.
Umnak Pass
Nikolski
FOX IS.
Is. of the Four Mountains
Seguam I.
Amlia I.
ALEUTIAN ISLANDS
PACIFIC OCEAN
GULF OF ALASKA
YUKON TERR.
KLONDIKE REGION
Dawson
Yukon R.
Ft. Selkirk
Haines Jct.
Whitehorse
CANADA
ST. ELIAS MTS.
BRIT. COL.
Skagway
Haines
Juneau
Dry B.
GLACIER BAY NAT'L PARK & PRESERVE
Pelican
Sitka
Angoon
ADMIRALTY I.
Petersburg
Wrangell
COAST MTS.
STIKINE MTS.
Stikine R.
Stewart
ALEXANDER ARCHIPELAGO
C. Ommaney
Ketchikan
MISTY FJORDS
Metlakatla
Prince Rupert
Kitimat
Dixon Entr.
Hecate Str.
Graham I.
QUEEN CHARLOTTE IS.
Moresby I.
Swanson
Atlin
Mt. Fairweather 15,300 ft. (4663 m.)
GLACIER BAY NAT'L PARK & Gustavus PRESERVE
Cross Sd.
Chichagof I.
Hoonah
Lynn Canal
Admiralty I.
Baranof I.
Kake
Kuiu I.
Kupreanof I.
Etolin I.
Edna Bay
Klawock
Craig
Hydaburg
Dall I.
Revillagigedo I.
C. Muzon
Dixon Entrance
Telegraph Creek
BRIT. COLUMBIA
COAST MOUNTAINS
0 50 100 mi.
0 50 100 km.
BERING SEA
ALEUTIAN ISLANDS
Attu I.
NEAR IS.
Agattu I.
Kiska I.
RAT IS.
Amchitka I.
Semisopochnoi
Kanaga I.
Tanaga I.
Adak I.
ANDREANOF IS.
Atka I.
Amlia I.
PACIFIC OCEAN
Same scale as main map
© Copyright HAMMOND INCORPORATED, Maplewood, N. J.

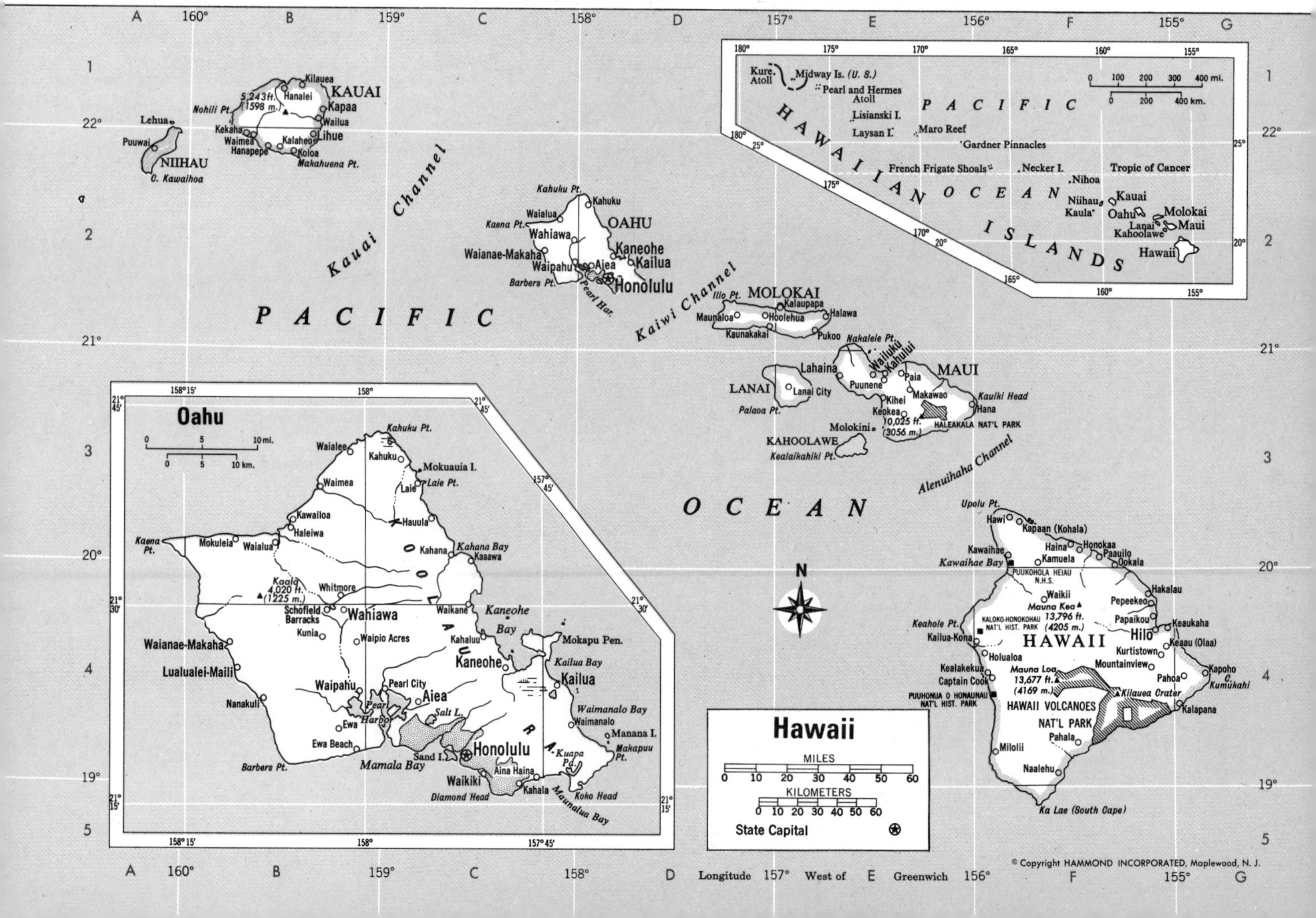
KAUAI
Kilauea
Hanalei
5,243 ft. (1598 m.)
Kapaa
Wailua
Lihue
Kalaheo
Koloa
Makahuena Pt.
Nohili Pt.
Kekaha
Waimea
Hanapepe
Lehua
Puuwai
NIIHAU
C. Kawaihoa
Kauai Channel
PACIFIC
OAHU
Kahuku Pt.
Kahuku
Waialua
Kaena Pt.
Wahiawa
Waianae-Makaha
Waipahu
Aiea
Kaneohe
Kailua
Honolulu
Barbers Pt.
Pearl Har.
Kaiwi Channel
MOLOKAI
Ilio Pt.
Kalaupapa
Halawa
Maunaloa
Hoolehua
Kaunakakai
Pukoo
Nakalele Pt.
Wailuku
Kahului
Lahaina
MAUI
Paia
Puunene
Makawao
LANAI
Lanai City
Palaoa Pt.
Kihei
Keokea
Kauiki Head
Hana
10,025 ft. (3056 m.)
HALEAKALA NAT'L PARK
Molokini
KAHOOLAWE
Kealaikahiki Pt.
Alenuihaha Channel
OCEAN
Upolu Pt.
Hawi
Kapaau (Kohala)
Haina
Honokaa
Paauilo
Ookala
Kawaihae
Kamuela
Kawaihae Bay
PUUKOHOLA HEIAU N.H.S.
Waikii
Mauna Kea 13,796 ft. (4205 m.)
Hakalau
Pepeekeo
Papaikou
Keahole Pt.
KALOKO-HONOKOHAU NAT'L HIST. PARK
Kailua-Kona
HAWAII
Hilo
Keaukaha
Keaau (Olaa)
Kurtistown
Mountainview
Holualoa
Kealakekua
Captain Cook
Mauna Loa 13,677 ft. (4169 m.)
Pahoa
Kapoho
C. Kumukahi
PUUHONUA O HONAUNAU NAT'L HIST. PARK
HAWAII VOLCANOES NAT'L PARK
Kilauea Crater
Kalapana
Pahala
Milolii
Naalehu
Ka Lae (South Cape)
Kure Atoll
Midway Is. (U. S.)
Pearl and Hermes Atoll
Lisianski I.
Laysan I.
Maro Reef
Gardner Pinnacles
French Frigate Shoals
Necker I.
Nihoa
Tropic of Cancer
Niihau
Kaula
Kauai
Oahu
Molokai
Lanai
Maui
Kahoolawe
Hawaii
PACIFIC OCEAN
HAWAIIAN ISLANDS
0 100 200 300 400 mi.
0 200 400 km.
Oahu
0 5 10 mi.
0 5 10 km.
Kahuku Pt.
Waialee
Kahuku
Mokuauia I.
Laie Pt.
Laie
Waimea
Kawailoa
Haleiwa
Hauula
Kaena Pt.
Mokuleia
Waialua
Kahana
Kahana Bay
Kaaawa
Kaala 4,020 ft. (1225 m.)
Whitmore
KOOLAU RA.
Schofield Barracks
Wahiawa
Waikane
Kaneohe Bay
Kunia
Waipio Acres
Kahaluu
Mokapu Pen.
Waianae-Makaha
Lualualei-Maili
Kaneohe
Kailua Bay
Kailua
Waipahu
Pearl City
Aiea
Pearl Harbor
Salt L.
Nanakuli
Ewa
Ewa Beach
Waimanalo Bay
Waimanalo
Manana I.
Makapuu Pt.
Sand I.
Honolulu
Kuapa Pd.
Barbers Pt.
Mamala Bay
Waikiki
Aina Haina
Diamond Head
Kahala
Maunalua Bay
Koko Head
Hawaii
MILES
0 10 20 30 40 50 60
KILOMETERS
0 10 20 30 40 50 60
State Capital
Longitude 157° West of Greenwich 156°
© Copyright HAMMOND INCORPORATED, Maplewood, N. J.

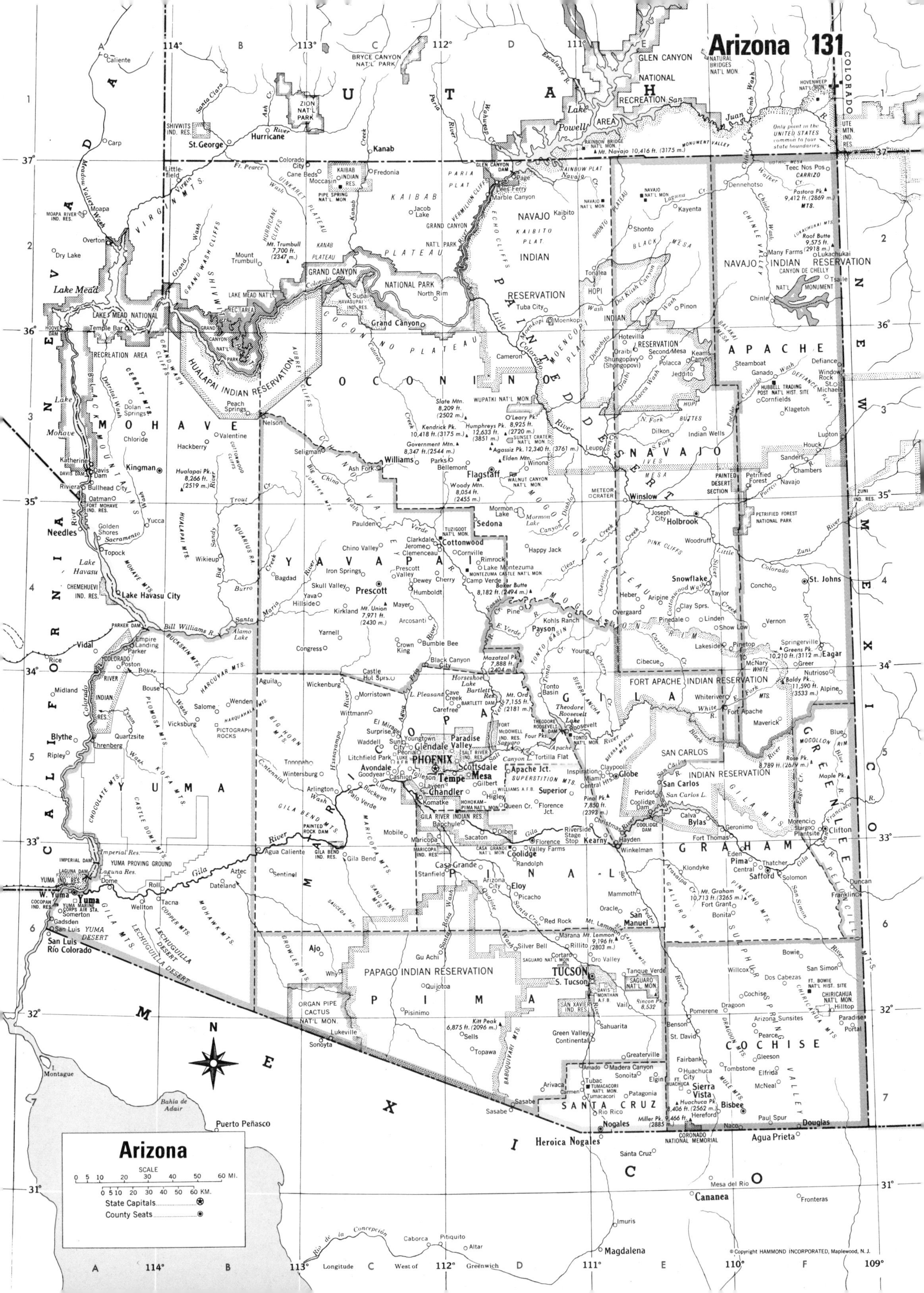
Arizona
SCALE
0 5 10 20 30 40 50 60 MI.
0 5 10 20 30 40 50 60 KM.
State Capitals
County Seats
UTAH
NEVADA
CALIFORNIA
NEW MEXICO
MEXICO
COLORADO
Only point in the UNITED STATES common to four state boundaries
MOHAVE
COCONINO
NAVAJO
APACHE
YAVAPAI
GILA
GREENLEE
GRAHAM
MARICOPA
YUMA
PINAL
PIMA
SANTA CRUZ
COCHISE
GLEN CANYON NATIONAL RECREATION AREA
GRAND CANYON NATIONAL PARK
LAKE MEAD NATIONAL RECREATION AREA
HUALAPAI INDIAN RESERVATION
NAVAJO INDIAN RESERVATION
HOPI INDIAN RESERVATION
FORT APACHE INDIAN RESERVATION
SAN CARLOS INDIAN RESERVATION
PAPAGO INDIAN RESERVATION
COLORADO RIVER INDIAN RES.
GILA RIVER INDIAN RES.
PETRIFIED FOREST NATIONAL PARK
ORGAN PIPE CACTUS NAT'L MON.
PAINTED DESERT
KAIBAB PLATEAU
COCONINO PLATEAU
MOGOLLON RIM
Lake Mead
Lake Powell
Lake Havasu
PHOENIX
TUCSON
Flagstaff
Prescott
Kingman
Yuma
Holbrook
St. Johns
Globe
Florence
Safford
Clifton
Nogales
Bisbee
Douglas
Winslow
Sedona
Williams
Needles
Lake Havasu City
Glendale
Tempe
Mesa
Scottsdale
Chandler
Casa Grande
Coolidge
Eloy
Sierra Vista
Tombstone
Willcox
Page
Tuba City
Kayenta
Chinle
Show Low
Payson
Wickenburg
Ajo
San Luis
Gila Bend
Humphreys Pk. 12,633 ft. (3851 m.)
Mt. Graham 10,713 ft. (3265 m.)
Mt. Lemmon 9,196 ft. (2803 m.)
Baldy Pk. 11,590 ft. (3533 m.)
Heroica Nogales
Agua Prieta
Cananea
Puerto Peñasco
Magdalena
Longitude West of Greenwich
© Copyright HAMMOND INCORPORATED, Maplewood, N.J.

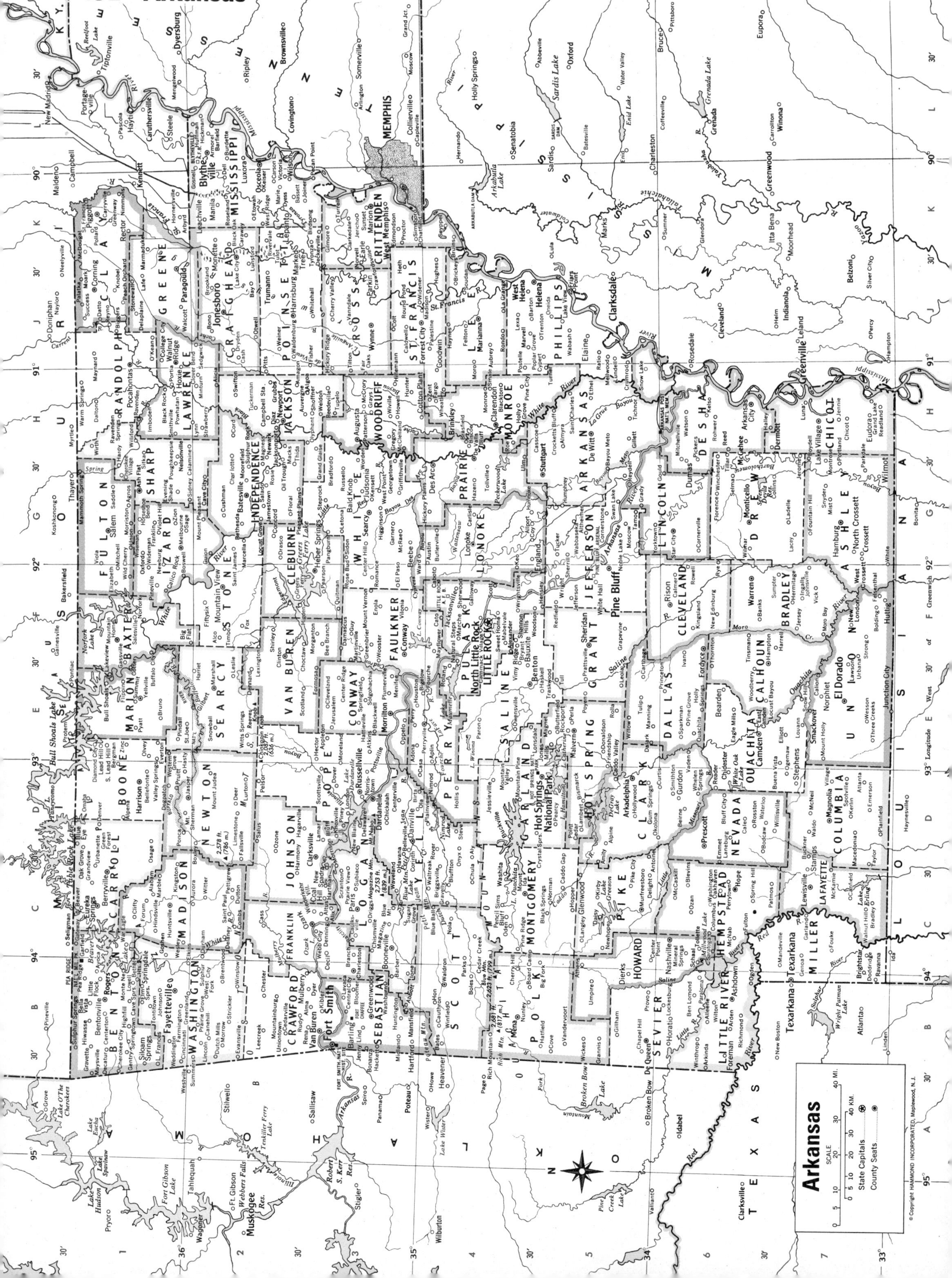
Arkansas
SCALE
0 5 10 20 30 40 MI.
0 5 10 20 30 40 KM.
State Capitals
County Seats
© Copyright HAMMOND INCORPORATED, Maplewood, N.J.
KY.
TENN.
MISSISSIPPI
LOUISIANA
TEXAS
OKLAHOMA
MISSOURI
Memphis
Little Rock
North Little Rock
Pine Bluff
Fort Smith
Fayetteville
Hot Springs National Park
Texarkana
El Dorado
Jonesboro
BENTON
CARROLL
BOONE
MARION
BAXTER
FULTON
RANDOLPH
CLAY
GREENE
LAWRENCE
SHARP
IZARD
STONE
SEARCY
NEWTON
MADISON
WASHINGTON
CRAWFORD
FRANKLIN
JOHNSON
POPE
VAN BUREN
CLEBURNE
INDEPENDENCE
JACKSON
CRAIGHEAD
MISSISSIPPI
POINSETT
CROSS
CRITTENDEN
ST. FRANCIS
LEE
PHILLIPS
MONROE
WOODRUFF
WHITE
FAULKNER
CONWAY
PERRY
YELL
LOGAN
SEBASTIAN
SCOTT
POLK
MONTGOMERY
GARLAND
SALINE
PULASKI
LONOKE
PRAIRIE
ARKANSAS
JEFFERSON
GRANT
HOT SPRING
CLARK
PIKE
HOWARD
SEVIER
LITTLE RIVER
HEMPSTEAD
NEVADA
OUACHITA
DALLAS
CLEVELAND
LINCOLN
DESHA
DREW
BRADLEY
CALHOUN
UNION
COLUMBIA
LAFAYETTE
MILLER
ASHLEY
CHICOT

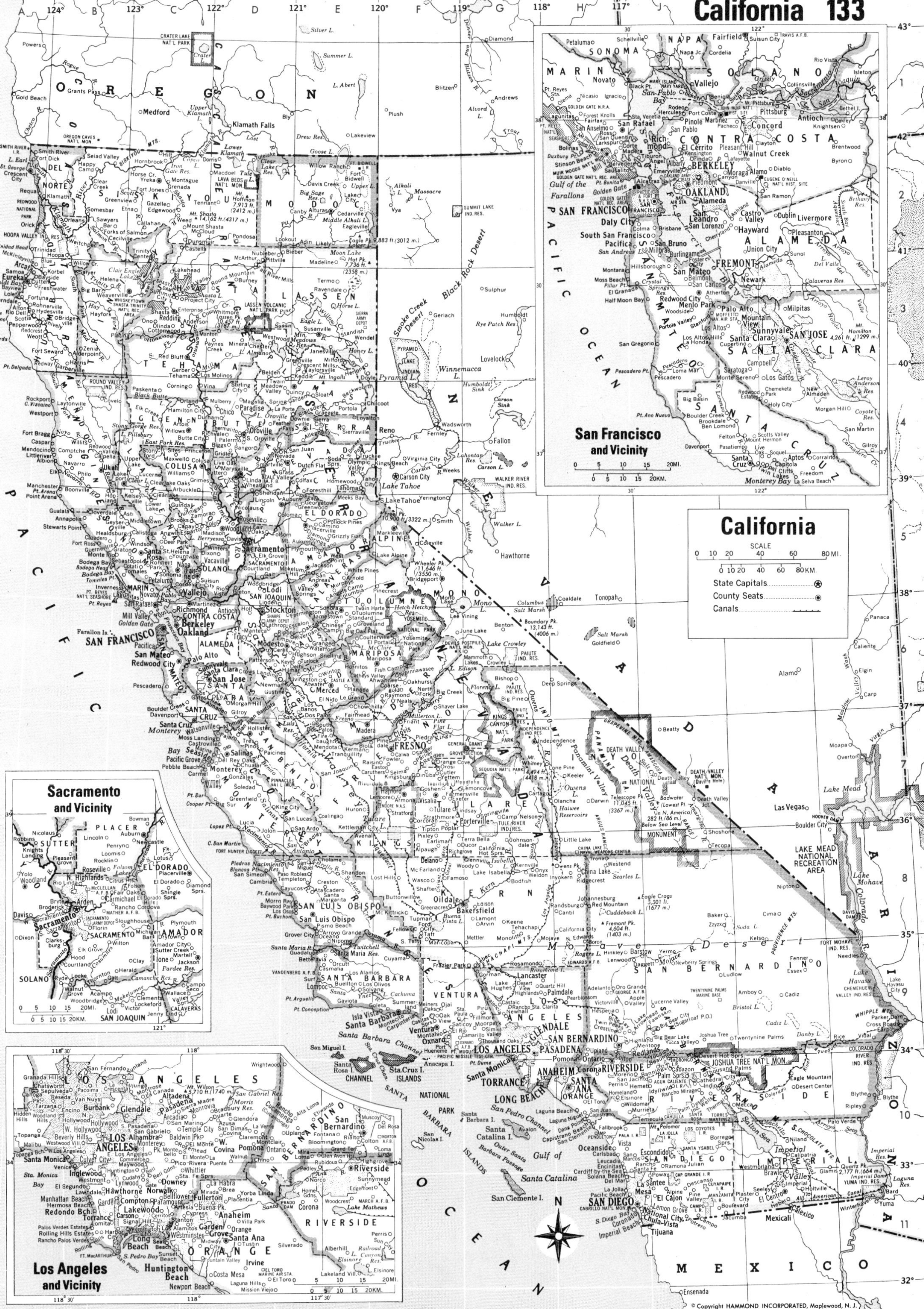
California
SCALE
0 10 20 40 60 80 MI.
0 10 20 40 60 80 KM.
State Capitals
County Seats
Canals
San Francisco and Vicinity
Sacramento and Vicinity
Los Angeles and Vicinity
OREGON
NEVADA
ARIZONA
MEXICO
PACIFIC OCEAN
Longitude 119° West of Greenwich 118°
SAN FRANCISCO
SACRAMENTO
LOS ANGELES
SAN DIEGO
FRESNO
Lake Tahoe
Mojave Desert
Death Valley
LAKE MEAD NATIONAL RECREATION AREA
Santa Barbara Channel
Gulf of Santa Catalina

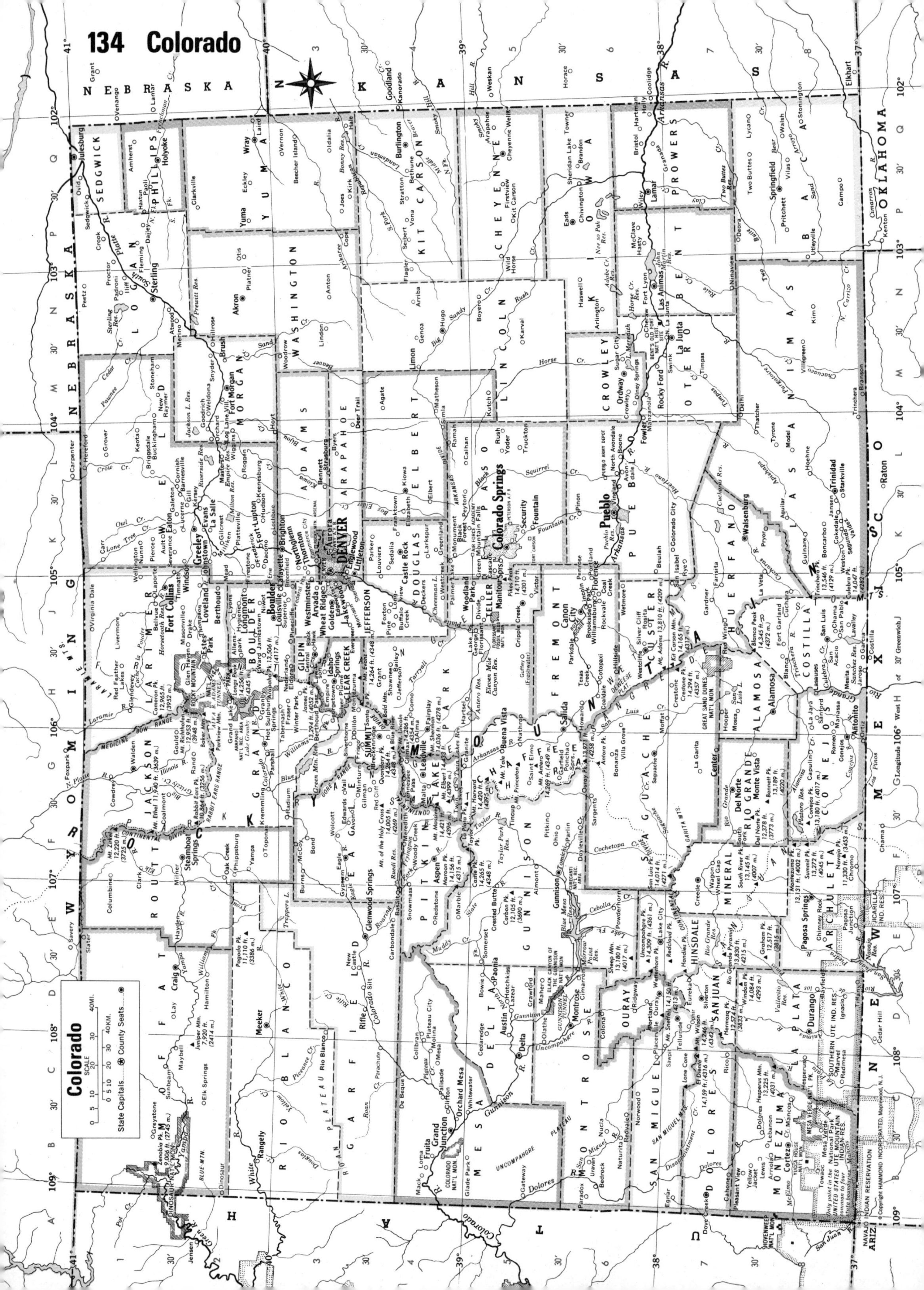
Colorado
SCALE
0 5 10 20 30 40 MI.
0 5 10 20 30 40 KM.
State Capitals ... County Seats
NEBRASKA
KANSAS
OKLAHOMA
NEW MEXICO
WYOMING
UTAH
ARIZ.
DENVER
Colorado Springs
Pueblo
Boulder
Fort Collins
Greeley
Grand Junction
Durango
Trinidad
Sterling
Lamar
La Junta
Alamosa
Glenwood Springs
Steamboat Springs
Gunnison
Montrose
Leadville
Cañon City
SEDGWICK
PHILLIPS
LOGAN
YUMA
WASHINGTON
MORGAN
WELD
LARIMER
KIT CARSON
CHEYENNE
LINCOLN
ELBERT
ADAMS
ARAPAHOE
DOUGLAS
EL PASO
KIOWA
PROWERS
BENT
OTERO
CROWLEY
PUEBLO
BACA
LAS ANIMAS
HUERFANO
CUSTER
FREMONT
TELLER
PARK
JEFFERSON
CLEAR CREEK
GILPIN
BOULDER
GRAND
JACKSON
ROUTT
MOFFAT
RIO BLANCO
GARFIELD
EAGLE
SUMMIT
LAKE
CHAFFEE
PITKIN
GUNNISON
SAGUACHE
ALAMOSA
COSTILLA
CONEJOS
RIO GRANDE
MINERAL
HINSDALE
ARCHULETA
LA PLATA
SAN JUAN
OURAY
MONTROSE
DELTA
MESA
SAN MIGUEL
DOLORES
MONTEZUMA
ROCKY MOUNTAIN NAT'L PARK
GREAT SAND DUNES NAT'L MON.
MESA VERDE NAT'L PARK
DINOSAUR NAT'L MON.
COLORADO NAT'L MON.
BLACK CANYON OF THE GUNNISON NAT'L MON.
Pikes Pk. 14,110 ft. (4301 m.)
Mt. Elbert 14,433 ft. (4399 m.)
CONTINENTAL DIVIDE
© Copyright HAMMOND INCORPORATED, Maplewood, N.J.

Connecticut
SCALE
0 5 10 15 MI.
0 5 10 15 KM.
State Capitals
MASSACHUSETTS
RHODE ISLAND
NEW YORK
LONG ISLAND
LONG ISLAND SOUND
ATLANTIC OCEAN
GARDINERS BAY
THE RACE
LITCHFIELD
HARTFORD
TOLLAND
WINDHAM
NEW LONDON
MIDDLESEX
NEW HAVEN
FAIRFIELD
SPRINGFIELD
WATERBURY
BRIDGEPORT
STAMFORD
NEW HAVEN
Longitude West of Greenwich
© Copyright HAMMOND INCORPORATED, Maplewood, N.J.

Florida
SCALE
0 5 10 20 30 40 50 MI.
0 5 10 20 30 40 50 KM.
State Capitals
County Seats
Canals
GEORGIA
ALA.
ATLANTIC OCEAN
GULF OF MEXICO
STRAITS OF FLORIDA
FLORIDA KEYS
Lake Okeechobee
Big Cypress Swamp
EVERGLADES NATIONAL PARK
Okefenokee Swamp
Tallahassee
Jacksonville
Gainesville
Ocala
Orlando
Tampa
St. Petersburg
Sarasota
Fort Myers
Naples
West Palm Beach
Fort Lauderdale
Miami
Miami Beach
Key West
Daytona Beach
St. Augustine
Pensacola
Panama City
NASSAU
DUVAL
BAKER
UNION
BRADFORD
CLAY
ST. JOHNS
PUTNAM
FLAGLER
VOLUSIA
ALACHUA
MARION
LEVY
DIXIE
GILCHRIST
COLUMBIA
SUWANNEE
HAMILTON
MADISON
TAYLOR
LAFAYETTE
JEFFERSON
LEON
WAKULLA
GADSDEN
LIBERTY
FRANKLIN
GULF
CALHOUN
JACKSON
CITRUS
SUMTER
LAKE
HERNANDO
PASCO
PINELLAS
HILLSBOROUGH
POLK
ORANGE
SEMINOLE
OSCEOLA
BREVARD
INDIAN RIVER
OKEECHOBEE
ST. LUCIE
MARTIN
PALM BEACH
BROWARD
DADE
MONROE
COLLIER
HENDRY
GLADES
HIGHLANDS
HARDEE
DE SOTO
MANATEE
SARASOTA
CHARLOTTE
LEE
Western Part of Florida
Same scale as main map
GULF OF MEXICO
ALABAMA
ESCAMBIA
SANTA ROSA
OKALOOSA
WALTON
HOLMES
WASHINGTON
BAY
JACKSON
CALHOUN
GULF
Longitude West of Greenwich
85° 84° 83° 82° 81° 80°
31° 30° 29° 28° 27° 26° 25°

Georgia
SCALE
0 5 10 20 30 40 MI.
0 10 20 30 40 KM.
State Capitals
County Seats
TENNESSEE
NORTH CAROLINA
SOUTH CAROLINA
ALABAMA
FLORIDA
GULF OF MEXICO
ATLANTIC OCEAN
SEA ISLANDS
ATLANTA
Augusta
COLUMBUS
Macon
SAVANNAH
Albany
Athens
Valdosta
Brunswick
Waycross
Rome
Tallahassee
JACKSONVILLE
CHATTANOOGA
COLUMBIA
APALACHEE BAY
OKEFENOKEE SWAMP
Longitude West of Greenwich
© Copyright HAMMOND INCORPORATED, Maplewood, N. J.

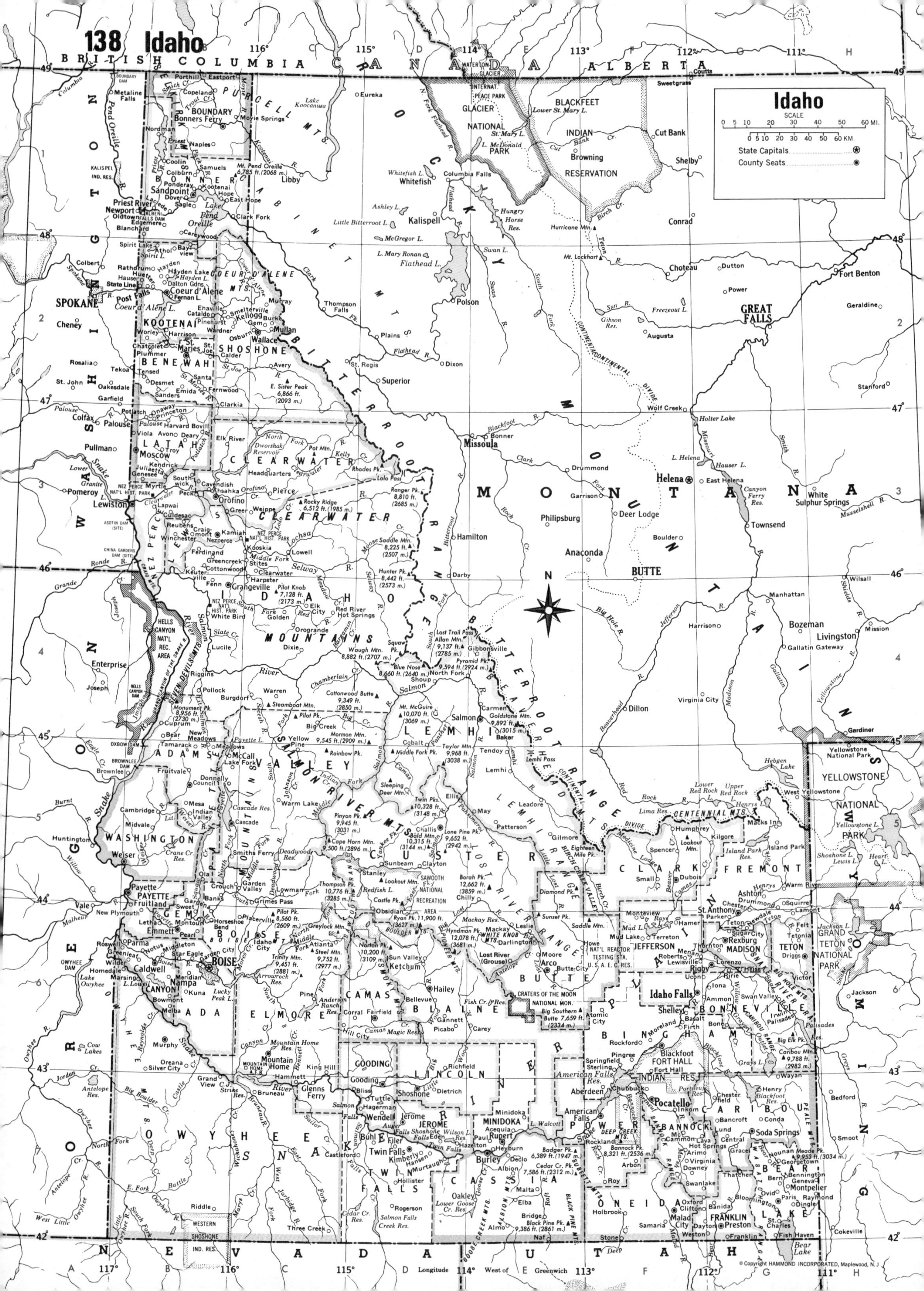
Idaho
SCALE
0 5 10 20 30 40 50 60 MI.
0 5 10 20 30 40 50 60 KM.
State Capitals
County Seats
BRITISH COLUMBIA
CANADA
ALBERTA
WASHINGTON
OREGON
NEVADA
UTAH
WYOMING
MONTANA
BOUNDARY
BONNER
KOOTENAI
BENEWAH
SHOSHONE
LATAH
CLEARWATER
NEZ PERCE
LEWIS
IDAHO
ADAMS
VALLEY
LEMHI
CUSTER
WASHINGTON
PAYETTE
GEM
BOISE
CANYON
ADA
ELMORE
CAMAS
BLAINE
BUTTE
CLARK
FREMONT
JEFFERSON
MADISON
TETON
BONNEVILLE
BINGHAM
GOODING
LINCOLN
JEROME
MINIDOKA
POWER
BANNOCK
CARIBOU
BEAR LAKE
FRANKLIN
ONEIDA
CASSIA
TWIN FALLS
OWYHEE
BOISE
Idaho Falls
Pocatello
Lewiston
Coeur d'Alene
Sandpoint
Moscow
Grangeville
Salmon
Twin Falls
Nampa
Caldwell
SPOKANE
Missoula
Helena
BUTTE
GREAT FALLS
GLACIER NATIONAL PARK
BLACKFEET INDIAN RESERVATION
YELLOWSTONE NATIONAL PARK
GRAND TETON NATIONAL PARK
CRATERS OF THE MOON NATIONAL MON.
SAWTOOTH NAT'L RECREATION AREA
HELLS CANYON NAT'L REC. AREA
FORT HALL INDIAN RES.
BITTERROOT RANGE
SALMON RIVER MTS.
CLEARWATER MOUNTAINS
LOST RIVER RANGE
LEMHI RANGE
ROCKY MOUNTAINS
CONTINENTAL DIVIDE
Longitude 114° West of Greenwich 113°
© Copyright HAMMOND INCORPORATED, Maplewood, N. J.

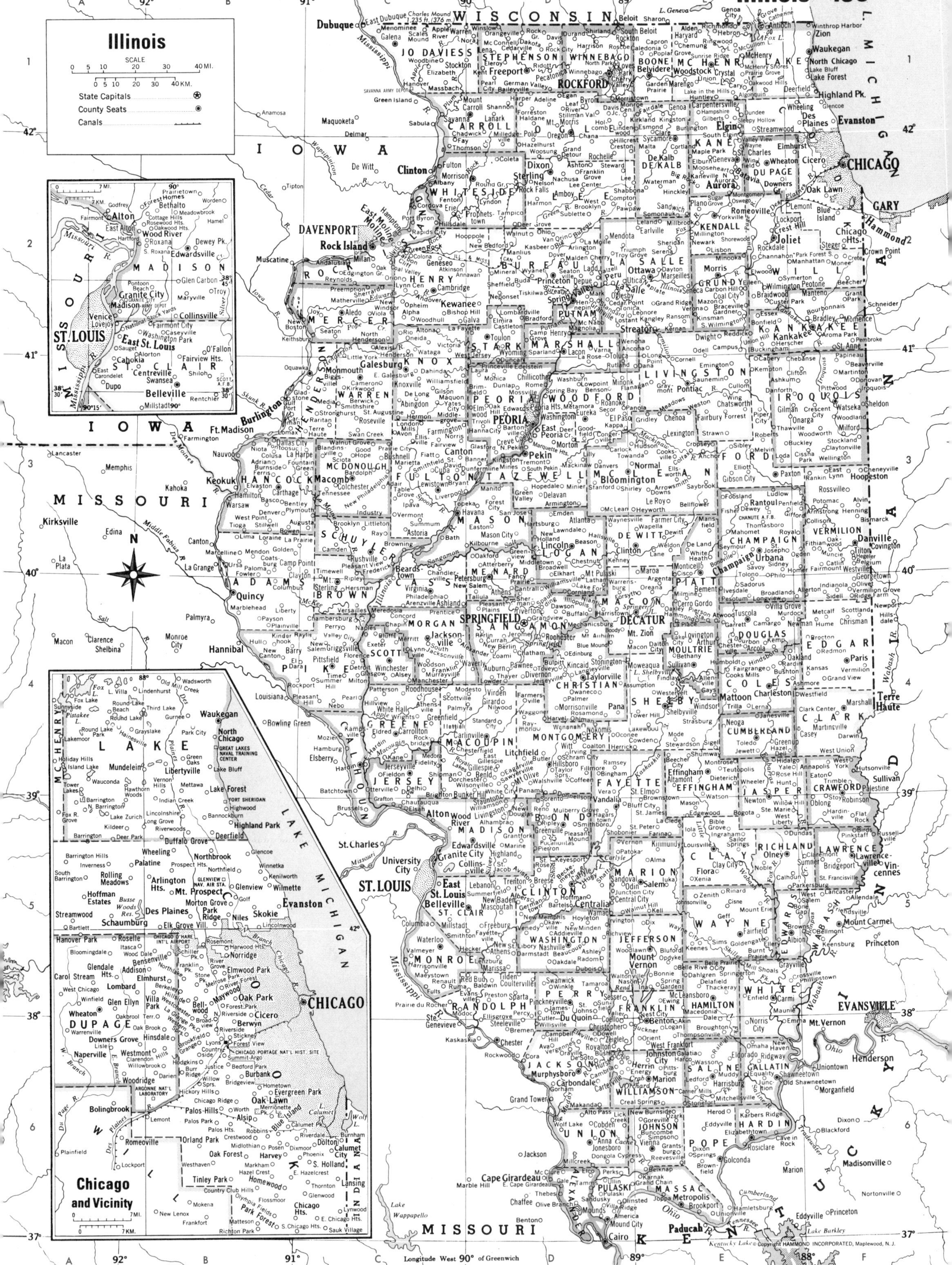
Illinois
SCALE
0 5 10 20 30 40 MI.
0 5 10 20 30 40 KM.
State Capitals
County Seats
Canals
WISCONSIN
IOWA
MISSOURI
KENTUCKY
INDIANA
LAKE MICHIGAN
CHICAGO
ROCKFORD
PEORIA
SPRINGFIELD
DECATUR
DAVENPORT
Rock Island
ST. LOUIS
EVANSVILLE
GARY
JO DAVIESS
STEPHENSON
WINNEBAGO
BOONE
MC HENRY
LAKE
CARROLL
OGLE
DE KALB
KANE
DU PAGE
COOK
WHITESIDE
LEE
KENDALL
WILL
ROCK ISLAND
HENRY
BUREAU
LA SALLE
GRUNDY
MERCER
PUTNAM
KANKAKEE
STARK
MARSHALL
KNOX
WARREN
HENDERSON
PEORIA
WOODFORD
LIVINGSTON
IROQUOIS
HANCOCK
MC DONOUGH
FULTON
TAZEWELL
MC LEAN
FORD
SCHUYLER
MASON
DE WITT
CHAMPAIGN
VERMILION
ADAMS
BROWN
CASS
MENARD
LOGAN
PIATT
MACON
MORGAN
SANGAMON
DOUGLAS
EDGAR
PIKE
SCOTT
CHRISTIAN
MOULTRIE
COLES
SHELBY
GREENE
MACOUPIN
MONTGOMERY
CUMBERLAND
CLARK
CALHOUN
JERSEY
FAYETTE
EFFINGHAM
JASPER
CRAWFORD
MADISON
BOND
CLAY
RICHLAND
LAWRENCE
ST. CLAIR
CLINTON
MARION
WAYNE
EDWARDS
WABASH
MONROE
WASHINGTON
JEFFERSON
RANDOLPH
PERRY
FRANKLIN
HAMILTON
WHITE
JACKSON
WILLIAMSON
SALINE
GALLATIN
UNION
JOHNSON
POPE
HARDIN
ALEXANDER
PULASKI
MASSAC
Chicago and Vicinity
0 7 MI.
0 7 KM.
Longitude West 90° of Greenwich
© COPYRIGHT HAMMOND INCORPORATED, Maplewood, N. J.

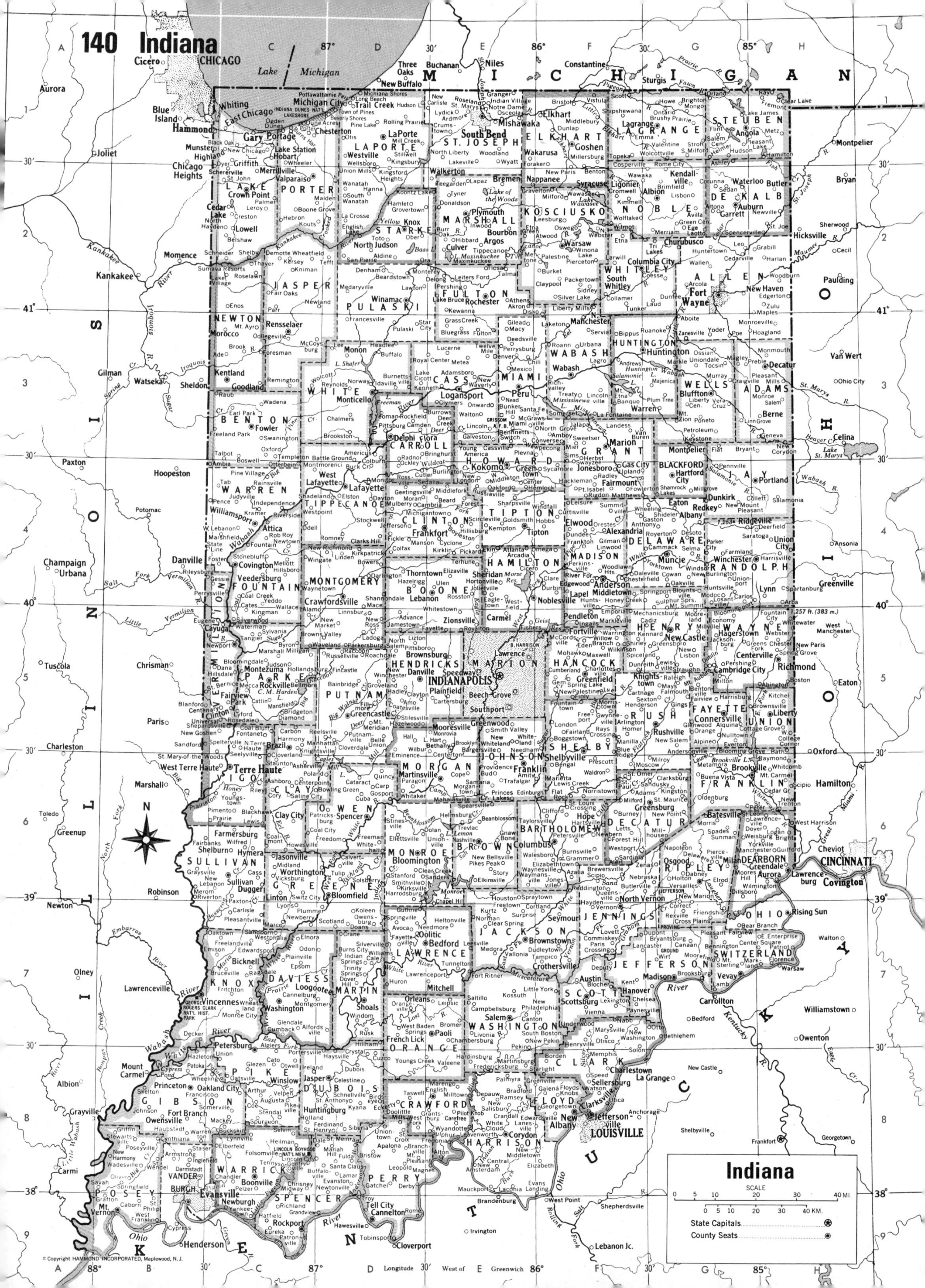

Indiana
SCALE
0 5 10 20 30 40 MI.
0 5 10 20 30 40 KM.
State Capitals
County Seats
Longitude West of Greenwich
M I C H I G A N
I L L I N O I S
O H I O
K E N T U C K Y
Lake Michigan
CHICAGO
INDIANAPOLIS
LOUISVILLE
CINCINNATI
Ohio R.
Wabash R.
LAKE
PORTER
LAPORTE
ST. JOSEPH
ELKHART
LAGRANGE
STEUBEN
DE KALB
NOBLE
KOSCIUSKO
MARSHALL
STARKE
JASPER
NEWTON
PULASKI
FULTON
WHITLEY
ALLEN
WABASH
MIAMI
CASS
WHITE
BENTON
CARROLL
HOWARD
GRANT
HUNTINGTON
WELLS
ADAMS
BLACKFORD
JAY
WARREN
TIPPECANOE
CLINTON
TIPTON
MADISON
DELAWARE
RANDOLPH
FOUNTAIN
MONTGOMERY
BOONE
HAMILTON
HENRY
WAYNE
VERMILLION
PARKE
PUTNAM
HENDRICKS
MARION
HANCOCK
RUSH
FAYETTE
UNION
VIGO
CLAY
MORGAN
JOHNSON
SHELBY
DECATUR
FRANKLIN
OWEN
MONROE
BROWN
BARTHOLOMEW
JENNINGS
RIPLEY
DEARBORN
OHIO
SULLIVAN
GREENE
LAWRENCE
JACKSON
JEFFERSON
SWITZERLAND
KNOX
DAVIESS
MARTIN
ORANGE
WASHINGTON
SCOTT
CLARK
FLOYD
HARRISON
CRAWFORD
DUBOIS
PIKE
GIBSON
POSEY
VANDERBURGH
WARRICK
SPENCER
PERRY

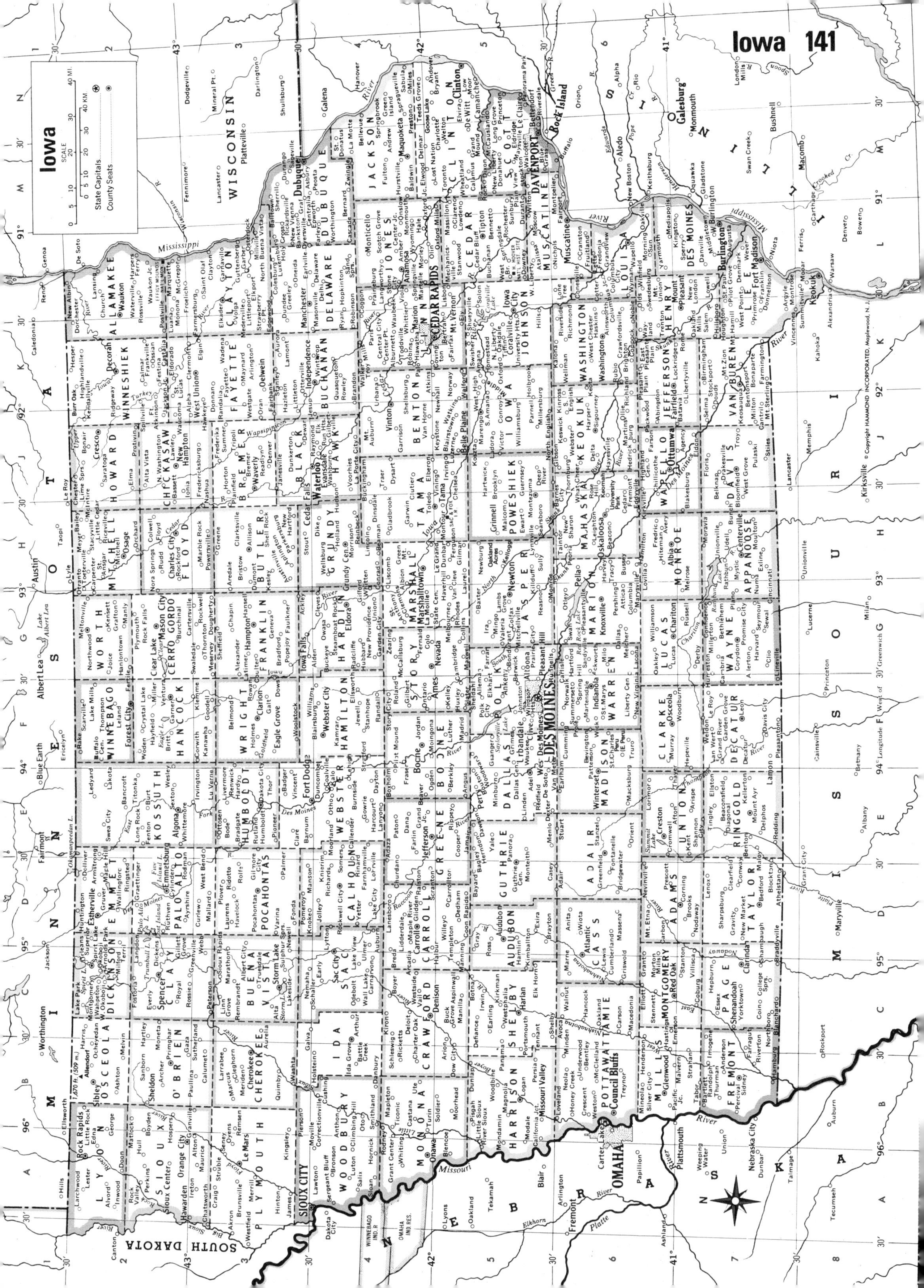
Iowa
SCALE
State Capitals
County Seats
MINNESOTA
WISCONSIN
ILLINOIS
MISSOURI
NEBRASKA
SOUTH DAKOTA
© Copyright HAMMOND INCORPORATED, Maplewood, N.J.

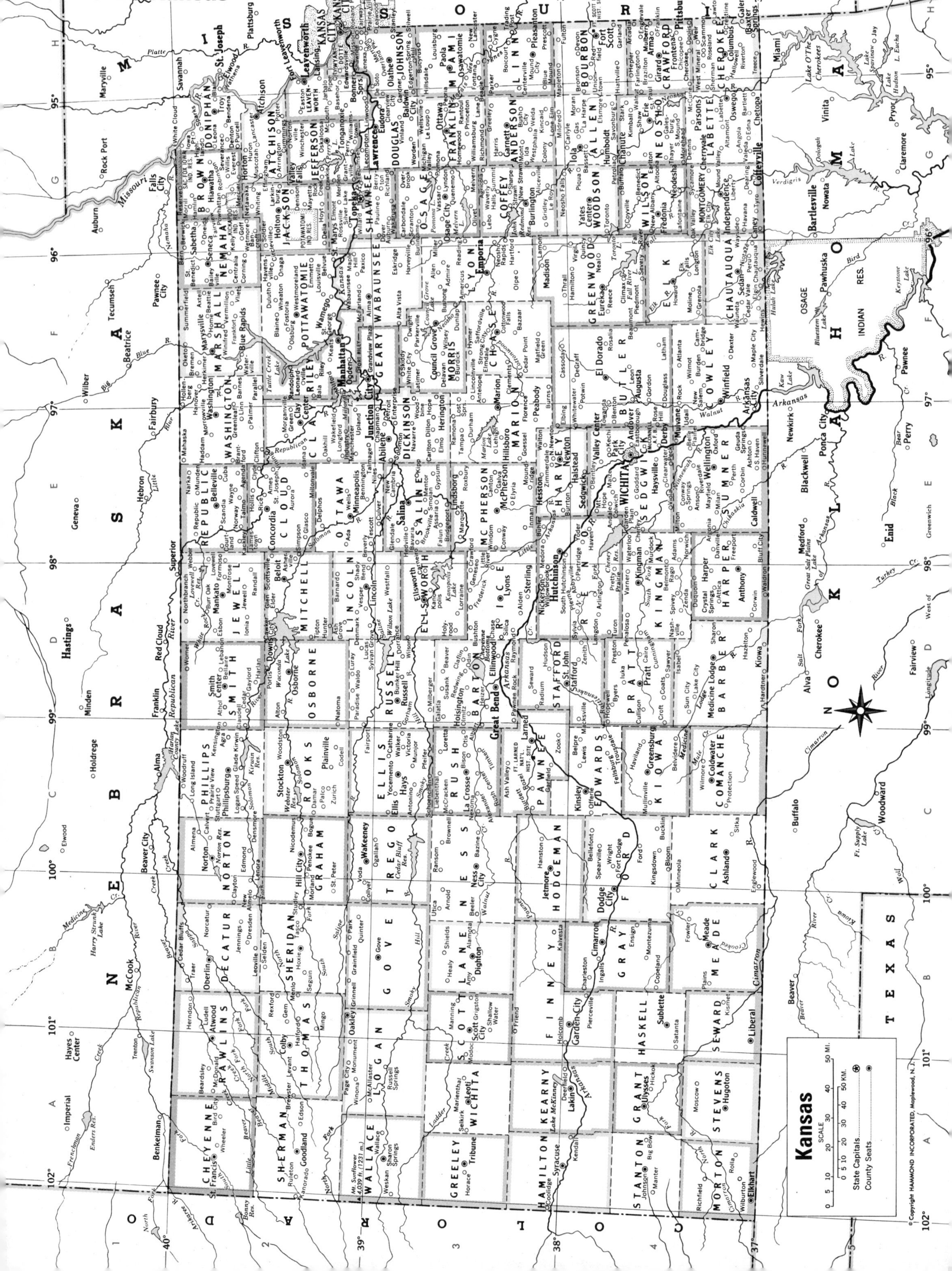
Kansas
SCALE
0 5 10 20 30 40 50 MI.
0 5 10 20 30 40 50 KM.
State Capitals
County Seats
© Copyright HAMMOND INCORPORATED, Maplewood, N.J.
NEBRASKA
MISSOURI
OKLAHOMA
COLORADO
TEXAS

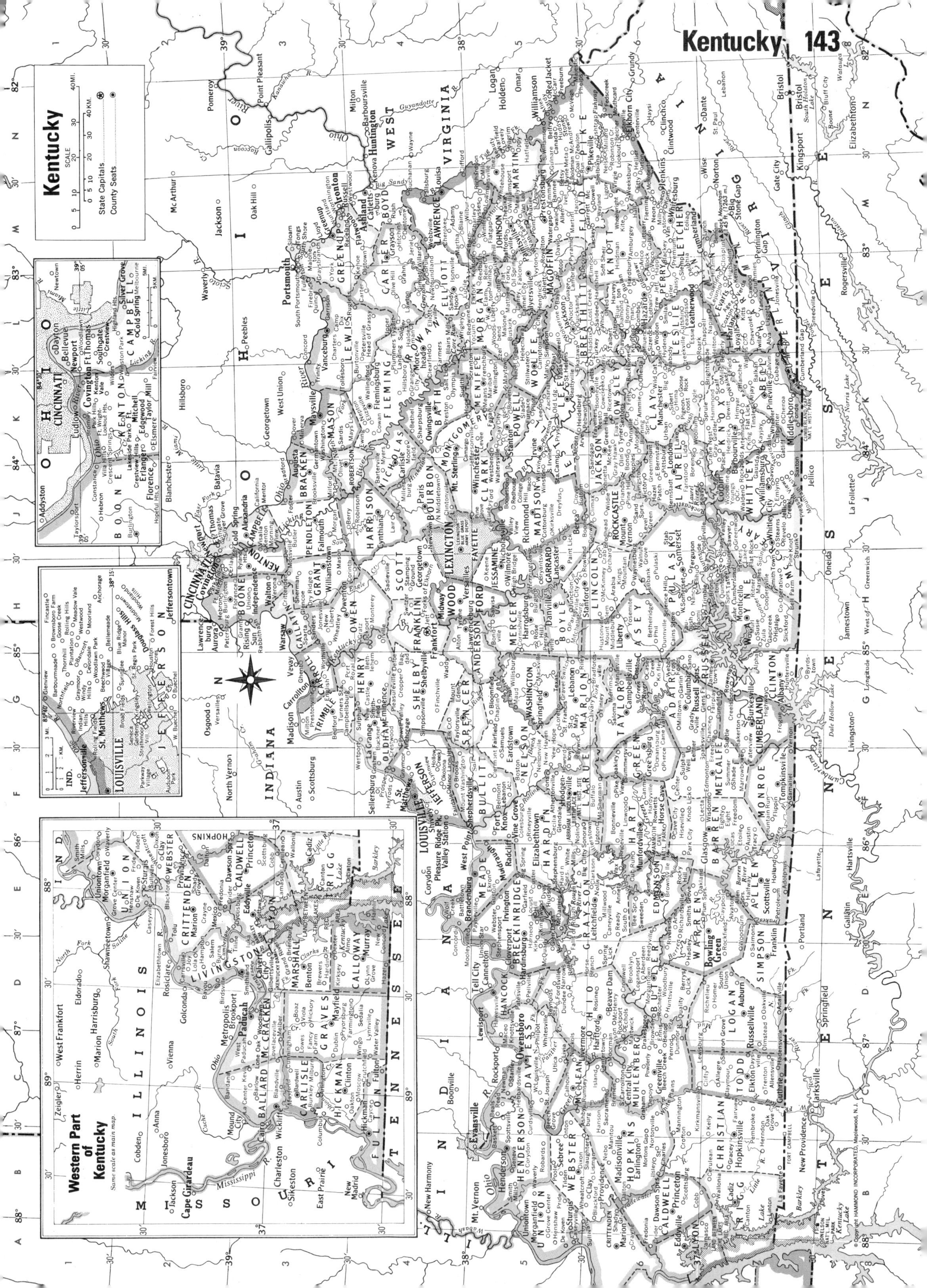
Kentucky
SCALE
State Capitals
County Seats
Western Part of Kentucky
Same scale as main map.
LOUISVILLE
CINCINNATI
© Copyright HAMMOND INCORPORATED, Maplewood, N.J.

New Orleans, Baton Rouge and Vicinity
Louisiana
SCALE
State Capitals
Parish Seats
Canals
GULF OF MEXICO
MISSISSIPPI
ARKANSAS
TEXAS
Longitude 91° West of Greenwich
© Copyright HAMMOND INCORPORATED, Maplewood, N.J.

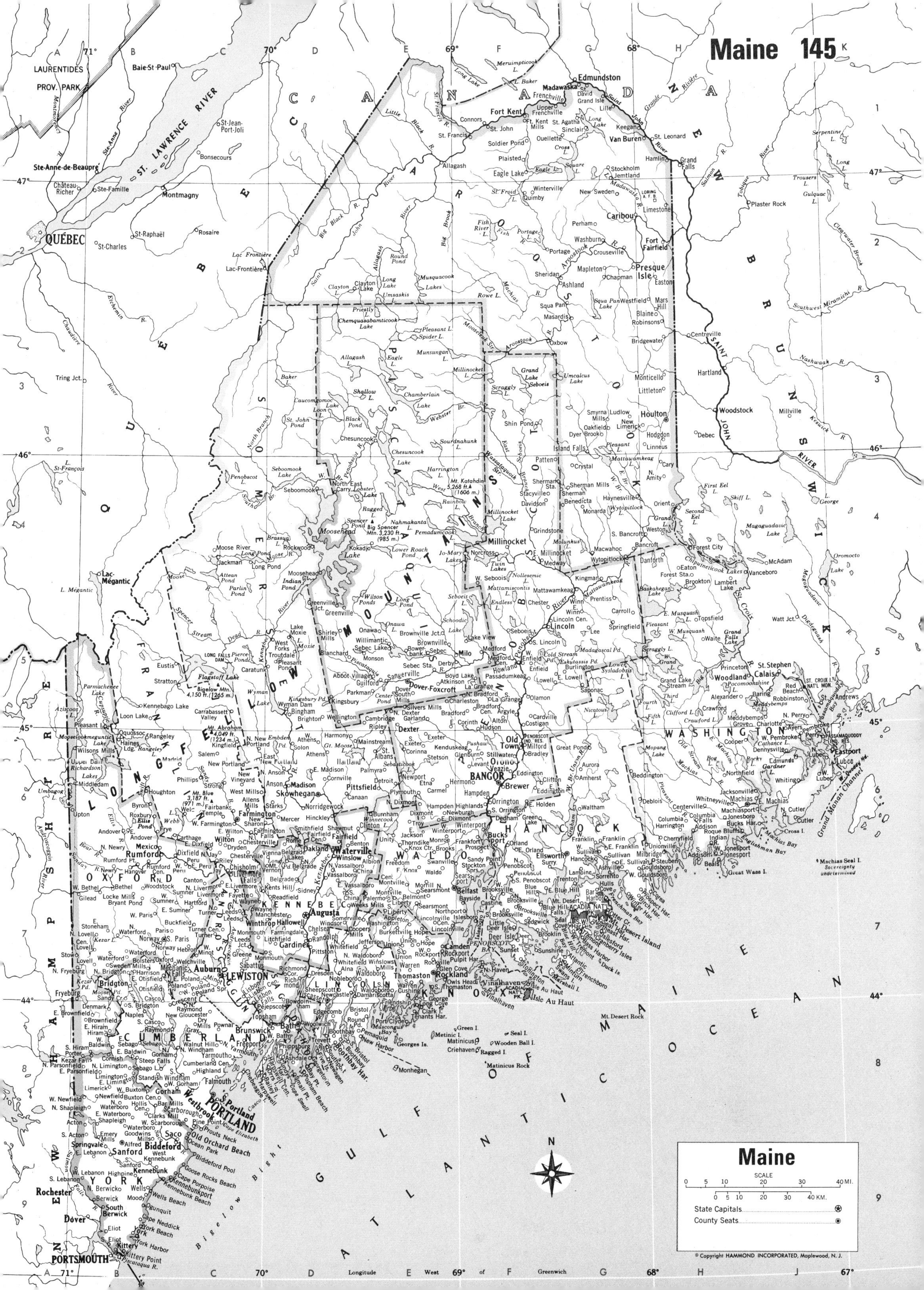

Maine
SCALE
0 5 10 20 30 40 MI.
0 5 10 20 30 40 KM.
State Capitals
County Seats
© Copyright HAMMOND INCORPORATED, Maplewood, N. J.
QUÉBEC
NEW BRUNSWICK
CANADA
NEW HAMPSHIRE
AROOSTOOK
PISCATAQUIS
PENOBSCOT
SOMERSET
FRANKLIN
OXFORD
ANDROSCOGGIN
KENNEBEC
WALDO
HANCOCK
WASHINGTON
CUMBERLAND
SAGADAHOC
LINCOLN
KNOX
YORK
LONGFELLOW MOUNTAINS
GULF OF MAINE
ATLANTIC OCEAN
ST. LAWRENCE RIVER
Augusta
PORTLAND
BANGOR
LEWISTON
Mt. Katahdin 5,268 ft. (1606 m.)
Mt. Desert Island
Isle Au Haut
Bigelow Bight
Grand Manan Channel
Longitude West of Greenwich

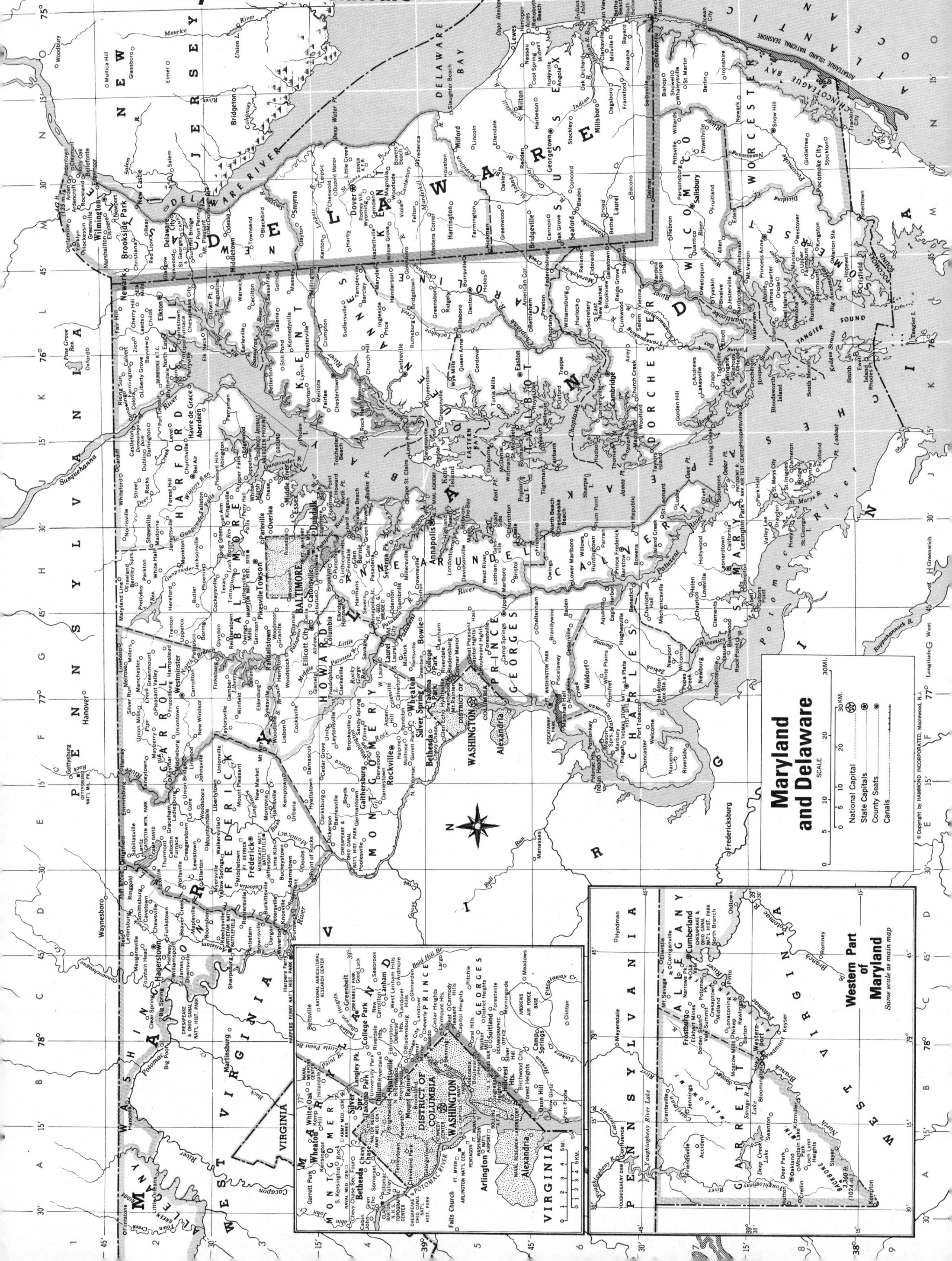

Maryland and Delaware
SCALE
National Capital
State Capitals
County Seats
Canals
© Copyright by HAMMOND INCORPORATED, Maplewood, N.J.
Western Part of Maryland
Same scale as main map
PENNSYLVANIA
NEW JERSEY
DELAWARE
WEST VIRGINIA
VIRGINIA
DISTRICT OF COLUMBIA
WASHINGTON
BALTIMORE
Annapolis
Dover
Wilmington
DELAWARE BAY
DELAWARE RIVER
ATLANTIC OCEAN
CHINCOTEAGUE BAY
TANGIER SOUND
CHESAPEAKE BAY
Potomac River

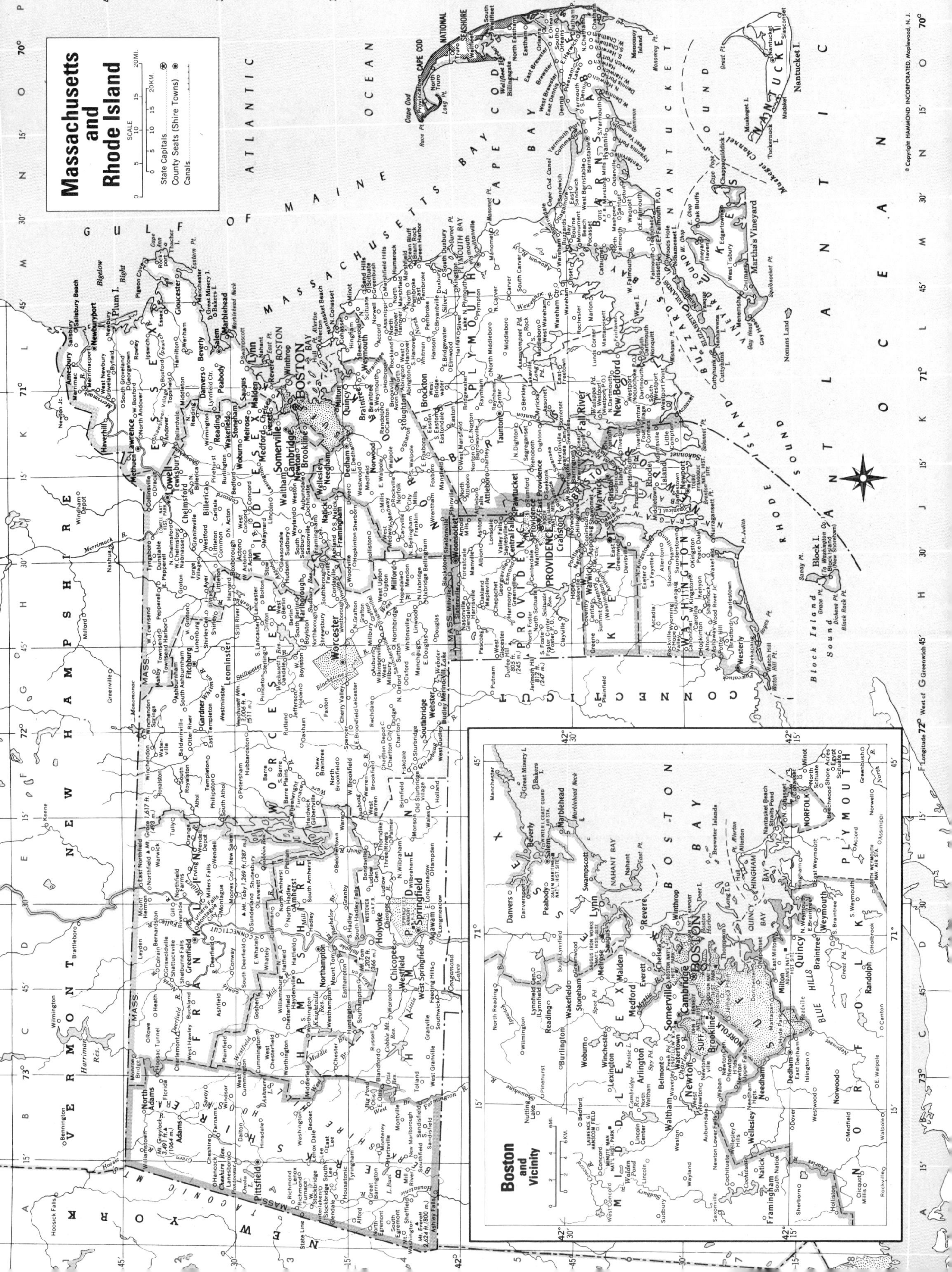
Massachusetts and Rhode Island
SCALE
0 5 10 15 20 MI.
0 5 10 15 20 KM.
State Capitals
County Seats (Shire Towns)
Canals
Boston and Vicinity
ATLANTIC OCEAN
GULF OF MAINE
MASSACHUSETTS BAY
CAPE COD BAY
NANTUCKET SOUND
RHODE ISLAND SOUND
Block Island Sound
NEW HAMPSHIRE
VERMONT
NEW YORK
CONNECTICUT
© Copyright HAMMOND INCORPORATED, Maplewood, N.J.

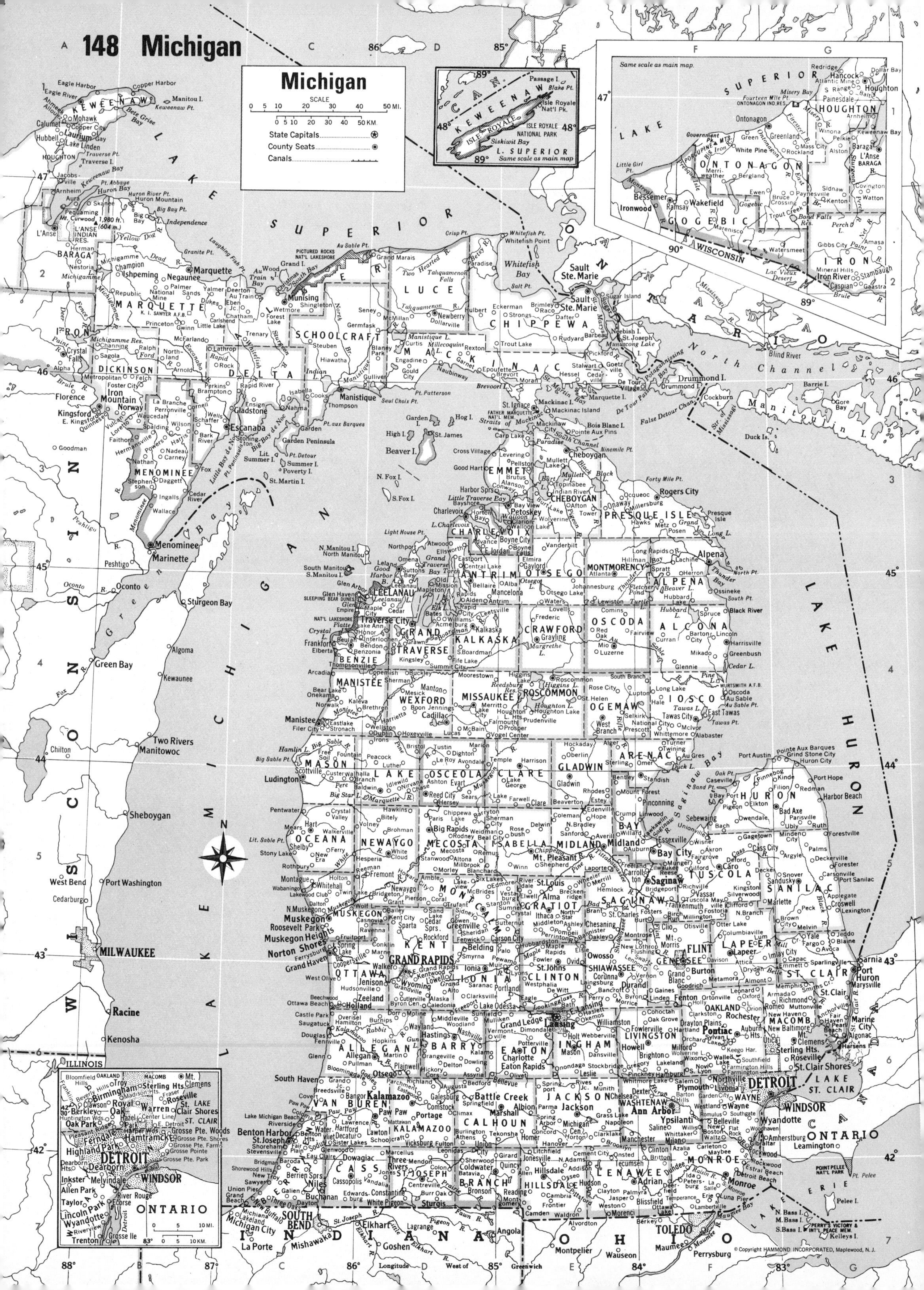
Michigan
SCALE
0 5 10 20 30 40 50 MI.
0 5 10 20 30 40 50 KM.
State Capitals
County Seats
Canals
ISLE ROYALE
ISLE ROYALE NATIONAL PARK
L. SUPERIOR
Same scale as main map
Same scale as main map.
LAKE SUPERIOR
LAKE MICHIGAN
LAKE HURON
LAKE ERIE
LAKE ST. CLAIR
ONTARIO
WISCONSIN
ILLINOIS
INDIANA
OHIO
North Channel
Manitoulin I.
Green Bay
Saginaw Bay
Thunder Bay
Grand Traverse Bay
KEWEENAW
HOUGHTON
ONTONAGON
GOGEBIC
IRON
BARAGA
MARQUETTE
ALGER
LUCE
CHIPPEWA
SCHOOLCRAFT
MACKINAC
DELTA
DICKINSON
MENOMINEE
EMMET
CHEBOYGAN
PRESQUE ISLE
CHARLEVOIX
ANTRIM
OTSEGO
MONTMORENCY
ALPENA
LEELANAU
GRAND TRAVERSE
KALKASKA
CRAWFORD
OSCODA
ALCONA
BENZIE
MANISTEE
WEXFORD
MISSAUKEE
ROSCOMMON
OGEMAW
IOSCO
MASON
LAKE
OSCEOLA
CLARE
GLADWIN
ARENAC
HURON
OCEANA
NEWAYGO
MECOSTA
ISABELLA
MIDLAND
BAY
TUSCOLA
SANILAC
MUSKEGON
MONTCALM
GRATIOT
SAGINAW
OTTAWA
KENT
IONIA
CLINTON
SHIAWASSEE
GENESEE
LAPEER
ST. CLAIR
ALLEGAN
BARRY
EATON
INGHAM
LIVINGSTON
OAKLAND
MACOMB
VAN BUREN
KALAMAZOO
CALHOUN
JACKSON
WASHTENAW
WAYNE
CASS
ST. JOSEPH
BRANCH
HILLSDALE
LENAWEE
MONROE
Lansing
Detroit
Grand Rapids
Flint
Windsor
Toledo
Milwaukee
© Copyright HAMMOND INCORPORATED, Maplewood, N.J.

Minnesota
SCALE
0 5 10 20 30 40 50 MI.
0 5 10 20 30 40 50 KM.
State Capitals
County Seats
Northeastern Part of Minnesota
Same scale as main map
MINNEAPOLIS
ST. PAUL
Duluth
Rochester
MANITOBA
ONTARIO
NORTH DAKOTA
SOUTH DAKOTA
IOWA
WISCONSIN
LAKE SUPERIOR
Lake of the Woods
Upper Red Lake
Lower Red Lake
Mille Lacs Lake
KITTSON
ROSEAU
LAKE OF THE WOODS
MARSHALL
KOOCHICHING
PENNINGTON
BELTRAMI
RED LAKE
POLK
CLEARWATER
ITASCA
SAINT LOUIS
LAKE
COOK
NORMAN
MAHNOMEN
HUBBARD
CLAY
BECKER
CASS
AITKIN
CARLTON
WILKIN
OTTER TAIL
WADENA
CROW WING
PINE
TODD
MORRISON
MILLE LACS
KANABEC
GRANT
DOUGLAS
TRAVERSE
STEVENS
POPE
STEARNS
BENTON
SHERBURNE
ISANTI
CHISAGO
BIG STONE
SWIFT
KANDIYOHI
MEEKER
WRIGHT
ANOKA
WASHINGTON
HENNEPIN
RAMSEY
CHIPPEWA
LAC QUI PARLE
YELLOW MEDICINE
RENVILLE
MCLEOD
CARVER
SCOTT
DAKOTA
SIBLEY
LINCOLN
LYON
REDWOOD
NICOLLET
LE SUEUR
RICE
GOODHUE
WABASHA
BROWN
PIPESTONE
MURRAY
COTTONWOOD
WATONWAN
BLUE EARTH
WASECA
STEELE
DODGE
OLMSTED
WINONA
ROCK
NOBLES
JACKSON
MARTIN
FARIBAULT
FREEBORN
MOWER
FILLMORE
HOUSTON
Copyright HAMMOND INCORPORATED, Maplewood, N. J.

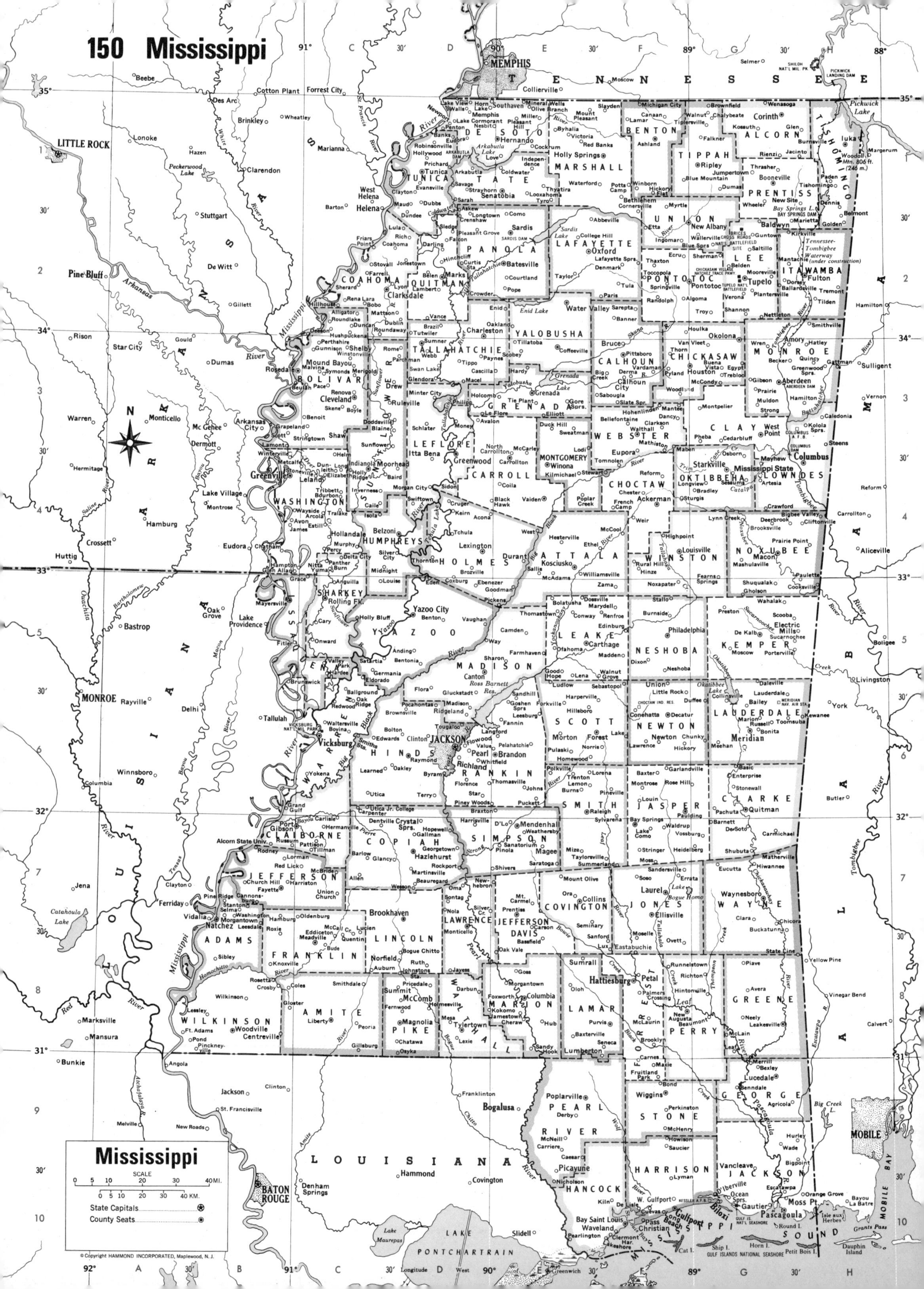
Mississippi
SCALE
0 5 10 20 30 40 MI.
0 5 10 20 30 40 KM.
State Capitals
County Seats
TENNESSEE
ARKANSAS
LOUISIANA
ALABAMA
MISSISSIPPI SOUND
LAKE PONTCHARTRAIN
MOBILE BAY
MEMPHIS
LITTLE ROCK
JACKSON
BATON ROUGE
MOBILE
DE SOTO
TUNICA
TATE
MARSHALL
BENTON
TIPPAH
ALCORN
TISHOMINGO
PRENTISS
UNION
LAFAYETTE
PANOLA
QUITMAN
COAHOMA
BOLIVAR
TALLAHATCHIE
YALOBUSHA
CALHOUN
PONTOTOC
LEE
ITAWAMBA
MONROE
CHICKASAW
GRENADA
SUNFLOWER
LEFLORE
CARROLL
MONTGOMERY
WEBSTER
CLAY
CHOCTAW
OKTIBBEHA
LOWNDES
WASHINGTON
HUMPHREYS
HOLMES
ATTALA
WINSTON
NOXUBEE
SHARKEY
YAZOO
MADISON
LEAKE
NESHOBA
KEMPER
ISSAQUENA
WARREN
HINDS
RANKIN
SCOTT
NEWTON
LAUDERDALE
CLAIBORNE
COPIAH
SIMPSON
SMITH
JASPER
CLARKE
JEFFERSON
LINCOLN
LAWRENCE
JEFFERSON DAVIS
COVINGTON
JONES
WAYNE
ADAMS
FRANKLIN
WILKINSON
AMITE
PIKE
WALTHALL
MARION
LAMAR
FORREST
PERRY
GREENE
PEARL RIVER
STONE
GEORGE
HANCOCK
HARRISON
JACKSON
GULF ISLANDS NATIONAL SEASHORE
© Copyright HAMMOND INCORPORATED, Maplewood, N. J.

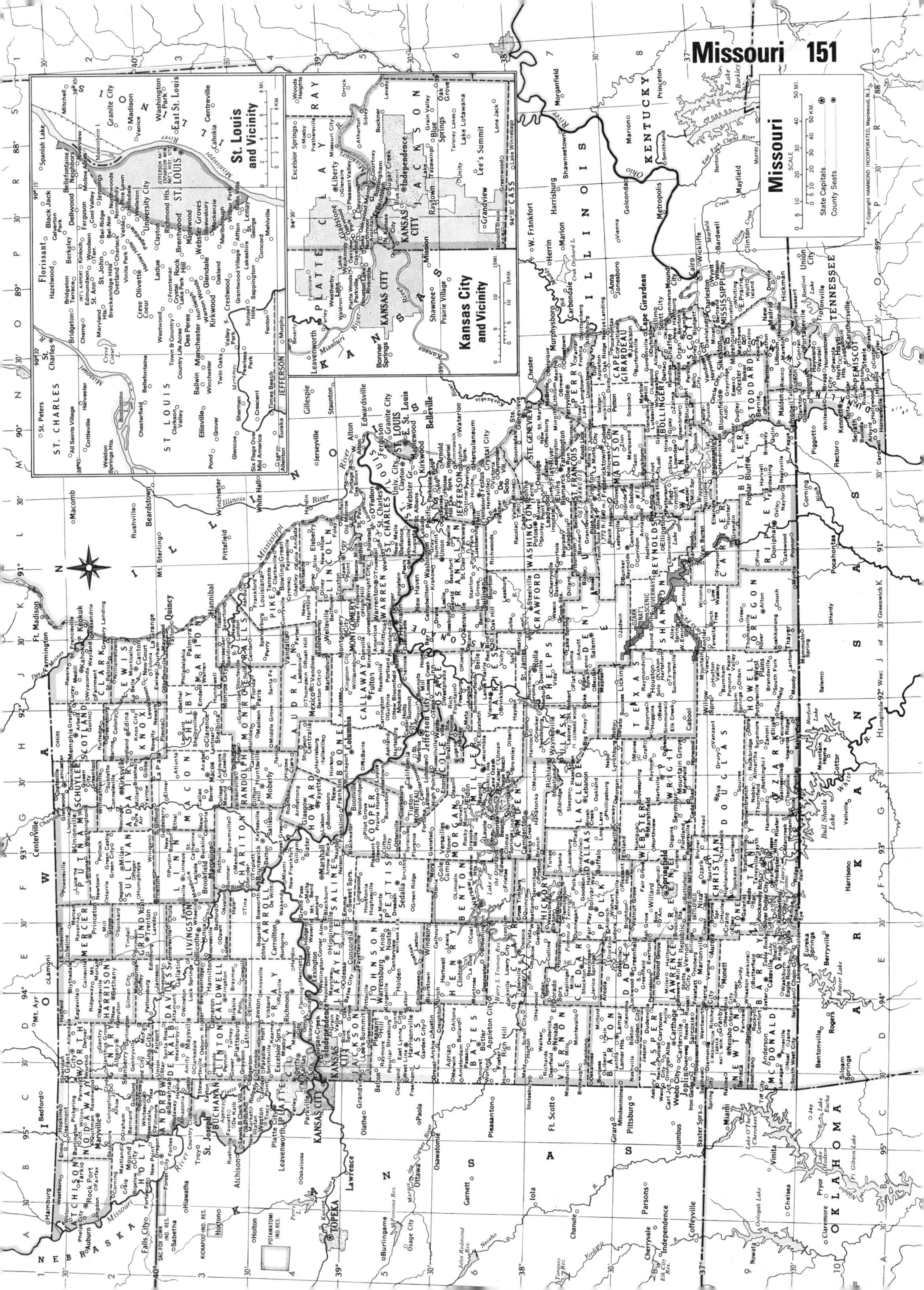
Missouri
SCALE
State Capitals
County Seats
© Copyright HAMMOND INCORPORATED, Maplewood, N.J.
St. Louis and Vicinity
Kansas City and Vicinity
ILLINOIS
KENTUCKY
TENNESSEE
ARKANSAS
OKLAHOMA
KANSAS
NEBRASKA
IOWA

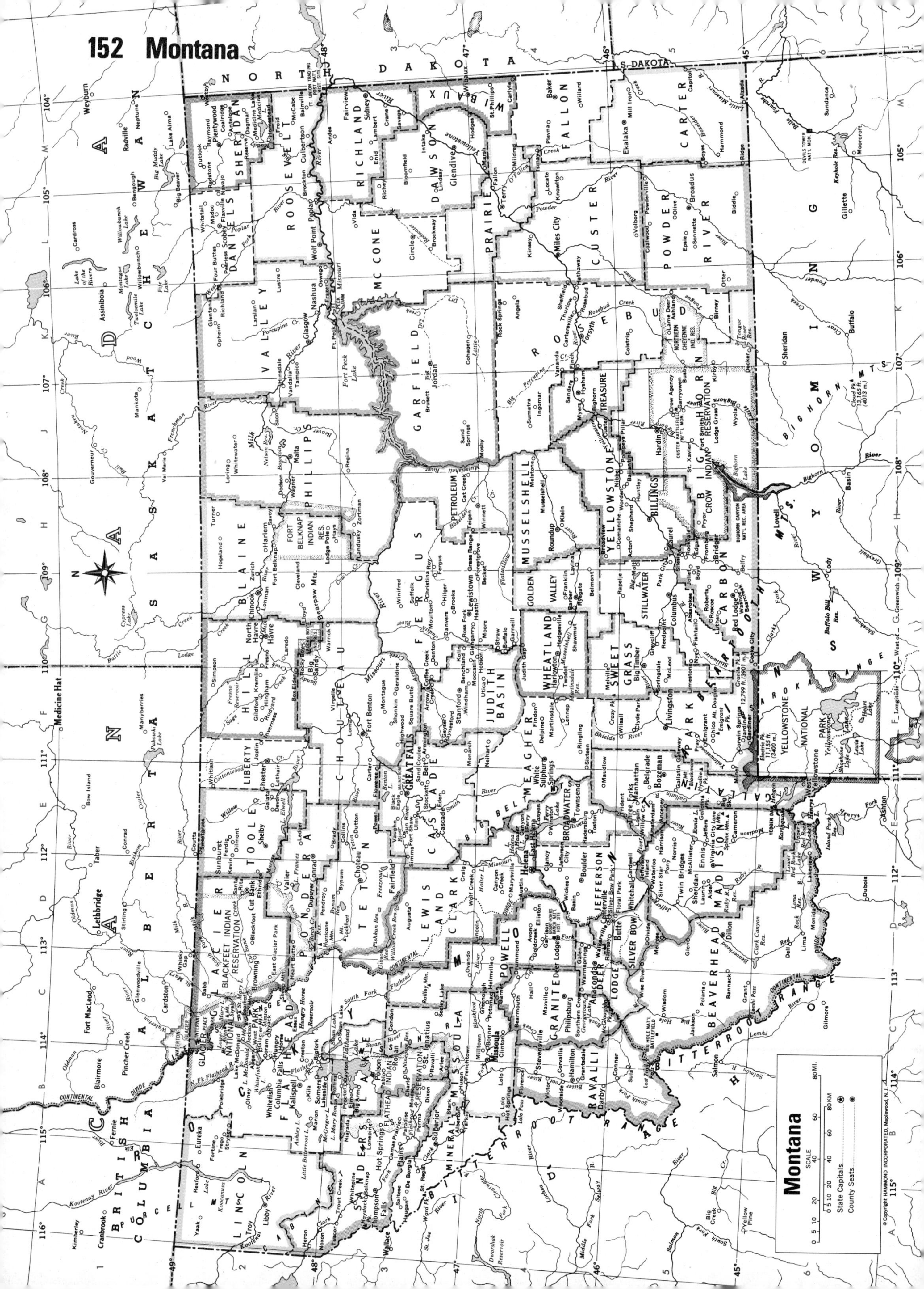
Montana
SCALE
0 5 10 20 40 60 80 MI.
0 5 10 20 40 60 80 KM.
State Capitals
County Seats
© Copyright HAMMOND INCORPORATED, Maplewood, N.J.
SASKATCHEWAN
ALBERTA
BRITISH COLUMBIA
NORTH DAKOTA
S. DAKOTA
WYOMING
IDAHO
SHERIDAN
DANIELS
ROOSEVELT
RICHLAND
DAWSON
WIBAUX
PRAIRIE
FALLON
CARTER
CUSTER
POWDER RIVER
MC CONE
GARFIELD
VALLEY
PHILLIPS
BLAINE
HILL
LIBERTY
TOOLE
GLACIER
PONDERA
TETON
CHOUTEAU
CASCADE
FERGUS
PETROLEUM
MUSSELSHELL
ROSEBUD
TREASURE
BIG HORN
YELLOWSTONE
GOLDEN VALLEY
WHEATLAND
JUDITH BASIN
MEAGHER
SWEET GRASS
STILLWATER
CARBON
PARK
GALLATIN
MADISON
BEAVERHEAD
SILVER BOW
JEFFERSON
BROADWATER
LEWIS AND CLARK
POWELL
DEER LODGE
GRANITE
RAVALLI
MISSOULA
MINERAL
SANDERS
LAKE
FLATHEAD
LINCOLN
YELLOWSTONE NATIONAL PARK
GLACIER NATIONAL PARK
BITTERROOT RANGE
BIGHORN MTS.
ABSAROKA RANGE
CONTINENTAL DIVIDE
Billings
Great Falls
Helena
Butte
Missoula
Bozeman
Kalispell
Havre
Miles City
Glendive
Lewistown

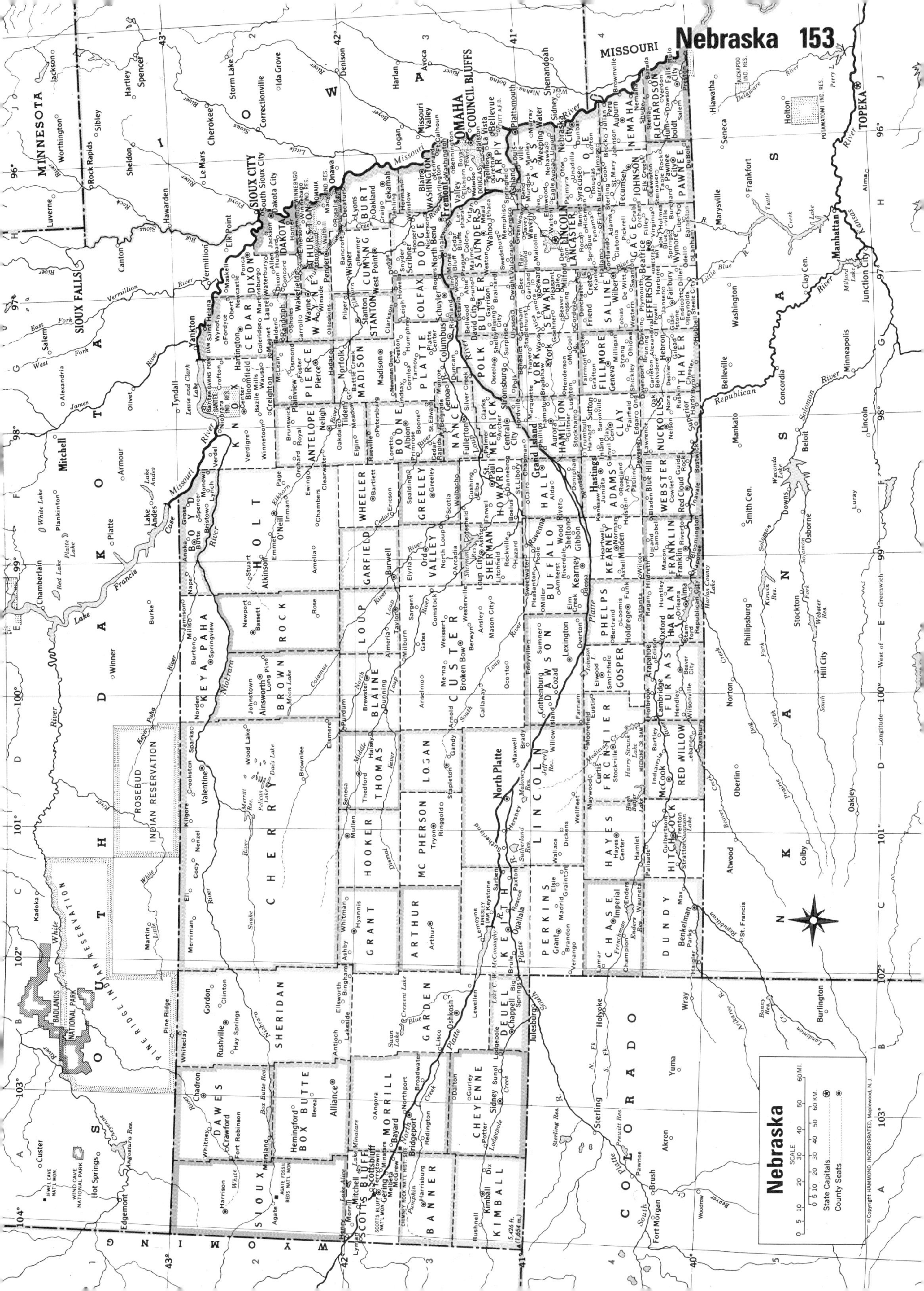
Nebraska
SCALE
0 5 10 20 30 40 50 60 MI.
0 5 10 20 30 40 50 60 KM.
State Capitals
County Seats
© Copyright HAMMOND INCORPORATED, Maplewood, N.J.
MINNESOTA
IOWA
MISSOURI
KANSAS
COLORADO
WYOMING
SOUTH DAKOTA
LINCOLN
OMAHA
COUNCIL BLUFFS
SIOUX CITY
SIOUX FALLS
TOPEKA
North Platte
Grand Island
Kearney
Hastings
Scottsbluff
ROSEBUD INDIAN RESERVATION
PINE RIDGE INDIAN RESERVATION
BADLANDS NATIONAL PARK
CHERRY
SHERIDAN
DAWES
SIOUX
BOX BUTTE
SCOTTS BLUFF
BANNER
KIMBALL
CHEYENNE
MORRILL
GARDEN
DEUEL
KEITH
ARTHUR
GRANT
HOOKER
THOMAS
BLAINE
BROWN
KEYA PAHA
ROCK
LOUP
GARFIELD
WHEELER
HOLT
BOYD
KNOX
CEDAR
DIXON
DAKOTA
THURSTON
WAYNE
PIERCE
ANTELOPE
BOONE
MADISON
STANTON
CUMING
BURT
WASHINGTON
DODGE
COLFAX
PLATTE
NANCE
GREELEY
VALLEY
CUSTER
LOGAN
MC PHERSON
LINCOLN
PERKINS
CHASE
DUNDY
HAYES
HITCHCOCK
FRONTIER
RED WILLOW
GOSPER
FURNAS
DAWSON
PHELPS
HARLAN
BUFFALO
KEARNEY
FRANKLIN
SHERMAN
HOWARD
HALL
ADAMS
WEBSTER
MERRICK
HAMILTON
CLAY
NUCKOLLS
POLK
YORK
FILLMORE
THAYER
BUTLER
SEWARD
SALINE
JEFFERSON
SAUNDERS
LANCASTER
GAGE
SARPY
CASS
OTOE
JOHNSON
PAWNEE
NEMAHA
RICHARDSON
DOUGLAS

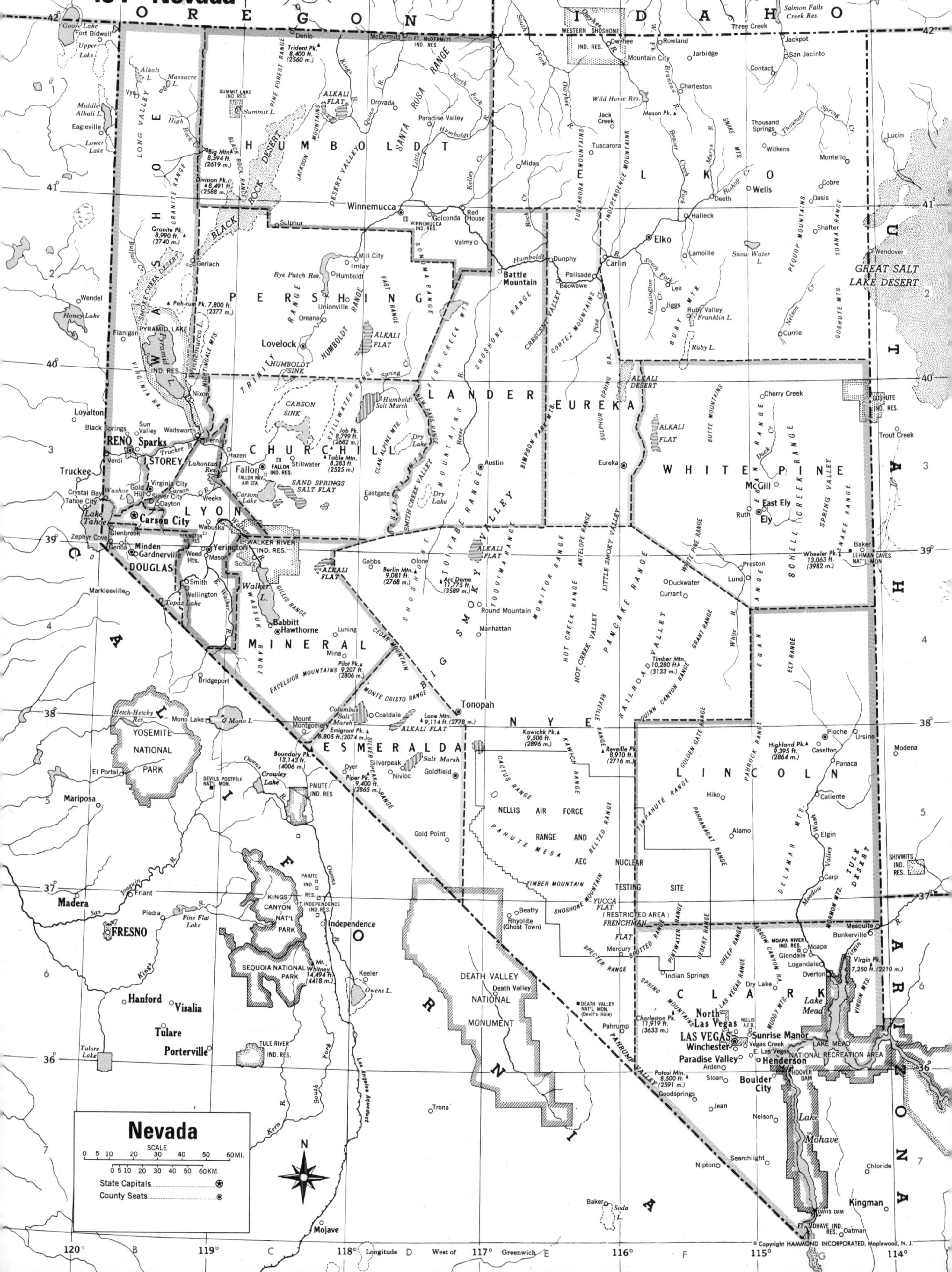
OREGON
IDAHO
UTAH
ARIZONA
CALIFORNIA
HUMBOLDT
ELKO
WASHOE
PERSHING
LANDER
EUREKA
WHITE PINE
CHURCHILL
STOREY
LYON
DOUGLAS
MINERAL
NYE
ESMERALDA
LINCOLN
CLARK
Carson City
RENO
Sparks
Winnemucca
Elko
Ely
East Ely
McGill
Ruth
Lovelock
Fallon
Battle Mountain
Austin
Eureka
Tonopah
Goldfield
Hawthorne
Babbitt
Yerington
Minden
Gardnerville
Pioche
Caliente
Panaca
LAS VEGAS
North Las Vegas
Henderson
Boulder City
Winchester
Paradise Valley
Sunrise Manor
Wells
Carlin
Jackpot
Owyhee
Mountain City
Gerlach
Denio
McDermitt
Mesquite
Bunkerville
Overton
Pahrump
Beatty
Rhyolite (Ghost Town)
Mercury
Indian Springs
Searchlight
Laughlin
Wendover
Lake Tahoe
Pyramid L.
Walker L.
Lake Mead
Lake Mohave
Honey Lake
Mono L.
Owens L.
BLACK ROCK DESERT
SMOKE CREEK DESERT
GREAT SALT LAKE DESERT
NELLIS AIR FORCE RANGE AND AEC NUCLEAR TESTING SITE
DEATH VALLEY NATIONAL MONUMENT
YOSEMITE NATIONAL PARK
KINGS CANYON NAT'L PARK
SEQUOIA NATIONAL PARK
LAKE MEAD NATIONAL RECREATION AREA
HOOVER DAM
DAVIS DAM
Wheeler Pk. 13,063 ft. (3982 m.)
Boundary Pk. 13,143 ft. (4006 m.)
Charleston Pk. 11,919 ft. (3633 m.)
Mt. Whitney 14,494 ft. (4418 m.)
Nevada
SCALE
0 5 10 20 30 40 50 60 MI.
0 5 10 20 30 40 50 60 KM.
State Capitals
County Seats
N
Longitude West of Greenwich
© Copyright HAMMOND INCORPORATED, Maplewood, N. J.

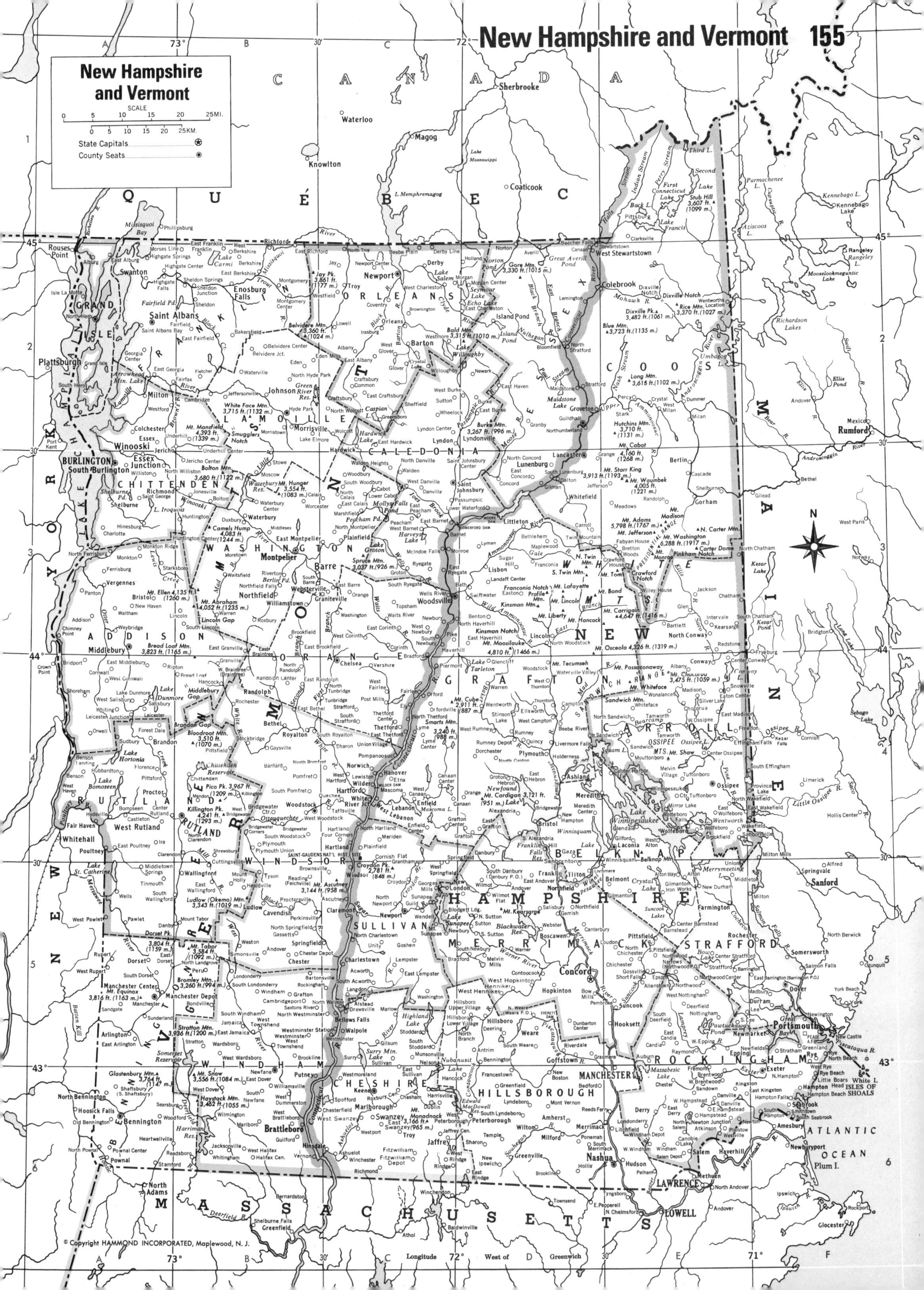
New Hampshire and Vermont
SCALE
0 5 10 15 20 25 MI.
0 5 10 15 20 25 KM.
State Capitals
County Seats
CANADA
QUÉBEC
NEW YORK
MAINE
MASSACHUSETTS
ATLANTIC OCEAN
VERMONT
NEW HAMPSHIRE
GRAND ISLE
FRANKLIN
ORLEANS
ESSEX
LAMOILLE
CALEDONIA
CHITTENDEN
WASHINGTON
ADDISON
ORANGE
RUTLAND
WINDSOR
BENNINGTON
WINDHAM
COOS
GRAFTON
CARROLL
BELKNAP
STRAFFORD
MERRIMACK
SULLIVAN
HILLSBOROUGH
CHESHIRE
ROCKINGHAM
Montpelier
Concord
Burlington
Manchester
Nashua
Portsmouth
Sherbrooke
Lake Champlain
L. Memphremagog
Lake Winnipesaukee
Connecticut R.
Mt. Washington 6,288 ft. (1917 m.)
Mt. Mansfield 4,393 ft. (1339 m.)
PRESIDENTIAL RANGE
ISLES OF SHOALS
Longitude 72° West of Greenwich
© Copyright HAMMOND INCORPORATED, Maplewood, N.J.

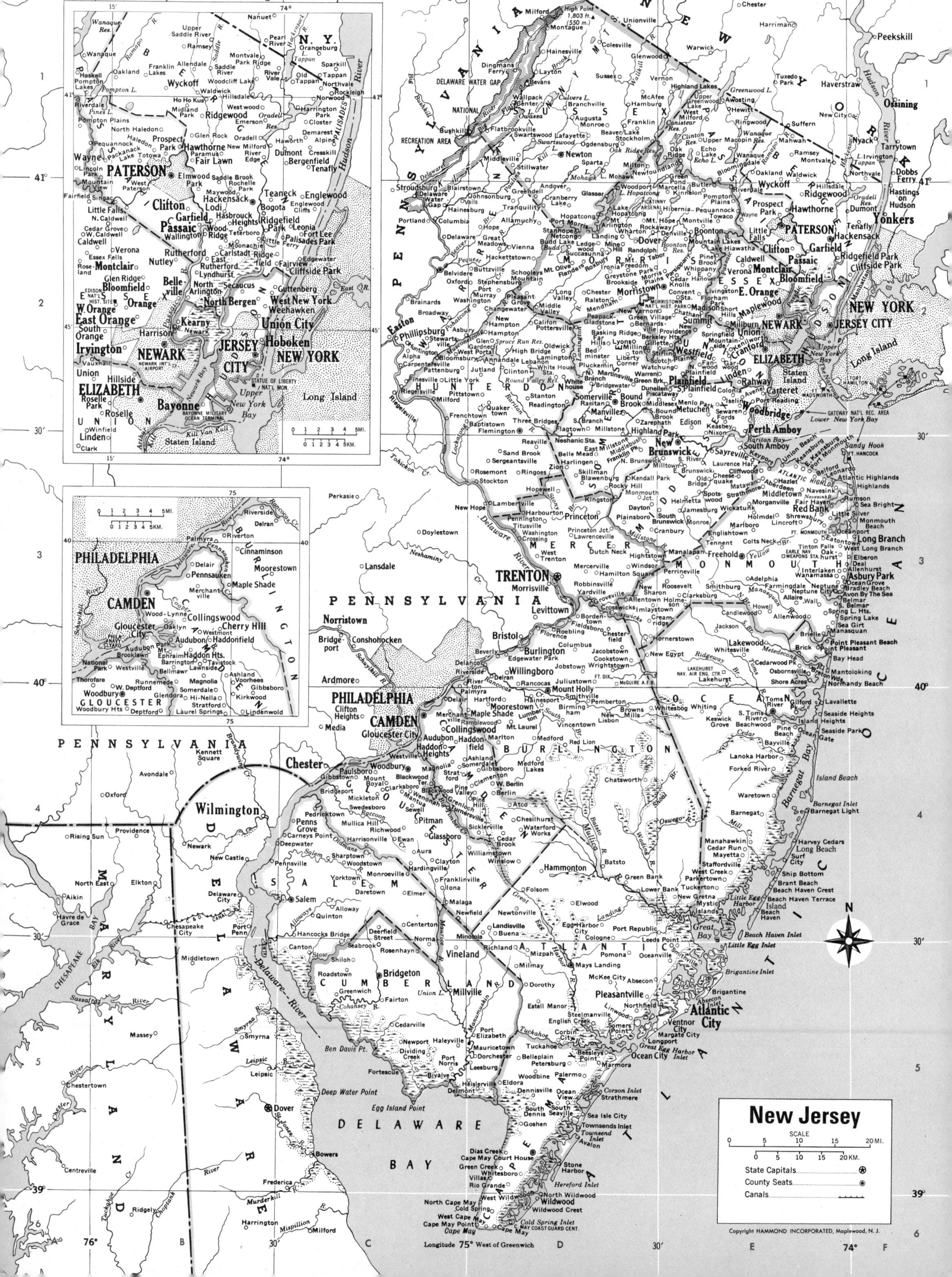
New Jersey
SCALE
0 5 10 15 20 MI.
0 5 10 15 20 KM.
State Capitals
County Seats
Canals
Copyright HAMMOND INCORPORATED, Maplewood, N. J.
Longitude 75° West of Greenwich
PENNSYLVANIA
NEW YORK
DELAWARE
MARYLAND
ATLANTIC OCEAN
DELAWARE BAY
SUSSEX
PASSAIC
BERGEN
WARREN
MORRIS
ESSEX
HUDSON
UNION
HUNTERDON
SOMERSET
MIDDLESEX
MERCER
MONMOUTH
OCEAN
BURLINGTON
CAMDEN
GLOUCESTER
SALEM
CUMBERLAND
ATLANTIC
CAPE MAY
TRENTON
NEWARK
JERSEY CITY
PATERSON
ELIZABETH
CAMDEN
PHILADELPHIA
NEW YORK
Atlantic City
Wilmington
DELAWARE WATER GAP NATIONAL RECREATION AREA
GATEWAY NAT'L REC. AREA
High Point 1,803 ft. (550 m.)
N
Long Island
Staten Island
0 1 2 3 4 5 MI.
0 1 2 3 4 5 KM.

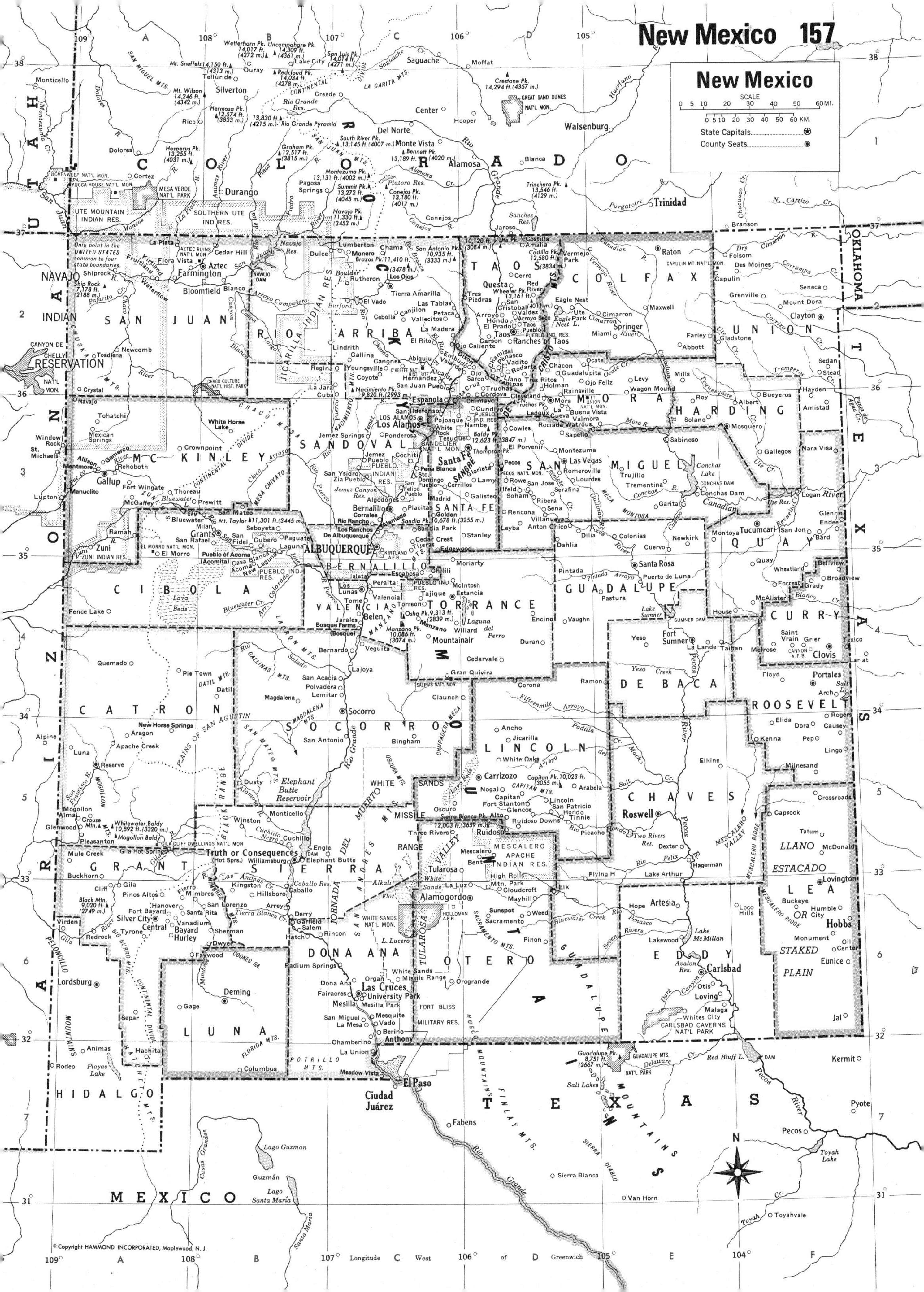
New Mexico
SCALE
0 5 10 20 30 40 50 60 MI.
0 5 10 20 30 40 50 60 KM.
State Capitals
County Seats
C O L O R A D O
U T A H
A R I Z O N A
O K L A H O M A
T E X A S
M E X I C O
SAN JUAN
RIO ARRIBA
TAOS
COLFAX
UNION
MORA
HARDING
MC KINLEY
SANDOVAL
LOS ALAMOS
SANTA FE
SAN MIGUEL
QUAY
CIBOLA
VALENCIA
BERNALILLO
TORRANCE
GUADALUPE
CURRY
DE BACA
ROOSEVELT
CATRON
SOCORRO
LINCOLN
CHAVES
SIERRA
GRANT
OTERO
LEA
EDDY
DONA ANA
LUNA
HIDALGO
Santa Fe
Albuquerque
Las Cruces
Roswell
Carlsbad
Farmington
Gallup
Clovis
Hobbs
Alamogordo
El Paso
Ciudad Juárez
LLANO ESTACADO
STAKED PLAIN
Longitude West of Greenwich
109° 108° 107° 106° 105° 104°
37 36 35 34 33 32 31

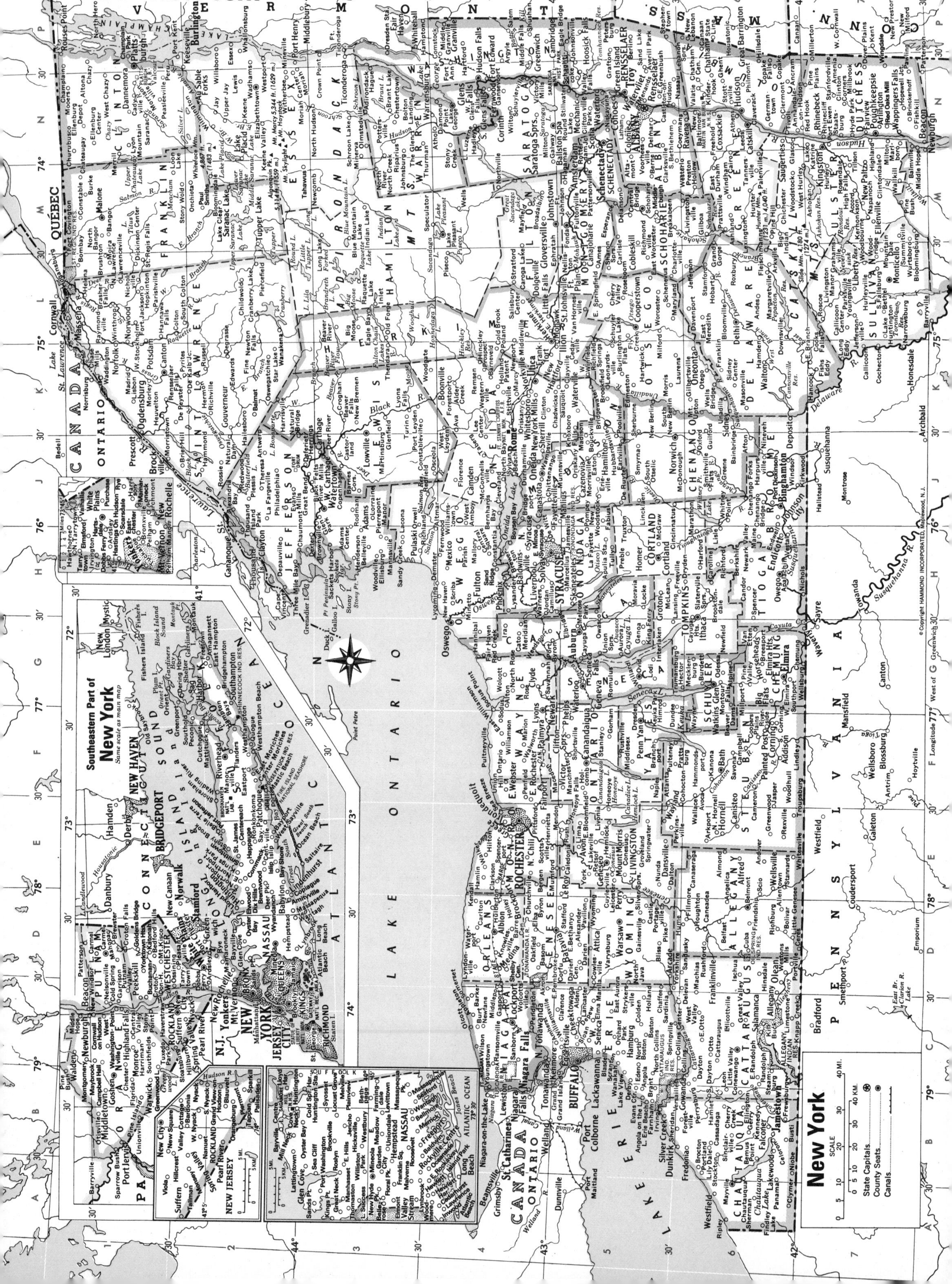
New York
SCALE
State Capitals
County Seats
Canals
Southeastern Part of New York
Same scale as main map
LAKE ONTARIO
CANADA
ONTARIO
QUÉBEC
PENNSYLVANIA
ATLANTIC OCEAN
LONG ISLAND SOUND
LAKE ERIE
© Copyright HAMMOND INCORPORATED, Maplewood, N.J.

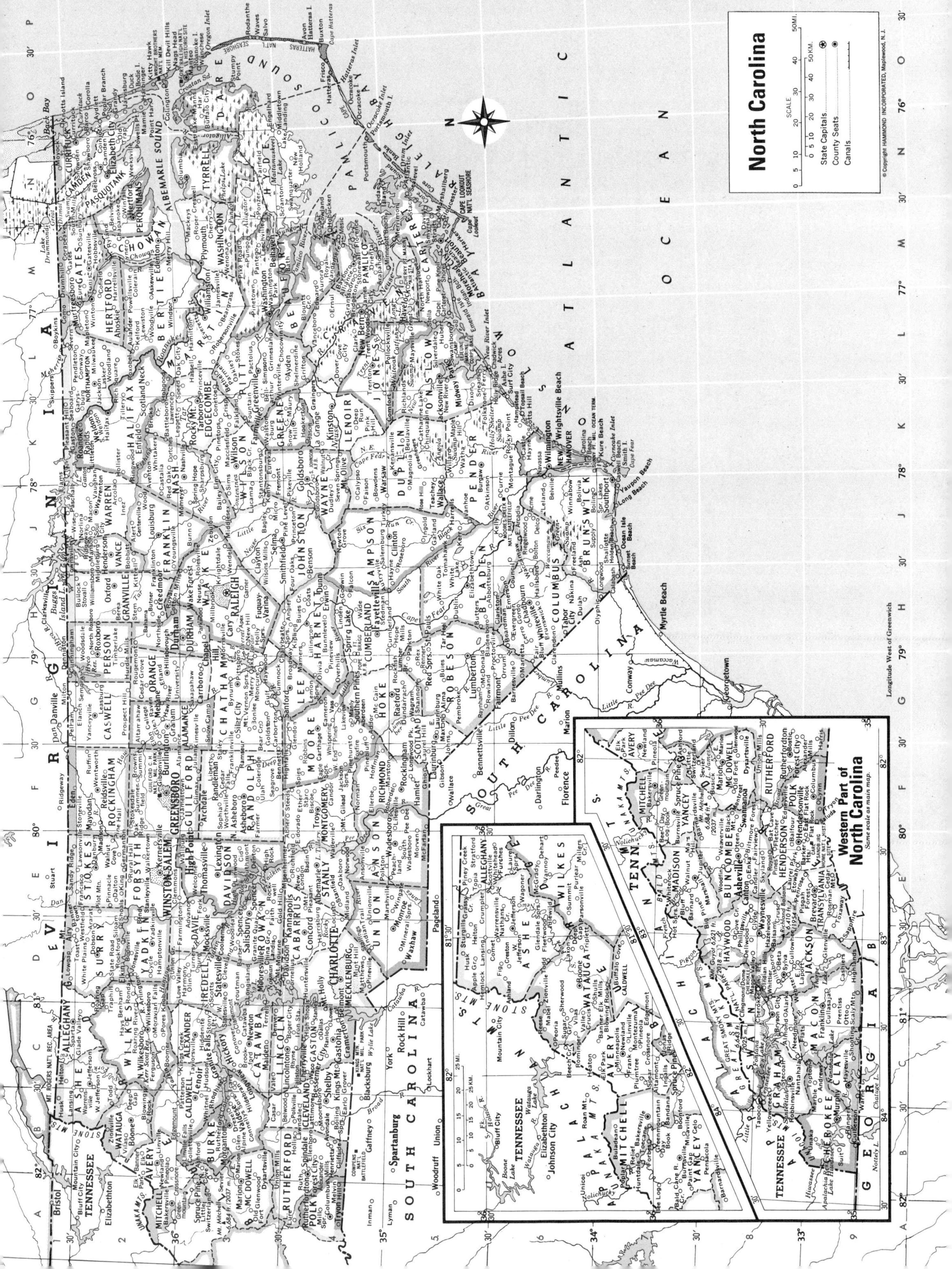
North Carolina
SCALE
0 5 10 20 30 40 50 MI.
0 5 10 20 30 40 50 KM.
State Capitals
County Seats
Canals
© Copyright HAMMOND INCORPORATED, Maplewood, N.J.
Western Part of North Carolina
Same scale as main map.
ATLANTIC OCEAN
VIRGINIA
TENNESSEE
SOUTH CAROLINA
GEORGIA
Longitude West of Greenwich

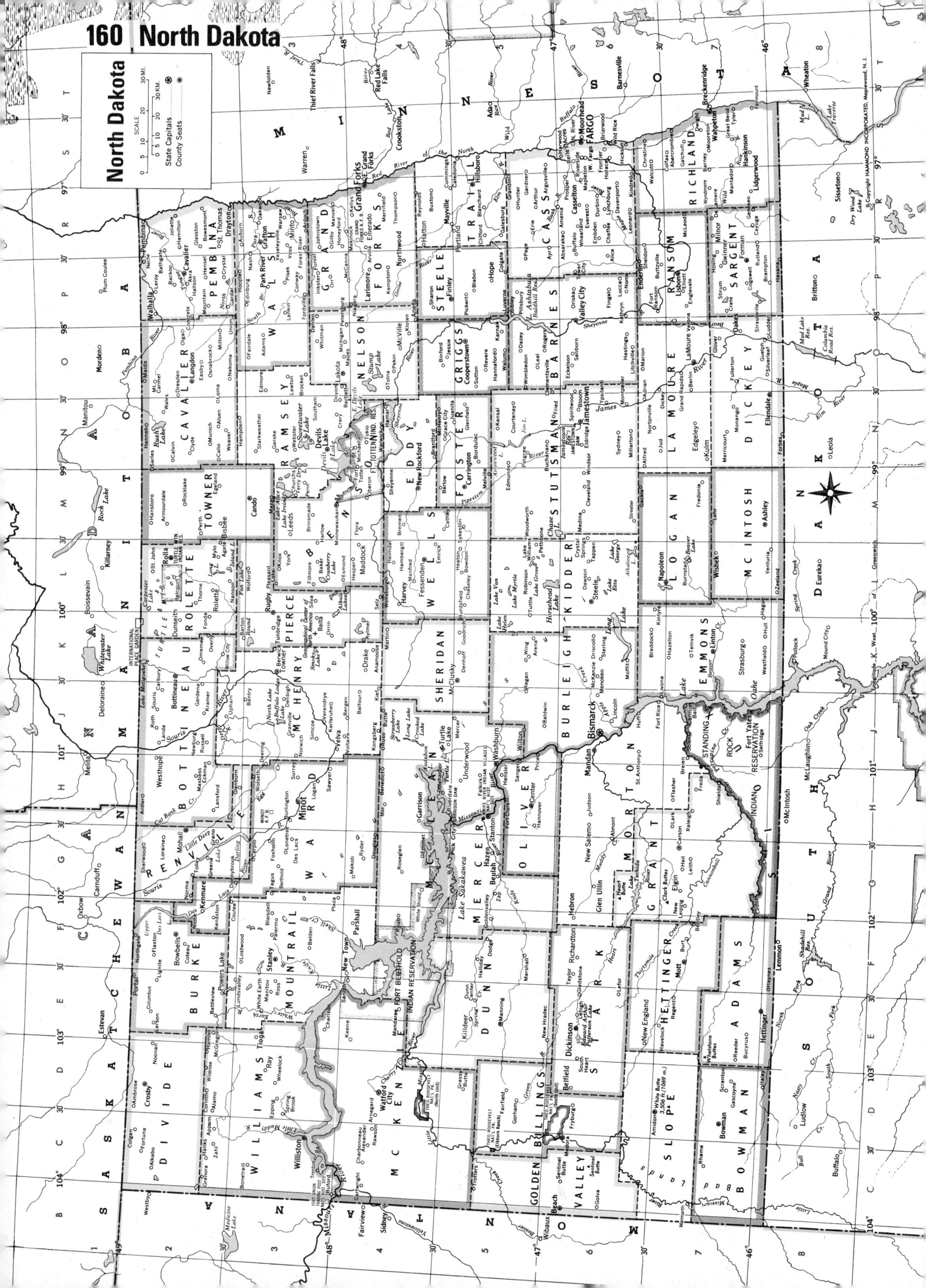
North Dakota
SCALE
0 5 10 20 30 MI.
0 5 10 20 30 KM.
State Capitals
County Seats
Copyright HAMMOND INCORPORATED, Maplewood, N. J.

MICHIGAN
INDIANA
PENNSYLVANIA
WEST VIRGINIA
KENTUCKY
ONTARIO
CANADA
LAKE ERIE
Lake St. Clair
DETROIT
Windsor
Toledo
CLEVELAND
Columbus
CINCINNATI
Dayton
Akron
Canton
Youngstown
Ohio River
Ohio
SCALE
0 5 10 20 30 40 MI.
0 5 10 20 30 40 KM.
State Capitals
County Seats
LAKE ERIE
KENTUCKY
© Copyright HAMMOND INCORPORATED, Maplewood, N. J.

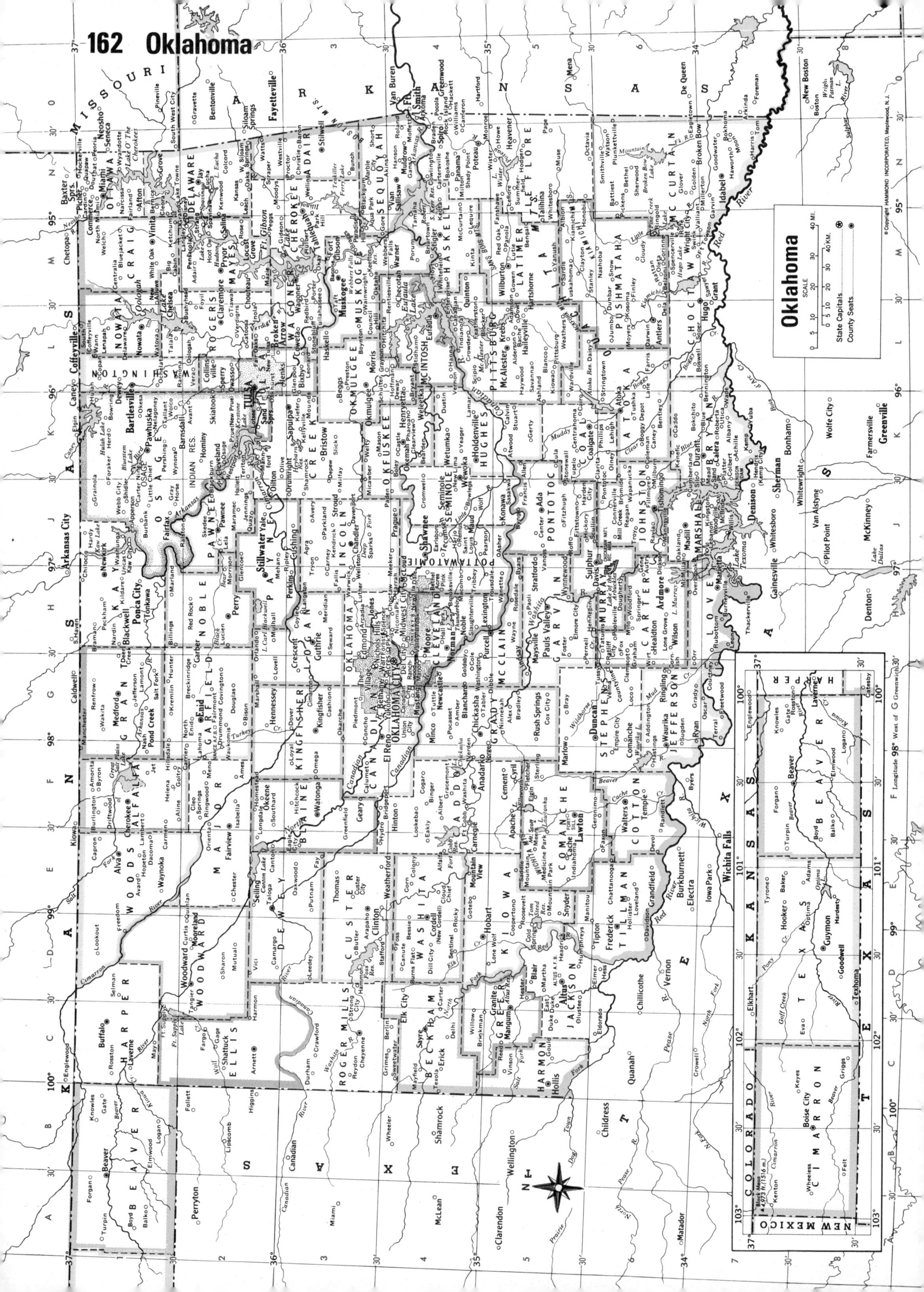
Oklahoma
SCALE
0 5 10 20 30 40 MI.
0 5 10 20 30 40 KM.
State Capitals
County Seats
© Copyright HAMMOND INCORPORATED, Maplewood, N.J.
Longitude 98° West of Greenwich

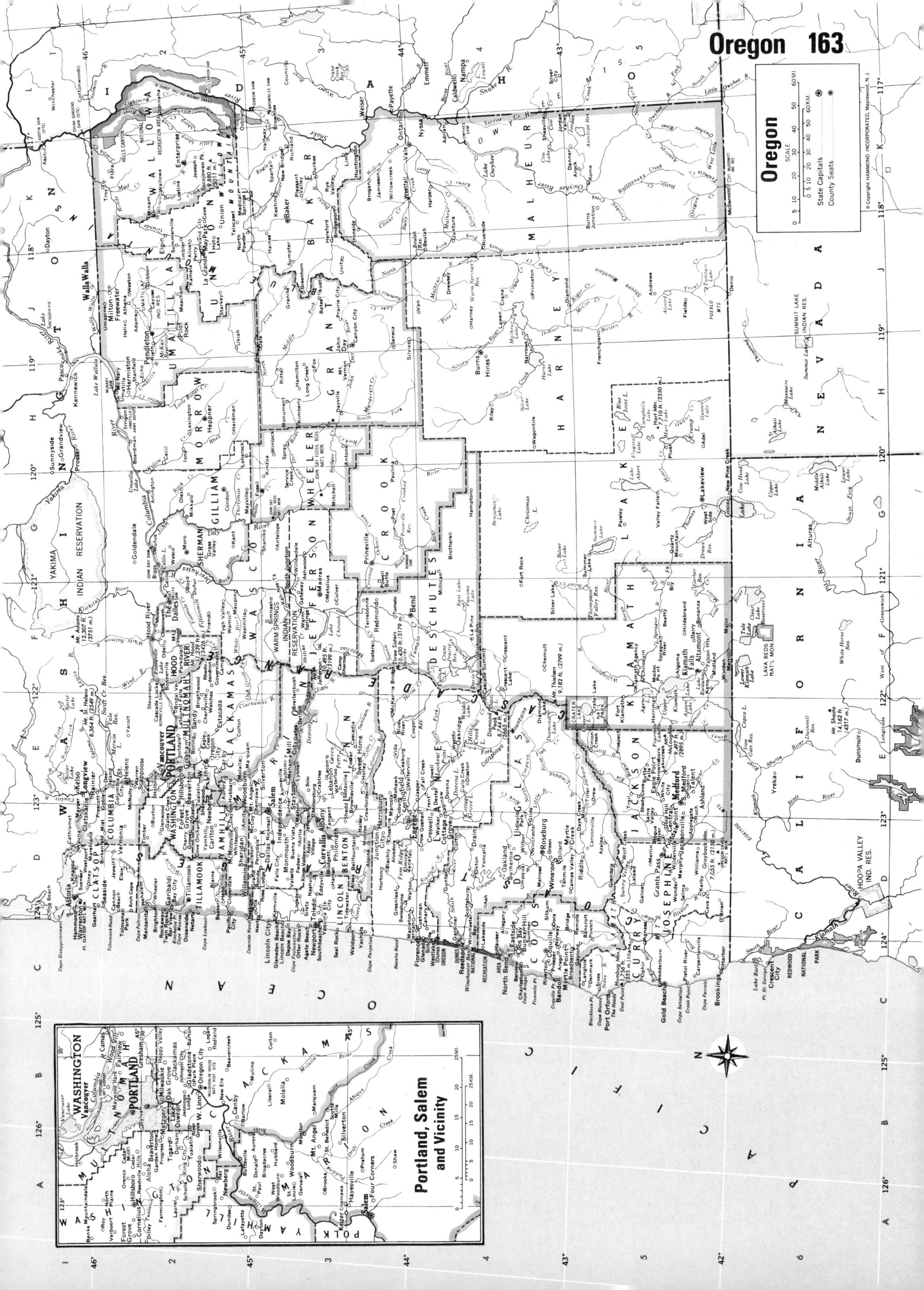
Oregon
SCALE
0 5 10 20 30 40 50 60 MI.
0 5 10 20 30 40 50 60 KM.
State Capitals
County Seats
© Copyright HAMMOND INCORPORATED, Maplewood, N.J.
Portland, Salem and Vicinity
PACIFIC OCEAN
WASHINGTON
IDAHO
NEVADA
CALIFORNIA
Portland
Salem
Eugene
Medford
Bend
Pendleton
Klamath Falls
Astoria
Coos Bay
Baker
La Grande
Burns
Lakeview
Roseburg
Corvallis
Albany
The Dalles
Ontario

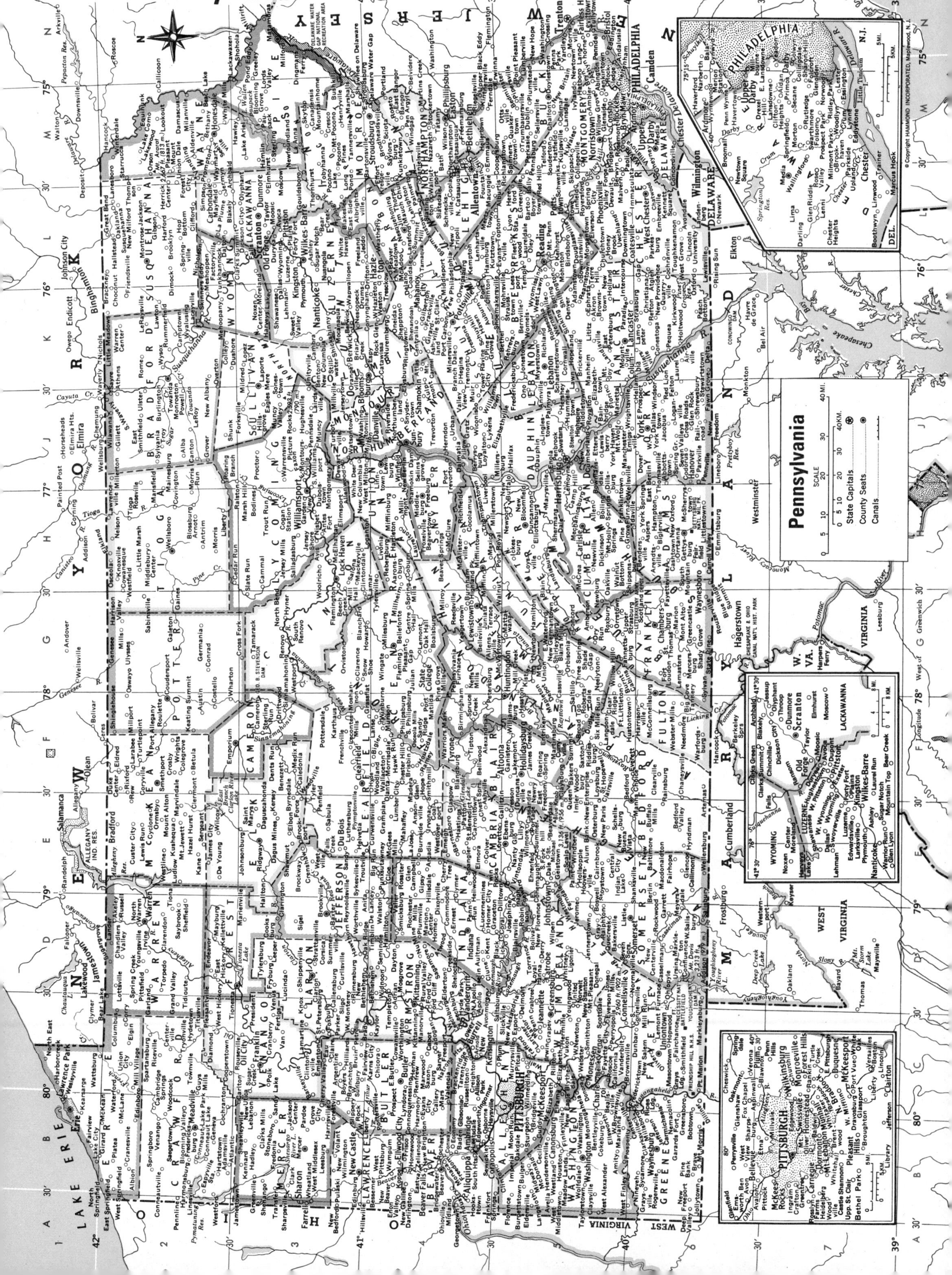
Pennsylvania
SCALE
State Capitals
County Seats
Canals
PHILADELPHIA
PITTSBURGH
LACKAWANNA
LUZERNE
WYOMING
LAKE ERIE
NEW YORK
NEW JERSEY
DELAWARE
MARYLAND
WEST VIRGINIA
VIRGINIA
OHIO
© Copyright HAMMOND INCORPORATED, Maplewood, N.J.

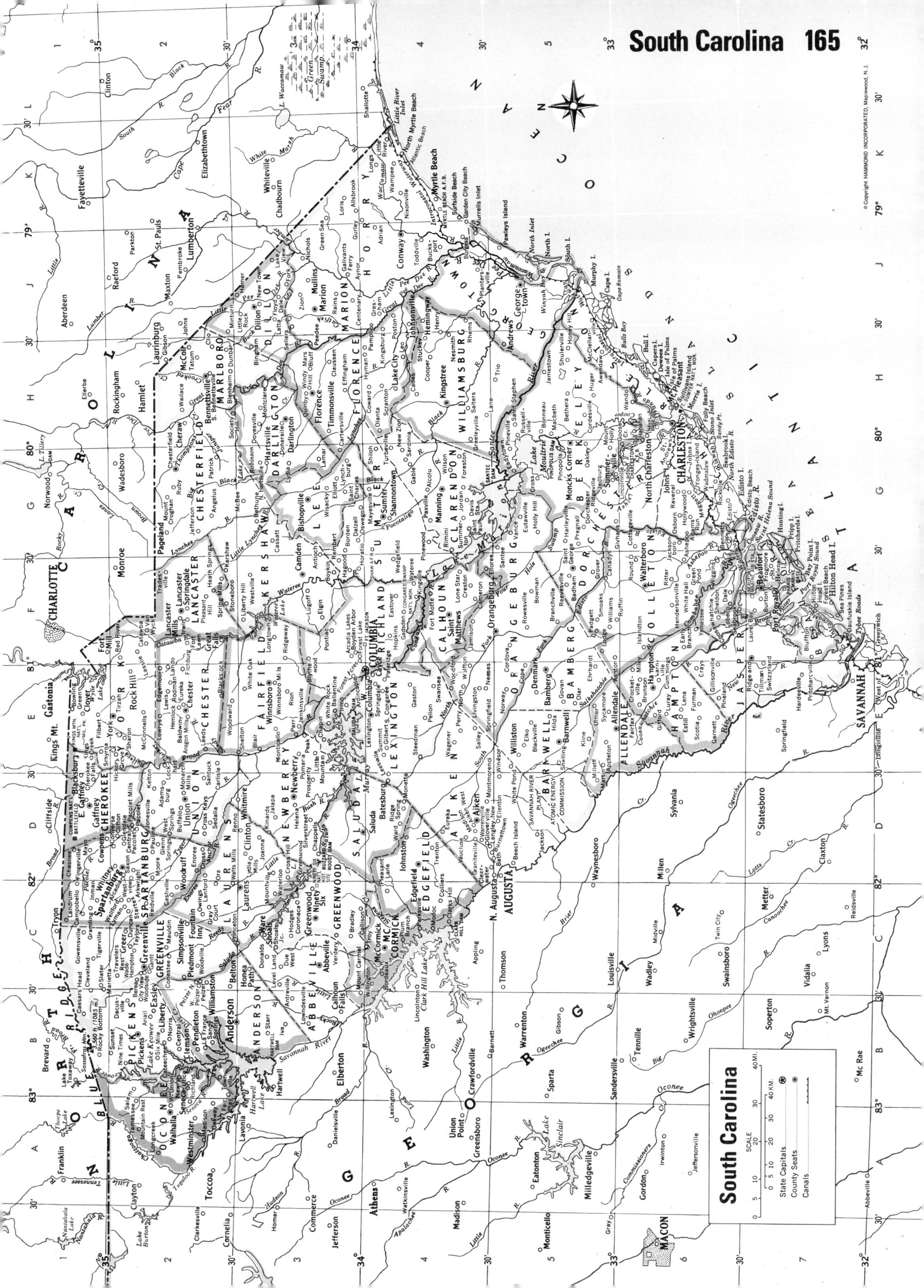
South Carolina
SCALE
0 5 10 20 30 40 MI.
0 5 10 20 30 40 KM.
State Capitals
County Seats
Canals
© Copyright HAMMOND INCORPORATED, Maplewood, N.J.
ATLANTIC OCEAN
NORTH CAROLINA
GEORGIA
BLUE RIDGE
COLUMBIA
CHARLESTON
CHARLOTTE
SAVANNAH
AUGUSTA
Greenville
Spartanburg
Rock Hill
Florence
Sumter
Myrtle Beach
Anderson
Orangeburg
Aiken
Beaufort
Georgetown
MACON

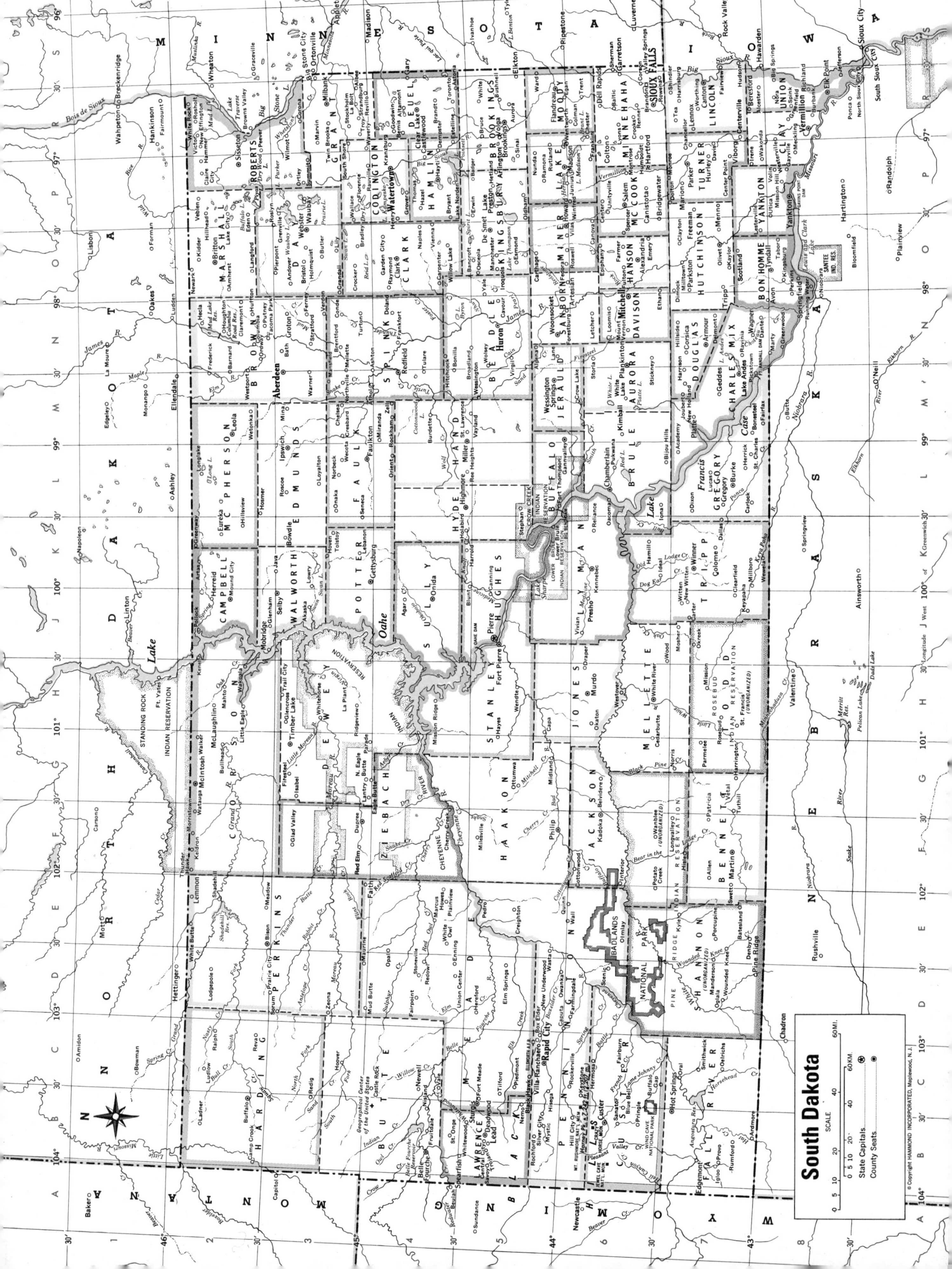
South Dakota
SCALE
0 5 10 20 40 60 MI.
0 5 10 20 40 60 KM.
State Capitals
County Seats
© Copyright HAMMOND INCORPORATED, Maplewood, N.J.
MINNESOTA
IOWA
NEBRASKA
WYOMING
MONTANA
NORTH DAKOTA
SIOUX FALLS
Pierre
Rapid City
Aberdeen
Watertown
Huron
Brookings
Mitchell
Yankton
Lake Oahe
STANDING ROCK INDIAN RESERVATION
CHEYENNE RIVER INDIAN RESERVATION
PINE RIDGE INDIAN RESERVATION
ROSEBUD INDIAN RESERVATION
BADLANDS NATIONAL PARK
Geographical Center of the United States
MT. RUSHMORE NAT'L MEM.
Harney Pk.
WIND CAVE NATIONAL PARK
JEWEL CAVE NAT'L MON.
Longitude West of Greenwich

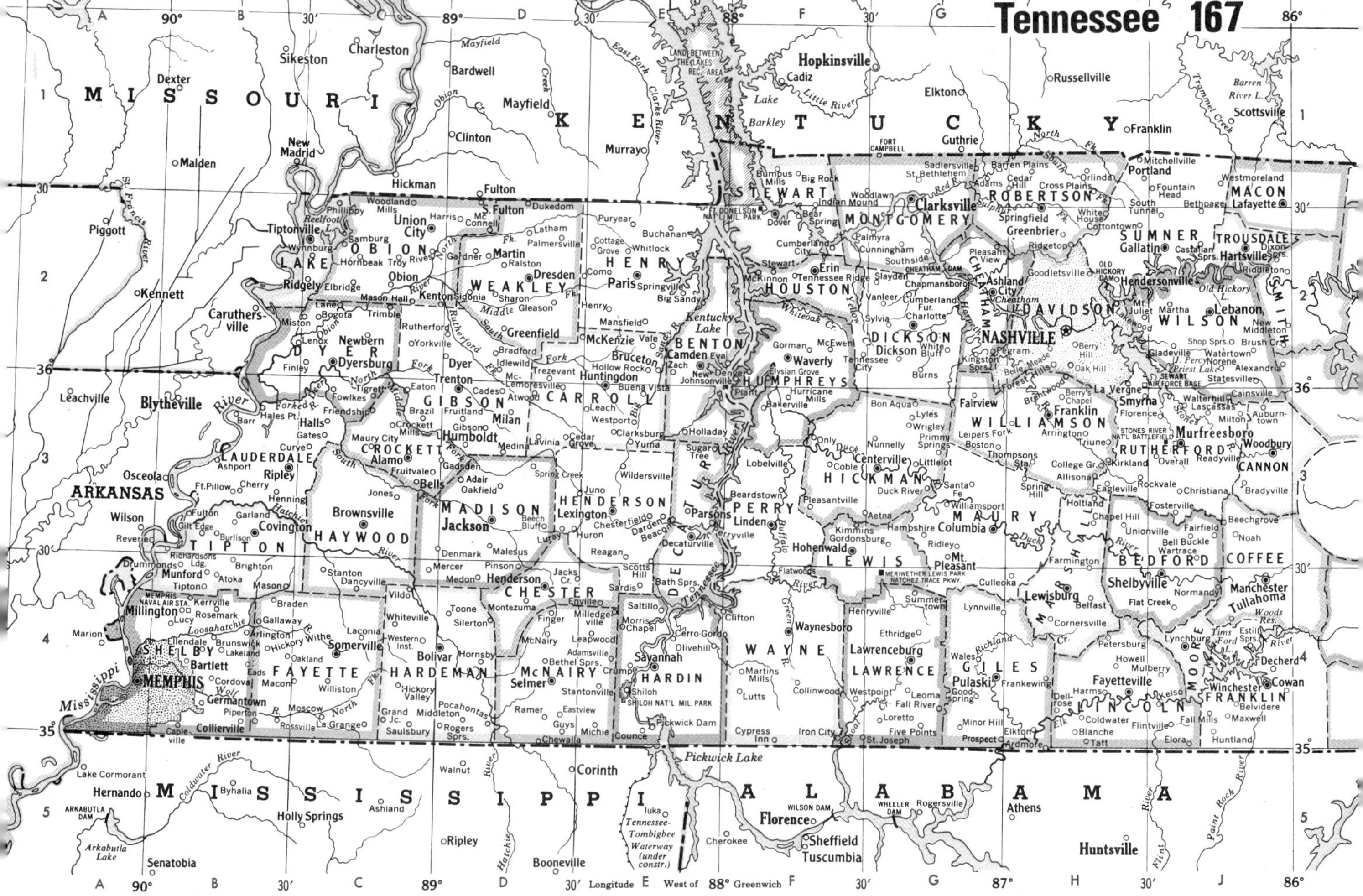
MISSOURI
KENTUCKY
ARKANSAS
MISSISSIPPI
ALABAMA
NASHVILLE
MEMPHIS
Longitude West of 88° Greenwich

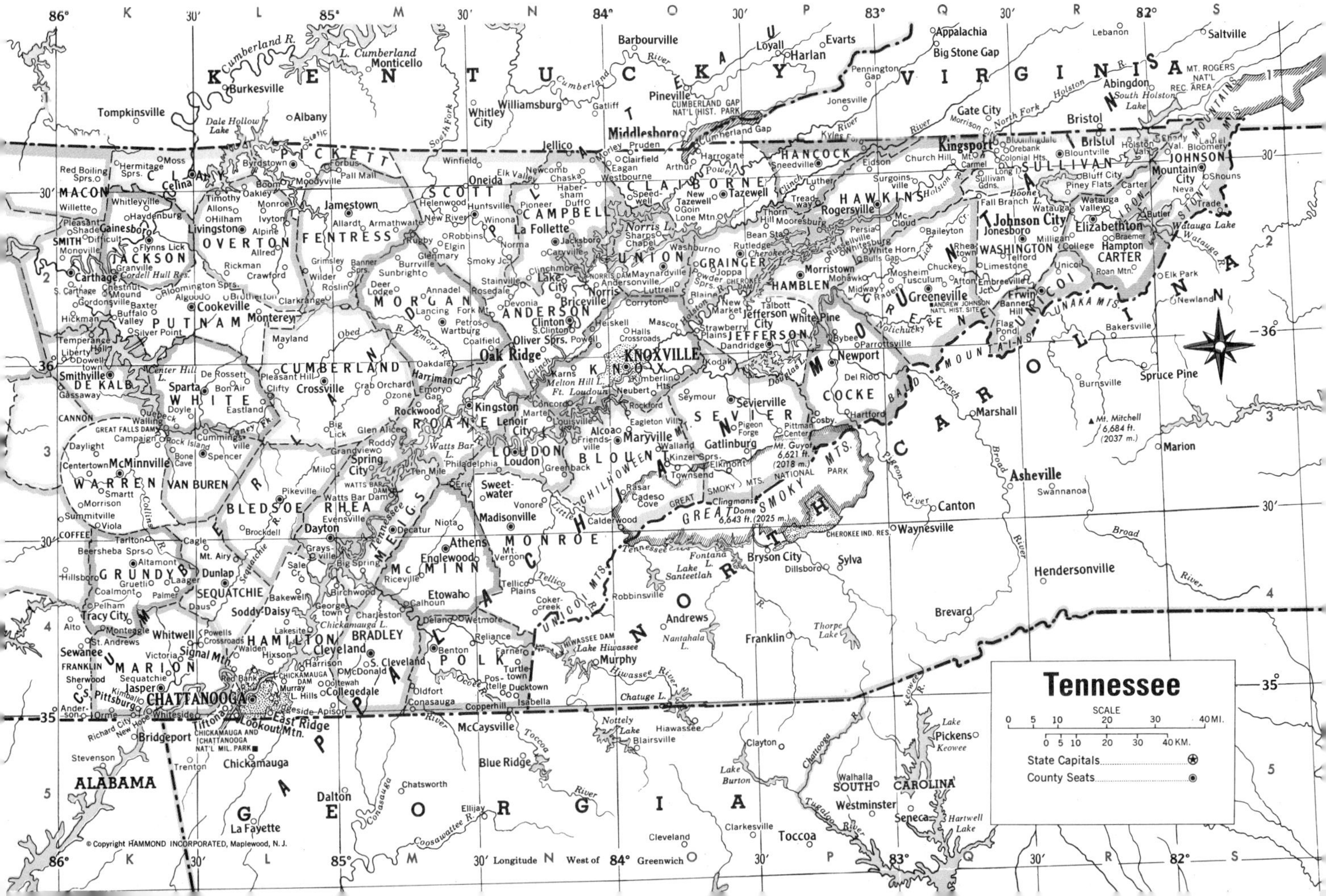
KENTUCKY
VIRGINIA
NORTH CAROLINA
GEORGIA
SOUTH CAROLINA
ALABAMA
KNOXVILLE
CHATTANOOGA
GREAT SMOKY MTS. NATIONAL PARK
Tennessee
SCALE
0 5 10 20 30 40 MI.
0 5 10 20 30 40 KM.
State Capitals
County Seats
Longitude West of 84° Greenwich

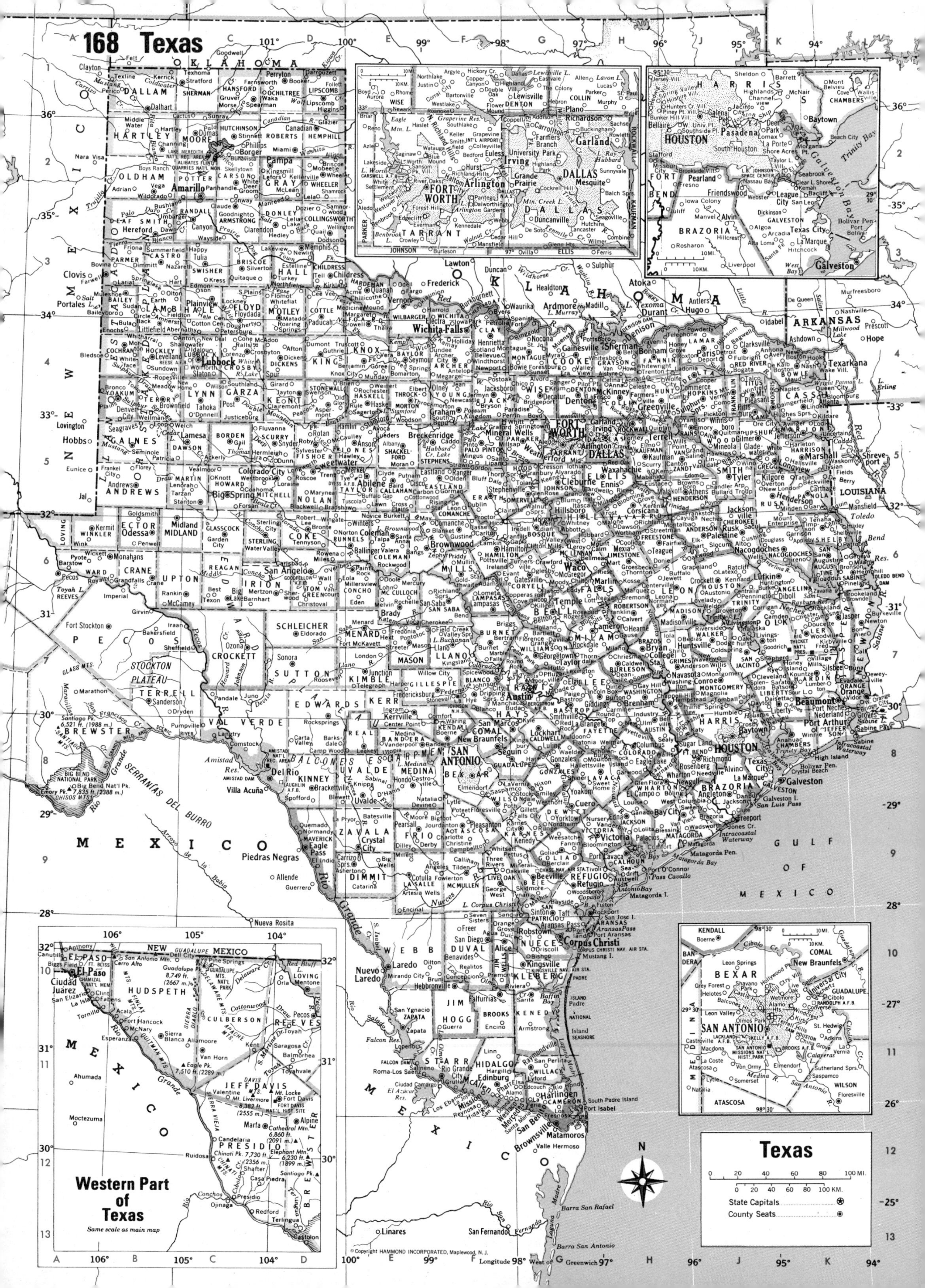
Texas
Western Part of Texas
Same scale as main map
State Capitals
County Seats
0 20 40 60 80 100 MI.
0 20 40 60 80 100 KM.
OKLAHOMA
NEW MEXICO
MEXICO
LOUISIANA
ARKANSAS
GULF OF MEXICO
HOUSTON
DALLAS
FORT WORTH
SAN ANTONIO
Austin
Corpus Christi
El Paso
Longitude 98° West of Greenwich 97°

© Copyright HAMMOND INCORPORATED, Maplewood, N. J.

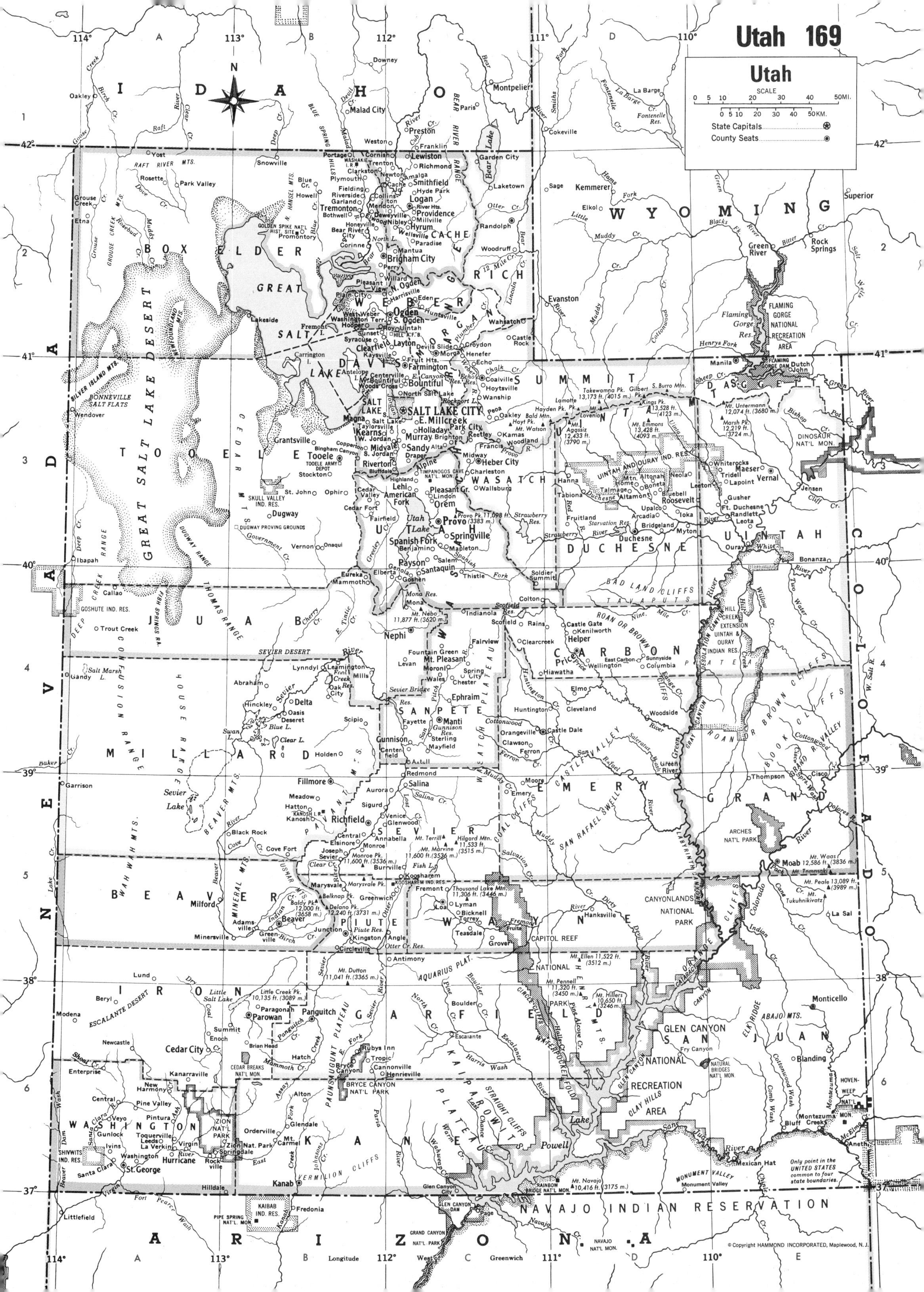
Utah
SCALE
0 5 10 20 30 40 50MI.
0 5 10 20 30 40 50KM.
State Capitals
County Seats
IDAHO
WYOMING
COLORADO
ARIZONA
NEVADA
BOX ELDER
CACHE
RICH
WEBER
MORGAN
DAVIS
SUMMIT
DAGGETT
SALT LAKE
TOOELE
UTAH
WASATCH
DUCHESNE
UINTAH
JUAB
CARBON
SANPETE
MILLARD
EMERY
GRAND
SEVIER
BEAVER
PIUTE
WAYNE
IRON
GARFIELD
SAN JUAN
WASHINGTON
KANE
GREAT SALT LAKE
GREAT SALT LAKE DESERT
SALT LAKE CITY
Ogden
Logan
Provo
Brigham City
Tooele
Heber City
Coalville
Morgan
Farmington
Randolph
Vernal
Duchesne
Nephi
Manti
Price
Castle Dale
Fillmore
Richfield
Junction
Loa
Beaver
Parowan
Panguitch
Moab
Monticello
St. George
Kanab
Manila
Evanston
Green River
Rock Springs
Kemmerer
FLAMING GORGE NATIONAL RECREATION AREA
DINOSAUR NAT'L MON.
ARCHES NAT'L PARK
CANYONLANDS NATIONAL PARK
CAPITOL REEF NATIONAL PARK
GLEN CANYON NATIONAL RECREATION AREA
BRYCE CANYON NAT'L PARK
ZION NAT'L PARK
CEDAR BREAKS NAT'L MON.
NATURAL BRIDGES NAT'L MON.
RAINBOW BRIDGE NAT'L MON.
NAVAJO INDIAN RESERVATION
BONNEVILLE SALT FLATS
Lake Powell
Sevier Lake
Utah Lake
Only point in the UNITED STATES common to four state boundaries.
Longitude
West of Greenwich
114°
113°
112°
111°
110°
42°
41°
40°
39°
38°
37°

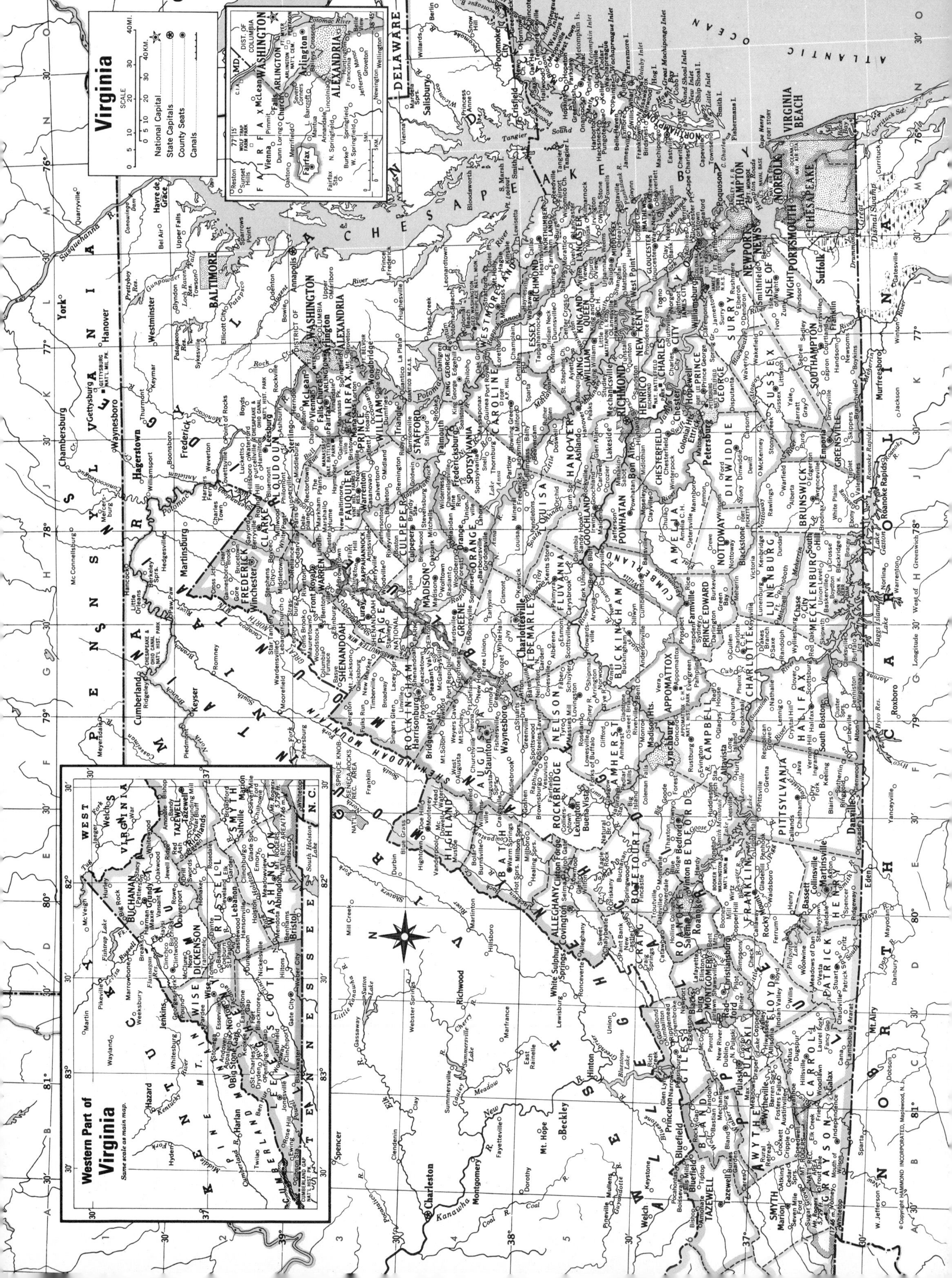
Virginia
SCALE
0 5 10 20 30 40 MI.
0 5 10 20 30 40 KM.
National Capital
State Capitals
County Seats
Canals
Western Part of Virginia
Same scale as main map.
ATLANTIC OCEAN
CHESAPEAKE BAY
© Copyright HAMMOND INCORPORATED, Maplewood, N.J.

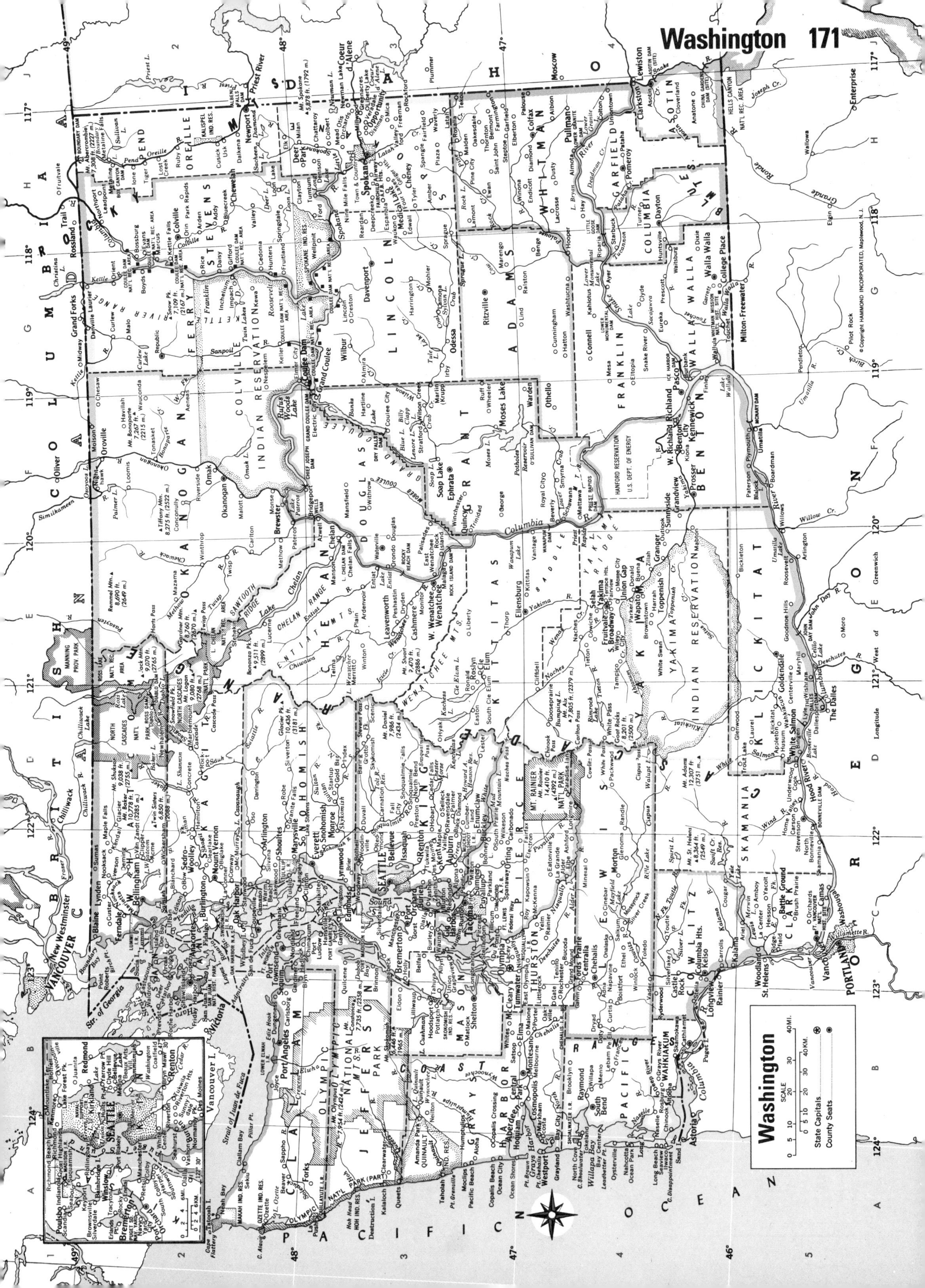
Washington
SCALE
0 5 10 20 30 40 MI.
0 5 10 20 30 40 KM.
State Capitals
County Seats
© Copyright HAMMOND INCORPORATED, Maplewood, N.J.
BRITISH COLUMBIA
IDAHO
OREGON
PACIFIC OCEAN
WHATCOM
SAN JUAN
SKAGIT
OKANOGAN
FERRY
STEVENS
PEND OREILLE
SPOKANE
LINCOLN
DOUGLAS
CHELAN
SNOHOMISH
ISLAND
CLALLAM
JEFFERSON
KITSAP
KING
KITTITAS
GRANT
ADAMS
WHITMAN
GARFIELD
ASOTIN
COLUMBIA
WALLA WALLA
FRANKLIN
BENTON
YAKIMA
KLICKITAT
SKAMANIA
CLARK
COWLITZ
WAHKIAKUM
PACIFIC
LEWIS
THURSTON
PIERCE
MASON
GRAYS HARBOR
Olympia
Seattle
Spokane
Tacoma
Vancouver
Yakima
Columbia
Snake R.

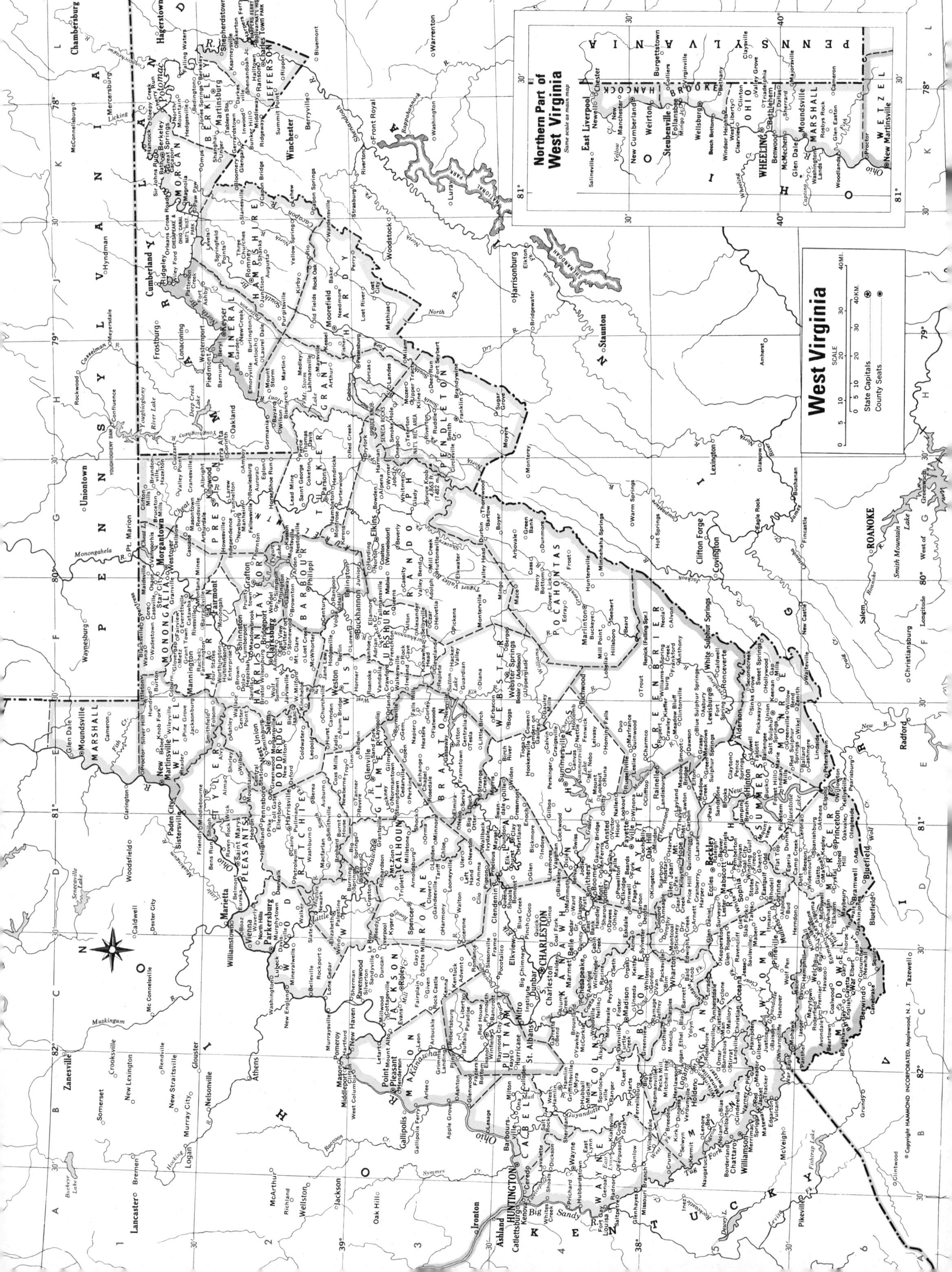
West Virginia
SCALE
0 5 10 20 30 40 MI.
0 5 10 20 30 40 KM.
State Capitals
County Seats
Northern Part of West Virginia
Same scale as main map
CHARLESTON
© Copyright HAMMOND INCORPORATED, Maplewood, N.J.

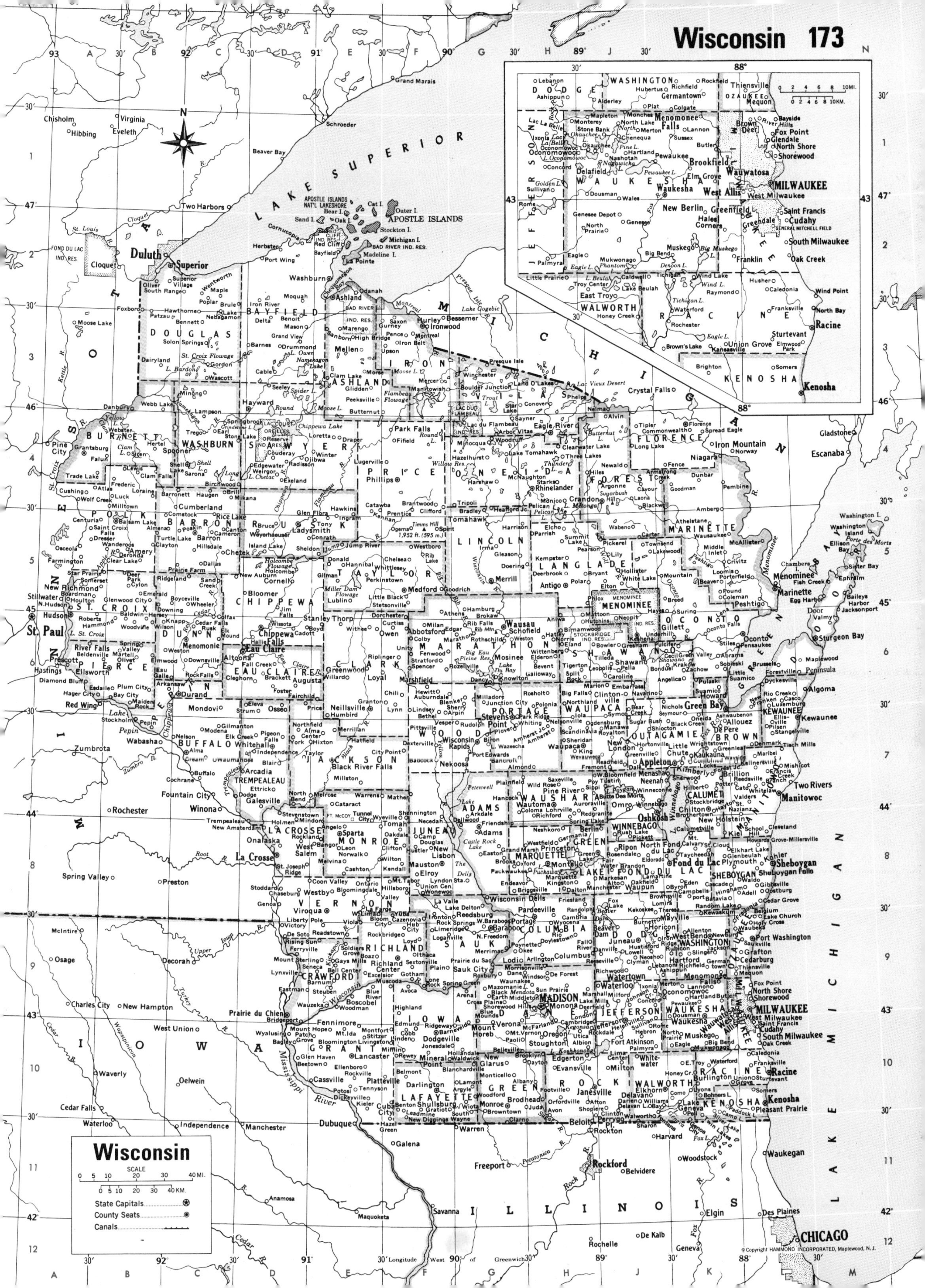
Wisconsin
SCALE
0 5 10 20 30 40 MI.
0 5 10 20 30 40 KM.
State Capitals
County Seats
Canals
LAKE SUPERIOR
LAKE MICHIGAN
GREEN BAY
APOSTLE ISLANDS
MINNESOTA
MICHIGAN
IOWA
ILLINOIS
Duluth
Superior
Ashland
Eau Claire
La Crosse
Wausau
Green Bay
Appleton
Oshkosh
Fond du Lac
Sheboygan
Manitowoc
Madison
Janesville
Beloit
Racine
Kenosha
MILWAUKEE
Waukesha
St. Paul
Rockford
CHICAGO
Dubuque
Longitude West 90° of Greenwich
© Copyright HAMMOND INCORPORATED, Maplewood, N. J.

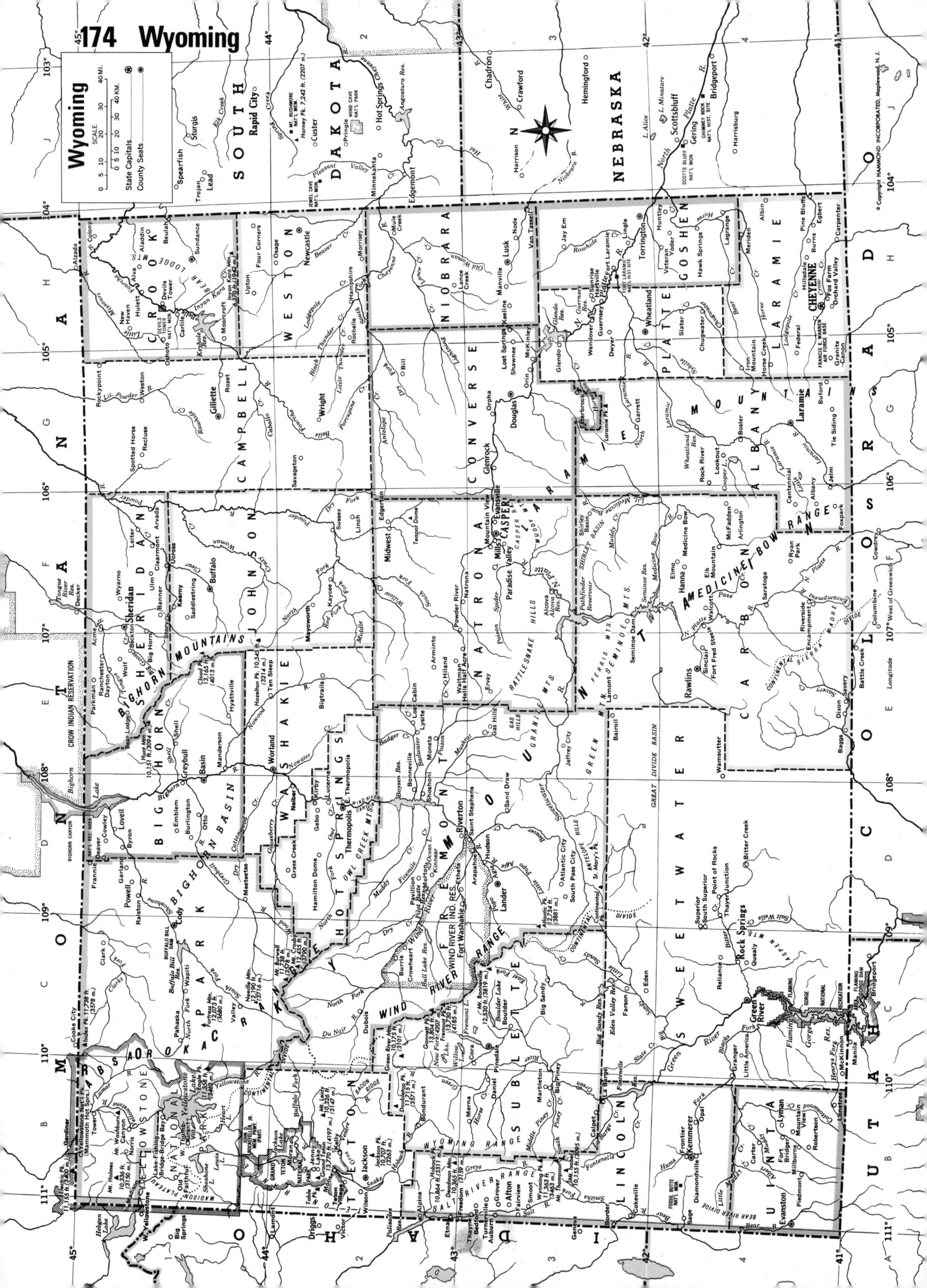
Wyoming
SCALE
0 5 10 20 30 40 MI.
0 5 10 20 30 40 KM.
State Capitals
County Seats
SOUTH DAKOTA
NEBRASKA
MONTANA
COLORADO
UTAH
IDAHO
CROOK
WESTON
NIOBRARA
GOSHEN
LARAMIE
PLATTE
CONVERSE
CAMPBELL
SHERIDAN
JOHNSON
NATRONA
ALBANY
CARBON
SWEETWATER
FREMONT
HOT SPRINGS
WASHAKIE
BIG HORN
PARK
TETON
SUBLETTE
LINCOLN
UINTA
CHEYENNE
Casper
Laramie
Rawlins
Rock Springs
Green River
Evanston
Kemmerer
Jackson
Lander
Riverton
Thermopolis
Worland
Cody
Sheridan
Buffalo
Gillette
Douglas
Lusk
Torrington
Wheatland
Newcastle
Sundance
Basin
Pinedale
BIGHORN MOUNTAINS
WIND RIVER RANGE
MEDICINE BOW RANGE
GREAT DIVIDE BASIN
YELLOWSTONE NATIONAL PARK
CROW INDIAN RESERVATION
WIND RIVER IND. RES.
© Copyright HAMMOND INCORPORATED, Maplewood, N.J.

	LAND AREA IN SQUARE MILES	POPULATION 1980	CAPITAL	LARGEST CITY	STATE FLOWER	STATE BIRD
Alabama	51,705	3,893,888	Montgomery	Birmingham	Camellia	Yellowhammer
Alaska	591,004	401,851	Juneau	Anchorage	Forget-me-not	Willow Ptarmigan
Arizona	114,000	2,718,425	Phoenix	Phoenix	Saguaro Cactus Blossom	Cactus Wren
Arkansas	53,187	2,286,435	Little Rock	Little Rock	Apple Blossom	Mockingbird
California	158,706	23,667,565	Sacramento	Los Angeles	Golden Poppy	California Valley Quail
Colorado	104,091	2,889,735	Denver	Denver	Rocky Mountain Columbine	Lark Bunting
Connecticut	5,018	3,107,576	Hartford	Bridgeport	Mountain Laurel	Robin
Delaware	2,044	594,317	Dover	Wilmington	Peach Blossom	Blue Hen Chicken
Florida	58,664	9,746,342	Tallahassee	Jacksonville	Orange Blossom	Mockingbird
Georgia	58,910	5,463,105	Atlanta	Atlanta	Cherokee Rose	Brown Thrasher
Hawaii	6,471	964,691	Honolulu	Honolulu	Hibiscus	Nene (Hawaiian Goose)
Idaho	83,564	944,038	Boise	Boise	Syringa	Mountain Bluebird
Illinois	56,345	11,426,596	Springfield	Chicago	Native Violet	Cardinal
Indiana	36,185	5,490,260	Indianapolis	Indianapolis	Peony	Cardinal
Iowa	56,275	2,913,808	Des Moines	Des Moines	Wild Rose	Eastern Goldfinch
Kansas	82,277	2,364,236	Topeka	Wichita	Sunflower	Western Meadowlark
Kentucky	40,409	3,660,257	Frankfort	Louisville	Goldenrod	Cardinal
Louisiana	47,752	4,206,312	Baton Rouge	New Orleans	Magnolia	Eastern Brown Pelican
Maine	33,265	1,125,027	Augusta	Portland	White Pine Cone and Tassel	Chickadee
Maryland	10,460	4,216,975	Annapolis	Baltimore	Black-eyed Susan	Baltimore Oriole
Massachusetts	8,284	5,737,037	Boston	Boston	Mayflower	Chickadee
Michigan	58,527	9,262,078	Lansing	Detroit	Apple Blossom	Robin
Minnesota	84,402	4,075,970	St. Paul	Minneapolis	Pink and White Lady's-Slipper	Common Loon
Mississippi	47,689	2,520,638	Jackson	Jackson	Magnolia	Mockingbird
Missouri	69,697	4,916,759	Jefferson City	St. Louis	Hawthorn	Bluebird
Montana	147,046	786,690	Helena	Billings	Bitterroot	Western Meadowlark
Nebraska	77,355	1,569,825	Lincoln	Omaha	Goldenrod	Western Meadowlark
Nevada	110,561	800,493	Carson City	Las Vegas	Sagebrush	Mountain Bluebird
New Hampshire	9,279	920,610	Concord	Manchester	Purple Lilac	Purple Finch
New Jersey	7,787	7,364,823	Trenton	Newark	Purple Violet	Eastern Goldfinch
New Mexico	121,593	1,302,981	Santa Fe	Albuquerque	Yucca	Road Runner
New York	49,108	17,558,072	Albany	New York	Rose	Bluebird
North Carolina	52,669	5,881,813	Raleigh	Charlotte	Flowering Dogwood	Cardinal
North Dakota	70,702	652,717	Bismarck	Fargo	Wild Prairie Rose	Western Meadowlark
Ohio	41,330	10,797,624	Columbus	Cleveland	Scarlet Carnation	Cardinal
Oklahoma	69,956	3,025,290	Oklahoma City	Oklahoma City	Mistletoe	Scissor-tailed Flycatcher
Oregon	97,073	2,633,149	Salem	Portland	Oregon Grape	Western Meadowlark
Pennsylvania	45,308	11,863,895	Harrisburg	Philadelphia	Mountain Laurel	Ruffed Grouse
Rhode Island	1,212	947,154	Providence	Providence	Violet	Rhode Island Red
South Carolina	31,113	3,121,833	Columbia	Columbia	Carolina (Yellow) Jessamine	Carolina Wren
South Dakota	77,116	690,768	Pierre	Sioux Falls	Pasqueflower	Ring-necked Pheasant
Tennessee	42,144	4,591,120	Nashville	Memphis	Iris	Mockingbird
Texas	266,807	14,229,288	Austin	Houston	Bluebonnet	Mockingbird
Utah	84,899	1,461,037	Salt Lake City	Salt Lake City	Sego Lily	Sea Gull
Vermont	9,614	511,456	Montpelier	Burlington	Red Clover	Hermit Thrush
Virginia	40,767	5,346,818	Richmond	Norfolk	Dogwood	Cardinal
Washington	68,139	4,132,180	Olympia	Seattle	Western Rhododendron	Willow Goldfinch
West Virginia	24,231	1,950,279	Charleston	Charleston	Big Rhododendron	Cardinal
Wisconsin	56,153	4,705,521	Madison	Milwaukee	Wood Violet	Robin
Wyoming	97,809	469,557	Cheyenne	Casper	Indian Paintbrush	Meadowlark

Acquisitions of Territory

OREGON COUNTRY
OREGON 1846
Treaty with Great Britain
WASHINGTON
IDAHO
MONTANA
WYOMING
NORTH DAKOTA
SOUTH DAKOTA
RED RIVER
Title Established 1818
MINNESOTA
LOUISIANA
1803
Purchased from France
NEBRASKA
IOWA
KANSAS
MISSOURI
OKLAHOMA
ARKANSAS
COLORADO
NEVADA
UTAH
CALIFORNIA
MEXICAN CESSION
1848
ARIZONA
NEW MEXICO
GADSDEN PURCHASE
1853
TEXAS
Annexed in 1845
WISCONSIN
MICHIGAN
ILLINOIS
INDIANA
OHIO
KENTUCKY
TENNESSEE
MISSISSIPPI
ALABAMA
GEORGIA
SOUTH CAROLINA
NORTH CAROLINA
VIRGINIA
WEST VIRGINIA
MD.
DEL.
PENNSYLVANIA
NEW JERSEY
NEW YORK
CONN.
R.I.
MASS.
VT.
N.H.
MAINE
UNITED STATES
1783
FLORIDA
1819
Treaty with Spain
ALASKA
1867
Purchased from Russia
HAWAII
Annexed in 1898

The United States in 1783 comprised the thirteen original states and included lands acquired by conquest during the Revolution and by the Treaty of 1783.

Rank by Area

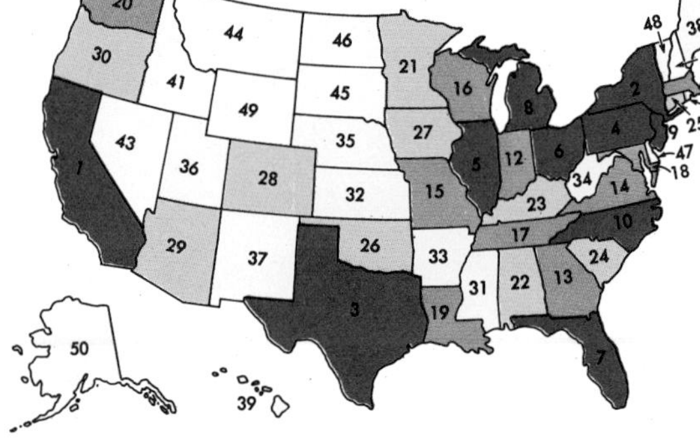

Rank by Population

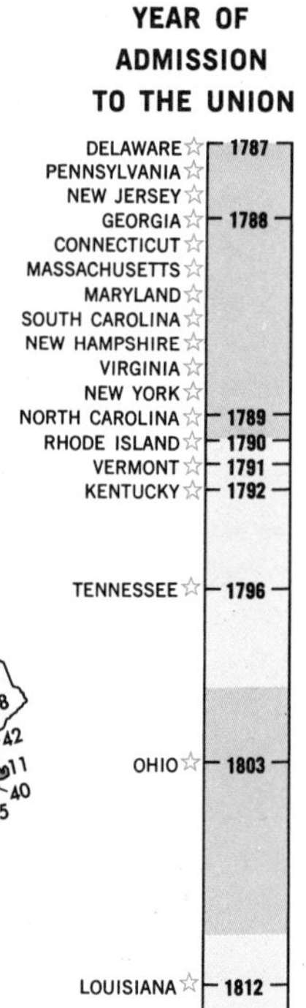
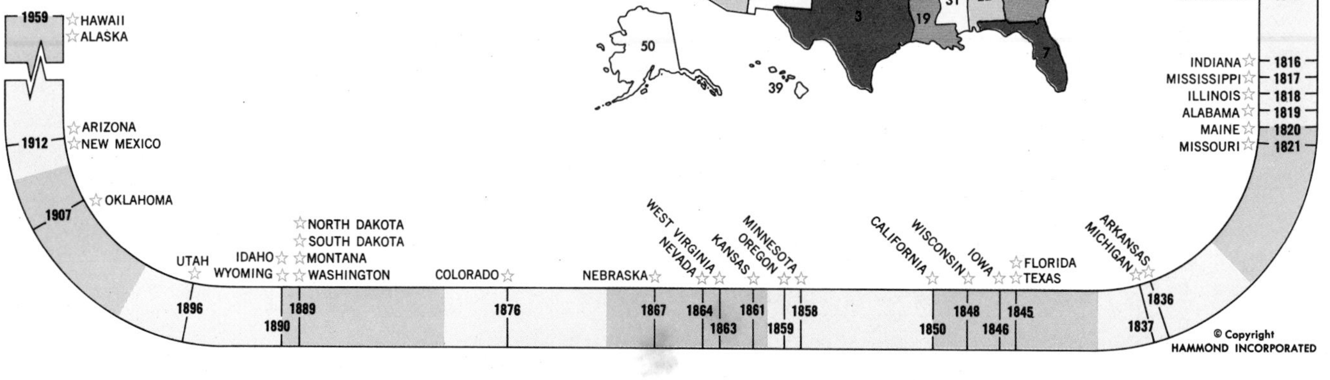
YEAR OF ADMISSION TO THE UNION
DELAWARE 1787
PENNSYLVANIA
NEW JERSEY
GEORGIA 1788
CONNECTICUT
MASSACHUSETTS
MARYLAND
SOUTH CAROLINA
NEW HAMPSHIRE
VIRGINIA
NEW YORK
NORTH CAROLINA 1789
RHODE ISLAND 1790
VERMONT 1791
KENTUCKY 1792
TENNESSEE 1796
OHIO 1803
LOUISIANA 1812
INDIANA 1816
MISSISSIPPI 1817
ILLINOIS 1818
ALABAMA 1819
MAINE 1820
MISSOURI 1821
ARKANSAS 1836
MICHIGAN 1837
FLORIDA 1845
TEXAS 1845
IOWA 1846
WISCONSIN 1848
CALIFORNIA 1850
MINNESOTA 1858
OREGON 1859
KANSAS 1861
WEST VIRGINIA 1863
NEVADA 1864
NEBRASKA 1867
COLORADO 1876
NORTH DAKOTA
SOUTH DAKOTA
MONTANA
WASHINGTON 1889
IDAHO
WYOMING 1890
UTAH 1896
OKLAHOMA 1907
ARIZONA
NEW MEXICO 1912
HAWAII
ALASKA 1959

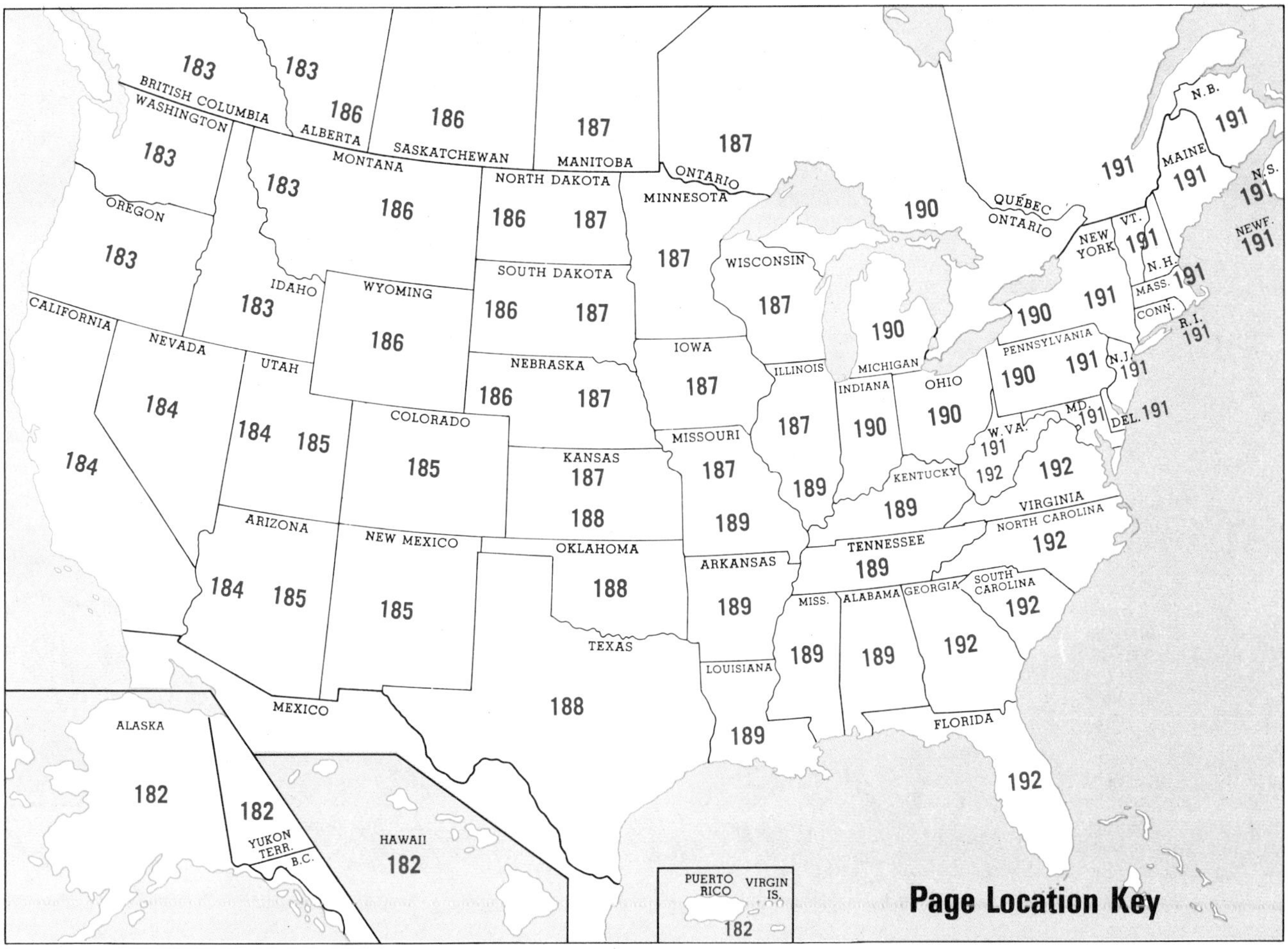
183
183
BRITISH COLUMBIA
WASHINGTON
183
186
ALBERTA
186
SASKATCHEWAN
187
MANITOBA
187
ONTARIO
MONTANA
183
186
OREGON
183
NORTH DAKOTA
186 187
MINNESOTA
187
SOUTH DAKOTA
186 187
IDAHO
183
WYOMING
186
CALIFORNIA
NEVADA
184
184
UTAH
184 185
COLORADO
185
NEBRASKA
186 187
IOWA
187
WISCONSIN
187
190
MICHIGAN
190
QUEBEC
ONTARIO
190
191
NEW YORK
190 191
VT.
191
N.H.
MAINE
191
N.B.
191
N.S.
191
NEWF.
191
MASS.
191
CONN.
R.I.
191
PENNSYLVANIA
190 191
N.J.
191
DEL. 191
MD.
191
ILLINOIS
187
INDIANA
190
OHIO
190
W. VA.
191
192
192
KENTUCKY
189
VIRGINIA
MISSOURI
187
189
189
KANSAS
187
188
ARIZONA
184 185
NEW MEXICO
185
OKLAHOMA
188
TENNESSEE
189
NORTH CAROLINA
192
ARKANSAS
189
SOUTH CAROLINA
192
MISS.
189
ALABAMA
189
GEORGIA
192
LOUISIANA
189
TEXAS
188
FLORIDA
192
MEXICO
ALASKA
182
182
YUKON TERR.
B.C.
HAWAII
182
PUERTO RICO
VIRGIN IS.
182
Page Location Key

Legend

- National Capitals ⊛
- Limited Access Highways
- Major Through Routes
- Ferries FY.
- Canals
- U.S. Interstate Route Numbers 95
- Trans-Canada Highway
- International Boundaries
- State and Provincial Capitals ⊛
- National Parkways
- Other Important Roads
- Mileage Between Dots 72
- Federal Route Numbers 2 2
- State and Other Route Numbers ② ②
- State and Provincial Boundaries

Points of Interest

- National Park/Preserve ◻
- National Monument ◻
- National Historical Park ▲
- National Historic Site △
- National Memorial Park ●
- National Memorial ⊙
- State/Provincial Park ◻
- National Forest/Forest Reserve ◻
- National Recreation Area ◻
- National Seashore/Lakeshore ◻ ≋
- National Military Park ⊗
- National Battlefield Park ⊠
- National Battlefield/Site ×
- Other Points of Interest ◻

NATIONAL PARKS

UNITED STATES

Acadia ....Maine
Arches ....Utah
Badlands ....South Dakota
Big Bend ....Texas
Biscayne ....Florida
Bryce Canyon ....Utah
Canyonlands ....Utah
Capitol Reef ....Utah
Carlsbad Caverns ......New Mexico
Channel Islands ....California
Crater Lake ....Oregon
Denali ....Alaska
Everglades ....Florida
Gates of the Arctic ....Alaska
Glacier ....Montana
Glacier Bay ....Alaska
Grand Canyon ....Arizona
Grand Teton ....Wyoming
Great Smoky Mts. ........N.C.-Tenn.
Guadalupe Mts. ....Texas
Haleakala ....Hawaii
Hawaii Volcanoes ....Hawaii
Hot Springs ....Arkansas
Isle Royale ....Michigan
Katmai ....Alaska
Kenai Fjords ....Alaska
Kings Canyon ....California
Kobuk Valley ....Alaska
Lake Clark ....Alaska
Lassen Volcanic ....California
Mammoth Cave ....Kentucky
Mesa Verde ....Colorado
Mount Rainier ....Washington
North Cascades ....Washington
Olympic ....Washington
Petrified Forest ....Arizona
Redwood ....California
Rocky Mountain ....Colorado
Sequoia ....California
Shenandoah ....Virginia
Theodore Roosevelt ......N. Dakota
Virgin Islands ....Virgin Islands
Voyageurs ....Minnesota
Wind Cave ....South Dakota
Wrangell-St. Elias ....Alaska
Yellowstone ....Wyo., Mont., Idaho
Yosemite ....California
Zion ....Utah

CANADA

Auyuittuq ....N. W. Terrs.
Banff ....Alberta
Cape Breton
Island ....Nova Scotia
Elk Island ....Alberta
Forillon ....Quebec
Fundy ....New Brunswick
Georgian Bay Islands ....Ontario
Glacier ....Br. Columbia
Gros Morne ....Newfoundland
Jasper ....Alberta
Kejimkujik ....Nova Scotia
Kluane ....Yukon Terr.
Kootenay ....Br. Columbia
Kouchibouguac ....New Brunswick
La Mauricie ....Quebec
Mount Revelstoke ....Br. Columbia
Nahanni ....N. W. Terrs.
Pacific Rim ....Br. Columbia
Point Pelee ....Ontario
Prince Albert ....Saskatchewan
Prince Edward Island ..........P.E.I.
Pukaskwa ....Ontario
Riding Mountain ....Manitoba
St. Lawrence Islands ....Ontario
Terra Nova ....Newfoundland
Waterton Lakes ....Alberta
Wood Buffalo ...Alta., N.W. Terrs.
Yoho ....Br. Columbia

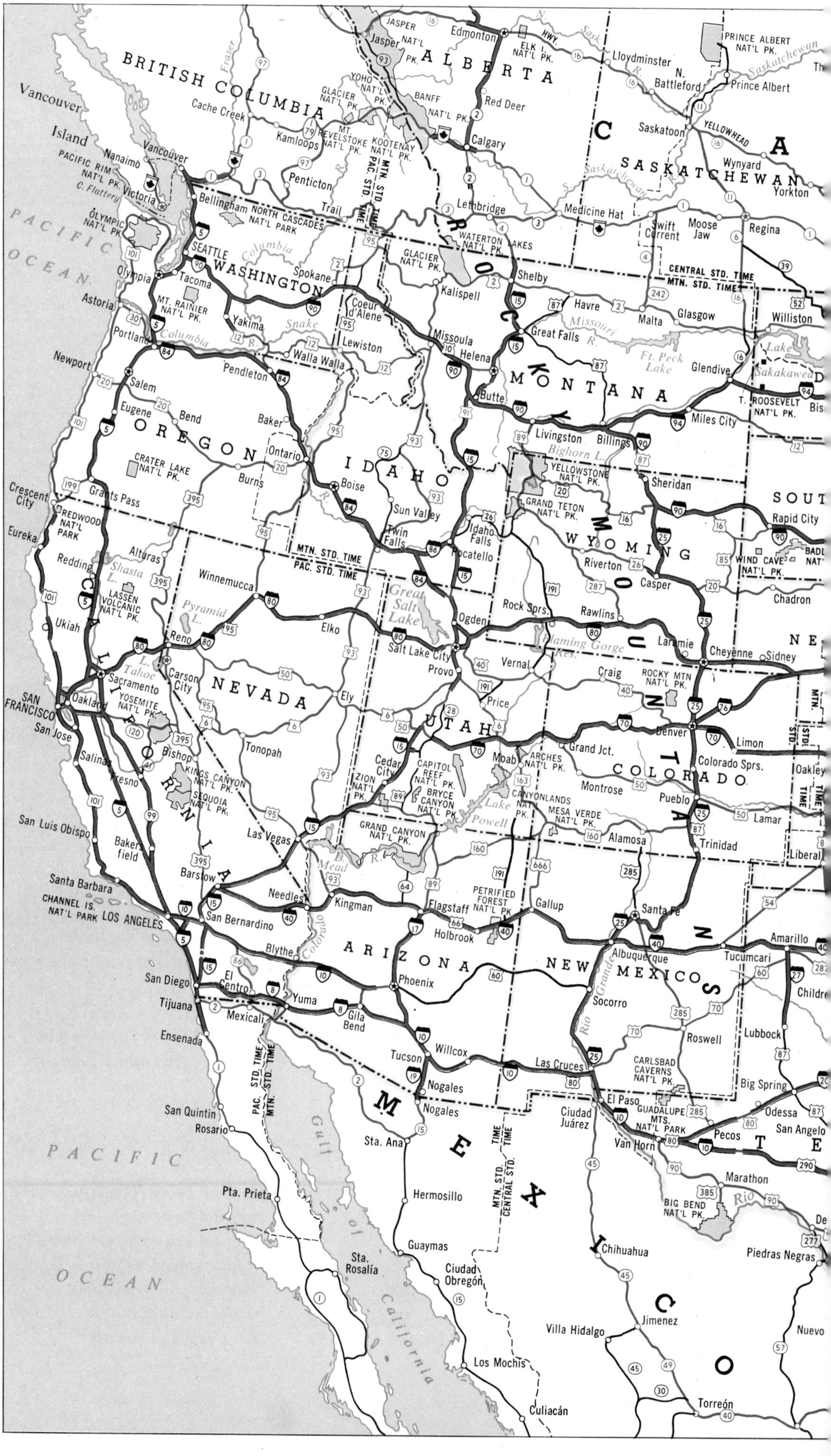

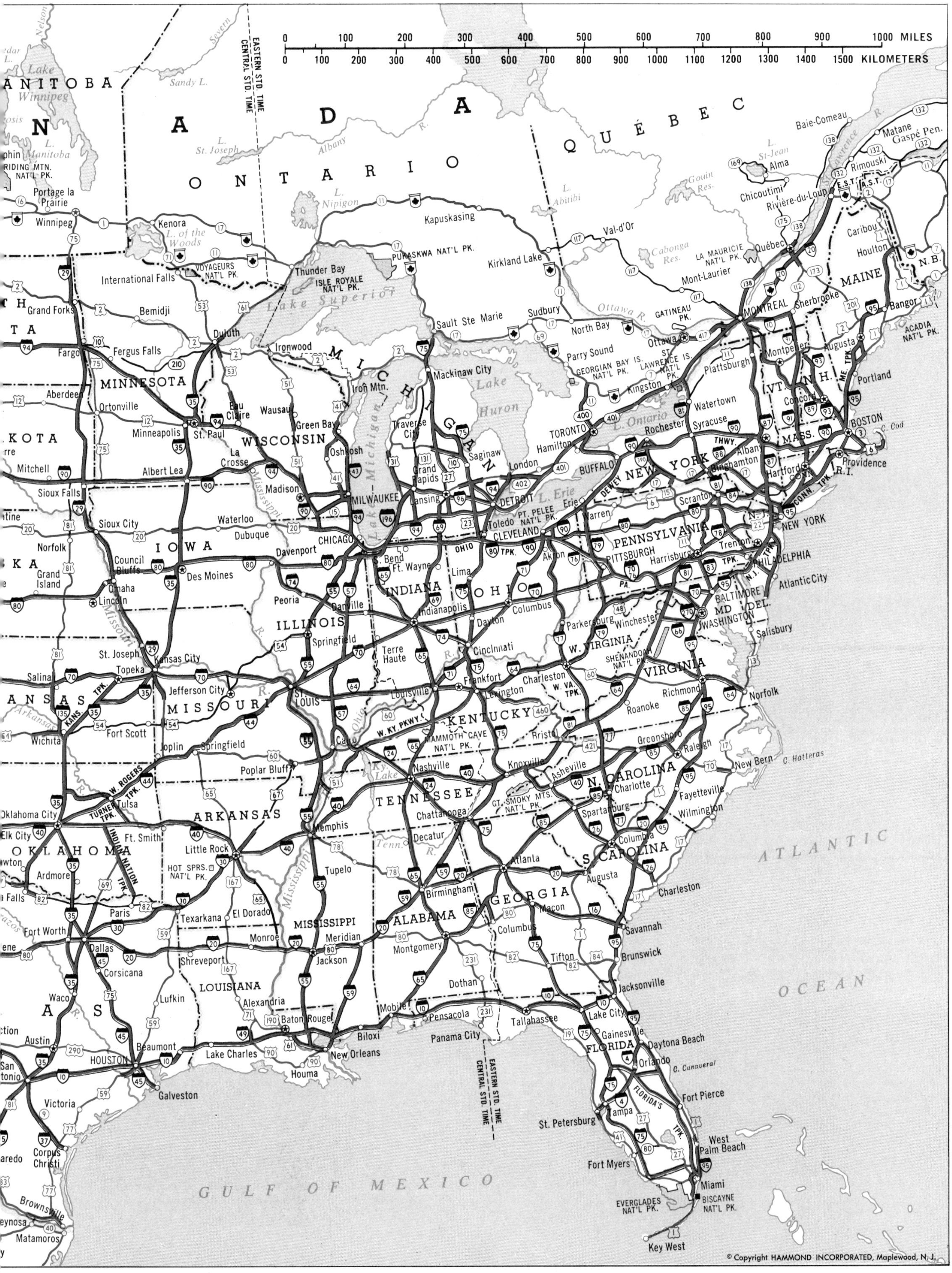
0 100 200 300 400 500 600 700 800 900 1000 MILES
0 100 200 300 400 500 600 700 800 900 1000 1100 1200 1300 1400 1500 KILOMETERS
EASTERN STD. TIME
CENTRAL STD. TIME
MANITOBA
Lake Winnipeg
L. Manitoba
RIDING MTN. NAT'L PK.
Portage la Prairie
Winnipeg
Kenora
L. of the Woods
VOYAGEURS NAT'L PK.
International Falls
Thunder Bay
ISLE ROYALE NAT'L PK.
Lake Superior
PUKASKWA NAT'L PK.
CANADA
ONTARIO
QUÉBEC
Sandy L.
L. St. Joseph
L. Nipigon
Kapuskasing
Kirkland Lake
Val-d'Or
L. Abitibi
Cabonga Res.
Gouin Res.
LA MAURICIE NAT'L PK.
Mont-Laurier
GATINEAU PK.
Sault Ste Marie
Sudbury
North Bay
Ottawa R.
Ottawa
Parry Sound
GEORGIAN BAY IS. NAT'L PK.
ST. LAWRENCE IS. NAT'L PK.
Kingston
L. Ontario
TORONTO
Hamilton
London
BUFFALO
L. Erie
PT. PELEE NAT'L PK.
Baie-Comeau
Matane
Gaspé Pen.
L. St-Jean
Alma
Chicoutimi
Rimouski
Rivière-du-Loup
E.S.T.
A.S.T.
Caribou
Houlton
Québec
MONTREAL
Sherbrooke
MAINE
N.B.
Bangor
ACADIA NAT'L PK.
Augusta
Portland
Montpelier
Plattsburgh
VT.
N.H.
Concord
ME. TPK.
BOSTON
C. Cod
MASS.
Providence
R.I.
Hartford
CONN. TPK.
Albany
Binghamton
Watertown
Syracuse
Rochester
THWY.
NEW YORK
DEWEY
Erie
Scranton
Warren
PENNSYLVANIA
PITTSBURGH
Harrisburg
Trenton
NEW YORK
PHILADELPHIA
N.J.
Atlantic City
BALTIMORE
MD
WASHINGTON
DEL.
Salisbury
Grand Forks
Bemidji
Duluth
Fargo
Fergus Falls
Ironwood
MINNESOTA
Aberdeen
Ortonville
Minneapolis
St. Paul
Eau Claire
Wausau
Green Bay
Iron Mtn.
Mackinaw City
Lake Huron
MICHIGAN
Lake Michigan
Traverse City
Saginaw
Grand Rapids
Lansing
DETROIT
Toledo
CLEVELAND
Akron
WISCONSIN
Oshkosh
La Crosse
Madison
MILWAUKEE
Albert Lea
Mitchell
Sioux Falls
Sioux City
Waterloo
Dubuque
Mississippi
IOWA
Norfolk
Council Bluffs
Des Moines
Davenport
CHICAGO
S. Bend
Ft. Wayne
Grand Island
Omaha
Lincoln
Peoria
ILLINOIS
Springfield
Danville
INDIANA
Indianapolis
Lima
OHIO
TPK.
Columbus
Dayton
Cincinnati
Terre Haute
Missouri
St. Joseph
Kansas City
Topeka
Salina
KANS. TPK.
Jefferson City
ST. LOUIS
MISSOURI
Wichita
Fort Scott
Joplin
Springfield
Louisville
Frankfort
Lexington
KENTUCKY
W. KY. PKWY.
MAMMOTH CAVE NAT'L PK.
Cairo
Charleston
W. VA. TPK.
Parkersburg
Winchester
W. VIRGINIA
SHENANDOAH NAT'L PK.
VIRGINIA
Richmond
Norfolk
Roanoke
Bristol
Greensboro
Raleigh
New Bern
C. Hatteras
N. CAROLINA
Charlotte
Fayetteville
Wilmington
Asheville
Knoxville
Nashville
TENNESSEE
GT. SMOKY MTS. NAT'L PK.
Chattanooga
Spartanburg
Columbia
S. CAROLINA
Charleston
Augusta
Poplar Bluff
W. ROGERS TPK.
Tulsa
TURNER TPK.
INDIAN NATION TPK.
Oklahoma City
Elk City
OKLAHOMA
Ft. Smith
ARKANSAS
Little Rock
HOT SPRS. NAT'L PK.
Memphis
Ardmore
Paris
Texarkana
El Dorado
Fort Worth
Dallas
Corsicana
Waco
Shreveport
Monroe
LOUISIANA
Alexandria
Lufkin
Austin
HOUSTON
Beaumont
Lake Charles
Baton Rouge
New Orleans
Houma
Galveston
San Antonio
Victoria
Corpus Christi
Laredo
Brownsville
Matamoros
Tupelo
MISSISSIPPI
Meridian
Jackson
Decatur
Birmingham
ALABAMA
Montgomery
Dothan
Mobile
Biloxi
Pensacola
Panama City
Tallahassee
Atlanta
GEORGIA
Macon
Columbus
Savannah
Tifton
Brunswick
Jacksonville
Lake City
Gainesville
Daytona Beach
FLORIDA
Orlando
C. Canaveral
FLORIDA'S TPK.
Tampa
St. Petersburg
Fort Pierce
West Palm Beach
Fort Myers
Miami
EVERGLADES NAT'L PK.
BISCAYNE NAT'L PK.
Key West
ATLANTIC OCEAN
GULF OF MEXICO

	Albuquerque, N. Mex.	Amarillo, Tex.	Atlanta, Ga.	Baltimore, Md.	Bangor, Maine	Birmingham, Ala.	Boise, Idaho	Boston, Mass.	Buffalo, N.Y.	Butte, Mont.	Charlotte, N. C.	Chicago, Ill.	Cincinnati, Ohio	Cleveland, Ohio	Dallas, Tex.	Denver, Colo.	Detroit, Mich.	El Paso, Tex.	Fargo, N. Dak.	Houston, Tex.	Jacksonville, Fla.	Kansas City, Mo.	Little Rock, Ark.	Los Angeles, Calif.	Louisville, Ky.	Memphis, Tenn.	Miami, Fla.	Milwaukee, Wis.	Minn.-St. Paul, Minn.	New Orleans, La.	New York, N.Y.	Oklahoma City, Okla.	Omaha, Nebr.
Albany, N.Y.	2114	1825	988	321	366	1091	2584	170	283	2344	750	807	707	466	1702	1844	536	2168	1462	1824	1117	1268	1360	2930	827	1217	1468	894	1223	1476	147	1569	1295
Albuquerque, N. Mex.	•	289	1429	1884	2433	1276	980	2232	1781	1040	1669	1285	1405	1516	650	432	1580	270	1310	844	1662	791	901	805	1328	1032	1986	1390	1223	1145	2056	545	892
Amarillo, Tex.	289	•	1143	1595	2144	985	1279	1963	1524	1237	1380	1071	1123	1319	361	422	1295	417	1056	604	1373	577	612	1091	1039	743	1697	1144	979	859	1756	263	648
Atlanta, Ga.	1429	1143	•	671	1215	155	2292	1070	876	2158	259	707	467	692	820	1431	726	1429	1343	841	315	823	541	2254	428	366	665	804	1114	517	863	880	1006
Austin, Tex.	774	485	938	1571	2221	783	1749	2012	1571	1814	1187	1140	1133	1383	197	907	1372	592	1307	161	1085	727	507	1385	1042	646	1403	1224	1161	519	1771	480	884
Baltimore, Md.	1884	1595	671	•	632	800	2440	400	366	2151	421	690	497	348	1393	1625	510	2025	1367	1452	794	1062	1102	2669	602	951	1143	772	1100	1153	192	1339	1153
Bangor, Maine	2433	2144	1315	632	•	1407	2900	233	652	2642	1049	1174	1094	827	2019	2189	892	2573	1828	2107	1426	1630	1718	3238	1198	1594	1773	1271	1589	1747	450	1902	1639
Billings, Mont.	1024	1001	1875	1924	2406	1782	607	2213	1754	237	2037	1234	1528	1579	1352	579	1503	1291	621	1595	2190	1065	1474	1300	1564	1532	2547	1171	831	1853	2062	1195	857
Birmingham, Ala.	1276	985	155	800	1407	•	2201	1210	932	2018	415	661	499	742	660	1327	743	1288	1308	673	427	716	386	2073	362	247	765	748	1069	359	988	741	926
Boise, Idaho	980	1279	2292	2440	2900	2201	•	2722	2268	452	2433	1726	1963	2082	1637	867	2011	1267	1228	1825	2615	1446	1833	887	1993	1913	2901	1763	1446	2140	2568	1489	1267
Boston, Mass.	2232	1967	1070	400	233	1210	2722	•	458	2442	821	974	861	640	1815	2012	707	2401	1631	1874	1201	1436	1492	3037	964	1340	1539	1060	1387	1556	211	1733	1467
Buffalo, N.Y.	1781	1524	876	366	652	932	2268	458	•	1988	733	520	428	186	1406	1537	249	1950	1177	1502	1080	980	1066	2586	537	924	1431	610	937	1248	367	1249	990
Butte, Mont.	1040	1237	2158	2151	2642	2018	452	2442	1988	•	2266	1468	1783	1813	1586	815	1737	1310	858	1829	2427	1302	1711	1158	1790	1769	2784	1408	1068	2077	2317	1413	1086
Charleston, W. Va.	1594	1325	519	391	1018	589	2197	781	439	2327	303	483	202	268	1119	1369	357	1670	1119	1201	671	796	752	2341	266	615	1043	561	880	936	566	988	905
Charlotte, N.C.	1669	1380	259	421	1049	415	2433	821	733	2266	•	765	475	578	1055	1609	664	1688	1419	1139	388	987	776	2474	467	637	746	854	1180	781	613	1119	1180
Chattanooga, Tenn.	1356	1067	118	662	1282	145	2140	1063	775	1972	320	590	343	592	807	1317	605	1439	1234	838	441	694	456	2197	275	317	788	686	995	514	854	811	886
Cheyenne, Wyo.	545	533	1468	1656	2147	1374	766	1954	1501	711	1644	967	1192	1320	880	101	2515	809	823	1143	1899	657	1053	1182	1187	1127	2240	1019	821	1376	1782	702	491
Chicago, Ill.	1285	1071	707	690	1174	661	1726	974	520	1468	765	•	294	345	936	1018	269	1466	657	1092	1017	505	652	2106	304	548	1377	87	418	929	828	826	465
Cincinnati, Ohio	1405	1123	467	497	1094	499	1963	861	428	1783	475	294	•	244	984	1171	251	1505	956	1081	783	600	625	2226	108	487	1133	385	717	820	635	901	700
Cleveland, Ohio	1596	1319	692	348	827	742	2082	640	186	1813	578	345	244	•	1219	1351	168	1754	999	1335	971	789	884	2427	351	737	1322	433	760	1060	486	1096	818
Columbia, S.C.	1655	1366	215	509	1140	371	2558	910	806	2278	94	759	527	664	1045	1687	733	1644	1416	1040	294	1045	749	2486	512	607	645	898	1226	713	694	1137	1205
Columbus, Ohio	1472	1220	563	392	994	592	2023	757	332	1789	503	311	108	140	1080	1228	186	1619	968	1205	867	668	762	2292	218	618	1213	404	737	959	546	937	765
Dallas, Tex.	650	361	820	1393	2019	660	1637	1815	1406	1568	1055	936	984	1219	•	784	1182	624	1110	243	1029	498	330	1410	876	468	1327	1063	964	500	1642	212	672
Denver, Colo.	432	422	1431	1625	2189	1327	867	2012	1537	815	1609	1018	1171	1351	784	•	1305	668	901	1028	1790	613	962	1162	1143	1058	2100	1039	845	1284	1788	616	537
Des Moines, Iowa	1032	786	916	1013	1520	854	1397	1328	866	1189	1085	330	584	688	704	674	614	1160	491	948	1255	207	581	1788	585	627	1598	358	254	1028	1165	566	139
Detroit, Mich.	1580	1295	726	510	892	743	2011	707	249	1737	664	269	251	168	1182	1305	•	1716	926	1307	1039	750	859	2419	363	726	1387	357	690	1077	626	1068	744
Duluth, Minn.	1380	1141	1193	1179	1585	1150	1540	1392	933	1109	1244	487	787	836	1113	1000	757	1506	251	1357	1518	608	996	2088	795	980	1870	406	152	1382	1315	968	518
El Paso, Tex.	270	417	1429	2025	2573	1288	1267	2401	1950	1310	1688	1466	1505	1754	624	668	1716	•	1453	753	1641	946	961	793	1513	1092	1994	1557	1351	1119	2175	682	1027
Fargo, N. Dak.	1310	1056	1343	1367	1828	1308	1228	1631	1177	858	1419	657	956	999	1110	901	926	1453	•	1364	1684	636	1045	1935	951	1061	2008	573	239	1479	1485	900	436
Fort Wayne, Ind.	1395	1181	633	528	1026	606	1882	845	394	1624	629	156	154	199	1035	1179	159	1559	819	1147	943	604	691	2224	207	568	1287	251	580	962	670	907	629
Fort Worth, Tex.	616	340	859	1367	2038	696	1615	1847	1438	1543	1087	968	1011	1248	31	759	125	588	1110	261	1061	534	371	1441	919	512	1398	1082	964	531	1667	212	701
Grand Forks, N. Dak.	1387	1133	1287	1415	1897	1385	1305	1705	1254	913	1496	734	1033	1076	1187	978	1003	1530	77	1441	1751	713	1122	1990	1028	1138	2085	650	316	1039	1552	984	513
Grand Rapids, Mich.	1462	1248	781	631	1017	736	1903	840	381	1645	857	167	306	278	1160	1207	148	1755	834	1278	1106	663	829	2355	364	694	1439	262	601	1124	763	1003	659
Great Falls, Mont.	1227	1224	2097	2113	2595	2026	610	2375	1923	158	2458	1423	1717	1768	1586	803	1692	1497	744	1831	2412	1301	1698	1316	1991	1768	2757	1322	988	2086	2247	1419	1035
Greensboro, N.C.	1762	1473	352	328	1316	507	2408	718	640	2292	93	749	469	485	1148	1626	571	1764	1425	1232	481	1030	824	2537	492	687	839	836	1167	874	520	1174	1156
Hartford, Conn.	2169	1869	966	297	332	1108	2634	101	387	2376	711	908	753	582	1755	1901	648	2288	1565	1791	1092	1327	1396	2947	866	1242	1440	995	1324	1464	113	1632	1373
Houston, Tex.	844	604	841	1452	2107	673	1825	1874	1502	1829	1139	1092	1081	1335	243	1028	1307	753	1364	•	924	744	439	1554	981	572	1242	1163	1211	358	1678	458	917
Indianapolis, Ind.	1313	1034	539	565	1136	492	1853	931	486	1674	586	188	104	300	921	1057	277	1425	840	1031	852	491	571	2131	114	444	1197	276	601	839	716	778	591
Jackson, Miss.	1062	777	400	998	1635	243	2063	1446	1115	1968	668	747	678	924	411	1219	931	1040	1271	433	597	613	257	1864	573	210	920	826	1062	182	1232	587	882
Jacksonville, Fla.	1662	1373	315	794	1426	427	2615	1201	1080	2427	388	1017	783	971	1029	1790	1039	1641	1684	924	•	1138	821	2427	766	672	345	1123	1440	568	979	1195	1349
Kansas City, Mo.	791	577	823	1062	1630	716	1446	1436	980	1302	987	505	600	789	498	613	750	946	636	744	1138	•	409	1620	523	467	1491	564	461	846	1214	357	208
Las Vegas, Nev.	587	876	2015	2478	3074	1861	688	2841	2396	877	2268	1876	1996	2221	1238	901	2140	716	1656	1445	2249	1416	1488	288	1939	1631	2628	1902	1708	1733	2630	1140	1401
Lincoln, Nebr.	834	590	1005	1211	1697	938	1240	1550	1048	1080	1211	576	758	876	635	613	845	1017	459	885	1360	222	631	1662	745	689	1713	557	289	1068	1304	430	58
Little Rock, Ark.	901	612	541	1102	1718	386	1833	1492	1066	1711	776	652	625	884	330	962	859	961	1045	439	821	409	•	1698	531	139	1161	727	833	434	1283	350	623
Los Angeles, Calif.	805	1091	2254	2669	3238	2073	887	3037	2586	1158	2474	2106	2226	2427	1410	1162	2419	793	1935	1554	2427	1620	1698	•	2161	1823	2737	2145	1996	1916	2823	1353	1698
Louisville, Ky.	1328	1039	428	602	1198	362	1993	964	537	1790	467	304	108	351	876	1143	363	1513	951	981	766	523	531	2161	•	365	1078	392	712	719	759	808	707
Madison, Wis.	1312	1091	842	834	1318	805	1685	1127	664	1330	909	144	443	493	1007	975	417	1508	506	1194	1178	493	747	2101	449	636	1507	78	267	1065	990	875	423
Memphis, Tenn.	1032	743	366	951	1594	247	1913	1340	924	1769	637	548	487	737	468	1058	726	1092	1061	572	672	467	139	1823	365	•	1017	632	852	399	1142	482	671
Miami, Fla.	1986	1697	665	1143	1773	765	2901	1539	1431	2784	746	1377	1133	1322	1327	2100	1387	1994	2008	1242	345	1491	1161	2737	1078	1017	•	1463	1771	878	1327	1518	1671
Milwaukee, Wis.	1390	1144	804	772	1271	748	1763	1060	610	1408	854	87	385	433	1063	1039	357	1557	573	1163	1123	564	727	2145	392	632	1463	•	334	1034	922	905	501
Minn.-St. Paul, Minn.	1223	979	1114	1100	1589	1069	1446	1387	937	1068	1180	413	717	760	964	845	690	1351	239	1211	1440	461	833	1996	712	852	1771	334	•	1251	1246	818	364
Mobile, Ala.	1277	988	369	1040	1672	235	2270	1439	1167	2148	628	896	734	977	627	1399	978	1263	1411	510	405	846	437	2037	597	350	687	983	1402	140	1232	787	1021
Montréal, Que.	2161	1876	1268	597	363	1324	2592	321	383	2309	1018	841	821	577	1759	1881	576	2331	1502	1883	1384	1326	1435	2995	828	1302	1732	941	1263	1637	395	1662	1320
Nashville, Tenn.	1247	972	251	732	736	201	2002	1126	717	1907	422	452	289	532	700	1187	544	1320	1092	810	577	556	359	2047	180	220	916	542	853	536	929	702	761
New Orleans, La.	1145	859	517	1153	1747	359	2140	1556	1248	2077	780	929	820	1060	500	1284	1077	1119	1479	358	568	846	434	1916	719	399	878	1034	1251	•	1353	684	1065
New York, N.Y.	2056	1756	863	192	450	988	2568	211	367	2317	613	828	635	486	1642	1788	626	2175	1485	1678	979	1214	1283	2823	759	1142	1327	922	1246	1353	•	1519	1293
Norfolk, Va.	1962	1673	592	249	881	753	2561	543	561	2342	321	874	600	531	1433	1892	699	2009	1531	1460	661	1193	1097	2795	693	958	1013	961	1287	1101	441	1535	1311
Oklahoma City, Okla.	545	263	880	1339	1902	741	1489	1733	1249	1413	1119	826	901	1096	210	616	1068	682	900	458	1195	357	350	1353	808	482	1518	905	818	648	1519	•	477
Omaha, Nebr.	892	646	1006	1153	1639	926	1267	1467	990	1086	1180	465	700	818	672	537	744	1027	436	917	1349	208	623	1698	707	671	1671	501	364	1065	1293	477	•
Philadelphia, Pa.	1915	1694	771	99	541	897	2450	303	360	2226	521	758	571	425	1540	1726	578	2091	1415	1589	889	1121	1197	2741	682	1057	1230	853	1176	1239	91	1436	1219
Phoenix, Ariz.	449	727	1888	2310	2882	1697	1020	2703	2348	1141	2126	1753	1854	2061	1021	826	2027	401	1726	1158	2053	1238	1337	389	1776	1470	2388	1833	1671	1527	2479	989	1325
Pittsburgh, Pa.	1636	1379	737	230	819	763	2156	576	220	1927	523	459	278	127	1260	1427	287	1803	1116	1364	893	850	914	2194	398	786	1237	550	877	1113	363	1145	918
Portland, Oreg.	1461	1737	2735	2847	3295	2658	435	3039	2671	653	2880	2131	2413	2519	2057	1285	2425	1709	1590	2282	3070	1901	2284	994	2437	2367	3414	2069	1721	2591	2959	1926	1700
Providence, R.I.	2232	1932	1037	368	276	1176	2757	44	456	2444	777	976	811	642	1818	1964	705	2351	1633	1854	1155	1390	1459	2999	935	1318	1503	1066	1389	1529	176	1695	1441
Québec, Que.	2333	2048	1426	765	228	1496	2764	390	533	2470	1176	1002	1027	738	1911	2043	738	2492	1764	2045	1542	1488	1597	3157	1058	1475	1897	1089	1420	1810	544	1806	1482
Rapid City, S. Dak.	831	799	1575	1605	2089	1498	952	1982	1493	552	1714	915	1231	1278	1108	401	1225	1080	536	1352	1932	743	1164	1399	1238	1245	2284	858	576	1573	1764	873	534
Reno, Nev.	1036	1324	2471	2641	3147	2416	427	2978	2512	842	2649	1970	2187	2323	1695	1040	2249	1167	1639	1888	2560	1665	2030	476	2213	2083	3021	2003	1797	2199	2818	1529	1500
Richmond, Va.	1877	1586	545	144	773	697	2473	543	473	2254	292	786	512	443	1333	1754	611	1937	1443	1353	646	1105	984	2709	575	845	994	877	1204	1057	330	1345	1223
Sacramento, Calif.	1117	1406	2611	2781	3287	2556	545	3118	2652	982	2789	2110	2327	2463	1835	1180	2389	1267	1779	2020	2700	1805	2170	387	2353	2223	3161	2143	1937	2339	2958	1669	1640
St. Louis, Mo.	1057	783	553	804	1379	503	1701	1188	723	1536	738	291	338	540	651	863	513	1167	812	801	881	254	357	1862	267	294	1222	371	553	699	961	523	453
Salt Lake City, Utah	612	908	1976	2110	2616	1857	363	2419	1965	428	2121	1443	1661	1784	1262	512	1719	880	1215	1453	2237	1118	1444	730	1656	1570	2603	1502	1246	1773	2278	1112	953
San Antonio, Tex.	719	512	1023	1649	2299	861	1704	2099	1651	1749	1254	1223	1230	1470	275	947	1448	568	1378	197	1141	773	578	1380	1124	711	1439	1314	1234	575	1863	477	943
San Diego, Calif.	815	1087	2172	2668	3240	2043	963	3061	2637	1212	2450	2118	2241	2446	1291	1201	2416	742	1943	1491	2320	1605	1695	122	2143	1829	2618	2191	2046	1864	2851	1349	1716
San Francisco, Calif.	1132	1420	2563	2884	3371	2409	654	3182	2728	1069	2835	2183	2424	2527	1773	1267	2482	1196	1873	1955	2787	1893	2032	403	2425	2162	3193	2203	2001	2278	3054	1692	1720
Savannah, Ga.	1683	1380	254	640	1269	409	2546	1048	971	2345	240	951	660	818	1017	1717	914	1653	1597	1029	154	1112	795	2482	640	657	506	1038	1352	641	830	1156	1298
Seattle, Wash.	1511	1800	2843	2733	3205	2703	529	3095	2629	615	2992	2031	2451	2511	2136	1377	2444	1785	1505	2354	3115	1904	2273	1177	2427	2362	3451	2045	1673	2645	2944	1975	1657
Shreveport, La.	836	547	637	1296	1940	477	1844	1736	1308	1796	892	867	879	1127	186	981	1078	813	1212	239	829	567	216	1631	751	322	1180	970	1386	316	1486	366	776
Sioux Falls, S. Dak.	1082	838	1196	1215	1699	1116	1295	1499	1045	895	1370	525	890	870	844	655	794	1217	230	1110	1539	390	799	1817	897	858	1861	507	221	1265	1353	644	187
Spokane, Wash.	1336	1559	2531	2515	2990	2420	391	2804	2390	318	2584	1716	2159	2176	1928	1067	2085	1617	1208	2164	2818	1617	2018	1249	2167	2082	3191	1751	1386	2383	2671	1651	1513
Springfield, Ill.	1086	861	652	753	1316	602	1688	1134	675	1507	749	196	302	489	766	832	443	1284	857	915	946	295	464	1982	282	390	1317	280	481	796	914	637	421
Tampa, Fla.	1738	1449	464	986	1620	552	2753	1383	1263	2551	583	1187	948	1166	1106	1928	1201	1746	1807	1007	194	1280	939	2607	865	782	248	1268	1578	644	1176	1264	1493
Topeka, Kans.	801	551	898	1133	1701	787	1433	1510	1051	1279	1058	568	688	862	509	557	841	947	604	759	1203	71	479	1549	593	538	1562	633	532	929	1288	342	168
Toronto, Ont.	1815	1530	975	465	683	1031	2246	462	99	1972	832	495	540	296	1391	1540	235	1951	1161	1542	1275	985	1094	2654	598	961	1530	582	913	1347	486	1303	979
Tucson, Ariz.	454	674	1746	2380	2887	1605	1191	2686	2235	1245	2005	1739	1842	2037	951	845	2005	317	1746	1070	1958	1255	1278	512	1749	1417	2311	1819	1677	1436	2517	941	1341
Tulsa, Okla.	658	374	832	1230	1791	680	1569	1597	1143	1498	1066	702	753	953	277	691	930	791	840	522	1123	247	291	1458	687	426	1461	792	779	706	1374	110	399
Vancouver, B.C.	1660	1949	2992	2882	3303	2852	674	3168	2878	764	3141	2247	2541	2504	2259	1526	2505	1934	1654	2503	3264	2053	2422	1328	2576	2511	3600	1612	1822	2794	3023	2121	1803
Walla Walla, Wash.	1208	1527	2570	2566	3045	2430	260	2938	2449	390	2670	1871	2187	2234	1858	1104	2181	1476	1248	2049	2833	1631	2000	1092	2194	2162	3204	1814	1458	2369	2720	1708	1384
Washington, D.C.	1904	1591	640	39	673	767	2440	440	372	2153	383	687	497	362	1403	1640	516	2040	1357	1448	754	1057	1058	2739	605	917	1105	784	1105	1150	226	1330	1149
Wichita, Kans.	620	359	978	1293	1832	830	1663	1673	1206	1327	1186	711	817	1012	386	512	969	744	731	629	1309	202	472	1384	744	549	1206	792	650	840	1436	168	309
Winnipeg, Man.	1658	1444	1587	1570	1803	1541	1443	1812	1377	875	1622	857	1151	1227	1328	1065	1149	1621	215	1611	1896	851	1260	2033	1161	1428	2212	786	462	1713	1683	1208	643

DISTANCES ARE APPROXIMATE AND HAVE BEEN COMPUTED OVER MAJOR THROUGH ROUTES

	Philadelphia, Pa.	Phoenix, Ariz.	Pittsburgh, Pa.	Portland, Oreg.	Rapid City, S. Dak.	Reno, Nev.	Richmond, Va.	St. Louis, Mo.	Salt Lake City, Utah	San Antonio, Tex.	San Diego, Calif.	San Francisco, Calif.	Savannah, Ga.	Seattle, Wash.	Spokane, Wash.	Tampa, Fla.	Washington, D.C.
Albany, N.Y.	233	2536	457	2999	1784	2798	472	1016	2251	1962	2894	3009	981	2928	2623	1331	367
Albuquerque, N. Mex.	1915	449	1636	1461	831	1036	1877	1057	612	719	815	1132	1683	1511	1336	1738	1904
Amarillo, Tex.	1694	727	1379	1737	799	1324	1586	783	908	512	1087	1420	1380	1800	1559	1449	1591
Atlanta, Ga.	771	1888	737	2735	1575	2471	545	553	1976	1023	2172	2563	254	2843	2531	464	640
Austin, Tex.	1681	993	1411	2301	1257	1759	1479	876	1386	78	1334	1787	1160	2274	1974	1168	1563
Baltimore, Md.	99	2310	230	2847	1605	2641	144	804	2110	1649	2668	2884	640	2733	2515	986	39
Bangor, Maine	541	2882	819	3295	2089	3147	773	1379	2616	2299	3240	3371	1269	3205	2990	1620	673
Billings, Mont.	1992	1258	1693	890	323	982	2040	1307	570	1513	1354	1208	2029	835	553	2314	1919
Birmingham, Ala.	897	1697	763	2658	1498	2416	697	503	1857	861	2043	2409	409	2703	2420	552	767
Boise, Idaho	2450	1020	2156	435	952	427	2473	1701	363	1704	963	654	2546	525	391	2753	2440
Boston, Mass.	303	2703	576	3039	1982	2978	543	1188	2419	2099	3061	3182	1048	3095	2804	1383	440
Buffalo, N.Y.	360	2348	220	2671	1493	2512	473	723	1964	1651	2637	2728	971	2629	2390	1263	372
Butte, Mont.	2226	1141	1927	653	552	842	2254	1536	428	1749	1212	1069	2345	615	318	2551	2153
Charleston, W. Va.	481	2042	233	2619	1457	2389	309	538	1865	1363	2409	2615	536	2618	2265	884	355
Charlotte, N.C.	513	2126	523	2880	1714	2649	292	738	2121	1254	2450	2835	240	2992	2584	583	383
Chattanooga, Tenn.	757	1808	618	2668	1420	2359	545	433	1829	1022	2146	2515	373	2598	2290	586	611
Cheyenne, Wyo.	1727	924	1427	1211	300	995	1708	910	457	1068	1257	1209	1722	1279	1032	1992	1658
Chicago, Ill.	758	1753	459	2131	915	1970	786	291	1443	1223	2118	2183	951	2031	1716	1187	687
Cincinnati, Ohio	571	1854	278	2413	1231	2187	512	338	1661	1230	2241	2424	660	2451	2159	948	497
Cleveland, Ohio	425	2061	127	2519	1278	2328	443	540	1784	1473	2446	2547	818	2511	2176	1166	362
Columbia, S.C.	604	2086	599	2995	1726	2697	362	742	2166	1250	2448	2771	142	2985	2676	492	412
Columbus, Ohio	472	1929	184	2478	1239	2269	473	413	1716	1372	2307	2475	720	2445	2117	1058	390
Dallas, Tex.	1540	1021	1260	2057	1108	1695	1333	651	1262	275	1291	1773	1017	2136	1928	1106	1403
Denver, Colo.	1726	826	1427	1285	401	1040	1754	863	512	947	1201	1267	1717	1377	1067	1928	1640
Des Moines, Iowa	1088	1449	799	1819	637	1638	1105	349	1089	983	1835	1851	1217	1766	1574	1403	1041
Detroit, Mich.	578	2027	287	2425	1225	2249	611	513	1719	1448	2416	2482	914	2444	2085	1201	516
Duluth, Minn.	1254	1830	954	1771	688	1956	1273	676	1395	1389	2188	2084	1435	1677	1385	1681	1179
El Paso, Tex.	2091	401	1803	1709	1080	1167	1937	1167	880	568	742	1196	1653	1785	1617	1746	2040
Fargo, N. Dak.	1415	1726	1116	1590	536	1639	1443	812	1215	1378	1943	1873	1597	1505	1208	1807	1357
Fort Wayne, Ind.	595	1842	302	2287	1071	2126	614	356	1572	1269	2200	2339	814	2187	1872	1099	528
Fort Worth, Tex.	1593	1044	1305	2078	1235	1663	1364	701	1239	268	1358	1734	752	2148	1903	1138	1434
Grand Forks, N. Dak.	1492	1803	1193	1645	613	1694	1520	889	1649	1455	1920	1928	1674	1459	1162	1884	1434
Grand Rapids, Mich.	738	1975	442	2308	1092	2147	750	478	1626	1412	2364	2389	966	2208	1893	1281	643
Great Falls, Mont.	2181	1273	1882	779	558	1000	2209	1533	585	1736	1370	1226	2351	701	413	2561	2108
Greensboro, N.C.	420	2219	430	2973	1807	2742	452	831	2224	1347	2543	2928	333	3085	2677	676	290
Hartford, Conn.	201	2592	474	3039	1823	2818	445	1070	2351	1976	2932	3091	937	2939	2624	1287	340
Houston, Tex.	1589	1158	1364	2282	1352	1888	1353	801	1453	197	1491	1955	1029	2354	2164	1007	1448
Indianapolis, Ind.	639	1750	355	2307	1122	2074	620	239	1544	1176	2134	2331	766	2312	1959	1005	567
Jackson, Miss.	1153	1456	972	2506	1453	2104	944	505	1685	614	1789	2203	603	2601	2263	678	1000
Jacksonville, Fla.	889	2053	893	3070	1932	2697	646	881	2237	1141	2320	2787	154	3115	2818	194	754
Kansas City, Mo.	1121	1238	850	1901	743	1665	1105	254	1118	773	1605	1893	1112	1904	1617	1280	1057
Las Vegas, Nev.	2537	338	2274	1016	1129	446	2514	1677	449	1319	337	583	2256	1193	1070	2325	2429
Lincoln, Nebr.	1213	1293	918	1712	569	1460	1270	473	931	930	1658	1683	1259	1790	1461	1465	1207
Little Rock, Ark.	1197	1337	914	2284	1164	2030	984	357	1444	578	1695	2032	795	2273	2018	939	1058
Los Angeles, Calif.	2741	389	2194	994	1399	476	2709	1862	730	1380	122	403	2482	1177	1249	2607	2739
Louisville, Ky.	682	1776	398	2437	1238	2213	575	267	1656	1124	2143	2425	640	2427	2167	865	605
Madison, Wis.	908	1748	602	2034	780	1925	930	361	1387	1282	2139	2145	1095	1956	1673	1306	835
Memphis, Tenn.	1057	1470	786	2367	1245	2083	845	294	1570	711	1829	2162	657	2362	2082	782	917
Miami, Fla.	1230	2388	1237	3414	2284	3021	994	1222	2603	1439	2618	3193	506	3451	3191	248	1105
Milwaukee, Wis.	853	1833	550	2069	858	2003	877	371	1502	1314	2191	2203	1038	2045	1751	1268	784
Minn.-St. Paul, Minn.	1176	1671	877	1721	576	1797	1204	553	1246	1234	2046	2001	1352	1673	1386	1578	1105
Mobile, Ala	1140	1648	1106	2705	1601	2316	914	644	1881	707	1918	2400	506	2710	2455	522	1031
Montréal, Que.	480	2603	603	2830	1756	2825	725	1073	1295	2024	2942	3029	1225	2774	2486	1571	601
Nashville, Tenn.	838	1690	568	2457	1295	2227	625	295	1674	949	2051	2409	508	2495	2173	908	697
New Orleans, La.	1239	1527	1113	2591	1573	2199	1057	699	1773	575	1864	2278	641	2645	2383	644	1150
New York, N.Y.	91	2479	363	2959	1764	2818	330	961	2278	1863	2851	3054	830	2944	2671	1176	226
Norfolk, Va.	348	2437	400	3012	1859	2734	88	930	2352	1575	2733	3059	507	3024	2775	859	195
Oklahoma City, Okla.	1436	989	1145	1926	873	1529	1345	523	1112	477	1349	1692	1156	1975	1651	1264	1330
Omaha, Nebr.	1219	1325	918	1700	534	1500	1223	453	453	943	1716	1720	1298	1657	1513	1493	1149
Philadelphia, Pa.	•	2430	294	2921	1703	2724	240	881	2188	1772	2769	2951	736	2862	2624	1083	136
Phoenix, Ariz.	2430	•	2085	1273	1238	762	2332	1492	688	978	358	794	2046	1510	1419	2134	2331
Pittsburgh, Pa.	294	2085	•	2599	1395	2427	312	599	1902	1521	2493	2645	745	2511	2267	1045	229
Portland, Oreg.	2921	1273	2599	•	1237	566	2924	2113	807	2190	1115	669	3051	173	366	3225	2904
Providence, R.I.	267	2655	539	3135	1891	2941	506	1137	2419	2039	3013	3168	1006	3007	2692	1352	402
Québec, Que.	635	2765	735	2994	1937	2987	869	1251	2457	2168	3120	3190	1368	2934	2646	1720	762
Rapid City, S. Dak.	1703	1238	1395	1237	•	1224	1771	984	686	1263	1466	1454	1828	1183	870	2011	1624
Reno, Nev.	2724	762	2427	566	1224	•	2737	1906	531	1744	565	227	2703	760	779	2798	2666
Richmond, Va.	240	2332	312	2924	1771	2646	•	842	2264	1579	2638	2964	499	2936	2687	842	107
Sacramento, Calif.	2864	902	2567	544	1364	140	2877	2046	671	1758	509	87	2792	717	834	2896	2806
St. Louis, Mo.	881	1492	599	2113	984	1879	842	•	1381	927	1906	2133	841	2102	1868	1030	804
Salt Lake City, Utah	2188	688	1902	807	686	531	2264	1381	•	1341	784	755	2236	869	738	2416	2123
San Antonio, Tex.	1772	978	1521	2190	1263	1744	1579	927	1341	•	1306	1779	1227	2265	2113	1229	1641
San Diego, Calif.	2769	358	2493	1115	1466	565	2638	1906	784	1306	•	526	2381	1292	1343	2457	2737
San Francisco, Calif.	2951	794	2645	669	1454	227	2964	2133	755	1779	526	•	2792	858	921	2943	2886
Savannah, Ga.	736	2046	745	3051	1828	2703	499	841	2236	1227	2381	2792	•	3063	2772	352	604
Seattle, Wash.	2862	1510	2511	173	1183	760	2936	2102	869	2265	1292	858	3063	•	288	3250	2752
Shreveport, La.	1394	1221	1161	2226	1309	1885	1183	582	1460	389	1549	1990	831	2344	2129	923	1246
Sioux Falls, S. Dak.	1283	1481	984	1580	343	1472	1311	632	941	1119	1865	1696	1473	1526	1213	1683	1212
Spokane, Wash.	2624	1419	2267	366	870	779	2687	1868	738	2113	1343	921	2772	288	•	2942	2500
Springfield, Ill.	841	1533	551	2121	955	1872	810	99	1374	1062	1900	2133	906	2133	1825	1154	765
Tampa, Fla.	1083	2134	1045	3225	2011	2798	842	1030	2416	1229	2457	2943	352	3250	2942	•	947
Topeka, Kans.	1214	1250	921	1863	727	1645	1176	321	1086	794	1534	1847	1183	1833	1658	1351	1128
Toronto, Ont.	460	2262	320	2626	1410	2465	572	748	1954	1683	2613	2678	976	2600	2312	1424	477
Tucson, Ariz.	2377	123	2486	1396	1246	912	2286	1457	820	881	422	921	1970	1666	1523	2063	2360
Tulsa, Okla.	1304	1113	1010	2037	932	1713	1288	412	1194	554	1475	1790	1106	2026	1830	1213	1214
Vancouver, B.C.	3008	1656	2657	319	1329	906	3082	2250	1015	2411	1438	995	3209	146	288	3396	2881
Walla Walla, Wash.	2659	1222	2318	281	956	622	2643	1832	596	1992	1214	849	2821	273	157	2977	2479
Washington, D.C.	136	2331	229	2904	1624	2666	107	804	2123	1641	2737	2886	604	2752	2488	947	•
Wichita, Kans.	1361	1040	1070	1854	729	1542	1318	460	1020	634	1410	1730	2821	1842	1642	1386	1283
Winnipeg, Man.	1615	1941	1316	1523	751	1854	1643	1105	1430	1602	2260	2088	1808	1444	1156	2014	1541

	AVERAGE TEMPERATURE IN °F				AVERAGE RAINFALL IN INCHES			
CITY	JAN	APR	JUL	OCT	JAN	APR	JUL	OCT
Albany, N.Y.	23	46	72	51	2.5	2.8	3.5	2.8
Albuquerque, N. Mex.	35	56	79	58	0.4	0.5	1.2	0.8
Amarillo, Texas	36	56	78	59	0.6	1.5	3.0	2.2
Anchorage, Alaska	12	37	58	36	0.8	0.4	1.9	1.9
Atlanta, Ga.	45	60	79	62	4.4	4.5	4.7	2.4
Augusta, Maine	20	43	70	49	3.5	3.3	3.4	3.4
Birmingham, Ala.	47	63	82	66	5.0	4.5	5.2	3.0
Boise, Idaho	29	50	75	52	1.3	1.2	0.2	0.8
Boston, Mass.	30	48	74	55	3.9	3.8	2.9	3.1
Buffalo, N.Y.	25	44	70	51	2.8	3.0	2.6	3.0
Butte, Mont.	15	38	63	42	0.4	0.9	1.2	0.7
Charleston, S.C.	50	65	81	66	2.5	2.9	7.7	2.8
Charlotte, N.C.	43	60	79	63	3.5	3.4	4.8	2.7
Cheyenne, Wyo.	25	43	70	48	0.6	1.7	1.9	0.9
Chicago, Ill.	26	49	76	55	1.9	3.0	3.4	2.8
Cincinnati, Ohio	34	54	77	58	3.7	3.5	3.5	2.2
Cleveland, Ohio	28	47	72	53	2.7	3.4	3.3	2.4
Dallas. Texas	46	65	85	68	2.3	4.0	1.9	2.7
Denver, Colo.	29	46	73	51	0.6	2.1	1.5	1.0
Detroit, Mich.	27	48	74	54	1.9	3.1	2.7	2.6
El Paso, Texas	43	63	82	64	0.5	0.2	1.6	0.9
Fargo, N. Dak.	6	43	71	47	0.5	1.7	3.5	1.1
Great Falls, Mont.	22	44	69	48	0.7	1.0	1.3	0.8
Honolulu, Hawaii	73	74	79	78	3.8	1.3	0.4	1.8
Houston, Texas	54	69	83	71	3.8	3.2	4.3	3.8
Jacksonville, Fla.	56	69	83	71	2.5	3.6	7.7	5.2
Juneau, Alaska	25	38	55	42	4.0	2.9	4.5	8.3
Kansas City, Mo.	32	56	82	60	1.4	3.6	3.2	2.9
Las Vegas, Nev.	44	65	90	67	0.6	0.2	0.5	0.3
Los Angeles, Calif.	56	62	73	67	3.1	1.2	.01	0.4
Memphis, Tenn.	42	61	81	63	6.1	4.6	3.5	2.7
Mexico City, D.F.	54	64	62	59	0.2	0.5	4.9	1.4
Miami, Fla.	67	74	82	78	2.0	3.9	6.8	8.2
Milwaukee, Wis.	21	44	69	50	1.8	2.5	3.0	2.1
Minneapolis, Minn.	12	44	72	49	0.7	1.9	3.3	1.6
Montréal, Que.	16	43	71	49	1.2	2.8	4.0	3.2
New Orleans, La.	55	68	82	70	3.8	4.6	6.7	2.8
New York, N.Y.	33	51	77	58	3.3	3.4	3.7	3.1
Oklahoma City, Okla.	37	60	83	63	1.3	3.1	2.4	2.5
Omaha, Nebr.	22	52	79	56	0.8	2.6	3.4	1.7
Philadelphia, Pa.	32	52	76	56	3.3	3.4	4.2	2.8
Phoenix, Ariz.	50	67	90	71	0.7	0.3	0.8	0.5
Pittsburgh, Pa.	29	49	72	53	3.0	3.1	3.9	2.5
Portland, Oreg.	38	52	67	54	5.4	2.1	0.4	3.6
Rapid City, S. Dak.	24	45	72	50	0.4	1.9	2.3	1.0
Reno, Nev.	30	48	68	49	1.2	0.5	0.3	0.5
Richmond, Va.	39	58	78	59	3.5	3.2	5.6	3.0
St. Louis, Mo.	32	55	78	58	2.0	3.7	3.3	2.9
Salt Lake City, Utah	27	50	77	52	1.4	1.8	0.6	1.2
San Antonio, Texas	52	68	84	71	1.7	2.8	2.1	2.5
San Diego, Calif.	55	62	70	66	2.0	0.8	.01	0.5
San Francisco, Calif.	51	56	59	61	4.0	1.3	.01	0.7
San Juan, P. Rico	74	77	80	80	4.7	3.7	6.3	5.8
Seattle, Wash.	38	49	65	52	5.7	2.4	0.8	4.0
Spokane, Wash.	25	47	71	49	2.4	0.9	0.4	1.6
Tampa, Fla.	61	71	82	75	2.1	2.8	8.6	2.8
Toronto, Ont.	25	45	72	51	1.3	2.3	2.9	2.4
Vancouver, Br. Col.	37	48	64	50	6.6	2.8	1.4	5.4
Washington, D.C.	37	56	78	59	3.0	3.2	4.2	3.1
Winnipeg, Man.	0	38	68	43	.01	0.8	2.7	1.2

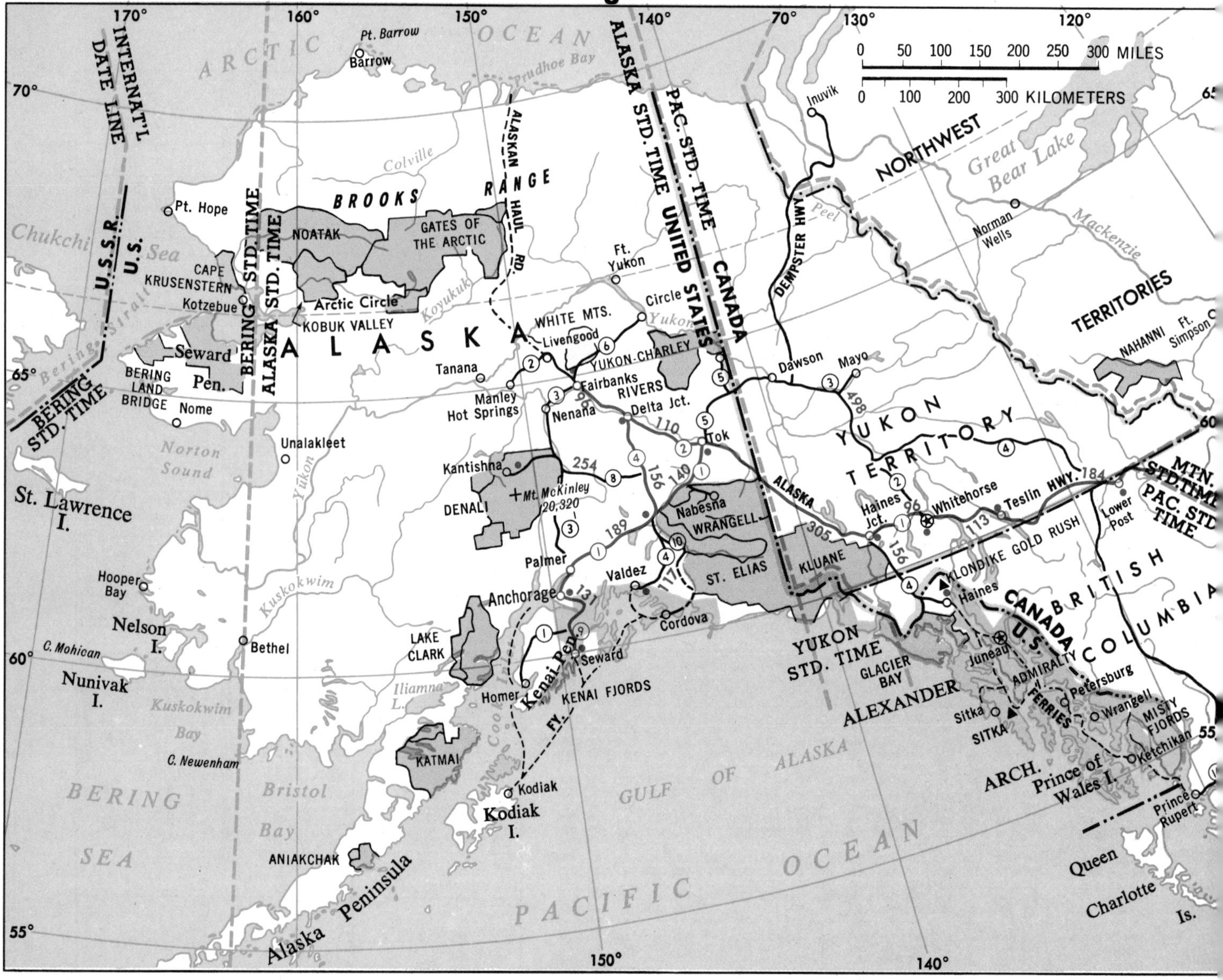
ARCTIC OCEAN
Pt. Barrow
Barrow
Prudhoe Bay
INTERNAT'L DATE LINE
ALASKA STD. TIME
PAC. STD. TIME
UNITED STATES
CANADA
0 50 100 150 200 250 300 MILES
0 100 200 300 KILOMETERS
Inuvik
NORTHWEST
TERRITORIES
Great Bear Lake
Norman Wells
Mackenzie
Peel
DEMPSTER HWY.
Colville
BROOKS RANGE
ALASKAN HAUL RD.
Pt. Hope
NOATAK
GATES OF THE ARCTIC
Chukchi Sea
U.S.S.R.
U.S.
BERING STD. TIME
CAPE KRUSENSTERN
Kotzebue
Arctic Circle
Koyukuk
KOBUK VALLEY
Ft. Yukon
Circle
Yukon
WHITE MTS.
Livengood
YUKON-CHARLEY RIVERS
ALASKA
Seward Pen.
BERING LAND BRIDGE
Bering Strait
Nome
Tanana
Manley Hot Springs
Nenana
Fairbanks
Delta Jct.
Tok
Dawson
Mayo
YUKON TERRITORY
NAHANNI
Ft. Simpson
Norton Sound
Unalakleet
Yukon
St. Lawrence I.
Kantishna
DENALI
Mt. McKinley 20,320
Nabesna
WRANGELL
ALASKA HWY.
Haines Jct.
Whitehorse
Teslin
Lower Post
MTN. STD. TIME
PAC. STD. TIME
KLUANE
ST. ELIAS
KLONDIKE GOLD RUSH
Haines
Palmer
Valdez
Anchorage
Hooper Bay
Kuskokwim
Cordova
Nelson I.
Bethel
C. Mohican
Nunivak I.
LAKE CLARK
Kenai Pen.
Seward
Homer
KENAI FJORDS
Iliamna L.
YUKON STD. TIME
GLACIER BAY
Juneau
ADMIRALTY
BRITISH COLUMBIA
CANADA
U.S.
Petersburg
Wrangell
MISTY FJORDS
Ketchikan
Sitka
SITKA
ALEXANDER ARCH.
FERRIES
Prince of Wales I.
Prince Rupert
Kuskokwim Bay
C. Newenham
KATMAI
Cook Inlet
Kodiak
Kodiak I.
GULF OF ALASKA
BERING SEA
Bristol Bay
ANIAKCHAK
Alaska Peninsula
PACIFIC OCEAN
Queen Charlotte Is.

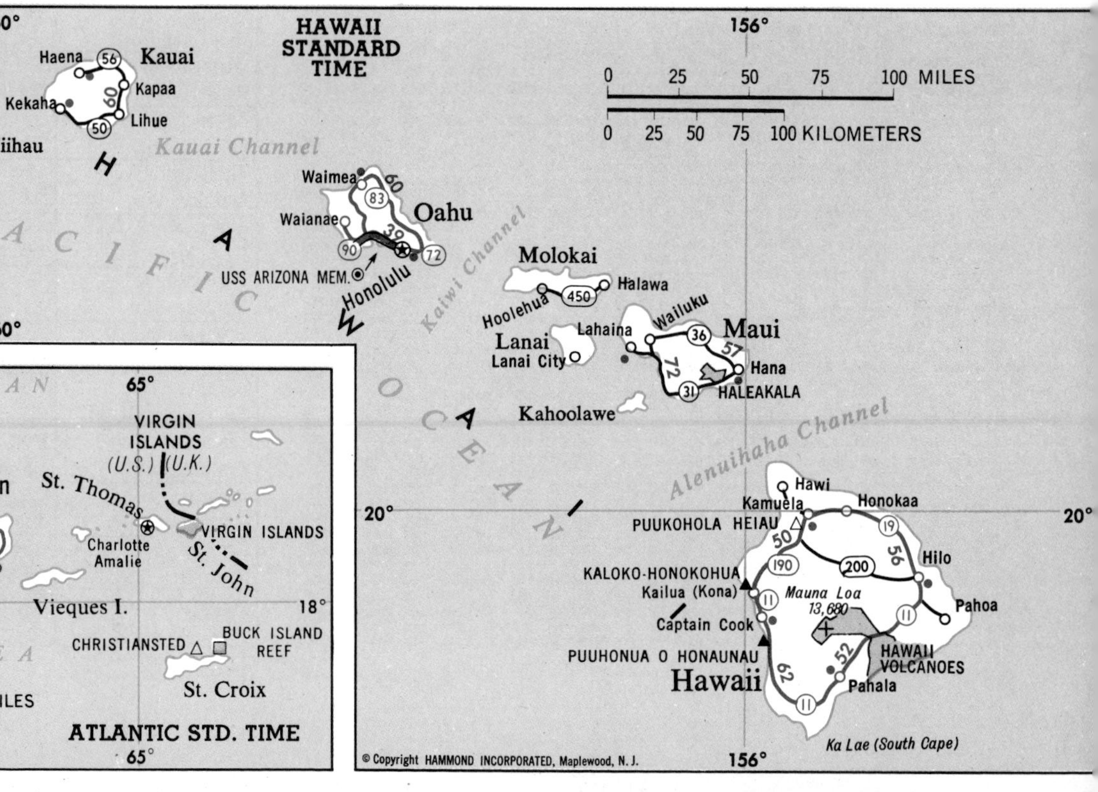
HAWAII STANDARD TIME
0 25 50 75 100 MILES
0 25 50 75 100 KILOMETERS
Haena
Kauai
Kapaa
Kekaha
Lihue
Niihau
Kauai Channel
HAWAII
Waimea
Waianae
Oahu
USS ARIZONA MEM.
Honolulu
PACIFIC OCEAN
Kaiwi Channel
Molokai
Halawa
Hoolehua
Lahaina
Wailuku
Maui
Lanai
Lanai City
Hana
HALEAKALA
Kahoolawe
Alenuihaha Channel
Hawi
Kamuela
Honokaa
PUUKOHOLA HEIAU
KALOKO-HONOKOHUA
Kailua (Kona)
Hilo
Mauna Loa 13,680
Pahoa
Captain Cook
PUUHONUA O HONAUNAU
HAWAII VOLCANOES
Hawaii
Pahala
Ka Lae (South Cape)

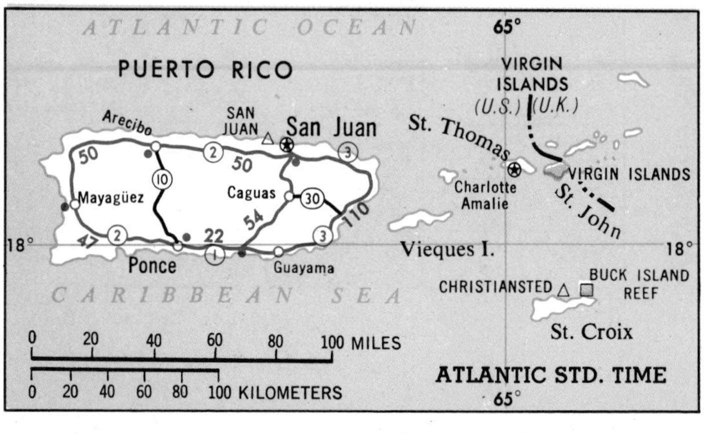
ATLANTIC OCEAN
PUERTO RICO
Arecibo
SAN JUAN
San Juan
VIRGIN ISLANDS
(U.S.) (U.K.)
St. Thomas
Charlotte Amalie
VIRGIN ISLANDS
St. John
Mayagüez
Caguas
Ponce
Guayama
Vieques I.
CHRISTIANSTED
BUCK ISLAND REEF
St. Croix
CARIBBEAN SEA
0 20 40 60 80 100 MILES
0 20 40 60 80 100 KILOMETERS
ATLANTIC STD. TIME

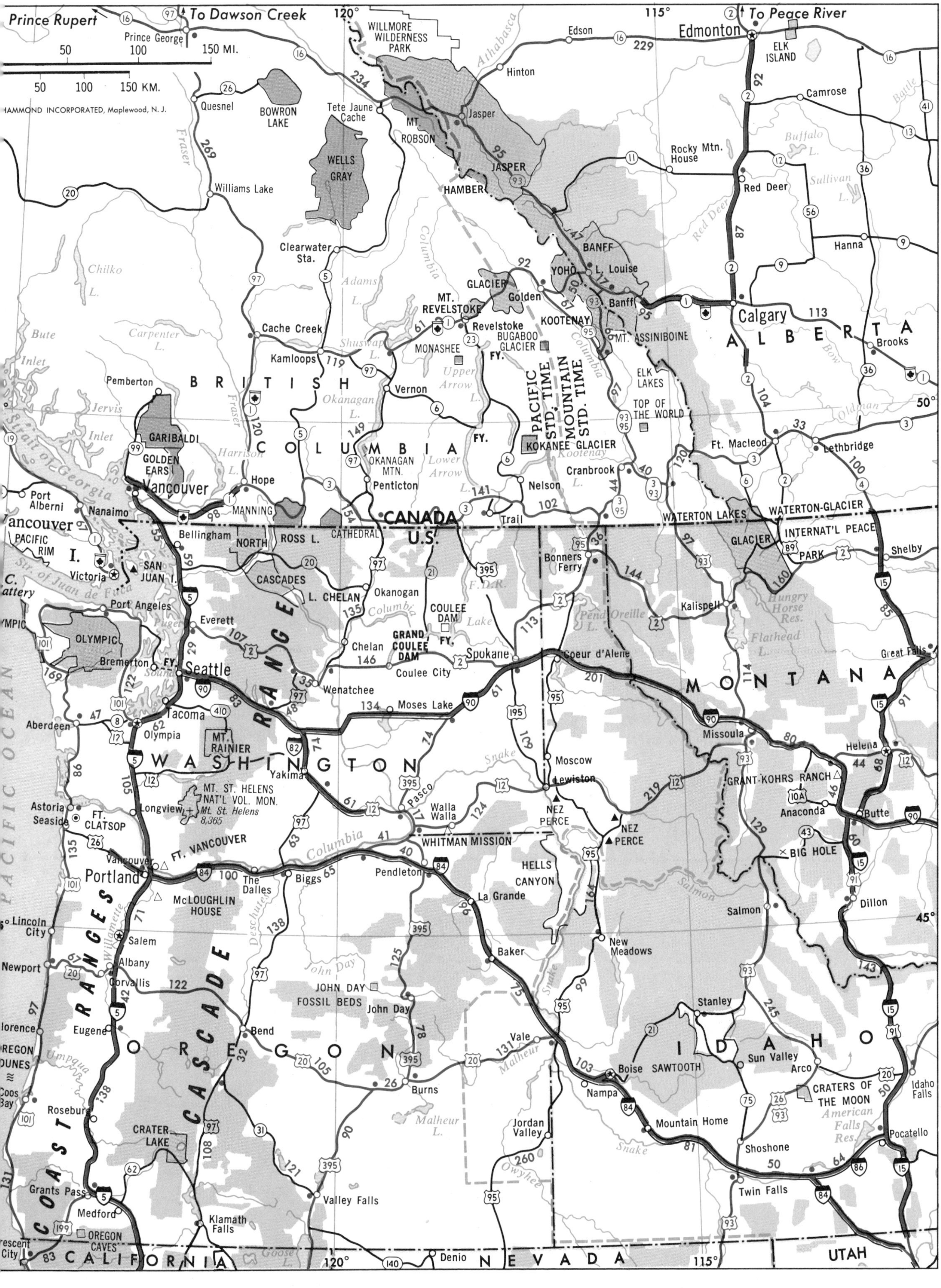
Prince Rupert
To Dawson Creek
Prince George
50 100 150 MI.
50 100 150 KM.
HAMMOND INCORPORATED, Maplewood, N. J.
WILLMORE WILDERNESS PARK
Edson
Edmonton
To Peace River
ELK ISLAND
Hinton
Quesnel
BOWRON LAKE
Tete Jaune Cache
Jasper
MT. ROBSON
WELLS GRAY
JASPER
Camrose
Rocky Mtn. House
Red Deer
Williams Lake
HAMBER
Hanna
Clearwater Sta.
BANFF
YOHO
L. Louise
GLACIER
Golden
Banff
Calgary
MT. REVELSTOKE
Revelstoke
KOOTENAY
BUGABOO GLACIER
MT. ASSINIBOINE
Cache Creek
MONASHEE
ALBERTA
Brooks
Kamloops
Pemberton
BRITISH COLUMBIA
Vernon
PACIFIC STD. TIME
MOUNTAIN STD. TIME
ELK LAKES
TOP OF THE WORLD
GARIBALDI
KOKANEE GLACIER
Ft. Macleod
Lethbridge
GOLDEN EARS
OKANAGAN MTN.
Hope
Cranbrook
Vancouver
Penticton
Nelson
Port Alberni
Nanaimo
MANNING
Trail
WATERTON LAKES
WATERTON-GLACIER INTERNAT'L PEACE PARK
CANADA
U.S.
Victoria
PACIFIC RIM
Bellingham
NORTH CASCADES
ROSS L.
CATHEDRAL
SAN JUAN I.
GLACIER
Shelby
Bonners Ferry
Okanogan
L. CHELAN
Port Angeles
COULEE DAM
Kalispell
OLYMPIC
Everett
Chelan
GRAND COULEE DAM
Spokane
Coeur d'Alene
Great Falls
Bremerton
Seattle
Coulee City
Wenatchee
MONTANA
Aberdeen
Tacoma
Moses Lake
Olympia
MT. RAINIER
Missoula
Helena
WASHINGTON
Moscow
Lewiston
Yakima
GRANT-KOHRS RANCH
MT. ST. HELENS NAT'L VOL. MON.
Longview
Astoria
Seaside
FT. CLATSOP
Pasco
Walla Walla
NEZ PERCE
Anaconda
Butte
WHITMAN MISSION
FT. VANCOUVER
Vancouver
Portland
The Dalles
Biggs
Pendleton
HELLS CANYON
BIG HOLE
McLOUGHLIN HOUSE
La Grande
Salmon
Dillon
Lincoln City
Salem
Baker
New Meadows
Newport
Albany
Corvallis
JOHN DAY FOSSIL BEDS
John Day
Stanley
Florence
Eugene
Bend
OREGON
IDAHO
Vale
Sun Valley
Arco
Boise
SAWTOOTH
Nampa
CRATERS OF THE MOON
Idaho Falls
Burns
Coos Bay
Roseburg
CRATER LAKE
Jordan Valley
Mountain Home
Pocatello
Shoshone
Twin Falls
Grants Pass
Medford
Valley Falls
Klamath Falls
OREGON CAVES
Crescent City
CALIFORNIA
Denio
NEVADA
UTAH
PACIFIC OCEAN
COAST RANGES
CASCADE RANGE

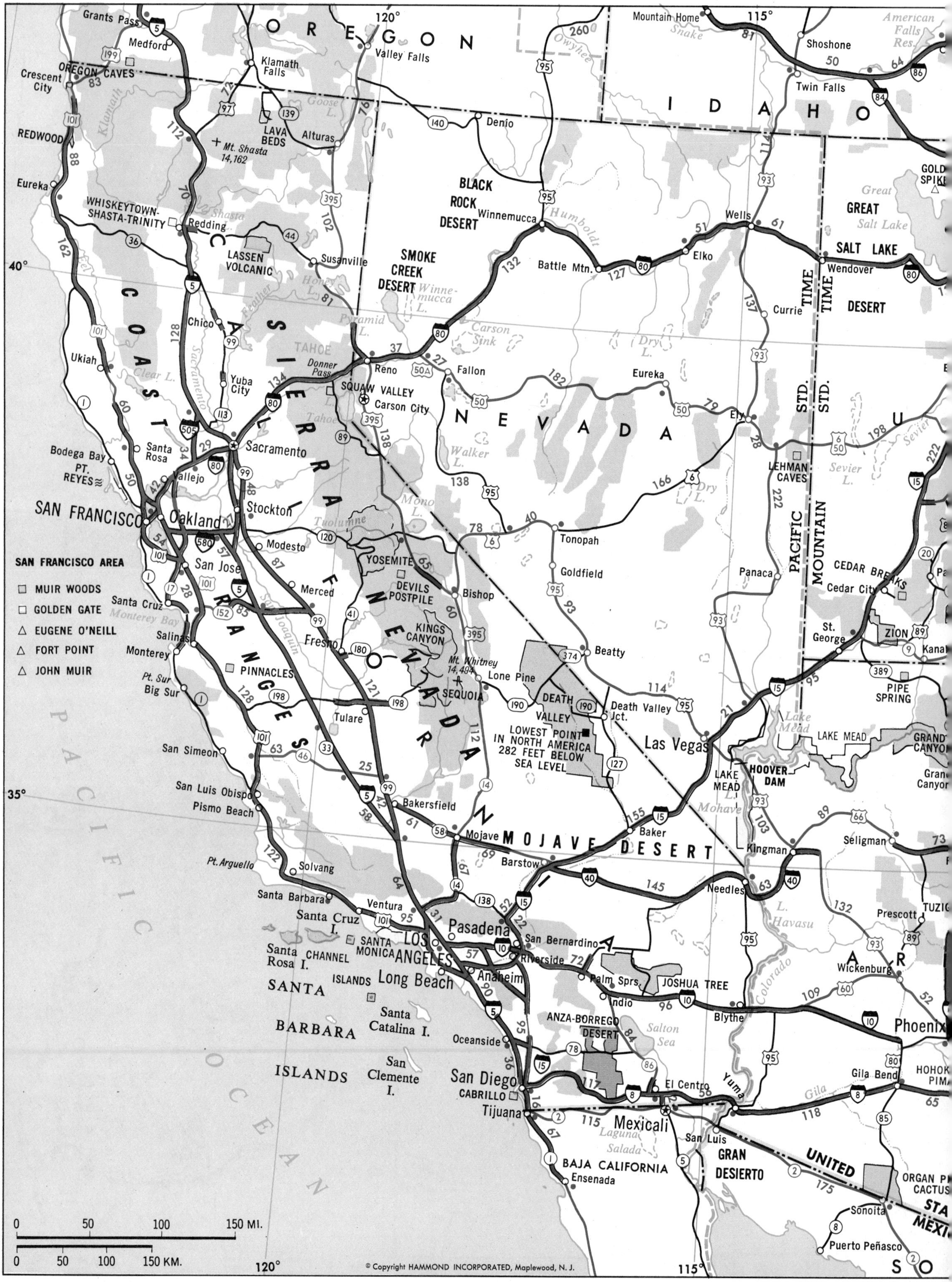
OREGON
IDAHO
NEVADA
Grants Pass
Medford
OREGON CAVES
Crescent City
Klamath Falls
Valley Falls
LAVA BEDS
Alturas
Mt. Shasta 14,162
REDWOOD
Eureka
WHISKEYTOWN-SHASTA-TRINITY
Redding
LASSEN VOLCANIC
Susanville
Mountain Home
Snake
Shoshone
American Falls Res.
Twin Falls
Denio
BLACK ROCK DESERT
Winnemucca
SMOKE CREEK DESERT
Wells
Elko
Battle Mtn.
GOLDEN SPIKE
Great Salt Lake
GREAT SALT LAKE DESERT
Wendover
Currie
PACIFIC STD. TIME
MOUNTAIN STD. TIME
COAST RANGES
SIERRA NEVADA
Chico
Yuba City
Ukiah
Clear L.
TAHOE
Donner Pass
Reno
Fallon
SQUAW VALLEY
Carson City
Eureka
Ely
Pyramid L.
Carson Sink
Walker L.
Mono L.
LEHMAN CAVES
Sevier L.
Bodega Bay
PT. REYES
Santa Rosa
Sacramento
Vallejo
SAN FRANCISCO
Oakland
Stockton
Modesto
SAN FRANCISCO AREA
MUIR WOODS
GOLDEN GATE
EUGENE O'NEILL
FORT POINT
JOHN MUIR
San Jose
Santa Cruz
Monterey Bay
Salinas
Monterey
YOSEMITE
DEVILS POSTPILE
Merced
Bishop
Tonopah
Goldfield
Panaca
CEDAR BREAKS
Cedar City
St. George
ZION
Kanab
KINGS CANYON
Fresno
Mt. Whitney 14,494
Lone Pine
SEQUOIA
PINNACLES
Pt. Sur
Big Sur
Beatty
DEATH VALLEY
Death Valley Jct.
LOWEST POINT IN NORTH AMERICA 282 FEET BELOW SEA LEVEL
PIPE SPRING
Tulare
Las Vegas
Lake Mead
LAKE MEAD
GRAND CANYON
San Simeon
San Luis Obispo
Pismo Beach
Bakersfield
HOOVER DAM
Mohave
Kingman
Seligman
Mojave
MOJAVE DESERT
Baker
Barstow
Needles
Pt. Arguello
Solvang
Santa Barbara
Ventura
Santa Cruz I.
SANTA MONICA
LOS ANGELES
Pasadena
San Bernardino
Riverside
Anaheim
Long Beach
Santa Rosa I.
CHANNEL ISLANDS
SANTA BARBARA ISLANDS
Santa Catalina I.
San Clemente I.
Palm Sprs.
JOSHUA TREE
Indio
Blythe
L. Havasu
Colorado
Prescott
TUZIGOOT
Wickenburg
Phoenix
ANZA-BORREGO DESERT
Salton Sea
Oceanside
San Diego
CABRILLO
Tijuana
El Centro
Yuma
Gila Bend
Gila
HOHOKAM PIMA
Mexicali
Laguna Salada
San Luis
GRAN DESIERTO
BAJA CALIFORNIA
Ensenada
UNITED STATES
MEXICO
ORGAN PIPE CACTUS
Sonoita
Puerto Peñasco
PACIFIC OCEAN
120°
115°
40°
35°
0 50 100 150 MI.
0 50 100 150 KM.
© Copyright HAMMOND INCORPORATED, Maplewood, N. J.

WYOMING
COLORADO
NEBRASKA
KANSAS
OKLA.
NEW MEXICO
TEXAS
CHIHUAHUA
Casper
Douglas
Lusk
Crawford
Lander
Rawlins
Medicine Bow
Laramie
Cheyenne
Rock Springs
Kemmerer
FOSSIL BUTTE
Evanston
FLAMING GORGE
Flaming Gorge Res.
FT. LARAMIE
AGATE FOSSIL BEDS
Alliance
Hyannis
Thedford
Scottsbluff
SCOTTS BLUFF
CHIMNEY ROCK
Ogallala
North Platte
Sidney
Niobrara
Platte
Salt Lake City
TIMPANOGOS CAVE
Vernal
DINOSAUR
Maybell
Steamboat Springs
Estes Park
Greeley
Sterling
McCook
Wray
Fort Morgan
St. Francis
Oberlin
ROCKY MTN.
SHADOW MTN.
Meeker
Boulder
Denver
Goodland
Oakley
Limon
Price
Green River
Grand Junction
Glenwood Sprs.
Aspen
Mt. Elbert 14,431
FLORISSANT FOSSIL BEDS
Colorado Springs
Pikes Peak 14,110
Cheyenne Wells
Big Sandy
ARCHES
COLORADO
Moab
BLACK CANYON OF THE GUNNISON
Gunnison
CURECANTI
Pueblo
BENT'S OLD FORT
Lamar
Garden City
Dodge City
La Junta
Arkansas
Hanksville
CANYONLANDS
CAPITOL REEF
Monticello
GREAT SAND DUNES
Walsenburg
Alamosa
NATURAL BRIDGES
HOVENWEEP
Cortez
MESA VERDE
Durango
Trinidad
GLEN CANYON
RAINBOW BRIDGE
Mexican Hat
YUCCA HOUSE
Cimarron
Liberal
Page
NAVAJO
Kayenta
AZTEC RUINS
Farmington
Raton
CAPULIN MTN.
Boise City
CANYON DE CHELLY
Cebolla
Taos
Dalhart
ALIBATES FLINT QUARRIES
LAKE MEREDITH
Cameron
CHACO CANYON
Los Alamos
FT. UNION
BANDELIER
Santa Fe
PECOS
Las Vegas
Pampa
Amarillo
Shamrock
WUPATKI
HUBBELL TRADING POST
Ganado
Gallup
SUNSET CRATER
Grants
Albuquerque
Tucumcari
Canadian
WALNUT CANYON
Winslow
PETRIFIED FOREST
EL MORRO
Vaughn
Clovis
Childress
MONTEZUMA CASTLE
Plainview
Show Low
Datil
SALINAS
Socorro
Carrizozo
Roswell
Lubbock
Brownfield
TONTO
Globe
GILA CLIFF DWELLINGS
Truth or Consequences
Lovington
Lamesa
CENTRAL STD. TIME
MTN. STD. TIME
CASA GRANDE
Alamogordo
WHITE SANDS
Artesia
Hobbs
Sweetwater
Big Spring
Carlsbad
Midland
Tucson
SAGUARO
Lordsburg
Deming
Las Cruces
CARLSBAD CAVERNS
Odessa
FT. BOWIE
CHIRICAHUA
El Paso
CHAMIZAL
GUADALUPE MTS.
Tombstone
Ciudad Juárez
Pecos
San Angelo
TUMACACORI
Bisbee
CORONADO
Douglas
Nogales
Rio Grande
Gila
Black
110°
105°
100°
40°
35°

To Saskatoon
To Prince Albert
RIDING MTN.
Fort Qu'Appelle
Qu'Appelle
Ft. Macleod
Medicine Hat
Swift Current
Moose Jaw
Regina
Broadview
Lethbridge
CYPRESS HILLS
Old Wives L.
SASKATCHEWAN
ALBERTA
Frenchman
Milk
Assiniboia
Weyburn
MOOSE MTN.
Virden
Brand
WATERTON-GLACIER
INTERNAT'L PEACE
PARK
GLACIER
CANADA
CENTRAL STD. TIME
Estevan
Souris
TURTLE MTN.
INTERNAT'L PEACE GARDEN
UNITED STATES
MTN. STD. TIME
Hungry Horse Res.
Shelby
Havre
Marias
Malta
Nashua
Fort Peck
Ft. Benton
Missouri
Williston
Minot
FT. UNION TRADING POST
Watford City
Lake Sakakawea
Great Falls
Fort Peck L.
Lewistown
Jordan
THEODORE ROOSEVELT
MONTANA
NORTH
KNIFE RIVER INDIAN VILLAGES
Helena
Canyon Ferry L.
Glendive
Anaconda
Harlowton
Yellowstone
Dickinson
Bismarck
Butte
Musselshell
Miles City
Custer
Livingston
Bozeman
Billings
Tongue
Bowman
Lemmon
Dillon
Yellowstone
CUSTER BATTLEFIELD
Buffalo
Grand
Mobridge
BIGHORN CANYON
Broadus
YELLOWSTONE
W. Yellowstone
Cody
Sheridan
Powder
DEVILS TOWER
Faith
Oahe
Yellowstone L.
Bighorn
Belle Fourche
SOUTH D
Snake
IDAHO
GRAND TETON
Worland
Buffalo
Gillette
Lead
MT. RUSHMORE
Cheyenne
Pierre
Idaho Falls
Jackson
Wind
JEWEL CAVE
Rapid City
Wall
Murdo
Custer
Pocatello
WYOMING
Midwest
Cheyenne
WIND CAVE
BADLANDS
White
Lander
Casper
Lusk
Douglas
Crawford
Valentine
Niobrara
GOLDEN SPIKE
Logan
Bear L.
FOSSIL BUTTE
Kemmerer
Green
Rawlins
Medicine Bow
FT. LARAMIE
AGATE FOSSIL BEDS
Alliance
Hyannis
Brigham City
Scottsbluff
Thedford
Ogden
Evanston
Rock Springs
FLAMING GORGE
Flaming Gorge Res.
Platte
SCOTTS BLUFF
CHIMNEY ROCK
Laramie
NEBR
Sidney
Ogallala
North Platte
Salt Lake City
Cheyenne
TIMPANOGOS CAVE
Vernal
DINOSAUR
Maybell
Steamboat Springs
Sterling
Provo
Utah L.
Estes Park
Greeley
Eureka
White
Meeker
SHADOW MTN.
ROCKY MTN.
Fort Morgan
Wray
McCook
Price
Colorado
Boulder
St. Francis
Oberlin
UTAH
Green River
Grand Junction
Glenwood Sprs.
Denver
Republican
Goodland
Richfield
ARCHES
COLORADO
Aspen
Mt. Elbert 14,431
FLORISSANT FOSSIL BEDS
Limon
Moab
Colorado Springs
Oakley
COLORADO
© Copyright HAMMOND INCORPORATED, Maplewood, N. J.

MANITOBA
Winnipeg
Gimli
Pine Falls
Portage La Prairie
NOPIMING
WHITESHELL
L. Winnipeg
SPRUCE WOODS
Morris
Lac Seul
Sioux Lookout
Kenora
Dryden
Minnitaki L.
Sturgeon L.
Eagle L.
Lake of the Woods
EASTERN STD. TIME
CENTRAL STD. TIME
ONTARIO
Lake Nipigon
Geraldton
Long L.
Marathon
Isle St. Ignace
PUKASKWA
SIBLEY
Thunder Bay
Atikokan
QUETICO
Ft. Frances
International Falls
VOYAGEURS
Rainy L.
Upper Red L.
Lower Red L.
Vermilion L.
GRAND PORTAGE
Grand Marais
ISLE ROYALE
LAKE SUPERIOR
Copper Harbor
Keweenaw Pen.
Keweenaw Bay
Houghton
Devils Lake
Grand Forks
Carrington
Bemidji
Hibbing
Virginia
Grand Rapids
Leech L.
Silver Bay
APOSTLE ISLANDS
Duluth
Superior
Ashland
Ironwood
Marquette
Munising
PICTURED ROCKS
Iron Mtn.
Escanaba
Fargo
Moorhead
Wadena
Brainerd
Mille Lacs L.
Fergus Falls
Breckenridge
MINNESOTA
St. Cloud
St. Croix Falls
Rice Lake
Rhinelander
Menominee
Aberdeen
Ortonville
Willmar
St. Paul
Minneapolis
WISCONSIN
Wausau
Chippewa Falls
Eau Claire
Marshfield
Stevens Point
Appleton
Green Bay
Manitowoc
Manistee
Ludington
Oshkosh
L. Winnebago
Sheboygan
Fond du Lac
Watertown
Huron
Brookings
PIPESTONE
Pipestone
Mankato
Faribault
Rochester
Winona
Tomah
La Crosse
Wisconsin Dells
Mitchell
Worthington
Fairmont
Albert Lea
Austin
Spirit Lake
Sioux Falls
Spencer
Mason City
Charles City
EFFIGY MOUNDS
Prairie du Chien
Madison
MILWAUKEE
Racine
Kenosha
Janesville
Beloit
Waukegan
Evanston
CHICAGO
INDIANA DUNES
Gary
Ft. Dodge
Waterloo
Dubuque
Freeport
Rockford
Elgin
Aurora
O'Neill
Sioux City
Carroll
Ames
IOWA
Marshalltown
Cedar Rapids
HERBERT HOOVER
Clinton
Davenport
Rock Island
CHICAGO PORTAGE
Joliet
Norfolk
Newton
Des Moines
Iowa City
Ottawa
Kankakee
Columbus
Fremont
Omaha
Council Bluffs
Osceola
Ottumwa
Galesburg
Peoria
Burlington
Bloomington
Grand Island
Lincoln
Kearney
Hastings
HOMESTEAD
Keokuk
ILLINOIS
Danville
Champaign
LINCOLN HOME
Springfield
Decatur
Kirksville
Bethany
Quincy
Jacksonville
Macon
Hannibal
Mattoon
Terre Haute
IND.
Smith Center
Marysville
St. Joseph
Belleville
MISSOURI
Moberly
KANSAS
Junction City
Topeka
Kansas City
Independence
Columbia
Lawrence
Alton
ST. LOUIS
E. St. Louis
Vincennes
Flora
Missouri
Mississippi
Des Moines
Iowa
Platte
Loup
Elkhorn
Republican
Solomon
Kansas
Chariton
Illinois
Kaskaskia
Wabash
Red R. of the North
Sheyenne
James
Big Sioux
Little Sioux
Minnesota
St. Croix
Cedar
Wolf
Green Bay
LAKE MICHIGAN
0 50 100 MI.
0 50 100 KM.
95°
90°
50°
45°
40°

COLORADO
Gunnison
CURECANTI
Colorado Springs
Pueblo
Cheyenne Wells
Big Sandy
Arkansas
BENT'S OLD FORT
Lamar
GREAT SAND DUNES
Rio Grande
La Junta
Walsenburg
Alamosa
Purgatoire
Trinidad
Raton
CAPULIN MTN.
Cebolla
Taos
Los Alamos
FT. UNION
BANDELIER
Santa Fe
PECOS
Las Vegas
Albuquerque
Tucumcari
Rio Grande
Vaughn
Clovis
SALINAS
Socorro
NEW MEXICO
Carrizozo
Roswell
Pecos
Alamogordo
WHITE SANDS
Artesia
Lovington
Hobbs
Carlsbad
CARLSBAD CAVERNS
GUADALUPE MTS.
El Paso
C. Juárez
MTN. STD. TIME
CENTRAL STD. TIME
Oakley
Hays
Smoky Hill
KANSAS
Great Bend
FT. LARNED
Garden City
Arkansas
Dodge City
Liberal
Cimarron
Junction City
Topeka
Salina
McPherson
Hutchinson
Newton
Emporia
Pratt
Wichita
El Dorado
Chanute
Wellington
Arkansas
CHEROKEE STRIP LIVING MUS.
Coffeyville
KANSAS TPK.
Boise City
Dalhart
ALIBATES FLINT QUARRIES
LAKE MEREDITH
Canadian
N. Canadian
Amarillo
Pampa
Shamrock
Woodward
Alva
Enid
Ponca City
Bartlesville
Oologah L.
CIMMARON TPK.
Tulsa
Keystone L.
TURNER TPK.
OKLAHOMA
Guthrie
Clinton
Oklahoma City
Muskogee
Washita
Norman
Shawnee
Canadian
Lawton
H.E. BAILEY TPK.
CHICKASAW
Ardmore
L. Texoma
Durant
Denison
INDIAN NAT. TPK.
Childress
Vernon
Red
Plainview
Lubbock
Brownfield
Wichita Falls
Seymour
Lamesa
Denton
Greenville
Brazos
Mineral Wells
Dallas
Ft. Worth
Sweetwater
Big Spring
Midland
Odessa
Abilene
Colorado
Corsicana
Palestine
TEXAS
Pecos
San Angelo
Waco
Trinity
Van Horn
Ft. Stockton
Temple
Lampasas
FT. DAVIS
Sheffield
Sonora
Marfa
Marathon
CHIHUAHUA
Rio Grande
LYNDON B. JOHNSON
Fredericksburg
Austin
New Braunfels
HOUSTON
Presidio
U.S. MEXICO
AMISTAD
Amistad Res.
Del Rio
BIG BEND
COAHUILA
Uvalde
San Antonio
SAN ANTONIO MISSIONS
Colorado
Eagle Pass
Piedras Negras
Victoria
Matagorda Bay
Beeville
Nueva Rosita
Rio Grande
Nueces
Corpus Christi
Nuevo Laredo
Laredo
Kingsville
PADRE ISLAND
Nuevo Laredo
Laredo
Salado
Kingsville
TEXAS
PADRE ISLAND
Falcon Res.
NUEVO LEÓN
Sabinas Hidalgo
Marte R. Gomez Res.
Laguna Madre
McAllen
Harlingen
Reynosa
PALO ALTO BATTLEFIELD
MONTERREY
Matamoros
Brownsville
105°
100°
35°
30°

MISSOURI
ILLINOIS
IND.
KENTUCKY
TENNESSEE
ARKANSAS
MISSISSIPPI
ALABAMA
GA.
N.C.
LOUISIANA
FLORIDA
GULF OF MEXICO
Independence
Kansas City
Columbia
Jefferson City
ST. LOUIS
JEFFERSON NAT'L EXPANSION MEMORIAL
Alton
Belleville
Vincennes
GEORGE ROGERS CLARK
Bedford
Maysville
Frankfort
Morehead
Lexington
MTN. PKWY.
Louisville
New Albany
LINCOLN BOYHOOD
Elizabethtown
Evansville
Henderson
Owensboro
BLUEGRASS PKWY.
A. LINCOLN BIRTHPLACE
Mt. Vernon
Marion
Flora
Clinton
Collins
Nevada
Rolla
L. of the Ozarks
OZARK NAT'L SCENIC RIVERWAYS
Springfield
WILSON'S CREEK
Joplin
G. W. CARVER
Willow Sprs.
Poplar Bluff
Cape Girardeau
Sikeston
Paducah
W. KY. PKWY.
MAMMOTH CAVE
Hopkinsville
Bowling Green
CUMB. PKWY.
Corbin
CUMBERLAND GAP
Middlesboro
BIG S. FORK
Clarksville
Martin
FT. DONELSON
Nashville
STONES RIVER
Murfreesboro
Crossville
Morristown
Knoxville
GREAT SMOKY MTS.
Chattanooga
CHICKAMAUGA & CHATTANOOGA
Clayton
PEA RIDGE
Harrison
Fayetteville
BUFFALO NAT'L RIVER
Mtn. View
Paragould
Jonesboro
Dyersburg
Blytheville
Newport
Jackson
W. Memphis
Memphis
Forrest City
Selmer
SHILOH
Corinth
Pulaski
Florence
RUSSELL CAVE
Huntsville
Decatur
Ft. Smith
Conway
Jacksonville
Waldron
Little Rock
HOT SPRINGS
Hot Sprs. Nat'l Pk.
Pine Bluff
ARKANSAS POST
Holly Sprs.
BRICES CROSS ROADS
TUPELO
Tupelo
NATCHEZ TRACE PKWY.
Clarksdale
Grenada
Greenwood
Greenville
Columbus
Tuscaloosa
Birmingham
Bessemer
Jasper
Anniston
Gadsden
Rome
Marietta
Atlanta
Griffin
La Grange
HORSESHOE BEND
Opelika
Columbus
TUSKEGEE INST.
ANDERSONVILLE
Texarkana
Camden
Fordyce
Dumas
Magnolia
El Dorado
Kosciusko
Meridian
Selma
Montgomery
Minden
Shreveport
Longview
Carthage
Monroe
Ruston
Vicksburg
VICKSBURG
Jackson
Winnfield
Natchitoches
Laurel
Waynesboro
Grove Hill
Greenville
Troy
Albany
Dothan
Bainbridge
Andalusia
Natchez
McComb
Hattiesburg
Alexandria
Crestview
Chattahoochee
Tallahassee
Mobile
Poplarville
Baton Rouge
Gulfport
Biloxi
GULF IS.
Pensacola
Fort Walton Beach
Panama City
Apalachicola
C. San Blas
C. St. George
Jasper
BIG THICKET NAT'L PRESERVE
Opelousas
Lafayette
New Iberia
Lake Charles
Beaumont
Port Arthur
Pasadena
Galveston
Galveston Bay
New Orleans
JEAN LAFITTE
Houma
Buras
Delta of the Mississippi
Atchafalaya Bay
EASTERN STD. TIME
CENTRAL STD. TIME
0 50 100 150 MI.
0 50 100 150 KM.
95°
90°
85°
35°
30°
© Copyright HAMMOND INCORPORATED, Maplewood, N. J.

ONTARIO
Geraldton
Hearst
Kapuskasing
Cochrane
Lake Abitibi
Timmins
Noranda
Val-d'Or
Kirkland Lake
Thunder Bay
Marathon
Isle St. Ignace
SIBLEY
GRAND PORTAGE
ISLE ROYALE
PUKASKWA
MISSINAIBI LAKE
Michipicoten I.
LAKE SUPERIOR
Chapleau
Grand Marais
CENTRAL STD. TIME
EASTERN STD. TIME
Keweenaw Pen.
Copper Harbor
Houghton
Keweenaw Bay
Ironwood
Marquette
PICTURED ROCKS
Munising
Sault Ste. Marie
Sudbury
Temiscaming
North Bay
Iron Mtn.
Escanaba
Manistique
FATHER MARQUETTE
Rhinelander
St. Joseph I.
Drummond I.
Manitoulin I.
Mackinac I.
KILLARNEY
ALGONQUIN
Pembroke
WISCONSIN
Wausau
Beaver I.
Cheboygan
Menominee
GEORGIAN BAY IS.
MUSKOKA LKS.
Stevens Point
SLEEPING BEAR DUNES
Traverse City
Alpena
LAKE HURON
Georgian Bay
Green Bay
Appleton
Frankfort
Grayling
Bruce Pen.
Manistee
Oshkosh
Manitowoc
Cadillac
Tawas City
Owen Sound
Orillia
KAWARTHA LKS.
Peterborough
Fond du Lac
Ludington
Baldwin
Wis. Dells
Sheboygan
Midland
Harbor Beach
Goderich
Oshawa
Madison
Mt. Pleasant
Saginaw
Bay City
Kitchener
Toronto
LAKE ONTARIO
MILWAUKEE
Muskegon
Grand Rapids
Flint
Port Huron
London
Hamilton
St. Catharines
Niagara Falls
Janesville
Beloit
Racine
Kenosha
Lansing
Sarnia
Buffalo
Freeport
Rockford
Waukegan
Kalamazoo
Pontiac
T. ROOSEVELT INAUGURAL
Evanston
Benton Harbor
Ann Arbor
DETROIT
Chatham
Elgin
Aurora
CHICAGO
INDIANA DUNES
Jackson
Windsor
Jamestown
Olean
CHICAGO PORTAGE
Dearborn
LAKE ERIE
PT. PELEE
Erie
Joliet
Gary
Elkhart
South Bend
Toledo
PERRY'S VICTORY AND INTERNAT'L PEACE MEM.
CLEVELAND
Warren
Meadville
Wellsboro
Ottawa
Kankakee
Plymouth
Ft. Wayne
Lorain
OHIO TPK.
Youngstown
Parma
Logansport
Huntington
Findlay
Williamsport
Bloomington
Lima
Akron
Du Bois
State College
ILLINOIS
Danville
Kokomo
Marion
Mansfield
Canton
Champaign
Lafayette
Anderson
Muncie
PENNSYLVANIA
Altoona
Pittsburgh
Decatur
Indianapolis
OHIO
Columbus
Wheeling
JOHNSTOWN FLOOD
ALLEGHENY PORTAGE R.R.
Harrisburg
Mattoon
Terre Haute
Springfield
Dayton
Richmond
Zanesville
PENNA.
INDIANA
Lancaster
Uniontown
Bedford
FT. NECESSITY
Hagerstown
ANTIETAM
Morgantown
Chillicothe
Columbus
Vincennes
W. H. TAFT
MOUND CITY GROUP
Marietta
Clarksburg
Cumberland
Flora
Cincinnati
Parkersburg
Winchester
HARPERS FY.
GEORGE ROGERS CLARK
Bedford
Portsmouth
WASHINGTON
Elkins
Maysville
WEST
SKYLINE DRIVE
SHENANDOAH
Evansville
New Albany
Frankfort
Ashland
Huntington
VA.
LINCOLN BOYHOOD
Charleston
Fredericksburg
Henderson
Louisville
Morehead
Owensboro
Lexington
VIRGINIA
Staunton

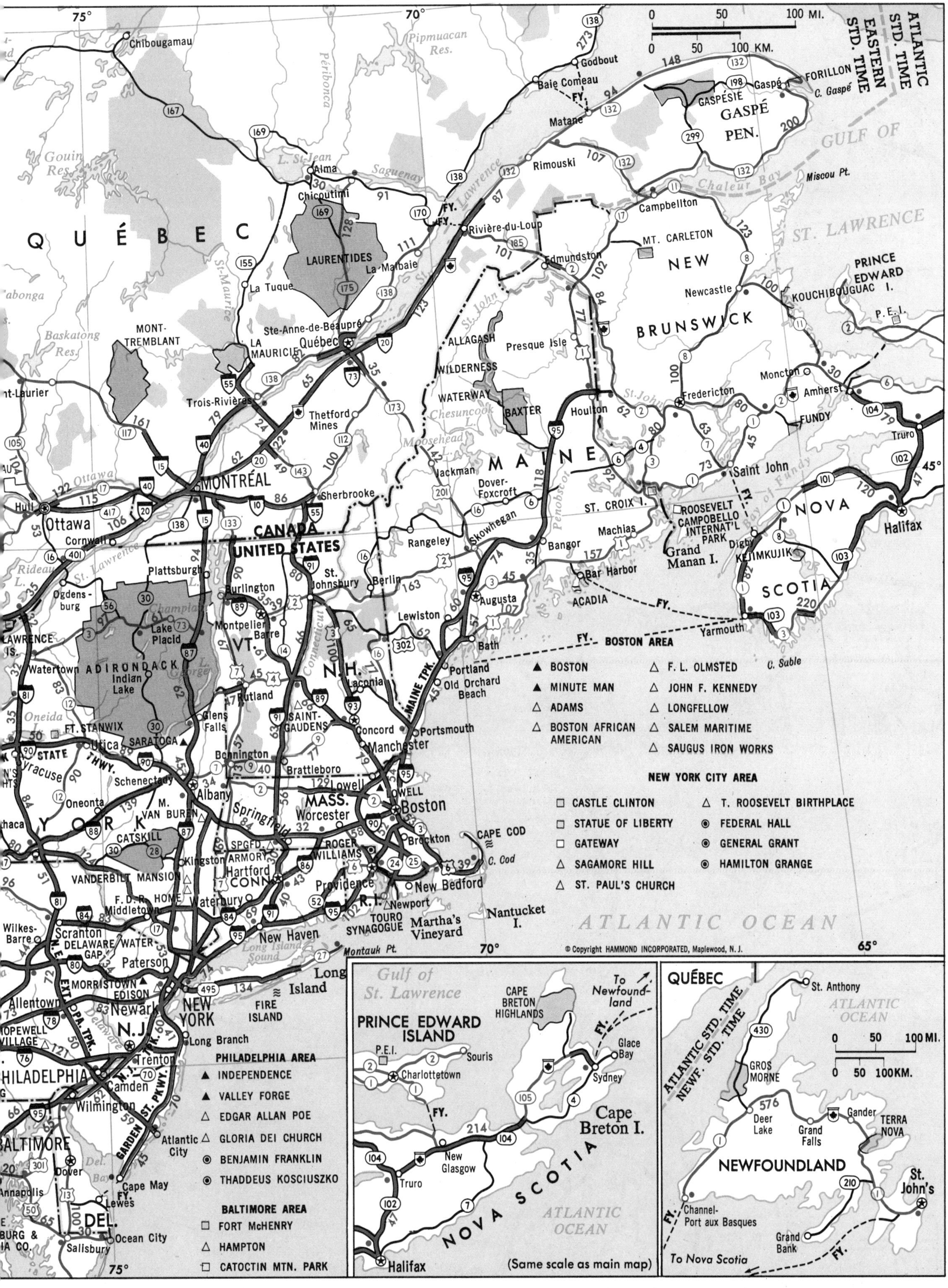
0 50 100 MI.
0 50 100 KM.
ATLANTIC STD. TIME
EASTERN STD. TIME
QUÉBEC
Chibougamau
Gouin Res.
L. St-Jean
Alma
Saguenay
Chicoutimi
Péribonca
Pipmuacan Res.
Godbout
Baie Comeau
FY.
Matane
GASPÉSIE
GASPÉ PEN.
Gaspé
FORILLON
C. Gaspé
GULF OF
ST. LAWRENCE
Rimouski
Chaleur Bay
Miscou Pt.
Campbellton
MT. CARLETON
NEW BRUNSWICK
Newcastle
KOUCHIBOUGUAC
PRINCE EDWARD I.
P.E.I.
LAURENTIDES
La Malbaie
Rivière-du-Loup
Edmundston
La Tuque
St-Maurice
abonga
Baskatong Res.
MONT-TREMBLANT
LA MAURICIE
Ste-Anne-de-Beaupré
Québec
ALLAGASH WILDERNESS WATERWAY
Presque Isle
BAXTER
Chesuncook L.
Moosehead L.
Fredericton
Moncton
Amherst
FUNDY
Truro
Houlton
St. John
Trois-Rivières
Thetford Mines
Sherbrooke
MONTRÉAL
Ottawa
Hull
Cornwall
Rideau L.
MAINE
Jackman
Dover-Foxcroft
Saint John
Bay of Fundy
NOVA SCOTIA
Halifax
Digby
KEJIMKUJIK
Yarmouth
C. Sable
ST. CROIX I.
ROOSEVELT CAMPOBELLO INTERNAT'L PARK
Grand Manan I.
Machias
Bangor
Penobscot
Bar Harbor
ACADIA
Skowhegan
Rangeley
CANADA
UNITED STATES
Plattsburgh
Ogdensburg
St. Lawrence
Burlington
Champlain
Lake Placid
Montpelier
Barre
St. Johnsbury
Berlin
Lewiston
Augusta
Bath
Portland
Old Orchard Beach
MAINE TPK.
ADIRONDACK
Watertown
Indian Lake
L. George
VT.
N.H.
Laconia
Connecticut
Rutland
SAINT-GAUDENS
Concord
Portsmouth
Manchester
Glens Falls
Oneida L.
FT. STANWIX
SARATOGA
Utica
STATE THWY.
Syracuse
Schenectady
Albany
Bennington
Brattleboro
Lowell
MASS.
Boston
Worcester
Springfield
Oneonta
M. VAN BUREN
YORK
CATSKILL
SPGFD. ARMORY
ROGER WILLIAMS
Brockton
CAPE COD
C. Cod
Kingston
Hartford
CONN.
Providence
R.I.
Newport
New Bedford
VANDERBILT MANSION
F.D.R. HOME
Middletown
Waterbury
TOURO SYNAGOGUE
Martha's Vineyard
Nantucket I.
ATLANTIC OCEAN
Wilkes-Barre
Scranton
DELAWARE WATER GAP
New Haven
Long Island Sound
Montauk Pt.
Paterson
Long Island
MORRISTOWN
EDISON
Allentown
Newark
NEW YORK
FIRE ISLAND
N.J.
Long Branch
Trenton
PHILADELPHIA
Camden
Wilmington
GARDEN ST. PKWY.
Atlantic City
BALTIMORE
Dover
Annapolis
Cape May
Lewes
DEL.
Ocean City
Salisbury
75° 70° 65° 45°
BOSTON AREA
▲ BOSTON
▲ MINUTE MAN
△ ADAMS
△ BOSTON AFRICAN AMERICAN
△ F. L. OLMSTED
△ JOHN F. KENNEDY
△ LONGFELLOW
△ SALEM MARITIME
△ SAUGUS IRON WORKS
NEW YORK CITY AREA
□ CASTLE CLINTON
□ STATUE OF LIBERTY
□ GATEWAY
△ SAGAMORE HILL
△ ST. PAUL'S CHURCH
△ T. ROOSEVELT BIRTHPLACE
◉ FEDERAL HALL
◉ GENERAL GRANT
◉ HAMILTON GRANGE
PHILADELPHIA AREA
▲ INDEPENDENCE
▲ VALLEY FORGE
△ EDGAR ALLAN POE
△ GLORIA DEI CHURCH
◉ BENJAMIN FRANKLIN
◉ THADDEUS KOSCIUSZKO
BALTIMORE AREA
□ FORT McHENRY
△ HAMPTON
□ CATOCTIN MTN. PARK
© Copyright HAMMOND INCORPORATED, Maplewood, N. J.
Gulf of St. Lawrence
PRINCE EDWARD ISLAND
P.E.I.
Souris
Charlottetown
CAPE BRETON HIGHLANDS
To Newfoundland
Glace Bay
Sydney
Cape Breton I.
New Glasgow
Truro
Halifax
NOVA SCOTIA
ATLANTIC OCEAN
(Same scale as main map)
QUÉBEC
ATLANTIC STD. TIME
NEWF. STD. TIME
St. Anthony
ATLANTIC OCEAN
0 50 100 MI.
0 50 100 KM.
GROS MORNE
Deer Lake
Grand Falls
Gander
TERRA NOVA
NEWFOUNDLAND
St. John's
Channel-Port aux Basques
Grand Bank
To Nova Scotia

OHIO
WEST VIRGINIA
VIRGINIA
KENTUCKY
TENN.
NORTH CAROLINA
SOUTH CAROLINA
GEORGIA
FLORIDA
ALA.
IND.
MD.
D.C.
DEL.
N.J.
APPALACHIAN MTNS.
ATLANTIC OCEAN
GULF OF MEXICO
Cincinnati
Portsmouth
Parkersburg
Winchester
WASHINGTON
Annapolis
Dover
Cape May
FY.
Lewes
Maysville
Ashland
Huntington
Charleston
Elkins
Frankfort
Louisville
Lexington
Morehead
BLUEGRASS PKWY.
MTN. PKWY.
A. LINCOLN BIRTHPLACE
Prestonsburg
Beckley
Staunton
Fredericksburg
T. STONE
FREDERICKSBURG & SPOTSYLVANIA CO.
G. WASHINGTON BIRTHPLACE
Charlottesville
Ocean City
Salisbury
ASSATEAGUE ISLAND
SKYLINE DRIVE
SHENANDOAH
W. VA. TPK.
Bluefield
Roanoke
Lynchburg
APPOMATTOX C. H.
Richmond
RICHMOND
M. L. WALKER
COLONIAL
Williamsburg
JAMESTOWN
Newport News
Norfolk
Virginia Beach
Petersburg
PETERSBURG
B. T. WASHINGTON
CUMB. PKWY.
Corbin
CUMBERLAND GAP
Middlesboro
BIG S. FORK
Bristol
Johnson City
A. JOHNSON
Danville
Buggs Island L.
BLUE RIDGE PKWY.
Winston-Salem
GUILFORD C. H.
Greensboro
Durham
Raleigh
Roanoke Rapids
Elizabeth City
WRIGHT BROTHERS
FT. RALEIGH
Rocky Mount
Williamston
Wilson
CAPE HATTERAS
C. Hatteras
Pamlico Sd.
Crossville
Morristown
Knoxville
GREAT SMOKY MTS.
Mt. Mitchell 6,684
Hickory
Salisbury
Asheville
Goldsboro
New Bern
Fayetteville
Chattanooga
CHICKAMAUGA & CHATTANOOGA
C. SANDBURG HOME
COWPENS
KINGS MTN.
Charlotte
Rockingham
Clayton
Greenville
Spartanburg
Rock Hill
Lumberton
MOORES CREEK
Morehead City
C. Lookout
CAPE LOOKOUT
Onslow Bay
Wilmington
C. Fear
Rome
Hartwell Res.
Greenwood
NINETY SIX
Florence
Marietta
Atlanta
Athens
Clark Hill Res.
Columbia
CONGAREE SWAMP
Myrtle Beach
L. Marion
Georgetown
Griffin
L. Sinclair
Augusta
Orangeburg
La Grange
Macon
OCMULGEE
C. Romain
Charleston
FT. SUMTER
Opelika
Columbus
Dublin
Statesboro
Yemassee
Savannah
Hilton Head I.
FT. PULASKI
Skidaway I.
Ossabaw I.
ANDERSONVILLE
Cordele
Albany
Baxley
Jesup
Sapelo I.
FT. FREDERICA
Dothan
Waycross
Brunswick
Sea Island
Jekyll I.
Bainbridge
Thomasville
Valdosta
CUMBERLAND ISLAND
Tallahassee
Perry
Live Oak
Jacksonville
FT. CAROLINE
CASTILLO DE SAN MARCOS
St. Augustine
FT. MATANZAS
Apalachicola
C. St. George
Gainesville
Ocala
L. George
Daytona Beach
De Land
CANAVERAL
C. Canaveral
Orlando
FLORIDA'S TPK.
Clearwater
Tampa
Lakeland
Melbourne
St. Petersburg
DE SOTO
Sarasota
Sebring
L. Kissimmee
Fort Pierce
EASTERN STD. TIME
CENTRAL STD. TIME
0 50 100 MI.
0 50 100 KM.
© Copyright HAMMOND INCORPORATED, Maplewood, N. J.
WASHINGTON, D.C. AREA
CHESAPEAKE & OHIO CANAL
CLARA BARTON
FORD'S THEATER
PENNSYLVANIA AVENUE
SEWALL-BELMONT HOUSE
ARLINGTON HOUSE
JEFFERSON MEMORIAL
LINCOLN MEMORIAL
NATIONAL CAPITAL PARKS
NATIONAL MALL
NATIONAL VISITOR CENTER
PISCATAWAY PARK
ROCK CREEK PARK
T. ROOSEVELT ISLAND
WHITE HOUSE
WOLF TRAP FARM PARK
WASHINGTON MONUMENT
MANASSAS
MONOCACY
FORT WASHINGTON PARK
FREDERICK DOUGLASS HOME
GREENBELT PARK
J. F. KENNEDY CENTER
L. B. JOHNSON MEM. GROVE
Fort Myers
Belle Glade
L. Okeechobee
West Palm Beach
MAR-A-LAGO
Naples
C. Romano
BIG CYPRESS NAT'L PRESERVE
EVERGLADES
Fort Lauderdale
Miami Beach
Miami
BISCAYNE
C. Sable
Flamingo
Key Largo
Florida Keys
Straits of Florida
FT. JEFFERSON
Key West
(Same scale as main map)

INDEX OF THE WORLD

This index, arranged in strict alphabetical order, includes grand divisions, countries, states, colonial possessions, major geographical areas, cities, towns and other features (both physical and man-made). Page number and index keys are given for the map on which they are shown at the largest scale. Note that inset maps continue the sequence of the keys from the main map. Population figures, where available, are also included for countries, some internal political divisions and for cities and towns. An asterisk preceding the population denotes that it represents an area larger than the city proper (i.e., metropolitan area, municipality, etc.).

LIST OF ABBREVIATIONS

A.F.B.	Air Force Base
Afghan.	Afghanistan
Ala.	Alabama
Alg.	Algeria
Alta.	Alberta
Antarc.	Antarctica
arch.	archipelago
Arg.	Argentina
Ariz.	Arizona
Ark.	Arkansas
A.S.S.R.	Autonomous Soviet Socialist Republic
Austr.	Australia
aut.	autonomous
Bah.	Bahamas
Bang.	Bangladesh
Belg.	Belgium
Bol.	Bolivia
Bots.	Botswana
Braz.	Brazil
Br., Brit.	British
Br. Col.	British Columbia
Bulg.	Bulgaria
Calif.	California
Camb.	Cambodia
Can.	Canada
cap.	capital
Cent. Afr. Rep.	Central African Republic
chan.	channel
Chan. Is.	Channel Islands
Col.	Colombia
Colo.	Colorado
Conn.	Connecticut
C. Rica	Costa Rica
Czech.	Czechoslovakia
D.C.	District of Columbia
Del.	Delaware
Dem.	Democratic
Den.	Denmark
depr.	depression
des.	desert
dist.	district
Dom. Rep.	Dominican Republic
E.	East, Eastern
Ecua.	Ecuador
E. Ger.	East Germany
El Sal.	El Salvador
Eng.	England
Equat. Guin.	Equatorial Guinea
est.	estuary
Eth.	Ethiopia
Fed.	Federal, Federated
Fin.	Finland
Fla.	Florida
for.	forest
Fr.	France, French
Fr. Poly.	French Polynesia
Ft.	Fort
Ga.	Georgia
Ger.	Germany
Greenl.	Greenland
Gt.	Great
Guad.	Guadeloupe
Guat.	Guatemala
Guy.	Guyana
har., harb.	harbor
Hond.	Honduras
Hung.	Hungary
isl., isls.	isle, island, islands
Ill.	Illinois
Ind.	Indiana
Indon.	Indonesia
Int'l	International
Ire.	Ireland
Isr.	Israel
isth.	isthmus
Iv. Coast	Ivory Coast
Jam.	Jamaica
Kans.	Kansas
Ky.	Kentucky
La.	Louisiana
Leb.	Lebanon
Lux.	Luxembourg
Madag.	Madagascar
Man.	Manitoba
Mass.	Massachusetts
Maur.	Mauritania
Md.	Maryland
Mex.	Mexico
Mich.	Michigan
Minn.	Minnesota
Miss.	Mississippi
Mo.	Missouri
Mong.	Mongolia
Mont.	Montana
Mor.	Morocco
Moz.	Mozambique
mt., mtn., mts.	mount, mountain, mountains
N., No.	North, Northern
N. Amer.	North America
Nat'l Pk.	National Park
N. Br.	New Brunswick
N.C.	North Carolina
N. Dak.	North Dakota
Nebr.	Nebraska
Neth.	Netherlands
Neth. Ant.	Netherlands Antilles
Nev.	Nevada
Newf.	Newfoundland
N.H.	New Hampshire
Nic.	Nicaragua
N. Ire.	Northern Ireland
N.J.	New Jersey
N. Korea	North Korea
N. Mex.	New Mexico
Nor.	Norway
N.S.	Nova Scotia
N.W.T.	Northwest Territories (Canada)
N.Y.	New York
N.Z.	New Zealand
Okla.	Oklahoma
Ont.	Ontario
Oreg.	Oregon
Pa.	Pennsylvania
Pak.	Pakistan
Pan.	Panama
Papua N.G.	Papua New Guinea
Par.	Paraguay
P.D.R. Yemen	People's Democratic Republic of Yemen
P.E.I.	Prince Edward Island
pen.	peninsula
Phil.	Philippines
Pk.	Park
plat.	plateau
Pol.	Poland
Port.	Portugal, Portuguese
P. Rico	Puerto Rico
prom.	promontory
prov.	province, provincial
pt., pte.	point, pointe
Que.	Québec
reg.	region
Rep.	Republic
res.	reservoir
R.I.	Rhode Island
riv.	river
Rom.	Romania
S.	South, Southern
sa.	serra, sierra
S. Africa	South Africa
S. Amer.	South America
São T. & Pr.	São Tomé & Príncipe
Sask.	Saskatchewan
S.C.	South Carolina
Scot.	Scotland
S. Dak.	South Dakota
Sen.	Senegal
Sing.	Singapore
S. Korea	South Korea
S. Leone	Sierra Leone
Sol. Is.	Solomon Islands
Sp.	Spain, Spanish
S.S.R.	Soviet Socialist Republic
St., Ste.	Saint, Sainte
St. Chris.-Nevis	St. Christopher-Nevis
str.	strait
St. Vinc. & Grens.	Saint Vincent & The Grenadines
Switz.	Switzerland
Tanz.	Tanzania
Tenn.	Tennessee
terr.	territory
Thai.	Thailand
Trin. & Tob.	Trinidad & Tobago
Tun.	Tunisia
U.A.E.	United Arab Emirates
U.K.	United Kingdom
Upp. Volta	Upper Volta
Urug.	Uruguay
U.S.	United States
U.S.S.R.	Union of Soviet Socialist Republics
Va.	Virginia
Ven., Venez.	Venezuela
V.I. (Br.)	Virgin Islands (British)
V.I. (U.S.)	Virgin Islands (U.S.)
Viet.	Vietnam
vol.	volcano
Vt.	Vermont
W.	West, Western
Wash.	Washington
W. Ger.	West Germany
W. Indies	West Indies
Wis.	Wisconsin
W. Samoa	Western Samoa
W. Va.	West Virginia
Wyo.	Wyoming
Yugo.	Yugoslavia
Zim.	Zimbabwe

A

B

C

H

L

M

N

O

S

GLOSSARY OF GEOGRAPHICAL TERMS

A. = Arabic Camb. = Cambodian Ch. = Chinese Dan. = Danish Du. = Dutch Finn. = Finnish Fr. = French Ger. = German Ice. = Icelandic It. = Italian Jap. = Japanese Nor. = Norwegian Per. = Persian Port. = Portuguese Russ. = Russian Sp. = Spanish Sw. = Swedish Turk. = Turkish

Å	Nor., Sw.	Stream
Abajo	Sp.	Lower
Ada, Adasi	Turk.	Island
Altiplano	Sp.	Plateau
Älv, Alf, Elf	Sw.	River
Arrecife	Sp.	Reef
Baai	Du.	Bay
Bahía	Sp.	Bay
Bahr	Arabic	Marsh, Lake, Sea, River
Baia	Port.	Bay
Baie	Fr.	Bay, Gulf
Bañados	Sp.	Marshes
Barra	Sp.	Reef
Belt	Ger.	Strait
Ben	Gaelic	Mountain
Berg	Ger., Du.	Mountain
Bir	Aarbic	Well
Boca	Sp.	Gulf, Inlet
Bolshoi, Bolshaya	Russ.	Big
Bolsón	Sp.	Depression
Bong	Korean	Mountain
Bucht	Ger.	Bay
Bugt	Dan.	Bay
Bukhta	Russ.	Bay
Burnu, Burun	Turk.	Cape, Point
By	Dan., Nor., Sw.	Town
Cabo	Port., Sp.	Cape
Campos	Port.	Plains
Canal	Port., Sp.	Channel
Cap, Capo	Fr., It.	Cape
Catarátas	Sp.	Falls
Central, Centrale	Fr., It.	Middle
Cerrito, Cerro	Sp.	Hill
Ciénaga	Sp.	Swamp
Ciudad	Sp.	City
Col	Fr.	Pass
Cordillera	Sp.	Mt. Range
Côte	Fr.	Coast
Cuchilla	Sp.	Mt. Range
Dağ, Dagh	Turk.	Mountain
Dağlari	Turk.	Mt. Range
Dal	Nor., Sw.	Valley
Darya	Per.	Salt Lake
Dasht	Per.	Desert, Plain
Deniz, Denizi	Turk.	Sea, Lake
Desierto	Sp.	Desert
Eiland	Du.	Island
Elv	Dan., Nor.	River
Emi	Berber	Mountain
Erg	Arabic	Dune, Desert
Est, Este	Fr., Port., Sp.	East
Estrecho, Estreito	Sp., Port.	Strait
Étang	Fr.	Pond, Lagoon, Lake
Fjørd	Dan., Nor.	Fiord
Fleuve	Fr.	River
Gebel	Arabic	Mountain
Gebirge	Ger.	Mt. Range
Gobi	Mongol	Desert
Gol	Mongol, Turk.	Lake, Stream
Golf	Ger., Du.	Gulf
Golfe	Fr.	Gulf
Golfo	Sp., It., Port.	Gulf
Gölü	Turk.	Lake
Gora	Russ.	Mountain
Grand, Grande	Fr., Sp.	Big
Groot	Du.	Big
Gross	Ger.	Big
Grosso	It., Port.	Big
Guba	Russ.	Bay, Gulf
Gunto	Jap.	Archipelago
Gunung	Malay	Mountain
Higashi, Higasi	Jap.	East
Ho	Ch.	River
Hoek	Du.	Cape
Holm	Dan., Nor., Sw.	Island
Hu	Ch.	Lake
Hwang	Ch.	Yellow
Île	Fr.	Island
Insel	Ger.	Island
Irmak	Turk.	River
Isla	Sp.	Island
Isola	Sp.	Island
Jabal, Jebel	Arabic	Mountains
Järvi	Finn.	Lake
Jaure	Sw.	Lake
Jezira	Arabic	Island
Jima	Jap.	Island
Joki	Finn.	River
Kaap	Du.	Cape
Kabir, Kebir	Arabic	Big
Kanal	Russ., Ger.	Canal, Channel
Kap, Kapp	Nor., Sw., Ice.	Cape
Kawa	Jap.	River
Khrebet	Russ.	Mt. Range
Kiang	Ch.	River
Kita	Jap.	North
Klein	Du., Ger.	Small
Kô	Jap.	Lake
Ko	Thai.	Island
Koh	Camb., Khmer	Island
Köping	Sw.	Borough
Körfez, Körfezi	Turk.	Gulf
Kuh	Per.	Mountain
Kul	Sinkiang Turki	Lake
Kum	Turk.	Desert
Lac	Fr.	Lake
Lago	Port., Sp., It.	Lake
Lagôa	Port.	Lagoon
Laguna	Sp.	Lagoon
Lagune	Fr.	Lagoon
Llanos	Sp.	Plains
Mar	Sp., Port.	Sea
Mare	It.	Sea
Meer	Du.	Lake
Meer	Ger.	Sea
Mer	Fr.	Sea
Meseta	Sp.	Plateau
Minami	Jap.	Southern
Misaki	Jap.	Cape
Mittel	Ger.	Middle
Mont	Fr.	Mountain
Montagne	Fr.	Mountain
Montaña	Sp.	Mountains
Monte	Sp., It., Port.	Mountain
More	Russ.	Sea
Muong	Siamese	Town
Mys	Russ.	Cape
Nam	Burm., Lao	River
Nevado	Sp.	Snow covered peak
Nieder	Ger.	Lower
Nishi, Nisi	Jap.	West
Nizhni, Nizhnyaya	Russ.	Lower
Nor	Mong.	Lake
Nord	Fr., Ger.	North
Norte	Sp., It., Port.	North
Nos	Russ.	Cape
Novi, Novaya	Russ.	New
Nusa	Malay	Island
O	Jap.	Big
Ö	Nor., Sw	Island
Ober	Ger.	Upper
Occidental, Occidentale	Sp., It.	Western
Oeste	Port.	West
Oriental	Sp., Fr.	Eastern
Orientale	It.	Eastern
Ost	Ger.	East
Ostrov	Russ.	Island
Ouest	Fr.	West
öy	Nor.	Island
Ozero	Russ.	Lake
Pampa	Sp.	Plain
Paso	Sp.	Pass
Passo	It., Port.	Pass
Pequeño	Sp.	Small
Peski	Russ.	Desert
Petit	Fr.	Small
Pic	Fr.	Mountain
Pico	Port., Sp.	Mountain, Peak
Pik	Russ.	Peak
Pointe	Fr.	Point
Poluostrov	Russ.	Peninsula
Ponta	Port.	Point
Presa	Sp.	Reservoir
Proliv	Russ.	Strait
Pulou, Pulo	Malay	Island
Punta	Sp., It., Port.	Point
Ras	Arabic	Cape
Ría	Sp.	Estuary
Río	Sp.	River
Rivier, Rivière	Du., Fr.	River
Rud	Per.	River
Saki	Jap.	Cape
Salto	Sp., Port.	Falls
San	Ch., Jap., Korean	Hill
See	Ger.	Sea, Lake
Selvas	Sp., Port.	Forest
Serra	Port.	Mts.
Serranía	Sp.	Mts.
Severni, Servernaya	Russ.	North
Shan	Ch., Jap.	Hill, Mts.
Shima	Jap.	Island
Shoto	Jap.	Islands
Sierra	Sp.	Mountains
Sjö	Nor., Sw.	Lake, Sea
Spitze	Ger.	Mt. Peak
Sredni, Srednyaya	Russ.	Middle
Stad	Dan., Nor., Sw.	City
Stari, Staraya	Russ.	Old
Su	Turk.	River
Sud, Süd	Sp., Fr., Ger.	South
Sul	Port.	South
Sungei	Malay	River
Sur	Sp.	South
Tagh	Turk.	Mt. Range
Tal	Ger.	Valley
Tandjong, Tanjung	Malay	Cape, Point
Tso	Tibetan	Lake
Val	Fr.	Valley
Velho	Port.	Old
Verkhni	Russ.	Upper
Vesi	Finn.	Lake
Vishni, Vishnyaya	Russ.	High
Vostochni, Vostochnaya	Russ.	East, Eastern
Wadi	Arabic	Dry River
Wald	Ger.	Forest
Wan	Jap.	Bay
Yama	Jap.	Mountain
Yug, Yuzhni, Yuzhnaya	Russ.	South, Southern
Zaliv	Russ.	Bay, Gulf
Zapadni, Zapadnaya	Russ.	Western
Zee	Du.	Sea
Zemlya	Russ.	Land
Zuid	Du.	South